The Handbook on Religion and Communication

Global Handbooks in Media and Communication Research

Series Editors: Janet Wasko (University of Oregon, USA) and Karin Wilkins (University of Miami, USA)

The Global Handbooks in Media and Communication Research series is co-published by Wiley Blackwell and the International Association for Media and Communication Research (IAMCR). The series offers definitive, state-of-the-art handbooks that bring a global perspective to their subjects. These volumes are designed to define an intellectual terrain: its historic emergence; its key theoretical paradigms; its transnational evolution; key empirical research and case study exemplars; and possible future directions.

Already published

The Handbook of Diasporas, Media, and Culture edited by Jessica Retis and Roza Tsagarousianou

The Handbook of Political Economy of Communications edited by Janet Wasko, Graham Murdock, and Helena Sousa

The Handbook of Global Media and Communication Policy edited by Robin Mansell and Marc Raboy

The Handbook of Media Audiences edited by Virginia Nightingale

The Handbook of Development Communication and Social Change edited by Karin Gwinn Wilkins, Thomas Tufte, and Rafael Obregon

The Handbook of Media Education Research edited by Divina Frau-Meigs, Sirkku Kotilainen, Manisha Pathak-Shelat, Michael Hoechsmann, Stuart R. Poyntz

Coming Soon

The Handbook of Conflict and Peace Communication edited by Sudeshna Roy

About the IAMCR

The International Association for Media and Communication Research (IAMCR) (http://iamcr.org) was established in Paris in 1957. It is an accredited NGO attached to UNESCO. It is a truly international association, with a membership representing over 90 countries around the world and conferences held in different regions that address the most pressing issues in media and communication research. Its members promote global inclusiveness and excellence within the best traditions of critical research in the field. The current president of the IAMCR is Janet Wasko.

The Handbook on Religion and Communication

Edited by

Yoel Cohen
Paul A. Soukup

WILEY Blackwell

Registered Office
John Wiley & Sons Ltd, The Atrium, Southern Gate, Chichester, West Sussex, PO19 8SQ, UK

Editorial Office
9600 Garsington Road, Oxford, OX4 2DQ, UK

For details of our global editorial offices, customer services, and more information about Wiley products visit us at www.wiley.com.

A catalogue record for this book is available from the Library of Congress

Hardback ISBN: 9781119671558; ePub ISBN: 9781119671589; ePDF ISBN: 9781119671602; obook ISBN: 9781119671619

Cover image: © MarcosMartinezSanchez/E+/Getty Images; Jackie Niam/iStock/Getty Images Plus/Getty Images; hadynyah/E+/Getty Images
Cover design by Wiley

Set in 11/13pt Dante by Integra Software Services Pvt. Ltd, Pondicherry, India

Contents

Contributors

Jason Bartashius is an early career researcher. He holds a PhD in global studies (Sophia University) and an MA in Asian religion (University of Hawaii at Manoa). Jason's research examines the intersections of religion and gender in cinematic representations as well as discourses on the phenomenon of migration. He has published essays in *Culture and Religion* and public scholarship in *Religion Dispatches*. In addition to his academic work, Jason has bylines in *The Japan Times*, *Kyoto Journal*, and *Honolulu Civil Beat*.

Piotr S. Bobkowski is a professor in the William Allen White School of Journalism and Mass Communications at the University of Kansas. He holds a doctorate in mass communication from the University of North Carolina at Chapel Hill. His current work focuses on journalism education, student media, and information and data literacy. He previously studied the motives and consequences of individuals sharing personal information in online media, including religious self-disclosure.

Rohit Chopra is an associate professor of communication at Santa Clara University. His research centers on the relationship of globalization, media, and culture. He is the author, most recently, of *The Gita for a Global World: Ethical Action in an Age of Flux* (Westland, 2021) and *The Virtual Hindu Rashtra: Saffron Nationalism and New Media* (HarperCollins, 2019). He is currently working on a book on the mediated memories of religious violence in Mumbai in 1992–1993 and another book on global cities in Europe, the United States, and South Asia as media archives of cultural history and memory.

Lynn Schofield Clark is a distinguished university professor of media, film and journalism studies at the University of Denver, where she is also director of the Estlow International Center for Journalism and New Media. She is a digital/mobile media studies researcher with a focus on feminist, critical race and indigenous theories, youth voice, youth journalism, family communication, and participatory politics. She authored *Young People and the Future of News* (with Regina Marchi, Cambridge University Press, 2017, winner of the Nancy Baym and the James W. Carey book awards), *The Parent App* (Oxford University Press, 2013), and *From Angels to Aliens: Teenagers, the Media, and the Supernatural* (Oxford University Press, 2003, winner of the NCA Ethnography book award). She is also affiliate faculty with the DU Center on American Politics and with the Joint Doctoral Program in Religious Studies (University of Denver/Iliff School of Theology). Professor Clark was a research fellow at Sodertorn University in Sweden (2022), was an affiliate professor with the University of Copenhagen's Department of Media, Cognition and

Communication (2014–2020), and was a visiting fellow at the Royal Melbourne Institute of Technology in Australia (2014). She served as president of the international Association of Internet Researchers (2019–2021) and as president of the International Society for Religion, Media and Culture (ISMRC) (2015–2017).

Yoel Cohen is a full professor (emeritus) on the faculty of the School of Communication, Ariel University, Israel (School Chairman, 2009–2011). A graduate of London University, he completed his doctorate at City University London on British foreign policy and the media. His research interests include religion and news, media and religion in Israel and Judaism, media and the City of Jerusalem, and foreign news and foreign correspondents. He is the author of many publications on media and religion, including the books *God, Jews and the Media: Religion and Israel's Media* (Routledge, 2012); editor of *Spiritual News: Reporting Religion around the World* (Peter Lang Publishers, 2018); and co-editor of *The Handbook of Religion and Communication* (Wiley, 2023). Other books include *Media Diplomacy: The Foreign Office in the Mass Communication Age* (Frank Cass, 1986) and *The Whistleblower of Dimona: Vanunu, Israel and the Bomb* (Holmes & Meier, 2003). His research articles have appeared in *Harvard International Journal of Press/Politics, Gazette, Asian Communication Research, Journal of Media and Religion, Israel Affairs, Review of International Studies, The Journal of Arab and Muslim Media Research, Religion and Social Communication, The International Encyclopaedia of Communication Theory and Philosophy, The International Encyclopaedia of Media Effects,* and *The Encyclopaedia of Religion, Communication and Media.* He was editor, Israel media, *Encyclopaedia Judaica.* He is a convenor of the Religion and Communication working group of the International Association of Media and Communication Research.

Monica Crawford (MA, University of North Carolina) is a graduate student at the Hussman School of Media and Journalism at the University of North Carolina-Chapel Hill. Her research revolves around gender representation, journalism practice, and sports media. She is a top student paper award winner for the LBTQIA+ Interest Group at the Association for Education in Journalism and Mass Communication.

Míriam Díez Bosch is a journalist and theologian. She is a professor and vice dean of research, postgraduate and international relations at the Blanquerna School of Communication and International Relations Blanquerna at the Ramon Llull University of Barcelona. She is director of Blanquerna Observatory on Media, Religion and Culture and of Global Engagement at Aleteia. org; vice-president of the Catalonia Religion Foundation; director of Catalonia's Chair on Freedom of Religion and Belief; vice-president of the International Society for Media, Religion and Culture; and a member of the steering committee of the Institute for Migration Studies at the Comillas Pontifical University of Madrid and of the ARC advisory board of the Center for the Anthropology of Religion and Cultural Change at the Sacro Cuore University of Milan. She writes regularly in newspapers including *El Punt Avui* and *El Nacional.*

Johannes Ehrat is a professor emeritus in the Faculty of Social Sciences, Pontifical Gregorian University, Rome. His research interests include semiotic, film theory, semiotic of the public sphere, and religious communication in world religions (Judaism, Christianity, Islam, Hinduism, Chinese religiosities). This synthetic effort necessitated developing a semiotic–pragmatic theory of religions founded on time cognition, and not ontologically ("does God exist?"), or on essentialist grounds.

Hadi Enayat is a visiting lecturer at SOAS and the Aga Khan University in London. He is a political sociologist whose main interests are in the areas of religion and international relations, the sociology of law, and secularism studies. He worked as a journalist for the Cairo-based *Al-Ahram Weekly* from 1992 to 1994. He has also worked in the area of refugee rights with the London-based nongovernmental organization *Praxis* from 2005 to 2007. His book *Law, State and Society in Modern Iran* (Palgrave Macmillan, 2013) won the 2013 Biennial Mossadegh Prize. He is co-editor (with Mirjam Kuenkler) of *The Rule of Law in the Islamic Republic of Iran: Power, Institutions and Prospects for Reform* to be published by Cambridge University Press. He is co-author (with Mohamed Keshavjee) of *Rethinking Sharia: Critical Debates in Political Context*, to be published by Bloomsbury.

Mark Fackler is a professor of communications emeritus, Calvin University in Grand Rapids, Michigan. He is co-author of the first edition of the celebrated text *Media Ethics: Cases and Moral Reasoning* (in its 12th edition). Among his other publications is *The Handbook of Media and Mass Communication Theory* (co-edited with Robert Fortner). He has taught in East Africa and published on East African media, and taken many American students to that part of the continent for exposure to its beauty, hospitality, and its leaders. His PhD is from the Institute of Communications Research at the University of Illinois, Champaign-Urbana.

John P. Ferré is a professor of communication at the University of Louisville, where he teaches courses on historical, ethical, and religious dimensions of media. In addition to numerous articles and reviews, he has published several books, including *A Social Gospel for Millions: The Religious Bestsellers of Charles Sheldon, Charles Gordon, and Harold Bell Wright* and *Channels of Belief: Religion and American Commercial Television*. A past president of the American Journalism Historians Association, he serves on the editorial boards of *Journal of Media and Religion*, *Journal of Media Ethics*, and *Journalism History*.

Robert S. Fortner entered the academy as a professor after completing his PhD in the Institute of Communications Research at the University of Illinois. He has taught at Northwestern University, Drake University, the State University of New York, George Washington University, Calvin University, the American University in Bulgaria, Hope College, and Palm Beach Atlantic University. He maintains his connection to the University of Illinois as a research scholar. He has also taught courses at the University of Addis Ababa and Uganda Christian University, and lectured at universities in Kenya, Russia, Bulgaria, Hungary, Mongolia, and Taiwan. He has written or edited 13 books. His areas of research include international communication, political economy, new technologies and implications for human life, philosophy of technology, cultural history, intercultural communication, and communication ethics, especially in the global arena. His latest book examines *Ethics in the Digital Domain*. He has also worked extensively with many international organizations in more than 40 countries, including many in postconflict situations.

Stephen Garner is academic dean and a senior lecturer in theology at Laidlaw College in Auckland, New Zealand. His research and teaching concerns theology, technology, and ethics; religion, media, and popular culture; and public and contextual theology. He is co-author (with Heidi Campbell) of *Networked Theology: Negotiating Faith in Digital Culture* (Baker Academic, 2016) and is co-chair of the American Academy of Region Human Enhancement and Transhumanism program unit and a board member of the Global Network for Digital Theology.

Myna German, PhD is a Full Professor in the Mass Communications, Visual and Performing Arts Department at Delaware State University. She is a former Chair of Mass Communications and working journalist. She writes in the areas of Religion and Media, the Literature of Communications, Tourism and Marketing. She holds dual degrees in Communications and Business. She is the author of two literary books and two academic books.

Damian Guzek is an associate professor in the Institute of Journalism and Media Communication at the University of Silesia in Katowice, Poland. He researches communication, religion, and politics. His research is driven by questions related to media consumption and digital media, religions, and politics. After a doctorate in Katowice, he conducted his postdoc at Uppsala University as well as a research internship at the University of Edinburgh. He was also a visiting fellow at Keele University and team member of the "Illiberal turn" project conducted at Loughborough University.

Mary E. Hess is a professor of educational leadership at Luther Seminary, where she has taught since 2000. She holds a BA in American studies from Yale, an MTS in theological studies from Harvard, and a PhD in religion and education from Boston College. As an educator straddling the fields of media studies, education, and religion, Hess has focused her research on exploring ways in which participatory strategies for knowing and learning are constructed and contested amidst digital cultures – in particular in dialogic forms of organizational development, and the challenges posed to communities by oppressive systems such as racism, classism, sexism, and so on. Her most recent book, co-written with Stephen S. Brookfield, is *Becoming a White Antiracist: A Practical Guide for Educators, Leaders and Activists* (Stylus Publishers, 2021).

Chiung Hwang Chen is a professor of communication, media, and culture at Brigham Young University-Hawai'i. Her research interests include media-related religion, gender, and race issues, as well as cultural studies in the Pacific and Chinese-speaking regions.

Heidi Ippolito is a PhD student in the Joint Doctoral Program at the University of Denver and Iliff School of Theology. She holds an MLitt in theology, imagination, and the arts from the University of St. Andrews in Scotland and a BA in cinema-television (critical studies) at the University of Southern California. Her interdisciplinary dissertation project examines how religion and storytelling shape online communities through a case study on QAnon, *The Matrix* films, and Internet memes.

Felicia Katz-Harris is the senior curator and curator of Asian and Oceanic folk art at the Museum of International Folk Art, in Santa Fe, New Mexico. Her exhibitions include *Yōkai: Ghosts and Demons of Japan*; the award-winning *Dancing Shadows, Epic Tales: Wayang Kulit of Indonesia*; and *Sacred Realm: Blessings and Good Fortune Across Asia*, which explored diverse ways that material religion empowers and blesses people in physical and spiritual realms of life. Her research and writing focus on decoloniality in museum practice, museum anthropology, material religion and ritual, and expressive culture in Asian contexts. She has a Master's degree in anthropology from Arizona State University, she studied art history at Visva Bharati University in West Bengal, language at Universitas Gadjah Mada in Yogyakarta, and is earning her PhD in ethnology at the University of New Mexico.

Mary Catherine Kennedy is an assistant professor of instruction in the Department of Management in the College of Business at Ohio University in Athens, Ohio. Her research interests include interpersonal communication; the intersection of religion, media, and marketing; social media management; and sport communication.

Keval J. Kumar is an adjunct professor at MICA, Ahmedabad, India. Formerly, he was reader and chair of Pune University's Department of Communication and Journalism, a professor and director at Symbiosis Institute of Media and Communication, and a senior lecturer in English at Sathaye College, Mumbai. He has also taught at Ohio State University, Siegen University, Jacobs University Bremen, and Bahrain Technical Institute. He holds a doctorate from the University of Leicester. He is the author of *Mass Communication in India* (Jaico Books, 5th Ed.), *Media Education, Communication and Public Policy: An Indian Perspective* (Himalaya) and co-author of *Environmentalism and the Mass Media: The North–South Divide* (Routledge). He has contributed "entries" to three international encyclopedias of communication (Wiley Blackwell-ICA), and over 75 research papers to edited books and academic journals. He was chair of the media education section of the International Association of Media and Communication Research (IAMCR) from 1998 to 2006 and chief adviser to NCERT for media studies in 2004. He is a member of the Board of Studies for Media and Communication Studies, Pune University and an associate member of ORBICOM. His research interests include communication theory, media education, cultural studies, political communication and religious communication.

Anthony Le Duc, SVD, is a priest in the Society of the Divine Word. He holds a bachelor's degree in molecular and cell biology and Asian studies from University of California, Berkeley, a Master of Divinity from Catholic Theological Union (Chicago), and a doctorate in religious studies from Assumption University, Thailand. In addition to teaching at Lux Mundi National Major Seminary of Thailand, he is the executive director of the Asian Research Center for Religion and Social Communication, St. John's University, Thailand, and the editor-in-chief of its scholarly journal, *Religion and Social Communication*. His current research and published books and articles primarily deal with the intersection between religion and contemporary issues such as ecology, migration, and technological development.

Josep Lluís Micó is a professor of journalism at the Ramon Llull University and dean at the Blanquerna School of Communication and International Relations Blanquerna, where, previously, he was director of the bachelor's degree in journalism, as well as the director of the university Master's degree in advanced journalism and reporting at Blanquerna-Godó Group. He has led national and international research projects and has participated in innovation initiatives with technological giants such as Google and Facebook. In the classroom, he teaches and practices with the students the same genres and formats that, later, he applies in media or groups such as "La Vanguardia," Prensa Ibérica, and RTVE: new journalism, massive data visualization, and branded journalism. He has won several essay and article awards and has appeared on numerous digital influencer lists in the electronic music and fourth industrial revolution categories.

Knut Lundby is a professor emeritus in media studies, at the Department of Media and Communication, University of Oslo, Norway. He is dr.philos. with a dissertation in sociology of religion. Lundby is among the founding members of the international research community on media, religion, and culture, and edited *Rethinking Media, Religion, and Culture* (with Stewart M. Hoover, Sage, 1997). He is editor of and contributor to *Mediatization: Concept, Changes, Consequences* (Peter Lang, 2009), *Religion Across Media* (Peter Lang, 2013), and the *Handbook on Mediatization of Communication* (De Gruyter Mouton, 2014). He directed the research projects Engaging with Conflicts in Religious Environments (2014–2018), published in *Contesting Religion. The Media Dynamics of Cultural Conflicts in Scandinavia* (open access, De Gruyter, 2018). Among his research essays is "Issues with Research on the Mediatization of Religion" in *Contemporary Challenges in Mediatization Research* (edited by Katarzyna Kopecka-Piech and Göran Bolin, Routledge, 2022).

Jim McDonnell was director of the Catholic Communications Centre, London, from 1990 to 2002 and a consultor on the Vatican's Pontifical Council for Social Communication until 2005. Since 2002, he has run his own PR and communications consultancy. He has been involved in and written extensively on the changing world of religion and media since the early 1980s as well as being on the organizing committee of several European TV festivals of religious programs. Among his essays is "Putting Virtue into the Virtual: Putting Ethics into the Infosphere," *Media Development*, 3, 2018. He is a board member of the World Association for Christian Communication.

Joel Mayward is an assistant professor of Christian ministries, theology and the arts at George Fox University in Oregon, United States. He has a PhD from the Institute for Theology, Imagination and the Arts, University of St. Andrews, and has published articles in academic journals such as *Pro Ecclesia, Horizons, Theology, ARTS, Journal of Religion and Film*, and *Journal for Religion, Film and Media*. A professional freelance film critic, he is the author of *The Dardenne Brothers' Cinematic Parables: Integrating Theology, Philosophy, and Film* (Routledge, 2022).

Joseph Muyangata is a lecturer in cross-cultural missions at Apostolic Faith Mission Theological Seminary, Harare, Zimbabwe. His research interests include culture, media, and religion in African religions and Christianity; health, communication, and religion; and theology. He holds a Master's in practical theology from Chester University, UK.

Carlo Nardella is a tenured assistant professor of sociology in the Department of Social and Political Sciences at the University of Milan, Italy. His research is primarily concerned with issues of social construction of reality and social change, with particular attention to cultural factors and communication. Specifically, he has focused on the interrelationships between religion and marketing, the use of religious symbols in commercial advertising, the relationship between Catholicism and the media, the adaptation of religious buildings to new uses, popular religiosity, and the role of religion in the legitimization of the European Union. Nardella is author of a book on the use of religious symbolism in Italian advertising and guest editor of two journal special issues. He is currently at work on a book, *Symbolic Economy*, with Routledge. Recipient of the British Sociological Association's Peter B. Clarke Memorial Prize and nominee for the Harvard Society of Fellows, Nardella was visiting scholar at the University of Pennsylvania's Annenberg School for Communication and the University of Colorado Boulder's College of Media, Communication and Information.

Allan Novaes, PhD (Pontifical Catholic University of São Paulo, Brazil), is an associate professor at the School of Theology, at the Digital Games Program, and in the Master's in Health Promotion Program, at the Adventist University of São Paulo (Brazil). His research interests are religion and communication, youth studies and religion, Adventist studies, and thanatology and religion. His publications include articles in *Religion Online: How Digital Technology Is Changing the Way We Worship and Pray* (Praeger/ABC Clio) and chapters in the Theology, Religion and Pop Culture series (Fortress Academics/Lexington Books). Presently, he is vice-president for Research and Institutional Development at the Adventist University of São Paulo (Brazil).

Gnana Patrick, PhD, professor and head of the Department of Christian Studies, University of Madras, holds a doctorate in Christian studies. He was awarded a postdoctoral fellowship in 2004 to carry out research on Asian religions and cultures in Hong Kong Chung Che College. He was awarded the Fulbright–Nehru Visiting Lecturer Fellowship in 2013 and taught a course on Public Religion: Learning from Indian and American Experiences at the Divinity School, Harvard University. He co-edited (with Elisabeth Schussler Fiorenza) *Negotiating Border – Theological Explorations in the Global Era* (ISPCK, 2008). His other publications include *Religion and Subaltern Agency* (2003); *Wings of Faith – Public Theologies in India* (2013); *Oral Traditions and Theology* (1996); and *Resonances (Tamil), Indian Christianity and Its Public Role* (edited, 2019), and *Public Theology – Indian Concerns, Themes and Perspectives* (Fortress Press, 2020). He has penned 90 research articles, published in various peer-reviewed journals. He served as the chief editor of *Indian Journal of Christian Studies* from 2012 to 2016. He was given the Best Researcher Award by the University of Madras in 2017–2018. Presently he is the dean of research, the University of Madras.

Gregory P. Perreault (PhD, Missouri) is a scholar of journalism and multimedia journalism professor at Appalachian State University. His research extends to journalistic epistemology, hostility in journalism, and digital labor. He is an Observatory of International Research-ranked scholar in the field of communication and serves as book review editor for *Journalism and Mass Communication Quarterly*.

Mildred F. Perreault (PhD, Missouri) is an assistant professor of media and communication at East Tennessee State University. Perreault's research and teaching expertise are in crisis communication, journalism, community–media relations, and media writing. She has been published in *American Behavioral Scientist, Journal of Media and Religion, Games and Culture, Disasters, Communication Studies, Journalism Practice*, and *Journalism Education*.

Alba Sabaté Gauxachs is a journalist, professor of journalism, and coordinator of the Global Communication Management Degree at the Blanquerna School of Communication and International Relations Blanquerna at Ramon Llull University (Barcelona). She is deputy director at the Blanquerna Observatory on Media, Religion and Culture, a member of the Global Board of Directors at the World Association for Christian Communication, a predoctoral visiting researcher at Boston College in 2018, a fellow at the King Abdullah bin Abdulaziz International Centre for Interreligious and Intercultural Dialogue in 2019, a fellow at the United Nations Alliance of Civilizations in 2020, a member of the research team of the Catalonia's Chair on Freedom of Religion and Belief, a contributor at Catalunya Religió, and assistant editor of the journal *Trípodos*.

Paul A. Soukup, S.J., has explored the connections between communication and theology since 1982. His publications include *Communication and Theology* (World Association for Christian Communication, 1983); *Christian Communication: A Bibliographical Survey* (Greenwood, 1989); *Media, Culture, and Catholicism* (Sheed & Ward, 1996); *Mass Media and the Moral Imagination* with Philip J. Rossi (Sheed & Ward, 1994); and *Fidelity and Translation: Communicating the Bible in New Media* with Robert Hodgson (Sheed & Ward, 1999). This latter publication grows out of his work on the American Bible Society's New Media Bible. In addition, he and Thomas J. Farrell have edited four volumes of the collected works of Walter J. Ong, S.J., *Faith and Contexts* (Scholars Press, 1992–1999). These volumes have led him to examine more closely how orality–literacy studies can contribute to an understanding of theological expression. Most recently, he has published a book of biblical meditations on communication, *Out of Eden: 7 Ways God Restores Blocked Communication* (Pauline Books and Media, 2006) and edited a collection of essays applying Ong's thought, *Of Ong and Media Ecology: Essays in Communication, Composition, and Literary Studies* (Hampton Press, 2012). A graduate of the University of Texas at Austin (PhD, 1985), Soukup teaches in the Communication Department at Santa Clara University, holding the Pedro Arrupe, S.J., university chair.

Amanda Sturgill is an associate professor of journalism, media analytics, and interactive media at Elon University in North Carolina. Her doctorate from Cornell University focuses on communication technology and organizational behavior. She studies the ways ideological groups use newer technologies. A former head of the Association for Education in Journalism and Mass Communication's Religion and Media Interest Group, her publications include articles in *Religion Online: How Digital Technology Is Changing the Way We Worship and Pray* and *Mind the Gap: Global Learning at Home and Abroad*. She authored *Detecting Deception: Tools for Fighting Fake News* and *We Are AltGov: Social Media Resistance from the Inside*.

Johanna Sumiala is an associate professor of media and communication studies at the Faculty of Social Sciences, University of Helsinki. She is one of the founders of the Helsinki Research Hub on Religion, Media and Social Change and past president of the International Society for Religion, Media and Culture. In recent years Sumiala's work has focused on theoretical and empirical analyses of mediations and mediatizations of religion and death in digital media. Her research on media and communications is inspired by social theory and anthropology, ritual studies, and digital ethnography. Sumiala is author of several books and journal articles. Her most recent books include: *Mediated Death* (Polity, 2021), *Hybrid Media Events: The Charlie Hebdo Attacks and Global Circulation of Terrorist Violence* (2018, Emerald, co-authored with K. Valaskivi, M. Tikka, & J. Huhtamäki), and *Media and Ritual: Death, Community and Everyday Life* (Routledge, 2013). She is a series editor of the Routledge Studies in Religion and Digital Culture.

Teemu Taira is a senior lecturer in the study of religion at the University of Helsinki. He has published extensively on atheism, media, and methodological issues in the study of religion, including *Media Portrayals of Religion and the Secular Sacred* (with Kim Knott and Elizabeth Poole) (Ashgate, 2013), *Taking "Religion" Seriously: Essays on the Discursive Study of Religion* (Brill, 2022), and *Atheism in Five Minutes* (Equinox, 2022). For more information, see teemutaira.wordpress.com.

Ruth Tsuria is an assistant professor at Seton Hall University. Her research investigates the intersection of digital media, religion, and feminism with a focus on developing theoretical tools to understand online discourse and interrogate the relationship between technology and society; discourse and power. She has published articles in various academic outlets, such as *The International Journal of Communication*, *The Communication Review*, and *Social Media + Society*. She has presented her research at national and international communication, media, and religion conferences. She received the Network for New Media, Religion, and Digital Culture's Digital Religion Research Award, and Religion in Society's "Emerging Scholar" award. She is currently working on a book *Holy Women, Pious Sex, Sanctified Internet: New Media in the Jewish Bedroom*.

Robert A. White is a past professor in the PhD program in communication and development at the University of Nairobi, professor in communication and development for 20 years at the Gregorian University in Rome, and director of the PhD program in development studies at Tangaza University in Nairobi, Kenya. He is co-author of the book *Normative Theories of the Media* (University of Illinois Press, 2009), which won the Luther Mott prize as the outstanding book of the field of journalism and mass communication in the United States. He is the past director of the journal *African Communication Research*.

Daniella Zsupan-Jerome is director of Ministerial Formation and Field Education at St. John's University School of Theology and Seminary in Collegeville, Minnesota, United States. Her research explores the intersection of social communication, digital culture, and pastoral theology. She has served as a consultant to the United States Conference of Catholic Bishops' Committee on Communications, as an educational consultant to the Catholic Media Association, and as a tutor for the Vatican's Dicastery for Communication's Faith Communication in the Digital World project. Key publications include: *Connected Toward Communion: The Church and Social Communication in the Digital Age* (Liturgical Press, 2014); *Evangelization and Catechesis: Echoing the Good News Through the Documents of the Church* (Twenty-Third Publications, 2017); and *Authority and Leadership: Values, Religion, Media* (co-editor, Blanquerna, 2017).

Introduction

Academics have studied communication and religion for some 40 years, but the area only slowly received recognition in the wider area of mass media studies. Media studies grew from the social sciences and like all social sciences initially emphasized empirical or even scientific methods and a secular orientation. Not surprisingly, it took time to incorporate elements like belief and spirituality into the schema of social scientists, who had little interest in studying religious doctrine or theology. However, they did pay attention to religious institutions and more so now to the place of religion in popular culture and to the rise of online religion.

If empty church pews in Western Europe and emptying ones in North America suggest a decline in organized religious activity, religion has not disappeared but has changed. Indeed, many factors have combined to raise the profile of religion in communication circles. The twentieth century witnessed considerable developments in religiosity: shifting allegiances to the historical Christian Churches, rising membership in Evangelical Christianity, the growth of public Islam, the decline of Church authority in traditionally Catholic countries, religious scandals touching on sexuality or on finances, and a globalization of non-Western religions. The place of religion vis-à-vis traditional media sources like the press, radio, television, and film has changed with traditional media expressing more critical views and giving less "soft" coverage of religion and religious groups, and with governments and media companies offering less free access to broadcasting. In the more recent past, new media offer new means to communicate and portray religion, with literally thousands of websites and Twitter feeds devoted to religion.

Religious groups have undergone a kind of communication conversion. In almost all the areas that media and religion scholars investigate, religious groups themselves have taken to communication media and communication practices, including advertising and public relations. Religious groups have also accepted that the digital media can communicate religious experience, using media in which voice and individuals converge with text, in a two-way process. Thus, the new media have a role in creating religious identity. Parallel to this has been a shift toward religious themes about spirituality and values and away from religious institutions. Those religious groups with recognised or official teachers – the Vatican Pontifical Council on Social Communication, the US National Council of [Christian] Churches, Islamic imams, synagogue organizations in Judaism, and so on – have recognized this phenomenon and offered a variety of instructions on media use. Communication studies have taken note.

Acts of terrorist violence carried out in the name of religion provide another development that has raised scholarly interest in religion and communication. While the attacks of 9/11 may remain the most visual act, satellite communications going back to the 1970s have enabled religion-related violence to reach a global audience. Digital media also enable religious hate speech to spread widely, whether such speech targets Christians, Muslims, Jews, or religious minorities. This phenomenon, too, merits scholarly attention.

The Handbook on Religion and Communication, First Edition. Edited by Yoel Cohen and Paul A. Soukup.
© 2023 John Wiley & Sons Ltd. Published 2023 by John Wiley & Sons Ltd.

On the positive side, the same technologies that allow instant access to religious violence also allow religious leaders to reach out with messages of peace, as have the Pope, the Dalai Lama, and the Chief Rabbis or Chief Imams of different countries. Interreligious meetings promoting harmony, such as meetings of different religious heads, receive wide media attention.

But the digital era threatens religious authority. If in the past, a person's religious beliefs were regarded as a private matter and one directed by religious teachers – priests, rabbis, imams, pastors, gurus, etc. – this has changed radically by the beginning of the twenty-first century. Audiences frankly discuss their religious beliefs on social networks; people seek religious advice or counsel online; the most eloquent (or demanding) voices become authoritative ones. Religious controversies become public controversies.

Yet it would be wrong to look at contemporary intersections between religion and popular culture only or primarily through the prism of new media and digital media. Even in today's digital age, old media, interpersonal communication, and material religion (to name just a few kinds of communication) still play important roles. Against the background of these developments, the *Handbook of Religion and Communication* aspires to map out the wider interactions of communication, religious identity, and behavior.

Given the international orientation of the International Association for Media and Communication Research (IAMCR), the *Handbook of Religion and Communication* aims to go beyond a Western locus, which has characterized research on media and religion in the past, to embrace faith traditions in other regions like Asia and Africa. The international approach also finds expression in the contributors to the Handbook, who include past and present members of the IAMCR's Religion and Communication working group as well as younger scholars new to the IAMCR.

Lynch (2005) identifies three different ways in which popular culture, including communication, interacts with religion: first, popular cultural texts and practices have shaped the beliefs, structures, and practices of religious groups; second, religion is represented in the wider culture; and third, religious groups interact with wider popular culture. Following that general schema, the Handbook discusses themes such as religion and evangelism in public culture and the ways that a media culture has begun to shape religious practice, evidenced in the styles of televangelists or in online religion. Second, it asks how religion is itself represented in wider culture, in film (fiction and documentary), in entertainment, and in media coverage of religion news. Finally, exploring how religious groups interact with wider popular culture, the book addresses issues such as religious authority and challenges from media, notably the new media. Not infrequently, the three ways in which popular culture interact with religion overlap, particularly in how far religions have taken on the trappings of commercialism in their own communication practices (pp. 20–42).

More specifically, the *Handbook of Religion and Communication* divides the material into eight parts. It opens with theoretical material on how scholars have approached the study of communication and religion; the theoretical and theological grounding for religious uses of communication; and overviews of doctrinal discussions of how the major faiths of the world view mass media and, in particular, ethical media conduct. The second part presents reviews of how major religious traditions, including Christianity, Islam, Judaism, Buddhism, Hinduism, Sikhism, traditional African religions, Jainism, and Confucianism, view communication media. The third part shifts the focus to the different kinds of religious communication sponsored by religious groups: broadcasting, televangelism, public relations, crisis communication, and web-based media. Part IV highlights how religious groups also use other media in their pastoral ministry, expressions of piety, and religious education.

The last four parts of the Handbook focus more on media. The essays in Part V look at media institutions facing religion: the mediatization of religion; news coverage of religion; and the views of religion in entertainment media, in film, and in documentary cinema. Part VI offers functional perspectives on the ways in which religious communication serves various religious functions, whether in fostering the social functions of religious belief, creating meaning, celebrating rituals, or marking death. Part VII presents different cultural perspectives, with essays examining religious communication as it interacts with gender and race, material religion, sexuality, authority, and community development. Finally, Part VIII looks at how new media have influenced religious communication.

*

The process of preparing this Handbook suggests a few things about the state of the study of communication and religion. The attempt to include non-Western religions as well as countries in the Global South revealed a general lack of scholarly material. While there are some publications, these have not received the same attention as those addressing other areas of the world. Similarly, much of the published work addresses the Abrahamic faiths – a bias to the West still remains.

Second, the impact of mediatization appears uneven – very strong in the West and in some non-Western countries as Chapter 18 demonstrates, but less so in the periphery or in villages where traditional religions seem untouched by media and depend on face-to-face contact. This indicates some room for continued research and theoretical development.

Third, because the research only reports what appears in the media, we scholars may miss a good deal of activity in communication and religion. If some of the branches of Abrahamic faiths, for example, discourage media use, how do they engage any kind of media and religion? How do nonmediated forms of communication shape these religious communities and individuals? Here Chapter 28 on material religion can offer some guidance.

Finally, we must acknowledge that we remain heirs of the social science tradition in media studies, which still seems hesitant to engage religion unless religion "looks like" material for the social sciences. The area of religion and communication remains comfortable with a sociology of religion perspective, which provides valuable insights and resources for study, but has it missed other approaches to religion? Similarly, our communication heritage has not shaken its origins in Western studies, with US and European perspectives present from the beginning and still exerting powerful influences.

This makes for a promising future since neither communication nor religion will likely disappear. If digital media are any indication, religious institutions and individuals will likely invent new ways to appropriate both old and new communication techniques.

Yoel Cohen
Jerusalem

Paul Soukup
Santa Clara, California

Reference

Lynch, G. (2005). *Understanding theology and popular culture*. Blackwell.

Part I
Theoretical Background

1

Academic Approaches to Communication, Media, and Religion

Lynn Schofield Clark and Heidi Ippolito

Introduction

Today's interdisciplinary research at the intersection of communication, media, and religion draws on several academic fields and traditions. In this chapter we trace the ways that scholars have addressed themselves to foundational questions in this subfield, including: What is religion? What is communication? What is (or are) media, and how are we to understand the processes of mediation? We explore scholarship that has given shape to this interdisciplinary subfield, considering how scholars have grappled with what has been termed *the material turn* and later *the epistemological* and *axiological turns*. We conclude by considering how a dialogue with new perspectives has given rise to new areas of inquiry. We note the particular urgency with which some in the field are now turning to religious, existential, and value-centered questions of communication, media, and technology, in response to the toxicity of the social as well as the physical and material realms. This emergent approach suggests that critical scholarship in this area may be viewed as a crucial foundation for the social and cultural change that is considered necessary for the future of the earth and for humanity itself.

Background to the Field

The story of scholarly inquiry into the fields of communication, media, and religion might be dated to one of the earliest works in the tradition of Western philosophy: that of Titus Lucretius, who, a century before the Common Era, authored an epic poem titled, *De Rerum Natura*: On the Nature of Things. The 7200-line poem, admired by the ancient Roman writers Virgil and Cicero, takes as its focus the explanation of life, the sensations, and the natural world. It develops these explanations through the lens of Epicureanism, a materialist philosophy that favored what today would be termed scientific explanations over supernatural ones. Explanations are at the heart of studies in communication, media, and religion, and over the centuries as these have evolved, so have human understandings of the sciences and the supernatural. In Lucretius's day, although

The Handbook on Religion and Communication, First Edition. Edited by Yoel Cohen and Paul A. Soukup.

divine intervention and references to the gods, Fates, or souls formed the basis for explanations, Lucretius instead emphasized the role of empirical observation, advocating for the gathering of evidence in the development of knowledge and understanding. He also spoke to a concern that remains particularly relevant: the question of how to conceptualize the relationship between human beings and their technologies, understood as materials and tools. Today, scholarship into religion, communication, and media continues to reflect on the relationships between human beings, technological tools, and causal explanations of the cosmos. Lucretius's work thus offers an interesting starting point for the traditions of Western and Eastern scholarship from which today's interdisciplinary studies have grown.

What Lucretius does not address, of course, are the fundamental categories and assumptions that today structure inquiry in this interdisciplinary field. We therefore begin the chapter with a set of definitions, raising the questions of: What is religion? What is communication? What is (or are) media, and how are we to understand the processes of mediation? In order to set the context for the rest of this volume, we describe the debates that currently shape inquiry into each of these areas, noting what is at stake now in complementary fields of inquiry and then considering the questions that are foregrounded through these approaches within the interdisciplinary field of religion, communication, and media.

What Is Religion?

The concept of religion seems to emerge in late antiquity Rome, beginning around the third century CE, approximately 400 years after the origins of Lucretius's writings. The Latin word *religio* did not have a counterpart in other (i.e. non-European) languages. In Hebrew, equivalent concepts refer to ethnicity, religion, or nation. In Southeast Asian cultures, the word *dharma* is a key concept with multiple meanings that have references to the ordering of the universe, cosmic law and order, personal conduct, and proper religious practice. The "three teachings" of Confucianism, Taoism, and later Buddhism are understood as nonexclusive and intertwined with the popular or folk religions related to ancestor rituals that most Chinese citizens practice, even as the government of China officially endorses state atheism. And Ibn Sina's philosophical accounts of God, reality, and Being dominated intellectual thought in the medieval Islamic world, separating the Islamic religious sciences from what were understood as the medicine and rational sciences of the Ancients.

Whereas philosophical systems of thought such as Confucianism, Vedic philosophy, Taoism, Buddhism, Judaism, Platonism, Stoicism, and Zoroastrianism developed long before the Common Era, religion as a particular field of study is generally viewed as a European development related to the specific cultural experience of Christianity and to the consolidation of political and religious authority in the Roman Catholic Church. Christianity became the official religion of the Roman Empire in 380 CE, with religious leaders establishing precepts or laws of the Church. By the fifth century CE, the Christian biblical canons of the Old and New Testaments and select religious practices, laws, and beliefs had been codified and standardized as the laws of the land. In the medieval era, religion, philosophy, and knowledge also came to warrant cultural exchange. During the era characterized as the Islamic Golden Age between the eighth to the fourteenth century CE, scholars from various parts of the Islamic world gathered and translated ancient knowledge into Syriac and Arabic, and translations from Arabic into Latin then informed the philosophies of the medieval Latin world. In that latter context of the Roman Empire, studies of the practices, moral tenets, and scriptures that differed from those of the Christian canon came to be understood as studies of other religions. Today these earliest studies of "other" religions are viewed as reflective of Europe worldviews. Interlocking systems of Christianity, colonialism, and power in Europe, North and South America, and elsewhere in the early Modern world further deepened the Othering of differing cultures, with the ideals of Christianity thus understood as providing justification for conquest, conversion, exploitation, and land theft. In the context of domination by non-Muslim imperial powers, Muslim reform took place in locations such as Indonesia and Malaya as a means of embracing modernism in response to transportation, social mobility, and technological change. These critiques of the roots of religious and specifically of Christian colonialist thought and its relation to systems of power in modernity form the foundation for the current epistemological and axiological turns in studies of media and religion described further later in the chapter.

Several late-nineteenth-century European scholars of religion can be considered particularly foundational in contemporary studies at the intersection of communication, media, and religion. Emile Durkheim, Max Weber, and William James were each less interested in the comparative studies of religion dominant in the travelogs and writings of the time than in how organizational commitments such as those of religion reinforced social cohesion, providing a foundation for studies of the role of media in relation to religious organizations that continues today. In the mid-twentieth century, the work of Mircea Eliade brought together the comparative with concerns of the sacred and profane, introducing scholarship on religion and myth that informed later scholarship on media and myth. And in the shadow of scientific and technological advances, sociologist Peter Berger and others argued that religion and the sacred would wane as the result of a general "disenchantment of the world," an approach that informed religion and media scholarship focused on the role of media in processes of secularization and sacralization. Late-twentieth- and early twenty-first-century scholars such as Jonathan Z. Smith, Talal Asad, Jose Casanova, and Tomoko Masuzawa critiqued much twentieth-century scholarship on religion for its Western academic assumptions, further sowing the seeds for the epistemological and axiological turn in media and religion that we discuss later in the chapter.

Also in the last decades of the twentieth century, the concept of lived religion emerged as feminist scholarship and ethnographic methodologies came to the fore in studies of religion. This strand of scholarship became particularly influential in contemporary discussions of communication, media, and religion in the 1990s and beyond, following the material turn that was taking place across various scholarly fields described later. Often challenging dichotomous categories of the sacred and profane and critiquing the earlier focus on organized religion at the expense of studying the practices of individuals and groups affiliating with religions, the lived religion approach as developed by scholars such as Nancy Ammerman, Robert Orsi, David D. Hall, and Meredith McGuire grounded work in the practices, perspectives, visual cultures, material objects, cultural histories, and lived experiences of those studied.

Debates about the nature and definition of religion remain robust in the field of religious studies. Some scholarship on communication, media, and religion takes established religious organizations and affiliations as a starting point for analysis and some continues to theorize the role of media in social change in relation to processes of secularization and sacralization. Other scholarship considers the relationships between religions and societal myths and political ideologies, and still other scholarship centers on common practices, worldviews, ethics, and geopolitical commitments of individuals or groups who affiliate with religion. Since the turn of the new millennium, scholars interested in religion increasingly have also grappled with critiques of the legacies of colonialism and questions of societal ethics emerging in the wake of heightened environmental disasters, thus also informing a new strand of existential media scholarship related to the epistemological and axiological turn.

Whereas differing strands of thought in the studies of religion were developing particularly in the United States and Europe throughout the late nineteenth and twentieth centuries, many conversations among those in positions of Christian religious leadership at the time focused on concerns about the "secular" nature of popular media. This concern, drawn upon by mid-twentieth-century communication and media scholars, informed some of the earliest studies in the interdisciplinary area of religion, communication, and media as we will see.

What Is Communication?

The field of communication studies itself claims roots in the ancient Greek and Roman traditions of rhetoric and persuasion, as deliberative communication was understood as an essential component of the democratic polis. In the European Middle Ages, drawing on ancient Hebrew and Christian traditions, communication became central to ideas of connection and communion between humans and the divine. Grammar, rhetoric, and logic were foundational for European education during the fourteenth to seventeenth centuries, as was Christianity, and thus a long tradition exists that links studies of rhetoric with homiletics – the study of writing and preaching sermons. In the Islamic world, communication was linked with the concept of *da'wah*, which refers to the preaching of Islam and the call to submit to Allah as well as to the desire to pursue respectful dialogue.

In nineteenth-century European and colonial North and South American writings, communication also was understood largely in relation to human interaction. It was not until World War II that the study of communication coalesced as a field, – and one that at the time was rooted in examinations of the then relatively new broadcast medium of radio. In the shadow of concerns regarding Hitler's use of radio, sociologist Paul Lazarsfeld and political scientist Harold Lasswell conducted influential studies of propaganda, with Lasswell coining the first model that shaped understandings of communication when he raised the question, "Who says what to whom in what channel to what effect?" Lazarsfeld developed a large research program and oversaw the production of a series of publications that became influential in the field, including his *Personal Influence* (Katz & Lazarsfeld, 1955), which was foundational for what was to become known as the media effects tradition. Communication was thus defined in the early to mid-century United States in relation to information exchange, persuasion, media effects, and public opinion; research that is today considered foundational to the Western field of communication studies as it is traditionally concerned with the relationship between information and the functioning of Western democratic society. State-run or government- and self-censored communication media outlets remain the norm in many countries around the world, including in North Korea, Eritrea, Saudi Arabia, Ethiopia, Azerbaijan, Vietnam, Iran, Myanmar, Cuba, and Russia. In such contexts, studies of communication and media have been tightly related to state aims. Approaching communication as a potential tool for political, social, and economic development, therefore, has been an idea exported from the West to places throughout Latin America, Africa, and Asia, along with technologies, capitalism, democracy, and ideas of progress. Such work would come to be critiqued in the neo-Marxist scholarship of the 1960s,1970s, and 1980s, as formerly colonized nations fought for independence from asymmetrical power relations. In the 1980s, 1990s, and early in the new millennium, communication scholars began to reject the dichotomous assumptions of cultural imperialism, favoring instead terms such as globalization and cultural hybridity. In the West, ideas of hegemony and consent came to the fore in communication and cultural studies beginning in the 1960s, and concepts of propaganda gave way to concerns with spaces for resistance and spaces of dominance.

By the 1960s, in part due to specialization of research in US university and institutional settings, the study of interpersonal communication emerged as a field separate from the study of what was then known as mass communication. Drawing on earlier work in persuasion and on humanistic approaches within the field of psychology, scholars primarily in the United States, Europe, and Australia began studying relationships, social interaction, and the human desire for uncertainty reduction. When feminist standpoint theory developed in the 1980s, with its claim that the social groups with which people are affiliated significantly shape knowledge and understanding, it significantly shaped the field of communication studies. With its attention to a Marxist critique of patriarchal theories and of systemic oppressions that devalue women's ways of knowing, this approach further informed developments in related interdisciplinary areas of critical race and queer theory, which in turn added critiques to performance studies and intercultural communication, each of which is recognized as a subfield in communication studies.

Whereas much of mainstream communication studies had focused on development and democracy at the mid-century with the utilization of social scientific methods, the subfield of interpersonal communication studies followed a humanistic path, described by communication scholar John Durham Peters (2001) as the project of reconciling self and other. Yet Peters also argued provocatively that the study of interpersonal communication was not different from that of mass communication in that in both instances there may be invisible, absent, or misunderstood audiences. Peters and other communication scholars have suggested that communication scholarship must continue to navigate the blurred lines between public and private, self and other, digital and analog, virtual and material, machine and human, even if the dust never settles on where these lines are drawn.

What Is Media?

In the US context, concerns with the technologies of communication had first arisen in relation to desires for heightened efficiencies. Seeking to assist US engineers in performing their jobs at the Bell Telephone company, mathematician Claude Shannon and scientist Warren Weaver in 1948 proposed that human communication can be broken into six components: sender, encoder, channel, noise, decoder, and receiver – an approach that remains influential in some fields but is critiqued as failing to take the contexts of communication into consideration.

As Shannon and Weaver's information exchange model of communication flourished in the mid-twentieth-century United States and defined media as a term largely interchangeable with the electronic communication technologies of radio and then television, different traditions were developing elsewhere. In Europe, a group of scholars and dissidents who came to be known as the Frankfurt School had been working in the shadow of the emergent capitalist, fascist, and socialist systems of the 1930s. Due to their sense that social theory and social scientific approaches were inadequate for the moment, they explored semiotic, socio-cultural, and critical traditions. With their studies of commercial culture and the culture industries, as Theodor Adorno termed them, these scholars, including Max Horkheimer, Ernst Bloch, Erich Fromm, Walter Benjamin, and Herbert Marcuse, offered scathing critiques of the relationships between antisemitism, authoritarianism, and capitalism. In contrast to the US tendency to understand media as technologies responsible for transporting messages, European and Latin American scholars approached media and technologies as welded to capitalist and dominant ideological systems. Their critiques of dominant capitalist culture were taken up by the European, Latin American, and US New Left in the 1960s and 1970s, as scholars and activists supported civil and political rights, feminism and gay rights, and protested the Vietnam War. In the East, however, scholars of the 1980s and 1990s began to develop the Islamicization of communication theory, centering ideas of *da'wah* and embracing a "prophetic science" that sought to uphold the relationships between humans and Allah while also foregrounding ethical concerns related to media effects and specifically to Western imperialism and commercialization. Islamic communication theories, and Asian communication theories as well, have been particularly concerned with countering the dominance of Western media systems while also seeking to reclaim the philosophical heritage of Eastern and Islamic thinking that has given shape to Western scientific and intellectual traditions.

With television as the dominant medium of concern at mid-century, studies of the media had come to be structured in relation to three categories: media texts, media producers, and media audiences. In the 1970s and 1980s, theorists began unpacking the relations between these categories, again focusing on media as interlocking processes of culture rather than as distinct contexts. In the UK, cultural theorists and historians Raymond Williams, Richard Hoggart, and Stuart Hall theorized the relationship between culture, power, and the elite, fascinated with the idea of popular culture as a site of struggle and of negotiation. Their work gave rise to the tradition known as cultural studies that explores the ways that political, economic, and social forces converge, are given shape, and are interpreted in relation to technologies, practices, and messages of the media. Stuart Hall credited feminist scholarship with a key shift in cultural studies, moving studies toward a closer examination of the everyday. This initiated a rethinking of how power functioned, encouraging scholars to examine the connections between what happened in the private and public realms.

In Latin America, Jesús Martín-Barbero (1992) focused on the ways some media audiences gave voice to their own local concerns, challenging the power of the international media industries. Criticizing Latin American universities for their adoption of the development assumptions of the North and West, Martín-Barbero argued for a shift in media studies from a focus on the technologies of the media to social processes: from the media to *mediations*, as the subtitle of his most renowned book phrases it. In Latin America, and also in Europe, mediation came to refer to the processes through which social production and reproduction occur, and directed scholarly attention to the networks of technologies, social actors, and technological protocols that served as the interface for these processes. An approach of mediation encouraged communication scholars to consider communication processes in relation to social movements, meanings, and collective cultural practices.

In Canada, the 1960s and 1970s saw the rise of a different tradition that challenged the information model of communication. Marshall McLuhan (1964) famously argued that the medium is the message, drawing attention to the ways that the technologies do not transparently transmit messages, but rather mediate, or give shape to and transform them. Although McLuhan's ideas achieved popular success and were quite influential in the field of education, they did not find much resonance outside the scholarly contexts of North American communication and media studies, as they were viewed as apolitical. By the first decade of the twenty-first century, however, the media landscape was undergoing drastic changes, both with the emergence of Google, Facebook, Apple, Amazon, and Netflix as primary distributors of media content (including user-generated content), and the US relaxed regulation environment that had led to the explosion of talk radio and the consolidation of radio and television interests along increasingly polarized lines. At that time, questions of immersion in a media ecology, drawing upon McLuhan, Neil Postman (1985), and others, gained traction once again. As the term "media" no longer served as a proxy for broadcast television and radio, new debates arose around whether or not the rise of mass forms of communication in conjunction with modernity had changed societies via processes of what European scholars Fredrich Krotz, Andrea Hepp (2012), Knut Lundby (2014), and Stig Hjarvard (2013) had theorized as *mediatization*. Studies of mediation have focused on the ways in which meaning is mediated, sometimes, but not only, via technologies. In contrast, studies of mediatization focus on the ways that the logics and prerogatives of differing (but particularly the broadcast) media industries have become entwined with and influence other institutions of society.

Media and the Digital Turn

By the first decade of the second millennium, the social media platforms of Facebook, Twitter, YouTube, and later Instagram and TikTok, had become vital sites for the rise of user-generated content. Whereas early writings on social media and the Internet, such as the influential scholarly work of Manuel Castells and the popular works of Clay Shirky and Howard Rheingold, were sometimes utopian in tone and celebrated the plurality of expressions present online, others in media studies, with its long tradition of analyzing the media industries and their relation to other societal systems of power, began to question the extent to which new platforms ushered in new power relations. Jose van Dijck's (2013) historical analysis of Facebook, Twitter, Flickr, YouTube, and Wikipedia revealed the ways that the owners of these platforms purported to embrace free expression and democratic values while their business practices instead favored profits and diminished transparency. Other works on "platformization" explore the ways that new platforms increasingly broker distribution and thereby change relationships of work, leisure, time, and the flow of commerce. Studies by Amanda Lotz (2018, 2022) and Mareike Jenner (2018) focus on the rising popularity and influence of entertainment-based streaming services like Netflix, Amazon Prime, and Hulu, noting that whereas once content distribution was dictated by structured time slots and advertising incentives, television has shifted to an unstructured format, shedding traditional legacy practices and embracing streaming service platforms. Likewise, the film industry has had to shift attention to include digital downloads alongside theatrical box office numbers. Meanwhile, YouTube and TikTok have emerged as dominant distribution channels of user-generated content, particularly among younger audiences.

In these new spaces, content finds new audiences, and cultural storytelling shifts from the dominant lowest-common-denominator approach to niche-style delivery. Those in media studies observed that just as virtual spaces cater to individual users, the stories that gain popularity on Netflix are able to reach both wide and niche audiences. Moreover, content now travels across a variety of platforms, garnering audiences, and generating profits as part of what scholar Henry Jenkins (2006) refers to as *convergence culture*.

Religion, Communication, and Media Studies

It was in the 1970s that both US and European scholars in communication first began to identify studies of communication, media, and religion as a subfield, with some drawing connections between their work and the nineteenth-century scholars who had studied religion and society before them. Also in the 1970s and 1980s in the United States and Europe, several scholars within Christian traditions were taking up the challenge of exploring the role of media, and specifically television, on Christianity and on Christian faith communities. At the time, Christian religious leaders were voicing concerns that echoed those of secularization and profane culture, sometimes placing concerns in the then widely accepted framework of media effects. In the mid-1960s, French philosopher Jacques Ellul had argued that modern communication technologies created a threat to both religion and to human freedom. In 1971, the Catholic Church issued its first pastoral instruction that centered on social communication. Titled *Communio et Progressio: On the means of social communication* and written by the order of the Second Vatican Council, the document set out to delineate the proper use of communication in a manner that would support "the unity and brotherhood of man," proposing that the incarnation – a term that refers to the belief that God sent his son Jesus to earth – should be understood as God's *communication* with humans.

The document speaks of access to information – to inform and to be informed – as a human right. Drawing on these ideas, French Catholic religious educator Pierre Babin (1978) placed Catholic religious formation in dialogue with McLuhan's work, seeking to leverage what he termed the audiovisual language in his efforts to make the catechism relevant for young people (Babin & McLuhan, 1978). Walter Ong (1982), a student of McLuhan's and also a Catholic, explored the transition from orality to literacy and the effect of this on human consciousness while also considering the various effects of technology on the Christian Church. United Methodist minister and professor of theology William Fore (1970), also responding to both Ellul's and McLuhan's thought, wrote an early history of religion on television in the late 1970s. Whereas he offered critiques of television's violent and sexual content, art historian Gregor Goethals (1981, 1990) offered her visual analyses suggesting that television was largely at odds with Christianity, themes later picked up in the work of Christian scholars William Romanowski (1996, 2002) and Quentin Schultze (1991, 2003).

The work of US communication scholar James Carey (1989) was to become particularly influential for scholars working in communication, media, and religion who sought to challenge the dominant paradigms of McLuhan's sweeping view, Ellul's pessimism, and the behavioral focus within the school of media effects. Carey's interest in the mythic dimensions of media had led him in the late 1970s to synthesize the work of religious scholar Mircea Eliade, anthropologist Clifford Geertz, and German philosopher Ernst Cassirer, who had argued that humans are *animal symbolicum*, or symbol-creators. UK scholar Roger Silverstone (1981) also drew upon Eliade's observations regarding myths in the late 1970s and 1980s, noting that myths have always been communicated through dramatic storytelling, which is the primary form for film and television, and thus, television and film inevitably communicate mythic themes. In the 1990s, theologians Frances Ford Plude and Mary Hess, among others, built on these themes as a means of developing what Plude termed a *communication theology* and what Hess integrated into innovations in Christian education.

As noted earlier, the emergence of feminist theory as well as queer and critical race theories had shaped studies of both media and religion beginning in the 1960s and 1970s. Feminism's influence in religious studies led to an examination of bodies, material practices, and intersectionalities in identity, much as feminism did in media studies. Yet at the time, many scholars in communication and media studies embraced critiques of religion as patriarchal. Following Freud, Althusser, and the Frankfurt School theorists, such scholars understood religion as regressive and inherently conservative. This contributed to a marked scholarly indifference toward religion, which was almost universally equated by these scholars with Christianity.

Nevertheless, in the 1980s and 1990s, several scholars drew upon critical media traditions to examine the phenomena of televangelism. Australian Peter Horsfield and American scholars Stewart Hoover and Quentin Schultze each wrote early and influential studies of the commercial, religious, and political roles of these cultural phenomena, situating them in relation to debates of secularization. Hoover, following other American media scholars such as Judith Buddenbaum, also focused on coverage of religion in the US news media and, building on the insights of Geertz and Carey, explored the ways that media industries inadvertently challenged religious authority in the definition of meaning and myth for religious adherents. Disputing both the universalizing approach to religion and the secularization hypothesis, Hoover (1984, 2006), along with Horsfield (1984, 2015) in Australia, Knut Lundby (1987, 2021) in Norway, and Alf Linderman (1997) in Sweden, worked across the fields of religious studies and media studies to bring the fields into conversation with one another in the late 1980s through the early 2000s (see also Hoover & Lundby, 1997). Others were also working in this new interdisciplinary space at the intersection of media studies, religious studies, and cultural studies, notably media and cultural studies scholar Marie Gillespie (1995) in her work on the reception of Hindi television among South Asians in London, and American religious historians David Morgan (1997, 2005) in his work on popular religious imagery and Colleen McDannell (1995) on lived religion and popular domestic culture. In the late 1990s and early 2000s, several European and North American anthropologists and scholars adopting anthropological methods also focused attention on the intersections of lived religion, narrative, and commercial media. In the field of anthropology, Faye Ginsburg (1998) explored the coverage of religion and the abortion debate in the United States, while Birgit Meyer (2009) focused on film, modernity, and popular religious belief in Ghana; Arvind Rajagopal (2001) explored television and Hindu nationalism; and Lila Abu-Lughod (1997) analyzed Egyptian women and politics in relation to television and religious and cultural practices. In communication and media studies, Rosalind Hackett (1998) considered media and new religious movements in Nigeria; Lynn Schofield Clark (2003) focused on popular culture and the formation of religious and non-religious identity among US adolescents; Mia Lovheim (2011) explored young people, nascent digital media practices, and belief in Sweden; Mara Einstein (2008) considered the relationships between religious groups and brand culture; and Purnima Mankekar (1999) analyzed television, womanhood, and postcolonial India. In the sociology of religion, Wade Clark Roof (2001), Robert Wuthnow (1996), Nancy Ammerman (2014), and Robert Bellah (1967) gave attention to the role of media and narrative in religious and national identity or civil religion. And in religious studies, Gordon Lynch (2005), Johanna Sumiala (2006), Christopher Partridge (2006), and others challenged ideas of Western society as secular, developing theories that grappled with the roles that technologies played in processes of sacralization while exploring emergent rituals and rites associated with human life and with death.

Religion, Communication, and Media: The Material Turn

The influence of anthropological attention to the everyday across a variety of fields was thus in alignment with a broader *material turn* in the humanities and social sciences away from postmodernism's crisis of representation and toward an enhanced interest in the role of objects, and by extension the role of popular culture, in signification and in everyday life. This turn invited further understanding across various religious traditions as well as deeper connections between religions and how they are created, practiced, communicated (mediated), and re-mediated. Scholars noted earlier as well as S. Brent Plate, Manuel Vásquez, Jessica Moberg, and others teased out the material dimension of religions, exploring how beliefs intermingle with rituals, objects, senses, spaces, and bodily experiences. Challenging an understanding of material bodies, technological tools, and other modes of mediation as *separate from* or merely *used by* religious practitioners, these material aspects of life came to be seen as *co-creators* with religion. In this sense, concepts earlier associated with media studies, including the concept of mediation, came to have influence in a rethinking of religions and religious practices. According to Meyer's (2009) theory of mediation, people encounter the transcendental through technologically mediated sensational forms. In other words, particular forms of media change over time, but the experiential dimension of religious phenomena remains constant. Similarly, Plate's (2014) book *History of Religion in 5 ½ Objects* traces religious history and definitions through seemingly everyday objects, teasing out the agentive relationship between objects and those who make, use, possess, caress, and taste them. Human bodies also become sites for defining religion, with scholars such as Angela Zito (1997) pointing to Chinese traditions of the body as medium for sacrifice and performance and others working through affect theory, new materialism, and tattoo and body modification studies.

In the 1970s, scholar of religion Jonathan Z. Smith (1975) first linked the material and techno-logical aspects of canonization with industrial modes of production, calling attention to the cor-porate and industrial aspects of religious material mediation. This is echoed by historians of religion at the end of the millennium who turned attention to the emergence of the book as a material object and the role of religion in the rise of both the commercial press and of literacy. In religious studies, Manuel Vásquez (1998, 2010) in El Salvador and David Chidester (2005) in South Africa, and, in the United States, Diane Winston (2000, 2009), Thomas Tweed (1997), Robert Orsi (2010), S. Brent Plate (2005, 2017), Sarah Pike (2001), and Jane Iwamura (2011) con-sidered the roles of popular culture and popular religion in collective religious identities and practices. The material turn incorporates conversations about individuals, industries, belief, materiality, and changes in technology. With the material turn, as well as the turn toward the digital in media studies, the question of "How are audiences using media and practicing reli-gion?" was adjusted to become "How do the material aspects of media affect their use?" Heidi Campbell's (2005) formative work on the use of communication technologies among differing religious communities led to her analysis of the religio-social shaping of technology, while Gary Bunt's (2003, 2009) analyses of online fatwas and E-Jihad and Chris Helland's (2000) categoriza-tions of "online religion" and "religion online" each laid the groundwork for others to consider how religious institutions and individual practitioners translated rituals and fostered community online. Video games and later social media became central to studies of digital Hinduism and digital Buddhism, with work by Kerstin Radde-Antweiler and Xenia Zeller (2018) as well as Dheepa Sundaram (2019) providing insights. Jeremy Stolow's (2019) historical contextualization of how technologies have been understood in relation to varied religious practices brought media and material history studies into conversation with one another, while scholars in North and South America, northern and southern Europe, Australia, South America, the Middle East, Africa and Asia explored social media practices in relation to ideas of religious identity, community, and authority.

Decolonizing Religion, Communication, and Media: The Epistemological and Axiological Turns

Questions of what it means to be human closely relate to questions of epistemology, or of how we know what we think we know. The first epistemological turn took place in the seventeenth century as Rene Descartes, Thomas Hobbes, Blaise Pascal, and later Immanuel Kant rejected divine explanations and favored scientific ones, ushering in empirical study and following in the earlier footsteps of Lucretius, as noted at the beginning of this chapter. In the last decades of the twentieth century and the beginning of the twenty-first, scholars across a range of fields began to grapple with the colonial and imperialist contexts that have shaped the epistemologies of Western rational thought. This in turn has raised axiological concerns, or concerns with both the goodness and worth of human actions and with the evaluation not of how societal arrangements are but of how they ought to be.

Research, as Indigenous scholar of the Maori Linda Tuhiwai Smith (2021) has argued, is inex-tricably linked to European imperialism and colonialism. This is because, as Peruvian sociologist Aníbal Quijano (2000) and Argentinian semiotician Walter Mignolo (2007) have observed, racism is the only way to explain the justifications given for the economic and political subordination of Indigenous people by Europeans that began with the colonial relations of the sixteenth century, extended through the enslavement of Africans, and continues to exist today. Such relations of subjugation and colonization have long-term negative psychological effects, as French West

Indian political philosopher Frantz Fanon (2008) noted in 1952. Not only were Black people dismissed by whites, Fanon argued, but they also felt themselves inferior, and thus both groups have discounted the knowledge rooted in the Black lived experience. Scholars such as Kenya's Ngũgĩ wa Thiong'o (1992) built on Fanon's work, calling for a decolonizing of the mind, and Fanon is considered a key figure in the legal school of thought known as critical race theory that criticizes all US laws as implicated in maintaining white supremacist systems of power relations.

Inspired by Michelle Alexander's (2010) work comparing our current prison system in the United States with the Jim Crow-Era laws that kept Black Americans subjugated, sociologists and media scholars Safiya Umoja Noble (2018) and Ruha Benjamin (2019) have argued that communication technologies, while appearing neutral, are in actuality deepening, and hiding, racial discrimination and systemic oppression. Biases are coded into algorithms and in fact into all aspects of technology, as evidenced in the ways that search engines, facial recognition software, smart devices, and virtual assistants are imagined and deployed. Discrimination is the default, these and other scholars argue, and thus what poses as technological benevolence must be questioned, and justice must be reimagined.

Thus scholarship at the intersection of communication, media, and religion in the beginning of the third millennium increasingly focused on media and religious systems in relation to power and governance, as exemplified in work such as Andrea Stanton's (2013) analysis of the role of government-sponsored radio in shaping Arab political and social life in the context of British colonialism; Pradip Thomas's (2010) focus on questions of secularism and the limitations to freedom of thought in India; Rianne Subijanto's (2011) studies of media resistance to Dutch East Indies imperialism (now Indonesia) and Merlyna Lim's (2012, 2017) explorations of the more recent rise of hate and nationalism in Indonesia; Mona Abdel-Fadil's (2019) studies of the ways that Muslim and Christian conflicts on Facebook strengthen in-group bonds; Marwan Kraidy's (2017) examination of the Islamic State's image warfare along with Carol Winkler and Kareem El Damanhoury's (2022) examination of the relationships between Jihad magazines and radicalization; and works by Kristin Peterson (2022), Ruth Tsuria (2017), Evelina Lundmark (2017), Giulia Evolvi (2019), and others who have focused on religious-informed activism and resistance in personal and in public spaces. The once-optimistic approaches to communication technologies in the service of democracy and enhanced human understanding have given way to concerns regarding disinformation campaigns that deepen societal distrust and may feed radicalization.

The axiological is also the focus of concern in the work of Kevin Healey and Bob Woods (2020), who have evoked a "prophetic imagination" and "resistance thinking" to critique the rising corporate and technological powers of Silicon Valley that envision themselves as benevolent custodians of a techno-utopic future. Healey and Woods draw upon both Buddhism's focus on personal transformation and the Judeo-Christian concern for social justice, issuing a collective call for civic mindfulness and for the humane design of emerging technologies. Noting that the prophetic language is related to Christian as well as Buddhist frameworks, they look at what it means to have ethical media, particularly in an age when the issue of trust looms large, especially in relation to religious, governmental, and corporate authority.

Amanda Lagerkvist's (2018) edited volume, *Digital Existence: Ontology, Ethics and Transcendence in Digital Culture*, has moved the axiological discussions of ethics forward in additional ways. Tracing the philosophical roots of Søren Kierkegaard, Martin Heidegger, and Hannah Arendt to frame current existential *conditions, experiences*, and *strivings* of digital culture, Lagerkvist asks whether we use and make tools or whether we emerge through and are mutually co-constituted by our tools. Her discussion of *existential experiences* relates digital meaning-making and shared vulnerability to what Heidegger calls "the thrownness" as well as Kierkegaard's description of the groundlessness of our existence. How, she asks, are scholars to think about ethics within virtual realms that alter traditional experiences of time and space into a sensation of "groundlessness"?

Amit Pinchevski's (2019) work on the relationship between media and trauma is equally provocative. He is interested in how both images of trauma and the words used to describe those images such as "flashes" and "burned in" are more than metaphors and figures of speech but rather provide "epistemological scaffolding." This scaffolding, in turn, may provide the keys to unlocking affective responses that lead to healing. Whereas this work may be understood in relation to the axiological turn, other scholarship, such as Gregory Grieve's (2014) work on Buddhist meditation apps and Jin Park's (2016) attention to discourses of healing in Korean television, similarly address a widened sphere of healing as part of the existential experience of what it means to be human.

Such work becomes particularly important in the contemporary context that sees people in various contexts leaving traditional organized religion. As Finnish scholar Teemu Taira (2019) has argued, as stories of such departures become more commonplace in fictional content as well as in personal digital spaces, it becomes easier for the non-religious to find ways to live comfortably in what are in many places still largely religious societies.

At the same time, in the midst of heightened awareness of the effects of climate change, including displacement, forced migration, and continued health crises, future scholarship in the area of religion, communication, and media can be expected to continue to grapple not only with how the field's key terms are understood, but with what those terms imply in the context of a world increasingly focused on questions not of religion's but of humanity's continued existence.

Conclusion

This chapter opened the conversation of interdisciplinary studies of religion, communication, and media with a discussion of definitions and of questions at the intersection of these fields. In the chapters that follow, scholars explore each of these areas in greater depth in an effort to address the subfield's need for more attention to voices and experiences emerging from outside the Western and Christian contexts that have largely shaped scholarship to date.

Today, debates in the fields of communication and media focus on whether communication might be studied scientifically in relation to message and information exchange and comprehension, and/or how the study of literary and other forms of communication demand an understanding of the ideological and political systems in which they are embedded. Scholarship on communication and media is also concerned with issues of transparency, privacy, memory, and the ownership of information, as well as with debates about the role of narrative and voice in democratic processes and the authenticity of communication messages in the context of an ever-more encapsulating commercial culture. Communication and media scholars are interested in issues of difference, conflict, and contestation, particularly as these play out in rational and agonistic publics as well as in authoritarian and nondemocratic settings. This becomes even more crucial as nationalism and fascism continue to rise globally. In the wake of the continued rise of populism around the world, scholarship in media, religion, and culture turned to explorations of religious nationalism, with scholars exploring the intersections of political and religious ideologies and their roles in the rise of misinformation and disinformation circulated for political influence. As local populist factions blossomed into national movements with the help of algorithms and mysterious black box regulations from Facebook, Twitter, and YouTube, conspiratorial ideas emerge from niche corners of the Internet and are given acknowledgment and legitimacy by mainstream news outlets. Scholarship in media, religion, and communication is now turning to the ways that fears surrounding immigration, mass shootings, pandemics, masks, and vaccines are inflamed by social media sharing, pushing online conversations into in-person spaces with near-religious fervor.

We conclude this chapter by observing that a key question that promises to shape research in the area of religion, communication, and media is this: Is communication a *human right?* And what does it mean to protect that human right in the contemporary era? Communication is named as a human right in the Universal Declaration of Human Rights (UDHR), first adopted by the United Nations in 1947. The UDHR commits nations to recognizing all humans as "born free and equal in dignity and rights." Article 19 of the UDHR states that everyone "has a right to freedom of opinion and expression," including the right to "seek, receive and impart information and ideas through any media regardless of frontiers." As noted early, the Pontifical Council for Social Communication (1971) similarly affirmed a human right to information. As communication technology evolves, our *access* to these technologies and to technologies that allow muted voices to be heard must also evolve in equitable ways. And as our offline and online lives become more interconnected, hindrances that limit access to information and to the ability to share information become human rights concerns.

The question of communication as a human right, as well as the turn to the material and to the axiological, give rise to new questions: How do we navigate justice and morality amidst increasingly splintered online environments? What is lost as individual opinions and perspectives take the place of the public and the collective? How are communication rights related to other basic human needs that are increasingly threatened in an era of rapid climate change, globalization, and heightened inequities?

Finally, in media studies and in related fields, the material and axiological turns in the contexts of intensified globalization and heightened climate change have led to a focus on the consequences of technological materiality. This in turn has brought attention to aging infrastructures and to the physical impact of commercial excesses, waste, and technological detritus, all of which belie earlier assumptions of "clean" technologies that could be designed for efficiency with little to no cost to humans or nature. As the global Covid-19 pandemic challenged institutions, governments, and businesses to adjust creatively to remote work, it also exposed deep inequities and disconnects in health care, supply chain issues, migration patterns, and the costs of essential work. Such concerns have spurred a renewed interest in the relationships between technological tools and what it means to be human, particularly in the shadow of accelerated artificial intelligence. Now, perhaps more than ever, there is an urgent need for a more holistic account of the interdependence between humans, technologies, and the natural world in which we live.

References

Abdel-Fadel, M. (2019). The politics of affect: The glue of religion and identity in social media. *Journal of religion, media and digital culture, 8*(1), 11–34.

Abu-Lughod, L. (1997). The interpretation of culture(s) after television. *Representations, 59,* 109–134. https://doi.org/10.2307/2928817

Alexander, M. (2010). *The new Jim Crow: Mass incarceration in the age of colorblindness.* New Press.

Ammerman, N. T. (2014). Finding religion in everyday life. *Sociology of Religion, 75*(2), 189–207. https://doi.org/10.1093/socrel/sru013

Babin, P., & McLuhan, M. (1978). *Autre homme, autre chrétien à l'âge électronique.* Editons du Chalet.

Bellah, R. N. (1967). Civil religion in America. *Daedalus, 96*(1), 1–21. https://doi.org/10.1162/001152605774431464

Benjamin, R. (2019). *Race after technology: Abolitionist tools for the new Jim Code.* Polity.

Bunt, G. (2003). *Islam in the digital age: E-jihad, online fatwas and cyber Islamic environments.* Pluto Press.

Bunt, G. (2009). *iMuslims: Rewiring the house of Islam.* University of North Carolina Press.

Campbell, H. (2005). *Exploring religious community online: We are one in the network.* Peter Lang.

Carey, J. W. (1989). *Communication as culture: Essays on media and society.* Unwin Hymay.

Chidester, D. (2005). *Authentic fakes: Religion and American popular culture*. University of California Press.

Clark, L. S. (2003). *From angels to aliens: Teenagers, the media, and the supernatural*. Oxford University Press.

Einstein, M. (2008). *Brands of faith: Marketing religion in a commercial age*. Routledge.

Fanon, F. (1952/2008). *Black skin, white masks*. Grove Press.

Fore, W. F. (1970). *Image and impact: How man comes through in the mass media*. Friendship Press.

Gillespie, M. (1995). *Television, ethnicity and cultural change*. Routledge.

Ginsburg, F. (1998) *Contested lives: The abortion debate in an American community*. University of California Press.

Goethals, G. (1981). *The TV ritual: Worship at the video altar*. Beacon Press.

Goethals, G. (1990). *The electronic golden calf: Images, religion, and the making of meaning*. Cowley.

Grieve, G. (2014). *Buddhism, the internet, and digital media: The pixel in the lotus*. Routledge.

Hackett, R. I. J. (1998). Charismatic/Pentecostal appropriation of media technologies in Nigeria and Ghana. *Journal of Religion in Africa, 28*(3), 258–277.

Healey, K., & Woods, R. (2020). *Ethics and religion in the age of social media: Digital proverbs for responsible citizens*. Taylor & Francis

Helland, C. (2000). Online religion/religion online and virtual communitas. In J. K. Hadden, & D. E. Cowan (Eds.), *Religion on the internet: Research prospects and promises* (pp. 205–224). JAI Press.

Hepp, A. (2012). *Cultures of mediatization*. Polity Press.

Herbert, D. E. J., Greenhill, A., & Gillespie, M. (Eds.). (2013). *Social media, religion, and spirituality*. Walter de Gruyter.

Hjarvard, S. (2013). *The mediatization of culture and society*. Routledge.

Hoover, S. M. (2006). *Religion in the media age*. Routledge.

Hoover, S. M., & Lundby, K. (1997). *Rethinking media, religion, and culture*. Sage Publications.

Horsfield, P. (1984). *Religious television: The American experience*. Longman.

Horsfield, P. (2015). *From Jesus to the internet: A history of Christianity and media*. Wiley & Sons.

Iwamura, J. (2011). *Virtual orientalism: Asian religions and American popular culture*. Oxford University Press.

Jenkins, H. (2006). *Convergence culture: Where old and new media collide*. New York University Press.

Jenner, M. (2018). *Netflix and the re-invention of television*. Palgrave Macmillan.

Katz, E., & Lazarsfeld, P. (1955). *Personal influence: The part played by people in the flow of mass communications*. The Free Press.

Kraidy, M. (2017). The projectilic image: Islamic State's digital visual warfare and global networked affect. *Media, Culture & Society, 39*(8), 1194–1209.

Lagerkvist, A. (Ed.). (2018). *Digital existence: Ontology, ethics and transcendence in digital culture*. Routledge.

Lim, M. (2012). Life is local in the imagined global community: Islam and politics in the Indonesian blogosphere. *Journal of Media and Religion, 11*(3), 127–140.

Lim, M. (2017). Freedom to hate: Social media, algorithmic enclaves, and the rise of tribal nationalism in Indonesia. *Critical Asian Studies, 49*(3), 411–427.

Lindeman, A. (1997). Making sense of religion in television. In S. M. Hoover, & K. Lundby (Eds.), *Rethinking media, religion, and culture* (pp. 263–281). Sage.

Lotz, A. (2018). *We now disrupt this broadcast: How cable transformed television and the internet revolutionized it all*. MIT Press.

Lotz, A. (2022). *Netflix and streaming video: The business of subscriber-funded video on demand*. Polity.

Lovheim, M. (2011). *Personal and popular: The case of young Swedish female top bloggers*. Uppsala University.

Lundby, K. (1987). The collectivity of faith. A sociological study of processes of dissolution in the Norwegian folk church. DPhil Thesis, University of Oslo.

Lundby, K. (Ed.). (2014). *Mediatization of communication*. De Gruyter Mouton.

Lundmark, E. (2017). This is the face of an atheist: Performing private truths in precarious publics. PhD Dissertation, Uppsala University.

Lundmark, E. (2021). *Religion I medienes grep: medialisering I Norge*. Universitetsforlaget.

Lynch, G. (2005). *Understanding theology and popular culture*. Blackwell.

Mankekar, P. (1999). *Screening culture, viewing politics: An ethnography of television, womanhood, and nation in postcolonial India*. Duke University Press.

Martín-Barbero, J. (1992). *Communication, culture, and hegemony*. Sage.

McDannell, C. (1995). *Material Christianity*. Yale University Press.

McLuhan, H. M. (1964). *Understanding media: The extensions of man*. McGraw Hill.

Meyer, B. (Ed.). (2009). *Aesthetic formation – Media, religion and the senses*. Palgrave Macmillan.

Mignolo, W. D. (2007). Introduction: Coloniality of power and de-colonial thinking. *Cultural Studies*, *21*(2–3), 155–167. https://doi.org/10.1080/09502380601162498

Morgan, D. (1997). *Visual piety*. University of California Press.

Morgan, D. (2005). *The sacred gaze*. University of California Press.

Noble, S. U. (2018). *Algorithms of oppression: How search engines reinforce racism*. New York University Press.

Ong, W. J. (1982). *Orality and literacy: The technologizing of the work*. Methuen.

Orsi, R. (2010). *The Madonna of 115th street: Faith and community in Italian Harlem, 1880–1950*. Yale University Press.

Park, J. (2016). Healed to imagine: Healing discourse in Korean popular culture and its politics. *Culture and Religion*, *17*(4), 375–391.

Pike, S. (2001). *Earthly bodies, magical selves*. DeGruyter.

Partridge, C. (2006). *The re-enchantment of the West: Alternative spiritualities, sacralization, popular culture and occulture* (2 Vols.). T & T Clark Publishers.

Peters, J. D. (2001). *Speaking into the air: A history of the idea of communication*. The University of Chicago Press.

Pinchevski, A. (2019). *Transmitted wounds: Media and the mediation of trauma*. Oxford University Press.

Plate, B. (2005) *Walter Benjamin, religion and aesthetics: rethinking religion through the arts*. Routledge.

Plate, B. (2017). *Religion and film: Cinema and the re-creation of the world*. Columbia University Press.

Plate, S. B. (2014). *History of religion in 5 ½ objects: Bringing the spiritual to its senses*. Beacon Press.

Pontifical Council for Social Communication (1971). *Communio et progressio*: On the means of social communication. Vatican. Retrieved May 10, 2022, from https://www.vatican.va/roman_curia/pontifical_councils/pccs/documents/rc_pc_pccs_doc_23051971_communio_en.html

Postman, N. (1985). *Amusing ourselves to death: Public discourse in the age of show business*. Penguin.

Quijano, A. (2000). Coloniality of power, Eurocentrism, and Latin America. *Nepantla: Views from the South*, *1*(3), 533–580.

Radde-Antweiler, K. and Zeller, X. (2018). *Mediatized religion in Asia: Studies on digital media and religion*. Routledge.

Rajagopal, A. (2001). *Politics after television: Religious nationalism and the reshaping of the India public*. Cambridge University Press.

Romanowski, W. (1996). *Pop culture wars: Religion and the role of entertainment in American life*. InterVarsity Press.

Romanowski, W. (2002). *Eyes wide open: Looking for God in popular culture*. Brazos Press.

Roof, W. C. (2001). *Spiritual marketplace: Baby boomers and the remaking of American religion*. Princeton University Press.

Schultze, Q. J. (2003). *Televangelism and American religion: The business of popular religion*. Wipf and Stock.

Schultze, Q. J., Anker, R. M., Bratt, J. D., Schultze, Q., Zuidervaart, L., & Worst, J. (1991). *Dancing in the dark: Youth, popular culture, and the electronic media*. Wm Eerdmans Publishing.

Smith, J. (1975). *Map is not territory: Studies in the history of religions*. University of Chicago Press.

Stanton, A. (2013). *This is Jerusalem calling: State radio in mandate Palestine*. University of Texas Press.

Stolow, J. (2013). *Deus in machina: Religion, technology, and the things in between*. Fordham University Press.

Sumiala, J. (2006). Implications of the sacred in media studies. In J. Sumiala-Seppänen, K. Lundby, & R. Sakolangas (Eds.), *Implications of the sacred in (post)modern media* (pp. 11–29). Nordicom.

Subijanto, R. (2011). The visibility of a pious public. *Inter-Asia Cultural Studies*, *12*(2), 240–253.

Sundaram, D. (2019). Instagram your Durga Puja! Social media, hashtags and state-sponsored cultural marketing. In X. Zeiler (Ed.), *Digital Hinduism* (pp. 107–127). Routledge.

Taira, T. (2019). Media and communication approaches to leaving religion. In D. Enstedt, G. Larsson, & T. Mantsinen (Eds.), *Handbook of leaving religion* (pp. 335–348). Brill.

Thiong'o, N.Wa. (1992). *Decolonizing the mind: The politics of language in African literature*. East African Publishers.

Thomas, P. (2010). *Political economy of communications in India: The good, the bad, and the ugly*. Sage Publications.

Tsuria, R. (2017). New media in the Jewish bedroom: Exploring religious Jewish online discourse concerning gender and sexuality. PhD Dissertation, Texas A & M University.

Tuhiwai Smith, L. (2021). *Decolonizing methodologies: Research and indigenous peoples.* Bloomsbury.

Tweed, T. (1997). *Our lady of the exile: Diasporic religion at a Cuban Catholic shrine in Miami.* Oxford University Press.

Tweed, T. (2005) *The American encounter with Buddhism, 1844–1912: Victorian culture and the limits of dissent.* University of North Carolina Press.

van Dijck, J. (2013). *The culture of connectivity: A critical history of social media.* Oxford Press.

Vasquez, M. (2010) *More than belief: A materialist theory of religion.* Oxford University Press.

Vasquez, M. (1998) *The Brazilian popular church and the crisis of modernity.* Cambridge University Press.

Winkler, C., & El Damanhoury, K. (2022). *Proto-state media systems: The digital rise of Al-Qaeda and ISIS.* Oxford University Press.

Winston, D. (2000, 2009). *Red-hot and righteous: The urban religion of the Salvation Army.* Harvard University Press.

Winston, D. (2009) *Small screen, big picture: Television and lived religion.* Baylor University Press.

Wuthnow, R. (1996). *Christianity and civil society: The contemporary debate.* T & T Clark.

Zito, A. (1997) *Of body and brush: Grand sacrifice as text/performance in eighteenth-century China.* University of Chicago Press.

Selected Readings

Campbell, H. (2010). *When religion meets new media* (1st ed.). Routledge.

Campbell, H. (Ed.). (2013). *Digital religion: Understanding religious practice in new media worlds.* Routledge.

Forbes, B. D., & Mahan, J. (2017). *Religion and popular culture in America* (3rd ed.). University of California Press.

Hoover, S. M. (2006). *Religion in the media age.* Routledge.

Hoover, S. M., & Echchaibi, N. (Eds.). (2021). *Media and religion: The global view.* De Gruyter.

Horsfield, P. (2015). *From Jesus to the internet: A history of Christianity and media.* Wiley & Sons.

Meyer, B. (Ed.). (2009). *Aesthetic formation – Media, religion and the senses.* Palgrave Macmillan.

2

Communication, Media, and Religion Research
Theoretical Roots

Stephen Garner

Introduction

Relationships between religion and communication are myriad, complex, and deeply embedded in many facets of human cultures and societies. For those outside of religious or spiritual communities, interest in these relationships might take on sociological, political, and anthropological dimensions as the place and impact of religions in the contemporary world are articulated and explored. For those within religious communities, there is often a deeply held perspective that sees communication, specifically between the divine, humanity, and the world, as foundational to understanding and living wisely and well in the everyday world. Thus, the study of the relationship between religion and communication is significant for a range of people and communities, for both those of faith and those who do not hold to a particular religious or spiritual perspective.

In the academic context, religion and communication embraces scholarship addressing both religious and secular contexts. In the religious context, research and scholarship focus on how a particular religious tradition negotiates and uses new media and technology, formal education and training, and effective methods of communication to the wider world. In the secular context, much of the work on religion and communications comes from the areas of sociology, religious studies, anthropology, and media studies, including the recent work on digital religion. Each of these contexts has developed a number of approaches for exploring these relationships, with significant crossover taking place. This chapter will first sketch the most significant development in communications and media studies – the shift from instrumental to cultural approaches – and then consider three different domains of religion and communication: religion and digital culture; public theology; and religion and popular culture. In the first, we examine the parallel fields of digital religion and digital theology and see where they cross over with the religious-social shaping of technology methodology. In considering public theology, we consider the quest for effective and persuasive communication by religious communities in the public sphere; finally, when examining religion and popular culture, we look to frameworks and methods for identifying and analyzing different relationships in both secular and religious contexts.

Given the breadth of both religion and communication a narrower focus will be employed at times with reference to Christianity, but with some examples from other religious and spiritual

The Handbook on Religion and Communication, First Edition. Edited by Yoel Cohen and Paul A. Soukup.
© 2023 John Wiley & Sons Ltd. Published 2023 by John Wiley & Sons Ltd.

traditions also included. We begin with how communications and media studies have moved from more instrumental approaches to a broader cultural approach that underpins much of the work in this area currently with particular impact on the religion, media, and culture scholarly community.

Communications and Media as Instrumental Tool and/or Cultural Expression

Horsfield (2008) sums up the different ways people approach communication in religious contexts by noting that scholars typically approach media in a dualistic fashion (pp. 111–122). People might first engage media and communication through an instrumental lens describing media as a tool to be wielded to achieve expected outcomes, and second, through a cultural lens that sees all of society and culture as mediated in some way. Horsfield identifies the instrumental approach emerging from the rise of mass media in the early parts of the twentieth century with the development of newspapers, magazines, cinema, and radio, and then television from the mid-twentieth century. As these forms developed, scholars questioned the power and influence that those who used and controlled mass media have in areas such as politics and commerce. Moreover, people sought to understand how media might function as a tool and, if so, what processes might aid that (pp. 111–113). What Hoover (2006b) calls the "dominant" or "effects" tradition emerged – one that focused on how individuals and audiences received particular forms of media, their messages, and the effects that reception had (pp. 29–32). In summary, people understood media to operate in a simple, linear cause-and-effect way, and this instrumental approach developed a longevity and ubiquity to become the dominant tradition of communications and media studies.

Horsfield (2008) notes that this approach appealed in various ways. First, it connected to a common-sense pragmatism that saw the world as the place where human beings can, with the right tools, control a process of cause and effect, or in some cases resist it if necessary. Second, the instrumental approach doesn't need complex media theories: if you understand media as a tool to be applied through tightly defined processes, you can apply it without having to know how it works. And finally, by focusing on the mechanics of using media, questions about media power, ownership, the social functions of media, and the values embedded in it can be ignored (p. 112).

White (1997) emphasizes this latter point about the value-laden quality of technology and media in her reflections on technology and worship. White identifies technology as a socio-technical system comprising three parts: the technological (in this case, media artifact) produced by some process; the special knowledge required to produce such an artifact; and the set of cultural values foundational to directing human knowledge and agency to produce both processes and artifacts (p. 16). The presence of certain technological artifacts and the processes to produce them is shaped by what the culture of the day determines as valuable, which in itself can become a kind of self-reinforcing narrative connected to things such as technological progress and the quest for efficiency at the expense of human beings common to Ellul's long-term sociological analysis of technology (1962, pp. 394–395; 1964, pp. 3–22; 1990, pp. 35–76).

Within the context of religion and communication this instrumental approach appears in particular methods of evangelism, with televangelism of particular interest with its use of television to produce an easily consumed religious product. But even this, which seems like an obvious candidate for instrumentalization, isn't necessarily able to be understood in this way. While one might expect that televangelism optimistically deepened personal faith, or more pessimistically, generated wealth and influence across a broad demographic, in fact the effects were much more limited. Televangelism appealed to those whose preexisting values in the mainstream media it reinforced, and didn't tend to attract people from outside of that community, or redistribute funds from existing religious communities to the televangelist (Hoover, 2006, p. 308).

Clearly this instrumental approach, while helpful in some ways, did not address some significant matters. The approach ran into a number of issues or concerns from the mid part of the twentieth century when researchers raised a number of questions that a simple value-neutral mechanism for communication could not address. Hoover (2006), for example, notes a constant concern about things like the effect of media violence on audiences, as well as questions around how the media shaped "individual psychological effects, political and civil engagement, adult socialization, and ethnic and gender roles and identities" (pp. 112–113; see also Horsfield, 2008, pp. 112–113; Mitchell, 2007; Andison, 1977; Ferguson, 2009).

Out of these concerns and others, engagement with media and communication that focused more on social and cultural dynamics developed alongside the ongoing instrumental approach. This new approach took a cultural view of media, introducing terms such as mediatization; the view saw all society and culture as a mediated phenomenon, in which media forms a contributive part. Horsfield (2008) describes this:

> Given the interrelatedness of these cultural processes, media should be understood not as instruments carrying a fixed message but as sites where construction, negotiation, and reconstruction of cultural meaning takes place in an ongoing process of maintenance and change of cultural structures, relationships, meanings, and values. (p. 113)

Similarly, Hoover (2006b) describes this push toward social and cultural dynamics:

> This becomes a more subtle and nuanced contrast with traditional "effects"-oriented media theory in a number of ways. Along with the various valences of culturalist media studies in general, it wants to look at the media from the perspective of media audiences and individual and collective meaning-making, rather than from the perspective media institutions or texts. It wants to understand things in terms of the media objects as symbolic resources rather than as determinative ideological constructions. It wants to propose that the important questions may be in the realm of meaning-making rather than the "impact" of media on *behavior*. There is also a more fundamental, and interesting, contrast in that what I am developing here – a view that sees media in terms of their *integration into daily life* rather than in terms of their *effects on it*. (pp. 40–41)

As we shall see later in this chapter, this alternative trajectory plays out in how descriptions of relationships between religion and popular culture are described, as well as in how the impact of technology and media on religion in digital contexts is shaped. This shift requires a reframing of the questions around religion and communication: questions such as how religious groups use media and communications; how the mass media represent religion; and, more importantly, how religion and religious practice become themselves a dynamic social construction as part of these mediatization processes. Thus, for Horsfield (2008) the key questions become, "not how does religion use media but how are media and religion interrelated? How is what we know as religion constructed, shaped, practiced, and transformed by the different media practices within which it is embodied?" (p. 114). With these questions in mind, we turn now to some specific approaches engaging communications, media, and religion.

Religion and Communication in Digital Media and Culture

Digital communications and media and digital culture represent a significant development in the area of religion and communication. The widespread, though uneven, adoption of mobile and Internet technologies, influenced significantly by global communications and media industries, has reshaped notions of the local and global. It highlights how people at a grassroots level can significantly participate in global contexts, as well as how global media influences shape local expressions of culture (Tudoroiu, 2014, pp. 346–365; Einstein, 2008). Religious communities are not immune to this interplay of the local and the global, both in the messages and cultures they convey, and in their own use of those same technologies.

This engagement with communication technologies stands as part of a long history of negotiations around technologies by religious communities. In his work considering the interaction of media across the breadth of Christian history, Horsfield (2015) comments that media and Christianity exist as a:

> symbiotic cultural phenomenon that inform and are integral to each other. Christianity is a mediated phenomenon; there is no aspect of Christianity that can exist except as it is being communicated. At every step of the way, how it communicates itself becomes an inextinguishable part of what Christianity is, whether that communication be through oral speech and physical performance, silence, smells, writing, physical phenomena, visual artifacts, song and dance, printing, architecture, or electronic media. (p. 8)

The late twentieth century saw religious communities beginning to reflect in depth on the emerging digital landscape. Driven in part by practitioners using these nascent digital technologies for everyday religious contexts such as sermon preparation, Bible study, online evangelism and mission, and even monastic life, wider institutional reflection emerged (Hutchings, 2007, pp. 244–245). Such publications included some from the World Council of Churches (Arthur, 1998; Lochhead, 1997), as well as some from the Vatican (Pontifical Council for Social Communication, 2002a, 2002b). For example, a Vatican document on Internet ethics (Pontifical Council for Social Communication, 2002a) stressed that the use of technology and media is "by persons to persons for the integral development of persons" while one on the Church and the Internet (2002b) added, "although the virtual reality of cyberspace cannot substitute for real interpersonal community, the incarnational reality of the sacraments and the liturgy, or the immediate and direct proclamation of the gospel, it can complement them, attract people to a fuller experience of the life of faith, and enrich the religious lives of users" (n. 5). Similar reflection also took place in other faith communities such as Islam and Judaism, with Bunt (2005) commenting about Islamic communities:

> The impetus to go online in the name of Islam has intensified. Particularly significant is the growth in materials in languages other than English, previously the dominant language of Muslim online discourse. Coupled with developments in terms of accessibility, cheaper technology, and software, it has become easier for individuals not just to be passive readers, but to go online and disseminate their own opinions. Equipped with basic technical skills and access, it is straightforward to create a website or e-mail list. To this can be added Islamic symbols and quotes from the Qur'an, photos of Mecca, and – in some cases – images of "spiritual leaders." (p. 69)

Bunt has done significant work in this area (see Bunt, 2000, 2003, 2009, 2018). Campbell (2015) has done similar work on Judaism.

In the academic space, investigation and reflection on digital communications and media took two trajectories. The earlier trajectory is "digital religion," which typically involves the study of religion, communications, and media in one or more religious communities from the standpoint of disciplines such as anthropology, sociology, and communication and media studies. The other trajectory, "digital theology," tends to be performed by participants or members of a religious or spiritual community as they reflect critically on how digital communications and media shape their own and their community's religious life, faith, and practices. Examples of digital religion include Brasher (2001), Campbell (2005), Højsgaard and Warburg (2005), Dawson and Cowan (2004), Soukup (1996), Soukup and Hodgson (1997), Helland (2000), Cowan and Haddon (2000), Cowan (2005), and Davis (1999).

Echoing the cultural approach to media studies noted earlier, Campbell (2017) describes a main focus of the digital religion space.

> Yet most scholars in this field share an understanding that the Internet should be approached not just as a technological tool or force, but as a social context and space where culture is made and negotiated. Digital Religion studies draw on this understanding by approaching the Internet and other forms of new media as technologies which create unique mediated contexts, spaces, and discourses where religion is performed and engaged. (p. 16)

Methodologically, Campbell identifies three distinct approaches that underpin work being done in the area of digital religion: mediatization; the mediation of meaning; and the religious-social shaping of technology.

In the first instance (mediatization), researchers focus on how media and communications technologies interact with social and cultural change, and in the case of digital religion, how that social and cultural change impinges upon religion and religious communities. Drawing upon the work of Lundby (2014) and Lövheim (2011), Campbell (2017, pp. 18–19) notes that by treating media as a set of tools by which humans communicate, one part of digital religion seeks to explain how media shape wider public perceptions of religion and how religious communities and institutions respond to, are shaped by, and use media. Moreover, digital religion examines how media, and particularly media institutions, shift the locus of interpretation of the place and function of religion and religious institutions, and of interpreters of cultural meaning, from those religious institutions toward the media institutions, which themselves may then become agents of social change and secularization.

This process of mediatization, where media might destabilize religious authority and identity as well as provide new avenues for religious expression, connects to the second focus of digital religion, the mediation of meaning. Campbell links this to the work of Hoover (2006b), who sees the media serving "as a reservoir from which people draw meaning to help explain, represent, and even assimilate religious ideals and beliefs within the contemporary society" (Campbell, 2017, p. 19). Human beings as individuals and groups consume and interpret media in ways their religious faith commitments and practices both shape while they themselves are shaped by the dialogue between religious faith and the messages mediated to them via media about the world. As seen later, this also connects to the way in which Lynch (2005) and Green (2002) see popular culture functioning as a lens through which everyday meaning and culture is explored and created. This intersection of digital media, popular culture, and religion also appears in the work of others, particularly Wagner (2012), who examines the formation of ritual in online spaces such as games and the variety of digital experiences that attempt to replicate both the geographies and experiences of pilgrimage (see also Garner, 2020b, 2013).

Digital religion's third approach, the one that also grounds digital theology, appears in Campbell's (2017) own religious-social shaping of technology (pp. 20–21). This approach, she argues, is a variation on the tradition of social shaping of technology that sees the broader structures of societal worldviews, history, and belief systems shaping how individuals and communities negotiate technology. In the religious context, Campbell sees those belief systems not only representing wider society but also the particularities of distinct religious communities as they engage with, adopt, and use media and technology. Campbell (2017) has applied this approach to Christian, Jewish, and Muslim communities, both in digital religion and digital theology contexts (Campbell & Garner, 2016). After briefly surveying digital theology, we will return to this approach.

Recently, Phillips et al. (2019) have categorized digital theology activity into four, sometimes overlapping, categories: mediated education; digitally enabled research; theologically resourced engagement with digital culture; and theological ethical engagement with digital technology and culture. Mediated education considers how didactic theological communication happens in relation to digital media including academic theological training as well as the use of digital media for education in discipleship, spiritual formation, and catechesis (Anthony, 2014; Crowley, 2014; Garner, 2019; Hess, 2005; Hess et al., 2014; Hodge, 2010; da Silva, 2019). Second, digitally enabled theological research uses digital communications and media to carrying out aspects of textual analysis of biblical and historical documents, data visualization, analysis of religious digital media, and demographic analyses (Ford et al., 2019; Houghton & Smith, 2016; Parker, 2003; Phillips, 2020; Siker, 2017). Third, digital theology provides a context in which theology is done, fostering a genuinely reflexive dialogue between digital culture and theology, where theology seeks to offer insights into the human creation of digital culture and digital culture offers back the human experience of engaging and living within those digital worlds (Byers, 2013; Schmidt, 2020; Spadaro, 2014). The previously mentioned religious-social shaping of technology might be a tool to use in this category, which would then bridge into the final category of digital theology, which adds a theological–ethical critique of digital technology and culture seeking to offer both Church and world *phronesis*, a kind of practical wisdom, for living well in digital and media cultures (Campbell & Garner, 2016; Delicata, 2015; Garner, 2020a; Lewis, 2018; Ott, 2019; Stoddart, 2008).

Digital theology and digital religion intersect in one area methodologically: the religious-social shaping of technology approach proposed by Campbell (2010). Campbell's approach is a multi-stage process involved with the observation and analysis of a religious community as it negotiates technology and media (pp. 57–63). It pays attention to technology and media possessing both instrumental and cultural dynamics (pp. 45–48), shaped by the earlier work of those like Christians (1997; see also Monsma et al., 1986). Campbell (2010) succinctly describes this approach as follows:

> The religious-social shaping of technology is put forth under the premise that while religious communities function similarly to other forms of social community – in that their choices related to technology are socially negotiated – they are also constrained by unique factors that need to be highlighted and considered. A unique element of the religious-social shaping of technology is that it seeks to explore in more detail how spiritual, moral, and theological codes of practice guide technological negotiation. Thus it calls for a deeper awareness of the role history and tradition play in religious communities' processes of negotiation. (p. 59)

The first stage contributes to the development of a thick description of the religious community negotiating new technology and media. In this stage, researchers ask about how the community currently uses technology and media including how it historically negotiated the adoption of that technology and media, and what impact the adoption or rejection had on the community. Adding to that developing description, in the second stage, the researcher explores the core values and beliefs defining the religious community with particular emphasis on the dominant social and religious values shaping the community and how those are interpreted and contextualized in their application to faith and life. With that thick description developed, the next stage investigates how a religious community negotiates new technologies and media in light of their historical tradition and beliefs, key criteria used for evaluating its use and adoption, asking who and what has authority in making those decisions. Following that negotiation, a further longitudinal stage can take place that examines the use and effects of the technology or media adopted or rejected, how the community narrates its decision-making process, how core beliefs and values might have been affected, and what implications for further negotiations with technology and media might take place in the future.

Campbell's religious-social shaping of technology is an approach that bridges both the digital religion and digital theology spaces. On the one hand, it allows those outside of a religious community to examine how that community negotiates and uses communications technology and media, while, on the other, it allows a more self-reflective way by a religious community as part of its own negotiation of new or existing communications technologies and media. Similarly, Helland's (2000) helpful typology of religion-online and online-religion might function in both digital religion and digital theology spaces. The former, religion-online, recognizes that religious communities replicate their physical ecclesiology, communication, and organization in digital spaces, while online-religion highlights that individuals or communities may experience or form new kinds of religious or spiritual experiences in those same spaces.

Public Theology as Religious Communication

A dimension to religion and communication, which takes a variety of approaches, addresses how religious communities interact with notions of the "public," asking specifically how religious communities communicate persuasively and intelligibly in public spaces such as government, business, local communities, educational institutions, and civil society. While this might connect to sharing the faith through evangelism and mission, it primarily concerns shaping public opinion and policy for a perceived public good. Within the Christian community, Graham et al. (2005) argue for two main strands in engaging the public. First, an apologetic strand examines the questions raised in wider society, seeks to articulate answers to these questions by drawing on the riches of a faith tradition, and supplies appropriate wisdom in a form suitable for the public consumption. Second, a dialectical strand seeks to enrich existing theological thinking by gleaning insight from secular thought, in turn speaking back into the secular world (p. 139). Both approaches fall under the broad term public theology, which has developed over the past 50 years or so, and which sits alongside other areas such as political theology and civil religion. Within the Christian tradition, Forrester (2004) described public theology as:

> theology which seeks the welfare of the city before protecting the interests of the Church, or its proper liberty to preach the Gospel and celebrate the sacraments. Accordingly, public theology often takes "the world's agenda," or parts of it, as its own agenda, and seeks to offer distinctive and constructive insights from the treasury of faith to help in the building of a decent society, the restraint of evil, the curbing of violence, nation-building, and reconciliation in the public arena, and so forth. It strives to offer something that is distinctive, and that is gospel, rather than simply adding the voice of theology to what everyone is saying already. Thus it seeks to deploy theology in public debate, rather than a vague and optimistic idealism which tends to disintegrate in the face of radical evil. (p. 6)

In order to achieve these goals, theologians raise questions about the form of this engagement between faithful agency and wider society and, in particular, about how they might communicate effectively to the publics involved. Should one take a "common-currency" approach where they mute God-talk to find some common ground with other groups through the use of a common secular discourse, or should one attempt to "outnarrate" competing narratives within the public square by offering a "distinctive discourse" rooted in the language of faith? Perhaps, as Marshall comments, following Gascoigne (2001), one should not introduce God too early to the conversation as it may act as a barrier to being heard, but at the same time not leave God out so much as to lose the religious identity of one's message. Therefore, "Christians must be able to speak the language of political discourse effectively, albeit with a foreign accent" (Marshall, 2005, p. 17). (For an example of public theology from the faith tradition of Judaism, see Unger, 2019.)

The affirmation of the world setting the agenda for this discourse may sit uncomfortably with religious communities that see the world as at best marred by human self-interest and at worst as the location of demonic activity, but this agenda-setting forms part of a constructive dialogue between the religious community, its faith and traditions, and the world it wants to affect. Within the Christian context, Stackhouse (2004) argues that the heart of public theology is a community of faith, informed by scripture and tradition, which is committed to reading the "signs of the times" and acting for the common good for society (p. 284). Starting with the concerns of the world aligns with Tillich's method of correlation, which we shall consider shortly. The starting point is not always the world's agenda and problems, as sometimes a particular sacred text, creed, confession, or the practice of worship provides an impetus for public engagement. Public theology, therefore, exists within a contested space of ideas and messages. In the West, current liberal democracies promote, in theory, access to public space for democratic participation and preserve that in various legislative forms. Access to this space, though, does not guaranteed that people will choose to hear a particular message, or that the message and messenger will be free from critique and the consequences of articulating their opinion (Beckerlegge, 2001). Moreover, for any message articulated by a religious person or group to be persuasive it needs both credibility and intelligibility to a wider public that no longer holds the religions and their sources to authoritative, unique, or a public truth (Marshall, 2005, p. 12).

Not only is the public space itself contested, but also the very definition of the "public." One of the most frequently cited definitions of "public" in relation to religious engagement and communication comes from Tracy (1981), who identified three distinct spaces or "publics" to which religion needs to provide both an accessible and coherent account of itself in its cultural context and to self-reflectively revise theology in light of that context. Three public spaces exist – society, the academy, and the Church – into which theologians speak to offer a:

> public response bearing meaning and truth on the most serious and difficult questions, both public and communal, that any human being or society must face: Has existence any ultimate meaning? Is a fundamental trust to be found amongst the fears, anxieties and terror of existence? Is there some reality, some force, even some one, who speaks a word of truth that can be recognized and trusted? (pp. 3–6)

Three dimensions comprise society for Tracy: a technocultural realm concerning economics and technological application; the realm of polity concerning social justice and politics; and the realm of culture concerned with primarily art, philosophy, and religion. The academy consists primarily of the university, the activities of its various disciplines (including theology), and its activity as a public reflective voice. The Church functions as the community of moral and religious discourse, into which the theologian speaks, and possesses both sociological and theological characteristics. Tracy further argues that theology, to function well, must function as public discourse in these three areas (pp. 6–31).

Other publics might include the state (local government, national government, state welfare), civil society (charities, faith communities, voluntary bodies), and the market (business, finance, corporations). In in some cases, people use "public" to mean anything outside of a religious community or secular in nature. But churches and other religious communities also represent a form of public, within which particular language, symbols, and traditions shape the messages addressed to those within those communities. For example, communication in a sermon or homily locates itself within the "public" of public worship, while communication at a youth event or through religious mass media represents different or overlapping publics. Similarly, interfaith dialogue and events represent a form of public that combines different religious publics, sometimes awkwardly. In all cases, though, there remains a need for communication intelligible and comprehensible to those publics, communication that credibly provides reasons for hearing, reflecting on, and then potentially acting on it for the good of individuals and communities.

Of course, public theology does not stand alone in bringing religious communication into trajectory to promote the public good, a goal shared by the related areas of both civil religion and political theology. Each is concerned in its own way with what Stackhouse (2004) identifies as "[t]he goal of finding a more inclusive, genuinely ecumenical and catholic way of identifying a valid, viable inner convictional and ethical framework on which to build the moral and spiritual architecture of our increasingly common life" (p. 277). Public theology should not be subsumed into either civil religion, which desires the creation of symbols or structures that express the core values of a community cultivated into a set of norms by which all must conform, or a political theology where religion is infused by a particular political ideology and theology becomes the servant of politics. Rather, argues Stackhouse, public theology seeks to critique and reform the values that underpin civil religion, while at the same time rejecting the utopianism of political theology. It does this because it is realistic about both the potential for reform as well as the abuse of power and the establishment of self-interest. Public theology may use political and social theories, but those should seek to serve society, not the other way around (p. 284).

Public theology as a reformist movement rejects the conservatism of civil religion as well as the revolutionary thrust of political theology because it is realistic about what it might achieve at any one time. But one must be careful that this is not an impotent realism, but something intelligible and creditable responding to what Graham et al. (2005) identify as the questions, anxieties, and challenges of living within a pluralistic and fallen world (p. 139).

Tillich (1953) proposed a method of correlation that utilizes theology to make "an analysis of the human situation out of which the existentialist questions arise, and it demonstrates that the symbols used in the Christian message are the answers to these questions" (p. 70). Falling within the apologetic strand of public theology, it offers something positive and constructive from the riches of a religious tradition into the public square. For Tillich, human existence in the everyday world raises questions, particularly ontological questions, which find expression in philosophy, the arts, social sciences, and other forms of human expression. Tillich understands that these questions arise out of the human awareness of finitude, transience in this world, and the possibility of nonbeing. Human beings live between being as they ought to be and being as they should not be, which Tillich describes as a distinction between the realms of salvation and creation. By bringing existential questions into dialogue with theology, Tillich argues, the symbols of Christianity, which are revelation sourced outside our reality, point to God as the answer to these questions, while at the same time those answers correlate to our experience of finitude and potential nonbeing. Theology must draw upon the symbols of revelation found within the Christian tradition to answer those questions in a form and language that connects with the situation of people in the everyday world (pp. 67–73). If it does this, Tillich contends that "Being human means asking the questions of one's own being and living under the impact of the answers given to this question. And, conversely, being human means receiving answers to the question of one's own being and asking questions under the impact of the answers" (p. 62). Thus, Tillich's method of speaking into the world reflects layers of communication and dialectic between God and world, God and humanity, humanity and the world, humanity and God, and humanity with itself. In some ways, he finds a distinct similarity between the way in which popular culture texts raise existential questions as described by Vanhoozer (2007) with his hermeneutical keys, and the theological and pastoral responses to those texts in the language of the people raising them.

Of course, these are just several possible approaches for religious communities to speak into the world around them to promote a common good. One of the key aspects of this form of religious communication is the community's own understanding of their religious faith, which will be of varying degrees of depth. So alongside this public theology stand related strands of religious instruction, self-reflection, and a deepening, critical understanding of the faith tradition they are part of and that shapes motivation to speak and act in the world. This forms a parallel educative, formational, and proclamatory task of addressing the public of the religious community to educate and inform that community of faith as to the dimensions and features of their own theology, to show the implications and trajectories of that faith, and then make it their own. Thus public theology has a twofold movement whereby the top-down source of revelation provides the norm, but that norm is realized through the personal convictions present in the community of faith (Stackhouse, 2004, p. 291).

Religion, Theology, and Popular Culture

Religion and communication embrace not just a single-direction trajectory from religion to communication and media, but myriad relationships between those things. This holds particularly for the relationships between religion and popular culture, where various disciplines explore how religions, religious ideas and symbols, and religious and spiritual practices are represented in popular culture and how those representations and interpretations influence religion and society.

Popular culture most commonly refers to examples of films, television shows, popular music, and video games that permeate and shape everyday life. This everyday nature of popular culture highlights its pervasiveness in communities, as well as the meaning-making that takes place through consuming and producing it. Forbes (2005) notes that popular culture is often set against other things such as "high culture," representing the culture and cultural endeavors affirmed by an elite such as an opera or classics of literature; or "folk culture," incorporating the oral ideas, customs, and expressions of smaller family and community groups. For Forbes, popular culture is culture and cultural artifacts communicated in a plethora of ways to large, widespread audiences, typically through mass media (pp. 2–3). Lynch (2005) frames his understanding of popular culture as "the shared context, practices, and resources of 'everyday life'" (p. 13). By emphasizing the broad, everyday world, Lynch asserts that examining popular culture deals not only with its "texts" or cultural artifacts, but also with the study of how these things are produced and "consumed" in society. This approach, focused on a cultural approach to media, gives insight into the wider structures, patterns, and activities of meaning-making taking place in everyday life. It also highlights, as Forbes does, that popular culture exists within and alongside other competing and complementary cultures (Lynch, 2005, pp. 15–16). Drawing these threads together, Green (2002) gives a helpful and succinct definition of popular culture as "that subsection of mass media which are appropriated by people in their daily lives and remodeled as the raw material through which they communicate their values and enthusiasms, and through which they connect to others" (p. 156). In considering how religion and popular culture interact with one another, and how that engagement with religion and popular culture might occur, the next sections will describe three approaches: (i) Forbes' typology helpful for locating different relationships between religion and popular culture; (ii) Lynch's three-fold scheme of auteur, documentary, and audience-reception approaches; and (iii) Vanhoozer's method of cultural exegesis for use within faith communities.

Forbes' Typology

Forbes (2005) proposes four key relationships that cover the dominant interactions between popular culture and religion: religion in popular culture; popular culture in religion; popular culture as religion; and religion and popular culture in dialogue (pp. 9–17). Religion in popular culture is perhaps the most obvious; it specifically examines popular culture to identify aspects of religion present in it (pp. 10–12). This includes overt uses of religious locations such as churches, mosques, or synagogues; particular religious symbols such as crucifixes or menorah; the use of sacred texts; and the use of religious characters such as priests, rabbis, monks and nuns, and imams, as well as everyday people of faith. This category also incorporates religious themes and symbols that, while significant, might not be as apparent to nonreligious viewers as to religious ones. For example, *Batman v Superman: Dawn of Justice* (2016) features a Christian religious tableau at the end of the film representing Superman, Batman, Wonder Woman, and Lois Lane as Jesus, the beloved disciple, Mary, and Mary Magdalene, respectively, complete with three crosses silhouetted on the horizon. To those familiar with the Christian Easter story the imagery is apparent, but perhaps not so for others. Similarly, religious themes of forgiveness, salvation, judgment, hope, and exodus feature, not necessarily overtly but in the background. In another example, Forbes points to what he notes as the "American Monomyth," a similar but different structure to Joseph Campbell's "Hero's Journey," which draws upon Judeo-Christian messianic imagination to dominate popular cultural narratives in America. Developed by Lawrence and Jewett (2002), this plot structure can be summarized as:

> A community in a harmonious paradise is threatened by evil; normal institutions fail to contend with this threat; a selfless superhero emerges to renounce temptations and carry out the redemptive task; aided by fate, his decisive victory restores the community to its paradisal condition; the superhero then recedes into obscurity. (Lawrence & Jewett, 2002, p. 6, cited in Forbes, 2005, p. 11)

Alongside religion in popular culture, Forbes identifies a category in which religious communities use and incorporate popular culture into their language, practices, and communal life (pp. 12–13). This can appear in the appropriation of particular styles of music or performance into worship (Romanowski, 2005, pp. 103–122). the use of advertising and marketing techniques (Einstein, 2008, pp. 95–119), the delivery of homilies or worship services in formats that communicate better to those raised on YouTube clips and "TED Talks," Bibles repackaged in teenage magazine styles (Blyth, 2021), as well as a plethora of podcasts and religious television shows, films, and contemporary music that mirror wider popular culture but with more overt religious messages (Hoover, 2006b, pp. 45–83).

Forbes' (2005) final categories (popular culture as religion and religion and popular culture in dialogue) focus less on how religion and popular culture are present in each, respectively, and more on how popular culture functions in religious contexts (pp. 14–16). Popular culture as religion points to how participation in popular culture can provide the kinds of identity markers, meaning-making, and community often associated with religious communities. Lynch (2005) also picks up on this when he notes functionalist approaches to religion that emphasize its social function of unifying communities around shared beliefs and values, an existential function orienting people's lives in the everyday world through supplying meaning, and a transcendent function where religious experience might happen through popular culture (pp. 27–33). Thus, playing and following sports or eSports, cosplay, fan communities, distilling wisdom about life from TV shows or music, immersive video games, and exploring ethical and moral issues through popular cultural texts can all replace or complement functional religious definitions (Riess, 2004; Garner, 2020b, pp. 93–108; Wagner, 2012). Forbes (2005) suggests religion and popular culture in dialogue takes place when religious communities engage with issues highlighted by popular culture in some way, such as violence, racism, anxiety about technology, and identity, as well as values narrated by popular culture. This may lead to affirmation or resistance to those value-laden narratives, using popular culture to support religious ventures (evangelism, discipleship, and mission), and seeking to reshape or "redeem" popular culture from a theological or religious perspective (pp. 15–16). This category of religion and popular culture interaction lends itself to the development of approaches that move beyond the categorizations that Forbes presents and into a deeper analytical engagement with popular culture.

Lynch's Scheme

Lynch (2005) highlights three approaches for engaging with popular culture from a theological perspective (whether for a desire to understand how religion functions in a world shaped by popular culture, how popular culture might function as a religious surrogate, how evangelism through popular culture works, or how popular culture might serve as a site for theological reflection) (pp. 20–42). Lynch, himself, is particular interested in how popular culture shapes the rhythms of everyday life for people, connecting back to Green's (2002) observation that popular culture is a matrix through which people express, reflect on, and embody particular values and narratives. Lynch (2005) proposes three approaches to analyzing popular culture: author-focused, text-based, and audience reception (pp. 112–117).

The author-focused or *auteur* approach concentrates on the person or persons who created the particular aspect of popular culture with a view to understanding the background, motivations, power dynamics, and, where available, the hermeneutical location of the creators of those texts. The text-based or documentary approach focuses on particular cultural texts, such as a film or song, to identify particular worlds, values, and meanings narrated in those texts. This includes themes discerned in song lyrics or the way a television show represents and reflects on certain contemporary or historical matters. Finally, the audience-reception approach examines how individuals and communities receive and respond to a popular cultural text. At one level this might be the meaning created in the space between screen and audience, while at another level how cultures of fandom and spirituality emerge from the text (Jenkins, 2006; Riess, 2004; Wilcox & Lavery, 2002). This latter approach fits well with Lynch's concern with popular culture's everyday rhythms and feeds back nicely into Forbes' category of popular culture and religion in dialogue.

Vanhoozer and Cultural Exegesis

Vanhoozer (2007) suggests that we need all three of Lynch's approaches for a deeper analysis of popular culture in order to bring it into genuine theological critique. Drawing on biblical hermeneutics, Vanhoozer highlights three worlds of a cultural text that need to be analyzed: the world behind the text; the world in the text; and the world before the text. Each of Lynch's approaches forms a component of a larger analytical framework where we read texts both on their own terms (to avoid reading into them something that isn't there) and in light of the Christian story (p. 44). Having read, watched, or listened to the text on its own terms, the analyst develops a thick description of the text by drawing on disciplines such as history, economics, film and media studies, social sciences, and theology. Similar to the author-focused approach, this approach asks questions about the world behind the text including: Who made this text? Why was this text made? What do we know about the creator? Whose interests or power does the text serve? That leads into a documentary or text-based phase, which examines the world within the text to see what meanings and values it promotes and how it communicates them to readers, listeners, or viewers. This includes identifying key aspects of the form of the text (e.g. the effects of genre), as well as the meanings, values, and ethos narrated (pp. 45–52). The final step of developing this thick description draws on social sciences and media and cultural studies, as well as on the narratives of consumers and users of the cultural material in order to examine the world before the text and how people consume, receive, and respond to the text in question. Using an audience-reception approach, insights into how people appropriate the text and how it shapes people's everyday rhythms of life and perception of the world are incorporated into the description. The heart of Vanhoozer's approach recognizes that cultural texts communicate "root metaphors," typically a single hermeneutical key that is then used to interpret the world, which through the telling of a story asks the receiver to incorporate that metaphor into your life and to then live accordingly (pp. 52–55).

Each of the approaches sketched earlier falls into the cultural approach to media and communication, though aspects of each might also display instrumental aspects whether through categorical rigidity in classifying religion and popular culture relationships or through applying a particular analytical approach in a mechanical way to every text without attention to nuance or needed flexibility. Each provides a helpful way into thinking about how religion and popular culture might interact with helpful entry points for those within and outside of particular religious communities.

Conclusion

This chapter has highlighted both the diversity and complexity of relationships between religion and communication, and has surveyed a number of more specific areas and their approaches and methodologies. In particular, the movement away from treating communications and media as cause-and-effect instruments or tools toward more mediatized and cultural understandings of media appears with increasing frequency in academic engagement with religion, communications, and media. This movement proves helpful in locating religion and communication not merely in the global mass media context, but also rooting the expression of religious communication in the everyday world.

Methodologies such as Campbell's religious-social shaping of technology, Tillich's method of correlation, and Vanhoozer's cultural exegesis demonstrate how religion and communication approaches designed for a particular context also become available for use in a variety of faith-based and secular contexts. Moreover, as fields such as digital religion and digital theology mature, dialogue between each of those fields as well as wider interdisciplinary engagement will help shape a deeper understanding of how new media will negotiate its global and everyday contexts.

Methods shaped by Western research frameworks and notions of religion dominate current scholarly methodologies in the area of religion and communication. As these fields continue to develop within the wider global context of religion, engagement between religion and communication will require perspectives and approaches located in other cultures, and in particular the Global South. This will bring much-needed alternative notions of religious communication, religion, and understandings of human communities and cultures to sit alongside and in dialogue with current scholarship and to truly reflect both religion and communication as global and local phenomena.

References

Andison, F. S. (1977). TV violence and viewer aggression: A cumulation of study results 1956–1976. *Public Opinion Quarterly, 41*(3), 314–331. https://doi.org/10.1086/268390

Anthony, J. (2014). Dreidels to Dante's Inferno: Toward a typology of religious games. In H. Campbell, & G. P. Grieve (Eds.), *Playing with religion in digital games* (pp. 25–46). Indiana University Press.

Arthur, C. (1998). *The globalization of communications: Some religious implications.* World Council of Churches.

Beckerlegge, G. (2001). Computer-mediated religion: Religion on the internet at the turn of the twenty-first century. In G. Beckerlegge (Ed.), *From sacred text to internet* (pp. 219–264). Ashgate.

Blyth, C. (2021). *Rape culture, purity culture, and coercive control in teen girl Bibles.* Routledge.

Brasher, B. E. (2001). *Give me that online religion.* Jossey-Bass.

Bunt, G. R. (2000). *Virtually Islamic: Computer-mediated communication and cyber Islamic environments.* University of Wales Press.

Bunt, G. R. (2003). *Islam in the digital age: E-Jihad, online fatwas, and cyber Islamic environments.* Pluto Press.

Bunt, G. R. (2005). Negotiating Islam and Muslims in cyberspace. *Concilium, 1,* 68–77.

Bunt, G. R. (2009). *iMuslims: Rewiring the house of Islam.* University of North Carolina Press.

Bunt, G. R. (2018). *Hashtag Islam: How cyber-Islamic environments are transforming religious authority.* The University of North Carolina Press.

Byers, A. J. (2013). *Theomedia: The media of God and the digital age.* Cascade Books.

Campbell, H. (2005). *Exploring religious community online: We are one in the network.* Peter Lang.

Campbell, H. (2010). *When religion meets new media.* Routledge.

Campbell, H. (2015). *Digital Judaism: Jewish negotiations with digital media and culture.* Routledge.

Campbell, H. (2017). Surveying theoretical approaches within digital religion studies. *New Media & Society, 19*(1), 15–24. https://doi.org/10.1177/1461444816649912

Campbell, H., & Garner, S. (2016). *Networked theology: Negotiating faith in digital culture.* Baker.

Christians, C. G. (1997). Religious perspectives on communication technology. *Journal of Media and Religion, 1*(1), 37–47. https://doi.org/10.1207/S15328415JMR0101_5

Cowan, D. E. (2005). *Cyberhenge: Modern pagans on the internet.* Routledge.

Cowan, D. E., & Haddon, J. K. (2000). *Religion on the internet: Research prospects and promises.* JAI.

Crowley, E. D. (2014). "Using new eyes": Photography as a spiritual practice for faith formation and worship. *Dialog, 53*(1), 30–40. https://doi.org/10.1111/dial.12086

da Silva, A. A. (2019). Catechesis in the digital age: From transmission to sharing. *Communication Research Trends, 38*(4), 11–20.

Davis, E. (1999). *Techgnosis: Myth, magic, mysticism in the age of information.* Serpent's Tail.

Dawson, L. L., & Cowan, D. E. (Eds.). (2004). *Religion online: Finding faith on the internet.* Routledge.

Delicata, N. (2015). Natural law in a digital age. *Journal of Moral Theology, 4*(1), 1–24.

Einstein, M. (2008). *Brands of faith: Marketing religion in a commercial age.* Routledge.

Ellul, J. (1962). The technological order. *Technology and Culture, 3*(4), 394–421. https://doi.org/10.2307/3100993

Ellul, J. (1964). *The technological society* (J. Wilkinson, Trans.). Vintage Books.

Ellul, J. (1990). *The technological bluff* (G. W. Bromiley, Trans.). Eerdmans.

Ferguson, C. J. (2009). Media violence effects: Confirmed truth or just another X-file? *Journal of Forensic Psychology Practice, 9*(2), 1–41. https://doi.org/10.1080/15228930802572059

Forbes, B. D. (2005). Introduction: Finding religion in unexpected places. In B. D. Forbes, & J. H. Mahan (Eds.), *Religion and popular culture in America* (pp. 1–20). University of California Press.

Ford, D. G., Mann, J. L., & Phillips, P. M. (2019). *The Bible and digital millennials.* Routledge.

Forrester, D. B. (2004). The scope of public theology. *Studies in Christian Ethics, 17*(2), 5–19. https://doi.org/10.1177/095394680401700209

Garner, S. (2013). Lament in an age of new media. In M. J. Bier, & T. Bulkeley (Eds.), *Spiritual complaint: Theology and practice of lament* (pp. 228–245). Pickwick Publications.

Garner, S. (2019). Imaging Christ in digital worlds: Continuity and discontinuity in discipleship. *Communication Research Trends, 38*(4), 21–30.

Garner, S. (2020a). Duties, consequences or virtues? Theological ethics for social media. In G. Ulshöfer, & M. Wilhelm (Eds.), *Theologische Medienethik im digitalen Zeitalter [Theological media ethics in the digital age]* (pp. 187–203). Kohlhammer-Verlag.

Garner, S. (2020b). Sacred pilgrimage in playful, digital spaces. In J. Tucker, & P. Halstead (Eds.), *Sports and play in Christian theology* (pp. 93–108). Lexington Books/Fortress Academic.

Gascoigne, R. (2001). *The public forum and Christian ethics*. Cambridge University Press.

Graham, E. L., Walton, H., & Ward, F. (2005). *Theological reflection: Methods*. SCM Press.

Green, L. (2002). *Technoculture: From alphabet to cybersex*. Allen and Unwin.

Helland, C. (2000). Online-religion/religion-online and virtual communitas. In D. E. Cowan, & J. K. Hadden (Eds.), *Religion on the internet: Research prospects and promises* (pp. 205–223). JAI.

Hess, M. E. (2005). *Engaging technology in theological education: All that we can't leave behind*. Rowman & Littlefield Publishers.

Hess, M. E., Gallagher, E. V., & Turpin, K. (2014). Forum: A new culture of learning. *Teaching Theology & Religion, 17*(3), 227–246. https://onlinelibrary.wiley.com/doi/10.1111/teth.12235

Hodge, D. W. (2010). Role playing: Towards a theology of gamers. In C. Detweiler (Ed.), *Halos and avatars: Playing video games with God* (pp. 163–175). Westminster John Knox Press.

Højsgaard, M. T., & Warburg, M. (Eds.). (2005). *Religion and cyberspace*. Routledge.

Hoover, S. M. (2006a). Media. In H. R. Fuchs Ebaugh (Ed.), *Handbook of religion and social institutions* (pp. 305–319). Springer.

Hoover, S. M. (2006b). *Religion in the media age*. Routledge.

Horsfield, P. (2008). Media. In D. Morgan (Ed.), *Key words in religion, media and culture* (pp. 111–122). Routledge.

Horsfield, P. G. (2015). *From Jesus to the internet: A history of Christianity and media*. Chichester. John Wiley & Sons, Ltd.

Houghton, H. A. G., & Smith, C. J. (2016). Digital editing and the Greek New Testament. In C. Clivaz, P. Dilley, & D. Hamidović (Eds.), *Ancient worlds in digital culture* (pp. 110–127). Brill.

Hutchings, T. (2007). Creating church online: A case-study approach to religious experience. *Studies in World Christianity, 13*(3), 243–260. https://doi.org/10.3366/swc.2007.13.3.243

Jenkins, H. (2006). *Fans, bloggers, and gamers: Exploring participatory culture*. New York University Press.

Lawrence, J. S., & Jewett, R. (2002). *The myth of the American superhero*. W. B. Eerdmans.

Lewis, B. (2018). Social media, peer surveillance, spiritual formation, and mission: Practising Christian faith in a surveilled public space. *Surveillance & Society, 16*(4), 517–532. https://doi.org/10.24908/ss.v16i4.7650

Lochhead, D. (1997). *Shifting realities: Information technology and the church*. World Council of Churches.

Lövheim, M. (2011). Mediatisation of religion: A critical appraisal. *Culture and Religion, 12*(2), 153–166. https://doi.org/10.1080/14755610.2011.579738

Lundby, K. (Ed.). (2014). *Mediatization of communication*. De Gruyter Mouton.

Lynch, G. (2005). *Understanding theology and popular culture*. Blackwell.

Marshall, C. (2005). What language shall I borrow? The bilingual dilemma of public theology. *Stimulus, 13*(3), 11–18.

Mitchell, J. P. (2007). *Media violence and Christian ethics*. Cambridge University Press.

Monsma, S. V., Christians, C. G., Dykema, E. R., Leegwater, A., Schuurman, E., & Van Poolen, L. (1986). *Responsible technology: A Christian perspective*. W. B. Eerdmans.

Ott, K. M. (2019). *Christian ethics for a digital society*. Rowman & Littlefield.

Parker, D. C. (2003). Through a screen darkly: Digital texts and the New Testament. *Journal for the Study of the New Testament, 25*(4), 395–411. https://doi.org/10.1177/0142064X0302500401

Phillips, P., Schiefelbein-Guerrero, K., & Kurlberg, J. (2019). Defining digital theology: Digital humanities, digital religion and the particular work of the codec research centre and network. *Open Theology, 5*(1), 29–43. https://doi.org/10.1515/opth-2019-0003

Phillips, P. M. (2020). *The Bible, social media and digital culture*. Routledge.

Pontifical Council for Social Communication. (2002a). Ethics in internet. Vatican. Retrieved February 20, 2011, from http://www.vatican.va/roman_curia/pontifical_councils/pccs/documents/rc_pc_pccs_doc_20020228_church-internet_en.html

Pontifical Council for Social Communication. (2002b). The church and internet. Vatican. Retrieved February 20, 2020, from http://www.vatican.va/roman_curia/pontifical_councils/pccs/documents/rc_pc_pccs_doc_20020228_church-internet_en.html

Riess, J. (2004). *What would Buffy do?: The vampire slayer as spiritual guide*. Jossey-Bass.

Romanowski, W. D. (2005). Evangelicals and popular music: The contemporary Christian music industry. In B. D. Forbes, & J. H. Mahan (Eds.), *Religion and popular culture in America* (pp. 103–122). University of California Press.

Schmidt, K. G. (2020). *Virtual communion: Theology of the internet and the Catholic sacramental imagination*. Lexington Books/Fortress Academic.

Siker, J. S. (2017). *Liquid scripture: The Bible in a digital world*. Fortress Press.

Soukup, P. A. (Ed.). (1996). *Media, culture, and Catholicism*. Sheed & Ward.

Soukup, P. A., & Hodgson, R., Jr. (Eds.). (1997). *From one medium to another: Communicating the Bible through multimedia*. Sheed & Ward.

Spadaro, A. (2014). *Cybertheology: Thinking Christianity in the era of the internet* (M. Way, Trans.). Fordham University Press.

Stackhouse, M. L. (2004). Civil religion, political theology and public theology: What's the difference? *Political Theology, 5*(3), 275–293. https://doi.org/10.1558/poth.5.3.275.36715

Stoddart, E. (2008). Who watches the watchers? Towards an ethic of surveillance in a digital age. *Studies in Christian Ethics, 21*(3), 362–381. https://doi.org/10.1177/0953946808096816

Tillich, P. (1953). *Systematic theology* (3 Vols., Vol. 1). James Nisbet & Co.

Tracy, D. (1981). *The analogical imagination: Christian theology and the culture of pluralism*. Crossroad Publishing Company.

Tudoroiu, T. (2014). Social media and revolutionary waves: The case of the Arab spring. *New Political Science, 36*(3), 346–365. https://doi.org/10.1080/07393148.2014.913841

Unger, A. (2019). *A Jewish public theology: God and the global city*. Lexington Books.

Vanhoozer, K. J. (2007). What is everyday theology? How and why Christians should read culture. In K. J. Vanhoozer, C. A. Anderson, & M. J. Sleasman (Eds.), *Everyday theology: How to read cultural texts and interpret trends* (pp. 15–60). Baker Academic.

Wagner, R. (2012). *Godwired: Religion, ritual, and virtual reality*. Routledge.

White, S. J. (1997). *Groundwork of Christian worship*. Epworth Press.

Wilcox, R., & Lavery, D. (2002). *Fighting the forces: What's at stake in Buffy the vampire slayer*. Rowman & Littlefield.

Selected Readings

Bosch, M. D., Soukup, P. S. J., Sanz, J. L. S. M., & Zsupan-Jerome, D. (Eds.). (2017). *Authority and leadership: Values, religion, media*. Ramon Llull University.

Campbell, H. (2017). Surveying theoretical approaches within digital religion studies. *New Media & Society, 19*(1), 15–24. https://doi.org/10.1177/1461444816649912

Campbell, H. (2015). *Digital Judaism: Jewish negotiations with digital media and culture*. Routledge.

Hoover, S. M. (2006). *Religion in the media age*. Routledge.

Horsfield, P. G. (2015). *From Jesus to the internet: A history of Christianity and media*. John Wiley.

Morgan, D. (2008). *Key words in religion, media and culture*. Routledge.

White, R. A. (2007). The media, culture, and religion perspective: Discovering a theory and methodology for studying media and religion. *Communication Research Trends, 26*(1), 3–24.

3

Theology and Communication

Paul A. Soukup S.J.

In its most general sense, theology refers to the study of God (the divine) and how humans relate to God. Historically, many academic programs take Christianity as a default and apply its label, "theology," in an analogical manner to other religious traditions and their reflections on beliefs. This works well for "religions of the Book" (Judaism, Christianity, and Islam), which share early traditions, but less so for religions of Asia where, for example, Buddhism and Confucianism do not center their teachings on the divine. This also poses a challenge in comparing how religious movements frame teachings on communication derived from the study of God and human relations with God. Ethical behavior (a prohibition against lying, for instance) emerges clearly in different religious traditions. But ethics, while in some cases deduced from theology, is not the same as theology; ethical systems can exist independently of theology. In religious traditions, teachings on communication based on theology also serve a more pragmatic end in determining how to use contemporary communication technologies and practices.

When religious groups apply theological reflection to communication, they typically focus first on divine communication (referred to as revelation or the ways in which the divine communicates with humanity) and second on human communication: on the effects of the divine communication on believers, on the human response to the divine through prayer or worship, or on the use of media such as recitation, texts, and images. Because religions have preserved their heritages in texts, many of the groups offer guidance for theological interpretation of those texts. Reflecting the transitions from oral to writing cultures, some give precedence to recitation while maintaining texts as an aid to memory. Religious groups also hold collections of the interpretations of key scholars in special regard, generating commentaries on the commentaries themselves. For the "religions of the Book," the status and use of images to depict the divine, prophetic figures, or other human figures has generated controversy, with each tradition determining a theological response. Decisions reached in these older debates often form the basis for the adoption and guidelines for the use of newer communication technologies, particularly the audiovisual ones.

This chapter does not intend a full introduction to the theological teachings of the religions included here, nor even a complete treatment of theological discussion of communication. It will briefly introduce the major religions that have addressed communication, their key theological groundings for communication, some principles of interpretation and theological argument, and some major points of theology applied to communication. The chapter will not address teachings on prayer or worship but simply note that all religions have such traditions. The chapter

The Handbook on Religion and Communication, First Edition. Edited by Yoel Cohen and Paul A. Soukup.

begins with religions of the book (in the chronological order of their emergence) and then Hinduism, one Asian religion with a theological tradition. The teachings of nontheistic world religions on communication appear in discussions of communication ethics in Chapter 4. The fact that other theistic religions do not appear in this chapter indicates only that they do not have any extensive theological discussion of communication.

Judaism

Contemporary Judaism exists in several broad groupings (Orthodox, Conservative, and Reform), with agreement on the main tenets of belief and disagreement on religious observances and on methods of interpretation. Judaism regards itself as a revealed religion and thus holds the existence of God (the creator) and the possibility that God communicates with humans as central beliefs (Cohen, 2012, p. 15). The key divine revelations occur in the Hebrew Bible and in the commandments and statutes communicated to Moses and recorded in the Pentateuch (Kohler & Lauterbach, 1906). Much of Jewish theology starts with the Bible and exists in the form of commentaries upon the biblical texts (or its translations – *Targum*), *Midrash* (exegetical readings), commentaries upon the commentaries themselves (often named for the rabbis who authored them), or statements of the Law (*Halakha, Shulkhan Arukh*). Jewish theological method consists of reflection, discussion, and interpretations of these texts with scholars and rabbis drawing their theological conclusions from them. The focus on text and commentary establishes a powerful tradition of communication at the very heart of Jewish theology. Like all religious reflection on belief, Jewish thought has shifted over the centuries from a medieval rationalism and a mystical tradition of prayer (*Kabbalah*) to more contemporary intellectual idioms. An older and currently renewed central focus in Jewish theology is on God's covenant, a belief that highlights "the communal character of so much of Jewish religion" and recognizes "highly intricate ways of structuring and directing relationships both interhuman and divine-human" (Novak, 1990, p. 315). Such a view implies the role and value of communication. Prayer and ritual also reinforce the value of communication (Cohen, 2012, p. 16).

Some describe Jewish theology as itself a kind of communication. This communication has evolved over some 6000 years from direct communication between God and the patriarchs and Moses, and later with the Jewish prophets. Communication also characterized the Jewish Temple periods, notably between the High Priest and God. With the destruction of the Second Temple in 70 CE, belief (or *emunah*) – a less direct form of communication – and prayer, along with the growth of the synagogue and the role of the rabbi, replacing the sacrificial order of the Temple, have existed as the prime form of divine communication to this day. In one sense, with the sacred writings as a start, Judaism is "an ongoing, few thousand years old, *conversation*" (Gronbacher, 2017, italics original), with no central authority or binding decisions. "In searching for a single idea that expresses the nature of halackhah ... we might settle upon the word, 'conversation'" (Washofsky, 2010, p. xxii), a conversation that involves both the "Written Torah" and the "Oral Torah (*Torah Shebal Peh*), a collection of laws and teachings that extend, expound, and supplement the biblical mitzbot" (p. xviii). "Under the three broad headings of God, Torah, and Israel," "discussions about revelation, the nature of God, morality, liturgy, ritual, blessings, scripture scholarship, observance – and a whole host of other issues – takes place" (Gronbacher, 2017). The main groupings of contemporary Judaism diverge on the components of such discussions. "How we understand Jewish attitudes ... will depend on whether ... we take the Torah to be the only relevant text, or whether our understanding of Judaism incorporates the 'oral law,' the Talmud" (Jones, 2006, p. 101) and how open the groups are "to the possibility and the desirability of religious innovation and creativity" (Washofsky, 2010, p. xxvii). Against that background, a Jewish theological attitude to communication takes outline. The covenantal and conversational traditions place a value on communication in all its forms, with writings dating from the earliest periods. Jewish communities embraced the nascent mass media, from book publishing to newspapers, with Jewish thinkers playing important roles in public life.

Images (central to so much contemporary communication) receive much discussion in Jewish theology. Multiple places in the Hebrew Bible prohibit the making of images, a practice the scriptures connected with idolatry (Exodus 20:3–6; Leviticus 26:1; Numbers 33:53; Deuteronomy 4:16). Many commentators extended this teaching against making images of God to making images of people or things that could be used in worship (Shulkhan Arukh, 2000; chapter 11). However, the prohibition does not seem uniform, with some prohibiting only sculpture (in accordance with the biblical ban on "graven images") but allowing other arts. Key counterexamples appear in archeological sites: the mosaic images in the third-century synagogue of Dura Europos (Goethals, 1999, p. 137; Silver, 2010) and a synagogue at Na'aran (Barber, 1997). Barber (1997) argues from the selective destruction of images at the latter site and from surviving polemic literature that Jewish communities turned away from images not for theological but for cultural reasons (to differentiate themselves from Christian practices). Bland (2001) concludes that while medieval Jews "railed against idolatry," "they did not construe the Second Commandment to mean that all visual images were forbidden," basing this conclusion on practices of Jewish communities (p. 7). Jewish theology shows itself to be much more nuanced in its attitudes toward images, though the ultra-Orthodox will more likely reject them. Jewish theology does reject some images in contemporary media (film, television, the Internet), not on the basis of idolatry, but on the basis of sexual modesty (Cohen, 2012, p. 18).

Cohen (2012) reports a number of theological opinions about the practices of contemporary media, ranging from the right to know, which supports accountability but prevents slander (pp. 18–22); the sanctity of communication, which addresses everything from preserving religious texts to copyright (pp. 22–24); and the use of media on the Sabbath, which may or may not constitute forbidden work (pp. 25–28). The protection of religious texts proves a thorny issue, for example, when online media display and then erase texts – something forbidden with written texts. Frost and Youngblood (2014) raise the issue of whether virtual participants can establish a quorum for communal prayer (p. 51).

The Covid-19 restrictions on in-person gatherings made some of these questions very real. Wechsler (2020) describes wrestling with whether traditional rabbinical guides allowed online worship. The theological discussions and decisions about such contemporary issues differ based on the school of thought of the rabbis and congregations. "The Reform movement seems better situated for diving into practicing religion online. Rabbi Scott Sperling reinforces this idea, pointing out that Reform congregations 'have always been early adopters of any means of communication that allowed greater numbers of human beings to learn from and share opinions with one another'" (Frost & Youngblood, 2014, p. 51).

Christianity

Like Judaism, Christianity in all its forms (Orthodox, Catholic, Protestant) accepts both the possibility and the fact that the divine can communicate with humans. Drawing on a biblical theology of revelation, Christianity affirms in its creeds that God does indeed reveal the divine to people, through the act and consequences of creation, through prophets, in the scriptures, and most completely in Jesus Christ. In the Roman Catholic Church's formulation at the Second Vatican Council, *Dei Verbum*, the Council:

teaches that God "chose to reveal Himself and to make known to us the hidden purpose of His will by which through Christ, the Word made flesh, man might in the Holy Spirit have access to the Father and come to share in the divine nature" (no. 2). God realized His plan "by deeds and words having an inner unity" and also a clear historical pattern. First He revealed Himself through created realities (no. 3); second He undertook the formation of a special people to acknowledge Him as "the one living and true God, provident father and just judge" and to wait for "the Savior promised by Him"; third ... "Jesus perfected revelation by fulfilling it through his whole work of making Himself present and manifesting Himself through His words and deeds, His signs and wonders, but especially through His death and glorious resurrection from the dead and final sending of the Spirit of truth" (no. 4). (Mirus, 2010)

The Catholic Church also maintains that the Church alone offers authoritative interpretation of the word of God through a teaching office descended from the apostles of Jesus. Though other Christian denominations do not accept this position of Catholic authentic interpretation, they do accept the necessity of theological understanding of revelation and have their own guidelines for interpreting revelation. The Orthodox, for example, vest interpretive authority in Ecumenical Synods (Mastrantonis, 2015).

Christianity, with its identification of the Incarnation (or enfleshment) of the divine in Jesus Christ, used the first- and second-century BCE Judeo-Greek terminology of the Word (*logos* or λόγος) to describe the divine and the incarnate divine. This language in the prologue to the Gospel of John starts the Christian tradition on the theological path to use the human practices and language of communication to describe God and to claim a connection between human communication and the divine (Pelikan, 1971, chapter 5; Yenson, 2019). Among the early Christian theologians developing this theme we find Augustine (fourth to fifth century CE), who justified the application of rhetorical tools to the interpretation of biblical texts (in his *De Doctrina Christiana*) and who further offered an understanding of the nature of God in the communication terms of the Word (*De Trinitate*). Several centuries later, John of Damascus also drew on the Incarnation of the Word to justify the use of images in Christian worship (Pelikan, 1974, pp. 120, 122), arguing that God's taking on human form sanctified the human image, noting that the humanity of the Christ formed an image of God; therefore, artists could use human images to depict the incarnate Word as well as human saints. Orthodox and Catholics share this position. The debate continued for centuries and played a role in the writings of the Protestant reformers in the sixteenth century (Jensen, 2000, p. 3). Emphasizing the Word, many of them banned images from their worship and from their churches. However, they quickly embraced the relatively new mass communication technology of the printing press as a way to disseminate God's Word in the Bible more widely and more quickly (Eisenstein, 1979; Pelikan, 1974).

The Christian tradition, influenced by a logos theology, has proven itself open to all manner of communication, from preaching and interpretation to the written or printed word through all art forms to new media. Christianity, unlike many other religious traditions, has also embraced translation so that peoples of any language can experience God's word in their own tongues (Noss, 2007).

These theological starting points bear fruit in different ways in Christianity. Among the Christian Churches, the Roman Catholic Church has a long tradition of theological reflection both on interpretation, as seen earlier, and on communication technologies. Documents from the nineteenth century indicate a defensive posture against misinformation spread by mass printing. More positively, the Catholic Church established Vatican Radio in 1931 with the theological motivation of proclaiming the gospel to the world (Pius XII, 1957, no. 7). Initially led by concerns for moral behavior and positive example (as in Pius XI's, 1936 document *Vigilanti Cura* on film and morals), later-twentieth-century documents such as *Miranda Prorsus* (Pius XII, 1957) added a positive theological message to the moral warnings about film, television, and radio, adding a duty to preach God's message in any way (Ephesians 3:8–9). Radio, film, and television presented the possibility of Christian teaching, education, the service of truth and virtue, as well as the involvement of all people in forming judgments. In 1971, the Vatican office for social (or mass) communication, published *Communio et Progressio*, a detailed statement on communication (Pontifical Council for Social Communication, 1971). The document begins with an extended theological understanding of communication, seeing contemporary media as "gifts from God," with the aim of promoting human community and progress. It draws its conclusions about communication from the model of the Incarnation. "Communication is more than the expression of ideas and the indication of emotion. At its most profound level it is the giving of self in love" as seen in Christ (no. 11). Drawing on this theology, the document presents an optimistic view of communication and asserts that people have a human right to communicate (both in access to information and in expressing themselves). Consistent with the centuries-old acceptance of images, the document accepts artistic expression in the images of film and television. Later Catholic documents on the Internet and other new media maintain a blend of regarding communication media and expression as consistent with God's creation, with human dignity, and with moral obligation (Pontifical Council for Social Communication, 2000). In addition to the Vatican documents, regional conferences of Catholic bishops in Latin America and Asia have also added their theological teaching on communication, reflecting the particular circumstances of their regions, usually arguing for greater access and more accurate representation, again based on the theological principles of the Incarnation (Eilers, 2014).

Orthodox Christianity's statements on communication have focused more generally on communication or dialogue between Christian denominations (McPartlan, 2009) and more specifically on social media guidelines. These guidelines for clergy and laity stress respect, protection of children, and the separation of personal opinion from Church teaching (Orthodox Church in America, 2018).

Led by the pragmatic need to participate in the communication culture of the twentieth and twenty-first centuries, individual Catholic theologians also contributed to religious understanding of media and the Church's role in contemporary media. The literature here is extensive and addresses revelation, the use of images, the practices of media, and the nature of the Christian Church (for summaries, see Eilers, 2014; Soukup, 1983, 1993, 2006; 2011, 2019; Zsupan-Jerome, 2014). The writings of Dulles (1972, 1974, 1989) stand out for his equating of the Church with communication: "The more I think about the matter, the more convinced I become that communications is at the heart of what the Church is all about. The Church exists in order to bring [people] into communion with God and thereby to open them up to communication with each other" (Dulles, 1972, p. 6). Every decision about the Church, he maintains, is a communication decision.

While not as extensive, writing from other Christian denominations also offers a theological understanding of communication. The World Council of Churches, in its general assemblies of the 1960s, 1970s, and 1980s wrote regularly of communication and the need to relate to the media "in a matter which is pastoral, evangelical, and prophetic" (quoted in Soukup, 1989, p. 81; see the list of citations in Soukup, 1989). The World Association for Christian Communication has also issued regular reflections on "Christian Principles of Communication" (1986). The US National Council of Churches offers its own theological reflection as a critique of a mass media culture (summarized in Fore, 1987), arguing that from a theological perspective, mass media can take on the role of a kind of counter-Christianity and so stand in need of critique.

Starting in the 1930s and 1940s, Evangelical Christian Churches embraced radio (and later television) seeing these mass media as a way to fulfill the "Great Commission" in which Jesus tells the disciples to "go and proclaim the good news to all the nations" (Matthew 28:19). Given their independent structures, these churches never developed a common theological approach beyond the urgency of the task. However, individual preachers – particularly among the television evangelists in the 1980s and 1990s – followed what Schultze (1990) calls an "experiential theology," one that stresses a "health and wealth" approach pleasing to its audience members (p. 44). Schultze explains:

> The experiential theologies of the electronic church are not taken from the historic creeds and confessions of the Christian church, from the writings of highly influential theologians, or even from the traditions of established denominations and churches. Instead, the electronic church stakes its theological claims on the experiences of its members as reported and interpreted in the broadcasts and writings of its charismatic leaders. This gives the electronic church an especially strong ahistorical quality; the gospel is usually interpreted in terms of the contemporary culture, rather than the culture being viewed through the eyes of the historic Christian gospel. (p. 44)

Fore (1990) expands on this experiential theology, noting that its features include authoritativeness of presentation, individualism, mainstream American values, the belief systems of viewers, a competition between God and the devil, and an eschatology that portends the coming judgment of God (p. 138). The theology finds its ground in a "traditional Christian conservatism, which deals with the Bible literally, accepts a supernatural world, and worships a God who acts in an anthropomorphic way in response to human appeals" (p. 138).

Similar theological messages appear in the radio and television evangelists of Central and South America, Africa, and India (see Chapter 11), as these preachers either trained in the United States, have an affiliation with US groups, or imitate what they have seen in the US televangelist preaching.

Overall, the Christian Churches have embraced mass communication and new media, following a theological path established at the very beginning of Christianity by equating the divine action in the world with "the Word," which extends to all communication technologies. Pragmatically Christianity seeks to spread that Word, though it also depends on the scriptural word for a critique of communication practices and a guide to communication behavior.

Islam

Islam in its two main branches (Sunni and Shia) accepts revelation, as shown in God's acts and communications to the prophets and recorded in the Qur'an and the hadith or collections of sayings of Prophet Muhammad (Renard, 2014, pp. 3–12). "Islam is a communicative religion. The Islamic God is a communicative God Who takes keen interest in the affairs of His creatures. As such Allah, has communicated to humanity through a progression of prophets from Adam to the last Prophet – Muhammad (PBUH)" (Khalil, 2016, p. 23). In fact, Islam holds that "God's self-disclosure is the bedrock and fundamental 'presupposition' of any 'theological' activity" (p. 164). Like Judaism and Christianity, its theology contains hermeneutic principles and methods that ground its activity (Renard, 2014, pp. 47–58). Renard points out that Islamic theologians have "developed an intense interest in the 'circumstances of revealed messages' (*asbab an-nuzul*) into an essential hermeneutical tool ... [and] have long discussed a question raised in Qur'an 3:7 about levels of interpretation"; in addition they note that as "God tailors revelatory communication to humanity's limited capacity to receive ultimate truth, He therefore reserves the right to 'abrogate' earlier messages in favor of refinements needed to move the community of believers further toward full understanding" (p. 47).

In developing the theological tradition, medieval Islamic scholars set out methods to make decisions based on the Qur'an and hadiths and to verify the hadith readings as genuinely from the Prophet. Bahri (2018) explains how this aspect of theology functions:

> The status and quality of a hadith, whether it can be accepted or rejected, depends on the sanad and the mate of the hadith. If the sanad of a hadith has fulfilled certain conditions and criteria, so is the case, then the hadith can be accepted as a proposition to do something or establish a law on something. However, if the conditions are not met, then the hadith is rejected and cannot be used as proof.
>
> The quality of a hadith can only be concluded after the existence of complete information and data about the narrators and the composition of the hadith text through criticism of the hadith studied (p. 268).

Once scholars have accepted a hadith, they can then use it in establishing principles for given cases, such as communication practices or ethics. Bringing the older practice to bear, Usman and Wazir (2018) caution that people posting hadiths on social media should apply similar principles to judge the quality of a hadith before they post.

A central theological justification for Islamic communication practices comes from the concept of *da'wah*. Umar (2019) explains that *da'wah* "is derived from the root word '*Da'awah* which means 'call' or 'invitation.'" The word "commonly appears in the Qur'an and Hadith, classical Muslim texts, and contemporary theological or ideological texts, written and spoken" (p. 205). Commentators and scholars have interpreted it differently:

> Bala (2015) technically sees *da'wah* as communicating and informing people the right path, guiding and showing the way to religion (of Islam) and its counsel in accordance with the statement of Allah:
>
> In another definition, the word refers to inviting ourselves and all others to obey Allah and His laws, which were given to the mankind through a long chain of messengers and prophets. The word *da'wah* used to refer to the call made by Allah (SWT) to mankind through his Noble prophet Muhammad (PBUH), call made by man to Allah (SWT), in his supplications, and call made by man to his fellow men to come wholeheartedly to the *Deen* (Religion of Islam). (Hussain, 2009; Umar, 2019, p. 205)

The concept ultimately justifies the use of various communication media by Islam since this theological principle imposes the obligation to spread Islam. For example, Umar (2019) concludes that "the most effective and efficient channel of disseminating *da'wah* programmes to the wide public at large is by the use of mass media" (p. 208). Hidayaturrahman and Putra (2019) and Ibahrine (2014) make much the same case for the use of social media, with a look at theological opinions on both sides of the issue.

Following the example of the approval of poetry by the Prophet Mohammad, Islam embraces a variety of communication forms including recitation, writing, poetry, and storytelling (Renard, 2014, p. 270). More broadly, scholars list characteristics of the Prophet's communication that should guide all communication: "tact," "good advice," "well-formed debate," "purifying the intention," "knowing the audience," "talk when needed," "narration," "analogy," and nonverbal communication (Usman et al., 2019, pp. 379–381). Historically, Islam has not hesitated to make use of communication resources, ranging from paper- and book-making to libraries, the printing press, postal communication, and cinema (Mowlana, 2003, p. 314).

While Islam may use communication media, its scholars seek guidance as to what is allowed, basing teachings on the Qur'an and the hadith (Khalil, 2016, p. 25), and drawing on several principles: "monotheism (*tawhid*), doctrine of responsibility, guidance and ... the idea of Islamic community (*Umma*), and, finally the principle of piety (*taqwa*)" (p. 28). Other commentators add the principle of *amrbi al-ma'ruf wa nahy'an al munkar* (commanding the right and prohibiting the wrong) to this list (Mowlana, 2003, p. 312; UKEssays, 2018). But even here scholars can disagree (Pasha, 1993), leading to the application of philosophical or cultural reasoning (Khiabani, 2007) as well as metaphorical readings of the *hadiths* (Thurston, 2015, p. 1072). As an illustration of such reasoning in favor of media use, Thurston (2015) gives the case of a Salafi community in Nigeria and radio; in choosing broadcasting, they "were also likely influenced by the electronic media engagement of Salafi scholars like Saudi Arabia's Shaykh 'Abd al 'Aziz ihn Bāz (1910–1999). Ihn Bāz delivered fatāwā (edicts) on the program '*Nūr 'ala al-Darb* (Light on the Path)' on Saudi radio" (p. 1067). Their practice of translating sermons from Mecca on live broadcasts found further support in community realities: "This focus on orality and electronic media is a deliberate strategic choice: Inuwa explained in one 'Al Azkar' episode, broadcast October 14, 2011, that because few Kano residents read newspapers or attend lectures in mosques, it was important to propound 'righteous speech (Hausa: *maganar adalci*)' on the radio" (p. 1067).

A complex case arises with images. Like Judaism, Islam connects images with idolatry; this forms the base of a prohibition of communication through images, based on hadiths condemning representation of living forms and the Qur'an's opposition to idolatry (Department of Islamic Art, 2001). Allen (1988) argues for a nuanced interpretation, drawing on other hadiths where the Prophet objected only to figural representations in worship, but then adds, "The traditional Muslim theological objection to images, which may have been observed more in the breach than in ordinary life, was eventually codified in a quite rigid form and extended to the depiction of all animate beings" (p. 19), citing a hadith that painters will be subject to condemnation on the day of judgment. In Allen's view the ban moved from one concerned with idiolatry (making images for worship) to a ban on sculpted images to a ban on all figural images. Soğanci's (2004) literature review argues for seven different approaches, each justifying or forbidding depicting living beings based on different readings of the tradition. Naef (2007) also argues for different opinions about images coming from different groups within Islam ("reformers," "fundamentalists," and "revolutionary Islamists"). Citing Naef's book, Seker (2007) concludes, "It is only in modern times that scholars have given imagery much thought, in view of the flood of images created by new techniques and media – film, photography, television, portrait painting."

A second area where Islamic theology touches on communication arises with ethical guidelines, which scholars derive primarily from theology (the Qur'an, the hadiths, and principles outlined earlier). Renard (2014) lists four key concerns of Islamic ethical teaching:

> First, an articulation of an overarching principle of Muslim ethics emphasizes active, socially engaged moral responsibility for all. Second,… The Prophet also functions as the paragon of ethical conduct and virtue… Third, concerns over the appropriate religious motivation and demeanor required of anyone elevated to leadership of Muslim communities throughout history have led to an important genre known as the "mirror for princes." Finally, philosophers and theologians alike have written numerous volumes known generically as the "science of character and comportment" (*'ilm-al-akhlāq*). Intended for the "average" person, not just for rulers, their topics include general canons of virtuous behavior as well as detailed analyses of how one identifies "sin." (p. 368)

Each of these four strands leads to an explication of communication guidelines, whether for interpersonal communication (Khalil, 2016) or media use. Mowlana (2003) further describes how Islamic ethical guidelines for communication draw on the secular ethics of the Greek tradition that influenced medieval Islamic scholars. He explains the two approaches:

the rationalist, which subscribed to rational opinion (*ra'y*), argued that where there is no clear guidance from the Qur'an or tradition, the Islamic judges and lawyers might make their own rational judgements on moral and ethical questions. The traditionalist insisted that ethical and moral judgements can be based only on the Qur'an and tradition. (p. 310)

Using the contemporary categories of communication rights, Mowlana notes:

According to these three sources [Qur'an, traditions, hadith] the basic rights of communication in Islam include the following: (1) the right to know, (2) the right to read (*igra*), (3) the right to write (*ghalam*), (4) the right to speak (*khutbah*), (5) the right to knowledge (*ilm*), (6) the right to consult (*showra*), (7) the right to disseminate (*tabligh*) and (8) the right to travel (*hijrah*) (p. 312)

In a review of the literature on the theological grounding of Islamic communication ethics, Bahri (2018) focuses on the doctrine of responsibility and maintaining information accuracy as well as on how scholars have developed and criticized teachings. In another example, Usman et al. (2019) offer a helpful illustration of theological reasoning suggested to evaluate viral news in the online world, explaining that:

the concept and understanding of *tabbayun* (investigating) to the sender and messages are [of] much importance to be applied in any form of communication situation as reminded in *al-Hujurat* verse 6, "O you who have believed, if there comes to you a disobedient one with information, investigate, lest you harm a people out of ignorance and become, over what you have done, regretful." (p. 382)

Their case study continues for several pages of citations from the hadiths, offering a good example of theological reasoning.

Hinduism

Like all non-Abrahamic religions, Hinduism suffers under the methods of Western theology through which many view religion. That can limit one's understanding of Hinduism even as it provides a framework to consider Hinduism's theological approach to communication. Acknowledging this weakness but for consistency, this section looks at the concepts of the divine, revelation, interpretation, and communication in Hinduism.

Hinduism does accept a divine principle but expresses that differently. It has sacred books, but these have functions somewhat different from that of the religions of the book. Konsky and her colleagues offer this background:

Hinduism is not a monolithic entity; instead it is a family of religions with the main philosophy centering around Brahman (supreme power), Jeeva (living being), Maya (ignorance)... Hindus believe in merging the "self" with the Supreme power known as Brahma. The sages or religious pundits have arrived at one central concept: The physical world is temporal; and, all peoples' worldly desires are doomed to frustration, which is the cause of all human sufferings... A second underlying belief is real peace can be achieved by controlling one's desires and by focusing the mind on one enduring ultimate reality, God. (Konsky et al., 2000, p. 238)

Hinduism honors ancient sacred texts, the Vedas, which they regard as revelation (Bhattacharyya, 2015, p. 4). The Vedas themselves reflect Hinduism's geographical and temporal origins.

Bhattacharyya (2015) describes them: "It is widely regarded that the *Rg* Veda is the oldest available text of the Indian civilization which is followed by the other three Vedas, *Yajurveda* (The Book of Rituals), *Samaveda* (The Book of Songs), and *Atharvaveda* (The Book of Applications). The Vedas are supposed to be *apauruseya*, that is, not attributable to human beings" or a form of revelation (p. 4). Scholars divide these texts

> into two groups: *śruti* and *smrti*. *Śruti* means "that which is heard," while *smrti* means "that which is remembered." In this classification, the term *śruti* is reserved for those texts that are believed to be revealed, while *smrti* is used for texts with identifiable human authors, regarded as secondary in authority to the *śruti*. While the distinction is helpful for surveying the scriptures of Hinduism, it is important to keep in mind that many *smrti* texts are understood by particular traditions to be revealed and enjoy considerable authority and prestige within those communities. The four Vedas (*Rg*, *Sāma*, *Yajur* and *Atharva*), however, are widely acknowledged by Hindus to be *śruti* and acceptance of the authority of the Vedas is commonly regarded as necessary for Hindu orthodoxy, even though such acceptance may be merely formal and nominal. (Rambachan, 2019, p. 17)

Rambachan (2019) explains that some texts act as commentary upon other texts, with varying degree of doctrinal acceptance. And, as implied in the name, *śruti*, Hinduism values an oral tradition. Jacobs (2012), quoting Lipner (1994), argues "that when written the sacred language of the Vedas, 'loses its vitality; the sacred word springs to life and exerts power when it is spoken and heard'" (p. 136).

"While the Vedas are regarded as the root source of every Hindu principle, the essence of the principles has been explained to the after-generations through the later scriptures such as the *Puranas*, the *Upanisads*, the *Dharmaśāstras*, the later commentaries by various scholars and also extant literature such as the *Rāmāyana*, the *Mahābhārata* and the *Bhagavad Gita*" (Bhattacharyya, 2015, p. 4). The multiplicity of sacred texts and the spread of Hinduism throughout India have led to a number of schools of Hindu thought, usually clustered around the teachings of a guru or interpreter. Hindery (1978) describes one such tradition, rooted in the Vedas, of Brahmanic authority of interpretation, especially of laws (p. 75). Whatever the level of acceptance, Hinduism does possess a set of various commentaries or scholars' interpretation of the sacred Hindu texts. Few, if any, write about a Hindu theology of communication, but one can infer theological approaches from ethical teaching and from communication practices.

In his comparative studies of Hindu ethics, Hindery (1976, 1978) demonstrates a pluralism in Hindu ethics, noting ethical teachings in each of the key texts. He argues that Hinduism deals with morality rooted in universal virtues (1978, p. 203), with appeals to authority important only in the neo-Brahmanic tradition (pp. 204, 207), and with a central ethos of life affirmation (p. 205). Creel (1975) identifies three key ethical principles: respect for all persons (p. 167), social solidarity (p. 168), and social welfare (168). Several contemporary writers apply these to communication (usually interpersonal communication but extensible to communication media). Aryani (2018) notes that religious ethical principles apply to both vertical and horizontal communication:

> Communication in the vertical aspect is done, especially when Hindus carry out ritual activities on certain days, especially on holy days of Hinduism and on the implementation of *pujawali* (the implementation of religious ceremonies)… Communication in the horizontal aspects associated with the implementation of Hinduism occurs in various forms, such as interpersonal communication, social communication, and group communication. All forms of communication aim to succeed the implementation of religious activities. (p. 148)

Moral communication actions "deal with the norms that must be followed in order to realize a harmonious life" as well as the deeds that implement them (p. 148). Adhikary (2010) begins with the assertion that "various Hindu texts consist of inquisition/exposition on communication" (p. 76). Commenting on those texts, he concludes, "The goal of communication as envisioned in Hinduism is certainly achieving commonness or mutual understanding. But the goal would not be limited to just this extent. Just as Hinduism always emphasizes to achieve all of the *purushartha chatustayas* (i.e., four goals of life: *artha* [wealth], *kama* [desire], *dharma* [righteousness], and *moksha* [liberation])," so too must communication serve these goals (p. 79). Communication serves the religious ends of Hinduism when it assists worship and helps people to live harmoniously.

Hindu communication practices show this and other implicit theological thinking at work. Despite the preference for the oral performance of the Vedas, Hinduism does make use of other communication forms: writing, images used in rituals, and – by extension – film and television. The oral stems from the chanting and performance of the scriptures, which occurs in worship but also in devotion. "For lay members … reciting from their scriptures is part of their religious practice, but the predominant medium for both individual and collective religious expression is the singing of devotional poetry in vernacular languages" (Qureshi, 1995, p. 139). Indeed, some professional singers and their clans have become an accepted part of the culture – the *kīrtankār*. Marcus (1995) describes performances of wandering musicians (*bābā*) (p. 168ff.), but more relevant for communication media, of recorded religious music (of a genre called *bhajan*). While the recordings lose the context of the performance, people use them to accompany *pūjā* (private religious rituals) (pp. 175ff.). Marcus (1995) concludes, "Whether contained within a live performance in a traditional setting or in a recent cassette release, the texts of devotional songs continue to practice of retelling and reinterpreting traditional myths, legends, and philosophy" (p. 182).

Hinduism embraced images, first in temples and then in homes. Rambachan (2019) explains the "context of the widely shared Hindu teaching that, in a properly consecrated icon, God becomes accessible for worship… According to Rāmānuja (eleventh century), the foremost Vaisnava theologian, the icon embodiment (*arcāvatāra*) is one of the five ways in which God manifests" (p. 11). This theological conclusion has led to the widespread acceptance of most subsequent communication forms in Hindu life. What began with carved images continued with "a rich iconography" of paintings and later printed reproductions (Jacobs, 2012, p. 138). In fact, with print technology, even the humblest families could have a "god poster" at home, something that "had a significant impact on the devotional practices of many Hindus" (p. 139), allowing for devotional practices apart from temples. Smith (1995) terms the devotions away from temples "omnipraxy," explaining in these words: "For those who see in god posters a positive theophany – that is, among those for whom the god posters function as 'real' images—many unprecedented, remarkably widespread and democratized, even innovative and idiosyncratic, rituals have crept into common usage" (p. 37). The acceptance of god posters indirectly connects to the rise of graphic novels of the lives of saints (Hawley, 1995).

From these beginnings, other media use developed:

> Film has continued the process of widening distribution begun by the proliferation of printed images. India has developed what might be identified as a unique genre of film, known as mythologicals, which derive their narratives from the rich storehouse of Hindu mythology. The visual conventions of god posters have influenced the visual style of mythological films. (Jacobs, 2012, p. 140)

Another preparation for such religious films comes from oral performance where "a performer, usually called a *kathāvācak* or *vyās*, is invited by an individual patron or community to retell or discourse on a sacred story … such storytellers were often hired on a long-term basis to narrate the entire epic in daily installments" (Lutgendorf, 1995, p. 227). The episodic nature of these performances indirectly led to one of the longest running television programs in India, Ramanand Sagar's 78-episode *Ramayan*, based on the religious epic, the *Rāmāyana* (p. 217). Lutgendorf sees a theological development in the "long historical process" of "orthodox iconography and ethos" and the combination of "orthodox and heterodox currents of devotionalism" (p. 246). Several commentators recount how viewers in movie theaters prostrated themselves before the images of the gods on the screen (Barnouw & Krishnaswamy, 1980, p. 15) and how "in many homes the watching of *Ramayan* has become a religious ritual, and the television set ... is garlanded, decorated with sandalwood paste and vermillion, and conch shells are blown" (Melwani, 1988, p. 56).

Without any formal theological debate, Hindu popular usage embraced printed images, audio recordings, film, and television.

Conclusion

These four major theistic religions make communication central, whether in prayer and worship or in the use of communication media to pass on their beliefs. Each judges the appropriateness of communication media according to principles derived from their sacred books, creating at least an implicit theology for communication.

References

Adhikary, N. M. (2010). *Sancharyoga*: Approaching communication as a *vidya* in Hindu orthodoxy. *China Media Research*, *6*(3), 76–84.

Allen, T. (1988). Aniconism and figural representation in Islamic art. In *Five essays on Islamic art* (pp. 17–37). Solipsist Press. Retrieved April 28, 2021, from http://sonic.net/~tallen/palmtree/fe2.htm

Aryani, N. L. (2018). Implementation of communication ethics in building social harmony. *International Journal of Social Sciences and Humanities*, *2*(1), 147–156. http://sciencescholar.us/journal/index.php/ijssh

Bahri, S. (2018). Hadiths about communication ethics: Study of hadiths about responsibility and maintaining information accuracy. *Budapest International Research and Critics Institute Journal*, *1*(4), 265–276. https://doi.org/10.33258/birci.v1i4.118

Bala, A.A. (2015) The role of dawa'h in the introduction and spread of Islam in Hausaland (northern Nigeria). *Journal of Humanities and Social Sciences*, *20*(8), 204–211.

Barber, C. (1997). The truth in painting: Iconoclasm and identity in early-medieval art. *Speculum*, *72*(4), 1019–1036.

Barnouw, E., & Krishnaswamy, S. (1980). *Indian film*. Oxford University Press.

Bhattacharyya, K. K. (2015). Conceptualizing a value-based communication system: Towards a synergy between Hindu and Islamic perspectives. *International Journal of Dharma Studies*, *3*(5), 1–14. https://doi.org/10.1186/s40613-015-0015-3

Bland, K. P. (2001). *The artless Jew medieval and modern: Affirmations and denials of the visual*. Princeton University Press.

Cohen, Y. (2012). *God, Jews, and the media*. Routledge.

Creel, A. B. (1975). The reexamination of "Dharma" in Hindu ethics. *Philosophy East and West*, *25*(2), 161–173. https://www.jstor.org/stable/1397937

Department of Islamic Art. (2001). Figural representation in Islamic art. In *Heilbrunn Timeline of Art History*. The Metropolitan Museum of Art. 2000–. Retrieved April 28, 2021, from http://www.metmuseum.org/toah/hd/figs/hd_figs.htm

Dulles, A. (1972). The church is communications. *Multimedia International*, *1*, 1–18.

Dulles, A. (1974). *Models of the church*. Doubleday.

Dulles, A. (1989). Vatican II and communications. In R. Latourelle (Ed.), *Vatican II: Assessment and perspectives, twenty-five years after (1962–1987)* (Vol. 3, pp. 528–547). Paulist Press.

Eilers, F.-J. (2014). *Communicating church: Social communication documents, an introduction.* Logos Publications.

Eisenstein, E. L. (1979). *The printing press as an agent of change: Communications and cultural transformations in early-modern Europe.* Cambridge University Press.

Fore, W. F. (1987). *Television and religion: The shaping of faith, values, and culture.* Augsburg Publishing House.

Fore, W. (1990). "Living church" and "electronic church" compared. In R. Abelman, & S. M. Hoover (Eds.), *Religious television: Controversies and conclusions* (pp. 135–146). Ablex Publishing Corporation.

Frost, J. K., & Youngblood, N. E. (2014). Online religion and religion online: Reform Judaism and web-based communication. *Journal of Media and Religion, 13*(2), 49–66. https://doi.org/10.1080/15348423.2014.909190

Goethals, G. T. (1999). The imaged word: Aesthetics, fidelity, and new media translations. In P. A. Soukup, & R. Hodgson (Eds.), *Fidelity and translation: Communicating the Bible in new media* (pp. 133–172). Sheed & Ward.

Gronbacher, G. E. (2017). Jewish theology – A primer (especially for Christians) – Part I. Patheos. Retrieved April 16, 2021, from https://www.patheos.com/blogs/opentablejudaism/2017/02/18/jewish-theology-primer-especially-christians-part

Hawley, J. S. (1995). The saints subdued: Domestic virtue and national integration in *Amar Chitra Katha.* In L. A. Babb, & S. S. Wadley (Eds.), *Media and the transformation of religion in South Asia* (pp. 107–134). University of Pennsylvania Press.

Hidayaturrahman, M., & Putra, D. I. A. (2019). The role of technology and social media in spreading the Qur'an and hadiths by Mubalig. *Dinika: Academic Journal of Islamic Studies, 4*(1), https://ejournal.iainsurakarta.ac.id/index.php/dinika/article/view/1858

Hindery, R. (1976). Hindu ethics in the Rāmāyana. *The Journal of Religious Ethics, 4*(2), 287–322. https://www.jstor.org/stable/40014906

Hindery, R. (1978). *Comparative ethics in Hindu and Buddhist traditions.* Motilal Banarsidass Publishers.

Hussain, M. Y. (2009). *Reading in Islamic Daawah.* International Islamic University Press.

Ibahrine, M. (2014). Islam and social media. LSE. Retrieved April 28, 2021, from https://blogs.lse.ac.uk/mec/2014/10/28/islam-and-social-media

Jacobs, S. (2012). Communicating Hinduism in a changing media context. *Religion Compass, 6*(2), 136–151. https://doi.org/10.1111/j.1749-8171.2011.00333.x

Jensen, R. M. (2000). *Understanding early Christian art.* Routledge.

Jones, M. (2006). Judaism, theology and the human rights of people with disabilities. *Journal of Religion Disability & Health Disability & Health, 10*(3–4), 101–145. https://doi.org/10.1300/J095v10n03_08

Khalil, A. I. A. E.-F. 2016. The Islamic perspective of interpersonal communication. *Journal of Islamic Studies and Culture, 4*(2), 22–23. https://doi.org/10.15640/jisc.v4n2a3

Khiabani, G. (2007). Is there an Islamic communication? The persistence of 'tradition' and the lure of modernity. *Critical Arts, 21*(1), 106–124. https://doi.org/10.1080/02560040701398814

Kohler, K., & Lauterbach, J. Z. (1906). Theology. Jewish Encyclopedia. Retrieved April 16, 2021, from https://www.jewishencyclopedia.com/articles/14362-theology

Konsky, C., Kapoor, U., Blue, J., & Kapoor, S. (2000). Religion and communication: A study of Hinduism, Buddhism, and Christianity. *Intercultural Communication Studies, 10*(2), 235–253.

Lipner, J. (1994). *Hindus: Their religious beliefs and practices.* Routledge.

Lutgendorf, P. (1995). All in the (Raghu) family: A video epic in cultural context. In L. A. Babb, & S. S. Wadley (Eds.), *Media and the transformation of religion in South Asia* (pp. 217–253). University of Pennsylvania Press.

Marcus, S. (1995). On cassette rather than live: Religious music in India today. In L. A. Babb, & S. S. Wadley (Eds.), *Media and the transformation of religion in South Asia* (pp. 167–185). University of Pennsylvania Press.

Mastrantonis, G. (2015). The fundamental teachings of the Eastern Orthodox Church. Greek Orthodox Archdiocese of America. Retrieved January 18, 2022, from https://www.goarch.org/-/the-fundamental-teachings-of-the-eastern-orthodox-church

McPartlan, P. (2009). The Ravenna agreed statement and Catholic-Orthodox dialogue. *The Jurist: Studies in Church Law and Ministry, 69*(2), 749–765. https://doi.org/10.1353/jur.2009.0027

Melwani, L. (1988). Ramanand Sagar's Ramayan serial re-ignites epic's values. *India Worldwide,* (February), 56–57.

Mirus, J. (2010). Vatican II on divine revelation. Catholic Culture. Retrieved April 14, 2021, from https://www.catholicculture.org/commentary/vatican-ii-on-divine-revelation/?repos=6&subrepos=0&searchid=2228176

Mowlana, H. (2003). Foundation of communication in Islamic societies. In J. Mitchell, & S. Marriage (Eds.), *Mediating religion: Conversations in media, religion, and culture* (pp. 305–315). T & T Clark.

Naef, S. (2007). *Bilder und Bilderverbot im Islam. Vom Koran bis zum Karikaturenstreit* [Images and the image Ban in Islam: From Koran to caricature debate]. C.H. Beck Verlag.

Noss, P. (2007). *A history of Bible translation*. American Bible Society.

Novak, D. (1990). Jewish theology. *Modern Judaism, 10*(3), 311–323.

Orthodox Church in America. (2018). Social media guidelines for clergy and lay leaders of the Orthodox Church in America. OCA. Retrieved January 18, 2022, from https://www.oca.org/holy-synod/statements/holy-synod/social-media-guidelines-for-clergy-and-lay-leaders-orthodox-church-in-ameri

Pasha, S. (1993). Towards a cultural theory of political ideology and mass media in the Muslim world. *Media, Culture and Society, 15*(1), 61–79. https://doi.org/10.1177/016344393015001005

Pelikan, J. (1971). *The Christian tradition: A history of the development of doctrine, Volume 1: The emergence of the Catholic tradition (100–600)*. University of Chicago Press.

Pelikan, J. (1974). *The Christian tradition: A history of the development of doctrine. Vol. 2: The spirit of Eastern Christendom (600–1700)*. University of Chicago Press.

Pius XI. (1936). *Vigilanti cura*. Vatican. Retrieved May 7, 2021, from http://www.vatican.va/content/pius-xi/en/encyclicals/documents/hf_p-xi_enc_29061936_vigilanti-cura.html

Pius XII. (1957). *Miranda prorsus*. Vatican. Retrieved May 7, 2021, from http://www.vatican.va/content/pius-xii/en/encyclicals/documents/hf_p-xii_enc_08091957_miranda-prorsus.html

Pontifical Council for Social Communication. (1971). *Communio et progressio*. Vatican. Retrieved May 7, 2021, from http://www.vatican.va/roman_curia/pontifical_councils/pccs/documents/rc_pc_pccs_doc_23051971_communio_en.html

Pontifical Council for Social Communication. (2000). Ethics in communications. Vatican. Retrieved May 9, 2021, from http://www.vatican.va/roman_curia/pontifical_councils/pccs/documents/rc_pc_pccs_doc_20000530_ethics-communications_en.html

Qureshi, R. B. (1995). Recorded sound and religious music: The case of Qawwālī. In L. A. Babb, & S. S. Wadley (Eds.), *Media and the transformation of religion in South Asia* (pp. 139–166). University of Pennsylvania Press.

Rambachan, A. (2019). *Essays in Hindu theology*. Fortress Press.

Renard, J. (Ed.). (2014). *Islamic theological themes: A primary source reader*. University of California Press. Retrieved April 13, 2021, from http://www.jstor.org/stable/10.1525/j.ctt6wqbpp

Schultze, Q. (1990). Defining the electronic church. In R. Abelman, & S. M. Hoover (Eds.), *Religious television: Controversies and conclusions* (pp. 41–52). Ablex Publishing Corporation.

Seker, N. (2007). Aniconism in Islam. Nimet Seker. Retrieved April 28, 2021, from https://nimetseker.wordpress.com/archiv/english/aniconism-in-islam

Shulkhan Arukh. (2000). Shulkhan Arukh. Part II: Yoreh De'ah, Chapter 11 – Idolatry. Project Genesis. Retrieved April 19, 2021, from https://torah.org/learning/shulchan-aruch-classes-chapter11/

Silver, C. (2010). Dura-Europos: Crossroad of cultures. *Archeology*. Retrieved April 20, 2021, from http://www.archaeology.org/online/features/dura_europos

Smith, H. D. (1995). Impact of "God posters" on Hindus and their devotional traditions. In L. A. Babb, & S. S. Wadley (Eds.), *Media and the transformation of religion in South Asia* (pp. 24–50). University of Pennsylvania Press.

Soğanci, I. O. (2004) Islamic aniconism: Making sense of a messy literature. *Marilyn Zurmuehlen Working Papers in Art Education*, Vol. 2004, Article 4. Retrieved April 28, 2021, from https://doi.org/10.17077/2326-7070.1376

Soukup, P. A. (1983). *Communication and theology: Introduction and review of the literature*. [Reprint: London: Centre for the Study of Communication and Culture, 1991]. World Association for Christian Communication.

Soukup, P. A. (1989). *Christian communication: A bibliographical survey*. Greenwood Press.

Soukup, P. A. (1993). Church documents and the media. *Concilium: revue internationale de théologie, 250*, 71–79.

Soukup, P. A. (2006). Recent work in communication and theology. In J. Srampickal, G. Mazza, & L. Baugh (Eds.), *Cross connections: Interdisciplinary communication studies at the Gregorian University: Saggi celebrativi per il xxv anniversario del CICS* (pp. 121–146). Editrice Pontificia Universita Gregoriana.

Soukup, P. A. (2011). Recent writing on communication and theology. *Media Development, 58*(3), 3–8.

Soukup, P. A. (2019). Some past meetings of communication, theology, and media theology. *Culture–Media–Theology, 38*(3), 25–46.

Thurston, A. (2015). The Salafi ideal of electronic media as an intellectual meritocrat in Kano, Nigeria. *Journal of the American Academy of Religion, 83*(4), 1058–1083. https://www.jstor.org/stable/43900150

UKEssays. (2018, November). The Islamic communication. UK ESSAYS. Retrieved April 24, 2021, from https://www.ukessays.com/essays/cultural-studies/the-islamic-communication.php?vref=1

Umar, K. A. (2019). Mass media as essential instrument for Da'wah (Islamic Propagation). *Journal of Humanities and Social Science, 19*(6), 204–211.

Usman, A. H., Sailin, R., & Mutalib, M. F. M. A. (2019). The prophetic arts of communication: Some reflections on humanity. *Humanities & Social Sciences Reviews, 7*(4), 377–384. https://doi.org/10.18510/hssr.2019.7449

Usman, A. H., & Wazir, R. (2018). The fabricated hadith: Islamic ethics and guidelines of hadith dispersion in social media. *The Turkish Online Journal of Design, Art and Communication – TOJDAC*, 804–808. Special Edition. https://doi.org/10.7456/1080SSE/114

Washofsky, M. (2010). *Jewish living: A guide to contemporary reform practice* (rev. ed.). URJ Press.

Wechsler, D. (2020). On Friday, the rabbi became a televangelist. Chizuk Amuno congregation. Retrieved April 20, 2021, from https://www.chizukamuno.org/2020/03/on-friday-the-rabbi-became-atelevangelist

World Association for Christian Communication. (1986). Christian principles for communication. *Communication Resource, 8*.

Yenson, M. L. (2019). Jacques Dupuis and Chalcedon. *Theological Studies, 80*(2), 271–292. https://doi.org/10.1177/0040563919836241

Zsupan-Jerome, D. (2014). *Connected toward communication: The church and social communication in the digital age.* Liturgical Press.

Selected Readings

Beckerlegge, G. (Ed.). (2001). *Religion today: Tradition, modernity and change: From sacred text to internet.* Ashgate.

Creel, A. B. (1975). The reexamination of "Dharma" in Hindu ethics. *Philosophy East and West, 25*(2), 161–173. https://www.jstor.org/stable/1397937

Gronbacher, G. E. (2017). Jewish theology – A primer (especially for Christians) – Part I. Patheos. Retrieved April 16, 2021, from https://www.patheos.com/blogs/opentablejudaism/2017/02/18/jewish-theology-primer-especially-christians-part

Khalil, A. I. A. E.-F. (2016). The Islamic perspective of interpersonal communication. *Journal of Islamic Studies and Culture, 4*(2),22–23 https://doi.org/10.15640/jisc.v4n2a3

Renard, J. (Ed.). (2014). *Islamic theological themes: A primary source reader.* University of California Press. Retrieved April 13, 2021, from http://www.jstor.org/stable/10.1525/j.ctt6wqbpp

Soukup, P. A. (1983). *Communication and theology: Introduction and review of the literature.* World Association for Christian Communication. [Reprint: London: Centre for the Study of Communication and Culture, 1991].

Soukup, P. A. (2006). Recent work in communication and theology. In J. Srampickal, G. Mazza, & L. Baugh (Eds.), *Cross connections: Interdisciplinary communication studies at the Gregorian University: Saggi celebrativi per il xxv anniversario del CICS* (pp. 121–146). Editrice Pontificia Universita Gregoriana.

4

Religious Traditions and Ethics in Communication

Robert S. Fortner

Introduction

The major religious traditions of the world see communication through different ethical lenses, leading to alternative theoretical and practical assumptions on this universal human activity. This chapter compares five significant religions and their treatment of ethics in communication: Buddhism, Christianity, Hinduism, Islam, and Judaism. Among them they claim 3.9 to 5.2 billion adherents, or approximately 50–70% of the global population. (Estimates of the number of Buddhist adherents vary widely.) Most of the remainder of people either claim no religion or adhere to Chinese folk or tribal religions, Shamanism, or Animism.

The bases of comparison among the five religions examined in this chapter include the assumed or declared purpose of communication, the principles that govern the use of communication, and the values espoused for communication practice. Inherent in these three aspects of communication are ethical perspectives. Finally, the chapter examines the relationship between each theistic/idealist theory and prevailing nontheistic theory. In some areas the religions have similar or compatible aspects, while in others they differ widely. The similarities should not surprise the reader. Three of the religious traditions included here are often referred to as "Abrahamic" in origin, referencing the Jewish patriarch in the scriptures that Judaism, Islam, and Christianity all accept as sacred. Hinduism, as an offshoot of Buddhism, shares some convictions about communication but also significant differences. There are two major forms of Islam (Shia and Sunni), but also minorities such as Sufis and Bahais. Judaism has ultra-Orthodox, Orthodox, and liberal interpretations. Tibetan Buddhists acknowledge two major approaches, Mahayana and Tantric, both paths to the middle way (Madhyamika), while Christianity is perhaps the most fragmented, including Catholic, Orthodox, Protestant ("liberal"), and evangelical approaches. Even breaking down such traditions this way fails to capture all the nuances of faith traditions' ethics, but as this chapter addresses communication and not theology, it will deal with some of these differences in a general way that may fail to capture some of the particularities of these major divisions.

The Handbook on Religion and Communication, First Edition. Edited by Yoel Cohen and Paul A. Soukup.
© 2023 John Wiley & Sons Ltd. Published 2023 by John Wiley & Sons Ltd.

The Assumed or Declared Purpose of Communication and the Ethics of Purpose

All these religious traditions share the purpose of connecting with an ethereal other. For Buddhists this other is the Buddha. For other traditions it is their God. Such communication allows the members of these faiths to petition, praise, experience, worship, or share their situation with the Buddha or their respective deity. Doing so is, ipso facto, ethical in all these traditions.

Beyond such deity talk lie other purposes for human communication. Some of these purposes are ritualistic, connective, altruistic, and instrumentalist. Hinduism, for instance, proposes the purpose of communication is commonness or oneness (Adhikary, 2014, pp. 65, 67). Communication results in achieving communion or bonding (p. 68; see also Choudhury & Bhattacharyya, 2014). Similarly, Buddhism recognizes communication as the means to avoid conflict by being mindful of its potential sources and seeking a "middle way" that will result in meditation (Chuang, 2006, p. 13). "In many ways the Buddhist idea of communication is one of silence not chatter, of meditation not polemics, of harmony not friction, of cooperation not competition, of peace not hostility" (Merrill, 2009, chapter 1). Although communion and meditation are not synonymous, both result in a more common understanding than might otherwise prevail. These are both connective purposes with altruism (denial of the self, or attention to the other) being paramount. Both Hinduism and Buddhism focus on the practice of "right speech" (ethical speech): that which both "furthers the practice of the speaker and contributes to the well-being of others and the world." Such speech is intentional and "rejects mindless chatter, gossip, slander, and lies" (Lasater & Lasater, 2009, p. 9).

In a less straightforward way, Judaism views culture and religion as essentially synonymous and if we take James Carey's point (1989, chapter 1) that culture is communication, then religion = culture = communication. Judaism focuses on the relationship between God and a chosen people. The Jewish Bible is thus not merely a book of laws and regulations, but a chronicle of relationship beginning with creation. Jewish communication theory assumes that the most significant purpose of communication is the talk of God to his people. Although interactive, it is also dominated by the words of God and his people's response to those words. Obedience to the revealed word is ethical, while disobedience is not only unethical, but will lead to unwanted consequences. What is important is what is passed on (Cohen, 2012, chapter 2). Transmission is the focus, with prophets the most significant vehicle for the messages transmitted. Jews are expected to inculcate God's commands for their behavior into daily routines such that they can be seen by others. Communication, then, is a process of revelation, by which God reveals what is concealed from human knowledge (Rohr Jewish Learning Institute, 2017, p. 5). Often what is revealed are ethical expectations for both belief and behavior.

Judaism also has a strong dialogic tradition as part of its emphasis on oral communication. "Jewish tradition teaches that dialogue is a sacred activity" (Chanin et al., 2006, p. 3). This focus has biblical roots and interpretations that emphasized the dialogue between Yahweh and his chosen people.

Maimonides, an important Jewish ethicist writing in the thirteenth century, blended his understanding of the Torah with "his knowledge of Greek philosophy and particularly of Aristotelian ethics" (Gorfinkle, 1912, p. 5). Maimonides agreed with the standard opinion – made clearest by Immanuel Kant – that the ability to choose good instead of bad was a function of humans' rationality. Reason, he wrote allowed people to "discriminate between proper and improper actions" (1912, p. 43). Numerous moral virtues included "moderation, liberality, honesty, meekness, humility, contentedness, courage, and other virtues akin to these" (1912, p. 50). Such virtues would also apply to efforts of people to communicate.

A modern theoretical and ethical focus on dialogue appears in Martin Buber and Emanuel Levinas's work in the mid-twentieth century. Buber emphasized the necessity of allowing people to define themselves in any relationship to others so that any objectification of the other might be avoided. In his best-known work, *I and Thou*, Buber claimed (1970) that people's very personhood (the "I") only existed because of the other ("Thou") (p. 80). Anyone who objectified the other treated them as "it," a thing that could be controlled. To truly encounter the other the I must understand that they are in the process of becoming, who they are is dynamic, not static, and they cannot be understood by attributing characteristics to them (age, gender, color, etc.) in the effort to make sense of them. Dialogue can only occur between two self-defining individuals.

Levinas (2006) also drew on the Jewish dialogic tradition in his writings about the other. He argued that people must encounter the naked face of the other, untainted and undefined by culture, to truly recognize the human responsibility of one for the other. It is through seeing the other that a person comes to know their own true humanity and can exist in the society of others. Communication is defined in the intimate relationship of other to other in mutual responsibility for one another.

Islam and Christianity accept the significance of the Jewish scriptures (what Christians call the Old Testament) within their own traditions. With a common basis, these faiths "share a fundamentally core vision about humanity's relationship with God" and "the necessity of universal ethics to order human relationships" (Karim & Eid, 2014, chapter 1). Each of these three traditions, as noted earlier, is also fractured. Although the basic theology may be similar within the subtraditions, the interpretation each of them applies to their scripture often creates different primary purposes.

First, Islam. The differences among Sunni, Shia, and Sufi perspectives on Islam are theological. They concern the issue of the legitimate successor to the Prophet Muhammad. There are no different perspectives on communication based on these histori-theological differences. "Islam is a communication-based religion. Allah created man with a basic function to communicate" (Khalil, 2016, p. 23). Humans must communicate because they live in society, which requires communication to succeed. Because communication "is linked with faithfulness, cleanliness of heart and mind, honor and prestige ..., it is the responsibility of Muslims to fight against evil and preach for virtues through effective communication" (p. 23). This makes Islam an evangelical and ethical religion ..., it is the responsibility of Muslims to fight against evil and preach for virtues through effective communication (p. 23). This makes Islam an evangelical and ethical religion.

Because people are individuals in society, they must then be integrated into the community of faithful (Umma). This is one of the principal ethical functions or purposes of communication, to facilitate that integration (Khalil, 2016, p. 26). Hamid Mowlana (1996, p. 41) writes that there are four main principles defining Tabligh (propagation) that make the shared culture of the Umma possible: monotheism, responsibility, guidance and action, and piety. Mowlana (2007) argues, too, that Islamic communication order requires the breaking of idols and dependence on outsiders, and the destruction of myths (p. 28). Such myths are often based on dualism, or the separation of religion and politics, which is not possible in Islam.

One early communication restriction in Islam was the demand that the Qur'an be read only in Arabic, the original language of the Prophet and of scripture. One reason for this was the inability of other languages to accurately translate the original Arabic. As time has passed, however, other languages, such as Farsi and Urdu, have been accepted as languages that can effectively carry the meaning of the Qur'an (see Jaffery, n.d.). The Qur'an has been translated into other languages, too, but these are not accepted as official.

As mentioned earlier, Islam is an evangelical religion. "Islamic propagation is an integral part of Islam. It is obligatory for every Muslim to be involved in Islamic propagation activities"

(Haque, 2016, p. 1). Thus, Islam is willing to propagate its tenets and practices in the minds of non-Muslims to build the Ummah. This impulse to proselytize has justified the use of propaganda by Muslims, most recently in the efforts of Al-Qaeda and ISIS to recruit adherents by spreading their ideologies and increasing sympathy for people and jihad, especially among Muslims around the world (Napitupulu, 2020).

Next, Christianity. The dominant foundation for theorizing about communication within the Christian tradition, the transportation analogy, posits that communication is the process of information transfer and that the Word as revealed in scripture is so powerful that once it is delivered, it will have the desired effect, which most routinely is proselytization. In this analogy, people are empty vessels that can be filled with the Word of God to attract new converts. All the different subtraditions within Christianity have strong attachments to the theory of persuasion that emerges from this foundation as all have a proselytizing focus in ministry. For instance, the papal encyclical, *Evangelii Gaudium* (Pope Francis, 2013, section III), declares that Christians "have the duty to proclaim the Gospel without excluding anyone," but with the caveat that "It is not by proselytizing that the Church grows, but 'by attraction.'" Quoting Pope John Paul II, preaching the Gospel "'is the first task of the Church.' Indeed, 'today missionary activity still represents the greatest challenge of the Church' and 'the missionary task must remain foremost.'" However, the overall tenor of this encyclical indicates significant attention to those already within the Church who may have their faith dulled or shattered by life events and who need revitalization.

However, other theoretical perspectives exist within the Christian tradition. There is also a strong emphasis on ritual communication, especially among Roman Catholic, Orthodox, Anglican, and Presbyterian believers. Such communication provides regularized opportunities for adherents to strengthen their connection to the divine by engaging in rituals such as prayer, worship, communion (Mass), marriage, and baptism (christening) among others, which all occur in defined space and time to remind attendees of their relationship with God. Although all subtraditions within Christianity also practice such rituals, they are more apparent and routinized within some and more fluid or spontaneous in others. Often the difference in practices rests on the degree to which the holy spirit is defined as a major player in the activity. The spirit is presumed in the more charismatic and Pentecostal subtraditions to lead to spontaneous outbursts among spirit-filled attendees, a situation unlikely to occur in highly liturgical practices. I can only write of different tendencies within subtraditions here, since there are elements of both foundations in all of them to a greater or lesser degree, making definitive claims about one subtradition or another problematic.

Roman Catholicism is organized more hierarchically than other Christian groups. It accepts the Pope (the Bishop of Rome) as the highest authority within the Church and his pronouncements on moral issues and good order will be taken into account as those in other dioceses and parishes conduct the Church's business. Other traditions also have hierarchies, but they (other than Orthodox Church) do not have a singular pope but operate more collectively and sporadically, and some subtraditions are organized into self-governed independent congregations or lack any systemic organization altogether. So, communication within the universal Church occurs in several different ways, leading to varying assumptions about the purpose of communication.

What theories develop from these different subtraditions? First, similar to Judaism, there is a focus on dialogue. To some that is dialogue with God in prayer. Others emphasize the necessity of dialogue in declarations of faith across cultural divides (see Cameron, 1991, p. 2). Still others focus on the ability to learn the requirements of faith by participating in question and answer catechism classes. The end sought is happiness. Thomas Aquinas (1964) affirmed this focus of Aristotle's Nichomachean ethics, acknowledging that although people had different opinions as to what happiness was, they all agreed that it was "apparent and obvious among the objects of sense" (Lecture 4). The exercise of power, which to Augustine of Hippo originated with God, also influenced Aquinas (although Augustine disagreed with Aristotle on this point), leading him to recognize the naturalness of human society and the existence of natural law that humans could know through reason. Those activities or beliefs that were good were so as a result of fulfilling their telos (purpose or plan) (Dimmock & Fisher, 2017, chapter 4). It was the powerful, such as monarchs, however, that could best know natural law (presumably because they best exhibited full rationality), which they would impose on common people as its trustee. He thus affirmed the hierarchical commitment of the Catholic Church (Tim, 2012).

Aquinas explored how people unknowledgeable about a particular subject might come to know about it. This resulted from both divine revelation and right speaking. People could bring enlightenment to the unknowing by adroit speech (Boland, 2006, p. 290). Their understanding of ethics was by and large a mimetic process, requiring a mentor or model whom they could emulate (Hibbs, 2007, p. 2). This could not be the sole means of ethical knowledge, however. It also had to be revealed to them by God (Aquinas, 1947).

Second, there is an emphasis on proclamation. This instrumentalist view of the role and use of communication concentrates on the necessity of declaring faith commitments in such a way that others will be persuaded to adopt that faith. This emphasis has also resulted in Christians adopting virtually every new means of communication developed to spread their message (see Schultze, 1991). This is especially true of those considered "fundamentalists" (implying a literal and uncontextualized interpretation of scripture) and charismatics who, within the Protestant subculture, preach a "health and wealth" gospel that concentrates on the material blessings that claimed to be the result of belief in Jesus Christ as the Son of God (see Coleman, 2000).

Third is the commitment to solitude and contemplation. The most prominent advocate for these practices is Thomas Merton, a Trappist monk in the Roman Catholic faith. Merton proposed these practices as the means to commune or hear God so that a person could learn how to love others (see Merton, 1958, 1961). Love, Merton thought, was the only thing that Christians need communicate to one another. Being able to demonstrate love resulted from the willingness to listen to God.

Fourth is the ability to communicate through the practice of ritual both in worship activities and through art. This is not unique to Christianity, as all religious traditions have rituals that their adherents perform at important times in their lives (even daily in the case of Muslims). In the Roman Catholic tradition, the Mass serves as the focal point of communication and includes the liturgy of the Word and the liturgy of the Eucharist. Up until the 1960s, the Mass was always celebrated in Latin, so most participants were largely observers since they did not speak this ancient language. In the 1960s, however, Vatican II allowed the Mass to be celebrated in vernacular languages, opening it up to people's understanding participation for the first time. Roman Catholic churches also are typically replete with symbolism, especially cathedrals that have stained glass and statuary celebrating saints of the faith. This is also true of Orthodox churches and Anglican/ Episcopal churches, although less universally. Practicing communion with God using liturgical devices that do not change, sometimes over centuries, creates a connection within the religious traditions that use them. They allow people to connect with God, with one another, and with those who have preceded them in their faith (see Gingerich, 2018; Patheos, n.d.).[3]

Each ritual comprises one or more discursive events (Foucault, 1972). Such events allow people to connect both to a deity or ideal, and with others similarly engaged in space or across time to create communities of the faithful. People engage in discursive events using time-honored practices, using the same language, symbols, chants, songs, and moves as those who preceded them in earlier ages. In the Roman Catholic tradition, for instance, people cross themselves in the same fashion, dab holy water on their foreheads, and chant the same words as people hundreds of years before. In Islam people engage in ritual cleansing before entering the mosque, line up in single-sex rows to pray five times each day in response to a call to prayer, and bow in unison in prayer. Such practices are to bring believers closer to God and to one another as they engage in discourse together.

Principles Governing the Use of Ethical Communication

How should a person communicate ethically? There are various approaches, including petition and praise that acknowledge dependence of a higher power (usually in prayer), prophecy, teaching, artistic expression including iconography, and memorization of prayers and catechisms. Muslims use the call to prayer that occurs five times per day, usually over loudspeakers; Christians use bells or carillons to call parishioners to worship; and Jews use the shofar (ram's horn) to signal the Rosh Hashanah holydays (see Fortner, 2011). All traditions expect that adherents will communicate ethically. This means that they will respect the dignity of all human beings, protect the innocent from harm, and tell the truth in communication (see Christians & Traber, 1997).

In addition to these universals, religions have their own communication practices. Buddhists communicate in a state of mindfulness. This requires that adherents consciously choose when to speak and when to listen, being willing to stay silent even when their first impulse might be to interject their thoughts into a conversation. This is to prevent regret for having said something that might immediately be regretted. It also requires that even the reticent interlocutor have the courage to speak up when necessary, especially on behalf of absent or silent others (Sofer, 2018). Sarah McLean (referenced by Kane, 2015) says that "Mindfulness means being present with what you are doing, while you are doing it, with a nonjudgmental attitude … it can be the way one is engaged in activity." In communication this means that people are aware of what they're saying (and its ethical implications), practicing observation instead of evaluation and paying close attention to others purposefully.

Hindu communication practices are intertwined with identity owing to the ethnic fragmentation of the South Asian population and the large diaspora of Indians around the world. In London, for instance, Tamil Hindus use sonic elements (gongs, drums, etc.) to demarcate processional space during outdoor rituals. These elements help sacralize the space through "sonorous and auspicious music that speaks directly to the deities" (David, 2012, p. 449).

Another perspective on communication is that it constitutes an inward search for meaning that leads to self-awareness, freedom, and finally to truth (Dissanayake, quoted in Singh, 2017, p. 37). Sacred sound syllables developed and were the basis of Vedic rituals to achieve this self-awareness (p. 37). Vedic sages declared self-knowledge the basis of all knowledge, which required an emphasis on intrapersonal communication. The ancient texts of Hinduism are all presented in dialogue form, with one interlocutor being more knowledgeable than the other. The end of communication is to reach the same level of understanding, with one the teacher and the other the learner (Choudhury & Bhattacharyya, 2014).

Much of Jewish communication practice focuses on the Torah and related Jewish law. Unlike the Buddhist focus on silence, however, Jewish communication is replete with interruption. Cooperative overlapping characterizes Jewish communication, not from the rudeness of interruption, but from genuine interest and appreciation, according to Tannen (2000). This everyday practice aligns with what Cohen described as the relationship between written texts and oral teaching about those texts. "Oral teaching refers not to a fixed corpus, but rather to each scribe's prerogative to provide a performative explanation of the written material that he passed down" (Weiss, 2012, p. 79). This practice of intermixing the written with the oral performance as created by scribes is what Cohen referred to as "multiplicity" (Weiss, 2012, chapter 2). Such multiplicity, in Jewish tradition according to Cohen, was due to the fact that "There is something inherently lacking in the written text considered in itself. A written text has a static existence outside of any particular individual; in contrast, each instance of the oral teaching cannot be separated from the performative interpretation of a particular individual at a particular time" (Weiss, 2012, p. 81).

Multiplicity in delivery of God's word to his chosen people is thought to establish a living and more concrete relationship between the two.

How are Christians to practice communication ethically? There are two positions on this question. The first is the transportation model/instrumentalist position in which communication is defined as the movement of symbols (including words, their expression, the intent of the initiator, nonverbal elements, etc.) from one person to another. Ethics is to define the message shared, the fidelity of the message as it arrives, and its persuasive content. The second is the ritual/communal position that sees communication as the practice of ritual (dialogue, artistic expression, rites of various kinds, all repeated in practice to cement relationships in community) to enable conflict resolution, the creation of common understandings, beliefs and commitments, etc.

In the first position, Christians "are convinced that if they faithfully preach the gospel to their audiences, then it assuredly will bear fruit [conversions, Church growth, deeper commitments]. Their confidence – based on knowledge of another's needs and situation ... – is founded in the power of the word, not in their efforts to build relationship and intimacy" (Fortner, 2007, p. 66). This evangelical approach to communication gives the impression that anyone who is not part of an existing tribe is an outsider "who needs to be saved or morally or politically converted to one or another cause" (Soukup, 2008, p. 264). There is concern in such an approach to communication about the response of the audience however, with an expectation that communicators will be sensitive to the ability of their audience to understand their message (see Kraft, 1991, chapter 2). As Soukup (2006) explains, "communication appears as a sacred trust, motivated not by the power of one partner to dominate the other, not by any desire to monopolize the conversation, but by the desire to let conversational partners speak what most concern them" (p. 38). It "is founded in the power of the word, not in their efforts to build relationship and intimacy" (Fortner, 2007, p. 66). This evangelical approach to communication gives the impression that anyone who is not part of an existing tribe is an outsider who needs to be saved or morally or politically converted to one or another cause (Soukup, 2008, p. 264). There is concern in such an approach to communication about the response of the audience however, with an expectation that communicators will be sensitive to the ability of their audience to understand their message (see Kraft, 1991, chapter 2). As Soukup (2006) explains, communication appears as a sacred trust, motivated not by the power of one partner to dominate the other, not by any desire to monopolize the conversation, but by the desire to let conversational partners speak what most concern them (p. 38).

Kristal R. Simpson (2019) argues that the principles that should govern true Christian communication are:

- "Principle 1: Effective Christian communication involves monitoring what is said.
- Principle 2: Effective Christian communication entails being mindful of the emotion or feelings behind our spoken words.
- Principle 3: Effective Christian communication requires us to examine our tone of voice.
- Principle 4: Effective Christian communication consists of checking the motivation behind our words."

The focus here is on the Christian speaker's words and the emotion and meaning behind them. This is an entirely transportation-focused instrumentalist approach to communication (see also https://www.christiancommunicators.com). Stackhouse (2003) argues that:

> As a form of Christian discourse, apologetical conversation ought to follow principles of communication patterned after the ministry of Jesus Christ. First, the apologist has to offer both verbal proclamation (message) and living testimony (life) to his or her neighbor. Second, communication must always be full of both grace and truth, rather than emphasizing one at the expense of the other.

Third, apologetics should be undertaken as an act of love both to God and to one's neighbor; all other purposes, whether to win the argument, try out new success tactics, and so on, must never compromise the love to God and neighbor as one's foremost concern. Fourth, keeping love to God and neighbor central means the apologist will always take an audience seriously on its own terms and seek out common ground between herself and her audience – which requires a cultivation of the art of listening.

Again, the focus here is on what is said and how it is said to the other. Smith (1992) on practicing communication as a Christian begins simply, "This is a book about proclamation" (p. 7). That is the transportation in a nutshell.

The ritual approach's main differences in approaching communication are, first, that no one is "the other." Anyone who participates in the discursive event(s) practiced in the ritual is one with the practice. People may be excluded from the ritual itself depending on their perceived status within the body, but once the event(s) begin, everyone shares an equal place. Second, ritual-based communication is iterative, while transportation-based theory is singular. The "power" in ritual is its repetition and practice, whereas in transportation theory it inheres in the words and conviction of the initiator in an exchange. Third, time in ritual is recursive (cyclical) and polychronic, unlike transportation, which is progressive and monochronic. Recursive time repeats over and over – as do rituals – and progressive time is a series of unique events. Polychronic time is more fluid, providing time for possible expansion of activities within the structure of ritual (potentially multiple discursive events), while monochronic time pays little attention to history or past events. In monochronic time it's possible to reinvent the wheel (see Nash, 2020)!

One perspective that emerged from ritual theory writ large is media ecology. This theoretical position was initially laid out by Harold A. Innis (the teacher) and Marshall McLuhan a Canadian Catholic scholar (the student). Subsequently, one of McLuhan's students and a main proponent of this approach to understanding communication was the Jesuit scholar, Walter J. Ong. Since rituals depend on the means of communication (even the Mass is dependent on the oral tradition that both McLuhan and Ong explored), the idea that the means used to communicate affects what we communicate requires a comprehensive understanding of communications media. McLuhan (1964) called media "extensions of man," arguing that each medium extended a basic human ability. Radio extended people's hearing capability, television their sight, and the computer their nervous system. Ong (1971) provided a more detailed and nuanced approach to this issue. He said that, "Sound exists only when it is going out of existence" (2015, p. 63). This short sentence indicates part of the necessity of ritual: rituals occur through sound and visuals, but these disappear – if not recorded – immediately. So they require repetition to keep them fresh and to encourage recall. Oral peoples, he continues (p. 64), "consider words to have magical potency," and "commonly think of names (one kind of words) as conveying power over things." These are the roots of the evangelical understanding of communication – a powerful, mystical means to proselytize. Up until the Industrial Revolution and romanticism, he writes (1971), "Western culture in the intellectual and academic manifestations can be meaningfully described at rhetorical (public speaking based) culture" (p. 9). "Speech, oral or textual, is always a hermeneutic event in the sense of an interpretive event" (2017, p. 27). Romanticism made the idea of "otherness" a primary trope (1971, p. 239) that reified the idea that there is a difference between one's self and others, thus justifying both the evangelical impulse to convert "the other" and the creation of a bifurcated culture comprising the "ins" and "outs," whether this was a religious tradition, a political party, an ethnic group, etc.

Many rituals practiced across the religious traditions examined here celebrate some mythic event ("the meaning of the original Greek mythos, something uttered, especially a story," Ong, 2017, p. 107). This is true of the Jewish Passover, Christian Christmas, Easter, and Pentecost, the

Islamic attributions of the Quran to the angel Gabriel's dictation to Muhammed, the feats of the various Hindu gods, and the sayings of the Buddha. Stories are all based in mythic events. Ong's attention to such matters across his career established a connection between his faith and interpretation of culture based on the character of communication occurring within them.

Ethical Values Espoused in Communication

In addition to the universal values mentioned previously, additional ones vary from tradition to tradition. Buddhism and Hinduism pay significant attention to ancestors when practicing communication. Hindus honor ancestors (Mayatitananda, 2005) and both Hindus and Buddhists believe in reincarnation so their communication is careful not to act or speak in such a way that might compromise their futures. Buddhists are particularly careful in their treatment, not only of human beings, but all living creatures, and they work for nonconflict solutions to problems and espouse peace as a central virtue. Both Hindus and Buddhists value all living creatures and espouse a sanctity of life perspective that is driven by ideas of reincarnation.

Jewish believers are conscious of their claimed status as a chosen people in their communication. They are not evangelically minded for the most part as being Jewish is simultaneously a religious condition, an ethnic condition, and a national condition– at least for Zionists. They tend to be more insular in their sacred communication, but not in their secular roles. Many are involved outside their Jewish community in the professions, business, academia, and the arts.

Christian communication values include all those mentioned in the Christian Bible, including truth, compassion and love, humility, thankfulness, peace, patience, kindness, goodness, faithfulness, gentleness, and self-control (see Gal. 5:22–23). The animating principle for such practices has changed over time, with notions of natural law that all would recognize by the exercise of rationality being replaced by emphasis on the "Golden Rule." Philosophically this is a movement from Thomas Aquinas (1947) to Immanuel Kant (1873), with communication scholars in the Christian tradition often pointing to Kant's categorical imperative that requires people to treat others as ends (independent agents who choose for themselves) rather than means (those who can be used to achieve one own's ends). This is the duty of those who would act ethically (Kant, 1873). The idea that people are all independent with their own defined ends (thus equal in value) emerged from Kant's reading of Rousseau, who changed his opinion of the "ignorant masses" to one in which all people had inherent worth. Such attitudes and attributes are to characterize any effort in dialogue, preaching, creating art and entertainment, service to others, and efforts to edify or teach.

Islam values the lineage of the faith, with Shiites and Sunnis having different interpretations of the correct lineage, which has led to much tension across the Middle East where large numbers of both traditions commingle. They value repetition in communication, personified by the five pillars of the faith, which includes daily prayer, a pilgrimage to Mecca at least once during a lifetime, alms giving, fasting during the holy month of Ramadan, and a declaration of faith. "The most important beliefs and religious practices were identified by Prophet Muhammad himself. Thus, there is general agreement on them among all Muslims. It provides an interesting comparison since modern Jews and Christians do not have similar uniformity in their belief systems. Christians, for example, have numerous creeds, but Jews do not have any universally agreed-upon beliefs. Different Jewish religious streams mostly agree over the 613 written commandments in the Bible – notwithstanding differences regarding the oral law tradition as well as later Rabbinic law" (Iman, 2013).

Relationships between Theistic/Idealistic Theory and Nontheistic Theory

The last part of this chapter briefly explores the relationships that connect the theistic/idealistic theories discussed and nontheistic theories that have influenced current understandings of communication within these traditions. Few doubt that Christian-based theories have been heavily influenced by Western communication theories, and especially empirically based American contributions (see Fortner, 2007, chapter 2, for a more complete analysis). Jewish communication theory is similar, in the sense that Jewish scholars either were trained in Western institutions or Israeli ones that were accepted as members of the Western scholarly community. Although Christianity developed in the Middle East from Jewish roots, it quickly became synonymous with the West as it took hold in the Roman Empire during the first century (see Holland, 2019). It is less clear, however, how Buddhist, Hindu, and Islamic theories relate to nontheistic ones.

Buddhist and Hindu theories of communication developed in Asia, but, as Wimal Dissanayake (2003) warned, "so far we have examined communication largely in terms of Western optics, approaches, and visions" (p. 18). What was needed, he said, was studies that developed from non-Western viewpoints. Yoshitaka Miike (2002) agreed, writing, "Throughout the 20th century, the field of communication studies has been one-sidedly dominated by the US Eurocentric anthropocentered, individualistic, efficiency-oriented, positivistic theory and research. Conventional academic views of communication have been skewed by Western frames of reference" (p. 1). Efforts to provide Asian perspectives on communication theory began in the 1980s (see Dissanayake, 1988; Kincaid, 1987). Although there have been efforts to have theory influenced by theology, for the most part in Asia it is theory that precedes theology, the result of most Asian communication scholars having been educated in the United States or UK (see Chuang & Chen, 2003; Narula & Roy, 2017).

The same problem exists for Islamic theory. Mowlana pioneered the development of Islamic-based theory so that theory itself could be de-Westernized (Khiabany, 2003, p. 415). Hussain (2016) took the position that some Western communication theories could be Islamized, indicating the precedence of theory over theology, although he did provide principles for religious communication. Yusoff (2016) also wrote that the basics of communication theory were all developed in the West, but they underestimated "the social function of communication and ignore the role of social structure and culture" (p. 10), emphasizing the effect of communication on individuals (the so-called empirical approach to communication – transportation model). Islamic communication scholars, however, also were careful not to stray too far from the accepted stimulus–response behavioral Western paradigm (Kasmani et al., 2017). Within the Islamic tradition, too, scholars worried that some were putting the value of exceptionalism ahead of the actual effort to understand possible similarities between Islamic theory and Western ones (see Khibany, 2007).

Conclusion

This chapter began with the perspective that there were many elements of theory that were similar across different religious traditions. It has tried to illuminate both these similarities and the unique perspectives on communication that have emerged within five major religious traditions. It is not an exhaustive effort, but one based in examining the ethics embedded in three basic issues in communication. Although ethics vary from one religious tradition to another, they are not so different that they would not be recognized by those who do not share religious convictions. This also suggests why theories may not seem as different as we might expect, since not only are the basic ethical commitments similar to one another, but those who have articulated theories ostensibly emerging from different perspectives have relied on similar methodologies and assumptions inherited from Western communication theory. It is likely that future scholars will continue to develop perspectives that take as their starting point theology and associated ethics as they apply to communication questions.

References

Adhikary, N. M. (2014). Mahatma Gandhi and the *Sadharanikaran* model of communication. *The Journal of University Grants Commission, 3*(1), 63–76. https://www.academia.edu/30988649/Mahatma_Gandhi_and_the_Sadharanikaran_Model_of_Communication

Aquinas, T. (1947). *Summa theologica* (Fathers of the English Dominican Province, Trans.). Benziger Brothers, Publishers. Retrieved January 13, 2021, from https://ccel.org/ccel/aquinas/summa/summa.i.html

Aquinas, T. (1964). *Commentary on the Nichomachean ethics* (C. I. Litzinger, Trans.). Henry Regnery Company. Retrieved January 13, 2021, from https://isidore.co/aquinas/Ethics.htm https://isidore.co/aquinas/english/Ethics.htm.

Boland, V. (2006). Truth, knowledge and communication: Thomas Aquinas on the mystery of teaching. *Studies in Christian Ethics, 19*(3), 287–304. https://www.researchgate.net/publication/249764323_Truth_Knowledge_and_Communication_Thomas_Aquinas_on_the_Mystery_of_Teaching

Buber, M. (1970). *I and thou* (W. Kaufmann, Trans.). Charles Scribner's Sons.

Cameron, A. (1991). *Christianity and the rhetoric of empire: The development of Christian discourse.* University of California Press.

Carey, J. W. (1989). *Communication as culture: Essays on media and society* (Rev. ed.). Routledge.

Chanin, M., Colflesh, M., Epstein, S. S., & Schoenfeld, R. (2006). *Dialogue in the Jewish tradition.* Jewish Dialogue Group.

Choudhury, B. L., & Bhattacharyya, K. K. (2014). Communication from Indian perspective with special reference to Nātyashāstra. *Dev Sanskriti, 4*, 62–72. https://archive.org/stream/CommunicationFromIndianPerspectiveWithSpecialReferenceToNatyashastra_2014/Communication%20from%20Indian%20Perspective%20With%20Special%20Reference%20to%20N%C4%81tyash%C4%81stra_djvu.txt

Christians, C. G., & Traber, M. (Eds.). (1997). *Communication ethics and universal values.* Sage Publications.

Chuang, R. (2006). Tibetan Buddhism, symbolism, and communication implications in the [post]modern world. *Intercultural Communication Studies, 15*(1), 12–23. https://www-s3-live.kent.edu/s3fs-root/s3fs-public/file/02-Rueyling-Chuang.pdf

Chuang, R., & Chen, G.-M. (2003). Buddhist perspectives and human communication. *Intercultural Communication Studies, 12*(4), 65–86.

Cohen, Y. (2012). *God, Jews and the media: Religion and Israel's media.* Routledge.

Coleman, S. (2000). *The globalization of charismatic Christianity: Spreading the gospel of prosperity.* Cambridge University Press.

David, A. (2012). Sacralising the city: Sound, space and performance in Hindu ritual practices in London. *Culture and Religion, 13*(4), 449–467. https://www.researchgate.net/publication/263534621_Sacralising_the_City_Sound_Space_and_Performance_in_Hindu_Ritual_Practices_in_London

Dimmock, M., & Fisher, A. (2017). Ethics for A-level. OpenBook Publishers. Retrieved May 22, 2021, from https://books.openedition.org/obp/4422

Dissanayake, W. (Ed.). (1988). *Communication theory: The Asian perspective.* Asian Mass Communication Research and Information Center.

Dissanayake, W. (2003). Asian approaches to human communication: Retrospect and prospect. *Intercultural Communication Studies, 12*(4), 17–37. https://citeseerx.ist.psu.edu/viewdoc/summary?doi=10.1.1.567.6317.

Fortner, R. S. (2007). *Communication, media, and identity: A Christian theory of communication.* Rowman & Littlefield Publishers, Inc.

Fortner, R. S. (2011). The ethics of a very public sphere: Differential soundscapes and the discourse of the streets. In R. S. Fortner & M. Fackler (Eds.), *Handbook of global media and communication ethics* (Vol. 2, pp. 973–991). Wiley-Blackwell.

Foucault, M. (1972). *The archaeology of knowledge and the discourse on language* (A. M. Sheridan Smith, Trans.). Vintage Books.

Gingerich, B. (2018). What is Catholicism? History, tradition & beliefs. Christianity.com Retrieved May 22, 2012, from https://www.christianity.com/church/denominations/what-is-catholicism.html

Gorfinkle, J. I. (1912). Introduction. In J. I. Gorfinkle (Ed.), *The eight chapters of maimonides on ethics: A psychological and ethical treatise* (Trans., pp. 1–33). Columbia University Press.

Haque, M. S. (2016). Information and communication technology in Islamic propagation. *Institutional Journal of Information and Communication Technology Research, 6*(8), 1–5. https://www.researchgate.net/publication/305620421_Information_and_Communication_Technology_in_Teaching_and_Learning_Among_Islamic_Education_Teachers_The_Roles

Hibbs, T. S. (2007). *Aquinas, ethics, and philosophy of religion: Metaphysics and practice.* Indiana University Press.

Holland, T. (2019). *Dominion: How the Christian revolution remade the world.* Basic Books.

Hussain, M. Y. (2016). Islamization of communication theory. *Media Asia, 13,* 32–36.

Iman, M. (2013). Core values of Islam. The Religion of Islam. Retrieved December 24, 2020, from https://www.islamreligion.com/articles/10256/core-values-of-islam

Jaffery, R. (n.d.). Islam and the role of language. Retrieved December 9, 2020, from https://www.islamicinsights.com/religion/islam-and-the-role-of-language.html

Kane, C. (2015, September 2). How to communicate like a Buddhist – Mindfully and without judgment. *The Washington Post.* Retrieved December 19, 2020, from https://www.washingtonpost.com/news/inspired-life/wp/2015/09/02/how-to-communicate-like-a-buddhist-mindfully-and-without-judgment

Kant, I. (1873). The metaphysics of morals, Part II. In T. K. Albert (Trans.), *Critique of practical reason and other works on the theory of ethics.* Longmans, Green and Company.

Karim, K. H., & Eid, M. (2014). Imagining the other. In M. Eid & K. H. Karim (Eds.), *Re-imagining the other: Culture, media, and Western-Muslim intersections* (pp. 1–21). Palgrave Macmillan.

Kasmani, F., Yusoff, S. H., Kanaker, O., & Abdulla, R. (2017). The Islamic communication paradigm: Challenges and future directions. *Advanced Science Letters, 23*(5), 4787–4791.

Khalil, A. I. A. E.-F. (2016). The Islamic perspective of interpersonal communication. *Journal of Islamic Studies and Culture, 4*(2), 22–37.

Khiabany, G. (2003). De-Westernizing media theory, or reverse Orientalism: 'Islamic communication' as theorized by Hamid Mowlana. *Media, Culture & Society, 25,* 415–422.

Khibany, G. (2007). Is there an Islamic communication? The persistence of tradition and the lure of modernity. *Critical Arts: A Journal of South-North Cultural Studies, 21*(1), 106–124.

Kincaid, D. L. (Ed.). (1987). *Communication theory: Eastern and Western perspectives.* Elsevier Academic Press.

Kraft, C. H. (1991). *Communication theory for Christian witness* (Rev ed.). Orbis Books.

Lasater, J. H., & Lasater, I. K. (2009). *What we say matters: Practicing nonviolent communication.* Rodmell Press.

Levinas, E. (2006). *Humanism of the other* (N. Poller, Trans.). University of Illinois Press.

Maimonides. (1912). *The eight chapters of Maimonides on ethics: A psychological and ethical treatise* (J. I. Gorfinkle, Ed. and Trans.). Columbia University Press.

Mayatitananda, S. S. (2005, July 1). Honoring ancestors. *Hinduism Today.* Retrieved January 21, 2022, from https://www.hinduismtoday.com/magazine/july-august-september-2005/2005-07-honoring-ancestors

McLuhan, M. (1964). *Understanding media: The extensions of man.* McGraw-Hill Education.

Merrill, J. (2009). Tenzin Gyatso, the Dalai Lama: Universal compassion. In C. G. Christians & J. C. Merrill (Eds.), *Ethical communication: Moral stances in human dialogue* (pp. 11–16). University of Missouri Press.

Merton, T. (1958). *Thoughts on solitude*. Farrar, Straus and Giroux.

Merton, T. (1961). *The new man*. Farrar, Straus and Giroux.

Miike, Y. (2002). Theorizing culture and communication in the Asian context: An assumptive foundation. *Intercultural Communication Studies*, *11*(1), 1–21.

Mowlana, H. (1996). *Global communication in transition: The end of diversity?* Sage Publications.

Mowlana, H. (2007). Theoretical perspectives on Islam and communication. *China Media Research*, *3*(4), 23–33.

Napitupulu, T. G. (2020). The Influence of ICT development on cyber terrorism activities. Case studies: Propaganda by terrorist groups such as Al-Qaeda and ISIS. Retrieved December 9, 2020, from https://www.researchgate.net/publication/346425084_The_Influence_of_ICT_Development_on_Cyber_Terrorism_Activities_Case_Studies_Propaganda_by_Terrorist_Groups_Such_as_Al-Qaeda_and_ISIS

Narula, S., & Roy, S. (2017). Alternative views on the theory of communication: An exploration through the strands of Buddhism. *Journal of Mass Communication and Journalism*, *7*(3), 354–357.

Ong, W. J. (1971). *Rhetoric, romance, and technology: Studies in the interpretation of expression and culture*. Cornell University Press.

Ong, W. J. (2015). *Orality and literacy: The technologizing of the word* (30th Anniversary Ed.). Routledge.

Ong, W. J. (2017). *Language as hermeneutic: A primer on the word and digitization*. Cornell University Press.

Patheos. (n.d.) Rites and ceremonies. Patheos. Retrieved May 22, 2012, from https://www.patheos.com/library/roman-catholicism/ritual-worship-devotion-symbolism/rites-and-ceremonies

Pope Francis. (2013). *Evangelii gaudium*: Apostolic exhortation on the proclamation of the gospel in today's world. Papal Encyclicals Online. Retrieved December 14, 2020, from https://www.papalencyclicals.net

Rohr Jewish Learning Institute. (2017). *Communication: Its art & soul*. The Rohr Jewish Learning Institute.

Schultze, Q. J. (1991). *Televangelism and American culture: The business of popular religion*. Wipf and Stock, Publisher.

Simpson, K. R. (2019). Four principles of effective Christian communication. Krystal R. Simpson. Retrieved December 22, 2020, from https://krystalrsimpson.com/four-principles-of-effective-christian-communication-2

Singh, S. (2017). Communication from Indian perspective – With special reference to Vedic spiritual tradition. *Dev Sanskriti*, *10*, 35–41.

Smith, D. K. (1992). *Creating understanding: A handbook for Christian communication across cultural landscapes*. Zondervan Publishing House.

Sofer, O. J. (2018). *Say what you mean: A mindful approach to nonviolent communication*. Shambhala Publications.

Soukup, P. A. (2006). *Out of Eden: Seven ways God restores blocked communication*. Pauline Books & Media.

Soukup, P. A. (2008). Considering a Catholic view of Evangelical media. In Q. J. Schultze & R. H. Woods Jr. (Eds.), *Understanding Evangelical media: The changing face of Christian communication* (pp. 263–273). IVP Academic.

Stackhouse, J. G. (2003). Principles of Christian communication. *Humble apologetics: Defending the faith today*. Oxford Scholarship Online. Retrieved December 22, 2020, from https://oxford.universitypressscholarship.com/view/10.1093/0195138074.001.0001/acprof-9780195138078-chapter-8#

Tannen, D. (2000). Interrupters: Linguist says it's the Jewish way. Lecture at Georgetown University. Retrieved January 21, 2022, from https://www.jweekly.com/2000/05/12/interrupters-linguist-says-it-s-jewish-way

Tim. (2012). Thomas Aquinas vs Saint Augustine, May 14, 2012. *Philosophy & Philosophers*, May 14, 2012. Retrieved January 21, 2022, from https://www.the-philosophy.com/thomas-aquinas-saint-augustine

Weiss, D. H. (2012). *Paradox & the prophets: Herman Cohen and the indirect communication of religion*. Oxford University Press.

Yusoff, S. M. (2016). Western and Islamic communication model: A comparative analysis on a theory application. *Journal of Islamic Social Sciences and Humanities*, *7*, 7–20.

Selected Readings

Bassin, S. (n.d.) The limits of communication. Reform Judaism. Retrieved July 4, 2022.

Fortner, R. S. (2007). *Communication, media, and identity: A Christian theory of communication*. Rowman & Littlefield Publishers, Inc.

Kane, C. (2016). *How to communicate like a Buddhist*. Hierophant Publishing.

Luu, T. Q. (2012). Some thoughts on Buddhism and communications. Some thoughts on Buddhism & Communication .... quangduc.com. Accessed July 4, 2022.

Muhammad, M. S., & Yahaya, A. G. (2020). Conceptualizing the principles of social media engagement: teachings from selected verses of Surah Al-Hujuraat. *Islamic Communication Journal*, *5*(1), 1–18.

Muhammad, N., & Omer, F. (2016). Communication skills in Islamic perspective. *Al-Idah*, *33*, 1–7.

Part II
Theological Perspectives

5

Christianity and the Mass Media

Mary Catherine Kennedy

As a religious tradition, Christianity has adapted to and transitioned with technological advancements in all the major eras of mass communication history, dating back to the rise of printing and up to the current state of the mass media, with Christians seeing communication advancements as God-given opportunities to spread the gospel message. However, appropriating media use in churches arguably cheapens Christianity in some way and creates a fantasy world that lures people away from truth and the divine (Togarasei, 2012).

During the oral era, information circulated by word of mouth and preaching. With the printing press, religious texts were some of the first publications made available to the masses. Christian denominations adopted technological advancements to best reach their congregants; the success of the Protestant Reformation may be attributed to decisions made by Martin Luther and his contemporaries at the outset of the written era. To be sure, Gaillardetz (2007) is cautious about the downsides of technological advancements, which include less in-person engagement and people becoming so totally engrossed in virtual communities that they ignore or completely miss opportunities for encounters with the divine. Nevertheless, as technologies developed and advanced, the major Christian denominations adapted and adopted new technology in order to keep up with the changes of the broader culture, in essence to meet their flocks where they are.

Looking at the overlapping scholarship in technology and society and religion and media is important to understanding the relationship between Christianity and the media. Lim (2012) cites the works of Heidegger and Marx who see technology not solely in its instrumental use and as standing in an external relationship with human beings as he begins to build a case for understanding how changes and advancements in technology have impacted Christianity over time. Indeed, De Vries (2001), like some other scholars, suggests that political, cultural, and economic forces have reinvented and even reshaped religious identity. To best understand how Christian denominations approach traditional and new media over time, one should acknowledge that religion and media are deeply intertwined with cultural life and how people make meaning in their lives. Religion has become "mediatized" – where today's understanding of what it means to be religious, especially in a Christian context, is shaped by the media in important ways (cf. Chapter 18). Some signs of this occurring include how often people turn to the media as a key source of information about religious issues. This grants the media power to shape how people understand religious issues. Because of this, the media not only dictate how religious information is dispensed and experienced, but, as Lim (2012) argues, media also take on "social functions that used to be performed by religious institutions, such as societal rituals,

The Handbook on Religion and Communication, First Edition. Edited by Yoel Cohen and Paul A. Soukup.
© 2023 John Wiley & Sons Ltd. Published 2023 by John Wiley & Sons Ltd.

moral orientation, and community formation" (pp. 190–1). Arguably this is more noticeable in the social age ushered in by Internet technology, but the use of the advanced printing technologies in the sixteenth century also led to major shifts in how Christianity itself was understood and practiced because of changes that took place in the wider culture. However, religious communities could not just jump on the bandwagon and embrace a new form of media without first considering the tradition and theology dating back centuries.

In their discussion of the development of printing, Horsfield and Teusner (2007) identify four conditions that aided the success of the new technology: the development of the technology itself, the development of the supporting materials for the industry, a means of distribution, and the right social conditions. They suggest that "the development of printing did not instigate changes in Christianity, but Christianity was affected by [the] changes taking place in the wider culture" (p. 283). For example, the Reformation spearheaded by Luther took off because he capitalized on the advantages that printing afforded in order "to construct an alternative Christianity that addressed the social momentum of the time" (pp. 283–284). Key moments in history worked in Luther's favor, such as economic factors that allowed him to become the best-selling author of his time: Horsfield and Teusner suggest that many of his titles were sold by name recognition alone. One of the reasons for this was his decision to print religious texts in the vernacular as opposed to Latin. The Catholic Church continued to produce content in Latin, which "limited the audience of their message and limited their capacity to counter the influence of Luther's ideas in the wider marketplace where they were having their greatest effect" (p. 286). Indeed, the introduction of the printing press and mass production of religious texts in the vernacular led to people feeling more empowered to challenge the Church's authority and teaching (Lim, 2012).

While printing was a means for Christian mission groups to publish materials like the Bible, especially the New Testament by Protestant groups, beginning in the Reformation and continuing to this day, even more important than the emergence of the printing press was the shift into the electronic age in the early twentieth century. The shift to electronic means of communication had more profound impacts because of the shift in how people understood time and space since these media created a sense of immediacy (Horsfield, 2015). As broadcast became the norm, the 1970s saw the emergence of televangelists (see Chapter 11) who ushered in a new way of spreading the gospel message through broadcast. Televangelism has especially been successful in international missions where for evangelicals, broadcast communication technologies better served "the Great Commission" to preach the gospel to all the nations. For Catholics, broadcast communication technologies allowed for further extension of the call to imitate Christ with personalities like Archbishop Fulton Sheen appearing on television to discuss a variety of moral issues of the time. During the print era, factors like time and geography limited religious institutions in connecting with people in distant places. As electronic and digital technology evolved, Christian institutions were eventually able to embrace the changes and eliminate some of the barriers, especially in reaching missionary territories. Electronic media seemed instantaneous and able to transcend distance as the world entered an era of globalization. The media helps people to make meaning about the world; so if religious institutions are present in these spaces, people would seek out information to understand more about their surroundings and state in life, including engaging with technology to find answers to questions about religion. Religion has an impact on other structures, and the media plays an important role in a definitive way.

Hoover (2005) discussed glocalization in his research on Christian televangelism in remote places like Barbados and Hawaii. His study maintained that television technology in particular greatly helped Christian mission work in places that had yet to be reached, mainly owing to the lack of infrastructure to support the advancements being made in media and technology in larger nations. De Witte (2003) notes that television and film "can make things and persons more beautiful and attractive than they really are, while at the same time presenting them as true and accessible" (p. 174), still other factors to consider with the success of televangelism. Television has undoubtedly been an important Christian missionary tool that is beginning to converge with new methods of dissemination like digital media. Yet Christianity in the media age would be challenged by new media technologies – becoming spaces where religious information is shared by everyday users instead of coming only from religious institutions. Much like with the development of the printing press making it possible for more voices to enter the public sphere to comment on religious issues, the advent of Internet technology continues to complicate things for Christian institutions with regard to control of content and messages.

The Internet – like printing technology before it – emerged at a time when social, political, economic, and cultural changes within the broader culture shifted how people perceived the world around them, thereby enabling changes and differences in interpretation, understanding, and expressions of faith. For example, technology changes the way church leaders and congregants connect. *TIME Magazine's* landmark 1996 cover story "Finding God on the Web" (Ramo, 1996) questioned how communities form and emerge, raised concerns about theological debates, and acknowledged the question of authority in online spaces, all of which are arguably still debated today (Hutchings, 2010). In the early days of the Internet, Christian communities emerged that allowed people to share in fellowship online. This led to a new way of thinking about how churches met and ministered to their flocks, which include viewing the Internet as a spiritual network, a worship space, a missionary tool, a space to maintain religious identity through connections made, and a functional technology.

Nevertheless, it is important to question how religious movements' use of media in any era to spread their message has an impact on religious practice (De Witte, 2003). As more religious communication shifted online, the concerns of those interested in religious community formation online were relegated to the formation of social networks, the active participation of community members, and keeping a balance between control and participation. Hutchings (2010) notes that institutions (churches themselves) typically employ methods of one-to-many communication while congregants in groups exercise more grassroots interaction. But these grassroots interactions become causes for concern, especially for religious groups where authorities need some control of the messages being sent. This has been an ongoing issue for at least a decade. The scope of new media has made it so that religious institutions must make sure the faithful have accurate messages regarding matters of faith with the multitude of messages people encounter on a daily basis in online spaces.

Factors that played a role in the Internet's development – its enabling conditions (Horsfield & Teusner, 2007) – were technological innovations, increased access, diminished trust in institutions that once spread news, and the availability of open-source content. Additionally, many scholars have noted that religious communities that form online complemented religious practice offline as opposed to being a replacement for it. Virtual space can provide an area to explore religious expression in different ways; however, it lacks what a physical church can provide, especially when it comes to the sacramental life. But perhaps the biggest question has been that of authority with online communication (Horsfield & Teusner, 2007). In the early days of Web 2.0 technology, users embraced social media because it gave a voice to the voiceless, but those same freedoms come with the cost of giving a voice to those who may oppose authority or have differing views. Today's Christian institutions face the same issues that the Catholic Church faced with the advent of printing when the institution insisted on maintaining publication in Latin instead of embracing the vernacular: failure to adapt to new media will necessarily limit its potential in spreading the gospel beyond traditional offline Christianity.

Online communities and their discussions become the home for new expressions of faith. People seem to flock to online spaces to form meaningful connections with others that are not bound by geography. Additionally, people can "build important relationships, find belonging, and enhance their religious life" in these spaces (Horsfield & Teusner, 2007, p. 293). For example, a community of Catholic users emerged on Twitter that is now known as "Catholic Twitter," and users within the community engage with one another primarily in the online space, but occasionally meet up at large religious conferences (pre-Covid) or host their own meet-ups. In addition to discussing issues related to Catholicism, couples have met and gotten married and business partnerships have flourished because of the formation of the community within social media space. In the future, we will likely see even more connections being facilitated in these online spaces as the world continues to grapple with the impacts of the Covid-19 pandemic.

In the Western world in particular, religious faith is increasingly discredited in the public sphere and people distrust religious figures more and more because of rampant news stories of scandal and of terrorist acts carried out by religious groups (Tatarnic, 2005). Still, faith remains a topic of discussion in the public sphere across media eras. As new media platforms developed, new topics of interest related to studying religion online emerged, including examining social networks, the active participation of users, and the balance between control and participation. These are issues that Christian denominations have grappled with across the ages and will be examined in detail in the next sections of this chapter. The sections will look at Roman Catholicism, Orthodox Christianity, and Protestantism.

Roman Catholicism

Describing itself as founded by Jesus Christ, the Catholic Church notes that other later Christian churches – including those discussed in the next subsections – were formed from Catholicism at various points in history. Catholic theology sets the institution apart from other Christian denominations (Campbell, 2010). Indeed, the Church "as a source for the interpretation of Scripture, authority of the Pope as Christ's representative on earth and source of apostolic succession, the importance of the seven sacraments, a belief in Purgatory, and the Veneration of Mary" (p. 13) are all teachings that separate Catholicism from Protestantism and the Orthodox Church.

The Catholic Church has embraced the digital world and encourages lay Catholics and members of Church hierarchy to do so as well (Kennedy, 2019). The Vatican, the home to the Pope and the headquarters of the institutional Church, oversees a variety of both traditional and digital media outlets whose "main objective is communicating the message and mission of the Catholic Church worldwide" (p. 14). These channels include an official newspaper, radio station, television station, and news outlet. The formal establishment of communications offices within the Catholic institution date back to the 1930s with the founding of Vatican Radio and the growing popularity of the cinema; as new media emerged over time, the Vatican created more offices to provide direction and clarity on how the inevitable secular issues that would arise coincided with Catholic teaching (Kennedy, 2019). In the United States, Catholic television programming featuring Archbishop Fulton Sheen began in 1952, and by the mid-1980s, Mother Angelica founded the Eternal Word Television Network (EWTN). EWTN has become the largest religious media network in the world with audiences in 140 countries. In addition to television programming, EWTN also has radio and newspaper holdings. The network has the largest privately owned shortwave radio station that seeks to evangelize listeners around the world; they are affiliated with more than 500 stations globally (EWTN Radio, 2021). EWTN Catholic Radio offers free programming to local stations to help answer questions that listeners (both Catholic and non-Catholic) might have. In 2011 the network acquired the *National Catholic Register*, a national Catholic newspaper (established, in 1927), and now owns the Catholic News Agency with bureaus in the United States, Latin America, and Europe.

The Catholic Church has used radio since Guglielmo Marconi himself set up the Vatican's first radio network in the 1930s. Since then and even still today, the Church uses radio technology to reach Catholics around the world. In the Philippines, Radio Veritas, a Catholic radio network, has operated for over 50 years with over 50 radio stations and three small television stations and reaches an audience of nearly 70 million (Jones, 2017). Programming includes Mass, retreats, national religious celebrations, international Catholic events, and Vatican news in addition to music and children's programming. When locations in the Philippines experienced political unrest, Catholic radio stations helped promote peace by providing a space for dialogue between government and rebel militias (Jones, 2017). Additionally, stations provide commentary on important political and social issues, allowing for the discussion of Catholic values to circulate in the public sphere. Radio has the capacity to reach even the most remote locations and has a lasting impact on diverse audiences because it doesn't require as much of an infrastructure as Internet networks.

The Church was an early adopter of Internet technology, with the Vatican launching its website in 1995 (Campbell, 2010). As early as 1990, Pope John Paul II encouraged the faithful to embrace new media with his message for World Communications Day, explaining:

> With the advent of computer telecommunications and what are known as computer participation systems, the Church is offered further means for fulfilling her mission. Methods of facilitating communication and dialogue among her own members can strengthen the bonds of unity between them. Immediate access to information makes it possible for her to deepen her dialogue with the contemporary world. In the new "computer culture" the Church can more readily inform the world of her beliefs and explain the reasons for her stance on any given issue or event. She can hear more clearly the voice of public opinion, and enter into a continuous discussion with the world around her, thus involving herself more immediately in the common search for solutions to humanity's many pressing problems. (John Paul II, 1990, para. 8)

The Pope – the central authority within the Roman Catholic Church – encourages the use of new media for promoting religious education, disseminating news, and reinforcing the mission of the Church.

The Second Vatican Council in 1962 saw the Church grapple with the effects of modernity as members of the flock began to fall away in increasing numbers. Communicating in online spaces challenged hierarchical structures, in part because of the opportunity for transparency and accessibility to the Catholic Church (Kennedy, 2019). On the other hand, in 2002, just before the world ushered in the era of Web 2.0 and its popular social media sites, the Vatican's Pontifical Council for Social Communications issued two reports that offered recommendations for the ethical use of new media. These reports reflected on Catholic social teaching and social justice issues and provided suggestions to those in leadership roles within the Church "on how to use the internet in ways that glorify God and further the work of the Church" (Campbell, 2010, p. 37). Staying relevant to all members in a world overloaded with information presents a key challenge to the Catholic institution. As a result of the popularity of digital media, top-down guidelines are necessary to help control the message when it comes to theological issues and matters of Church teaching. Zuspan-Jerome (2014) suggested that formation on the human, spiritual, intellectual, and pastoral levels be made available to both Church leaders and laity as they began reaching out to the flock on new platforms. As social media became more popular and social networks online continued to emerge, the Church set out to capitalize on the active participation of its flock in these spaces as it sought to find balance between letting participation evolve organically and finding ways to control the message and narrative. Use of social media also trickles down to the parish level as the popularity of social media platforms continues and millennials and members of Gen Z begin entering the workforce.

Today, bishops, priests, deacons, seminarians, and religious sisters have a presence on social media platforms like Twitter and TikTok where they can live their vocation and connect with young Catholics who have questions about the faith. For example, @TheHappyPriest, Fr. Cassidy Stinson, who began his Twitter presence as @TheHappySeminarian and changed his handle on the day of his ordination from seminarian to priest, engages not only his parishioners in Virginia but also other priests and many young lay Catholics. Another example is The Daughters of St. Paul (known as the Media Nuns): Sr. Theresa Altheia Noble (@pursuedbytruth) is "at the fore-front of reviving the ancient discipline of *memento mori* ('remember your death')" (Pursued by Truth, n.d.) through both tweets using the hashtag #mementomori and the publication of a meditative journal geared toward helping readers to meditate through scripture reflections on their inevitable death. These examples show how media use at the parish level can inspire media use through frequent engagement in social media spaces.

Lay Catholics have begun to embrace social media in an effort to engage in evangelization. Much of this active participation can be attributed to engagement with other like-minded indi-viduals in social media space and the encouragement users receive from engaging with ordained and professed social media users like priests, deacons, and religious sisters. Begun in blogs, these grassroots efforts have transitioned to other platforms like Twitter, Instagram, TikTok, and even Clubhouse (e.g. The Catholic Club). In these spaces, everyday users encounter the gospel mes-sage through informative content and collaborative conversations. Young Catholic TikTok users crave more than the snappy viral content, which includes dances, memes, and challenges, on the platform: these users formed a community where they sought not only to defend the faith but to evangelize to other users. "Unafraid to speak their mind" (Escobar, 2020), users encourage dia-logue among their followers. Because of the deeper involvement at the grassroots level and the delicacy some topics demand, experts still stress the need for social media users to remember that "everyone has equal access to multiple channels, making it incredibly loud … [and] hard to dis-cern which voices are important and need to be heard" (para. 15). These members remind the Church to be active in online spaces.

Orthodox Christianity

The Orthodox Church, encompassing Greek-speaking Christians in the eastern Mediterranean, and the Roman Catholic (Latin-speaking) Church split in the Great Schism of 1054. "Officially it was the result of a disagreement between Pope Leo IX and the then Patriarch of Constantinople, about the nature of papal authority and doctrinal disputes over the understanding of the relationship between God and Jesus" (Campbell, 2010, p. 13). While the Churches hold many similar beliefs, they do dis-agree on issues related to the papacy, how saints are venerated, and the use of religious icons.

The second largest Christian communion globally (after Roman Catholicism), Orthodox Christians have historically faced suppression that has had an impact on how they relate to the modern world. Orthodox Christianity has a mixed response to communication technology. For example, the monks and pilgrims who seek refuge on Mount Athos, a peninsula in Greece consid-ered the spiritual heart of Eastern Orthodox Christianity, willingly leave the advancements of the modern world behind as a matter of discipline and asceticism. But for the communion of self-headed national and self-ruled churches that make up the Orthodox Church in the world, the relationship to the mass media is more complicated. There is no central authority figure for Orthodox Christians, like the Pope in the Catholic Church: the Patriarch of Constantinople, prob-ably the most well-known Orthodox figure and the senior-most bishop of the Orthodox Church, has authority that only extends to his territory; decisions about media take place locally.

Much of the Orthodox Christian community uses digital media and other forms of communication to reach their congregants both in Eastern Europe and in Greece. Each of the Orthodox communities has a different relationship with media, drawing upon on the church's relationship with the government of the specific geographic area. For example, the Orthodox Church in Eastern Europe did not enjoy freedom to communicate with the faithful until the 1990s after the fall of communism there; before governments controlled the churches and limited their ability to have any place in society. The Russian Orthodox Church became one of the most trusted entities in Russia in this time after working carefully on its image and hiring lay people to manage their image and media presence. In 2000, the Holy Synod of the Russian Orthodox Church issued a declaration that explained "how the church should relate to broader secular society in the post-communist era, including how the church relates to the media" (Turner, 2019, p. 114). However, with widely available Internet in Russia, some people still support the idea of state control of online spaces, which can make it difficult for the Russian Orthodox Church to have great impact there. Suslov (2016) notes a "common-trope for self-positioning of the Church is that the Russian Orthodox Church is a state-shaping religion, and as such it weaves its own historical narrative with the narrative of the Russian State. Thus, the Orthodox religion in Russia has an ineliminable political and geo-political component." The Church does have "its own sense of mission, ideological agenda, and doctrinal grounds…, which provide for a possibility … to raise an independent and oppositional voice" (pp. 2–3). This distinction helps it continue as a trusted entity as the Russian Church treads forward into the digital domain.

In contrast, the Orthodox Church has been a prominent fixture of Greek life since it gained independence from the Ottoman Empire in the 1800s. Owing to its prominence in the area, the Greek Orthodox Church spent less time cultivating an image in the media than did the Russian Church, and its image has declined in the twentieth century. In regions where Orthodox Christianity is not widely practiced, like in the West, the parish website is more common than in the Roman Catholic and Protestant Churches because it serves as a point of contact not only for the faithful, but also for those interested in Orthodox Christianity and considering conversion (Turner, 2019).

Even though Orthodox churches have used media to reach their congregants, they have expressed skepticism. In 2016, several Orthodox churches met for the Great and Holy Council of the Orthodox Church to discuss matters of shared concern regarding "problems of humanity" (Orthodox Church, Great and Holy Council, 2016, para. 4). One document concerned the relationship of the Church, its congregants, and the media. In a section about the Church's mission to witness love through service, the Council writes:

> Mass media frequently operates under the control of an ideology of liberal globalization and is thus rendered an instrument for disseminating consumerism and immorality. Instances of disrespectful – at times, blasphemous – attitudes toward religious values are cause for particular concern, inasmuch as arousing division and conflict in society. The Church warns her children of the risk of influence on their conscience by the mass media, as well as its use to manipulate rather than bring people and nations together. (Orthodox Church, Great and Holy Council, 2016, section F, para. 8)

Even though not all of the autocephalous churches were represented at the Council, most congregations that did not participate do hold similar views (Turner, 2019). This complicated relationship of the Orthodox Church with the media is one that the institution grapples with: "Some patriarchs acknowledge that media is a means of reaching far more people than would be possible through normal means, and the use of media is an appropriate extension of the traditional proclamation of the Gospel message" (p. 116). To have no presence at all also means that the institution would not control their own narrative.

Similar to the Catholic Church, some of Orthodox sacramental life, like the reception of communion, cannot be experienced in the digital realm. However, other elements of spirituality translate better to online spaces, such as lighting virtual candles or following the liturgy on electronic devices (Turner, 2019). The Orthodox Church has a variety of websites that host liturgical texts in their original languages and in local vernaculars, making it possible for ordinary users to access a full library of religious material. Veneration of icons holds an important role in the Orthodox liturgical tradition, and some icons are considered to be miraculous. Historically, highly trained artists who follow specific rules and techniques produce icons. Advancements in technology have made icons more accessible because they can be more easily reproduced, but there are questions about whether these mass-produced icons are legitimate for veneration. "For the faithful such icons, even if printed out on a sheet of paper, are often regarded as acceptable for veneration since theologically speaking, to be true, it is not the image itself that is venerated but the saint" (p. 117). Additionally, digital technology has made it possible to simulate pilgrimages to important spiritual locations throughout the Middle East.

Orthodox Christians have access to media outlets officially sanctioned by the Church through partnerships; in addition, some Orthodox clergy and lay members maintain presences in new media space. Oftentimes this use of media aligns with the spirit of the institutional Orthodox Church, but it can also manifest a spirit of criticism. Turner (2019) notes the anonymity that online communication provides its users, which makes it easier for them to "share information that might be embarrassing, or otherwise suppressed by the official segments of the Church" (p. 120). Sometimes this type of content dissemination is unproductive, but it can shed light on major issues happening within the Church that hierarchs need to address. It also serves as a venue for more voices to be heard about important topics in Orthodox spirituality.

Protestantism

The Protestant Church grew out of the Reformation associated with Martin Luther's nailing his 95 theses on the church door in Wittenberg, Germany in the sixteenth century. His writings challenged teachings in the Catholic Church and rallied others throughout Europe, resulting in new religious groups associated with "Protestant" Christianity, as Lutherans, Presbyterians, and Baptists. Early Protestant theology draws upon five fundamental principles of faith including the Bible being the only source of authority for believers, justification by faith alone, access to God through Jesus only, and the mission of life being to glorify God (Campbell, 2010, p. 14). Protestants have no central authority figure like the Pope, so many voices emerge as potential authorities on a variety of subjects. These voices can contradict one another: for example, when it comes to use of new technologies like the Internet, some more conservative Protestant groups oppose it, arguing that it can take believers further away from God because of the artificiality of the online world, while other Protestant groups argue that Protestants should use the latest tools in the spirit of St. Paul, who is lauded as "the first 'cyberapostle' … who used the technology of his day to be virtually present in different churches as well as eras" (p. 38). Like the Catholics and the Orthodox, most branches of Protestantism acknowledge concerns with using new media technology but embrace it as a way to connect with followers where they are.

Many Protestant denominations today have overlap in their core beliefs, but their theology and practices have diverged, with Protestantism further divided into two groups in North America and Western Europe especially: "mainline, who trace their roots back to the Reformation, and evangelical churches that are marked by more fundamentalist interpretations and applications of the Bible" (Campbell, 2010, p. 14). Mainline Protestant groups consist of both liberals and evangelicals: the groups differ on theological issues related to original sin, eternal damnation, and biblical inspiration (Balmer & Winner, 2002; Sturgill, 2019). Groups associated with the mainline denominations include the United Church of Christ, the United Methodist Church, the Episcopal Church, the Presbyterian Church in the United States, the Christian Church, the American Baptist Church, and the Evangelical Lutheran Church (Sturgill, 2019). Despite its value for evangelizing, conservative groups of Christians and evangelicals fear the Internet as antithetical to Christianity, encouraging "anti-Christian values" (Campbell, 2010).

The spread of charismatic and Pentecostal churches (that is those that stress the direct action of the Holy Spirit and forms of worship that include praise and speaking in tongues, recalling the first Christian Pentecost) outside of the Western world depended on broadcasting. In the 1990s, Christian groups, particularly those of charismatic and Pentecostal backgrounds, bought airtime on both private television channels and FM radio stations across Africa. In Ghana, for example, religious programming makes up a large percentage of radio and television programming, especially on weekends (De Witte, 2003). While radio and television stations are legally required to be based on secular practice, the charismatic and Pentecostal churches have the financial resources to dominate the airwaves. Stations often employ charismatic pastors to provide entertainment programming. Religious broadcasting plays an important role. It brings religious discourse into the public sphere alongside political and economic discourses, and thus creates a diversity of ideas regarding issues like morality and human rights.

Radio and television broadcasts are popular ways for other countries in Africa to utilize the existing media structures for religious content. Pentecostals in southern Africa (Zimbabwe and Botswana especially) see the media as a way to reach worshipers and spread the gospel message (Togarasei, 2012). The programming found on television and radios in Botswana and Zimbabwe differs from televangelism in the United States and even Ghana. In Zimbabwe, media laws dictate state approval for programming while in Botswana, media laws are more relaxed. Churches do not have their own radio and television stations in either country, but they can acquire airtime to promote events, run special programs, and play music.

The evangelical community has a long history with media engagement and remains active in all forms of media, including online platforms, print and broadcast publications, and film both in producing its own media and in influencing mainstream media (Peverill-Conti & Thibault, 2007). Evangelical groups in the West like Focus on the Family and Saddleback Church create diversified media content. For example, Focus on the Family publishes podcasts and other on-demand content as a way to reach listeners on mobile devices. Saddleback Church installed large screens (jumbotrons) to help massive audiences feel more connected to church leader Rick Warren as he preached, which found new uses for video and parallel outlets that can exist separately. Video broadcasts also allowed megachurches like Saddleback to provide content to remote locations, which breaks down geographic barriers. According to Peverill-Conti and Thibault, "in all cases, the use of media is based on supporting and promoting the 'Great Commandment' ... and the 'Great Commission' ... in order to create purpose driven churches all over the world connected by technology" (Peverill-Conti & Thibault, 2007, para. 26). Critics of evangelical Christians have long been concerned about the monetization of content in the name of Christianity.

Mainline Protestant churches (both liberals and evangelicals) have embraced new media for a variety of functions. Online spaces afford church congregations a fresh outlook because the denominations can separate themselves from the physical constraints of a church campus and "attract visitors without the reputation of the denomination" (Sturgill, 2019, p. 29). Sturgill (2019) describes how mainline Protestant groups use new media on denominational, congregational, and individual levels. At the denominational level, mainline groups offer news and information about the denomination itself, spiritual formation guidelines and evangelism efforts, and opportunities for faith-based activities in real-life communities. At the congregational level, content varies, but usually centers on diversity and inclusion, portrayed through photo-heavy content geared toward retaining existing members. Additionally, larger individual congregations tend to invite their members to stream services online, which "makes sense in these denominations where place-based practices and sacraments are not as important as they are in faiths" (p. 32) that require in-person attendance for the reception of sacraments (i.e. Catholicism). Streaming also makes sense for older congregations whose members may be homebound. At the individual level, the media use pastors or other leaders who form and maintain relationships with church congregants. Since new media provide good tools for creating and maintaining relationships, the mainline denominations have suggested best practices for both leadership and for church-related accounts. It has required church leaders to remain up-to-date with new media technology. These include rules like asking for permission before posting photos of congregants in order to protect their privacy and having policies in place for communicating with youth members. Sturgill notes that "encouraging congregants to participate in worship by checking in or tweeting may become more common as the constant engagement with technology becomes further diffused and more accepted by society" (p. 36). Given the complexities all religious groups encountered in the face of the global Covid-19 pandemic, even the smallest of religious groups were forced to think outside of the box to reach their flocks during strict lockdowns in 2020.

Like in Catholicism, there is a grassroots effort of everyday users making Christian content for their followers on a variety of social media platforms. The youngest of these users are on TikTok. Analytics for popular hashtags related to Christianity (e.g. #Jesus, #Bible, #Christian) reveal billions of views and hundreds of thousands of posts dedicated to Christian content (TikTok, 2021).

Future Directions and Conclusions

Despite the rise of secularization and an increased distrust of organized religion and religious officials, many people still adhere to a faith tradition as a moral compass in their lives. The media, for better or worse, also serve as a guide to many people, and sometimes the messages promoted in the media directly compete with religious values or are highly critical of religious institutions. While some Christian groups see media use as a distraction from the divine, most in Catholic, Protestant, and Orthodox circles have embraced media as a necessary part of their ministry. Religious institutions cannot break from centuries of theology and tradition, so they only slowly adopt many of the advancements experienced in the modern age, especially if these do not align with doctrine, teaching, or belief systems. These views also serve to provide guidelines and parameters for media use, especially in institutions with central authority figures like in the Catholic and Orthodox Churches. Hoover (2013) acknowledges a need for religious institutions to adapt to changes resulting from technological advancement. There is a need for "a more nuanced view of the digital" that takes a multidimensional and layered approach to understanding concepts like authenticity and authority, which are issues that all facets of the Christian institution must contend with as they utilize new media technology. He concludes that religious institutions should be less concerned about the content that is shared in digital space: "While the content is important, churches should place more attention on the spiritual experience of the user in the digital space because users are flocking to new media spaces in search of answers and community" (p. 266).

Tatarnic's (2005) discussion of Christianity and television suggests that the Church has the opportunity to capitalize on the uncertainty of our times: People are searching for answers. The Church can provide these answers by being vulnerable, too. Tatarnic suggests that churches need to consider how to minister to people in a mediated world – especially to those wounded from engaging with the media in a variety of ways. Indeed, Christian institutions should position themselves in such a way that they can provide a safe haven for those who are searching. Evangelization efforts hinge on providing care, meeting the pastoral needs of the faithful, and those who seek to spread the Christian message.

References

Balmer, R. H., & Winner, L. F. (2002). *Protestantism in America*. Columbia University Press.

Campbell, H. A. (2010). *When religion meets new media*. Routledge.

De Vries, H. (2001). In media res: Global religion, public spheres, and the task of contemporary comparative religious studies. In H. De Vries, & S. Weber (Eds.), *Religion and media: Cultural memory in the present* (pp. 3–42). Stanford University Press.

De Witte, M. (2003). Altar media's *living word*: Televised charismatic Christianity in Ghana. *Journal of Religion in Africa, 33*(2), 172–202.

Escobar, A. (2020, September 26). Catholic 'influencers' are using TikTok for community and evangelization. National Catholic Reporter. Retrieved March 8, 2021, from https://www.ncronline.org/news/media/catholic-influencers-are-using-tiktok-community-and-evangelization

EWTN Radio. (2021). Catholic radio. EWTN Radio. Retrieved April 17, 2021, from https://www.ewtn.com/radio

Gaillardetz, R. R. (2007). *Transforming our days: Finding God amid the noise of modern life*. Liguori Publications.

Hoover, S. M. (2005). Islands in the global stream: Television, religion, and geographic integration. *Studies in World Christianity, 11*(1), 125–143.

Hoover, S. M. (2013). Concluding thoughts: Imagining the religious in and through the digital. In H. A. Campbell (Ed.), *Digital religion: Understanding religious practice in new media worlds* (pp. 266–268). Routledge.

Horsfield, P. (2015). *From Jesus to the internet: A history of Christianity and media*. Wiley-Blackwell.

Horsfield, P., & Teusner, P. (2007). A mediated religion: Historical perspectives on Christianity and the internet. *Studies in World Christianity, 13*(3), 278–295.

Hutchings, T. (2010). The internet and the church: An introduction. *The Expository Times, 122*(1), 11–19.

Jones, K. J. (2017). Faith, hope, and community: Catholic radio at work in the Philippines. Catholic News Agency. Retrieved May 31, 2022, from https://www.catholicnewsagency.com/news/37149/faith-hope-community-catholic-radio-at-work-in-the-philippines

Kennedy, M. C. (2019). Roman Catholicism in the digital age. In A. E. Grant, A. F. C. Sturgill, C. H. Chen, & D. A. Stout (Eds.), *Religion online: How digital technology is changing the way we worship and pray, Volume 2: Faith groups and digital media* (pp. 10–27). Praeger ABC-Clio.

Lim, F. K. G. (2012). Mediating Christianity in contemporary Asia. *Studies in World Christianity, 18*(2), 189–203.

Orthodox Church, Great and Holy Council. (2016). The mission of the church in today's world. Holy Council. Retrieved February 19, 2021, from https://www.holycouncil.org/-/mission-orthodox-church-todays-world

Paul, J., II. (1990). The Christian message in a computer culture: Message of the Holy Father John Paul II for the 24th World Communications Day. Vatican. Retrieved March 8, 2021, from http://www.vatican.va/content/john-paul-ii/en/messages/communications/documents/hf_jp-ii_mes_24011990_world-communications-day.html

Peverill-Conti, G., & Thibault, M. (2007). Evangelicals and the media. MIT Communications Forum. Retrieved March 7, 2021, from http://web.mit.edu/comm-forum/legacy/forums/evangelicals.html

Pursued by Truth. (n.d.) Homepage. Retrieved March 7, 2021, from https://pursuedbytruth.com

Ramo, J. C. (1996, December 16). Finding God on the web. *TIME Magazine*. Retrieved March 7, 2021, from http://content.time.com/time/subscriber/article/0,33009,985700-1,00.html

Sturgill, A. F. C. (2019). Mainline Protestantism and the internet. In A. E. Grant, A. F. C. Sturgill, C. H. Chen, & D. A. Stout (Eds.), *Religion online: How digital technology is changing the way we worship and pray, Volume 2: Faith groups and digital media* (pp. 28–38). Praeger ABC-Clio.

Suslov, M. (2016). *Digital orthodoxy in the post-Soviet world: The Russian Orthodox Church and Web2.0.* distributed by Columbia University Press.

Tatarnic, M. S. (2005). The mass media and faith: The potentialities and problems for the church in our television culture. *Anglican Theological Review, 87*(3), 447–465.

TikTok. (2021). #Jesus. TikTok. Retrieved March 8, 2021, from https://www.tiktok.com

Togarasei, L. (2012). Mediating the Gospel: Pentecostal Christianity and media technology in Botswana and Zimbabwe. *Journal of Contemporary Religion, 27*(2), 257–274.

Turner, J. (2019). Orthodoxy Christianity in the digital age. In A. E. Grant, A. F. C. Sturgill, C. H. Chen, & D. A. Stout (Eds.), *Religion online: How digital technology is changing the way we worship and pray, Volume 2: Faith groups and digital media* (pp. 111–125). Praeger ABC-Clio.

Zuspan-Jerome, D. (2014). *Connected toward communion: The Church and social communication in the digital age.* Liturgical Press.

Selected Readings

Herbert, D. (2011). Why has religion gone public again?: Towards a theory of media and religious re-publicisation. In G. Lynch, J. Mitchell, & A. Strhan (Eds.), *Religion, media and culture: A reader.* Routledge.

Hoover, S. M., & Clark, L. S. (2002). *Practicing religion in the age of the media: Explorations in media, religion, and culture.* Columbia University Press.

Klassen, P. E., & Lofton, K. (2013). Material witnesses: Women and the mediation of Christianity. In M. Lovheim (Ed.), *Media, religion and gender.* Routledge 52–65.

Lovheim, M., & Hjarvard, S. (2019). The mediatized conditions of contemporary religion: Critical and future directions. *Journal of Religion, Media and Digital Culture, 8*(2), 206–223. https://doi.org/10.1163/21659214-00802002

Meyer, B. (2004). Christianity in Africa: From African independent to Pentecostal-charismatic churches. *Annual Review of Anthropology, 33,* 447–474.

Stahle, H. (2022). *Russian Church in the digital era: Mediatization of orthodoxy.* Taylor & Francis.

Wilfred, F. (2014). *The Oxford handbook of Christianity in Asia.* Oxford University Press.

6

Communication in Judaism and Islam

Yoel Cohen and Hadi Enayat*

Introduction

Judaism and Islam arose centuries apart in the Middle East and Arabia; both witness to one God, a God who interacts with humanity. Both stress communication in its various forms and consequently each teaches about and practices communication. And because of their scope, both also appear in and use contemporary media. Beginning with the more ancient Judaism and finishing with Islam, this chapter introduces the communication teaching of each religious group, examining ethical guidelines for communication, then looking at the ways that the different religions use communication media.

Judaism

Jewish Communication Ethics

Language, speech, and communication play a central role in Judaism. The only knowledge of God that humanity enjoys are through His acts and messages. Hebrew is not only a language, connecting sender and receiver, but is itself power-laden. The Hebrew Bible (Genesis 1:3) in recounting, "And God said: 'Let there be light,'" shows that communication in Hebrew enjoys the power to create and act. The biblical account of the world being called into existence through mere divine utterance emphasizes this and leads Jews to call Hebrew the "holy language." Communication and language form the essence of Judaism.

Communication has changed over the centuries. The prophets – from the Patriarchs Abraham, Isaac, and Jacob through to Moses and beyond – fulfilled a primary role as messengers of God (Haggai 1:13), as witnesses of God's power and mercy. The prophet was more than a messenger, but also a participant standing in the presence of God (Jeremiah 15:19). His communication was not neutral but comprised ethical monotheism, a religion of morality. Since the end of Jewish prophecy in the fourth century BCE, faith replaced prophecy as the staple ingredient of the relationship between the Jewish People and God. Any Jewish theological study of communication became reduced to belief (*emunah*). After the destruction of the Temple in 70 CE, oral prayers

The Handbook on Religion and Communication, First Edition. Edited by Yoel Cohen and Paul A. Soukup.
© 2023 John Wiley & Sons Ltd. Published 2023 by John Wiley & Sons Ltd.

fulfill important roles also, enabling the congregant to become a participant in humanity's relationship to God. A clue to the centrality of speech appears in the *Vidduy* prayer, or Confession on the Day of Atonement (*Yom Kippur*) prayer services, where over a quarter of the Jew's confession relates to the abuse of speech. All this demands that human speech should be performed in a dignified manner – free of violence, threats, or nonpeaceful statements.

As the written source of Judaism, the Bible is the revelation of a 4000-year-long relationship between God and his chosen people. In chronicling often-dramatic events such as the early Israelite history in Egypt, the Exodus, and the capture of the Promised Land of Canaan, the Bible does not differ much from the news media. That the only knowledge of God that humanity enjoys through His acts and messages, was, for example, reflected in the Israelite passage through Sinai to Canaan: God's presence through the pillar of fire and the Divine Cloud of protection. And, within the Tabernacle, and later the First Jewish Temple in Jerusalem, God communicated through the breastplate (*hoshen*) worn by the High Priest. Similarly, God's satisfaction was expressed through fire from Heaven which consumed the offerings, and the Divine Presence (*Shekhinah*) inside the Tabernacle and Temple.

Judaism encourages social interaction. The commandments aimed to establish a just society by the standards of the day and distinctive in its service of God. Thus, Jewish ethics seek to build peace and harmony, including dialogue, and be a channel for strengthening family ties, notably between parents and children, and friends.

Judaism and mass media developed separately, with wide time spans between one and the other. While the first newspapers began in the seventeenth century CE, Judaism as a system of belief had long concluded its formative period with the end of the prophets. Bible texts themselves and rabbinical discussions – collected in rabbinic texts like the Mishna and Talmud – may be used to extrapolate principles relevant to contemporary questions about mass media.

The Right to Privacy and the Right to Know

Perhaps the most significant contribution of Jewish thought to mass communications concerns regulating the transfer of or information sharing among people. The biblical edict (Leviticus 19:16) warning against being "a talebearer among your people" prohibits social gossip (*loshon hara*), that is, the divulging and publication of information that may damage another person's reputation (*loshon hara*). The same biblical verse continues "Do not stand idly by the blood of your neighbor," indicating that Judaism compares social gossip to character assassination. Judaism gives a superior weighting to an individual's name and social reputation.

Falk (1999) provides a complete Jewish schema of what information may be shared among people and what may not. For example, in his singular tome, "Hofetz Hayim," Rabbi Yisrael Meir Kagan of Radin, Poland, divided information into three categories (Ha-Cohen, 1873). Even positively speaking about a person (*rechilut*), and "neutral information" not besmirching a person, was, according to the *Hofetz Hayim*, forbidden. For the *Hofetz Hayim*, information had to have a social value: to bring knowledge about dangers to the attention of the public. Latter-day examples could be information about a pedophile, radiation, government corruption, or social discrimination. So, today, the primary value Western society gives to the right to know (weighted above the right to privacy) contrasts with Judaism, which gives greater weight to the right to privacy over the right to know (Cohen, 2012a, 2018), and suggests that in the eyes of the *Hofetz Hayim* "neutral information" fulfills no social value and should not be published.

According to the Talmud, while information known to less than three people may not be divulged – and is regarded as a profound breach of *loshon hara* – once that same information is known to more than three it is no longer in the private realm and is permissible. This raises questions for source–reporter relations in modern journalism because a politician leaking to a journalist carries out the grievous act of disclosing previously unknown information for political advantage, such as damaging a political opponent. Contemporary rabbis have nevertheless sought to reconcile the Jewish strictures on social gossip with modern ideas of public information in a democracy and the principle of the right to know. The views of the *Hofetz Hayim* may be contrasted with Rabbi Abraham Isaac Kook, Chief Rabbi in Palestine during the British mandate, who recognized the role of the fourth estate in critical reporting, enabling the citizenry to be informed about those elected to power, and about inappropriate behavior by public officials (Chwat, 1995; Feldman, 2015; Korngott, 1993).

A different interpretation of the juxtaposition in Leviticus 19:16 where the warning against being "a talebearer among your people" is followed by "Do not stand idly by the blood of your neighbor" holds that one has an obligation to inform society about something that is a danger to it. Indeed, the next verse (19:17) says "You shall admonish your fellow and do not bear a sin because of him." The Bible itself disclosed Moses' sin of smiting the Rock instead of speaking to the Rock, to bring forth water, which would have otherwise publicized a miracle and have been a means toward moral teaching. This led one rabbi, Azriel Ariel (2001), to articulate the Jewish religious concept of "social gossip by consent": by putting themselves forward for elected office and being in the public limelight elected politicians understand that they will be under public and media scrutiny. Examples include disclosures of information of corruption or sexual improprieties committed by rabbis. Rabbis set up high standards of moral conduct, and such disclosures defame the religion and even God (*hilul Hashem*). The provision of information about events and societies, which contributes to understanding and reduces conflict – while not generally identified as a peculiarly religious goal – is endorsed by Judaism.

Nevertheless, if social repair (*tikkun olam*) can be achieved through means other than media publicity – like turning to the police authorities – this is preferred. If there is no other way, the journalist has still to verify the information. Rumors are unsatisfactory bases for news reporting. Moreover, the goal of the journalist should accordingly be as a watchdog rather than scooping other media.

Privacy has a privileged status in Jewish thought. In a famous edict, Rabbenu Gershom imposed a prohibition not to read somebody's letter. Finklestein (1924) says that the Rabbenu Gershom edict developed in the Middle Ages when letters were transported by personal messengers. One's property, therefore, includes information about oneself, and the right to privacy includes what information is not publicly known about a person. In discussing the concept of *hezek re'iyah* – or causing damage by prying into somebody's home – the Talmud says that in, for example, a courtyard between two dwellings, there is a religious obligation to construct a fence between the two to ensure the privacy of the occupants. Thus, engaging in a web search that discloses private information not available from a casual Googling is religiously questionable. Warhaftig (2009) is concerned that the computer which records the surfing behavior of the user enables outside interests to gain access without authorization to data about a user's economic standards, bank data, tastes, even medical problems. Arguably, in the age of the computer, the individual partly gives up their right to privacy. Another question raised by Warhaftig concerns photography. Is it permitted to photograph somebody without their knowledge? Should the object of a photograph receive financial remuneration? Is it permitted to photograph the person, such as in an informal private pose, which may draw popular appeal but embarrasses the individual? Yet, notwithstanding the importance that Judaism gives to privacy, there is no Jewish law of privacy per se (Meir, 2014).

One solution is to redefine or refocus contemporary debate about the threat to privacy upon the individual. Washofsky (2014, p. 120), advancing the Reform school of Progressive *Halakhah*

(Jewish religious law), proposes that "man show restraint before he shares his life with the virtual universe, to consider the potential outcome of one's actions before one posts, uploads text or tweets." Separating oneself more from Big Brother and data control and accepting an obligation of the individual to take self-responsibility is not dissimilar from the original biblical injunction for Jews: to build the ideal community in the image of God.

Related to the Jewish laws regarding social gossip but a separate command comes the requirement to be accurate in passing information, including for news reporters to be accurate. Without it, honesty and credibility in interpersonal relations cannot be assumed. Indeed, prior to the invention of paper, literacy, and printing, social relations drew heavily upon the integrity of the individual. In *Proverbs* (2:19) "the lip of truth shall be established forever; a lying tongue is but for a moment," the Bible ascribes importance to providing accurate information. So important is truth that lying is tantamount to idol worship. For example, 10 of the 12 spies whom Moses sent into the Land of Canaan from the Sinai Desert to "spy out the Land" (Numbers 13) sinned because they deliberately falsified their observations about the Promised Land (Liebes, 1994). The requirement of accuracy takes on added importance in strategic communications, like advertising and public relations. In commerce, Leviticus (25:17) instructs "In selling, do not be extortionate." Judaism prohibits a trader, in promoting his products, from creating a false impression (*genevat daat*). The good aspects of a project may – indeed, in Judaism's view, should – be shown. But showing the defects of the product of one's competitor is not far from being slanderous and false (Cohen, 2012b; Levine, 1981).

Judaism, therefore, offers principles about the threat to secrecy characterized by the digital age. Whereas in the pre-Internet era, rules of reporting by professional journalists could be enforced, ordinary people blogging in social media like Facebook lack training in these Jewish strictures on interpersonal communication. Bloggers are required to take into account the damage that can be caused online where potentially thousands of people can read it. Care should be taken in social media not to provoke criticism or bullying or insulting.

But while Judaism's discussion on speech goes beyond the question of privacy to emphasize that message content should neither damage nor slander, it does not discuss whether the presentation of facts paints an accurate and objective record of an event – short of demanding that the communicator does not possess bad intentions. There is even less supervision in Judaism of the visual image given that pictures can be interpreted in different ways. As a result, there may be numerous images constructed of the same event with different meanings. In the visual age of television and digital communication Judaism does not offer guidelines for the construction of the image or picture to be accurate.

The penumbrum of accurate information is the prohibition not to "steal" information. Judaism provides a separate moralistic view about the ownership of information (Weisfish, 2010) and may have influenced contemporary standards regarding copyright ownership. The command in the Ten Commandments "Do not steal" (Exodus 20:13) may be interpreted as not limited to physical objects but extending to ideas such as artistic creation. With the exception of common information in the public arena, Judaism recognizes information as a commodity. The Bible and information about public events are not subject to copyright. But an exclusive news report, which uncovers new facts and was prepared exclusively by one reporter, is the property of the reporter and the news organization for whom they work.

The question of modern copyright has received renewed attention by rabbis in the digital age. What are the implications of the world wide web for ownership of information in light of the proliferation of downloading and copying texts? Here some rabbis draw upon the Jewish law principle that once an owner has given up possession of an object that has gone missing, it does not have to be returned to its rightful owner. While individual rabbis have suggested that the world wide web is like an open river, the fact that some programs may be accessed or down-loaded only following payment suggests that copyright exists no less in the age of the Internet.

A separate media-related prohibition in Jewish law refers to pronouncing the Holy Name of God, the Tetragrammaton (Exodus 20:7). This acknowledges that no word can capture the awe-some, infinite power of the creator. Texts such as prayer books have, by tradition, been buried in a cemetery. To overcome the problem, Hebrew religious newspapers do not print the Tetragrammaton.

Another area where the Judaism regulates media behavior concerns Sabbath observance. As a celebration of God's creation of the world in seven days, as described in the opening chapter of the Book of Genesis, the fourth of the Ten Commandments requires the Jew to observe and rest on the Sabbath day. In effect, this limits the use of electronic media – like radio, television, and the Internet – on the Sabbath, because turning on electricity during the Sabbath is regarded by *halakhah* in Orthodox and Conservative Judaism as an act of "creation." The prohibition of using electrical media on the Sabbath has taken on a new dimension because in the international time zone, the Sabbath – a dusk to dusk 24-hour period – falls at different times in different regions, raising the intriguing question of whether a Jewish website (especially a commercial one) may or may not be accessed on the Sabbath.

The Production and Consumption of Mass Media

Given that the media's construction of events is determined by news values and public interest rather than a mystical order recording divine events and miracles, a gap necessarily exists bet-ween the media's view and the traditional view of Judaism. If past dramatic events in Jewish history (the biblical Exodus from Egypt, for example) fulfill criteria for dramatic media interest, the event itself is not occurring today. How does a journalist who by training is a critical ratio-nalist write about miracles of God, "interventions" in the natural cycle of nature? News media are not supposed to be conveyers of religion, distant religious stories, and events done in the past, but focus on the present. So, too, the Internet era.

Psychological and ideological news values play important roles in the construction of news in the Israeli media. Religions that are closer, or, more proximate to Israeli audiences, namely Judaism, receive greater coverage. Religious crises are defined as news. Religious elites, whether individuals like leading rabbis or institutions like the Chief Rabbinate or most recognized *yeshivot* (educational institutions of higher learning, Talmudical institutions), are more likely to be defined as newsworthy than lesser souls or less significant institutions. Religion stories with public or political dimensions are the most covered subject in the Israeli media, with religious political parties the biggest single category. Religion-related news on the news pages comprises mostly conflict-related developments and reflects the tensions between Judaism and modern statehood. Much of the tension between the religious and secular centers around the question of whether the state of Israel should be based upon Jewish religious law (*halakhah*) or be a secular democracy. A major issue concerns observance of the Sabbath by public institutions. Attempts by Orthodox groups and political parties to exert influence that public transport and places of entertainment should not operate on the Sabbath and holy days are widely covered. Other mat-ters concern personal status (which is in the hands of the religious courts) including (i) religious conversion and the extent of study and commitment demanded of a convert, with the Orthodox rabbis charging that non-Orthodox rabbis perform superficial conversions; (ii) the *aguna*, or a husband of a couple who have separated and refuses to give his wife a divorce, or a husband who disappeared as a result of armed conflict; and (iii) the laws of divorce – also monopolized by the

Orthodox – and that Orthodox rules of procedure provide substantial advantages to the man in a case of dispute. Other news stories relate to public funding for religious institutions, distributed by state-sponsored local religious councils. Membership by non-Orthodox representatives like the Reform and Conservative religious is necessary in order to win financial allocations for non-Orthodox synagogues, schools, and social services. An issue of religious freedom that arguably has generated the most media spin concerns feminist groups and non-Orthodox Jewish movements that want to perform their own prayer services at the *Kotel* or Western Wall on the Temple Mount, Jerusalem.

Most key news organizations in the mainstream media have specialist religion reporters with the result that most of the religion writing is done by a handful of individuals, which gives them an immense responsibility and influence. The religion affairs reporter in the Israeli media has invariably covered only the Jewish religion – in contrast to other countries where religious affairs reporters cover the gamut of religions. The level of a reporter's background knowledge has an impact on the work. Given a lack of formal source-media channels, the work of the religion affairs reporter is to locate the centers of power within the Haredi world – the key rabbis – and to develop a network of tipsters, aides, cronies, religious teachers, and students close to them. Haredi rabbis have unclear lines of contact with the media, with many viewing the nonreligious media as *treifah* (the term used for nonkosher food), but with a few recognizing the need to talk to the "devil."

Religious Israelis tend to view journalists as antireligious, with over 50% of respondents in a 1995 poll saying that at least some journalists were antireligious (Smith poll, Haredi Image in the media, April 1995). Another study found that a majority of Israelis felt that the media were inclined to be neutral (Cohen, 2005). A perceived bias results less from a specific biased news report but more from the volume of coverage that religious communities receive. There is no proportionate relationship in coverage between the amount of coverage that different Jewish religious streams receive and their size in the population. The Haredim or Ultra-Orthodox (10% of the Israeli Jewish population) are media stars both because of their visibility, with their distinct black garb, and because of their political clout. The lower amount of religion content concerning Modern Orthodox (20% of the Jewish population) may be explained by the fact that since the 1967 war the Modern Orthodox community is taken up today less with specifically religious issues (like "Who is a Jew?") and has become increasingly characterized by the nationalist task of settling the biblical territories of Judea, Samaria, and Gaza captured in the war.

The Haredi Media

Jewish ethics are most visible in Israel's religious media. Both the Haredim and Modern Orthodox outlooks respect the values of freedom of expression and the freedom of the press. Characterized by a style of life of social withdrawal, or constructing cultural walls to limit outside, non-Torah influences, Haredi political parties and Haredi rabbis have created their own alternative newspapers and radio stations. The biblical dictum that "the Israelite camp in the Wilderness in which God walked shall be holy ... that God should not see anything unseemly and turn himself away from you" (Deuteronomy 23:15) should accordingly be reflected in media content. Perhaps a preoccupation of mass media with sexuality (in particular, visual media like cinema, television, and the Internet) focuses different religious streams in Judaism upon the question of sexual modesty. The Haredi media have incorporated certain standards foreign to mainstream journalism. There are no pictures of women. Haredi radio stations not only do not have women singing but even limit interviews with them. In the case of some Haredi newspapers even the first names of

Haredi women reporters and writers are written with only their initials (Baumel, 2005). Television is banned. As a result of the religious strictures on social gossip, there is an absence of gossip columns in the Haredi media. Bans by Haredi rabbis on their followers accessing secular media, such as television, have been broadly accepted by the Haredi community. But computers and mobile technology have successfully challenged Haredi rabbinical hegemony, and Haredi rabbis have led a mostly losing battle against the Internet, partly because of the very centrality of the computer in general, and the Internet in particular, in modern life (Cohen, 2011, 2012c, 2015, 2017, 2018). Haredim have sought to create their own online cultural ghettos by isolating the Internet to "kosher sites." Moreover, Covid-19 and the need for information not provided in the Haredi media because of low newsgathering resources led some Haredim to search in the secular media.

Yet the basic feature of the cultural ghetto still exists. The traditional offline frameworks of Jewish life (the synagogue, the yeshiva, and the Jewish home) remain paramount for Haredi Jews no less today. Indeed, Jewish study has been enhanced through the application of technology like Torah educational websites, and even online *yeshivot* and online *shiurim* (religious lessons).

The Modern Orthodox Media

The Modern Orthodox, who account for an estimated 15–20% of the Israeli Jewish population, hold a view that Judaism and modernity do not inherently conflict. Media literacy, rather than censorship, is theoretically, at least, key. This community interprets sexual modesty in a more enlightened manner, and nonprovocative pictures of women, for example, are run of the mill in their media. They impose limits for this community in the artistic expression of love and sexuality in visual media.

Diaspora Jewish Media

In the Jewish diaspora, which numbers eight million Jews, weekly Jewish newspapers, Jewish radio stations, and Jewish Internet are agents of religious identity. The state of Jewish media differs from country to country and has depended upon several variables including the economic sustainability of Jewish media, local political conditions where Jewish media were allowed to exist, the level of professionalism among Jewish journalists in the media, and audience levels and changing news values drawing Jewish audience interest such as the establishment and subsequent years of Israel or anti-Semitism (Cohen, 2019). In the United States, the largest Jewish community outside of Israel, after the heyday of quality Yiddish papers at the turn of the twentieth century, the Anglo-Jewish press has engaged in little of its own reporting and, even in the case of the wealthier papers, there has been little or no investigative journalism. Primarily, the American Jewish press seeks to convey local Jewish information, promote local communal involvement, and, if necessary, defend Jews against their enemies. On the one hand the American Jew is confident and successful, but on the other feels a need to present an image of communality. Much of the news published both in the US Jewish press – as well as in the Jewish press elsewhere – has come from the New York based-Jewish Telegraphic Agency. Community surveys show that between one-third and two-thirds of identifying Jews in the United States read a Jewish newspaper (Sheskin, 2001).

Today, the diaspora media play an important role in generating ties between Israel and diaspora Jews, and are a major source of information and interpretation of events concerning Israel. Clearly, national media rather than the Jewish media are the main source of information for reporting developments involving Israel, albeit mostly of a security and military nature. The Jewish media are less critical and cover a broader gamut of issues such as internal Israeli politics, the economy, religion, and society.

As a virtual form of communications knowing no boundaries, the Internet is relevant to any study examining the flow of information among both Israelis and Jewish communities in the diaspora. The Internet has created a revolution in accessibility to information about Judaism, Jewish-related matters, and Israel. The sponsors of Internet sites may be broken into grassroots groups and individuals, organizational news, and commercial. Religious content in the grassroots group and individual category includes the Bible, commentaries, the Talmud, and Jewish law codes. Sites enable the Jewish surfer in far distant communities to participate in Jewish studies and hear inspirational talks about the *Torah*. The "virtual rabbi" replies to *sheiltot* (Jewish law questions) and offers counseling (Cohen, 2012c, 2016). It also provides such basic information about community structures like listings of synagogues, schools, kosher restaurants, and places of Jewish historical interest.

Islam

Islamic Communication Ethics

This discussion of Islam also starts with the importance of oral communication. The Prophet Muhammad received the Qur'an – which means "recitation" – not as a written text but in oral form, and the beauty of the recitation can be a moving experience for listeners. Although many regard the Qur'an as a book, most Muslims interact with it in its orally recited form ideally in a sonorous Arabic voice. For example, Muslims always recite it in its original Arabic form at mosques and at public events such as funerals and weddings even to non-Arabic-speaking audiences. Indeed, for Muslims, listening to the Qur'an is a form of communion with God (Nelson, 2002, pp. 257–261). Once the Qur'an was compiled as a book in 650 CE the question of who had the authority to understand and communicate its message became highly contested, but it was generally the religious scholars (*ulama*) who took up this role. As we shall see further later, however, their position as the most authoritative communicators of the meaning of the scriptures has been challenged in the modern era.

In general, Muslim ethics place a great deal of emphasis on speech, making it equivalent to acts in the eyes of God. According to this perspective, communication plays a role in the development and progress of both the individual and the community, and is important for realizing the ultimate goal of serving God within the divine scheme of creation. The Qur'anic vision of ethical communication is that all communication should be conducive to the duty all Muslims have of "promoting goodness and combating evil" (*al bi-I maruf wa-n nahy al-munkar*). Both the individual and community have a responsibility to work within the confines of this principle. To abstain from communication to further the good and the righteous course is considered immoral (Ayish & Sadig, 1997, p. 123; Sadig, 2017).

The Qur'an cites several situations in which communication is immoral. For example, the most fundamental ethical principle of Islamic communication is truthfulness. Thus, telling lies is as evil as worshiping idols (*shirk*), which is the worst offense Muslims can commit. This finds justification in a prophetic hadith that states: "He who deceives us is not one of us" (Sahih Muslim Book 1, Hadith 190). Because truthfulness is a dialogical concept, both the speaker and the recipient of messages are obliged to seek the truth. Incomplete or sketchy information – "fake news" – needs to be investigated further and verified. "Oh, ye who believe! If a wicked person comes to you with any news, ascertain the truth, lest ye harm people unwittingly" (Qur'an 49:6). The principle of *taqqiya* (expedient dissimulation) is endorsed by the Shi'ites but only to conceal their association with their faith when revealing it would result in danger (Enayat, 1982, p. 179).

Another ethical principle of Islamic communication is respect for others and the social recognition of another human's dignity, regardless of that person's gender identity or indeed any other aspect of their identity (Ayish & Sadig, 1997, p. 114). The following Qur'anic verse reflects this:

> Let not some man among you laugh at others. It may be that the latter are better than the former. Nor let some women scoff at others. It may be that the latter are better than the former. Nor defame nor be sarcastic to each other, no call each other by offensive nicknames. (Qur'an, 49:11)

Respect for others includes the right to privacy. For example, Muslims are not allowed to enter each other's homes without permission. Nor should Muslims spy on each another or try to extract secret information from others, even if they are involved in acts that are deemed sinful. Religious scholars who advocate respect for privacy often cite the anecdote about 'Umar Ibn al-Khattab, the second Caliph, who entered a house by climbing over the wall and caught another engaging in wrongdoing. The man protested that whereas he had sinned once, 'Umar had sinned three times: he had spied when God had prohibited spying; he had entered through the roof, against the command to enter the house by its door; and he had failed to greet the inhabitants when entering the house, as God had commanded. 'Umar let the man be, ordering him to repent (Zubaida, 2011, pp. 165–166).[1]

Gossip or backbiting is another sin that violates human dignity. "And do not … Speak ill of each other behind their backs. Would any of you like to eat the flesh of his dead brother? Nay, you would abhor it" (Qur'an 49:12). Indeed, when an absent person is accused, the listener is obliged to defend the accused, because the listeners must act as defender of those accused in their absence. This principle is reinforced by a prophetic hadith that states: "If anyone defends his brother who is slandered in his absence it will be his due from Allah to set him free from the fire of hell."[2]

Humor (laughter, fun, joking) is permissible as long as it does not violate the principles of respect and privacy outlined earlier and is not blasphemous. Humor should take place according to the principles of civilized manners (*adab*). Some have argued that this is a very restricted activity in Islam owing to the inherent puritanism of monotheistic religions that cannot accept moral ambiguity or the absence of a final truth – hallmarks of humor and comedy (Morreall, 2009, p. 147). Others have argued that Islam, like other Abrahamic religions, has developed mystical traditions that delight in the nuances of a "comic vision" and at poking fun at clerical orthodoxies (Ramsay & Alkhedar, 2020, p. 91).

What of freedom of speech? Many in the West perceive Muslims to be especially sensitive to religious offense. If this assessment is accurate – and as Rex Adhar points out, it is by no means easy to measure and compare offensiveness experiences among various faiths, creeds, and identities – why might this be the case (Adhar, 2014, p. x)? Talal Asad suggests that criticism is perceived as an attempt to "seduce" Muslims from their living relationship with God and so might be regarded as akin to a kind of "violence" (Asad, 2009, p. 33). It is, according to this view, impossible to remain passive when confronted with blasphemy. Furthermore, Saba Mahmood argues that to insult the Prophet is to harm Muslims themselves in ways similar to racial assault though not entirely reducible to it (Mahmood, 2009, p. 78). Thus, speech is regulated in Islamic law and for some this is an issue that pits freedom of speech against the intolerance of Islam (Hallaq, 2009). Yet no society protects freedom of speech absolutely and various forms of speech such as Holocaust denial are subject to legal censure in some Western states.

How is the issue of freedom of speech articulated in Islamic law? In classical *fiqh* (Islamic juris-prudence) a number of rules restrict the liberal notion of religious of speech, especially in con-nection with religion. These include punishments for apostasy (*ridda*), blasphemy (*sabb Allāh* and *sabb al-rasūl*), heresy (*zandaqa*), hypocrisy (*nifāq*), and unbelief (*kufr*). The punishments for these crimes are harsh, ranging from capital to various forms of corporal punishment. The majority of scholars have, for example, prescribed the death penalty for apostasy based on the *adīth* "whoever leaves his religion, kill him." Moreover, many Muslims see insulting the Prophet as a punishable offense. But the mainstream *fiqhi* positions in this sphere have been challenged by Muslim reformers who have often pointed to Qur'anic verses such as *Sūrat al-Baqara* (2:56) "There is no compulsion in religion" to defend religious freedom. Others have questioned the authenticity of the aforementioned *adīth* cited to justify the death penalty for apostasy "whoever leaves his reli-gion, kill him" as a weak *adīth*. Others still have argued that that this *adīth* was directed at trea-sonous individuals, since at that time citizenship was defined by religion – as it was in Christendom. Thus, leaving your religion and leaving your political community constituted treason. Since in the era of the nation-state religious and political citizenship are no longer conjoined, then chang-ing one's religion – and the speech-acts involved in doing this – should not be punished as they do not constitute treason. Likewise, some argue that securing a conviction for blasphemy had to involve demonstrating an intent of treason by the accused. Simply insulting or ridiculing the Prophet was not deemed enough by a majority of Muslims jurists (Rabb, 2012, pp. 146–147).

Who Speaks for Islam? Changing Modes of Communication and the Fragmentation of Religious Authority

We now turn to a more sociological focus to discuss the changing modes of communication in modernity and how this has led to the fragmentation of religious authority in Islam. In order to understand how the modern forms of print, digital, and social media have helped to forge sources of authority for wider constituencies in the contemporary age, we need to briefly explore the traditional sources of religious authority in Islam. Unlike Christianity, Islam does not have a cen-tralized hierarchical institution to establish orthodoxy for its adherents. But the foundational religious texts do need interpreters who wield authority (Turner, 2007). In Sunni Islam, as well as in Judaism, there are not usually formal initiations into a "priesthood" or religious leadership, as is the case in Catholicism, Protestantism, and Shia Islam. In the absence of an officially sanc-tioned set of religious actors to claim exclusive religious authority, God and the Prophet embody the "authoritative center" in Islam (Abu El-Khadl, 2001, p. 11). However, God does not speak directly to humans and the Prophet is no longer alive; God speaks via the Qur'an, and the Prophet through volumes of collections of prophetic narrations. Prior to the advent of modernity, states were not powerful enough to define religion across vast geographic domains and most of the population was illiterate. Thus, the traditional scholars (ulama) mainly spoke for Islam and had a monopoly on religious authority and education. The ulama's central role was by virtue of their scholarship; their "competent human agency to discover God's law" (Hallaq, 2003, pp. 252, 258). Transmission of Islamic teachings occurred mainly through mosques, madrassas, or in person.

This structure underwent a paradigm shift in the wake of European colonization and the formation (often imposition) of the modern nation-state. This process of modernization led to institutional differentiation and specialization, with various organizations and functions splitting off from Islam, the ulama, and their authority (Zubaida, 2005, p. 439). Increasingly spheres that were under the control of the ulama such as law, education, and religious endowments (*waqf*) were co-opted by the modern state, which also (in most countries) imposed state control over mosques and *madrasas*. Large areas of the law and education were secularized and those that remained Islamic were now largely under state control. The ulama no longer commanded a monopoly over exclusive religious authority and increasingly modern states and the ulama in their employment – such as state-sponsored muftis – would speak for Islam. A mufti is a Muslim religious scholar who is empowered to give rulings (*fatwa*) on religious matters. (For a useful discussion of state-sponsored muftis, see Skovgaard-Petersen, 2004.) This undermining of traditional religious authority happened in conjunction with the introduction of print capitalism, rising rates of literacy, and the emergence of a public sphere of newspapers, books, and novels that created a new society with a different, and more skeptical, approach to religion and religious authority (Yildirim, 2019, p. 10).

But if print capitalism has broken the monopoly of religious scholars on Islamic knowledge, the predominance of television and digital media has further accelerated the fragmentation of religious authority. Through contemporary media, works of exegesis and jurisprudence can be stored and accessed by users in multi-media format. The Internet, for instance, has enabled particular religious individuals and communities to circulate and publicize their message through a proliferation of religious websites, blogs and forums, DVDs, and e-books. Thus, there is now a cacophony of religious voices and a kind of bidding war between traditionally trained ulama, state-sponsored muftis, bearded jihadists, and self-taught lay Muslims – often Muslim youth and Muslim women. Two features of this new landscape stand out: televangelism and social media.

The Impact of Digitization on the Religious Sphere: Televangelism

Televangelism (see Chapter 11), which uses satellite television/the Internet as a medium of preaching, has gained popularity in recent years. Televangelism, historically a product of US evangelical churches, combines religion and entertainment and can be conceived of as one manifestation of the predominance of "infotainment" in contemporary media culture. For infotainment, which appears in politics as well as in religion, Van Zoonen has observed "the celebrity politician of television does not have to depend on anyone else except his own talent as a performer" (Van Zoonen, 2005, p. 79). Televangelism reflects the rise of the celebrity culture. In a similar way to public figures such as popular artists and politicians, televangelists have become media celebrities with thousands of fans and followers on social media networks (El-Naggar, 2014, p. 192).

By the 1990s televangelism had been adopted by Muslims in various contexts, in Egypt, Pakistan, and Indonesia as well as in the United States and the UK. A characteristic feature of this Islamic televangelism is that it promotes self-development and "pious neoliberalism" (Atia, 2012; El-Naggar, 2014). For example, the Egyptian televangelist Amr Khaled – not trained in a traditional *madrasa* – preaches in colloquial Arabic and Egyptian slang, coupling moving speeches laced with emotional stories of Prophet Mohammed with a call for civic responsibility and professional success. He is known as "the cool preacher, the Islamist in jeans who knows how to talk to young people in a language they understand" (Atia, 2012). His website is the third most popular Arabic site in the Middle East, and in 2005 it got more hits worldwide than Oprah Winfrey's site (Shapiro, 2006). Khaled articulates the ethos of a pious neoliberal; his success lies in how seamlessly he blends religion, self-help, and management training often more appealing to middle-class Egyptians than the radical messages of Islamist ideologies. He particularly appeals to the well-to-do Egyptians who desire a spiritual and fulfilling life that does not shun materialism and consumerism. For Khaled and his followers, the best model of success is capitalism melded with Islamic social values (Atia, 2012, p. 816). Khaled's emphasis on productive time resonates with Max Weber's (1992) considerations on time in his *Protestant Ethic and the Spirit of Capitalism*.

In a similar vein to Khaled, two popular televangelists in Indonesia, Abdullah Gymnastiar (popularly known as Aa Gym) and Arifin Ilham, promote religion as a means of personal development. Aa Gym integrates his religious message with advice on personal development and business management (e.g. promoting communicative skills and networking). He has three mottos: "start with yourself," "start with small things," and "start now" (El-Naggar, 2014, p. 194). Both the Egyptian and the Indonesian new-style preachers or *dai* present themselves as ordinary, middle-class Muslims. In doing this they disavow any claim to classical Islamic scholarship or traditional religious authority and instead "model a 'born again' piety in their entertainment-rich preaching and in the how-to books and DVDs spun off from their televised 'Islam lite' preaching" (Howell, 2010, p. 226).

As a religious phenomenon, the dominant form of Islamic televangelism, with its focus on individual change and professional/business success, is very much geared to the ethos of corporate capitalism and consumerism. We should note that an anticapitalist expression of Islam – Islamic liberation theology – with an emphasis on social justice and antiracism is being articulated by some Muslim youth particularly in the United States and to a lesser extent Europe and the Middle East. However, this phenomenon does not tend to find expression through televangelism but more in the form of music, especially Muslim rap music, often inspired by Malcom X (Aidi, 2014). However, as Aidi notes, owing to the radical incompleteness of Malcom X's thought, different Muslim factions – from Saudi Salafis, to the Iranian government and urban Muslim youth – project diametrically opposite political visions onto him in order to try and co-opt his legacy (Aidi, 2014, pp. 233–245).

The Impact of the Internet and Social Media on the Religious Sphere

Like other regions, countries with a Muslim majority have witnessed a rapid diffusion and adoption of social media platforms such as Twitter, Facebook, Snapchat, Instagram, and YouTube in recent decades. The use of these different platforms varies from country to country but generally speaking social media have become the dominant source of news in the region – especially in the Arab world, with some countries having among the highest use of social media platforms in the world (Radcliffe & Abuhmaid, 2020, pp. 8–9). In connection with Islamic knowledge, YouTube has been particularly important and content about Islam on this platform far exceeds that of other faiths. In 2012, more than 5000 Islamic religious and lifestyle-themed videos were published on YouTube every week (Ibarhine, 2014).

Muslims can now access millions of judgments and *fatwas* on everyday issues from the permissibility of using alcohol-based cleaning products to sexual advice – in dozens of languages. Much of the most popular advice is characterized by a humorous tone targeted at digital natives (young people who have grown up in the digital age). Increasingly, *fatwas* (religious opinions) are issued by lay Muslims. In some cases, this takes the form of charismatic individuals who use platforms like Instagram and YouTube to deliver Islamic sermons to tens of thousands of people, a much greater reach than traditionally trained imams. Additionally, Muslims are forming their own online spaces and networks outside traditional mosque structures – spaces they use to talk more openly. As one young Muslim put it: "Online, I can be whatever Muslim I choose to be… I am not labeled, I don't define my faith by what mosque I go to or what sheikh I listen to. I am just a Muslim – the way Allah intended me to be" (quoted in Kesvani, 2019, p. 13). Young British Muslims who once sat through mosque lectures from Pakistani or Bangladeshi imams reciting passages from the Qur'an now communicate with self-taught liberal Muslim scholars such as Salmaan Saleem, a 48-year-old optician from Birmingham on YouTube channels such as Epic Islamic Lectures (Kesvani, 2019, p. 20). Instead of learning only about prayer, young Muslims now discuss issues of piety, spirituality, and mental wellbeing. Indeed, for many, social media have become an ideal platform, the new mosque or *madrasa*, for the dissemination of Islamic belief.

Moreover, the Internet has become a place where voices can compete for authority, and debates between Islamic traditionalist and nontraditionalist voices can take place. One example is the issuing of *fatwas* online – now commonly referred to as *e-fatwas*. Whereas in the past, the traditional route for getting *fatwas* was through formally educated scholars, *fatwas* are now offered through websites where scholars associated with the website respond to questions. This means that new media have opened up spaces where a variety of actors can claim religious authority. An example is a *fatwa* issued by the European Council for Fatwa and Research in 1999 that permitted the use of a loan in order to solve one's housing situation. This *fatwa* radically reshaped the prohibition of *riba* (usury) imposed by traditional interpretation of Islamic law by the means of *hāja* (need) in which the European Muslims potentially find themselves when trying to find housing (Sisler, 2007, p. 210). Published by Islamonline.net and Islamonline.net, the *fatwa* triggered a debate on the Internet, and influenced subsequent *fatwas*, for example, one issued later by Al-Azhar University – widely seen as the most authoritative traditional Sunni institution globally. Similar debates and *fatwa*-borrowings appear in many other cases. The public nature of the process opens a larger space for criticism and allows lay Muslims to construct the Islamic public sphere (Sisler, 2007, p. 210). The phenomenon of *e-fatwas* and the debate they helped to generate testifies to the creation of a global public sphere where some Islamic interpretations may be discussed, contested, and negotiated in chat rooms and websites. It also demonstrates that Islam in Europe can shape and/or reshape the dominant interpretations of Islam in some Muslim-majority contexts. Whether *fatwas* are issued by religious institutions such as Al-Azhar University or independent organizations such as the European Council for Fatwa and Research, cyberspace has become an important forum where religious knowledge can be disseminated, contested, and negotiated, undermining or asserting the authority of particular actors (El-Naggar, 2014, p. 204).

Social media have also had a knock-on effect in debates about gender roles and sexuality. Muslim women have responded to sexist behavior with websites such as Side Entrance, which juxtaposes photographs of extravagant prayer halls reserved for men with the often dismal spaces set aside for women at the back or even sometimes in the basement of mosques. In 2018, women used #MosqueMeToo to share stories of sexual abuse and assault in mosques. Kesvani (2019) writes about how once-taboo subjects like abortion are discussed on Tumblr (pp. 81–86). The Internet has also encouraged the emergence of gay and lesbian Muslim groups. There is a Queer Jihad website; the movement is especially strong in California, where Muslims participate in the San Francisco Gay Pride parade. Around these new practices and movements, a host of websites have been constructed to offer advice, much of which of course is innovative rather than conservative (pp. 223–228).

Traditionalist scholars warn of the dangers of following unreliable advice from these web-based auto-didactic Muslims, referring to them pejoratively as "Sheikh Google" (Pandith, 2019). For instance, Abdul Aziz Al Shaikh, Grand Mufti of Saudi Arabia, has adopted a critical stance toward social media platforms such as Facebook and Twitter because, he says, they disseminate lies and may destroy established relationships in the real world. In a similar vein, religious authorities in some Islamic countries issued *fatwas* against the use of social media like Twitter, arguing for its incompatibility with *shari'a* because of trading accusations and promoting lies.

But while some Islamic religious leaders advise their followers not to use social media platforms, the overwhelming majority of scholars and preachers capitalize on the effectiveness and efficiency of social media in engaging with the community of believers and enhancing their fidelity and loyalty. Indeed, only very few voices condemn the use of the new digital media as wholly incompatible with Islamic practices. In fact, some religious leaders called for the launch of *shari'a*-compliant social media platforms as an alternative to Facebook and Twitter. Consequently, a number of these platforms have emerged (Muxlim.com, SalamWorld, and Muslimsocial.com), though their adoption rate is relatively low.

Despite some fragmentation of religious authority, traditional forms of authority continue to be important in local Muslim communities, where memorization and recitation play a central role in religious revivalism and in sustaining the cohesion of local communities.

Notes

*   Yoel Cohen authored the section on Judaism; Hadi Enayat authored the section on Islam.
1   From the hadith collection Al-Mustardak compiled by al-Nishapuri in 1002 (CE).
2   Prophetic hadith reported by Abu Darda from the Sunan al-Tirmidhī, 1931.

References

Abu El-Khadl. (2001). *Speaking in God's name: Islamic law, authority and women.* Oneworld Publications.
Adhar, R. (2014). Foreword. In E. Kolig (Ed.), *Freedom of speech and Islam* (pp. xi–xiv). Routledge.
Aidi, H. (2014). *Rebel music: Race, empire and the new Muslim youth.* Vintage Books.
Ariel, A. (2001). Loshon HaRah B'Maarekhet Tzibnori Democrati [The place of social gossip in the public democratic system]. *Tzohar 5–6*
Asad, T. (2009). Free speech, blasphemy, and secular criticism. In T. Asad, W. Brown, J. Butler, & S. Mahmood, *Is critique secular? Blasphemy, injury, and free speech* (pp. 20--64). Fordham University Press.
Atia, M. (2012). "A way to paradise": Pious neoliberalism, Islam, and faith-based development. *Annals of the Association of American Geographers, 102*(4), 808–827.
Ayish, M. I., & Sadig, H. B. (1997). The Arab-Islamic heritage in communication ethics. In C. Christians, & M. Traber (Eds.), *Communication ethics and universal values* (pp. 105–127). Sage Publications.
Baumel, S. (2005). *Sacred speakers: Language and culture among the Haredim in Israel.* Berghahn.
Chwat, A. (1995). *Itonim V'Hadashot Mitzva O Isur* [Newspapers and news: Religious obligation or prohibition]. T'lalei Orot.
Cohen, Y. (2005). Religion News in Israel. *Journal of Media & Religion, 4*(3), 179–198. https://doi.org/10.1207/s15328415jmr0403_4
Cohen, Y. (2011). Haredim and the Internet: A hate-love affair. In M. Bailey, & G. Redden (Eds.), *Mediating faiths: Religion and socio-cultural change in the twenty-first century* (pp. 63–71). Ashgate.
Cohen, Y. (2012a). *God, Jews and the media: Religion and Israel's media.* Routledge.
Cohen, Y. (2012b). God, religion, and advertising: A hard sell. In A. Hetsroni (Ed.), *Advertising and reality: A global study of representation and content* (pp. 73–90). Continuum.
Cohen, Y. (2012c). Jewish Cybertheology. *Communication Research Trends, 31*(1), 4–14.
Cohen, Y. (2015). The Israeli rabbi and the Internet. In H. Campbell (Ed.), *Digital Judaism: Jewish negotiations with digital media and culture* (pp. 183–203). Routledge.
Cohen, Y. (2016). On-line Judaism: Potential and limits. In M. D. Bosch, J. L. Mico, & J. M. Carbonell (Eds.), *Negotiating religious visibility in digital media: Religion in the digital era* (pp. 183–205). Ramon Llull University.
Cohen, Y. (2017). The media challenge to Haredi rabbinic authority in Israel. *Essachess, 10*(2), 113–128.
Cohen, Y. (2018). Jewish law and ethics in the digital era. In M. Price, & N. Stremlau (Eds.), *Speech & society in turbulent times: Freedom of expression in comparative perspective* (pp. 150–168). Cambridge University Press.
Cohen, Y. (2019). Communications and media history. In D. P. Bell (Ed.), *The Routledge companion to Jewish history and historiography* (pp. 585–596). Routledge.
El-Naggar, S. (2014). The impact of digitization on the religious sphere: Televangelism as an example. *Indonesian Journal of Islam and Muslim Societies, 4*(2), 189–211.
Enayat, H. (1982). *Modern Islamic political thought.* University of Texas Press.

Falk, E. (1999). Jewish laws of speech: Toward multicultural rhetoric. *The Howard Journal of Communications*, *10*, 15–28. https://doi.org/10.1080/106461799246870

Feldman, D. Z. (2015). *False facts and true rumors: Lashon Hara in contemporary culture*. Maggid.

Finklestein, L. (1924). *Jewish self-government in the middle ages*. Phillip Feldheim.

Ha-Cohen, I. M. (1873). *Chofez Hayim*. (For an English edition, see Pliskin, Z. (1975). *Guard your tongue: A practical guide to the laws of Loshon Hara based on the Chofetz Hayim*. Aish HaTorah).

Hallaq, W. B. (2003). Juristic authority vs. state power: The legal crises of modern Islam. *Journal of Law and Religion*, *19*(2), 243–258.

Hallaq, W. B. (2009). *An introduction to Islamic law*. Cambridge University Press.

Howell, J. (2010). Sufism on the silver screen: Indonesian innovations in Islamic televangelism. *Journal of Indonesian Islam*, *2*(2), 225–239.

Ibarhine, M. (2014). Islam and social media. LSE Middle East Centre Blog, October 28. Retrieved February 27, 2021, from https://blogs.lse.ac.uk/mec/2014/10/28/islam-and-social-media

Kesvani, H. (2019). *Follow me Akhi: The online world of British Muslims*. Hurst Publishers.

Korngott, E. M. H. (1993). Tafkido shel Itonei, Ha-Iton¨Bimah Le-Vikukhim, Ziburiim, Pirsum Khashud B'Iton, Tviot Nezikin ul Hotzaat Dibah B-Iton [The role of the journalist, The newspaper: A platform for public disputes, The publication of rumors in a newspaper, Legal action for slander in a newspaper]. In E. M. H. Korngott *Or Yehezkel [The light of Ezekiel: Contemporary issues in Jewish law]* Petach Tiqva.

Levine, A. (1981). Advertising and promotional activities as regulated in Jewish law. *Journal of Halakha and Contemporary Society*, *1*(1), 5–37.

Liebes, T. (1994). Crimes of reporting: The unhappy end of a fact-finding mission in the Bible. *Journal of Narrative and Life History*, *4*(1–2), 135–150. https://doi.org/10.1075/jnlh.4.1-2.08cri

Mahmood, S. (2009). Religious reason and secular affect: An incommensurable divide? In T. Asad, W. Brown, J. Butler, & S. Mahmood (Eds.), *Is critique secular? Blasphemy, injury, and free speech* (pp. 64–100). University of California Press.

Meir, A. (2014). Internet privacy in Halachah. Jewish Action. Retrieved February 21, 2022, from https://jewishaction.com/religion/jewish-law/internet-privacy-halachah

Morreall, J. (2009). *Comic relief: A comprehensive philosophy of humour*. Wiley Blackwell.

Nelson, K. (2002). The sound of the divine in daily life. In D. L. Bowen, & E. A. Early (Eds.), *Everyday life in the Muslim Middle East*. (pp. 257–261) Indiana University Press.

Pandith, F. (2019). Muslim millennials and the lure of "Sheikh Google". *Tufts Magazine*. Retrieved March 6, 2021, from https://tuftsmagazine.com/issues/magazine/muslim-millennials-and-lure-sheikh-google

Rabb, I. (2012). Negotiating speech in Islamic law and politics: Flipped traditions of expression. In A. M. Emon, M. Ellis, & B. Glahn (Eds.), *Islamic law and international human rights law* (pp. 144–168). Oxford University Press.

Radcliffe, D., & Abuhmaid, H. (2020). Social media in the Middle East: 2019 in review. *SSRN Electronic Journal*. Retrieved March 2, 2021, from https://www.researchgate.net/publication/338539787_Social_Media_in_the_Middle_East_2019_in_Review/citation/download

Ramsay, G., & Alkhedar, M. (2020). *Joking about jihad: Comedy and terror in the Arab world*. Hurst Publishers.

Sadig, H. B. (2017). Islamic universals and implications for global communication ethics. *The Journal of International Communication*, *23*(1), 36–52.

Shapiro, S. M. (2006). Ministering to the upwardly mobile Muslim. *The New York Times Magazine*. Retrieved February 21, 2022, from https://www.nytimes.com/2006/04/30/magazine/ministering-to-the-upwardly-mobile-muslim.html

Sheskin, I. (2001). How Jewish communities differ. North American Jewish Data Bank. City University of New York. Retrieved June 26, 2022, from https://www.jewishdatabank.org/content/upload/bjdb/711/How_Jewish_Communities_Differ_Sheskin_2001_FullReport.pdf

Sisler, V. (2007). The Internet and the construction of Islamic knowledge in Europe. *Masaryk University Journal of Law and Technology*, *1*(2), 205–217.

Skovgaard-Petersen, J. (2004). A typology of state muftis. In Y. Y. Haddad, & B. F. Stowasser (Eds.), *Islamic law and the challenges of modernity* (pp. 81–98). Altamira Press.

Smith poll. Haredi image in the media. April 1995.

Turner, B. S. (2007). Religious authority and the new media. *Theory, Culture & Society*, *24*(2), 117–134.

Van Zoonen, L. (2005). *Entertaining the citizen: When politics and popular culture converge*. Rowman & Littlefield.

Warhaftig, I. (2009). *Tzin'at Adam [The right to privacy in Jewish law]*. Institute for Halacha & Law.

Washofsky, M. (2014). Internet, privacy, and progressive Halakhah. In W. Jacob (Ed.), *The Internet revolution and Jewish law* (pp. 81–142). Solomon B Freehof Institute of Progressive Halakhah.

Weber, M. (1992). *The Protestant ethic and the spirit of capitalism*. Routledge.

Weisfish, N. M. (2010). *Copyright in Jewish law*. Feldheim.

Yildirim, A. K. (2019). The new guardians of religion: Islam and religious authority in the Middle East. Centre for Middle East Studies, Rice University. Retrieved February 21, 2022, from https://www.bakerinstitute.org/media/files/files/25ca754a/cme-pub-luce-intro-031119.pdf

Zubaida, S. (2005). Islam and secularization. *Asian Journal of Social Science*, *33*(3), 438–448.

Zubaida, S. (2011). *Beyond Islam: A new understanding of the middle East*. I. B Tauris.

Selected Readings

Aidi, H. (2014). *Rebel music: Race, empire and the New Muslim youth*. Vintage Books.

Anderson, J. W., & Eickleman, D. (2000). *New media in the Muslim world: The emerging public sphere*. Indiana University Press.

Baumel, S. (2002). Communication & change: Newspapers, periodicals and acculturation among Israeli Haredim. *Jewish History*, *2*(16), 161–187. https://www.jstor.org/stable/20101467

Cohen, Y. (2012). *God, Jews & the Media: Religion & Israel's media*. Routledge.

Falk, E. (1999). Jewish laws of speech: Toward multicultural rhetoric. *The Howard Journal of Communications*, *10*, 15–28. https://doi.org/10.1080/106461799246870

Kesvani, H. (2018). *Follow me Akhi: The online world of British Muslims*. Hurst Publishers.

Oppenheimer, S. (2001). Journalism, controversy, and responsibility: A halakhic analysis. *The Journal of Halacha & Contemporary Society*, Spring, XLI.

Rabb, I. (2012). Negotiating speech in Islamic law and politics: Flipped traditions of expression. In A. M. Emon, M. Ellis, & B. Glahn, *Islamic law and international human rights law* (pp. 144–168). Oxford University Press.

7

Religious Communication in Asia

Anthony Le Duc and Keval J. Kumar*

This chapter examines religion and communication in Asia. As a large, heavily populated region, Asia has many religions; thus, the chapter addresses Buddhism, Confucianism, Hinduism, Jainism, the Bhakti tradition, and Sikhism – religions that appear throughout the areas. (The chapter does not address Christianity and Islam since other chapters do so.) Asian religions were never uniform and monolithic; they were, and continue to be, characterized by numerous sects and cults, and centered on orthopraxy rather than orthodoxy. They are largely "open" faith systems, nondoctrinal and often nonsectarian too, and their historical evolution through the early, medieval, and modern periods focused on the use of the varieties of forms of oral and traditional media, and later of modern mass media and the new digital media.

In each case, the chapter introduces the religion and its general approach to communication, any ethical teachings that touch on communication, and its use of communication and digital communication technologies.

Buddhism

Buddhism has an undisputed historical founder, Siddhartha Gautama, who lived about 500 years BCE in what is now Nepal and India. An enormous corpus of written records represents 45 years of teaching and preaching, preserved in the oral tradition.

The Buddha as Communicator

Dissanayake (2014, p. 227) calls the Buddha a "communicator par excellence" and asserts that the success of Buddhism was owed primarily to the Buddha's ability to communicate his teachings in such a way that his audience could easily understand. After his enlightenment, the Buddha resisted the temptation to enter directly into *nibbāna* (*nirvana*) because of his conviction that he was "born into the world for the good of the many, for the happiness of the many, for the advantage, the good, the happiness of gods and men, out of compassion for the world" (quoted from *Digha Nikaya* by Pratt, 1928, p. 9).

The Handbook on Religion and Communication, First Edition. Edited by Yoel Cohen and Paul A. Soukup.
© 2023 John Wiley & Sons Ltd. Published 2023 by John Wiley & Sons Ltd.

The Buddha trained monks and nuns, conducted public preaching, and gave individual counseling sessions. He tailored his communication to the psychological, social, and intellectual background of the people to whom he was communicating and made abundant use of "parables, allegories, tropes, wit, humor, innovative narrative strategies, parallelisms" (Dissanayake, 2014, p. 227). Several characteristics describe his communication style. First, the Buddha was respectful of his listener, who represented the full spectrum of castes and classes. However, he recognized the humanity in every individual, "The venerable Gautama bids everyone welcome, is congenial, conciliatory, not supercilious, accessible to all" (quoted from *Digha Nikaya* by Pratt, 1928, p. 10).

Just as the Buddha was cognizant of the disposition and state of each person he encountered, he was equally aware of himself. He was forthright in stating his own superior state not out of vanity but simple objectivity. In the *Anguttara Nikāya*, the Buddha speaks of himself:

> I am one whose behavior is purified and I claim: "I am one whose behavior is purified. My behavior is purified, cleansed, undefiled." My disciples do not cover me up with respect to my behavior, and I do not expect to be covered up by my disciples with respect to my behavior. (A.3.126)

The Buddha asserted the same about his livelihood, dhamma (dharma) teaching, explanations, knowledge, and vision. Nevertheless, in another situation when the disciple Sariputta extolled, "Such faith have I, Lord, that methinks there never was nor will be nor is now any other greater or wiser than the Blessed One," the Buddha was quick to remind the overly enthusiastic pupil that he had never known any other Buddha of the past, or of the future. Even the mind of Buddha that he knew in the present could not be entirely penetrated so as to be able to make grand and bold claims (quoted in Smith, 1991, p. 90). This clear-headedness, transparency, and objectivity characterized the Buddha's communication throughout his mission. At the end of his life, the Buddha affirmed, "I have not kept anything back" (quoted in Suzuki, 1981, p. 2). Nonetheless, unlike the Brahmins of his time, the Buddha advised his disciples never to adopt ideas simply because they have been spoken about by figures of authority or because they have been passed down by tradition (A.1.189).

Because the Buddha's primary mission was to help people achieve liberation, he limited his communication to practical matters deemed not as idle theorizing and useless speculation. He demonstrates this in his parable of the man who has been struck by a poisoned arrow. When this happens, it is useless for the physician to make inquiries about the identity, physical traits, or social status of the perpetrator or the victim, nor about the qualities of the bow and arrow. What is important is how to save the victim. Therefore, metaphysical questions not immediately related to the matter of rebirth, old age, death, and suffering need not be considered because they are not useful for the situation at hand (*Majjhima Nikaya, Sutta 63*). Indeed, a "noble silence" was as much a part of the Buddha's communication strategy as his spoken instructions, either because he refused to engage in fruitless speculation or because of the mental state of the person with whom he was in dialogue (Thich Nhat Hanh, 2014, epub version).

Buddhist Communication Ethics

After the Buddha achieved enlightenment, he communicated the Four Noble Truths to five ascetics. These Truths essentially diagnose the true human condition, present a vision for healing, and propose the path for the realization of that vision. The first two Noble Truths (the diagnosis part of Buddhist pedagogy) describe the essence of mundane life as unsatisfactory because of the existent reality of the impermanence of all things in the world. The Buddha gave these realities a common descriptive name – suffering or unsatisfactoriness (*Dhammacakkappavattana Sutta*, SN.5.11). The second Truth locates the root of this unsatisfactoriness in the ignorance of the true nature of reality, causing one to crave (*tanhā*) things that do not bring about lasting happiness because of their impermanence. The Buddha listed three kinds of craving: craving for sensual pleasure, craving to become, and craving to get rid of unwanted things. The Buddha presented a vision of hope contrary to the condition of suffering. That vision appears in the third Noble Truth, which declares that human beings need not be enslaved by this perpetual cycle of unsatisfactoriness; that one can put an end to the suffering in one's life by achieving freedom from the various desires mentioned earlier. One can realize this vision of eternal bliss by practicing the Noble Eightfold Path with its threefold training of morality, concentration, and wisdom in order to attain freedom.

In the *Nidāna Sutta* of the *Saṃyutta*, the Buddha extolls the Noble Eightfold Path as the "ancient road travelled by the Perfectly Enlightened Ones of the past," which leads to cessation of aging and death – volitional formations (S.II.12). It leads to "suffering's appeasement" (S.II.15), cessation of form, feeling, perception, consciousness, clinging (S.III.22), and cessation of *kamma* (*karma*) (S.IV.35). It is the raft that takes one to "the further shore, which is safe and free from danger" (S.IV.35), that is, *nibbāna* itself. Bodhi (2012) notes, "The path translates the Dhamma from a collection of abstract formulas into a continually unfolding disclosure of truth. It gives an outlet from the problem of suffering with which the teaching starts. And it makes the teaching's goal, liberation from suffering, accessible to us in our own experience, where alone it takes on authentic meaning" (p. v).

Communication in context of Buddhism is part and parcel of the Buddhist project to eliminate suffering for sentient beings as laid out in the Four Noble Truths and the Noble Eightfold Path. The evaluative criterion is whether the act of communication contributes to reduced suffering for the person performing the act as well as the person(s) affected by the act. Thich Nhat Hanh (2014) asserts that communication is not neutral because it impacts our karma. "Our communication is what we put out into the world and what remains after we have left it. In this way, our communication is our karma. The Sanskrit word karma means 'action,' and it refers not just to bodily action but to what we express with our bodies, our words, and our thoughts and intentions." Therefore, communication, in the Buddhist understanding, includes unspoken thoughts. Thoughts, the moment they are produced, can have either positive or negative effects on the thinker as well as those around the thinker. While many have emphasized the third (right speech), fourth (right action), and fifth (right living) elements in the Noble Eightfold Path as especially pertinent to Buddhist communication ethics, the fact that thinking is already a communicative act affirms that the first two elements of right view and right thought are equally important to a well-rounded Buddhist communication approach (see also, Aryal, 2019–2020).

The Buddha gave four precepts for right speech (Bodhi & Thera, 2000, 10, 17, 10 [PTS5, 262]), including abstaining from false, slanderous, unkind speech, and instead practicing truthful, peaceful, friendly, and helpful speech. While the precepts directly pertain to speech, they easily generalize to communication as a whole. Telling the truth, refraining from exaggerating, being consistent, and using peaceful, nonviolent communication are all conducive to reducing personal and collective harm and suffering. The life of the Buddha shows that skillful communication does not mean communicating in the same way with everyone irrespective of each person's disposition and emotional and intellectual state. Restructuring the message to render it appropriate to the individual or silence on a matter does not imply hiding or bending the truth.

The seventh element of right mindfulness in the Noble Eightfold Path has received much attention in the field of communication. "Mindful communication" and "mindful journalism" have appeared in both Asian and Western societies, with books, research papers, seminars, and workshops gaining popularity in the corporate world – both Apple and Google have hosted talks on "mindful work," "mindful leadership," and "mindful connection." Thich Nhat Hanh himself gave a presentation at Google on mindfulness to the great enthusiasm of his audience.

Within communication, mindful journalism describes the concept in the field of journalism. Gunaratne (2015) says that its elements derive from the Buddhist phenomenology in teachings and sermons of the Buddha, the rules and regulations governing monastic life, and Buddhist commentaries that constitute the Buddhist canon (p. 1). Gunaratne says that mindful journalism is "not profit making but truthful reporting without institutional restraints that might defile the clarity of the trained journalist's mind" (p. 5). Mindful journalism can co-exist with other genres and become a "formidable example of enlightened journalism" for other genres that aim to produce commercially driven news (p. 1). Pearson and Senarath (2015), despite grounding mindful journalism in fundamental Buddhist teachings, do not propose that those who practice mindful journalism need become Buddhists (p. 156). Rather, mindful journalism is a specific instance of mindful communication in the public interest (Pearson, 2015, p. 171).

Buddhism and Modern Mass Communication Technology

Communication technology both facilitates the propagation of religious teachings to adherents and allows for evangelization of nonadherents (Le Duc, 2017, p. 44). Buddhism throughout history has used technological developments to communicate its teachings to the masses (Veidlinger, 2015, p. 6). The Buddha himself traveled throughout India to proclaim his message. Buddhist monks and lay missionaries took advantage of the Silk Road to carry their message to Central Asia and China. They translated Buddhist teachings into a variety of languages. The printing press evolved in Chinese Buddhist monasteries during the Tang Dynasty (618–907 CE) where Mahayana texts such as the Diamond Sutra and the Lotus Sutra were carved into wooden blocks from which multiple copies were printed (You, 2010, pp. 56–62). Buddhist communicators continue to use printed materials. For example, the Dalai Lama's website lists 131 of his books. The late Vietnamese zen monk Thich Nhat Hanh published more than 100 books. From the Theravada tradition, the Thai scholar monk Phra Prayudh Payutto wrote extensively on the Pali Canon.

Western writers like Bhikkhu (Bodhi 2012) translated into English four great Pali-suttas and authored many other books and essays on a variety of topics; Bhikkhu Nanamoli (1995) translated some of the most difficult Buddhist texts into readable English, notably the fifth-century commentary on Buddhist teachings and practice by Buddhaghosa entitled *Visuddhimagga* (*The Path of Purification*); and Thanissaro Bhikkhu, representing the Thai forest tradition, publicized translations of dhamma talks and translated the *Dhammapada* as well as over 1000 suttas of the *Sutta Pitaka*.

Chinese Buddhist monks began to make use of radio in 1950 when the Venerable Cihang gave a dharma talk on Taipei's Minben radio station. Soon after, the Venerable Nanting had his own regular radio broadcast "The Voice of Buddhism" (Pham, 2017, p. 49). These efforts led to the establishment of a Buddhist dharma broadcasting division by the Buddhist Association of the Republic of China in 1953. Buddhist communicators in Taiwan incorporated television beginning with the Venerable Hsing Yun's dharma program "Sweet Dew" (p. 50).

In Thailand, Buddhist radio and television broadcasts by various monks and from various temples remain a staple in the life of the predominantly Buddhist country. In addition, Buddhist beliefs, images, and tropes are abundantly incorporated into the content produced for television as well as cinema. One can hardly watch a Thai television drama series without hearing a reference to kamma falling from the mouth of a character commenting on life events. The depiction of beautiful and exotic temples and meditation centers in entertainment programs also contributes to attracting foreigners to visit Thailand to see the temples or even enroll in a short-term meditation course. This introduces Buddhism to a completely new audience.

Buddhist Communication in the Digital Age

Digital technology has put the Theravada Pali Canon and Mahayana texts in multiple languages within reach of anyone with internet access. The *Journal of Buddhist Ethics* established in 1994 was the first online peer-reviewed journal in religious studies (Prebish, 2016, p. 82). Online information and Buddhist content are abundant, as evidenced by a simple Google search. A variety of writings, radio programs, television programs, lectures, etc. appear on a single website. Apps promoting Buddhist teachings, mindfulness, meditation, and inspirational sayings can be downloaded from app stores, including "Insight Time" with 45 000 free meditation sessions complete with ambient music. For a membership fee, users gain access to special mediation courses lasting 7–10 days (Maina, 2022).

Buddhist leaders of all levels use the internet to spread the dhamma, including the Dalai Lama, who tweets to his nearly 20 million followers non-religion-specific messages, addressing common human issues, concerns, and aspirations, which therefore reverberate easily with a global audience (Le Duc, 2020, p. 112).

The Dalai Lama is not alone in recognizing the potential of information and communication technology to promote Buddhist thought and teachings to the masses. For example, in Thailand, where Buddhism accounts for 90% of the population, many Buddhist-oriented schools have explored ways to adapt the dhamma to the contemporary milieu in order to generate greater accessibility and garner more interest from younger audiences (Schedneck, 2021, p. 285). "Monk celebrities" in Thailand try to appeal to a wider contemporary audience with more entertaining content and humor. However, the reception of their communication strategies among the Buddhist faithful has been mixed (Schedneck, 2021).

Yamcharoen (2015) found that Thais tend to follow Buddhist personalities that appeal to them, accessing Buddhist content via mobile phones and preferring interesting and simplified content rather than abstract and dry presentations of Buddhist teachings. In addition, Yamcharoen also identified long-term patterns of Buddhist communication, including: (i) supporting individuals and organizations in promoting Buddhist values; (ii) providing Buddhist communicators with better technological skills; (iii) promoting knowledge of integrated communication and public relations via integrated online communication; (iv) producing a new generation of Buddhist communicators to the society; (v) working to reduce the rural–urban digital divide to ensure more equal access to Buddhist content; and (vi) encouraging the older generation to be good role models in displays of faith and behavior (see also, Phra Thanit Sirivathano, 2015).

In summary, the history of Buddhist communication has always played out in a variety of ways, from the ancient paths of India, to the Silk Road of Central Asia, to the information highway of the digital age. In every instance, the fundamental purposes have remained the same: to eliminate suffering in the world and to support the human desire to achieve lasting happiness and liberation.

Confucianism

Confucianism, a system of thought variously described as a philosophy, a way of life, a worldview, a religion, or a culture, is named after Kung Fu-tzu, or Kung the Master, born in the sixth century BCE in the principality of Lu in the modern Shandong Province of China. Confucianism has characterized the life of a large segment of people in Asia and beyond for several thousand years, and began with an intellectual convinced that he had a divine mission to re-establish the social order of his time. Despite government resistance, Confucius never gave up on teaching his disciples, spending the last years of his life editing the classics of China's past in an effort to provide a way out of social and political conflict due to human moral decline, especially among those in power. Confucius' pedagogical regimen consisted of lessons in civics, literature, mathematics, history, music, propriety, divination, and sports. This comprehensive and integrated method for human beings to transform themselves from the inner core started with the individual undertaking a self-effort that would contribute positively to the entire society. In communication style, Confucius shared similarities with Socrates, preferring to engage students with questions and conversations rather than giving lectures (Smith, 1991, p. 174).

Confucian Ethical Worldview

Ethical human communication in the Confucian paradigm requires a process of personal self-cultivation and transformation in order to be imbued with qualities that characterize full self-realization. Through a proper education and consistent learning, the individual embodies the following essential qualities: Ren (仁, benevolence, humaneness); Yi (义; 義, righteousness, justice); Li (礼; 禮, propriety, rites); Zhi (智, wisdom, knowledge); and Xin (信, sincerity, faithfulness) (Runes, 1983, p. 338). These qualities demonstrate being in relationship with others and the desire to act toward others virtuously as their dignity deserves. Whether in formal religious ceremonies or in mundane daily routines, actions must be carried out with precision and intention in accordance with each particular context. Confucius taught, "Do not look at what is contrary to *li*, do not listen to what is contrary to *li*, do not speak what is contrary to *li*, and do not make any movement that is contrary to *li*" (*Analects*, 12.1).

One imbued with these qualities is appropriately called a *junzi* (君子) – the paradigmatic model of Confucian personality, who embodies the highest degree of moral excellence and is free from any sign of depravity, ill-will, and pettiness. Translated variously as "superior person," "exemplary person," and "profound person," *junzi* communicates the image of one who has received a proper education and has the ability to establish in oneself the unity of knowledge and action. Indeed, education and character, in the Confucian paradigm, are integrally connected to one another, supporting and informing one another. According to Confucius, a *junzi* has nine wishes (Nadeau, 2014, p. 45): (i) to have a clear vision; (ii) to be able to listen well; (iii) to have a gentle appearance; (iv) to exhibit reverential expressions; (v) to be true to one's word; (vi) to be conscientious of one affairs; (vii) to make inquiries when in doubt; (viii) to regret having lost one's temper; and (ix) to consider carefully before attaining something (*Analects*, chapter 10).

While Confucian self-transformation is first and foremost to achieve self-realization, to be authentically human is not simply about the acquisition of knowledge and skills for selfish purposes. While self-cultivation takes the individual as the point of departure, the self exists within an interconnected and ever-expanding network of human relations – starting with the family and going toward the community, the world, and indeed the cosmos. According to Tu (n.d.), "Self-realization as a communal act presupposes a personal commitment for harmonizing the family, governing the state, and bringing peace to the world. The full realization of personhood entails the real possibility of transcending selfishness, nepotism, parochialism, nationalism, and anthropocentrism" (p. 79). Thus, authentic humanity is ever conscious of the four essential dimensions of the shared human experience: self, community, Earth (nature), and Heaven.

According to Tu, authentic humanity calls for the integration of the body, heart, mind, soul, and spirit of the self. This integration results in actions and interactions that promote harmony at all levels. As Smith (1991) remarks, "In shifting the center of one's empathic concern from oneself to one's family one transcends selfishness. The move from family to community transcends nepotism. The move from community to nation overcomes parochialism, and the move to all humanity counters chauvinistic nationalism" (p. 200). Indeed, the conscious move to the transcendent overcomes egotistical anthropocentrism leading to what Tu (2013) calls an "anthropocosmic" vision of reality (p. 6).

Although Confucianism serves an all-encompassing role, it is usually not identified as a religion by its adherents. Religion, for many East Asians, is associated with institutional teaching or schools of instruction, and is organizational and sectarian. Instead, Confucianism is thoroughly diffused in people's lives, more like the air that East Asians breathe (Nadeau, 2014, p. 21). Even though regional historical and political forces have suppressed certain aspects of Confucian thought and practices, or judged them outdated and oppressive, the Confucian worldview and its values still largely govern the way East Asians perceive themselves and their relationships with others. Many in East Asia continue to perform family-oriented rituals rooted in Confucian teaching, making regular offerings to ancestors even if they do not explicitly identify themselves as Confucian. In Communist Vietnam, the government sanctions and organizes ceremonies annually to pay tribute to the legendary Hung kings who Vietnamese people consider to be their national ancestors. Although students in East Asia no longer pore over Confucian classics and memorize sayings by the beloved sage, Confucianism remains very much a part of the social and spiritual fabric of East Asian societies as the ancient teachings get re-contextualized for the contemporary age.

Confucianism and the Media

While Confucian teachings have been communicated through literature and traditions throughout the centuries, the modern age has commonly transmitted Confucian values through movies and dramas. Some media scholars attribute the success of Korean dramas as part of the "Hallyu" Korean wave in East Asian markets to "cultural proximity" (Yang, 2008, p. 109). Cultural proximity refers to the cultural resemblances that enable people from different countries to appreciate and receive what each has to offer. This theory explains the popularity of Korean dramas among the Chinese audience, who can relate to the depiction of "Neo-Confucian social concepts … awakening a respect for traditional values lost under communism" (Kim, 2007, p. 127). In Japan, cultural proximity refers to a consciousness of the similarities between the Korean and Japanese cultures, with the latter once perceiving the former as backward and underdeveloped (Kim et al., 2007, p. 1351). However, seeing Confucian aspects embedded in the Korean culture as depicted in the dramas, Japanese people began to see Koreans in a new light. In Vietnam and Taiwan, countries profoundly influenced by Confucianism, the audiences easily connect with the widely watched Korean dramas and the cultural elements and social traditions portrayed. While cultural proximity may explain this popularity in the region, other explanations are needed to account for the popularity in countries where Confucianism is not the prevalent worldview, for example, the United States and South Asian countries. Whatever the reason, the reach of the Korean wave means that Confucianism has been introduced to entirely new audiences.

Although Confucian values continue to influence contemporary Asian society, China has also seen a revival of Confucianism, signified by the release of the movie *Confucius* in 2009 to commemorate the 60th anniversary of the founding of the People's Republic of China and the 2560th birthday of Confucius. Although Hollywood productions outgrossed *Confucius* 2.5 times per day during its theatrical release (Lafraniere, 2010), the fact that the movie was made at all was remarkable, considering that during the Cultural Revolution, Confucius's teachings were banned by Mao Zedong, who ordered his family home destroyed.

Various communication genres have portrayed the positive values of Confucianism, but others have shed light on controversial elements of Confucian social systems, especially pertaining to the role of women in a hierarchical Confucian society. In Vietnamese society, the four virtues required of a married woman (work, manner, speech, and ethics) remain deeply ingrained in the consciousness of women who marry as well as of men who expect these virtues from their wives. Songs about mothers are regularly composed and continue to be popular even in the modern pop culture. In addition, the depiction of the struggles and suffering of women in loveless arranged marriages and dealing with dictatorial and sometimes drunken gambling husbands is a staple in Vietnamese dramas and comedy. The 1993 critically acclaimed film by Tran Anh Hung, *The Scent of Green Papaya*, depicts a Vietnamese woman as a hardworking, patient, and kind person who has to deal with such a husband. She can only quietly accept her fate and suffering. Confronting this reality, Vietnamese find themselves torn between feeling distaste for such apparent inequality and injustice, and admiration for the strength of Vietnamese women upholding Confucian values.

In summary, while Confucianism is academically categorized as a world religion, its organizational structure differs significantly from other religions, even Buddhism, which has temples and sanghas that serve as the official face of institutional Buddhism. Thus, communication and transmission of Confucian thought and worldview over the centuries have been implemented primarily through formal education, traditional practices, social inculcation, and literature rather than through individuals affiliated with religious institutions. In the modern age, Confucian values and practices appear in various media such as films, plays, television drama, and music. Through the ongoing portrayal of elements of Confucianism in modern media, this worldview continues to influence the way East Asians perceive and communicate about themselves. At the same time, the portrayals also facilitate opportunities for deeper critique about unjust elements embedded in Confucian thought and practices as well as creating opportunities for dialogue with other religious systems in matters relevant to the contemporary milieu.

Hinduism, Jainism, Sikhism

Role of Communication in Hinduism

The religious scenario of India has been, and continues to be, diverse, eclectic, and syncretic. The religion with the largest population is Hinduism, though it is not a religion in the Semitic tradition: it has no known founder, no doctrines that have to be mandatorily accepted, no single sacred book, no leader or head, and no specific rituals and practices that are absolutely essential. Indeed, there is no word for religion in Sanskrit and most modern Indian languages. The closest word for religion in Indian languages is "dharma," which refers to obligations and duties rather than to a set of beliefs and practices. Middle class Hindus describe their religious practices as those of Sanatan Dharma (Eternal Order or Eternal Path). The word Hindu or Hinduism itself came into general use only in the nineteenth century, and was a geographical term in Persian, referring to people who lived in the region beyond the Indus. It took on religious connotations later (Thapar, 2014, p. 119). The notion of a Hindu and Muslim community as defined today was tied to the British Census, and emerged from colonial views of Indian society (Thapar, 2014, p. 120). Thapar (2014) therefore urges that Hinduism is better seen as "a mosaic of religious sects" rather than as a single uniform religion along the lines of a monotheistic Judeo-Christian type of religion (p. 129), in terms of personal devotion to deities of local cult shrines, or to gurus, *faqirs* (Hindu or Muslim religious ascetics), *pirs* (Muslim saints), and other holy men and women (p. 52). Section 2 of the Hindu Marriage Act of 1955 defines a Hindu as one who is not a Muslim, Christian, Buddhist, Jain, Sikh, Parsi (Zorastrian), or Jew. But the Vishwa Hindu Parishad, World Hindu Council (VHP) of America defines Hindus as "all those who believe, practice, or respect the spiritual and religious having roots in Bharat. Thus, Hindu 'includes Jains, Budhas [*sic*], Sikhs and Dharmic people, and the many different sects within a Hindu ethos'" (Andersen & Damle, 2018, p. 51, citing the VHP's website).

The Puranas are collections of popular literature on a host of religious and secular subjects including philosophy, theology, astronomy, cosmology, folk stories, love tales, humorous tales, and several others. They comprise over 400 000 verses in diverse literary genres. The verses are generally classified after deities like Vishnu. There are altogether 18 Puranas. They were composed by a host of authors during the post-Vedic period and transmitted orally from generation to generation over centuries before they were put down in writing on palm leaves, with little or no consistency in the versions that were passed on. Brahmins did not have a monopoly on them either as authors or transmitters. They were written in Sanskrit, but also in several other Indian regional languages. The Jain Puranas, for instance, were in Ardhamagadhi. Access to them was open to all castes, unlike the Vedas which the lower caste population was prohibited from reading or even listening to.

Role of Communication in Jainism

Buddhism and Jainism, the main "shramanas," arose around the sixth century BCE to challenge the degrading humiliation of the lower-caste Hindus, and also the ritual-obsessed and animal-sacrificing Brahmins, who lorded over the whole populace. Gautama Buddha (567–187 BCE) and Mahavira (fifth century BCE), founders of Buddhism and Jainism, respectively, turned their backs on these practices and gathered a following, largely of the lower castes, laying emphases on asceticism, detachment from the ways of the world, the righteous life, and adherence to the Four Noble Truths. They eschewed worship of idols and images, even belief in a divine Creator, and of course the degrading caste system. Both acknowledged the right of women to be nuns (Thapar, 2014, p. 133). Buddhism propagated the Sangha or Buddhist Order, a community of monks, while Jainism emphasized the tradition of 24 Tirthankars (or ford-makers), "enlightened beings who appear periodically in the world to create a crossing or 'ford' over the waters of rebirth" (Long, 2011, p. 159). They did not see the need for the intervention of a deity or deities, and established monasteries, universities, and schools for the education of all castes. Both Buddhists and Jains denied deity as well the divine sanction of the Vedas, and rejected the existence of a soul; these tended to be splinter groups breaking away from the main organization, the Sangha (Thapar, 2014, p. 143). In addition, the Buddhist ethic envisaged social behavior as being determined by ethical norms conducive to well-being, irrespective of caste and divine sanction (p. 132), The Buddha's dhamma was a universal ethic of family and community privileging nonviolence, tolerance, and respect for the individual; these values applied to all with no intervention of deity (p. 132).

Sikhism and Its Communication

Sikhism rose to prominence in the early sixteenth century as the culmination of developments in Indian religious experience. Its founder, Guru Nanak, came under the influence of the Bhakti movement and the Sufi saints; even as a young man he was inclined to meditation and the religious life. It was during one such period of meditation and prayer at a riverside that he was blessed with a mystical moment in which he felt called to a new spiritual life. God had spoken to him in this epiphany. "There is no Hindu, there is no Mussalman," were the first words he proclaimed (Singh, 1963/2011, p. 31). He then went on to travel extensively in north and western India, and later to Mecca and Iraq, all the while exchanging religious ideas with Hindu, Jain, Muslim, Sufi, and Bhakti saints and holy men. Gradually, he gathered around him followers from both Hindu and Muslim sects; they called themselves "Sikhs" (learners, disciples). Sikhism was born out of a wedlock between Hindus and Muslims after they had known each other for a period of nearly 900 years (p. 17). Like Islam and Christianity, it was strictly monotheistic and opted for the *namamarg, the path of the Divine Word* (which is integral to *bhaktimarg*, the path of devotion) rather than the Brahminical Hindu's paths of *karma* (action) or *jnan* (knowledge). Nanak summed up his message in three commandments: *kirt karo, nam japo, vand cako* – work, worship, give in charity. He stressed the role of *sat sang* (truthful companionship).

Rather than mass media, the Sikh tradition favors interpersonal communication and the written word.

They formed strong communities, met at places of worship, which came to be called "gurudwaras" (temples, churches), and sang hymns, recited prayers, and gave discourses inspired by Bhakti and Sufi traditions. Most significantly, they ate together in a free community kitchen (*Guru ka langar*, or just *langar*), irrespective of caste or social status. The institution of the "langar" was to break the vicious hold of caste (Singh, 1963/2011, p. 40). *Seva*, or voluntary work, would mark the cooking and serving of food, and the care of the gurudwara. Sikhs would greet each other not with a Hindu namaste or Muslim Salaam Aleikum, but with the words *sat kartaar* (true creator), which later evolved into *sat sri akaal* (p. 45).

A succession of nine gurus followed; the ninth guru, Arjun, compiled these many discourses, hymns, and prayers into the Adi Granth Sahib, which became the holy book of the Sikhs. The first edition of the Granth Sahib was put together by Guru Arjun; later gurus added their own selection of hymns and prayers, with the ninth guru adding his own selection, and declaring that the holy book itself would be the tenth and last guru. The monumental compendium emerged as the single sacred scripture of the Sikhs, who bow before it and read, recite, sing, and listen to it with the greatest reverence. It comprises hundreds of hymns composed by Nanak and the eight gurus, as well as those written by 16 Bhaktas and Sufis from different parts of the country. Kirtan (hymn singing) in the vernacular Punjabi replaced the recitation of Sanskrit *shlokas* (verses) and the script adopted was Gurmukhi.

Media and Communication Ethics

Each of the major religions in India has ethical principles that apply to both interpersonal and mass media, though many developed these for the print media. The major Indian religious traditions stress the key values of pluralism (*anekantavada*) and nonviolence (*ahimsa*). Jain philosophy, for instance, affirms the "many-sided doctrine" or "doctrine of nonabsolutism" (*anekantavada*) and the corresponding relativistic epistemology affirmed in its "doctrine of perspectives" (*nayavada*) and its doctrine of conditional predication or "maybe doctrine" (*syadvada*). This complex of doctrines is seen by many contemporary Jains as an extension into the intellectual realm of the principle of nonviolence (Long, 2011, p. 159). Both these values are the basis of the three guiding principles: right belief, right knowledge, and right conduct (Shah, 2019, p. 141). Given the oral nature of Jainism, Shah (2013) sees a slow acceptance of the use of media, but one that acknowledges a right of freedom of speech in the propagation of religious truths.

Hinduism sees the goal of communication as oneness, or commonness (Adhikary, 2014, pp. 65, 67) and proposes the principle of right speech (or ethical speech) – speech that contributes to the well-being of others (see Chapter 4). Hinduism also values three ethical principles: respect for all persons, social solidarity, and social welfare (Creel, 1975, pp. 167–168), Others (e.g. Aryani, 2018) apply these to different forms of communication, whether ritual, interpersonal, social, or group. Much of the writing about Hinduism and communication does not address specific ethical concerns with the mass media, so some teachings must be deduced from practices. As noted in the text that follows, Hinduism certainly employs a range of media, with the implication that gurus do not forbid reading, watching, or listening to anything (Luthra, 2001). Chopra (2018) discusses whether Hinduism favors free speech, noting both treatises that defend free speech and others, particularly by B. R. Ambedkar, which argue that Hinduism is incompatible with freedom of speech.

Indian Religions and the Mass Media

Religious communities in India readily took to the mass media to propagate their faiths, often competing with each other to convert or reconvert but also to reinforce the faiths of believers. The printing press and the profession of journalism came in handy in the eighteenth century for Christian missionaries from Europe; the earliest print efforts involved the printing of the Bible and catechisms for new converts and potential converts to the various denominations of Christianity (see also, Pinto, 2007), but the Hindus, Muslims, Buddhists, Jains, and Sikhs were not far behind. Social reformers like Raja Ram Mohan Roy, Bal Gangadhar Tilak, and others launched newspapers in English and vernacular languages to counter the Christian missionary effort. The Nawal Kishore Press launched its printing and book publishing press in Lucknow in 1858 (Stark, 2007), as did Motilal Banarsidass Publishing House (owned by a Jain family) in 1903 in the city of Lahore but later moving to Mumbai. Both ventures have served English and Hindi readers of popular and scholarly literature in Indology, Buddhology, Jainism, and other subjects for more than a century.

But for conservative Hinduism perhaps the most successful publishing venture was the Gita Press, established in the 1920s, first in Calcutta but later shifting to Gorakhpur in the United Provinces (the present State of Uttar Pradesh). The primary goal of this venture/mission was to counter Christian missionary propaganda (Mukul, 2015, p. 416) with the monthly Hindu religious journal called *Kalyan* (meaning beneficent), which published its inaugural issue in Bombay in 1926 but moved to its permanent editorial office and printing house the following year. A hundred years on, *Kalyan* continues a regular publication schedule, with its mission of propagating a conservative form of nationalist Hinduism. It has played no small role in "the making of Hindu India", the subtitle of Mukul's scholarly work on the beginnings, the history, and present activities of the Gita Press (Mukul, 2015). But it was not the journal in both its Hindi and English versions that promoted "Hindi, Hindu, and Hindustan" and Hindu rightist organizations like the RSS, the Hindu Mahasabha, the Jan Sangh, the VHP, and the BJP. The Gita Press was foremost in printing and publishing Hindu religious epics like the Ramayana and the Mahabharata, and texts like the Puranas, Upanishads, and other popular literature in their original Sanskrit but also in Hindi and English and other Indian languages, distributing millions of copies of these attractively produced and low-priced texts, often funded by Marwari businessmen. The publications actively promoted, and continue to do so even today, the caste system, gender segregation, Hindu masculinity, the prohibition of widow remarriage and inter-caste marriage, and the Muslim community as "the other" (Mukul, 2015, p. 416). Most of the publications have now gone online.

Another publisher dedicated to promoting and popularizing Hindu epics and mythology was India Book House, Bombay, and its editor, Anant Pai, a Kerala Brahmin (Pritchett, 1997). It opted for the popular comic genre, combining full-color illustrations and text to carry a story forward. Since the 1980s it has published more than 500 titles; all the titles are now available as an app, ACK Comics, besides the usual hard copy versions.

Even secular publishers like Bennett Coleman & Co. Ltd. (The Times of India group), carry columns on religious communication, relating religious and spiritual topics to Indian indigenous faith traditions, and occasionally to Abrahamic traditions as well. Similarly, the *Sunday Express* carries a regular column "Dalitality," which takes up issues of concern to Dalits, many of whom are Neo-Buddhists. Dalit Camera and Dalit Desk in the online space serve a similar purpose.

Radio, Music, and Television

Radio and television broadcasting have served as religious communication in India since the 1950s. Christian evangelists transmitted their radio broadcasts using transnational platforms like FEBA (Far East Broadcasting Association) and Radio Veritas (Thomas, 2008) since All India Radio (AIR), the public broadcasting service, and Vividh Bharati, AIR's commercial service, hold a monopoly under Indian government regulatory law. AIR, however, early on discriminated against some religiously inspired music: K. V. Keskar, the Minister of Information and Broadcasting in the 1950s, banned "Muslim-inspired music," allowing only classical (Hindu) traditions (Thomas, 2015, p. 36).

Indian television does allow for religious broadcasting by both domestic and foreign religious communities on channels and networks under license from the Ministry of Information and Broadcasting. In fact, religious broadcasting had its beginnings with the public television broadcaster, Doordarshan, which produced and transmitted nationally episodes of the Hindu religious epic, the Ramayana, in 1987 and 1988. Rajagopal (2001) unveils the role that this serial played in the emergence of the Ram Temple movement and the consequent rise of Hindu nationalism and the BJP. The TV serial was revived during the national lockdown prompted by the Covid-19 pandemic in mid-2019. The Hindu Right has used the epic as propaganda in its nationalistic enterprises to support religious nationalists (Thomas, 2015, p. 35).

More than 76 around-the-clock television channels, dedicated exclusively to religion, make up the televangelical scene in India. Around 50 of these channels, owned and run by various Hindu sects, gurus, and babas (religious teachers), and prominent temples and pilgrim centers operate. The largest clutch of channels is promoted by Baba Ramdev, the most renowned yoga guru and Ayurveda evangelist. Ramdev leads hundreds of followers in live yoga sessions beamed around the country every day, and also gives discourses on physical and spiritual well-being. The channels also promote branded herbal products. Religion and commerce, as in global charismatic televangelism, are thus bound together to reduce faith to a commodity, and devotees to consumers, following the charismatic ideals of health, prosperity, and success (James, 2010). Thomas (2008) came to a similar conclusion about Christian televangelism in India. Minority religious groups like the Neo-Buddhists, Jains, and Sikhs own two channels each and use them for transmitting both recorded and live discourses, the singing of bhajans and hymns, and other types of spiritually uplifting programs.

The audiocassette revolution in India during the 1970s and 1980s (Manuel, 1993) and the videocassette one during the 1980s and 1990s (Kumar, 2021) opened up the recorded music industry to India's diverse religious communities; bhajans, hymns, kathas, and other forms of religious participation took on a new life. The monopoly of the Gramaphone Company of India and the two public broadcasters, Doordarshan and AIR, gave way to small-scale enterprises like T-Series and Tips Industries (Kumar, 2021; Manuel, 1993; Marcus, 1997).

The Indian film industry is obsessed with themes that relate to Hindu mythology. The mythological genre, from the very first silent film, Dadasaheb Phalke's *Harishchandra*, has proved successful at the box office. Popular social films are replete with religious motifs (Derne, 1997, p. 191). A 1984 National Film Archive of India study found that ten films had been devoted to portraying Mira's life, four each for Tulsidas and Surdas, and smaller numbers for Nanak, Kabir, and Ravidas (Hawley, 1997, p. 131n).

Indian Religions Online

Helland (2000) distinguishes between "online religion" and "religion online": "religion online" represents established and official religious communities; "online religion" expresses individual and personal religious beliefs and experiences. Both types have a significant presence in the Indian media. An instance of "religion online" is the Pūjā (or worship), which Hindus of all sects conduct in temples and at home. In temples, Brahmin priests generally perform the Pūjā in an elaborate manner that involves the clashing of cymbals, the beating of drums, the blowing of conch shells, and the offering of food, flowers, and incense, and the presence of a congregation, though the last is not mandatory. In homes, elders in the family perform this ritual, though without the elaborations. The digital era has made the e-puja extremely popular, particularly during the ongoing Covid-19 pandemic. Pūjās in large temples are uploaded on platforms and applications; worshippers can participate by animated graphics of flowers, incense, and the sound of cymbals. The virtual religious experience is no doubt different but most worshippers seem to believe that they are as efficacious as the offline Pūjā. Scheifinger (2013) argues that the key element of a Pūjā is *darshan* – the exchange of gazes between a deity and the worshipper – and this ritual can take place as effectively in cyberspace. Rani surveys the varied uses of online media by four prominent temples of South India (Rani, 2016). Rituals such as the Pūjā are not part of Buddhism, Neo-Buddhism, Jainism, and Sikhism. The reading of scriptures, listening to religious discourses, and the singing of hymns are given prime importance among these faiths.

The Hindu Right has the most pervasive presence online, in the form of websites, social media accounts, and applications. However, it has to compete with other fundamentalist religious groups like the Islamists and Christian evangelists. The scholarly work of Chaturvedi (2016), Sam and Thakurta (2019), Chopra (2019), Bhatia (2022), and others has uncovered this dark side of online media in the context of a "masculine" Hindu nationalism.

Jainism "can employ digital communication to propagate its set of routine activities that most Jains can follow to create better and deeper understanding of Jainism" (Shah, 2019, p. 148), though this process is still new to its adherents. Shah (2019) found evidence of Jain texts online, but her informants noted that "any method which makes use of electronic connection is not recommended" due to a stress on interpersonal channels (pp. 155–156).

The online space does allow minority groups (especially religious minorities) access to communication audiences otherwise unavailable. Thomas (2015) calls for attention to online Islamic films from India as examples of the widening religious communication sphere in India.

Interreligious Conflict and Media

Religious communication in India has faced pressures in a diverse country. The Pew Research Centre's (2020) survey of nearly 30 000 adult Indians from different faiths found that an overwhelming majority of the respondents said they believed in God, visited places of worship, and prayed regularly. A majority of followers (53%) of all faiths also said that religious diversity benefits the country, they were proud to be Indian, and that it was important to be tolerant and to respect other religions; only 24% held that religious diversity is harmful. However, the survey revealed some disturbing attitudes. Those respondents who were BJP voters said that to be "truly Indian" one had to be Hindu and be able to speak in Hindi, implying that non-Hindus like Muslims, Christians, Buddhists, Jains, Sikhs, tribals, and Dalits were not true Indians; nor were those who did not speak Hindi. Interestingly, Buddhists, Jains, and Sikhs are appropriated into the Hindu fold since their religions are deemed to be indigenous; tribal religions too are accepted into the same fold, much against their will.

This manifests India's generally poor record of using mass media to foment religious violence. The Sangh Parivar, its parent organization, the RSS, and its over 40 affiliates aggressively promote anti-Muslim and anti-Christian sentiments through the traditional media, the mass media, and the digital social media, with the primary objective of uniting the various sects and cults of Hindus against the minority communities, and of perpetuating their hegemonic political power at the national, regional, and local levels. Global indexes on freedom of religion, human rights, and press freedom place India nearly at the bottom (Patel, 2021). Interreligious dialogue appears to be the only way forward but must occur not only at the local level but on a media level.

Note

*   Anthony Le Duc authored the sections on Buddhism and Confucianism; Keval J. Kumar authored the sections on Hinduism, Jainism, and Sikhism.

References

Adhikary, N. M. (2014). Mahatma Gandhi and the *Sadharanikaran* model of communication. *The Journal of University Grants Commission, 3*(1), 63–76.

Andersen, W., & Damle, S. (2018). *The RSS: A view to the inside.* Viking.

Aryal, K. (2019–2020). Buddha's teachings and roots of nonviolent communication. *Aanekaant: A Journal of Polysemic Thought, 11*, 63–70.

Aryani, N. L. (2018). Implementation of communication ethics in building social harmony. *International Journal of Social Sciences and Humanities, 2*(1), 147–156. https://doi.org/10.29332/ijssh.v2n1.105

Bhatia, K. V. (2022). Hindu nationalism online: Twitter as discourse and interface. *Religions, 13*(739), 1–17. https://doi.org/10.3390/rel13080739

Bodhi, B. (Trans.) (2012). *The numerical discourses of the Buddha: A complete translation of the Anguttara Nikaya* (annotated edition). Wisdom Publications.

Bodhi, B., & Thera, N. (2000). *Numerical discourses of the Buddha: An anthology of suttas from the Anguttara Nikaya.* Altamira Press.

Chaturvedi, S. (2016). *I am a Troll: Inside the secret world of the BJP digital army.* Juggernaut.

Chopra, R. (2018). Free speech, traditional values, and Hinduism in the internet age: Indian and global trends. In M. E. Price, N. Stremlau, & L. Morgan (Eds.), *Speech and society in turbulent times: Freedom of expression in comparative perspective* (pp. 237–254). Cambridge University Press.

Chopra, R. (2019). *Virtual Hindu rashtra: Saffron nationalism and new media.* HarperCollins.

Creel, A. B. (1975). The reexamination of "Dharma" in Hindu ethics. *Philosophy East and West, 25*(2), 161–173. https://doi-org/10.2307/1397937

Derne, S. (1997). Market forces at work: Religious themes in commercial Hindi films. In L. A. Babb, & S. S. Wadley (Eds.), *Media and the transformation of religion in south Asia* (pp. 191–216). Motilal Banarsidass.

Dissanayake, W. (2014). *The idea of verbal communication in early Buddhism.* S. Godage and Brothers.

Gunaratne, S. A. (2015). Introduction. In S. A. Gunaratne, M. Pearson, & S. Senarathm (Eds.), *Mindful journalism and news ethics in the digital era: A Buddhist approach* (pp. 1–17). Routledge.

Hawley, J. S. (1997). The saints subdued: Domestic virtue and national integration in Amar Chitra Katha. In L. A. Babb, & S. S. Wadley (Eds.), *Media and the transformation of religion in south Asia* (pp. 107–136). Motilal Banarsidass.

Helland, C. (2000). Religion online / online religion and virtual communitas. In J. K. Hadden, & D. E. Cowan (Eds.), *Religion on the internet: Research prospects and promises* (pp. 205–224). JAI Press / Elsevier Science.

James, J. D. (2010). *McDonaldisation, masala McGospel and Om economics: Televangelism in contemporary India.* Sage Publications.

Kim, S. S., Agrusa, J., Lee, H., & Chon, K. (2007). Effects of Korean television dramas on the flow of Japanese tourists. *Tourism Management, 28,* 1340–1353. https://doi.org/10.1016/j.tourman.2007.01.005

Kim, Y. (2007). The rising East Asian 'wave': Korean media go global. In D. K. Thussu (Ed.), *Media on the move: Global flow and contra-flow* (pp. 135–152). Routledge.

Kumar, K. J. (2021). *Mass communication in India* (5th ed.). Jaico Books.

Lafraniere, S. (2010 January 29). *China's zeal for "Avatar" crowds out "Confucius". The New York Times.* Retrieved July 24, 2022 from https://www.nytimes.com/2010/01/30/business/global/30avatar.html

Le Duc, A. (2017). Buddhism and the ecology in the digital age. *Journal of International Association of Buddhist Universities, 10*(2), 40–51. https://so06.tci-thaijo.org/index.php/Jiabu/issue/view/15570

Le Duc, A. (2020). *Religion and society in the digital age: Interreligious and intercultural contexts.* Eliva Press.

Long, J. D. (2011). Jain philosophy. In W. Edelglass, & J. L. Garfield (Eds.), *The Oxford Handbook of World Philosophy.* Oxford University Press.

Luthra, R. (2001). The formation of interpretative communities in the Hindu diaspora. In D. Stout, & J. Buddenbaum (Eds.), *Religion and popular culture: Studies on the interaction of worldviews* (pp. 125–139). Iowa University Press.

Maina, T. (2022). *Top 5 Buddhist apps you should check out in 2022.* Afritech News. Retrieved June 30, 2022 from https://afritechnews.com/buddhist-apps

Manuel, P. (1993). *Cassette culture: Music and technology in north India.* Chicago University Press.

Marcus, S. L. (1997). On cassette rather than live: Religious music in India. In L. A. Babb, & S. S. Wadley (Eds.), *Media and the transformation of religion in South Asia* (pp. 167–188). Motilal Banarsidass Publishers Private Limited.

Mukul, A. (2015). *Gita Press and the making of Hindu India.* Harper Collins.

Nadeau, R. L. (2014). *Asian religions: A cultural perspective.* Wiley Blackwell.

Nanamoli, B. (Trans.) (1995). *The middle discourses of the Buddha: A new translation of the Majjhima Nikāya.* Buddhist Publication Society.

Nussbaum, M. C. (2007). *The clash within: Democracy, religious violence, and India's future.* Permanent Black.

Patel, A. (2021). *Price of the Modi years.* Westland Books.

Pearson, M. (2015). Journalism and mental cultivation. In S. A. Gunaratne, M. Pearson, & S. Senarathm (Eds.), *Mindful journalism and news ethics in the digital era: A Buddhist approach* (pp. 162–177). Routledge.

Pearson, M., & Senarath, S. (2015). Journalism and ethical conduct. In S. A. Gunaratne, M. Pearson, & S. Senarathm (Eds.), *Mindful journalism and news ethics in the digital era: A Buddhist approach* (pp. 143–161). Routledge.

Pew Research Centre. (2020). Retrieved September 26, 2022, from https://www.pewresearch.org/religion/2021/06/29/religion-in-india-tolerance-and-segregation

Pham, Q. A. (2017). Buddhist television in Taiwan: Adopting modern mass media technology for dharma propagation, Doctoral dissertation, University of California.

Phra Thanit Sirivathano. (2015). The model and process of Buddha-Dhamma communication through social media of Buddhist monks in Thailand. *Journal of International Buddhist Studies, 6*(2), 85–88.

Pinto, R. (2007). *Between empires: Print and politics in Goa.* Oxford University Press.

Pratt, J. B. (1928). *The pilgrimage of Buddhism and a Buddhist pilgrimage.* Macmillan.

Prebish, C. S. (2016). Online peer-reviewed journals in Buddhism. In G. P. Grieve, & D. Veidlinger (Eds.), *Buddhism, the internet, and digital media: The pixel in the lotus* (pp. 79–92). Routledge.

Pritchett, F. W. (1997). The world of Amar Chitra Katha. In L. A. Babb, & S. S. Wadley (Eds.), *Media and the transformation of religion in South Asia* (pp. 76–106). Motilal Banarsidas.

Rajagopal, A. (2001). *Politics after television: Hindu nationalism and the reshaping of the public in India.* Cambridge University Press.

Rani, P. (2016). A study of the usage of online media in selected Hindu temples in South India. *Religion and Social Communication, 14*(2), 140–164.

Runes, D. D. (Ed.) (1983). *Dictionary of Philosophy.* Philosophical Library.

Sam, C., & Thakurta, P. G. (2019). *The real face of Facebook in India: How social media have become a propaganda weapon of disseminator of disinformation and falsehood.* Paranjoy.

Schedneck, B. (2021). Educational philosophies and celebrity monks: Strategies for communicating Buddhist values to Thai Buddhist youth. *Journal of Global Buddhism, 22*(2), 273–289. https://doi.org/10.5281/ZENODO.5764613

Scheifinger, H. (2013). Hindu worship online and offline. In H. Campbell (Ed.), *Digital religion: Understanding religious practice in new media worlds* (pp. 121–127). Routledge.

Shah, B. (2019). Types of communication strategies in Jainism: A study of Jain mendicants, educators and lay persons. *Religion and Social Communication, 18*(1), 140–164.

Shah, K. (2013). Jainism: Its philosophical tradition and the re-adaptation through media and communication. *Religion and Social Communication, 11*(1), 33–46.

Singh, K. (1963/2011). *A history of the Sikhs Volume 1 (1469–1839).* Oxford University Press.

Smith, H. (1991). *The world's religions: Our great wisdom traditions.* HarperOne.

Stark, U. (2007). *An empire of books: The Nawal Kishore press and the diffusion of the printed word in colonial India.* Permanent Black.

Suzuki, B. L. (1981). *Mahayana Buddhism 1948* (rev. ed.). Allen & Unwin. (Original work published 1948).

Thapar, R. (2014). *The past as the present: Forging contemporary identities through history.* Aleph.

Thich Nhat Hanh. (2014). *The art of communicating.* HarperOne.

Thomas, P. (2015). Contested religion, media, and culture in India: Explorations, old and new. *Economic and Political Weekly, 50*(18), 32–39. http://www.jstor.org/stable/24481909

Thomas, P. N. (2008). *Strong religion, zealous media: Fundamentalist Christianity in South India.* Sage Publications.

Tu, W. M. (2013). Spiritual humanism. Hangzhou International Congress, "Culture: Key to Sustainable Development", May 15–17, 2013.

Tu, W. M. (n.d.). *Ecological implications of Confucian humanism.* Retrieved July 24, 2022 from http://msihyd.org/pdf/19manuscript_tu.pdf

Veidlinger, D. (2018). Introduction. In G. P. Grieve, & D. Veidlinger (Eds.), *Buddhism, the internet, and digital media: The pixel in the lotus* (pp. 1–20). Routledge.

Yamcharoen, N. (2015). Buddhist communication styles for new generation in present-day Thailand. *Asian Social Science, 11*(2), 174–180. https://doi.org/10.5539/ass.v11n2p174

Yang, J. (2008). The Korean wave (hallyu) in East Asia: A comparison of Chinese, Japanese, and Taiwanese audiences who watch Korean TV dramas. *Development and Society, 41*(1), 103–147. https://www.jstor.org/stable/deveandsoci.41.1.103

You, Y. (2010). *The Diamond Sutra in Chinese culture.* Buddha's Light Publishers.

Selected Readings

Agrawal, B. C. (2013). Influence of religious telecast in a multi-religious India: An analysis of Hindu and non-Hindu television viewers. *Religion and Social Communication, 11*(1), 1–21.

Gunaratne, S. A., Pearson, M., & Senarath, S. (2015). *Mindful journalism and news ethics in the digital era: A Buddhist approach.* Routledge.

Hall, D. L., & Ames, R. T. (1987). *Thinking through Confucius.* SUNY Press.

Harvey, P. (2000). *An introduction to Buddhist ethics: Foundations, values and issues.* Cambridge University Press.

Jeffrelot, C. (2021). *Modi's India: Hindu nationalism and the rise of ethnic democracy.* Context.

Marcos, F. G. (2022). *Communication in the analects of Confucius*. Peter Lang.

Mukul, A. (2015). *Gita Press and the making of Hindu India*. Harper Collins Publishers.

Thapar, R. (2014). *The past as the present: Forging contemporary identities through history*. Aleph.

Thich Nhat Hanh. (2018). *The art of communicating*. Harper Collins.

Yum, J. O. (1988). The impact of Confucianism on interpersonal relationships and communication patterns in East Asia. *Communication Monographs*, *55*(4), 374–388.

8

African Religions and Communication

Joseph Muyangata and Mark Fackler

Understanding African religions presents challenges no less complex than understanding religious beliefs and practices anywhere else, except perhaps that African traditional religions (ATR) commonly do not have the advantage (for researchers) of historical documents, confessions, learned scholarship, reports of theological debate and discourse, seminaries or universities dedicated to the intellectual defense of beliefs, or the extent of missionary activity and data associated with the monotheistic religions.

To note at the start affiliation data, in the east, middle, and south of Africa, Christianity holds the majority of those who practice a religion. In the north and west, Islam leads. Nowhere on the continent does ATR command a large membership (10% in the west, 0.4% in the north, 6–8% in the east, middle, and south). Liberia is ATR's most populous nation (10%). Somalia leads with Islam (99.8%), and in the Christian population, the DRC (95%) (ARDA, 2010).

The monotheistic faiths in Africa have established media outposts and media training. Catholic-, Protestant-, and Islamic-funded universities offer bachelor to doctoral degree programs in media theory and production, with graduates working in religious media but also in the major media houses. Magazines, tribal language radio, and film production have developed industries with centers in the large urban, primarily English-speaking metroplexes: Lagos, Nairobi, Kampala, and Johannesburg. Christian use of media followed from its emphasis on teaching a written Bible, translated from the start into local languages, and published throughout the continent by United Bible Societies supported from the West. Christianity has always been a religion of the Word. Islam's sense that Arabic is the pure revelation of God has kept its holy book from widespread distribution, but that is changing. Vernacular translations have appeared, along with numerous new worship centers.

This chapter will address ATRs in some detail, including their approaches to communication ethics. Next the chapter will review some of the research on religion and Christianity and Islam. Since the African context for these latter two appears in other chapters (see Chapters 5 and 6), we will offer only brief summaries here, noting the use of digital media.

African Traditional Religions

ATRs are strong on oral culture, ritual, ancestor veneration, prophets and preachers, and the usual questions of human life associated with religious belief: Who is the self? How does the person relate to other persons? Where is divine presence manifest in the life of the clan, tribe, region? Where does

The Handbook on Religion and Communication, First Edition. Edited by Yoel Cohen and Paul A. Soukup.
© 2023 John Wiley & Sons Ltd. Published 2023 by John Wiley & Sons Ltd.

God live, and what matters to God? How may God be made an ally in the struggle to live, raise children, find food, and to die? How does homage to God recharge hope that tomorrow may be a better day in light of the conflicts, scarcities, and setbacks of the hour? All religions deal with these core human issues, which are finally distilled to the two fundamental communication questions: Does God speak, and if so, what is the report? Does God hear, and under what conditions? For the purposes of this chapter, "God" refers to theological constructs of various kinds, diverse, complex, and disputed. "God" is the divine being of holy books, historic confessions of faith, academic theology, and traditional religions for which there is little documentation but centuries of oral tradition. The use of "God" for all expressions of religious belief in this chapter is meant to denote and recognize the pursuit of the ineffable by people of all walks of life. This chapter respects the many ways people for millennia have sought to communicate meaningfully, effectively, and often angrily with the divine being. Religion is, among other things, the story of humanity, joys and sorrows, oppressions and liberations, hopes, dreams, ambitions, and an enduring search for God's peace.

On the African continent, all scholars agree, God has been speaking for a very long time. For how long, only forebears of prehistory can say, though we of the third millennium are free to imagine. John Mbiti (1969), the Anglican cleric whose scholarship celebrated ATR as precursor to imported faiths (Christianity, Islam, Buddhism, others), famously wrote: "Wherever the African is, there is religion" (p. 108) (see Odozor, 2019 for a thorough review of ATR theology and morality).

First on the continent were ATRs and these communities still carry significant religious and cultural weight, from the Cape to Saharan sands. Details of the many ATRs are beyond the scope of this chapter, but all share these elements: a sense of meaningful personhood; a critical case for communitarian solidarity; and a mystical internal home where God holds serene sovereignty and mostly does not wish to be disturbed. All religious faiths seek to communicate a way of life to succeeding generations, if not to wider, trans-tribal publics. This chapter discusses communication trends in African religions, with the proviso that change can happen quickly (such as the cell phone phenomenon of the early 2000s) and any report such as this needs updating by the week.

Meaningful personhood on the African continent is deeply religious. The birth of a child is reason to celebrate both the greatest of a group's resources and the blessings of Deity. Christian theology celebrates birth as the emergence of a life-long plan developed by God (Psalm 22:10). A birth is never explained as mere chromosomes assembling or zygotes blending. ATRs likewise celebrate birth and include in its process "veritable birth" (Beller, 2001, p. 1), when the newborn is given a name in front of the community. By this process, "the community is the place of true birth" (Bujo, 1997, quoted in Beller, p. 49). Naming a baby situates the person that child is prescribed to become, always with reference to defining "the being" of the child (Bujo, 1997, p. 17). Note here the contrast with Western assumptions that the proper role of media is to examine leaders, in effect to teach subscribers and viewers how to name their lords, whether political overseers or the meaning-makers of culture: artists, poets, and musicians. Film-makers and radio talk personalities are increasingly influential in this advisory and naming role. Early on, ATRs establish a person's role and identity, which is then lived out in dialogue with the community and in accord with primal community investment. In the village, all women of child-bearing age are mothers-with-authority for all children; likewise adult males are fathers of all and thus children are never independent personages seeking an identity in an I–It world (cf. Buber, 1971).

A child raised in cultures where ATR thrives may receive the name of their season of birth (seasons being God's various inclinations toward providing abundance or drought), or of an admired forebear (ancestors being active, living presences, remembered by names, revered in death), prophets or respected leaders (many Old Testament names where Christianity dominates), and even some names seemingly carelessly given, such as Judas and Absalom. Theophoric names predict a relationship the child is believed to establish for themselves and their community with Deity (Beller, 2001, p. 1). Thus, at birth and through communal rites of naming, an identity is created with which mediated messaging may eventually reckon. At birth, however, the vital reckoning is the person with Deity and the people living on Deity's land.

"Through the ages, religion has been for Africans the normal way of looking at the world and experiencing life itself" (Mbiti, 1975, p. 14). An Anglican clergyman, Mbiti argued decisively on behalf of ATRs as one of the three major faiths on the continent alongside Christianity and Islam. Mbiti aggressively dismissed claims that diminished the relevance or sophistication of ATRs, which follow no sacred book, organize no synods or denominations, change with the generations, and seem to outsiders quite taken with fanciful and discredited notions of healing and ancestor reverence. Mbiti sought to correct these misjudgments. African religion, he insists, has its theology, ethics, ceremonial protocols, sacred objects and places, and leaders, just as other faiths, but more: at no time in the past was African religion "introduced"; it always was. At no time was a reformation of religion fought over, or an Enlightenment invented, threatening tenets long believed. Even among converts to Christianity and Islam (and there are millions, he acknowledges), Africans retain their religion alongside the practices and teachings of newer arrivals. This "very pragmatic and realistic" religion changes with circumstances, yet stabilizes in custom, dance, language, marriage and family, and concepts of the hereafter.

Unlike the monotheistic faiths, ATR does not actively seek converts. There are neither missionaries nor founders, neither mega-church preachers, nor reformers. Beliefs are elastic, changing with "the historical changes in the lives of the people" (Mbiti, 1975, p. 16). Old ways are recalled if important to life, forgotten if not. Memory goes deep, but history for its own sake requires resources unavailable to rural adherents. To know African religions, Mbiti asserts, one must know the language that carries the message, the names that perpetuate belief across generations, the riddles and proverbs short and easily memorized, that capture key concepts and reinforce central claims. Religion "is seen in all aspects of life; it influences all areas of life; it has been largely responsible for shaping the character and culture of African peoples throughout the centuries" (p. 30).

ATRs are inherently syncretistic. Most professing Muslims and Christians still use forms of ritual and practice from Indigenous religions though they deny adherence to traditional spokespersons. Olupona (2015) assumes that the number of followers of ATR has dwindled as Islam and Christianity have spread, their influence magnified through strategic media usage. While Christianity dominates the east and south, Islam the north, and ATR is strongest in the central states of Africa, there are no geographic dividing lines. Forms of these religions appear everywhere, even in mono-religious states, which formally do not allow variances, and reflect beliefs and practices before the Christian and Islamic colonization of Africa (Olupona, 2015). These varied movements are bounded by ethnic identity and geography. For example, the Yoruba religion has historically been centered in southwestern Nigeria, the Zulu religion in southern Africa, and the Igbo in southeastern Nigeria. While most features of ATR and its practices show similarities, presenting the appearance of a unitary portrait (Olademo, 2008, p. 3), the situation is more complex, with some adopting exotic and foreign practices.

While Mbiti portrays ATR as generous, the benevolent precursor and communal partner to Christianity and Islam, other researchers are dubious of ATR's innocence. Mosely (2004) describes aspects of ATR as magic, witchcraft, telepathy, clairvoyance, psychokinesis, and precognition – the fearful dark side of close relationships, particularly in the case of witchcraft, whose practitioners injure not by technique or training, but with "an inherent quality. A witch performs no rite, utters no spell, and possesses no medicine. An act of a witch is a psychic act" (Evans-Pritchard, 1937, p. 21).

Mokgobi (2014) notes that in all African regions, traditional healers are resourceful and play a pivotal role in peoples' sense of well-being. They are the medical knowledge storehouses (Yeboah, 2000). Traditional healers are also educators in culture, cosmology, and spirituality. "They serve as counselors, social workers, and psychotherapists as well as custodians of indigenous knowledge systems" (Mills et al., 2005, p. 466). Healers are commonly known as diviners, now coming up in media spaces, social and mainstream. Olupona (2015) notes that diviners go through a long education and apprenticeship. Yoruba diviners, for example, draw on Indigenous knowledge by consulting Ifa, a treasure trove of knowledge handed down "from Babalawo (Ifa diviner) to Babalawo for centuries." This knowledge is guarded, revealed only to solve problems, and largely outside media coverage, allowing for continuity, mystery, and veneration.

Still, there is a market for the imaginative perusal of this knowledge. The film industry in Nigeria (Nollywood) feeds these themes of fear and the paranormal with a vengeance. In a typical story, a lover takes a bold risk to win the affection of a paramour, only to be threatened with unlimited terror, then to be rescued via the intervention of a virtuous piece of magic, as the vanquished evil intruder retreats and the happy couple slides into lover's paradise. One can imagine the superstition of this type of narrative becoming a deterrent to ATR followers (even followers of all faiths). In a world perceived to be full of pernicious and malevolent powers, a billboard or tweet could carry the omen that destroys one's family and health. Competing themes – Mbiti versus Western anthropology – present a dynamic area of research, slowed to a snail's pace by the obvious requirements of language acquisition and intimacy born through "living among" over time.

Why would Africans following a traditional religious life resist the influence of mass media? Sociologists at the Catholic University of East Africa described the secularization of African culture – its flight from traditional beliefs and values. Adding research results to comments in prior paragraphs here, Shorter and Onyancha (1997) cite startling differences in the cultures projected by major media and the traditional values of ATR.

News media sets its cannons on competitive politics. Elections are about speeches (promises made beyond capacities to fulfill), money give-aways, institutions (schools, policing, hospitals, international nongovernmental organizations), and immediacy (today matters most, then tomorrow). ATRs sail quite different oceans. Speeches that matter come from prophets and preachers whose promises stretch well beyond the limited horizon of media, from ancestors to newborns, from harvest to the afterlife, from health and prosperity to supremacy over evil spirits lurking, scheming, gleaming with malice. Of what account is political rhetoric in the context of a search for more rain or more children, or relief from blindness or chronic pain? Money matters for everyone, but money in traditional culture is not for investment growth or retirement savings; money is to be shared widely, for a people's only safety net is the capacity of a village to sustain and replenish its workers and its mothers. Money is not an end in itself, not worth a life of labor, not fungible apart from herds and grains. Institutions likewise have little appeal: schools take children away from families for a process of alienation and estrangement. Schools produce children "smarter" than parents and ancestors, thus useless to the village, where decisions depend not on literacy or the deposit of wisdom found in the library of the humanities, but on palaver, the process of unified vision and community action. Immediacy is perhaps the outlier, the most foreign of media values to ATR followers: rain matters; gestation; a youth's courage during circumcision and then as "warrior" guarding sheep and cows; older people silently bearing their final pains; the God's pleasure ambiguously revealed in a chain of events or mystic utterances. These priorities do not comport with hours and minutes; they flow through time as clouds pass over distant hills, as stars traverse the night sky.

Music from old Zaire (now the Democratic Republic of the Congo, DRC) and from Congo Brazzaville is famous throughout East Africa, more popular by far than local music.

"Much of the dancing that goes with the music is sexually explicit" by traditional standards (Shorter & Onyancha, 1997, p. 72). Of major media, television and video have created the greatest cultural wave threatening traditional shorelines. In the early days of entertainment television, viewing was communal – one working TV set for rooms full of viewers. Now sets are accessible even in the tin roof, mud, and thatch dwellings of the urban poor. Programming is abundant with Western themes and moods. "To watch television is to enter an ideal world which has little to do with the real Africa… The medium is a major instrument of globalization and cultural homogeneity. Television is basically about money and control. It commercializes everything it touches" (Aylward, 1918, p. 75). ATRs sustain the social order with emphasis on food supply, nurture of children, enduring marriages, and communal flourishing under the watching eyes of ancestors and Deity. Admittedly, negative social and personal values show up; no social network is flawless. Yet the cosmos encountered on screen is of a different order, the sociologists conclude:

> TV advertisements initiate us into another cosmology, into a philosophy of consumer materialism and economic rationalism… People are taught to crave for products they do not need and cannot afford… The primary concern of TV advertisements is not our well-being or the proper upbringing of our children. (Aylward, p. 75)

The analysis is telling. If ATR raises legitimate doubts concerning its fringe claims to supernatural knowledge and access, on this point its teaching resonates full-throated: children growing into responsible adulthood equates to community survival. If media viewing threatens that growth, little wonder ATR followers place major media in the camp of the foreigner and interloper. Youth are attracted no doubt, while ATRs try to keep watch over the vulnerable adolescents who are its future. A social-cultural movement called "the liberal West's new, post-Judean-Christian values agenda" is not only divisive in the developed world (Mead, 2022, p. A15): the values gap is pronounced and explicit among African nations short on almost every life need the West takes for granted.

Obvious differences and ideational conflicts are evident between followers of ATRs, Christian believers, Islamic loyalists, and other religious communities. Mass media require sufficient resources to be profitable, even for government-owned media, which need their own loyal constituents to justify existence and maintain hegemony over messaging. Mass media's relentless quest to acquire and retain listeners/viewers/readers drives these enterprises toward sources of wealth, consumers, entrepreneurs, and educated elites (Beller, 2001, p. 101). Farmers, bricklayers, *walezi* (guardians, babysitters), and herbal healers rarely walk with that cosmopolitan constituency.

Communication Ethics and ATRs

Few media theorists/ethicists have had greater influence in the last half-century than Clifford Christians of the University of Illinois' Institute of Communication Research. His incorporation of Ubuntu as a research theme in the early 2000s energized his advocacy for a communitarian ethic worldwide (Christians, 2004). On this theme, ATRs left the starting gate centuries earlier and have lived the experience of communitarianism even as the term waited for academic expression and media application.

Christians based much of his admiration for Ubuntu on the work of Thaddeus Metz of the University of Johannesburg, who presumed in his setting an ontology of universal human dignity that focused not on persons as individuals, but the space and energy between them, the mediating space, the infinite, dynamic measure of the distance between. Metz (2012) had noted three conceptions common among precolonial peoples living below the Sahara (p. 37), nearly all of whom perceived the world through categories of traditional religion. First among the essential conceptions of African Ubuntu: human beings possess a spiritual nature articulated and celebrated in worship of the divine. Only humans have this divine orientation, thus "human rights" are primal, and all humans deserve the common respect these rights entail. "Since human beings have something akin to a soul, an immaterial substance that will survive the death of the body, they are the most special things on the planet" and deserve priority among other living beings for the "entitlements to life, liberties, resources, and the like" (Metz, 2014, p. 312). Perhaps to the surprise of Western ethicists, ATRs had laid the foundation of what was beginning to be a universal moral claim. Second, Metz identified a "capacity for life-force," a vital energy, a "liveliness" that persuades on its own terms apart from theological references. Humans uniquely possess "creativity, confidence, and strength" and show by these aspects alone a "superlative inner worth, a dignity" (p. 313). As the Deities of traditional religions project these qualities or mirror the projected creativities and confidences of those gathered to pay them homage, we see the moral life and communicational pattern of traditional religions in a harmony nearly absent from social media today. An earlier, mystical, pre-Enlightenment movement on a continent unheralded for progressive social ethics is shaming the West's communicational vulgarity without asking for its remorse or change, as if to say, you get what you ask for. Third, the Ubuntu tradition provides a rationale for communal relationships. With a robust view of community and a marked absence of Enlightenment notions of individual rights and liberties, ATR presents a stark contrast to worldviews of major media consumers, efficiency experts, bureaucrats, drive-time radio commentary, and highway billboards, to name a few examples. Life in cosmopolitan Africa is a rush of individual competition for status, amusement, money, and influence, things common to the materialist ethos everywhere. Life in rural areas is a walk along a rocky path, always with conversation – an informal communication network as conscious of symbolic meaning as any other, now aided by a cell phone and often two, one for the nearest tower, the second for the end of the path and a different service provider.

Christians (2019) concludes that "ontologically, human dignity denotes the special status of the human species … dignity [as] an inalienable property, a non-contingent implication of one's status as human" (p. 195). Media have a duty to facilitate the recognition and development of human dignity by weaving into its narrative "the verbal and visual symbols of everyday life, images, representations, and myths [that] make social relations meaningful for us and locate us in time and space" (p. 200). By any measure, major media have a long moral recovery ahead to meet this ambitious mandate.

Yet prior to the academy's declarations of mass media obligations and critiques of their immense industrial footprint is the foundational medium for humankind and the most exercised among ATR followers: orality. Among ATRs, the break-out from rural-interpersonal to urban media-cosmopolitan has been much retarded for reasons related to its oral culture, its sense of consciousness, and the secularism of media, especially entertainment media but also the generally negative attitude of major media executives and producers toward religious belief, expressed consistently in programing, commentary, and news coverage.

Oral culture and ATR are interwoven and embedded, a substance indissoluble. Ong (1967) expounded orality with an approach nearly reverential: life expressed itself in voice and sound, prior to sight and smell. His famous reference to buffalos – dangerous when heard – evoked oral images of primal culture as surely as did his literary exposition of the Gospel of John's "Word made flesh." For Ong, sound was more than decibel or signal. Oral communicators emphasized poetry, agonistic confrontation, and memory. Ong (1982) drew distinctions between the modern West and an era before mediated images and rapid transportation. Ong described communities that rehearsed values in couplets (enchanted evening, healthy body, good sport) and songs that everyone memorized and sang as community recreation. Ellul (1885) likewise gave priority to hearing over sight, auditory over the visual, in social relationships: "Images fall into a pattern with respect to each other, but sounds do not. Instead, sounds contradict each other and cancel each other... Sounds produce incoherence. The noises I hear form no panorama of the world" (quoted in McLuhan & McLuhan, 1988, p. 13).

Goody (2000) referred to writing as a technology of the intellect. Humans categorize and interact with the world based on syllogisms and listing behavior. Literacy enables this component of human life; oral culture does not. Goody's research distinguished pristine oral culture from writing cultures with an oral element. In the former, being alone, eating alone, or communicating with oneself was regarded as suspicious behavior, a prelude to nefarious activity, possibly witchcraft (p. 24).

Like Goody (1968), Ong conducted some of his research on oral culture in West Africa, where he found communal life in extremis, perhaps to the level at which his own communion had always worked but rarely arrived. "Sound unites groups of living beings as nothing else does," wrote Ong (1967, p. 122) soon after colonial powers vacated Africa and regional democracy took its first faltering steps. Ong (1974, p. 150) recalled from one of his visits to Cameroon "the most exotic feature" of a tribal liturgy. It was not the setting, the homilies, or the vestments but the oyenga, "the drawn-out, piercing shriek ... high-pitched ... sustained as long as breath could hold ... piercing through the choir." Voiced only by women, the *oyenga* brought listeners to attention in the present. For Ong this was the equivalent of bells in the Roman liturgy, "but more insistent and demanding" because it was voice.

In the African village, Ong found a theory of word and self that points human sound-making toward hopeful ends: the village palaver, talk that unifies a group's vision and resources and thus binds the community as such. Congolese theologian Benezet Bujo (1997, p. 56) describes the palaver – what he calls an African philosophical "Other" – as open, continuous interpretation of communal norms, ready "to pay attention to past experiences of the ancestors ... and to confront them with the claims of modern time." Palaver is roundabout, overlapping, redundant, inefficient, celebrative, and agonistic. Its participants must be embedded in communal history and committed to promoting life. The palaver never stops until the last story is finished; the last parable expounded. This is not Western bar-talk: idle prattle, casual cajoling, rapid chatter preventing break-ins. Bujo's palaver calls for long pauses, time to reflect, the slow gathering of consensus that takes a tortoise's pace toward decision. Oral culture in Africa appears like a collage of opinion and narrative enjoyed for its own sake in open-ended time. Yet not without purpose and progress. A Kikuyu proverb says, "He is clever who has listened to advice" (marginal note to Psalm 112, Oasis International, 2012, p. 871).

ATRs tend to create and re-create premodern social structures: intense group loyalty, fear or ignorance of outside-the-group beliefs, group cohesion in terms of shared essential services, isolation from mass media resources and careers, and, in many places, weak access to the Internet. ATR adherents become the forgotten, overlooked populations of national planners who for decades have adopted the development model of industrialization and monetization of social relations. In her authoritative summary of media development, Bourgault (1995) describes the attitudes of planners toward people left behind by modern media, and by implication, still further behind modernity, its pleasures and freedoms, by adherence to outworn religious perspectives:

> Africans were believed to be clannish, present-tense oriented, superstitious, and ill-adapted to change. They were capable of loyalty only to their own kin... They quaked before powerful forces of good and evil. They clung excessively to tradition. (p. 228)

In a paradoxical turn, planners thus intended to use mass media "to reconstitute African peoples for the modern world." The "structural distortions" of this media assault on primitive ideologies – assisted vigorously by the United Nations Educational, Scientific and Cultural Organization (UNESCO) and other aid organizations – accrued to the benefit of elites until the leadership class realized that access to media among traditional people could "awaken the masses" (p. 228). How would this Catch-22 be resolved? The answer involved a wholesale clearing of traditional norms and ideas along the lines of Western secularism: abandon tribal medical practices; release labor from family "business" to industry; create personal wealth following examples profiled in media accounts; provide for children's futures not by more children but through the storage of labor's capital; and finally privatize or surrender the pre-scientific Weltanschauung that heretofore had been the traditionalists' unquestioned birthright. The result at long last was recognition that "the materialist values and consumerist lifestyles … brought about a sense of purposelessness and a feeling of personal and political alienation" (p. 231). Major media and their social-change campaigns came and went, with little effect.

Yet one small corner of mass media seems immediately available and relevant to the semi-literate traditionalists of ATR. The gateway to this "corner" is not public debate per se, not polemic rationalizations, not heftier theology. It is common play, the first public activity humans learn and practice (Fackler & Obonyo, 2014, pp. 726–740). We play because play is the first order of human business, wrote Huizinga (1950). Before inventing alphabets or institutions, churches or academies, we humans created play as the golden mean of instinct and will, a sensate, essential part of human activity. From play came ritual, poetry, music and dance, political campaigning and warfare. The rules of play are the origins of international law. "Once they are broken, society falls into barbarism and chaos" (p. 173).

Major media also play. In headlines, news columns, feature stories, interviews, the "game" of power and privilege is the germ of news reportage. Elites of entertainment, sport, business, and religion rise to prominence as players in a roughly ruled game, culture. Through media, culture elites maintain and transform relationships, generate wealth, and make clear the ambitions and assumptions that coagulate community. The "most read" part of print media in East Africa are editorial cartoons, which depict in play form the contests woven through a culture and lived out on street corners, river banks, posh luncheons in Euro-style hotels, and kiosks inside slums. Cartoonists play with satire and hyperbole. In cartoons, those without political power challenge parliamentarians and police chiefs. Children show wisdom higher than priests. Women hold the power of a military general. On city streets, hawkers and vendors proliferate, the lowest, easiest targets for arrest and confiscation. In cartoons they outwit the Keystone Cops every time. Cartoons push out the bellies of the white-shirt-and-tie crowd. In cartoons, pretense and posturing are smacked with the scorn they deserve, the simple word or gesture the honor it needs. Common sense resides with the people who must accommodate a leader's childish appetites. Viewers/readers of cartoons take their comforts knowing that, at the end of the day, "Wanjiku" (the common villager) will eat at their own fire and sleep near their own people. Political, business, even religious leaders will trip over their exaggerated foibles and general tomfoolery. One need not read cartoons; they draw the laugh of convivial understanding by exaggerated image and preposterous mockery. One "reads" this medium together with street-corner comrades; laughter is never solitary. The cartoon is passed around, smudged with city grime, the residue of urban reading. The cartoon says it all, even if news columns and editorial commentary cannot. Why should cartoonists draw, or children sketch in the dirt, or villagers snicker and pass the page to others? Cartoons create palaver with refreshing spontaneity, a much-needed antidote to ennui and a release from state terror.

At the turn of the millennium, former UNESCO Director General Federico Mayor (2001) wrote:

> We cannot fail to observe the increase in soul-sickness at the very heart of the most prosperous societies, bet protected from misfortune. The heart itself seems prey to a curious void. Indifference and passivity grow. There is an ethical desert. Passions and emotions are blunted. People's eyes are empty and solidarity evaporates... Long-term vision is discredited. Now and then we are truly sick at heart. (p. 5)

Add to this the grim titles of scholarship on Africa: *Continent in Chaos* (Ayyitey, 1994), *A Continent Self-Destructs* (Schwab, 2002), *Kenya, Between Hope and Despair* (Branch, 2011), and *The Sacrifice of Africa* (Katangole, 2010). Why, Katangole asks, after so much aid, international and domestic, is the politics of greed, state brutality, hunger, and corruption still the story of Africa (p. 9)?

For solutions, Mayor (2001) called for four "contracts" (p. 20). The third he called the cultural contract, focusing on education, languages, and media access. Katangole (2010) called for a refreshment of story, a recovery and restatement from the people themselves, of a cultural past and a hopeful future (p. 18). In this, religious leaders from all communions join Mayor, Katangole, and communications scholars pressing for a third way between Enlightenment liberalism and lost-in-time traditionalism, a way toward a communication of *shalom* – *emayiana* – as the Maasai say: a story not of fatally ill cultures but of people engaged in the difficult, timeless work of building a future more secure, joyful, and prosperous than the present.

In terms of communication theory and strategy, that way forward may be through playful points of light generated by cartoonists and leaders with a lifted heart who want us to see something new, to reach for just-beyond-the-possible, and as that reach draws sweat and toil, then to laugh, to see the humor in our striving, to enjoy the walk. Cartoonists let us attend, one step removed. In this sense, they invite us to play. In the cartoon, all we know about culture comes to bear on everything we should be as cultural participants, everything worth becoming: a community with vision, ideals, and obstacles, none of them so great that they cannot succumb to laughter and eventual change.

Cartoonists draw for hope and play, life skills shared by all religions and beyond, each drawing a small step closer to *shalom* – a media ripe for entry and experiment. Traditionalists and the major religious communions alike know the grin that shares this common dream: freedom for the other, justice to protect the other, time to restore the other.

Christianity

Religious followers, while many may aspire to economic power or political control, are raised on an agenda of values contrary to the normal fare of mass media. For Christians, a cruciform life imitating the servant-sacrifice of Jesus presents a case of cultural resistance to media values. Elements of the ambitious "electronic Church" often convey what missiologists refer to as the "health and wealth gospel": live well, support the preacher and the Church, and riches will follow. This obvious aberration from historic Christendom is widely criticized for its excesses, though open-air healing rallies attract thousands who hope beyond hope for relief and a touch of prosperity.

Protestant and Catholic communions use media prodigiously, energetically, and often thoughtfully. Obviously there can be much to criticize: the materialization of the message, claims to certainty that trigger uncertainty, false claims to piety that cover wrongful behavior, and offers of answers to prayer by preachers speaking passionately on behalf of God without the power to fulfill. Ihejirika (2009, p. 19) cites "glamorous house magazines, handbills, posters, billboards, T-shirts, caps, fashion, music" as a few examples of creative, sensational marketing of the faith.

Jeffress (2008) notes the increasing role of multimedia technologies in the Church. The goal for media technology is to strengthen and enhance everyday activities and communication. Lovrick (2017) agrees, "Preachers in various Christian denominations use audio-visual technology in their sermons and homilies. PowerPoint, video clips, and even hologram imagery have found their way to the pulpit." Media technology is the fastest tool to advertise and disseminate information as to where people in need could easily access help. In her dissertation Witte (2013) writes, "Many scholars of preaching advocate reshaping the sermon from a purely oral genre to a multimedia genre that resonate more clearly and powerfully to the current multimedia culture" (p. 2). The modern-day preachers have mastered marketing themselves through these media technologies, giving a huge rise to televangelism (see Chapter 11).

This can give rise to the bizarre. A Zimbabwean pastor, known popularly as Pastor Talent, associated with Victory World International Ministries, won huge media attention after posting a video showing him on his phone saying: "Hello, is this heaven? I have a woman here, what do you have to say about her?" The pastor had plans to launch a television show called *Heaven Online* where viewers could listen in on his phone calls with God. Soon after, however, Pastor Talent withdrew his offer of access to Heaven, saying the time is not right (Laing, 2017).

The use of various media is not only exclusive to the Pentecostals and Protestant Christians of Africa. The Catholic Church has since come out of their church buildings and are now prophetically bringing their message using different media platforms including social media (Ihejirika, 2009).

There are also tragic times of total religious collapse, such as the complicity of churches in the Rwanda genocide of 1994. The Christian tradition calls for repentance of these wrongs. Yet the media universe of Christendom has much to commend it, from print to Internet: courageous good news well beyond the scope of this article to document.

Islam

Islam, despite its historic divisions based on succession and Koranic interpretation, presents a multi-form response to Western secularism/degenerative values. In nearly all cases, Islamic values question or outright reject the progressivism of media lifestyles and aspirations (for a revisionist presentation of Islamic values, in particular on matters of speech freedom and toleration in the context of the Sudan, see Sadig, 2010).

Islamic ministries have used television, radio, newspapers, and magazines to propagate teachings to youth, professionals, and intellectuals. Reviewing African religious media, Ihejirika (2009) notes:

> Evidence of a new focus in Muslim media is the attraction of Arabic-based satellite television channels like Al Jazeera and Al Arabiya, for the Muslim faithful in Africa. Part of this attraction, according to Abubakar (2008), is the use of Arabic in their broadcasts which eliminate the possibility of distorting true Islamic teaching. (Ihejirika, 2009, p. 35)

Thus, the widening use of media and inevitable distortions of the Prophet's teaching is countered by the purity of one language for all time and all people, a remarkable solution that immediately conjures a future of debate and diversity. Islam has also used television, radio, newspapers, and magazines to propagate its teachings as they are produced in different categories, such as for children, youths, and adults, and for different levels, such as the layman, professionals, intellectuals, and scientists, addressing varying needs and interests. The future of Islam in Africa should be carefully watched by communications specialists and scholars.

Islam is growing very fast (Ibahrine, 2014). Its digital platforms largely impact the everyday social life of Muslims in Africa. This includes and is not limited to including their religiosity, preaching, religious practices, and issuing *fatwas* (religious decrees). The aim is to build border-less communities among the Muslims. Ibahrine (2014) further notes that, "Social media have become an invaluable means to pursue the path of *da'wah* and the dissemination of the Koran" (p. 737). Faithful Muslims tweet Qur'anic verses and the sayings from the Prophet as part of religious rituals and habits. This has been done for special events like Ramadan and on the occasion of Haj, where pilgrims tweet feeds as a way of sharing their rituals and spiritual experience with other Muslims and their families. Facebook, Twitter, WhatsApp, and YouTube have been very useful tools in mediating Islam. Ishak and Sohilin (2012, p. 263) argue, "As much as the media can disrepute the general Muslim population and Islam, it can also restore and further inform the public of the true image of the religion." Media become the best tool for the proper propagation and understanding of Islam.

Conclusion

Media and religion have great popularity in the African landscape as the rituals, experiences, services, and personal activities of the religious adherents are heralded on both mainstream media and social media. These have occupied a central position in the African religious discourse in recent years, mainly among Christians, Muslims, and the ATRs. Media use by these religious groups has also led to their explosion in terms of numerical growth and also in their presence being felt in places those religions could not reach physically in Africa. Nonetheless, media abuses have also been noted, hence the need to guard against them and create a healthy media-religious platform that aims to build an authentic and positive use of media among the religious faithful.

References

Abubakar, A. (2008, July 10–12). Not lost in translation and no subtitle: Global pan-Islamism, Al-Jazeera satellite broadcast, and Nigeria's non-Arabic speaking audience. Paper presented at the International Conference on New Media and Religious Transformations in Africa. Abuja, Nigeria. African Communication Research.

ARDA. (2010). Association of religious data archives. ARDA. Retrieved July 29, 2022, from thearda.com

Ayyitey, G. (1994). *Continent in chaos*. St. Martin's Griffin.

Beller, R. (2001). *Life, person and community in Africa*. Paulines.

Bourgault, L. (1995). *Mass media in sub-Saharan Africa*. Indiana University Press.

Branch, D. (2011). *Kenya: Between hope and despair, 1963–2011*. Yale University Press.

Buber, M. (1971). *I and thou*. Simon & Schuster (Touchstone).

Bujo, B. (1997). *The ethical dimension of community*. Paulines.

Christians, C. (2004). Ubuntu and communitarianism in media ethics. *Ecquid Novi: African Journalism Studies, 25*(2), 235–256. https://doi.org/10.1080/02560054.2004.9653296

Christians, C. (2019). *Media ethics and global justice in the digital age*. Cambridge University Press.

Ellul, J. (1885). *The humiliation of the word*. Eerdmans.

Evans-Pritchard, E. E. (1937). *Witchcraft, oracles, and magic among the Azande*. Clarendon.

Fackler, M., & Obonyo, L. (2014). Play theory and public media: A case study in Kenya editorial cartoons. In R. Fortner, & M. Fackler (Eds.), *The handbook of media and mass communication theory* (pp. 726–739). Wiley.

Goody, J. (1968). *Literacy in traditional societies*. Cambridge University Press.

Goody, J. (2000). *The power of the written tradition*. Smithsonian Institution Press.

Huizinga, J. (1950). *Homo ludens*. Beacon.

Ibahrine, M. (2014). Islam and social media. In K. Harvey (Ed.), *Encyclopedia of social media and politics* (pp. 737–741). Sage Publications.

Ihejirika, W. (2009). Research on media, religion and culture in Africa: Current trends and debates. *African Communication Research, 2*(1), 1–60 DOI: 10.1057/9781137264817_9.

Ishak, M. S. B. H., & Sohilin, M. S. (2012). Islam and media. *Asian Social Science, 8*(7), 263–269 DOI: 10.5539/ass.v8n7p263.

Jeffress, M. S. (2008). The role of multimedia tools in preaching according to recent homiletics texts: Toward a healthy theology of the convergence of multimedia tools and preaching. Paper presented to the meeting of the Evangelical Homiletics Society, Birmingham, AL. Retrieved July 30, 2022, from https://www.academia.edu/32081228/The_Role_of_Multimedia_Tools_in_Preaching_according_to_Recent_Homiletics_Texts_Toward_a_Healthy_Theology_of_the_Convergence_of_Multimedia_Tools_and_Preaching

Katangole, E. (2010). *The sacrifice of Africa*. Eerdmans.

Laing, A. (2017, May 24). Zimbabwean pastor 'talks to God on his mobile phone'. *The Times*. Retrieved July 30, 2022, from https://www.thetimes.co.uk/article/zimbabwean-pastor-talks-to-god-on-his-mobile-phone-j6hsbmdb7#:~:text=A%20Zimbabwean%20pastor%20has%20courted,Hello%2C%20is%20this%20heaven%3F%E2%80%9D

Lovrick, P., Deacon. (2017, May 16). Media technology in preaching: A Catholic response. Homiletic & Pastoral Review. Retrieved July 30, 2022, from https://www.hprweb.com/2017/05/media-technology-in-preaching

Mayor, F. (2001). *The world ahead*. Palgrave.

Mbiti, J. (1969). *African religions and philosophy*. Praeger.

Mbiti, J. (1975). *Introduction to African religion* (2nd ed.). Waveland.

McLuhan, M., & McLuhan, E. (1988). *Laws of media*. University of Toronto Press.

Mead, W. R. (2022, July 11). Wokeness is Putin's weapon: Russia and China capitalize on the West's moral and political confusion. *Wall Street Journal*. Retrieved July 30, 2022, from https://www.wsj.com/articles/wokeness-is-putins-weapon-ukraine-western-values-abortion-climate-change-human-rights-protectionism-decadence-xi-jinping-revisionist-powers-11657569787

Metz, T. (2012). African conceptions of human dignity. *Human Rights Review, 13*(1), 13–37 https://doi.org/10.1007/s12142-011-0200-4.

Metz, T. (2014). Dignity in the Ubuntu tradition. In M. Dunwell (Ed.), *The Cambridge handbook of human dignity: Interdisciplinary perspectives* (pp. 310–318). Cambridge University Press.

Mills, E., Cooper, C., & Kanfer, I. (2005). Traditional African medicine in the treatment of HIV. *Lancet, 5*(8), 465–467. https://doi.org/10.1016/S1473-3099(05)70172-9

Mokgobi, M. G. (2014). Understanding traditional African healing. *African Journal for Physical Health, Education, Recreation, and Dance, 20*(Suppl 2), 24–34.

Mosely, A. (2004). Witchcraft, science and the paranormal in contemporary African philosophy. In L. M. Brown (Ed.), *African philosophy: New and traditional perspectives* (pp. 136–156). Oxford.

Oasis International. (2012). *NTL Africa study bible*. Tyndale House.

Odozor, P. I. (2019, February 21). The essence of African traditional religion. *Church Life Journal: A Journal of the McGrath Institute for Church Life*. Retrieved July 30, 2022, from https://churchlifejournal.nd.edu/articles/the-essence-of-african-traditional-religion

Oladaemo, O. (2008). Theology of African traditional religion. National Open University of Nigeria. Retrieved July 30, 2022, from https://docslib.org/doc/3199124/theology-of-african-traditional-religion

Olupona, J. (2015, October 6). The spirituality of Africa. *The Harvard Gazette*. Retrieved July 30, 2022, from https://news.harvard.edu/gazette/story/2015/10/the-spirituality-of-africa

Ong, W. (1967). *The presence of the word*. Yale University Press.

Ong, W. (1974). Mass in Ewondo. *America, 28*, 148–151.

Ong, W. (1982). *Orality and literacy: The technologizing of the word*. Methuen.

Sadig, H. B. (2010). Ustadh Mahmoud Mohammed Taha and Islamic reform. In R. Fortner, & M. Fackler (Eds.), *Ethics and evil in the public sphere* (pp. 235–245). Hampton.

Schwab, P. (2002). *A continent self-destructs*. Palgrave.

Shorter, A., & Onyancha, E. (1997). *Secularism in Africa*. Paulines.

Witte, A. C. (2013). Preaching and technology: A study of attitudes and practices. PhD Dissertation, Graduate College of Bowling Green State University.

Yeboah, T. (2000). Improving the provision of traditional health knowledge for rural communities in Ghana. *Health Libraries Review, 17*, 203–208. https://doi.org/10.1111/j.1471-1842.2000.00297.x

Selected Readings

Buzo, B. (1997). *The ethical dimension of community*. Paulines.

Christians, C. (2019). *Media ethics and global justice in the digital age*. Cambridge.

Magesa, L. (1997). *African religion*. Paulines.

Mbiti, J. (1990). *African religions and philosophy* (2nd ed.). Heinemann.

Ogude, J., & Nyairo, J. (Eds.). (2007). *Urban legends, colonial myths: Popular culture and literature in East Africa*. Africa World Press.

Paris, P. (1995). *The spirituality of African people*. Augsburg.

Shaw, M., & Gitau, W. (2020). *The Kingdom of God in Africa* (rev ed.). Langham Global Library.

Shorter, A., & Onyacha, E. (1997). *Secularism in Africa*. Paulines.

9

Atheism and the Media

Teemu Taira

If one follows discussions concerning the relationship between atheism/atheists and the media, one may have heard someone suggesting that atheism is ubiquitous in the media. This claim is often made by a religious person who thinks that the media do not cover their group, community, or tradition favorably, fairly, or frequently. This person may also state that media professionals are atheists themselves or at least share the views and values of atheists rather than theirs. However, one may have also heard someone saying that atheism is absent from the media. This claim is frequently presented by atheists who do not see their group presented in media coverage. These two suggestions seem to contradict each other. However, on closer inspection, both claims can be true. Atheism can be considered ubiquitous in the media and largely invisible at the same time – present in the views and values of the journalists and other media professionals and inscribed in the logic of how the media work, but also almost absent in the coverage. This conundrum requires nuanced qualification, for there remains a tension between the two claims. However, it is good way to start thinking about the relationship between atheism and the media.

In what follows, I shall explore different areas where atheism, atheists, and media interact and overlap or are in conflict with each other. Atheism and media come in many forms. Most atheists are not organized and do not have a presence in the media as such; as will be seen, the media presence of atheism is primarily composed of organized atheists and a few celebrities and public intellectuals who tend to be more critical of religion than typical atheist individuals. Similarly, it should be kept in mind that the word media is plural. Here the emphasis will be on the traditional news media, especially in the first half of the chapter, but then the examination will be extended to other types of media, including entertainment media (films in particular) and online virtual environments, addressing select websites and social media that have been significant for the recent proliferation of atheism and atheists.

The word atheism has several meanings, but for the purposes of this overview I shall combine two typical understandings. First, atheism refers to a stated lack of belief in the existence of God, gods, or similar supernatural forces. Lack itself is not enough; it needs to be articulated one way or another – otherwise newborn babies would count as atheists, too. Second, atheism is an identification that people may apply to themselves, no matter their exact definition of the term. The most obvious case is when both of these two understandings apply. Much weaker cases are those where only one applies. I include all these under the term atheism, but I am mostly writing about atheists who are clear about their stated lack of theistic beliefs and who are likely to accept the term atheist as their self-identification.

The term atheism overlaps with other terms. In the past decade and a half, nonreligion has become a rival term used in self-identification, surveys, and media. Here I consider such terms

The Handbook on Religion and Communication, First Edition. Edited by Yoel Cohen and Paul A. Soukup.

practically synonymous in the media discourse, but acknowledge their difference as identity categories and as academic terms. However, none is a more specific term, because it has been established to signify a person with no religious affiliation. Another related term, secularism, is also somewhat different, because religious people can politically be secularists if they support the separation of religion from politics and the state, although it often refers to a belief system that is nonreligious in orientation.

While these rough working definitions do apply, it is worth remembering that there are multiple forms of atheism, nonreligion, and secularism. They differ according to countries and regions, as well as within areas. Atheism and secularism differ in India, Iran, Turkey, the Netherlands, France, Germany, the UK, the United States, Canada, and postsocialist countries (Berg-Sørensen, 2013; Bullivant & Ruse, 2013; Rectenwald et al., 2017), but generally atheism is relatively uncommon in many parts of Africa, Asia, and Latin America (Keysar & Navarro-Rivera, 2013).

Mainstream News Media and Approaches to Atheism

Despite regional variations, it is fair to suggest that the media "got secularism" (Cimino & Smith, 2014a) and atheism in the first decade of the twenty-first century in an unprecedented manner. Excluding the former and contemporary socialist and Communist countries (Froese, 2004; Yao & Liu, 2018), atheism had not been a widely discussed item in mainstream media as part of the "normal" landscape of religions and worldviews. In Muslim-majority countries, atheism has largely been an imagined enemy situated in the allegedly hedonistic and morally corrupt "West," with no real local representatives. In North America and Europe, atheism has been often seen as a threat to "our" society, as exemplified in the 1960s when the founder of American Atheists, Madalyn Murray O'Hair, was identified by *Life* magazine as the most hated woman in the United States, in the 1980s when atheists and Communists were labeled the enemies of Christian America by President Reagan himself, or in twentieth-century Finland where atheism was associated with its Communist neighbor (i.e. the Soviet Union) and perceived as threatening the existence of an independent, culturally Lutheran country. Atheism has also been seen as a minor phenomenon, condensed into the stereotype of the aggressive "village atheist" who always opposes what the rest decide to do (Schmidt, 2017). More positively, atheism has had a legitimate role among artists, scholars, intellectuals, and the media elite, as long as they have kept it to themselves.

It was not until the twenty-first century that atheism became an increasingly normal part of the everyday media landscape, being one possible viewpoint among others, in liberal democratic societies. Although its spokespersons (and some of its most eloquent opponents) are typically highly educated men in the natural sciences, their message addresses ordinary people much more directly than before and without explicit references to class struggles. There has been an increase in stories about atheism and atheists in news media (for examples from British, Finnish, and North American newspapers, see Knott et al., 2013, p. 103; Taira, 2012, p. 27; 2019a; Cimino & Smith, 2014b, pp. 88–93); this is partly due to the activity of outspoken "New Atheists" (Cimino & Smith, 2014a). In addition, the narrative about the rise of the "nones" began to form soon after the publication of "New Atheist" bestsellers in the 2000s, particularly in the United States but also in a more secular Europe. This was largely due to surveys where people reported having no religious affiliation. Some of them believe privately or individually, some are indifferent toward religion, and some are antireligious. In the media, however, the nones started to look like a homogeneous group that is growing fast and becoming the second biggest religious group after Christianity in several countries (Ramey, 2019). Arguably, a positive feedback loop was created: the media attention encouraged people to identify themselves as nones, which provided further reason for the media to write about nones. Moreover, this drove some nones to get organized and join various atheist, secular, and humanist groups. This was not an orchestrated project, but it worked in favor of what Richard Dawkins had hoped for in his *The God Delusion* (2006) – namely, that people would come out as atheists and nonreligious and encourage others to do so – knowing well that the media attention would follow.

Conservative Christians often claim that the mainstream news media has pro-atheist and liberal biases. One of the reference points for such a claim is a 2008 report from the politically conservative US-based Media Research Center. According to the report based on data from 2007, about 80% of feature stories about atheism were positive, and 71% of feature stories about Christian-themed stories gave an atheist's perspective on Christianity or atheism was mentioned as a counterpoint. This report analyzed 105 stories but only 21 feature stories about atheism, and, although the material was based on different sources, the selection did not contain the most conservative examples. The main data consisted of weekly magazines, such as *Time*, *Newsweek*, and *US News and World Report*. The feature stories in such publications were often informative and investigative rather than judgmental, especially if contrasted with popular tabloids. Furthermore, the data collection period arguably represented the high point in introductory news coverage of atheism, thanks to the publication of four books: Sam Harris's *Letter to a Christian Nation* (2007), Christopher Hitchens's *God Is Not Great* (2007), Richard Dawkins's *The God Delusion* (2006), and Daniel Dennett's *Breaking the Spell* (2006). Harris's first bestseller, *The End of Faith*, had already come out in 2004. This is the period when magazines and other media outlets were starting to grasp the "New Atheism" phenomenon. That name had been coined just a year earlier, in a *Wired* magazine story written by Gary Wolf in 2006 (Wolf, 2006). The overall conclusion of the report is at odds with most academic studies on the topic, but it reflects the claims that right-wing and conservative pro-Christian media often spread (Knott et al., 2013).

Scholars have suggested that religion is becoming more mediatized, as a larger segment of the population encounters religion through mainstream media than in face-to-face meetings. In a comparison between media institutions and religious communities, it is obvious that the former are more secular than the latter (Hjarvard, 2013). However, even if mediatization were to foster secularization, it would not yet necessarily lead to people turning into atheists. As Bruce (2002) argues, the most likely outcome of secularization (wherever that takes place) is indifference, not explicit and/or antireligious atheism. The media may well diminish the overall authority of religious leaders and institutions in secularizing regions, but there is little evidence of explicitly atheist bias in the media content itself (Taira, 2020).

Media biases tend to follow the society in question, meaning that in relatively liberal societies the majority of mainstream media outlets reflect and promote such values. However, even in liberal societies the media coverage is not particularly favorable for the antireligious viewpoints that many atheist activists wish to promote (Knott et al., 2013; Taira, 2015, 2020), and in some cases atheists are left outside of "religious programming" that is typically obligatory for public service broadcasting (Karis, 2018). How, then, is atheism represented in mainstream media?

There is a relative absence of atheism in media coverage, as most atheists do not appear in the media in that role. They are not easy to find, because only a small minority are organized. Atheists do not necessarily have a meeting place where journalists could go, whereas visiting a mosque or a synagogue is often a decent start for a news story. Furthermore, when news organizations have religion correspondents to cover news about religion, atheism is not automatically on their radar. And if it is, some atheists see this as problematic, since they do not want to be represented as atheists or as one group among religions. This is why the coverage of atheism tends to be dominated by two types of representatives: celebrity atheists and campaigning associations.

Celebrity atheists are frequently scientists interested in contributing to the public discussion, comedians, or otherwise established media persons. Campaigning associations contain secular societies, humanist groups, freethinkers, and atheists, and it depends primarily on national context which are most visible and what type of differences their public activities have. While some celebrities transcend national borders (particularly the most famous Anglophone atheists) and have become international media phenomena, most associations are visible in the media nationally and some only locally. Taken together, the visibility of those who represent atheism has increased, but the media rarely supports their views (Knott et al., 2013; Taira, 2015). They are, however, capable of raising issues for conversation so that atheist viewpoints are heard. While atheists do manage to affect what the media discusses, it is typical that the mainstream media favors the viewpoints of dominant religious institutions more than those of atheists. In their study of British media, Knott et al. (2013) conclude that the "media's normative position is the middle-ground between a campaigning atheism and an Evangelical or literalist Christianity" (p. 117) and they continue that the "media is rarely anti-religious," although Christianity is occasionally mocked; the media allows Christians to operate as moral specialists and representatives of the common good, but atheists are never in those roles (p. 117). In the US context, Cimino and Smith (2014b) suggest likewise that "mainstream media coverage remains problematic," as stories "often paint atheists as aggressive and belligerent" (p. 91). The situation is frequently worse when examples outside Europe and North America are examined. For instance, in Tunisia, where Islam is a state religion, the news media tend to portray atheists as Satan-worshipers, subsuming the former in the latter, in accordance with Islamic pressure-groups whose aim is to eradicate atheism from the country (Slima, 2021).

Left outside of media coverage in most countries are those ordinary atheists who are not celebrities or who do not speak with the voice of leading associations. This is important to note, as no atheist speaks for all atheists in the same way as a religious clergyperson may represent at least their congregation or church. It is understandable that the media gives more space for those atheists who are articulate and able to speak eloquently for the atheist cause, but this also means that the media struggles to communicate the variation within atheism. The majority of atheists do not actively campaign against religious institutions or hold antireligious views; most are rather indifferent toward religious issues. They do not necessarily approve of the presence and power of religious institutions in society, but the majority accept that individuals have every right to practice their religion.

Are Media Professionals Atheists?

It is common for religious people to assume that media professionals are atheists, especially if their coverage does not please them. Similar thoughts have been aired by scholars too. For instance, Berger et al. (2008, p. 60) write that Dawkins speaks to a significant minority, and "they will also be clustered in certain professions, notably *the media*." Although they do not explicitly claim that media professionals are atheists – they simply argue that Dawkins has appeal to media professionals – that is largely implied in their comment. They are not completely wrong, but this common assumption about atheistic media professionals should be nuanced.

Most of the studies on media professionals who frequently report about religion have been based on the United States. The studies from the 1990s did not reveal major differences in the religious outlook of media professionals and the population in general (Buddenbaum, 1998). More recent research shows that while media professionals in general tend to be less religious than the rest of the population, the "focused producers" (i.e. those who frequently cover religion in their profession) are more religious than media professionals in general (Weaver et al., 2007; Winston & Green, 2012). Winston and Green (2012) found that more than half of focused producers considered religion extremely important and almost all were affiliated with a religious tradition. By contrast, only 20% of all media professionals held religion to be extremely important, even though a large number (87%) also belonged to a religious tradition (Taira, 2015, pp. 111–112). Although people with no religious affiliation are overrepresented among media professionals, they are underrepresented among the focused producers of religion-related media content. The share of atheists is even smaller, as many people not affiliated with a religion believe in God.

Some studies of different European countries have touched upon this issue and their tentative evidence – though based on small samples – points toward a similar conclusion: media professionals who cover religion are far from the stereotypical antireligious atheist (Taira, 2015). If there is a link between personal convictions or attitudes and media content, it is hard to conclude that the media professionals who cover religion (including atheism) would be particularly biased in favor of atheism. It remains an open question whether religiosity of media professionals in general – being more likely to be atheists than the rest of the population – has a significant impact on how atheism is covered in the media.

The personal religiosity and attitudes of media professionals are only a part of the story. Multiple factors contribute to how media professionals deal with religion – for example, editorial policy, ownership, education, and the pressure to produce publishable stories in a short time frame. The editorial policies of news outlets structure the viewpoints of individual journalists, particularly in matters relevant for the outlets themselves, and in some cases the owners dictate the take on the topic. This means that economic and political issues, more often than religion, are controlled by the editors-in-chief and owners. However, in cases where the owners are known for representing a particular religion (such as Catholics in the case of *The Daily Telegraph* in the UK) or where a significant part of the readership represents a particular religion (such as Laestadians, a Protestant revival movement, in the case of *Kaleva* in the area of Oulu in Finland), there are limits to how fierce the journalistic critique toward a particular religious institution or movement can be. It is also the case that the style, genre, and discursive practices of the outlet determine the extent to which atheism is prevalent. For instance, in the context of newspapers, broadsheets typically have a respectful approach to religion and atheism, but they also publish investigative, skilled, and sometimes critical analyses, whereas tabloids tend to support the dominant religion among their readers, taking a position against atheists, even when also publishing mocking stories about hypocritical religious leaders. This means that media outlets and their operating logic condition a certain type of coverage, which is rarely only positive or negative, but even then there is a greater tendency to support the familiar religion rather than atheist activism, especially in societies where a particular religion is established or followed by the majority of the population.

An additional factor is that in the age of newspaper crises, media companies have reduced the number of religion reporters. This is changing how religion and atheism are covered, but it is too early to be sure exactly how. It is likely that religion will not have a special section in the news or that professionals who cover such a section will cover several other areas, too, as the issue is not only about the religion beat: "all specialty beats at newspapers, including the environment, health, and education, are suffering as newspapers, with shrinking budgets, allocate an increasing fraction of their diminished newsroom staffs to general assignment jobs" (Paulson, 2009). This does not mean that atheism or antireligion is becoming a dominant viewpoint among the journalists, but it may mean that professionals have less special knowledge concerning religion and atheism.

How Do Atheists Interact with the Mainstream Media?

If it is the case that atheists do not always get the mainstream media coverage they would like to have, there are several ways in which atheists still utilize the media logic for their own purposes. One of the main tactics is to send press releases to media professionals. A problem with this is that the media do not necessarily find it newsworthy to publish stories on the basis of such releases; they often need to include more general information than what might be interpreted as simply an advertisement for an atheist group.

A good example of successful work with press releases is the Finnish web portal *Eroa kirkosta* (Resign from the Church). Launched in 2003, it is run by atheist activists, and its main service is to provide people with a means to unsubscribe from membership in a religious community in Finland. Three quarters of a million Finns have used the service and currently most resignations take place via this website. The website records the resignation numbers and collects information about the reasons people give for their decision. The people who run the website make press releases and sometimes the mainstream media publish them with few changes. The media find them interesting, and it would be very laborious for the journalists to get such information otherwise. This is an example where a few atheists are able to feed the media with stories that favor them.

Another tactic is to send letters to the editor. This traditional way of contributing to public discussion and opinion formation may seem old-fashioned in the era of social media, but it continues to have weight, particularly in the highly appreciated newspapers. Many printed newspapers have become rather slim, and they have reduced the space reserved for readers' letters. The ones that get published are seen as more significant than they would have been a couple of decades ago, when many newspapers printed several pages of readers' letters every single day. When Pope Benedict XVI came to the UK in 2010, Dawkins and a group of atheists, public intellectuals, and celebrities signed a letter that was published in *The Guardian* on the first day of the papal visit, suggesting that the Pope should not be honored with a state visit. The opinion of Dawkins and others was already known by many, and they could have aired their views on social media without any effort, but publishing a letter in a valued newspaper had symbolic value and it played into media logic: the letter itself became a news item for several papers and news outlets (see Knott et al., 2013, p. 168).

Although writing a letter to the editor still has value, as it has more weight than a random comment in a discussion forum, a lot of such opinion sharing takes place on social media, particularly Twitter and Facebook. While Facebook functions better for internal interaction among those who already agree about the need for such activism, thus being an example of bonding, Twitter is better for reaching a wider external audience. As many news stories nowadays originate from social media posts, it is a relevant channel for interacting with and reacting to the mainstream media – in terms of both feeding potential topics for media and journalists and responding to what has already been published.

Media campaigns are one of the most effective tactics in getting attention. They are often connected with court cases, particularly in the United States. There has been an increase in such attempts in the past couple of decades when groups have aimed to achieve a recognizable position in American public life (Wexler, 2019). Take The Satanic Temple (TST), for example. TST is a practically secularist and atheist organization, whose fifth "fundamental tenet" underlines that "beliefs should conform to one's best scientific understanding of the world." For TST, Satan is a symbol, not a figure that should be conflated with the Satan of theistic Satanism. Since its early days in 2013, it has launched several court cases, most of them pending at the time of writing (Laycock, 2020). As part of these cases, it has sought media attention and shown a high-level understanding of what media professionals find to be an interesting story to cover. Furthermore, a relatively popular and acclaimed documentary, *Hail Satan!*, was made in 2019 about TST (directed by Penny Lane).

Laycock (2020) classifies TST's tactics into three types: legalistic, Satanic philanthropy, and Satanic culture jamming. They all have a media dimension but in different ways. The first refers to attempts to take cases to court, and such cases often attract the media's interest. Satanic philanthropy consists of TST's civic engagement in helping people in various locales, for instance. This is interesting for the media, because that is not what "evil Satanists" are supposed to do. Satanic culture jamming refers to performances whose primary goal is to seek attention (from the media) by shocking the audience. Largely because of its media skills, the group enjoys a disproportionately great deal of success. TST's media strategy has been successful because it has appropriated the controversial figure of Satan and at the same time has been active in civic engagement. While media attention toward Satanism is not new, here the relevant point is that it would be much more difficult for different atheistic groups, including humanists, secularists, and freethinkers, to get the attention that TST and its nontheistic Satanic predecessors have received quite easily.

It is not that atheistic groups are not trying to get their activities covered, but there have not been many large-scale media campaigns. The multinational atheist bus campaign in 2009 and following years is an exception. This originated in the UK when the British Humanist Association, Dawkins, and comedian Ariane Sherine (who created the idea) bought bus advertisements stating: "There's probably no God. Now stop worrying and enjoy your life." The UK and 14 other countries where the campaign took place in some form or was planned to take place have been examined in detail, including the media responses (Tomlins & Bullivant, 2017).

The whole campaign aimed at media attention. In the UK, only a small minority saw any of the buses, but many heard about the campaign and the slogan used in it, because the advertisement was discussed widely in the media. The pattern was generally similar in those countries where the campaign was not disrupted. The mainstream media reported it as an interesting story but did not openly support it. The overall attitude was reserved. There was space for supportive individual voices, but also for those who vehemently opposed the campaign or thought that it had little or no purpose (Taira, 2017).

In some cases, religious actors reacted negatively to the campaign, such as in Spain, where Catholic bishops produced a press release that accused it of blasphemy and damaging religious freedom. In Canada and the UK, however, some religious people openly supported it (Tomlins & Bullivant, 2017; see also Knott et al., 2013, pp. 105–106). In other contexts, such as Brazil – the only Latin American country where a version of the campaign took place – the news media were silent about the event and the online publicity did not reach the mainstream media (Montero & Dullo, 2017). The main organization there, the Brazilian Association of Atheists and Agnostics, struggles to get its message through in the traditional news media in general.

Audiovisual Representations of Atheism

Only some of the campaigns have been effective, and from the media and communication perspective, an at least equally relevant phenomenon is the proliferation of atheistic documentaries in the twenty-first century. Examples include *Atheism: A Rough History of Disbelief* (2004–2007, also known as *A Brief History of Disbelief*), *The Atheism Tapes* (2004), *The God Who Wasn't There* (2005), *The Root of All Evil?* (2006), *The Enemies of Reason* (2007), *The Four Horsemen* (2008), *Religulous* (2008), *Faith School Menace* (2010), and *The Unbelievers* (2013). These documentaries address from the atheistic perspective the question of how humans should live. None of them targets specific groups but religiosity in general. Moreover, although the documentaries promote atheism, they do not describe the atheistic lifestyle in detail; instead, they focus on what is wrong with religion.

Several of these documentaries refer to 9/11 and Islamic terrorism explicitly, and many of them address more mundane worries about the organization of education in a particular country. The production has revolved around a small number of atheistic celebrities. For example, Dawkins has been involved in more than half of the films mentioned above. In addition, the development of media technologies, particularly in terms of distribution, has facilitated their reach. Many of the documentaries have been broadcast on television, it is possible to buy them as DVDs, and some can be watched via video-streaming services. Contemporary documentaries generally have potential for broad dissemination at very low cost, and their form is sufficiently entertaining. As Nichols (2017) argues, "Documentary has become the flagship for a cinema of social engagement and distinctive vision" (p. 1). One could add that documentary film has also become one of the means by which atheistic media activism takes place and reaches public discussion concerning religion (Taira, 2022).

Despite the resurgence of interest in the documentary genre, fiction films are typically more popular. However, in one of the few overviews of atheism and film, Nina Power (2013) notes that "surprisingly little has been written about the relationship between atheism and film at the formal or conceptual level" (p. 727). This is still true. There are also relatively few descriptions of atheism in individual films. One notable popular exception is *Inherit the Wind* (1960), based on the so-called Scopes Monkey Trial of 1925. In addition, there are several atheistic directors whose works have been addressed in studies focusing on atheism and film, such as David Cronenberg, Pier Paolo Pasolini, Sergei Eisenstein, and Dziga Vertov (Power, 2013). However, some of them reflect a sympathetic approach to religion by an atheist, as in the case of Pasolini's *The Gospel According to St. Matthew* (Il Vangelo secondo Matteo, 1964). Moreover, one finds popular films that are interpreted as critiques of religion (Blizek, 2013), and some of them have drawn accusations of blasphemy, such as *Monty Python's Life of Brian* (1979, dir. Terry Jones) and *The Last Temptation of Christ* (1988, dir. Martin Scorsese), but they do not address atheism as such (Taira, 2022). More recent relevant examples are *Contact* (1997, dir. Robert Zemeckis), in which the main protagonist is a sympathetic character whose atheist identity has a role in the plot; a biographical drama film about Madalyn Murray O'Hair, *The Most Hated Woman in America* (2017, dir. Tommy O'Haver); and *The Ledge* (2011), whose director Matthew Chapman advertised it as the first American pro-atheist feature film with an openly atheist hero (Walsh, 2011).

Does the Online Media Environment Lead People to Become Atheists?

So far it has been suggested that although atheists have found ways to interact with the media and use the channels appropriate for them, the mainstream media does not offer special support for the atheist cause. It may facilitate the processes in which people become atheists, but social media and more limited "micropublics" have been even more relevant. There are several ways in which they may lead people to become atheists and sustain the atheistic identity.

Some celebrity atheists provide an example and encouragement for individuals. The "New Atheists" have worked hard to bring atheism and criticism of religion into public debates. They have published best-selling books that people have found inspirational, and they have participated in several debates that are available on YouTube, for example. Although it is not clear how big an influence the views of celebrity intellectuals have had on people who have become atheists, some have stated that the mediated activism of Dawkins and others has contributed to their decision to abandon religion (Cimino & Smith, 2014b; Kontala, 2016, p. 108).

Not completely unlike the secularist press in Victorian England, websites – containing information about atheism and like-minded people – can empower people to become atheists if they have doubts but are otherwise uncertain about "coming out" (Nash, 2002). Some bloggers, such as American biology professor Paul Zachary "PZ" Myers and his Pharangyla blog, spread the message of atheism effectively, whereas websites such as WikiIslam focus on a specific tradition and its problems. There are several websites where exit stories and conversation narratives are shared. Some of these are connected to atheist activism, such as the Richard Dawkins Foundation for Science and Reason, which has a Convert's Corner where people can leave testimonies on how they became nonreligious or atheists. Others are not explicitly atheist; rather, they focus on sharing the narratives of people who have left a particular tradition, such as Mormonism (Avance, 2013) or Islam (Enstedt & Larsson, 2013; Taira, 2019b).

Particularly in some Asian and African contexts where information about atheism is limited in the public sphere and the mainstream media, and where identifying as atheist is harmful or dangerous, the Internet has proved to be a game-changer for many individuals. For example, Candice Breitz's seven-channel art installation *Love Story* (2016) includes an interview with Farah Abdi Mohamed (an assumed name), who explains how he became an atheist and a refugee. He escaped Somalia in 2012 because he feared being killed as an atheist in an Islamic country. He arrived first in Cairo, Egypt, and then fled to Europe. He was afraid that the Muslim community would isolate him if he did not believe, so rather than talking to other people, he started to look up information on the Internet. Soon he found many people who had doubts and he became very happy that he was not alone. He also found the terms "atheism" and "atheist" on the Internet. In Somalia, he was afraid to type such words into the search engine and he always emptied the browser cache after doing so. This testimony is an example of a general pattern, where becoming an atheist can be a slow and rocky process, with the Internet playing an important facilitating rather than constitutive role (Taira, 2021).

Some of the examples may give the impression that the Internet and social media are liberatory units isolated from the more pro-religious mainstream media. In some cases that is correct, especially in societies where public expression of atheism is not allowed or tolerated, but in liberal democratic societies it is more common that there is interaction and convergence between the mainstream media and different websites or discussion forums. People begin to share their views anonymously in a discussion forum and become empowered to go public about their experiences (Nash, 2002). When the news media give space for their experiences, it makes it slightly easier for those in doubt to leave a movement, recognize that they are not alone with their feelings, or at least realize that the leaders of the movement may struggle to justify some of their practices (Taira, 2019b, pp. 340–341).

These are examples of how the media can stimulate people to become atheists or abandon their religion, even when the news media's general approach to religion is supportive. In addition to these, the overall role of the logic of the Internet and social media has been discussed by scholars. The Internet and social media have become ubiquitous in the everyday life of a significant part of the world's population since the mid-2000s. Their relation to religion is far from a settled issue, as they have allowed new religious expressions to flourish while also making possible the thriving of atheistic online communities. Generally, it can be said that the Internet tends to favor a short-term attention span (surfing and browsing from one page to another), and it makes it easy to find information that challenges one's inherited truths and beliefs (Zuckerman, 2014, pp. 71–72). In that sense, the Internet and social media are potentially "liberatory" from closed communities and their teachings. It is therefore common to find stories about people who have found support for their atheism online, especially by people who live in strongly religious countries where public declarations of atheism are not allowed or even information about atheism is not available outside the Internet (Nieuwkerk, 2018; Taira, 2019b, 2021; Whitaker, 2014).

Many of these nations are in Africa and Asia, also being Muslim-majority countries. There are famous examples from Indonesia, where stating one's atheism on Facebook has resulted in a prison sentence and serious threats by Muslims (Taira, 2021). In Indonesia and several other Muslim-majority countries, and in Hindu-dominated India, atheism does not figure much in the mainstream media, at least in a neutral or positive manner. Despite the relative freedom of the media, they and journalists are often financially dependent on the majority groups. In such a situation, online forums have developed strong supportive networks for atheists and also served as arenas providing tools for potential counter-narratives that would change the role and status of atheism (Atack, 2014; Binder, 2020; Khatib, 2018; Schäfer, 2016). Furthermore, in post-Soviet contexts, the online environment has made it possible to challenge the existing presence of old, Soviet-style atheist representations in favor of more Western-style ones (Louw, 2019).

If the Internet supports people in becoming atheists, it can also help people maintain their identity, despite the fact that only a very small minority of those who abandon religion turn into atheist activists. Thanks to the Internet and social media, atheists are not left alone with their views, because they are able to find like-minded people and forums – even algorithms may take care of that – and receive positive feedback for their atheism. However, some scholars have noted that social media's atheist echo chamber does not constitute only a supportive, happy family. Laughlin (2016) suggests that there are significant limits to Internet-mediated atheism. The Internet offers some semblance of the communal for atheists, but web-based atheism is more of an example of a temporary discourse than a movement, community, or institution, as it depends on the attention it gets. When attention decreases or is not continually maintained, the community practically ceases to exist. Furthermore, the community may prove to be internally divided, as demonstrated by Laughlin (2016) and Lundmark (2019). The latter also shows how atheist women vloggers (video bloggers) in the United States have constituted their own atheist counter-public against what they consider too male-dominated and sometimes even sexist atheist online communities.

Future Prospects

This chapter has mapped the complex relations between atheism and the media, suggesting that mainstream media content and media professionals are not as supportive of atheism and atheists as people often think they are, but revealing at the same time how the mainstream media's attention-seeking logic, which increasingly favors opinion and commentary rather than traditional and more expensive news content (see Meltzer, 2019), tends to provide a space for controversies and conflict between religious people and atheists. Furthermore, atheist activities in online environments have successfully contributed to this situation. Overall, the media may provide opportunities for doubters to "come out" as atheists, but it would be an exaggeration to suggest that the media are the main or even a key factor in people becoming atheists.

"New Atheism" was a fresh phenomenon in the first decade of the twenty-first century, and the most famous international campaigns following that exposure were widely reported. Enthusiasm and increasing interest lasted for several years, but in the early 2020s the attraction has plateaued. Hitchens passed away in 2011. Turning 80 years old in 2022, Dennett is only occasionally involved in commenting on religion. And although Dawkins – aged 81 in 2022 – has continued his antireligious activism on Twitter and other media forms, people are paying less attention to him than 10–15 years ago. Harris is younger (55 in 2022) and rather actively involved in public debates on religion, but he has lost some former supporters owing to Internet controversies. No new celebrities of the same caliber have replaced them or filled the media space they have left behind. This may give us reasons to focus more on local (national and regional) contexts and the convergence between the mainstream media and social media in researching and theorizing mediated atheism.

After all the examples from different parts of the world and thematic explorations of relations between atheism/atheists and the media, it may come as a surprise how little research has been done on this. What is also problematic is that atheism, secularism, and nonreligion have not yet become standard parts of textbooks about religion and media (see Arthur, 1993; Mahan, 2014; Stout, 2012). Likewise, handbooks about atheism barely mention news media (Bullivant & Ruse, 2013; Martin, 2007; see, however, Cimino & Smith, 2014a). Currently, there is plenty of research focusing on religion and the media as well as atheism and nonreligion, but few scholars have dedicated their focus to atheism and the media. That is why it would be forced to construct any established canon in the study area, although some useful examples – many of them already mentioned in this chapter – should facilitate future studies.

Regarding the mainstream news media, Silk's (1995) more than 25-year-old study on making news of religion in the United States is still a good example of how nuanced research can challenge the assumptions about the atheistic news media. Silk shows how the news production concerning religion is "unsecular," meaning that the media present religion from a religious point of view, primarily because religious values are embedded in American culture at large. If religious values and institutions lose their hold on society, it might change the balance in the media too. More recently, Knott et al. (2013) examined how media portrayals of religion and the secular have changed in British media from the early 1980s to early 2010s. Writing extensively about atheism and atheists, they include these as a significant part of the changing media landscape regarding religion. There are also some studies that expand and update their findings by focusing more specifically on atheism and atheists in mainstream media (Taira, 2015, 2020).

There are some studies highlighting the relevance of digital and social media. For example, scholars have examined the role of the Internet for individual atheists and secularist communities, particularly in the United States (Addington, 2019; Cimino & Smith, 2014b; Nash, 2002). Lundmark (2019) has studied how American women vloggers construct precarious counter-publics through their performatives, and Laughlin (2016) has theorized the relevance of virtual spaces for atheist micropublics. Taira (2019b, 2021b) has written several articles mapping the potential importance of the Internet and social media for atheists, and Chalfant (2020) is one of the few who has emphasized the relevance of the role of the media in studies on atheism. Studies focusing on Asia, Africa, and Muslim-majority countries usually highlight social media (Schäfer, 2016; Whitaker, 2014).

To conclude, atheism is easily seen as ubiquitous in the media, especially if one assumes that the media do not support one's own religious values and viewpoints. Atheism is also seen as almost absent from the media, because its visibility is relative and limited primarily to select celebrity atheists and a few campaigning associations. Studies on media portrayals of atheism and atheists in liberal democratic societies suggest that the media are far from supportive of atheism or atheists as such, especially the most antireligious forms, but favor individual freedom as opposed to the assumed limitations conservative (religious) groups try to impose on people. However, media logic may in fact favor the erosion of religious authorities, and that is one of the reasons why people may perceive that the media are in service of atheism. Practically all studies of atheism in online environments highlight its significance in terms of forming and sustaining atheist identity, and such environments are particularly relevant in societies in which mainstream media expressions of atheism are limited or suppressed. Several of these findings and suggestions can be contested and nuanced, but in order to do so convincingly, scholars should do more research on the topic.

References

Addington, A. (2019). Building bridges in the shadow of steeples: Atheist community and identity online. In R. Cragun, C. Manning, & L. Fazzino (Eds.), *Organized secularism in the United States* (pp. 135–149). De Gruyter.

Arthur, C. (Ed.), (1993). *Religion and the media: An introductory reader*. University of Wales Press.

Atack, E.-L. (2014). *Indonesian atheists, marginalised communities, and the internet as a tool for empowerment and action* Indonesia Studies Program. Monash University.

Avance, R. (2013). Seeing the light: Mormon conversion and deconversion narratives in off- and online worlds. *Journal of Media and Religion, 12*(1), 16–24. https://doi.org/10.1080/15348423.2013.760386

Berger, P., Davie, G., & Fokas, E. (2008). *Religious America, secular Europe: A theme and variations*. Ashgate.

Berg-Sørensen, A. (Ed.), (2013). *Contesting secularism: Comparative perspectives*. Ashgate.

Binder, S. (2020). Storytelling and mediation: The aesthetics of a counter-narrative of atheism in South India. In D. Johannsen, A. Kirsch, & J. Kreinath (Eds.), *Narrative cultures and the aesthetics of religion* (pp. 219–245). Brill.

Blizek, W. (2013). Using movies to critique religion. In W. Blizek (Ed.), *The Bloomsbury companion to religion and film* (pp. 39–48). Bloomsbury.

Bruce, S. (2002). *God is dead: Secularization in the west*. Blackwell.

Buddenbaum, J. (1998). *Reporting news about religion: An introduction for journalists*. Iowa State University.

Bullivant, S., & Ruse, M. (Eds.). (2013). *The Oxford handbook of atheism*. Oxford University Press.

Chalfant, E. (2020). Material irreligion: The role of media in atheist studies. *Religion Compass, 14*(3), e12349. https://doi.org/10.1111/rec3.12349

Cimino, R., & Smith, C. (2014a). How the media got secularism – With a little help from the new atheists. Oxford Handbooks Online. Oxford University Press. https://doi.org/10.1093/oxfordhb/9780199935420.013.15. Retrieved February 23, 2022, from https://www.oxfordhandbooks.com/view/10.1093/oxfordhb/9780199935420.001.0001/oxfordhb-9780199935420-e-15?rskey=AFY8bD&result=1

Cimino, R., & Smith, C. (2014b). *Atheist awakening: Secular activism and community in America*. Oxford University Press.

Dawkins, R. (2006). *The God delusion*. Black Swan.

Dennett, D. C. (2006). *Breaking the spell: Religion as a natural phenomenon*. Penguin.

Enstedt, D., & Larsson, G. (2013). Telling the truth about Islam? Apostasy narratives and representation of Islam on WikiIslam.net. *CyberOrient, 7*(1), 64–93. https://cyberorient.net/2013/05/10/telling-the-truth-aboutislam-apostasy-narratives-and-representations-of-islam-on-wikiislam-net

Froese, P. (2004). Forced secularization in Soviet Russia: Why an atheistic monopoly failed? *Journal for the Scientific Study of Religion, 43*(1), 35–50. https://doi.org/10.1111/j.1468-5906.2004.00216.x

Harris, S. (2004). *The end of faith: Religion, terror, and the future of reason*. W. W. Norton & Company.

Harris, S. (2007). *Letter to a Christian nation*. Alfred A. Knopf.

Hitchens, C. (2007). *God is not great: How religion poisons everything*. Twelve.

Hjarvard, S. (2013). *The mediatization of culture and society*. Routledge.

Karis, T. (2018). Secular voices on air: The British debate on *thought for the day*. *Journal for Religion, Media and Digital Culture, 7*(3), 329–345. https://doi.org/10.1163/21659214-00703006

Keysar, A., & Navarro-Rivera, J. (2013). A world of atheism: Global demographics. In S. Bullivant, & M. Ruse (Eds.), *The Oxford handbook of atheism* (pp. 553–586). Oxford University Press.

Khatib, H. (2018). Atheists in Muslim majority countries: Between inclusion and exclusion. Sicherheitspolitik-blog, Retrieved February 23, 2022, from https://www.eurasiareview.com/27052018-atheists-in-muslim-majority-countriesbetween-inclusion-and-exclusion-oped

Knott, K., Poole, E., & Taira, T. (2013). *Media portrayals of religion and the secular sacred: Representation and change*. Ashgate.

Kontala, J. (2016). *Emerging non-religious worldview prototypes: A faith-Q-sort-study on Finnish group-affiliates*. Åbo Akademi University Press.

Laughlin, J. (2016). Varieties of an atheist public in a digital age: The politics of recognition and the recognition of politics. *Journal of Religion, Media and Digital Culture, 5*(2), 315–338. https://doi.org/10.1163/21659214-90000084

Laycock, J. (2020). *Speak of the devil: How the Satanic Temple is changing the way we talk about religion*. Oxford University Press.

Louw, M. (2019). Atheism 2.0: Searching for spaces for atheism in contemporary Kyrgyzstan. *Central Asian Affairs*, 6(2–3), 206–223. https://doi.org/10.1163/22142290-00602007

Lundmark, E. (2019). *"This is the face of an atheist": Performing private truths in precarious publics*. Uppsala University.

Mahan, J. (2014). *Media, religion and culture: An introduction*. Routledge.

Martin, M. (Ed.). (2007). *The Cambridge companion to atheism*. Cambridge University Press.

Meltzer, K. (2019). *From news to talk: The expansion of opinion and commentary in U.S. journalism*. SUNY.

Montero, P., & Dullo, E. (2017). Brazil: The invisibility of the Brazilian bus campaign. In S. Tomlins, & S. C. Bullivant (Eds.), *The atheist bus campaign: Global manifestations and responses* (pp. 50–80). Brill.

Nash, D. (2002). Religious sensibilities in the age of the internet: Freethought culture and the historical context of communication media. In S. Hoover, & L. S. Clark (Eds.), *Practicing religion in the age of the media* (pp. 276–290). Columbia University Press.

Nichols, B. (2017). *Introduction to documentary* (3rd ed.). Indiana University Press.

Nieuwkerk, K. v. (2018). Nonbelieving in Egypt. In K. van Nieuwkerk (Ed.), *Moving in and out of Islam* (pp. 306–332). University of Texas Press.

Paulson, M. (2009). Religion reporting is losing its prominence in American newspapers. *The Boston Globe*. Retrieved February 23, 2022, from http://archive.boston.com/news/local/massachusetts/articles/2009/09/13/religion_reporting_is_losing_its_prominence_in_american_newspapers

Power, N. (2013). Film. In S. Bullivant, & M. Ruse (Eds.), *The Oxford handbook of atheism* (pp. 727–734). Oxford University Press.

Ramey, S. (2019). Nostalgia and the discourse concerning "nones". In V. Touna (Ed.), *Strategic acts in the study of identity: Towards a dynamic theory of people and place* (pp. 21–47). Equinox.

Rectenwald, M., Almeida, R., & Levine, G. (Eds.). (2017). *Global secularisms in a post-secular age*. De Gruyter.

Schäfer, S. (2016). Forming 'forbidden' identities online: Atheism in Indonesia. *ASEAS – Austrian Journal of South-East Asian Studies*, 9(2), 253–268. https://doi.org/10.14764/10.ASEAS-2016.2-5

Schmidt, L. E. (2017). *Village atheists: How America's unbelievers made their way in a godly nation*. Princeton University Press.

Silk, M. (1995). *Unsecular media: Making news of religion in America*. University of Illinois Press.

Slima, Y. B. (2021). Tunisia. In S. Bullivant, & M. Ruse (Eds.), *The Cambridge history of atheism*. Cambridge University Press.

Stout, D. (2012). *Media and religion: Foundations of an emerging field*. Routledge.

Taira, T. (2012). More visible but limited in its popularity: Atheism (and atheists) in Finland. *Approaching Religion*, 2(1), 21–45. https://doi.org/10.30664/ar.67489

Taira, T. (2015). Media and the nonreligious. In K. Granholm, M. Moberg, & S. Sjö (Eds.), *Religion, media, and social change* (pp. 110–125). Routledge.

Taira, T. (2017). Finland: The recognition and rearticulation of atheism in public discourse. In S. Tomlins, & S. C. Bullivant (Eds.), *The atheist bus campaign: Global manifestations and responses* (pp. 139–156). Brill.

Taira, T. (2019a). From Lutheran dominance to diversity: Religion in Finnish newspapers 1946–2018. *Temenos: Nordic Journal of Comparative Religion*, 55(2), 225–247. https://doi.org/10.33356/temenos.87827

Taira, T. (2019b). Media and communication approaches to leaving religion. In D. Enstedt, G. Larsson, & T. Mantsinen (Eds.), *Handbook of leaving religion* (pp. 335–348). Brill.

Taira, T. (2020). The negotiation of religious authorities in European journalism. In K. Radde-Antweiler, & X. Zeiler (Eds.), *The Routledge handbook of religion and journalism* (pp. 95–108). Routledge.

Taira, T. (2021). The internet and the social media revolution. In S. Bullivant, & M. Ruse (Eds.), *The Cambridge history of atheism* (pp. 1024–1039). Cambridge University Press.

Taira, T. (2022). Atheistic documentaries and the critique of religion in Bill Maher's *Religulous*. In T. Eaghll, & R. King (Eds.), *Representing religion in film* (pp. 27–39). Bloomsbury.

Tomlins, S., & Bullivant, S. C. (Eds.). (2017). *The atheist bus campaign: Global manifestations and responses*. Brill.

Walsh, S. (2011). New atheist movie 'The Ledge' evangelizes godlessness. CNN Belief Blog. Retrieved February 23, 2022, from https://religion.blogs.cnn.com/2011/07/08/new-atheist-movie-the-ledge-evangelizes-godlessness

Weaver, D., Beam, R., Brownlee, B., Voakes, P., & Wilhoit, G. C. (2007). *The American journalist in the 21st century: U.S. news people at the dawn of the millennium.* Lawrence Erlbaum Associates.

Wexler, J. (2019). *Our non-Christian nation: How atheists, satanists, pagans, and others are demanding their rightful place in public life.* Redwood Press.

Whitaker, B. (2014). *Arabs without God: Atheism and freedom of belief in the Middle East.* Create Space Independent Publishing Platform.

Winston, D., & Green, J. (2012). *Most Americans say religion coverage too sensationalized.* USC Annenberg. Retrieved February 23, 2022, from https://annenberg.usc.edu/most-americans-say-media-coverage-religion-too-sensationalized

Wolf, G. (2006). The church of the non-believers. *Wired.* Retrieved May 24, 2021, from https://www.wired.com/2006/11/atheism

Yao, Q., & Liu, Z. (2018). Media and religion in China: Publicizing gods under an atheistic governance. In Y. Cohen (Ed.), *Spiritual news: Reporting religion around the world* (pp. 179–198). Peter Lang.

Zuckerman, P. (2014). *Living the secular life: New answers to old questions.* Penguin.

Selected Readings

Barnett, C. R. (2021). Film and television. In S. Bullivant, & M. Ruse (Eds.), *The Cambridge history of atheism* (pp. 740–759). Cambridge University Press.

Bird, S. E. (2009). True believers and atheists need not apply: Faith and mainstream television drama. In D. Winston (Ed.), *Small screen, big picture: Television and lived religion* (pp. 17–41). Baylor University Press.

Chalfant, E. (2020). Material irreligion: The role of media in atheist studies. *Religion Compass, 14*(3), e12349. https://doi.org/10.1111/rec3.12349

Cimino, R., & Smith, C. (2014). How the media got secularism – With a little help from the new atheists. *Oxford Handbooks Online.* Oxford University Press. https://doi.org/10.1093/oxfordhb/9780199935420.013.15

Knott, K., Poole, E., & Taira, T. (2013). *Media portrayals of religion and the secular sacred: Representation and change.* Ashgate.

Laughlin, J. (2016). Varieties of an atheist public in a digital age: The politics of recognition and the recognition of politics. *Journal of Religion, Media and Digital Culture, 5*(2), 315–338. https://doi.org/10.1163/21659214-90000084

Taira, T. (2021). The internet and the social media revolution. In S. Bullivant, & M. Ruse (Eds.), *The Cambridge history of atheism* (pp. 1024–1039). Cambridge University Press.

Part III

Religions as Actors

10

Religious Broadcasting: An Overview, 2000–2021

Jim McDonnell

Introduction

The first religious broadcast, a service from Calvary Episcopal Church, Pittsburgh, United States, took place a century ago in January 1921. A year later in December 1922, the BBC broadcast its first religious talk. Since those days, a myriad of churches, religious groups, and individual preachers have embraced, some cautiously, others with enthusiasm, radio, television, the Internet, and now social media. How that adaptation occurred and the importance and relevance of religious broadcasting today vary from continent to continent.

This overview focuses on traditional forms of over-the-air religious broadcasting as developments in online and digital broadcasting are covered elsewhere in this Handbook. It also concentrates on the broadcasting of religious programs rather than studies of how religion or religious themes appear in broadcasting more generally. The chapter is organized into four main sections. After (i) a review of the research literature, the chapter surveys (ii) the current state of religious broadcasting around the world, (iii) audiences and programs, with a short (iv) conclusion.

Global Varieties of Religious Broadcasting: A Literature Review

A review of the literature indicates that traditional religious broadcasting is still a force in a world increasingly dominated by digital media. The number of studies that focus on religious radio, for example, is quite striking. There are, as might be expected, some striking gaps. The number of studies of Black religious broadcasting is still relatively few. The attention given to evangelical or, increasingly, Islamic broadcasting, is not matched by the number of studies of broadcasters from other religious traditions, Buddhism for example. Catholic TV and radio broadcasting, for another example, appears on every continent and offers a fertile field waiting to be explored more fully by scholars.

Examining religious broadcasting over the past two decades, and drawing upon extensive surveys by Biernatzki (1991), Soukup (2002), and White (2007), provides a basis from earlier research. Also helpful are surveys of Africa by Ihejirika (2009b), of Latin America by Sierra Gutiérrez

The Handbook on Religion and Communication, First Edition. Edited by Yoel Cohen and Paul A. Soukup.
© 2023 John Wiley & Sons Ltd. Published 2023 by John Wiley & Sons Ltd.

(2008), and of Spain by Fuente-Cobo and Carabante-Muntada (2018). Unfortunately, German research is not represented in this survey (the journal *Communicatio Socialis* is an essential resource) but Karis (2016) provides a starting point for literature in Dutch and German.

North America

American scholars continue to explore the relationship between televangelism and its audience in a range of studies, many following an ethnographic approach (M. F. Frederick, 2015; M. Frederick, 2009; Rouse et al., 2016; Walton, 2009; Ward, 2016). Taylor and Chatters (2011) studied the religious media use of Afro-Americans, Black Caribbeans, and non-Hispanic Whites. Other researchers continue to take close interest in the changing linguistic, rhetorical, and performance strategies of televangelists (Armstrong et al., 2005; Hangen, 2002; Tomaselli & Shepperson, 2002). The importance of radio (and gospel music) in nourishing the evangelical interpretative community from 1920 to 1960 is elucidated, using historical ethnography, by Ward (2014, 2017), who also calls for more scholarly attention to the economics of the electronic Church in both TV and radio sectors (Ward, 2018).

A number of historical studies examine the pioneers of US religious broadcasting (Farney, 2018; Hajkowski, 2009; Pavuk, 2007) while Rosenthal (2001, 2007) documents the skeptical attitudes of mainstream Protestant denominations to the new medium of television. Fortner (2005) offers a rare comparative historical study of Church attitudes to broadcasting in Britain, Canada, and the United States between 1919 and 1945. McGowan (2008, 2009) analyses interactions between churches, broadcasters, and regulators in English-speaking Canada, and Pagé (2002) looks at the evolution of religious radio programming in Catholic Québec from 1931 until 1983. Faassen (2011) argues against continuing the historical obligation mandating balance in Canadian religious broadcasting.

Latin America

The rise of the Latin American electronic Church stimulated a range of research on the broadcasting strategies of individual Brazilian Churches (Fajardo, 2014; Miguel, 2013; Mora, 2008). Sierra Gutiérrez (2008) offers a comprehensive research survey on Brazilian "tele-faith." Smith and Campos (2005) analyze the interplay between politics and religion in their study of Pentecostal preachers in Brazil and Guatemala; Placeres (2017) does the same in a study of Brazilian Catholic TV networks. In Mexico there are studies of religious radio in Chiapas State (Martínez Mendoza et al., 2015; Toledo Lorenzo & Castañeda Seijas, 2018; Villar Pinto et al., 2013) and, in and around Mexico city, by Reyna Ruiz (2007, 2012, 2014).

Europe

Krückeberg (2008) surveys the radio work of Protestant Churches across Europe. Fuente-Cobo and Carabante-Muntada (2018) describe Spanish religious broadcasting while Santos Diez and Pérez Dasilva (2014) look at Catholic radio stations. Malherbe (2017) surveys religious broadcasting in France. McCarthy (2007) offers an insider's view of religion on Irish public television. Specialized religious radio and satellite channels in the UK are examined by Hunt (2011) and Cooper and Macaulay (2015).

From a central European perspective, Jenča et al. (2013) consider the role of religious broadcasting in a public service and Velics and Doliwa (2015) ask if religious broadcasters pose a risk to the diversity of Hungarian and Polish community radio sectors. There are a number of studies on Polish Catholic radio stations and their audiences (Burdziej, 2008; Doliwa, 2014; Gajdka, 2013; Guzek, 2015; Wilk, 2018). Religious broadcasting in Romania is covered by Tudor and Bratosin (2018) and in Russia by Khroul (2018).

Recent years have seen moves toward more pluralism and diversity in public broadcasting across European countries (McDonnell, 2004). Guyot (2009) and Oliva (2006) in France explore the balance between the principles of neutrality (laicité) and pluralism in allocating television time to religious groups. In Italy Provvidenza (2008) investigates Catholic Church influence on the public broadcaster, RAI (Radiotelevisione italiana), and the lack of pluralism. Lövheim and Axner (2011) and Stjernholm (2019) analyze how Swedish public media try to create a space for discussing religion including Islam. Karis (2016) compares how well German and Dutch public broadcasting have adapted to growing diversity of belief.

Moves to reflect a more diverse range of beliefs in the UK challenge assumptions about the nature and relevance of religious broadcasting (McDonnell, 2009). The BBC's efforts to adapt to changing public expectations and a growing diversity of religions is documented by Noonan (2011, 2012, 2013, 2014). Wallis (2016, 2020) finds a growing divide between producers with less understanding or sympathy for religion, and Church expectations. There is now an ongoing debate around demands to open up BBC Radio 4's short reflection slot, *Thought for the Day*, to humanist and secular speakers (Karis, 2018). Karis and Buss (2018) compare the UK arguments to those around secularism in Nepal. A previous controversy in 1955 is covered by Brown (2012). Scholars have also investigated BBC interwar religious broadcasting (Bailey, 2007), collective worship for schools from 1940 to 1975 (Parker, 2015), and early attempts to promote a more biblically authentic image of Jesus (Veldman, 2017). Lynch (2000) reveals how from 1926 to 1951, Irish public radio learned from the BBC how to retain editorial control over religion while keeping the Church at arm's length.

Cohen (2015) and Combeau (2018) tell the history of Le Jour de Seigneur, the oldest religious program on French television. There are histories of Radio Renascença, the successful Church-owned Portuguese commercial station (Ribeiro, 2002), and the Radio COPE (Cadena de Ondas Populares Españolas) network in Spain (Sánchez Redondo, 2001). Gómez García (2009) reveals how the Franco regime incorporated Catholic programming into its own propaganda. Italian audience studies explore the appeal of the broadcast Jubilee 2000 religious ceremonies to Italian viewers (Martelli et al., 2003; Martelli, 2004; Martelli & Cappello, 2005) and broadcast Masses as television events (Zordan, 2014). In Sweden, Alvarsson (2018) conducted a participant ethnographic study of a small local charismatic "tele-church," while Linderman (2002) provides a more general overview.

Africa and Middle East

Ihejirika (2009b) offers a wide-ranging survey of religion, media, and cultural studies in anglophone sub-Saharan Africa from 1987. He and others highlight the rise of home-grown Pentecostalism and its growing media involvement in Nigeria, Ghana, Uganda, and elsewhere (Asamoah-Gyadu, 2005; De Witte, 2011, 2012; Ihejirika, 2005, 2006; Jenga, 2017). Obayi and Edogor (2016), Ukah (2015), and Yusuf et al. (2020) cast critical eyes on the Nigerian broadcasting regulatory system. Though religious ownership of broadcast licenses is forbidden, Pentecostal and Islamic broadcasters can still access many broadcast outlets.

Religious broadcasting in Anglophone and Francophone West African countries is surveyed by Bathily (2009), and in East Africa by Rambaud et al. (2007). Religious radio in Ghana and Benin, Burkina Faso, and Togo is covered by Damome (2014, 2018) and Grätz (2011, 2014). The complex relationship between religious groups and the South African Broadcasting Corporation (SABC) is covered by Hackett (2006) and Scharnick-Udemans (2017), and Scharnick-Udemans (2018) also considers the influence of the SABC's only Islamic magazine TV program, *An Nur* (The Light).

Haron (2002, 2015) charts the history of Muslim community stations in South Africa, and Brennan (2015) that of the Muslim radio station Voice of Mombasa in Kenya between 1947 and 1966. Studies of Islamic media in Mali (Schulz, 2012), South Africa (Ingram, 2015), and Kenya (Ndzovu, 2019) reveal how women and women preachers are challenging the traditional authority of male broadcasters. Ng'atigwa (2014) compares a Catholic and an Islamic radio station in Tanzania concluding that they perpetuate the "othering" tendency of religions and may threaten national peace and unity. More positively, Frahm-Arp (2012) studied a South African commercial radio program that brings people together across faith divides. Ihejirika (2009a) surveyed Muslims who felt marginalized in Port Harcourt, Nigeria. Most blamed broadcasters for preferring Christian programs to Islamic ones, but others criticized religious leaders for being slow to put the Islamic message on air. In Ghana, White and Assimeng (2016) found a positive effect on viewers of one televangelism program. In Zimbabwe, Anglicans use the imaginative creations they borrow from televangelism to shape their local identity (Lundby, 2002).

The growth and influence of Arab Islamic satellite channels in the Middle East and North Africa is covered by Galal (2015) and Hroūb (2012). The latter also has essays on mainstream channels, Salafist channels and preachers, Christian broadcasting, and Jewish programs on Israeli television. Arab and Turkish Islamic channels compete in a crowded commercial satellite market, which means preachers have to find new televisual ways, such as talk shows, to reach diverse younger audiences (Hadj-Moussa, 2014; Özçetin, 2019; Skovgaard-Petersen, 2011). How Arab Muslims in the Nordic countries and elsewhere integrate Islamic TV into their lives is explored by Galal (2012, 2014) and Mellor (2014). Sonay (2018) investigates how the growth of Islamic radio in Turkey has been influenced by the power of the AKP (Adalet ve Kalkınma Partisi).

Asia and the Pacific

Thomas (2008) surveys Christian broadcasting in India and takes a detailed look at the influence of the satellite televangelist network God TV in Chennai. US televangelism in India is studied by James (2010), who distinguishes between global, local, and "glocal" (the fusion of Indian and US programs). Audiences for religious television are studied by Agrawal (2013, 2014) in India; by Pernia et al. (2006) in the Philippines; and in Pakistan by Biberman et al. (2016) and Kazi (2021). Indonesian researchers explore the growth in popularity of television preachers (Howell, 2008; Muzakki, 2012) and the rise of conservative Salafist radio stations (Sunarwoto, 2016; Yakin, 2018). Attitudes of producers in British and Malaysian Islamic television channels are compared by Karim and Fadilah (2018).

Siagian et al. (2016) reveal how editorial policies regulate Islamic TV programming in Malaysia and Indonesia, and Kong (2006) examines Singaporean regulatory policies designed to preserve multireligious harmony. In Australia Horsfield (2006) considers the issue of mandatory religious broadcasting on commercial television while historical relations between the Churches and regulators are studied by Healey (2005), Potts (2018), Griffin-Foley (2008), and Lee (2017) documents the important political and social role of two Korean Protestant broadcasters, the Christian Broadcasting System (CBS) and Far East Broadcasting Company (FEBC), up to broadcasting liberalization in 1990.

International Broadcasting

The expansion of international radio and satellite broadcasting has presented US radio and TV evangelists with new opportunities to extend their reach and influence. Kay (2009) describes how American televangelism intersects with and influences Pentecostal churches in different countries. Thomas and Lee (2012) bring together essays on the impact of US televangelism on other cultures and religious traditions – Islamic, Hindu, Buddhist – in the context of economic and cultural globalization. To find out what made Adventist World Radio (AWR) popular in Tanzania, Vernon (2013) analyzes over 25 years of audience correspondence. Ngô (2009) investigates how FEBC shortwave broadcasts succeeded in converting northern Vietnamese Hmong to evangelical Christianity. The global socio-political impact of US televangelists is framed by Serazio (2009) as an exercise in soft power. The expansion of post-Second World War shortwave international evangelical broadcasting is explored by Stoneman (2017) and Skelchy (2020). The best historical account of Vatican Radio in English is still Matelski (1995), while Perin (2018) writes about the use of Vatican Radio as a propaganda tool, especially during the Second World War.

Conclusion

Despite this ongoing work, other areas still await investigation, including comparative and cross-cultural studies of religious broadcasting. Fortner's (2005) study of the United States, Canada, and the UK stands out here, but other examples are Damome's (2014) survey of religious radio in Africa, Karis (2016) on German and Dutch public media, Hroūb (2012) on Arab broadcasting, and Thomas and Lee (2012) on global televangelism. More willingness to cross religious, cultural, and linguistic boundaries could greatly enrich our knowledge and understanding.

Finally, as every reviewer knows, there are the gaps that arise from the limitations of the reviewer and the format. There are the limitations of language, time, the lack of space, and the inevitable failure to include studies that were simply missed. Research on religious broadcasting, apart from Islamic, in Asia-Pacific is somewhat sparse. I hope, however, that this compilation will prove helpful and encourage others to correct, supplement, and expand its findings.

The Current State of Religious Broadcasting

In spite of the global diversity of religious broadcasting, one can identify four main models of religious broadcasting:

1. Religious broadcasting that is part of a public or state broadcasting system.
2. Broadcasting linked to individuals or groups aiming to win (proselytize or evangelize) new adherents and available on dedicated private religious channels.
3. Broadcasting affiliated with a Church or religion with the objectives of promoting its values, nourishing the faith of practicing members, and/or evangelizing available on private generalist or dedicated channels.
4. Broadcasting affiliated with a Church or religion providing some religious or devotional programs as a part of the output of a local community channel.

These models are found in every region, but the exact configuration is historically and culturally conditioned by different political, legal, economic, and social structures. Nearly every country in the world has a media system in which the public can access a range of local or international private and government controlled or owned public channels. Countries differ in how they regulate access to the airwaves, and on what obligations and restrictions they impose on broadcasters, e.g. regarding ownership, proselytizing, advertising, on-air fundraising, relations with other religions, etc.

European Religious Broadcasting

Broadcasting in European countries was regulated as a state or public service from the beginning, and religious broadcasting was part of the system. In nearly all countries Churches and other religious groups are allocated limited airtime on public TV channels on a confessional basis to produce a certain number of their own programs (Katsirea, 2008). In France, for example, time is allocated each Sunday to Catholic, Protestant, Orthodox, Jewish, and Muslim groups. In addition, most of the public broadcasters also air other programs on religious topics. Similar kinds of arrangements apply in many other European countries, for example, Belgium, Finland, Switzerland, Germany, and the Netherlands. In the UK, Ireland, Austria, Norway, Sweden, and Denmark religious groups do not have direct access, but public broadcasters produce religious programs for all. The Catholic Church dominates religious public broadcasting output in many countries including Ireland, Italy, Spain and Portugal, Slovakia, Slovenia, Croatia, Poland, and Hungary, though a variety of other religious groups also have access. The Orthodox Church has a privileged position in Russia, Greece, Bulgaria, and Romania.

In addition to public broadcasters, there are a growing number of private religious radio and TV channels available by satellite, cable, and a growing number only on the Internet. International evangelistic channels and their local offshoots abound, run by US Christian televangelists such as Trinity Broadcasting Network (TBN) and Christian Broadcasting Network (CBN), Adventists, and the Catholic Eternal Word Television Network (EWTN). There are also local groups such as Premier Radio in the UK, and the populist Catholic Radio Maryja and TV Trwam in Poland, as well as a variety of state and private channels serving Muslim communities across the region.

Church-supported radio is found in many countries, notably in Italy, Poland, Portugal (Radio Renascença), Spain (Radio COPE), and France (where over 140 Christian radio stations belong to two federations, RCF and COFRAC (Communauté francophone des radios chrétiennes)). There are also a number of Jewish stations. The international Radio Maria network has opened around 25 radio stations across the continent. Catholic Church-supported TV stations include KTO in France, TRECE (13TV) in Spain, and the SAT2000 satellite channel in Italy.

Religious Broadcasting in the Americas

In contrast to Europe, the dominant form of religious broadcasting across the Americas is varieties of televangelism on dedicated private commercial channels. In the United States, Christian televangelists are increasingly consolidated into large media groups, such as the TBN and Daystar TV networks, the Salem Media Group for talk radio, and American Family Radio for gospel music. In addition, there are hundreds of radio stations serving different religious communities, some affiliated with Churches and others with charismatic preachers like Kenneth Copeland, Joel Osteen, and Rick Warren.

Canadian audiences are also exposed to US religious channels as well as the home-grown Catholic channel Salt and Life and the family-oriented channel VisionTV, which carries a range of religious content from different faith groups. In addition, the Canadian public broadcaster CBC (Canadian Broadcasting Corporation)/Radio-Canada broadcasts regular religious programming.

In Latin America, US and home-grown varieties of televangelism and the rise of large Pentecostal Churches have posed a challenge to the dominance of the Catholic Church. The controversial Universal Church of the Kingdom of God in Brazil, for example, controls a radio network and, through its ownership of Record TV, has expanded its reach across Latin America and globally. There are also Catholic TV networks linked to the Church or founded by religious entrepreneurs, which offer a charismatic alternative to the Pentecostals. There are also numerous dedicated commercial religious TV channels and others affiliated with bodies like universities, for example, UCV or Canal13 in Chile. Across the continent there are varieties of Protestant evangelical and Catholic local radio stations, many of which are also community stations. The Radio Maria network is also active.

Religious Broadcasting in Africa

In sub-Saharan Africa, local radio linked to a Church, a charismatic televangelist, or an Islamic preacher is still the most important and widespread medium for religious broadcasting, though television, and latterly the Internet, are fast growing in importance. Catholic, evangelistic, and Pentecostal outlets are increasingly networked via satellite and the Internet with sustaining programs provided by global broadcasters like TransWorld Radio, Vatican Radio, TBN, and, in French Africa, COFRAC. Many of these stations, especially those affiliated with the historic Churches, are also engaged in community activities. Most national and state/public broadcasters in Africa, notably the SABC, offer some form of coverage or airtime to religious groups.

In North Africa and the Middle East state broadcasters and associated approved Islamic channels, e.g. al Nas, formerly a Salafi channel, are dominant. Islamic channels and preachers out of favor with current regimes broadcast by satellite from abroad (Ghanem, 2020). Christians can also access a range of foreign channels including the ecumenical Christian TV channel SAT7, headquartered in Cyprus.

Israel offers religious coverage of Jewish, Christian, Islamic, and Druze festivals on public radio and TV, and there are dedicated religious radio stations and satellite channels available. Proselytizing of Jews is forbidden. Lebanon hosts a range of radio and TV channels often connected to political or religious groups, including the TV channels Télé-Lumière (Christian) and NBN (National Broadcasting Network; Shia).

Religious Broadcasting in Asia-Pacific

Religious broadcasting in the region is highly complex and is much influenced by its multicultural and multireligious nature. Many governments exert strict control over religious broadcasting (Peyrouse, 2010), especially where there are inter-religious or inter-ethnic tensions. State/public broadcasters promote approved versions of religion and culture, e.g. Islam in Pakistan, Islam and Orthodoxy in Central Asian countries like Turkmenistan and Uzbekistan, and Buddhism in Thailand. Singapore allows a limited expression of Islamic broadcasting to serve the Malay population but otherwise pursues a policy of secular neutrality banning all free to air religious outlets.

In India, there are many varieties of spiritual and religious channels as well as Church outlets. In the Philippines, the Catholic Church runs a radio network of around 50 stations and its own TV channel; Pentecostal and Protestant Churches also own their own broadcast media. In Japan one local radio station is part owned by the Catholic Society of St. Paul and there are other Christian radio stations. In Korea, where unusually over 50% of the population are nonbelievers, there are Buddhist, Protestant, and Catholic radio and TV broadcasters. Across all Asian regions religious content is widely available by satellite and online.

The Australian public broadcaster, ABC (Australian Broadcasting Corporation), follows the BBC model of religious broadcasting, and there is a country network of evangelical radio stations as there is in New Zealand, where public radio also broadcasts church services. In the Pacific region faith-based, mostly Christian, stations make up 50% of all community radio outlets and there are a large number of other dedicated religious stations, linked to specific Churches or televangelists (Austin, 2014).

Religious Audiences and Programs

All religious broadcasters are interested in the size and composition of their audiences, but detailed audience data are valuable and not publicly available. Broadcasters prefer to publicize their reach, engagement with audiences, and the number of different media platforms on which they can be found.

In 2014 around 20% of US adults claimed to have watched or listened to religious (that is Christian) TV, radio, or music in the previous week. Black Protestants and White evangelicals were the heaviest users and weekly TV viewing increased with age, with one-third over 50 years old (38% over 65) compared with 15% under 50 years (Pew Research, 2014). Black Christians are significantly more frequent users than non-Hispanic Whites (Taylor & Chatters, 2011). Christian TV mostly appeals to women over 60, born-again Christians, African Americans, people with limited education and income, and people in the southern United States (Barna Group, 2005, 2020). The pattern is similar elsewhere: older female audiences form the core audience in Brazil for the Rede Vita TV network (Sierra Gutiérrez, 2008) and religious radio in Poland is most popular with older age groups (Burdziej, 2008; Wilk, 2018). Televangelists of all faiths create and serve audiences who value their broadcasting affiliations as markers of belonging to a parallel or alternative subculture (Burdziej, 2008; Cooper & Macaulay, 2015; Grätz, 2014; Guzek, 2015; Hroūb, 2012; Thomas & Lee, 2012; Ward, 2016).

In Africa and the Caribbean, Pentecostal televangelists have been successful in reaching across the age range and the gender divide. Young, educated, upwardly mobile, urban people are attracted by a mix of entertainment, versions of the prosperity gospel, and aspirational teaching (M. F. Frederick, 2015; De Witte, 2011). Elsewhere, younger Muslims in Pakistan, the Maghreb, Arab countries, and Europe watch and evaluate the various views of charismatic Islamic television preachers (Biberman et al., 2016; Galal, 2014; Hadj-Moussa, 2014; Kazi, 2021; Mellor, 2014).

How does the media experience itself affect viewers and listeners? It seems liturgies are mediatized as viewers experience them more as televised events than sacred acts (Martelli, 2004; Martelli et al., 2003; Martelli & Cappello, 2005; Zordan, 2014). People used to radio start to judge the same program as a spectacle when it moves to TV (Stamm, 2012). Evidence for the direct influence of religious media is relatively sparse. In India, a moderate or low influence of religious TV was found among both Hindus and non-Hindus, though Muslims reported strengthened belief after watching (Agrawal, 2013, 2014). The success of FEBC shortwave broadcasts in converting Hmong listeners in northern Vietnam is explained by the congruence of Protestantism with core Hmong beliefs and by its association with modernity (Ngô, 2009).

Religion on public channels generally attracts a relatively small proportion of the overall audience. In Europe the BBC is exceptional in the amount and range of its religious programming across radio and TV (over 7000 hours a year) but it is still a small part of its output (BBC, 2017). However, relatively few BBC users, mostly older people (aged 55+) regularly tune in to religious programs (Ofcom, 2020) and average viewing of religious programs on the main UK public TV channels is about three hours per week (Ofcom, 2011). However, occasionally, individual religious programs will attract sizable audiences across a wider range.

Some audiences of public and generalist channels want fewer or even no religious programs, as in Scandinavia (Lundby, 2018, p. 93), but others want more. BBC audiences identify religious programs as worship, documentaries about issues, discussions and interviews, debates, lifestyle documentaries, and entertainment. Documentaries have the widest appeal; worship is the most polarizing. The term religion is off-putting (BBC, 2017). Similar kinds of audience reactions were found in Norway (Lundby, 2017, p. 258). UK viewers expect and want worship, personal stories and witness, informative and issue-based documentaries, and debates (Ofcom, 2005; Viney, 1999). Interestingly, religious TV viewers in the Philippines also have a diverse definition of religious programs, watching for entertainment, to satisfy curiosity, and to pass the time (Pernia et al., 2006).

In the early years of religious broadcasting the dominant genres were talks, broadcasts of church services, and hymn singing. These are still a staple of public and private broadcaster schedules across the globe. The BBC's *Thought for the Day* and *Das Wort zum Sonntag* in Germany, both long-running brief daily religious reflections, are still broadcast. Gospel music is a mainstay of evangelical radio programs in the United States and elsewhere.

These formats are supplemented by others: entertainment and documentary programs; popular films on religious subjects; advice and talk shows by Islamic, Christian, and other televangelists; and presentations on spirituality and mindfulness. In practice, regulators and religious broadcasters count any program with a religious or ethical theme, while televangelists consider religious programs to be any compatible with and supportive of their religious values and beliefs (Ward, 2016).

Interestingly, during the Covid pandemic year of 2020 broadcasters found that in uncertain and anxious times religious programs were attracting larger audiences. The rebroadcast by Indian public television of the Hindu *Ramayana* and *Mahabharata* epics of the 1990s during a lockdown period proved to be a huge popular success (Deepak, 2020). The BBC's *Songs of Praise* saw a 29% jump in weekly viewing to 1.2 million (Ashworth, 2021). And a US survey noted an increase in religious (and news) viewing in March 2020 as the first wave of Covid encouraged more people to stay at home (Advanced Television, 2020). Also, many public broadcasters have put on extra religious services and other programs (BBC, 2020; RTE, 2021).

Conclusion: Future Trends in Religious Broadcasting

The future of religious broadcasting is already here. Like broadcasting generally, it is mutating under the influences of digital technology, the end of spectrum scarcity, the Internet, mobile phones, social media, and streaming. All broadcasters, from the largest to small community stations, are becoming multiplatform. This trend will only continue and intensify. Platforms can be purely digital (mobile, social media, web, etc.) or combinations of digital and linear TV and radio. The international Catholic broadcaster Radio Veritas Asia, for example, is now completely online. On the other hand, though Vatican Radio has set up a 24-hour web radio service, it still serves populations in Africa and Asia by shortwave broadcasts in 41 languages (Watkins, 2021). As usual with media developments, older media will continue to coexist with the new.

Religious broadcasters have also to adjust their business models as audience behavior changes. Younger age groups in the United States are rapidly abandoning cable and satellite pay TV to access content through online media (Rainie, 2021), and ways have to be found to attract a new generation of viewers and listeners as well as continuing to serve older loyal audiences. Declining church attendance and more people professing no religious belief in Europe and the United States contrast with the continuing growth and influence of religion in Asia-Pacific, Latin America, and Africa. Religious broadcasting, in every one of its forms, will have to adapt to the changing patterns and demographics of belief in different regions of the world.

References

Advanced Television. (2020). US TV audiences turn to news and religious content. Advanced Television, April 15. Retrieved February 25, 2022, from https://advanced-television.com/2020/04/15/us-tv-audiences-turning-to-news-religious-content

Agrawal, B. C. (2013). Influences of religions telecast in a multi-religious India: An analysis of Hindu and non-Hindu television viewers. *Religion and Social Communication, 11*(1), 5–21.

Agrawal, B. C. (2014). Influences of religious telecast in a multi-religious India: An analysis of Hindu and Muslim television viewers. *Religion and Social Communication, 12*(1), 54–69.

Alvarsson, J.-Å. (2018). Televangelism in Sweden – now? Is channel 10 in Älmhult in fact a telechurch? In J. Moberg, & J. Skjoldli (Eds.), *Charismatic Christianity in Finland, Norway, and Sweden* (pp. 213–238). Palgrave Macmillan. https://doi.org/10.1007/978-3-319-69614-0_9

Armstrong, R. N., Hallmark, J. R., & Williamson, L. K. (2005). Televangelism as institutional apologia: The religious talk show as strategized text. *Journal of Media and Religion, 4*(2), 67–83.

Asamoah-Gyadu, J. K. (2005). Anointing through the screen: Neo-Pentecostalism and televised Christianity in Ghana. *Studies in World Christianity, 11*, 9–28.

Ashworth, P. (2021). BBC: "New approach" to religious programming will better serve faith communities. *Church Times*, March 19. Retrieved February 25, 2022, from https://www.churchtimes.co.uk/articles/2021/19-march/news/uk/bbc-new-approach-to-religious-programming-will-better-serve-faith-communities

Austin, L. (2014). Faith-based community radio and development in the South Pacific Islands. *Media International Australia, 150*(1), 114–121.

Bailey, M. (2007). "He who has ears to hear, let him hear": Christian pedagogy and religious broadcasting during the inter-war period. *Westminster Papers in Communication and Culture, 4*(1), 4–25. http://doi.org/10.16997/wpcc.70

Barna Group. (2005). More people use Christian media than attend church. Barna Group. Retrieved February 25, 2022, from https://www.barna.com/research/more-people-use-christian-media-than-attend-church

Barna Group. (2020). Do Americans replace traditional church with digital faith expressions? Barna Group. Retrieved February 25, 2022, from https://www.barna.com/research/worship-shifting

Bathily, A. (2009). *Médias et religions en Afrique de l'Ouest.* Institut Panos Afrique de l'Ouest.

BBC. (2017). Religion and ethics review. BBC. Retrieved February 25, 2022, from http://downloads.bbc.co.uk/aboutthebbc/insidethebbc/howwework/reports/pdf/religion_and_ethics_review.pdf

BBC (2020). BBC unveils plans to support and represent faith communities during unprecedented times. BBC. Retrieved February 25, 2022, from https://www.bbc.co.uk/mediacentre/latestnews/2020/religion-coronavirus

Biberman, Y., Gul, S., & Ocakli, F. (2016). Channelling Islam: Religious narratives on Pakistani television and their influence on Pakistani youth. *Asian Affairs: An American Review, 43*(3), 78–97. https://doi.org/10.1080/00927678.2016.1202712

Biernatzki, W. E. (1991). Televangelism and the religious use of television. *Communication Research Trends*, *11*(1), 1–30.

Brennan, J. R. (2015). A history of Sauti ya Mvita (Voice of Mombasa) Radio: Public culture and Islam in coastal Kenya, 1947–1966. In R. I. J. Hackett, & B. F. Soares (Eds.), *New media and religious transformations in Africa* (pp. 19–38). Indiana University Press.

Brown, C. G. (2012). "The unholy Mrs Knight" and the BBC: Secular humanism and the threat to the "Christian nation" c.1945–60. *The English Historical Review*, *128*(525), 345–376. https://doi.org/10.1093/ehr/ces001

Burdziej, S. (2008). Voice of the disinherited? Religious media after the 2005 presidential and parliamentary elections in Poland. *East European Quarterly*, *42*(2), 207–221.

Cohen, E. (2015). Présence et manifestations du religieux dans la télévision des années cinquante. *Histoire, Monde et Cultures religieuses*, *33*, 13–20. https://www.cairn.info/revue-histoire-monde-et-cultures-religieuses-2015-1-page-13.htm

Combeau, Y. (2018). *L'Évangile en direct. "Le Jour du Seigneur", 70 ans d'histoire de l'émission la plus ancienne du monde*. CFRT/Presses de la Renaissance.

Cooper, M., & Macaulay, K. (2015). Contemporary Christian radio in Britain: A new genre on the national dial. *The Radio Journal*, *13*(1+2), 75–87. https://doi:org/10.1386/rajo.13.1-2.75_1

Damome, E. (2014). *Radios et religions en Afrique subsaharienne*. Presses Universitaires de Bordeaux.

Damome, E. (2018). Religions et médias au Ghana et au Togo. *Revue française des sciences de l'information et de la communication*, *13*. https://doi.org/10.4000/rfsic.3710

De Witte, M. (2011). Business of the spirit: Ghanaian broadcast media and the commercial exploitation of Pentecostalism. *Journal of African Media Studies*, *3*(2), 189–204.

De Witte, M. (2012). Television and the gospel of entertainment in Ghana. *Exchange*, *41*(2), 144–164.

Deepak, V. (2020). Reruns of religious dramas comfort Indians in dire times. ABC News, May 23. Retrieved February 25, 2022, from https://abcnews.go.com/Entertainment/wireStory/reruns-religious-dramas-comfort-indians-dire-times-70845871

Doliwa, U. (2014). Religious radio stations in Poland: A community-oriented Catholic ghetto? A case study of Radio Niepokalanów. In M. Oliveira, G. Stachyra, & G. Starkey (Eds.), *Radio: The resilient medium* (pp. 205–220). Centre for Research in Media and Cultural Studies.

Faassen, M. (2011). A fine balance: The regulation of Canadian religious broadcasting. *Queen's Law Journal*, *37*(1), 303–337.

Fajardo, A. (2014). Manoel de Melo e o pioneirismo na utilização dos meios de comunicação de massa para propagação do pentecostalismo. In D. M. de Oliveira (Ed.), *Pentecostalismos em diálogo* (pp. 169–181). Fonte Editorial.

Farney, K. D. (2018). "A [radio] tower of strength": Walter A. Maier, broadcasting, and gospel proclamation. *Lutheran Mission Matters*, *26*(2), 240–261.

Fortner, R. S. (2005). *Radio, morality and culture: Britain, Canada, and the United States (1919–1945)*. Southern Illinois University Press.

Frahm-Arp, M. (2012). Radio and religion: A case of difference and diversity. In L. Gunner, D. Ligaga, & D. Moyo (Eds.), *Radio in Africa* (pp. 208–222). Wits University Press.

Frederick, M. (2009). Reading race and American televangelism. In S. Stein (Ed.), *The Cambridge history of religions in America* (pp. 631–647). Cambridge U.P. https://doi.org/10.1017/CHOL9780521871082.031

Frederick, M. F. (2015). *Colored television: American religion gone global*. Stanford University Press.

Fuente-Cobo, C., & Carabante-Muntada, J. M. (2018). Media and religion in Spain. *Journal of Religion, Media, and Digital Culture*, *7*(2), 175–202. https://10.1163/21659214-00702003

Gajdka, K. (2013). Roman Catholic broadcasting radio stations in Poland. *Revista Romana de Jurnalism si Comunicare*, *2–3*, 26–33.

Galal, E. (2012). Belonging through believing: Becoming Muslim through Islamic programming. In S. Hjarvard, & M. Lövheim (Eds.), *Mediatization and religion: Nordic perspectives* (pp. 147–160). Nordicom.

Galal, E. (2014). Audience responses to Islamic TV: Between resistance and piety. In E. Galal (Ed.), *Arab TV-audiences: Negotiating religion and identity* (pp. 29–50). Peter Lang.

Galal, E. (2015). Conveying Islam: Arabic Islamic satellite channels as new players. In R. I. J. Hackett, & B. F. Soares (Eds.), *New media and religious transformations in Africa* (pp. 171–189). Indiana University Press.

Ghanem, T. (2020). Muslim media in the post-Arab Spring: The curious case of Egypt. Maydan, March 18. Retrieved February 25, 2022, from https://themaydan.com/2020/03/muslim-media-in-the-post-arab-spring-the-curious-case-of-egypt

Gómez García, S. (2009). Entretenimiento y fe en las ondas. Las emisiones religiosas de Radio Nacional de España durante el primer franquismo (1939–1959). *Estudios sobre el Mensaje Periodístico, 15*, 261–276.

Grätz, T. (2011). "Paroles de vie": Christian radio producers in the Republic of Benin. *Journal of African Media Studies, 3*(2), 161–188. https://doi.org/10.1386/jams.3.2.161_1

Grätz, T. (2014). Christian religious radio production in Benin: The case of Radio Maranatha. *Social Compass, 61*(1), 57–66. https://doi.org/10.1177/0037768613513943

Griffin-Foley, B. (2008). Radio ministries: Religion on Australian commercial radio from the 1920s to the 1960s. *Journal of Religious History, 32*(1), 31–54.

Guyot, J. (2009). Mediating religious matters on PSB television in Europe. *Hyper Article en Ligne – Sciences de l'Homme et de la Société*, 10670/1.db65y7.

Guzek, D. (2015). 'Religious Radio Families' between the social and economic needs. *Romanian Journal of Journalism and Communication/Revista Română de Jurnalism 'I Comunicare, 49*, 33–39.

Hackett, R. I. J. (2006). Mediated religion in South Africa: Balancing air-time and rights claims. In B. Meyer, & A. Moors (Eds.), *Media, religion, and the public sphere* (pp. 166–187). Indiana University Press.

Hadj-Moussa, R. (2014). Maghrebi audiences: Mapping the divide between Arab sentiment, Islamic belonging, and political praxis. In E. Galal (Ed.), *Arab TV-audiences: Negotiating religion and identity* (pp. 71–94). Peter Lang.

Hajkowski, S. (2009). Father Justyn and the Rosary Hour. *U.S. Catholic Historian, 27*(3), 59–82.

Hangen, T. J. (2002). *Redeeming the dial: Radio, religion, and popular culture in America*. University of North Carolina Press.

Haron, M. (2002). The South African Muslims making (air) waves during the period of transformation. *Journal for the Study of Religion, 15*(2), 111–144.

Haron, M. (2015). Muslim community radio stations: Constructing and shaping identities in a democratic South Africa. In R. I. J. Hackett, & B. F. Soares (Eds.), *New media and religious transformations in Africa* (pp. 82–98). Indiana University Press.

Healey, A. (2005). A critical alliance: ABC religious broadcasting and the Christian churches (1932–1977). *Journal of the Australian Catholic Historical Society, 26*, 15–28.

Horsfield, P. (2006). Down the tube: Religion on Australian commercial television. *Media International Australia, 12*(1), 136–148. https://doi.org/10.1177/1329878X0612100116

Howell, J. (2008). Sufism on the silver screen: Indonesian innovations in Islamic televangelism. *Journal of Indonesian Islam, 2*(2), 225–239.

Hroūb, K. (Ed.). (2012). *Religious broadcasting in the Middle East*. Hurst Publishers.

Hunt, S. (2011). Transformations in British religious broadcasting. In M. Bailey, & G. Reddan (Eds.), *Mediating faiths* (pp. 25–36). Ashgate.

Ihejirika, W. (2009a). Muslim minorities and media access in a predominantly Christian city: The case of Port Harcourt, Nigeria. *Journal of African Media Studies, 1*(3), 469–491.

Ihejirika, W. (2009b). Research on media, religion, and culture in Africa: Current trends and debates. *African Communication Research, 2*(1), 1–60.

Ihejirika, W. C. (2005). Media and fundamentalism in Nigeria. *Media Development, 52*, 38–44.

Ihejirika, W. C. (2006). *From Catholicism to Pentecostalism: The role of Nigerian televangelists in religious conversion*. University of Port Harcourt Press.

Ingram, B. (2015). Public Islam in post-apartheid South Africa: The Radio Islam controversy. *Critical Research on Religion, 3*(1), 72–85. https://doi.org/10.1177/2050303215577490

James, J. (2010). *McDonaldisation, masala McGospel and Om economics: Televangelism in contemporary India*. Sage Publications.

Jenča, I., Sekerešová, Z., & Zárubová, H. (2013). Religious broadcasting as public service. *European Journal of Science and Theology, 9*(6), 61–70.

Jenga, F. (2017). Pentecostal broadcasting in Uganda. *Journal of Communication & Religion, 40*(4), 53–71.

Karim, N. K. A., & Fadilah, A. A. (2018). Religiopolitical and sociocultural factors shaping creative decisions in the production of British and Malaysian Islamic television. *Malaysian Journal of Communication, 34*(1), 300–315.

Karis, T. (2016). Religious diversity as a media regulation issue: The changing frameworks in German and Dutch public broadcasting regulation. In C. Richter, I. Dupuis, & S. Averbeck-Lietz (Eds.), *Diversity in transcultural and international communication* (pp. 69–90). LIT Verlag.

Karis, T. (2018). Secular voices on air: The British debate on Thought for the Day. *Journal of Religion, Media and Digital Culture, 7*(3), 329–345.

Karis, T., & Buss, J. (2018). Introduction: A comparative study on notions of the secular in the debate on Thought for the Day in the United Kingdom and the Nepali debate on secularism. *Journal of Religion, Media and Digital Culture, 7*(3), 320–328.

Katsirea, I. (2008). *Public broadcasting and European law. A comparative examination of public service obligations in six member states.* Kluwer.

Kay, W. K. (2009). Pentecostalism and religious broadcasting. *Journal of Beliefs and Values, 30*(3), 245–254. https://doi.org/10.1080/13617670903371555

Kazi, T. (2021). *Religious television and pious authority in Pakistan.* Indiana University Press.

Khroul, V. (2018). Religious media dynamics in Russia after 'perestroika' (1991–2017). *Kultura – Media – Teologia, 33,* 39–62.

Kong, L. (2006). Religion and spaces of technology: Constructing and contesting nation, transnation, and place. *Environment and Planning A, 38*(5), 903–918. https://ink.library.smu.edu.sg/soss_research/1718

Krückeberg, S. (2008). *Die Hörfunkarbeit evangelischer Kirchen in Europa zu Beginn des 21. Jahrhunderts.* Christliche Publizistik Verlag.

Lee, S. (2017). A history of religious broadcasting in Korea from a religious politics standpoint: Focusing on the period of a Protestant broadcasting monopoly. *Journal of Korean Religions, 8*(2), 11–31.

Linderman, A. (2002). Religious television in Sweden: Toward a more balanced view of its reception. In S. M. Hoover, & L. S. Clark (Eds.), *Practicing religion in the age of the media* (pp. 295–304). Columbia University Press.

Lövheim, M., & Axner, M. (2011). Halal-TV: Negotiating the place of religion in Swedish public discourse. *Nordic Journal of Religion and Society, 24*(1), 57–74.

Lundby, K. (2002). Between American televangelism and African Anglicanism. In S. M. Hoover, & L. S. Clark (Eds.), *Practicing religion in the age of the media* (pp. 328–344). Columbia University Press.

Lundby, K. (2017). Public religion in mediatized transformations. In F. Engelstad, H. Larsen, J. Rogstad, & K. Steen-Johnsen (Eds.), *Institutional change in the public sphere: Views on the Nordic model* (pp. 241–262). De Gruyter Open Poland.

Lundby, K. (Ed.). (2018). *Contesting religion: The media dynamics of cultural conflicts in Scandinavia.* De Gruyter.

Lynch, B. (2000). Steering clear: Broadcasting and the church, 1926–1951. *New Hibernia Review, 4*(2), 26–39.

Malherbe, C. (2017). Comment les religions ont trouvé leur place à la radio et la television. La revue des medias. Retrieved February 27, 2022, from https://larevuedesmedias.ina.fr/comment-les-religions-ont-trouve-leur-place-la-radio-et-la-television

Martelli, S. (2004). La visibilizzazione della religione in TV. Tra popolo "fedele" ed audience da primato. *Sociologia della comunicazione, 25*(1–2), 155–169.

Martelli, S., Capello, G., & Molteni, L. (2003). *Il Giubileo 'mediato': Audience dei programmi televisivi e religiosità in Italia.* Franco Angeli.

Martelli, S., & Cappello, G. (2005). Religion in the television-mediated public sphere transformations and paradoxes. *International Review of Sociology, 15*(2), 243–257.

Martínez Mendoza, S., Cordero Fernández, F., & Villar Pinto, H. (2015). Expansión y presencia de la radio libre en Chiapas, un fenómeno de la globalización. *Correspondencias & Análisis, 5,* 153–171.

Matelski, M. J. (1995). *Vatican Radio: Propagation by the airwaves.* Praeger.

McCarthy, D. (2007). Religious broadcasting at national level. *The Furrow, 58*(11), 608–615.

McDonnell, J. (2004). Public broadcasting, religion, and diversity: Irish religious broadcasting in a European context. Broadcasting Committee, Church of Ireland. Retrieved February 27, 2022, from https://www.ireland.anglican.org/news/861/public-broadcasting-religion-and-diversity

McDonnell, J. (2009). From certainty to diversity: The evolution of British religious broadcasting since 1990. In H. Geybels, S. Mels, & M. Walrave (Eds.), *Faith and media: Representation and communication* (pp. 151–178). Peter Lang.

McGowan, M. G. (2008). Air wars: Radio regulation, sectarianism, and religion broadcasting in Canada, 1922–1938. *Historical Papers: Papers of the Canadian Society of Church History.* Retrieved February 27,

2022, from https://historicalpapers.journals.yorku.ca/index.php/historicalpapers/article/view/39154/35500 (Accessed 20 January 2021).

McGowan, M. G. (2009). The Fulton Sheen affair: Religious controversy, nationalism, and commercialism in the early years of Canadian television, 1952–1958. *Historical Studies, 75*, 221–238.

Mellor, N. (2014). Religious media as a cultural discourse: The views of the Arab diaspora. In F. Galal (Ed.), *Arab TV-audiences* (pp. 95–114). Peter Lang.

Miguel, G. (2013). Producción mediática y religiosidad: Dinámicas transnacionales de las comunicaciones evangélicas. *Religião e Sociedade, 33*(2), 37–57. https://doi.org/10.1590/S0100-85872013000200003

Mora, G. C. (2008). Marketing the 'health and wealth gospel' across national borders: Evidence from Brazil and the United States. *Poetics, 36*(5–6), 404–420. https://doi.org/10.1016/j.poetic.2008.06.008

Muzakki, A. (2012). Islamic televangelism in changing Indonesia: Transmission, authority, and the politics of ideas. In P. N. Thomas, & P. Lee (Eds.), *Global and local televangelism* (pp. 45–63). Palgrave Macmillan.

Ndzovu, H. J. (2019). Broadcasting female Muslim preaching in Kenya. *African Journal of Gender and Religion, 25*(2), 14–40.

Ng'atigwa, F. X. (2014). "Othering" and "others" in religious radio broadcasts in Tanzania: Cases from Radio Maria Tanzania and Radio Imaan. *The Journal of Religion and Popular Culture, 26*(2), 230–243.

Ngô, T. (2009). The short-waved faith: Christian broadcasting and the transformation of the spiritual landscape of the Hmong in Northern Vietnam. In F. K. G. Lim (Ed.), *Mediating piety* (pp. 139–158). Brill.

Noonan, C. (2011). 'Big stuff in a beautiful way with interesting people': The spiritual discourse in UK religious television. *European Journal of Cultural Studies, 14*(6), 727–746.

Noonan, C. (2012). The BBC and decentralisation: The pilgrimage to Manchester. *International Journal of Cultural Policy, 18*(4), 363–377. https://doi.org/10.1080/10286632.2011.598516

Noonan, C. (2013). Piety and professionalism: The BBC's changing religious mission (1960–1979). *Media History, 19*(2), 196–212.

Noonan, C. (2014). 'Not a museum piece': Exploring the 'special' occupational culture of religious broadcasting in Britain. *International Journal of Media and Cultural Politics, 10*(1), 65–81. https://doi.org/10.1386/macp.10.1.65_1

Obayi, P. M., & Edogor, I. O. (2016). Nigerian audiences' perception of Pentecostal churches' ownership of satellite television channels. *Global Journal of Arts Humanities and Social Sciences, 4*(3), 12–28.

Ofcom. (2005). Religious programmes: A report of the key findings of a qualitative research study. Ofcom. Retrieved February 27, 2022, from https://www.ofcom.org.uk/__data/assets/pdf_file/0016/40255/religious-programmes.pdf

Ofcom. (2011). PSB report 2011-information pack. C-PSB viewing. Ofcom. Retrieved February 27, 2022, from https://www.ofcom.org.uk/__data/assets/pdf_file/0034/74896/psb-viewing-c.pdf

Ofcom. (2020). Annual report on the BBC 2019/20. Ofcom. Retrieved February 27, 2022, from https://www.ofcom.org.uk/__data/assets/pdf_file/0021/207228/third-bbc-annual-report.pdf

Oliva, A.-M. (2006). Emissions religieuses et service public audiovisuel. *Droit et Cultures, 51*, 103–112.

Özçetin, B. (2019). Religion on air: The birth and transformation of religious broadcasting in Turkey. *Middle East Journal of Culture and Communication, 12*(2), 236–252.

Pagé, P. (2002). Cinquante ans d'émissions religieuses à la radio québécoise (1931–1983). *Études d'histoire religieuse, 68*, 7–23. https://doi.org/10.7202/1006733ar

Parker, S. G. (2015). Mediatising childhood religion: The BBC, John G. Williams, and collective worship for schools in England, 1940–1975. *Paedagogica Historica, 51*(5), 614–630. https://doi.org/10.1080/00309230.2015.1013559

Pavuk, A. (2007). Constructing a Catholic church out of thin air: 'Catholic Hour's' early years on NBC radio. *American Catholic Studies, 118*(4), 37–67.

Perin, R. (2018). Vatican Radio and modern propaganda. In G. Vian (Ed.), *Le pontificat romain dans l'époque contemporaine* (pp. 65–85). Ed. Ca' Foscari.

Pernia, E. E., San Pascual, M. R., & Kwon, D. H. (2006). Religion in the box: Viewership of religious television programs in the Philippines. *Journal of Communication and Religion, 29*(2), 484–510.

Pew Research. (2014). Religion and electronic media. Pew Research Center. Retrieved February 27, 2022, from https://www.pewforum.org/2014/11/06/religion-and-electronic-media

Peyrouse, S. (2010). Why do Central Asian governments fear religion? A consideration of Christian movements. *Journal of Eurasian Studies, 1*(2), 134–143. https://doi.org/10.1016/j.euras.2010.04.006

Placeres, G. (2017). Confluencia politica, religiosa e midiatica: Os lacos das redes paulistas de televisao catolica no congresso nacional. *Espaço e Cultura* (42), 5–25. https://doi.org/10.12957/espacoecultura.2017.46720

Potts, J. (2018). The 'radio service': Religion and ABC national radio. *Radio Journal, 16*(2), 159–171. https://doi.org/10.1386/rjao.16.2.159_1

Provvidenza, S. (2008). Prime considerazioni in tema di pluralismo religioso nel sistema radiotelevisivo italiano. *Stato, Chiese e pluralism confessionale, 12,* 1–62. https://www.statoechiese.it/it/contributi/prime-considerazioni-in-tema-di-pluralismo-religioso-nel-sistema-radiotelev

Rainie, L. (2021). Cable and satellite TV use has dropped dramatically in the U.S. since 2015. Pew Research Center. March 17. Retrieved February 27, 2022, from https://pewrsr.ch/3vAc7Yz

Rambaud, B., Tudesq, A., & Lenoble-Bart, A. (2007). Médias chrétiens en Afrique de l'Est. *Histoire et missions chrétiennes, 4*(4), 115–129. https://doi.org/10.3917/hmc.004.0115

Reyna Ruiz, M. (2007). Los programas religiosos en la radio del Valle de México: Un primer acercamiento. *Revista Versión, 17,* 289–305.

Reyna Ruiz, M. (2012). Resonancias de fe: Los programas religiosas en la radio Mexicana. *Revista Versión, 21,* 53–82.

Reyna Ruiz, M. (2014). La religión mediada: Sintonizando a Dios en la radio mexicana. *Cultura y religión, 8*(1), 65–82.

Ribeiro, N. (2002). *A Rádio Renascença e o 25 de abril.* Universidade Católica Editora.

Rosenthal, M. (2001). 'This nation under God': The broadcast and film commission of the National Council of Churches and the new medium of television. *The Communication Review, 4*(3), 347–371. https://doi.org/10.1080/10714420109359474

Rosenthal, M. (2007). *American Protestants and TV in the 1950s.* Palgrave Macmillan.

Rouse, C. M., Jackson, J. J. L., & Frederick, M. F. (2016). Black Christian redemption: Contested possibilities. In J. J. L. Jackson, & C. M. Rouse (eds.), *Televised redemption: Black religious media and racial empowerment* (pp. 33–54). NYU Press. https://doi.org/10.2307/j.ctt1bj4r3n.5

RTE. (2021). RTE extends additional religious content until end of June. RTE. Retrieved February 27, 2022, from https://about.rte.ie/2021/02/01/rte-extends-additional-religious-content-until-end-of-June

Sánchez Redondo, M. I. (2001). *Historia de la COPE (1959–1983).* Fundación Universitaria San Pablo CEU.

Santos Diez, M. T., & Pérez Dasilva, J. Á. (2014). Las radios católicas españolas. *Revista de estudios sociales, 50,* 140–154. https://revistas.uniandes.edu.co/doi/10.7440/res50.2014.14

Scharnick-Udemans, L.-S.-S. (2017). A historical and critical overview of religion and public broadcasting in South Africa. *Journal for the Study of Religion, 30*(2), 257–280.

Scharnick-Udemans, L.-S.-S. (2018). Biographies and the mediatisation of religion. *Religion and Education, 45*(1), 110–124. https://doi.org/10.1080/15507394.2017.1407623

Schulz, D. E. (2012). Equivocal resonances: Islamic revival and female radio 'preachers' in urban Mali. In L. Gunner, D. Ligaga, & D. Moyo (Eds.), *Radio in Africa* (pp. 63–80). Wits University Press.

Serazio, M. (2009). Geopolitical proselytizing in the marketplace for loyalties: Rethinking the global gospel of American Christian broadcasting. *Journal of Media and Religion, 8*(1), 40–54. https://doi.org/10.1080/15348420802670934

Siagian, H. F., Mustari, & Ahmad, F. (2016). The position of Da'wah messages and ethics in Malaysian and Indonesian television programs. *Malaysian Journal of Communication, 32*(2), 749–769.

Sierra Gutiérrez, L. I. (2008). Tele-faith: Mediated religion in Brazil. *Communication Research Trends, 27*(1), 3–23.

Skelchy, R. P. (2020). The afterlife of colonial radio in Christian missionary broadcasting of the Philippines. *South East Asia Research, 28*(3), 344–362. https://doi.org/10.1080/0967828X.2020.1803761

Skovgaard-Petersen, J. (2011). Islamic fundamentalism in Arab television: Islamism and Salafism in competition. In U. Mårtensson, J. Bailey, P. Ringrose, & A. Dyrendal (Eds.), *Fundamentalism in the modern world* (Vol. 2, pp. 264–291). Tauris.

Smith, D. A., & Campos, L. S. (2005). Christianity and television in Guatemala and Brazil: The Pentecostal experience. *Studies in World Christianity, 11*(1), 49–64. https://doi.org/10.3366/swc.2005.11.1.49

Sonay, A. (2018). Local media in Turkey: The growth of Islamic networks in Konya's radio landscape. *Middle East Critique, 27*(2), 127–140. https://doi.org/10.1080/19436149.2018.1433585

Soukup, P. (2002). Media and religion. *Communication Research Trends*, 21(2), 3–37.

Stamm, M. (2012). Broadcasting mainline Protestantism: The Chicago Sunday Evening Club and the evolution of audience expectations from radio to television. *Religion and American Culture*, 22(2), 233–264.

Stjernholm, S. (2019). Muslim religious oratory on Swedish public service radio. *Journal of Contemporary Religion*, 34(1), 57–73.

Stoneman, T. (2017). Global radio broadcasting and the dynamics of American Evangelicalism. *Journal of American Studies*, 51(4), 1139–1170. https://doi.org/10.1017/S0021875816002000

Sunarwoto. (2016). Salafi Dakwah Radio: A contest for religious authority. *Archipel*, 91, 203–230. https://doi.org/10.4000/archipel.314

Taylor, R. J., & Chatters, L. M. (2011). Religious media use among African Americans, Black Caribbeans, and Non-Hispanic Whites. *Journal of African American Studies*, 15(4), 433–454. https://doi.org/10.1007/s12111-010-9144-z

Thomas, P. N. (2008). The changing nature of Christian broadcasting in India. In *Strong religion, zealous media: Christian fundamentalism and communication in India* (pp. 105–132). Sage Publications.

Thomas, P. N., & Lee, P. (Eds.). (2012). *Global and local televangelism*. Palgrave Macmillan.

Toledo Lorenzo, D., & Castañeda Seijas, M. Y. (2018). Dios en el micrófono: Radio cultural vida en Ocosingo, Chiapas. *Revista Cultura y Religión*, 12(1), 115–132.

Tomaselli, K., & Shepperson, A. (2002). "Speaking in tongues, writing in vision": Orality and literacy in televangelistic communications. In S. Hoover, & L. Clark (Eds.), *Practicing religion in the age of the media* (pp. 345–360). Columbia University Press.

Tudor, M., & Bratosin, S. (2018). The Romanian religious media landscape: Between secularization and the revitalization of religion. *Journal of Religion, Media, and Digital Culture*, 7(2), 223–250.

Ukah, A. (2015). Managing miracles: Law, authority, and the regulation of religious broadcasting in Nigeria. In R. I. J. Hackett, & B. F. Soares (Eds.), *New media and religious transformations in Africa* (pp. 245–265). Indiana University Press.

Veldman, M. (2017). Dressed in an angel's nightshirt: Jesus and the BBC. *Journal of British Studies*, 56(1), 117–137. https://doi.org/10.1017/jbr.2016.117

Velics, G., & Doliwa, U. (2015). Voice of the church: A debate about religious radio stations as community broadcasters. *Media and Communication*, 3(4), 76–90. https://doi.org/10.17645/mac.v3i4.344

Vernon, D. L. (2013). International religious radio broadcasting: The reactions of local listeners to a global message. *Michigan Academician*, 41(3), 355–376. https://doi.org/10.7245/0026-2005-41.3.355

Villar Pinto, H. A., Martínez Mendoza, S., & Cordero Fernández, F. J. (2013). El púlpito electrónico: La radio religiosa en Chiapas. *Razón y palabra*, 83, 466–502.

Viney, R. (1999). Religious broadcasting on UK television: Policy, public perception, and programmes. *Cultural Trends*, 36, 3–28.

Wallis, R. (2016). Channel 4 and the declining influence of organized religion on UK television. The case of Jesus: The evidence. *Historical Journal of film, Radio and Television*, 36(4), 668–688. https://doi.org/10.1080/01439685.2015.1132821

Wallis, R. (2020). Genesis of the bible documentary: The development of religious broadcasting in the UK. In H. K. Bond, & E. Adams (Eds.), *The Bible on television* (pp. 16–39). Bloomsbury.

Walton, J. L. (2009). *The ethics and aesthetics of Black televangelism*. NYU Press.

Ward, M. (2014). Give the winds a mighty voice: Evangelical culture as radio ecology. *Journal of Radio and Audio Media*, 21(1), 15–133.

Ward, M. (Ed.). (2016). *The electronic church in the digital age: Cultural impacts of evangelical mass media*. Praeger.

Ward, M. (2017). *The Lord's radio: Gospel music broadcasting and the making of Evangelical culture, 1920–1960*. McFarland & Company.

Ward, M. (2018). Digital religion and media economics: Concentration and convergence in the electronic church. *Journal of Religion, Media and Digital Culture*, 7(1), 90–120.

Watkins, D. (2021). Vatican Radio celebrating 90th anniversary with new services. Vatican News, February 9. Retrieved February 27, 2022, from https://www.vaticannews.va/en/vatican-city/news/2021-02/vatican-radio-90th-anniversary-statement-web-radio.html

White, P., & Assimeng, A. (2016). Televangelism: A study of the 'Pentecost Hour' of the Church of Pentecost. *HTS Teologiese Studies/Theological Studies*, 72(3), 1–6. https://doi.org/10.4102/hts.v72i3.3337

White, R. A. (2007). The media, culture, and religion perspective. *Communication Research Trends, 26*(1), 3–24.

Wilk, D. (2018). Role and room for social broadcaster with Radio Fara as an example. *Social Communication, 4*, 16–29. https://doi.org/10.2478/sc-2018-0012

Yakin, A. U. (2018). Salafi Dakwah and the dissemination of Islamic Puritanism in Indonesia: A case study of the radio of Rodja Ulumuna. *Journal of Islamic Studies, 22*(2), 205–236. https://doi.org/10.20414/ujis.v22i2.335

Yusuf, I. U., Usman, M., & Ibrahim, A. M. (2020). A comparative study of BRTV and NTA Maiduguri regarding their compliance with Nigeria Broadcasting Code on religious programming. *Informasi, 50*(1), 71–84. http://doi.org/10.21831/informasi.v50i1.29106

Zordan, D. (2014). Screening piety, invoking fervour: The strange case of Italy's televised Mass. *Journal of Religion, Media and Digital Culture, 3*(1), 56–83.

Selected Readings

Frederick, M. F. (2015). *Colored television: American religion gone global*. Stanford University Press.

Geybels, H., Mels, S., & Walrave, M. (Eds.). (2009). *Faith and media: Representation and communication* (pp. 151–178). Peter Lang.

Hroūb, K. (Ed.). (2012). *Religious broadcasting in the Middle East*. Hurst Publishers.

Ihejirika, W. (2009b). Research on media, religion, and culture in Africa: Current trends and debates. *African Communication Research, 2*(1), 1–60.

Sierra Gutiérrez, L. I. (2008). Tele-faith: Mediated religion in Brazil. *Communication Research Trends, 27*(1), 3–23.

Thomas, P. N., & Lee, P. (Eds.). (2012). *Global and local televangelism*. Palgrave Macmillan.

Ward, M. (Ed.). (2016). *The electronic church in the digital age: Cultural impacts of evangelical mass media*. Praeger.

11

Religious Personalities and Televangelism

Paul A. Soukup S.J.

Many people experience the confluence of religion and communication in terms of a television preacher. Most literature refers to a "televangelist," a term borrowed from Christianity (Bekkering, 2011, 2018; Burhani, 2020; Floden, 2016; Moll, 2012; Saleh, 2012; Thomas, 2012), whether or not the tradition seeks to evangelize. Because the phenomenon of television preaching spread widely and rapidly, many have studied it, a few from a global perspective (Thomas & Lee, 2012), but most concentrating on particular locations, with classic studies focused on the United States (Bruce, 1990/2019; Frankl, 1986; Hadden & Swann, 1981; Horsfield, 1984) and later ones on different parts of the world (James, 2010a; Okon, 2011; Walton, 2009). Methodologies range from the descriptive (Dabney, 1980) and historical (Floden, 2016) to uses and gratifications audience studies (Ableman, 1987) to content analysis of programming (Haigh & Brubaker, 2018).

This chapter focuses on people – the televangelists – rather than on the phenomenon, presenting a brief history, then an introduction to some of the participants, and finally some theoretical commonalities.

Historical Background

Televangelism depends on broadcast media. The printed mass media may have made religious leaders – like Martin Luther, Erasmus, or John Wesley – well known, but print did not give them an immediacy with large numbers of people. Only radio created a true mass media preacher. In this form, the religious leader meets the congregation not in a church, synagogue, temple, mosque, or meeting house, but in a virtual electronic world. The form, born in Christian circles in the United States in the 1920s, had spread around the world by the end of the twentieth century.

The United States, with its focus on independent communication businesses and constitutionally guaranteed freedom of religion, opened religion to entrepreneurial creativity, with independent religious broadcasting beginning in the 1920s. Evangelical (Baptist, Pentecostal) churches recognized the impact of radio for publicity; following a guest appearance on Chicago radio, Paul Rader began a weekly broadcast of his Gospel Tabernacle Church on WBBM in 1922, and the radio exposure drew people to his church. Other parts of the United States experienced the same thing, with some religious broadcasters achieving local or national fame. In Los Angeles, Rev. Aimee Semple McPherson became the first woman to preach on radio; in 1923 she established

The Handbook on Religion and Communication, First Edition. Edited by Yoel Cohen and Paul A. Soukup.
© 2023 John Wiley & Sons Ltd. Published 2023 by John Wiley & Sons Ltd.

a radio station at her church, the Angelus Temple (Comstock, 1927; McGloughlin, 1967). Across town, at the Trinity Methodist Church, Rev. Robert "Fighting Bob" Shuler set up station KGEF. In addition to the usual preaching, he gained a huge audience by denouncing the sins of public officials, business leaders, and entertainers, an audience so large that other stations could not compete at the hour of his program (Aikman, 1930; Duncan, 1964).

A reorganization of the broadcast spectrum and the enforcement of technical standards eliminated many religious radio stations in favor of commercial operators. Acknowledging this loss of business investment by the churches, the 1934 US Federal Communications Act required stations to set aside time for "public service" broadcasts, a category that included education and religion. The emerging US radio networks reserved Sunday mornings for the three large centralized religious groups in the United States: Protestants, Catholics, and Jews. These groups typically used an educational or dramatic format. Because the Catholics relied on one preacher, Fulton Sheen became a well-known voice of Catholicism in the United States, with a program that successfully made the transition to television and continued into the 1950s. Evangelical churches, too small to qualify for free network time and disqualified from station ownership, bought radio time; unlike the larger religious groups, they used worship formats like the revival meetings that characterized their public evangelization. Such formats, which included music, preaching, and Bible study proved well suited to radio. By the end of the 1940s, a number of regular radio preachers had achieved public renown. Public exposure made religious radio personalities famous, much as film roles did for movie stars. The radio era in the United States saw the rise of celebrity preachers, including Charles Swindall, W. A. Criswell, and Rex Humbard, whose main preaching took place on radio and later television.

Early radio saw the creation of new forms of religious practice in the development of approaches that continue to the present time. First, with churches serving as studios, the evangelical radio preachers structured their religious services or events for the radio; in-church services took place for broadcast. Second, and in contrast, liturgical religious groups (Catholic, Orthodox, Anglican, Lutheran) emphasized existing events, to which radio or television might listen in. The Pope provides an example: while he makes radio or television appearances, he typically does so in the context of public events. Interestingly, the Pope, with the Catholic Church's own Vatican Radio, seldom personally uses it, appearing only when the station carries religious services in Rome. Similar practices characterized the Anglican Communion, which rarely broadcast services, but instead featured performances by choirs around the UK. In the evangelical world, preachers, like the renowned revivalist Billy Graham, occasionally appeared on radio, but focused on an in-person revival ministry taking place in large public gatherings independently of radio.

Three later phenomena shaped the rise of the celebrity preachers. First, a number of evangelical or Pentecostal churches (which emphasize a literal interpretation of the Bible) sought to obey the "Great Commission" – "Go make disciples of all nations" (Matthew 28:19) – by establishing shortwave radio stations for international broadcasting of the Christian gospel (Freed, 1968, 1980). These included FEBC and HCJB, two of the largest in the world (Neely, 1980; Skelchy, 2020) as well as more local stations such as EWLA in West Africa (Stoneman, 2012). Many of their broadcasts feature a single evangelist, supported by a choir. International evangelical radio introduced this kind of programming around the world. Second, an evangelical denomination in the United States formally authorized radio as a form of ministry.

"Televangelism" first appeared in 1958 as the title of a proselytization project of the Southern Baptist Convention that combined dramatic television programs with efforts to engage viewers in person. "Televangelist" was introduced in 1975 to describe an emerging type of American television preacher, the most successful of whom built powerful parachurch organizations. (Bekkering, 2011, p. 101)

Third, the development of cable television in the United States made a great number of television channels available; eager to gain programming, US cable companies welcomed religious programming. Low-cost formats (preacher, choir) and satellite distribution around the country made the programming affordable. The 1980s saw the establishment of key televangelists on US cable television: Pat Robertson, Jim and Tammy Bakker, Rex Humbard, Jimmy Swaggart, and Robert Schuller (Bekkering, 2011, pp. 105–106).

Religious Groups

Televangelists have spread widely in the past 25 years. Most are Christian, but the phenomenon appears in Islam, Hinduism, Buddhism, and Judaism.

Christianity

Divided into several branches with some theological differences (see Chapters 3 and 5), Christianity, particularly its nonliturgical and independent evangelical churches emphasizing the "Great Commission," has seen the largest number of televangelists, starting in the United States and spreading around the world. In an admittedly incomplete list, Wikipedia includes 165 names from the different branches of Christianity. Many of these pastors share a common and somewhat stylized background story, which includes a call by God (sometimes from a sinful life, perhaps plagued by alcohol or drugs), a dramatic conversion or a blessing by God with a special talent (for preaching or healing), the foundation of a church, and the beginnings of a broadcast ministry (Bakker & Lamb, 1976; Dabney, 1980; Epp, 1952, 1964; Fuller, 1940; Robertson & Buckingham, 1972; Sinitiere, 2012; Strober & Tomczak, 1979; Voskuil, 1983).

Presenting developments in celebrity preaching, Bekkering (2011) identifies the following key US-based televangelists moving from local televangelism to more global kinds via the Internet: "Kenneth Copeland, Creflo Dollar, Joyce Meyer, and Benny Hinn. In addition, … the websites of Juanita Bynum, Paul Crouch, Marilyn Hickey, Brian Houston, T.D. Jakes, Joel Osteen, Rod Parsley, Oral Roberts, and Robert Tilton; all preachers with active television ministries" (p. 107). More are choosing online video over broadcast or as a complement, using platforms like Streaming Faith, LightSource, Cross.tv, and Tangle (p. 108). As background, Bekkering provides other demographic information about those who have moved their ministries online:

> In addition to the American ministries, one broadcast originated from New Zealand, and another from Nassau, in the Bahamas. Of the broadcasting ministries, 12 were non-denominational, 10 appeared to be linked with various denominations from the Baptist tradition, three identified with the Church of God, and one belonged to the African Methodist Episcopal church. (p. 110)

Spurred by the US denominations, Christian televangelism early on became international, as examples from Brazil and Guatemala illustrate. Initially, televangelists used shortwave radio or paid local stations to carry broadcasts recorded in the United States. Later they became local, as occurred in Brazil with the Seventh-Day Adventist program, *The Voice of Prophecy*, which recruited Roberto Rabello as its local radio evangelist in the 1940s (Bessa, n.d.). Television evangelism followed, using a similar pattern of imports from the United States (which could afford to buy time on Brazilian commercial television stations), and the growth of an indigenous model rooted in evangelical and Assemblies of God churches. In the 1980s Nilson do Amarai Fanini began a television ministry on 88 stations around the country. However, his larger enterprises ultimately failed financially. Edir Macedo, the founder of the Universal Church of the Reign of God (IURD), bought Fanini's television interest and turned it into the seed capital to create a media empire to fund his religious works, leading the "the most successful 'religious enterprise' in the global South" (Smith & Campos, 2005, p. 57). Macedo's IURD includes local churches in smaller cities, mega-churches in large cities, radio, television, newspapers, and online sites. Macedo's brother-in-law, R. R. Soares, has also become a well-known televangelist in Brazil, with his International Church of God's Grace and his own television strategies whose format differs from both Protestant worship and other televangelists (p. 59). A third well-known Brazilian Pentecostal television ministry, the Apostolic Church of Rebirth in Christ, differs from the others in being headed by a husband and wife team, Estevan and Sonia Hernandes Filho, and geared to a youth audience (p. 60).

Brazilian broadcast ministries extend beyond Pentecostalism. Caio Fabio, Jr., a Presbyterian television preacher had a successful ministry in the 1990s, even influencing political figures like Anthony Garotinho, who combined an evangelical ministry with his political career (Smith & Campos, 2012, p. 213). Perhaps inspired or challenged by Pentecostal churches, the Catholic charismatic renewal movement established its own television ministries led by televangelist priests Padre Eduardo Dougherty, S.J. (an American-born missionary), Padre Marcelo Rossi, and Padre Jonas Abib (Cleary, 2009, pp. 126–127). Rossi and another priest, Father Reginaldo Manzotti, anchor their television ministries with a music ministry that has led to top-selling albums, making a point to donate any sales proceeds to charity (Cobo, 2010). Unusually for Catholics, these programs feature not liturgical but praise and worship formats.

Guatemala became another center of Western hemisphere televangelism. Influenced by US churches and sometimes educated there, four preachers have dominated: Jorge H. López (succeeded by his son, Alex), Fernando Solares, Harold Caballeros, and Carlos "Cash" Luna. The first three evangelists' programs focus on worship – praise songs, testimonies, healings, and emotional messages – indigenous spirituality, telethons, and social services. Luna's program proclaims a prosperity gospel and uses unabashed fundraising (Smith & Campos, 2005, pp. 50–54).

In Africa, Ghana, Uganda, and Nigeria have produced televangelists. Like the Central and South American ministries, those in Ghana grew out of the evangelical movement in the 1950s–1970s and "the exposure to the media ministries of such American televangelists as Oral Roberts, T. L. Osborn, Benny Hinn, Morris Cerullo, Kenneth Hagin, and Kenneth Copeland within the same period" (Asamoah-Gyadu, 2005, p. 12). The American influence not only led to television ministries but also, according to Asamoah-Gyadu (2005), served "to erode denominational loyalties to historic mission churches in Ghana" (p. 12). The two leading television figures are the father of charismatic Christianity in Ghana, Archbishop Nicholas Duncan-Williams and Bishop Charles Agyin-Asare. Asamoah-Gyadu lists other noteworthy televangelists:

> In addition to the "Voice of Inspiration" [Duncan-Williams], "God's Miracle Hour" and "Your Miracle Encounter" [Agyin-Asare], there is also: "Living Word" hosted by Pastor Mensa Otabil of the International Central Gospel Church; "Mega-Word," hosted by Bishop Dr Dag Heward-Mills of the Lighthouse Chapel International; "Power in His Presence," hosted by Bishop Sam Korankye Ankrah of the Royal House Chapel (also known as International Bible Worship Center); "Treasures of Wisdom," hosted by Pastor Gordon Kisseih of Miracle Life Gospel Ministry International, Tema, Ghana; "Let the Prophet Speak," hosted by Pastor Isaac Nana Anto of the Conquerors Chapel International; and "Solid Rock," hosted by the only female charismatic pastor among the popular lot, Pastor Christy Doe Tetteh of the Solid Rock Chapel International. (p. 20)

The programs, modeled on the successful formulas of other televangelists, feature entertainment, strong pastoral personalities, and audience participation.

Uganda's path to televangelism resembles that in the United States, with the national broadcaster setting aside time for the major religious groups (Catholic, Anglican, Muslim); its decision in 1994 to allow private stations opened the door to other religious groups and allowed a greater share of broadcast hours (Jenga, 2017, p. 56). Some 20 years later, Pentecostal churches ran 16 of 20 religious stations in Kampala, receiving the highest ratings, almost twice as high as the next religious station, run by the Catholic Church (p. 61). "[I]ndigenous Pentecostal pastors such as Jackson Ssenyonga, Joseph Sserwada, David Kiganda, and Robert Kayanja, who own broadcast media houses, seem to dominate religious broadcasting in Kampala" (p. 61). Jenga (2017) notes that "Pentecostal broadcasting has also been used by pastors to enlarge their public profiles. Through use of emotional advertising techniques, pastors market themselves as 'anointed men of God'; and their religious events as 'miracle packed' or 'power-filled'" (p. 65). Like other broadcast evangelists, the Ugandans combine Ugandan tradition, "searching for blessings and financial breakthroughs" with personality-driven branding, entertainment, and praise songs (p. 68).

Nigeria also has televangelists, though Ihejirika (2012) distinguishes them from the US model in that these ministers first served in established churches before turning to broadcast ministries. The programs feature worship services, healings, and the casting out of demons. Ihejirika comments:

> In Nigeria, as in many other African countries, religious broadcasting is synonymous with Pentecostalism (Hackett, 1998; Ihejirika, 2005). As Asamoah-Gyadu (2005) rightly noted: "visual media and material culture are important for the charismatic movements, because, as world-affirming/accommodating movements the images of well being and prosperity used are meant to underscore the efficacy of the gospel of prosperity they preach" (p. 346). (Ihejirika, 2012, p. 180)

Since Nigerian law limits religious ownership of stations, many of the Pentecostal preachers make use of satellite and cable television channels. Most religious satellite channels

> belong to prominent Nigerian televangelists including Daystar, belonging to the Daystar Bible Church; the Deeper Christian Life Ministry (DCLM); Emmanuel TV – Pastor Joshua of the Synagogue of all Nations; Matthew Ashimolowo's Kingsway International Christian Centre (KICC); Mountain of Fire Ministries (MFM); LoveWorld – Pastor Chris Oyakilome's Christ Embassy; and Dove TV – Pastor Enoch Adeboye's Redeemed Christian Church of God. (p. 181)

More and more of these ministries have also turned to online models in order to bypass the legal restrictions on station ownership. The Pentecostal preachers have gained great visibility in the country. "It has made many of them like Enoch Adeboye, Chris Oyakhilome, Tunde Bakarc, Matthew Ashimolowo, Chris Okotie, and T. B. Joshua household names" (p. 182). Factors setting the Nigerian media evangelists apart include a very public opposition to Islam (Pastor Ayo Oritsejafor) and overt political ambitions for the pastors (Chris Okotie, Tunde Bakare, Enoch Adeboye, and Oritsejafor) (pp. 182–188).

Satellite broadcasting, which brought international televangelism to India in the 1990s, quickly led to a growth of local television preachers from various Christian groups. James (2010) reports that, at the time of his writing at least 10 24-hour Christian networks existed. "Some of these include: Shalom, Divine, New Hope, Ashirwad, Power Vision, Amboli (Catholic), and Rainbow. Angel TV, a 24-hour charismatic television network, based in the south has programs in Malayalam, Tamil, Telugu, English, and even one in Chinese" (p. 108). Several of the Indian televangelists gained local fame, including Brother Dhinakaran and his son, Dr. Paul Dhinakaran of the television program *Jesus Calls* (p. 112). The program, aired on 15 local channels, supports a ministry of prayer towers modeled on the work of US televangelist Oral Roberts. "Theologically, the Dhinakarans, like Roberts, preach and teach a charismatic theology, which includes the concept of prosperity, healing, and power encounters" (p. 116). In recent years, the ministry has expanded to address the Indian diaspora, with offices in the United States, Canada, Europe, and Dubai where people can donate to support the ministry. Dhinakaran differs from the US televangelists culturally and perhaps theologically by focusing on a collectivist gospel – looking at the group rather than the individual (Groen, 2019–2020, p. 29). Another well-known ministry, Gospel for Asia, features K. P. Yohanan and his television program, *Athmeeya Yatra*. The program promotes fundraising for a wide range of social needs such as "disaster relief, sinking wells, supplying water to villages, building orphanages and schools" (pp. 120–121).

Islam

Both Sunni and Shia Islam (see Chapter 6), particularly in Egypt, Mali, Indonesia, India, Kuwait, Pakistan, and the United States, have seen the rise of Islamic preachers on television and online in the past 25 years, coinciding with the availability of satellite or cable television and of the Internet. All major branches of Islam have televangelists, indicating that Islamic theology accepts this form of preaching. Many of the sources attribute both the idea of using television and the formats used to the inspiration of the Christian televangelists. Moll (2010) notes that Abu-Haibah, an Egyptian producer, "was impressed by Christian televangelism, telling an interviewer that he 'believ[ed] that if we did this with Islam it would be a new experience for Islam.'" Echchaibi (2011) echoes this:

> This new generation of spokespersons of Islam has been loosely labeled the "Islamic televangelists," the "preachers of air-conditioned Islam," or the "face of cool Islam"... Inherent in these labels is a conviction that this contemporary mediation of Islam is simply mimicking or importing the religious performance genre that helped popularize American evangelical Christianity through the adoption of modern mass media. (pp. 26–27)

Floden (2020), however, notes that "these individuals can trace their roots to earlier preachers who used newspapers, radio, and cassettes, as well as the phenomenon of popular storytellers from the medieval period." The present-day show formats often combine music, talk-show interviews, advice giving, storytelling, and recitation. While acknowledging the similarity of the program formats to that of Christian televangelists, Echchaibi (2011) points out that Islam has long made use of electronic formats such as audiocassettes of recorded sermons and recitations, forms that also appear in the broadcast materials.

The literature lists several studies of Islamic televangelists, with a bibliography by Floden (2020), which includes a documentary by Derouet (2009) that features many of them, and a collection edited by Hroub (2012) that provides some context for their television ministries.

Amr Khaled offers a representative figure. Neither a scholar nor a jurist, he is a ʿda-iyia or "caller to Islam" and seeks to address a younger audience. Beginning on an Egyptian satellite channel:

> the preaching style Khaled first developed on this show [*Words from the Heart*] – since copied with equal success by other young *duʾah* [callers] – continues to define the phenomenon known as *al-duah al-gudud* (the new preachers) – an easy-going yet energetic performance that is in colloquial Egyptian, the linguistic register of everyday life and conversation, and that makes frequent rhetorical use of allusions to popular culture and contemporary issues among youth, utilizing a format that is part US evangelical show, part US therapeutic talk show. (Moll, 2012, p. 21)

His show aims to teach "ordinary people" about religion and often uses the genre of Islamic storytelling. His success has inspired others like Moez Massoud and Mustafa Hosni (Saleh, 2012, p. 76). In addition to these, a more conservative televangelism reflects the Salafi school of Islam, with televangelists such as Abboud al-Zumur (p. 76). Other influential television presences include the Egyptian Yūsuf al-Qaradāwī (Floden, 2016, p. 19), representing formally trained religious scholarship; Ahman al-Shugairi, a Saudi whose program applies Islam to a wide range of topics (p. 30); and Tariq al-Suwaidan, a Kuwaiti preacher addressing business and religion (p. 35).

In the non-Arab Islamic world, the television and radio preachers of Mali present two illustrative models, both connected to reform movements. Noting that "one figure stands out," Schulz (2006) introduces the "charismatic preacher Cheick Cherif Ousmane Madani Haidara, whose mesmerizing voice pervades streets, market life, and domestic settings in the capital, Bamako, in San, and in Segu" (p. 210). Cherif Haidara, like many popular teachers began with audiocassettes and moved to local radio (being blocked by the government from national radio or television). Cherif Haiara, often criticized by establishment figures as poorly educated, has captured the public with his call for moral reform. The desire for moral reform based on a deeper knowledge of Islam motivates a group of female radio evangelists in Mali. Often addressing women's groups, they provide commentary and instruction. Addressed by the title *hadja*, and broadcasting on local radio stations, "The *hadjas* often stress that they are not Muslim 'teachers' (singular, *karamògò*) and do not voice independent interpretations but merely offer 'moral lessons' (*ladili*), a category of edifying speech in which older women are expected to engage" (Schulz, 2012, p. 24). Schulz (2012) introduces two – Hadja Salimata and Hadja Amina – as examples of female radio preachers who highlight cultural and gender issues in Mali. The experience of both the male and female preachers also points up the oppositional nature of these popular radio evangelists.

Indonesia saw a growth in broadcast religion after 1999 with the deregulation of television. Independent channels promoted a kind of preaching different from state-sponsored religious programming.

> The first of this model of preacher and the one who established the formula of *tuntunan* (religious advice) combined with *tontonan* (entertainment; a show), was Abdullah Gymnastiar (popularly known as Aa Gym)… Other star-status televangelists of the period, like Yusuf Mansur and Jefry Al Buchori ("Uje"), had somewhat different television routines, but all in one way or another offered light entertainment along with simple religious advice. (Howell, 2014, p. 237; see also Floden, 2016)

Even more serious preachers like Arifin Ilham incorporated entertainment. Howell (2014) sees these television ministries as part of a larger movement that incorporated mass rallies and other lay-run movements. In describing them, she compares the strategies behind them to that of the Christian televangelists, seeing a "fluidity" in their respective communities resulting from the medium – television – more than from any theological or copycat considerations (p. 240). Both groups try to create a community through viewing, coupled with in-person prayer meetings, the sale of religious goods, and branding in their respective cultures. Like their Christian counterparts in the United States, these "new preachers" relied not so much on their education (sometimes little formal religious training) as on their conversion stories to justify their television ministries and to connect them to their audiences (Burhani, 2020, p. 156). Muzakki (2012) adds several others to the list of Indonesian Islamic television preachers: K. H. Aainuddin MZ, Qurrata A'yun, Mamah Dedeh, Ahmad Al-Habsyi, Nur Maulana, and Soleh Mahmud (p. 45), noting the presence of several women in the group. Like other commentators, Muzakki argues that their popularity depends less on Islamic learning than on audience identification, pointing to the "negative public sentiment [that] arose over the practice of polygamy by Aa Gym," resulting in his loss of standing in the televangelist world (p. 51).

India's Islamic television figures reflect the complex religious situation in India. Like their Christian counterparts, they make use of satellite television channels to broadcast globally, often from stations outside of India.

> Mumbai-based Zakir Naik is currently the most popular Indian Islamic televangelist… His Islamic satellite television channel Peace TV … addresses mainly a Salafi public – Sunni Muslims who claim to follow the ideas and practices of the pious ancestors (*al-salaf al salih*) and advocates returning to the Quran and Sunnah by using *ijtihad*, independent reasoning. (Eisenlohr, 2017, p. 876)

Though banned by the Indian government in 2012, he continues on some channels and online. Citing the scriptures of Islam, Hinduism, and Christianity, he often invites other religious leaders to debates within a program format that also includes recitation, meditation, and interpretation or teaching (p. 876). The other major Islamic preaching comes from the "World Islamic Network (WIN), a Shi'ite media center established in 1991" (p. 878), which focuses less on a single preacher than on trained scholars, using a number of program formats including news, interviews, and phone-in questions (p. 879). Neighboring Pakistan has also produced a well-known Islamic television evangelist, Aamir Liaquat, who later used his television fame to anchor a political career (PARHLO, n.d.).

A rising star among the Islamic television preachers coming from the United States uses YouTube rather than satellite channels, although his popularity "secured him some airtime on the UK-based Islamic Channel, which is accessible in 132 countries" (Echchaibi, 2011, p. 26). Ali Ardekani or "Baba Ali represents one of the youngest generations of Muslim televangelists in the West. Although he was born in Iran, he grew up in the US in a non-religious family and converted to Islam as a young adult" (El Naggar, 2017, p. 2). His videos "revolve around the social life of Muslim youth from finding a spouse online to dealing with co-workers to responding to anti-Muslim rhetoric" (p. 2). His program format – a combination of entertainment, comedy, and Islamic teaching – betrays the influences of both Western pop culture and the YouTube media forms. He follows the characteristics of other popular Islamic television preachers: ordinary clothing, colloquial language, everyday topics, entertainment forms, and – in Baba Ali's case especially – an appeal to youth and the use of English (p. 4). His work also points to a new direction of televangelism (of all religious groups): the move to online program distribution, freeing preachers from the sometimes quite steep satellite and cable television expenses (see also Boy et al., 2018; El-Nawawy & Khamis, 2009; Hew, 2019).

Hinduism

By far the largest religious group in India, Hinduism (a noncentralized and theologically diverse group – see Chapter 3) has televangelists. Though resisted by the Hindu right, which "has insistently argued, Hinduism by default is a non-evangelical religion" (Chakrabarti, 2012, p. 157), other Hindu groups developed a Hindu televangelism in response to the Christian presence on television, to "mobilize Hindus" through "television channels like *Aastha, Sanskar, Maharishi, Sadhna, Jagran,* and *Om Shanti* [which] all feature Hindu televangelists" (James, 2010, p. 120). James (2010) cites one Indian scholar, who

> sees a direct link between the upsurge of Christian televangelism and the growth of Hindu televangelism. Professor Pavarala, firstly, sees the Hindu channels as a "social oddity" as Hinduism historically does not have a tradition of discourse like the Judeo-Christian faiths. Secondly, Pavarala

describes Hindu channels as "imitative and reactive" in that they are "aping Christian television and reacting to the hyper-Hindu sentiment of the ... Government." (p. 129)

Key Hindu television preachers include Baba Ramdev, Sri Ravi Shankar, Swami Sukubutananda, Guru Oshu, Aasaram Bapu, Divya Maharaas Leela, and Prajapita Bhramakumaris. Ramdev first attracted attention when he appeared on Sanskar; television executives from the larger rival channel Aastha "realized that Ramdev's appeal lay in making yoga accessible and, for that matter, teachable through television. This accessibility is at the heart of Ramdev's own discourse around yoga" (Chakrabarti, 2012, p. 156). James (2010) notes that "Ramdev, who teaches and demonstrates his *pranayam* (breath control) techniques, has cashed in on television to build a huge religious enterprise" with its own ashram, pharmacies, and television channels (p. 128). He has also developed some loose connections with leading political parties (Chakrabarti, 2012, p. 159). His programs include both yoga techniques and political commentary.

Other Hindu television personalities take different approaches. James (2010) describes how some model themselves on their Christian counterparts:

> It is interesting to note that two out of the 10 Hindu programs involve teachers or priests who move around the stage, like the Charismatic televangelists; and two out of 10 teach in English, both using a "three point sermon" outline, a popular technique used by Christian preachers. Swami Sukubutananda, who is known for his "relax your mind, transform your mind" rhetoric, communicates with passion like the American Charismatic televangelists. Sukubutananda is one of the few Hindu televangelists who speaks in English as his audience extends to Indians in the diaspora, in Switzerland, USA, and England as well. (p. 123)

Others mix instruction with prayer (Guru Yashpal Sudhanshu), simply meditate during the program (Sai Baba), recite mantras (Divya Maharaas Leela), or demonstrate yoga positions (Sonalia Guswari). In contrast to the mostly male Christian televangelists, the latter two Hindu televangelists are female (p. 124). James reports that a content analysis of two of the Hindu channels indicates that 55% of the time addresses yoga and meditation, 35% prayer and worship, and 5% preaching from Hindu texts (pp. 124–125).

Sri Ravi Shankar uses satellite television and markets supporting materials to a worldwide audience. He also has made good use of YouTube as a distribution medium. "Shankar's Art of Living Seminars are based on fees which consist of 'differently priced packages for each city and more expensive advance courses in big cities'" (James, 2010, p. 128). Nayar (2015), quoting Joseph, argues that his fame as a teacher comes

> in part because the movement provides "a yogic alternative to going to a shrink, stigmatized even today in India as an evidence of mental imbalance" (Joseph, 2011). Instead, the modern affluent of India pay for advice on how to breathe, meditate, and manage stress; they participate in "a brand of Hindu philosophy that is secular in nature," and frequently proffered in the form of "stock phrases ('Do not fall in love, rise in love')." (Nayar, 2015, p. 450)

Deepak Chopra has developed a presence both on Hindu channels and around the world with his "mind and body healing therapies based on *Aryuveda* – the traditional system of Indian medicine" (James, 2010, p. 128). Chopra combined his medical training with his knowledge of traditional medicine to become one of the most financially successful Hindu televangelists in the West. Nayar (2015) sees him as offering a "simplified Hinduism," drawing from various sources to appeal to a Western audience (pp. 450–451).

Buddhism

While Buddhism does not embrace evangelism but welcomes a wide range of practices, contemporary forces (including migration to dense urban areas and the presence of Christian televangelists) have influenced practices such that teachers have employed television and live-streaming to lead meditation sessions; this in turn led to growing fame for the teachers involved (Tricycle, 2020). Buddhist practices in countries like Thailand have moved into television programs as ways to reach more people (Feungfusakal, 2012). The Thai Global Buddhist Network (Dhammakaya media channel) began as a satellite channel and, after government restrictions on local television, is now available worldwide on YouTube. Though the channel features regular teachers, it tends not to list them by name. One group that does, Da-Ai TV, focuses on Master Zheng-Yan, who founded the Tzu-Chi movement in Taiwan. "Da-Ai TV, established as a non-profit-making TV network in 1998, is broadcast globally to more than 25 countries, from Asia to America, Africa, and Europe, via terrestrial broadcast signals, and satellite, as well as webcasting via its official website." Its programming includes Master Zheng-Yan's lectures, dramas (often based on her life or those of other key figures), news, educational material, health information, and so on (Liao, 2013, p. 289). In their review of digital religion in China, Xu and Campbell (2018) note a growing number of online Buddhist sites and the existence of celebrity teachers: "Some religious leaders, celebrities, or common followers are utilizing social media platforms, especially through Weibo and WeChat … [for] promoting online religious communication and dissemination" (pp. 270–271). However, government restrictions make it difficult for any sustained development of celebrity preachers or teachers. Other Buddhist teachers outside of Asia also distribute their teaching online, as does Tara Brach, an American psychologist and Buddhist teacher.

Judaism

None of the three main branches of Judaism engages in the kind of evangelism pioneered by the Christian televangelists; while not discouraging conversion of Gentiles, Judaic theology does not support a proactive evangelical agenda to Gentiles but rather focuses on other, assimilated, Jews. Reformed Jews are more comfortable with technology while the ultra-Orthodox ban it in some situations. However, Judaism has a number of celebrity rabbis, mostly from the Orthodox and Reform branches, who use online video or one of the proliferating "ask-a-rabbi" sites. Typically, these sites feature rabbis who answer questions posed by visitors, either to their local synagogue or to one of the larger sites. One Israeli rabbi, Amnon Yitzchak, has parlayed media appearances to become what Rosenthal (2003) called "a religious lecturer, aspiring tele-rabbi, and all-round media provocateur" whose "audience is composed of Israeli Jews who define themselves as Sephardic or Mizrahi – belonging to the 'Eastern' Jewry that immigrated to Israel from Morocco, Iran, Iraq, Yemen, Egypt, and Syria in the 1950s." Yitzchak encourages a "repentance revolution" and often presents himself as at odds with mainstream Israeli media.

A number of rabbis have developed followings to their video sermons. Several have material on https://en.meirtv.com, which hosts a variety of rabbis leading Torah study and others on the (interreligious) television site, HolyTV.co, a site founded by Mona Bijoor as a community platform open to any belief system (Wasserman, 2020). Rabbi Jonathan Aaron of Temple Emanuel in Beverly Hills appears on HolyTV as well as on YouTube. Rabbi Daniel Bortz, the self-proclaimed "millennial Rabbi," ministers through "jteen" of San Diego and has videos on most major platforms (https://www.rabbibortz.com). Another, Shmuley Boteach, a rabbi identified with the Chabad or Lubavitch branch of the Haredi Hassidic branch of Orthodox Judaism became "the first Orthodox rabbi to be a full participant in celebrity culture" (Ungar-Sargon, 2014), appearing with his own show on the TLC channel in the United States.

Kinds of Programs

Televangelists typically use media channels as they become available. Today they appear on radio; broadcast, cable, satellite, and online television channels like YouTube; and social media like Facebook and TikTok. Evangelical churches pioneered the mix of entertainment, preaching, and talk formats first in the US markets, probably because those formats fit well with both existing programming and religious purposes. Here, both religion and media exerted pressures to shape the programming. Churches ruled out formats such as comedies, and the audience expectation of the television medium ruled out long lecture formats. Some church groups (notably Catholics and Lutherans in the United States) experimented with dramatic forms; while these had some success, the nature of the form did not lead to a focus on any individual preacher.

By the end of the development period for cable television, a recognizable program format had developed, to the point that new mega-churches modeled their worship services on these formats, which consist of music, Bible proclamation, preaching, testimonials, interviews, and sometimes healings. Mega-churches, like Saddleback Church in the United States and Hillsong Church in Australia (and their affiliated churches around the world) have produced celebrity pastors like Rick Warren, Brian and Bobbie Houston, and Carl Lentz through outreach programs, though they are not known as televangelists, since they do not have a specific television ministry. As televangelism has spread throughout the world and to other religious groups, different countries and religions have reshaped the program formats to fit denominational and local preferences, but almost all merge entertainment with religion and fundraising. In addition to welcoming prayer requests and providing religious information, televangelist websites offer products for online purchase including books and recorded sermons; some sites run nonreligious advertising (Bekkering, 2011, p. 112).

Conclusion

Televangelism has spread to most major religions throughout the world because its model – television formats combining preaching and other religious content with entertainment usually delivered via satellite channels, focusing on a charismatic preacher – has proven easily adaptable, so that even groups that do not support an evangelical theology find it an acceptable form for reaching believers. Several trends emerge, some arising from the format, some from religious tradition, some from the changing media world.

First the format: many of the studies cited in this chapter include analyses of program content and note that in addition to preaching, teaching, or interpreting texts, the programs include entertainment elements. This makes sense since television lends itself to entertainment, moving even religious discourse into an entertainment format (Postman, 1985). Many religious groups adapt forms of entertainment from their worship traditions such as singing, dancing, or reciting, for example. Where religions do not have a tradition of such forms, television preachers might add them from secular sources. Because television can incur high costs, many televangelists include fundraising in their programs, either through direct appeals for donations or through the sales of branded items. Christian evangelical groups are more likely to allow this to influence their religious message, preaching a "prosperity gospel" that promises worldly success (Thomas, 2012, p. 237). The television format also takes advantage of the affordances of the digital world that allows a seamless transition to streaming and social media (Haigh & Brubaker, 2018). Several other factors work to make the form popular. Televangelism cultivates the central role of the preacher. This leads to the development of a parasocial relationship, much like those manifested in the cult of film or television stars. Bekkering (2011) refers to these as "parapersonal bonds" and then highlights a limitation: "Despite the establishment of parapersonal bonds between television ministries and their audiences, televangelists were unable to form religious communities around their personalities, as the unidirectional nature of television communication did not allow viewers to interact with each other" (p. 106). Other viewers watch because they find the programs unobjectionable compared with other television fare (Ableman, 1987). In some of the African churches, people tune in as an extension of their regular worship, as the televangelists broadcast from church services (Ihejirika, 2012; Jenga, 2017), thus enjoying a "shared ritual of viewing" (Bekkering, 2011, p. 106). For the non-Christian groups, the form offers a nonlocal or more universal sense of religion.

Second, religious tradition also influences televangelism. As noted, the form proves more successful with nonliturgical Christian groups and with non-Christian groups whose religious practice involves instruction by an imam, minister, rabbi, or guru. This factor cuts across religions and predicts which denominations will be more likely to embrace televangelists. Religions that value a charismatic style of leadership also tend to embrace televangelists as do groups whose theology highlights greater emotional response to the divine. On the other hand, televangelism raises a number of problems for religious groups. Thomas (2012) decries the "commodification of religion" (p. 239) and an increased global market for one kind of religious discourse and attendant religious goods. Bekkering points out that this form of religion promotes individualism, as worshipers do not have strong bonds to a community. The form also has spawned less religiously motivated imitators, particularly as it has moved to online formats. Without the costs associated with television broadcasting, a number of individuals without religious training and unaffiliated with any tradition put themselves forward as "influencers" or teachers. The research for this chapter turned up a number of comments warning the websurfer about some individuals who falsely represent their traditions. Finally, though not reported in this chapter, scandals (often financial and sometimes sexual) have embroiled televangelists from almost all traditions.

Third, Web 2.0 and social media have presented new opportunities for televangelism. As reported earlier in the chapter, a number of ministries make use of YouTube and other online channels like Roku (Roettgers, 2011) as low-cost worldwide distribution systems. The features of social media also allow them to overcome the isolation and lack of community and to reinforce the parasocial interactions with the evangelist. A number have taken to other social media like TikTok (Seo, 2020). The ease of such technology has also led other religious groups into the online evangelization world as happened with the Church of Jesus Christ of Latter-day Saints in Brazil (Weaver, 2019). The televangelist model also allows television celebrities to indirectly promote religion, as occurs with at least one popular Mormon commentator in the United States (Brooks, 2010).

Televangelism has affected religious practice globally. First it marks the beginnings of shifting religious practice from a church, synagogue, mosque, or other gathering place to a virtual experience in the home, something only increased by public health restrictions during the Covid-19 pandemic. In short, it reinforces the mediatization of religion (see Chapter 18) and the cultural importance of media. Second, it challenges religious leadership and authority by promoting religious teachers who bypass traditional training and ordination in favor of conversion experiences or personal charisma. In effect, televangelists promote "independent churches," that is, religious groups without traditional connections to theological leadership, whether in Christianity,

Judaism, Islam, or Hinduism. Third, some (Bekkering, 2011; Fore, 1990; Schultze, 1990; Thomas, 2012) argue that the televangelists distort religious content in favor of television ratings and business models, arguing that their ministries are businesses first and religious centers second. Fourth, the high-profile successes of televangelists have led to imitation both by other religions and by local religious groups imitating their formats in face-to-face gatherings; in other words, they have led to a homogenization of religious practices and to changes in prayer or liturgical rites in some places. Fifth, the success of the televangelists points to religion's involvement in a wider media ecology. Their success highlights the interaction of urbanization (guiding people separated from traditional worship), education (stressing emotional appeal over theology), technology (with new communication replacing face-to-face contact), and entertainment.

While some academic research examines televangelist programming, historical growth, audience motivations, and business models, more work remains in exploring audience numbers and growth, resilience and religious commitment, and responses by established religious groups.

References

Ableman, R. (1987). Religious television uses and gratifications. *Journal of Broadcasting & Electronic Media*, *31*(3), 293–307. https://doi.org/10.3366/swc.2005.11.1.90.1080/08838158709386665

Aikman, D. (1930). Savonarola in Los Angeles. *American Mercury*, *21*(4), 423–430.

Asamoah-Gyadu, J. K. (2005). Anointing through the screen: Neo-Pentecostalism and televised Christianity in Ghana. *Studies in World Christianity*, *11*(1), 9–28 https://doi.org/10.3366/swc.2005.11.1.9.

Bakker, J., & Lamb, R. P. (1976). *Move that mountain!* Logos International.

Bekkering, D. (2018). *American televangelism and participatory cultures: Fans, brands, and play with religious "fakes"*. Palgrave Macmillan.

Bekkering, D. J. (2011). From 'televangelist' to 'intervangelist': The emergence of the streaming video preacher. *The Journal of Religion and Popular Culture*, *23*(2), 101–117. https://doi.org.10.3138/jrpc.23.2.101

Bessa, L. D. (n.d.). The voice of prophecy – Brazil. EDSA: Encyclopedia of Seventh-Day Adventists. Retrieved February 21, 2021, from https://encyclopedia.adventist.org/article?id=AI9O&highlight=The|voice|of|prophecy

Boy, J. D., Uitermark, J., & Wiersma, L. (2018). Trending #hijabfashion: Using big data to study religion at the online-urban interface. *Nordic Journal of Religion*, *31*(1), 22–40. https://doi.org/10.18261/issn.1890-7008-01-02.

Brooks, J. (2010). America's first Mormon televangelist. Religion Dispatches. Retrieved June 1, 2021, from https://religiondispatches.org/americas-first-mormon-televangelist/

Bruce, S. (1990/2009). *Pray TV: Televangelism in America* (reissued 2019 by Taylor and Francis). Routledge, Chapman, and Hall.

Burhani, A. N. (2020). Muslim televangelists in the making: Conversion narratives and the construction of religious authority. *The Muslim World*, *110*(2), 154–175. https://doi.org/10.1111/muwo.12327

Chakrabarti, S. (2012). The avatars of Baba Ramdev: The politics, economics, and contradictions of an Indian televangelist. In P. N. Thomas, & P. Lee (Eds.), *Global and local televangelism* (pp. 149–170). Palgrave Macmillan.

Cleary, E. L. (2009). *How Latin American saved the soul of the Catholic church*. Paulist Press.

Cobo, L. (2010, May 28). Priests become a hit-making trinity in Brazil. Reuters. Retrieved February 22, 2021, from https://www.reuters.com/article/us-brazil/priests-become-a-hit-making-trinity-in-brazil-idUSTRE64S06T20100529.

Comstock, S. (1927). Aimee Semple McPherson: Prima donna of revivalism. *Harpers Magazine*, *156*, 11–19.

Dabney, D. (1980). God's own network: The TV kingdom of Pat Robertson. *Harpers*, *261*(1563), 33–52.

Derouet, T. (Dir. 2009). *Muslim televangelists: Voices of Islam's future*. Journeyman Pictures.

Duncan, R. (1964). "Fighting Bob" Shuler: The holy terror. *Los Angeles*, *8*(3), 38–41, 65–67, 72.

Echchaibi, N. (2011). From audio tapes to video blogs: The delocalization of authority in Islam. *Nations and Nationalism, 17*(1), 25–44. https://onlinelibrary.wiley.com/doi/10.1111/j.1469-8129.2010.00468.x

Eisenlohr, P. (2017). Reconsidering mediatization of religion: Islamic televangelism in India. *Media, Culture & Society, 39*(6), 869–884. https://doi.org/10.1177/0163443716679032

El Naggar, S. (2017). 'But I did not do anything!' – Analysing the YouTube videos of the American Muslim televangelist Baba Ali: Delineating the complexity of a novel genre. *Critical Discourse Studies.* https://doi.org/10.1080/17405904.2017.1408477

El-Nawawy, M., & Khamis, S. (2009). *Islam dot com: Contemporary Islamic discourses in cyberspace.* Palgrave Macmillan.

Epp, T. H. (1952). *Adventuring by faith.* Back to the Bible Publishers.

Epp, T. H. (1964). *Twenty-five years of adventuring by faith.* Back to the Bible Publishers.

Feungfusakal, A. (2012). Urban logic and mass meditation in contemporary Thailand. In P. N. Thomas, & P. Lee (Eds.), *Global and local televangelism* (pp. 219–233). Palgrave Macmillan.

Floden, T. (2020). Muslim television preachers. Oxford Bibliographies. https://doi.org/10.1093/OBO/9780195390155-0273. Retrieved April 28, 2021, from https://www.oxfordbibliographies.com/view/document/obo-9780195390155/obo-9780195390155-0273.xml#:~:text=Prominent%20examples%20of%20Muslim%20television,Naik%20of%20India%2C%20Abdullah%20Gymnastiar%20

Floden, T. B. (2016). *Televangelists, media duʿā, and ʿulamā': The evolution of religious authority in modern Islam* (unpublished doctoral dissertation). Georgetown University.

Fore, W. (1990). "Living church" and "electronic church" compared. In R. Abelman, & S. M. Hoover (Eds.), *Religious television: Controversies and conclusions* (pp. 135–146). Ablex Publishing Corporation.

Frankl, R. (1986). *Televangelism: The marketing of popular religion.* Southern Illinois University Press.

Freed, P. E. (1968). *Towers to eternity.* Word Books.

Freed, P. E. (1980). *Let the earth hear.* Thomas Nelson Publishers.

Fuller, J. E. (1940). *The Old Fashioned Revival Hour and the broadcasters.* The Fellowship Press.

Groen, D. (2019–2020). Christian televangelism in India: Influence of globalization and technological advancements on religion Unpublished Master's Thesis), Leiden University. Retrieved March 16, 2022, from https://studenttheses.universiteitleiden.nl/access/item%3A2662648/view

Hackett, R. I. J. (1998). Charismatic/Pentecostal appropriation of media technologies in Nigeria and Ghana. *Journal of Religion in Africa, 28*(3), 258–277. https://doi.org/10.1163/157006698X00026

Hadden, J. K., & Swann, C. E. (1981). *Prime time preachers: The rising power of televangelism.* Addison-Wesley.

Haigh, M. M., & Brubaker, P. J. (2018). Social media and televangelists: Examining Facebook and Twitter content. *Journal of Religion, Media and Digital Culture, 7*(1), 29–49. https://doi.org/10.1163/25888099-00701003

Hew, W. W. (2019). On-offline dakwah: Social media and Islamic preaching in Malaysia and Indonesia. In K. Radde-Antweiler, & X. Zeiler (Eds.), *Mediatized religion in Asia: Studies on digital media and religion* (pp. 89–104). Routledge.

Horsfield, P. (1984). *Religious television: The American experience.* Longman Publishing Group.

Howell, J. D. (2014). Christendom, the ummah, and community in the age of televangelism. *Social Compass, 61*(2), 234–249. https://doi.org/10.1177/0037768614524322

Hroub, K. (2012). *Religious broadcasting in the Middle East.* C. Hurst & Co.

Ihejirika, W. C. (2005). Media and fundamentalism in Nigeria. *Media Development, 52*, 38–44.

Ihejirika, W. C. (2012). From televisuality to social activism: Nigerian televangelists and their socio-political agenda. In P. N. Thomas, & P. Lee (Eds.), *Global and local televangelism* (pp. 173–199). Palgrave Macmillan.

James, J. D. (2010). *McDonaldisation, masala, McGospel, and om economics: Televangelism in contemporary India.* Sage Publications.

Jenga, F. (2017). Pentecostal broadcasting in Uganda. *Journal of Communication and Religion, 40*(4), 53–71.

Joseph, M. (2011) Spiritualism made for the modern age: Letter from India. *New York Times* (July 7), 2.

Liao, P.-R. (2013). Imagining a 'human Bodhisattva' via televisual discourse: Media platform of the Tzu-Chi organisation. *Contemporary Buddhism, 14*(2), 284–297. https://doi.org/10.1080/14639947.2013.832083.

McGloughlin, W. G. (1967). Aimee Semple McPherson: "Your sister in the king's glad service". *Journal of Popular Culture, 1*(3), 192–217. https://doi.org/10.1111/j.0022-3840.1967.0103_193.x

Moll, Y. (2010). Islamic televangelism: Religion, media, and visuality in contemporary Egypt. *Arab Media & Society*, 10, 1–27. https://www.arabmediasociety.com/islamic-televangelism-religion-media-and-visuality-in-contemporary-egypt

Moll, Y. (2012). Storytelling, sincerity, and Islamic televangelism in Egypt. In P. N. Thomas, & P. Lee (Eds.), *Global and local televangelism* (pp. 21–44). Palgrave Macmillan.

Muzakki, A. (2012). Islamic televangelism in changing Indonesia: Transmission, authority, and the politics of ideas. In P. N. Thomas, & P. Lee (Eds.), *Global and local televangelism* (pp. 45–63). Palgrave Macmillan.

Nayar, S. J. (2015). Hinduism. In J. C. Lyden, & E. M. Mazur (Eds.), *The Routledge companion to religion and popular culture* (pp. 440–459). Routledge.

Neely, L. (1980). *Come up to this mountain: The miracle of Clarence W. Jones & HCJB.* Tyndale House Publishers.

Okon, G. (2011). Televangelism and the socio-political mobilization of Pentecostals in Port Harcourt metropolis: A KAP survey. *Politics and Religion*, 5(1), 61–80. https://www.researchgate.net/publication/273135326_RELIGION_MEDIA_AND_POLITICS_IN_AFRICA_61_TELEVANGELISM_AND_THE_SOCIO-POLITICAL_MOBILIZATION_OF_PENTECOSTALS_IN_PORT_HARCOURT_METROPOLIS_A_KAP_SURVEY

PARHLO. (n.d.) Introduction – Dr. Aamir Liaquat Hussain. PARHLO. Retrieved February 26, 2021, from https://www.parhlo.com/dr-aamir-liaquat-hussain

Postman, N. (1985). *Amusing ourselves to death: Public discourse in the age of show business.* Penguin.

Robertson, P., & Buckingham, J. (1972). *Shout it from the housetops.* Logos International.

Roettgers, J. (2011). Jesus loves Roku: Televangelism in the age of web TV. Gigaom. Retrieved March 2, 2021, from https://gigaom.com/2011/02/04/jesus-loves-roku-televangelism-in-the-age-of-web-tv

Rosenthal, M. (2003). Israel's tele-rabbi. *Religion in the News*, 6(2). https://www3.trincoll.edu/csrpl/RINVol6No2/Israel's Tele-rabbi.htm.

Saleh, I. (2012). Islamic televangelism: The Salafi window to their paradise. In P. N. Thomas, & P. Lee (Eds.), *Global and local televangelism* (pp. 64–83). Palgrave Macmillan. https://doi.org/10.1057/9781137264817_4

Schultze, Q. (1990). Defining the electronic church. In R. Abelman, & S. M. Hoover (Eds.), *Religious television: Controversies and conclusions* (pp. 41–52). Ablex Publishing Corporation.

Schulz, D. E. (2006). Promises of (im)mediate salvation: Islam, broadcast media, and the remaking of religious experience in Mali. *American Ethnologist*, 33(2), 210–229. Retrieved March 15, 2022, from https://www.jstor.org/stable/3805412

Schulz, D. E. (2012). Dis/embodying authority: Female radio "preachers" and the ambivalences of mass-mediated speech in Mali. *International Journal of Middle East Studies*, 44(1), 23–43. https://www.jstor.org/stable/41474979

Seo, R. (2020). Meet the TikTok generation of televangelists. Christianity Today. Retrieved March 2, 2021, from https://www.christianitytoday.com/ct/2020/november/meet-tik-tok-generation-z-televangelists-seo.html

Sinitiere, P. L. (2012). Preaching the good news glad: Joel Osteen's tel-e-vangelism. In P. N. Thomas, & P. Lee (Eds.), *Global and local televangelism* (pp. 87–107). Palgrave Macmillan.

Skelchy, R. P. (2020). The afterlife of colonial radio in Christian missionary broadcasting of the Philippines. *South East Asia Research*, 28(3), 344–362. https://doi.org/10.1080/0967828X.2020.1803761

Smith, D. A., & Campos, L. S. (2005). Christianity and television in Guatemala and Brazil: The Pentecostal experience. *Studies in World Christianity*, 11(1), 49–64.

Smith, D. A., & Campos, L. S. (2012). God's politicians: Pentecostals, media, and politics in Guatemala and Brazil. In P. N. Thomas, & P. Lee (Eds.), *Global and local televangelism* (pp. 200–218). Palgrave Macmillan.

Stoneman, T. (2011). Radio missions: Station ELWA in West Africa. *International Bulletin of Missionary Research*, 26(4), 200–204 https://doi.org/ 10.1177/239693931203600407.

Strober, J., & Tomczak, R. (1979). *Jerry Falwell: Aflame for God.* Thomas Nelson Publishers.

Thomas, P. N. (2012). Whither televangelism: Opportunities, trends, challenges. In P. N. Thomas, & P. Lee (Eds.), *Global and local televangelism* (pp. 223–246). Palgrave Macmillan.

Thomas, P. N., & Lee, P. (Eds.). (2012). *Global and local televangelism.* Palgrave Macmillan.

Tricycle. (2020). Introducing free online practice sessions. Tricycle. Retrieved February 28, 2021, from https://tricycle.org/trikedaily/online-meditation

Ungar-Sargon, B. (2014). Celebrity rabbi, heal thyself. Tablet. Retrieved March 1, 2021, from https://www.tabletmag.com/sections/news/articles/shmuley-boteach

Voskuil, D. (1983). *Mountains into goldmines: Robert Schuller and the gospel of success*. William B. Eerdmans.

Walton, J. L. (2009). *Watch this! The ethics and aesthetics of black televangelism*. New York University Press.

Wasserman, T. (2020). Holy TV founder sees religion as a social (media) experience. Forbes. Retrieved March 1, 2021, from https://www.forbes.com/sites/toddwasserman/2020/11/19/why-holy-tv-founder-sees-religion-as-a-social-media-experience/?sh=3bb53e59d821

Weaver, S. J. (2019). These Latter-day Saint social media influencers have impacted millions. Here's the secret to their success. Church News. Retrieved March 2, 2021, from https://www.thechurchnews.com/members/2019-11-03/social-media-brazil-nicole-luz-wesley-merces-165901

Xu, S., & Campbell, H. A. (2018) Surveying digital religion in China: Characteristics of religion on the Internet in Mainland China. *The Communication Review*, *21*(4), 253–276, https://doi.org/10.1080/10714421.2018.1535729

Selected Readings

Bekkering, D. (2018). *American televangelism and participatory cultures: Fans, brands, and play with religious "fakes"*. Palgrave Macmillan.

Bekkering, D. J. (2011). From 'televangelist' to 'intervangelist': The emergence of the streaming video preacher. *The Journal of Religion and Popular Culture*, *23*(2), 101–117. https://doi.org.10.3138/jrpc.23.2.101.

Bruce, S. (1990). *Pray TV: Televangelism in America*. Routledge, Chapman, and Hall, (reissued 2019 by Taylor and Francis).

Burhani, A. N. (2020). Muslim televangelists in the making: Conversion narratives and the construction of religious authority. *The Muslim World*, *110*(2), 154–175. https://doi.org/10.1111/muwo.12327

Horsfield, P. (1984). *Religious television: The American experience*. Longman Publishing Group.

Howell, J. D. (2014). Christendom, the ummah, and community in the age of televangelism. *Social Compass*, *61*(2), 234–249.

Hroub, K. (2012). *Religious broadcasting in the Middle East*. C. Hurst & Co.

Ihejirika, W. C. (2012). From televisuality to social activism: Nigerian televangelists and their socio-political agenda. In P. N. Thomas, & P. Lee (Eds.), *Global and local televangelism* (pp. 173–199). Palgrave Macmillan.

James, J. D. (2010). *McDonaldisation, masala, McGospel, and om economics: Televangelism in contemporary India*. Sage Publications.

Thomas, P. N., & Lee, P. (Eds.). (2012). *Global and local televangelism*. Palgrave Macmillan.

12

Public Relations and Advertising

Carlo Nardella

Religion and marketing have grown more closely intertwined as religious institutions seek economic resources in competition with other religions by employing the codes and techniques of advertising and public relations. In the United States, this phenomenon has existed for some time, but more recently it assumed unprecedented intensity, frequency, and a remarkable spread. Research using a range of theoretical perspectives and research methods, and addressing diverse national and social contexts, has led to a key conclusion: we can think of something called the "marketing of religion." While neither fund-raising nor religious marketing is new or a repositioning of existing tools, the marketing of religion signals a new dimension in religious organizations' approaches, which regard both the faithful and nonfaithful as part of a broad audience of consumers.

This phenomenon sits in the context of a wider historical and social change, one marked by the emergence of competition among religious actors, and the need for those actors to ensure survival in a competitive environment. Berger (1967) identified the dynamics at its origin as essentially concerning two levels. First, pointing to endogenous factors within the religious dynamic, the processes accounting for the change substantially depend on (i) the proliferation of religious organizations and groups, fueled by structural secularization and socio-cultural pluralism, which has (ii) created the conditions for the existence of a variety of equally possible religious choices, and, by reducing the efficiency of religious institutions in exercising social control, has (iii) made it possible for individuals to privately make their own choices in matters of religion. Second, the sociologists account for some exogenous factors, such as the rise of the economy as a central sector of society driving social change, more specifically those sectors formed by capitalist and industrial processes, whose pervasive influence has produced a general process of rationalization, with significant consequences of both a collective and individual nature (see Wilson, 1966).

The key sector is therefore the economy, with its underlying general process of rationalization, understood in a Weberian sense, which implies the use of a highly rationalized bureaucracy influencing "both the religious organizations' internal and their external social relations" (Berger, 1967, p. 140). Internally, the logic of bureaucracy dominates both the administration and the "day-to-day operations" with which religious organizations define their essential objectives to survive as well as the ways to achieve them (e.g. by attracting members, funds, and public support). Externally, "the religious institutions deal with other social institutions as well as with each other through the typical forms of bureaucratic interaction," such as public relations with

The Handbook on Religion and Communication, First Edition. Edited by Yoel Cohen and Paul A. Soukup.

potential customers, lobbying with politicians, and advertising campaigns aimed at raising funds from private or public sources (p. 153).

Pluralism, both as an institutional fact and a cultural aspect, appears essential (Berger, 1967, p. 127; on pluralism as a concomitant of secularization, see Berger & Luckmann, 1966). In a mutual cause–effect relationship, pluralism reacts with other phenomena of the privatization of choices, norms, and general orientations toward social values and behaviors, creating particular adaptations in the configuration and behavior of the religious organizations and their theological systems in a knock-on effect (Berger has drawn attention to this point, developing some intriguing hypotheses; Berger, 1967, pp. 155–171; 1969).

Within a process of mutual interdependence between secularization, rationalization and pluralism, religious institutions have gone from being monopolies to becoming "marketing agencies" in competition with each other. The result, according to Berger, is a situation in which:

> the religious tradition, which previously could be authoritatively imposed, now has to be *marketed*. It must be "sold" to a clientele that is no longer constrained to "buy." The pluralistic situation is, above all, a *market situation*. In it, the religious institutions become marketing agencies and the religious traditions become consumer commodities. And at any rate a good deal of religious activity in this situation comes to be dominated by the logic of market economics. (Berger, 1967, p. 138)

Having identified some modern trends driving the shift toward marketing religion, one should not draw the hasty conclusion that we see a brand new phenomenon. Campbell's (1987) analysis of the origin of consumerism shows that consumer-oriented cultures and lifestyles are not recent. Similarly, Moore's (1994) historical study of the commodification of religion in the United States underlines that the mix of religion with commercial logics is not an exclusively modern or twentieth-century phenomenon. We can easily find examples of commercial aspects of religion in past times: Moore points to the growth of markets and fairs in cathedral towns, in whose profits the Church shared; the sale of indulgences attacked by Martin Luther; and the spread of Protestantism among urban merchants in Europe. On the other hand, that religion has found it necessary to embrace techniques of commercial expansion should not be seen as an authentic residue of a past left virtually unchanged. Moore notices that this phenomenon has changed fundamentally over time, identifying in this regard a watershed moment in the "transformations of market societies in the 19th century," which "transform[ed] the issues, changing the whole texture and meaning of activities labeled 'spiritual'" (p. 7).

This is true in particular for the United States, which prohibits a state Church while leaving its citizens free to pursue and practice their own belief sets, a society that is organized (since at least the 1790s) according to a free market logic, with a history of competition between religious institutions, and between religious and other cultural institutions. This offers another reason to study the commercial component of religion and its relationship with the tools of marketing communications, such as advertising and public relations. We first focus attention on how and why religious organizations have offered their products "for sale" in this specific national context.

A Historical Overview

Religious and commercial spheres mixed in nineteenth-century America. Between 1800 and 1830, the mass production of Bibles introduced the sale of religious books to a profit-based market with little distinction between business and nonbusiness (Moore, 1994). Missionary organizations, like the American Tract Society and the American Bible Society (funded primarily by

Presbyterian and Congregational laymen), aimed for large-scale printing and distribution of the Bible and other religious tracts. To this end, they developed innovative printing techniques and found new ways to sell their message to consumers by borrowing the advertising and publicity techniques employed by merchants. These included hiring artists, engravers, and illustrators to increase the appeal of their materials and advertising religious texts as an enjoyable read: "tracts were 'short,' 'interesting,' 'striking,' 'clear', 'plain,' 'pungent,' and 'entertaining,' the same adjectives picked up by copywriters to sell popular serials and fiction" (p. 20; see also Nord, 1984).

McDannell (1995) describes the commercial expansion of the book trade in the first half of the nineteenth century, the competition between religious and nonreligious publishers, and the sale of religious titles alongside novels and other nondevotional books. McDannell also notes that, by the 1830s, the innovations introduced by the missionary and tract societies to sell the Bible helped make it not just a book but also an artifact with a specific use value for those who owned it. This combined social meanings with the practice of reading and praying, aesthetics, taste, identity, and social status. For this reason, many displayed the Bible at home. This explains the increasing attention that publishers paid to its material aspect, such as the size, the quality of the leather binding, the paper, and the color of the illustrations – all to entice possible buyers. The Bible fit in with other "religious objects" that had similar use values, as, for example, glasses etched with the Lord's Prayer, wooden Noah's Arks, Bible puzzles, wax and porcelain crosses, and bookmarks with religious mottoes. These demonstrated the marketing success of Christian organizations like the Gospel Trumpet Company (the publishing house of the Church of God, later called Warner Press), whose religious products influenced the aesthetics of American Protestant homes until the mid-twentieth century.

Between 1870 and 1930 merchants, retailers, craftsmen, and trade associations worked to transform Christmas, Easter, and Valentine's Day into "consumer rites" for specialized goods for the holidays – from Valentines to greeting cards to floral decorations, millineries, and groceries (Schmidt, 1995). The economic reorientation of the religious calendar began with Christmas among the Protestant churches, with advertising convincing the public that this holiday was an occasion for consumption, a task largely completed by 1900. Previously, Christmas had known little commercialization: Schmidt (1991) reports that, from 1800 to 1820, hymns and religious poems occupied more space in newspapers than the few advertisements for holiday gifts (p. 890). (For other aspects of the commercialization of Christmas, see Belk, 1987; Nissenbaum, 1997.)

Other factors affecting the transformation of Christmas into a consumer celebration included an endorsement of advertising by at least a part of the American Protestant clergy, both to encourage seasonal sales and to provide a means for reaching the public. Moore (1994) notes the convergence of two seemingly disconnected situations in the early twentieth century. First, advertisements for Christmas gifts created strong associations between "the 'miracle' of Santa Claus and his reindeer" and "the 'miracle' at Bethlehem and the gifts that the three kings carried to the Christ child" (p. 206). Second, liberal Protestant leaders looked benignly upon such associations as their vision about how to build a just and good society involved a large-scale use of advertising and other techniques of efficient business management. Indeed, advertising became a key area for American liberal Protestant churches, and the target for heavy investment from the late 1890s to the early 1930s.

These advertising investments paved the way for the commercialization of Christmas and the turning of churches into business-like organizations to manage growth. By the end of the 1930s, for example, books designed to improve church activities through advertising became part of a growing body of literature (Case, 1921; Reisner, 1913; Stelzle, 1908). These early works argued that advertising and publicity – terms used interchangeably – could expand church attendance and reach people who were not likely to come to church. Case (1921) mixed faith and business by collecting suggestions from both ministers and people working in the advertising profession. He offered churches and their leaders practical information on how to create slogans able to spark people's curiosity, get church news in the papers, and lay out a church bulletin with maximum eye-catching effect (Moore, 1994, p. 214). Reisner (1913), too, promoted cultivating relationships with newspaper editors and reporters to gain publicity (Butler, 2020, p. 49). These books stressed reaching new "consumers" by telling them what the church had for sale; simply waiting for people to come to church on their own initiative was no longer a viable option.

Turning Points and Underlying Trends

The 1960s mark a turning point in applying marketing tools to religion. At this time, switching to another faith, or to no faith at all, became more common and accepted among the American population (McLeod, 2007; Roof, 1993). Religious practice and belonging rested on personal choice rather than social pressure; other external constraints no longer guaranteed stable audiences for religious institutions. Hence, they increasingly turned to advertising to fill the church pews. This change, however, did not fully manifest itself until the end of the 1980s (Einstein, 2008). Evidence of this appears in the slow but continuous increase in academic publications on the subject – virtually nonexistent until that time, with the exception of the seminal work of Culliton (1959) – which began to appear in both marketing and religious journals. These publications differed from Case (1921) and the others appearing 50 years before, in that the latter aimed toward finding solutions to religious institutions' practical problems in becoming more successful, while the former highlighted how "scientific" marketing concepts could be effectively applied in religious contexts.

Several authors contributed to this line of research: for example, Healy and DeLozier (1978) proposed a marketing plan to allow religious organizations to carry out their mission efficiently; Anderson et al. (1984) developed a marketing model that incorporated the 4Ps of product, price, place, and promotion; and Carman (1987) created a mathematical model to suggest promotional expenditure plans to religious organizations. Wrenn (1993) analyzed the distinctive characteristics of religious organizational marketing with respect to commercial enterprise marketing, and Mehta and Mehta (1996) identified factors determining worshipers' church satisfaction (see Cutler, 1992, and Cutler and Winans, 1998, for a more comprehensive review of this literature).

This literature broadened in the 1990s from a narrow focus on marketing issues to a wider emphasis on improving the "business." This became possible when academics and marketing experts addressed pastors and other local church leaders to provide them with practical knowledge on modern marketing methodologies and techniques to use to implement their church growth (Barna, 1992; Shawchuck et al., 1992; Stevens et al., 2006).

Whatever the advantages of a marketing communications approach for churches, clergy members do not always favor marketing in religion. Although religious marketing appears more often in the United States, we have seen that religious specialists do not always embrace the idea that marketing tools apply in the same way to a religious organization as to a business corporation. A series of studies (mainly in the 1980s) explored whether American religious communities actually held a prejudice against some of the main marketing techniques, especially advertising. Several studies found the opposite, with support for marketing in religion in North Carolina (Dunlap et al., 1983), California (Gazda et al., 1984), Texas (Moncrief et al., 1986), and nationally (McDaniel, 1986, 1989). Most of these showed that clergy approved advertising in telephone directories, billboards, newspapers, and direct mailing as well as by door-to-door canvassing. The clergy were more open to advertising than the general public, although clergy preferred not to use the term "marketing" in referring to these activities.

Subsequent studies used these empirical findings as a starting point to guide research, shifting the object of study from the perceived appropriateness of marketing religion to frequency and perceived effectiveness. Over half of large US Southern Baptist churches used newspaper, telephone directory, direct mail, radio, and television advertising (Hines, 1996); Midwestern Episcopal, Presbyterian, and Lutheran churches frequently used telephone directory advertising, monthly newsletters, bulletins, and brochures, as well as home visits, telephone calls, and direct mail to people who visited the church (Webb et al., 1998). Comparing the perceived effectiveness of marketing communication categories (personal contact, print, and broadcast) with their purpose (recruiting new members or retaining current members), Webb and colleagues (1998) found that pastors perceived personal contact methods most effective to retain churchgoers, but print and radio advertising more effective for recruitment, while rejecting television advertising as ineffective for both purposes. Vokurka et al. (2002) noted that churches in urban areas as opposed to rural areas more likely used marketing communication media and experienced growth. This study confirmed that pastors felt home visits and telephone calls were the most effective means of outreach to church visitors. The preference for more personal forms of communication may account for US pastors' willingness to include various online-based media, such as websites, podcasts, Facebook, Twitter, and YouTube among the primary means used for growing their churches, as the Internet became available. American Christian church leaders can now broadcast messages to anyone who follows their page (Webb, 2012). Many of them have embraced Twitter as a space for communication among congregants, as well as for building relationships. In addition, half of Webb's sample of 1000 Protestant churches used Facebook as a ministry aid in 2010.

The Pole of Consumers

The United States shows a well-established relationship between the growth needs of churches (not only Protestant) and a range of communication tools traditionally employed by marketers – a tie strengthened since the 1990s. The early 2000s saw some changes linked to the emergence of a new approach to marketing based on the creation of symbolic meanings around products and services with the aim of turning them into useful tools for people to communicate and interact. These changes affecting the commercial communication sphere also had an impact on religious communication. The use of marketing was no longer just a means for "selling" a message aimed at attracting different kinds of resources (new members, volunteers, donations, etc.), but also dominated the conceptualization of the religious message itself. Marketing communication methods and techniques shifted from external tools used by religious organizations to spread their ideas and influence outward to integral parts of their overall meaning systems.

Marketing communication as a "form" became autonomous with respect to its "content." Here the religious message is conceptualized directly within the communication: according to some scholars, this transformation allows religious institutions to exist and persist in a secularized world.

Einstein (2008) proposed that the proliferation of religious choices, the high level of media saturation, and the ubiquitous presence of advertising have led religious institutions to promote their products as "brands." This leads religious "producers" and their "consumers" to construct their own identities and interact with other users through "religious branding" or "faith brands" (pp. 92–94). These consist of religious products and services (books, religious courses, spiritual practices, etc.) that, like their secular counterparts, serve to distinguish them from others in the marketplace and assist consumers in making a personal connection with the product. They are usually associated with their creators, namely pastors, televangelists, and other religious leaders, who become faith brands themselves (more than their churches). Einstein notes that when it comes to faith brands, public relations, rather than advertising, forms the predominant tool of promotion both because consumers tend to more readily accept information circulated using public relations materials (such as press releases, media kits, and other printed materials) than information put across in advertising messages, and because the production and diffusion of these materials have a relatively lower cost. The application of public relations strategies to the commercialization of religious products and services, dubbed "Christian PR," emerged in connection with the campaigns of two American consultants: Mark DeMoss, who worked with televangelist pastor Jerry Falwell during the 1980s (Saroyan, 2006), and Larry Ross, who launched Rick Warren in the early 2000s. Warren founded a mega-church and authored the best-selling book, *The Purpose Driven Life*, which Einstein analyzed as a perfect example of a "faith brand." Its main promotional tool was a church course titled "40 Days of Purpose," which through a public relations kit (videos, sermons, songs, reading materials) demonstrated how to create a church capable of applying the principles illustrated in the 40 chapters of the book. Before becoming a fully fledged course, "40 Days of Purpose" was the 2002 public relations campaign launched to promote sales of the book. It consisted of a series of public meetings, lasting 40 days, in which all the enrolled churches were expected to buy stocks of the book (at a discounted price) to allow all of the faithful to follow. The success was immediate: just a year after its launch, 1.5 million Americans from 4500 churches had enrolled in the course (Einstein, 2008, p. 128).

The advent of the Internet had an impact on the implementation of religious branding strategies. Religious use of advertising, public relations, and other promotional tools and online activities extends beyond technical matters and includes a new dimension in the church approach to the faithful and marks a substantial change affecting religious organizations. The use of marketing, and online marketing in particular, highlights that it is no longer just a question of producing and commercializing specific symbolic goods (or "faith brands" in Einstein's terminology), but rather of ensuring that these goods are used and valued.

The key consensus, which users assign to religious products, concerns the extent to which users evaluate their real or potential use as important (Guizzardi, 2014). This accentuates user relations, as religious organizations must now recognize their relative autonomy to escape the goods on offer and to attribute to them new meanings and functions (which may differ from those defined by their religious producers), as well as to combine partial uses and meanings in other forms. From this perspective, the relationships between religion and marketing need updating: three poles (not just religion and marketing) play their parts. A third variable, which I call the "pole of consumers," appears (Nardella, 2014). Religious actors must address this collective subject in addition to their capital of consensus (increased or held by means of marketing tools) in order to recognize its relative autonomy, and to accept thereby the partial loss of hegemony that this recognition entails.

This challenges traditional religious institutions because, just like all organizations define "what their product stands for," they hardly *decide* to give up complete control of this definition (Einstein, 2014). These same processes work in the commercial world too, something reflected in the tendency for marketing companies to engage in meaning co-creation processes that give rise to "consumer tribes" (Cova & Cova, 2002) or "consumer communities" (Muniz & O'Guinn, 2001). These groups revolve around symbols and rituals celebrating commercial brands, at times even raising them to cult status (Muniz & Schau, 2005). From this point of view, if the Internet and social media offer unprecedented opportunities to involve people in the use of religious products, transforming them through the symbolic potential they incorporate into tools of identification, distinction, and belonging, it is equally true that the religious actors often do not widely take up these opportunities in part because of how Internet-based marketing communication tools are employed. As examples of such social media use in the United States Einstein

(2013, 2014) analyzes the "I'm a Mormon" campaign run by the Church of Jesus Christ of Latter-day Saints starting in the summer of 2010 and the online activities implemented by the Episcopal Church in the same period. While she interprets the former as an example of a campaign that, despite existing in the online space, goes against social media logic because it is top-down communication, the online marketing strategy developed by the Episcopal Church recognizes the consumer's autonomy by allowing confrontation, discussion, and even disagreement with the church in the debate developed on its social media.

European Developments

Religious marketing has found practical applications in other national contexts. In Europe, for example, this sector sees advertising and public relations regularly employed as promotional tools by many religious actors. Some differences exist with the American situation: the application of marketing techniques and methods in religion began more recently in Europe and uses these instruments differently. European religious organizations often devote a significant proportion of their advertising to raising funds, and less to increasing attendance numbers.

The Italian Catholic Church, which embraced advertising for the first time in the early 1990s, provides an example. Its first advertisement appeared in spring 1990: a national television commercial showed two baskets of bread and fish side by side, while a voiceover reminded the audience of the welfare services provided by the Church. The Italian case long remained unique in Europe because of a fund-raising context resulting from a new concordat between the Vatican and the Italian government, signed in 1984. As of 1990, the state abolished *congrua* (i.e. the parish priest's official stipend), through which it financed the clergy and other activities of the Catholic Church, and established a system based on competition between different state-accredited religious groups for the distribution of public funds collected through citizen choices on tax returns. One consequence of this change was the Catholic Church's adoption of advertising techniques to convince Italian citizens to donate their tax preferences to the Church – an example soon followed by other Italian religious organizations including several Protestant denominations, the Orthodox Church, and the Italian Jewish community. Another effect appears in the content of the religious advertisements themselves, in which references to values of solidarity toward the poorest and the marginalized mix with references to religious belonging and national identity; the messages also demonstrate the effectiveness of previous donations and identify future projects. The legal change meant that the Italian Catholic Church had to turn to the public, and not only to its faithful, for economic resources. The Church accepted competition with other institutions, lost its symbolic monopoly in Italy, and revealed economic activity as a key function of the Church. In other words, "religious marketing" now exists in Italy in spite of a critique that commercialization desacralizes elements of the Church's identity and actions. (This critique appears, for example, in Pope John Paul II, 1991, when while reflecting on the free market and its legitimacy, the Pope writes, "[T]here are goods which by their very nature cannot and must not be bought or sold. Certainly the mechanisms of the market offer secure advantages... Nevertheless, these mechanisms carry the risk of an 'idolatry' of the market, an idolatry which ignores the existence of goods which by their nature are not and cannot be mere commodities," No. 40.)

The Catholic Church's position has changed over time, shifting toward a more favorable view of religious marketing (and advertising in general), although its acceptance still appears far from certain. The Pontifical Council for Social Communication (1997) examined the then realities of advertising through the lens of ethics, offering thoughts on best practices. Its document, which came in response to what the Vatican perceived as a radical change, strictly links praxis (i.e. what to do) and knowledge (i.e. of the criteria for determining what to do and who can legitimately define these criteria). The main drive for this change came from the development of new advertising methods and the emergence of new professional figures, such as marketing directors and brand managers, who over those years began to gain credit and autonomy as representatives of new, central sectors of the economy. In addition, nonmarginal economic processes played a role, principally the development of new markets with an interdependence between production sectors and communication techniques, whose aim was to obtain consumers' consensus in a context of increasing plurality, diversification, and intersection of the commercial goods and services for sale. Beyond the economic actors' interests, cultural and political processes came into play too, ultimately affecting the position of advertising professionals, who started testing and pushing the limits of advertising in the highly competitive battle to capture consumers' attention.

The Pontifical Council (1997) held that, while considered morally neutral, advertising could lead to problematic situations when inducing "people to act on the basis of irrational motives ('brand loyalty,' status, fashion, 'sex appeal,' etc.)," becoming a "tool of the 'phenomenon of consumerism'" (No. 10). The solution proposed lay in a formula of "ethically correct behavior," defining a reality in which advertisers had the responsibility to "do what is morally right," that is, by creating a message that "respect[s] and uphold[s] the rights and interests of their audiences" and serves "the common good" (No. 18). By interpreting the advertising profession as "ethically responsible," the Church gave the advertiser–consumer relationship a paternalistic nature, in which, by virtue of their technical knowledge and position as carriers of "moral responsibility," the advertising professionals could decide what was good for consumers on their behalf (for a critique, see Ringold, 1998). At the same time, consumers lost autonomy and freedom to make their own choices (Brenkert, 1998). The relative formulas of "truthfulness in advertising" and "dignity of the human person" (Pontifical Council, 1997, Nos. 15–16) nevertheless contained two different, if not conflicting, parts. On the one hand, they recognized the importance of dialogue and left the decision to the consumer's "interior freedom"; on the other hand, the Catholic Church did not renounce its symbolic power; that is, the power to propose the criteria according to which the advertisers had to exercise their profession with the aim, in turn, of reflecting those same criteria on the public. Only in such cases, according to the council's argument, could the advertising profession prove to be useful in a positive sense (Cohen, 2012b).

But, while recognizing the importance of advertising in contemporary societies, the Catholic Church clearly indicated the existence of a knowledge system, owned and controlled by the Church itself, which legitimized a hierarchical order between the religious field and the marketing field. Hence, marketing took a subordinate position along with the economic goods that it promoted. Despite accepting advertising as a new and important social "force," the Church seemed unwilling to give autonomy to advertisers, and to the users (or "pole of consumers") even less so, in order to maintain its hegemonic position.

Since the early 2000s, the growing use of brand-based messages in advertising has made the situation more complex. This is also evident from the fact that, contrary to the Pontifical Council's indications – which asked advertisers to help consumers make prudent decisions based on rational information – today's advertisements use symbolic meanings alone to create positive associations with products and services, and to instill confidence as to the promoted goods' ability to provide consumers with resources framed in terms of emotional experiences. Advertisers appear free to use as little product information as they choose and encourage consumers to substitute emotion for reason in their purchasing decisions. The pinnacle of this activity, the so-called "brand heaven" (Kunde, 2000), offers a consistent and authentic commercial message that encourages involvement and delivers values. Advertisers do this in a combination of ways, including the use of religious symbols, which advertisers incorporate in their messages, creatively and pretty much unreservedly, in order to accomplish a whole host of commercial tasks (see Mallia, 2009; Nardella, 2012). And yet, since its 1997 document on ethics and advertising, the Church's position on advertising practices has remained unchanged.

After this digression into ethics, let us return to the advertising practices of the Church. The use of advertising has some longer-term implications for the organizational life of the Catholic Church. First is the slow but inevitable twist of religious messages toward the logics and linguistic codes of commercial communication, responding to needs ranging from the transformation of complex content into effective slogans to the creation of specific "faith brands" whose use value the public must recognize. The Italian Catholic Church, for example, has started using the Internet and social media to increase interactivity in its promotional strategies. For example, the tax preference commercials are now integrated with videos and documentaries on Church-controlled websites and Facebook pages, in which people and groups tell of the concrete impact of funds raised through previous campaigns. Second, the Church decided to systematically draw on the expertise of advertising agencies and marketing companies, with technical skills extraneous to the religious field: when the Italian Catholic Church chose advertising as its primary means for collecting the financial resources deriving from the tax system, it hired Saatchi & Saatchi to produce all of its campaigns, from the first advertisement aired in 1990 through to today's television commercials. On closer inspection, this collaboration highlights a further aspect not usually considered in the analyses, marking a difference in how the Catholic Church has managed the use of advertising with respect to other means of mass communication. While its use of mass media (newspapers, radio, and television) led to the establishment of an internal apparatus, composed of professional "religious work" figures assigned the specific task of directly or indirectly managing most of the Church's traditional (Soukup, 2005) and digital (Golan & Martini, 2019) media, the use of marketing has not led to the development of similar organizational features. Why? A possible explanation could lie in the sort of "taboo of making things explicit" (Bourdieu, 1998, p. 120) hidden behind the relationship of the Catholic Church, and all traditional religious institutions in general, with the economy (and consequently with marketing, which could be viewed as the economy's cultural and communicative system). The upshot is that the "economic" aspect is mostly left implicit or strongly euphemized. For example, the Italian Episcopal Conference's Service for the Promotion of Economic Support of the Catholic Church is a communication office, objectively a marketing agency. However, the systematic use of euphemisms hides this. Using advertising to convince individuals to give their tax preferences to the Church becomes "asking for ecclesial participation and co-responsibility," the relative monetary exchange becomes a "gift exchange," the funds gathered thanks to advertising become "tools of good work."

In other European countries the Catholic Church puts more emphasis on public relations than on advertising; this results from its constant effort to monitor and strengthen the organization's image (Sulkowski et al., 2022). Baster et al. (2018) confirmed that, in England and Wales, public relations have become the main tool that this institution uses to communicate and leverage its "brand equity" more effectively and generate high levels of "brand loyalty" among its members – not surprisingly, these authors propose the existence of a specific "Catholic brand." They also report that while this tendency prevails at a national level, local English and Welsh churches use the equivalent of display adverts and other marketing techniques. Lastly, none of these public relations, marketing, or advertising initiatives appears to present a personality for the "church brand" as their core product. Of course, this does not mean that a "brand personality" could not be used as a promotional tool by the Catholic Church: making a persona's life, opinions, and successes newsworthy would bring the religious organization onto the media agenda. The marketing literature has already identified examples of "brand personality" in the figures of the Pope and Mother Teresa (see, for example, Alpion, 2007).

Emerging Trends in the Middle and Far East

The religions of the Middle and Far East as well as new religious/spiritual milieus also employ advertising. An overall example of the interaction between religion and marketing in Islam appears in the halal industry of products permitted by Islam, which now goes beyond food to include pharmaceuticals, cosmetics, toiletries, and services such as banking, insurance, and tourism, giving life to "a new market of consumer products, advertising, and commercial media programming ... increasingly labeled 'Islamic'" (Echchaibi, 2012, pp. 31–32). The literature around this new phenomenon tends to focus more on advertising than public relations (Ariffin et al., 2016; Behboudi et al., 2014). Studies show that, in terms of content, Islamic advertising pays particular attention to the ethical dimension by trying to create credible, simple, and humane messages (Shafiq et al., 2017). Studies also emphasize the importance that Islamic symbols and motifs play in these advertisements and, more generally, in the marketing communications directed to the halal market segment (Yousaf, 2014). Islamic advertising messages vary depending on the country, type of target audience, and time of the year. For example, in conservative Islamic countries such as Saudi Arabia and Malaysia, advertisers carefully consider Islamic taboos and other sensitive cultural issues like women's clothing when they develop their communication strategies (Waller & Fam, 2000). Focusing on Saudi society, Cader (2015) verifies that advertisers make sure they do not offend or violate the Islamic creed to avoid a negative brand image. Islamic advertising also pays particular attention to the religious identity of consumers and, to this end, especially during Ramadan, incorporate the religious cues to which Muslim consumers are more responsive (see Aydin & Hasiloglu, 2019; for a comprehensive review, see Mamun et al., 2021).

Judaism also occupies a position in this debate. Levine (1981) argues that projecting the quality of a good or service is regarded positively in Judaism. But drawing upon the biblical verse "In selling ... do not be distortionate" (Leviticus 25:17), Judaism prohibits the trader, in promoting products, from creating a false impression or *genevat daat*. A trader is required to divulge to a prospective customer all defects in his product. A trader is permitted to draw the buyer's attention to the good features of a product as long as these are accurate.

Marketing has become an issue in Israel in two spheres. First, advertising should treat the audience in a respectful and nondeceptive way. Cohen (2012a) observes that in Israel some Orthodox Jewish groups, such as the Haredi Jewish community, act as pressure groups – by means of censorship and the threat or actual use of boycott actions – to ensure that advertising messages show more sensitivity (p. 156). This has two main consequences. On the one hand, advertisements appearing in Haredi-controlled media only promote certain products considered "kosher" by the community, such as mobile phones with no access to the Internet, a disabled text-messaging function, and avoidance of "offensive representations" (e.g. Haredi media do not feature advertisements containing women). On the other hand, advertising professionals consider the Haredi community a lucrative market segment for goods ranging from milk products to books, travel, education, and health services (p. 166). Over time, the marketing of products and services aimed at Haredi consumers has developed more sophisticated and creative advertising patterns; Israeli agencies have established offices and departments with staff specialized in developing marketing solutions for this market segment. One solution involves promoting goods and services in a way that makes them appear "kosher" even if they are manufactured outside the Haredi community (Cohen, 2017). Israeli advertisers obtain this result by employing images and slogans, such as visual or verbal representations of rabbis endorsing the product.

The second sphere involves the promotion of Judaism through advertising and public relations. Cohen (2012a) underlines that many rabbis have come to recognize the importance of using mass and digital media to sell their message and increase synagogue attendance and religious commitment; a few have even become media celebrities themselves. Cohen's survey of 300 rabbis in the early 2010s provides empirical confirmation of this trend. More than three-quarters of respondents agreed positively that it was important to appear in the media (p. 174). Several Jewish movements make active use of the Internet as a means to build an effective religious marketing strategy. One of these is the Habad-Lubavitch community, one of the largest branches of Hasidic Judaism and one of the largest Jewish Orthodox movements worldwide, which controls Chabad.org, a website founded in the 1990s by a young rabbi, Yosef Kazen, as the continuation of an electronic discussion network named Fidonet, published worldwide since 1988 (Fishkoff, 2003). With more than 50 million different visitors per year and tens of thousands of articles covering all areas of Judaism, Chabad.org is the world's largest Jewish faith-based website. Another online source is the MyKehilla (literally "my community") website, which enables synagogue communities to keep in touch and strengthen ties with their members by providing a weekly schedule of online religious services, Torah lectures, and other synagogal events. Finally, online rabbinical counseling, a relatively new digital tool, has received attention across the Jewish world since the Internet grew in popularity with Jewish groups other than the ultra-Orthodox. This service provides live consultation on Jewish legal teachings from panels of rabbis via specific websites, such as Kipa, Moreshet, Moriah, Jewish Answers, and Project Genesis (Cohen, 2015).

These developments do not necessarily imply that religious marketing has become an integral and fully accepted part of Judaism. It faces significant limits and obstacles, especially in Israel. An example is an advertising campaign in 1999 jointly created by two non-Orthodox groups (i.e. the Conservative and Reformist movements), which are not officially recognized. The campaign, distributed nationwide, consisted of 350 radio ads with the slogan "There is more than one way to Judaism" to promote the existence of alternatives to the dominant Jewish Orthodox groups. Despite resistance by the Israeli Broadcasting Corporation (a public station controlled by different political parties including orthodox religious parties), which refused to run the advertisements, the campaign was released on the radio following an appeal to the Israeli Supreme Court, but on condition that the slogan, considered offensive by the Israeli Broadcasting Authority, was removed.

The interaction between religiosity and commerce appears among Asian religions too. Symbolic economies drive the production and veneration of Buddhist monuments and other religious places in Thailand and its neighboring regions (Askew, 2008). A brisk retail market of Hindu ritual paraphernalia has developed in Singapore (Sinha, 2011). Religious practices associated with Chinese popular religion are monetized during spiritual festivals in Malaysia and China (DeBernardi, 2008). The religious entrepreneurs who deal with these particular types of goods rely upon pricing, marketing, advertising, and other profit-making strategies similar to those used by commercial retailers (Sinha, 2011).

The marketing efforts of "new religious movements" from Scientology and ISKCON to Wicca and New Age, have come to exemplify the market-based consumerism characterizing religious traditions. Their widespread presence in almost all continents has led to the development of a parallel and alternative religious market and, along with it, a new sector in the construction of religious images, narratives, and symbolic references. In many ways syncretic, it uses communication methods and techniques borrowed from different domains, ranging from marketing to advertising, media, and entertainment, and it combines and integrates them in new forms within a religious dimension that hence loses its traditional boundaries, or at least sees a widening of the gray border areas. Various examples appear, from advertisements for Scientology and the Kabbalah Center in the United States (Einstein, 2008, 2011), through the events of the International Christian Fellowship in Europe (Favre, 2014), to the performances of Pentecostal churches and charismatic communities in Latin America and Africa (Adebayo & Zulu, 2019; Benyah, 2018), which attract the faithful through television and radio preachers, mass shows, mega events, and musical performances by singing priests.

Concluding Hypotheses

Although different religious traditions embrace marketing tools in different ways, marketing concepts and practices definitely apply to religions. And yet, the situation remains to some extent paradoxical, at least from the point of view of the religious institutions themselves. As Voas (2014) pointed out: "no doubt 'Mother Teresa' became a brand, and that brand was successfully deployed for charitable purposes, but many people would be offended by the suggestion that there was anything conscious about the way her name and image became a trademark for altruism" (p. xviii). Indeed, not all religious organizations admit to being "enterprises" with a specific economic dimension and, for this reason, they function in a sort of permanent denial of this aspect, which, if recognized, runs the risk of diminishing or annulling their symbolic capital and assigning new powers to other groups. In this view, the symbolic capital possessed by religious institutions must remain the only valid capital supplying interpretative contents. Bourdieu (1998) made reference to this "misrecognition" using the expression "double game" adding that "the truth of religious enterprise is that of having two truths: economic truth and religious truth, which denies the former" (p. 204). Accordingly, a scientific analysis of religion should always employ "two words, superimposed on each other, as if in a musical chord: apostolate/marketing, faithful/clientele, sacred service/paid labor, and so forth" (p. 204).

This consideration raises a knotty issue in the debate: if advertising, public relations, and other marketing communication methods have become so important for religious actors, what consequences occur? The answers rely on different hypotheses. The secularization thesis can explain the adoption of marketing techniques by religious organizations, as well as the commercialization of religious products and services: religions are losing their authority, while other institutions in the world of the economy and consumption become dominant. From this perspective, consumer culture appears ascendant, while religions must adapt in order to compete in a marketplace with multiple sources of meanings. But an opposite answer, which radically denies secularization, can also be found if one accepts the axiom that religious demand is an independent variable, located at the level of the individual, and not subject to relevant variations over time. This solution postulates that overall religious demand is (and will always be) constant, shifting the explanation for the ongoing changes to the level of the religious institutions, which have the task of capturing and, possibly, raising the demand for religion by adopting increasingly sophisticated marketing communication techniques and methods.

References

Adebayo, R. O., & Zulu, S. P. (2019). Miracle as a spiritual event and as a marketing tactic among neo-charismatic churches: A comparative study. *Journal for Christian Scholarship*, 55(1–2), 105–125. http://hdl.handle.net/10321/3332

Alpion, G. (2007). *Mother Teresa: Saint or celebrity?* Routledge.

Anderson, S. J., Rountree, W. D., & Dunlap, B. J. (1984). A proposed marketing model for religious organizations: An empirical evaluation. *Proceedings of the Southern Marketing Association*, 86–88.

Ariffin, S. K., Ismail, I., & Shah, K. A. M. (2016). Religiosity moderates the relationship between ego-defensive function and attitude towards advertising. *Journal of Islamic Marketing*, 7, 15–16. https://doi.org/10.1108/JIMA-11-2014-0074

Askew, M. (2008). Materializing merit: The symbolic economy of religious monuments and tourist-pilgrimage in contemporary Thailand. In P. Kitiarasa (Ed.), *Religious commodifications in Asia: Marketing Gods* (pp. 89–119). Routledge.

Aydin, O., & Hasiloglu, S. B. (2019). An evaluation of used objects in bank tv commercials in Ramadan. *Journal of Islamic Marketing, 10*(4), 1219–1229. https://doi.org/10.1108/JIMA-05-2018-0093

Barna, G. (1992). *Finding a church you can call home.* Regal Books.

Baster, D., Beresford, S., & Jones, B. (2018). The 'brand' of the Catholic church in England and Wales: Challenges and opportunities for communications. *Journal of Public Affairs, 19*(e1881), 1–2. https://doi.org/10.1002/pa.1881

Behboudi, M., Vazifehdoust, H., Najafi, K., & Najafi, M. (2014). Using rational and emotional appeals in online advertisements for Muslim customers. *Journal of Islamic Marketing, 5*, 97–24. https://doi.org/10.1108/JIMA-07-2012-0039

Belk, R. W. (1987). A child's Christmas in America: Santa Claus as deity, consumption as religion. *Journal of American Culture, 10*(1), 87–100. https://doi.org/10.1111/j.1542-734X.1987.1001_87.x

Benyah, F. (2018). Commodification of the gospel and the socio-economics of neo-Pentecostal/Charismatic Christianity in Ghana. *Legon Journal of the Humanities, 29*(2), 116–145. https://doi.org/10.4314/ljh.v29i2.5

Berger, P. L. (1967). *The sacred canopy: Elements of a sociological theory of religion.* Doubleday.

Berger, P. L. (1969). *A rumor of angels: Modern society and the rediscovery of the supernatural.* Doubleday.

Berger, P. L., & Luckmann, T. (1966). Secularization and pluralism. *International Yearbook for the Sociology of Religion, 2*, 73–86.

Bourdieu, P. (1998). *Practical reason: On the theory of action.* Stanford University Press.

Brenkert, G. G. (1998). Ethics in advertising: The good, the bad, and the church. *Journal of Public Policy & Marketing, 17*(2), 325–331. https://doi.org/10.1177/074391569801700217

Butler, J. (2020). *God in Gotham: The miracle of religion in modern Manhattan.* Harvard University Press.

Cader, A. A. (2015). Islamic challenges to advertising: A Saudi Arabian perspective. *Journal of Islamic Marketing, 6*, 166–187. https://doi.org/10.1108/JIMA-03-2014-0028

Campbell, C. (1987). *The romantic ethic and the spirit of modern consumerism.* Basil Blackwell.

Carman, J. M. (1987). Rules for church promotion decisions. *Decision Sciences, 18*(Fall), 598–616. https://doi.org/10.1111/j.1540-5915.1987.tb01549.x

Case, F. H. (1921). *Handbook of church advertising.* Abingdon Press.

Cohen, Y. (2012a). *God, Jews and the media: Religion and Israel's media.* Routledge.

Cohen, Y. (2012b). God, religion, and advertising. In A. Hetsroni (Ed.), *Advertising & reality: A global study of representation and content.* Continuum.

Cohen, Y. (2015). The Israeli rabbi and the internet. In H. A. Campbell (Ed.), *Digital Judaism: Jewish negotiations with digital media and culture* (pp. 183–204). Routledge.

Cohen, Y. (2017). The media challenge to Haredi rabbinic authority in Israel. *ESSACHESS – Journal for Communication Studies, 10*(2), 113–128.

Cova, B., & Cova, V. (2002). Tribal marketing: The tribalisation of society and its impact on the conduct of marketing. *European Journal of Marketing, 36*, 595–20. https://doi.org/10.1108/03090560210423023

Culliton, J. W. (1959). A marketing analysis of religion. *Business Horizons, 2*(1), 85–92. https://doi.org/10.1016/0007-6813(59)90046-1

Cutler, B. D. (1992). Religion and marketing. *Journal of Professional Services Marketing, 8*(1), 153–164. https://doi.org/10.1300/J090v08n01_12

Cutler, B. D., & Winans, W. A. (1998). What do religion scholars say about marketing? Perspectives from the religion literature. *Journal of Professional Services Marketing, 18*(2), 133–145. https://doi.org/10.1300/J090v18n02_09

DeBernardi, J. (2008). Commodifying blessings: Celebrating the double-yang festival in Penang, Malaysia and Wudang Mountain, China. In P. Kitiarsa (Ed.), *Religious commodifications in Asia: Marketing gods* (pp. 49–57). Routledge.

Dunlap, B. J., Gaynor, P., & Rountree, W. D. (1983). The viability of marketing in a religious setting: An empirical analysis. *Proceedings of the Southern Marketing Association, 45*–58.

Echchaibi, N. (2012). Mecca cola and burqinis: Muslim consumption and religious identities. In G. Lynch, J. Mitchell, & A. Strhan (Eds.), *Religion, media and culture: A reader* (pp. 31–39). Routledge.

Einstein, M. (2008). *Brands of faith: Marketing religion in a commercial age.* Routledge.

Einstein, M. (2011). The evolution of religious branding. *Social Compass, 58*(3), 331–338. https://doi.org/10.1177/0037768611412138

Einstein, M. (2013). Branding faith and managing reputations. In D. Rinallo, L. Scott, & P. Maclaran (Eds.), *Consumption and spirituality* (pp. 132–143). Routledge.

Einstein, M. (2014). From static to social: Marketing religion in the age of the internet. *Sociologica, 8*(3), 1–14. https://www.rivisteweb.it/doi/10.2383/79476

Favre, O. (2014). The International Christian Fellowship (ICF): A sociological analysis of religious event management. In J.-C. Usunier, & J. Stolz (Eds.), *Religions as brands: New perspectives on the marketization of religion and spirituality* (pp. 47–58). Ashgate.

Fishkoff, S. (2003). *The rebbe's army: Inside the world of Chabad-Lubavitch.* Schocken.

Gazda, G. M., Anderson, C. I., & Sciglimpaglia, D. (1984). Marketing and religion: An assessment of the clergy. *Proceedings of the Southern Marketing Association,* 78–90.

Golan, O., & Martini, M. (2019). Religious live-streaming: Constructing the authentic in real time. *Information, Communication & Society, 22*(3), 437–454. https://doi.org/10.1080/1369118X.2017.1395472

Guizzardi, G. (2014). The eternal struggle: Symbols, religion, marketing. *Sociologica, 8*(3), 1–17. https://www.rivisteweb.it/doi/10.2383/79480

Healy, D. F., & DeLozier, M. W. (1978). Developing a religious program. In M. W. Delozier, & A. Woodside (Eds.), *Marketing management: Strategies and cases* (pp. 753–769). Charles E. Merrill Publishing.

Hines, R. W. (1996). Church advertising practices and perceptions. *Journal of Ministry Marketing & Management, 2*(1), 81–95. https://doi.org/10.1300/J093v02n01_07

John Paul II. (1991). *Centesimus annus.* Vatican. Retrieved July 18, 2022, from https://www.vatican.va/content/john-paul-ii/en/encyclicals/documents/hf_jp-ii_enc_01051991_centesimus-annus.html

Kunde, J. (2000). *Corporate religion: Building a strong company through personality and corporate soul.* Prentice Hall.

Levine, A. (1981). Advertising and promotional activities as regulated in Jewish law. *Journal of Halakha and Contemporary Society, 2*, 5–37. http://hdl.handle.net/10822/791035

Mallia, K. L. (2009). From the sacred to the profane: A critical analysis of the changing nature of religious imagery in advertising. *Journal of Media and Religion, 8*(3), 172–190. https://doi.org/10.1080/15348420903091162

Mamun, M. A. A., Strong, C. A., & Azad, M. A. K. (2021). Islamic marketing: A literature review and research agenda. *International Journal Consumer Studies, 45*(5), 964–984. https://doi.org/10.1111/ijcs.12625

McDaniel, S. W. (1986). Church advertising: View of the clergy and general public. *Journal of Advertising, 15*(1), 24–29. https://doi.org/10.1080/00913367.1986.10672985

McDaniel, S. W. (1989). The use of marketing techniques by churches: A national survey. *Review of Religious Research, 31*(1), 175–182. https://doi.org/10.2307/3511188

McDannell, C. (1995). *Material Christianity: Religion and popular culture in America.* Yale University Press.

McLeod, H. (2007). *The religious crisis of the 1960s.* Oxford University Press.

Mehta, S. S., & Mehta, G. B. (1996). Marketing of churches: An empirical study of important attributes. *Journal of Professional Services Marketing, 13*(1), 53–64. https://doi.org/10.1300/J090v13n01_06

Moncrief, W. C., Lamb, C. W., Jr., & Hart, S. H. (1986). Marketing the church. *Journal of Professional Services Marketing, l*(4), 55–63. https://doi.org/10.1300/J090v01n04_07

Moore, R. L. (1994). *Selling God: American religion in the marketplace of culture.* Oxford University Press.

Muniz, A. M., Jr., & O'Guinn, T. C. (2001). Brand community. *Journal of Consumer Research, 27*(4), 412–432. https://doi.org/10.1086/319618

Muniz, A. M., Jr., & Schau, H. J. (2005). Religiosity in the abandoned Apple Newton brand community. *Journal of Consumer Research, 31*(4), 737–747. https://doi.org/10.1086/426607

Nardella, C. (2012). Religious symbols in Italian advertising: Symbolic appropriation and the management of consent. *Journal of Contemporary Religion, 27*(2), 217–240. https://doi.org/10.1080/13537903.2012.675689

Nardella, C. (2014). Studying religion and marketing: An introduction. *Sociologica, 8*(3), 1–15. https://www.rivisteweb.it/doi/10.2383/79475

Nissenbaum, S. (1997). *The battle for Christmas.* Alfred A. Knopf.

Nord, D. P. (1984). The evangelical origins of mass media in America, 1815–1835. *Journalism Monographs, 88.*

Pontifical Council for Social Communication (1997). Ethics in advertising. Vatican. Retrieved July 18, 2022, from https://www.vatican.va/roman_curia/pontifical_councils/pccs/documents/rc_pc_pccs_doc_22021997_ethics-in-ad_en.html

Reisner, C. F. (1913). *Church publicity: The modern way to compel them to come.* Pilgrim Press.

Ringold, D. J. (1998). A comment on the Pontifical Council for Social Communications' ethics in advertising. *Journal of Public Policy & Marketing, 17*(2), 332–335. https://doi.org/10.1177/074391569801700218

Roof, W. C. (1993). *A generation of seekers: The spiritual journey of the baby boom generation.* HarperCollins.

Saroyan, S. (2006, April 16). Christianity, the brand. *New York Times Magazine.* Retrieved July 19, 2022, from https://www.nytimes.com/2006/04/16/books/christianity-the-brand.html

Schmidt, L. E. (1991). The commercialization of the calendar: American holidays and the culture of consumption, 1870–1930. *The Journal of American History, 78*(3), 887–916. https://doi.org/10.2307/2078795

Schmidt, L. E. (1995). *Consumer rites: The buying and selling of American holidays.* Princeton University Press.

Shafiq, A., Haque, A., Abdullah, K., & Jan, M. (2017). Beliefs about Islamic advertising: An exploratory study in Malaysia. *Journal of Islamic Marketing, 8,* 409–429. https://doi.org/10.1108/JIMA-02-2015-0018

Shawchuck, N., Kotler, P., Wrenn, B., & Rath, G. J. (1992). *Marketing for congregations: Choosing to serve people more effectively.* Abingdon Press.

Sinha, V. (2011). *Religion and commodification: Merchandizing diasporic Hinduism.* Routledge.

Soukup, P. A. (2005). Vatican opinion on communications. In C. Badaracco (Ed.), *Quoting God: How media shape ideas about religion and culture* (pp. 233–245). Baylor University Press.

Stelzle, C. (1908). *Principles of successful church advertising.* Fleming H. Ravell.

Stevens, R. E., Loudon, D. L., Wrenn, B., & Cole, H. S. (2006). *Concise encyclopedia of church and religious organization marketing.* Routledge.

Sulkowski, L., Ignatowski, G., & Seliga, R. (2022). Public relations in the perspective of the Catholic church in Poland. *Religions, 13*(2), 1–2. https://doi.org/10.3390/rel13020115

Voas, D. (2014). Preface. In J.-C. Usunier, & J. Stolz (Eds.), *Religions as brands. New perspectives on the marketization of religion and spirituality* (pp. xvii–xix). Ashgate.

Vokurka, R. J., McDaniel, S. W., & Cooper, N. (2002). Church marketing communication methods. *Services Marketing Quarterly, 24*(1), 17–32. https://doi.org/10.1300/J396v24n01_02

Waller, D. S., & Fam, K.-S. (2000). Cultural values and advertising in Malaysia: Views from the industry. *Asia Pacific Journal of Marketing and Logistics, 12*(1), 3–16. https://doi.org/10.1108/13555850010764613

Webb, M. S. (2012). Diversified marketing media and service offerings prove successful for nondenominational churches. *Services Marketing Quarterly, 33*(3), 246–260. https://doi.org/10.1080/15332969.2012.689940

Webb, M. S., Joseph, W. B., Schimmel, K., & Moberg, C. (1998). Church marketing: Strategies for retaining and attracting members. *Journal of Professional Services Marketing, 17*(2), 1–6. https://doi.org/10.1300/J090v17n02_01

Wilson, B. (1966). *Religion in secular society.* Watts.

Wrenn, B. (1993). The role of marketing for religious organizations. *Journal of Professional Services Marketing, 8*(2), 237–249. https://doi.org/10.1300/J090v08n02_21

Yousaf, S. (2014). Promotion mix management: A consumer focused Islamic perspective. *Journal of Marketing Communications, 22,* 215–231. https://doi.org/10.1080/13527266.2014.888575

Selected Readings

Cohen, Y. (2012). God, religion, and advertising. In A. Hetsroni (Ed.), *Advertising & reality: A global study of representation and content.* Continuum.

Einstein, M. (2008). *Brands of faith: Marketing religion in a commercial age.* Routledge.

Kitiarsa, P. (Ed.). (2008). *Religious commodifications in Asia: Marketing gods.* Routledge.

Moore, R. L. (1994). *Selling God: American religion in the marketplace of culture.* Oxford University Press.

Sandikci, O., & Rice, G. (Eds.). (2011). *Handbook of Islamic marketing.* Edward Elgar Publishing.

Schmidt, L. E. (1995). *Consumer rites: The buying and selling of American holidays.* Princeton University Press.

Stolz, J. and Usunier, J.-C. (2019). Religions as brands? Religion and spirituality in consumer society. *Journal of Management, Spirituality & Religion, 16*(1), 6–31. https://10.1080/14766086.2018.1445008.

13

"Survival and Salvation"
Religious Situational Crisis Communication Strategies

Gregory P. Perreault, Mildred. F. Perreault, and Monica Crawford

In May 2022, the Southern Baptist Convention (SBC) published a report from an investigation into their own denomination. The report details the SBC's extensive efforts to cover up sexual abuse allegations against their pastors (Graham & Dias, 2022). According to the report:

> For many years, a few senior [executive committee] leaders, along with outside counsel, largely controlled the EC's response to these reports of abuse. They closely guarded information about abuse allegations and lawsuits, which were not shared with EC Trustees, and were singularly focused on avoiding liability for the SBC to the exclusion of other considerations. In service of this goal, survivors and others who reported abuse were ignored, disbelieved, or met with the constant refrain that the SBC could take no action due to its policy regarding church autonomy – even if it meant that convicted molesters continued in ministry with no notice or warning to their current church or congregation. (Guidepost Solutions, 2022)

This report and the ensuing news coverage are just the latest examples of how religious crisis communication at times occurs: through attempts to hide or dismiss the crisis altogether. While crisis communication often involves a collective response, different faiths give different degrees of agency depending on their monotheistic/polytheistic perspectives on God, control, and the natural world. While many of our examples in this chapter come from monotheistic religions, it is important to understand the difference in worldview associated with monotheistic and polytheistic religious practices when thinking about crisis response.

There are numerous other avenues for crisis communication. Across faiths, religious organizations, individuals, and stakeholder groups have encountered crises that affect their reputations (Morehouse, 2020; Perreault et al., 2017; Spaulding, 2018). Situated within the larger disciplinary umbrella of crisis communication, religious crisis communication deals specifically with these sorts of scandals.

The Handbook on Religion and Communication, First Edition. Edited by Yoel Cohen and Paul A. Soukup.
© 2023 John Wiley & Sons Ltd. Published 2023 by John Wiley & Sons Ltd.

Crisis Communication Across Faiths

Religious crisis communication stretches back across history with crisis communication reflected in large-scale moments tied to institutions – largely the Roman Catholic Church – for example, through the Inquisition and the Catholic Counter-Reformation (Dalton, 2020) and through responses from American Muslim communities following the terrorist attacks on September 11, 2001 (Fadda-Conrey, 2011). While this chapter primarily deals with monotheistic and Abrahamic faiths (Islam, Judaism, and Christianity), it is helpful to understand how these faiths orient themselves to their communities and to the community outside their faith. While all faiths experience crises, most differences rely on the faiths' understanding of power and control. For example, in relationship to the Covid-19 pandemic, faith leaders in Abrahamic faith spaces emphasized the importance of taking action to help others as a key tenet of their faith – as well as the value placed on human life (Elsanousi et al., 2020). Similar approaches have been taken to environmental crises (Campbell, 2020; Sayem, 2021). While often crisis communication involves reputational (individual or organizational) crises, Abrahamic faiths identify the agency of individual congregation members in creating a collective response. In addition to their understanding of the role of humans and God, their need to make things right in the world differs from polytheistic religions. For example, in polytheistic religions (i.e. Buddhism, Hinduism, Confucianism) or even more ancient religious practices (i.e. Greek, Roman, Egyptian), where there are multiple entities that control the world, the power of people to change specific circumstances comes with differing degrees of agency (Assman, 2004; Campbell, 2020).

Huang (2019) argues that while religion can provide structure for society, as a sociological and political force, it can also provide a countercultural perspective and justification for unacceptable actions. The degree to which a congregant or believer sees their agency in a crisis can be dictated by their belief system and associations with organized religious practice (Sayem, 2021). In polytheistic religions like Hinduism, there is a connection to multiple lifetimes and less of a collective governing of religion from congregation to congregation. This is why in cultures where people practice Buddhism and Hinduism individual actions and responses might be valued less, and believers might be held less accountable for their actions in the public sphere, but their actions might have more serious implications for their affiliation to smaller religious communities as well as their spiritual life (White, 2006). These challenges are also evident in communities where two forms of religion collide. For example, in Ukraine the tensions between Christian religion and paganistic traditions (Lesiv, 2017), and South American Indigenous practices and Catholicism (Burns, 2021).

Situational Crisis Communication Theory

Prior research has reflected on the value of viewing organizational crisis communication through the lens of situational crisis communication theory, and indeed it would seem the most relevant framework to employ for such research given that religious organizations respond to crisis in a similar manner to other types of organizations. Coombs (2007) developed situational crisis communication theory (SCCT) to address how organizations can most effectively manage crises. Within his framework, crisis managers can take specific steps to assess the level of reputational threat in crises and make strategic decisions for postcrisis responses with the goal of maintaining the "organization's survival through and after the crisis" (Morehouse & Austin, 2022, p. 107). SCCT has been an essential intervention in crisis communication research because it allows researchers to find evidence-based solutions for crises rather than just relying on case study analyses. Coombs (2007) defines a crisis as "a sudden and unexpected event that threatens to disrupt an organization's operations and poses both a financial and reputational threat" (p. 164).

Within the SCCT framework, there are three types of crises and three broad crisis response strategies, which have multiple subcategories. The three types of crises or "crisis clusters" are victim crises, accidental crises, and intentional crises (Perreault & Perreault, 2021). A victim crisis implies that the crisis happens to the organization, and it is, in essence, a victim. A common example of this kind of crisis would be a natural disaster, workplace violence, or rumors (Coombs, 2007). In an accidental crisis, the organization has no intention of or control over the event happening (Coombs, 2007). This would likely be a "technical error that causes harm or a product that causes harm" (Morehouse & Austin, 2022, p. 108). On the other hand, in an intentional crisis, the organization "knowingly placed people at risk" (Coombs, 2007, p. 168), which is the type of crisis that carries the most reputational threat. Each of these three types of crises requires different levels of crisis response strategies, which broadly fall into the categories of *deny*, *diminish*, or *rebuild* (Morehouse & Austin, 2022).

These are similar to strategies taken widely at the organization level with *apologia theory* (Coombs et al., 2010). Apologia theory states that an organization or individual will take a specific stance in relationship to the crisis depending upon the perceived risk and long-term impact of that crisis. Coombs and colleagues drew from the work of Dionisopolous and Vibbert (1988), who found there were essentially four strategies that could be used in crisis response strategies by corporations:

1. Denial
2. Bolstering
3. Differentiation
4. Transcendence

When employing the *deny* strategy, organizations attempt to prove that they are not involved in the perceived crisis (Coombs, 2007). For example, if the crisis is rumor-based, the organization would release a statement explaining that rumors are false, and they have been wrongly associated with the crisis. The *diminish* strategy involves an attempt to argue that the "crisis is not as bad as people think or that the organization lacked control over the crisis" (Coombs, 2007, p. 171). Organizations using this strategy often justify why or provide excuses for why they are involved in the crisis. Finally, organizations employing the rebuild strategy often offer a full apology for the crisis and remind stakeholders of the positive impact their organization has had and will continue to have in the future. Coombs (2007, p. 172) writes that "the key is to offset the negatives from the crisis" with positive information.

Religious Communication

Religious communication scholars contend a gap exists in the literature revolving around religion and crisis communication (Morehouse & Austin, 2022; Spaulding, 2018). Spaulding (2018) points out that, in many ways, religious organizations like churches operate similarly to other secular organizations that encounter crises. For example, pastors of churches are akin to CEOs of companies in that they are thought leaders of organizations and are looked to as leaders during moments of crisis. Thus, SCCT could be applied to religious organizations as well. However, when studying religious crisis communication, it is important that one considers the impact that religious beliefs and faith might have on stakeholders' perceptions of the crisis. As Morehouse (2020) writes, "ignoring the religious context and influence of faith and God limits our collective understanding of stakeholder motivations and values within discourse of renewal specifically, but also within crisis communication and public relations research overall" (p. 269). In a later experiment testing the impact of religious rhetoric in postcrisis responses, Morehouse and Austin (2022) found that participants representing a general public audience held more positive views of an organization if that organization did not include religious rhetoric in their crisis responses. On the other hand, participants who exhibited high levels of religiosity viewed crisis response statements that utilized religious rhetoric favorably when presented with an intentional crisis. Therefore, Morehouse and Austin (2022) suggest that scholars using SCCT in religious contexts should pay specific attention to stakeholders' religious identities as well as the type of crisis and potential reputational threat to the organization.

Hence, and following the guidance of Spaulding (2018, p. 29), who utilized a "quasi-case study approach to add richness" to the SCCT model, in this chapter we aim to place discussions of religious crises and ensuing communications in the framework of SCCT, a prominent theory within the broader crisis communication field. The following sections break our discussion of religion and crisis communication into three broad categories, admitting failure, using a moderated response, and reinforcing dominant narratives, which roughly correlate with SCCT's rebuild, diminish, and deny strategies. Despite the differing types of crises discussed in the following sections, each one involves a relationship with religion that affects the response strategy or stakeholder perceptions.

Admitting Failure

Perhaps one of the most prominent religious crises of recent history is the Catholic Church sex abuse scandal, which the *Boston Globe* broke in 2002. Journalists and investigators from the John Jay College of Criminal Justice eventually uncovered thousands of cases of sexual abuse of children by priests dating back decades within the Catholic Church and an extensive operation by the Church to settle the cases quietly (Barth, 2010). Despite the initial secrecy of legal settlements at the time of their occurrence, after the *Boston Globe's* story broke, the US Conference of Catholic Bishops (USCCB) accepted full responsibility for their failure to maintain the safety of the children within their congregations following the reports: "As bishops, we acknowledge our mistakes and our role in that suffering, and we apologize and take responsibility for too often failing victims and or people in the past" (USCCB, 2002, p. 3).

The USCCB then implemented a zero-tolerance policy regarding priests with past or present instances of sexual harassment (Barth, 2010). Furthermore, over the course of time, the Catholic Church has admitted failure both more prominently and with greater resolve to reckon with its own shortcomings. Upon his election to Pope in 2013, Pope Francis called for a decisive decision on sexual abuse within the Church and, in a 2021 visit to France, stated "I would like to express to the victims my sadness and pain for the trauma that [victims] suffered... It is also my shame, our shame, my shame, for the incapacity of the church for too long to put them at the center of its concerns" (Associated Press, 2021).

The USCCB's post-2002 response to the sexual harassment crisis within the Catholic Church and their ultimate admission of complete failure and apology exhibit a key step in the rebuild strategy for crisis management. The rebuild strategy is especially effective in religious crisis communication, as Morehouse and Austin (2022) show through their experimental study. Morehouse and Austin (2022) found that whether the crisis was accidental or intentional, crisis responses using the rebuild strategy led to the most positive outcomes. For religious organizations rooted in Christianity, the rebuild strategy might be so effective because when using it, organizations take responsibility for their actions and ask for forgiveness, both of which are core values in the Christian faith (Morehouse & Austin, 2022).

Nonoffending stakeholder groups related to the organization at the root of the crisis can also play a role in the rebuilding process. In her study on Leadership Roundtable, Morehouse (2020) found that the organization utilized the discourse of renewal in their crisis response messaging. Conversant with Coombs's (2007) rebuilding strategy, the discourse of renewal framework involves taking ownership of a crisis. However, rather than potentially compensating victims, engaging in a discourse of renewal involves seeing the crisis as "an opportunity for renewal" (Morehouse, 2020, p. 245). In the discourse of renewal framework, an organization's core values drive the emphasis on optimism for the organization's future (Seeger & Padgett, 2010). For an organization like Leadership Roundtable, which is made up of members of the Catholic faith, their religious values affected their decisions on how to communicate ethically in the wake of a crisis (Morehouse, 2020).

In both the USCCB and Leadership Roundtable's crisis management strategies, Church leaders and stakeholders admitted to the Catholic Church's failure to properly address instances of sexual abuse and organizational management related to the sexual abuse crisis. While admitting failure and offering an apology is an important step in SCCT's rebuilding strategy (Coombs, 2007), the continued prominence of sexual abuse cases throughout the Catholic Church globally leaves one to wonder if and when the Church will be able to fully rebuild or renew its reputation. For example, in 2019, the Associated Press reported that despite promises to create an extensive list of clergy members who have committed sexual abuse, the Church left at least 900 known sex offenders off their list (Lauer & Hoyer, 2019). Reporting in Europe from 2021 and 2022 has also exposed hundreds of thousands of instances of sexual abuse by clergy members in Italy, France, and Germany (Amante & Pullella, 2022; Breeden, 2021; Horowitz Law, 2022).

Moderated Response

Scholarly literature on more nuanced, complex cases sheds light on the ways in which a moderated crisis response might prove more beneficial (Knight et al., 2009; Morehouse & Spaulding, 2022; Perreault et al., 2017). Using SCCT verbiage, a moderated response could include statements diminishing the severity of the crisis or distancing the organization from the cause of the crisis (Coombs, 2007).

One instance of a moderated approach is the conflict between the Church of Jesus Christ Latter-day Saints (LDS) and the US Jewish Holocaust survivors community over posthumous baptism. Posthumous baptism is a common tradition within the Mormon Church whereby, through a proxy baptism, the deceased is granted the option to become Mormon. This drew controversy given that as a "religious ritual done to someone without his or her expressed permission" (Perreault et al., 2017, p. 142), numerous Jewish victims of the Holocaust were baptized. Through a case study analysis of the coverage of the conflict, Perreault et al. (2017) used narrative theory to illustrate how journalists worked to de-emphasize the themes of conflict in media coverage of the negotiations. This unique case of a minority religion versus minority religion conflict (rather than majority–minority) resulted in news coverage that attempted to de-emphasize the conflict themes within the stories rather than rely on them as often happens in journalism (Perreault et al., 2017; see also Kananovich & Perreault, 2021; Hume & Perreault, 2022; Perreault et al., 2021; Perreault & Meltzer, 2022; Thomson et al., 2018).

Media coverage plays an important role in crisis communication (Coombs, 2007) often employed strategically to mediate between two groups, two positions.

The moderated approach is also a strategy that has been employed by nonreligious organizations when faced with a religious crisis. For example, Fonterra is a New Zealand dairy company that became entangled in the Muhammad Cartoon crisis (Knight et al., 2009; Morehouse & Spaulding, 2022). The controversy started when a Danish newspaper *Jyllands-Posten* published a set of cartoons that at one point illustrated Muhammad with a bomb in his turban. The original cartoons and then ensuing republished versions by other newspapers around the world led to a boycott of Danish products in multiple Middle Eastern countries. Eventually, three Australian-owned newspapers in New Zealand republished the cartoons, and Fonterra began to devise a crisis management plan for the boycotts that would likely follow (Knight et al., 2009).

Fonterra refrained from making statements explicitly about the cartoons for fear of unnecessarily involving themselves in the conflict. For example, one spokesperson for Fonterra included in the study by Knight et al. said, "We made statements available to sales staff saying that Fonterra is a company that is respectful of all religions, it does not support the position taken by an editor of one of New Zealand's many newspapers" (quoted in Knight et al., 2009, p. 11). Throughout their response, Fonterra attempted to avoid "direct public comment as far as possible" (Knight et al., 2009, p. 14) effectively distancing themselves from a conflict that they unintentionally became involved in. The decision to publish the Muhammad cartoons in an Australian-owned newspaper in New Zealand to begin with is especially interesting given the context of the study by O'Donnell et al. (2017) on baseline knowledge of Islam in Australia. Through a survey study with Australian government officials and crisis communicators, they found that "approximately 78% of participants considered that they knew little to nothing about Islam and Muslims; 22% considered they knew a reasonable amount; but none considered they knew a lot" (O'Donnell et al., 2017, p. 28). These findings, coupled with the original decision to publish the cartoons, provide further evidence for the urging from religious crisis communication scholars to incorporate identity and religious beliefs as factors in crisis response decisions.

Reinforcing the Dominant Narrative

SCCT calls for the denial strategy when an organization is the victim of the crisis; however, much of the religious crisis communication literature centers around case studies of the religious sex abuse crises – crises in which religious groups are clearly not a victim (Morehouse & Austin, 2022). In some cases, though, churches or religious organizations fall under the victim category when they are involved in rumor-based scandals. Spaulding (2018) considered four different scandals involving evangelical pastors who allegedly engaged in same-sex behavior. Given the evangelical stance against homosexuality embraced by the Religious Right, these potential same-sex actions would require successful image repair tactics for the pastors to maintain their positions within church leadership. One of the four cases Spaulding (2018) analyzed was that of Eddie Long, who was a bishop and senior pastor of New Birth Missionary Baptist Church. In 2010, four former members of the church accused and pursued legal action against Long for forcing them to engage in sexual contact with him on overnight trips. Despite the four men's testimonies, there was no additional evidence or proof of their claims, allowing Long to deny that "he was the man being portrayed in the media" (Spaulding, 2018, p. 35). Long left any mention of detail out of his denial, though, and even though he "did use a denial response, it is unclear what he was specifically denying" (Spaulding, 2018, p. 35). Throughout the scandal, Long maintained his position in the church and did not end his marriage; therefore, his decision to deny the accusations and reinforce his dominant narrative that he was not the "man being portrayed in the media" (Spaulding, 2018, p. 35) was ultimately a success.

It is worth noting that religious organizations have at times found the *deny* strategy difficult to employ given pressure from the press. However, as the number of religion specialists in journalism has declined, religious organizations have created their own in-house news teams designed, to some degree, to help provide organizations the means to respond to crises. Independent journalists often regard journalists on such teams as not overly dissimilar in reporting, but in cases where they are tasked with reporting on their own religious organization journalists see them as a robust public relations team (Perreault & Montalbano, 2022).

In general, the role of the *deny* strategy is to lean into the dominant narrative of the religious organization. By denying the crisis, this allows groups to double down on their initial strategy, reaffirming the value of their perspective. For example, when faced with the Syrian refugee crisis, *Christian Today* – a publication representing the views of right-wing, nondenominational Christians in the UK – essentially sought to deny the humanitarian crisis by denying Syrian refugees their humanity. *Christian Today* reported on the Syrian refugees' stay in Austria in this way, as described by Perreault and Paul (2019):

> Muslim refugees were described as a "horde" who "left their dirt in Austria" and treated the country's Christian residents with "vileness"… The refugees were attributed with leaving behind "an orgy of garbage and feces of unparalleled dimensions." The article sourced the German news source *Unzen Suriert* as saying that, furthermore, the refugees called the Christian women of Austria "Christian whores." This is an explicit orientalist frame that dehumanizes the refugees by likening them to barbarians (e.g., "hoard") and treating them as unclean (e.g., leaving their "dirt" and "garbage and feces"). (p. 290)

The dehumanizing, xenophobic reporting of *Christian Today* appears as a representation more broadly of the organization's need to diminish the crisis.

Similarly, in 2020, US-based international evangelical ministry Young Life came under fire for hiding antiqueer policies until after young people had become invested in the ministry. Young Life professes to minister to "all young people, wherever they live or whomever they are" (Young Life, 2022), but in the midst of the hashtag campaign #dobetteryounglife, many former students and staff came forward with stories of discrimination based on race, gender, and sexuality. As with the Syrian refugee crisis, Young Life responded largely by denying the crisis, and reaffirming its values. In 2021, Young Life even adopted the name of the hashtag for its own website (e.g. "dobetter.younglife.org") and headed the website with a video on its inclusive outreach to young people. It issued an apology on the website that in a sense expressed sadness for the experiences of Young Life members while denying culpability. Yet in that same apology, it doubled down on its policies for staff:

> Like all religious organizations, Young Life expects that those seeking leadership positions support Young Life's beliefs, tenets, and policies on a wide range of theological issues… One of those issues is human sexuality, and Young Life is confident – with continued study, prayer and reflection – that our theology is faithful to God's vision for this important aspect of the human experience. (Young Life, 2021)

Simply put, denial crisis strategies need not simply reflect a denial of the crisis, but can also reflect a denial of the accusers, the accusers' good faith, and the accusers' humanity.

Religious Celebrities

In religious crisis communication, prominent religious individuals face a different set of cultural expectations than religious organizations. Again, applying SCCT, it is worth considering the interactions between people and communities. In the current era, social media often dominate these conversations; the role of social media influencers and direct communication via social media have given all religious celebrities a direct line to their publics. These parasocial relationships are consistent with other parasocial relationships in that influencers use them for advertising, engagement, teachings, and even at times indoctrination (Golan et al., 2021; Smith et al., 2021). Similarly online and offline communication by religious communicators can facilitate "religious activities, including storytelling, learning, and enlightenment" (Ratcliff et al., 2017; Smith et al., 2021). Davies and Hobbs (2020) found that religious influencers use public relations principles similar to organizations. In addition religious celebrities share curated content online, and engage in co-creation of information with those who follow them (Golan et al., 2021; Lou, 2021; Lou & Yuan, 2019). In addition, their influence is built on a shared identity or covenantal relationship with those who they engage with online and offline. These covenantal relationships are characterized by "mutual trust and co-responsibility, two-way communication, dedication to a particular human good or need, and a public pledge to serve that need" (Tilson & Venkateswaran, 2006, pp. 114–115). The culture of religious celebrities, or celebrities who are religious, and influencers is not something that is new because of social media. For example, The Beatles popularized Hinduism in the 1960s by sharing with the Western world what they learned while abroad and also upset many in the evangelical Christian religious movement (Sullivan, 1987).

There are however ethical challenges when these celebrities act and their voice differs from that of the religious organization with which they are affiliated. Similarly, religious influencers can make an impact beyond a certain organization or affiliation. For example, influencers often have great impact when speaking to a greater cause like human rights (i.e. gender equality, the rights of children, immigration, or even prochoice and antiabortion stances), which can influence people to purchase certain things or engage in certain conversations (Djafarova & Rushworth, 2017; Schouten et al., 2020).

Admitting Failure

Beth Moore is a religious theologian who has worked to bring her offline presence online (Golan et al., 2021). Her first Bible study was published in 1995, but she was an early adopter of social media in 2005 and has been on Twitter since 2009. Often offline engagement allows for influencers to hold a position of leadership by reiterating their teachings and connecting with their following online. As a teacher, and woman, Beth Moore has used her knowledge of the Bible as a way to discuss issues such as domestic abuse, gender inequality, and ethics (Moore, 2016).

Moore (2018) responded to those who criticized her in "A letter to my brothers" where she uses biblical teaching and scripture to further her argument for a deeper evaluation of their gendered faith perspectives and alignment with political candidates. This is a similar approach she took in her response to the policy on complementarianism (the idea that men and women have different specific roles in the Church). After stating in March 2021 she would no longer affiliate with the SBC, she openly apologized to her followers in a Tweet:

> "I plead your forgiveness for how I just submitted to it and supported it and taught it." … "Let me be blunt" Moore tweeted. "When you functionally treat complementarianism – a doctrine of MAN – as if it belongs among the matters of 1st importance, yea, as a litmus test for where one stands on inerrancy & authority of Scripture, you are the ones who have misused Scripture. You went too far." (Shimron & Smietana, 2021)

While many people sided with the SBC and decided to stop using Moore's Bible studies in their churches, many followers chose to rethink the way they interpreted this scripture based on her reputation and consistency of message.

Moore's responses to the political issues around Trump and the controversies of theology in Southern Baptist churches notably call her followers to action, but also demonstrate how she was changing her actions while remaining consistent in her beliefs. This is consistent with the apologia theory often used in public relations and crisis communication. Moore was more established in this space than other evangelical women theologians like Jen Hatmaker and the late Rachel Held Evans (Payne, 2017), and therefore had to make statements over time to define her position; that noted, the sales of her Bible studies and those of Lifeway media plummeted after her initial statements against the SBC in 2015 (Payne, 2017). Moore was able to use this response as a way to reform her own brand and identity as well as claim agency for herself and her followers (Rae, 2022).

Diminish

The phrase "it's not that big of a deal" is not something often seen in religious circles, but what is observed is a couching of the crisis into a misinterpretation by the public. Often religious influencers work to disengage with the public and reframe the crisis as a trial or challenge (Perreault & Perreault, 2019). For example, in the case of the Duggar family, famous for the TLC (The Learning Channel) show *19 Kids and Counting* and later the spin-off show *Counting On*, this tactic reared its head in a very clear way. Josh Duggar – the eldest son of the family, which was associated with the evangelical Quiverfull movement – molested several underage girls in 2006. It later was revealed that his sisters were included in this group. It was also revealed his parents had not done much to address the issue and had primarily relied on religious teachings to address his misbehavior. In August 2015, Josh was found to be cheating on his wife Anna, when the extramarital affair website Ashley Madison was reported on for a data leak. The 2006 charges also resurfaced.

In 2015, Josh's two married sisters, Jill Dillard and Jessa Seewald, were very active on social media, specifically on Instagram posting photos of themselves and biblical phrases to deflect their involvement; they were also interviewed on Fox News about their brother's arrest (Perreault & Perreault, 2019; Diulio & Arendt, 2018). However, in 2015, the family's website and TLC's official communication differed in their approach, using official statements (Perreault & Perreault, 2019).

The family's shows were both canceled by TLC, the first in 2015 and the second in June 2021. In March 2021, Josh was found to be in possession of child pornography. He was convicted in December 2021. In response his sisters spoke to CNN about their journey with the molestation and following crises (Respers France, 2021).

The surfacing of subsequent reputational crises for their family and their belief system meant they had to take ownership of their faith but not his actions. This is demonstrated in their response after the conviction; another married Duggar sister Jinger Vuolo released this statement on her Instagram account:

> We are saddened for the dishonor this has brought upon Christ's name. Josh claims to be a Christian. When a professing follower of Jesus is exposed as a hypocrite, the response of many will be to challenge the integrity of Jesus himself.

We are thankful to God for exposing Josh's actions and to a legal system committed to protecting the innocent and punishing the guilty in this case. We are grateful for justice. We are praying for further justice, vindication, protection, and healing for all those who have been wronged. (Vuolo, 2021)

Comments were blocked on this Instagram post but it had more than 166 000 likes. That said, Josh's sisters Jessa, Jill, Jinger, and Joy-Anna Forsythe have been involved in a legal case of their own since 2017 regarding the release about their 2006 molestation to the news media, which caused their show *Counting On* to be canceled by TLC (Rawden, 2022). This has meant their communication since 2017 about the issue has been limited. In March 2022, Josh was sentenced to 12 ½ years in federal prison. This meant they could no longer deny the allegations and had to acquiesce to apologizing in order to salvage the perceptions of their followers.

Denial

Perhaps one of the most egregious examples of denial is when Warren Steed Jeffs the president of the Fundamentalist Church of Jesus Christ of Latter-day Saints (FLDS Church) was prosecuted for child abuse and as an accessory to rape in Texas in 2011. In Jeffs and his followers' official statements, he denied that what he did was wrong, maintained consistency that marrying off girls and young women to older men was a religious practice, and noted that "spiritual marriage" was not the business of the court but of God (Caron et al., 2011).

While denying or reframing the crisis is a strategy that is not always positively received by followers and appears to have a negative impact long term, it is often consistently practiced and predictable when examining the individual or their brand or an act of "brand standing" (Capizzo, 2019; Garrett, 2011). This is consistent with the Benoit (1995) differentiation strategy; that is, the undesirable action is described as another "similar but less desirable" action (Benoit, 1995, p. 24).

But often religious leaders and businesses will deny their actions or try to justify their actions as part of their religious beliefs (because religion is protected by the First Amendment of the US Constitution). This was the case with Truett Cathy's (owner of Chick-Fil-A) 2015 statement against LBGTQ+ marriage (Singal et al., 2016). This has also has been common practice for international nonprofit Samaritan's Purse's founder Franklin Graham in his response to backing candidates, controversial political issues, immigration, gay marriage, and gender discrimination (Pitofsky, 2020). Graham has experienced a backlash through online organization and petitions, which has caused him to lose credibility with a large number of evangelical Christians. While these statements admit doing something the unaffiliated public might perceive as wrong, within a religious community they use the common beliefs and practices of their community to justify their actions or unsavory stances.

Summary and Application

The ways in which religious organizations and people respond to crises merit much more study. A search of studies on religious reputation management and public relations strategies is limited and often does not consider how religion spills into other sectors of public life like politics, healthcare, education, and public engagement. As social media have become the mainstream form of engagement for religious leaders and communicators, there is much more involvement from followers, and these publics often beg their leaders and influencers to respond to issues. Even though they use similar tactics to communicate in public-facing settings, churches and church communicators may use communication differently internally and with those they have direct relationships with in ways that may "influence one another's spiritual beliefs and well-being" (Golan et al., 2021, p. 250).

Many religious organizations and celebrities emphasize denial crisis communication strategies when first confronted with a crisis – this is a natural response given that a values-focused organization would naturally prefer to use crises as opportunities to reaffirm their values. However, largely the literature reflects that these strategies, far from effectively dismissing the crises, often exacerbate the crises. While religious organizations and religious celebrities clearly make claims that extend beyond humanity, this does not negate that they are in essence human organizations run by humans, for humans. Effective strategies more often involve admitting failure. The fear for religious organizations and individuals is that admitting failure will necessarily curtail their normative claims.

The degree to which the organization or individual is responsible or the fact that the crisis is a broader societal crisis can change the way a religious organization responds. Depending on the claims being made, this may be the case (e.g. it is hard to imagine an admission of failure from Young Life that would not diminish its claim of being inclusive of young people); however, evidence points toward the debilitating effects of attempting to dismiss crises. Often the implications of these crises are felt at the religious institutional level as well as the organizational and individual level. For example, in the case of the Duggars, the reputation of the family, the evangelical Quiverfull movement, and Josh Duggar himself would seem to have been more damaged by his initial dismissal of the crisis. Duggar's need to admit later that he and his parents had lied in initially dismissing the crisis ended up compounding the crisis and creating challenges for other family members. What challenges surface require different approaches, as with any crisis. However, application of SCCT and observations of public reception are vital in crisis communication strategies both online and in more internal settings with parishioners, donors, and followers.

While dismissal would seem to be the most expedient and value-affirming crisis response, it's also largely the most damaging crisis response in the long term. So regardless of what type of response religious organizations and individuals take, they have a connection to their followers, parishioners, and even those with a cultural or historical relationship to their religions.

References

Amante, A., & Pullella, P. (2022, May 19). Italy's Catholic Church at crossroads over sexual abuse investigation. Thomson Reuters. Retrieved July 1, 2022, from https://kfgo.com/2022/05/19/italys-catholic-church-at-crossroads-over-sexual-abuse-investigation

Assmann, J. (2004). Monotheism and polytheism. In S. I. Johnston (Ed.), *Religions of the ancient world: A guide* (pp. 17–31). The Belknap Press of Harvard University Press.

Associated Press. (2021). Pope expresses 'shame' at scale of clergy abuse in France. Associated Press. Retrieved June 30, 2022, from https://apnews.com/article/pope-francis-europe-vatican-city-sexual-abuse-sexual-abuse-by-clergy-610dedf949d7f1c71b35faaebfbb8df4

Barth, T. (2010). Crisis management in the Catholic Church: Lessons for public administrators. *Public Administration Review, 70*(5), 780–791. https://doi.org/10.1111/j.1540-6210.2010.02205.x

Benoit, W. L. (1995). Sears' repair of its auto service image: Image restoration discourse in the corporate sector. *Communication Studies, 46*(1–2), 89–105. https://doi.org/10.1080/10510979509368441

Breeden, A. (2021, October 5). Over 200,000 minors abused by clergy in France since 1950, report estimates. The New York Times. Retrieved July 1, 2022, from https://www.nytimes.com/2021/10/05/world/europe/france-catholic-church-abuse.html

Burns, E. B. (2021). Cultures in conflict: The implication of modernization in nineteenth-century Latin America. In E. B. Burns, T. E. Skidmore, & V. Bernhard (Eds.), *Elites, masses, and modernization in Latin America, 1850–1930* (pp. 11–78). University of Texas Press.

Campbell, H. A. (2020). Religion in quarantine: The future of religion in a post-pandemic world. Retrieved August 22, 2022, from https://hdl.handle.net/1969.1/188004.

Capizzo, L. (2019). Managing intractability: Wrestling with wicked problems and seeing beyond consensus in public relations. Unpublished doctoral dissertation) University of Maryland, College Park.

Caron, C., Canning, A., Jindelan, K., & Toboni, G. (2011, July 29). Sect leader Warren Jeffs defends polygamy, threatens court with 'sickness and death' from God. ABC News. Retrieved June 30, 2022, from https://abcnews.go.com/US/warren-jeffs-speaks-court-defends-polygamy/story?id=14191589

Coombs, W. T. (2007). Protecting organization reputations during a crisis: The development and application of situational crisis communication theory. *Corporate Reputation Review, 10*(3), 163–176. https://doi.org/10.1057/palgrave.crr.1550049

Coombs, W. T., Frandsen, F., Holladay, S. J., & Johansen, W. (2010). Why a concern for apologia and crisis communication? *Corporate Communications: An International Journal, 15*(4), 337–349. https://doi.org/10.1108/13563281011085466

Dalton, J. M. (2020). *Between popes, inquisitors and princes: How the first Jesuits negotiated religious crisis in early modern Italy*. Brill.

Davies, C., & Hobbs, M. (2020). Irresistible possibilities: Examining the uses and consequences of social media influencers for contemporary public relations. *Public Relations Review, 46*(5), 101983. https://doi.org/10.1016/j.pubrev.2020.101983

Dionisopolous, G. N., & Vibbert, S. L. (1988). CBS vs Mobil oil: Charges of creative bookkeeping. In I. H. R. Ryan (Ed.), *Oratorical encounters: Selected studies and sources of 20th century political accusation and apologies* (pp. 214–252). Greenwood.

Diulio, A., & Arendt, C. E. (2018). #CancelTheDuggars and #BoycottTLC: Image repair or exploitation in reality television. *Public Relations Review, 44*(2), 224–235. https://doi.org/10.1016/j.pubrev.2017.12.001

Djafarova, E., & Rushworth, C. (2017). Exploring the credibility of online celebrities' Instagram profiles in influencing the purchase decisions of young female users. *Computers in Human Behavior, 68*, 1–7. https://doi.org/10.1016/j.chb.2016.11.009

Elsanousi, M., Visotzky, B. L., & Roberts, B. (2020, April 9). Love your neighbour: Islam, Judaism and Christianity come together over COVID-19. World Economic Forum. Retrieved June 30, 2022, from https://www.weforum.org/agenda/2020/04/religions-covid-19-coronavirus-collaboration

Fadda-Conrey, C. (2011). Arab American citizenship in crisis: Destabilizing representations of Arabs and Muslims in the US after 9/11. *MFS Modern Fiction Studies, 57*(3), 532–555. https://doi.org/10.1353/mfs.2011.0068

Garrett, P. D. (2011). *Brand standing*. University of Melbourne, Victorian College of the Arts.

Golan, G., Morehouse, J., & English, A. E. (2021). Building relationships with the faithful: Examining church communicators perceptions of social media influencers in their OPR strategy. *Journal of Public Relations Research, 33*(4), 250–266. https://doi.org/10.1080/1062726X.2021.2011729

Graham, R., & Dias, E. (2022, May 22). Southern Baptist leaders mishandled sex abuse crisis, report alleges. The New York Times. Retrieved July 1, 2022, from https://www.nytimes.com/2022/05/22/us/southern-baptist-sex-abuse.html

Guidepost Solutions. (2022, May 15). Report of the independent investigation: The Southern Baptist Convention executive committee's response to sexual abuse allegations and an audit of the procedures and actions of the credentials committee. Guidepost Solutions. Retrieved July 1, 2022, from https://static1.squarespace.com/static/6108172d83d55d3c9db4dd67/t/628a9326312a4216a3c06 79d/1653248810253/Guidepost+Solutions+Independent+Investigation+Report.pdf

Horowitz Law. (2022, March 4). New child sexual abuse, coverup lawsuit filed against Diocese of Alexandria. KALB. Retrieved July 1, 2022, from https://www.kalb.com/2022/03/04/new-child-sexual-abuse-coverup-lawsuit-filed-against-diocese-alexandria

Huang, H. L. (2019). What is religious misconduct: A typological analysis of the crimes motivated by polytheistic religion, using the Chinese folk religion as an example. *International Journal of Criminology and Sociology, 8*, 55–67. https://doi.org/10.6000/1929-4409.2019.08.07

Hume, H., & Perreault, G. (2022) Media and mass shootings: Field theory in CNN news coverage of the Columbine high school and Parkland high school mass shootings. *Electronic News, 16* (3), 147–163. http://doi.org/10.1177/19312431221111380

Hung, C. J. F. (2005). Exploring types of organization – public relationships and their implications for relationship management in public relations. *Journal of Public Relations Research, 17* (4), 393–426. https://doi.org/10.1207/s1532754xjprr1704_4

Kananovich, V., & Perreault, G. (2021). Audience as journalistic boundary worker: The rhetorical use of comments to critique media practice, assert legitimacy and claim authority. *Journalism Studies, 22*(3), 322–341. https://doi.org/10.1080/1461670X.2020.1869912

Knight, J. G., Mitchell, B. S., & Gao, H. (2009). Riding out the Muhammad cartoons crisis: Contrasting strategies and outcomes. *Long Range Planning, 42*(1), 6–22. https://doi.org/10.1016/j.lrp.2008.11.002

Lauer, C., & Hoyer, M. (2019, October 3). 100s of accused priests living under radar with no oversight. Associated Press. Retrieved July 1, 2022, from https://apnews.com/article/crime-sexual-abuse-by-clergy-sexual-abuse-sexual-assault-the-reckoning-6109dc3f9e744298ae3fd5fe607f0a3c

Lesiv, M. (2017). Blood brothers or blood enemies: Ukrainian pagans' beliefs and responses to the Ukraine-Russia crisis. In K. Rountree (Ed.), *Cosmopolitanism, nationalism, and modern paganism* (pp. 133–155). Palgrave Macmillan.

Lou, C. (2021). Social media influencers and followers: Theorization of a trans-parasocial relation and explication of its implications for influencer advertising. *Journal of Advertising, 51*(1), 1–18. https://doi.org/10.1080/00913367.2021.1880345

Lou, C., & Yuan, S. (2019). Influencer marketing: How message value and credibility affect consumer trust of branded content on social media. *Journal of Interactive Advertising, 19*(1), 58–73. https://doi.org/10.1080/15252019.2018.1533501

Moore, B. (2016 October 9). Twitter post. Retrieved July 1, 2022, from https://twitter.com/BethMooreLPM/status/785119502769852418?s=20

Moore, B. (2018). A letter to my brothers. The LPM Blog. Retrieved July 1, 2022, from https://blog.lproof.org/2018/05/a-letter-to-my-brothers.html

Morehouse, J. (2020). Stakeholder-formed organizations and crisis communication: Analyzing discourse of renewal with a non-offending organization. *Journal of International Crisis and Risk Communication Research, 3*(2), 243–274. https://doi.org/10.3316/INFORMIT.101450860937217

Morehouse, J., & Austin, L. L. (2022). The impact of religion in situational crisis communication theory: An examination of religious rhetoric and religiosity. *Journal of Media and Religion, 21*(2), 105–123. https://doi.org/10.1080/15348423.2022.2059327

Morehouse, J., & Spaulding, C. (2022). Advancing research on crisis communication and religion. In Y. Jin, & L. L. Austin (Eds.), *Social media and crisis communication* (pp. 256–266). Routledge.

O'Donnell, K., Ewart, J., & Alston-Knox, C. (2017). Baseline knowledge of Islam and Muslims: A study of Australian government crisis communication officials. *Salus Journal, 5*(2), 16–35. https://doi.org/10.3316/informit.809153853618529

Payne, L. (2017 October 12). Why female theologians take flak in the public square: The potential rewards of celebrity culture are many, but so are the risks. Christianity Today. Retrieved July 1, 2022, from https://www.christianitytoday.com/ct/2017/october-web-only/why-female-theologians-take-flak-in-public-square.html

Perreault, G., & Meltzer, K. (2022). Metajournalistic discourse and reporting policies on white nationalism. *Journal of Communication Inquiry*. Advance online publication. https://doi.org/10.1177/01968599211072452

Perreault, G., & Montalbano, K. (2022). Covering religion: Field insurgency in United States religion reporting. *Journalism*. Advance online publication. https://doi.org/10.1177/14648849211073220

Perreault, G., & Paul, N. (2019). Narrative framing of the Syrian refugee crisis in British religious news. *Journal of Religion, Media and Digital Culture, 8*(2), 276–297. https://doi.org/10.1163/21659214-00802005

Perreault, G., Peters, J., Johnson, B., & Klein, L. (2021). How journalists think about the first amendment vis-à-vis their coverage of hate groups. *International Journal of Communication, 15* 2021. https://ijoc.org/index.php/ijoc/article/view/17930

Perreault, G. P., Duffy, M., & Morrison, A. (2017). Making a Mormon?: Peacemaking in US press coverage of the Mormon baptism for the dead. *Journal of Media and Religion, 16*(4), 141–152. https://doi.org/10.1080/15348423.2017.1401410

Perreault, M. F., & Perreault, G. (2019). Symbolic convergence in the 2015 Duggar scandal crisis communication. *Journal of Media and Religion, 18*(3), 85–97. https://doi.org/10.1080/15348423.2019.1678945

Perreault, M., & Perreault, G. (2021). Responding to video game moral panic: Persuasive messaging in the video game industry's response to news coverage of mass violence. In S. G. Schartel Dunn, & G. S. Nisbett (Eds.), *Innovations and implications of persuasive narrative* (pp. 179–193). Peter Lang.

Pitofsky, M. (2020 September 9). 11,000 sign petition to remove Franklin Graham as charity's CEO after convention prayer. The Hill. Retrieved July 1, 2022, from https://thehill.com/blogs/blog-briefing-room/news/514857-11000-sign-petition-to-remove-franklin-graham-as-charitys-ceo

Rae, S. J. (2022). Considering the agency of faith in reimagining narrative and shared space in Beth Moore's departure from the Southern Baptist Convention. MA Thesis, Georgia State University Scholar Works. https://doi.org/10.57709/28834706

Ratcliff, A. J., McCarty, J., & Ritter, M. (2017). Religion and new media: A uses and gratifications approach. *Journal of Media & Religion, 16*(1), 15–26. https://doi.org/10.1080/15348423.2017.1274589

Rawden, J. (2022, 20 January). When the Duggar sisters could finally settle their molestation report lawsuit. Cinema Blend. Retrieved July 1, 2022, from https://www.cinemablend.com/television/when-the-duggar-sisters-could-finally-settle-their-molestation-report-lawsuit

Respers France, L. (2021, December 14). Josh Duggar's siblings speak out about his conviction. CNN. Retrieved July 1, 2022, from https://www.cnn.com/2021/12/14/entertainment/josh-duggar-conviction-siblings/index.html

Sayem, M. A. (2021). Lynn White, Jr.'s critical analysis of environmental degradation in relation to faith traditions: Is his "the historical roots of our ecological crisis" still relevant? *Journal of Ecumenical Studies, 56*(1), 1–23. https://doi.org/10.1353/ecu.2021.0004

Schouten, A. P., Janssen, L., & Verspaget, M. (2020). Celebrity vs. influencer endorsements in advertising: The role of identification, credibility, and product-endorser fit. *International Journal of Advertising, 39*(2), 258–281. https://doi.org/10.1080/02650487.2019.1634898

Seeger, M. W., & Griffin Padgett, D. R. (2010). From image restoration to renewal: Approaches to understanding postcrisis communication. *The Review of Communication, 10*(2), 127–141. https://doi.org/10.1080/15358590903545263

Shimron, Y., & Smietana, B. (2021, April 7). On the heels of her split with Southern Baptists, Beth Moore apologizes for supporting a theology that restricts women. She tweets: "I plead your forgiveness for how I just submitted to it and supported it and taught it". Washington Post. Retrieved July 1, 2022, from https://www.washingtonpost.com/religion/2021/04/07/beth-moore-women-complementarianism

Singal, M., Krawczyk, M., & Beal, J. (2016). Clashing values, firm identity, and changing social norms: The case of Chick-fil-A. SAGE Business Cases. International CHRIE.

Smith, B. G., Hallows, D., Vail, M., Burnett, A., & Porter, C. (2021). Social media conversion: Lessons from faith-based social media influencers for public relations. *Journal of Public Relations Research, 33*(4), 231–249. https://doi.org/10.1080/1062726X.2021.2011728

Spaulding, C. (2018). Evangelical Christian crisis responses to same-sex sex scandals. *Journal of Media and Religion, 17*(1), 28–40. https://doi.org/10.1080/15348423.2018.1463717

Sullivan, M. (1987). 'More popular than Jesus': The Beatles and the religious far right. *Popular Music, 6*(3), 313–326. https://doi.org/10.1017/S0261143000002348

Thomson, T. J., Perreault, G., & Duffy, M. (2018). Politicians, photographers, and a Pope: How state-controlled and independent media covered Francis's 2015 Cuba visit. *Journalism Studies, 19*(9), 1313–1330. https://doi.org/10.1080/1461670X.2016.1268929

Tilson, D. J., & Venkateswaran, A. (2006). Toward a covenantal model of public relations: Hindu faith communities and devotional–promotional communication. *Journal of Media and Religion, 5*(2), 111–133. https://doi.org/10.1207/s15328415jmr0502_3

United States Conference of Catholic Bishops. (2002). Promise to protect: Pledge to heal: Charter for the protection of children and young people [Revised 2011]. USCCB. Retrieved July 1, 2022, from https://www.usccb.org/resources/Charter-for-the-Protection-of-Children-and-Young-People-2018-final%281%29.pdf

Vuolo, J. (2021, December 10). Instagram post. Instagram. Retrieved August 22, 2022, from https://www.instagram.com/p/CXUUxBHvHEn.

White, D. G. (2006). Digging wells while houses burn? Writing histories of Hinduism in a time of identity politics. *History and Theory, 45*(4), 104–131. https://doi.org/10.1111/j.1468-2303.2006.00387.x

Young Life. (2021). For all kids–Do better Young Life. Young Life. Retrieved July 1, 2022, from https://dobetter.younglife.org

Young Life. (2022). For every kid. Young Life. Retrieved July 1, 2022, from https://younglife.org/get-involved/for-every-kid

Selected Readings

Morehouse, J. (2020). Stakeholder-formed organizations and crisis communication: Analyzing discourse of renewal with a non-offending organization. *Journal of International Crisis and Risk Communication Research, 3*(2), 243–274. https://doi.org/10.3316/INFORMIT.101450860937217

Morehouse, J., & Austin, L. L. (2022). The impact of religion in situational crisis communication theory: An examination of religious rhetoric and religiosity. *Journal of Media and Religion, 21*(2), 105–123. https://doi.org/10.1080/15348423.2022.2059327

Morehouse, J., & Spaulding, C. (2022). Advancing research on crisis communication and religion. In Y. Jin, & L. L. Austin (Eds.), *Social media and crisis communication* (pp. 256–266). Routledge.

Perreault, M. F., & Perreault, G. (2019). Symbolic convergence in the 2015 Duggar scandal crisis communication. *Journal of Media and Religion, 18*(3), 85–97. https://doi.org/10.1080/15348423.2019.1678945

Spaulding, C. (2018). Evangelical Christian crisis responses to same-sex sex scandals. *Journal of Media and Religion, 17*(1), 28–40. https://doi.org/10.1080/15348423.2018.1463717

14

Web Presence

Amanda Sturgill

The World Wide Web has served as a useful resource for religious organizations from the very beginnings of publicly available web protocols. The uses of websites vary as much for the faithful as they do for those in any other area of life, and religious organizations vary in their adoption of web technologies. This chapter looks at characteristics of the web that relate to faith communities in general. Factors include the types of groups creating and maintaining web presences, the audiences, and the purposes. The technology itself presents affordances and limitations, both technological and theological. We will also consider the present state of web usage in major faith traditions.

The expression of faith can be personal and corporate. Some faith groups maintain hierarchical organization as, for example, Christian faith communities that are, themselves, members of larger associations or denominations. These larger associations create and maintain their own web presences that remain somewhat distinct from those of individual faith communities, though logos and messaging around matters of faith can be similar. Local temples, congregations, and groups also maintain presence on the web. In some cases, where a faith group lacks formal organization, a para-organization may provide information and education about a faith and its beliefs. Finally, individual adherents sometimes maintain presences – anything from a fully hosted website to a templated blog that gives public expression to individual thoughts and interpretations of faith.

Public communication intends a public, something no less true for faith group websites. Sometimes, a website can target internal audiences, adherents to a particular faith itself. Other sites appear to target seekers looking for a faith to elucidate life's purpose or the curious who look for information about the structure of a faith's organizations, practices, and beliefs. Often, sites attempt to serve a mix of audiences, sometimes with all information publicly available and sometimes with a division between public and password-protected information, intended only for insiders.

Communication requires not only an audience, but also a purpose. Across faiths perception of the affordances of particular modes of communication can significantly differ. Presence on the web complements and is complemented by the actions of religious communities in other online spaces such as apps, electronic mail, and social media. Sturgill's (2004) early work of looking at the web presence for faith communities by studying the websites of Southern Baptist churches led to her proposing a dichotomy between information about the faith community as an organization and information about the faith itself. This made sense when looking at an evangelical faith – after all, a central call for evangelicals is to follow the biblical edict to make disciples. But she found that the faith communities tended, instead, to provide information about the institution itself. Topics included church location, staff credentials, and meeting times. In the intervening years, both the expressions of faith on the web and its study have diversified considerably. Individual faith communities appear on the web along with larger organizations

The Handbook on Religion and Communication, First Edition. Edited by Yoel Cohen and Paul A. Soukup.
© 2023 John Wiley & Sons Ltd. Published 2023 by John Wiley & Sons Ltd.

like denominations. It doesn't stop there. Sites provide information and connection for people interested in a faith, and whole online faith communities exist entirely through the web. The threads of organizational and institutional types of information persist, but the diversity of faith life online demands new research categories. Campbell (2013) organized a volume on the topic around the themes of authority, authenticity, community, identity, ritual, and religion (p. 12). Some of those same themes appear here in the light of advances in technology that further democratize web spaces in terms both of creation of religious web spaces and of their use by the faithful and by others. Faith communities have a set of common uses for their websites. Advertising and branding create the digital impression that the faith community makes, thanks to the coherence of the message as well as abilities in message formation and in technology use. Education is closely related. Communities linked with all faiths can and do use the web for instruction on the tenets of the belief, whether for adherents, for external audiences, or for both. There are also instrumental uses. Websites can facilitate two-way and multi-way communication, through something as simple as an e-mail link or as complex as ongoing message board discussions. The Covid-19 pandemic's lockdowns and other pressure to restrict face-to-face meetings accelerated a trend toward an instrumental use of the web in the practice of faith itself, as faith communities wrestled with whether individual worship, corporate worship, and ritual were advisable or even permissible online. Can religious sentiment be shared and can religious faith be enacted through a web browser that restricts some potential for faith expression? You can see a votive candle online, but you can't smell it or feel its heat. The browser also allows for new connectivity, as a homebound adherent can participate in religious education and discussion with those able to attend. When it comes to practice of religion, the web can appear as a both an opportunity and a threat, and faith groups have responded to it in both ways.

Historically, a web presence required skill, although services and technologies have developed to fill some of those gaps. There are several advantages to moving faith activities online. Multimedia content can allow users to experience words, images, and music even though not physically present at a meeting, or even if those users never attend meetings. This allows for new connectivity, as a homebound adherent can participate in worship with those able to attend. Disability can limit accessibility, though: a small motor-related issue can make it difficult to select something with a click; a screen reader for the blind needs a properly encoded site; the hearing impaired need transcripts to take advantage of sound files of religious services or teachings. Although guidance on best practices for disability access exists, church website creators or managers may not know of or follow those guidelines. Creating and maintaining a website requires technical skill, and this can create issues. Groups that have skilled laypeople or funds to hire experts can create content that is more engaging both to audiences and search engines, which can increase visibility and allow communities to grow in membership, creating a sort of religious digital divide. The services that make sites easier to develop and maintain tend to provide templates that create standardized faces for the faith communities who use them.

Finally, the democratizing nature of the web creates issues for more hierarchical faiths. When apostolic succession or other paths of training create expertise, it is troublesome when this expert expression looks the same as amateur assessment. When a faith community sets itself apart from daily life for religious purposes, the choice to engage online at all can allow adherents to access "contaminating" information. And although a web presence can permit a faith community to appear as a suggested answer in a search engine query, this is not all good news. Search engines use proprietary criteria to determine the resource most likely to satisfy the user, and the results may not fit how adherents of a faith would like to see themselves presented. For example, a search for Scientology may lead to a site critical of Scientology's claims.

Faith communities on the web interact within themselves. They also act toward and sometimes with others on the outside. At the same time, those outside of faith communities can become part of their digital audience, with all the attributes of those audiences that bless, perplex, and vex digital media creators. The members of these audiences have agency – they can choose to pay attention and to stop paying attention, to interact, to lurk, or to lampoon. Faith communities balance a tension between the needs of the audience, the message, and the technology when they create and maintain presence on the web.

Christianity

While Christians vary in their focus on evangelism, spreading of the faith is a central concern, either in terms of social justice or proclamation – both vehicles through which they propagate faith. Affiliated websites let Christian groups share their faith with potentially large external audiences. At the congregational level, websites are a way for individual churches to define themselves for those audiences (Cox, 2014, p. 221) and can help bring in potential new members (Webb, 2012). Pastors of mainline Protestant denominations like Methodist, Lutheran, and United Church of Christ say their web presence is a tool to fight shrinking numbers in the pews (Webb, 2012).

Mainline denomination websites offer resources to find opportunities for community service and social justice initiatives, and directories of local faith communities; denomination-level websites commonly offer search features or directories to enable people to find those local parishes. The quality of mainline Protestant faith communities' websites vary, often because of the demands of maintaining the technology. Shrinking numbers and graying congregations make it difficult for some churches to have the latest technologies. Small mainline congregations sometimes have a basic static website, focusing on giving sufficient information for an interested person to physically locate them, with the site created or maintained by a congregational volunteer.

On the other side of the digital divide, better-resourced churches provide opportunities to interact online (forums, live chats) on up-to-date sites in terms of technology and design, with frequently refreshed content. Despite the challenges of creating and maintaining a web presence for older and poorer mainline congregations, there are advantages to them doing so. For example, the particular concerns of the elderly related to the Covid-19 pandemic led to websites becoming a nexus for keeping congregations connected without in-person services. The pandemic increased the incentive for all faith organizations to try live streaming; people could find web addresses for the streamed content on existing church signage. This ability to participate online makes sense in denominations where place-based practices and sacraments are not as important as in faiths requiring pilgrimages or immersion baptism. They also make sense for older congregations with more homebound members.

Some racial division exists in Christian churches in the United States, with some denominations de facto having primarily white members and others drawing members from Black, Hispanic, or other communities. The denominational web presences are similar. In other countries, mainline expression shows the tension between reinforcing the Church as an institution and using the Church to change the institutions around it. For example, Kim (2007) finds similarities between a mainline Korean mega-church and the populist Christianity offered by evangelical mega-churches elsewhere, with website elements that show "order, elite culture, and formality." The church's online presence focuses on Church authority in the form of the pastor, who is represented in several different ways on the homepage. Chinese Protestants use the web to "construct and defend alternative communities" (Dunn, 2007, p. 447). In Australia, web pages provide a space for Church positionality on political matters when it comes to statements in support of Aboriginal rights (Heathcote, 2017).

Evangelical Protestants have enthusiastically adopted web usage, as they did with most communication technologies over time, seeing technology as a way of spreading their faith (Sturgill, 2006). Around the world, from the denomination level to that of a single ministry within a congregation, slick, multimedia websites are popular for presenting the faith's story to seekers who explore a low-commitment introduction in a digital space. An informational web network for Christian churches in Latin America, for example, echoes the goals of evangelical churches and serves as an example of both social relations and human psyche, offering support through collective intelligence, described as being transcendent (Soberón Mainero, 2010). Moschetti (2010), describing Latin American Christianity, notes that "Today, we find in digital media apt resources for representing the relationship with God" (p. 24, my translation). Globally, denominational websites usually focus externally, with information on church history, leadership, and governance being common front-page fodder. Statements of belief are common, as are search features to find local congregations. Technically sophisticated denominational sites feature analytics, modern development strategies including search engine optimization, and engaging, inviting, and attractive contents, with a multimedia blend of photographs, text, and video. Denominations vary in the extent to which they offer the most modern web experience. Some offer multimedia and responsive web design for all devices, while others are more text based and would be difficult to use on a phone or tablet. When it comes to individual congregations, large, well-funded churches have web masters as a part of a media team for the church, and the sites feature custom-produced videos and graphics. For example, see the website of Saddleback Valley Community Church, which has multiple, large campuses in southern California. The site has links to multimedia resources and even a church app to download. Similar racial division appears in evangelical churches, and the web presences are also similar.

Smaller congregations often depend on volunteers or staff members to create and update websites on a part-time basis, but they can also use companies like Ekklesia and Ministry Design, which provide templates, technical support, and hosting, to make that job easier. Though some view evangelicals as similar, it is interesting to note that these services offer interface design in a variety of themes with names like Augustine, Tubman, and ten Boom – all names that resonate with evangelicals from different traditions and with varying worship styles. Churches using these services tend to have technologically modern, easy-to-use, and frequently updated websites because the web master can focus on the content alone. For example, the First Baptist Church of tiny Muleshoe, Texas (population fewer than 6000 with at least 15 churches), has a site that uses the Online Church Solutions service to create an attractive, functional website. In contrast, in the town of Walnut Grove, on the North Carolina / Virginia border (fewer than 2000 residents and 21 churches), the 100-year-old Peniel Pentecostal Holiness Church has a site, which at the time of writing, did not use modern web design, did not work well on mobile devices, and did not have its security configured properly, though it provided links to sermons and recorded live streams. Congregational websites exist for evangelical churches around the world. Hackett (2009) found that Pentecostal websites in Africa were predominately from Nigeria. Although Pentecostal churches have both male and female leadership, African churches with websites were more likely to be headed by males.

Some evangelical churches are organized into larger affiliations and denominations, but the affiliation doesn't seem to influence how smaller associations and congregations choose to develop, form, and act. The evangelical concept of priesthood of the believer implies that individual adherents can and do understand and manage their relationship with the divine. An acceptance of some sort of notion of apostolic succession (Cross & Livingstone, 2005) or other transmission of authority through divine selection of leadership (the Church of Jesus Christ of Latter-day Saints, n.d.) leads some branches of Christianity to be hierarchical and male in their leadership—something that appears online as well.

The Church of Jesus Christ of Latter-day Saints (the Mormons) has a frequently updated messaging strategy that includes use of mass media tools influenced by denomination-level policy. The Church used to offer separate online experiences for internal and external audiences through sites with different URLs, http://LDS.org for adherents and http://mormon.org for others. These sites now both redirect to http://www.churchofjesuschrist.org. The former redirects to the home page of the site, which has information about events for members as well as links to spiritual development materials like blog posts and videos. Mormon.org redirects to an inside page targeting spiritual seekers with information about how to join, how to download an app offering a spiritual growth experience, and more. Generally, the Church has a modern website both in design and in web technology usage. The denomination coordinates messaging strategy and branding at all levels, with changes resulting from rebranding in the name of the group, a decision made at the top of the highly hierarchical faith. President Russell M. Nelson, considered a living prophet by adherents (Dias, 2019), announced in 2018 that members should not use LDS or Mormon to refer to themselves or to their faith.

Eilers (2009) notes that communication has characterized the Roman Catholic Church for hundreds of years, with the goal of "social communication" an explicit one since the Second Vatican Council in the 1960s. Roman Catholics had some of the first web presence for a faith group. The first web server came online in 1990 (CERN, n.d.) and by the time the web was five years old, Chabad (Harmon, 1998) and the Roman Catholic Church (Traditio, 1994) both had presences. This illustrates the robust relationship between religious faiths and the communication technologies they see as valuable opportunities to share religious truths or to gain converts. The Vatican's official website appears in 10 languages (in 2022) and is conservative in both appearance and content. The muted tones in the background lend an air of seriousness to information that includes facts about historical pontiffs or the writings and speeches of the current one, alongside a feature that displays the latest papal tweet. Interestingly, a visit in 2021 showed that the site uses neither mobile-friendly design nor modern Internet security.

Roman Catholic web presence at the local level occurs through individual parishes or through individual clergy or lay leaders. As evangelical churches do, some Catholic parishes rely on services that help with site set up, training, and hosting. Some of the same companies work for multiple types of faiths, but services like The Catholic Web Company offer creative services tailored for Catholics. Interestingly, a tab on that company named The Church & Internet legitimizes the services in two ways: by pointing out the usefulness of a web presence in general and with a reminder that the Holy See has embraced the Internet for some religious purposes. eCatholic also offers web design services and offers inspiration in the form of "Best of" lists for parishes, schools, and more. The ratings are based on form more than function. One review reads:

> Good websites are a reflection of an organization, its brand, and story. The Basilica of Saint Louis' new custom website both tells the story of this historic church, as well as creates an experience similar to walking through the actual front doors. The selection of site colors, background patterns, and imagery were as if pulled from the exact interiors of the church. (Kern, 2020)

That basilica website focuses primarily on information to encourage and allow visitors to come to the physical parish. An interesting feature offers the chance to purchase vigil candles online that people at the church will light there on your behalf. Another service called Parishes Online offers a searchable list of church publications like Sunday bulletins from various congregations. This kind of service can provide a web presence for parishes that are too small or the lack funding to launch a full website.

The differences between the web presences of the Vatican and those of individual congregations is especially interesting as Roman Catholicism also has a hierarchical faith tradition, with the Holy See in Rome at the top and an array of cardinals, bishops, and archbishops playing important roles as both administrators and arbiters of the faith. Through their theological training, these leaders and local priests are understood as having the authority to act on behalf of the divine. This relationship is tested, though, by a desire to keep in line with the determination by Church authorities of what constitutes religious truth. The Vatican's formal communications come through offices for a variety of media including the web; Pope Francis consolidated a Secretariat for Communications in 2015. While not strictly a web-based action, the Pope tweets in multiple languages and his English-language feed, @Pontifex, had more than 18 million followers in 2021. Like the Pope, other individual Roman Catholic personalities also share on social media and create web presence through blogs. Many Catholic priests blog, some with amusing titles like "Bonfire of the Vanities" for Fr. Martin Fox from Ohio. Other Church figures blog as well, like the Benedictine sisters, who maintain iBenedictines and provide a global ministry from a cloistered life.

Orthodox Christian churches are also hierarchical. Heads of each branch maintain web presences. Perhaps fitting with a more structured faith group, help for individual churches comes from within, with denominational support for faith communities in providing sites with carefully created messages for what appear to be mostly internal audiences. The Greek Orthodox Archdiocese of America has a Department of Information Technology that states its mission is "to aid in proclaiming the Gospel of our Lord and Savior Jesus Christ," suggesting an expectation that those outside the faith may also be paying attention. Most of the content, though, seems targeted at those inside. For example, the department offers tools for local parishes like a Sunday bulletin builder and e-mail listserv product as well as centralized services like online games for children that local sites can link. A Department of Internet Ministries offers some related features like tools to stream parish services on Roku or Apple TV and religious content that can be easily embedded in local parish sites. It also offers web hosting for parishes. Outside of the patriarchate, the business Orthodox Christianity offers an index of web tricks and tools, while Orthodox Web Solutions offers to help manage a local site for a fee, prominently stating "Coding knowledge not required." Further toward serving existing believers, Turner (2019) notes that there are limited instances in which interactive, online practice of religion goes beyond reading scripture or watching sermons or other interpretations. For example, online communion (bring your own bread and wine) is available in some cases. Online practice can become an issue, though, as questions arise about the legitimacy of digital icons, two-dimensional images of Christ, important events in church history, or saints that are found in churches and used in prayer (Turner, 2019).

Judaism

Within the Jewish tradition, different streams of faith practice have different types of web presence. For example, the most conservative, the ultra-Orthodox (Haredim) differs from the Modern Orthodox in their entire approach to the Internet. For the Haredi, who make up about 10% of Israel's population, Internet use in general is complicated. Possible conveniences of modern life and the Internet's potential for faith development compete with fear of contaminating the minds of a people who choose to set themselves apart. Orthodox websites exist, some of which provide information like directories of Jewish groups and sometimes provide training for participation in ceremonies and in rituals as well as other types of education. Other sites provide news, interaction, and even access to dating. Sites like The Orthodox Union have a modern, usable design with many links to teachings and programs.

Still, some see the web as a threat to the purity of belief of adherents. Ultra-Orthodox Rabbi Mordecai Blau told the BBC "The Internet is a catastrophe... It's liberal, open, and it's a terrible danger" (BBC News, 2016), representing a view that information offered away from the center of the faith is harmful. But in that same article and several like it, authors discuss how more ultra-Orthodox men are seeking employment in Israel's technology sector as Israel reduces child subsidies, making a life of a large family and full-time religious study untenable. Golan (2015) writes that the Haredim have a dualist perspective on new media, seeing both inherent risk and potential. For the Modern Orthodox, while sacred texts are still primary, the attitude toward new communication technologies is more prosaic. There is a belief that the Internet has potential as a part of modern life, but that it also conveys some of the negatives of modernity like easy access to pornography. So, media literacy, parental guidance, and automated filtering all play a role in online safety for adherents. Outside pressures to adopt Internet technologies persist, and the Covid-19 pandemic saw a rapid adoption of online services (Cohen & Scheer, 2020).

The web is less contentious for Jews identifying with the Conservative Movement. Instead of rabbinical prohibitions against web use, web spaces offer resources to rabbis and to adherents alike. For example, the Rabbinical Assembly offers a blog, resources for leading services, readings and prayers, and job listings for rabbis, as well as articles on matters like converting to Judaism and kosher food laws for others interested in learning about the faith. A section on social justice includes perspectives on everything from healthcare to civil rights, with online and offline resources. In the conversion section, the site notes that "a supportive Jewish community that takes Judaism seriously, within which one can grow ... is essential." The value of community is also a feature of the United Synagogue of Conservative Judaism site, a modern, graphical site where the first tab offers help to "strengthen my congregation" and the third, ways to connect with peers. This includes a link to a digital community called The Commons, designed to build community among leaders in Conservative Judaism.

Reform Jews have no strictures against web use for adherents, seeing the web as a way of sharing the faith with others. ReformJudaism features tabs at the top of the page for beliefs, actions, and an about page with historical context, all focused for external audiences. The page can serve a mix of audiences. From the idea that "Judaism must change and adapt to the needs of the day to survive" (Union for Reform Judaism, n.d.), Reform Jews see that new technologies for communication can be a part of that change and adaptation. Golan (2015) writes that the frame is inclusive adoption. "Inclusive adoption refers to building legitimacy through framing new media as a vital part of modern times and most fitting form to express and transmit religious knowledge and beliefs" (p. 136). This appears on sites like those from the World Union for Progressive Judaism and on ReformJudaism, both of which take advantage of new media affordances like multimedia, interactivity, and social media links on their websites.

Because they lack centrally determined authoritative resources, individual Jewish faith communities turn to private companies for web development. For example, the web design service Synagogue Websites creates web presence for synagogues of all types and has a portfolio that makes it easy to compare the distinctive features of each. Shul Cloud offers a similar service, touting the ability to easily manage accounts receivable. Some Orthodox Jewish communities in the United States do maintain synagogue websites. Similar to other faith traditions, they offer photos of group activities, information about the clergy, calendars, descriptions of programming, etc. There is often membership information and, in some cases, an online membership application. Links provide access to educational materials as well as information on in-person educational sessions. New Jersey's congregation Ahavat Achim even offers multiple audio files for visitors to experience and practice songs used in worship. Several sites also link to community resources like kosher restaurants to enable faith practice in the larger community. Although Orthodox Jewish leaders have been known to disapprove of online meetings for prayers (Davidson, n.d.), the Covid-19 pandemic has caused the question to be revisited (Sharon, 2020).

Conservative and Reform synagogues have met the pandemic challenge in part through online services (Dolstein, 2020). Tsuria (2019) notes that Conservative Jews hold congregation as a core value. Her small study of synagogue websites noted similarities in visual design, with white and blue or earth tone color schemes being popular as were photos of the community engaging with each other. They present organizational information (Sturgill, 2004) as a way of understanding and finding the community in real life. The sites she studied were less likely to have online learning resources or online engagement opportunities like discussion features. In contrast, some reform synagogues prominently feature online engagement activities like Congregation Shaare Emeth with an online Trivia Night or the Upper Valley Jewish Community, offering teens an online Passover seder with a chance to learn about the impacts of the fashion industry on labor and justice. Richart (2019) writes "In the United States, the dispersed, decentralized nature of Reform Judaism and the often geographically separate of Reform Jews also facilitates digital media use in religious practice as a repository for religious resources and Jewish education and as a means of communication between congregations and membership" (p. 162). Some virtual communities exist. For example, a group called Stretnutie uses the web for the maintenance of a community for Czech émigrés who now live in Israel, North America, and Australia, as well as around Europe (Salner, 2021).

Islam

As a diverse faith with multiple streams of belief and types of in-person practice, Islam's diversity plays out on the web as well. As Bunt noted in 2009, the dichotomy of religion online vs. online religion matters in Muslim expression on the web. In terms of religion online, the practice of Islam includes considering opinion and guidance from faith leaders but also the pressures of government in places where Islam is a state religion (Mellor et al., 2011). Idid and Hashim (1989, as cited in Ghani, 2011) note that different types of Muslim media (including media for Muslims in Muslim and non-Muslim countries) focus both internally and externally on the faith. Externally, websites proselytize the faith in some circumstances. The site Islamicity, which describes itself as "The Global Muslim e-Community," is an example of a seeker-friendly, English-language site with educational links like "Understanding Islam" and practical links like a calculator to determine times of prayer. The site is run by Hadi, a US charitable organization, and sells both products and memberships that it says will "help promote the splendors of Islam to thousands of visitors." Other sites like Islamweb and Islamreligion offer the seeker portions of larger sites devoted to articles about Islamic thought, resources, and issues. The sites appear in varied languages and, interestingly, have some differences in content between the versions.

Islamic websites serve believers as well. Sites like Quran.com provide training in the faith through things like an online Qur'an with translation and interpretation, and support for individual practice with tools such as prayer time and fast time calculators. Islam values purity among the faithful (Özdemir & Frank, 2000), and the web provides information and opportunities for interaction and collaboration for the internal audience. For Muslims who cannot find in-person teaching from faith leaders in person, prominent faith leaders support websites. For example, the offices of Ayatollah Sistani, a noted Shia cleric and Nobel prize nominee, supervise the Ahlulbayt (a.s.) Global Information Center, which publishes several websites, include http://al-shia.org, which has on its landing page the chance to select versions in 29 different languages. Interestingly, the versions differ in more than language, with notably divergent graphic design and user experiences. The Spanish-language version begins with links to teaching on the prophet Muhammed, while the English-language version begins with a scripture quotation and a quotation from its interpretation by an imam. Third-party sites also support other Muslim media, including an affiliate of *Sisters* magazine, a women's magazine for Muslims, a UK site for the *Little Explorers* magazine for Muslim children, or the site for MyVoice, which has articles for Muslim youth on many themes – from fashion to overcoming imposter syndrome to the Muslim pilgrimage, the Hajj. Because of concerns about rectitude and purity of information, Arab Muslims were slower to adopt the Internet overall than were other religious groups worldwide (Mellor et al., 2011), but the trajectory and forms of faith expression online for Muslims worldwide continue to grow.

Buddhism

Buddhism, practiced both in Asia and in the diaspora, differs in its in-person experience between the regions. While a resident of any city in Thailand may expect on any given morning to encounter Theravada Buddhist monks in their saffron robes walking on the road with their begging bowls, a resident of a city in Europe or Canada may have to drive a long distance to find a Buddhist temple of any sort. In both Asia and in the diaspora, people use digital technology to find information and help for those who seek engagement with it. Ostrowski (2006) writes about the online presence of Buddhists in the United States, noting that American Buddhism in general tends to be more inclusive than that practiced in parts of Asia. One aspect of inclusivity is making teachings available, and the cybersangha, or online Buddhist community, is one way of making the teachings more open. Ostrowski surveyed visitors to online Buddhism resources and found that about one-third of the respondents indicated that they used online resources because there were no in-person temples near them. Elements of Buddhist sites are seeker focused, with introductions to Buddhism and guides on how to meditate. Buddhism does not have a central authority, so web presences vary, but the faith's notion of *upaya*, or expedience, allows for different organizations to provide resources for seekers in the faith. As Veidlinger (2015) notes, the Buddha himself believed that clear communication is essential to ensure success of teachings.

Websites are portals for communication of Buddhist teachings. For example, the Buddha Dharma Education Association, which sprang from a meditation center in Australia, runs BuddhaNet, which compiles resources for learning about and practicing Buddhism. The site features a news feed, links to an online magazine, audio of educational talks and meditation aids, e-books, a link to a monastery/retreat center in New South Wales, and more. A prominent display ad promotes a downloadable app version of a nonsectarian World Buddhist Directory, a searchable database also found on the website. The Triratna Buddhist Community (*Triratna* being a Sanskrit term expressing the Buddha, the *Dharma* (teachings), and the *Sangha* (the people) – three aspects of Buddhist faith) offers The Buddhist Centre, which includes a Dharma toolkit designed to allow individual acts, but also to include opportunities for joining with others in meditation and in livestreamed talks. Some Buddhist centers, monasteries, and temples also maintain an online presence. For example, Amaravati Monastery in Hertfordshire, UK, maintains a website that offers links to personal meditation retreat experiences, videos, podcasts, and e-books. As with other faiths, smaller groups tend to have a less sophisticated web presence, lacking up-to-date technology or using a simpler design. For example, the Arizona Buddhist Temple, at the time of writing, did not adapt to mobile devices, required lots of scrolling, and was largely text based. The site offered links to Dharma talks on video and podcast, meeting opportunity times, and even several vegan recipes.

Hinduism

Hinduism is also widely practiced in the diaspora (Mitra, 2019), and web presence for Hindu interest and Hindu temples offers practice for adherents separated from physical temples. The faith has no central authority and a diverse set of practices, with common beliefs including a cycle of rebirths and the possibility of release from it. Oral tradition has been important from the early days (Jacobs, 2010, p. 2), even being seen as an advantage. Retelling stories makes them relevant for modern audiences. In this mode. Dr. A. V. Srinivasan runs his own site, which provides information and links and, at the time of writing, had a promotion for the book *Hinduism for Dummies* on the home page. Kuaui's Hindu Monastery runs a similar page, Himalayan Academy, with opportunities to read and learn from texts and articles and to look and listen to talks as well as other informative videos and audio. A "Live Spiritually" portion offers advice for learning Hindu practice on your own. The Hindu American Foundation in the United States also provides general information at an eponymous website that features Hinduism basics, including information for school children. They also have information on government policy issues they say are of interest to Hindus including civil and human rights and religious liberty.

The online presence reflects three areas of Hindu temple practice: digital *darshan*, online rituals, and virtual Hinduism. Digital *darshan* takes a ritual practice of beholding the sacred image and applies it in the virtual world. The act of following hyperlinks can become positive action toward beholding. Online ritual takes the practice of the *pūjā*, a set of actions that allows communion with the divine, and moves it online. In some cases this means contracting for someone onsite to perform the rituals in your place. In these cases, the sites act as a sort of virtual priest (Mallapragada, 2010). The web can also affect the value of the temple itself, Scheifinger (2010) writes. Considering the digital *pūjā*, he notes that it shifts power differentials, diminishing the role of the temple authorities and priests. In this way, the physical temple itself declines in importance (Scheifinger, 2009). Temples have, in some cases, reimagined themselves as online spaces. For example, the Austin Hindu Temple livestreamed events during the pandemic. Varanasi, India's Shrikashi Viswanth temple, has an official website that offers online services for purchase as well as booking for an onsite guest house.

New Religious Movements

As faith organizations, new religious movements face a conundrum of sorts, with a desire to gain legitimacy through communications and a desire to keep secret knowledge a secret. Investigation of the websites of 392 new religious movements (NRMs) (Sturgill, 2019b) found that movement sites did have belief-oriented content as well as organizational content. Most sites had some sort of history or background of the group, and many had an NRM mission statement, a logo, or both – features that would presumably appeal to the external audience. Belief-oriented content included online readings and lessons. Organizational information included descriptions of organizational structure as well as contact information. Opportunities to interact online were uncommon. It's worth noting that many sites had some content restricted to "members only."

An example of an NRM website is the International Society of Krishna Consciousness, the Hare Krishnas, which has a website using modern web technology. The site includes a feed of news stories mentioning the faith. The site also provides one-way communication, with a live chat feature for nonpublic, two-way communication. The site also provides links for information on local temples. Some, like the temple in Cartago, Costa Rica, do maintain a website, but instead use Facebook to provide local information like events, videos and even educational documents. Others like the temple in London offer their own sophisticated and attractive website that offers a "spiritual community in the heart of London." Other NRMs permit online practice of the faith. For example, adherents of Eckankar can experience the Hu sound online through assorted organization websites or through many videos on YouTube.

For some NRMs, a single entity is all there is of the faith. In these cases, the NRM web presence supplies information targeted toward impression management for the external audience. The belief that they have a secret knowledge makes them less likely to want to share it online and for others; past criticism and suspicion has made them more circumspect. For example, the successor group to the Branch Davidian church maintains a website that primarily offers explanations of the church's failings in following David Koresh and new success with new leadership. The Heaven's Gate UFO cult, known for its mass suicide in 1997, has a website that continued to exist at the time of writing, flashing "Red Alert" at the top and stating, "If you study the material on this website you will hopefully understand our joy and what our purpose here on Earth has been. You may even find your 'boarding pass' to leave with us during this brief 'window.'" The site is maintained by Heaven's Gate members who did not participate in the ritual suicide (Harding, 2017). In other cases, the web is about outreach. For example, Dunn (2007) examines the Eastern Lightning NRM, which considers a Chinese woman a manifestation of a returned Christ, now on Earth to perfect followers and bring about the apocalypse. The group reaches out to the West through Google Ads and a website, run from the United States and in English, that explains the group's motivations and immediately invites the visitor into educational live chat.

Web-Only Faith Groups

The web is the only home for other faith movements, some of which seem serious to adherents and like parody to others. For example, The Church of the Latterday Dude has more than a quarter of a million ordained clergy, but ordination only requires a free web form. As the faith describes itself:

> Although Dudeism makes use of a lot of humor and satire, we are totally serious in our belief that it is "the religion for its time and place." Or, we're as serious as anyone can be about a "belief." One of the core tenets of Dudeism is that everything is "just, like, your opinion, man" and so everything has to be up for debate. Unlike other religions, we're open to suggestions. In this way, Dudeism could be considered an "open source religion." (Dudeism FAQ, n.d.)

The interactions with Dudeism take place mostly online, through the website and also through social media. In the same way, The Temple of the Jedi Order (Temple, n.d.) and other Jedi organizations, which promote a faith using principles from the Star Wars series of movies, exist primarily online. The Temple of the Jedi Order offers faith information and training programs as well as opportunities to interact with other practitioners on onsite forums. Other sites like Jedi Church mostly redirect users to Facebook for forums to contact others who practice. Futurists considering the development of artificial intelligence (AI) have, in some cases, decided that self-aware AI will be so far superior to humans that it will, effectively, be a deity (Sturgill, 2019a). Some have started online faith communities in preparation. For example, the Way of the Future Church existed online from 2017 to 2021 and offered information for "Humans United in support of AI, committed to peaceful transition to the precipice of consciousness" (Korosec, 2021). The Turing Church also exists online, with a website that functions as a blog on transhumanist topics and that links to engagement opportunities including Facebook groups and a Discord channel for audio or video conversation. The website describes it as "a group of seekers at the intersection of science and religion, spirituality and technology, engineering and science fiction, mind and matter. Hacking religion, enlightening science, awakening technology." Because these new faith ideas don't have the history of an institution, they are more open to participatory development of the faith, its principles and practices.

Finally, some websites are made by the faithful themselves, in particular sites that are intended as criticism or warning about particular faiths. For example, QuitMormon offers a free service designed to automate parts of resigning membership in the Church of Jesus Christ of Latter-day Saints, which the site says can be a lengthy process with lots of unwanted contact from Church leaders. On the other hand, FAIR, a product of the Foundation for Apologetic Information and Research, says it exists to defend the Church of Jesus Christ of Latter-day Saints against online detractors, who can be found in multiple areas online including social media and message boards. The website Spiritual Abuse is run by an individual who says she "felt led to take an active role in exposing abuse in churches and to specifically help those who left the United Pentecostal Church." The dated-looking site includes links to personal experience blogs, a link to an online support group, and other resources. Operation Clambake, found at the aptly named Xenu.net, links resources opposing Scientology, and The Underground Bunker does the same. Stop Baptist Predators highlights news related to sexual abuse in connection with the Southern Baptist Church. Antireligious content appears on third-party websites as well. For example, the social media site Reddit has multiple posts that purport to explain sex abuse in the Roman Catholic Church or to offer insight from users who claim to be priests, abuse victims, and the like. They sometimes link to other user-generated resources like a site that offers a clickable map leading to diocese-by-diocese records of abuse cases, with clickable references offered in support.

Conclusion

Across faiths, the web has presented tremendous potential, but also raised tremendous questions for faith communities. Carefully guarded beliefs and traditions that seek to explain the origin and meaning of life run up against technological and social evolution at a speed greater than the faithful have had to contend with before. The audience for religious messages now exists well beyond the door of the worship center and can become quite personal, as that audience can access a site from their phone. At the same time, faith communities can worry about attracting and serving those external audiences. And all audiences can talk back, share, and remix messages. Faith community responses vary depending on how the community is structured. More hierarchical faiths are carefully guarding messages and devoting resources to enable local sites to stay in line with what is seen as a winsome and accurate presentation. Technology represents both an affordance and a challenge, as religious doctrine, education, and even practice can be widely and conveniently accessed online, but the type of skill to create the opportunities is different from the training of most faith leaders. Well-resourced faith groups have a real opportunity to excel in the creation and promotion of online presence, which could mean a self-perpetuating and worsening digital divide that may change the landscape of offline faith expression as well. Miniaturization of technology, algorithmic selection of information, and the deconstruction of information from its context endemic to social media will likely increase the tensions between the faithful and the web in the future.

References

BBC News. (2016, September 8). The ultra-Orthodox Jews combining tech and the torah. *BBC News*. Retrieved March 3, 2022, from https://www.bbc.com/news/magazine-37300929

Bunt, G. R. (2009). *IMuslims: Rewiring the house of Islam*. University of North Carolina Press.

Campbell, H. (Ed.). (2013). *Digital religion: Understanding religious practice in new media worlds*. Routledge.

CERN. (n.d.). A short history of the web. CERN. Retrieved March 3, 2022, from https://home.cern/science/computing/birth-web/short-history-web

Cohen, T., & Scheer, S. (2020, April 20). Israel's ultra-Orthodox Jews take to internet in coronavirus lockdown. Reuters. Retrieved March 2, 2022, from https://www.reuters.com/article/us-health-coronavirus-israel-ultraorthod/israels-ultra-orthodox-jews-take-to-internet-in-coronavirus-lockdown-idUSKCN225265

Cox, S. D. (2014). *American Christianity: The continuing revolution*. University of Texas Press.

Cross, F. L., & Livingstone, E. A. (Eds.). (2005). Apostolic succession. In *The Oxford dictionary of the Christian church* Oxford University Press. Retrieved March 2, 2022, from https://www.oxfordreference.com/view/10.1093/acref/9780192802903.001.0001/acref-9780192802903

Davidson, B. (n.d.). Will the synagogue ever go virtual? Why a Skype minyan is not OK. Chabad.org. Retrieved March 2, 2022, from https://www.chabad.org/library/article_cdo/aid/1783077/jewish/Will-the-Synagogue-Ever-Go-Virtual.htm

Dias, E. (2019, June 29). "Mormon" no more: Faithful reflect on church's move to scrap a moniker. *The New York Times*. Retrieved March 2, 2022, from https://www.nytimes.com/2019/06/29/us/mormon-church-name-change.html

Dolstein, J. (2020, April 24). For now, online services mean many synagogues are seeing greater attendance. *The Times of Israel*. Retrieved March 2, 2022, from https://www.timesofisrael.com/for-now-online-services-mean-many-synagogues-are-seeing-greater-attendance

Dudeism. (n.d.). Frequently asked questions. Retrieved March 2, 2022, from https://dudeism.com/faq

Dunn, E. C. (2007). Netizens of heaven: Contesting orthodoxies on the Chinese Protestant web. *Asian Studies Review*, 31(4), 447–458. https://doi.org/10.1080/10357820701710740

Eilers, F.-J. (2009). Church and social communication. In H. Geybels, S. M. Hans, & M. Walrave (Eds.), *Faith and media: Analysis of faith and media: Representation and communication* (pp. 39–51) (Gods, Humans, and Religions, No. 17). P.I.E. Peter Lang.

Ghani, Z. (2011). The uniformity of broadcast media in the Muslim world during the age of globalization. *ISLAMIYYAT*, 33, 53–58. https://oarep.usim.edu.my/jspui/bitstream/123456789/4208/1/The%20Uniformity%20of%20Broadcast%20Media%20in%20the%20Muslim%20World%20During%20the%20Age%20of%20Globalization.pdf

Golan, O. (2015). Legitimation of new media and community building amongst Jewish denominations in the U.S. In H. Campbell (Ed.), *Digital Judaism: Jewish negotiations with digital media and culture* (pp. 137–144). Routledge Taylor & Francis Group.

Hackett, R. J. (2009). The new virtual (inter) face of African Pentecostalism. *Society*, 46(6), 496–503.

Harding, N. (2017, April 4). Mass suicide survivors who stayed behind to keep death cult's bizarre teachings alive for 20 years. *Mirror*. Retrieved March 2, 2022, from https://www.mirror.co.uk/news/weird-news/two-decades-after-heavens-gate-10158830

Harmon, A. (1998, December 13). Yosef Kazen, Hasidic rabbi and web pioneer, dies at 44. *The New York Times*. Retrieved March 2, 2022, from https://www.nytimes.com/1998/12/13/nyregion/yosef-kazen-hasidic-rabbi-and-web-pioneer-dies-at-44.html

Heathcote, C. (2017). The politically correct pulpit. *Quadrant Magazine*, 6(3), 32–35.

The Church of Jesus Christ of Latter-day Saints. (n.d.). How are prophets called? LDS Church. Retrieved March 2, 2022, from https://www.churchofjesuschrist.org/study/friend/2016/04/how-are-prophets-called

Jacobs, S. (2010). *Hinduism today: An introduction*. Bloomsbury Publishing Plc.

Kern, D. (2020). Inspired design: Best Catholic websites of 2020. eCatholic. Retrieved March 3, 2022, from https://ecatholic.com/blog/best-catholic-websites-of-2020

Kim, K. (2007). Ethereal Christianity: Reading Korean mega-church websites. *Studies in World Christianity*, 13(3), 208–224.

Korosec, K. (2021, February 18). Anthony Levandowski closes his church of AI. TechCrunch. Retrieved March 3, 2022, from https://techcrunch.com/2021/02/18/anthony-levandowski-closes-his-church-of-ai

Mallapragada, M. (2010). Desktop deities: Hindu temples, online cultures and the politics of remediation. *South Asian Popular Culture, 8*(2), 109–121. https://doi.org/10.1080/14746681003797955

Mellor, N., Rinnawi, K., Dajani, N., & Ayish, M. I. (2011). *Arab media: Globalization and emerging media industries*. Polity.

Mitra, S. (2019). Hinduism goes online: Digital media and Hinduism in the diaspora. In A. E. Grant, D. A. Stout, C. H. Chen, & A. F. C. Sturgill (Eds.), *Religion online: How digital technology is changing the way we worship and pray* (Vol. 2, pp. 199–218). Praeger.

Moschetti, W. (2010). Del púlpito a las redes sociales. *Chasqui, 112*(13901079), 23–26. https://dialnet.unirioja.es/servlet/oaiart?codigo=5791229

Ostrowski, A. (2006). Buddha browsing: American Buddhism and the internet. *Contemporary Buddhism, 7*(1), 91–103.

Özdemir, A., & Frank, K. (2000). Cleanliness and purity. In *Visible Islam in modern Turkey* (pp. 170–179). Palgrave Macmillan.

Richart, A. (2019). Reform Judaism in the digital age. In A. E. Grant, D. A. Stout, C. H. Chen, & A. F. C. Sturgill (Eds.), *Religion online: How digital technology is changing the way we worship and pray* (Vol. 2, pp. 160–169). Praeger.

Salner, P. (2021). Emigration, home, identity: An ethnological examination of the identity of Jewish emigrants from Czechoslovakia. *Occasional Papers on Religion in Eastern Europe, 41*(2), 51–68. https://digitalcommons.georgefox.edu/ree/vol41/iss2/5/

Scheifinger, H. (2009). The Jagannath Temple and online darshan. *Journal of Contemporary Religion, 24*(3), 277–290. https://doi.org/10.1080/13537900903080402

Scheifinger, H. (2010). Internet threats to Hindu authority: Puja-ordering websites and the Kalighat temple. *Asian Journal of Social Science, 38*(4), 636–656.

Sharon, J. (2020, March 20). Orthodox Tel Aviv synagogue begins virtual online prayer services. *The Jerusalem Post*. Retrieved March 3, 2022, from https://www.jpost.com/israel-news/orthodox-tel-aviv-synagogue-begins-virtual-online-prayer-services-621427

Soberón Mainero, L. (2010). Cultura digital en clave de comunión. *Chasqui, 112*(13901079), 19–22. http://www.redalyc.org/articulo.oa?id=16057456003

Sturgill, A. (2004). Scope and purposes of church web sites. *Journal of Media and Religion, 3*(3), 165–176. https://doi.org/10.1207/s15328415jmr0303_3

Sturgill, A. (2006). Evangelicalism. In D. Stout (Ed.), *Encyclopedia of religion, communication and media* (pp. 136–140). Routledge.

Sturgill, A. (2019a). Artificial intelligence: Its future uses in religious compassion. In A. E. Grant, D. A. Stout, C. H. Chen, & A. F. C. Sturgill (Eds.), *Religion online: How digital technology is changing the way we worship and pray* (Vol. 1, pp. 57–66). Praeger.

Sturgill, A. (2019b). New age and new religious movements and the internet. In A. E. Grant, D. A. Stout, C. H. Chen, & A. F. C. Sturgill (Eds.), *Religion online: How digital technology is changing the way we worship and pray* (Vol. 2, pp. 267–276). Praeger.

Temple of the Jedi Order. (n.d.). IRS exemption letter. Temple of the Jedi Order. Retrieved March 3, 2022, from https://www.templeofthejediorder.org/images/TOTJO-IRS-Exemption-Letter.pdf

Traditio. (1994). Traditional Roman Catholic network, including the official Catholic directory of traditional Latin Masses. Traditio.com. Retrieved March 3, 2022, from www.traditio.com

Tsuria, R. (2019). Conservative Judaism in the digital age. In A. E. Grant, D. A. Stout, C. H. Chen, & A. F. C. Sturgill (Eds.), *Religion online: How digital technology is changing the way we worship and pray* (Vol. 2, pp. 144–159). Praeger.

Turner, J. (2019). Orthodox Christianity in the digital age. In A. E. Grant, D. A. Stout, C. H. Chen, & A. F. C. Sturgill (Eds.), *Religion online: How digital technology is changing the way we worship and pray* (Vol. 2, pp. 111–125). Praeger.

Union for Reform Judaism. (n.d.). What we believe. Union for Reform Judaism. Retrieved March 3, 2022, from https://urj.org/what-we-believe

Veidlinger, D. (2015). Introduction. In G. P. Grieve, & D. Veidlinger (Eds.), *Buddhism, the internet, and digital media: The pixel in the lotus* (pp. 1–22). Routledge.

Webb, M. S. (2012). Church marketing: Building and sustaining membership. *Services Marketing Quarterly, 33*(1), 68–84. https://doi.org/10.1080/15332969.2012.633440

Selected Readings

Campbell, H. (2011). Internet and religion. In M. Consalvo, & C. Ess (Eds.), *The handbook of internet studies* (pp. 232–250). Wiley.

Campbell, H. A. (2012). Understanding the relationship between religion online and offline in a networked society. *Journal of the American Academy of Religion, 80*(1), 64–93. https://doi.org/10.1093/jaarel/lfr074

Grant, A. E., Sturgill, A. F., Chen, C. H., & Stout, D. A. (Eds.). (2019). *Religion online: How digital technology is changing the way we worship and pray [2 volumes]*. ABC–CLIO.

Helland, C. (2016). Digital religion. In D. Yamane (Ed.), *Handbook of religion and society*. Springer. https://doi.org/10.1007/978-3-319-31395-5_10

Stout, D. A. (2013). Internet. In *Media and religion: Foundations of an emerging field* (pp. 73–84). Taylor and Francis.

Part IV

Individual Religious Communication

15

Pastoral Ministry and Communication

Daniella Zsupan-Jerome

Given the practical nature of pastoral ministry, this field of theological action is a natural conversation partner for the study of media and communication. Pastoral ministry "does" theology, and interpersonal engagement, whether mediated or face to face, is an essential part of this work. When it comes to training and formation for pastoral work, communication skills, interpersonal skills (what some traditions call "human formation"), media literacy, and media awareness from both a technical and cultural perspective are essential components for understanding communication for pastoral ministry.

This chapter gives an overview of the conversation between pastoral ministry and communication. Key themes that drive this chapter include understanding the scope of pastoral ministry; identifying the role of theology in pastoral communication; understanding the essential role of communication within pastoral ministry; exploring various kinds of pastoral ministries of communication and various kinds of approaches to media through pastoral communication; and examining the shift in pastoral ministry from an instrumental view of media as broadcasting tools to a cultural view of media, especially digital media, as a milieu in which to encounter and engage people.

What is Pastoral Ministry?

Pastoral ministry is individual and collective action stemming from the credal foundations of a faith community in response to a spiritual need. The faith community expressing itself through acts of service and care is "pastoral," especially when these acts are carried out in a professional or official capacity by its leaders or by those delegated to serve in particular roles. In other words, pastoral ministry goes beyond the performance of good works generally required of people of faith. It is intentional work on behalf of the faith community. It expresses the beliefs and values of the faith community in action as carried out by a formal representative of that community in service to a particular spiritual need. In general, pastoral ministry finds expression in activities such as preaching and teaching the faith, leading worship practices, moral and spiritual counseling, work for justice and peace, care for people in particular challenging situations (illness, poverty, grief, separation from a spouse), care for particular age groups (youth, young adult, senior), or care for particular life circumstances (parenting, married couples; Eilers, 2009, p. 13).

The Handbook on Religion and Communication, First Edition. Edited by Yoel Cohen and Paul A. Soukup.

The imperative to serve in response to a spiritual need exists in different religious traditions, whether teaching, counseling, leading worship, or providing care for people in particular life stages or circumstances. The term "pastoral" comes from the Latin *pastor*, meaning shepherd, which provides a generative metaphor for understanding this theological activity. While Latin roots imply a Christian framework, not only Christianity but also Judaism and Islam consider the image of the shepherd significant for understanding pastoral ministry, especially as a shepherd caring for a flock, protecting it from predators, and ensuring that it finds good pasture (Long & Ansari, 2018, p. 110; Sheer, 2008; Winstanley, 1986). The shepherd metaphor has biblical foundations in both the Hebrew and Christian scriptures (Ezekiel 34, John 10) as well as Islamic hadiths (Al Adab Al-Mufrad 212, 214).

Other religious traditions may not use the shepherd image but also esteem this kind of service. Buddhism calls for a posture of right livelihood that reveres all life and works for the benefit of others along these lines. Awareness of suffering is integral to the process of spiritual enlightenment. Engaged Buddhism is even more intentional along these lines about service to others in response to suffering as inherent to religious practice (Monett, 2005). In Hinduism, there is a deep sense of interconnectedness and a consequent obligation to the world around us, the common good. Hindus are called to act for the good of others, which is not only socially responsible but also spiritually purifying (Shipman, 2020).

Ministry is a term that in the theological context implies service. As noted, it is an activity done on behalf of the faith community and stemming from the faith community's credal identity: a minister is a person serving a need while also representing who the community is and what the community believes. People of faith are generally called to perform good works, such as works of mercy and charity in Christianity, *mitzvot* in Judaism, *sadaqat* in Islam, the Ten Good Deeds in Buddhism, or good actions to clear karmic debts in Hinduism. Ministry is distinct from these in that it is carried out in an official or formal capacity by a person in a leadership role. The leadership role may result from ordination, consecration, delegation, appointment, or call; it may be a formal or volunteer role. The distinction here is that the minister, whether the head of the faith community or a volunteer parent teaching religious education, is a person acting on behalf of the community to perform a service in a public, professional role, as opposed to privately expressing one's personal faith. Ministry therefore also implies some formation, training, and recognition of a person by the community to carry out a particular service.

Pastoral ministry is a general umbrella term that implies service carried out in a variety of ways, whether in the context of religious education, worship, social justice, community building, and, to some extent, counseling and healthcare. In all of these the aim of the minister is to provide spiritual care and to communicate in words and actions the core, life-giving beliefs and values of the faith tradition as they pertain to a particular life circumstance. Such spiritual care, of course, cannot be separated from physical, emotional, or intellectual care as these are naturally intertwined, and the minister's work will in reality respond to the needs of the whole person. At the same time, stressing the spiritual impetus of ministry work helps to distinguish the minister from a counselor, social worker, teacher, life coach, community leader, or other secular role.

The Role of Theology in Communication

Undergirding pastoral or service work is the core theological self-understanding of the faith community. As an activity, pastoral ministry emerges from the credal identity of a faith community. It is a concrete and practical expression of the beliefs of the community offered in service of a spiritual need. As such, pastoral ministry is fundamentally rooted in the theology held by the faith community; it is a practical expression of that theology through pastoral action. Along these lines, when thinking about communication or any other activity in the context of pastoral ministry, naming the theological foundations helps focus the activity as an authentic expression of service in a particular community. When it comes to pastoral ministry and communication, the most relevant theological foundation is that of divine revelation, or the study of how we understand God's communication to humankind. Depending on the religious tradition, the study of divine revelation considers the content of divine revelation as well as the "method" or manner by which God communicates (see Chapter 3).

In Christian pastoral ministry, successful communication represents more than just a well-honed human skillset. Christian theology understands communication as a concept founded in divine revelation, in God's self-communication to humankind. In Christianity, God communicates: in and through the created world, in and through the salvation history of the relationship between God and people over time, and in the most significant way through the incarnation of God's Word in the person of Jesus Christ. God's Holy Spirit continues to animate the communication of the story of Jesus as the fundamental mission of the Christian Church. Communication therefore is essentially a theological act that reveals how God relates to the world. Communication between persons, especially when carried out in the context of pastoral ministry, therefore is an opportunity to reflect what Christians believe about God's self-communication to humankind. This theological impetus embraces both the content and method of communication. Because of the Christian belief in the incarnation of the divine Word in the *person* of Jesus Christ, revelation cannot be distilled to a set of teachings but must also include the living witness and example of the life of Jesus Christ. As such, Christian theology reflects on the content *and* manner of God's communication, while Christian pastoral ministry strives to communicate the tradition in both the content and method of engaging with people.

The concept of divine revelation or the idea that God communicates to humankind is also relevant in Judaism, Islam, and Hinduism. Judaism reveres God's self-communicating act to Moses and to the people in the context of the Exodus:

> The essence of revelation according to the Old Testament or the Hebrew Bible as it is called in the Jewish tradition consists precisely of this self-communication of God to His people as He makes himself known to them (Ex. 64:2) and speaks to them (Ex. 25:22). The word of God is spoken in a special way to Moses (Ex. 20:18). God's word to Israel is His most precious gift; in it He communicates himself: "I am the Lord" (Gn. 28:13; Ex. 6:2, 6:29) and "there is no other" (Is. 45:5). (Beki, 2005, p. 192)

In the understanding and sharing of this revelation, it is the books and the commandments, the content, that takes central role. As Beki (2005) describes (quoting Maimonides), the manner of God's revelation remains a mystery: "'We believe,' says Maimonides, 'that the Torah reached Moses from God in a manner that is described in Scripture figuratively by the term "word" and that nobody has ever known how it took place except Moses himself to whom the word reached'" (p. 192). Thus, as compared to the Christian theology of revelation described earlier, the Jewish understanding of God's self-communication centers more on content than on the manner by which God's self-communication took place. Pastoral ministry in the Jewish context therefore may still value excellent interpersonal communication skills such as listening and ability to dialogue, but unlike Christian ministry it does not necessarily root these in a theology of *how* God has communicated.

Divine revelation in Islam is similar to the biblical approaches listed earlier in that Allah communicates to humankind through a series of events and encounters. Revelation in Islam is characteristically mediated, meaning that God's Word has angelic messengers who share it, and human messengers, prophets, who hand it on. Along these same lines, the prophets, as inspired communicators, have a most significant role in Islam; principal among them is of course Mohammed. The inspired manner by which prophets receive divine revelation is called *wahy*:

> The primary verse that explains the types and categories of *wahy* is Allah's statement: "It is not possible for any human being that Allah should speak to him, unless it be by inspiration, or from behind a veil, or (that) He sends a Messenger to reveal what He will by His Permission. Verily, He is the Most High, Most Wise" (42:51). Moreover, "It is for Us to collect it and recite it. When we have recited it, then follow its recitation" (75:17–18). Also, "And if any of the idolaters seeks your protection, then grant him protection, so that he may hear the word of Allah" (9:6). (Beki, 2005, pp. 195–196)

Islam refers to Allah's communicating but at the same time asserts that this is a veiled, mysterious process through which the prophet is inspired. Like Judaism, Islam insists on a level of reverential mystery around God and on a formality about how humans engage in a divine encounter. Along these lines, pastoral ministry in Islam also would not root human interpersonal communication skills in a theological foundation.

Like sacred texts in Christianity, Judaism, and Islam, the Hindu Vedas also are revered as content passed on to humankind through divine revelation. The Hindu concept of *Shruti*, Sanskrit for "what is heard," is a distinct classification for those sacred texts that have been divinely revealed to sages, as opposed to *Smriti*, which is human interpretation of these divinely revealed texts. *Shruti* is considered more authoritative than *Smriti*, though both are integral to the overall tradition. The experience of revelation in Hinduism is inner and contemplative; one needs to be properly disposed through contemplative spiritual practice to receive it. In this sense, divine revelation lovingly seeks a human communication partner, and is personal and compassionate. This understanding of revelation colors pastoral practice in terms of compassionate listening, and ministry of presence and acceptance (Swami Sarvaananda, 2009).

Buddhism is distinct in that its sacred teachings originate from a human founder, Siddhartha Gautama, called the Buddha or the Enlightened One. Instead of receiving communication from the divine, Buddhism understands revelation as inner enlightenment through spiritual discipline. While divine revelation does not frame the concept of communication in Buddhist thought, the practice of communication, including truth telling and right speech, is strongly emphasized (Konsky et al., 2000, p. 242).

On the most practical level, all these traditions would certainly value good communication skills in pastoral work as a professional skillset when working with people.

Pastoral Ministry and Communication

Communication is an interpersonal event that is fundamental to pastoral ministry. Pastoral ministry is the faith tradition, represented by the minister, engaging with people in need to provide spiritual care. Communication is the relational act between persons built on the sharing of information, and it assumes that the communication partners, in this case, pastoral ministers, have the ability to turn with openness to the other and enter into a mutual exchange. Therefore, how a minister engages with people and turns to others with attentiveness matters. This is manifest in listening skills, dialogical skills, clarity, and coherence, all built on the basic premise of entering into communication not with a bullhorn but with a handshake. In other words, an apt pastoral minister is aware that communication is first and foremost a relational act, a way to engage with people, that gives context to the exchange of particular information. Good or bad communication skills can make or break the efficacy of pastoral work, and can even render the pastoral work authentic or inauthentic in the perception of the broader community. Any substantive ministry formation program is thus attentive to honing good interpersonal communications skills as part of its curriculum.

Eilers (2009) identifies five general areas of communication relevant to pastoral ministry: interpersonal communication, group communication, traditional communication, mass media, and multimedia (pp. 167–198). Interpersonal communication is the person-to-person activity that forms the basic communicative activity of pastoral work. It includes skills like the ones noted earlier and more, all with the fundamental goal of engaging well with people. Good interpersonal communication in pastoral ministry is an acquired skill, depending on the development of a number of internal dispositions, including the emotional, intellectual, archetypal (psychological), existential, and spiritual, in order to be able to relate pastorally with another person (pp. 168–169). These internal dispositions all have an impact upon how a person relates to other people, and awareness of these allows a person to grow professionally in their interpersonal skills, including communication. Developing these dispositions is generally part of formation or training for ministry work.

Closely related to one-on-one interpersonal communication is group communication. Eilers (2009) defines group communication as "the communication of a small group of people where everybody can see, act and react immediately to anybody around" (p. 172). Group communication may be face to face or mediated by teleconferencing or video technology. When it comes to pastoral ministry, group communication presents a situation in which managing group dynamics becomes integral to the overall task of the pastoral minister, whether it is about inviting and honoring the participation of all members, staying on task during the time allotted, or navigating conflict or discord.

Traditional communication according to Eilers closely relates to cultural expressions of popular piety, such as storytelling, songs, dance, drama, art, and visual expression as well as communal celebrations, processions, and pilgrimages. These examples encompass rich and meaningful ways in which a particular culture tells its communal story. These also often resonate with people on a deeply personal and emotional level. As the goal of pastoral ministry is to serve people in their actual lives, fluency in these traditional ways of communication is essential for authentically encountering people where they are and engaging them meaningfully when it comes to their spiritual needs. For example, a particular hymn, song, image, or devotion may speak more profoundly in a situation of pastoral care like grief than a series of informative statements about the faith.

Mass media extend human communications beyond the physical limitations of time, space, and distance, and deliver information to larger and farther audiences than what is possible face to face. For Eilers these media include the press and news media, print publications, radio, television, film, and video, as he places the Internet and digital media into a separate category. The mass media offer pastoral ministry the opportunity to extend certain kinds of spiritual care into contexts isolated by distance or physical limitation, such as prisons, nursing homes, mission territories spread out over a large geographic area, or other contexts where a face-to-face encounter is not possible. The mass media can also help "bring home" the spiritual presence and care of the faith community by enabling believers to access faith-based content outside of the locus of the faith community: one can view, listen or read at home, or while driving, traveling, working, etc. While the mass media truly extend the reach of a ministry, at the same time, it is important for pastoral ministry to recognize the challenges of the mediated presence these mass communication channels bring. For example, since the advent of televised religious services, faith communities have debated whether and how viewing a service is distinct from attending one face to face (Zukowski, 1993, pp. 13–15). Media literacy helps equip pastoral ministers with the ability to continue to reflect on these questions as well as to guide communities of faith to do the same.

With the emergence of mass-mediated faith content, it thus becomes increasingly important for media literacy to become part of pastoral formation and religious education as a whole.

This need for media literacy and media awareness also figures into Eilers's fifth area of media for pastoral ministry: multimedia, including the Internet, websites, and email. Today we might label this area digital media instead and include social media and mobile media as significant components therein. As with mass media, digital media extend the presence and availability of faith content and particular kinds of pastoral ministry beyond face-to-face opportunities. Unlike mass media, however, the digital media are fluid and porous when it comes to identifying the sender and the receiver of a particular message. Digital media invite the presence and active participation of people while they access content, becoming content producers themselves to varying degrees. For pastoral ministry this shift toward ubiquitous participation is important, because it implies that anyone, not just the designated pastoral minister, can communicate the faith, and do so in a broad range of ways. The authority of designated pastoral ministers as sole or official faith communicators is shifting to find itself alongside new kinds of religious authorities in digital culture (Soukup, 2017, p. 39). In this context, a comprehensive religious education that includes media literacy becomes all the more important.

Pastoral Ministries of Communication

Effective interpersonal communication is fundamental for pastoral ministry as it is for any related social service field in which people interact with people in contexts of care. At the same time, pastoral ministry relates to communication in a number of other, distinct ways. Among the various religious traditions and across denominations therein, pastoral ministry finds expression in a number of ways, particularly in a communication or media-related context. One example, especially in the Protestant and evangelical Christian context, is "media ministry" or "multimedia ministry," which indicates a specialized area of ministry that deals with the use of technology in support of both the worship experience and overall mission of a faith community. Media ministers or media pastors are persons especially qualified and skilled in media production, audiovisual technology, sound, lights as well as digital media. Comparable roles exist in Reform Judaism in the congregational staff who manage the website or other relevant media need (Frost & Youngblood, 2014, p. 51). Since the advent of the Covid-19 pandemic, the need to rely on technology to extend a faith community's presence and ministry has become ubiquitous, placing new emphasis on the importance of these media ministry roles.

Another way communication forms a distinct area of ministry is through the role of communication directors, communication managers, or communication officers for a particular community of faith. These can exist on a congregational level and would be comparable to a media minister, but broader in scope in terms of carrying responsibility for a communications strategy and its implementation for that particular community. Communication directors, managers, and officers can also exist in administrative roles in the broader institutional leadership structure and serve to manage the formal and public communication and public relations of the faith community as an institution. In the Christian context, these roles would oversee and implement communication strategy on the regional, diocesan, or national level. Communication directors, managers, and officers often bring a journalism, public relations, or marketing background to service in the faith-based context.

A third category of communication and ministry is expressed through the work of media professionals who work for a specifically faith-based media organization, whether in journalism, publishing, broadcasting, or digital presence. The degree to which their service may be labeled a pastoral ministry depends on the organization's identity, mission, and affiliation with a faith community. For example, Roman Catholic dioceses will often have a newspaper, magazine, or television or radio broadcast, and thus the media professionals who create these would directly serve under the mission of the diocese. Other media organizations claim a faith identity but function independently from ecclesial structures, though they may invite an official representative of the faith community to serve as a board member or consultant. Such independent faith-based media outlets will also offer a statement of faith to indicate credal identity, thus holding their employees to a ministerial standard, however informal.

Faith-based media professionals also can vary in terms of the formality of their platform. While some serve in traditional publications or media outlets, others have created new platforms altogether. In the digital context, those with a spiritual message can easily create a public platform and gain an audience. For example, in the Hindu context, online *satsangs*, or meditation and conversation gatherings, can come together in response to the website or social media invitation of a spiritual teacher. In a similar vein, a blog or a YouTube channel established by an adherent to any faith can gain a large following and exert influence outside of traditional authority structures.

Under the umbrella of faith-based media professionals is the distinct category of media-based faith leaders. In other words, these are people who extend their ministry or services specifically through the media, and today, this means primarily through digital media. One can seek out and request online the services of a minister across the religious traditions: connecting with an imam for counseling, studying with a rabbi to understand the tradition, seeking pastoral support from a Buddhist chaplain, or prayers or rituals services from a Hindu Pandit to perform a *pūjā* on behalf of a believer, or pastoral care from a Christian "internet" pastor, such as the Rev. Frycklund of the Lutheran Church of Sweden, who has the web as her designated parish (Gray, 2021).

Whether serving as a media minister, a communication director, manager, or officer, or a media professional, the service to the community rendered through these roles could be properly considered pastoral if consistent with the overall goal of offering spiritual care outside the overall mission and identity of the faith tradition. While setting up lighting or an audiovisual system, offering a press release, updating the website or social media, or working on a radio show may seem entirely secular activities, if the activity is offered in service of the spiritual care and flourishing of believers, placing these activities into the category of pastoral work is appropriate.

Pastoral Communication

In addition to relating pastoral theology and ministry *to* communication, scholars like Eilers identify a unique communication category within the life of a faith community or church, called "pastoral communication." Pastoral communication, according to Eilers (2009) is "communicating for pastoral care, 'shepherding,' building up, maintaining, and deepening of faith. It is more specifically and in a strict sense, the *communicatio intra Ecclesiam*, the inner ecclesiastical communication for the members of the Church or those in preparation to become members" (p. 14). He distinguishes pastoral communication from evangelizing communication; pastoral communication concerns the internally directed communicative activity of the Church, whereas evangelizing communication is directed outward, sharing the story, beliefs, and values of the community beyond the community's boundaries. This internal emphasis to pastoral communication is relevant insofar as it shapes the language, depth of content, and communication partners or voices involved. Pastoral communication as internal communication includes preaching, teaching, worship, fellowship, care, and counseling, and is performed by leaders of the faith community across the board: from bishop to priest to lay professionals in ministry.

As noted earlier, pastoral theology and ministry concerns the actual lives of people as it seeks to provide a spiritual service in various circumstances of need. As Eilers (2009) notes, "all activities of pastoral theology, which, as practical theology, are applied to the lives of people, have a communication dimension" (p. 94). Pastoral communication recognizes and focuses in on this fundamental communication dimension as integral to any pastoral activity. Recalling the shepherd metaphor above, "if pastoral theology in general is the theology of how the 'good shepherd' treats his flock, pastoral communication considers the communication dimension of this activity and concern" (p. 94). In practical terms, pastoral communication is about how people communicate and relate with fellow members of the faith community as part of pastoral ministry. Along these lines, pastoral communication is concerned with both the content and method of the communication of the faith in response to a spiritual need. The sharing of the faith as communication is a total act that includes the relational act between persons as well as the message – what is shared.

Media, Ministry, and Digital Culture

How pastoral ministry approaches the reality of the various communications media is another relevant question for pastoral ministry as related to communication. With the advent of digital media, the question of media in ministry is shifting yet again. In the digital context, the media themselves are changing in that it is increasingly difficult to separate each of them from digital media. Print media exist in traditional print, and electronic forms like e-books and e-zines; radio and television broadcasts stream online; more and more films are released through streaming services instead of theaters; the press likewise is ubiquitously present online, including on social media, while social media itself has become a news source. In addition to all of these, digital media offer information in their own distinct ways, whether through social media, podcasting, blogging, or vlogging, which rest on traditional media forms re-presented in novel ways. Keeping the Internet or the digital as a distinct media category apart from other media forms no longer holds. In light of this, future approaches to media in ministry may become increasingly integrated and porous as well.

The advent of digital media has led pastoral ministry to shift its overall appreciation of the media from an instrumental to a cultural approach. The increasing ubiquity of broadcast and electronic media throughout the twentieth century challenged pastoral ministry to initially embrace an instrumental approach, asking how various media could *be of use* to particular ministry efforts. Through this instrumental approach, pastoral ministry sought the ways the media can serve the effort of sharing the message, beliefs, and values of a particular faith community, whether internally or externally. In this instrumental approach, the media are regarded as tools for communicating something better, faster, broader, more clearly, and more efficiently. Radio or television broadcasting a service reaches people who cannot physically be present; disseminating a printed version of a story or teaching not only reaches a broad audience but also sustains the memory of the tradition by keeping a record. Media in this regard served as tools to extend our human capabilities for communication over time, distance, space. In this context, pastoral ministers generally approached communications media with a question or problem to solve: how to reach more people, how to reach a particular population, how to provide access to particular information. Through this instrumental approach, the media remain passive and lack opportunities for direct engagement and dialogical interaction with other readers and audience members (Lytle, 2013, p. 71).

This instrumental approach can persist when considering today's digital media as well. Whenever we consider the digital media as tools and gadgets that help attain a goal in ministry, this mindset remains consistent with the approach described earlier. However, appraising the digital media only instrumentally is increasingly inadequate, as these communication technologies have ushered in a shift that is not only technical but properly cultural. Digital communication has shaped the way we think, relate to one another, and make assumptions about access to information and to resources as we navigate life. It has also engendered a kind of participatory culture (Jenkins et al., 2009) in which having a voice and the ability to express oneself publicly has become an accepted element of life in today's society. For pastoral ministry, this transition from digital tools to digital culture has meant broadening the scope of the conversation from examining a set of tools to reflecting on the way people think and relate. This cultural approach recalls again the need for developing the internal dispositions fundamental for relating well to others, as listed under the interpersonal communication category presented by Eilers. In digital culture, pastoral ministry is discerning again how to relate well to people in a society that has come to hold particular assumptions about communication, information, and social connections. Further than that, pastoral ministry as a ministry of spiritual care has the particular goal to discern the spiritual dimensions of life that arise in digital culture, whether opportunities or challenges, and to respond to these creatively in this cultural context.

While digital culture has certainly had an impact on the practice of ministry, nothing brought this question to the forefront like the 2020 Covid-19 pandemic, which, during lockdowns around the world, necessitated the question of pastoral ministry through digital communication. For some communities of faith, this was the first time, while others enhanced already existing resources. Online or live streamed worship services and religious formation events are now more familiar across religious tradition, whether online *satsangs* or mediated *pūjā* in Hinduism, online *dharma* talks in the Buddhist context, virtual *Shabbat* services, Masses, Divine Liturgies, and Sunday services. When it comes to pastoral ministry and communication, the pandemic highlighted the relevance of the question, and encouraged ministers across religious traditions to think more intentionally about communication methods and technologies. Moving forward, significant questions post-Covid will be to what extent pastoral outreach can remain technologically mediated, and to what degree pastoral practices will return face to face.

References

Beki, N. (2005). The concept of revelation according to the Bible and the Qur'ān. *Journal of Academic Studies [Akademik Araştırmalar Dergisi]*, 7(26), 191–210.

Eilers, F.-J. (2009). *Communicating in ministry and mission* (3rd ed.). Logos/Divine Word Publications.

Frost, J. K., & Youngblood, N. E. (2014). Online religion and religion online: Reform Judaism and web-based communication. *Journal of Media and Religion*, 13(13), 49–66. https://doi.org/10.1080/15348423.2014.909190.

Gray, A. (2021). Sweden: Internet pastor engages faith seekers online. The Lutheran World Federation. Retrieved March 17, 2022, from https://www.lutheranworld.org/news/sweden-internet-pastor-engages-faith-seekers-online

Jenkins, H., Clinton, K., Purushotma, R., Robinson, A. J., & Weigel, M. (2009). Confronting the challenges of participatory culture: Media education for the 21st century. MacArthur Foundation. Retrieved March 17, 2022, from https://www.macfound.org/media/article_pdfs/JENKINS_WHITE_PAPER.PDF

Konsky, C., Kapoor, U., Blue, J., & Kapoor, S. (2000). Religion and communication: A study of Hinduism, Buddhism, and Christianity. *Intercultural Communication Studies, 10*(2), 235–251. https://web.uri.edu/iaics/files/15-Catherine-Konsky-Usha-Kapoor-Janet-Blue-Suraj-Kapoor.pdf

Long, I. J., & Ansari, B. (2018). Islamic pastoral care and the development of Muslim chaplaincy. *Journal of Muslim Mental Health, 12*(1), 109–121. http://dx.doi.org/10.3998/jmmh.10381607.0012.105.

Lytle, J. A. (2013). *Faith formation 4.0. Introducing an ecology of faith in a digital age.* Morehouse.

Monett, M. (2005). Developing a Buddhist approach to pastoral care. *Journal of Pastoral Care and Counseling, 59*(1–2), 57–61. https://doi.org/10.1177/154230500505900106.

Sheer, C. (2008). Bikkur Holim: The origins of Jewish pastoral care. *Journal of Health Care Chaplaincy, 15*(2), 99–113. doi: 10.1080/08854720903152497.

Shipman, A. (2020). Hinduism and chaplaincy. Relating core concepts to spiritual care. *Convergence Magazine, 3*(2), 4–13. https://convergenceoncampus.org/wp-content/uploads/2020/05/ConvergenceMagazine-May2020Final.pdf

Soukup, P. A. (2017). Authority, new media and the church. In M. Diez Bosch, P. Soukup, J. L. Micó, & D. Zsupan-Jerome (Eds.), *Authority and leadership: Values, religion, media* (pp. 31–40). Blanquerna Observatory.

Swami Sarvaananda. (2009). The Hindu chaplain. *Hinduism Today.* Retrieved March 17, 2022, from https://www.hinduismtoday.com/magazine/july-august-september-2009/2009-07-the-hindu-chaplain

Winstanley, M. T. (1986). The shepherd image in the scriptures a paradigm for Christian ministry. *The Clergy Review, 71*(June), 197–206.

Zukowski, A. A. (1993, April 17). Should the Mass be televised? *America, 168*, 13–15.

Selected Readings

Bingaman, K. A. (2018). *Pastoral and spiritual care in a digital age: The future is now.* Lexington Books

Campbell, H., & Tsuria, R. (2021). *Digital religion: Understanding religious practice in digital media* (2nd ed.). Routledge.

Kurlberg, J., & Philips, P. M. (2020). *Missio dei in a digital age.* SCM Press.

Roberto, J. (ed.). (2022). *Digital ministry and leadership in today's church.* Liturgical.

16

Piety, Religious Identity, and the Media

Damian Guzek and Piotr S. Bobkowski

Introduction

While the role of religion in the lives of individuals across the globe is diminishing (Ingelhart, 2021), the presence of religion in the media appears to be increasing (Knott et al., 2013), and religious traditions may be transforming under the influence of the media (Günter, 2016; Hjarvard, 2016). These three shifts contribute to "progressive secularization," that is, a distancing away from a society imbued with religion to a society where religion is an option alongside antireligion and no religion (Casanova, 1994; Künkler et al., 2018; Taylor, 2007). Drawing on Bellah's (2007) reading of Taylor's (2007) work, this movement also includes the distancing of public institutions from religious norms and the influence of religion, the decline of individual religious practices, and the withdrawal of religion and faith from the social imagination.

Secularization, which boils down to the displacement of religion in society and individual life, is driven to some extent by the media. Intuitively, the growth of the media, including in religious life, does not seem to go hand-in-hand with secularization. More religion in the media suggests something of a progressive republicization (Herbert, 2015) or desecularization (Hjelm, 2012). In practice, it is the media, with a clear relationship to piety and religious identity, that drive the movement at each level of secularization.

Based on a review of research published over the past decade on media, piety, and religious identity, this chapter argues that secularization does not manifest uniformly in the media but, rather, that it is a multidimensional condition. We identify two distinct dimensions of secularization in the media: media content that illustrates the weakening of religious identities, and content that illustrates individuals' agency to determine their religious identities. This latter dimension comprises two further subdimensions, as individuals use the media to embrace and communicate both orthodox and unorthodox religious identities. Before discussing each of these themes, we begin by defining piety and religious identity, and describe how different approaches to the study of religion and spirituality have opened up understanding of their role in communication and media.

The Handbook on Religion and Communication, First Edition. Edited by Yoel Cohen and Paul A. Soukup.

Decoding Piety

Media and religion offer two approaches to understanding what piety is and what it means to consider somebody a pious person. The first approach rests on the media coverage of pious people and pious rituals. The second approach considers the performance of pious practices mediated through digital entities. To understand the differences between these two approaches, we start with a reflection on the meaning and place of piety within an increasingly individualized and highly diverse world of contemporary religion.

At the individual level, piety begins and takes place within a person, and communicates something about the person (Gökarıksel & Secor, 2013). Piety refers to the attributes that testify to a person's engagement in the meaning-making process that makes one pious. These attributes can include an individual's attire (Gustavsson et al., 2016), rhetoric (Jennings, 2016), or physical presence at the source of the holy (Knott, 2005; Suykerbuyk, 2020). Piety goes back and forward as a result of individual agency, personal values, and preferences (Morgan, 1998).

On a communal level, people can express piety with the same attributes as at the individual level; it concerns groups of people participating in ritual or mass action. Individual agency loses meaning in this context and, instead, a person's actions are a kind of representation of or even substitution for group actions (Etengoff & Rodriguez, 2020).

Therefore, from a social perspective, individual and communal piety encompasses two of the three levels of the scale of social activity: the micro and the meso dimensions. At the macro dimension, however, the phenomenon of piety becomes problematic. Some religious rituals are celebrated throughout the world, such as Muslim pilgrims converging on Mecca during the Hajj, or Christians celebrating Easter on the same day. In these instances, however, individuals perform many actions all at once rather than participating in one global ritual that expresses piety.

Since we touch on the phenomenon of piety at the micro and meso levels of the social structure, we can assume that piety can manifest itself in various ways, such as in the dominance of the individual form, the supremacy of the group, but also through multiple forms of their entanglement. Thus, our premise is that whenever there is an analysis of the relationship between piety and the media, it takes place at the intersection of what co-creates individual and collective identity.

Religious Identity as a Field of Study

Religious identity can be the key to understanding differences between distinct beliefs and spiritual traditions (Werbner, 2010). The questions driving such a positioned term include the meaning of religious identity, its origin and dynamics of change, research achievements on this phenomenon, and current findings.

Much of the literature understands religious identity simply as a point-in-time self-identification with a particular religious tradition (Bell, 2010). Using a developmental perspective, it may be more appropriate to understand religious identity as a process in which "individuals develop their own personal sense of religious and/or spiritual identity over the course of their lifetime" (Etengoff & Rodriguez, 2020, p. 1).

Our understanding of religious identity encompasses both religiosity and spirituality, which are often presented as a dichotomy in the scientific study of religion. This perspective tends to associate religion with rituals and traditions while relating spirituality to an individual's personal faith and ethical beliefs. But this dichotomy can connect religious identity and piety. At the individual and group levels, piety is directly associated with religiosity. In addition, at the individual level, piety also may be related to the expression of human spirituality.

Researchers have proposed a number of theories to account for the origins of religious identity, including ones rooted in biology, environment, and society. Some have speculated that individuals' propensity to be religious is embedded in their genes. However, mapping the human genome has not brought positive results in this area (Cole-Turner, 1992). Instead, a link between religiosity and the use of neurotransmitters responsible for the serotonin-binding potential has been noticed (Borg et al., 2003). The environmental approach understands the origins of religious identity in social learning of religious patterns from parents (Petro et al., 2018). One thesis proposes that initially all people are atheists and, depending on the character of their parental socialization, develop a religious identity or religious fanaticism (Humphrey, 1998). The social approach understands religious identity as emerging from an interaction between an individual's external cultural context and internal motivations (Bronfenbrenner, 1979), resulting in a practice-based cultural activity (Belzen, 1999; Etengoff & Rodriguez, 2020).

Combining these three approaches provides a meaningful view of the characteristics of religious identity. Religious identity turns out to be a contextual creation, formed both by changing environmental factors and the limitations of our bodies.

Three Faces of Secularization

Having found that, by definition, piety and religious identity function at the intersection of what is private and belonging to the interior of human being, and what is shown and collective, we turn to describing three dimensions of secularization in the media based on research findings published over the past decade. The first dimension concerns the media's role in advancing secularization and transformations in religion that are shaped by the media. The second and third dimension concern the individual's role in determining their religious identity. This includes, first, the extent to which one's religious identity is shaped by religious orthodoxy, and second, the extent to which it is shaped by religious unorthodoxy, including irreligion. In all, these three dimensions place the digital sphere as the cornerstone of piety. Piety as an expression of religious and spiritual identity and, as the practice of action, reveals one's entanglement in the world of the media.

Media Forcing Secularization

Secularization theory constitutes a prominent lens through which researchers today understand the cultural place of religion and, by extension, piety and religious identity. Broadly speaking, secularization theory holds that the role of religion in orienting and guiding people's lives is declining, as evidenced by longitudinal studies such as the World Values Survey and the European Values Study (Ingelhart, 2021b). Across the globe and especially in developed countries, over time these surveys have registered drops in how much individuals report believing in a higher power, attending religious services, engaging in personal religious practices like prayer, and adhering to religious teachings.

Table 16.1 illustrates this trend using responses to a World Values Survey question asking respondents whether they identify as a "religious person" (Haerpfer et al., 2021). These data come from six waves of the survey, conducted every few years between the early 1990s and late

2010s. In about one-third of the 28 countries included in the table, the data suggest downward trends in the proportions of these countries' populations that identify as religious. These include Australia, with a decline from 59% in the mid-1990s to 37% in the late 2010s; Chile with a decline from 77 to 50%; Colombia with a decline from 85 to 74%; Japan with a decline from 26 to 16%;

Table 16.1 Estimated proportion of each country's population answering affirmatively to the question, "Independently of whether you go to church or not, would you say you are a religious person?" across six waves of the World Values Survey (adapted from Haerpfer et al., 2021)

	Wave 2 1990–4	Wave 3 1995–8	Wave 4 1999–2004	Wave 5 2005–9	Wave 6 2010–14	Wave 7 2017–20
Argentina	73	81	84	81	72	74
Australia	–	59	–	52	42	37
Belarus	41	70	–	–	63	36
Brazil	88	85	–	88	81	75
Chile	77	74	71	65	52	50
China	5	–	15	24	13	16
Colombia	–	85	–	80	83	74
Georgia	–	89	–	97	97	96
Germany	–	47	–	43	51	52
India	84	80	80	78	92	–
Iraq	–	–	87	55	84	77
Japan	26	24	27	24	25	16
Jordan	–	–	86	92	81	80
Mexico	75	65	77	75	75	70
Peru	–	82	88	82	84	82
Philippines	–	84	80	–	81	85
Poland	–	94	–	95	88	86
Romania	–	84	–	93	83	82
Russia	56	64	–	74	61	80
Slovenia	–	69	–	73	69	69
South Africa	83	80	79	81	–	–
South Korea	–	–	31	30	33	16
Spain	70	69	63	46	41	49
Sweden	29	33	39	33	32	27
Switzerland	74	57	–	65	–	48
Turkey	75	79	80	83	85	72
Ukraine	–	64	–	81	68	65
United States	82	81	83	72	68	59

Note: This table omits (i) Wave 1, which surveyed only 10 countries, and (ii) countries in which this question was asked fewer than four times over the seven waves of the survey.

and the United States with a decline from 82 to 59%. Proportions of populations that identify as religious in other countries appear either stable (e.g. Philippines, Slovenia) or increasing (e.g. Russia) over these three decades. Note that the table includes only countries in which this question was asked four or more times across the World Values Survey waves.

Declines in the role of religion in individuals' lives have been attributed to advances in science and education, to urbanization and the weakening of social ties, and to decreases in socioeconomic and health-related insecurities (Ingelhart, 2021). Global data echo more granular analyses from individual countries like the Netherlands (Kregting et al., 2018). Ingelhart (2021) has argued that as threats to survival have decreased and life expectancies have risen, increasing numbers of people see religious moral teachings meant to bolster fertility (e.g. antigender and LGBT equality) as irrelevant and repressive. In the United States, for instance, support for LGBT rights and marijuana legalization distinguish nonreligious young adults from their religious peers (Putnam & Campbell, 2010).

The most marked declines in religiosity in recent years have been found among younger cohorts (Pew Research Center, 2018), and young people's use of digital media has accompanied these declines. Using the Internet may be associated with the weakening of religious identities through exposure to ideological diversity (McClure, 2017). US survey data show that individuals who report "surfing" the Internet more are less likely to have a religious affiliation than those who surf the Internet less. Those who surf the Internet more also are more likely than those who spend less time on the Internet to support religious pluralism, specifically, to believe that different religions are true and that adherents to different religions "worship the same God" (McClure, 2017, p. 489).

In Poland, the profound decline in young people's engagement with religion is directly associated with their use of digital media to organize social actions against the pro-religious government and the patriarchal social system (Guzek, 2021). In 2020, young Poles took to the streets after the Constitutional Court, the country's highest judicial body, curtailed the already restrictive right to abortion. The spontaneous protests, which took place across the country, were organized in a coherent form on social media, and were also recorded and broadcast live on social media platforms. Many of the protests culminated in front of Catholic churches and cathedrals, registering young people's displeasure with the Catholic Church, which plays a prominent role in shaping the politics of the governing Law and Justice party. These protests illustrated the essence of Ingelhart's (2021) argument about what drives secularization, that is, young people turning away from religious traditions over their regressive social stances. The protesters' use of social media to organize, document, and promote their actions illustrates the key role that media play in advancing secularization.

In addition to facilitating the weakening of religious institutions, digital media also propel media–religion phenomena unique to secularization, namely, mediatization, banal religion, and the secular sacred. The mediatization of religion refers to the changing nature of religion as a result of the way the media transform and present religion (Hjarvard, 2016). Mediatization (see Chapter 18) was developed in studies on the relationship between media, technology, and their culture in Scandinavian countries. This work noted the rise of religion in the media, which suggested a desecularizing trend, that is, a retreat from secularization and a re-establishment of religion (Berger, 1999; Hjelm, 2012). Studies on media-driven changes in religion and spirituality showed the opposite, however. The increasing religious content in the media had nothing in common with the control or influence of religious actors, and the representatives of religious traditions had no power to intervene with the media. Live broadcasts from papal pilgrimages, for example, presented during the Catholic "World Youth Day" in Cologne in 2005, where media narratives bore a specific relation to questions of religion, focused on the performance of social rituals instead of highlighting traditional Catholic language and imagery (Hepp & Krönert,

2010). This illustrates the process of mediatizing religion, that is, the shifting of religion owing to its representation in the media. As a result of mediatization, the institutional religious perspective loses its force. In the space vacated by institutional religion, so-called banal religion occupies the sphere of mediated religion. Banal religion refers to mediated representations or experiences of religion where the object of religion is limited or has no relationship to its origin's institutional religion (Hjarvard, 2012). A crucifix worn on a necklace as a fashion accessory and without religious meaning is an example of banal religion. Banal religion traces maintain their religious dimension, but their original symbolism or primary supernatural features are absent (Guzek, 2019; Nybro Petersen, 2013).

The secular sacred, a third phenomenon, refers to the imposition of secular motifs on traditionally religious observances or practices (Knott et al., 2013). In British media, for instance, the observance of traditionally Christian holy days like Christmas or Easter focuses on families celebrating together instead of on explicitly religious themes (Knott et al., 2013). Practices of piety, likewise, have found their secular counterparts in observation, characterized by comparing religious commitment and material content and meaning at the same time. The secular sacred also manifests in public rituals that the media facilitate, organizing reflexive and engaged social responses that address instances of social stress. The mediated mourning rituals following the 2015 mass shootings at the Charlie Hebdo satirical newspaper offices and at a Jewish deli, hybridized analogue and digital wholly secularized expressions (Sumiala et al., 2018). In contrast to the earlier religious practices covered in traditional media broadcasts (Dayan & Katz, 1994; Sumiala, 2013), in the digital world both ordinary users and media outlet editors undertook narratives that consisted of new forms and formats. In the media, performing mourning rituals and expressing one's piety consisted of using a simple hashtag in social media posts, #jesuischarlie, or of using comments, posts, tweets, and blogs to express one's grief (Sumiala, 2017).

In sum, the media serve as a mechanism that advances secularization. At the individual level, ideas espoused in the media can inform one's religious and spiritual selves. Across countries and cultures, the media appear to be activating and supporting perspectives that undermine traditional religious teachings and promote alternatives to religious identity. The media help individuals participate in collective expressions of religious disenfranchisement, as the case of the Polish youth protests illustrates. At the same time, while religion is not disappearing from the media, the media are secularizing the meaning of traditionally religious concepts and practices. The media thus model secular language and ideas that groups can use in reference to religious observances or practices, and that individuals can then apply to or perform in their own lives, expressing their secularized pieties.

Reinforcing Orthodox Religious Identities

While the media serve as tools of secularization, they also provide places where individuals negotiate religious identity and piety expressions. These identities and practices need not veer away from conventional religious traditions, however. Several recent case studies illustrate how television and social media reinforce orthodox religious teachings and structures, leaving seemingly little room for personal expression and religious moderation.

Within the boundaries of a religion's orthodoxy, the media can inform individuals' negotiations about identity and piety. Religious television talk shows in Pakistan, for example, feature debates between religious scholars who represent different sectarian traditions, and who address call-in questions from viewers about proper Muslim practices (Kazi, 2018). Despite the seeming differences between the various religious leaders who appear on these shows, these programs do not veer outside established orthodoxy. The plurality of the religious teachings represented on the shows enables viewers to tailor their practices to match their preferences and media content they consume elsewhere, and even to forgo some beliefs or practices on which the religious scholars do not reach consensus. These apparent choices, however, remain fixed within the confines of male-dominated mainstream Muslim movements.

In other cases, such as Zimbabwe, public media taken over by political forces and their propaganda approach present new types of narratives on religion and piety. By limiting public discourse in this country to issues associated with so-called "inventing traditions," public media outlets promote rules and rituals congruent with an ideology of the ruling Patriotic Front (ZANU-PF) party. Constantly repeated norms and values broadcast through different media types imply the continuity of these narratives with the historical past (Tarusarira, 2020). The steady streams of media coverage present state interventions and editors' decisions on which genre to explore concerning the nation's history. A similar situation, evident through an Iranian talent competition, refers to performing piety as a complex conglomerate of notions. Through Ermia's TV broadcasting of music competitions, its complex media environment demonstrates the tension between traditional Iranian and Western counterparts. These oppositions work toward dichotomies "between reality and fabrication, homeland and diaspora, secularity and piety, and religion and politics" (Hemmasi, 2017, p. 431).

Social media, similarly, can reinforce religious orthodoxy while mimicking the organizing processes of socially progressive collective action. In Indonesia, for instance, Young Muslim Women's Groups, which connect thousands of members through Instagram and other social platforms, communicate dress, conduct, and aspiration norms for young Muslim women (Beta, 2019). Religious influencers in these groups model for young women the ideals of religious piety, financial prosperity, and motherhood. Social media content can organize Young Muslim Women's rallies at which young women promote the wearing of long dresses and veils or oppose the observance of Valentine's Day, for instance. These social media groups, therefore, establish benchmarks of piety with which young Muslim women are expected to align, and organize collective action that bolsters conservative religious practices and structures.

Another case study examined institutionally unauthorized social media accounts that present religious teachings and aspire to aligning themselves with religious orthodoxy to strengthen their authoritativeness and influence. Because social media allow anyone to promulgate religious teaching, even when they have little to no religious training, such online democratization of religious authority can undermine official religious positions. An analysis of several social media platforms used for religious teaching in Indonesia, however, found that contrary to the expectation that religiously unauthorized social media would undermine religious orthodoxy, these platforms supported traditional Islamic teaching (Solahudin & Fakhruroji, 2020). Moreover, in a reciprocal relationship between religious authorities and the owners of the online platforms and social media accounts, both sides sought to collaborate, to establish relationships and harness each other's influence to represent authoritative Islamic teaching in the digital space.

Online forums serve as a location for individuals to explore their religious identities. The starting point for many digital media users is the need to extend their participation in the religious community beyond the physical church building, as the example of Germany and Poland illustrates (Kołodziejska & Neumaier, 2017). Believers join online forums to discuss their approaches to religion and the meanings of the rituals they practice. The dynamics of such forums show their users expressing the processes of individualization that lead them to enter the digital communities of their choice. In some of these communities, individuals can question the value of traditionally understood authority and the rituals associated with it. Communities discuss practices of piety within religious traditions and reflect on what can be approached from the group position as well as from individual members' everyday life contexts (Kołodziejska, 2018).

Two examples from Europe indicate that piety, as belonging to the realm of private life, gains visibility and becomes an argument in the public space (Evolvi, 2019). The first concerns the problem of banning the hijab in public spaces in France. Young Muslim women see their veils as manifestations of their private lives more than as public religious actions. Paradoxically, therefore, Muslim women appear in the public space "by insisting on the private character of their religious practices" (Evolvi, 2019, p. 161). Catholics, meanwhile, publicly express their antigender equality views by transferring their piety and religious convictions from the individual level to activities in the public sphere. Catholics in Europe, for example, organize themselves for public prayers and discussions to combat what they define as gender ideology. Their approach is nonnegotiable and full of commitment. These different approaches that negotiate piety across public and private spheres reflect the performative value of religious activities and religious visibility (Hjelm, 2015; Marín, 2015).

Using social media to deepen one's religious identity or to engage in expressions of piety can be a fraught experience, however. Husein and Slama (2018) examined how Indonesian Muslims negotiate the conflict between online religious practices and Islamic proscriptions against public expressions of piety. They focused on two practices that have become common in recent years: online Qur'an reading groups and social media charity appeals. Hosted on WhatsApp, the Qur'an reading groups connect individuals, primarily women, who dedicate themselves to reading one section of the scripture per day. The groups serve not only as an accountability mechanism but also as a safety net, as members take over the reading responsibilities of members who cannot fulfill their commitment on any particular day. Online charity appeals, meanwhile, consist of individuals' testimonials on Facebook or other social media that describe their charitable donations, that point to the financial prosperity they have experienced in return, and that encourage others' generosity with the expectation of similar returns. Both of these practices can appear to constitute *riy* (public worship for the purpose of gaining recognition for one's piety). Because Islamic theology strongly discourages *riy*, some Muslims who participate in Qur'an reading groups or who post online charity appeals seek the guidance of religious scholars about how to engage in the public religious practices while not engaging in *riy*. This case study illustrated the unique circumstances and negotiations that the public nature of mediated piety can precipitate.

Religious piety sometimes enters into a relationship with politics and the military. The example of religious discourse on militant God-willed service in Russia refines the model. Through media materials and religious sermons, representatives of the Orthodox Church in Russia reread the idea of military service as a state duty, meaning a pious expression of commitment both to the country and to the Church. Such a case is associated with the collaboration and fusion of the activities of both parties, which "led to the emergence of hybrid forms of church-military interactions on structural, institutional, or aesthetic levels" as well as on their liturgy (Knorre & Zygmont, 2020, p. 6).

Some religious authorities provide guidance to members of their religious communities about how to present themselves, religiously and otherwise, on social media. The Church of Jesus Christ of Latter-day Saints (LDS) encourages its members to use social media to dispel misconceptions about LDS and about being Mormon, to proselytize, and to use social media wisely and in limited quantities (Kimmons et al., 2017). According to Kimmons et al. (2017) LDS proscription about using social media with wisdom results in LDS members engaging in less uncivil rhetoric than non-LDS social media users. Consequently, computational and sentiment analyses of a large dataset of Twitter accounts showed that users who explicitly identified as LDS generated tweets that were more civil and more positive in tone than those posted by users who did not so identify. This study illustrates that religious teaching and online identification with a religious tradition can shape how users present themselves on social media.

Sometimes the opposite happens, for example, when mediating piety may clash with the media audiences. A refined example of this occurs in Malaysia. Islamic-themed films find it difficult to become popular among the country's religious audiences owing to the incongruent choice of fashion present within these productions. Most often, the Sunni Muslim middle-class audience is offered movie productions, films, and dramatic series, whose characters wear clothes representing a different mentality for Islam. While the characters are depicted as highly pious, the audience seems to be much more liberal. Ultimately, these films are not very popular (Zainal, 2019).

In sum, the media, including television and social media, reinforce religious orthodoxy. While the formats used, like television talk shows and influencer-driven social media groups for young women, can mimic media practices that are often used to promote progressive ideas, the case studies discussed here use formats to uphold traditional beliefs and practices. Even as religious convictions appear to be retreating in many parts of the globe, often aided by the media, these case studies illustrate that in some cases today's media also are being harnessed to buttress conventional religious institutions and structures.

Religious Unorthodoxy and the Digital World

In addition to reinforcing religious orthodoxy, the media also facilitate and portray the growth of unorthodox religious identities, or religious "peculiarities," which shape modern piety in the context of secularization. Our discussion of these unorthodox identities focuses on three spheres: "nones," that is, the nonreligious; fully digital churches and religious practices; and digitally embedded practices of mourning.

Over time, surveys of religious identity have noted a growth in the category of "none," "nonreligious," or "unaffiliated" (Pew Research Center, 2019). In the United States, the unaffiliated account for almost one-quarter of the population (Pew Research Center, 2019). The Internet and social media facilitate an abundance of identities and meanings of being nonreligious. Studies show that nonreligion is not a straightforward identity. Sizable proportions of survey respondents who identify as nonreligious report believing in God, while some of those who say that they are religious also identify as atheists, agnostics, or as having doubts about the existence of God (Smith & Cragun, 2019, Table 16.1). The Internet legitimizes the process of religious and nonreligious tinkering (Berger et al., 1974; McClure, 2017) by exposing users not only to a multiplicity of individuals who ascribe to unique and sometimes contradictory identities and belief systems, but also to nonreligious individuals who live meaningful and fulfilled lives. The Internet also facilitates the cultivation of new nonreligious communities modeled on religious practices such as the Sunday Assembly, founded in 2013, and constituting several dozen congregations in Europe and the United States (Smith & Cragun, 2019; Smith, 2017).

For some individuals who identify as nonreligious, particularly for those who are in the process of becoming nonreligious, online communities and social media can offer social support. Some online communities specialize in providing spaces in which individuals share their religious exit narratives, also referred to as extimonies or nonreligious comings-out (Starr et al., 2019). An analysis of deconversion narratives posted in one online forum for ex-Christians showed that exiting religious faith involves intellectual, emotional, and social negotiation and development. Posters indicated that exposure to Internet content that undermined their religious convictions, such as debates about whether God exists or whether creationism is real, precipitated their initial critical questions about religion, and played a role in their subsequent quests toward religious departures. Being nonreligious can be a stigmatized identity in many parts of the world (Lundmark, 2019). In addition to being a place of exploration and debate, online communities for the nonreligious can function as safe spaces for presenting as religious nones (Jürgens & Stark, 2017; Lundmark & LeDrew, 2019; Robards, 2018). The ex-Christian forum figured centrally in the deconversion narratives posted on the forum as a safe space in which individuals processed their religious doubts and their future post-Christian identities, and where they received support from others who concurrently or previously pursued similar deconversion journeys (Starr et al., 2019).

The Internet also enables hybrid nonorthodox religious practices with digitally organized religious spaces. Connecting networks with traditional worship has led to a situation where fully independent online churches have given way to extensions of local churches, religious communities, and religious institutions that create churches online (Hutchings, 2017b). Research in this area has focused on the existence of these entities and the "material status" of digital practices (Lagerkvist, 2017; Lagerkvist & Peters, 2018). The existential approach means putting a vulnerable human being at the center, which determines all human practices (Ess, 2020; Hoskins, 2017). The material status of digital practices rests on the assumption that rituals, through digital media, present similarities in the function and shape of the religious sphere as compared with nonvirtual objects and practices (Hutchings, 2017a). Their difference comes down to a different degree of engagement in a pious practice. Sometimes music offers a means of mediation within this process. The example of Karnatik music from India shows that music mediated through different sources of communication plays an integral part in rituals traditionally associated with a Hindu temple. In terms of current religious conditions, it becomes more of a "divine language" for expressing the people's relation to the Almighty than simply tonal music (Narayanan & Periyasamy, 2020).

With some religious institutions and practices operating fully online, the Internet also exposes religious seekers to orthodox religious practices and ways of expressing piety new to them. Burton (2020) described a group of young adults in the United States who call themselves Weird Christians, and who are drawn to ritually rich practices like the Catholic Latin Mass, the medieval Episcopal Rite I, the Liturgy of the Hours, and the tradition of women wearing veils in religious settings. The mainstreaming of virtual religious services precipitated by the Covid-19 pandemic enabled these young adults to discover and experience rituals online with which they previously were unfamiliar. While to a Christian historian there may be nothing less weird than the Latin Mass, the mysteriousness and artistry of these traditional rituals appear to manifest the transcendent for these young adults to a degree that less ritually abundant post-Vatican II Catholicism, or mainline and evangelical Christian services, do not.

The final example of a practice that involves engaging in the virtual space is digital mourning (see Chapter 26). People mourn online through the use of social media, applications, blogs, multiplayer role-playing games, and visits to memorial websites (Haverinen, 2017). The traditional rituals related to grief, considered a "sequestered death," have given way to the public exposure of mourning (Wright, 2014). Within the process, emotion has been moved online together with the memory (Giaxoglou & Döveling, 2018; Simpson, 2019). Grief itself has also acquired a communal notion that is no longer just an individual issue owing to its increased dimension (Babis, 2021).

Digital media facilitate the development and dissemination of unorthodox religious identities, expressions, and spaces, including ones that intentionally position themselves outside of religious institutions. While the decision to leave a religious tradition is an individual one, some go through a shift in identities in the context of a collective, that is, in digital forums that support religious disaffiliation and exit narratives. Unorthodox religious identities and expressions of piety also are evident in wholly online churches, among religious seekers who discover traditional rituals in online venues, and among mourners who express their grief online. In each of these instances, individuals curate a religious identity and practices that appear unique and individual yet connect to those of a group, however loose that collective might appear.

Conclusions

There is little doubt that the relevance of religious traditions is decreasing in many parts of the world, especially in developed countries. At the same time, religions continue their presence in the media, both on conventional platforms like television and in digital media like online social networks. This persistent presence of religious identities and piety practices in the media shape today's religion–media juncture and, more broadly, inform how religions are understood by those who adhere to and reject them.

The trends this chapter reviews show secularization as a multidimensional condition. Secularization does not simply mean that religions and religious identities are waning. Instead, religious identities and expressions of piety today take on diverse forms in the media, from the secularized and banal, to orthodox, to the nonreligious, seemingly new, and unorthodox. A key lesson of this chapter is that acknowledging the force of secularization cannot equate dismissing religious identities as irrelevant. In each of the case studies discussed here, religious traditions propel individuals or groups toward or away from identities, practices, and actions that are imbued with religious meaning.

Hoover (2020) recently echoed this chapter's key takeaway – that adherence to secularization theory should not lead to dismissing religion's cultural and political influence. Examining two religious media events executed by US President Donald Trump in June 2020, Hoover (2020) argued that journalists, public intellectuals, and scholars miss the depth of religious forces today and thus are unable to adequately explain some social, political, and cultural events. In the midst of nationwide protests opposing police brutality against Black people, President Trump first held up a Bible in front of a boarded-up Episcopal church. Protesters had been forcibly removed from Lafayette Square – the space between the White House and the church – shortly before this event, enabling Mr. Trump to walk to the church from the White House. The next day, he and First Lady Melania Trump posed for photos at the Catholic St. John Paul II National Shrine. Analyzing these events and their media coverage, Hoover (2020) asserted that journalists and political observers largely missed the full extent to which mediated religious symbolism animates such social, political, and cultural developments. Hoover (2020) identified secularization theory and two related notions – that religion is about "faith, belief, doctrine, piety, discipline, and spirituality" as opposed to "social and cultural politics," and that religious symbols are self-evident and closed to interpretation – as the mechanisms that limit intellectuals' ability to perceive and account for religions' sociopolitical influence (p. 4510).

While some may dismiss the influence of religious identity and ideology as innocuous, the dark side of religion persists, and it can be amplified by digital media. A last case study illustrates that the media can foment collective animosity against the religious other. Hindu WhatsApp groups in India have been used to propagate misinformation and hate speech against the Muslim minority (Nizaruddin, 2021). The Covid-19 pandemic precipitated narratives in publicly accessible WhatsApp groups that blamed Muslims for the proliferation of the virus. In some instances, mainstream news organizations picked up misinformation that first appeared on WhatsApp. The WhatsApp groups, meanwhile, regularly disseminated mainstream media narratives that cast the Muslim minority in a negative light.

In all, these examples of religious symbols and expressions intersecting the political sphere, as well as the three dimensions of secularization discussed in this chapter, suggest that religious identities and expressions of piety deserve to be considered seriously as driving cultural forces. Understanding religious identity and piety in the media can help make sense of how religion and nonreligion shape individual and group action, and facilitate communication across religious divides.

References

Babis, D. (2021). Digital mourning on Facebook: The case of Filipino migrant worker live-in caregivers in Israel. *Media, Culture & Society, 43*(3), 397–410. https://doi.org/10.1177/0163443720957550.

Bell, D. M. (2010). Religious identity. In D. A. Leeming, K. Madden, & S. Marlan (Eds.), *Encyclopedia of Psychology and Religion* (pp. 776–778). Springer. https://doi.org/10.1007/978-0-387-71802-6_821.

Bellah, R. N. (2007, October 19). Secularism of a new kind. The Immanent Frame. Retrieved March 23, 2022, from https://tif.ssrc.org/2007/10/19/secularism-of-a-new-kind

Belzen, J. A. (1999). The cultural psychological approach to religion: Contemporary debates on the object of the discipline. *Theory & Psychology, 9*(2), 225–229. https://doi.org/10.1177/095935439992004.

Berger, P. L. (Ed.). (1999). *The desecularization of the world: Resurgent religion and world politics.* Eerdmans.

Berger, P. L., Berger, B., & Kellner, H. (1974). *The homeless mind: Modernization and consciousness.* Vintage Books.

Beta, A. R. (2019). Commerce, piety and politics: Indonesian young Muslim women's groups as religious influencers. *New Media & Society, 21*(10), 2140–2159. https://doi.org/10.1177/1461444819838774.

Borg, J., Andrée, B., Soderstrom, H., & Farde, L. (2003). The serotonin system and spiritual experiences. *The American Journal of Psychiatry, 160*(11), 1965–1969. https://doi.org/10.1176/appi.ajp.160.11.1965.

Bronfenbrenner, U. (1979). Contexts of child rearing: Problems and prospects. *American Psychologist, 34*(10), 844–850. https://doi.org/10.1037/0003-066X.34.10.844.

Burton, T. I. (2020, May 8). Christianity gets weird. *New York Times.* Retrieved March 23, 2022, from https://www.nytimes.com/2020/05/08/opinion/sunday/weird-christians.html.

Casanova, J. (1994). *Public religion in the modern world.* University of Chicago Press.

Cole-Turner, R. (1992). Religion and the human genome. *Journal of Religion and Health, 31*(2), 161–173. https://doi.org/10.1007/BF00986794.

Dayan, D., & Katz, E. (1994). *Media events: The live broadcasting of history.* Harvard University Press.

Ess, C. (2020). *Digital media ethics* (3rd ed.). Polity Press.

Etengoff, C., & Rodriguez, E. M. (2020). Religious identity. In S. Hupp, & J. D. Jewell (Eds.), *The encyclopedia of child and adolescent development* (pp. 1–10). Wiley-Blackwell. https://doi.org/10.1002/9781119171492. wecad458.

Evolvi, G. (2019). *Blogging my religion: Secular, Muslim, and Catholic media spaces in Europe.* Routledge.

Giaxoglou, K., & Döveling, K. (2018). Mediatization of emotion on social media: Forms and norms in digital mourning practices. *Social Media + Society, 4*(1), 1–4. https://www.doi.org/10.1177/2056305117744393.

Gökarıksel, B., & Secor, A. (2013). "You can't know how they are inside": The ambivalence of veiling and discourses of the other in Turkey. In P. Hopkins, L. Kong, & E. Olson (Eds.), *Religion and place: Landscape, politics and piety* (pp. 95–114). Springer.

Günter, T. (2016). The mediatization of religion – As temptation, seduction, and illusion. *Media, Culture & Society, 38*(1), 37–47. https://doi.org/10.1177/0163443715615659.

Gustavsson, G., van der Noll, J., & Sundberg, R. (2016). Opposing the veil in the name of liberalism: Popular attitudes to liberalism and Muslim veiling in the Netherlands. *Ethnic and Racial Studies, 39*(10), 1719–1737. https://doi.org/10.1080/01419870.2015.1124126.

Guzek, D. (2019). *Mediatizing secular state: Media, religion and politics in contemporary Poland.* Peter Lang. https://doi.org/10.3726/b15404.

Guzek, D. (2021). La protesta delle donne in Polonia nel 2020 tra religione, politica e comunicazione digitale. *Religioni E Società, 36*(99), 102–105. https://doi.org/10.19272/202131301011.

Haerpfer, C., Inglehart, R., Moreno, A., Welzel, C., Kizilova, K., Diez-Medrano, J., Lagos, M., Norris, P., Ponarin, E., & Puranen, B. (2021). *World Values Survey time-series (1981–2020) cross-national data-set.* JD Systems Institute & WVSA Secretariat. Data File Version 2.0.0 https://doi.org/doi:10.14281/18241.15.

Haverinen, A. (2017). *Digital death: Online mourning rituals and practices.* Routledge.

Hemmasi, F. (2017). "One can veil and be a singer!" Performing piety on an Iranian talent competition. *Journal of Middle East Women's Studies, 13*(3), 416–437. https://doi.org/10.1215/15525864-4179034.

Hepp, A., & Krönert, V. (2010). Religious media events: The Catholic "World Youth Day" as an example for the mediatization and individualization of religion. In N. Couldry, A. Hepp, & F. Krotz (Eds.), *Media events in a global age* (pp. 265–282). Routledge.

Herbert, D. (2015). Theorising religious republicisation in Europe: Religion, media and public controversy in the Netherlands and Poland 2000–2012. In K. Granholm, M. Moberg, & S. Sjö (Eds.), *Religion, media, and social change* (pp. 54–70). Routledge.

Hjarvard, S. (2012). Three forms of mediatized religion: Changing the public face of religion. In S. Hjarvard, & M. Lövheim (Eds.), *Mediatization and religion Nordic perspectives* (pp. 21–44). NORDICOM.

Hjarvard, S. (2016). Mediatization and the changing authority of religion. *Media, Culture & Society, 38*(1), 8–17. https://doi.org/10.1177/0163443715615412.

Hjelm, T. (2012). Desecularization. In C. R. Wade (Ed.), *Encyclopedia of global religion & society* (pp. 293–294). Sage Publications.

Hjelm, T. (2015). Is God back? Reconsidering the new visibility of religion. In T. Hjelm (Ed.), *Is God back? Reconsidering the new visibility of religion.* Bloomsbury.

Hoover, S. M. (2020). Myth "today": Reading religion Into research on mediated cultural politics. *International Journal of Communication, 14*, 4508–4532. https://ijoc.org/index.php/ijoc/article/view/16122

Hoskins, A. (2017). *Digital memory studies: Media pasts in transition.* Routledge.

Humphrey, N. (1998). What shall we tell the children? *Social Research, 65*(4), 777–805. https://www.jstor.org/stable/40971287

Husein, F., & Slama, M. (2018). Online piety and its discontent: Revisiting Islamic anxieties on Indonesian social media. *Indonesia and the Malay World, 46*(134), 80–93. https://doi.org/10.1080/13639811.2018.1 415056.

Hutchings, T. (2017a). Augmented graves and virtual Bibles: Digital media and material religion. In T. Hutchings, & J. McKenzie (Eds.), *Materiality and the study of religion: The stuff of the sacred* (pp. 85–99). Routledge.

Hutchings, T. (2017b). *Creating church online: Ritual, community and new media* (1st ed.). Routledge.

Ingelhart, R. F. (2021). *Religion's sudden decline: What's causing it, and what comes next?* Oxford University Press.

Jennings, J. T. (2016). Mixed reactions: How religious motivation explains responses to religious rhetoric in politics. *Political Research Quarterly, 69*(2), 295–308. https://doi.org/10.1177/1065912916636690.

Jürgens, P., & Stark, B. (2017). The power of default on Reddit: A general model to measure the influence of information intermediaries. *Policy & Internet, 9*(4), 395–419. https://doi.org/10.1002/poi3.166

Kazi, T. (2018). Religious television and contesting piety in Karachi, Pakistan. *American Anthropologist, 120*(3), 523–534. https://doi.org/10.1111/aman.13061.

Kimmons, R., McGuire, K., Stauffer, M., Jones, J. E., Gregson, M., & Austin, M. (2017). Religious identity, expression, and civility in social media: Results of data mining Latter-Day Saint Twitter accounts. *Journal for the Scientific Study of Religion, 56*(3), 637–657. https://doi.org/10.1111/jssr.12358.

Knorre, B., & Zygmont, A. (2020). Militant piety" in 21st-century Orthodox Christianity: Return to classical traditions or formation of a new theology of war? *Religions, 11*(1), 1–17. https://doi.org/10.3390/rel11010002.

Knott, K. (2005). *The location of religion: A spatial analysis.* Routledge.

Knott, K., Poole, E., & Taira, T. (2013). *Media portrayals of religion and the secular sacred: Representation and change.* Ashgate.

Kołodziejska, M. (2018). *Online Catholic communities: Community, authority, and religious individualization.* Routledge.

Kołodziejska, M., & Neumaier, A. (2017). Between individualisation and tradition: Transforming religious authority on German and Polish Christian online discussion forums. *Religion, 47*(2), 228–255. https://doi.org/10.1080/0048721X.2016.1219882.

Kregting, J., Scheepers, P., Vermeer, P., & Hermans, C. (2018). Why God has left the Netherlands: Explanations for the decline of institutional Christianity in the Netherlands between 1966 and 2015. *Journal for the Scientific Study of Religion, 57*(1), 58–79. https://doi.org/10.1111/jssr.12499.

Künkler, M., Madeley, J., & Shankar, S. (Eds.). (2018). *A secular age beyond the West: Religion, law and multiple secularities in Asia, the Middle East, and North Africa.* Cambridge University Press.

Lagerkvist, A. (2017). Existential media: Toward a theorization of digital thrownness. *New Media & Society, 19*(1), 96–110. https://doi.org/10.1177/1461444816649921.

Lagerkvist, A., & Peters, J. D. (2018). *Digital existence: Ontology, ethics and transcendence in digital culture.* Routledge.

Lundmark, E. (2019). *"This is the face of an atheist": Performing private truths in precarious publics.* Department of Theology, Uppsala University.

Lundmark, E., & LeDrew, S. (2019). Unorganized atheism and the secular movement: Reddit as a site for studying "lived atheism". *Social Compass, 66*(1), 112–129. https://doi.org/10.1177/0037768618816096.

Marín, F.-X. (2015). Islam and virtual reality: How Muslims in Spain live in the cyberspace. In M. D. Bosch, J. L. Micó, & J. M. Carbonell (Eds.), *Negotiating religious visibility in digital media* (pp. 81–90). Facultat de Comunicació I relacions Internacionals Blanquerna Universitat Ramon Llull.

McClure, P. K. (2017). Tinkering with technology and religion in the digital age: The effects of internet use on religious belief, behavior, and belonging. *Journal for the Scientific Study of Religion, 56*(3), 481–497. https://doi.org/10.1111/jssr.12365.

Morgan, D. (1998). *Visual piety: A history and theory of popular religious images.* University of California Press.

Narayanan, J., & Periyasamy, D. S. (2020). The musical language of piety: The semiotics of visual media in shaping the divine status of Karnatik music. *Quarterly Review of Film and Video, 39*(8), 1–19. https://doi.org/10.1080/10509208.2020.1796180.

Nizaruddin, F. (2021). Role of public WhatsApp groups within the Hindutva ecosystem of hate and narratives of "CoronaJihad". *International Journal of Communication, 15*, 1102–1119. https://ijoc.org/index.php/ijoc/article/view/16255

Nybro Petersen, L. (2013). Danish female fans negotiating romance and spirituality in the Twilight saga. In M. Lövheim (Ed.), *Media, religion, and gender: Key issues and new challenges* (pp. 171–196). Routledge.

Petro, M. R., Rich, E. G., Erasmus, C., & Roman, N. V. (2018). The effect of religion on parenting in order to guide parents in the way they parent: A systematic review. *Journal of Spirituality in Mental Health, 20*(2), 114–139. https://doi.org/10.1080/19349637.2017.1341823.

Pew Research Center. (2018). The age gap in religion around the world. Pew Research Center. Retrieved March 25, 2022, from https://www.pewforum.org/wp-content/uploads/sites/7/2018/06/Religious Commitment-FULL-WEB.pdf

Pew Research Center. (2019). Religious landscape study. Pew Research Center. Retrieved March 25, 2022, from https://www.pewforum.org/religious-landscape-study

Putnam, R. B., & Campbell, D. E. (2010). *American grace: How religion divides and unites us.* Simon & Schuster.

Robards, B. (2018). "Totally straight": Contested sexual identities on social media site Reddit. *Sexualities, 21*(1–2), 49–67. https://doi.org/10.1177/1363460716678563.

Simpson, K. (2019, November 3). Should we be warning against digital mourning? Medium. Retrieved March 25, 2022, from https://medium.com/the-public-ear/should-we-be-warning-against-digital-mourning-b9bf112f3057

Smith, J. M. (2017). Can the secular be the object of belief and belonging? The Sunday assembly. *Qualitative Sociology, 40*(1), 83–109. https://doi.org/10.1007/s11133-016-9350-7.

Smith, J. M., & Cragun, R. T. (2019). Mapping religion's other: A review of the study of nonreligion and secularity. *Journal for the Scientific Study of Religion, 58*(2), 319–335. https://doi.org/10.1111/jssr.12597.

Solahudin, D., & Fakhruroji, M. (2020). Internet and Islamic learning practices in Indonesia: Social media, religious populism, and religious authority. *Religions, 11*(1), 1–19. https://doi.org/10.3390/rel11010019.

Starr, C., Waldo, K., & Kauffman, M. (2019). Digital irreligion: Christian deconversion in an online community. *Journal for the Scientific Study of Religion, 58*(2), 494–512. https://doi.org/10.1111/jssr.12599.

Sumiala, J. (2013). *Media and ritual: Death, community and everyday life.* Routledge.

Sumiala, J. (2017). "Je suis Charlie" and the digital mediascape: The politics of death in the Charlie Hebdo mourning rituals. *Journal of Ethnology and Folkloristics, 11*(1), 111–126. https://doi.org/10.1515/jef-2017-0007.

Sumiala, J., Valaskavi, K., Tikka, M., & Huhtamäki, J. (Eds.). (2018). *Hybrid media events: The Charlie Hebdo attacks and the global circulation of terrorist violence.* Emerald Publishing Limited.

Suykerbuyk, R. (2020). *The matter of piety: Zoutleeuw's Church of Saint Leonard and religious material culture in the low countries (c. 1450–1620).* Brill.

Tarusarira, J. (2020). When piety is not enough: Religio-political organizations in pursuit of peace and reconciliation in Zimbabwe. *Religions, 11*(5), 1–16. https://doi.org/10.3390/rel11050235.

Taylor, C. (2007). *A secular age*. Harvard University Press.

Werbner, P. (2010). Religious identity. In M. Wetherell, & C. T. Mohanty (Eds.), *The SAGE handbook of identities* (pp. 233–257). Sage Publications.

Wright, N. (2014). Death and the internet: The implications of the digital afterlife. *First Monday, 19*(6). https://doi.org/10.5210/fm.v19i6.4998.

Zainal, H. (2019). The irony of Islamization: Sexuality, piety, and power on Malaysian screens. *Continuum, 33*(1), 16–36. https://doi.org/10.1080/10304312.2018.1536778.

Selected Readings

Hjelm, T. (2015). Is God back? Reconsidering the new visibility of religion. In T. Hjelm (Ed.), *Is God back? Reconsidering the new visibility of religion*. Bloomsbury.

Hoover, S. (2006). *Religion in the media age*. Routledge.

Ingelhart, R. F. (2021). *Religion's sudden decline: What is causing it, and what comes next?* Oxford University Press.

Knott, K., Poole, E., & Taira, T. (2013). *Media portrayals of religion and the secular sacred: Representation and change*. Ashgate.

Künkler, M., Madeley, J., & Shankar, S. (2018). *A secular age beyond the West: Religion, law and multiple secularities in Asia, the Middle East and North Africa*. Cambridge University Press.

Smith, J. M., & Cragun, R. T. (2019). Mapping religion's other: A review of the study of nonreligion and secularity. *Journal for the Scientific Study of Religion, 58*(2), 319–335.https://doi.org/10.1111/jssr.12597

17

Youth, Education, and Media

Mary E. Hess

Introduction

Many have raised concern over the past three decades about the challenges facing youth growing up amidst pervasive digital media (Gauntlett, 2008; Seiter, 2005; UNICEF, 2017; Watkins, 2009). Coupled with the clear diminishment of participation in religious communities (Smith & Snell, 2009), the topic of youth and education in the context of religion and communication is a deeply fraught one. Durka (2015) writes:

> In this millennium we are witnessing the collision of people of faith and new thresholds, both of which require new ways of seeing, speaking, and acting. The collisions occur when communities of faith or factions within them become estranged. Also, boundaries separating religious groups have become more porous in this globalized contemporary world. There are many who worry that such blurring of identity weakens religious belonging especially among youth. (p. ix)

Given the uncertainties at the time of writing these lines (during the Covid-19 pandemic, and the uncertainties in how youth, educators, and religious communities interacted with communication), the chapter will focus instead on identifying arenas of challenge and pointing to emerging responses to those challenges.

In exploring youth and education (particularly in its religious forms), it is instructive to clarify a specific definition of *communications media*. The definition that is most useful in education is of *media* as the plural form of the word *medium*, with the connotation of "a condition or environment in which something may flourish" (Merriam-Webster Online, 2022). This definition allows us to consider *communications media* as the various environments in which meaning flourishes, whether they are, for example, books, religious rituals and traditions, online social networks, music forms, video games, and so on (Hess, 2015).

Boys (1989) formulated a key definition of religious education: "Religious education is the making accessible of the traditions of the religious community and the making manifest of the intrinsic connection between traditions and transformation" (p. 193). Meaning-making and communication are, therefore, central to the task, and the definitions of "education" (the root of which is *educare* – to draw out) (Conde-Frazier, 2017, p. 230) and "religion" (the root of which is *religare* – to bind together) (Swidler, 2014, p. 7) draw attention to this. So, it is both a drawing out and a binding together.

The Handbook on Religion and Communication, First Edition. Edited by Yoel Cohen and Paul A. Soukup.
© 2023 John Wiley & Sons Ltd. Published 2023 by John Wiley & Sons Ltd.

Given these dynamics, one of the more challenging aspects of discussing communication, religion, and education with youth in the twenty-first century is that the environments in which we make meaning are constantly shifting and changing. Digital media profoundly reshape three dynamics in particular: (i) as authority is flattened, (ii) authenticity becomes a key criterion for authority, and (iii) what constitutes agency is consistently being challenged (Hess, 2015). All three of these dynamics – authority, authenticity, and agency – lie at the heart of psychological and social development as children emerge from childhood into their youth and young adulthood (Kegan, 1982).

In education it is necessary to ask who is participating, who isn't, and why? Who has authority to shape meaning in these spaces? What constitutes authentic communication in both religious and nonreligious settings? And how do such settings shape learning? As Cortes (2000, p. 168) writes, "as an anarchically democratic arena, cyberspace provides opportunities for people to cross intercultural bridges. Conversely, it can draw them into narrow, constricting perceptual and attitudinal tunnels." How do religious communities invite participation, without creating ideological enclosures (Hull, 1985)?

These media raise a broad and deep range of questions and we need to pay attention to the arenas of interpersonal communication, as well as communication within and between communities. It is useful to think in terms of three main sets of challenges within learning, religion, and media. The first, most personal, has to do with how primary caregivers support a vivid sense of relationship with the divine with their children and youth. The most immediate and long-lasting experiences of authority begin in the ways in which primary care givers interact with the children in their care (Rizzuto, 1979). Foster (2012, p. 125) writes of a form of imagination that "enables us 'to attend to the deep meaning of things' that eventually lead us into a deeper knowledge of God and our relationship to the world around us." How are families to do this?

The second challenge lies in formal educational spaces, whether understood as schools and/or communities of faith. Much has been discussed, in particular about specific developmental dynamics (Buchanan & Gellel, 2015, 2019; Turpin & Walker, 2014; Wimberly et al., 2020). Questions of authenticity build upon and compete with differing experiences of authority.

The third and final set of challenges concerns youth and the kinds of learning necessary for them to have personal agency while being both deeply rooted in and loyal to a specific community of faith, but also generously open to relationship with persons across multiple faiths in a world that is fraught with divisions around economics, justice, identity, meaning, and so on (Rosenak, 1987). Youth face overwhelming pressures concerning consumerism and commodification, and the need to help youth move from forms of agency that describe them as "undeveloped consumers," to more positive forms of agency, which Meyers (2018, p. 7) has labeled "called co-creators," is central.

Persons, Transcendence, Media: How Is Authority Constructed and Experienced?

The first challenge lies within the most immediate forms of relational connection. Learning, particularly when understood as "drawing out," requires first and foremost trusted relationships grounded in effective communication (Buchanan & Gellel, 2015). Is authority experienced as loving and relational or harshly disciplinary and autocratic? Religious communities vary greatly in how they design and implement learning for families at this level. There is as yet no consensus on how best to shape learning that either arises within mediated spaces or draws on digital media within families. How a particular religious community understands what it is to be a person and how it understands the human relationship to the divine lie at the heart of religious identity formation.

In Christianity, for example, God speaks and the world comes into existence. God is understood first and foremost as communicating within God's very being, and then from the three persons of the Trinity (God, Jesus Christ, the Holy Spirit), in various ways with God's creation. God's relationship within Godself is an essential element of Christian belief, and from it grows the understanding that human persons arise from God's desire to be *in relationship* and *to communicate* with God's beloved community (Scharer & Hilberath, 2008). To communicate requires being in relationship. The relationship necessarily begins with God, who creates the person (D'Souza, 2016).

Judaism shares much in common with Christianity, not least being the Hebrew Bible's insistence on God's covenantal relationship with God's chosen people. Yet Jewish thought concerning human persons, communication, and learning differs distinctly from Christian thought. In Jewish thought, for instance, there is a long tradition of viewing the relationship between human beings and God as one of disputation and study. From the Torah and the Book of Psalms through the Talmud and Mishnah, the record of human beings arguing with God is carefully recorded. Human experience is an important piece of data in this study, and humans are bound by God into a covenant that establishes God's deep relationality with humanity for all time (Neusner & Avery-Peck, 2003, pp. 379–381). As with Christianity, there are many forms of Jewish community and many interpretations of Judaism that are emerging in the midst of digital communication (Yael, 2015). Some of these forms come alive in interpreting Jewish religious law (*Halakhah*), in particular its application to the contemporary era – including questions regarding engaging media (Rosenthal, 2014).

Like Judaism and Christianity, Islam also has deep engagement with sacred text, in this case, the Qur'an. Divine authority rests even more profoundly in this scripture, with many communities within Islam only engaging with the text in its Arabic version regardless of their vernacular languages. Yet even within Islam there are many communities that interpret scripture in vastly diverse ways (Goldberg, 2020) and digital communications media further expand the possibilities (Benson, 2015). Muslim interpretations of the revelation of Allah in the Qur'an inform and influence religious ritual. For example, prayers offered five times a day place communicating with God at the heart of a Muslim's life, making religious practice a key form of media in this community (Selçuk & Valk, 2012).

Hinduism and Buddhism also share a deep commitment to religious practice as a medium for communicating with a divine power but neither link so easily to a specific holy text (Largen, 2009, 2011). Indeed, even more than the Abrahamic tradition (Islam, Judaism, and Christianity), the Hindu and Buddhist traditions speak of multiple communities, multiple texts, and a striking diversity of practices (Clooney, 2010). Within Hinduism and Buddhism, faith practices themselves form the primary medium in which meaning is constructed (Largen, 2009, 2011). It is not possible to speak of a single, authoritative Hindu "text," although there are particular song cycles, epic poems, among other religious texts, which have been at the heart of certain streams of Hindu practice. Instead, members of Hindu communities trace their beliefs and practices through the lineage of specific teachers, or gurus. Authority is vested in these concrete relationships. Transcendence regularly touches human lives, often with unanticipated results, and parents (and other primary caregivers) become essential partners for helping children to interpret and respond to such divine action (Clooney, 2018). Here again, the practices of communication require paying attention to a divine reality that communicates with human reality and shapes and grounds it (Heft, 2006; Yust et al., 2005).

In each of these religious communities there are diverse responses to emerging forms of digital media, responses that often hinge on the extent to which they regard a particular medium as able to carry meaning for a community in light of its convictions. In religious communities, acceptance of a specific communication medium emerges because adherents find key evocations of their meaning and practices in that medium. In other segments, there is condemnation and an imperative to refuse contact with anything emerging within that medium.

One striking example of these dynamics that earned global attention was the universe of books, games, and movies that constituted the Harry Potter phenomenon. To the extent that parents saw this universe as supporting the religious convictions they wanted their children to embrace – care for each other, collective action, love being stronger than death, and so on – they welcomed their children's immersion in it. To the extent that parents saw these media as carriers of dangerous viruses – particularly that of evil embodied in the form of witches and wizards – they shunned the series, and tried to prevent their children from engaging in it (Hess, 2008). Under those interpretations lie deeper assumptions about authority. The belief that naming something calls it into being – a clear definition of one form of authority often found within conservative evangelical Christian spaces – meant that parents were clearly frightened by the Harry Potter universe (Maddux, 2010). A differing understanding of authority, one mediated by practice, a respect for authentic meaning found in metaphor and analogy, as well as a keen interest in human agency, lie beneath the ways in which other Christian communities embraced the series (Lyons, 2017).

Regardless of the specific interpretation of authority, or the kinds of authenticity and agency that flow from it, the question of how primary caregivers should support learning the specifics of their communities' claims to relationship with transcendence in the midst of digital forms of communication cannot be contained solely within the confines of family and home. Religious traditions offer guidance to their adherents, but in the twenty-first century that guidance exists within a context of competing authorities, inside and outside of specific faith communities. Who has authority, and what kind of authority, within a community to determine what are acceptable practices in relation to various media? These questions can have strikingly different answers within the same tradition, let alone between traditions. Increasingly the guidance that parents and other primary caregivers look toward is found in nonreligious contexts.

Youth, Religion, and Media and Shifting Notions of Authenticity

A key element in the maturation and growth of young people comes as they form peer groups and move beyond the authority and constraints of their immediate family caregivers and into settings bounded by school and other communities of practice that may include religion, but even more frequently center on sports, workplaces, and so on. The challenges for supporting religious identity as people grow and mature only become more complicated. As Osmer and Schweitzer (2003) note:

> The problematics of contemporary religious education go beyond the "external" relationship of the church and religious education in public educational institutions. Even in the churches themselves, there are internal ambiguities about religious education. Is religious education to be viewed primarily as a ministry in the church or as discipline in the academy? (p. 11)

Authority is once again in question, and more and more of the broader social environs stress authenticity as a key criterion for authority. Mercer (2008) writes, describing two subjects in her study of adolescent girls, that "Julie and Liza, standing in radically different locations theologically and politically, nevertheless held in common an important concern about faith. Both girls craved authenticity" (p. 15). Yet what constitutes authenticity in market-driven spaces?

Consider, for example, the rise of social media sites like Facebook, where the primary "product of such spaces are the users themselves through the mechanisms associated with the monetization of identity in advertising" (Rheingold, 2012). Young people are particularly vulnerable at their stage of development to enticement around self-creation (Subrahmanyam et al., 2001). The questions that communities must deal with include questions of media practices. What should be considered "private," for instance, and what "public"? Or is it more appropriate to think in terms of the "personal" and the "collective" (Thomas & Seely Brown, 2011)? What advice does a religious community or tradition offer on such questions (Lytle, 2013; Schein, 2019)? Might there be guiding frameworks for making such decisions? Communities of faith have very different responses to these questions, but they tend to cluster in two areas.

One cluster of responses marks clear dividing lines between what is "in" the community and what is "outside" the community. Religious communities with such clear boundaries tend to support specific kinds of social media that exist within "their" community. This might be termed a more "bounded set" framework for determining what is authentic. The second cluster of religious responses is made up of people of faith from various traditions that use more broad-based or "secular" media, including sites such as Facebook. These communities do not mark their external boundaries with the same degree of sharpness but tend instead to rely on their central values for guidance and identity. Authenticity flows from what might be termed a "centered set" frame (Guder, 1998).

In the first instance, people expect their institutional authorities to play a strong role in determining whether a particular site is an appropriate environment (Hess, 2019; Maddux, 2010). In the second instance, members of the community are expected to make their own decisions, albeit in relationship to community norms, about which environments are the most appropriate (Hess, 2017a, 2017c), which feel most authentic. There is literature, for instance, on how to help adolescents engage with the movies they love, in ways that "help girls practice theological questioning" (Parker, 2017, p. 168).

In the case of online games, for example, we may ask whether it is appropriate to choose resources for children's education from the broad array of games available on the Internet, or is it better to choose resources that carry the imprimatur of a particular institutional authority (boyd, 2014; Clark, 2013)? What advice should a faith community offer families regarding children's participation in Internet activities (Drescher, 2011; Gould, 2015; Lytle, 2013)? A simple search for "children's video games" with a religious adjective ("Christian," "Muslim," "Jewish," etc.) results in thousands of links. The search for "educational" appears endless.

Addressing this question is far more complicated than simply examining a site's content, because the underlying rules that shape a game's interaction actually define the forms of identity that are supported or contested (Zeiler, 2014). Indeed, parents and primary caregivers rarely pay close attention to the mechanics of a game, however, worrying instead about issues of privacy and control. For example, does a child have to ask a parent's permission to play? Or can anyone sign up to be involved? Are there consequences for behaving badly on a site – using obscenities or bullying – and are such consequences determined and enforced by adults, or by the children who are involved? Caregivers here are expressing concern about authority, without understanding that experiences of authenticity are profoundly in play.

The decision to allow children or youth to participate tends to rest on the varying forms of authority in faith communities raised earlier in this chapter: "Who has authority?" and "What kind of authority?" Both questions are crucial in communities of faith, and they point to basic questions about how a given religion speaks about children and childhood, and how parental obligations are understood (Browning & Bunge, 2009).

In religious traditions with a few key scriptures and strict hierarchical leadership, the challenge posed by media available through global digital networks has proven overwhelming, as, for example, the challenge to its authority experienced by the global Roman Catholic Church (Horsfield, 2012; Soukup, 2017). In the past, the most authoritative statements issued within the Roman Catholic Church appeared first in Latin within the Vatican and were then communicated to conferences of bishops, who then communicated them to local dioceses, who then, eventually, had priests who communicated them to parish members. Along the way the documents would be translated into the vernacular of each context and would be interpreted by Church officials within those contexts. Now, in an era of digital communications media, these documents appear on the Vatican's website and can be downloaded, translated, and distributed quickly by news media and other organizations who have little or no contact with Church authorities. Local congregational members often engage these texts themselves in advance of, or even absent from, any conversation with their local church leaders, and parents find themselves relying on journalists (whether religious or otherwise) for advice concerning such statements. Often what "feels right" (perhaps is "authentic") becomes the dominant criterion.

Religious communities who do not have such centralized ways of communicating – Protestant and Reform Christians, the many and diverse Jewish traditions, Hindu and Buddhist teachers who claim lineages through thousands of gurus – find themselves ever more marginalized in public discussions, and struggle to find ways to offer authoritative guidance to parents. Many of these communities have found themselves trying to develop support for building awareness of their traditions for children who regularly play various video games. Planet Minecraft (https://www.planetminecraft.com), for instance, is a website that calls itself a "family friendly community that shares and respects the creative works and interests of others," and supports many diverse communities who build spaces within the Minecraft software. Planet Minecraft has forums for multiple religious communities, including Jewish, Muslim, Hindu, and Buddhist, where participants share examples of the temples, sacred spaces, and other artifacts they are creating to support religious presence. Yet there is no "authoritative" or institutionally sanctioned presence in this website. The people who upload their creations label them, and it is up to the user to decide if they are adequately descriptive.

Yet another example of such a challenge arises around the sharing of music. Most religious traditions have vivid forms of music in which they have imbued their beliefs and practices. Music, then, is a key medium for religious practice. Yet digital tools make it possible to easily record and share music. Here again are many challenges with regard to music: Are there forms of music, for instance, that are sacred and as such must only be shared in the context of prayer and worship? What about music that was made to be sung communally, that is composed for and by a specific community? Can that music be lifted from the community and shared more widely? Who gets to decide? On what grounds? Is there an ethics of music sharing? Much of the time, youth are more adept at accessing and sharing music than are the adults around them, and many times these questions are not answered well within religious communities let alone within the larger educational contexts youth inhabit.

Religious schools in particular, and across faith traditions, have tended to enforce fairly strict rules about engagement with music. In some cases, these rules are intended to prevent youth from even listening to music deemed problematic. Yet one research finding within the broader world of youth and education in relation to communications media indicates that the most effective way to help youth develop critical engagement with music sharing issues has been to help them to develop and produce music themselves (Jenkins et al., 2016). Media educators, for instance, often invite youth to do various kinds of "mash-ups" – taking a song and putting new words to it (Collier, 2020). This is a longstanding common practice. In the age of the Internet it may even be *required* in identity formation, given the global circulation of multiple materials that come to bear markers of authenticity (Couture et al., 2015).

Scholars across the world are excited about the new opportunities to create and collaborate together, drawing on elements of preexisting content (Jenkins, 2006; McClure, 2011; Shirky, 2009). Some of the more creative videos available on YouTube are precisely the homemade productions that bring together elements of previous videos (Collier, 2020). Such mash-ups, however, not only pose interesting questions for intellectual property law but also familiarize people with practices that are more about creation than consumption. Again, given the extent to which communities of faith are concerned with who has authority, and what kinds of authority are being exercised, this more radical form of democratization has proven problematic. If the forms of media that a community has determined as appropriate are no longer easily controlled by those authorities, who controls them? Further, what does it mean when authenticity becomes the key criterion for their use? Womanist theologian and religious educator Evelyn Parker (2017) describes the elements of authentic identity that emerge from her research with African-American girls. She notes that:

> African-descended women [must] be clear and authentic about their identity. An authentic identity keeps one moored to one's core values, beliefs, and practices. it also sustains a person during stressful and stormy times in life. A key to thriving amid tumultuous environments of sexism, racism, and heteronormativity is an authentic identity. (p. 93)

Yet what is authentic? And how is the divine to be encountered outside the confines of a particular community of faith, or at least without institutional framing? As noted at the beginning of this chapter, if there ever were clear answers to these questions they certainly no longer exist amidst global disruption.

Youth, Media, Education, and the Shaping of Agency

A third realm in which youth, religious education, and communications media interact vividly is the public sphere. This is the place where there is some hope emerging. Youth have both historically and recently led the way in forms of varieties of public demonstration, advocacy, and even in some cases civil disobedience (Jenkins et al., 2016). This is a realm in which the shifting dynamics of authority and authenticity are clearly present, but agency is of particular importance (Rowe et al., 2017). Digital media are participatory media, and at their best can be spaces of creative collaboration (Jenkins et al., 2016). Scholars increasingly point to the necessity of supporting questions, of leading learning that is "inquiry-driven, project-based, and portfolio-assessed" (Hess, 2017a, p. 53). This is a form of learning that in many ways is very ancient, but in others is newly relevant precisely because of the affordances of digital communications media (Davidson, 2017).

The vast disruptions of Covid-19 led to a rapid increase in the use of digital technologies within learning spaces, as the necessity of physical distancing has forced the utilization of synchronous technologies to an extent and at a pace no one predicted in advance. As mentioned earlier, youth are often more adept at finding ways to utilize these technologies than are the adults around them, and we can see this in the rapid rise of youth-led political mobilization (Barron et al., 2014).

As youth grow up within increasingly polarized communicative practices, religious communities struggle to find ways to "give access to and make manifest" tradition and transformation (to return to Boys' definition). Arguments about God's Word, or ways in which one is to interpret God's commands, are that much more complicated in the pluralism made visible by digital communications media (Hoover, 2013).

When religious identity is based on much broader notions of what it is to be human and how one should navigate among competing claims in terms of human experience, is it possible, for instance, to determine the correct measures to take from a personal perspective? Can we argue from the good of the individual to the good of the community? Many religious scholars would argue no, and that we must make specific claims that arise from a community's beliefs (Heim, 2001). The challenge then becomes balancing competing claims in the midst of a larger community, or society at large (Pattyn, 2000).

Christianity and Judaism tend to disagree here. Christian religious educators more often point to a specific universal normative claim, while Jewish educators tend to emphasize specific contexts and specific problems. Along a different axis, Islamic educators move the discussion to a specific passage in the Qur'an that could apply to a situation. Different understandings of the medium of scripture may be one element in these distinctions, and these different understandings may also underlie disagreements about what constitutes ground for ethical action (Sacks, 2002). So how do youth make sense of these disagreements? Especially when they most often encounter them not within their own community, but in wider public spaces like social media, and other forms of communication media? Often the arguments represented there are at odds with how a specific religious community actually sees the conflict.

This is a key educational issue, and religious communities do not yet have consensus (even within a specific community) about how to handle this in educational terms, let alone in relation to how citizenship is defined in a given setting. Yet as Blum (2012) notes:

> as our society becomes more and more diverse, there is an increasing need for its citizens to gain this sense of shared humanity, appreciation of diversity, and greater comfort, ease, and trust with those who are different… Diversity-friendly capabilities enable citizens to better appreciate how their fellow citizens' group identities affect their life experiences and outlooks, while also rendering them better able to see those fellow citizens as individual. (p. 189)

In some ways, in specific circumstances, differing communities of faith, each from their own location, can find common ground in their specific understandings of transcendence, and the consequences of that transcendence for human agency. Thus, one faith community might argue that because God's Word became embodied through Christ in a community, then language matters, and the medium in which language is used matters (Fiorenza, 2015). Another community might argue that God's Word is best understood through a dialogue between scripture and a rabbi's efforts to make sense of scripture. Thus, language matters, and the medium (dialogue) in which it is used matters (Sacks, 2015). Yet another community might hold firmly to the belief that Arabic is the original language in which the holy text was heard, and thus the Qur'an must be read in that language, even as interpretation continues to unfold (Selçuk, 2013). These are arguments that are specifically located, but that make it possible to come to common agreements about communication practices that have religious elements (Moore, 2020).

The pervasiveness of communications media means the public are increasingly functioning somewhat like journalists, because the tools to create and distribute one's ideas are becoming so cheap and easy to use. The "public" is becoming the creator rather than simply the consumer of "news." This shift means the challenges of communications media in learning and knowing are becoming much more problematic. Thus 17-year-old Darnella Frazier digitally recorded and shared the death of George Floyd under the knee of Derek Chauvin, catapulting a specific incident of police brutality into a global catalyst for protest: a clear example of personal agency having global effect (Italie, 2020). This is a positive example, but there are at least as many negative examples (Tripodi, 2018).

Religious communities hope that by encouraging people to dig more deeply into the communication in which they are embedded, they might bring a more deeply faithful response to their public engagement (Hess, 2017b). As even more people flood into social networking spaces, engagement has become more responsible (Ofcom, 2020). Studies have shown, for example, that young people between the ages of 18 and 24 have a far more effective grasp of how to manage privacy policies on Facebook as compared with older users who are less familiar with social networking (boyd & Hargittai, 2010). Blogging sites with multiple authors and open comment demonstrate that community codes of practice may be drafted that regulate community interactions and that eventually may even be articulated in codes of conduct or institutionalized in the fabric of such sites' architecture (Benkler, 2006; Schimmel, 2011).

Beyond their engagement with specific public media, communities of faith are also beginning to work more intentionally on drawing on the specific media that are organic and integral to their own faith and using such media to reframe and recontextualize public media (Drescher, 2011; Gould, 2015; Hess, 2017c; Horsfield, 2015; Panzer, 2020). Christian theologian and former BBC reporter Jolyon Mitchell, for example, argues that "remembering practiced when participating in worship can transform how viewers reinterpret the images of violence that they see and then recall from the news" (Mitchell, 2007, p. 23).

Digital storytelling is a form of media education that increasingly is being picked up by faith communities as an active form of not only media literacy but also as active faith formation (Hess, 2019). In this process people of all ages engage in story-creating workshops in which they learn the basic elements of how to tell a story effectively (Lambert, 2009). People then record themselves telling that story and add sounds, music, and images to create additional resonance and offer other layers of meaning. Next, these story productions are edited into short videos shared using web streaming at sites such as Vimeo.com, YouTube.com, and so on. This process teaches people how specific media shape and construct meaning (Atay, 2020; Bell, 2010). At each stage of the process personal agency is activated, developing a degree of authenticity that conveys authority in the medium.

When the story prompts invite memories with explicit religious connections, the process takes on a formative character that can be very powerful in religious education (Hess, 2014). It has ramifications far beyond the specific boundaries of religious communities, as those who work with youth in restorative justice circles note:

> storytellers are themselves vindicated by the moral support that comes from others in the Circle. Their suffering and its impact on their lives are recognized and respected. Thus, the benefits of healing within the Circle are mutual: both those who tell their stories and those who listen gain from the sharing. The outcome is that the community strengthens its capacity to care for itself by providing this vital function. (Boyes-Watson, 2008, p. 170)

Conclusion

While it was unclear during Covid-19 what would emerge from the pandemic period, attending to issues of authority, authenticity, and agency remained an essential path through the thicket of conflicting challenges. Religious communities continued to struggle, as they have over centuries, with how to educate their youth in ways that remain loyal to the specificities of a tradition while yet remaining open to divine action. Turpin (2006) offers three criteria worth pondering:

A primary one is that the meaning system must contribute to decrease suffering of those who are rendered less powerful by the consumer system. The ability of the desires cultivated by the meaning system to be sustained within the limits of the earth's resources is a second criterion. A third is the meaning system's contribution to human fulfillment and flourishing and its adequacy to assist meaning making in the face of difficult circumstances. (pp. 226–227)

Jewish parents and school teachers remind us that the more robust our questioning of communications media, the more likely people will arrive at deep truth (Schein, 2019). Muslim parents and school teachers remind one that through learning and communication we can honor the Holy that is present at the heart of our representations (Selçuk, 2017). Buddhist teachers help young people learning to be monks to prioritize meditation, and to see digital games as playful ways to relax (Rath, 2018). Christian parents and school teachers encourage wonder about what it means to be faithful and authentic in digital communications media, and in what ways humans might be missing each other rather than encountering each other (Thompson, 2016). Indeed, all of these communities of faith struggle with learning what it means to embody communication with the divine. Recognizing and respecting transcendence requires human beings to retain humility and to shape practices in such a way as to be mindful of the ability to destroy as well as to create. Communication is at the heart of human being, and thus learning about and through communications media for better and for worse is at the heart of education in religious communities.

References

Atay, A. (2020). New media, new possibilities. In A. Atay, & D. Fassett (Eds.), *Mediated critical communication pedagogy* (pp. 61–74). Lexington Books.

Barron, B., Gomez, K., Pinkard, N., & Martin, C. (2014). *The digital youth network: Cultivating digital media citizenship in urban communities*. MIT Press.

Bell, L. (2010). *Storytelling for social justice: Connecting narrative and the arts in antiracist teaching*. Routledge.

Benkler, Y. (2006). *The wealth of networks: How social production transforms markets and freedom*. Yale University Press.

Benson, K. (2015). Private space, public forum: A netnographic exploration of Muslim American women, access, and agency in 'Islamic' cyberspace. In G. Messina-Dysert, & R. Ruether (Eds.), *Feminism and religion in the 21st century: Technology, dialogue, and expanding borders* (pp. 101–111). Routledge.

Blum, L. (2012). *High schools, race, and America's future: What students can teach us about morality, diversity, and community*. Harvard Education Press.

boyd, D. (2014). *It's complicated: The social lives of networked teens*. Yale University Press.

boyd, D., & Hargittai, E. (2010). Facebook privacy settings: Who cares? *First Monday, 15*(8). https://firstmonday.org/article/view/3086/2589

Boyes-Watson, C. (2008). *Peacemaking circles and urban youth: Bringing justice home*. Living Justice Press.

Boys, M. (1989). *Educating in faith: Maps and visions*. Harper & Row.

Browning, D., & Bunge, M. (Eds.). (2009). *Children and childhood in world religions: Primary sources and texts*. Rutgers University Press.

Buchanan, M., & Gellel, A. (Eds.). (2015). *Global perspectives on Catholic religious education in schools* (Vol. I). Springer.

Buchanan, M., & Gellel, A. (Eds.). (2019). *Global perspectives on Catholic religious education in schools* (Vol. II). Springer.

Clark, L. (2013). *The parent app: Understanding families in the digital age*. Oxford University Press.

Clooney, F. (2010). *Comparative theology: Deep learning across religious borders*. Wiley-Blackwell.

Clooney, F. (2018). *Learning interreligiously: In the text, in the world*. Fortress Press.

Collier, A. (2020, December 28). Young artists and activists wrapping 2020 in light. NetFamilyNews. Retrieved March 28, 2022, from https://www.netfamilynews.org/young-artists-activists-wrapping-2020-in-light

Conde-Frazier, E. (2017). Religious education for generating hope. *Religious Education, 112*(3), 225–230. https://doi.org/10.1080/00344087.2017.1309514

Cortes, C. (2000). *The children are watching: How the media teach about diversity.* Teachers College Press.

Couture, P., Mager, R., McCarroll, P., & Wigg-Stevenson, N. (Eds.). (2015). *Complex identities in a shifting world: Practical theological perspectives.* LitVerlag.

D'Souza, M. (2016). *A Catholic philosophy of education: The church and two philosophers.* McGill-Queen's University Press.

Davidson, C. (2017). *The new education: How to revolutionize the university to prepare students for a world in flux.* Basic Books.

Drescher, E. (2011). *Tweet if you ♥ Jesus: Practicing church in the digital reformation.* Morehouse Publishing.

Durka, G. (2015). Preface. In M. T. Buchanan, & A. M. Gellel (Eds.), *Global perspectives on Catholic religious education in schools* (Vol. I, pp. ix–xi). Springer.

Fiorenza, E. (2015). *Jesus: Miriam's child, Sophia's prophet: Critical issues in feminist christology.* Bloomsbury T & T Clark.

Foster, C. (2012). *From generation to generation: The adaptive challenge of mainline protestant education in forming faith.* Cascade Books.

Gauntlett, D. (2008). *Media, gender, and identity: An introduction.* Routledge.

Goldberg, T. (2020). Is this the other within me? the varied effects of engaging in interfaith learning. *Religious Education, 115*(3), 245–254. https://doi.org/10.1080/00344087.2020.1770014

Gould, M. (2015). *The social media gospel: Sharing the good news in new ways.* Liturgical Press.

Guder, D. (1998). *Missional church: A vision for the sending of the church in North America.* WB Eerdmans Publishing.

Heft, J. (Ed.). (2006). *Passing on the faith: Transforming traditions for the next generations of Jews, Christians, Muslims.* Fordham University Press.

Heim, M. (2001). *The depth of the riches: A trinitarian theology of religious ends.* Wm. Eerdmans Publishing Co.

Hess, M. (2008). Resisting the human need for enemies, or what would Harry Potter do? *Word & World, 28*(1), 47–56. https://digitalcommons.luthersem.edu/faculty_articles/92

Hess, M. (2014). A new culture of learning: Digital storytelling and faith formation. *Dialog, 53*(1), 12–22. https://doi.org/10.1111/dial.12084

Hess, M. (2015). Learning with digital technologies: Privileging persons over machines. *Journal of Moral Theology, 4*(1), 131–150. https://jmt.scholasticahq.com/article/11285-learning-with-digital-technologies-privileging-persons-over-machines

Hess, M. (2017a). Designing curricular approaches for interfaith competency, or why does learning how to live in a 'community of communities' matter? In E. Fernandez (Ed.), *Teaching for a multifaith world* (pp. 34–54). Pickwick.

Hess, M. (2017b). Exploring the epistemological challenges underlying civic engagement by religious communities. *The Good Society Special Issue: On Reintegrating Facts, Values, Strategies, 26*(2–3), 305–322. https://www.jstor.org/stable/10.5325/goodsociety.26.2-3.0305

Hess, M. (2017c). Gameful learning and theological understanding: New cultures of learning in communities of faith. In M. Bosch, P. Soukup, J. Sanz, & D. Zsupan-Jerome (Eds.), *Authority and leadership. values, religion, media* (pp. 191–200). Blanquerna School of Communication and International Relations Facultat de Comunicació i Relacions Internacionals Blanquerna.

Hess, M. (2019). Storying faith: The promises and contradictions of new media in Catholic religious education. In M. T. Buchanan, & A. M. Gellel (Eds.), *Global perspectives on Catholic religious education in schools* (Vol. II, pp. 357–368). Springer.

Hoover, S. (2013). Evolving religion in the digital media. In K. Lundby (Ed.), *Religion across media: From early antiquity to late modernity* (pp. 169–184). Peter Lang Publishing.

Horsfield, P. (2012). A moderate diversity of books? The challenge of new media to the practice of Christian theology. In P. Cheong, P. Fischer-Nielsen, S. Gelfgren, & C. Ess (Eds.), *Digital religion, social media and culture: Perspectives, practices, and futures* (pp. 243–258). Peter Lang.

Horsfield, P. (2015). *From Jesus to the internet: A history of Christianity and media*. John Wiley & Sons.

Hull, J. (1985). *What prevents Christian adults from learning?* SCM Press.

Italie, H. (2020). Teen who documented George Floyd death to receive PEN/Benenson Courage award. ABC 7 Eyewitness News. Retrieved March 28, 2022, from https://abc7chicago.com/darnella-frazier-gofundme-award-pen-america/7424532

Jenkins, H. (2006). *Convergence culture*. NYU Press.

Jenkins, H., Ito, M., & boyd, D. (2016). *Participatory culture in a networked era*. Polity Press.

Jenkins, H., Shresthova, S., Gamber-Thompson, L., Kligler-Vilenchik, N., & Zimmerman, A. (2016). *By any media necessary: The new youth activism*. New York University Press.

Kegan, R. (1982). *The evolving self: Problem and process in human development*. Harvard University Press.

Lambert, J. (2009). *Digital storytelling: Capturing lives, creating community*. Digital Diner Press.

Largen, K. (2009). *What Christians can learn from Buddhism*. Fortress Press.

Largen, K. (2011). *Baby Krishna, infant Christ: A comparative theology of salvation*. Orbis Books.

Lyons, P. (2017). *Teaching faith with Harry Potter: A guidebook for parents and educators for multigenerational faith formation*. Church Publishing.

Lytle, J. (2013). *Faith formation 4.0: Introducing an ecology of faith in a digital age*. Morehouse Publishing.

Maddux, K. (2010). *The faithful citizen: Popular Christian media and gendered civic identities*. Baylor University Press.

McClure, J. (2011). *Mashup religion: Pop music and theological invention*. Baylor University Press.

Mercer, J. (2008). *Girltalk, godtalk: Why faith matters to teenage girls – and their parents*. John Wiley & Sons.

Merriam-Webster Online. (2022). Medium. Merriam-Webster. Retrieved March 28, 2022, from http://www.merriam-webster.com/dictionary/medium

Meyers, J. (2018). *Liberating youth from adolescence*. Fortress Press.

Mitchell, J. (2007). *Media violence and Christian ethics*. Cambridge University Press.

Moore, M. (2020). Sacred, revolutionary teaching: Encountering sacred difference and honest hope. *Religious Education, 115*(3), 291–303. https://doi.org/10.1080/00344087.2020.1738044

Neusner, J., & Avery-Peck, A. (2003). *The Blackwell companion to Judaism*. Blackwell Publishing.

Ofcom. (2020, December 29). Children's media use and attitudes. Repeated studies from 2006 to the present across the UK. Ofcom. Retrieved March 28, 2022, from https://www.ofcom.org.uk/research-and-data/media-literacy-research/childrens

Osmer, R., & Schweitzer, F. (2003). *Religious education between modernization and globalization*. William B. Eerdmans Publishing Company.

Panzer, R. (2020). *Grace and gigabytes: Being church in a tech-shaped culture*. Fortress Press.

Parker, E. (2017). *Between sisters: Emancipatory hope out of tragic relationships*. Cascade Books.

Pattyn, B. (Ed.). (2000). *Media ethics: Opening social dialogue*. Peeters.

Rath, R. (2018). In Thailand Buddhist monks grapple with the meaning of video games. Vice. Retrieved March 28, 2022, from https://www.vice.com/en/article/7xegk4/thailand-buddhist-monks-video-games

Rheingold, H. (2012). *Net smart: How to thrive online*. MIT Books.

Rizzuto, A. (1979). *The birth of the living god*. University of Chicago Press.

Rosenak, M. (1987). *Commandments and concerns: Jewish religious education in secular society*. Jewish Publication Society.

Rosenthal, M. (2014). *Mediating religion, sanctifying media: Exploring the nexus of media practice and contemporary religious revival in Israel*. Walter De Gruyter.

Rowe, M., Ambrush, K., Anderson, N., & Arcus, C. (Eds.). (2017). Agency. *A special issue of the Journal of Media Literacy, 64*(1&2). http://www.aml.ca/wp-content/uploads/2017/03/JMLVo.64No.12-2017.pdf

Sacks, J. (2002). *Dignity of difference: How to avoid a clash of civilizations*. Continuum.

Sacks, J. (2015). *Not in God's name: Confronting religious violence*. Schocken Books.

Scharer, M., & Hilberath, J. (2008). *The practice of communicative theology: Introduction to a new theological culture*. Crossroad Publishing.

Schein, J. (2019). *Text me: Ancient Jewish wisdom meets contemporary technology*. Hamilton Books.

Schimmel, S. (2011). The blogosphere of resistance: Anonymous blogging as a safe haven for challenging religious authority and creating dissident communities. In S. Hoover, & M. Emerich (Eds.), *Media, spiritualities, and social change* (pp. 147–157). Continuum Publishing Group.

Seiter, E. (2005). *Internet playground: Children's access, entertainment, and mis-education*. Peter Lang.

Selçuk, M. (2013). Academic expertise, public knowledge, and the identity of Islamic religious education. *Religious Education, 108*(3), 255–258. https://doi.org/10.1080/00344087.2013.783313

Selçuk, M. (2017). God will tell you the truth regarding your differences. *Religious Education, 112*(4), 312–316. https://doi.org/10.1080/00344087.2017.1320500

Selçuk, M., & Valk, J. (2012). Knowing self and others: A worldview model for religious education in Turkey. *Religious Education, 107*(5), 443–454. https://doi.org/10.1080/00344087.2012.722473

Shirky, C. (2009). *Here comes everybody: The power of organizing without organizations*. Penguin.

Smith, C., & Snell, P. (2009). *Souls in transition: The religious and spiritual lives of emerging adults*. Oxford University Press.

Soukup, P. (2017). Authority, new media, and the church. In M. Bosch, P. Soukup, J. Sanz, & D. Zsupan-Jerome (Eds.), *Authority and leadership. values, religion, media* (pp. 31–39). Blanquerna School of Communication and International Relations Facultat de Comunicació i Relacions Internacionals Blanquerna.

Subrahmanyam, K., Kraut, R., Greenfield, P., & Gross, E. (2001). New forms of electronic media. In D. Singer, & J. Singer (Eds.), *Handbook of children and media* (1st ed., pp. 73–99). Sage Publications.

Swidler, L. (2014). *Dialogue for interreligious understanding: Strategies for the transformation of culture-shaping institutions*. Palgrave Macmillan.

Thomas, D., & Seely Brown, J. (2011). *A new culture of learning: Cultivating the imagination for a world of constant change*. CreateSpace Independent Publishing.

Thompson, D. (2016). *The virtual body of Christ in a suffering world*. Abingdon Press.

Tripodi, F. (2018). Searching for alternative facts: Analyzing scriptural inference in conservative news practices. Data&Society (Media Manipulation Research Initiative). Retrieved March 29, 2022, from https://datasociety.net/library/searching-for-alternative-facts

Turpin, K. (2006). *Branded: Adolescents converting from consumer faith*. The Pilgrim Press.

Turpin, K., & Walker, A. (2014). *Nurturing different dreams: Youth ministry across lines of difference*. Pickwick Publications.

UNICEF. (2017). Children in a digital world: The state of the world's children, 2017. UNICEF. Retrieved March 29, 2022, from https://www.unicef.org/reports/state-worlds-children-2017

Watkins, S. (2009). *The young and the digital: What the migration to social-network sites, games, and anywhere media means for our future*. Beacon Press.

Wimberly, A., West, N., & Lockhart-Gilroy, A. (Eds.). (2020). *From lament to advocacy: Black religious education and public ministry*. Wesley Foundry Books.

Yael, B. (2015). From telephone to live broadcast: Becoming a brick-and-mortar synagogue without walls. In G. Messina-Dysert, & R. Ruether (Eds.), *Feminism and religion in the 21st century: Technology, dialogue, and expanding borders* (pp. 130–140). Routledge.

Yust, K., Johnson, A., Sasso, S., & Roehlklepartain, E. (Eds.). (2005). *Nurturing child and adolescent spirituality: Perspectives from the world's religious traditions*. Rowman and Littlefield.

Zeiler, X. (2014). The global mediatization of Hinduism through digital games. In H. Campbell, & G. Grieve (Eds.), *Playing religion in digital games* (pp. 66–87). Indiana University Press.

Selected Readings

Boyd, D. (2014). *It's complicated: The social lives of networked teens*. Yale University Press.

Clark, L. (2013). *The parent app: Understanding families in the digital age*. Oxford University Press.

Hess, M. (2019). Storying faith: The promises and contradictions of new media in Catholic religious education. In M. T. Buchanan, & A. M. Gellel (Eds.), *Global perspectives on Catholic religious education in schools: Volume II, leading in a pluralist world*. Springer.

Hobbs, R. (2021). *Media literacy in action: Questioning the media*. Rowman & Littlefield.

Lyons, P. (2017). *Teaching faith with Harry Potter: A guidebook for parents and educators for multigenerational faith formation*. Church Publishing.

Wimberly, A., West, N., & Lockhart-Gilroy, A. (Eds.). (2020). *From lament to advocacy: Black religious education and public ministry*. Wesley Foundry Books.

Part V
Media Institutions

18

Mediatization

Knut Lundby

Introduction

The concept of mediatization refers to the societal transformations that are in interplay between the communication media and their environments. The mediatization of religion reshapes public religion in its encounter with, and dependence on, modern media.

The transformations may entail whole societies or smaller segments of them. The changes may appear gradually over time or may be launched through disruptions.

From his Northern European context, Stig Hjarvard (2012) identifies three forms of mediatized religion, "religious media," "journalism on religion," and "banal religion." The latter are a mixture of elements from religious traditions and symbolism in the popular media. Together, they change "the public face of religion" (p. 21).

All three forms are handled in other chapters of this handbook, although the transformations that are described may not be acknowledged as being the results of mediatization. "Religious media" are treated in Chapter 10 on religious broadcasting, Chapter 12 on public relations and advertising, and in Chapter 14 on the web presence of different religious institutions. "Journalism on religion" is covered in Chapter 19 on news and reporting on religion and in Chapter 22, on religion as documentary. The third form of mediatized religion concerns popular expressions, which are seen as religious content in entertainment (Chapter 20) and in film (Chapter 21).

This chapter takes a broader and more general perspective on mediatization. The emphasis is on how the mediatization of religion applies to various religious traditions. This chapter opens a window onto the mediatization of religion outside Europe and North America, the areas where the theory has primarily been developed and discussed (Lundby, 2009, 2014).

Technology Triggers

Mediatization research either observes the transformations from below, from ongoing symbolic and social interactions in society, or from above, through the encounter between media and other institutions. The former offers a cultural perspective, the latter an institutional approach.

While printed books came to change religious traditions (Eisenstein, 1979), early mediatization studies began with television (Schulz, 2004). However, mediatization studies concern the whole media environment, in contrast to changes that are identified with one new medium following another, as in "medium theory" (Krotz, 2014).

The Handbook on Religion and Communication, First Edition. Edited by Yoel Cohen and Paul A. Soukup.

Today, the transformations following the digital networked media are in the foreground. Internet searching, social media, and net-based media services, in particular through the use of smartphones, have intensified the fight for people's attention. The big American media tech companies have transformed national media economies in most of the world, with Chinese counterparts following suit. What attracted people and businesses as new means of communication through which to gain information and stay in touch with others turned out to be instruments in a new surveillance capitalism (Zuboff, 2019). The costs of connection are high. The massive automated collection of data, gained through the advanced algorithms used in searches and communication on the Internet, has "colonized human life" (Couldry & Mejias, 2019) and given the big information technology companies enormous power and influence.

Contrasting Approaches

In order to grasp the mediatization of various religious traditions it is necessary to take the most relevant theoretical road. Thus, a discussion of the different, partly competing, directions is needed.

The cultural, or social-constructivist, approach, as laid out by Friedrich Krotz (2009), regards mediatization as being a long-term process that goes back to the use of tools for communication in early human history. In contemporary society, "human beings construct their social and cultural reality by communicative action" (p. 24) with technological media. The sociologists Peter Berger and Thomas Luckmann (1966) explained "the social construction of reality." The media were not on their horizon at all. Today, this social construction is highly mediatized. Various technical media and infrastructures have become inherent parts of social interaction, as we communicate with networked devices. We thus need to grasp this "mediated construction of reality," Nick Couldry and Andreas Hepp (2017) argue.

The present all-encompassing digital and data processing influences lead into "deep mediatization" (Couldry, 2021; Hepp, 2020). Digital networked media offer new ways to build and reconstruct a range of "communicative figurations" (Hepp et al., 2018). From this perspective, (deep) mediatization of religion can be analyzed through the constellation of actors (in a religious field) who share a particular frame of reference (religion) with an ensemble of media in communicative practices within a radically changing media environment. In this mediatized lifeworld, the understanding of religion is constantly being redefined (Radde-Antweiler, 2019).

While this cultural approach builds an understanding of mediatization from below, the institutional approach starts – not really from above but, rather, from the meso level – by observing the interaction between various institutions in society. Hjarvard (2013, 2014a, 2014b) is the leading proponent of this approach to mediatization. Inspired by Anthony Giddens (1984), Hjarvard considers an institution to be "an identifiable domain or field of social life that is governed by a particular set of formal and informal rules, displays a particular structure, serves certain social functions, and allocates resources for action in various ways" (Hjarvard, 2014a, p. 130).

All institutions in modern societies depend on media technologies for their communication. There is no simple all-encompassing "media logic." Changes occur in encounters between the specific logics of media institutions and the logics of other institutions. "Institutional logics" encompass the ways in which institutions interpret and approach their environment. Mediatization processes are driven when the logic of the media influences the logics of other institutions, like religion (Hjarvard, 2014b, pp. 212–216). Other institutions become dependent on media and their logic for their functioning in contemporary society (2013, p. 17). The institutional take on mediatization is "primarily focusing on the 'structuring influence' of the logics of media institutions for social interaction within other domains of society" (Lövheim & Hjarvard, 2019a, p. 210) – in our case, within the domain of religion.

While the cultural approach observes institutionalization being built up through the processes of symbolic interaction, the institutional approach studies the exchange between existing institutions and the ways in which they are transformed. Both approaches are concerned with social interaction through media and communication technologies: the former observing how mediatization shapes social *figurations* and the latter stressing how mediatization makes *conditions* for social and cultural activity.

Institutions in a Nested Structure

The institutional and cultural approaches both acknowledge the necessity of institutions; however, they conceptualize them differently.

Media institutions "are ways of organizing communication," of keeping "the *possibilities* for social order" (Couldry, 2021, pp. 257–258). Instead, Hjarvard builds his argument from the encounter between institutional logics, as society become more deeply embedded in the dynamics of new communication technologies. The debate thus arises between the two on whether "media logic" is a fruitful concept or not.

"Religion" and "the media," as broad fields, are both part of the social order. Both are also exposed to conflicts and technological disruption. As institutions, both are frameworks for action "with relatively high stability" (Engelstad et al., 2017, p. 3). Social institutions are more general than specific organizations but need not be located on an overarching level of the social structure. "Often they form a nested structure, somewhat like Chinese boxes, with different levels of specification" (pp. 3–4). "The media," for example, encompass "the press," which, again, consists of particular newspaper institutions with their organization (Lundby, 2017, p. 246). Within "religion," there are different "religions" (e.g. Christianity, Islam) within which there are even more specific traditions (e.g. Christian denominations, Sunni and Shia Islam). These are institutions on various levels, and are to be distinguished from the organization of concrete Christian Churches, or the schools within Islam.

The task, here, is to disclose transformations in the interplay between, on the one hand, media institutions that are based in various technologies and, on the other, religious institutions within different traditions.

Moving Outside Europe

Recently, there has been considerable interest in mediatization theory around the globe. This also applies to the mediatization of religion. Within the frame of this chapter, this global turn can only be covered through selected cases. They will all be taken from outside Europe and North America. Studies in non-European and non-Christian settings may challenge the dominant understanding of mediatized religion (Lövheim, 2014).

This chapter leans toward the institutional approach. It concentrates on selected religious traditions. This leaves aside a range of religious and spiritual expressions. As the Brazilian scholar Luis Mauri Sa Martino states, the "process of mediatization, and the practice of religion in a mediatized environment, goes well beyond the borders of institutional religion itself" (2013, p. 14). There is thus more to be said about the mediatization of religion than could be covered in this handbook piece.

The communication sociologist Dan M. Kotliar (2020) challenges what he terms "data orientalism": how it is overlooked that "the power of algorithms perpetually flows back and forth – between East and West, South and North" (p. 919). While the research on data colonialism tends to focus on the influence of a few big American data companies, such algorithms are actually "developed in various geographical locations and used in highly diverse socio-cultural contexts" (p. 919). Echoing Edward Said's book *Orientalism* (1995), Kotliar attempts to grasp the algorithmic construction of the non-Western other.

Let's start the exploration in the "Orient," as the Eastern world, in relation to Europe and the Western world, used to be termed by the West. From Sikhism, out of India, the chapter moves to Asian Buddhism and Islam in Asian countries. Further to Orthodox Judaism, African Pentecostalism, and, finally, to charismatic Catholicism in Latin America. The aim is to allow for accounts of mediatized religion as they are seen from the East and the South.

Sikhism in the Punjab and Beyond

Sikhism is one of the youngest and smallest of the world religions. Like "Hinduism" and "Buddhism," "Sikhism" is a Western word, coined from a European perspective, but it is today used by Sikhs themselves. "Sikh" means a learner or disciple of the Guru. Their scriptures inspire "ordered harmony and unity, and a spiritual discipline" (Nesbitt, 2016, pp. 1–2). The Sikh community has a history that goes back to the first Guru at the end of the fifteenth century, and today Sikhism counts 25 million adherents (Mann, 2016). Sikhism is both a monotheistic religion and a national/ political identity. Both are shaped in mediatization processes. Sikhism originated in the Punjab in northern India. The Sikhs form a minority in Hindu-dominated India, making up no more than 2% of the population. However, in the Indian Punjab they make up a majority. They thus have a "homeland," but Sikhs are globally dispersed, on all continents owing to early, extensive migration to serve the British Empire overseas as soldiers and police and in other occupations (Jodhka & Myrvold, 2015, p. 1). Their sense of Sikh community is strong. They have developed "transnational practices and links" to "the 'homeland' of the Punjab in India, as well as within a global Sikh community" (p. 2). Beyond travel, Sikhs rely on the Internet and various media to stay in touch. To what extent have the media contributed to transforming Sikh lives and their religion?

Christina Myrvold (2018) gives a rare glimpse into the early mediatization of the Sikh community through her study of photography in colonial Punjab from the 1850s onwards. This then new media technology was applied by the British rulers "to collect scientific material for imperial knowledge and control of colonial subjects" (p. 45). They visualized Sikhs as warriors, royals, and rebels. In effect, they used the medium of photography to shape the images of Sikhs and to categorize them, thus to transform their life conditions through this mediatization. However, the new practices of photography also gave Sikhs themselves the tools with which to later challenge colonial rule.

Today, there are about half a million Sikhs living in the UK. In the contemporary transnational "Sikhscape" there are narratives of "Return" to the Punjab (Ferraris, 2012). Return may take place by going there through physical travel but could also happen at a distance through mediated interaction with smartphones, via websites, discussion forums, or YouTube videos. There are combinations, like a video made for family use, addressed to participants on a pilgrimage to the Punjabi area of Pakistan, organized by Sikhs in the UK (pp. 95–97). Ferraris also discusses two British television programs on Sikhs who travel back to the Punjab, thematizing identity "between diaspora and notions of homeland" (p. 100). These stories are mediatized accounts of Sikh identity.

Sikhism's media image "is predominantly male, and reports often suggest that it is a religion preoccupied with swords and turbans" (Nesbitt, 2016, p. 1). The turban is "the ultimate male symbol"; however, there is a "small, but highly visible identifiable trend of women wearing turbans," in particular, in the diaspora, observes Doris Jakobsh (2015, p. 131). This identity construction among Sikh women takes place in the mass media, and particularly on the Internet (p. 126). Jakobsh suggests that globalization and the increasing mediatization of the turban play key roles when the turban emerges as a central identity marker for Sikh women. The many image proofs that can be found when searching the world wide web using the search term "Sikh women" are indicative of a cultural shift (p. 131).

In conclusion, contemporary Sikhism is heavily mediatized, and has been slowly transformed in media communication to redefine Sikh identity and to uphold the Sikh community in a global setting.

Mediatizing Asian Buddhism

Buddhism has its roots in Asia (Cantwell & Kawanami, 2016). Siddhartha Gautama, born in India in 566 BCE, was recognized as the Buddha, the "Awakened One." Buddhists now make up 7% of the world's population (Eckel, 2005, p. 112). "Whereas many religions focus on the worship of God or other divine beings, Buddhists focus on the figure of the Buddha – a human being who discovered how to bring suffering to an end and escape the cycle of death and rebirth" (p. 133). Buddhist ethics inspire self-discipline, on the path "from the world of suffering to the achievement of *nirvana*" (p. 163).

The overwhelming majority of this world religion live in the Asian-Pacific region and belong to different Buddhist traditions. However, Buddhist communities, temples, and meditation centers are now found on all continents, with a significant growth in the West owing to both migration and conversions (Obadia, 2015, p. 346) – and to media influences. Mediatized Buddhism fits with contemporary individualism. Buddhist "themes, aesthetic figures, and symbols have been 'rearranged' to fit the settings of new host countries," the anthropologist Lionel Obadia observes (2015, p. 344). "Buddhist semantics, materialities, and aesthetics" are carried over into fields like "psychology, psychotherapy, self-help, and the like … with the practices of mindfulness being the most popular in contemporary societies. Further examples are the realm of medicine, the field of popular culture, and entertainment, … marketing and branding," the scholar of religion Inken Prohl (2020, p. 116) holds. Thus Buddhism "has aligned with the 'fluid' quality of globalization" (Obadia, 2015, p. 351). In many Asian countries there is a marked resistance against this global communication and the cultural export of Buddhism. However, Buddhist ideas and texts have been spread on the Internet. Mediatization is regarded as a "decisive process in the globalization of Buddhism" (p. 347). Obadia underlines the transformations of information and communication technologies with "the rise of new forms of religious transmission, textuality, and authority in the context of virtual networks" (p. 351).

The scholars of media, religion, and culture, Gregory Price Grieve, Christopher Helland, and Rohit Singh (Grieve et al., 2019), discuss the digitalization that conditions Buddhist social structures and practices (p. 140). They observed the Dalai Lama reading from old Tibetan Buddhist philosophy during the 33rd Kalachakra ceremony in Himalayan India in 2014. The event was shared on the Internet. This was not merely a transmission of "the same old analogue *dharma* in new digitized bottles," they observed. The teachings (*dharma*) were carefully adapted to the affordances of the new technologies (p. 141). Such transformation implies mediatization.

Grieve, Helland, and Singh test their case on Hjarvard's institutional theory of mediatization. Their aim is a "Buddhist reconditioning" of Hjarvard's perspective (p. 141). They hold that a

Buddhist theory of communication analyzes media practices "as the mutual conditioning of two or more communicators" (p. 151). They found that the Kalachakra ceremony and the digital technologies "mutually conditioned one another" (p. 140).

Interestingly, Lövheim and Hjarvard (2019) underline exactly the *conditions* of contemporary religion under mediatization, "how institutions form the conditions for social interaction and meaning making" (p. 208). The difference may be that Grieve, Helland, and Singh point to the circular conditions that are inherent to Buddhist ritual culture carried into mediatized forms by the digitalization, while Lövheim and Hjarvard point to the conditions for social interaction that are created through mediatization. They thus each start from their own end of the communication process.

Grieve, Helland, and Singh argue against Hjarvard's institutional approach to mediatization as being incompatible with Buddhist culture. In order to base their own argument, they set up a strawman by stating that Hjarvard follows a linear sender–receiver model of communication. This is quite misleading. Lövheim and Hjarvard find the study of the Buddhist case compatible with the institutional perspective on mediatization: "By emphasizing the communication logic of Tibetan Buddhism" they "perform an analysis of the interplay between an institutional religious logic as manifested in a particular time and space and a particular media institution, in this case an interactive ceremony using various forms of digital media technology." For Lövheim and Hjarvard, this is in line with "the institutional approach to mediatization as a multi-levelled, reciprocal process" (p. 219).

Mediatized Islam in Asia

In Asia, Islam (Bigelow, 2016) is the largest religion. About one in four Asians are Muslims. Islam has a stronghold in several Asian countries, in particular in Indonesia, Pakistan, and Bangladesh. In the two most populous countries in Asia, India and China, Muslims make up minorities that are under pressure from the governments and from the dominant religions. However, in terms of their numbers of people, these minorities are not small. For example, the 20 million Muslims in China make up a number that is on a par with the total population of Saudi Arabia (Ho, 2019, p. 42).

Wai-yip Ho (2019) discusses the mediatization of religion among young Muslims of the Hui minority in the northwestern part of China. Ho argues that the power of mediatization in China lies with the state and the transformations that are ordered by the government. The Hui youth supported official Chinese policies on development and on religion, which set the framework for their activities and their website. Their mediatized space thus became highly restricted. Their own suggestions for change were therefore limited. Still, in 2015, the state closed down all Muslim websites. Contrary to Western mediatization studies underlining the expanding autonomy and power of media institutions, Ho reminds us of the circumvention of mediatized religion by authoritarian states.

With the Internet, Asian Muslims could enter "Cyber-Islamic Environments" (Bunt, 2009). This global *Ummah* also helps Muslim diasporas to stay in touch with fellow believers in their home countries. The diasporas are also influenced by their host cultures. Yarry Panji Setianto (2015) tells how the small Indonesian Muslim diaspora in the United States mediatized Islamic practices. Their use of networked media to cope with issues that they face in America did not drive them toward secularization, as has often been assumed in mediatization theory (Hjarvard, 2011). Rather, their mediatized practices made these Muslim in the diasporas more religious. "When mediatization hits the ground," one has to realize the decentralized authority structure in Islam, which implies that the mediatization of religion "takes a complex form" (Couldry, 2014, p. 62).

In India, the satellite channel, Peace TV, was banned by the Indian government in 2012, but was still available on other platforms in the main cities. Peace TV is one of the two Islamic televangelist projects in India that were studied by Patrick Eisenlohr (2017). One is based in a Salafist Sunni tradition, the other in a Shia controlled set-up. Peace TV is the Sunni case, and it is run by the popular Indian Islamic televangelist Zakir Naik. He is a television performer applying new TV genres. He is not an Islamic scholar, but is a new kind of religious authority through his command of new media forms. Still, he "draws on established patterns of religious mediation in the narrow sense", that is, "interactions between Muslims and the divine" (p. 876). Since the form of Islamic communication, in this case, is being transformed, Eisenlohr finds this to be a mediatization of religion.

The Shia case, on the contrary, is not to be considered as a mediatization of religion, since the Islamic teachings strictly follow Shia rules, despite the use of modern communication technologies and the introduction of new televised genres. The case is the televangelism among Shia Muslims in Mumbai that is part of the large World Islamic Network. The programs and teachings for followers, in this Indian city, are given by traditionally trained Shia clerics, controlled by Ayatollah Ali al-Sistani in Najaf, Iraq. There is no transformation of the inherent Shia doctrines or the structures of religious authority.

Both cases fall within an institutional frame of religion. Eisenlohr (2017) finds Hjarvard's conception of mediatized religion too focused on the logic of media institutions. The social anthropologist argues that it is not only necessary to look at the media presence of religion in the public sphere, but that this must be combined with an understanding of the inner conception of the tradition's relation to the divine. This "religious mediation" has to be differentiated from "public religion." Both aspects must be considered in the mediatization of religion studies, he argues. One must look at the "processes of interaction between human actors and the divine, along with the institutions and authorities that sustain them" (p. 870).

Lövheim and Hjarvard (2019, pp. 217–218) counter this criticism. They point out that the distinction between public religion and religious mediation had already been made by David Herbert (2011). They argue that Eisenlohr's Sunni case plays into an institutional logic of the religious tradition. This, however, does not happen in the Shia case.

In countries where Islam makes up a majority, like Malaysia and Indonesia, Chinese Muslims have found space. Hew (2019) tells of two young Chinese converts who became popular Muslim preachers: Felix Siauw in Jakarta and Firdaus Wong in Kuala Lumpur. Both have a background in marketing, and both have high media competence. Both hold conservative Muslim values, but neither is trained as an Islamic scholar. They attain authority from their communication skills, practiced through combinations of on- and offline preaching events. Their performances differ somewhat, but both display Islam as both public religion *and* religious mediation. They thus both practice mediatized religion, as Eisenlohr found with the controversial television preacher Zakir Naik. Firdaus Wong, in Malaysia, even claims to be a follower of Zakir Naik.

In Shia-dominated Iran, the annual mourning and processions in the *Muharram* are an important ritual. This is when Iranian Shia Muslims commemorate the tragedy of Karbala in Iraq, where the Prophet Muhammad's grandson and his family were massacred, thus creating the split between Shia and Sunni Muslims. Narges Valibeigi (2019) explores how young Iranians take part in the *Muharram* through postings on Instagram. She follows Hjarvard's conceptualization of mediatization, which she finds fits perfectly for this religious event in contemporary Iran. "Traditional Shi'a Islam is still the main discourse for religious Iranians," Valibeigi (p. 186) admits. However, she details how the affordances of Instagram help young Iranians to form and express a mediatized Shia identity "in accordance with the genres of popular culture and individual lifestyle" (p. 187). The "traditional structure of the Iranian Shi'a community is [thus] under a perceptible transformation in the process of mediatization" (p. 166).

Resistance in Orthodox Judaism

"Judaism is a complex cultural system" (Kunin, 2016, p. 174). The historian and media scholar Menahem Blondheim (2015, p. 16) makes the point that Judaism, like digital technology, is binary: "Unlike other religions, it is a nationality, and unlike other nationalities, it is a religion." Today, the Jewish people number some 14 million worldwide. The majority are secular. Modern Judaism is divided among seven streams: five religious and two secular. Outside the United States, Orthodox Jews dominate. One-third of all Jews live in Israel (Kunin, 2016, pp. 174–175). Judaism in Israel "has histori-cally been highly mediatized," with media being both acclaimed and rejected (Tsuria & Campbell, 2019, p. 190). Modern Orthodox Jews, one-fifth of the Jewish population in the country, may adapt to modern media and to many other aspects of modern society. They have to handle dual loyalties, to the orthodox tradition on the one hand and to modernity on the other (Cohen, 2012, pp. 96–107). While they try to handle the dilemmas of mediatization, the ultra-Orthodox try to avoid them.

This exploration will concentrate on the smaller ultra-Orthodox branch in Israel, where they make up 8% of the Jewish population (Cohen, 2017, p. 114). Ultra-Orthodox Jews are critical of modern media as they give priority to Jewish tradition over modernity. They leave little or no room for individual choice. The body of law in religion has greater authority, and this is usually guarded by the rabbis (Kunin, 2016, pp. 196–199). On the right wing of ultra-Orthodoxy, Haredi commu-nities are cultural ghettos. Their rabbis created their own Haredi newspapers, which they censor. They reject television and other secular media so as to preserve traditional values (Cohen, 2017). Likewise, they have dubious relations with the Internet (Campbell, 2010, pp. 117–122). Despite Haredi rabbis condemning computers and the Internet, many of the faithful use these technol-ogies. The Chabad is an ultra-Orthodox Hasidic group within the Haredi movement, which is active in the United States as well as in Israel. Young Chabad members became web pioneers. These webmasters aimed to strengthen internal Chabad solidarity, "protecting and fortifying the enclave's boundaries" (Golan & Stadler, 2016, p. 72), while also sharing their outlook of Judaism with the world. Chabad webmasters undertake mediatizing work as they "'Chabadize' Judaism" (p. 85).

Menahem Blondheim and Elihu Katz (2016) regard the case of digital Chabad as touching "the interaction of God and humans" (p. 89), thus satisfying the second criterion of mediatized religion that has been set by Eisenlohr (2017), in addition to the encounter between media and religious institutions. Haredi websites, and other alternative Haredi media, have challenged the authority of Haredi rabbis (Cohen, 2017), thus mediatizing the Haredi movement. Tsuria and Campbell (2019) discuss the digital media use by ultra-Orthodox Jews in Israel in the light of institutional mediatiza-tion theory. They conclude that the encounters between the two institutional logics do not in them-selves provide a satisfactory explanation. One also has to take into account the religious traditions within the cultural context of the communication. They thus suggest supplementing the institu-tional theory of mediatized religion with the theory of the Religious Social Shaping of Technology (RSST), which Campbell (2010) has been instrumental in developing. "RSST argues that religious communities shape technology and mediatization claims that technology as a social institution shapes society" with its religious institutions, Tsuria and Campbell claim (2019, p. 192).

Prosperity Pentecostalism in Africa

Among the diversity of African religions, a variety of Christian Churches are highly visible, owing to the history of the colonial past that has been merged with indigenous religious traditions (Bongmba, 2012). African independent Churches have developed alongside mainline national versions of Catholicism and the Protestant denominations. During the past few decades, African initiated Churches have met competition from charismatic Pentecostalism. This religious change has occurred in parallel with the economic liberalism and media deregulation that has been pushed onto African states by Western institutions. The preachers of the Pentecostal–charismatic Churches promise success, health and prosperity to their, often deprived, followers. These Churches have a global outlook on new forms of communication. They apply the latest available media technology, inspired by the American mega-churches. Still, they are inherently African (Meyer, 2012).

The anthropologist Birgit Meyer (2004) studied the rise of these popular charismatic media movements as they took place in Ghana from the 1990s onwards. Ghana adopted democracy and liberalized the media sector, which opened up a new public sphere. The country's video-film industry took off. "Pentecostalism and video-films came together and articulate alternative, Christian imaginations of modernity" (p. 96). The commercialization of society fitted the charismatic religious style, which blended in with popular culture and people's relation to "old gods, witchcraft, and new spirits" (p. 96). With their expressive charismatic forms, this new Pentecostalism transformed the public sphere in Ghana. In her rich account of these developments, Meyer applied the term mediatization: "mediatization and commercialization have transformed Pentecostalism as an institutional form as well as … its place and role in society" (p. 105). This sounds like an institutional perspective on the mediatization of religion. However, this theory was launched some years later. Actually, Meyer turned against Hjarvard's view of the "media as agents of religious change," worried that "'the media' become the key institution that imposes its media-logic on other institutions, including religion" (2013, pp. 14–15). She admits that, with mediatization theory, "media formats and aesthetic conventions and modes of address" shape or transform politics, the economy and religion. However, to Meyer, this is merely the surface.

Meyer (2009) tries to go deeper into the transforming of religion by the use of the concept of "mediation." This, to her, implies that the media are "intrinsic to religion." She understands "religion as *mediation*" (2013, p. 2). The "media" encompass a range of mediators, from spirit mediums to computers (p. 8). Religion, she had already argued, in relation to her Ghanaian studies, "cannot be analyzed apart from the forms and practices of mediation that define it" (2004, p. 94). Mediation, in general, "is a process that produces a shared world to be inhabited, taken for 'real' and experienced as 'immediate'" (2013, p. 5). Religion "as a practice of mediation between humans and the professed transcendent … necessarily requires specific material media" (p. 8). The point is "to explore how the transition from one mode of mediation to another, implying the adoption of new mass media technologies, reconfigures a particular practice of religious mediation" (Meyer & Moors, 2006, p. 7).

In the institutional approach to mediatization, "mediation" simply means the ongoing communication by the technical media. The affordances of each specific medium put restrictions and open possibilities on the communication. Over time, or in disruptive incidents, the mediation may change the structural relation between the media and the other institutions involved, thus shaping the mediatized conditions of social interaction (Hjarvard, 2018).

The distinction between Meyer's "mediation of religion" and Hjarvard's "mediatization of religion" may be put like this: "The mediation perspective gives priority to the forms of *religion*, while the mediatization approach gives priority to the forms of *media*... In a mediation perspective, [the] transformation of religion is seen from inside the mediation practices of the actual religion, while the mediatization perspective sees transformations of religion from outside, through the media-saturated environment" (Lundby, 2013, p. 200).

Charismatic Catholicism in Latin America

The Catholic Church has played a major role in the development of Latin American culture since the arrival of the Spanish and Portuguese colonizers. Nearly 4 in 10 Catholics in the world live in Latin America. Francis is the first pope in history to come from the continent. However, affiliation and identification with Catholicism are declining (Wormald, 2014). Jesús Martín-Barbero, the Columbian scholar of communication and culture, noted, at the end of the 1990s, that Catholicism was no longer the religiosity of the less favored, of "the urban masses, the youth, and the popular classes" (1997, pp. 112–114).

Inspired by Martín-Barbero's pioneering work on "mediations" as countercultural communications against hegemonic power (1993), Latin American scholars adapted the mediatization of religion theory to fit their situation. Catholic communication researchers in Brazil were particularly active in this effort (e.g. Gomes, 2017). Martino (2013) stresses that in Latin America the mediatization of religion "cannot be understood outside the political conflicts and instabilities of the region" (p. 21). A total of 6 in 10 Brazilians are Catholics (Wormald, 2014, p. 14). Because of its size, Brazil is the country with the largest Catholic population. New Protestant charismatic Pentecostalism has been on the rise, and since the 1980s the hegemonic Catholic Church in Brazil has "lost visibility to its mediatized Pentecostal competitors, which had diligently invested in media communication" (Martino, 2013, p. 50).

There is also a considerable Catholic charismatic movement in Brazil, imported from the United States, and accepted by the Vatican (Cleary, 2011). This predominantly lay movement was reluctantly accepted by the bishops in Brazil in order to compete with the more commercialized Protestant Pentecostalism (Chesnut, 2010). The Catholic version, in contrast, connects the charismatic expressions to the eucharist and the Virgin Mary. However, their preaching and gatherings are just as mediatized. "Singing-priests" such as Marcelo Rossi in São Paulo, have been particularly successful (Preston et al., 2019). Rossi's position is built on charismatic authority, his own interpretations of Catholicism, and his ability to handle the media and create shows (Martino, 2013, pp. 83, 100–101). "His mass celebrations were like any pop music festival" (p. 37).

Latin American scholars have long been active in developing their own understanding of mediatization theory in encounters with European colleagues (Scolari et al., 2021). Eliseo Verón (e.g. 2014) is a key reference for the alternative Latin American effort (Scolari & Rodríguez-Amat, 2018). Verón goes as far back in history as Krotz (2009), with mediatization being a process that has existed since the beginning of humanity, when humans used the first tools for communication. Verón (2008) opposes Hjarvard's restriction of mediatization to high modern societies. He applies a semiotic and anthropological perspective on the human capability of semiosis, of making meaning by signs. The semiotic capacity of humans is expressed in what Verón (2014) calls "mediatic phenomena," material devices through which to externalize mental processes, that is, media phenomena, stone tools first. New technologies later allowed for new mediatic phenomena. Mediatization is, thus, "just the name for the long historical sequence of mediatic phenomena being institutionalized in human societies" (p. 3).

This conceptualization, institutionalized as mediatization, is quite different from the European-based institutional approach. The Latin American take proves useful in a study of those Pentecostal individuals who leave institutional Churches, but who remain charismatic in their own way (Souza & Matos, 2017). Many Pentecostals seek to defend conservative morals in activist political participation outside the Churches. "The evolution of Pentecostal semiosis is part of the growing ... interpenetration [of] mediatization logics" with digital media. In that way, "the Pentecostal mediatization arrive[s] at a stage in which the institutions depend on" the logics "of this new ambience" (p. 50). Perhaps the distance between institutional and mediatic approaches to mediatization is not that great?

Conclusion

These case studies from around the world all illustrate that institutional religious traditions are shaped in encounters with modern media, which they have to rely on for their communication in contemporary society. "Mediatization," and the competing concepts of "mediation," the "social shaping of technology," and "mediatic" phenomena, all try to capture the transformative power of technological media on communication in human collectives. With the modern media, all cases in this chapter relate to modernity. The limitation to twentieth-century European high modernity in Hjarvard's initial institutional theory of mediatization (2008) is not necessary. Countries in the global East and South each have their own form of modernity. Liberalization of a country's media system stimulates mediatization. However, China demonstrates that mediatization in authoritarian states may occur within a combination of advanced media technology and state control.

Religious traditions are cultural systems. With the mediatization of religion, individuals, groups, and institutions mix and rearrange traditional elements from "world religions" and redistribute them through modern media. The institutional approach to the mediatization of religion captures the transformative capacity of mediated communication that is based in religious traditions. This applies to the global East and South, as well as to the global North. The cases in this chapter, however, help to adjust the institutional approach by giving closer attention to the specific religious communication with the divine in the traditions that are studied here. The forms of mediatized religion vary, not just with the kind of modernity, but also with the conception of the religious.

References

Berger, P. L., & Luckmann, T. (1966). *The social construction of reality. A treatise in the sociology of knowledge.* Anchor Books.

Bigelow, A. (2016). Islam. In L. Woodhead, C. Partridge, & H. Kawanami (Eds.), *Religions in the modern world. Traditions and transformations* (pp. 237–276). Routledge.

Blondheim, M. (2015). The Jewish communication tradition and its encounters with (the) new media. In H. A. Campbell (Ed.), *Digital Judaism: Jewish negotiations with digital media and culture* (pp. 16–39). Routledge.

Blondheim, M., & Katz, E. (2016). Religion, communications, and Judaism: The case of digital chabad. *Media, Culture & Society, 38*(1), 89–95. https://doi.org/10.1177/0163443715615417

Bongmba, E. K. (Ed.). (2012). *The Wiley-Blackwell companion to African religions.* Wiley-Blackwell.

Bunt, G. R. (2009). *iMuslims: Rewiring the house of Islam.* The University of North Carolina Press.

Campbell, H. A. (2010). *When religion meets new media.* Routledge.

Cantwell, C., & Kawanami, H. (2016). Buddhism. In L. Woodhead, C. Partridge, & H. Kawanami (Eds.), *Religions in the modern world. Traditions and transformations* (pp. 73–112). Routledge.

Chesnut, R. A. (2010). Conservative Christian competitors: Pentecostals and charismatic Catholics in Latin America's new religious economy. *SAIS Review of International Affairs, 30*(1), 91–103. https://www.jstor.org/stable/27000213

Cleary, E. L. (2011). *The rise of charismatic Catholicism in Latin America.* University Press of Florida.

Cohen, Y. (2012). *God, Jews and the media: religion and Israel's media.* Routledge.

Cohen, Y. (2017). The media challenge to haredi rabbinic authority in Israel. *ESSACHESS. Journal for Communication Studies, 10*(2), 113–128. https://ssrn.com/abstract=3124458

Couldry, N. (2014). When mediatization hits the ground. In F. Krotz, & A. Hepp (Eds.), *Mediatized worlds: Culture and society in a media age* (pp. 54–71). Palgrave.

Couldry, N. (2021). Deep mediatization. Media institutions' changing relation to the social. In L. A. Lievrouw, & B. D. Loader (Eds.), *Routledge handbook of digital media and communication* (pp. 257–267). Routledge.

Couldry, N., & Hepp, A. (2017). *The mediated construction of reality*. Polity.

Couldry, N., & Mejias, U. A. (2019). *The costs of connection. How data is colonizing human life and appropriating it for capitalism*. Stanford University Press.

Eckel, M. D. (2005). Buddhism. In M. D. Coogan (Ed.), *Eastern religions. Origins, beliefs, practices, holy texts, sacred places* (pp. 110–211). Oxford University Press.

Eisenlohr, P. (2017). Reconsidering mediatization of religion: Islamic televangelism in India. *Media, Culture & Society, 39*(6), 869–884. https://doi.org/10.1177/0163443716679032

Eisenstein, E. L. (1979). *The printing press as an agent of change: Communications and cultural transformations in early-modern Europe*. Cambridge University Press.

Engelstad, F., Larsen, H., Rogstad, J., & Steen-Johnsen, K. (2017). Introduction: The public sphere in change: Institutional perspectives on neo-corporatist society. In F. Engelstad, H. Larsen, J. Rogstad, & K. Steen-Johnsen (Eds.), *Institutional change in the public sphere: Views on the Nordic model* (pp. 1–21). De Gruyter Open.

Ferraris, F. (2012). Narratives of "return"? Travels to Punjab in the contemporary transnational Sikhscape. In K. A. Jacobsen, & K. Myrvold (Eds.), *Sikhs across borders: Transnational practices of European Sikhs* (pp. 87–104). Bloomsbury.

Giddens, A. (1984). *The constitution of society: Outline of the theory of structuration*. Polity Press.

Golan, O., & Stadler, N. (2016). Building the sacred community online: The dual use of the internet by Chabad. *Media, Culture & Society, 38*(1), 71–88. https://doi.org/10.1177/0163443715615415

Gomes, P. G. (2017). *From media to mediatization. An evolving concept*. Editora Unisinos.

Grieve, G. P., Helland, C., & Singh, R. (2019). Digitizing Tibet. A critical Buddhist reconditioning of Hjarvard's mediatization theory. In K. Radde-Antweiler, & X. Zeiler (Eds.), *Mediatized religion in Asia. Studies on digital media and religion* (pp. 139–161). Routledge.

Hepp, A. (2020). *Deep mediatization*. Routledge.

Hepp, A., Breiter, A., Hasebrink, U. (Eds.). (2018). Communicative figurations: Transforming communications on times of deep mediatization. In Hasebrink, U., & Hepp, A. (Eds.), *Transforming communications – Studies in cross-media research* (Vol. 1). Palgrave Macmillan. http://library.oapen.org/handle/20.500.12657/27916

Herbert, D. (2011). Why has religion gone public again? Towards a theory of media and religious re-publicization. In G. Lynch, J. Mitchell, & A. Strhan (Eds.), *Religion, media and culture: A reader* (pp. 89–97). Routledge.

Hew, W. W. (2019). On-offline dakwah: Social media and Islamic preaching in Malaysia and Indonesia. In K. Radde-Antweiler, & X. Zeiler (Eds.), *Mediatized religion in Asia. Studies on digital media and religion* (pp. 89–104). Routledge.

Hjarvard, S. (2008). The mediatization of society. A theory of the media as agents of social and cultural change. *Nordicom Review, 29*(2), 105–134. https://doi.org/10.1515/nor-2017-0181

Hjarvard, S. (2011). The mediatization of religion: Theorizing religion, media and social change. *Culture and Religion, 12*(2), 119–135.

Hjarvard, S. (2012). Three forms of mediatized religion: Changing the public face of religion. In S. Hjarvard, & M. Lövheim (Eds.), *Mediatization and religion. Nordic perspectives* (pp. 21–44). Nordicom.

Hjarvard, S. (2013). *The mediatization of culture and society*. Routledge.

Hjarvard, S. (2014a). From mediation to mediatization: The institutionalization of new media. In F. Krotz, & A. Hepp (Eds.), *Mediatized worlds: Culture and society in a media age* (pp. 123–139). Palgrave.

Hjarvard, S. (2014b). Mediatization and cultural and social change: An institutional perspective. In K. Lundby (Ed.), *Mediatization of communication* (pp. 199–226). De Gruyter Mouton.

Hjarvard, S. (2018). The logics of the media and the mediatized conditions of social interaction. In C. Thimm, M. Anastasiadis, & J. Einspänner-Pflock (Eds.), *Media logic(s) revisited. Modelling the interplay between media institutions, media technology and societal change* (pp. 63–84). Palgrave Macmillan.

Ho, W.-Y. (2019). Religious mediatization with Chinese characteristics. Subaltern voices of Chinese Muslim youths. In K. Radde-Antweiler, & X. Zeiler (Eds.), *Mediatized religion in Asia. Studies on digital media and religion* (pp. 39–52). Routledge.

Jakobsh, D. R. (2015). Marking the female Sikh body: Reformulating and legitimating Sikh women's turbaned identity on the world wide web. In K. A. Jacobsen, & K. Myrvold Eds., *Young Sikhs in a global world. Negotiating traditions, identities and authorities.* [first published 2015 by Ashgate] (125–148). Routledge.

Jodhka, S. S., & Myrvold, K. (2015). Sikhism and its changing social structure. In B. Turner, & O. Salemink (Eds.), *Routledge handbook of religions in Asia* (pp. 63–75). Routledge.

Kotliar, D. M. (2020). Data orientalism: On the algorithmic construction of the non-western other. *Theory and Society, 49*(5–6), 919–939. https://doi.org/10.1007/s11186-020-09404-2

Krotz, F. (2009). Mediatization: A concept with which to grasp media and societal change. In K. Lundby (Ed.), *Mediatization: Concept, changes, consequences* (pp. 21–40). Peter Lang.

Krotz, F. (2014). Mediatization as a mover in modernity: Social and cultural change in the context of media change. In K. Lundby (Ed.), *Mediatization of communication* (pp. 131–161). De Gruyter Mouton.

Kunin, S. D. (2016). Judaism. In L. Woodhead, C. Partridge, & H. Kawanami (Eds.), *Religions in the modern world. Traditions and transformations* (pp. 173–206). Routledge.

Lövheim, M. (2014). Mediatization and religion. In K. Lundby (Ed.), *Mediatization of communication* (pp. 547–570). De Gruyter Mouton.

Lövheim, M., & Hjarvard, S. (2019). The mediatized conditions of contemporary religion: Critical status and future directions. *Journal of Religion, Media & Digital Culture, 8*(2), 206–225. https://doi.org/10.1163/21659214-00802002

Lundby, K. (2009). *Mediatization: Concept, changes, consequences.* Peter Lang.

Lundby, K. (2013). Media and the transformations of religion. In K. Lundby (Ed.), *Religion across media: From early antiquity to late modernity* (pp. 185–201). Peter Lang.

Lundby, K. (2014). Mediatization of communication. In K. Lundby (Ed.), *Mediatization of communication* (pp. 3–37). De Gruyter Mouton.

Lundby, K. (2017). Public religion in mediatized transformations. In F. Engelstad, H. Larsen, J. Rogstad, & K. Steen-Johnsen (Eds.), *Institutional change in the public sphere: Views on the Nordic model* (pp. 241–263). De Gruyter Open.

Mann, G. S. (2016). Sikhism. In L. Woodhead, C. Partridge, & H. Kawanami (Eds.), *Religions in the modern world: Traditions and transformations* (pp. 113–142). Routledge.

Martín-Barbero, J. (1993). *Communication, culture and hegemony: From the media to the mediations.* Sage.

Martín-Barbero, J. (1997). Mass media as a site of resacralization of contemporary cultures. In S. M. Hoover, & K. Lundby (Eds.), *Rethinking media, religion, and culture* (pp. 102–116). Sage Publications.

Martino, L. M. S. (2013). *The mediatization of religion: When faith rocks.* Ashgate.

Meyer, B. (2004). "Praise the Lord": Popular cinema and Pentecostalite style in Ghana's new public sphere. *American Ethnologist, 31*(1), 92–110. https://doi.org/10.1525/ae.2004.31.1.92

Meyer, B. (2009). From imagined communities to aesthetic formations: Religious mediations, sensational forms, and styles of binding. In B. Meyer (Ed.), *Aesthetic formations: Media, religion, and the senses* (pp. 1–28). Palgrave Macmillan.

Meyer, B. (2012). Christianity in Africa: From African independent to Pentecostal-charismatic churches. In E. K. Bongmba (Ed.), *The Wiley-Blackwell companion to African religions* (pp. 153–170). Wiley-Blackwell.

Meyer, B. (2013). Material mediations and religious practices of world-making. In K. Lundby (Ed.), *Religion across media. From early antiquity to late modernity* (pp. 1–18). Peter Lang.

Meyer, B., & Moors, A. (2006). Introduction. In B. Meyer, & A. Moors (Eds.), *Religion, media, and the public sphere* (pp. 1–25). Indiana University Press.

Myrvold, K. (2018). Visualizing Sikh warriors, royalties, and rebels. In K. A. Jacobsen, & K. Myrvold (Eds.), *Religion and technology in India: Spaces, practices and authorities* (pp. 43–74). Routledge.

Nesbitt, E. (2016). *Sikhism: A very short introduction* (2nd ed.). Oxford University Press.

Obadia, L. (2015). Buddhism. Modernization or globalization? In B. S. Turner, & O. Salemink (Eds.), *Routledge handbook of religions in Asia* (pp. 343–358). Routledge.

Preston, P., Mariz, C., & Carranza, B. (2019). Charismatic movement. In G. Ritzer, & C. Rojek (Eds.), *The Blackwell encyclopedia of sociology* (pp. 1–5). Wiley-Blackwell.

Prohl, I. (2020). Branding and/as religion. The case of Buddhist related images, semantics, and designs. In T. Brox, & E. Williams-Oerberg (Eds.), *Buddhism and business: Merit, material wealth, and morality in the global market economy* (pp. 111–127). University of Hawai'i Press.

Radde-Antweiler, K. (2019). Religion as communicative figurations – Analyzing religion in times of deep mediatization. In K. Radde-Antweiler, & X. Zeiler (Eds.), *Mediatized religion in Asia: Studies on digital media and religion* (pp. 211–223). Routledge.

Said, E. W. (1995). *Orientalism: Western conceptions of the Orient* (Originally published 1978). Penguin Books.

Schulz, W. (2004). Reconstructing mediatization as an analytical concept. *European Journal of Communication, 19*(1), 87–101. https://doi.org/10.1177/0267323104040696

Scolari, C. A., Fernández, J. L., & Rodríguez-Amat, J. R. (Eds.). (2021). *Mediatization(s): Theoretical conversations between Europe and Latin America.* Intellect Books.

Scolari, C. A., & Rodríguez-Amat, J. R. (2018). A Latin American approach to mediatization: Specificities and contributions to a global discussion about how the media shape contemporary societies. *Communication Theory, 28*(2), 131–154.

Setianto, Y. P. (2015). Mediatization of religion: How the Indonesian Muslim diasporas mediatized Islamic practices. *Journal of Media and Religion, 14*(4), 230–244. https://doi.org/10.1080/15348423.2015.1116268

Souza, C. R. P. D., & Matos, D. C. D. A. R. (2017). Between no churched and cyber Pentecostals: Religious *modus vivendi* in the society under mediatization. *ESSACHESS. Journal for Communication Studies, 10*(2), 33–51 https://papers.ssrn.com/sol3/papers.cfm?abstract_id=3124418.

Tsuria, R., & Campbell, H. A. (2019). Understanding Jewish digital media in Israel: Between technological affordances and religious-cultural uses. In K. Radde-Antweiler, & X. Zeiler (Eds.), *Mediatized religion in Asia: Studies on digital media and religion* (pp. 190–207). Routledge.

Valibeigi, N. (2019). Being religious through social networks: Representation of religious identity of Shia Iranians on Instagram. In K. Radde-Antweiler, & X. Zeiler (Eds.), *Mediatized religion in Asia: Studies on digital media and religion* (pp. 165–189). Routledge.

Verón, E. (2008). Mediatización de la política: Estrategias, actores y construcción de colectivos. In A. Mercier (Ed.), *La comunicación política* (pp. 63–72). La Crujía.

Verón, E. (2014). Mediatization theory: A semio-anthropological perspective and some of its consequences. *MATRIZes, 8*(1), 1–8.

Wormald, B. (2014). Religion in Latin America: Widespread change in a historically Catholic region. Pew Research Center. Retrieved April 1, 2022, from https://www.pewforum.org/2014/11/13/religion-in-latin-america

Zuboff, S. (2019). *The age of surveillance capitalism: The fight for a human future at the new frontier of power.* Profile Books.

Selected Readings

Couldry, N., & Hepp, A. (2017). *The mediated construction of reality.* Polity.

Eisenlohr, P. (2017). Reconsidering mediatization of religion: Islamic televangelism in India. *Media, Culture & Society, 39*(6), 869–884.

Hjarvard, S. (2013). *The mediatization of culture and society.* Routledge.

Lövheim, M., & Hjarvard, S. (2019). The mediatized conditions of contemporary religion: Critical status and future directions. *Journal of Religion, Media & Digital Culture, 8*(2), 206–225.

Radde-Antweiler, K., & Zeiler, X. (Eds.). (2019). *Mediatized religion in Asia. Studies on digital media and religion.* Routledge.

Scolari, C. A., Fernández, J. L., & Rodríguez-Amat, J. R. (Eds.). (2021). *Mediatization(s). Theoretical conversations between Europe and Latin America.* Intellect Books.

19

Reporting Religion News

Yoel Cohen

Religion news coverage in Western countries goes back to the first half of the nineteenth century, when changes in printing resulted in the rise of the mass circulation press. In the United States, the penny papers, which began in the 1830s, redefined news as daily reporting of events rather than mere commentary. In the redesigned newsroom with specialist reporters, one covered the churches. Scandals in the churches were part and parcel of news. In the past, journalism, in covering religion, sought to deal with the "challenge" of religion by regarding it as private matter. Much of the news in Western countries was local church news, with the press little inclined to critique religious leaders and institutions, or church doctrine. By the mid-twentieth century, Church public relations – mirroring the steady development of government public relations (see Chapter 12) – also took on an organizational dimension. The second half of the twentieth century showed a trend in Western countries for appointing specialist religion reporters, sometimes ex-church figures rather than professional journalists, who moved from general reporting to become specialist religion reporters. An overall decline in deference to authority in contemporary Western society has also affected religion, with the temptation to write candidly without reservation both about religious institutions and those at the helm, as well as about nonconformist trends such as new religious movements. Much religious news is secondary to a bigger nonreligious story, for example, politics or conflict. Moreover, of the small amount of raw religion coverage, not a little is superficial, and comprises more soft, human interest stories, as, for example, a story about a defrocked priest.

Much of the religion content focuses on the monotheistic faiths, and then mostly Christianity. Until the turn of this century, little content on Islam existed. Nonmonotheistic faiths – Hinduism, Buddhism – remain little covered in the Western press. By contrast stories on Hinduism and Buddhism do appear in the Asian press. For example, in the Indian media, Hinduism is a regular news subject (Kumar, 2003, 2018); and in the Japanese media, Buddhism and Shintoism are covered as culture stories, with little intentional bias against religion – rather, it is the ignorance of some reporters and lack of coverage itself that distorts the image of many religious people and religious communities.

One useful survey pointing to trends in religion news content came from Garrett-Medill (1999). A wide content analysis, it examined 2349 religion stories in newspapers, news magazines, national television, and local television in the United States, for the period October 1998 to April 1999. It did not include new media in the analysis so the results are only relevant to the traditional media. In the section on daily newspapers, which covered the *New York Times*, *Chicago Tribune* (both quality papers), and *Chicago Sun-Times* and *USA Today* (both

The Handbook on Religion and Communication, First Edition. Edited by Yoel Cohen and Paul A. Soukup.
© 2023 John Wiley & Sons Ltd. Published 2023 by John Wiley & Sons Ltd.

popular papers), the coverage overwhelmingly leaned toward monotheistic faiths: 59% of religion content in the daily newspapers dealt with Christianity, perhaps expected given that it is the dominant faith in America. Twenty percent of the coverage was of Judaism and 14% of Islam (both New York as well as Chicago have Jewish and Muslim communities of significant sizes), but only 2% for Hinduism, 2% for Buddhism, and 3% for other religions. In terms of national television (the evening news on US network television, ABC, CBS, and NBC) 64% of coverage concerned Christianity, 27% Judaism, and 9% Islam (Buddhism, Hinduism, others = 0%).

The latter half of the twentieth century brought about certain changes in religion news. With a decline in church attendances in Western Europe, as well as to a lesser degree in the United States, there was a reduction in news interest in religious institutions but an increase in interest in spirituality and religious values. This reflected the individual's quest and longing for tracing their roots and origin, and a desire to control personal destiny.

In the United States, an early study of 30 newspapers in 1982 found that a twofold increase in the number of newspapers in the United States gave more than 100 column inches to religion news each week, from 27% to 59% more than the previous decade (Dart & Allen, 1993). And in television, the ABC network was the first US television network to hire, in the 1990s, a full-time religion reporter, reflecting news interest in the subject. Individual radio stations followed suit, including National Public Radio. This has increased further in the age of the Internet, which is characterized by its interactive, and antihierarchical, nature.

Any discussion of religion news must take account of niche religious media, particularly given the limitations of the broad news media in covering religion. In the United States, noteworthy denominational publications include *Christianity Today* and the *National Catholic Reporter*. The denominational publications have developed parallel news websites. The Eternal World Network and Christian Broadcast Network (CBN) are television stations geared toward Roman Catholic and evangelical Christians, respectively.

The central, but sometimes "disguised role" that news agencies play in newsgathering is also true in religion news as wholesalers of news to newspapers, radio and tv stations, and news websites. In addition to religion coverage by mainstream news agencies like Associated Press (AP), Reuters, and Agence France Presse (AFP), as well as smaller agencies like Deutsches Press Alles (DPA), the Italian ANSA, and the Japanese Kydo agency – each of which covers religion alongside the rest of the news – other news agencies focus solely upon religion. Religion News Service covers the breadth of religions, while others focus upon a particular faith including Catholic News Service, the Catholic UCA Asia agency, the Jewish Telegraphic Agency (JTA), and the International Islam News Agency (IINA). These have correspondents, full time or part time, stationed in key religion capitals around the world, for example, Vatican City, Jerusalem, Mecca, etc. Some are independent; others are supported by faith institutions themselves, which raises questions about their editorial independence. Economic cuts have resulted in uncertainty in the denominational media, with Ecumenical News and Lutheran News Service closing.

In discussing religion news coverage, this chapter seeks to assess the subject from an international, comparative perspective. It will discuss the question of defining religion news; the background of journalists in covering religion; news sources for religion news; audience interest in religion news; and how new media change the manner in which religion is covered. Much of the quantitative research about religion and news has been carried out in the United States, reflecting how young the media–religion academic discipline is; this is necessarily also reflected in the discussion here.

Defining Religion News

In examining religion news, the initial question arises of whether the media's image reflects the reality of the religious event. For journalists, deciding whether something is news seems a matter of intuition – fresh, unpublished, interesting, or important, preferably all. But academic researchers define only a few happenings about religion in the world at any moment of the day as news. First, we must identify which news values underly the journalist's choice about an event and become news, and which do not. The news medium itself is a determinant. Television coverage of religion, for example, emphasizes visuals: religious buildings or shrines, symbols and practices, and people in religious dress.

Media researchers think about news criteria, going back to Galtung and Ruge's 1965 exploratory study. But to this day no single all-embracing theory of religious news values exists. The theory of Galtung and Ruge (1965) rested on examining coverage of international conflicts in the foreign press. They explained news as foreign events comprising at least one of three criteria: events culturally proximate to an audience; events about elites; and news about conflict or social breakdown. Building on this, religion is culturally proximate. Religion news of events closer – or, more "proximate" – to a religion of the audience will have a greater chance of being defined as news than less proximate ones.

Some of the hypotheses have become the basis for not a few theories about general news making. Richardson and Introvigne (2007), in discussing the role of ideology as a news factor, emphasize what interests the public audience. This raises the question of the proximity of ideology to theology. Westerstahl and Johansson (1994) argue that ideologies provide the main source of deviations in news reporting from objective criteria (pp. 168–169). Moreover, the media's role in legitimizing those in political power could translate into the media's role in legitimizing the power of religious organization, and their heads, or even indeed religious doctrine itself.

There are other factors in newsgathering, which apply no less to religion news than to other categories, like access for reporters, and events occurring in the space between issues of a newspaper or news bulletin, but this matters less in the age of nonstop news on the Internet.

Events include religious holy days. A "high" of religious proximity of events includes religious festivals – "calendar journalism." Examining religion news in Nordic countries 1988–2008, Niemalä and Christensen (2013) found that much of the religion reportage occurred during religious holy days, notably Christmas but also Easter and Eid at the end of Ramadan. Overall, they found more articles on religion at festival time in Iceland, Finland, and Norway than in Denmark and Sweden – the latter two countries are more secular. And, analyzing Israeli media coverage of the Jewish faith, which itself is characterized by a rich annual cycle of festivals and fasts, Cohen (2018a) found that the mainstream media coverage of holy days has a strong consumerist character, with little spiritual content, as distinct from the religious media; this meant that secular Israelis, drawing information about religion from the media rather than from formal religious institutions, had an image of the holy days somewhat distant from the original theology. A comparison between press coverage and Internet coverage did not show much difference, though the convergence of print, visual, and sound might have led to the expectation that coverage would have been greater on the Internet than in the printed press. Moore (1994) argued that commercialism has played an important part in the growth of Christianity itself in the United States.

The annual five-day pilgrimage of the Hajj – to Mecca and Medina in Saudi Arabia – marks the climax of the Muslim calendar. Its coverage is limited mostly to religion reporters from the Muslim faith, given that non-Muslims are prohibited by *sharia* from entering the two cities of

Islam. Physically demanding – particularly when the pilgrimage is held in the summer – coverage often depends on the reporter's feature reporting prior to, or following, the Hajj. The Kumkbh Mela festival at Madhya Pradesh features no less than 18 press centers, with state-of-the-art media technology for the press, radio, TV, and web reporters. With numerous Hindu religious organizations in attendance, together with a host of gurus and saints of one type or another, the reporter's visit goes well beyond witnessing and covering the Holy Dip to also engaging Brahmins, the Hindu priestly class. Yet some traditions in Hinduism occur in sacred privacy, necessarily distant from the eyes of enquiring journalists.

Religious elites – whether defined as individuals like leading clerics or as religious institutions – are more likely to be defined as newsworthy than lesser souls or less significant institutions. The criterion of elites as newsworthy is present in religion less in terms of interest in hierarchical figures in religious institutions, and more in terms of scandals, involving religious clerics "falling from grace." Audiences and reporters find a certain satisfaction in seeing those who claim to be holy failing to live up to the religious vow. Sex may appear to be a vital ingredient in the popular media. But over the past two decades the Catholic Church's crisis involving the molestation of thousands of children by priests has become a permanent news story of far greater proportions generating not only shock but even calling into question the authority of the Church itself. Beginning as a story in the Boston area covered by the *Boston Globe* in 2002, it developed to other areas in the United States, and eventually in other Western countries, with journalists appealing to the courts for records to be opened, and inviting readers to tell the newspaper accounts of their molestation as children. The newspaper published some 900 news stories in the first two years (Robinson, 2003). When the US Conference of Catholic Bishops held its annual meeting – an event that normally drew only 75 religion reporters – 700 media people attended. But the Church's failure to deal with the matter only exacerbated matters. Dixon (2004) argues that rather than seeking to repair its image, the Church was far more concerned with maintaining its authority over congregants, and with silencing efforts that threatened its orthodoxy and authority.

Conflict, crisis, socio-religious breakdown, the unusual, and interruption – criteria in determining news interest – occur in theological disputes. The story often lies in the conflicts or in the leaders or in the margin. Theological disputes include those paralleled outside a formal religious framework, and those in broader society. For example, disputes about the ordination of women or religious attitudes to sexuality mirror disputes in wider society about the status of women and alternative sexuality, respectively. Of course, religion sometimes plays a minor role in a general nonreligious story, like one on international conflict or politics. According to the Garrett-Medill survey (1999), 62, 42, 34, and 16% of religion stories on national or local US television, and in US daily newspapers, and news magazines, respectively, dealt with international conflicts in which religion was the secondary story. Similarly, 19, 18, 17, and 8% of religion coverage in fact primarily addressed politics in US newspapers, news magazines, national TV, and local TV respectively. And 13% of religion stories on US local TV were in fact about crime, with religion as a secondary story.

Longer-term religion processes, occurring outside the schedule of a newspaper or a news bulletin, are far more difficult to register. Faith and religious activity are less observed, and therefore less defined as news. Yet O'Neill and Harcup (2009) term these alternative media, and sought to go behind the events themselves to the processes of news, including in the case of religion, new religious trends, discussions of doctrine, and state–religious relations.

Unlike other news categories, religion news has its own special characteristics as a news theme because it rests on the spiritual and not solely on the rational. How is the infinite, the spirit, communicable? It reflects more generally a delayed recognition in the mass media discipline – itself characterized like all social sciences as purely scientific and secular in orientation; media studies has taken time to incorporate such nonrational elements as belief and spirituality into its schema. When religion takes a prominent place in a country's agenda, the news media often see this as an indication of a backward society. So, unlike other categories of news reporting, religion reporting faces an unresolved dilemma: news reporters require objectivity and rationality, and therefore fail to broach the question of the fabric of belief.

For example, consider a 1995 incident in India in which the Hindu deity Ganesha, one of the most loved of the Hindu gods, reportedly began to drink milk offered by devotees. The Reuters report of the incident carried the headline, "Idol drinks milk in Indian miracle scene." But the media faced the dual dilemma of reporting a news event that was called a "miracle" and that was (for many Western countries) in a minority religious tradition. For example, in editing the story, Canada's *Globe & Mail* altered the headline to read, "Milk slurping statue real to many Indians." Reuters itself alluded to the dilemma by headlining subsequent reports, "Rumors of milk drinking Hindu idols sweep India," and "Miracle reports in Hindu gods sweep India." Religion challenges the image of a secular reality held by many media workers. Where religion holds a central place in a particular society, news of the religion will be covered professionally or close to it. But where it is a minority religion (like Hinduism in the West), it receives attention only if it is bizarre or controversial (Mann, 2015).

"Framing" provides a structure to understand an event, suggesting cognitive and interpretive patterns, attempting to make meaning of an event and analyze its perceived causes. Frames help reduce complex issues to simpler terms; this influences the way an audience understands the issues behind an event. However, a frame employed by journalists may be deceptive because it implies a rational pattern, and the media frame may not truly reflect the event on the ground. Bisha and Ruge-Jones (2005) compare journalists' framing to a pastor's sermon. Both seek to frame their topics so that the audience understands the message. "Frames can be located in the communicator (the way you see the issue addressed in the Sunday's sermon), the text (the script of the sermon), the receiver (the pre-existing conceptions of members of the congregations), and the culture of the prevailing views on the issue in current ideology, and values etc." (p. 18). This, in turn, improves the chances that the audience will understand the news and that the religious body's interpretation will become the accepted one in the news. However, a journalist lacking knowledge of religious issues is very likely to report the event in the context of religious identity, a religious organization, or religious doctrine. In examining religion news, an initial question is whether the media's image reflects the reality of the event. The Garrett-Medill survey (1999), found that only one-third of religion stories in US news media (newspapers, news magazines, national TV) and only one-quarter of US local TV provided context to reports.

While news values have free rein in Western societies that value freedom of the press, this is not the case in other societies. Only an estimated one-third of countries have a totally free media in the Western tradition, but in other countries news values determining news content face governmental intervention and control. Since the collapse of the Soviet Union and its allied states in 1989–1990, the number of states that control news media has gone down, but many, most notably, China, North Korea, and Cuba, continue to restrict reporting. Many states, especially in the developing world, experience governmental controls of different sorts. In newly developing countries, the media not only report the news but take on a proactive role in national development, including influencing religion news reporting.

China, still characterized by an atheist ideology with religion regarded as backward and even antirevolutionary, does permit coverage of religion today, as long as it does not discriminate or insult people with religious beliefs, on the one hand, and does not encourage religious extremism, on the other hand. This necessarily affects the way religion news is reported in China. Examining religion content from 1996 to 2005 in *People's Daily*, the organ of the Communist Party, Yao and Liu (2018) found of 4749 articles, 19.1% framed religion as intolerant, 14% framed religion as politically active (something forbidden in China), and only 7.5% framed it as law-abiding. Yet websites and blogs by religious clerics, notably representing Islam and Buddhism, have flourished.

In the postcommunist period, from 1989, Russia has treated religion news more favorably. A 2015 decision of the Russian Parliament called upon journalists to provide greater coverage of religion inside Russia and abroad. Television is the main source of religion news. But there is little public interest in religion news owing to the communist era when religious activity was forbidden. And to the extent there is, it is mostly sensational news. With the Russian Orthodox Church an intrinsic part of Russian identity, the focus of coverage is on that Church, with far less coverage of other branches of Christianity. There is limited coverage of Islam, Buddhism, and Judaism.

Journalists: Religious Knowledge and Religion Background

Many have noted a perceived lack of religious knowledge among reporters (as distinct from specialized religion reporters) leading to superficiality and errors in reporting religion-related developments. Winston and Green (2015) found that less than one-fifth of all US journalists polled said they were "very knowledgeable" about religion, and 50% said that a major challenge was a lack of knowledge of religion. Such a lack of knowledge means that the reporter cannot provide a nuanced picture of moral, ethical, and value-laden religious elements. As one journalist-turned-priest, Christopher Landau, put it: "A lack of literacy that would be unacceptable in relation to politics or business is somehow tolerated when it comes to religion – which might make sense if religion news never made it onto mainstream outlets, but while it does, crass mistakes are potentially embarrassing" (Landau, 2012, p. 83).

However, many studies of journalists show that journalists are no less religious than the rest of their nation, having basic religious beliefs. Underwood (2002) found that of 422 US journalists surveyed, 73% said that religion or spirituality was "important" or "very important" in their life, 14% were indifferent, and 13% said religion was not important in their life. Underwood concluded, "it is important to recognize that today's journalists may reflect a strong religious orientation in their professional value system while not universally acknowledging their religiosity or even liking the idea that religious ideas might be operating in their work life" (p. 134). One should recognize the complicated manner in which "religion commingles with professional principles in the day to day operations of modern journalism" (p. 147).

The operations of a news organization divide between reporters ("news gatherers") and editors ("news processors"). Editors are no less important than the specialist reporters in the production of news because they act as gatekeepers, thereby influencing what events make the news pages, website, and broadcast news bulletins; the place of that news, from the front page headlines to the last page (in the case of the newspaper); and determining which items do not make it. The tension between reporters and editors is key in studying religion reporters, given the claim that news processors fail – if only as a result of limited space and air time – to give adequate weighting to the work of the religion reporters.

Key questions concerning religion reporters include background knowledge of religion, and concerns about whether a reporter's own religious background endangers journalistic objectivity. Much of the albeit limited quantitative research about religion reporters has been carried out in the US milieu. Surveying religion reporters in the US, Dart and Allen (1993) found that 76% of religion reporters agreed that religious studies were helpful in covering the religion beat and another 14% said they were essential to the job. The same survey showed that for US clergy and journalists 60% of clergy polled said that religion reporters should be actively religiously, while only 20% of journalists agreed. Buddenbaum (1988) found that only 25% of US religious reporters thought it preferable that a religious person should cover religion, 25% disagreed, and 50% were neutral. Yet there are limits. Asked whether a member of the clergy should cover it, no journalists were positive, 27% were neutral, and the remainder opposed the idea.

Buddenbaum's study of religion reporters (1988) in the United States found that only 10% reported no religious affiliation, 59% were Protestant, 21% were Roman Catholic, 6% other Christian traditions, 2% Jewish, and none from Islam. Only 2% were from other religions outside the Judeo-Christian faith. The 9/11 attacks underlined the relative lack of attention that the media in Europe and North America had given Islam. With almost no religion reporter belonging to Islam, the absence was sorely felt among Western news audiences seeking to understand *jihad* or seeking more general knowledge of and information about the faith.

To explore the religious beliefs of journalists worldwide, the Worlds of Journalism Project (2011) gathered data from 67 countries. Using an identical questionnaire made it possible to produce a precise picture of the issues. With the exception of Ireland, the majority of journalists in all West European countries, for example, reported possessing no religion or denomination. For example, 74% of journalists in Spain, 70% of journalists in Belgium, 61% in the UK, and 51% in Switzerland reported no religion or denomination. By contrast, some other regions showed higher levels: in Islamic countries, 99% of journalists in UAE, 82% in Indonesia, 79% in Bangladesh, 55% in Turkey, and 53% in Malaysia replied that they were Muslim. Regarding the importance of religion or religious belief, the survey found that on a scale of 5 to 1 (extremely important to not important at all) it could identify a pattern of journalists' religious belief. The mean varied between the different world regions and countries: Asia (3.98), Africa (3.6), Latin America (3.14), the United States (3.06), Europe (2.26), and Australia (2.06). Countries where religion or the religious belief of the journalist rated highest were Malawi (4.49), Sierra Leone (4.23), Malaysia (4.22), Kenya (4.19), Bhutan (4.19), and UAE (4.14). Countries rating lowest (toward "not important at all") were Switzerland (0.6), Tanzania (0.7), Ireland (2.1), Belgium (0.7), the UK (2.3), and Spain (3.4). For the related question of the influence of religious considerations on reporting (5 = extremely influential; 1 = not influential), the highest rating came from journalists in Malaysia (3.72), Bhutan (3.62), Malawi (3.44), Kenya (3.41), UAE (3.38), and Indonesia (3.02), and the lowest from Cyprus (1.24), Belgium (1.32), Canada (1.33), Switzerland (1.39), Germany (1.52), Ireland (1.55), and the Netherlands (1.70).

A reporter who specializes in a specific theme (politics, economics, defense, religion, etc.) possesses an advantage over the general reporter because of a background knowledge of the subject and a network of news sources. Like other specialists in their areas, the religion reporter can provide the background and explanation for news involving religion – a subject not adequately understood by most journalists. A news organization with its own religion reporter has a kind of religious literacy in the newsroom. Religion reporting by the specialist religion reporter often comes from a sympathetic view, given a tendency for religion reporters to be actively religious themselves. The specialist religion reporter has a singular influence in covering much of what their news outlet publishes about religion. But the absence of a religion specialist (the case with the vast majority of newsrooms) correlates with the absence of religious literacy. Several factors indicate the status of religion reporters: the employment of a religion specialist; full- or part-time employment status; the space religion stories receive; whether religion stories only run in a religion section once a week or whether they appear throughout the organization's news coverage; the autonomy enjoyed by the religion reporter; the gatekeeper; and whether the religion reporter may assign religion-related stories to other reporters in the newsroom (Cohen, 2018b).

In contrast to some other specializations in news journalism, religion has had an uncertain status in newsroom priorities. In the case of the US media, a rising religious coverage in the early twentieth century begins to decline (notably the printed press) in the last decades of the twentieth century and into the third decade of the twenty-first century, with the notable exception of the Roman Catholic Church's sex molestation scandals. The earlier period saw movement by the media away from coverage of religion news of a conflictual nature, such as Church–state relations, to an interest in longer-term trends in religious and spiritual behavior. Later, religion and belief/values sections began to appear, notably in regions with evangelical Christian communities; for example, the *Dallas Morning News* began an award-winning Faith and Values section in 1994 with five staff religion reporters and two editors, but it closed in 2007. In the third decade of the current century, smaller circulation daily papers in the United States, faced with major economic problems, began to cut the specialist religion reporter. Key US newspapers (notably the *New York Times* and *Washington Post*, and the key news agencies including AP and Reuters) had religion specialists. Appointments by the national television networks of a religion specialist at the end of the twentieth century proved to be short term. Only between 50 and 75 newspapers out of 1500 daily morning and evening papers in the United States have a full-time religion reporter (Buss, 1995; Steinfels, 1993). That few news organizations in Western countries have specialist religion reporters, and that many media systems, notably in non-Western countries, do not have financial resources for specialist reporters as a whole helps to explain the low priority religion appears to receive inside news organizations.

The developing world, South America, and parts of Africa and Asia show media interest in religion given a revival of Roman Catholicism and Pentecostal Christianity, even if limited resources in the media means they have few specialist religion reporters. In India, for example, few mainstream daily newspapers or TV news channels have specialist religion reporters, with news about religion covered by general staff/freelance reporters or correspondents. Other specialists (in crime, courts, education, politics, sports, and cinema) are responsible for religion stories related to their respective beats. Thus, the primary sources of religion-related news stories are a newspaper/news channel's own reporters/correspondents and stringers or national news agencies: Press Trust of India (PTI), United News of India (UNI), and international news agencies (Reuters, AP, Agence France Presse (AFP), Deutsche Presse Alles (DPA), and India Abroad News Service (IANS)). But there are some specialist religion reporters. The International Association of Religion Journalists (IARJ), founded by David Briggs, formerly AP's chief religion writer, has a membership of religion reporters in over 90 countries.

Another clue to the changing nature of religion news appears in its international dimension. News about religion has taken an international leap, including terrorism and conflict in the name of religion. True, Poole (2021), in an international comparative study of religion news in Australia, the UK, Canada, and Finland, showed that most religion news remained domestic, and international religion news remained a minority, but it was there and is increasing. This increased the need for foreign reporters to not only have knowledge of politics, foreign affairs, and economics but also of religion.

Source–Media Relations

Journalism is nonroutine: it is nonconformist, requiring news reporters (whether general reporters or specialists) to use creative means to gather the news. For religion news, clergy form a key source. Yet the level of openness of faith organizations to journalists remains varied. While most religions, in principle, see communication as an important goal, in order to spread the faith, the extent to which clerics are in practice open to a one-on-one dialogue with the media is often limited particularly in the case of religious groups characterized by a hierarchy. In the case of the Vatican, for example, the Roman Catholic Church was for centuries shrouded in secrecy, until the latter half of the twentieth century, when in the aftermath of Vatican II, and in particular the creation of the Pontifical Commission for Social Communication in 1964, the Vatican opened up more if only to spread the gospel outside the Church (Soukup, 2005). The level of trust that reporters have in clergy varies, but often remains lower than they have with other sources of news. The Worlds of Journalism Project (2011) found that on a 1 to 5 rating, the level of trust in religious leaders in the journalist's country rated on average only 2.59. This contrasted with 3.26 trust among journalists in the media themselves, 3.11 in the judiciary, 3.5 in the military, 3.22 in voluntary or charitable institutions, 2.86 in parliament, and 2.79 in the government. This varies from region to region. Thus, journalists' level of trust in religious leaders was lower in Western countries (2.11 in Switzerland, 2.09 in Greece) compared with some traditionally religious, non-Western countries, including Muslim countries like Indonesia (3.32) and Egypt (2.85), and strongly religious ones like Uganda 3.65 and Chile 3.15.

Audience Interest in Religion News

Editors determine what news to publish in part according to the level of interest among their audiences. Thus, in a competitive media market, religion news developments deemed not interesting will probably not pass the news threshold. Yet, precisely gauging audience interest in religion news poses difficulties. A decline in religious activity in West Europe and in North America led to a decline in religion interest. By contrast, the growth of different branches of Christianity, including Roman Catholicism and Pentecostalism in Latin America, Africa, and Asia, indicates greater audience interest in religion. We may draw a distinction in the case of any decline in religion in Western countries with a growing interest in spirituality. A 2010 poll of the US public showed that 52% said they "enjoyed keeping up a lot with religion news," and a further 35% with some religious news (Winston & Green, 2015, p. 16). A 1988 US survey showed similar results: 72% of the US public who regarded religion as important read about the subject in the press daily (Hoover et al., 1993). A 1986 BBC survey in the UK found a more predictable reaction. Asked about viewing a religious program, only 3% of highly religious viewers "switch off when a religious program appears on the tv," as compared to 48% of viewers who had "a very low religiosity." Similarly, 79% of highly religious viewers pay attention when it comes on, in contrast to 15% of those with "very low religiosity" (Svennevig et al., 1988).

Yet there was audience interest in some religious themes, and less in others. Winston and Green (2015 found that 39% of the respondents said they were interested "to a great deal" in spirituality, 37% in religion and American politics, and 31% in local church news. In contrast only 27% were interested to a great deal in religion and economy and business news; 16% in religion, arts, and entertainment, and 13% in religion and sport. In spite of the logic of journalists defining as news developments that interested their audiences, sometimes a dissonance occurred between the two sides. Thus, the 2010 US survey showed a 70% public interest in spirituality, religious experiences, and beliefs, but only 63% of journalists said that audiences prefer coverage of religious institutions, religious activities, and religious personalities (Winston & Green, 2015). In the UK, a 2008–2009 survey by Knott et al. (2013, p. 41) found that the majority of references to religion on television and in newspapers addressed conventional religion topics and 41% of the references were to common religion – to beliefs and practices associated with the supernatural. Just 3.5% referred to the secular sacred – to matters that were nonnegotiable and inviolate.

At a time of international significance, religion-related events may become a single all-encompassing subject on the news agenda. Thus, when Pope John Paul II, admired for his care and attention to the poor, the sick, and the disenfranchised, died in April 2005, Brown (2009) surveying the news in five continents with a poll of over 1700 persons, and found that 55% of people heard of the news of the death within the first 90 minutes and 69% within a four-hour period. Within eight hours, 97% of people had heard the news; 57% learned of the Pope's death from television. But 20% learned of the news from another person (Cohen, 2017), 12% from radio, and 9% from the Internet. Though the Internet may not have been the source for most people to hear the breaking news, 20% said it was the most reliable source (after television, 67%). Print media was a distant 5.5% (Brown, 2009).

The balance in reporting between the dominant religion of a country and minority religions forms another topic of investigation. Should coverage focus only on the main faith (often the official faith) or not? Examining Catholicism in the Brazilian media, do Nascimento Cunha (2021) proposes the notion of the "dominant religion," based on factors such as number of adherents, political position, privileges, and disqualification of the other results in that faith dominating the coverage. So, in the Brazilian case the media pushed other Christian groups including Pentecostalism or other religious to the margins. In research carried out in 2014 of religion content in Brazil's largest newspaper and in the news program of Globo Network, 73% of news coverage was of Christianity (Islam accounted for 19%), of which 77% concerned Catholicism. Moreover, all the articles on Catholicism were positive, whereas 82% of the articles on Islam and 72% of those on Protestant Christians were negative (do Nascimento Cunha, 2021, p. 297). A 1988 BBC study of viewing habits indicated that in the UK (where the Anglican Church is the official one, with the head of state as head of the Church) the public overwhelmingly favored equal coverage for all religions, not just Christianity (Svenning, Haldane, & Gunter, 1988, p. 56). However, when broken down by faith, Christian respondents appeared less inclined to agree (59%) in contrast to members of some of the minority religions in the UK (Hindus, 67%; Muslims, 76%; and Black Pentecostals, 80%) (Gunter & Viney, 1994, p. 93).

Should religious news be kept to religion pages and religion programs or included in the main pages? The BBC survey did not find a clear view: 40% of viewers said religion should be part of the regular coverage, in contrast to 47% who disagreed (Svenning, Haldane, & Gunter, 1988, p. 56).

Considerable dissatisfaction exists among the public with the news coverage of religion. Only 28, 32, and 36% rated the quantity of religion coverage in the US media in radio, newspapers and television, respectively, as good (Winston & Green, 2015). Similarly, the BBC survey found that while over two-thirds (74%) said that the quantity of coverage of religion coverage was "right," 19 and 2% said it was "too little" or "far too little," in contrast to 4 and 1% who said it was "too much" or "far too much." Asked to rate the level of satisfaction of religion news on a scale of 1 to 7 (with 7 being the most important) respondents to the Hoover survey (Hoover et al., 1993) found that satisfaction with the coverage of religion (4.32) was lower than with the coverage of transport (5.74), business (5.29), entertainment (5.18), education (5.00), food (4.99), health (4.76), the arts (4.67), and personal advice (4.39).

A major criticism of religion reporting alleges bias and stereotyping of religious people. Addressing this requires a distinction between intentional and unintentional bias. The former refers to a journalist attaching their own views, and the latter to the reality that in free societies characterized by freedom of the press, news coverage is not determined by an intentional desire to be balanced but rather is a product of covering interesting and important news within limited space or time. The professional standard in journalism of adhering to the principles of objectivity and accuracy and avoiding intentional bias remain cardinal if only because a journalist's superiors (editors and proprietors) demand it of journalistic employees. Much of the basis in religion reporting is of the second type.

The most frequent and most researched case of bias concerns the coverage in the West of Islam (e.g., Ahmed & Matthes, 2017; Ewart & O'Donnell, 2018; Pearson, 2017; Pintak & Franklin, 2013; Poole, 2002). Analyzing coverage of Islam in their research on the British media and religion, Knott et al. (2013) found a massive increase between 1982 and 2008 in the quantity of coverage of Islam: 33 media references to Islam in 1982 compared with 306 in 2008 (starting even before 9/11). And, in 2008, of 255 references to Islam, 141 dealt with militant action and 41 with extremism. By contrast only two each concerned mosques, Sufism, and Mecca. Against the background of terrorism by Muslims in the name of *jihad*, a frequent theme in coverage of Islam has been the question of the suitability of Muslims in Western society. Questions of asylum and refugees enter the public agenda in the West. But if the themes themselves are negative, the overall image of the Muslim is demonic. Beyond the standards of objectivity and balance (including reporting both sides of an issue), there is little which the editors can do because the overall image constructed appears negative.

The clergy – themselves a key section of "the public" – criticize media coverage as encouraging secularism and antireligion. Vanderbilt University's Freedom Forum (Dart & Allen, 1993) surveyed 988 Christian clergy, from 6 Christian denominations in the United States and 701 journalists, including 151 religion reporters in 1993. The results indicated that 58% of mainline Christian ministers, 70% of Catholic priests, and 91% Conservative Christians agreed that "religion coverage today is biased against ministers and organized religion." Two-thirds of clergy said that "news on religion gave an unfairly negative picture of clergy." (The same proportion of writers said so.) Three-quarters of the clergy agreed with the statement that most journalists "introduce their own selective perspective in religion studies rather than report objectively." More than half of the journalists disagreed, though 28.5% agreed. Of the clergy, 60% said that religion writers should be active in a religion (but fewer than 20% of journalists said so). Notwithstanding that much of the criticism of the media's religion coverage is valid, one can still ask whether some clergy fail to understand the newsgathering and news selection processes that determine the media's construction of the religion. On the other hand, many clergy favor the news media's more aggressive stance in their reporting about religious leaders: 71% of priests agreed, as did 80% of mainline ministers, but only 58% of conservative clergy did.

The Future of Religion Journalism and New Media

New media have begun a new era in all areas of news. But how new is it, and how has it altered the supply of religion news? Far more religion-related information exists today. Journalists lacking knowledge about religion or not understanding the nuances of religious disputes have easier access to factual information, including information about the sources themselves. If past theological disputes within religious organizations took place behind closed doors, these have become public events as they are played out in social media and blogging.

News organizations' activities have branched out to providing online services. Religion journalists and academic researchers can now make alternative perspectives available to wider publics through blogs, social media, and specialist religion news sites. For example, surveying the Danish public, Fischer-Nielsen (2012) found that 16% of the public turned to websites of newspapers and of TV stations for information about religion or spiritual issues. Broken down by age group, 25% of those aged 18–29 said so, with an incremental by age. However, with the 24/7 nonstop nature of news website journalism, fewer opportunities exist for reporters to engage in original reporting, such as tracing new religious trends and religious activities. And, with newsgathering increasingly bound to desktop editing, there is greater dependence on news agencies.

More independent voices beyond the major news organizations also find a place online. One of the early attempts to cover religion online, Belief.net focused entirely upon religion and spirituality and intended to provide the breadth of religion news that the general media failed to provide or that was only found in specialized religious periodicals. Launched in 1999 as an independent online religion news website, Beliefnet.org started as a serious religion news website but subsequently changed to a site focusing upon spirituality. It featured newsletters on a broad range of subjects from spirituality to faith, to religion institutional politics, culture, and religious holidays. From being a site originally dedicated to objective news it became one identified through its blogs with advocacy. In 2002 Belief.net filed for bankruptcy. The Belief.net case shows that while new media appear to offer spaces for numerous small initiatives, in practice they could not survive without becoming a part of a larger news empire, bound up with the wider commercial, non-religion-related, business empire. In 2007 Belief.net was bought out by Rupert Murdoch's media empire but sold in 2010 (Mason, 2012).

Religious institutions may also use digital topics and infrastructure to attract the attention of professional journalists to their causes. In a Danish example, Fischer-Nielsen (2012) found that 10% got information on religion and spiritual issues from religious websites. And, broken down, 18% of those aged 18–29 said so. Indeed, asked where you would look for an answer if you had a question concerning Christianity, 56% among all those surveyed replied "the Internet," in contrast to 37% "a pastor," 28% "the Bible," and 21% "books."

Smaller minority religions can find an online platform challenging the seeming monopoly of the single dominant religion in a country that characterized the earlier pre-Internet era. Given the criticism in the pre-Internet era of the lack or selective coverage of new religious movements (Richardson & van Driel, 1997), this change holds profound significance for media coverage of new religious movements. And this may even increase the recruitment of new members.

If the earlier era showed justified criticism about the quantity or lack of religion reporting in press, radio, and television, today the multiple channels of media communication point to an overplay of religion news. With social networks on religion becoming online pulpits for all – for citizen journalists, gurus, and fellow travelers – anxious to spread "the Word" with few, if any, pretensions to being objective, accurate, or balanced, this gives professional journalism an important role to guide the news consumer through claims, counterclaims, messages, disinformation, and fake news. All this encourages reporters to prove their mettle and be more competitive. Whatever the massive transformation which new media has caused to the flow of religion news, the latter is also influenced by other factors including economic change, media regulation, and cultural change.

Conclusion

The questions of whether journalists have a suitable background for covering religion, and of whether religion news sources are accessible to reporters, help address concerns regarding the quantity of religion news; other areas of news raise these doubts less frequently. Overall, the two do not fully answer the criticism regarding the quantity of religion news because the issue of editors' decisions in defining news being influenced by news values remains the chief factor. These questions influence the quality of religion reporting as distinct from the quantity. Given that much religion information is esoteric and that even adherents of a faith group may not fully understand doctrine (let alone those not observant or outside the faith), the need for reporters qualified to explain and commentate is crucial, even more so than in the case of other journalism specialists. Also, the flow of religion information to the public is not advanced if a cleric, who sits in a position of authority, does not recognize the principle of the right to know.

Clearly, the digital age affects the quantity of reporting because if in the past a lack of space or limited broadcast time shunted religion news aside or behind other types of news, today many more outlets for religion news and information exist, and news reporting takes on a 24/7 schedule. Indeed, audience interest in the subject will increase because of the multiplier effect: the more coverage, the more audience interest it generates for even more religion news and information. And this appetite puts pressure on the quantity scale. However, in response to the many unobjective channels for religion information on the Internet, there is an even greater need for objective religion reporting on news websites to guide the audience through the maze of claims, sponsored information, leaks, and fake news.

References

Ahmed, S., & Matthes, J. (2017). Media representation of Muslims and Islam from 2000 to 2015: A meta-analysis. *International Communication Gazette, 79*(3), 219–244. DOI:10.1177/1748048516656305

Bisha, R., & Ruge-Jones, P. (2005). Critically reading the other hand. *Currents in Theology & Mission.* February.

Brown, W. J. (2009). Mediated influence of Pope John Paul II. *Journal of Communication & Religion, 32*(1), 33–61.

Buddenbaum, J. (1988). The religion beat at daily newspapers. *Newspaper Research Journal, 9*(4), 57–70.

Buss, D. D. (1995). Religion and the press. *American Enterprise, 6*(6), 55–57.

Cohen, Y. (2017). Diffusion theories: News diffusion. In P. Rossler (Ed.), *International encyclopaedia of media effects.* Wiley-Blackwell Publishers.

Cohen, Y. (2018a). Holy days, news media and religious identity: A case study in Jewish holy days and the Israeli press and news websites. In Y. Cohen (Ed.), *Spiritual news: Reporting religion around the world* (pp. 303–321). Peter Lang Publishers.

Cohen, Y. (2018b). The religion reporter. In Y. Cohen (Ed.), *Spiritual news: Reporting religion around the world* (pp. 53–75). Peter Lang Publishers.

Dart, J., & Allen, J. (1993). *Bridging the gap: Religion and the news media.* The Freedom Forum. Retrieved May 27, 2002, from https://www.freedomforuminstitute.org/wp-content/uploads/2016/10/bridgingthegap.pdf

Dixon, M. A. (2004). Silencing the lambs: The Catholic church's response to the 2002 sexual abuse scandal. *Journal of Communication & Religion, 27*(1), 63–86.

do Nascimento Cunha, M. (2021). Journalism, religious intolerance and violence in Brazil. In K. Radde-Antweiler, & X. Zeiler (Eds.), *The Routledge handbook of religion & journalism* (pp. 296–310). Routledge.

Ewart, J., & O'Donnell, K. (2018). *Reporting Islam.* Routledge Publishers.

Fischer-Nielsen, P. (2012). The internet mediatization of religion & church. In S. Hjarvard, & M. Lovheim (Eds.), *Mediatisation and religion: Nordic perspectives* (pp. 45–61). Noridicom.

Galtung, J., & Ruge, M. (1965). The structure of foreign news. *Journal of Peace Research, 2*(1), 64–91.

Garrett-Medill Center for Religion and the News Media. (1999). *Media coverage of religion, spirituality, and values.* Northwestern University.

Gunter, B., & Viney, R. (1994). *Seeing is believing: Religion TV in the 1990s.* John Libbey.

Hoover, S., Hanley, B., & Radelfinger, M. (1993). Who reads religion news? *Nieman Reports, 47*(2), 42–49.

Knott, K., Poole, E., & Taira, T. (2013). *Media portrayals of religion and the secular sacred.* Ashgate.

Kumar, K. (2003). Spirituality in the Indian media. *Religion & Social Communication, 1*(1), 32–37.

Kumar, K. (2018). Reporting religion in Indian news media: Hindu nationalism, 'reconversions' and the secular state. In Y. Cohen (Ed.), *Spiritual news: Reporting religion around the world* (pp. 179–198). Peter Lang Publishers.

Landau, C. (2012). What the media thinks about religion: A broadcast perspective. In J. Mitchell, & O. Gower (Eds.), *Religion and the news* (pp. 79–88). Ashgate.

Mann, R. (2015). Hinduism in the news: The shifting role of religion and the media in Canadian public life. *Canadian Journal of Communication, 40*(1), 87–103. DOI:10.22230/cjc.2015v40n1a2892

Mason, D. L. (2012). Religion news online. In D. Winston (Ed.), *The Oxford handbook of religion and the American news media* (pp. 157–170). Oxford University Press.

Moore, R. L. (1994). *Selling God: American religion in the marketplace of culture.* Oxford University Press.

Niemalä, K., & Christensen, H. R. (2013). Religion in newspapers in the Nordic countries in 1988–2008. *Nordic Journal of Religion and Society, 26*(1), 5–24.

O'Neill, D., & Harcup, T. (2009). News values and selectivity. In K. Wahl-Jorgensen, & T. Hanitzsch (Eds.), *The handbook of journalism studies* (pp. 161–175). Routledge Publishers.

Pearson, M. (2017). Lessons from reporting Islam: An Australian newspaper's coverage of radicalisation. *Australian Journalism Review, 39*(1), 47–62.

Pintak, L., & Franklin, S. (2013). *Islam for journalists: A primer on covering Muslim communities in America.* Reynolds Institute/Newsbooks.

Poole, E. (2002). *Reporting Islam: Media representations of British Muslims.* Tauris.

Poole, E. (2021). Religion on an ordinary day in UK news: Christianity, secularism and diversity. DOI:10.1163/21659214-BJA10043. Taira, T., & Kyyro, J. Religion in Finnish newspapers on an ordinary: Criticism and support. DOI:10.1163/21659214-BJA10045. Weng, E, & Halafoff, A. Religion on an ordinary news day in Australia: Hidden Christianity and the pervasiveness of lived religion, spirituality and the secular sacred. DOI:10.1163/21659214-BJA10041. Helland, C & Michels, D.H., Religion in the news on an ordinary day: Diversity and change in English Canada. DOI:10.1163/21659214-BJA10050. Vanasse-Pelletier, Lefebvre S., & Khlifate I., Religion on an ordinary day in Quebec: Cultural Christianity, "threatening" Islam and the supernatural marketplace. DOI:10.1163/21659214-BJA10052. *Journal of Religion, Media and Digital Culture, 10*(2).

Richardson, J. T., & van Driel, B. (1997). Journalists' attitudes toward new religious movements. *Review of Religious Research, 39*(2), 116–136. https://doi.org/10.2307/3512177

Richardson, J. Y., & Introvigne, M. (2007). New religious movements, countermovements, moral panics, and the media. In D. D. Bromley (Ed.), *Teaching new religious movements* (pp. 91–112). Oxford University Press.

Robinson, W. V. (2003). Shining the globe's spotlight on the Catholic church. *Nieman Reports, 57*(1). https://niemanreports.org/articles/shining-the-globes-spotlight-on-the-catholic-church

Soukup, P (2005). Vatican opinion on modern communication. In C. Badaracco (Ed), *Quoting God: How media shape ideas about religion and culture.* Naylor University Press.

Steinfels, P. (1993). Constraints of the religion reporter. *Nieman Reports, 47*(2), 3–5, 55.

Svennevig, M., Haldane, I., & Gunter, B. (1988). *Godwatching: Viewers, religion and television.* John Libbey.

Underwood, D. (2002). *From Yah-weh to Yahoo!: The religious roots of the secular press.* University of Illinois Press.

Westerstahl, J., & Johansson, F. (1994). Foreign news: News values and ideologies. *European Journal of Communication, 9*(1), 71–89. DOI: 10.1177/0267323194009001004

Winston, D., & Green, J. C. (2015). *Most Americans say media coverage of religion too sensationalized.* (Report) USC Annenberg School of Communication and Journalism and the University of Akron. Ray C. Bliss Institute of Applied Politics.

Worlds of Journalism Project. (2011). Homepage. Retrieved May 27, 2022, from www.worldsofjournalism.org.

Yao, Q., & Liu, Z. (2018). Media and religion in China: Publicizing gods under atheistic governance. In Y. Cohen (Ed.), *Spiritual news: Reporting religion around the world* (pp. 199–215). Peter Lang Publishers.

Selected Readings

Cohen, Y. (Ed.). (2018). *Spiritual news: Reporting religion around the world.* Peter Lang Publishers.

Marshall, P., Gilbert, L., & Green Ahmanson, R. (Eds.). (2009). *Blind spot: When journalists don't get religion.* Oxford University Press.

Pintak, L. (2011). *The Arab journalist.* Tauris.

Radde-Antweiler, K., & Zeiler, X. (Eds.). (2021). *The Routledge handbook of religion and journalism.* Routledge.

Silk, M. (1998). *Unsecular media: Making news of religion in America.* University of Illinois.

20

Entertainment

Allan Novaes

"Entertainment" and "Pop Culture" as Concepts: Historical–Epistemological Context

The concepts of "entertainment" and "pop culture" generate tension with religion and religiosity. Both terms have multiple meanings and the very vagueness of the term entertainment and the related term pop culture impedes our discussion of the seeming gap between entertainment and religion. We should, therefore, attempt first to define entertainment and pop culture. Some define pop culture in very broad and subjective terms, such as "everyday life" and "mundane doings of people" (Waskul & Vannini, 2016, pp. 1–2), "unauthorized culture" (Parker, 2011, pp. 166–167), or simply as that which is not art or which demonstrates a lack of high culture (McKee, 2012, p. 9). The term entertainment also carries its own vagueness, which runs the gamut from the notion of scheduled and generally paid-for activities in the context of North American entrepreneurship in postindustrial capitalism (Trigo, 2008, pp. 25–26) to processes involving the provision of pleasure to a passive audience through external stimulation (Bates & Ferry, 2010, p. 15).

An academic perspective directly associates the concepts with the discussion about high culture and popular culture (folk culture), or mass culture in the West in the late eighteenth and early nineteenth century, derived from the Industrial Revolution and the massification of media technologies of the time. It is not possible here, in the specific discussion of religion and entertainment or popular culture, to revisit the debate on high culture and popular culture. Suffice it to say that debate about popular culture and entertainment, which included, for example, Matthew Arnold (1822–1888), in the last decades of the 1800s – for whom the working class would produce a degrading and immoral culture, influenced by market logic – undermined the edifying creations of the elite and of "high culture." Ideas of frivolity, transgression, rebellion, and criminality were associated with youth culture, and thus with pop culture. The term pop culture was born in this context, in the 1950s, when English cultural critics tried to understand – and, in a way, disqualify as sensationalist and transient – both the emergence of rock'n'roll and youth culture in its genesis.

There are five main theoretical antecedents of the terms pop culture and entertainment, without which we cannot properly understand their epistemological limits: (i) mass culture, (ii) cosmopolitan culture, (iii) society of the spectacle, (iv) youth culture, and (v) leisure. Entertainment and pop culture are cosmopolitan and of the "mass" or for the masses because they presuppose that the range of media technology extends to a global audience, given the process of urbanization and the development of communication systems, modes of consumption, and market logic,

The Handbook on Religion and Communication, First Edition. Edited by Yoel Cohen and Paul A. Soukup.
© 2023 John Wiley & Sons Ltd. Published 2023 by John Wiley & Sons Ltd.

so as to create communicational territorialities. The two terms can also be referred to as fruits of the society of the spectacle, in the sense that they are naturally geared to the logic of the spectacularization of life and the predominance of representation over reality. Moreover, pop culture and entertainment can be seen as emerging from youth culture – although not restricted to this age and social condition – because they articulate aspects such as speed, ephemerality, novelty, and volatility, offering a space in which collective identities are formed that interact with the universe of media narratives and symbols. Finally, the two terms are linked to the idea of leisure, in the sense that nonworking spaces would have a natural affinity for entertainment in its commercial, mass, trivial, and even vulgar form, as defined by Roberts (2004) when he pointed out that leisure can be characterized by the "Big Five" gambling, sex, alcohol, television, and annual holidays.

Pop Culture

In relation to the pop culture concept, three characteristics stand out.

First, pop culture is historically deeply connected to the mass media and it acts as an environment in which sounds, images, symbols, narratives, and media myths that are part of the construction of the social fabric of contemporary daily life are conveyed. Thus, pop culture can be designated as a synonym of "media culture," from the standpoint developed by Kellner (2020), and it is also configured as a convergent and transmediatic phenomenon, in terms of the concept of "convergence culture" by Jenkins (2006), which involves massive production in several media and platforms, such as cinema, television, games, comics, newspaper, magazines, social media, music, etc.

Second, in relation to the ideas of capital, industry, and merchandise, pop culture refers to the notion of "consumer society" as developed by Bourdieu (1930–2002) and Baudrillard (1929–2007), which consists of mass production, wide circulation and distribution of flows, and exacerbated consumption of material goods, marked by ephemerality and programmed obsolescence. "Pop" is also associated with the consumption of media content and experiences by large audiences on a global and cross-cultural level, also in connection with the concept of "consumer culture" as understood by McCracken (1990) and Featherstone (2007).

Third, pop culture can be understood as a new global worldview and as a complex contemporary urban mythology that, by articulating narratives and producing meanings, participates in the construction of collective identities and socio-affective bonds among its adepts/consumers. It can create fan communities (fandom) with the potential to transcend geographical and cultural boundaries, as evidenced by the concepts of "globalization of media communication" and "transcultural communication" by researchers such as Castells (2010) and Hepp (2015).

Entertainment

The concept of entertainment has two characteristics.

First, entertainment is predominantly linked to a business model centered on the interests of large consumer audiences, in order to minimize risks through processes such as production in consolidated popular genres, recycling of famous franchises (e.g. *Star Wars, Marvel, Game of Thrones*) and audience testing. Therefore, entertainment is an audience-centered commercial culture, a system driven by spectators/consumers' desires, hopes, and wishes, and by business models and strategies (Collis, 2017, p. 19; Dyer, 2002, p. 20).

Second, entertainment is a cultural form that has its own aesthetic system, which values elements promoting strong emotional responses from consumers – such as speed, spectacle, fun, and vulgarity – through its stories and frequent happy endings (McKee, 2012, p. 10; 2016, p. 11). Like all cultural productions, entertainment also has a symbolic value and, therefore, its consumption is focused on generating experiences and emotional engagement in the audience, somehow providing satisfaction and pleasure (McKee et al., 2014, p. 113).

Even if Meyersohn (1978, pp. 331–332) and others consider entertainment and popular culture as synonyms, this chapter treats them as different conceptual categories. However, in terms of the pop culture–religion and entertainment–religion relations, they are usually treated as interchangeable or equivalent concepts, since, from the perspective of the study of religious phenomena, they seem to translate the same processes, practices, and systems. Thus, even though this chapter recognizes the independence of the concepts, when, for didactic purposes, some equivalence is necessary, this will be done in order to generate more clarity in the description of the relations and interactions of religion with the concepts in question.

The Pop Culture–Religion and Entertainment–Religion Interface as Objects of Study

Despite the relevant historical background and the rich theoretical framework surrounding the terms pop culture and entertainment, both concepts have suffered a certain indifference from several fields of knowledge, according to Bourdieu's logic of social hierarchy of the objects of study. Bosshart and Macconi (1998, p. 3) state that there is no proportionality relation between the amount of entertainment produced and consumed and the amount of scholarly research on entertainment, while Gray (2012) defends the creation of the entertainment studies field beyond other already known names such as media studies or communication studies, for example, in an attempt to delimit the area and reinforce its relevance. Pop culture faced a similar situation. There has been, however, a growing recognition of the area in the past two or three decades as reflected in the number of academic programs as well as in the number of academic events and publications devoted to it.

However, this disqualifying treatment of pop and entertainment as objects of academic investigation remains when it comes to its relationship with the study of religion. This still occurs because while religion is generally associated with serious themes, processes, and practices, academia sometimes relegates pop culture and entertainment to the category of objects incapable of generating deep, quality scientific research because some consider them as part of the realm of triviality, futility, playfulness, and ephemerality, typical of moments of fun and leisure. Added to this is the fact that, especially from some strands of theological and religious studies, pop culture and entertainment are analyzed from conservative assumptions, such as the idea that pop culture is profane, perverse, and/or morally degrading (Freccero, 1999, p. 1; Klassen, 2014, p. 2).

In response to such views, Lynch (2005) and Clark (2007) have articulated a set of reasons why scholars should take the pop culture–religion interface seriously. I have adapted this set of reasons for this chapter in order to also include issues related to the entertainment–religion dialogue.

1. Since pop culture and entertainment, in their transcultural rationale of market and spectacularization, aim to reach a large number of people, they express the *zeitgeist* of an era. For this reason, the study of pop culture and entertainment, particularly in dialogue with religions, allows the researcher to transcend pop and amusement per se and reflect on geopolitical, cultural, philosophical, and existential issues that not only translate the feelings, beliefs, and ideas of an era, but also present the roles that religion plays at this juncture.

2. Studying pop culture and entertainment in its interface with religion consists of identifying and analyzing how religious traditions – with their adherents, rituals, and practices – are portrayed in the various forms and products made to entertain. Studies of this nature can provide an indication of researchers' biases and the concerns of contemporary society, pointing out which interests these representations of religion serve and which groups, sectors, or individuals these portrayals benefit or harm. With this, it is possible to associate certain ideological and political agendas in the way the religious phenomenon is portrayed in the most varied platforms of pop and entertainment, helping to diagnose the perpetuation of religious stereotypes and their implications in public life.

3. The study of pop and entertainment culture in dialogue with religion can result in the identification of products and practices that influence and have an impact on beliefs, processes, and rituals of religious institutions or groups. Studies of this nature assist researchers in understanding how religious movements engage with and appropriate pop culture and entertainment modes of communication and practices, what motivations and assumptions this relationship articulates, and how this interaction generates benefits and difficulties, raising complex religious issues.

4. Taking into account the social, existential, and transcendent functions of most religions, the study of pop culture and entertainment at the interface with religious phenomena is useful and relevant in the task of identifying whether and how practices and languages originally made to entertain can replace traditional religious forms and services – prayers, penance, fasting, etc. – as sources of affective bonding, sense of community, attribution of existential meaning, and, ultimately, as a means of encountering the transcendent.

5. Recognizing the foundational, normative, and proselytizing role that oral history and texts, considered sacred, play in various religious traditions, the study of symbols, icons, texts, and narratives from pop and entertainment culture has also been present in hermeneutical and literary approaches in the science of transmission and interpretation of sacred stories and texts. This occurs in studies that explore pop and entertainment narratives in relation to sacred texts, and also through the reading and analysis of theological themes present in productions originally made to entertain. Some studies even propose to explore pop culture and entertainment as a source and method to do theology (Taylor, 2008; Vanhoozer, 2007).

Pop Culture, Entertainment, and Religion: Key Theoretical Paradigms and Transnational Case Study Exemplars

In order to better understand the complex interaction between the religious phenomenon, pop, and entertainment, as well as to identify highlights and main examples of this relationship in the global context, I will revisit two classifications: the forms of relationship and dialogue between pop culture and religion elaborated by Forbes (2017), and the classification of theoretical–methodological approaches most employed in the study of media and religion proposed by Mitchell (2007). I have adapted both typologies, despite their nomenclature, and applied them to the pop culture–religion and entertainment–religion intersections.

Approaches on Religion and Pop Culture/Entertainment Intersection

For Mitchell (2007) under the various approaches in media and religion studies lie a number of assumptions, which I have named "dangers," "opportunities," "resources," and "audiences."

Dangers Category (the Iconoclastic Approach) and Opportunities Category (the Iconographic Approach)

One question that represents the dangers category, Mitchell's (2007, p. 37) iconoclastic approach, is: what are the threats and dangers that pop and entertainment offer to religions? This approach represents the resistance and distrust that many religious organizations exhibit when a technological change, such as the advent of a new media, occurs. The emergence of new communication technologies disrupts the control of information and knowledge dissemination previously established in religious institutions, which, in turn, may articulate narratives and discourses that demonize the use of certain media or disapprove of the assimilation of pop and entertainment languages in order to have greater influence over their membership, protecting and reinforcing dogma and orthodoxy. This approach has a great historical ballast, since, in the Western context, it goes back to the censorship that the Roman Catholic Church exercised on publications via the press in the context of the Protestant Reformation in the sixteenth century, in an attempt to safeguard the Holy See's monopoly of knowledge; it goes through the restrictions on various forms of leisure and entertainment advocated by the Puritans in seventeenth-century America, but also projects itself into the distrust and rejection of the mass media, such as cinema, radio, and television, by American evangelicals and other conservative Christians. As an example, Christian fundamentalists in the United States of the 1930s rejected radio; the major philosophical obstacle that believers had to overcome was the potential of this media for what was considered futile entertainment (Bendroth, 1996, p. 76).

This revulsion that many conservative and fundamentalist Christians projected onto the media and the entertainment industry fueled episodes such as the censorship of comic books that would induce children and young people to delinquency and crime – an accusation made by psychiatrist Fredric Wertham, which brought him all the way to the US Congress to share his ideas (Hajdu, 2009; Tilley, 2012; Wertham, 1954; Wright, 2003). This thinking was also responsible for fomenting moral panic on several occasions between the 1950s and 1990s – through the discourse of the dangerous presence of subliminal messages in movies, TV series, and cartoons, in video games and role-playing games, and in music albums of famous bands and artists, especially in North and Latin America (Janisse & Corupe, 2016; Laycock, 2015; Springhall, 1998; Vokey & Read, 1985). Such controversies also played out in the Nigerian film industry, made more complex in its representations of Christianity, Islam, and African Traditional Religions (Mitchell, 2009).

The opportunities, or iconographic approach category, appears in the question: what opportunities do pop and entertainment offer for religious communication? Rather than presenting concerns about interaction with pop culture and entertainment, this approach emphasizes the potential to reach new audiences. The assumption here is essentially utilitarian, so that the elements of pop and entertainment language are usually validated when they are shown to be useful and efficient for the process of transmitting religious content and for indoctrination. Many examples of utilitarian interactions in relation to media technologies and the appropriation of elements of pop and entertainment language exist. Mainline Protestants and evangelical Christians in North America use radio and television significantly, with great optimism toward technology and with a certain measurable success in reaching new audiences in the twentieth century (Schultze, 2013; Ward, 2013). Beyond electronic media, religious groups have made instrumental use of other elements of the entertainment universe as a tool for evangelization. Bronder (2020) addresses the use of comics as a catechetical tool for Catholic youth through the *Treasure Chest of Fun and Fact* series (1946–1972), while Weinstein (2009) points to the influence of Judaism in the creation of superhero comic book narratives such as *Superman*, *Batman*, and *Captain America*, among others. One of the most significant examples occurs in the era of the televangelists or electronic church phase, between the 1960s and 1980s in the United States, with great penetration and impact in Latin America, and in countries in Africa and Asia. This period was characterized by religious television programs that incorporated elements of entertainment and show business, with energetic and charismatic presentations that included jokes, musical performances, and other attractions, often emulating aspects of television genres consolidated in "secular" TV such as talk shows (Abelman & Hoover, 1990; Neuendorf, 1990).

Both approaches – iconoclastic and iconographic – portray a process typical of religious movements, especially in the scope of Christianity. Taking into consideration the context of the emergence and expansion of the press during the sixteenth century, as well as the emergence of cinema, radio, television, and the Internet in the twentieth century, one identifies a pattern of discourses and attitudes of resistance and integration of many Christian groups with the language of media and entertainment. This allows us to propose the existence of a sociotheological cycle of relations between media/pop culture/entertainment and religious organizations, especially those of Christian matrix, namely:

1. In the first phase, tension occurs. Tensions can be observed especially on the occasion of the emergence of new media genres, products, and/or technologies. On the one hand, this process produces curiosity, which leads to experimentalism and pioneering religious use of media for evangelistic purposes and, as a consequence, the rearticulation of religiosities in the media environment. However, on the other hand, the advent of new genres, products, and/or media technologies also often generates distrust and resistance to the new and unknown, resulting in rejection and "demonization" of the interaction between pop culture/entertainment and religions.

2. In the second phase, intersections occur. And although tension is still present in this and the next phase, but in a different way and with different intensity, the adoption of pop and entertainment practices and languages gradually gains acceptance if conventional metrics of evangelistic success are met – i.e. donations, conversions, visibility, etc. In this phase, the expansion of models of intersection of the religious with the pop demands from religious organizations a kind of regulation, so that the negotiation of what works or what is permissible is in accordance with institutional-religious parameters and codes. Thus, the negotiation of the religious universe with pop practices and languages gains more concrete contours, but still paradoxical to the extent that many times there is a posture of implicit and inherent condemnation of the pop universe. This happens, among other reasons, because the entertainment industry uses elements such as violence, eroticism, consumerism, and other topics thought of by many religions as typical of profane, materialistic, and/or excessively liberal agendas in morals and customs. Added to this are certain ideological incompatibilities between some religious doctrines and some assumptions and values associated with pop culture and entertainment products.

3. In the third phase, hybridization occurs. This is when the institutional regulation of the adoption of pop and entertainment practices and languages matures and consolidates. Thus, the ecclesiological–missiological model of a denomination merges with pop-media rationales and approaches, even though ambiguities, contradictions, and conflicts between entertainment rationales and the theological framework of the religious denomination in question are still present. In this phase there is a transition from the utilitarian paradigm of using the media as an evangelistic tool to the perspective of the mediatization of religion and the hybridization of religious practices with the media ecosystem.

Resources Category and Audiences Category

The resources category translates as approaches that do not see the media, pop, and entertainment as threats or opportunities for religious communication, escaping from a Manichean rationale. The question that typifies this approach is: what theoretical and methodological resources are available for those who want to go beyond the dangers and opportunities paradigms? In response to this question Mitchell (2007, p. 42) presents four academic views or "resources" from media and cultural studies, which are focused on: (i) the historical continuities and discontinuities of media technologies; (ii) the effects and impacts of media; (iii) the institutions and power structures that house media; and (iv) the audiences and reception processes of media content. These views basically describe the main theories, methods, and scholarly traditions employed in studies investigating the dialogue between media/pop culture/entertainment and religion.

Audience, given its predominance with regard to the theories and methods most frequently employed in recent decades, earns its own category in Mitchell's (2007 p. 42) classification, and its question is: what are the habits, routines, and practices that help audiences move from apathy and indifference to engagement? Unlike approaches that consider the media as a communication instrument or emphasize the power of the medium and message over the receiver, the category of audiences investigates how readers/listeners/viewers construct their own meanings from what they read/hear/watch, showing that they are an active part of the communication process. Once this is taken into account, it becomes easier to understand why many people seek spiritual nourishment and religious edification in the universe of pop and entertainment. Bhrugubanda (2018) describes a more complex interaction in south India where political groups engage religion's influence on cinema audiences, who often display devotional activity in the cinema just as they would in a temple. These practices of viewership flow into political practices of citizenship.

Relationships between Religion and Pop Culture/Entertainment

According to Forbes (2017), religion and pop culture relate to each other in at least four different ways, but only the first three will be dealt with here, as they are more frequent and explicit, namely, religion in pop culture, pop culture in religion, and pop culture as religion.

Religion in Pop Culture

This category consists of examples that characterize the presence of icons, symbols, characters, texts, and religious themes in the pop and entertainment universe. We can summarize them by the following questions: How does religion manifest itself in entertainment elements and expressions? How are religious institutions and movements and their leaders and faith practices portrayed in the various products of pop culture?

In this category research that investigates how religious groups are portrayed and represented in pop and entertainment products stands out. Many of the examples in this category are related to the film and religion relationship. This field of study has grown considerably in the past decades with two prevailing approaches: "using movies to interpret religion and using religion to interpret film" (Blizek, 2009, p. 8). From these two interpretative keys and taking into account the robustness of American cinema, many studies analyze the presence of religious icons, figures, organizations, and personalities in movies (Wright, 2007), including the study of religious themes in major pop franchises such as *Star Wars*, *Star Trek*, *Lord of the Rings*, and *Marvel* stories. Following in this direction of audiovisual fiction, television and streaming products also feature representations of religions and the religious. In addition to studies that address portrayals of the religious phenomenon in popular series (Das Gupta, 1989; Dwyer, 2006; Gittinger & Sheinfeld, 2020), the presence of the religious in television fiction programs in some countries is noteworthy, even if these examples could also be placed into the category "pop culture in religion," which will be discussed in the text that follows. This is the case with the emergence of subgenres in Brazilian telenovelas: the spiritualist telenovelas (Meigre e Silva, 2018), of Kardecist influence, popularized in the 1990s and 2000s by Globo TV, and the biblical telenovelas (Kanyat, 2019), aired by Record TV, from the 2010s until today, which consist of adaptations of the narratives of the Hebrew Bible and the Christian Bible from the perspective of Brazilian *evangélicos*. It also applies to Hindi religious film and television (Dwyer, 2006; Lutgendorf, 2002; Mankekar, 2002).

In addition to films, several other media genres also portray religion and the religious, namely: the representation of Christian and Hindu tradition, among others, in comic books (Brackett, 2015); the representation of Muslims and Jews in video games (Masso & Abrams, 2014; Šisler, 2014); and portrayals of mysticism in heavy metal subgenres (Coggins, 2018), among others.

Pop Culture in Religion

This category refers to the appropriation of aspects and elements of pop culture and entertainment by religious organizations and traditions. It takes into account the impact of pop on religious people, and how the logic of entertainment influences what they believe and how they operate. It can be translated through the following questions: How does the appropriation of marketing rationale and other media resources affect the way religious groups understand themselves and interact with society? Is it possible to speak of the existence of a religious pop culture?

The phenomenon of mega-churches in countries such as Brazil, South Korea, the United States, and Australia, among others, can be classified as one of the main examples of the pop culture in religion category because, as a successor of the electronic Church movement and heir to the legacy of the gospel industry, it can be understood as the apex of the synthesis between religion and the rationale of pop and entertainment (Coleman & Chattoo, 2019; von der Ruhr, 2019). The model of mega-churches seems to consider as central and core in their communicative–religious structure the practices and languages of pop, submitting their practices and processes to the rationale of entertainment in a more explicit and forceful way. Martino's (2013) typology, which classifies churches into high-mediated and low-mediated in their interaction with the media based on research in Christian churches in the UK, France, and Latin America, is useful to identify some of the conditions and elements necessary for this process of synthesis or hybridization between religion and the universe of pop and entertainment to occur in denominations, especially Christian ones. For Martino (2013, 2015), the relationships between religion and pop/entertainment culture result from tensions, intersections, and hybridizations. There is, however, since the 1970s in the United States and 1980s in other regions, such as Latin America, a progressive intertwining between pop practices and religious practices, especially in Catholicism and Protestantism. This approach of Catholic and Protestant denominations to pop culture, even if initially irregular and even reluctant, happened from the perspective of the instrumental–evangelistic use of media until it gradually became, in several cases, the media–religious modus operandi of some denominations, which adopted pop practices and languages in their liturgies, rituals, discourses, and evangelization practices.

Several studies point to this gradual change of relations – from distancing to approximation and even hybridization – between pop/entertainment culture and religion. Roman Catholicism shows several phases in the relationship with communication, especially from the analysis of encyclicals and papal bulls and ecclesiastic discourses and practices. In the first phase, the behavior of the Catholic Church was oriented toward the exercise of censorship and repression through the Index of Forbidden Books, passing through a second phase of suspicious acceptance of the new media, with vigilance over the press, cinema, and radio. Then, in a third phase, the need for an *aggiornamento* that emerges from the Second Vatican Council reflected on the relationship of the Catholic Church with communication, determining an imperative to evangelize through the media. Finally, a fourth and final phase appears in which Catholicism experiences a crossroads of challenges imposed by digital culture and the need to recognize communication as an articulating element of society (Kennedy, 2019; Puntel, 2011). Even other Christian traditions undergo this shift in interaction with the universe of pop and entertainment. This is the case of Seventh-day Adventism, whose text-centered and print-driven vocation resulted in a conflicting relationship with the universe of pop and entertainment, so that as they emerged, mass media and other technologies were demonized, being associated with bohemian life, secularism, and spiritual problems. However, Adventism's attitude is gradually becoming more flexible and integrated with media logic (Ellis, 2019; Novaes, 2019).

A similar process occurs in some of the Eastern religions. This is the case with Buddhism, which, according to Connely (2010), is predominantly present in the digital context through virtual worlds and games, mobile applications, websites, and social media. However, Buddhist scholars show concerns about the impact of adherents' engagement with the pop-media universe, since entertainment products and social media can easily be tools of distraction or addiction, getting in the way of maintaining an ideal mental state according to the logic of karma (McGuire, 2019).

It is important to note, however, that both the instrumental use and intersection of religious practices with the logic of the media environment happen in negotiated ways in religious groups. The nature and purpose of religious messages and practices demand the existence of rules and limits in the appropriation of pop, so that traits associated with eroticism, violence, narcotics use, and "profanity," among others, tend to be excluded.

Pop Culture as Religion

This category, aligned with the previous section's fourth reason to take pop culture and religion studies seriously, involves the argument that pop culture functions as religion or religiosity for various individuals, encompassing the following questions: In what dimensions and meanings can pop culture be compared with the rituals, values, and beliefs of religious adherents? In what ways can pop and entertainment narratives and practices help people find meaning and purpose in life, as well as build affective, communal, and religious bonds?

Although critics point to theoretical–methodological problems in the equivalence between pop culture/entertainment and religion (McCloud, 2003), scholars who point to this similarity usually do so on the basis of the forms and functions of religion (Chidester, 1996). They compare religious rites and symbols to entertainment activities like watching a movie, going to a music concert, or cheering for a favorite soccer team (religious forms) and attribute typical roles of religion to entertainment practices, such as conferring meaning and helping to deal with personal and existential dilemmas (religious functions). Comparisons like these appear in studies such as Lyden (2003), who proposes a method for viewing film as religion; Gaffney (2008), who compares the behavior of soccer fans of Rio de Janeiro and Buenos Aires teams with the devotion attitudes of religious adepts; Bhrugubanda (2018), who examines South Indian audiences' devotional responses to film portraying Hindu divinities; Uwah (2011), who shows how African films represent and invite responses to traditional African religion; and Lofton (2011), who presents in what dimensions the celebrity – in this case, Britney Spears – would be a divine figure and her fans the believers.

These studies have a common trait: they are based on the behavior and culture of fans (fandom), i.e. a subculture of fans of stories, elements, and characters from pop culture and the entertainment universe who share their affection and extend the experience through networks, conventions, and other forms of community bonding. One of the most popular examples of fan-created "fiction-based religion" is Jediism, a religious–mediatic movement based on George Lucas' *Star Wars* franchise, which seeks to live according to the Jedi Code and perform rituals to communicate with the Force (Davidsen, 2013, 2016).

From this perspective the cartographic–critical method for analyzing pop culture artifacts from the perspective of the science of religion and theology elaborated by Reblin (2020) deserves mention. This method has three typical elements for analyzing pop culture objects and products such as comics, games, series, and movies, among others: (i) language, (ii) contexts of production, and (iii) artistic expression. In language, the critic considers reading the artifact, that is, the plot and the narrative structure. The contexts of production involve the dynamics of the entertainment industry (internal context); its political, economic, social, cultural, and religious environment, which provide demands and agendas (external context); and, finally, the market context, which refers to the reception by the audience of what is produced and marketed. Finally, artistic expression takes into account the aesthetic–creative potential of the analyzed object, which involves the historicity or tradition of the narrative, that is, the place that the narrative occupies in the reception of the audience and in the fan community; and the critical analysis, which consists in the production of religious meanings derived from the pop artifacts.

Conclusion: Pop Culture, Entertainment, and Religion: Challenges and Perspectives

With a growing intellectual production in recent years, research on the pop culture/entertainment–religion interface is moving toward a legitimization in the academic world from an inherently interdisciplinary perspective, with contributions from sociology, anthropology, psychology, history, theology, religious studies, literary criticism, and communication and media studies (Clark, 2007).

This comprehensive nature allows us to outline at least four major challenges and future perspectives for this area of studies. First, after overcoming the resistance and mistrust about the academic potential of pop and entertainment in dialogue with the religious phenomenon as an object of study, we realize that research on religion in pop culture and pop culture in religion, in the terms of Forbes' classification, currently predominates. Research involving the category of pop culture as religion should deepen its theoretical and methodological consistency, dealing more carefully with the epistemological boundaries of strategic and basic concepts in the field of religion, such as devotion, faith, belief, spirituality/religiosity, and, the most complex and challenging, religion. This endeavor leads, consequently, to the continuous and in-depth revisiting of concepts articulated by the field of communication such as media, entertainment, and pop culture, among others.

Second, from a communication perspective, many studies on the pop culture/entertainment–religion interface start from the premise of production or reception of media content, probably with predominance of the second point. However, with the complexity of the pop-media eco-system in its dialogue with the religious phenomenon, there should be an increasing demand for research that, while focusing on one aspect or the other, integrates more the aspects of production and reception. More and more objects of study will need this union because of the intermingling of various theories, models, and interdisciplinary concepts. An example of this is Morgan's (2007) idea of the matrix of study, which involves the integration between analyses of production, distribution, and reception.

Third, even with the growing tendency toward hybridization between the processes and languages of religion and the logic of pop and entertainment, there will continue to be a great demand for studies that identify the attitudes of religions toward the pop-media universe, and the forms of negotiation between ecclesiastical codes and the forms and languages of entertainment. As each religious tradition has its own ethical–theological framework and its own set of narratives and premises, the interaction with pop culture and entertainment is, in essence, complex and unique. Therefore, studies that take into consideration core concepts such as identity, memory, and religious authority, among others, as Hoover (2016) and Campbell (2021) have done, should have plenty of space in the academic circuit.

Finally, studies based in a dialogue among pop, entertainment, and religion will be able to promote more equity and diversity in societal life. The perpetuation of stereotypes of ethno-religious groups, the labels attributed to religious organizations, and especially the discrimination against religious minorities and groups in vulnerable situations are still very recurrent when religion and the religious are portrayed by the language of pop and entertainment. Hopefully more studies will consolidate pop culture and entertainment as critical tools to confront stereotypes and as effective instruments for positive social change.

References

Abelman, R., & Hoover, S. (Eds.). (1990). *Religious television: Controversies and conclusions*. Ablex Publishing Corporation.

Bates, S., & Ferry, A. (2010). What's entertainment? Notes toward a definition. *Studies in Popular Culture*, *33*(1), 1–20. http://www.jogoremoto.pt/docs/extra/FjSXoz.pdf

Bendroth, M. (1996). Fundamentalism and the media, 1930–1990. In D. Stout, & J. Buddenbaum (Eds.), *Religion and mass media: Audiences and adaptations* (pp. 74–84). Sage Publications.

Bhrugubanda, U. M. (2018). *Deities and devotees: Cinema, religion, and politics in south India*. Oxford University Press.

Blizek, W. L. (2009). The future of religion and film. In W. Blizek (Ed.), *The Continuum companion to religion and film* (pp. 7–15). Continuum.

Bosshart, L., & Macconi, I. (1998). Media entertainment. *Communication Research Trends*, *18*(3), 3–8.

Brackett, J. (2015). Religion and comics. *Religion Compass*, *9*(12), 493–500. https://doi.org/10.1111/rec3.12167

Bronder, L. (2020). Capes and catechesis: The use of comic books to catechize Catholic youths. Honors Thesis, University of Dayton. Retrieved April 7, 2022 from https://ecommons.udayton.edu/uhp_theses/250

Campbell, H. (2021). *Digital creatives and the rethinking of religious authorities*. Routledge.

Castells, M. (2010). *The rise of the network society: The information age: Economy, society and culture* (Vol. 1). Wiley-Blackwell.

Chidester, D. (1996). The church of baseball, the fetish of Coca-Cola, and the potlatch of rock 'n' roll: Theoretical models for study of religion in American popular culture. *Journal of the American Academy of Religion*, *64*(4), 743–765. http://hdl.handle.net/20.500.11910/7766

Clark, L. (2007). Why study popular culture? Or, how to build a case for your thesis in a religious studies or theology department? In G. Lynch (Ed.), *Between sacred and profane: Researching religion and popular culture* (pp. 5–20). I.B. Tauris.

Coggins, O. (2018). *Mysticism, ritual and religion in drone metal*. Bloomsbury Academic.

Coleman, S., & Chattoo, S. (2019). Megachurches and popular culture: On enclaving and encroaching. In S. Hunt (Ed.), *Handbook of megachurches* (pp. 84–102). Brill.

Collis, C. (2017). What is entertainment? The value of industry definitions. In S. Harrington (Ed.), *Entertainment values: How do we assess entertainment and why does it matter?* (pp. 11–22). Palgrave Macmillan.

Connely, L. (2010). Virtual Buddhism: An analysis of aesthetics in relation to religious practice within Second Life. *Online: Heidelberg Journal of Religions on the Internet*, 4(1), 12–34. DOI:10.11588/heidok.00011295

Das Gupta, C. (1989). Seeing and believing: Science and mythology: Notes on the 'mythological' genre. *Film Quarterly*, 42(4), 12–18.

Davidsen, M. A. (2013). Fiction-based religion: Conceptualizing a new category against history-based religion and fandom. *Religion and Culture*, 14(4), 378–395. https://doi.org/10.1080/14755610.2013.838798

Davidsen, M. A. (2016). From *Star Wars* to Jediism: The emergence of fiction-based religion. In E. Van den Hemel, & A. Szafraniec (Eds.), *Words: Religious language matters* (pp. 376–389). Fordham University Press.

Dwyer, R. (2006). *Film the gods: Religion and Indian cinema*. Routledge.

Dyer, R. (2002). *Only entertainment*. Routledge.

Ellis, L. (2019). *Seventh-day Adventists and the movies: An historical and contemporary exploration of the conflict between Christianity and visual media*. Regent University.

Featherstone, M. (2007). *Consumer culture and postmodernism*. Sage Publications.

Forbes, B. D. (2017). Introduction: Finding religion in unexpected places. In B. D. Forbes, & J. Mahan (Eds.), *Religion and popular culture in America* (pp. 1–29). University of California Press.

Freccero, C. (1999). *Popular culture: An introduction*. New York University Press.

Gaffney, C. T. (2008). *Temples of the earthbound gods: Stadiums in the cultural landscapes of Rio de Janeiro and Buenos Aires*. University of Texas Press.

Gittinger, J., & Sheinfeld, S. (Eds.). (2020). *Theology and Westworld*. Lexington Books/Fortress Academics.

Gray, J. (2012). Entertainment and media/cultural/communication studies. In A. McKee, C. Collis, & B. Hamley (Eds.), *Entertainment industries: Entertainment as a cultural system* (pp. 1–6). Routledge.

Hajdu, D. (2009). *The ten-cent plague: The great comic-book scare and how it changed America*. Picador.

Hepp, A. (2015). *Transcultural communication*. Wiley-Blackwell.

Hoover, S. (Ed.). (2016). *The media and religious authority*. Pennsylvania State University.

Janisse, K., & Corupe, P. (2016). *Satanic panic: Pop-cultural paranoia in the 1980s*. FAB Press.

Jenkins, H. (2006). *Convergence culture: Where old and new media collide*. New York University Press.

Kanyat, L. C. (2019). A linguagem como mediação: Uma análise de discurso da expressão midiática telenovela bíblica. *Dispositiva*, 8(13), 85–101. https://doi.org/10.5752/P.2237-9967.2019v8n13p85-101

Kellner, D. (2020). *Media culture: Cultural studies, identity, and politics in the contemporary moment*. Routledge.

Kennedy, M. C. (2019). Roman Catholicism in the digital age. In A. Grant, A. F. C. Sturgill, C. H. Chen, & D. A. Stout (Eds.), *Religion online: How digital technology is changing the way we worship and pray* (Vol. 2). Praeger/ABC-Clio.

Klassen, C. (2014). *Religion and popular culture: A cultural studies approach*. Oxford University Press.

Laycock, J. (2015). *Dangerous games: What the moral panic over role-playing games says about play, religion, and imagined worlds*. University of California Press.

Lofton, K. (2011). Religion and the American celebrity. *Social Compass*, 58(3), 346–352. https://doi.org/10.1177/0037768611412143

Lutgendorf, P. (2002). A superhit goddess: Jai Santoshi Maa and caste hierarchy in Indian films. *Manushi*, 131, 10–16.

Lyden, J. C. (2003). *Film as religion: Myths, morals, and rituals*. New York University Press.

Lynch, G. (2005). *Understanding theology and popular culture*. Blackwell.

Mankekar, P. (2002). Epic contests: Television and religious identity in India. In F. D. Ginsburg, L. Abu-Lughod, & B. Larkin (Eds.), *Media worlds: Anthropology on new terrain* (pp. 134–151). University of California Press.

Martino, L. M. (2013). *The mediatization of religion: When faith rocks*. Routledge.

Martino, L. M. (2015). Like a prayer: Articulações da cultura pop na midiatização da religião. In S. Sá, R. Carreiro, & R. Ferraraz (Eds.), *Cultura pop* (pp. 57–71). EDUFBA/Compós.

Masso, I., & Abrams, N. (2014). Locating the pixelated Jew: A multimodal method for exploring Judaism in the shivah. In H. Campbell, & G. Grieve (Eds.), *Playing with religion in digital games* (pp. 47–64). Indiana University Press.

McCloud, S. (2003). Popular culture fandoms, the boundaries of religious studies, and the project of the self. *Culture and Religion*, 4(2), 187–206. https://doi.org/10.1080/01438830032000135674

McCracken, G. (1990). *Culture and consumption: New approaches to the symbolic character of consumer goods and activities*. Indiana University Press.

McGuire, B. (2019). Digital media and global Buddhism. In A. E. Grant, D. A. Stout, C. H. Chen, & A. F. C. Sturgill (Eds.), *Religion Online: How digital technology is changing the way we worship and pray* (Vol. 2, pp. 232–249). Praeger/ABC-Clio.

McKee, A. (2012). The aesthetic system of entertainment. In A. McKee, C. Collis, & B. Hamley (Eds.), *Entertainment industries: Entertainment as a cultural system* (pp. 9–19). Routledge.

McKee, A. (2016). *Fun! What entertainment tells us about living a good life*. Palgrave Macmillan. https://doi.org/10.1057/978-1-137-49179-4_3

McKee, A., Collis, C., Nitins, T., Ryan, M., Harrington, S., Duncan, B., Carter, J., Luck, E., Neale, L., Butler, D., & Backstrom, M. (2014). Defining entertainment: An approach. *Creative Industries Journal*, 7(2), 108–120. https://doi.org/10.1080/17510694.2014.962932

Meigre E Silva, M. V. (2018). Televisualidades da matriz religiosa espírita na telenovela brasileira. *Revista Extraprensa*, 12(1), 98–115. https://doi.org/10.11606/extraprensa2018.150469

Meyersohn, R. (1978). The sociology of popular culture: Looking backwards and forwards. *Communication Research*, 5(3), 330–338. https://doi.org/10.1177/009365027800500307

Mitchell, J. (2007). Questioning media and religion. In G. Lynch (Ed.), *Between sacred and profane: Researching religion and popular culture* (pp. 34–46). I.B. Tauris.

Mitchell, J. (2009). Decolonising religion in African film. *Studies in World Christianity*, 15(2), 149–161. https://doi.org/10.3366/e135499010900046x

Morgan, D. (2007). Studying religion and popular culture: Prospects, presuppositions, and procedures. In G. Lynch (Ed.), *Between sacred and profane: Researching religion and popular culture* (pp. 21–33). I.B. Tauris.

Neuendorf, K. (1990). The public trust versus the almighty dollar. In R. Abelman, & S. Hoover (Eds.), *Religious television: Controversies and conclusions* (pp. 71–83). Ablex Publishing Corporation.

Novaes, A. (2019). Seventh-day Adventists in the digital age. In A. E. Grant, D. A. Stout, C. H. Chen, & A. F. C. Sturgill (Eds.), *Religion online: How digital technology is changing the way we worship and pray* (Vol. 2, pp. 92–109). Praeger/ABC-Clio.

Parker, H. (2011). Toward a definition of popular culture. *History and Theory*, 50(2), 147–170. https://www.jstor.org/stable/41300075

Puntel, J. (2011). A Igreja a caminho, na comunicação. *Teocomunicação*, 41(2), 221–242. https://revistaseletronicas.pucrs.br/ojs/index.php/teo/article/view/9755

Reblin, I. A. (2020). Método cartográfico-crítico para análise de artefatos da cultura pop a partir da área de ciências da religião e teologia. *Rever: Revista de Estudos da Religião*, 20(3), 11–26. https://doi.org/10.23925/1677-1222.2020vol20i3a2

Roberts, K. (2004). *The leisure industries*. Palgrave Macmillan.

Schultze, Q. (2013). Evangelicals and the power of television. In R. Woods Jr. (Ed.), *Evangelicals Christians and popular culture: Pop goes to the gospel* (Vol. 1, pp. 119–141). ABC-Clio.

Šisler, V. (2014). From Kuma\War to Quraish representation of Islam in Arab and American video games. In H. Campbell, & G. Grieve (Eds.), *Playing with religion in digital games* (pp. 109–133). Indiana University Press.

Springhall, J. (1998). *Youth, popular culture, and moral panics: Penny gaffs to gangsta-rap, 1830–1996*. Martin's Press.

Taylor, B. (2008). *Entertainment theology: New-edge spirituality in a digital democracy*. Baker Academic.

Tilley, C. (2012). Seducing the innocent: Fredric Wertham and the falsifications that helped condemn comics. *Information & Culture, 47*(4), 383–413. https://doi.org/10.1353/lac.2012.0024

Trigo, L. G. (2008). *Entretenimento: Uma crítica aberta*. Editora Senac São Paulo.

Uwah, I. E. (2011). The representation of African traditional religion and culture in Nigeria popular films. *Politics and Religion, 5*(1), 81–102. https://doi.org/10.54561/prj0501081u

Vanhoozer, K. (2007). *Everyday theology: How to read cultural texts and interpret trends*. Baker Academic.

Vokey, J., & Read, J. D. (1985). Subliminal messages: Between the devil and the media. *American Psychologist, 40*(11), 1231–1239. https://doi.org/10.1037/0003-066X.40.11.1231

von der Ruhr, M. (2019). Megachurches in the religious marketplace. In S. Hunt (Ed.), *Handbook of megachurches* (pp. 131–149). Brill.

Ward, M. (2013). Air of the king: Evangelicals and radio. In R. Woods Jr. (Ed.), *Evangelicals Christians and popular culture: Pop goes to the gospel. Volume 1: Film, radio, television, and the internet* (pp. 101–117). ABC-Clio.

Waskul, D., & Vannini, P. (2016). Introduction: Popular culture as everyday life. In D. Waskul, & P. Vannini (Eds.), *Popular culture as everyday life* (pp. 1–17). Routledge.

Weinstein, S. (2009). *Up, up, and oy vey: How Jewish history, culture, and values shaped the comic book superhero*. Barricade Books.

Wertham, F. (1954). *The seduction of the innocent*. Rinehart.

Wright, B. (2003). *Comic book nation: The transformation of youth culture in America*. Johns Hopkins University Press.

Wright, M. (2007). *Religion and film: An introduction*. I.B. Tauris.

Selected Readings

Brackett, J. (2015). Religion and comics. *Religion Compass, 9*(12), 493–500. https://doi.org/10.1111/rec3.12167

Campbell, H., & Grieve, G. (Eds.). (2014). *Playing with religion in digital games*. Indiana University Press.

Forbes, B. D., & Mahan, J. (Eds.). (2017). *Religion and popular culture in America*. University of California Press.

Lynch, G. (Ed.). (2005). *Between sacred and profane: Researching religion and popular culture*. I.B. Tauris.

21

Religion and Film

Joel Mayward

The Cave

In Werner Herzog's 2010 3D documentary film, *Cave of Forgotten Dreams*, the eccentric German filmmaker visits Chauvet Cave in southern France, which contains on its walls some of the oldest human-painted images ever discovered. The 32 000-year-old visual depictions of animals and human figures appear to move on the cave walls depending on the angle of the light source, suggesting an early form of animation. Moreover, there is evidence on the cave floor of what appears to be a religious ceremonial mound and markings. When watching Herzog's immersive film and the awe-inspiring images appear to come alive on the underground walls in the flickering light, it is not difficult to imagine Chauvet Cave as an amalgamation of sacred temple and movie theater. Not unlike Plato's allegorical cave in *The Republic*, in this real-life subterranean proto-cinema, projected moving images and human meaning-making are linked. Indeed, the relationship between film and religion has existed since before the inception of the seventh art; as French film critic André Bazin once commented, "the cinema has always been interested in God" (Bazin, 1951, p. 237).

A few millennia after Chauvet's animators, the advent of cinema as a technical apparatus in the late nineteenth century prompted critical reflection on the medium's potential for depicting religious stories, as well as generating religious experiences. During the silent era, both American and European filmmakers depicted religious stories drawn from sacred texts, including numerous "Jesus films" (Lindvall, 2011, 2019; Shepherd, 2016). Writing in 1915, poet and film theorist Vachel Lindsay recognized cinema as a site for religious significance, alluding to biblical books when describing filmmakers as "prophet-wizards" with a divine vocation, providing an "immortal soul" to the apparatus that makes visible the invisible (Lindsay, 2000, p. 172). Similarly, European film theorists observed film's potential for accessing a spiritual dimension, such as Hugo Münsterberg's "soul psychology," Edgar Morin's magical "soul of the cinema" as "affective participation," and Germaine Dulac's description of cinema as an "art of spiritual nuance" capable of capturing the immaterial. Jean Epstein's concept of *"photogénie"* suggested that film somehow bridged the gap between the conscious and unconscious, allowing access to the human soul itself (Cooper, 2013, pp. 34–39, 44–45). Bazin could be considered the patron saint of both academic film studies and the scholarly discourse of "religion and film." A heterodox Roman Catholic, Bazin originally included a single illustration accompanying his foundational essay, "The Ontology of the Photographic Image": Giuseppe Enrie's 1931 photograph of the Turin Shroud, in which we can apparently see the face of Christ imprinted on the ancient cloth (Bazin, 1967, pp.

The Handbook on Religion and Communication, First Edition. Edited by Yoel Cohen and Paul A. Soukup.
© 2023 John Wiley & Sons Ltd. Published 2023 by John Wiley & Sons Ltd.

9–16). For Bazin, the shroud correlates to cinematic celluloid in that an image is seemingly miraculously copied onto the mediating film, a visible historical icon of the invisible transcendent God that appeals to our sense of faith as much as our rational belief. The shroud's material surface has objectively captured an image from out of time and space, but the religious significance of that image demands ongoing subjective interpretations, as does the photograph – the latter is an image of an image. Bazin's inclusion of the photograph discloses his understanding of photography and cinema as being "incarnational," as the photographic image is an "absent presence" of ontological reality itself, a literal snapshot of a religiously meaningful event in time allowing us to revisit this historical religious reality over and over again in subsequent ritualistic faith (Dalle Vacche, 2020, pp. 16–19).

Though later film scholars often dismissed them as overly "mystical," these early film theorists laid the foundation for contemporary religion and film discourse. Brent Plate observes three "waves" of critical approaches to the scholarly consideration of cinema and religion in English publications (Plate, 2017b, p. xv). The first wave, from the late 1960s to early 1980s, anchored in Paul Tillich's correlational theology of culture, focused mainly on European auteurs such as Carl Theodor Dreyer, Robert Bresson, and Ingmar Bergman, as well as Japanese filmmakers Akira Kurosawa and Yasujirô Ozu. Critics noted the capacity of these films to draw attention to the divine through a humanistic approach, a transcendence by way of immanence as they addressed the "ultimate concern" of human existence via aesthetic modes outside of the typical Hollywood productions. The second wave, emerging in the late 1980s as a reaction to the earlier emphasis on arthouse cinema and operating primarily from a religious studies paradigm, examined popular Hollywood films, as "this is what the masses watch and thus when we investigate popular films we find out something about mass culture in general" (Plate, 2017b, p. xv). In Plate's view these publications emphasized film narratives by using a literary hermeneutic to treat cinema as filmic "texts." Regarding this literary approach, Melanie Wright rightly wondered if this frequent conflation of film with texts is due to the privileging of sacred scriptures over other media; she questioned whether such text-based approaches truly engaged with film *qua* film at all (Wright, 2008, pp. 21–22). Thus, the third wave (late 1990s through the 2000s) moved away from literary models of interpretation toward cinema-specific models, as well as shifted away from narrative analysis toward audience reception and how film-viewing functions as a religious activity (Plate, 2017b, pp. xv–xvi).

In the past 25 years – perhaps in a fourth "wave" beyond Plate's overview – the academic subfield has produced peer-reviewed journals like the *Journal of Religion & Film* in the United States and the *Journal for Religion, Film and Media* in Europe, as well as collections of scholarly readers and companions, not to mention dozens of edited collections and monographs (Blizek, 2013; Lindvall, 2004, 2005; Lyden, 2009; Mitchell & Plate, 2007; Plate, 2017a). Over the years, myriad typologies have attempted to classify the various approaches between religion and cinema. In *New Image of Religious Film*, John May (1997) offers one such categorization from a Roman Catholic perspective: (i) *religious discrimination (heteronomy)*, where traditional Christian orthodoxy is the ultimate norm by which cinema is judged and often condemned; (ii) *religious visibility*, which considers "religious films" as those that have overt or distinctly religious or theological elements, such as films about saints or clergy, or the Bible on film, such as the "Jesus film" and "biblical epic" genres; (iii) *religious dialogue*, a back-and-forth dialectic between film and religion, and arguably the most popular methodological descriptor (see later in the chapter); (iv) *religious humanism (theonomy)*, a Tillich-inspired approach where humanistic themes and questions of transcendence expressed in cinema correlate to theological or religious concepts; and (v) *religious aesthetics (autonomy)*, a study of cinematic formal aesthetics rather than religious or ethical content, giving priority to the distinct cinematic medium in interpretive considerations and considering how films and film-going might generate a "transcendent" or "religious" experience through the distinctive audio-visual medium (pp. 17–37). Each of these approaches has its proponents and detractors, and most can be readily applied to various religious traditions as well as film theories.

Following in this typological tradition, and borrowing categories from Plate (2017a, pp. 2–3), I have structured this overview of the current field of religion and film into three general categories: (i) *religion in film*, or cinematic depictions of religious traditions and figures; (ii) *film in religion*, how religions have utilized or responded to film; and (iii) *film as religion*, where filmgoing and filmmaking function in religion-like ways as myth, ritual, and revelation. I include case studies in order to give a specific concrete example in each category, and I have focused the filmic examples to primarily twenty-first-century cinema, as there are already a plethora of religion and film resources with earlier examples. Likewise, I strive to emphasize twenty-first-century publications to give a sense of the contemporary academic discourse. Even as I offer a range of religions and films from across the globe, my own scholarly expertise and personal background are in Western Christianity and culture, and this perspective may influence my chosen illustrations. Still, the framework will hopefully apply to world religious cinema as well as to the West. Every typology or taxonomy has its limitations and blind spots, and certainly individual films and publications go beyond imposed categories and labels. Nonetheless, the following outline may help to identify and distinguish a film or method within the polyphonic religion and film conversation.

Religion in Film

"Religion *in* film" connotes the presence of religious characters, practices, locations, symbols, or texts within the diegetic world of a film. That is, religious elements appear explicitly *within* the onscreen movie, whether as the primary narrative or as a secondary element, either quite obvious or at other times, more opaque or allusive, requiring a discerning eye and ear. Academic studies on religion *in* film use both qualitative (Rankin, 2019; Settle & Worley, 2016) and quantitative (Brant, 2012; John, 2017) methods, ranging from focused critical analysis of individual films (Sison, 2012; Welch-Larson, 2021), to cataloging broader religious symbols or figures within a variety of movies (Chong, 2020), to focusing on religious themes with the films of auteurs such as Joel and Ethan Coen (Siegler, 2016), Terrence Malick (Barnett & Elliston, 2017), and Martin Scorsese (Barnett & Elliston, 2019).

When Mel Gibson's *The Passion of the Christ* arrived in cinemas in 2004, it marked a critical shift in the contemporary public reception of religious films, and sparked numerous academic commentaries (see Beal & Linafelt, 2006; Plate, 2004). The brutally violent biblical epic depicting the 12 hours before the death of Jesus drew from medieval Passion plays, Renaissance and Baroque paintings, and Gibson's own preferred bloodlust aesthetic and apparent anti-Semitic views. The film ultimately generated over US$622 million worldwide, making it one of the – if not *the* – most financially profitable religious films of all time. Yet its apparent success stands on the shoulders of the hundreds of other such "Jesus films" (see Tatum, 2013) and movies depicting religious figures, beginning with the Lumière brothers' first public screening of a motion picture in December 1895. Indeed, one of the primary examples of religion *in* film is the cinematic depiction of important religious figures. There have been filmic depictions of Jesus (e.g. *The Gospel According to St. Matthew* (1964), *Last Days in the Desert* (2015)), Moses (e.g. *The Ten Commandments* (1956), *Exodus: Gods and Kings* (2014)), the Prophet Muhammed (e.g. *The Message* (1976), *Muhammad: The Messenger of God* (2015)), the Buddha (e.g. *Buddha Dev* (1923), *Little Buddha* (1993)), and a myriad of deities based on Hindu epics (e.g. *Jai Santoshi Maa* (1975), *Sita Sings the Blues* (2008)). There are also various depictions of saints or revered religious figures as a type of "hagiopic" (see Grace, 2009), such as the plethora of films about Roman Catholic Saint Joan of Arc, ranging from Carl Th. Dreyer's iconic 1928 silent masterpiece, *The Passion of Joan of Arc*, to Bruno Dumont's pair of wonderfully absurdist postsecular musicals, *Jeanette: The Childhood of Joan of Arc* (2017) and *Joan of Arc* (2019).

There are many films directly about priests, nuns, and other clergy, such as *Spring, Summer, Fall, Winter … and Spring* (Ki-duk Kim, 2003), *Doubt* (John Patrick Shanley, 2008), *Calvary* (John Michael McDonagh, 2014), and *The Club* (Pablo Larraín, 2015). More on the periphery, clergy perform religious rituals in films – such as presiding over weddings or funerals, preaching a sermon, or hearing confession – and characters with religious backgrounds participate in such rituals. In the Coen brothers' *Hail, Caesar!* (2016), we witness movie producer and "fixer" Eddie Mannix (Josh Brolin) going to Catholic confession before he starts his day at work in a 1950s-era fictional Hollywood studio, which is producing a "tale of the Christ." In another scene, Mannix gathers together clergy from different traditions – Protestant, Catholic, and Orthodox Christians, as well as a Jewish rabbi – to see if the cinematic depiction of Jesus is theologically "up to snuff." Another example is the awkward Passover meal in the Safdies' *Uncut Gems* (2019), which features Jewish jeweler Howard Ratner (Adam Sandler) trying to placate his estranged wife Dinah (Idina Menzel) and his violent loan shark brother-in-law Arno (Eric Bogosian), whom Howard owes US$100,000. In *Hala* (2019, Minhal Baig), a 17-year-old Pakistani-American girl navigates her fidelity to her Muslim faith while growing up in suburban Chicago. And in *Wadjda* (Haifaa al-Mansour, 2012), the first feature film shot entirely in Saudi Arabia, a young Muslim girl participates in a Qur'an recital competition in order to win money to purchase a new bike.

Internal religious conflicts of interpretation appear in film. In the Israeli film *Gett: The Trial of Viviane Amsalem* (Ronit Elkabetz, Shlomi Elkabetz, 2014) the eponymous Viviane (Ronit Elkabetz) endures the bureaucracy of a religious court presided over by rabbis in order to request a "gett" (divorce). A similar premise, but in a Muslim context, is portrayed in Asghar Farhadi's *A Separation* (2011), as a wealthy estranged "secular" couple find themselves at odds with a religiously conservative working-class husband and wife in contemporary Iran. In Mauritanian-born Malian filmmaker Abderrahmane Sissako's 2014 *Timbuktu*, militant Islamic rebels occupy a more religiously progressive community, which leads to violent confrontations due to divergent Muslim postures. And in *Menashe* (Joshua Z. Weinstein, 2017), a Yiddish-language indie American film, a recently widowed Hasidic Jewish man must attempt to remarry in order to regain custody of his son per a ruling by his ultra-Orthodox rabbi.

Religious symbols and texts appear as props and tropes, such as a character making a sign of the cross, the presence of the Bible on a bookshelf or bedside table, or an ancestral shrine as part of the household *mise-en-scène*. Even if these latter elements go unacknowledged by both the diegetic characters and the film's audience, they nevertheless imbue the film with a distinct sense of religiosity – these religious moments are usually not in the film accidentally, and thus are worthy of attention and examination.

Religion is notably prominent in the horror film genre, which often employs cultic rituals, religious sects, and sacred texts to give the terrifying onscreen images and scenes a sense of spiritual (or demonic) gravitas (see Cowan, 2016; Dhusiya, 2019; Goldberg et al., 2020). The acclaimed horror films of American filmmaker Ari Aster, *Hereditary* (2018) and *Midsommar* (2019), both feature gruesome secretive cultic rituals at the center of their narratives, drawing heavily from *Rosemary's Baby* (Roman Polanski, 1968) and *The Wicker Man* (Robin Hardy, 1973), respectively. Likewise, Robert Eggers's 2015 horror film *The Witch* uses Puritan-era Protestant catechisms and dialect to make its spiritual dread more authentic and believable. The successful *Conjuring* horror franchise centers around the alleged real-life exploits of Christian paranormal investigators/exorcists, Ed and Lorraine Warren, and the various supernatural presences they encounter (including a demonic nun). Similarly, the *Raaz* films (2002, 2009, 2012, 2016) are a popular Bollywood supernatural horror series that blends Hollywood tropes with distinctly Hindu spirituality. The Persian-language supernatural psychological horror film *Under the Shadow* (Babak Anvari, 2016) features an Islamic mother and daughter being tormented by a djinn in 1980s war-torn Tehran. The spirits of the dead are also part of French-Senegalese filmmaker Mati Diop's *Atlantics* (2019), which incorporates elements of Muslim mysticism and bodily possession, as well as Guatemalan filmmaker Jayro Bustamante's *La Llorona* (2019), which uses indigenous Latin American folklore and the supernatural to address the genocide perpetrated against the Mayan population. And a dybbuk, a malicious spirit in Jewish mythology, is central to the horror films *Demon* (Marcin Wrona, 2015) and *The Vigil* (Keith Thomas, 2019), both of which premiered at the Toronto International Film Festival. A dybbuk also plays a small role in the sinister parable-like tale that opens Joel and Ethan Coen's darkly comic *A Serious Man* (2009), itself a quasi-adaptation of the Book of Job from the Hebrew Bible.

The Bible has generated its own subgenres of "Bible films" and "biblical epics," which have in turn spawned a considerable amount of scholarly attention (Babington & Evans, 1993; Burnette-Bletsch, 2016; Clayton, 2020; Reinhartz, 2013; Walsh, 2018; see also Page, n.d., www.biblefilms. blogspot.com). Rhonda Burnette-Bletsch offers a helpful 10-part classification of ways in which the Bible is used and represented in film (Burnette-Bletsch, 2016, pp. 5–11). These categories include: celebratory adaptations that attempt onscreen historical and cultural verisimilitude to biblical stories, such as traditional "sword-and-sandal" or peplum biblical epics; transposed adaptations that feature recognizable biblical storylines and characters, but transfer the story into a new context, such as Mil Rau's *The New Gospel* (2020), which transposes the gospel narratives into a contemporary Italian setting with Jesus as a Black migrant from Cameroon fighting for immigration rights in secular Europe; genre determinations, such as musicals or comedies, e.g. Jaco Van Dormael's *The Brand New Testament* (2015) about God as a slacker living in present-day Brussels; hagiography of "minor" biblical characters; secondary (or tertiary, etc.) adaptations, which depend upon novels and plays that are themselves adaptations of biblical stories, such as *The Young Messiah* (Cyrus Nowrasteh, 2016), which adapts an Anne Rice novel about the childhood of Jesus Christ; references to the Bible as a book or cultural icon, such as the postapocalyptic film *The Book of Eli* (The Hughes Brothers, 2010) where a blind warrior (Denzel Washington) protects the last known copy of the Bible; citations, quotations, or paraphrases of a biblical text, such as the explicit use of Jeremiah 11:11 in Jordan Peele's horror film *Us* (2019); paradigms that employ biblical narrative structures or character types within the context of an ostensibly nonreligious film, i.e. the use of a Christ-figure trope; allusions and echoes that indirectly (but intentionally) bring the Bible to mind, such as the use of "biblical epic" tropes and clear parallels to the biblical Exodus story in *War for the Planet of the Apes* (Matt Reeves, 2017), or the quasi-Nativity stories of Alfonso Cuarón's *Children of Men* (2006) and Eugène Green's *The Son of Joseph* (2016); and analogues, which differ from allusions in that audiences may discern potential biblical themes or parallels even when the filmmakers never overtly intended them, such as viewing Belgian filmmakers Jean-Pierre and Luc Dardenne's *Rosetta* (1999) or *Two Days, One Night* (2014) as postsecular depictions of the Stations of the Cross, or the Dardennes' *The Son* (2002) as a reimagining of the *Akedah*, the Abraham and Isaac narrative from Genesis 22.

Case Study: The Cinematic Noah

As a case study, consider the scriptural story of Noah (Genesis 5–9) and its recent cinematic depictions and adaptations. The most direct adaptation is Darren Aronofsky's 2014 film, *Noah*, which blends the genres of biblical epic and eco-disaster blockbuster (Burnette-Bletsch & Morgan, 2017). Aronofsky incorporated extra-biblical Jewish writings from the books of Enoch and

Jubilees, as well as rabbinic commentaries, creating a fascinating (and bonkers) cinematic mid-rash of the Noah myth. There are giant rock monsters, magical flaming swords, hallucinatory dream sequences, and a somewhat unhinged Russell Crowe as the eponymous ark-builder. Crowe's Noah is an antihero environmentalist, a "righteous" man of justice who is even willing to sacrifice his own family for the sake of caring for the Earth. The film is more akin to a fantasy epic like the *Lord of the Rings* trilogy (Peter Jackson, 2001–2003) than a biopic or hagiography. Like his 2017 biblical horror allegory, *mother!*, Aronofsky imbues the film with an environmental message about caring for the natural world.

In stark tonal contrast, the 2007 Tom Shadyac comedy film *Evan Almighty* stars comedian Steve Carell as the Noah character. Carrell portrays an American congressman commissioned by God (Morgan Freeman) to build an ark for an impending flood coming to Washington DC. The film bridges between what Adele Reinhartz categorizes as the Bible *on* film and the Bible *in* film: the biblical Noah is often referenced by characters in the film, even as the film itself is a modern-day depiction of the scriptural tale (Reinhartz, 2013, pp. 9–12). In this version, God tells Evan (Noah) that his Act of Random Kindness (ARK) saved his community. Where Aronofsky's *Noah* depicts an invisible God of justice and judgment, *Evan Almighty*'s deity is kindly, gracious, and approachable.

We may also consider parallels to Noah, which are not direct depictions but rather more suggestive and allusive. Consider modern eco-disaster films – *Deep Impact* (Mimi Leder, 1998), *The Day After Tomorrow* (Roland Emmerich, 2004), and *Geostorm* (Dean Devlin, 2017) – which parallel the biblical deluge and often subtly and indirectly refer to Noah. For instance, in *Deep Impact*, as a giant comet (named "God's Hand" in the film) heads to Earth, American citizens are selected via the "Ark National Lottery" to survive in an underground facility called the "ARK Cave Site." Other apocalyptic science-fiction films, such as *WALL·E* (Andrew Stanton, 2008), *Interstellar* (Christopher Nolan, 2014), and *Passengers* (Morten Tyldum, 2016), utilize a spacecraft (a cosmic ark of sorts) to save humankind from a catastrophic destruction on Earth. Even more implicit and allusive, Jeff Nichols's 2011 thriller film *Take Shelter* never directly references Noah, but the plot has strong parallels to the biblical story: an ordinary good man (Michael Shannon) has terrifying visions of a coming storm, prompting his obsession with creating a storm shelter in his backyard to protect himself and his family. Or consider Wes Anderson's 2012 *Moonrise Kingdom*. The film incorporates two diegetic performances of Benjamin Britten's 1958 opera *Noye's Fludde* as thematic bookends to the romantic story of two 12-year-olds in 1960s New England. When the preteens run away together, it prompts an island-wide rescue effort. A huge storm and flash floods force all of the characters to seek refuge in the town church during a Britten performance; the church serves as a type of "Noah's ark" for the various pairs and couples in the story. Anderson's distinctive symmetrical visual aesthetic is even Noahic: the deliberately proportional cinematic framing often creates images of characters as "two-by-two."

Film in Religion

We now turn to "film *in* religion," that is, how religions have used or responded to film, ranging from censorship to education to proselytizing, and gradations in between. Some religions restrict imagistic depictions, such as the commandment to "make no graven images or likenesses" of God in the Jewish Decalogue, or the Muslim injunction against depicting the Prophet in certain hadiths. Other religions, such as Buddhism, Jainism, and Hinduism, have included and celebrated images and image-making (statuary, symbols, iconography, etc.) as part of their practices. There is a vast spectrum of positions between the "pro-" and "anti-" extremes, exemplified by the ongoing iconoclast–iconodule debate within Christianity. Moreover, the advent of the "moving image" of cinema in the late nineteenth century further complicated such debates – how do the plethora of audio-visual forms and media (re)shape religious practices? In addressing this question, we initially look to Christianity for some examples of how these discussions have played out.

In 1910, Rev. Herbert A. Jump published a pamphlet for local New England churches titled, "The Religious Possibilities of the Motion Picture," where he described how the new technological apparatus (and possible art form) of the cinema could be used for giving religious instruction, missionary work, and sermon illustrations (Mitchell & Plate, 2007, pp. 14–24). Jump even proposed purchasing moving picture equipment to be owned and used by his church in Connecticut, essentially turning their local church building into a religious movie house. Though Jump's church-as-cinema enterprise did not come to fruition, the audio-visual form has become a mainstay within Christianity as a tool for evangelism and proselytizing, with a long history of distinctly Christian filmmaking in the United States (see Lindvall, 2011; Lindvall & Quicke, 2011). One significant example is *The Jesus Film* (John Krish and Peter Sykes, 1979) produced by Campus Crusade for Christ, described variously as "one of the greatest evangelistic success stories" and "the most-watched, and the most-translated film in world history," having apparently been viewed by over 6 billion people since its release (Merz, 2010, p. 111). Because of heavily marketing to conservative Christian audiences, the American contemporary "faith-based film" industry has likewise been quite lucrative despite (or perhaps because of) many faith-based films' problematic depictions of race and gender, the "preachy" tone of the screenplays, and the treatment of complex problems with rose-colored spiritualized simplicity (Moore, 2018). For instance, the Kendrick brothers' 2006 film *Facing the Giants* was made for only US$100,000, yet ultimately earned over US$10.1 million in American cinemas and sold over 2.5 million DVD copies, making *Facing the Giants* one of the most financially profitable films in cinema history based on return on investment. Many American Christian evangelical mega-churches have also directly engaged with popular films through the "At the Movies" Sunday sermon series, as well as various ministry small group discussion guides and books (for examples, see Larsen, 2017; Mayward, 2015). The popular evangelistic "Alpha Film Series" produced by Holy Trinity Brompton in London (www.alpha.org) is a 10-week series of sessions that aims to cover the basic tenets of Christian doctrinal beliefs through short films and postviewing discussions. Similarly, the "NOOMA" series of short films (2002–2009) feature mega-church pastor-turned-motivational speaker Rob Bell discussing topics about Christian spirituality in conjunction with poetic indie-aesthetic filmic narratives. And "BibleProject" (www.bibleproject.com), an Oregon-based nonprofit animation company established in 2014, produces short-form animated films to explain biblical stories and concepts. BibleProject currently has about 2 million subscribers and over 100 million views worldwide on their various channels. These examples point to how a religion may adopt a positive and receptive stance toward film by incorporating filmmaking and film-viewing into its practices and teachings.

But Christianity also shows a more negative response toward film through the practices of censorship, boycott, and outcry against the immoralities of "sinful" cinema, a predominant stance throughout the twentieth century. This kind of posture traces back to Code-era Hollywood and the Catholic "Legion of Decency" (Black, 1994; Walsh, 1996), as well as Protestant organizations like the Protestant Film Commission (Romanowski, 2012). A notable twenty-first-century example came in the volatile political climate of America in autumn 2020 with a call to "cancel" the French-Senegalese film *Cuties* (Maïmouna Doucouré, 2020) and its American distributor, Netflix, owing to conservative Christian audiences' perception that the film sexually exploited young preteen girls based on an ill-considered movie poster (Wilkinson & Romano, 2020). The film's reception became a political and religious shibboleth partly fueled by the quasi-religious

adherents of the QAnon conspiracy theory. The film addresses an 11-year-old girl from a traditional Senegalese Muslim immigrant family adopting unhealthy hyper-sexualized behaviors
owing to influences from social media videos and peer pressure; ironically, the film critiques the
very ideas and practices its loudest detractors condemned. In this way, the *Cuties* controversy is a
complex example of religion *in* film (traditional Islam depicted onscreen), film *in* religion (the
Christian censorship of *Cuties*), and film *as* religion (the onscreen preteen girls' worshipful imitation and idolization of the adult dance troupes they see in online videos).

Turning from Christianity and Islam, the onscreen depiction of Hindu gods and goddesses in
India generated a variety of responses from viewers, such as prostrations upon seeing the deities
or rituals preceding a film-viewing (Lutgendorf, 2012), as well as the phenomenon of the "possessed" female spectator (Bhrugubanda, 2019). Anjali Gera Roy (2020) observes a tension between encroaching global consumerism and traditional Hindu ethics, while the Bollywood film
Padmaavat (Sanjay Leela Bhansali, 2018) generated volatile protests from both Hindu and Muslim
groups across India owing to the questionable portrayals of both religions (the film is based on
an epic Sufi poem about a Muslim king's obsession with a beautiful Hindu princess). In the
United States, Plate (2017b, p. 158) observes that in the Sri Gaayatri Mandir temple in Minneapolis,
some of the *bhajans* (devotional songs) "have been borrowed from Hindi devotional films or are
sung in a Bollywood song style."

Gil Toffell (2018) presents a fascinating study of how the "picture houses" in Jewish neighborhoods of interwar Britain in the 1920s and 1930s contributed to a sense of communal politico-
religious identity. Moreover, both documentary and historical films have functioned as memorials
for Jewish individuals and communities addressing the collective trauma of the Shoah, especially
for third-generation Holocaust survivors (see Steir-Livny, 2019). And in Japan, Hayao Miyazaki's
anime films, such as *My Neighbor Totoro* (1988) and *Spirited Away* (2001), present a form of playful
"religion-entertainment" with motifs of Buddhism and Shinto animism (religion *in* film), but
also "appear to generate hermeneutic thinking and exegesis" and "elicit ... spiritual responses" in
viewers who reflect upon and subsequently enact Miyazaki's implicit spiritual beliefs in their own
religious praxis (film *in* religion; Thomas, 2007, pp. 86–87; see also Thomas, 2012). Whether
critics see such practices as the influence of entertainment-based consumer capitalism or as an
innovative cultural appropriation, various religions nevertheless employ audio-visual media in
their rites and rituals. As a case study of film *in* religion, we now turn to a Buddhist phenomenon
in Chinese cinema.

Case Study: Buddhist Pilgrimage and Paths of the Soul

Part arthouse film, part documentary, Chinese filmmaker Zhang Yang's *Paths of the Soul* (2015)
chronicles the account of ordinary Tibetan citizens undergoing a lengthy, arduous pilgrimage to
the holy site of Lhasa. The events take place over the course of an entire year as the band of travelers lay prostrate on the ground every few paces in an act of religious contemplation. The film's
Tibetan and Chinese titles refer to Mount Kailash, the pilgrims' sacred destination. Teng-Kuan
Ng offers an overview of the simple narrative:

> In a village in eastern Tibet, an old man, reflecting on his brother's recent death, wishes to perform
> a pilgrimage while he still can. His nephew agrees to take him. A band of 11 villagers forms, each
> motivated by different reasons for joining this merit-making trip. By day, they travel westward along
> China's longest highway. By night, they huddle to sleep in their big tent pitched by the road. Through
> rain and shine, gravelly roads and murky puddles, summer heat and wintry cold, the pilgrims faith-
> fully perform prostrations. Prone to the ground, then up, again and again, for 1,600 miles. (Ng, 2020)

Ng goes on to describe how, from a Buddhist perspective, the film "unfolds like a mandala" and "nirvana is realized through the pilgrims' simple faith and equanimity." Even as this is clearly a depiction of religion *in* film, what makes *Paths of the Soul* an example of film *in* religion (and, arguably, film *as* religion) is both the production and the reception within a contemporary "secular" Chinese context, particularly with regard to the faith and practices of Tibetan Buddhism. In an interview, Zhang describes how he was drawn to create *Paths* out of a state of spiritual "lostness and confusion" (*mimang hunluan*; Wang, 2015, p. 43). He employed a relatively small crew, and invited nonprofessional local villagers who

> had no idea what a movie was when he first found them, but who sincerely wanted to do the pilgrim-age themselves. With creative openness, he worked without a script, incorporating scenes as events spontaneously arose. [...] Due to the meager compensation, Zhang wanted everyone to find their own deeper motivations for participating, in order to experience filmmaking as a 'different kind of life.' (Ng, 2020)

In a sense, the movie production itself was the catalyst and means for the pilgrims to embark on this religious journey. *Paths of the Soul* thus blurs the lines between documentary and fictional filmmaking (as well as *film* and *religion*) as the process of making the film functioned as a kind of religious ritual for everyone involved. Indeed, Zhang makes explicit connections between the production and a pilgrimage: "It was a kind of spiritual practice [*xiuxing*] for me. It doesn't have to be linked to Buddhism. But it relates to one's sense of self. That year was a process of continual self-discovery" (Wang, 2015, p. 43). In this way, through *Paths of the Soul*, both Zhang and the villagers participated in a spiritual journey both in front of and behind the camera. Zhang's follow-up film, *Soul on a String* (2016), was also a Chinese Tibetan-language journey with overt Buddhist themes: a hunter killed by lightning is saved by Gautama Buddha, who orders the hunter to escort a treasure to a holy Tibetan location.

Beyond the production, *Paths of the Soul*'s reception demonstrates the impact of film on religion. Premiering at the Toronto International Film Festival in 2015, then released widely in China in the summer of 2017, the film quickly became the highest-grossing art film in Chinese history. Despite its quiet slow-paced aesthetic, more than two-thirds of residents in some major Chinese cities watched the film in the summer of 2017, beating out some Hollywood blockbusters at the box office. Ng observes that many viewers have responded to the film in "explicitly Buddhist terms." He states that this raises critical concerns about utilizing Tibetan Buddhism for commercial purposes, a critique evidenced by the numerous viewers who rushed to sign up for tours to Tibet and other Chinese sacred mountains which may demonstrate that "the film functions like an 'opium factory' for generating escapist, interpellative fantasies." However, the overall reception has been "overwhelmingly positive," as *Paths of the Soul* is viewed as "a testimony to the 'power of faith' (*xinyang de liliang*)," and "a focal point in the public discourse on the anomie of post-Mao society" (Ng, 2020). Indeed, Zhang's docudrama offers unique insights into the latent spiritual dynamics of Tibetan Buddhist in contemporary postsocialist China, and invites further study into the religious aspects of Chinese cinema.

Film as Religion

In a *Cahiers du cinéma* essay titled, "The Festival Viewed as a Religious Order," Bazin (1955) described his experience at the Festival de Cannes – arguably the most prestigious, exclusive, and well-renowned film festival in the world – as being comparable with "the foundation of a religious Order; fully-fledged participation in the Festival is like being provisionally admitted to convent life. Indeed, the Palace which rises up on the Croisette is nothing less than the present-day monastery of the moviemaker" (Bazin, 2009 [1955], pp. 11–19). In *Sight and Sound*, Nick Roddick (2010) describes attending Cannes as a pilgrimage, calling it "the cathedral of cinema, a massive edifice steeped in ritual and tradition that bestows solemnity on the most banal of things. The badges issued to the press are more hierarchical than the Catholic church." My own experience as a film critic at Cannes in 2019 echoes Bazin's and Roddick's sentiments:

> Beyond the films themselves, I was struck by the religious dynamic of Cannes bystanders' and tourists' worshipful treatment of the films' stars… Eager mobs of onlookers – many who would likely never see a single film during the festival – would wait for hours outside the Palais or the Hotel Martinez on the Croisette, craning their necks (and their phones) for a possible glimpse of a celebrity. The red carpet served as a sort of sacred site; only the most faithful and penitent (and properly attired) were allowed to make the brief pilgrimage up the red steps into the massive Grand Théâtre Lumière (and no selfies allowed!)… I confess, seeing Tilda Swinton, Isabelle Huppert, and Willem Dafoe in the flesh does bring with it a frisson of reverence, as if one has suddenly encountered a sacred or angelic figure. (Mayward, 2019, pp. 211–212)

Beyond noting depictions of religious themes in film or the utilization of movies within a religious tradition, studies in religion and film have also observed how film can function or operate in religion-like ways – this is film *as* religion. In his groundbreaking book *Film as Religion: Myths, Morals, and Rituals*, John Lyden (2019) makes a compelling case that film can serve a religious function in our present-day milieu. Lyden (as well as Plate, 2017a, p. 13) draws from Clifford Geertz's definition of religion: "(1) a system of symbols which acts to (2) establish powerful, pervasive, and long-lasting moods and motivations in men [*sic*] by (3) formulating conceptions of a general order of existence and (4) clothing these conceptions with such an aura of factuality that (5) the moods and motivations seem uniquely realistic" (Geertz, 1973, p. 90). Lyden uses Geertz's definition to persuasively argue that films and film-going may operate as a religion (Lyden, 2019, pp. 22–36). That is, through the immersive experience of imaginative onscreen worlds and narratives which affect viewers' minds and bodies, films may function as myth, ritual, and potential revelation. This section addresses each of these three aspects in turn.

The notion of film as myth draws on a wide variety of definitions and understandings of "myth." From Joseph Campbell's singular "monomyth" to Roland Barthes's multiple "mythologies," myths address and define cosmogony and creation, history and truth, goodness and evil – they tell us not just *where* we are from but also *who* we are, *why* we exist, and *how* we should act. Significantly, most (if not all) myths have a narrative structure and form; they are communicated as *stories* – indeed, often *the* Story – which generate and inform human meaning-making (the Greek *mythos* simply means "story"). Even as cinema is not limited or relegated to solely storytelling, popular contemporary film is still generally structured as emplotted narratives, even from a wide range of nations and cultures. In this regard, the link between myth and film is quite apparent, as cinema draws upon common or long-standing cultural myths, even as films and filmmakers also define their own mythologies.

One example of the myth-making capacities of film are the popularity of contemporary superhero movies, particularly the recent immense box office success of the Marvel Cinematic Universe (MCU). Beginning with *Iron Man* (Jon Favreau, 2008) and culminating with *Avengers: Endgame* (Joe and Anthony Russo, 2019) – the latter film broke numerous box office records – the MCU films trace a lengthy episodic tale filled with fantastical heroes and villains, quests and missions, romances and betrayals, all under the auspices of incredibly high stakes. Beyond the grander mythology of the MCU, these films also deliberately employ mythological and religious elements within them (religion *in* film). For instance, the Thor films – *Thor* (Kenneth Branagh, 2011), *Thor: The Dark World* (Alan Taylor, 2013), *Thor: Ragnarok* (Taika Waititi, 2017), and *Thor: Love and Thunder* (Taika Waititi, 2022) – explicitly draw from Norse mythology and feature the "God of Thunder" as a member of the Avengers. *Doctor Strange* (Scott Derrickson, 2016) similarly draws from various Eastern mystical traditions as an American medical doctor (Benedict Cumberbatch) travels to Nepal to learn the "Mystic Arts" from the Ancient One (Tilda Swinton), and thus become the Sorcerer Supreme. And *Black Panther* (Ryan Coogler, 2018) features the mythical African kingdom of Wakanda and its king, T'Challa (Chadwick Boseman); the film opens with a father telling his son the myth narrative of Wakanda, a narrative that imbues meaning both within the diegetic world, as well as a reimagining or "other-worlding" of a real-life utopia where Black lives truly matter. What still remains in question is how to distinguish "myth" from any other meaningful story – if such distinctions even can or should be drawn – both for individuals and for wider cultures. If we follow Barthes's (2012) view that *everything* can be a myth because "the universe is infinitely fertile in suggestions" for semiotic meaning-making (pp. 217–218), then filmmakers are certainly mythmakers.

In terms of ritual, my aforementioned Cannes experience is an example of how film-viewing and film-going can function as a kind of religious practice opening up the possibility of accessing a sense of the sacred. In this way, the movie screen is seen as a sacrament or altar, the movie theater as a kind of temple or church, the film festival as a sacred site for true disciples and believers. Plate (2017b) observes two religious-like "after-images" that can emerge from film-viewing: (i) cinema's capacity to create and re-create rites and rituals, and (ii) cinematic "pilgrimages" to various global locations "that have been made sacred because they have been framed and selected as part of a filmic world" (p. 155). For rituals and rites of passage, Plate notes the rise of film-themed weddings and b'nai mitzvah, such as a *Star Wars* wedding and a *"Titanic*-themed" bat mitzvah. Moreover, film audiences also create entirely new rituals, such as the midnight singalong viewings with all the campy accoutrements of *The Rocky Horror Picture Show* (Jim Sharman, 1975), a film that has earned the conspicuously religious moniker of being a "cult" movie. More recent "cult films" that have generated broader significance through a passionate fanbase include *The Room* (Tommy Wiseau, 2003), *The Babadook* (Jennifer Kent, 2014), and *Alita: Battle Angel* (Robert Rodriguez, 2019; see Mathijs & Sexton, 2020; Romano, 2017; Roy, 2017; White, 2019). New media technologies and digital forms of communication often shape such cult(ural) phenomena; the cult movie has evolved from midnight showings at indie theaters to sharing and viewing digital copies of films online or interacting on social media. Indeed, the advent of audio-visual social media forms, such as YouTube and TikTok, also allows for individuals to build up their own "cult" following by making well-liked and oft-shared short videos and films, "religious" and otherwise. This online change requires that we attend to the evolution of *how* audiences experience films.

A second film *as* religion practice is the pilgrimage to a location primarily because of the place's onscreen significance. For instance, tourism to New Zealand skyrocketed following the success of Peter Jackson's *Lord of the Rings* trilogy (2001–2003), as Tolkien fans traveled to see the "real-life" Middle-earth where the films were shot. Likewise, one can go on a Harry Potter-themed tour to locations throughout the United Kingdom where the popular wizard coming-of-age films were made, such as taking the "Hogwarts Express" (the Jacobite Steam Train) over the Glenfinnan Viaduct in Scotland on the way to the fictional Hogwarts. While we should draw important distinctions between a religious "pilgrim" and a secular "tourist," what is significant is how cinema's use of these locations to create meaningful fictional worlds has, in a sense, *made* those locations into "sacred" sites for the visitors – a movie, quite literally, has altered the landscape for diehard fans. And, as noted, the international film festival has become a site for pilgrimage for film critics and cinephiles who travel across the globe in order to be present at a film premiere or catch a glimpse of the stars.

Finally, film functions as a means of revelation, either by way of transcendent experience or some form of divine encounter. From a Christian theological perspective, Kevin Vanhoozer (2007) observes four doctrines that have special bearing on whether God reveals Godself in and through cultural artifacts such as cinema: (i) the incarnation of Christ as God entering into world history, (ii) the notion of "general revelation," (iii) the Protestant Reformed view of "common grace" and/or the Catholic view of "natural theology," and (iv) the *imago dei* or "image of God" uniquely present in human beings and their cultural meaning-making endeavors (pp. 42–43). In this way, film can be a means of divine encounter, where cinema takes on a "sacramental" capacity (see Detweiler, 2008). In a Buddhist view, the unique audio-visual dimensions of cinema can be "a medium for cultivating certain ways of being in the world that have previously been attained through ritual and contemplative practices" (Cho, 2017, p. 1). For instance, in the short films *Walker* (2012) and *Journey to the West* (2014) from Malaysian-Taiwanese auteur Tsai Ming-Liang, a man dressed in the red robes of a Tibetan Buddhist priest walks at an excruciatingly slow pace through bustling urban settings. This deliberately "slow cinema" attunes the viewer to both the pro-filmic world, as well as their own bodily and interior world as a form of contemplation or meditation via the film-viewing experience. In my own scholarship, I have argued for "theocinematics," a constructive synthesis of theology, phenomenology, and film theory that considers film as "theology in motion" (*theos* + *kínēma*) as a theological parallel to the "film-philosophy" practiced by philosophers such as Stanley Cavell (1979), Stephen Mulhall (2016), and Robert Sinnerbrink (2011). While others in Christian theology have also emphasized the value of film aesthetics – such as Gerard Loughlin's "cinematic theology" (2004) and Paul Schrader's "transcendental style in film" (2018) – I explore how film may function simultaneously as theological reflection *about* God and potentially sacramental experience *of* God. Indeed, we may discern religious or theological significance even within so-called "secular" films viewed as "cinematic parables" (see Mayward, 2020).

Similarly, experimental filmmaker Nathaniel Dorsky (2014) describes "devotional cinema" as not necessarily referring to specific religious forms, but rather as

> the opening or the interruption that allows us to experience what is hidden, and to accept with our hearts our given situation. When film does this, when it subverts our absorption in the temporal and reveals the depths of our own reality, it opens us to a fuller sense of ourselves and our world. It is alive as a devotional form.

Dorsky goes on to describe the "post-film experience," how there is *something* in cinema beyond intellectual or narrative content that can "produce health" through its "mystical implications; it can be, at its best, a way of approaching and manifesting the ineffable." In this way, film generates "revelation or aliveness" precisely through its aesthetics: lighting, editing, cinematography, montage, etc. Moreover, Dorsky suggests that that not only film-viewing, but filmmaking, can function as a religious or spiritual practice. This echoes Zhang Yang's approach to *Paths of the Soul*, as well as the view of seminarian and documentarian Macky Alston (2004), who describes filmmaking as a spiritual practice and vocational ministry, an "intention to answer a call, whether it be bringing people together through film or some more traditional form of ministry" (p. 83).

Case Study: Star Wars and Fandom

In 2012 – the same year Disney purchased Lucasfilm – John Lyden stated that "if there is any popular culture phenomenon that can be referred to as 'religion,' it would be the fandom associated with the *Star Wars* films" (p. 775). Since Lyden's statement a decade ago, the subsequent releases of *Episodes VII–IX – The Force Awakens* (J. J. Abrams, 2015), *The Last Jedi* (Rian Johnson, 2017), and *The Rise of Skywalker* (J. J. Abrams, 2019) – as well as the standalone *"Star Wars stories"* *Rogue One* (Gareth Edwards, 2016) and *Solo* (Ron Howard, 2018), as well as TV streaming series such as *The Mandalorian* (Jon Favreau, 2019–), have further cemented the *Star Wars* saga into the popular social imagination. Informed by Joseph Campbell's monomyth theories and borrowing heavily from silent sci-fi (e.g. *Metropolis* (Fritz Lang, 1927)) and Japanese samurai films (e.g. *The Hidden Fortress* (Akira Kurosawa, 1958)), *Star Wars* has generated its own myths and rituals as a "hyper-real" or "fiction-based" religion (Davidsen, 2016; Possamai & Murray, 2011). Recent scholarly books addressing the *Star Wars* mythos from theological (McDowell, 2017) and religious studies (Derry & Lyden, 2018) perspectives have noted that the "space opera" has generated a fandom culture marked by religious zeal. Some of this fandom has become militant, as seen in the strong negative "backlash" reactions of *Star Wars* fans toward Rian Johnson's *The Last Jedi*. Where professional film critics were largely positive on the film (myself included), some disgruntled and disappointed fans campaigned to lower the Rotten Tomatoes and Metacritic audience scores, as well as harassed actress Kelly Marie Tran online to the point where she left social media altogether (VanDerWerff, 2017). More positively, a number of fan activities bear the traits of a religion, including a sense of communal identity and belonging, a "canon" of filmic lore (one that continues to generate debates as to what is "in" the canon – Han shot first!), specific language and jargon bearing transcendent or spiritual significance ("May the Force be with you"), and various rituals and practices, such as fan conventions, reenactments, cosplay, and (of course) film-viewings and the subsequent post-film discussions, either in person or online.

Star Wars may be considered an example of religion *in* film in that the saga includes a fictionalized religious order, the Jedi. The emergence of "Jediism" as a real-world religion itself is an example of film *as* religion. Markus Altena Davidsen (2016) offers a helpful overview of Jediism, what he calls a "fiction-based religion," which is "a religion that uses fictional texts as its main authoritative, religious texts. That a text is authoritative for a religion means that its members use terminology, beliefs, practices, roles, and/or social organization derived from the authoritative text as a model for their own real-world religion" (p. 377). Where *Star Wars* fandom may employ myths and rituals, Jediism takes this a step further into the realm of spirituality and theology, where the Force is viewed as being more than mere filmic fantasy. Davidsen identifies a significant contingency of individuals and groups who appear to legitimately consider Jediism as their belief system and basis for social ethics. Based on census data and online social media groups, Davidsen proposes that there are an estimated 30 000 Jediists in the UK, Canada, Australia, and New Zealand combined (p. 381). Davidsen identifies various iterations of Jediism, ranging from a philosophical "spirituality" to a more animistic "religion," with the Temple of the Jedi Order even being recognized as a nonprofit religious group under Texas laws. He ultimately concludes that *Star Wars* fandom and Jediism should be viewed as distinct, with only the latter truly deserving the label of "religion" (contra Lyden).

Whether such fandom can be considered a "religion" or not depends on how one chooses to define "religion." Further qualitative research into the specific practices and beliefs of such fiction-based religions would be beneficial for understanding the cultural and sociological influence of popular films and media, as well as how human beings are undergoing the meaning-making process in our late-modern postsecular world, perhaps even pursuing "strange rites" within popular culture itself (Burton, 2020). As Lyden (2012) suggests, "studying the way that popular culture fandom mirrors religious practice may illuminate the changing nature of religion as much as it illuminates the practices of popular culture" (p. 783). In other words, we may better understand contemporary religious practices by looking at film reception, and vice versa.

A Religious New Wave in Film

When the rebellious French New Wave of the late 1950s and early 1960s emerged with provocative masterpieces from Godard, Truffaut, Rivette, and Varda, it had ripple effects across cinematic history. I want to suggest a religious new wave in film has emerged over the past two decades, films that rival spiritual classics from Ingmar Bergman, Maya Deren, or Andrei Tarkovsky for their existential and theo-religious profundity. Such religious new wave films include (in chronological order): Philip Gröning's *Into Great Silence* (2005), Carlos Reygadas's *Silent Light* (2007), Lee Chang-Dong's *Secret Sunshine* (2007), Tomm Moore and Nora Twomey's *The Secret of Kells* (2009), Jessica Hausner's *Lourdes* (2009), Asghar Farhadi's *About Elly* (2009), Xavier Beauvois's *Of Gods and Men* (2010), Lech Majewski's *The Mill and the Cross* (2011), Terrence Malick's *The Tree of Life* (2011), Vera Farminga's *Higher Ground* (2011), Rama Burshtein's *Fill the Void* (2012), Cristian Mungiu's *Beyond the Hills* (2012), Paweł Pawlikowski's *Ida* (2013), Ava DuVernay's *Selma* (2014), Deniz Gamze Ergüven's *Mustang* (2015), Avishai Sivan's *Tikkun* (2015), Tom McCarthy's *Spotlight* (2015), Laszlo Nemes's *Son of Saul* (2015), Ciro Guerra's *Embrace of the Serpent* (2015), Martin Scorsese's *Silence* (2016), Anne Fontaine's *The Innocents* (2016), Greta Gerwig's *Lady Bird* (2017), Paul Schrader's *First Reformed* (2018), Nadav Lapid's *Synonyms* (2019), and Terrence Malick's *A Hidden Life* (2019). This is just a smattering of evocative twenty-first-century cinematic depictions of (broadly Western) religions marked by a critical-yet-open posture toward tradition and transcendence. Yet this religious new wave in film is noticeable with regard for nearly all global religious traditions – there appears to be more religion *in* film than ever before.

We can also observe a "new wave" of scholarship on religion and film from the past decade. I want to draw attention to the following five trends: (i) A dismantling of dichotomies between "arthouse" and "popular," "realist" and "formalist" films, corresponding to an expanding awareness and engagement with world cinema, particularly national cinema outside of the North Atlantic context (John, 2017; Nayar, 2012; Plate, 2003; Sison, 2006, 2012). (ii) A renewal of phenomenological approaches and an increased focus on audience reception, giving greater attention to viewers' affect and emotions, as well as bodily responses to the cinematic experience (Balstrup, 2020; Knauss, 2007; Settle & Worley, 2016). (iii) Advancements in neuroscientific and psychological understandings of how human beings perceive and experience cinema, with an emphasis on cognitivism regarding film aesthetics and transcendent movie-going experiences (Callaway et al., 2020; Pasulka, 2016; see also Zacks, 2014). (iv) An increase in religious and theological considerations of cinema beyond hegemonic Christian perspectives, including a growing appreciation of nontraditional religions and spiritualities (Dwyer, 2006; Pak-Shiraz, 2017; Petersen, 2021; Suh, 2015; Weisenfeld, 2007; Zierler, 2017). (v) An emphasis on cinematic aesthetics, paying more attention to audio-visual styles and techniques – particularly in sound, cinematography, editing, and production design – rather than merely treating films as "texts" or visual stories (Callaway, 2012; Downing, 2016; Hamner, 2011; Ponder, 2017).

Even with these broadening horizons, the religion and film discourse still remains deficient when naming and defining its theoretical and methodological positions, particularly as it relates to film studies and the philosophical dimension of cinema. Indeed, the most common methodological descriptor in religion and film is the term "dialogue," where religion and film are brought into a sort of interdisciplinary back-and-forth conversation with one another. Yet the notion of "dialogue" is problematic, as it implies a distinct separation between the "secular" film and the "sacred" autonomy of religion, which is an unnecessary dichotomy in an increasingly pluralistic world characterized by postsecular cinema (see Bradatan & Ungureanu, 2014; Caruana & Cauchi, 2018). Additionally, despite stated good intentions, in practice the supposed dialogue is more often like a monologue, with religion typically having the first and last word on the subject. As

Stefanie Knauss rightly notes, scholars of religion studying film "tend to use religious concepts in order to think about film, but not the other way around, and typologies of the relationship between film and religion look at how religions or their representatives have reacted to film, but not at how films or their producers relate to religion" (Knauss, 2020, p. 84).

Recognizing that there can be no singular way to approach religion and film, I want to propose an alternative to the dialogical hegemony described: a methodology of *montage*. While "montage" is synonymous with "editing" in American film terminology, *editing* suggests trimming or removal, whereas the French *montage* connotes a creative constructive or assembly process between two or more images or sequences. Arguably the essential distinction of the cinematic form, montage is described by Bazin (1967) as "the creation of a sense or meaning not proper to the images themselves but derived exclusively from their juxtaposition" (p. 25). In this constructive way, both religion and film are brought together in tandem, and new meanings are generated for each discipline. Where "dialogue" tends to result in mere comparisons or analogies while each interlocutor can remain essentially unchanged, the fundamental goal of montage is the generation of multiple fresh understandings of reality, with both participants transformed by the encounter. Thus, scholars of religion must learn the language and terminology of film and media studies, while film and media scholars ought to grow in appreciation and knowledge of theological beliefs, sacred texts, and religious traditions. Through montage, perhaps the next wave of religion and film scholarship can employ cinematic metaphors and methodologies as a way of expanding our understanding of both fields. In other words, how might we view cinema religiously as well as view religion cinematically?

References

Alston, M. (2004). Filmmaking as spiritual practice and ministry. *CrossCurrents, 54*(1), 76–83.

Babington, B., & Evans, W. (1993). *Biblical epics: Sacred narrative in the Hollywood cinema.* Manchester University Press.

Balstrup, S. (2020). *Spiritual sensations. Cinematic religious experience and evolving conceptions of the sacred.* Bloomsbury.

Barnett, C., & Elliston, C. (2017). *Theology and the films of Terrence Malick.* Routledge.

Barnett, C., & Elliston, C. (2019). *Scorsese and religion.* Brill.

Barthes, R. (2012). *Mythologies* (R. Howard, & A. Lavers, Trans.). Hill and Wang.

Bazin, A. (1951). Cinéma et théologie. *Esprit, 19*(176), 237–245.

Bazin, A. (1967). *What is cinema?* (Vol. I, H. Gray, Trans.). University of California Press.

Bazin, A. (2009). The festival viewed as a religious order. In R. Porton (Ed.), *On film festivals (Dekalog³)* (pp. 11–19). Wallflower Press. (Original work published 1955)

Beal, T., & Linafelt, T., (Eds.). (2006). *Mel Gibson's Bible: Religion, popular culture, and The Passion of the Christ.* University of Chicago Press.

Bhrugubanda, U. (2019). *Deities and devotees: Cinema, religion, and politics in South India.* Oxford University Press.

Black, G. (1994). *Hollywood censored: Morality codes, Catholics, and the movies.* Cambridge University Press.

Blizek, W. (Ed.). (2013). *The Bloomsbury companion to religion and film.* Bloomsbury.

Bradatan, C., & Ungureanu, C. (Eds.). (2014). *Religion in contemporary European cinema: The postsecular constellation.* Routledge.

Brant, J. (2012). *Paul Tillich and the possibility of revelation through film.* Oxford University Press.

Burnette-Bletsch, R. (Ed.). (2016). *The Bible in motion: A handbook of the Bible and its reception in film.* De Gruyter.

Burnette-Bletsch, R., & Morgan, J. (Eds.). (2017). *Noah as antihero: Darren Aronofsky's cinematic deluge.* Routledge.

Burton, T. (2020). *Strange rites: New religions for a godless world*. PublicAffairs.

Callaway, K. (2012). *Scoring transcendence: Contemporary film music as religious experience*. Baylor University Press.

Callaway, K., Schnitker, S., & Gilbertson, M. (2020). Not all transcendence is created equal: Distinguishing ontological, phenomenological, and subjective beliefs about transcendence. *Philosophical Psychology*, *33*(4), 479–510.

Caruana, J., & Cauchi, M. (2018). *Immanent frames: Postsecular cinema between Malick and von Trier*. SUNY Press.

Cavell, S. (1979). *The world viewed: Reflections on the ontology of film*. (Enlarged, ed.). Harvard University Press.

Cho, F. (2017). *Seeing like the Buddha: Enlightenment through film*. SUNY Press.

Chong, K. (2020). *Transcendence and spirituality in Chinese cinema: A theological exploration*. Routledge.

Clayton, W. (Ed.). (2020). *The Bible onscreen in the new millennium: New heart and new spirit*. Manchester University Press.

Cooper, S. (2013). *The soul of film theory*. Palgrave Macmillan.

Cowan, D. (2016). *Sacred terror: Religion and horror on the silver screen*. Baylor University Press.

Dalle Vacche, A. (2020). *André Bazin's film theory: Art, science, religion*. Oxford University Press.

Davidsen, M. (2016). From *Star Wars* to Jediism: The emergence of fiction-based religion. In E. van den Hemel, & A. Szafraniec (Eds.), *Words: Religious language matters* (pp. 376–389). Fordham University Press.

Derry, K., & Lyden, J. (2018). *The myth awakens: Canon, conservatism, and fan reception of Star Wars*. Cascade Books.

Detweiler, C. (2008). *Into the dark: Seeing the sacred in the top films of the 21st century*. Baker Academic.

Dhusiya, M. (2019). *Indian horror cinema: (En)gendering the monstrous*. Routledge.

Dorsky, N. (2014). *Devotional cinema* (3rd ed.). Tuumba.

Downing, C. (2016). *Salvation from cinema: The medium is the message*. Routledge.

Dwyer, R. (2006). *Filming the gods: Religion and Indian cinema*. Routledge.

Geertz, C. (1973). Religion as a cultural system. In C. Geertz (Ed.), *The interpretation of cultures: Selected essays* (pp. 87–125). Basic Books.

Goldberg, E., Sen, A., & Collins, B. (Eds.). (2020). *Bollywood horrors: Religion, violence, and cinematic fears in India*. Bloomsbury.

Grace, P. (2009). *The religious film: Christianity and the hagiopic*. Wiley-Blackwell.

Hamner, M. (2011). *Imaging religion in film: The politics of nostalgia*. Palgrave Macmillan.

John, M. (2017). *Film as cultural artifact: Religious criticism of world cinema*. Fortress Press.

Knauss, S. (2007). The sensuality of sense: Reflections on the bodily dimension of filmic and religious experience. In S. Knauss, & A. Ornella (Eds.), *Reconfigurations: Interdisciplinary perspectives on religion in a post-secular society* (pp. 197–216). LIT Verlag.

Knauss, S. (2020). *Religion and film: Representation, experience, meaning*. Brill.

Larsen, J. (2017). *Movies are prayers: How films voice our deepest longings*. IVP Press.

Lindsay, V. (2000). *The art of the moving picture*. Modern Library.

Lindvall, T. (2004). Religion and film, part I: History and criticism. *Communication Research Trends*, *23*(4), 1–44.

Lindvall, T. (2005). Religion and film, part II: Theology and pedagogy. *Communication Research Trends*, *24*(1), 1–40.

Lindvall, T. (2011). *Sanctuary cinema: Origins of the Christian film industry*. NYU Press.

Lindvall, T. (2019). *God on the big screen: A history of Hollywood prayer from the silent era to today*. NYU Press.

Lindvall, T., & Quicke, A. (2011). *Celluloid sermons: The emergence of the Christian film industry, 1930–1986*. NYU Press.

Loughlin, G. (2004). *Alien sex: The body and desire in cinema and theology*. Blackwell.

Lutgendorf, P. (2012). Ritual reverb: Two "blockbuster" Hindi films. *South Asian Popular Culture*, *10*(1), 63–76.

Lyden, J. (Ed.). (2009). *The Routledge companion to religion and film*. Routledge.

Lyden, J. (2012). Whose film is it, anyway? Canonicity and authority in *Star Wars* fandom. *Journal of the American Academy of Religion*, *80*(3), 775–786.

Lyden, J. (2019). *Film as religion: Myths, morals, and rituals* (2nd ed.). NYU Press.

Mathijs, E., & Sexton, J. (Eds.). (2020). *The Routledge companion to cult cinema*. Routledge.

May, J. (Ed.). (1997). *New image of religious film*. Sheed and Ward.

Mayward, J. (2015). *Jesus goes to the movies: The youth ministry film guide*. The Youth Cartel.

Mayward, J. (2019). Festival review, 72nd Festival de Cannes: Finding faith in film. *Journal for Religion, Media and Film, 5*(2), 204–213.

Mayward, J. (2020). The fantastic of the everyday: Re-forming definitions of cinematic parables with Paul Ricoeur. *Horizons, 47*(2), 283–314.

McDowell, J. (2017). *The Gospel according to Star Wars: Faith, hope and the Force* (2nd ed.). Westminster John Knox.

Merz, J. (2010). Translation and the visual predicament of the "JESUS" film in West Africa. *Missiology, 38*(2), 111–126.

Mitchell, J., & Plate, S. B. (Eds.). (2007). *The religion and film reader*. Routledge.

Moore, R. (2018). "Take my film and let it be": Critics and consecration in faith-based cinema. *The Journal of Religion and Popular Culture, 30*(3), 143–164.

Mulhall, S. (2016). *On film* (3rd ed.). Routledge.

Nayar, S. (2012). *The sacred and the cinema: Reconfiguring the 'genuinely' religious film*. Bloomsbury.

Ng, T.-K. (2020). *The open road: Zhang Yang's "Paths of the Soul" and the contemporary Chinese quest for faith*. Paper presented at the American Academy of Religion Annual Meeting, Online. December 7.

Page, M. (n.d.). Bible films blog. Bible FilmsRetrieved April 14, 2022, from https://biblefilms.blogspot.com

Pak-Shiraz, N. (2017). *Shi'i Islam in Iranian cinema: Religion and spirituality in film*. I.B. Tauris.

Pasulka, D. (2016). "The fairy-tale is true": Social technologies of the religious supernatural in film and new media. *Journal of the American Academy of Religion, 84*(2), 530–547.

Petersen, K. (Ed.). (2021). *Muslims in the movies: A global anthology*. Harvard University Press.

Plate, S. B. (Ed.). (2003). *Representing religion in world cinema: Filmmaking, mythmaking, culture making*. Palgrave Macmillan.

Plate, S. B. (Ed.). (2004). *Re-viewing the passion: Mel Gibson's film and its critics*. Palgrave Macmillan.

Plate, S. B. (2017a). *Film and religion: Critical concepts in media and cultural studies*. Routledge.

Plate, S. B. (2017b). *Religion and film: Cinema and the re-creation of the world* (2nd ed.). Columbia University Press.

Ponder, J. (2017). *Art cinema and theology: The word was made flesh*. Palgrave Macmillan.

Possamai, A., & Murray, L. (2011). Hyper-real religions: Fear, anxiety, and late-modern religious innovation. *Journal of Sociology, 47*(3), 227–242.

Rankin, D. (2019). *Film and the afterlife*. Routledge.

Reinhartz, A. (2013). *Bible and cinema: An introduction*. Routledge.

Roddick, N. (2010). The annual pilgrimage. *Sight & Sound, 20*(7), 15.

Romano, A. (2017, 19 December). *The Room*: How the worst movie ever became a Hollywood legend as bizarre as its creator. Vox. Retrieved April 14, 2022, from https://www.vox.com/culture/2017/12/2/16720012/the-room-tommy-wiseau-backstory-explained

Romanowski, W. (2012). *Reforming Hollywood: How American Protestants fought for freedom at the movies*. Oxford University Press.

Roy, A. G. (2020). Consuming Bollywood. *Journal of Religion & Film, 24*(2), 1–40.

Roy, J. (2017, June 9). *The Babadook* as an LGBT icon makes sense. No, really. Los Angeles Times. Retrieved April 14, 2022, from https://www.latimes.com/entertainment/movies/la-et-mn-babadook-gay-icon-lgbt-history-20170609-story.html

Schrader, P. (2018). *Transcendental style in film: Ozu, Bresson, Dreyer*. University of California Press (Original work published 1972)

Settle, Z., & Worley, T. (Eds.). (2016). *Dreams, doubt, and dread: The spiritual in film*. Cascade Books.

Shepherd, D. (Ed.). (2016). *The silents of Jesus in the cinema (1897–1927)*. Routledge.

Siegler, E. (Ed.). (2016). *Coen: Framing religion in amoral order*. Baylor University Press.

Sinnerbrink, R. (2011). *New philosophies of film: Thinking images*. Continuum.

Sison, A. (2006). *Screening Schillebeeckx: Theology and third cinema in dialogue*. Palgrave Macmillan.

Sison, A. (2012). *World cinema, theology and the human: Humanity in deep focus*. Routledge.

Steir-Livny, L. (2019). *Remaking Holocaust memories: Documentary cinema by third-generation survivors in Israel*. Syracuse University Press.

Suh, S. (2015). *Silver screen Buddha: Buddhism in Asian and western film*. Bloomsbury.

Tatum, W. (2013). *Jesus at the movies: A guide to the first hundred years and beyond* (3rd ed.). Polebridge Press.

Thomas, J. B. (2007). *Shûkyô Asobi* and Miyazaki Hayao's. *Anime. Nova Religio: The Journal of Alternative and Emergent Religions, 10*(3), 73–95.

Thomas, J. B. (2012). *Drawing on tradition: Manga, anime, and religion in contemporary Japan.* University of Hawaii Press.

Toffell, G. (2018). *Jews, cinema and public life in interwar Britain.* Palgrave Macmillan.

VanDerWerff, E. (2017, December 19). The "backlash" against Star Wars: The Last Jedi, explained. Vox. Retrieved April 14, 2022, from https://www.vox.com/culture/2017/12/18/16791844/star-wars-last-jedi-backlash-controversy

Vanhoozer, K. (2007). What is everyday theology? How and why Christians should read culture. In K. Vanhoozer, C. Anderson, & M. Sleasman (Eds.), *Everyday theology: How to read cultural texts and interpret trends* (pp. 15–60). Baker Academic.

Walsh, F. (1996). *Sin and censorship: The Catholic Church and the motion picture industry.* Yale University Press.

Walsh, R. (Ed.). (2018). *T&T Clark companion to the Bible and film.* T&T Clark.

Wang, H. (2015). Faxian ziwo de chaosheng zhi lu – Gang renboqi daoyan chuangzuo tan [Discovering one's self via the path of pilgrimage: A conversation with the director of *Paths of the Soul* on its creative production]. *Beijing Dianying Xueyuan Xuebao*, (6), 41–43.

Weisenfeld, J. (2007). *Hollywood be thy name: African American religion in film, 1929–1949.* University of California Press.

Welch-Larson, S. (2021). *Becoming alien: The beginning and end of evil in science fiction's most idiosyncratic film franchise.* Cascade Books.

White, A. (2019, July 10). The cult of 'Alita: Battle Angel' – alt-right parable or neglected classic? The Independent. Retrieved April 14, 2022, from https://www.independent.co.uk/arts-entertainment/films/features/alita-battle-angel-alitaarmy-fandom-james-cameron-alt-right-a8984711.html

Wilkinson, A., & Romano, A. (2020, September 11). How Cuties, a French movie on Netflix, became part of America's culture war. Vox. Retrieved April 14, 2022, from https://www.vox.com/culture/21431237/cuties-cancel-netflix-controversy-explained

Wright, M. (2008). *Religion and film: An introduction.* I.B. Taurus.

Zacks, J. (2014). *Flicker: Your brain on movies.* Oxford University Press.

Zierler, W. (2017). *Movies and midrash: Popular film and Jewish religious conversation.* SUNY Press.

Selected Readings

Bradatan, C., & Ungureanu, C. (Ed.). (2014). *Religion in contemporary European cinema: The postsecular constellation.* Routledge.

Burnette-Bletsch, R. (Ed.). (2016). *The Bible in motion: A handbook of the Bible and its reception in film.* De Gruyter.

Knauss, S. (2020). *Religion and film: Representation, experience, meaning.* Brill.

Lyden, J. (2019). *Film as religion: Myths, morals, and rituals* (2nd ed.). NYU Press.

Mayward, J. (2022). *The Dardennes brothers' cinematic parables: Integrating theology, philosophy, and film.* Routledge.

Plate, S. B. (2017). *Religion and film: Cinema and the re-creation of the world* (2nd ed.). Columbia University Press.

Solano, J. R. (2021). *Religion and film: The basics.* Routledge.

Filmography

About Elly. Directed by Asghar Farhadi. 2009. Iran.

A Hidden Life. Directed by Terrence Malick. 2019. United States/UK/Germany.

Alita: Battle Angel. Directed by Robert Rodriguez. 2019. United States/Japan/Canada.

A Separation. Directed by Asghar Fardahi. 2011. Iran.

A Serious Man. Directed by Joel and Ethan Coen. 2009. United States.

Atlantics. Directed by Mati Diop. 2019. France/Senegal/Belgium.

Avengers: Endgame. Directed by Joe and Anthony Russo. 2019. United States.

Beyond the Hills. Directed by Cristian Mungiu. 2012. Romania/France/Belgium.

Black Panther. Directed by Ryan Coogler. 2018. United States.

Buddha Dev. Directed by Dhundiraj Govind Phalke. 1923. India.

Calvary. Directed by John Michael McDonagh. 2014. Ireland/UK.

Cave of Forgotten Dreams. Directed by Werner Herzog. 2010. Canada/United States/France/Germany/UK.

Children of Men. Directed by Alfonso Cuarón. 2006. United States/UK/Japan.

Cuties. Directed by Maïmouna Doucouré. 2020. France.

Deep Impact. Directed by Mimi Leder. 1998. United States.

Demon. Directed by Marcin Wrona. 2015. Poland/Israel.

Doctor Strange. Directed by Scott Derrickson. 2016. United States.

Doubt. Directed by John Patrick Shanley. United States.

Embrace of the Serpent. Directed by Ciro Guerra. 2015. Colombia/Venezuela/Argentina.

Evan Almighty. Directed by Tom Shadyac. 2007. United States.

Exodus: Gods and Kings. Directed by Ridley Scott. 2014. United States/UK/Spain.

Facing the Giants. Directed by Alex Kendrick. 2006. United States.

Fill the Void. Directed by Rama Burshtein. 2012. Israel.

First Reformed. Directed by Paul Schrader. 2018. United States/UK/Australia.

Geostorm. Directed by Dean Devlin. 2017. United States.

Gett: The Trial of Viviane Amsalem. Directed by Ronit Elkabetz and Shlomi Elkabetz. 2014. Israel/France/Germany.

Hail, Caesar!. Directed by Joel and Ethan Coen. 2016. United States.

Hala. Directed by Minhal Baig. 2019. United States.

Hereditary. Directed by Ari Aster. 2018. United States.

Higher Ground. Directed by Vera Farminga. 2011. United States.

Ida. Directed by Paweł Pawlikowski. 2013. Poland/Denmark/France/UK.

Interstellar. Directed by Christopher Nolan. 2014. United States/UK/Canada.

Into Great Silence. Directed by Philip Gröning. 2005. France/Switzerland/Germany.

Iron Man. Directed by Jon Favreau. 2008. United States/Canada.

Jai Santoshi Maa. Directed by Vijay Sharma. 1975. India.

Jeanette: The Childhood of Joan of Arc. Directed by Bruno Dumont. 2017. France.

Joan of Arc. Directed by Bruno Dumont. 2019. France.

Journey to the West. Directed by Tsai Ming-liang. 2014. Taiwan/France.

La Llorona. Directed by Jayro Bustamante. 2019. Guatemala.

Lady Bird. Directed by Greta Gerwig. 2017. United States.

Last Days in the Desert. Directed by Rodrigo Garcia. 2015. United States.

Little Buddha. Directed by Bernardo Bertolucci. 1993. Italy/UK/France/Liechtenstein.

Lourdes. Directed by Jessica Hausner. 2009). Austria/France/Germany.

Menashe. Directed by Joshua Z. Weinstein. 2017. United States.

Metropolis. Directed by Fritz Lang. 1927. Germany.

Midsommar. Directed by Ari Aster. 2019. United States/Sweden.

Moonrise Kingdom. Directed by Wes Anderson. 2012. United States.

mother!. Directed by Darren Aronofsky. 2017. United States.

Muhammad: The Messenger of God. Directed by Majid Majidi. 2015. Iran.

Mustang. Directed by Deniz Gamze Ergüven. 2015. Turkey/France/Germany/Qatar.

My Neighbor Totoro. Directed by Hayao Miyazaki. 1988. Japan.

Noah. Directed by Darren Aronofsky. 2014. United States.

Of Gods and Men. Directed by Xavier Beauvois. 2010. France.

Padmaavat. Directed by Sanjay Leela Bhansali. 2018. India.

Paths of the Soul. Directed by Zhang Yang. 2015. China.

Passengers. Directed by Morten Tyldum. 2016. United States/Australia.

Raaz. Directed by Vikram Bhatt. 2002. India.

Raaz: The Mystery Continues. Directed by Mohit Suri. 2009. India.

Raaz 3: The Third Dimension. Directed by Vikram Bhatt. 2012. India.

Raaz Reboot. Directed by Vikram Bhatt. 2016. India.

Rogue One: A Star Wars Story. Directed by Gareth Edwards. 2016. United States.

Rosemary's Baby. Directed by Roman Polanski. 1968. United States.

Rosetta. Directed by Jean-Pierre and Luc Dardenne. 1999. Belgium/France.

Secret Sunshine. Directed by Lee Chang-Dong. 2007. South Korea.

Selma. Directed by Ava DuVernay. 2014. United States.

Silence. Directed by Martin Scorsese. 2016. United States/UK/Taiwan/Japan/Mexico/Italy.

Silent Light. Directed by Carlos Reygadas. 2007. Mexico/France/the Netherlands/Germany.

Sita Sings the Blues. Directed by Nina Paley. 2008. United States.

Solo: A Star Wars Story. Directed by Ron Howard. 2018. United States.

Son of Saul. Directed by Laszlo Nemes. 2015. Hungary.

Soul on a String. Directed by Zhang Yang. 2016. China.

Spirited Away. Directed by Hayao Miyazaki. 2001. Japan.

Spotlight. Directed by Tom McCarthy. 2015. United States.

Spring, Summer, Fall, Winter...and Spring. Directed by Ki-duk Kim. South Korea.

Star Wars: Episode VII – The Force Awakens. Directed by J.J. Abrams. 2015. United States.

Star Wars: Episode VIII – The Last Jedi. Directed by Rian Johnson. 2017. United States.

Star Wars: Episode IX – The Rise of Skywalker. Directed by J.J. Abrams. 2019. United States.

Synonyms. Directed by Nadav Lapid. 2019. Israel/France/Germany.

Take Shelter. Directed by Jeff Nichols. 2011. United States.

The Babadook. Directed by Jennifer Kent. 2014. Australia/Canada.

The Book of Eli. Directed by Albert and Allen Hughes. 2010. United States.

The Brand New Testament. Directed by Jaco Van Dormael. 2015. Belgium/France/Luxembourg.

The Club. Directed by Pablo Larraín. 2015. Chile.

The Conjuring. Directed by James Wan. 2013. United States.

The Day After Tomorrow. Directed by Roland Emmerich. 2004. United States.

The Gospel According to St. Matthew. Directed by Pier Paulo Pasolini. 1964. Italy/France.

The Hidden Fortress. Directed by Akira Kurosawa. 1958. Japan.

The Innocents. Directed by Anne Fontaine. 2016. France/Poland.

The Jesus Film. Directed by John Krish and Peter Sykes. 1979. United States.

The Lord of the Rings: The Fellowship of the Ring. Directed by Peter Jackson. 2001. New Zealand/United States.

The Lord of the Rings: The Two Towers. Directed by Peter Jackson. 2002. New Zealand/United States.

The Lord of the Rings: The Return of the King. Directed by Peter Jackson. 2003. New Zealand/United States.

The Mandalorian. Created by Jon Favreau. 2019–. United States.

The Message. Directed by Moustapha Akkad. 1976. Lebanon/Libya/Kuwait/Morocco/UK/Saudi Arabia/Egypt.

The Mill and the Cross. Directed by Lech Majewski. 2011. Poland/Sweden.

The New Gospel. Directed by Milo Rau. 2020. Germany/Switzerland/Italy.

The Passion of Joan of Arc. Directed by Carl Theodor Dreyer. 1928. France.

The Passion of the Christ. Directed by Mel Gibson. 2004. United States.

The Rocky Horror Picture Show. Directed by Jim Sharman. 1975. UK/United States.

The Room. Directed by Tommy Wiseau. 2003. United States.

The Secret of Kells. Directed by Tomm Moore and Nora Twomey. 2009. Ireland/France/Belgium/Netherlands/United States/Denmark/Brazil/Germany/Austria/Hungary.

The Son. Directed by Jean-Pierre and Luc Dardenne. 2002. Belgium/France.

The Son of Joseph. Directed by Eugène Green. 2016. France/Belgium.

The Ten Commandments. Directed by Cecil B. DeMille. 1956. United States.

The Tree of Life. Directed by Terrence Malick. 2011. United States.

The Vigil. Directed by Keith Thomas. 2019. United States.

The Wicker Man. Directed by Robin Hardy. 1973. UK.

The Witch. Directed by Robert Eggers. 2015. United States/Canada.

The Young Messiah. Directed by Cyrus Nowrasteh. 2016. United States/South Korea.

Thor: Love and Thunder. Directed by Taika Waititi. 2022. United States.

Thor: Ragnarok. Directed by Taika Waititi. 2017. United States/Australia.

Thor: The Dark World. Directed by Alan Taylor. 2013. United States.

Thor. Directed by Kenneth Branagh. 2011. United States.

Tikkun. Directed by Avishai Sivan. 2015. Israel.

Timbuktu. Directed by Abderrahmane Sissako. 2014. Mauritania/France/Qatar.

Titanic. Directed by James Cameron. 1997. United States/Mexico/Australia/Canada.

Two Days, One Night. Directed by Jean-Pierre and Luc Dardenne. 2014. Belgium/France.

Uncut Gems. Directed by Josh and Benny Safdie. 2019. United States.

Under the Shadow. Directed by Babak Anvari. 2016. UK/Jordan/Qatar/Iran.

Us. Directed by Jordan Peele. 2019. United States.

Wadjda. Directed by Haifaa al-Mansour. 2012. Saudi Arabia/Netherlands/Germany/Jordan/UAE/United States.

Walker. Directed by Tsai Ming-liang. 2012. Hong Kong.

WALL·E. Directed by Andrew Stanton. 2008. United States.

War for the Planet of the Apes. Directed by Matt Reeves. 2017. United States/Canada/New Zealand.

22

Documentary Film and Religious Faith in Historical Perspective

John P. Ferré

In 1910, when patrons crowded into store-front nickelodeons to watch short actualities, Herbert Jump reflected on the potential that the popular new medium held for churches in *The Religious Possibilities of the Motion Picture*. The minister of New Britain, Connecticut's South Congregational Church, identified five ways that motion pictures could serve religious organizations. Jump suggested that churches open their sanctuaries and fellowship halls to provide their neighborhoods with wholesome entertainment. Movies could also serve Sunday schools by providing religious instruction. Similarly, films on travel and ethnology as well as those featuring the work of medical and industrial missions could assist the promotion of foreign and home missions. Films about health, child care, history, and civics could provide essential information to promote community education especially among immigrant populations because the language of film is universal, what he called "a sort of graphic esperanto." Finally, Jump envisioned films providing preachers in the pulpit with "pictorial, dramatic, and above all, interesting" sermon illustrations. Writing in the era of such creative silent movies as Sidney Olcott's *Ben-Hur* (1907), J. Stuart Blackton's *The Life of Moses* (1909), and D. W. Griffith's *A Drunkard's Reformation* (1909), Jump saw film as a medium of entertainment, education, outreach, and inspiration (Jump, 1910, pp. 23–25).

Most of the writing about religion and film in the century since Jump published his pamphlet has concerned fictional features, films that portray scriptures on screen, tell ostensibly religious stories, or infuse secular narratives with religious meaning, unlike documentaries about religion, which purport to be nonfiction expositions of actual events. Whether popular or scholarly, this literature typically offers theological interpretations of commercial movies, sometimes ostensibly religious, often not. This focus misses histories of nonfiction films about religion. As film historian Ian Aitken (2013, p. 1) points out, "Documentary film is the founding genre of the cinema," and religion was among its earliest subjects, but no history of documentaries about religion exists. *Activist Documentary Film in Pakistan: The Emergence of a Cinema of Accountability* is close, but none of the films author Rahat Imran (2016) discusses had much impact outside of Pakistan. Likewise, *The Amish and the Media* (Eitzen, 2008) includes a chapter on documentaries, but its tight focus leaves no room for explaining documentary films about religion beyond the Amish experience. Standard treatments of documentaries such as Erik Barnouw's *Documentary: A History of the Non-Fiction Film* (1993), Bill Nichols' *Introduction to Documentary* (2017), and Patricia Aufderheide's *Documentary Film: A Very Short Introduction* (2007) say little about religion.

The Handbook on Religion and Communication, First Edition. Edited by Yoel Cohen and Paul A. Soukup.

The Routledge Companion to Religion and Film says nothing about documentaries (Lyden, 2009). The *Bloomsbury Companion to Religion and Film* summarizes some recent documentaries about Jewish, Christian, and Muslim subjects, but without historical perspective (Blizek, 2013). Similarly, popular and academic articles offer contemporary analyses of individual documentaries including *Into Great Silence* (2005), *Religulous* (2008), and *Where in the World Is Osama Bin Laden?* (2008), but they do not address the broader history of documentaries about religion. That is, individual documentaries about religion have been studied in terms of their production, content, distribution, and audience, but their collective history has been overlooked.

In their *Companion to Contemporary Documentary Film*, co-editors Alexandra Juhasz and Alisa Lebow (2015) introduce a section on religion that has one chapter on documentaries about Buddhism (Fenner, 2015), another about Israeli documentaries (Morag, 2015), and a third on the 1987 Vietnamese documentary, *The Story of Kindness or How to Behave* (Wilson, 2015), by observing, "Religion is not the first theme that comes to mind when thinking about documentary film or, for that matter, scholarship about documentary" (Juhasz & Lebow, 2015, p. 337). They attribute the inattention to religion in documentary studies to a bent toward activism and social change and away from issues of spirituality. Just as documentaries avoid addressing "the spiritual quest at the heart of religion" and focus instead on institutional and material practices, Juhasz and Lebow (2015) point out that documentary studies which engage religion do so "from a critical, historical, aesthetic, cultural, and/or ethnographic position" (pp. 337–338).

However much documentaries about religion have shied away from the ineffable, they represent a consistent theme in the history of film. They examine a variety of traditions and subjects. Many of them became socially significant, important both in their time and for subsequent generations. And consistent with the history of documentary films in general, the earliest documentaries about religion were actualities and travelogues, followed by generations of expository, poetic, observational, participatory, and hybrid compositions. The history of documentaries about religion reveals how they have challenged generations of viewers with their images and perspectives on belief, expression, and behavior.

Silent Actualities and Travelogues

Just two years after the Lumière brothers exhibited their first film in Paris in 1895, the 46-second *Workers Leaving the Lumière Factory*, the Salvation Army in Melbourne, Australia, became the first religious group to produce its own films. Two dozen one-minute moving picture "actualities" of such events as children exercising and revivalists selling *The War Cry* on a city street were made to complement the slides and sound recordings that Herbert Booth, a son of Salvation Army founder William Booth, used to accompany his barnstorming lecture titled "Social Salvation." Joseph Perry, the cinematographer who made the movies for Booth, eventually worked for Australasian Films, the premier producer and distributor of films in Australia through the 1920s.

Inspired by the success of its sister mission in Australia, the Salvation Army in Britain began producing films of its own in 1903. The motivation was simple: the Salvation Army wanted a novelty to raise the low attendance at its meeting halls on weeknights. In the East End of London, for instance, Congress Hall had been reporting Saturday evening attendance of just 250 for an auditorium that could accommodate over 3000. But after 1906 when these services showcased movies, Congress Hall filled to capacity. Film services produced similar successes in other locations. Attendance at services in Northampton grew from 80 to 1000 and in Glasgow City Hall from several hundred to over 3000. The small admission fee that those in attendance paid made the film services remunerative (Rapp, 1996, pp. 165–170).

The films captured scenes from both home and abroad. A 1903 film showed homeless and unemployed men learning how to raise poultry and make bricks on the Salvation Army's 900-acre Hadley Farm in Essex. *Our Slummers at Work* showed a policeman breaking up an inner-city street brawl witnessed by Salvation Army officers. *William and Bramwell Booth at a "Field Day"* showed spirited open-air preaching. Salvation Army missionary work in India was featured in *Commissioner Higgins Visits Ahmedabad Girls' School*, with scenes of local schoolgirls with pompoms, and in *Salvation Army Parade in Indian Village*, which showed villagers of all ages riding in a cart or walking with farm implements, jars, or baskets. *Salvation Army in Lucerne* showed a Salvation Army member playing an accordion as *The War Cry* was being distributed on a busy street. Many of the films highlighted General Booth traveling in England, Wales, and Scotland as well as Palestine. By 1906, the Salvation Army had made 74 films about its activities in Britain, India, and Palestine (Rapp, 1996, pp. 170–172).

Cultural historian Dean Rapp (1996, p. 173) characterized these Salvation Army documentaries as "interest films" because they did not tell stories; their appeal, instead, was simply "to curiosity about the subject and fascination with movement." In the case of the interest films of the Salvation Army, the subjects and movements were simple: marching in parades, protesting outside pubs, touring in cars, preaching outdoors, distributing literature, and playing music. These documentaries ranged in length from 20 seconds (*Cadets Salute*) to nearly six minutes (*Salvation Army Printing Works*). Given their brevity, it is not surprising that they typically relied on stationary cameras and single shots and used few edits. Surviving films do not even have intertitles (p. 173). In their rush to produce moving pictures the Salvation Army paid little attention to technique.

Five years after establishing its Cinematograph Department, the Salvation Army eliminated it. By 1908, the novelty of interest films was waning and the demand for story-length commercial films was growing. The Salvation Army increasingly saw films as worldly and refused to participate in a pastime that, at the very least, distracted participants from sacred endeavors if it did not outright tempt viewers with visions of sin (Rapp, 1996, pp. 179–182). Other religious groups, however, refused to dismiss motion pictures outright. They may have renounced commercial efforts that traded in worldliness, but they saw great missionary promise in what film historian Terry Lindvall (2007) called "sanctuary cinema."

For example, the annual rally of the Foreign Christian Missionary Society held at Central Christian Church in Indianapolis, Indiana, set an attendance record with its multimedia presentation. Society President Archibald McLean used slides to illustrate missionaries and their schools in Africa and India and short films that showed animal sacrifices, Muslims praying at a mosque in Calcutta, and the King of Uganda going to church, accompanied by a large crowd (Lindvall, 2001, p. 16). Such success created so much demand for movies that churches and other community organizations could use that by 1910 movie distributor George Kleine published a 350-page *Catalogue of Educational Motion Pictures* that listed thousands of films arranged under headings including Agriculture, Fine Arts, Literary, History, and Religious (Jump, 1910, p. 31).

Reverend Jump's observation that motion pictures did "more for foreign and home missions than any agency yet utilized by our assiduous and ingenious missionary secretaries" would hold true throughout the silent film era (1910, p. 23). At the Centenary Celebration of American Methodist Missions, which was held at the state fairgrounds in Columbus, Ohio, during three weeks in the summer of 1919, over a million visitors watched films such as *Freeing Palestine* and *Methodized Cannibals* on a 10-story screen. The so-called Methodist World Fair also showed films in its eight international pavilions including scenes from missions in Africa and Asia and ethnographic studies of Egypt, Korea, and Mexico. The Hollywood filmmaker D. W. Griffith was even on hand to produce a documentary of the Methodist Centenary, *The World at Columbus*, to honor the memory of his devout Methodist mother and raise money for the denomination (Anderson, 2005).

The Methodist centenary solidified the place of documentaries in the service of Christian missions. Editors of *National Geographic* said that every missionary "ought to carry the best camera that can be had and ought to use it as often as he does his Bible" (Lindvall, 2007, p. 115). The next year, the Interchurch World Movement sent teams of filmmakers to North Africa and Asia to make newsreels about foreign missions for screening in commercial movie theaters. Eva Chappell, the organization's publicist, said, "The missionary, as these pictures will show, is, of necessity, a versatile man; the camera is as likely to catch him extracting the teeth of a wriggling native, or climbing the rigging of an elephant, or killing a boa constructor, or being stalked by a lion, as engaged in the performance of his more strictly ministerial duties." The promise of making a stockpile of exciting missionary newsreels collapsed, however, with the dissolution of the Interchurch World Movement in 1920 (Lindvall, 2007, pp. 92–93).

Still, promotion of religious documentaries continued. In 1921, *Educational Film Magazine* promoted *Sunrise for the Mono* produced by the Baptist General Board of Promotion. The Native American Mono tribe of central California "retains some of its most primitive customs, such as the pounding of acorns between flat stones for acorn mush," the review points out, but thanks to "the efforts of their missionary, J. E. Brendel, these Indians practically monopolize grape and hop picking and wood hauling" (Bollman, 1921, p. 19). A more effusive attestation of a religious documentary came from R. H. Rolofson, pastor of Vinton (Iowa) Presbyterian Church, who said that showing a missionary film about India filled his sanctuary as no other service about missions had ever done. "The day was talked of for weeks," Rolofson said. "In my pastoral experience I have never known a more valuable day for missions" (Rolofson, 1924, p. 267).

Enthusiasm for documentary film extended to Roman Catholics as well. In the late 1920s, Saint Joseph's Foreign Missionary Society made documentaries that showcased its medical and food relief programs in Kashmir and Punjab. The goal was to raise funds by showing British audiences how the Mill Hill Fathers propagated Catholic faith and improved the living conditions of villagers in rural India. The content of the Mill Hill films ranged from ethnographic scenes of village life including agricultural practices, tribal craftsmanship, and children at play to visuals of ruins, streets, and other elements of the local environment to views of interactions between missionaries and villagers and hospital patients, and to sights of festivities celebrating the work of the missions and the gratitude of the villagers. The visual anthropologist Annamaria Montrescu-Mayes points out that despite their imperialism, these documentaries offer "raw visual accounts of everyday life in India" (Motrescu-Mayes, 2017, pp. 131–132).

An important transitional documentary was produced after the German filmmaker Willy Rach received permission to film at the Catholic mission on Flores Island in eastern Indonesia in 1924. A priest at the Netherland seminary in Steyl edited Rach's footage into a two-hour narrative about Dutch missionaries who made the difficult journey to Flores to educate and convert the primitive people they found there. Along the way, the missionaries traveled rough terrain by horseback, slayed a Komodo dragon, and witnessed pagan practices and gambling, but they also saw nature's primal beauty and the potential of the native people, who learned to make furniture, raise livestock and poultry, cultivate seeds, and plant trees. An inter-title near the end of *Flores* says, "The Missionary: Bringer of Civilization." Next came a scene showing streams of local converts carrying rocks to build a church, after which the film showed a priest conducting a wedding ceremony before rushing away to pray over the body of a man who recently died. The Flores film marks the shift from religious interest films to narrative documentaries – in this case, with re-enacted scenes inserted to help propel the documentary's narrative plot (Ray, 2017).

Expository and Poetic Films with Sound

Newsreels, short documentary films of news, and timely feature stories bridged the eras of silent movies and talkies. Pathé News began to produce newsreels in 1910, and with the entry of *The March of Time* in 1935, several major companies including Fox, Hearst, Paramount, and Universal were making them, typically to be shown in a theater before a feature film. Television news ultimately replaced newsreels, which began their steady decline in the 1950s.

With newsreels, religion became less the focus of denominational outreach and promotion and more the occasional subject of interest of commercial enterprises. That is the clear impression in Raymond Fielding's (1972) history of newsreels. His analysis of newsreels in the United States from 1939 to 1948 shows sports (18.7%), foreign news (14.8%), and national defense (12.1%) receiving the most coverage and weather (0.6%), farming (0.4%), and health (0.4%) receiving the least. Religious news averaged 1% over this 10-year period, with a high of 2.3% in 1946 and a low of 0.4% in 1942 (p. 290). The Fox Movietone News Collection (n.d.) available online from the University of South Carolina shows that newsreels about religion covered ceremonies such as a Russian Orthodox procession, music at St. Patrick's Cathedral, and a Muslim prayer festival at a British mosque; exotic visuals, including whirling dervishes in Egypt and Shinto shrines in Japan; various personalities, such as the Hindu mystic Meher Baba, the Four Square Gospel celebrity Aimee Semple McPherson, and social reformer Charles H. Parkhurst; and the unusual, including child evangelists Helen Campbell and Mary Louise Page, the baptism of African Americans in the Mississippi River, and the head of the Association for the Advancement of Atheism, Charles Lee Smith, speaking on the rights of atheists after serving time in an Arkansas jail for distributing obscene, slanderous, or scurrilous literature (Fox Movietone News Collection, n.d.).

Of course, newsreels, like any other communication medium, are hardly objective or ideologically neutral. In her study of Italian newsreels about religion in the two decades after World War II, Giulia Evolvi (2018) shows that they depicted Catholicism as a moral resource for Italians. In those decades from 1946 to 1965, Italian movie theaters showed government-sponsored newsreels along with feature films. Italian newsreels about religion emphasized the Pope, political figures, religious assemblies, and traditional Catholic celebrations, only occasionally turning their attention to other religions, which they cast as exotic and premodern. By depicting Catholicism both as an element of Italian tradition and as a forward-looking participant in industrialism, Italian newsreels after World War II fostered the idea that Italy was "a good Catholic country" whose citizens embraced Catholic values without question.

The first film about religion to enter the canon of historically important documentaries was *Song of Ceylon*, the 1934 production by Basil Wright for the Ceylon Tea Propaganda Board. Film historian Richard Barsam (1973) called *Song of Ceylon* "a film of refined composition, rare power, and restrained impact" (p. 57). Wright's assignment was to make a film that about tea production in Ceylon (now Sri Lanka) that promoted the industry not with the hard sell of advertising, but with the soft sell of public relations. Wright took those instructions to heart, and made a 38-minute documentary that extols the island, its Sinhalese people, and the Buddhism that sustains them. The film has four parts. Part 1, "Buddha," begins with a scene of palm and palmetto leaves that open to worshipers climbing the mountain trail to Adam's Peak, where they eventually reach statues of Buddha at the top. Interspersed in their journey are majestic shots of surrounding nature. Robert Gardner, Director of the Film Study Center at Harvard University, said that the Buddha segment evoked "transporting spirituality … where stone, birds, air and water are joined to create an overwhelming atmosphere of holiness" (Gardner, 1988, p. 24). Part 2, "The Virgin Island," shows Sinhalese villagers in harmony with nature and with each other. Villagers share food with mendicant Buddhist monks, build houses, make pottery, harvest rice, fish along the seashore, and train children in traditional dance. Part 3, "The Voices of Commerce," features a voice-over reading of commodity prices and scenes of a shipyard and a business office juxtaposed with women harvesting tea by hand, suggesting that industrialization is literally just over the horizon from unspoiled nature and community. Part 4, "The Apparel of God," returns to ceremonial dance and the rendering of offerings to Buddha. Aided by an intricate soundtrack and reverent narration, the effect, by the exit at the end back through palm and palmetto, is one of a rural Buddhist paradise thriving beyond the incursion of empire, city, and industry.

In an interview near the end of his career, Wright observed that the arrival of television after World War II subsumed documentary. "Documentary belongs on the television screen," he said. But television differed from traditional documentary filmmaking. "When television came, all of the producers and directors of the documentary television were a new crew; a new generation," he said. "I tried to do some television, but couldn't work that fast" (Mareth & Bloom, 1980, pp. 75–76).

Like the newsreels about religion that preceded them, documentaries about religion that American television networks broadcast comprised a steady minority of programming on news magazines. Daniel Einstein of the UCLA Film & Television Archive compiled two thick compendiums of network television documentaries that list more than 200 episodes about religion from 1955 to 1989. Taken together, these episodes highlight the history of issues and personalities on the nation's social agenda. The 1950s included CBS's "Burma, Buddhism, and Neutralism" on *See It Now* and NBC's "The S-Bahn Stops at Freedom" on *Kaleidoscope*. The 1960s included the CBS News special, "Christmas in Vietnam," and "Religion in the Nuclear Age" on NBC's debate program, *The Nation's Future*. The 1970s included "Mother Teresa" on NBC's *Prime Time Sunday* and a CBS News special, "The Horror of Jonestown." The 1980s included "Onward Christian Voters" about the Religious Right on CBS's *60 Minutes* and "Priestly Sins" about pedophile priests on ABC's *20/20*. American television documentaries about religion between 1955 and 1989 highlight the nation's attention to the Cold War, power, corruption, and saintliness, among myriad other issues (Einstein, 1987, 1997).

Of course, network-produced documentary films about religion do not necessarily please viewers who are religious. Vociferous complaints were made in 1984, for instance, when the UK's Channel 4 broadcast the three-part *Jesus: The Evidence*, a deliberately provocative production that questioned the historicity of biblical accounts of Jesus. Critics of the documentary complained that the program was sensational, that it undermined Christian faith and tradition, and that it was imbalanced and misleading. Steve Goddard, editor of the evangelical *Buzz* magazine, used the publication to campaign against the documentary, which aired on Channel 4, calling it "London Weekend Television's £420,000 attempt to undermine the biblical view of Christ." The campaign helped to advertise the program, which was seen by 1.8 million viewers, a high number for a TV documentary about religion. The controversy over *Jesus: The Evidence* shows both the decline of influence that organized religion has over broadcasting in the UK and broadcasters who increasingly treat religion in terms of its commercial appeal rather than its heartfelt traditions and devotion (Wallis, 2016).

When television broadcasting began in Ireland in 1961, it included a religion documentary program called *Radharc*, meaning "view" or "vision" in Irish, which continued until 1996. Documentary films had been produced earlier in Ireland, of course, but most of them concerned agriculture or tourism. Radharc Films, the first independent television production company in Ireland, was run by two priests, Joseph Dunn and Des Forristal. Inspired by the parables of Jesus and cognizant of the need for popular appeal, Dunn proposed to his archbishop a magazine program that featured both serious content and entertainment. "To get viewers to watch items with really serious content it may be necessary to sugar the pill," Dunn (1986, p. 20) wrote. "By this I mean introduce items of quasi-religious or humorous nature." For its 35 years on RTÉ Television, Radharc presented viewers with films on issues including homelessness, poverty, prison life, and prostitution, alternating with the lighter fare of foreign missions, church openings, and pilgrimages to holy shrines (O'Brien, 2013).

Observational Documentary

By the 1960s, advances in sound and film technology enabled a new approach to documentary filmmaking. Affordable 16 mm cameras became light enough to hold, and, connected to portable sound recording equipment, enabled immediate synchronization of sound and picture.

Without heavy equipment, studios, and large crews, documentary makers could do their work far less intrusively and more spontaneously. They may not have become unseen fly-on-the-wall observers, but they were able to capture candid moments. This greater closeness and candor between filmmaker and subject led to what Nichols (2001) called observational documentary, whereby documentary narratives unfold without the guidance of commentary. Three significant documentaries about religion – *A Time for Burning* (1966), *Salesman* (1969), and *Marjoe* (1972) – exemplified this new approach, capturing events as they happened even if they sacrificed historical context and traditional narration (p. 34).

A Time for Burning (1966) is often cited as a prototype of observational documentary because co-directors William Jersey and Barbara Connell so successfully revealed the candid thoughts of their subjects, in this case, a white Lutheran congregation in Omaha, Nebraska, whose pastor was urging them to meet their Black neighbors. The filming occurred in 1965, the year that President Lyndon Johnson signed into law the Voting Rights Act eliminating barriers that prevented African Americans from voting. The civil rights movement was in full swing, and Bill Youngdahl, pastor of Augustana Lutheran Church, wanted 10 married couples from his church to volunteer to have dinner at the homes of 10 married couples from a nearby Black church. Few of Youngdahl's congregants had ever had a meaningful conversation with African Americans, much less broken bread with them, so he hoped that these dinners would be a first step toward acceptance and understanding.

It was not to be. Early in the documentary, Youngdahl talks with a Black barber, Ernie Chambers, who tells him that white Christians are hypocrites. Later, after Youngdahl says that he wants to understand the perspective of African Americans, Chambers replies, "If you listen and try to do something you'll get kicked out of your church. See, that's the way your people are."

Undaunted, Youngdahl meets with Augustana's social ministry committee. "You're asking for a pretty tough decision, and I'd just as soon put it off," says committee member Ray Christiansen. "This will split the church wide open." By the end of the meeting, Ray has had a change of heart and votes in favor of the interracial dinners. But the meeting with the church council the following night goes poorly. "Why be so revolutionary?" one council member asks, citing parishioners' worries "that this church might become integrated... They don't see why we should go and keep harping on this idea of civil rights." By the end of the film, less than two weeks later, Youngdahl has tendered his resignation following a scene accompanied by a cacophony of voices from earlier in the film. In a voice-over, Youngdahl reads from his letter. An accompanying scene shows a coat rack with a shelf of black hats. Jersey and Connell were not at the meeting where Youngdahl announced his resignation, so they made do by showing the hats of the men who asked him to leave (Edwards, 2020).

In a recent interview, co-director Jersey explained how his crew of three was able to get such raw footage. "They believed – and it was true – that I wasn't trying to hang them," Jersey said. "I was trying to understand them and let them say who they really were." Later he added, "I was able to convince people that it was OK for them to be who they really were" (Edwards, 2018).

Another classic expression of observational documentary about religion appeared two years after *A Time for Burning*. Edited down to 90 minutes from 100 hours of footage by Charlotte Zwerin, *Salesman* (1969) showed middle-aged Paul Brennan selling Bibles door to door in Boston and in Opa-locka, Florida, with three other Catholic representatives of the Mid-American Bible Company. Nicknamed "the Badger" because of his selling style, Brennan becomes increasingly frustrated as his sales decline.

The work is difficult. To cover territory efficiently, the team first meets with a parish priest who provides them with a list of communicants and their addresses. Then they split up, knocking on doors, gaining entrance, and making their pitches. The large illustrated Bible they sell costs US$49.99 and their customers are homemakers strapped for cash. It helps that they have a no-money-down "Christian honor plan" of six monthly installments. Many discomforting scenes show Brennan pushing Bibles that the women do not want and cannot afford but hesitate to turn down.

The salesman of the title is Brennan, but it could just as easily refer to his sales manager, Kennie Turner, who motivates his sales staff by inspiration and by intimidation. "Money is being made in the Bible business," he says at one staff meeting. "It's a fabulous business, it's a good business… The money is out there… Go out and get it." At another meeting, his salesmen stand and proclaim their goals for the coming year. One man says that he will triple his production. Another says that his wife convinced him to buy a big house and wants to have more children, so he will make US$35 000. Not to be outdone, a third says that he expects to make US$50 000. The applause increases with every promise.

Turner's motivational speeches typically become threatening. "You'll see some missing faces," he tells his gathered staff. "We eliminated a few men, not because we were mad at them, not because we didn't like them, and not because we didn't need the few sales that they made." In another meeting he said, "If a guy's not a success he's got nobody to blame but himself."

In order to get such candid footage, brothers Albert and David Maysles accompanied the salesmen with minimal equipment and no additional staff people. At the door, they followed the salesman's introduction by telling the homeowner, "We're doing a human interest story about this gentleman and his three colleagues. And we'd like to film his presentation." (They avoided the term "sales pitch.") Albert with a camera and David with his tape recorder were almost always welcomed with the salesman. Only one homeowner refused to sign a release at the end (Barnouw, 1993, p. 241).

There are no winners in *Salesman*. Door-to-door selling was in decline, most parishioners did not buy the coffee-table Bible, and those who did likely did not read it. Increasingly despondent, Brennen affects his mother's Irish brogue. "Yer fatha's on the fahce. He gets a good pinsion. He puts in a lot of time, but he gets his rewahd." With his Bible selling days at an end, he has little to show (Keough, 2020).

The third film from this period, *Marjoe*, blended observational documentary techniques with archival footage to expose fraud among Pentecostal revivalists. The film begins with a voice-over of Marjoe Gortner, the child evangelist who had been ordained at the age of three, preaching a sermon: "Just as sure as you're listening to me, just as sure as you're listening to an eight-year-old voice, just as sure as you're playing a record, it's just as sure that you're going to go to Hell if you're not saved."

The son of itinerant evangelists, Marjoe – named for Mary and Joseph – garnered publicity and free-will offerings wherever he and his parents went. He spent hours every day memorizing sermons with accompanying gestures and was punished if he made mistakes by being smothered by a pillow or having his head held under running water, measures that motivated the boy but left no mark. Gortner estimated that by the time he was 16, he had helped his parents take in US$3 million. Soon after his 16th birthday, his father absconded with the money.

Directors Howard Smith and Sarah Kernochan filmed *Marjoe* in 1971, when Gortner was 27 years old. Wanting to leave evangelism to become an actor, Gortner looked forward to the publicity he would receive from the documentary about his final revivals in California, Texas, and Michigan. The film shows Gortner preaching, strutting like Mick Jagger, and shaking hands with congregation members who have lined up to put cash – to "bring what you would to Jesus" – in a large plastic trash can. Gortner also shares tricks of the trade. He recalls a popular radio evangelist with the gift of prophecy who told his listeners that God wanted a lady who had put a US$10 bill into a cookie jar to mail it to his ministry, saying, "God will give you a reward such as you've never known before." That promise reaped a $2000 reward for the radio evangelist. Gortner also recalls applying a special ink on his forehead in the shape of a cross that turned red temporarily as he began to sweat. "I had that whole audience at one of the biggest meetings I ever had," he recalls.

Because *Marjoe*'s distributor believed that it would have a hostile reception in the Bible Belt, he refused to show the movie south of Des Moines. Nevertheless, *Marjoe* went on to win the Academy Award for Best Documentary Film of 1972. The documentary did end up launching an acting career for Gortner, who found parts in made-for-TV and formula TV serials (Hesse, 2014).

Participatory Documentary

Shoah, Claude Lanzmann's 1985 film about the Holocaust, is a prime example of what Bill Nichols called participatory documentary: rather than the fly-on-the-wall observational approach, participatory documentary emphasizes interactions between the filmmaker and the subjects. In the case of *Shoah* (the Hebrew word meaning devastation or annihilation) viewers see 9 1/2 hours of interviews between Lanzmann and survivors, witnesses, and sometimes perpetrators from across Nazi-occupied Poland – from Chełmno, where Jews were exterminated in gas vans, from the Treblinka and Auschwitz-Birkenau death camps, and from the Warsaw Ghetto (Nichols, 2001, p. 34).

The effect is powerful. In one scene, Lanzmann interviews Abraham Bomba, a barber who the Nazis forced to shear the hair of naked women and children in a gas chamber at Treblinka right before they were killed. (The hair was sent to Germany, where it was made into fabric.) Bomba says that with SS guards behind them, the barbers had two minutes per person. When he recalls another barber whose wife and sister enter the gas chamber, he stops. "I can't. It's too horrible. Please," Bomba says. He sniffs and wipes away tears, but says nothing for a more than minute. Lanzmann implores, "You have to do it. I know it's very hard. I know and I apologize." Minutes pass before Bomba agrees to speak again. He says that the women tried to talk with the husband, who could not tell them what was about to happen. All he could do, Bomba says, is "hug them and kiss them, because he knew he would never see them again."

For another interview, Lanzmann rented a train engine for Henryk Gawkowski like the one he used when he was 20 years old to transport some 18 000 Jews to their deaths in Treblinka. As he arrives once again in Treblinka, Gawkowski looks back at imaginary cattle cars and draws his finger across his throat, reenacting his message to the Jews he hauled. Gawkowski recalled being grateful for the vodka that the Nazis gave to the drivers of "special trains."

The interviews and the re-creations not only jog memories, but bring the past into the present. A survivor of Chełmno, who was forced to sing for his Nazi captors, is brought back and asked to sing the songs again. A prisoner who was forced to exhume bodies hastily buried in Ponary so that they could be incinerated unearthed the bodies of his family. Asked by Lanzmann how he recognized them, he said, "They'd been in the earth four months, and it was winter. They were very well preserved. So I recognized their faces, their clothes too." Hearing these memories spoken gives them a sense of presence that archival footage cannot do (Roscoe, 2013).

Lanzmann's work on *Shoah* was monumental. He spent 7 years tracking down subjects and interviewing them in 14 countries. He amassed 350 hours of footage, which took 5 years to edit into its final 9 1/2 hours of oral history. In an interview, Lanzmann compared editing *Shoah* to "being on the north face of a peak and having to invent the way up, to devise a route to the top" (Chevrie & Le Roux, 2016, p. 791).

Performative and Hybrid Documentary

Many recent documentary films are what Nichols (2001) called performative because they emphasize the filmmaker's personal engagement with the subject. In pursuit of the audience's emotional and social engagement, they appeal to the truth of experience, not to objectivity (p. 34). As Alisa Lebow (2008) explains in *First Person Jewish*, such documentaries are both subjective and relational, "involving many others in the project of constructing the self on screen" (p. xi). In general, performative documentaries about religion tend to serve as visual meditations on issues of community and identity.

A prime example of performative documentary is Pearl Gluck's *Divan* (2004) in which the filmmaker's search for a family heirloom serves as a means of coming to terms with her Hasidic Jewish upbringing and reconciling with her estranged father. The heirloom is her great-grandfather's couch that a great rabbi had slept on 1879. Finding and trying to buy this couch requires Gluck to learn about her heritage first hand, which she does by spending time with relatives while on a Fulbright scholarship to document Hasidic stories in Hungary and Ukraine.

The complication is that Gluck left the Hasidic community in Brooklyn to live with her mother in Manhattan after her parents divorced when she was a teenager. Bringing the divan home is Gluck's way to make peace with her father. She travels to Hungary, where she meets family and learns much more than she expected about customs, perspectives, and the Holocaust. Gluck does not get the couch, but she does rebuild a relationship with her father and reconcile her secular present with her ultra-Orthodox past. With humor and a soundtrack featuring klezmer, *Divan* relays a personal story of heritage and choice that has resonance far beyond ex-Hasidim.

Another first-person documentary about religion is the 2015 film *A Sinner in Mecca*, director Parvez Sharma's follow-up to his 2007 documentary about gay Muslims, *A Jihad for Love*. The previous documentary examined same-sex love among devout Muslims in Africa and the Middle East. In *A Sinner in Mecca*, Sharma turns the camera on himself. Haunted by memories of his deceased mother's disapproval of his homosexuality, Sharma decides to fulfill the fifth pillar of Islam and go on the Hajj, the pilgrimage to Mecca. "I am now faced with a crisis of faith," he says in a voice-over. "I need to prove that I can be a good Muslim and be gay."

The tension in the film comes both from Muslim homophobia and from the prohibition against taking unsanctioned video of the Hajj. But Sharma blends into the throng of pilgrims and records the video images on his cell phone, so he goes mostly unnoticed. Sharma participates in the rituals of the Hajj, circumambulating and touching the Kaaba in Mecca, traversing between the hills of Safa and Marwa, climbing Mount Arafat, and collecting pebbles at Muzdalifah. By the end of the experience, which includes the slaughter of a goat, Sharma says, "I have emerged from my Hajj a better Muslim" (Portwood, 2015).

The turn to performative documentary took place at a time when digital technology lowered the cost of making and distributing documentaries and raised the popularity of watching them. Documentary filmmakers felt free to make autobiographical films such as *Divan* and *A Sinner in Mecca*. They also felt free to combine expository, poetic, and observational modes to make documentaries the public found relevant and compelling. Such hybrid documentaries about Christianity include the 2006 film about indoctrination, *Jesus Camp*, and the 2007 film about homophobia, *For the Bible Tells Me So*. Jewish subjects have been treated in such hybrid documentaries as the 2016 film about a Holocaust survivor, *Big Sonia*, and the 2016 film about Israeli settlements in the West Bank, *The Settlers*. Interesting hybrid documentaries that focus on Islam include the 2005 film about sexism, *Me and the Mosque*, and the 2019 film about extremism, *Ghosts of Sugar Land*.

In *Representing Religions in World Cinema*, S. Brent Plate (2003) points out that "new media developments always carry with them the promise of a more democratic representation. This ... continues to hold true for newer film and video technologies. Not only do more people have access to receiving the new media, more people have access to producing with the new media" (p. 9). Plate's prophecy about indigenous film production has been realized more in feature films than in documentary films, at least in terms of international distribution. There are exceptions, of course – such as the Indian documentary filmmaker Benoy K. Behl, who has more than 6000 subscribers to his YouTube channel through which viewers watch his popular documentaries about Buddhism – but quality documentaries about religion throughout the world still tend to come from American directors. Donna Carole Roberts directed *Yemanjá: Wisdom from the African Heart of Brazil*, the story about Candomblé. Judy-Anne Goldman directed *Rise and Dream*, about a Christian and Muslim teenage band in the Philippines. The same pattern applies for the acclaimed documentaries about religion in Africa: *The Devil Came on Horseback* (2007, directed by Ricki Stern and Anne Sundberg), *Pray the Devil Back to Hell* (2008, directed by Gini Reticker), and *The Redemption of General Butt Naked* (2011, directed by Daniele Anastasion and Eric Strauss). Perhaps the popularity of such films will lead to increased local production of nonfiction films that explore religious beliefs and practices.

Conclusion

When Herbert Jump wrote *The Religious Possibilities of the Motion Picture*, he conceived of motion pictures as media for advancing the agenda of religious organizations. Whether fiction or nonfiction, motion pictures could fulfill a battery of public relations ministries: entertaining, educating, advertising, advocating, and inspiring viewers who would grow to see religious institutions as wellsprings of enlightenment for individuals and their communities. From the earliest documentary films made by the Salvation Army, many documentary films about religion were designed with that vision in mind. Documentaries in this mold have been instruments of the status quo, used to attract adherents and supporters and to convey the teachings and practices of religious groups.

But as newsreels and televised documentaries attracted audiences that were more interested in information and investigation than in apologetics and promotion, many nonfiction films about religion began to question and challenge the state of affairs. Exploiting the capabilities of the medium, such documentaries functioned more as prophets than as priests, calling out self-righteousness, malice, oppression, manipulation, hypocrisy, and bigotry. Documentaries that criticized beliefs and practices have seldom opposed religion as such; rather, they have highlighted the harms caused by religious perversion. Had Herbert Jump foreseen this development, he might have added reproof to the religious possibilities of the motion picture that he identified.

In many ways, the history of documentary films about religion serve as an index to well over a century of personages, events, perspectives, and concerns. What documentarians chose to film and not to film, what was preserved and what was discarded suggests a society's values. What viewers have written about documentaries adds layers of perception and meaning. And what later generations remember reveals both continuity and change in religious points of view. Having compound significance, documentary films about religion deserve extensive study as artifacts in the history of religion and media.

References

Aitken, I. (2013). Documentary film: An introduction. In I. Aitken (Ed.), *The concise Routledge encyclopedia of the documentary film* (pp. 1–16). Routledge.

Anderson, C. J. (2005). The world's fair of 1919: Ethnographic and technological exhibits on display at the centenary celebration of American Methodist missions. *Methodist History, 43*(4), 273–285. https://archives.gcah.org/bitstream/handle/10516/6641/MH-2005-July-Anderson.pdf

Aufderheide, P. (2007). *Documentary film: A very short introduction.* Oxford University Press.

Barnouw, E. (1993). *Documentary: A history of the non-fiction film* (2nd rev. ed.). Oxford University Press.

Barsam, R. (1973). *Nonfiction film: A critical history.* Dutton.

Blizek, W. L. (Ed.). (2013). *The Bloomsbury companion to religion and film.* Bloomsbury Academic.

Bollman, G. (1921). Review of films. *Educational Film Magazine, 5*(1), 19. https://archive.org/details/educational192122filmmwhitrich/page/n23/mode/2up?view=theater

Chevrie, M., & Le Roux, H. (2016). Site and speech: An interview with Claude Lanzmann about *Shoah.* In J. Kahana (Ed.), *The documentary film reader: History, theory, criticism* (pp. 784–793). Oxford University Press.

Dunn, J. (1986). *No tigers in Africa! Recollections and reflections of 25 years of Radharc.* Columba.

Edwards, R. (2018). Truth or consequences: Bill Jersey on the end of evangelicalism (Parts 1 and 2). The King's Necktie. Retrieved April 18, 2022 from. https://edwardsrobt.medium.com/truth-or-consequences-bill-jersey-on-the-end-of-evangelicalism-part-2-c11ed42c2977

Edwards, R. (2020). America against itself: A time for burning (again). The King's Necktie, 7. Retrieved April 18, 2022 from. https://edwardsrobt.medium.com/america-against-itself-a-time-for-burning-again-bd37baf10905

Einstein, D. (1987). *Special edition: A guide to network television documentary series and special news reports, 1955–1979.* Scarecrow.

Einstein, D. (1997). *Special edition: A guide to network television documentary series and special news reports, 1980–1989.* Scarecrow.

Eitzen, D. (2008). Reel Amish: The Amish in documentaries. In D. Zimmerman Umble, & D. L. Weaver-Zercher (Eds.), *The Amish and the media* (pp. 42–64). Johns Hopkins University Press.

Evolvi, G. (2018). The myth of Catholic Italy in post-fascist newsreels. *Media History, 24*(1), 71–85. https://doi.org/10.1080/13688804.2016.1207510

Fenner, A. (2015). Rising in the east, sett(l)ing in the west: The emergence of Buddhism as contemporary documentary subject. In A. Juhasz, & A. Lebow (Eds.), *A companion to contemporary documentary film* (pp. 341–365). John Wiley & Sons.

Fielding, R. (1972). *The American newsreel, 1911–1967.* University of Oklahoma Press.

Fox Movietone News Collection (n.d.). Fox Movietone News Collection. University of South Carolina Libraries. Retrieved April 18, 2022, from https://sc.edu/about/offices_and_divisions/university_libraries/browse/mirc/collections/fox_movietone_news_collection.php

Gardner, R. (1988). Basil Wright. *Anthropology Today, 4*(1), 24. https://www.jstor.org/stable/3032879

Hesse, J. M. (2014). A look back at *Marjoe,* the 1972 documentary about evangelical con men. Vice.com (December 23). Retrieved April 18, 2022, from https://www.vice.com/en/article/ppm45m/marjoe-director-sarah-kernochan-talks-about-her-incredible-doc-on-the-evangelical-conman-456

Imran, R. (2016). *Activist documentary film in Pakistan: The emergence of a cinema of accountability.* Routledge.

Juhasz, A., & Lebow, A. (2015). Introduction: Religion. In A. Juhasz, & A. Lebow (Eds.), *A companion to contemporary documentary film* (pp. 337–340). John Wiley & Sons.

Jump, H. A. (1910). *The religious possibilities of the motion picture.* South Congregational Church.

Keough, P. (2020, April 17). In 'Salesman,' a joyless reality of the American dream. Boston Globe. Retrieved April 18, 2022, from https://www.bostonglobe.com/2020/04/17/arts/salesman-joyless-reality-american-dream

Lebow, A. S. (2008). *First person Jewish.* University of Minnesota Press.

Lindvall, T. (2001). Missionaries and moving pictures. In T. Lindvall (Ed.), *The silents of God: selected issues and documents in silent American film and religion 1908–1925* (pp. 14–15). Scarecrow Press.

Lindvall, T. (2007). *Sanctuary cinema: Origins of the Christian film industry.* New York University Press.

Lyden, J. (Ed.). (2009). *The Routledge companion to religion and film.* Routledge.

Mareth, P., & Bloom, A. (1980). Basil Wright: An interview. *Film & History, 10*(4), 73–82. https://muse.jhu.edu/article/402943/pdf

Morag, R. (2015). The new religious wave in Israeli documentary cinema: Negotiating Jewish fundamentalism during the second *Intifada.* In A. Juhasz, & A. Lebow (Eds.), *A companion to contemporary documentary film* (pp. 366–383). John Wiley & Sons.

Motrescu-Mayes, A. (2017). Paradoxical legacies: Colonial missionary films, corporate philanthropy in South Asia and the Griersonian documentary tradition. In I. Aitken, & C. Deprez (Eds.), *The colonial documentary film in South and South-East Asia* (pp. 128–147). Edinburgh University Press.

Nichols, B. (2001). *Introduction to documentary*. Indiana University Press.

O'Brien, H. (2013). Ireland. In I. Aitken (Ed.), *The concise Routledge encyclopedia of the documentary film* (pp. 412–416). Routledge.

Plate, S. B. (Ed.). (2003). *Representing religion in world cinema: Filmmaking, mythmaking, culture making*. Palgrave Macmillan.

Portwood, J. (2015). On screen: The Middle East. *Advocate* (October/November), 24–25. https://www.advocate.com/print-issue/current-issue/2015/08/28/three-new-films-capture-lgbt-life-middle-east

Rapp, D. (1996). The British Salvation Army, the early film industry and urban working-class adolescents, 1897–1918. *Twentieth Century British History*, 7(2), 157–188. https://doi.org/10.1093/tcbh/7.2.157

Ray, S. (2017). Two films and a coronation: The containment of Islam in the Flores in the 1920s. In I. Aitken, & C. Deprez (Eds.), *The colonial documentary film in South and South-East Asia* (pp. 107–127). Edinburgh University Press.

Rolofson, R. H. (1924). Great Sunday evenings with pictures. *The Educational Screen*, 3(7), 266–268. https://archive.org/details/educationalscree03chicrich/page/n1/mode/2up

Roscoe, J. (2013). *Shoah*. In I. Aitkin (Ed.), *The concise Routledge encyclopedia of the documentary film* (pp. 839–841). Routledge.

Wallis, R. (2016). Channel 4 and the declining influence of organized religion on UK television: The case of *Jesus: The Evidence*. *Historical Journal of Film, Radio and Television*, 36(4), 668–688. https://doi.org/10.1080/01439685.2015.1132821.

Wilson, D. (2015). Tran Van Thuy's story of kindness: Spirituality and political discourse. In A. Juhasz, & A. Lebow (Eds.), *A companion to contemporary documentary film* (pp. 384–400). John Wiley & Sons.

Selected Readings

Aitken, I. (Ed.). (2013). *The concise Routledge encyclopedia of the documentary film*. Routledge.

Aufderheide, P. (2007). *Documentary film: A very short introduction*. Oxford University Press.

Lyden, J. (Ed.). (2009). *The Routledge companion to religion and film*. Routledge.

Nichols, B. (2017). *Introduction to documentary* (3rd ed.). Indiana University Press.

Wells, J. (2018). *How to film truth: The story of documentary film as a spiritual journey*. Cascade.

Filmography

A Drunkard's Reformation. Directed by D. W. Griffith. 1909. United States.

A Jihad for Love. Directed by Parvez Sharma. 2007. UK/France/Germany/Australia/United States.

A Sinner in Mecca. Directed by Parvez Sharma. 2015. United States.

A Time for Burning. Directed by Barbara Connell and William C. Jersey. 1966. United States.

Ben-Hur. Directed by Sidney Olcott and Frank Oakes Rose. 1907. United States.

Big Sonia. Directed by Todd Soliday and Leah Warshawski. 2016. United States.

"Burma, Buddhism, and Neutralism." Episode of CBS program *See It Now*. February 3, 1957. United States.

Cadets' Salute. Produced by Salvation Army Cinematograph. 1906. UK.

"Christmas in Vietnam." CBS News Special. December 28, 1965. United States.

Commissioner Higgins Visits Ahmedabad Girls' School. Produced by Salvation Army Cinematograph. 1904. UK/India.

Divan. Directed by Pearl Gluck. 2004. United States/Hungary/Israel/Ukraine.

Flores Film. Directed by Simon Buis. 1926. Indonesia/Netherlands.

For the Bible Tells Me So. Directed by Daniel Karslake. 2007. United States.

Freeing Palestine. Directed by Lowell Thomas. 1919. United States.

Ghosts of Sugar Land. Directed by Bassam Tariq. 2019. United States.

Into Great Silence. Directed by Philip Gröning. 2005. France/Switzerland/Germany.

Jesus Camp. Directed by Heidi Ewing and Rachel Grady. 2006. United States.

Jesus: The Evidence. Directed by David W. Rolfe. 1984. UK.

Marjoe. Directed by Sarah Kernochan and Howard Smith. 1972. United States.

Me and the Mosque. Directed by Zarqa Nawaz. 2005. Canada.

Methodized Cannibals. Produced by Burton Holmes Travel Pictures. 1918. United States.

"Mother Teresa." Episode of NBC program *Prime Time Sunday*. December 9, 1979. United States.

"Onward Christian Voters." Episode of CBS program *60 Minutes*. September 21, 1980. United States.

Our Slummers at Work. Produced by Salvation Army Cinematograph. 1906. UK.

Pray the Devil Back to Hell. Directed by Gini Reticker. 2008. United States.

"Priestly Sins." Episode of ABC program *20/20*. December 2, 1988. United States.

"Religion in the Nuclear Age." Episode of NBC program *The Nation's Future*. December 24, 1961. United States.

Religulous. Directed by Larry Charles. 2008. United States.

Rise and Dream. Directed by Judy-Anne Goldman. 2011. United States/Philippines.

Salesman. Directed by Albert Maysles and David Maysles. 1969. United States.

Salvation Army in Lucerne. Produced by Salvation Army Cinematograph. 1904. UK/Switzerland.

Salvation Army Parade in Indian Village. Produced by Salvation Army Cinematograph. 1904. UK/India.

Salvation Army Printing Works. Produced by Salvation Army Cinematograph. 1906. UK.

Shoah. Directed by Claude Lanzmann. 1985. France/UK.

Song of Ceylon. Directed by Basil Wright. 1934. UK/Sri Lanka.

Sunrise for the Mono. Produced by the Stereoptical Department of the Baptist General Board of Promotion. 1921. United States.

The Devil Came on Horseback. Directed by Ricki Stern and Anne Sundberg. 2007. United States/Sudan.

"The Horror of Jonestown." CBS News special. November 24, 1978. United States.

The Life of Moses. Directed by J. Stuart Blackton. 1909. United States.

The Redemption of General Butt Naked. Directed by Daniele Anastasion and Eric Strauss. 2011. United States/Georgia/Liberia.

"The S-Bahn Stops at Freedom." Episode of NBC program *Kaleidoscope*. November 2, 1958. United States.

The Settlers. Directed by Shimon Dotan. 2016. France/Germany/Israel/Canada.

The Story of Kindness or How to Behave. Directed by Van Thuy Tran. 1987. Vietnam.

The World at Columbus. Directed by D. W. Griffith. 1919. United States.

Where in the World Is Osama Bin Laden? Directed by Morgan Spurlock. 2008. France/United States.

William and Bramwell Booth at a "Field Day." Produced by Salvation Army Cinematograph. 1905. UK.

Workers Leaving the Lumière Factory. Directed by Louis Lumière. 1895. France.

Yemanjá: Wisdom from the African Heart of Brazil. Directed by Donna Carole Roberts. 2015. Brazil/Canada/United States.

Part VI
Functional Perspectives

23

The Role of Media in Creating Communities of Religious Belief and Identity

Myna German

Introduction

Today's digital diasporas form the latest version of a phenomenon through which communication has maintained and shaped the identity and the communities of peoples. Often supported by the Internet and its affiliated technologies – laptops, tablets, handheld devices, and mobile phones – contemporary migrants can easily remain connected with support structures of family and religion. But similar things happened, though on a different time scale in the past, through letters. Religious documents contained in books such as printed Bibles could be physically transported to the New World. Reflecting the origins of many migrants to north America, the King James version of the Bible was the most widely used religious document of the early American settlers (Campbell et al., 2014).

This chapter explores the role of communication media in supporting global communities of religious belief and identity, while touching on the relevant theories of media, social identity, and religion. It considers the development of media historically and ends with some practices and case studies from the Abrahamic traditions of Judaism, Christianity, and Islam, as well as some religions of Asia.

Religion and Social Community

Among their functions, both religion and communication media create community, enforce social order, and shape identity, often acting together. Manuscripts of the Bible, Koranic recitations, shared the narratives of the *Mahābhārata*, the teachings of the Buddha have all created communities of believers. The traditions themselves, whether shared by text or performance, often specify social ordering through ethical directives. Finally, the communities and the behaviors they enforce provide a source of identity for individual members, whether as a Jew, a Catholic, a Buddhist, a Muslim, or a Hindu. From a sociological perspective, some groups delineate levels of identity: priests, monks, laity; members of a caste; those who have participated in various religious works like the Hajj vs. those who have not. In its simplest sense, then, community refers to human groups organized around a common goal; for religious communities, that goal is belief and worship.

The Handbook on Religion and Communication, First Edition. Edited by Yoel Cohen and Paul A. Soukup.
© 2023 John Wiley & Sons Ltd. Published 2023 by John Wiley & Sons Ltd.

Religion fulfills a variety of functions through different kinds of communication. The first and most basic addresses meaning, often expressed in stories. Every culture has had a creation myth, a story that builds identity and speaks to where their civilization evolved from, geographically, spiritually. The Romans traced their city's founding to twin brothers Romulus and Remus. Indian people in Mumbai believed their ancestors emigrated from Kashmir, up in the Himalaya mountains (Beaver, 1994). The Hebrew Bible speaks about Moses and the Exodus from Egypt. Such origin stories speak to a hunger in people to know their ancestry, their roots, and their connection to the divine, even if these roots cannot always be explained or traced scientifically. Communication media and practices enable these stories.

People perceive the meaning of such narratives differently, as communication studies have demonstrated for almost all interaction. Accounting for this discrepancy are differences in culture, the mood of the perceiver, background, and life stages. Connected to this is the idea of salience, what communicators want to perceive reflects what issues are paramount in their mind. "Meaning" in religious communications involves religion, culture, and what context receivers have to incorporate the material they have gleaned. Meaning is understood in terms of a system (Campbell et al., 2014). In the mid-twentieth century, psychologists like Carl Jung focused on symbolism and meaning. After the 1950s, people studied the role of religion more as an expression of the structure of ideas, values, beliefs, and values of society (Davies, 1994, p. 13).

Second, religions play a role in creating community. Community constitutes the collective framework for making meaning. As sociologists and anthropological researchers study human behavior, religion as pattern can be observed like other human activities (Beaver, 1994). The community formation resembles a kind of socialization, with effects beyond religion. A congregant who attends the house of worship for social reasons is apt to be involved politically in the community, vote regularly, and support public institutions such as the newspaper or library. This tie to communication reinforces senses of community. Buddenbaum (1993, p. 2) notes that individuals who attend to news are more active in the political process. If one is well informed through the newspaper, one is more likely to participate in the community (Berelson, 1949; Lynd & Lynd, 1929).

In the past, going to church or synagogue, mosque, or another place of worship constituted a major time commitment and often facilitated seeing friends and neighbors, akin to involvement in a social club or community activity (Armfield, 2003, p. 13). Such group activity is more external and its motivation need not reflect the need for questing or comfort/security, although there could be some overlap. When the term "socialization" appears in this research, it does not reflect the degree to which an individual is "socialized" to church teachings, but rather the person's use for religion.

Third, religion represents a spiritual quest, a sense of embodied meaning. Religious "questers" today, according to Roof (1998, 2003), find religion in many places, including those previously assumed to be secular. Sylvan (2005) explains, "Implicit in this perspective is the notion that religion, in a broader and more fundamental sense, is the underlying substratum for all cultural activity and serves as the foundation for culture in general" (p. 13). Buddenbaum (1994) defines a "questor" as "having a religiously inspired world view and desire for belief-confirming information regardless of religious beliefs" (p. 3). In other words, the "questor" seeks the religious experience per se and may even try to be impartial to the "brand" of religiosity, selecting what suits personal needs without a firm or exclusive orientation. They tend to focus more on spiritual needs and derive satisfaction more related to inner psychological needs than social networking. This group is less likely to participate in temporal affairs and more in spiritual matters, using the house of worship as a base for this orientation (German, 2007).

Fourth, religion acts as a source of comfort or security. The "religion as comfort" orientation taps an intrinsic or God-centered approach to religion (Buddenbaum, 1994). It is similar to the "questor" mentality in that it is inner-oriented rather than societally oriented. Both groups possess characteristics that differentiate them from the more social mentality which in the past has driven an understanding of church attendance and community participation. The difference between the questor-oriented and the comfort-oriented religious individual is that the questor is open to investigating many different religions and is more of a seeker. The "religion as comfort" mentality revolves around satisfaction within one's faith, viewing it as the religious home, and this person is more of a "finder" than a "seeker" (German, 2007).

Religion and Identity

Religion also provides a sense of identity in two ways. First, members of a group draw a sense of identity from their group, something seen clearly in immigrant groups, for example, to maintain contact with families and religious traditions. Improvements in communication technology made this easier. Second, religion offers a sense of identity drawn from a connection with the deity.

Each person packages identity in terms of personally important categories along with the meanings attached to them (Deaux, 2008). According to one perspective, identity appears as a personal meaning system: existential, salient, central, and changing to reflect context. From another perspective, identity appears as a collective meaning system: shared reality, interpreting shared experience, and influencing goals and behavior (Deaux, 2008). The second clearly depends on communication media and, for the religious, religious communication. Without socially recognized identities, such as those drawn from religion, there are no socially situated individuals; in other words, most identities are "ascribed," "given," or "inherited" identities (German, 2007). So, people's identities are at once both personal and social (Festinger, 1957) and "cannot co-exist without feedback and judgement from others." In the contemporary world, marked by widespread communication, the central dilemma for individuals encountering multiple groups lies in deciding whose opinion matters more.

Religious self-categorization is a source of social identity and leads to the creation of in-groups and out-groups. Tajfel (1981) examined this in detail and concluded that in-groups will inflate their view of themselves to reduce dissonance and deflate their view of out-groups (Puddifoot, 1997). Social identity theory provides a lens through which to study the interrelationships of various groups, status hierarchies, and how individual identity is maintained within a group.

As a way of situating oneself in society, religion creates reference groups and self-definition. But communication media also create and rely on self-definition, as if to say in the United States, for example, "I am a Fox News watcher." Specific demographics are connected to being a Fox user (older, conservative, less educated) vs. an MSNBC viewer (younger, more liberal, more educated). To reduce dissonance (Festinger, 1957), audiences cluster around channels that reinforce the views that they already have. Hence, self-definition as a religious adherent and self-definition as a particular brand of media adherent often overlap, as in Christian evangelicals' support of Fox News Network in America. Simmel (1955, p. 17) noted, "a certain amount of ... outer controversy is organically tied up with the very elements that ultimately hold the group together." In other words, external turbulence and even discrimination foster identity in the group, which creates social bonds between the members, who need each other to survive. Many of these social bonds are reinforced by media, as they are by religion.

Since digitalization, many of these groups exist online and later morph into real-time associations. This follows an old pattern. Since the Chinese invention of paper 2400 years ago, communities of literacy have existed, replacing orality. Writing fostered creation of cultures of literacy and textuality (Stock, 1983). Innovations in communication paved the way for preservation and spread of religion. The two institutions of religion and media go hand-in-hand. Where earlier generations used communication media (a sacred text or shared music and ritual) to maintain identity, for many today the social media world is the communication world. The so-called discursive approach (Lamerichs & te Molder, 2003, pp. 451–473) shows this more clearly, by applying the approach of discursive psychology to online interaction, where language is viewed as talk-in-interaction. This means that it involves social action rather than cognition: the word is an act, and the language is an action. Speaking has the same meaning and relevance as action. Rather than regarding language as an abstract system of reference, this perspective considers as its focus what participants do with it (Lamerichs & te Molder, 2003).

The discursive approach to communication and language means, first, that identity is considered as a product of discourse. In fact, identities are narrated into being in everyday practices so that "they include the sometimes invisible exercise of power within our lives, especially effects on inequality, poverty, gender, race, and disability" (Wyn et al., 2005). Second, identity is defined as relational; identities are realized in the shifting patterns of our connections with others. In other words, various forms of information technologies have significance in identity formation because they deeply affect the forms and the processes through which social relationships are conducted, and they provide strong identity resources, particularly for children and young people (Atkinson & Nixon, 2005, pp. 387–409). Children and young people are more likely to be subjected to the influence of communication and information technologies because their identities are more fluid and flexible than adults' identities. They are still looking for identification, for their own personality, for their role. This is true also for adults, but during adolescence this search takes the shape of a struggle.

Finally, in studying identity formation processes, it is important to remember that the expression and performance of identities rest on cultural, symbolic, and material resources (Wyn et al., 2005). This means that each person who has access to informational technology and computer-mediated communication makes these tools less neutral because each approach embodies a culture, an education, a symbolic burden, and an economic condition that is individually and structurally crafted. When technology is used, it passes through an interpretation: it meets other identities and becomes culturally characterized (German & Banerjee, 2011).

This point of view helps in analyzing how identity (including religious identity) is influenced by the usage of communication media; this analysis takes into consideration the fact that identity construction is something that people actively do through communication (Lamerichs & te Molder, 2003, pp. 451–473). For example, some early research in this area found that anonymous online interactions seem to facilitate postmodern, fragmented, and multiple identities (Stone, 1995). Therefore, the type of language and what words mean have consequences for identity construction, characterizing the process not only in shape but in substance. Where communication supported religion in sustaining group identity in the past, now it challenges this religious function. Identity becomes more and more fluid, multiple, and changing, similar in some ways to communication speeding across the Internet.

From a global perspective, there are three co-existing factors. First, we attest to the development of a cultural homogenization, while the global postmodern era is leading to an erosion of natural identities. Second, national and other local or particularistic identities are being empowered as opposition against empowerment of more global identities. Third, as a consequence, national identities will diminish, and new identities of a hybrid character will take their place. This was not possible in the days of the printed newspaper alone, which required a brick-and-mortar distribution system. This leads to the creation of different typologies of identity: the "multiple" typology, which is the more representative of the postmodern paradigm; the "radicalized" one, reducing all the identities to only one fundamental identity; and the "cosmopolitan" one, characterized by a feeling of belonging to the world more than just to one country. The most common case is the one in which the individual is in balance between two cultures, acting like a bridge. So, the individual belongs to one culture for some aspects and to the other culture for other aspects. The same principle applies to belonging to a religion and to a communication culture, not through marriage but a hybridization within the individual.

Both of the sources of identity exercise their attraction on the individual, who, according to the contest and to the needs, will choose the more appropriate and convenient set of values, behaviors, and significances. A suitable example to explain the radicalized identity is the fundamentalist individual: in this case, the illusion of an only identity is promoted. To sustain the possibility of a unique identity is quite easy because it responds to some basic and common needs. This is what happens, for example, in the case of religious terrorists: a fragment of the entire and complex identity of an individual is taken, isolated, and transformed into a priority (Sen, 1995). Before examining how communication media can affect the formation of religious identity and community, let us briefly look in more detail at how communication interacts with religion.

Communication, Identity, Community, and Religion

Several factors play pivotal roles in understanding how religion interacts with communication media, in reporting or in personal practice, for example. How news media report religion helps to shape and define religious communities that were once shaped and defined only by the religious press. This section will look at three noteworthy theories: "mediatization," "uses and gratifications," and "uses and gratifications of religion." Livingstone (2009) suggests three levels of analysis: mediatization reflects the macro level (overarching, dealing with media and society); uses and gratifications, the micro level (dealing with the individual); and uses and gratifications of religion, the meso or middle level, dealing with the institutions of society, such as religion.

Macro Level: Mediatization

Mediatization theory (see Chapter 18) states that powerful media, government, and religious elites all interact and intersect to create confluences of power that shape society. Mediatization research engages with the complex relationship between changes in media and communication on the one hand and changes in various fields of culture and society on the other. The emergence of the concept of mediatization is part of a paradigmatic shift within media and communication research (Hepp et al., 2015).

Mediatization looks at the interplay among media, communications, culture, and society as a holistic societal force that cannot be dissected. Media is culture as it develops around lifestyles, elections, and politics, and the forces all intersect and influence each other. Hepp et al. (2015) describe the need for this kind of analysis:

> There is a strong need for such a move, given the increasing relevance of media to various fields of society If it is correct that media have become more important to different fields of (late) modern society such as politics, education, religion and science... What researchers can bring to such an interdisciplinary dialogue is the experience understanding processes of mediated communication ("mediation") and their transforming potential ("mediatization"). Furthermore, mediatization theory does place emphasis on the role of the media, but rather looks at all aspects of society holistically shaped by the interface of powerful institutions and audience-participants. (p. 316)

Religion reporters, for example, play the role of interpreters in their professional lives. While earlier reporters refrained from expressing religious bias, confining it to the religious press, now with evangelicalism and conservatism intertwined politically in the United States, it is possible for reporters to be seduced by the ideology of televangelists. Hence, their reporting is less objective in interacting with this segment and could influence other segments, such as elections, something unheard of in the less political days of religion reporting. A second example of the entanglement of media and religion comes from the evangelical embrace of new technologies to spread their message – in part, perhaps, because their initial self-perception was one of a marginalized minority – including being among the first to utilize the then-new technologies of movies, radio, and TV (Lindvall, 2004).

The media's gatekeeping function as described in agenda-setting theory depicts another shifting mediatization. Where once news organization placed issues in the national discourse and culture, now social media – with no overt ownership and where anyone, newscaster or not, can become an "influencer" with a following – displace the role of the commentator or journalist as gatekeeper and democratize media, while possibly making it less professional in its judgments. Similarly, religious leaders have lost some of their power as authority figures. Anyone can create a YouTube channel and become a televangelist.

In that sense, the "mediatization" of religion has already occurred, creating a patchwork of populist faiths. Anyone can post and become an "opinion leader" without ordination or official status. A knowledge hierarchy may develop on the website among regular posters, as it would on Quora.com, but no formal hierarchy exists between priest and congregant. More to the point here, such channels and groups shape the religious identity of their participants. Communities of shifting identity are born with no geographic parameters and known demographics.

Micro Level: Applying Uses and Gratifications Theories, Functionalist Theory

The twentieth century witnessed a difference of approach to the study of religion. Instead of asking the evolutionary question of how religion originated, discourse shifted to what "function" it served in society (Davies, 1994, p. 13) – what needs it met. Lin (1993, p. 224) summarizes the basic assumptions of uses and gratifications theory as follows: "The uses and gratifications perspective … assumes that media use behaviors are motivated by certain internal needs and specific gratification-seeking motives. With such self-fashioned intentions, audiences are able to dictate their content selection and use patterns for the purposes of fulfilling their gratification expectations." Scholars study media effects by viewing media consumers as active audience members who purposefully chose specific media programs in order to satisfy a "need" (Herzog, 1942). A "need" is a social or psychological desire, such as entertainment, information, escape, companionship, arousal, and more (Abelman, 1989; Papacharissi, 2008; Sundar & Limperos, 2013; Williams & Banjo, 2013).

The uses and gratifications approach investigates "(1) the social and psychological origins of (2) needs, which generate (3) expectations of (4) the mass media or other sources, which lead to (5) differential patterns of media exposure (or engagement in other activities), resulting in (6) need gratifications and (7) other consequences, perhaps mostly unintended ones" (Katz et al., 1974, p. 20). To put it simply, researchers seek to understand how and why people are motivated to use media: *what needs and expectations provide motivation*. Gratifications occur when needs are satisfied through consumption of media including books, radio, or television (Katz et al., 1974). The most common needs in uses and gratifications research include cognitive, affective, personal integrative, social integrative, and tension release (Sundar & Limperos, 2013). The most common goals in uses and gratifications research include diversion, personal relationships, personal identity, and surveillance (Papacharissi, 2008; Sundar & Limperos, 2013). All of these can be seen as providing motivation for behavior. However, there is a distinction between "function" and "uses" of media within the uses and gratifications framework. Media functions are the goals of media industries: to generate profit, media sell advertisements, and encourage media consumption by performing functions of informing, persuading, entertaining, etc. On the other hand, uses of media include the goals of media consumers (i.e. reinforce an identity, connect with friends, cure boredom) and are driven by needs and expectations, or motivations. This theoretical perspective supports the idea that people turn to media sources for key information related to their self-understanding.

Social media platforms have challenged the ways in which religious organizations communicate with their publics (Campbell, 2013) and thus their abilities to shape the identity of their adherents. Traditionally, pastors have addressed their flocks in sermons based on biblical teachings and thoughtful interactions. Now, many pastors and churches are also challenged with engaging their congregants in digital spheres, where competition for attention is fierce.

The two explanations for media impact on identity meet in religious uses and gratifications.

Meso Level: The Uses and Gratifications of Religion

Researchers have studied religious media uses and gratifications through television (Abelman, 1987, 1989), music (Williams & Banjo, 2013), and books (Woods et al., 2016). For example, Williams and Banjo (2013) conducted focus group interviews with college students to examine the uses and gratifications of religious music. Research suggests that uses and gratifications of religious media (music) include lifestyle reinforcement, connection to God, habit, and enculturation (Williams & Banjo, 2013). To our knowledge, little research has examined motivations for using religious *social media* content, though Campbell (2010, 2013) has begun to look at the issue. The question becomes: could the uses of online religious affiliation differ from typical uses and gratifications of media? Do people use these media to connect or for spiritual comfort or to gain a label in terms of social identity? Religion has various uses for various people: comfort in troubled times, social-leisure time activity, and the object of a spiritual quest. In that sense, its theoretical uses and gratifications mirror and extend functionalist theories in mass communications. The newspaper or web offers many gratifications such as entertainment, socialization, leisure time activity, and this has been studied, historically, in more detail since Bernard Berelson's famous (1949) study on missing the newspaper in a *New York Times* strike.

Religion and religious media offer many historical examples of communication media creating religious community and identity.

Examples from the History of Religion

Historical Christianity

While the biblical text provided a focus for Christian communities in the Eastern and Western Mediterranean, the printing press accelerated the process. The Bible, published in many vernacular languages thanks to the invention of the printing press by Johannes Gutenberg in around

1440, created a text common to religious groups (Campbell et al., 2020). The Reformation and Martin Luther's principles were quickly disseminated through the technology of the press and this aided in shaping the identity of reformation churches.

Evangelical and other Christianity

Centuries later, in the United States, evangelical Christians have been at the forefront of adopting and adapting to new technologies to spread their message – in part, perhaps, because their initial self-perception was one of a marginalized minority – including being among the first to utilize the then-new technologies of movies, radio, and TV (Lindvall, 2004). The televangelists (see Chapter 11) used cable television to shape the identity of a national community of viewers (Abelman, 1989).

Helland (2019) documents the emergence of what he terms religion-online in contrast with the emergence of online-religion. Religion-online arose as people and institutions learned to exploit the interactive elements of the Internet and the web (including chat rooms, hyperlinks, multimedia, etc.) in order to engage actively with one another in dialogue and – as is documented especially by Heidi Campbell and Stephen Jacobs – create new spaces and experiences of spirituality. In particular, Helland shows how diaspora communities (Jewish, Hindu, Muslim) have successfully used the web to shape their religious identity by developing virtual pilgrimages, virtual visits to important temples and religious sites, and ways of participating in important rituals online.

Hinduism

Jacobs (2007) points out that Hinduism has a long tradition of worship at home, including the *pūjā* rituals that constitute much of the ritual practice he documents in a Hindu Virtual Temple. The shift from a *pūjā* ritual already carried out in the home to one taking place through an Internet-connected PC in the home may thus be an easier step than for Western Christians, who tend to affiliate the sacred with the sanctuary as separate from the home. Bollywood films have made Hindu culture widely accessible, both to Easterners and Westerners.

Islam

The Hajj or the pilgrimage from Medina to Mecca in the 12th Islamic month in normal times draws people from all over the world. In the technological era it is captured on cell phones through footage and disseminated homeward, although this was never true historically. Details are posted on Arabic-language discussion boards. Abdullah (2007) points out that in the Middle Eastern context, the Internet is an especially important medium, not only because it provides venues for free expression, but because it thereby gives researchers insight into views and ideas that may not appear in government-controlled media. Abdullah (2007) prefaces her study by reminding us that, contrary to Western tendencies to conflate Islam with Arabs and Arab countries, most Arabs (defined as a specific ethnic group) are Muslims, while the majority of Muslims (people who choose Islam as their religion) are from non-Arab countries. The use of the discussion boards unites them into one community internationally, but there are major differences in customs between diaspora and converted Muslims and those who express Arab ethnicity.

Japan

Akira Kawabata and Takanori Tamura (2007) provide additional quantitative understanding of religion-online – first of all by way of a comparison between very low use of the Internet for religious purposes in Japan (2.5%) and very extensive use of the Internet in the United States for religious purposes (c. 64%). The Japanese, however, do not much employ online tools for religious identity. Kawabata and Tamura show that the contrast with the United States reflects important differences in the demographics between Japan and the United States. While large numbers of US citizens express at least some religious belief, in Japan, believers are much more likely to be older, and therefore less like likely to make use of the Internet. In addition, Kawabata and Tamura illustrate very different attitudes toward and understandings of what counts as "religion" in Japan that would further explain low reporting of religious usage of the Internet in Japan. For example, many respondents who do *not* identify themselves as "religious" nonetheless engage in what would otherwise be considered "religious" activities, such as annual family visits to family graves.

Independent religious identity

A good contemporary example of communication affecting the formation of religious identity comes from the online world: Beliefnet.com, a website community, brings together people seeking spirituality without joining an established house of worship. In the past, these communities existed, but were bounded by physical entities, such as ethnic newspapers like *The Jewish Week* or *Catholic Daily* or *Christian Science Monitor*. Beliefnet periodically runs surveys asking respondents to itemize religious beliefs and then categorizes them by computer into an existing religious framework. Beliefnet will ask in a survey questions like, "Do you tend to prefer earth-based religions over fundamentalist or proscribed religions?" or "Do you insist on religions where men and women are treated exactly equal?" or "How important is private prayer to you?"

Using algorithms, it decides which religion best suits a given user and spews out names like "neo-pagan" or "Universalist" that the inputter may never have considered, categorizing hitherto amorphous beliefs. The website is creating, through its algorithms, converts with an identity without ever sending out a missionary, priest, or rabbi. The user self-identifies and may seek out other websites with that orientation and hence a religion is made, but the seeker has never met anyone from that faith. This, however, makes it harder for established religious communities to keep adherents within its borders, despite parochial or religious school indoctrination. The youngster need look no further than the Internet to find competitive teachings and challenge what is taught in school.

Beliefnet publishes articles on inspiration, faith and prayer, yoga, and wellness, as well as on organized religions like Christianity. It helps the reader characterize religious beliefs apart from the organized variety found in more conventional spheres. The site reaches out to the unaffiliated – those who would show up on Pew Foundation surveys as "nones," those who profess no organized faith. However, they may consider themselves spiritual and their spirituality is eclectic, embodying many established faiths in a personalized mandala of beliefs. By comparison, the historical religious media only reached people who already identified with that faith. The websites, unlike other religious media, are international in scope.

In using the web, worldwide consumers are seeking a religious or spiritual experience that unites them with others such as in the cyber-church or recent Zoom meetings during the Covid-19 crisis, but they are also seeking to pick and choose from an array that is vast and defies stereotypical categories. Web religionists often like that it is race-neutral and demographics do not define the user but rather psychographics. In a sense, these international collaborations create new identity-generating organizations. For example, Soka Gokkai International Nichiren Buddhism attracts people from all over the world and has its own physical and online publications. Its members in 192 countries and territories study and put into practice the humanistic philosophy of Nichiren Buddhism. Soka Gakkai members strive to actualize their inherent potential while contributing to their local communities and responding to the shared issues facing humankind.

The advertisements on Beliefnet.com reflect the mosaic of psychographic characterizations, and ads focus on beads or incense, rather than a specific cross or Jewish star. *Yoga Journal* also cuts across demographic borders and has readers from various backgrounds who share a love of the activity of yoga. They unite the Muslim, Buddhist, and Hindu worlds, breaking down national borders and inviting cross-cultural contributions by writers.

This kind of religion is popular with Generation Z (the generation born between 1999 and 2018; Dorsey & Villa, 2020). Often shunning religious rituals and services, they turn to Internet sites that provide information about established religions and seem to be creating their own "amalgamated identities" (Banerjee, 2008; German & Banerjee, 2011). However, even these relatively recent patterns of religious and spiritual affiliation may be changing. Formerly confined to comfort, questing, and community, there is now a focus on individual needs and identity. Media contribute to these condensed identities, where the houses of worship are replaced by cyberspace. Additionally, in the past few years, the importance of understanding the differential effects related to the worldwide impact of Covid-19 of economic, political, and environmental pressures and challenges to health and well-being, physical and psychological, on these different generations and cohorts is becoming more salient.

Further research should address whether a system of worship implies a meeting in place as a form of social identity or whether identity could be individualistic, through the Internet. Even within individualistic amalgams, communities that know one another, greet each other, and share trials and tribulations do form online. In the early days of Compuserve, beta testing of chat rooms found that the same people visited at the same time, knew one another's avatar names, and knew who was genuine (or not) in their representation (German & Banerjee, 2011).

Conclusion

Mediated religion, those religious experiences aided by some form of information technology, has long helped to shape religious identity. The convergence of the two fields, media and religion, can never again be denied, along with the hegemony of the Internet among media technologies. Several theories describe the identity-shaping role of different media: mediatization, uses and gratifications, and religious uses and gratifications.

Today, religious websites create new religions at a supersonic rate, without gatekeepers or clergy. Anyone with a computer or smartphone can use a website to join a religion or cult, but with no official or recorded document such as a baptism certificate marking that affiliation or conversion, researchers have difficulty knowing precisely how many people belong to a particular religion, let alone defining its borders. Religious identity offers one way to measure this and presents a fruitful area of research.

Once the aspects of local community, adherence to priesthood, and house of worship membership are eradicated, religion shifts more to spiritual quest and away from socialization and use of leisure time as its driving forces. This creates a patchwork of religious loyalties yet to be understood fully, but it is still a drift away from large numbers of people, particularly younger generations, professing no religion. The lockdowns of the 2020–2021 pandemic forced people to pursue online-religion and gatherings and this trend might continue indefinitely unless localization kicks in to a greater degree after the crisis fades.

References

Abdullah, R. A. (2007). Islam, jihad, and terrorism in post 9/11. *Journal of Computer-Mediated Communication, 12*(3), 939–955. https://doi.org/10.1111/j.1083-6101.2007.00357.x.

Abelman, R. (1987). Religious television uses and gratifications. *Journal of Broadcasting & Electronic Media, 31*(3), 293–307. https://doi.org/10.1080/08838158709386665.

Abelman, R. (1989). "PTL Club" viewer uses and gratifications. *Communication Quarterly, 37*(1), 54–66.

Armfield, G. G. (2003). A structural equation model of religiosity's effect on mass media use and civic participation. Paper before Association of Educators in Journalism and Mass Communication (AEJMC), Kansas City, Missouri.

Atkinson, S., & Nixon, H. (2005). Locating the subject: Teens online @ ninemsn. *Discourse: Studies in the Cultural Politics of Education, 26*(3), 387–409. https://doi.org/10.1080/01596300500200276.

Banerjee, P. (2008). Amalgamated identities: New phenomenon or new paradigm? Reconceptualizing identity for an age of globalization. *International Psychology Bulletin, 12*, 10–15.

Beaver, R. P. (Ed.). (1994). *Eerdmans' handbook to the world's religions.* Wm. B. Eerdmans Publishing Co.

Berelson, B. (1949). What missing the newspaper means? In P. Lazarsfeld, & F. Stanton (Eds.), *Communication research, 1948–1949* (pp. 111–129). Harper & Row.

Buddenbaum, J. M. (1993). Religion, politics, and media use: A study of six Middletown congregations during the 1992 presidential campaign, Working Paper.

Buddenbaum, J. M. (1994). *Characteristics of readers of religious publications for political information.* Paper before the Association for Education in Journalism and Mass Communication, National Convention, Atlanta, Georgia, August.

Campbell, H. (2010). *When religion meets new media.* Routledge.

Campbell, H. (2013). *Digital religion: Understanding religious practice in new media worlds.* Routledge.

Campbell, R., Martin, C., & Fabos, B. (2014). *Media & culture: Mass communication in a digital age.* Macmillan Publishing.

Campbell, R., Martin, C., Fabos, B., & Harmsen, B. (2020). *Media essentials* (5th ed.). Bedford/St. Martin's.

Davies, D. (1994). The study of religion. In R. P. Beaver (Ed.), *Eerdmans' handbook to the world's religions* (pp. 10–21). Wm. B. Eerdmans Publishing Co.

Deaux, K. (2008). To be an American: Immigration, hyphenation, and incorporation. *Journal of Social Issues, 64*(4), 925–943. https://doi.org/10.1111/j.1540-4560.2008.00596.x.

Dorsey, J., & Villa, D. (2020). *Zconomy: How Gen Z will change the future of business – and what to do about it.* Harper-Collins.

Festinger, L. A. (1957). *A theory of cognitive dissonance.* Harper & Row.

German, M. (2007). *The paper and the pew: How religion shapes media choice.* University Press of America.

German, M., & Banerjee, P. (2011). *Migration, technology, and transculturation.* Lindenwood University Press.

Helland, C. (2019). Diaspora on the electronic frontier: Developing virtual connections with sacred homelands. *Journal of Computer-Mediated Communication, 12*(3), 939–955. https://doi.org/10.1111/j.1083-6101.2007.00357.x.

Hepp, A., Hjarvard, S., & Lundby, K. (2015). Mediatization: Theorizing the interplay between media, culture, and society. *Media, Culture & Society, 37*(2), 314–324. https://doi.org/10.1177/0163443715573835.

Herzog, H. (1942). Professor quiz: A gratifications study. In P. F. Lazarsfeld, & F. N. Stanton (Eds.), *Radio research 1941* (pp. 64–93). Duell, Sloan, and Pearce.

Jacobs, S. (2007). Virtually sacred: The performance of asynchronous cyber rituals in online spaces. *Journal of Computer-Mediated Communication, 12*(3), 939–955. https://doi.org/10.1111/j.1083-6101.2007.00357.x.

Katz, E., Blumler, J. G., & Gurevitch, M. (1974). Uses and gratifications research. In J. G. Blumler, & E. Katz (Eds.), *The uses of mass communications.* Sage Publications.

Kawabata, A., & Takanori, T. (2007). Online-religion in Japan: Websites and religious counseling from a comparative cross-cultural perspective. *Journal of Computer-Mediated Communication, 12*(3), 939–955. https://doi.org/10.1111/j.1083-6101.2007.00357.x.

Lamerichs, J., & te Molder, H. (2003). Computer-mediated communication: From a cognitive to a discursive model. *New Media & Society, 5*(4), 451–473. https://doi.org/10.1177/146144480354001.

Lin, C. A. (1993). Modeling the gratification-seeking process of television viewing. *Human Communication Research, 20*, 224–244.

Lindvall, T. (2004). Images have consequences: Preliminary reflections on the impact of the visual on the word. In C. Ess (Ed.), *Critical thinking and the Bible in the age of media* (pp. 213–236). University Press of America.

Livingstone, S. (2009). On the mediation of everything: ICA presidential address. *Journal of Communication, 59*(1), 1–18. https://doi.org/10.1111/j.1460-2466.2008.01401.x.

Lynd, R. S., & Lynd, H. M. (1929). *Middletown: A study in contemporary American culture.* Harcourt, Brace and Company.

Papacharissi, Z. (2008). *Uses and gratifications. An integrated approach to communication theory and research.* Harcourt Brace.

Puddifoot, J. E. (1997). Psychological reaction to perceived erasure of community boundaries. *Journal of Social Psychology, 137*(3), 343–355. https://doi.org/10.1080/00224549709595445.

Roof, W. C. (1998). Modernity: The religious and the spiritual. *The Annals of the Academy of Politics and Social Sciences, 558*(1), 211–224. https://doi.org/10.1177/0002716298558001016.

Roof, W. C. (2003). Toward an integrated analysis. In M. Dillon (Ed.), *The Oxford handbook of the sociology of religion* (pp. 137–149). Oxford University Press.

Sen, A. (1995). *Inequality examined.* Harvard University Press.

Simmel, J. (1955). *Conflict.* Free Press.

Stock, B. (1983). *The implications of literacy: Written language and models of interpretation in the eleventh and twelfth centuries.* Princeton University Press.

Stone, A. R. (1995). *The war of desire and technology at the close of the mechanical age.* MIT Press.

Sundar, S., & Limperos, A. (2013). *Uses & grats 2.0.* Cambridge University Press.

Sylvan, R. (2005). *Trance formation: The spiritual and religious dimensions of global rave culture.* Routledge.

Tajfel, H. (1981). *Human groups and social categories.* Cambridge University Press.

Williams, K. M., & Banjo, O. O. (2013). From where we stand: Exploring Christian listeners' social location and Christian music listening. *Journal of Media and Religion, 12*(4), 196–216. https://doi.org/10.1080/15348423.2013.845027.

Woods, R. H., Skarritt-Williams, K., Chan, C., Waters, K., & Agodzo, D. (2016). Motivations for reading the Left Behind book series: A uses and gratifications analysis. *Journal of Media and Religion, 15*(2), 63–77. https://doi.org/10.1080/15348423.2016.1177343.

Wyn, J., Cuervo, H., Woodman, D., & Stokes, H. (2005). Young people, wellbeing and communication technologies. *Melbourne, VicHealth, 12*(4), 196–216. https://doi.org/10.1080/15348423.2013.845027.

Selected Readings

Bradley, H. (1997). *Fractured identities: Changing patterns of inequality.* Polity Press.

Brubaker, P. J., & Haigh, M. M. (2017). The religious Facebook experience: Uses and gratifications of faith-based content. *Social Media + Society*, April–June, pp. 1–11. https://doi.org/10.1177/2056305117703723.

Giddens, A. (1991). *Modernity and self-identity: Self and society in the late modern age.* Polity Press.

Hewitt, J. P. (2000). *Self and society. A symbolic interactionist social psychology.* Allyn and Bacon.

Jenkins, R. (1996). *Social identity.* Routledge.

Mead, G. H. (1934). *Mind, self and society. From the stand point of a social behaviorist.* University of Chicago Press.

Woodward, K. (2000). *Questioning identity: Gender, class, nation.* Routledge and Open University Press.

24

Religion and Meaning

Johannes Ehrat

[W]hen you open the next new book on the philosophy of religion that comes out, the chances are that it will be written by an intellectualist who in his preface offers you his metaphysics as a guide for the soul, talking as if philosophy were one of our deepest concerns... If on the other hand, a man has had no religious experience, then any religion not an affectation is as yet impossible for him; and the only worthy course is to wait quietly till such experience comes. No amount of speculation can take the place of experience. (Peirce, 1960, CP1.654–6551)[1]

There is no more to religion *than* meaning; the "and" in our title sounds pleonastic. One may neglect dance technique in Bharatanāṭyam, but by failing to grasp the "sanskritized body" as embodiment of Śiva's cosmic dance in the devadāsī practice including śṛṅgāra-rasa – representation of sexual love through dance – one risks misunderstanding (similar to the British Raj, which felt compelled to repress devadāsīs as temple prostitutes).

Religious meaning is more labile, confusing, and demanding than other practices; and misunderstanding – even well-intended – was devastating, as the devadāsī's fate illustrates.

There are two temptations when attempting to appropriate such a delicate object: theories tending to prescribe and empiricism refusing to understand. Following meandering theories is as Sisyphean as it is fruitless; not even a general conception of religion has been agreed upon in religious studies. Empirical investigation is confined to observables in ritual practices. The scholarly haystack is replete with pointless case descriptions of scarcely comprehended practices, more descriptive – but less neat – than theories. One can resist religious studies knowing too much by sticking to what historical religions know about themselves. Knowing empirically, on the other hand, knows with, not against, religious practices. Material objects, abstracting experienced meaning methodologically, explain nothing of essence. The alternative must be theoretically empirical, synthetic effort, analyzing meaning as it arises from practice in different religions. Analytic synthesis is possible only because religious meaning always needs form – there is no formless experiencing of holiness. Only forms are communicable, taught, transmitted, interiorized. Intelligential analysis, then, comprehends general meaning forms, not reduceable to meta-research or annotated bibliography. Both temptations come into play when social sciences mirror religion: "theory-free method-driven" research, or material objects, reach spiritual meaning as little as functionalism, which pervades sociality with a theory construct "religion."

Meaning-aware social theories use methods capable of grasping meaning natively. Each of the two main traditions, Semiotic Pragmaticism[2] (Peirce, Mead, Chicago School, Symbolic

The Handbook on Religion and Communication, First Edition. Edited by Yoel Cohen and Paul A. Soukup.
© 2023 John Wiley & Sons Ltd. Published 2023 by John Wiley & Sons Ltd.

Interactionism) and phenomenological approaches (Husserl, Schütz, Ricœur, Berger, Giddens) have unique advantages. Subjectivity is central to Schütz' egology, which struggles with "objective meaning." Semiotic, not based on what-it-means-for-me, offers more granularity – and specificity for religious meaning. Practically, they differ more in method – immediate-consciousness vs. category-based logic (technically: signs). Conceptualizing meaning as signs appears to be less tangible experience than consciousness. Most people are used to Heideggerian, Buberian explorations of religious existence, whereas pragmatic religion is less known (except for James's infelicitous psychologism).

This chapter will first review the advantages of approaching religious meaning as a Sign system following Peirce's theory of Semiotics; then consider form, genre, and practice in religious Semiotics; next, examine Sign classes; and finally propose a semiotic grid of religious practices.

Religious Meaning as a Sign System

Several key advantages derive from understanding religious meaning as pragmatic and as a Sign system.

1. Religion is specific meaning.
What makes meanings different? Analyzed as Signs, meanings differ in-nature – not arbitrarily (Saussure) or through intentionality (Husserl). We relate differently to reals, or realities force us to relate through different modes (traditionally called Categories). From realism follows that meanings become *plurale tantum*. These different relation modes are habits; when analyzed, habits guided by reason condense to logic, and habitual universe appropriation operates as logical inference. Such operations are called Signs, which differentiate conducts. Religions, as varieties of conduct, are not simply meaningful but specifically so. Semiotic, the broadest frame for Sign analysis, comprehends all meanings, and can differentiate religious cognitive behaviors as species among other meaning types.

2. Sign as conduct: rendered by interpretations abstracted in time's continuity.
Pragmatic is when conceptions/Signs regulate conduct/habits: when conceptions differ, conduct differs; religious Signs – literally – mean different religion practices, from ethics to liturgy/meditation. Epistemologically, Semiotic is radical in comprehending everything as cognitive conduct, no thing is not already meaning. To compare reality with meaning – happening only in Signs – is literally meaningless. No other access to the real exists unless habit-mediated through Signs. Signs, however, are enormously variegated, even thoughts are Signs, which subsequent Signs can Interpret. Semioses can be classified, but Sign classes do not exist, for Signs are living, and no Sign starts *ab ovo* but instead contains its entire prehistory, chaining Interpretations of many Classes. Meaning chains have been long known as language figuration (metaphoric, metonymic, synecdoche, irony). Signs are iterative Interpretations, "grown symbols" (Peirce CP2.302), but searching for each Sign's archeology (hypothetically) leads only to an asymptotic "literality." Here and now, we live with full Signs' Interpretation chains, so that "percept" as imaginary initial spark is an abstraction.

Most religious meaning is incomprehensible without deep Interpretation chains. This applies most strikingly to Hindu mythology's ramifications and extensions, in narratives as much as in iconography. Similarly, the deceptively familiar Christian Eucharist (with its meaning rooted in sacrificing Egypt's primogeniture, the exodus, the promised land, betrayal, the Last Supper, Jesus' crucifixion, etc.) is a paradigm of complex meaning. It is not only incomplete with any of the aspects omitted, but no layer can claim any predominate Interpretative hold. Analytically, each Interpretation step ("Semiosis") continues the chain link in a distinctive way.[3] The Lord's Passover is used as key, among many others, in the Gospel Passion narratives woven into the Last Supper. Continuing through Eucharistic adoration and mysticism, all these meanings subsist in the Sign, although each has a different logical nature. Seeking an "original" meaning is as stupid as polemicizing "transubstantiation" (an ultimate philosophical Passover derivative) or extolling adoration. Religious iconoclasm provides a counter-illustration: here the problem consists of percepts yielding to images. Therefore, Moses needed to smash the golden calf, because manmade icons obstructed the immediacy of his face-to-face with The Holy Name. In short, Interpretations/practices can be rejected. All such passages really constitute different practices condensed in Interpretation variances.

3. Signs as living stimulate religious-meaning communication.
One should not be fooled into hoping for an easy access to religious meaning, especially nonnatively. No mundane object is stably referenceable. Core experiences are not reproduceable. God's "I am that I am" (Exodus 3:14) is totally unlike "this burning bush" (Exodus 3:2). Religious Signs have thus to cope with inherent, essential instability and irreproducibility. We shall see how these are compensated Semiotically – through form and genre. Imitates of instable meaning (e.g. "prophetic inspiration" narratives) present themselves as "direct lines to God" (especially with false prophets). Unstable religious meanings compensate by stabilizing practices through forms, establishing practice frameworks. Thus, scripture interpretation, the Magisterium, and Paradosis/Oral-Torah take charge of singularities (prophecies, inspiration, mysticism), interpreting them according to their respective forms. Once scripture interprets mystical gifts, their original singular meaning – to the mystic – results in Signs communicable to all.

Form saves religious meaning from subjective arbitrariness – as sociology is tempted to pigeonhole one's drawing meaning for one's life from religion. This truism, as old as Durkheim and as recent as Habermas ("authenticity validity claim"), emphasizes important blind spots in scientific comprehension of religious meaning, for their foundational epistemological limitations prevent communication/social sciences from reaching deeper into religious meaning. Positivism debates (cf. Luhmann, Popper, Adorno) continuously reveal the problematic nature of their object constitution *in se*. For "religion" that leaves what their range restricts them to, namely, repeatedly observables – "flies outside of the bowl, never finding out, how it feels to be a goldfish" (that uncharitable point made by W. Cantwell-Smith, the Nestor of religion comparativism). Battles over reductionism in religious studies have been fought a long time ago, but, still, there are still degrees of incomprehension. Geertz's *Thick Description* of religion proves there are nuances limiting understanding. That method introduces Semiotic-in-disguise, assigning decisive functions to symbols taken from Peirce; Geertz resists investigating religious symbolism *in se*, though. For the stubborn comprehension-refusenik Asad (1993), that was already too substantial; Geertz-Asad's dispute counts among classics – hilarious for *ad personam* invectives but a stalemate *in re*. While the debate went stale, Geertz took his own interpretative approach to religions by foregoing the internal complexities of the Sign triad. Keen anthropological observer that he was, mysticism/ḏikr could not escape his attention studying Moroccan Islam. Anthropological disciplinary constraints shortchanged his deeper comprehension of that "Symbol," which is actually Icon, pragmatically a highly unstable ḏikr imagination and practices. Asad, opposing mysticism, pegs Islam's essence to slavedom – Muslims bound to God as slaves through "unconditional obedience" (1993, p. 222), serving his Islam framework "command" better than "love" the key to Sufi-mysticism.

Carrying the idea of conception-guided (Sign-Interpreting) Conduct into social sciences helps obtain a more complete reality (love and order and wisdom) of what religions effectively practice through meanings that exceed mere interiority – exceed a mere (subject–object) Sign, exceed mere Interpretation. Each of these "essences" figures as central meaning in abstractions from the complete meaning. Once it was *sheer* piety[4] but thoroughly misunderstanding (bhakti, mere holy-sign – Qur'an, Hindu murti) that constituted religion. Then, *mere* ritual (à la Frits Staal, Daoist "pure sacrifice" qīng jiào 清醮). Or, *mere* Interpretation (rabbinic responsa-type "Ask the Rabbi"). The history of religion (including sinology, Indology) could show that lopsided perspectives of the three kinds dominated certain epochs. The defect is not error but overlooking the rest, for religion is concrete in being triadically whole, Categorically ((i) quality, (ii) existence, (iii) law), Pragmatically ((i) mysticism, (ii) order, (iii) wisdom), and in Signs ((i) aesthetic, (ii) ethic, (iii) logos). Some social scientists, Geertz, Milton Singer, Parmentier et al., understood well what this completeness meant for "symbolism" (Semiotic) and sociality (Pragmatic). Semiotic's advantage is lost in "semiotics,"[5] though.

Logical forces controlling pragmatic are differentiated according to their logical nature and can be classified; transubstantiation theory is not adoration, but both mean Eucharist, as described earlier. Appreciating difference in meanings makes one observe what exactly Signs have to operate to construct meaning. The idea is simple: the sign is not the "thing," but it stands for it. So, its "standing" first needs construction material (sound, marks, etc.); second, its "standing for" must be determined (from woof to "chien" /狗); third, its "for" must be explained (from imitation to zoology, even imitating a dog must know it). In relating the three, one constructs meaning, but evidently zoology cannot build on woof woofity. So, the nature of each of the three Correlates matters. All possible con-tri-nations are classes of all possible Signs. In forming habits of behavior one relates these three: a (i) word (acoustic, written) tells one what one (iii) must do with (ii) this-here ([beware of biting] dog!). So with religion: (i) temple dance (Bharatanāṭyam) (ii) expresses the devadāsī's śṛṅgāra-rasa (and a knowledgeable audience appreciates through bhakti), and one (iii) sees Śiva's cosmic dance. This is religious practice, analytically dissected, holistically experienced. Sign classes must not be construed as hidden functionalism, nor semiologically as Signs through convention. Religion must remain historical-cultural experience; rightly understood Sign classes must describe, but never prescribe and thus produce a methodological artifact.

What Value, Then, Does Semiotic Add from Approaching Religion through Signs?

Analyzing and sorting Semioses, the very ferment of religious-meaning-as-experienced, is not moot, but useful.[6] However, Semiotic anthropologist Parmentier (2016, pp. 48–61) rightly warned of applying Sign classification 1:1 to social science. Signs are overrefined descriptors of actually used meaning to fit the latter's comparatively coarse purpose. The richly textured meaning used in social interaction is invariably reduced by social science into starkly simplified aggregates. Parmentier, in one of his illustrations belabors a semiotic/anthropological problematization of presence: the Mandylion, extendable to other acheiropoieta (e.g. the Vera Icona "Veronica," in St. Peter's or the Turin Shroud). The real problem is not as in Parmentier's elucubrations the presentic. He tries to typify a religious behavior where signs presentify the Unseen ("No man hath seen God at any time" 1 John 4:12 "Thou canst not see my face: for there shall no man see me, and live" Exodus 33:20). Anthropologists might want to lump cross-religion darśana-type rituals, under penalty of sacrificing the Judeo-Christian meaning nuance that divinity is never "here-now-I" – not even in the "image of the invisible God" (Colossians 1:15), whose Sudarium is proto-typos of all such icons-cum-legends. Pilgrims beholding the Vera Icona do not therefore behave like catchers of Krishna's gaze (darśana cf. Diana Eck, 1998) in a Ratha Jātrā of Jagannātha/Juggernaut. Only religious anthropological/comparatist theory suppresses meaning subtleties, which do control actual religious Conduct (in the sense of Peirce's Pragmatic Maxim).

While every science generalizes by means of abstraction, religion is not a true/false relation to existing objects (in space), but to reality-in-time. Technically speaking, religious meaning abstracts time ("prescissive abstraction"); anthropology abstracts space ("hypostatic abstraction"), coming up with variations distributed spatially.

Religious meaning is given in dharma/Vedic cosmology – Brahman; anthropology belabors caste/jajmani systems.

Semiotic adds insight, *first*, by accounting for *the* unique feature of religious meaning: the bivalent true/false-dyadic relation – existence – is intrinsically absent. What is meaning of Signs which don't stand for? In(-nowhere-)dicate? Is the Second Correlate in the triad of God Signs empty? How can Semiotic as a general theory of meaning handle those? Because reality is not identical with existence! In Peirce's parlance, Possibility and Necessity are Reals as much as Existence. God is real, but does not exist, wherefor one can't indicate "this is" God (and that not). Non-Existence extends to all major related concepts such as, e.g. Messiah (hidden end-time savior al-mahdī in Shīʿah Islam, Sabbateans in Judaism), kingdom of God (Luke 17:20f), resurrection (yaum al-qiyāma), Last Judgment (yaum ad-dīn), the *"well-guarded tablet"* Q43:22 or Heavenly Qurʾn, Daoist Ghost money, karma-economy with Brokaw's (1991) merit-ledgers 功過格, etc. Conversely, nothing in religious meaning – *pace* Parmentier – necessitates bivalent, factual existence (*hic-nunc-ego*), not even history of salvation (the *nunc* is the Pessah-seder-Haggadah-at-reading, not Moses' Red Sea). Cosmological temporality of post-Vedic religions and Daoism result in similar nonindexical Signhoods.

Religious temporality, ἔσχατα-logic (cf. Heidegger, infra), differs from (various cognitive aspects of) experienced time – time after time, and before – Garden-Eden; analogously, post-Vedic cosmogony in Brahman's primordial sacrifice of Puruṣa (Kuiper, 1970) – and since Vedic time is cyclic, also the end-time. What for Vedas "is" time, consequently turns into transcendent cosmological order in the immanent, i.e. dharma. Exploring religious Semiosis in depth here would lead too far into Semiotic theory and is left for another occasion (Ehrat, 2021).

Second – this is our focus here – Semiotic *appreciates* the historical, cultural givenness of religions. Signs per se are not deduced meaning (like a Kantian a priori) but grasp all possible thought formally – empty, not actual – Sign-using experience. Form presents two affordances: (i) specific religions generate specific traditions of Sign uses, but we still can tell the difference from not-religion. (ii) Interpretation-types persist as tradition, warding off religious meaning flattened into subjectivity. (Ad1) Meaning remains rich, not a sterile structure, nor the ever same social function (like Parsons' "latency"). (Ad2) Religions evolve, despite contrary affirmations. Technically, Signs iteratively Interpret Signs of the same Object – "symbols grow" (Peirce, CP2.302). Historical religions constitute Interpretation chains grown through the ages simultaneous with counter-Interpretations – internal or external phobias: heterodoxies or apologetics. As forms, transmissions occur as text genres *and* practices (both constituting webs/constellations): Peirce's Pragmatic Maxim assigns Signs the role of a conduct rule; conversely, in understanding/inventing conduct, one uses/creates Signs.

Sparking the chain of meaning is construable as one seminal ur form, from which a historical religion generates its unique array of interpretative practices, and which holds together the gamut of diverse generative upshots over its long unfolding through the ages. One can leave the genre/generation idea quite vague, as it is not a Hegelian dialectic but a historic-contingently evolving tradition, Interpretations of Interpretation. Even today's temple Buddhism in China and its tantric variety in Tibet are rooted in one form (the root Semiosis). Not that this ur form is still ready at hand; it needs to be reconstructed (Peirce, CP4.235) from today's pragmatic forms. Islamic ur form, e.g. is in Muhammad's words receiving from Ǧibrīl (the Archangel Gabriel) God's command "in clear Arab language" (Q26:193–195).

Form, Genre, Practice

Our concern coincides with the central Poetics/narratology problem of generative principles: form seed, "seminal genre," Genette's *architexte*, but cognizant of Miller's (1984) situating genre as social practice. Since its Platonic-Aristotelian *exordium*, Poetics understood narrating, not by configuring actions into text *ad libitum*, but by following teleological principles. Analogous to narration generation, religions communicate their meaning through their own generative forms. Setting aside theologoumena like revelation, technically a religion's history initiates with something to be communicated, and how. This initial mode becomes canonical for all further forms. Inspirational events without such congenial form remain fleeting and are forgotten. In order for such a singular unrepeatable moment in a lone inspired subject to survive, it had to have a communicable form into which it managed to transform itself. The term "genre" signals a cultural form of time, as Ricœur described narrative teleology (cf. Ehrat, 2005); conversely, the manner how a culture ("vulgar time") exists as temporality, forms narrative.

At their very core, religious meanings practice time; see, for example, the core of Augustine's analysis of God's time – "eternity." Both temporalities, narrative and – *a fortiori* – the "eternal," need forms, but different ones. Time culturally exists as form only, transforming perception of passing into telos (or another logic such as experiment sequences becoming a law of nature). Narrative temporality is culturally privileged, which allowed religions to repurpose it, sometimes by mythologically narcotizing teleology for time after time. That strata overlay remains inherently ambiguous and in danger of being misunderstood and reduced to something more manageable (Ramayana TV serials for instance). Vedas and purāṇas created religion-as-mythos, whose ambiguity resides in the interpretation strata. Doniger (1973) distinguishes four: "(1) story, occasionally of the shaggy dog variety … (2) the divine level… Above this is the (3) cosmic level of the myth… And below it, shading off into folklore, is the (4) human level, the search for meaning in human life…" (p. 2 cf. pp. 11–12), and no level and interpretation can claim to be the unique key.

Combining divine, cosmic, narrative, Mythos achieves as genre – generative figuration. Parousia is another genre, a cultural time figuration, traversal to all other culture temporalities, profoundly bewildering the Thessalonians – 2Th 2:1ff. To Heidegger's *Einleitung* (1975, Bd. 60, pp. 98–110), seven years before *Sein und Zeit* – we owe this stupendous phenomenology of two time registers, meshed and diverse. Myth and Parousia constitute simultaneously text configuration (*architexte*) and communication of trans-ordinary, religious experience-as-time. How? *Via negativa*, by keeping orderly/ordinary time experience at bay with improbable tales ("shaggy dog").

Muslims admire the Qurʾan's inimitability (iʿğāz): it couldn't be Muhammad's own mundane confabulation. Aesthetic text experience, therefore, proves Muhammad's prophethood; and that text is divinity's highest expression by communicating unknowables (al-iḫbār ʿan al-ġuyūb). Sunna and Shia attributed wonderous knowing-of-heavenly-origin to the Qurʾan, Muhammad, and Shiite imams (Nagel, 2010, p. 223, cf. 257) – against eleventh-century muʿtazilite rationalists. The end-times – the foremost unknowable – are in/through the Qurʾan text. Mystics and Shiites insisted on interpreting it as shrouding coming events, not as ʿUṯmān's imperial rule-book (the fourth caliph ʿUṯmān the redactor of the Qurʾan as we know it today).

Eschatology clearly is Christianity's core inspiration, the link to everything else, particularly the gentile mission, which in the fullness of time fulfills God's repeated promises prophesied in Isaiah 2, etc. The missionary ur genre is homily. After Roman armies destroyed Jerusalem's Temple (Isaiah's aim of the peoples' pilgrimage), Judaism defined itself ethnically – *a fortiori* by distancing from messianism (Schäfer, 2010), both Christian and Bar Kochba's varieties. Talmudic genre practice thus substituted for sacrifice. Subtextually, though, messianism persisted in Midrash, kabbalah, and hekhalot (Arbel, 2003) literature (Daniel 7). Even living messiahs – following Scholem – have reappeared until Shabbatai Zevi and hassidic Haredim.

Once religions succeeded in giving communication form to their specific temporality, each spawned further strictly/loosely origin-linked Sign forms. Novel forms generate new meanings. Inventing *le roman* – as literary theory/Poetic knowledge – didn't simply replicate diegesis or tragedy. Analogously, televangelism, although a remotely generatively descendant from Paul's eschatological mission to the gentiles, isn't plainly homily (Thessalonians may hardly recognize the likes of Oral Roberts, though).

Seminal forms and their descendant texts and practices remain fragile figurations to keep religious temporality intact – some defending religious integrity less successfully. Hare Krishna relates to Hindu bhakti as much as the evangelical prosperity cult does to St. Francis. Meaning, nevertheless, stays irremediably form bound, so that form changes entail different meanings. *Habent sua fata libelli*, religions evolve with their practices, losing meaning irretrievably, creating others audaciously, but never subjectively/arbitrarily: form keeps steady through evolution because it in-forms (more inert) social practice; neither evolution occurs haphazardly or arbitrarily.

Parmentier we saw despaired with meaning subtlety: Sign classes achieved, questioning useful applications in the anthropological toolbox. Indeed, when messy social practice turns to logic through Signs/form, that is a far cry from science, Peirce's paradigm in *"methods of fixing our beliefs."* Science undoubtedly is Semiotically/cognitively controlled conduct; action-in-general is – presumably, but without being fallibilistically constrained by truth. Where would – *a fortiori* – "conceiving practical bearings"[7] control religious meaning? Parmentier might concede the general idea of a logical-rule-constituted society; religions, however, never claimed to have invented rules – enlarged through ampliative reasoning (further "generalizing" symbols) – such as science invents and corrects laws. Religious practices' temporal, nonexistential logic also rules science as an in-the-long-run-hope, but with different corrective truths.

Both are aided by logic's "uberty" (Peirce, EP2:463–474), more productive but less secure than mere deduction. Abductive inference regulating conduct means, first, receiving on the fly many mental associations as candidates for making meaning; and then, in a second step, selecting among those the best; this is risky/unnecessary but it rewards with novelty. As religious conduct, thus is inspiration; even if blindly following commandments, in reality God commands. God, wherefor, is never deducted into immanence, but found, creatively. To illustrate that inherent creativity – operative across religions – there are various classical religious acts:

> *Finding God's will.* One might well profess to do what God wills and not oneself, but no one receives verbatim instructions, and is thus forced to interpret signs (from dreams to miracles) in the immanent, indicating God's design.
>
> *Mitzvot* (oral and written Torah) appears to be clear-cut and unmistakable to-dos and not to-dos, but their far from arbitrary invention is contingent upon an extensive set of cautious exegetical rules.
>
> *Dharma* (even the notoriously controversial Laws of Manu) interprets a cosmic order, not social caste stratification, through authoritative brahmins, layered commentators of guru authorities; it is creativity contained by authority.
>
> *Ḥudūd Allāh* God's boundaries, *al-amr* (Q3:152) God's command, and similar (cf. Nagel, 2001, p. 268) are couched in an attitude of passively receptive obedience, exemplarily Muhammad's.
>
> *Chinese practices* are more than body-cultivation technologies. They include nèidān, Inner Alchemy, talismanic healing techniques, etc., all based on a transcendental cosmology

(wàidān 外丹). Combinatorics especially of the Yijing 易經 Book of Changes is intriguing in its creative complexity.

Religious creativity isn't pure fancy, though; Interpretation proceeds creatively by rules and canonical templates/models from both channels and enables creative reinterpretation. Creation – after community reception – branches into morals and what, as historical institutions and communities, become hallmarks of their religion. Sometimes popular practices, unpredictable and creative, overcame the resistance of instituted leadership. Conversely, thearchic or hierarchic leadership survived only through popular renewal; branches also became splits, which happened in all religions except Hinduism, which instituted its singular mythological inclusivity, that is, prior to Hindutva. Growing religious meaning creatively is of deeper importance than institutional regulation.

Sign Classes

In institutions' tug-of-war with inspiration, Sign classes construe meaning both ways – logically. Technically, Sign (iii) relations Interpret previous (i) Signs of the same (ii) object. (i) becomes the First Correlate in the new triad, novel meaning enters into the Third, Sign use in the Second. Instead of pegging meaning – easier to deal with for an anthropologist – Sign-classes subtleties are creativity's avenues.

Such abstract description sounds less dramatic than, say, Revivalists' inventing "hitting the sawdust trail" (Balmer, 2004, p. 602). That gave stale repentance ideas in Protestantism – the public nature of sin and probity in Quakerism – new, tangible meaning. It continued in Billy Graham's stadium and television crusades, adopted later by many televangelists, adding in each evolutionary step new meaning facets. The mission "non-oratory" homilia through the first pagan communities of Christ's disciples is but the remotest ancestor; for homily, while evolving from synagogal derashot (sermons) (Stockhausen, 2008, p. 70), carefully avoids rhetorical craft. Its style is conversation, of a trembling evangelist, with nobodies. The Second Epistle of Clement, really an oral homily, not an epistle, addresses pagans literally as nothings (εκαλεσεν γαρ ημας ουκ οντας 2 Cl1.8), former stone-worshippers (2 Cl1.6). Although the late-first/early-second-century text's author is not Clement, Peter's fourth successor, but today is assumed to be *adespotos* (anonymous); Corinth's Pauline community still freshly recollected its conversion from paganism. To that corresponds Paul's role in fear and trembling (1 Corinthians 2:3), a far cry from an Asianic *grandiloquus* orator, even beneath *humilis* rhetoric (Siegert, 2008, pp. 25–26). The choice in missionary communication is very conscious, between trembler and nobodies, who thus are linked to those hitting the sawdust trail (less so, admittedly, the connection of trembler with grandiloquent televangelists). That form choice irremediably defined two complementary roles, once and for all, clearly departing from what other religions define as their role complements functionally analogous to nobodies and tremblers. These chosen form, and role constraints should negatively exclude, reject, or at least marginalize violent, asymmetric, manipulative persuasion. History provides lots of counter-examples, of course, but at least this makes clearer what is more genuine: St. Francis or the Crusaders. Eschatological temporality is a meaning expressed better in patience than in assault.

The evolution of religious meaning practices amounts to argumentation and results in evolved forms (Sign classes). Classification affords accounting for subtle variation of religious meaning but, more importantly, alerts to less spectacular practices. Hindutva, for example, may top

Hinduism literature rosters. The bulk of communication studies, though, tends to ignore that religious dance corporality continues to express devotion, even in today's Bollywood productions. Firstness-determined Signs such as devotion and corporality Semiotic cannot not notice.

All meaning (again technically) relates a First stand-for (Representamen, Sign) to a Second user's situation (Object) to a Third idea (Interpretant); Hindu practice relates (i) a sacred gesture (pūjā, mudrā, bhāratanāṭyam-dance movement-asanas, darśan-look) to (ii) sacralized space (bhakti, life dedication, temple, Rāmcaritmānas, Ramayan tele-visioning) to (iii) divine intervention (dharma, union, possession: as Kālī's thag/thug or Santoshī Mā's devotee in the homonymous 1975 film, or 2006 tele-serial). Certainly, both the Hindu pantheon and communication studies are mindblowingly convoluted and complex; using the triadic sign relation, though, the meaning of Hindu practices unfolds logically.

A First is either simple or rule-based. Pūjā consists mostly of gestures as simple as offering food, bathing, and garland adorning. That can only enter into simple Second Subject–Object relations, "drinking" auspicious divine views – darśana of the third eye – starting one's mornings at the household altar (cf. Babb's, 1981; Eck's, 1998, many descriptions). A simple Third completes the triad relating to auspiciousness or grace. Lutgendorf (1990) describes a quite similar Semiosis, Ramayan TV serial spectatorship, devotees' screen-touching and drinking Rama's look. Likewise, bhāratanāṭyam, devotion-bhakti-in-dance, sacred corporality of devadāsīs, which in all its sophistication is simple bodily bhakti. It can then become nātyaśāstra-teaching reflecting the assistants' identification with mythos as अभिनय abhinaya, not a simple sign, but – a Third – the cosmic–corporeal order. In view of its Hindutva ideologization (Sanskritization) – another complex Third – the famous dancer Ananya reacted critically with "how do I secularize my body?" (Chatterjea, 2004, p. 107). Attempting to disentangle from ideology, she saw only the solution to liberate it from religion itself "causing a fissure in the seemingly inevitable relationship between the forms and movement aesthetic" (p. 106). Abhinaya sans codification? How, seeing the intimate entwining of dance, body, and devotion? Her attempt, conversely, shows how effective entanglement is; in Bhāratanāṭyam practice, she had to conclude soberly, de-sanskritizing is quasi-destructive. Interpretation networks can certainly extend in various other directions; the point of this illustration is merely to prove the very different grip of different Classes. Once Thirds with complex Sign usage chains operate (hindutva or de-sanskritization), simple pūjā-type devotion is hard to recuperate.

Analogous recodification examples abound. Scholem, a contemporary Kabbala authority, for example, is no longer a Kabbalist, but at a scholarly thaumaston-distance – two quite different meanings. What made Sephardi Judaism continue to cultivate the Kabbala, which some of the Ashkenazi (or European) school after Sabbatianism transmuted into Hasidism (Scholem, 1954, pp. 325–350)? The answer can be a historian's, or Ba'al Shem Tov's, suffered apprehension of Frankism. Hidden divinity as Firstness-dominated Semiosis, as Kabbala or as hasidic messianism, is a simple Sign, whereas Talmudic rejection is a complex discourse. *A fortiori*, so outsider perspectives, as in some communication studies treat "ultra-Orthodox" (a pejorative term) Tremblers/Haredim as Martian-look-alikes, speaking hyperbolically. Is down/degrading misunderstanding inevitable if one cannot appreciate simple meaning forms linking Haredi to millenary messianic mysticism?

So, here is the point of Semiotic Sign classification to understand religious meaning and praxis in its differences. Of three Correlates:

- The First, sign material, cannot be neglected – this could justify material culture studies (often failing to exploit their vantage fully).
- The Second, relates Interpreters to their intended Object. Religious Secondness is quite tricky, for God is never at hand, and all miracles, portents, inspirations, and talismans intend yonder.

– Third Correlates function as corrals in order to keep Interpretation religious: this draws the line between Mauss-Malinowski's gift economy concept and Buddhists or Hindus performing their caste-determined dāna-duties (Parry, 1986). Correlates divide into (iii) general rule-based, (ii) *hic-nunc-ego* presence-based, and (i) mere-characteristic-based. Holy books (rules, grammar analogous) are unlike darśana third eyes, and are unlike mantra chanting: (ii) chanters relate to meditation Objects; (i) viewing a deity connects devotees auspiciously. (iii) Torah students relate to divine Law. (iii) Law is the idea of Talmud, (ii) whereas Moses' Sinai revelation is Shekhinah Presence of the Holy Name, the idea guiding Iconicity is limited to devotion (dangerous, thus leading to aniconism).

It is worth mentioning that it is only as a triad of all Correlates that meaning is concrete, or better, communicable, that social conduct is performed. Studies describing religious practices merely as material, therefore, are not rendering religiously practicable practices, neither do those exclusively interested in ideologies (Hindutva, Jihad). If such practices are practiced as mere ideology, they have turned political and ceased to be religious. Avoiding Peirce's exact, albeit extravagant, terminology, it does not help the uninitiated to understand Hare Krishna chants as Rhematic–Iconic–Qualisign Triad, but the cognitive and behavioral principles should be clearer. (Thus, Woody Allen's *Hannah and Her Sisters* could not understand Hare Krishna chanting performance, because of his intellectual quest for what occurs after death, although, granted, neurosis generates comic effects.)

Synthetic Panorama of Religious Meaning Communication Types: Semiotic Grid of Religious Practices

A meaningful haystack of religious practices contradicts meaning, which reflects our ways of thought, or what counts as order. We cognitively behave in our universe through types that range from rigor (laws) to freedom (imagination). Types order religious practices into meaning classes: from Posek responsum to dervish trance. Behaving religiously grasps the ordered totality to select one meaning, as speaking a sentence selects one tense-person-mood from grammar's totality. For meaning, Sign classification constitutes that totality, which every competent actor grasps and which synthesizes each religion from where practitioners competently select. Religions compare as coherent totalities/syntheses/com-positions, but afford surprisingly similar positions across compositions. Given the subtlety of Sign classification – concurring with Parmentier – such similarity is reasonable only to a certain depth, after which all social behavior becomes "messy." Messiness enables innovation, though, technically it enables relational–constructivity/degeneracy of Sign triads: each new Interpretation adds ("ampliative reasoning") or reduces meaning. We discuss both dimensions of religious meaning, grafting generativity onto order and genre onto grammar.

Mantra chanting is a degenerate triad of dharma, degenerate of cosmology (degeneration/complexity reduction is never logically compelling, that is, necessary; it constitutes only three grades – sentiment from ethic from cosmic order. From cosmology exist many other degeneration chains). Mantras are meaning derived even in their musical form (as Annette Wilke and Oliver Moebus, 2011, showed) and simple practice, not songs/music (for practitioners, only for tourists). Without cohering to a meaning universe that regulates social behavior and that knows about a comprehensive order, mantras become mood muzak. Contrariwise, Staal is known for declaring ritual/mantras as meaningless, but his "position is an astute piece of gamesmanship: a spirited and entertaining defense of a weak position. Vulnerable from all sides, he holds it well enough to set the protocols, stay in the game, protect every vulnerable point with clever feints, and, from all appearances, win a draw" (Hiltebeitel, 1994, p. 125). Coherence means logically persistent, but not attended, co-presence – volitional attention constructively shiftable. Collections merely lump together religious practices, sometimes even taxonomically. Semiotic construes order via meaning constructedness – all possible thought through abstraction – but doesn't accomplish the concrete thinking. Only when factually and historically situated can it be shown that religions practice this, and not that other, meaning. This especially concerns how subtly practices (and so meanings) can vary: even tent revivals becoming televangelism cannot be Semiotically deduced, but merely observed and described, namely, after some creative community's invention.

Once created, type/genre might be imitated – or avoided – by other religions, otherwise, how would "Islamic televangelist" shows appear on Egyptian, Indonesian, etc., television? Or neo-pentecostalist "health and wealth" transmogrify into outright prosperity cults, especially in karma-economy environments. In Thai Buddhism, "engined by the large-scale merit-making industry, the prosperity cult of phuttha phanit represents a religo-cultural [sic] space where popular Buddhism has converged with market economy, consumers' practices and the quest for personal and cultural identities" (Kitiʿāsā, 2008, pp. 120–121).

Order is smarter than collecting cases, which alone makes practices describable. Ordering is antipodal to fragmenting the religion symbol along disciplinary corrals (material culture, communication, film, television, dance studies, etc.), because religious meaning practices are so overarching: post-Vedic religions, for example, from mantras the self-same meaning passes into temple theater (Sullivan, 2010), dance (Falcone, 2016), Bollywood mythologicals (Dwyer, 2006), Ramayan serials (Lutgendorf, 1990), even Hindutva Ekatmata Yātrā pilgrimages converging in Ayodhyā (Katju, 2003, p. 43). By splitting symbol continua, one risks losing the key to religious understanding.

Now, for religious symbols – being historical-social-empirical – the logical order cannot simply mean Sign-classes-order. Meaning, for which communities invented forms/genres, doesn't hinge merely on one fundamental inspiration, but contingent circumstances forced reflexions and responses. Novel historical/cultural environments – not chance – impel religions to invent novel practices and variegated meaning. Religion universally subsists as worshiping but also as organized community, in determinate relations to norms/power, contrasting with the Other. Another process sets in – also universally – once respective seminal genres became classical/authoritative counter-inventions needing compensating ossified authority weight: mysticisms compensate legalisms; Šīʿa's Hidden Imam contrasts Kalifs; eschatological churches contrast structure; messianism contrasts rabbinism; saṅgha ascetism contrasts temple Buddhism (compensation patterns adapt over epochs). Genres of compensating practices – immediately recognizable – contrast substantially from authority Signs/practices. Religious legalism constitutes an argument class of Semiosis, whereas compensating mystics invariably use First classes (corporality, senses, imagination). Indeed, Firsts protect mysticism guaranteeing that authoritative-discursive-structural Semioses cannot abduct and abuse it.

While unusable for *prescribing*, Semiotic is quite suited for *describing* meaning that Sign users had historic-contingently constructed, limiting semioticians to the effectively observed and its constructive-degenerative evolutionary order. All present-day meaning (re-)produced by religions came from canonical practices/scriptures as seedbeds. Such progeny can be considered in two respects: (i) generatively as genres constellate through each other's positioning; and (ii) functionally as fulfilling different meaning communication. As mere practice arrangements both overlap.

Semiotic-technically speaking, genres constitute standardized Sign usages with one of the Sign triad's Correlates dominating, as illustrated earlier with Bhāratanāṭyam (Firstness), dharma (Secondness), and mythology (Thirdness). The functional genre for establishing relation beyond the world-immanent (transcendence, liturgy, prayer, etc.), for example, prefers Firstness-dominated Semioses. Mysticism – not exactly the same function – uses similar Sign processes, but without a social/ritual meaning compound: ḏikr, for example, in Islam contrasts for historical/political/ideological/confessional reasons with the religious sociality in the seminal genre command/al-amr Q3:152, as Interpreted by the Sunna/majority. Unfortunately, older Peirceanizing studies described religious practices as plain "icon," "index," "symbol," which in reality they never were – instead, they are complex Semiotic interpretation chain constructions. That rich growth stays with religious Signs, and branching meaning exploits this constructively/degeneratively.

By tabulating connected forms, two things come into view: (i) how the core *generates* lesser forms, and/or (ii) by serving different *functions*, how forms unfold. Both are mere groupings – using Sign classification – under different perspectives.

1. *Genetic*: After inducing their magnetic field of meaning forms, religions cast material usage forms of textual genres. These texts constitute the originary rhetoric, specific discursivities for specific religions. Naturally religions produce a wealth of genre traditions but not infinite kinds.

How – to illustrate the principle – would Christians cast the gifts of the Holy Spirit into reproduceable form? Prophecy and glossolalia – practiced intensely in Pauline communities, continuing among charismatics and Quakers – proved to be impractical (Paul corralled them with other, communicable charisms); the genre, far from disappearing, became more stable as mystics' autobiographies, religious order charisms, and even Spiritual Exercises. Spectacular (tele-)evangelist prophesies have their root in this genre, but also distinctive neo-Pentecostalist prayer forms as they spread to Africa, encountering, and sometimes merging with, witchcraft (Rio et al., 2017).

At the other end of that derivation from the core, Less of the Same, namely lesser in rank, less demanding, than the seminal genre, one can group forms that constitute accommodations of religions to their day-to-day practices. Weaker forms complement, but do not change meaning; communities practice frequently more quotidian meaning, still generated by the *architexte*.

- *Islam,* while instantiating divine "commanding good and forbidding evil" (Q9:112) in *fatwa* genres, cultivates rich allocution genre arrays. From authoritative Friday sermon ḫuṭba lay miracle-tellers qāṣṣ to daʿwa, the latter dominate contemporary communication forms as Maghreb cassette-preachers, cyber-daʿwa, or missionary Tablīghī-Jamāʿat. In synthesis, the entire genre spectrum constructs complementary roles of God-derived authority and observants.
- *Christianity* analogously, with the homily as its quotidian subform – "conversation" without rhetorical artifice (cf. *supra*) – constructs complementary roles through lacking authority. Homily is still in the orbit of the mission to the gentiles and gift of the Holy Spirit, but has moved to a stance less in awe of the eschatological moment.
- *Rabbinic* halacha has its foremost instantiation in Talmudic discourse; synagogal genres (derashah), though, construct quotidian meaning, a holy people complementing halachic Interpreters (Stemberger, Himmelfarb). This role configuration obtains to present-day Orthodox Jewish practices.
- *Hinduism* allocates genres entirely differently when mythology is seminal, contrasted with practices dharmas of non-Vedic traditions (avaidika Jains, Buddhists), thus the myth-telling principal form is quotidianly complemented by bhakti fervor. Ramayan TV serials, numerous studies show, encounter their audiences' fervid devotion: these replicate complementary roles in consumption patterns of pūjā sacrifice, dance, and theater.
- *Sinosphere* (Sadao) religiosities constellate genres specifically based on thearchy ideas, contrasted by Kleeman's Licentious Cults 淫祀 yínsì (sacrifices by whom was not authorized).

Central genres are rites, but quotidianity communicates (Inner and Outer) alchemy. Today, nonlicencedness continues in many deviant sects resembling Aum Ōmoto, and what was alchemy transmuted into self-cultivation, Qigong, etc. Role complementarity is nuanced, but "official" and "amoral cult" practices still relate.

2. *Functional*: All religions, in their specific manner, pattern communicational functions.

Communication is necessarily directed, from the communal/individual subject to certain others. In that relation, religious origin specifies both poles, *ego* and *alter*, quite differently from mundane communication. Religious subjectivity – devout souls or chosen people – has no other quality than being in relation to its divine alterity. This alterity informs also – as the divine alterity's altern – *ego*, mundane communication directed to the outside of religion (exclusive you), to all (inclusive we), to us (exclusive we). That is what Roman *re-ligio* meant before Tertullian's abduction of the term as trans-ethnic, that is, with a gentile focal point.

Unlike nonreligion, the foremost Otherness is not intra-mundane. In Platonistic understanding, transcendent alterity is not even really other but *interior intimo meo et superior summo meo* (Augustine, Confessions III,6,11). Subject–Object differentiation, as Peirce's Secondness Category contemplates, is thus bracketed. Mystics cannot separate what is theirs from God's. The primordial function for religious communication is directed to nowhere direction, literally "climb beyond hither," that is, transcend from the immanent (some might prefer the term sacrality).

Genre: weaker/lesser than Shechinah is temple liturgy, quotidian sacredness-at-hand, which in turn sacralizes the Aaronite priesthood into temporary trans-mundanity. In Himmelfarb's theory, the weak genre after the temple destruction is Israel's holiness – in ethnic, ethical, and sacral regard; again, a Sign of a peculiar religious I-Thou-Secondness.

No religion leaves it to arbitrariness how to reach divinity/nirvana but establishes practices that are learned, transmitted, and ordered as ritual or ascetic texts/genres. Attaining Buddhahood, tathagata, or arhat status separates Pure-Land, Maitreya-Future-Buddha Buddhism from other Mahāyāna and Theravāda Buddhisms, but constitutes luxuriant theories and complexity, as well as being the foundation of various "millennial" Salvationist movements in the Sinosphere.

Islam appears to stand out with its ḫuṭba-centered Friday service. Mystical nondifferentiation, however, is outsourced to Sūfī esoterism and ḏikr Allāh ecstasy – again, there are notorious, conflictual cases of mystics' identification with God.

Communication with the beyond is not arbitrary; neither are the other communication functions (i) *ad extra*, (ii) *ad omnes*, and (iii) *ad intra*:

1. Externally, meaning is presented *outward*. Some religions avoid *ad extra*: Judaism sticks to its ethnic delimitation, whereas the originary Christian impulse is mission. Pre-hindutva-Hinduism had no notions of conversion, but the Arya-Samaj movement "repurposed" Shuddhi-rituals to "re-vert" to Hinduism as competition with daʿwa and missionaries. Analogously, Chinese thearchy had no real outside, so outside rites could be licensed; recent Buddhist and Salvationist missionaries were (post-)colonially inspired. *Daʿwa*, instead, has become so central to Islam that in its most extreme forms it amounted to Jihad/ǧihād: Boko-Haram's full name is ǧamāʿat ahl as-sunna li-d-daʿwa wa-l-ǧihād. Direction from whom to whom? Communicating a specific meaning is not analogous to didacticism, the asymmetric impartation by knowers to not knowers. The perversion of *daʿwa* (the present-day synonym for terrorism) indicates perils of falsely constructed religious *ego-ʾīmān* to the wrong *alter-kāfir*. What does it mean to prohibit coerced conversion (Q2:256), or even inciting conviction overpersuasively, if not the respect of a special alterity of outsiders addressed by sinners/ deficient/not accomplished? Outsiders are unlike secular transaction target audiences. There

is no good reason for attracting them religiously if not by divine mandate or karunā/compassion – not for any self-gain.

2. Ethic, generally, posits claims concerning all; no ethic is meaningful as mere description of "our customs" but only as a normativity claim binding the all-inclusive "us." The exclusive "us" is the hallmark of *ad intra* communication directed at "our community." Why would religions extend their own meaning to everybody, either as a norm or as coercion? *Ad omnes* (or universal) approaches vary. More restricted to the Umma, Caliphs assert their authority universally under the Islamic premise that Allah mandates "commanding good and forbidding evil" (Q9:112). Problems with such universal indiscriminateness arise from disenchantment à la Max Weber: religion and state legitimization always identified functionally, except solely in modernity. Premodern ethics, religion, and power are essentially identical. Asad's coercion/order conception of Islam applies to all other extra-modern socialities, although without his power emphasis. No sooner had religion dissociated from other normativities than ethic functional communication imposed itself. As a collectively binding decision appeal, ethic now functions socially. Leaving aside Weber's disenchantment thesis of capitalism and Protestant ethics, there is a place for pragmatic meaning experienced comprehensively through religious temporality. Post-Vedic dharma may be the most tangible. There is – inherent to this temporality – no restriction: it presupposes to be universally experienceable. How norms are discovered is a post-Kantian aporia that stems from strict severance of cognitive from pragmatic reasoning. Peirce succeeded in reuniting both as cognitive behavior, at the price of Critical Common-sensism, which is miniscule truth theory without absolute claims. In the frame of Pragmaticism, religious pragmatic as revisable Common-sense is deconfined from community bounds but still not coercible as absolute truth.

3. *Ad intra* communication is directed to "us" exclusively. Its necessity might also be owed to the modern fracture of universal normativity, now enshrined in the separation of private from public spheres. Religions are expected to communicate functionally *inward*, for establishing community conduct, specific to each religion. This is more of a problem for the public sphere with its growing tendency to monopolize normativity, encroaching on other normativities. Burqa legislation in France shows the uneasy cohabitation of human rights with a state monopoly of power. Sharia is expected to yield to state law, leaving to mosques matters of ethic, moral, and custom in matrimonial (UK, India), dietary, purification practices, etc. However, periodical outbursts of states encroaching on communities, or the lack thereof, prove private/public separation controversial and fraught. Ambedkar's Dalit unsuccessfully advocated encroaching on Hindu caste marriage and other bondage rules. However, customs within religious communities form inevitably, and they are supported by common identity in the relational alterity from God. Rules can be as complex, exhaustive as halakha, or as loose as in chiliastic groups.

Conclusion

Religious meaning, in the singular, can as such only be grasped synthetically, unless one advocates a Parsons-like functionalism, where latent meaning is deduced. If one recognizes religions as empirical-historical, though, one has to reckon with innumerable manifestations. These might not be constituted by design or planification, but that does not mean that they are illogical. This contribution employed mainstream literary genre theory, which Miller (1984) expressed as "typified rhetorical actions based in recurrent situations," thus, taking seriously that "discourses that are complete, in the sense that they are circumscribed by a relatively complete shift in rhetorical situation" (p. 159), we applied it to religions as historical bodies. Semiotic Pragmatic supplied the logical scaffolding for synthesis as one meaning, a coherent whole.

Notes

1   This chapter builds on the analysis of meaning proposed by the American philosopher Charles Sanders Peirce. For background, see Deledalle (2000), Liszka (1996), and Peirce (1991). "Peirce's conception of the sign is triadic, which entails its forming part of a potentially never-ending, at any rate continuous dynamics reflected in many of life's occurrences… The sign is identified as comprising a first – called a representamen – which stands for a second – its object – to a third – its interpretant—, the latter in turn becoming a representamen of the same object to another interpretant and so on ad infinitum, thus creating an endless series of interrelated signs that Peirce referred to as semiosis or 'meaning-making'" (Stecconi, personal communication; see also Stecconi, 2009).

Stecconi offers an example drawn from translation that illustrates the concepts used by Professor Ehrat in this chapter: "The term Bible, for instance, is a representamen (or material embodiment, or sign) used to represent (or refer to) what the Bible in itself actually is or said to be (Word of God, Sacred Scripture, Good Book, etc) (and that it is regardless of whether it is being referred to or not), i.e. – in semiotic terms – as an object. Now the latter (the Bible as object) in itself cannot be approached: it is the sign's dynamical object, and can only be thought through its representation in the sign, namely the immediate object (that is the specific instance of Bible in view – a particular translation for example). From thence the need to interpret the object via the interpretant, since this is the only way to take into account the connection between the representamen and the object it stands for. The immediate interpretant may be defined as what is immediately, though somewhat vaguely, interpreted. The dynamical interpretant as the actual response that is triggered. And the final interpretant as the sum of the consequences brought about by the sign. The interpretant then indefinitely turns into a representamen; likewise, the Bible and its interpretations are ever evolving and always need a new translation or exegesis, thereby falling in line with the logical continuity of Peircean semiosis.

"This basic definition is to be considered in the light of Peirce's phaneroscopy, which holds that anything resorts to one of the following modes of being: firstness (what is in itself), secondness (what exists in response to something else), and thirdness (what relates a first to a second – often in the form of a rule or law. These three phaneroscopic categories then combine with (1) the monadic mode of apprehension of the representamen, (2) the dyadic relation of the representamen to its dynamical object, and (3) the triadic relation of the representamen to its dynamical object and to its final interpretant, so as to form the main three trichotomies of the sign. These trichotomies are then to be associated with one another abiding by the law of categories (a third logically comprises a second and a first, and a second comprises a first – not the other way around)" (Stecconi, personal communication).

2   The upper case is used when terms in Peircean Semiotic have a usage different from common usage. I am grateful for Francis Coffey's corrections and critique.

3   In the technical Peircean term: Representamen/Sign/First Correlate in either constructive or degenerative Semiosic Correlation.

4   That "Protestant" outlook on religions was the main factor for Groot's and others' meticulous but thorough misunderstanding of Chinese "religion," which was gleefully held against European Orientalists.

5   NB semiotics ≠ Semiotic, and is epistemologically irreconcilable (cf. Ehrat, 2005). Semiological communication studies became sterile code-differentiation acrobatics, or, as Leone (2014) diagnosed, hot air "*aria fritta*" (p. 93). "Code"-binges *à la* Eco made "*applied semiotics*" deterring and didn't yield many insights. In short, Peircean Semiotic is neither arbitrary code nor structure, but Conduct, as earlier.

6   Using Peirce on religion is/has been done in quite different ways, his vastly extended theory architecture being the culprit. The later Peirce complemented metaphysical upshots from Categories (from where Semiotic and Pragmatic originated much earlier). Metaphysic – albeit derivative general Reality theories

(Tychism, Anancism, Agapism Peirce CP6.302) – served certain theologians for positioning God into its apex – Idealism in Peircean disguise. In this way, Semiotic/Pragmatic remains in sublunary realms of actual cognitive conduct. A theory of God's Reality, derived from ways in which it is experienced, isn't needed and would nonapophatically prove difficult.

Resisting even Peirce's own religion-philosophical lead to think God through cognitive evolution (along the famous "Neglected Argument"), in the realm of God-thought we leave cognitive Discovery to historical religions. Peirce's "method of science" – the orderly convergence of adequate opinions of an unlimited community of researchers – shares "musement," Galileo's "lume naturale," Abduction (Peirce CP6.477–6.488) with religions, which, however, establish their own kind of eliminatory procedures. While the final state of investigation is absolute truth, present as ideal in Discovery, speculating about a final state of religion – in philosophical terms – remains moot. Ideals of ever-higher-adequacy-opinion governing religious Abductive inferences are inconceivable. Conceiving of religion metaphysically hinges too much on analogies with scientific Discovery. If we account for what is dissimilar between scientific and religious discovery, little commonality is left: Agapism-as-Religion is pantheism, but not living, developing, reforming, reviving religions, whose home-grown finality is eschatology, not progress.

7   To quote the Pragmatic Maxim: Peirce CP5.402 "Consider what effects, that might conceivably have practical bearings, we conceive the object of our conception to have. Then, our conception of these effects is the whole of our conception of the object."

References

Arbel, V. D. (2003). *Beholders of divine secrets: Mysticism and myth in the Hekhalot and merkavah literature.* SUNY Press.

Asad, T. (Ed.). (1993). *Genealogies of religion: Discipline and reasons of power in Christianity and Islam.* Johns Hopkins University Press.

Babb, L. A. (1981). Glancing: Visual interaction in Hinduism. *Journal of Anthropological Research, 37*(4), 387–401.

Balmer, R. H. (2004). *Encyclopedia of evangelicalism* (rev. and expanded ed.). Baylor University Press.

Brokaw, C. J. (1991). *The ledgers of merit and demerit: Social change and moral order in late imperial China.* Princeton University Press.

Chatterjea, A. (2004). In search of a secular in contemporary Indian dance: A continuing journey. *Dance Research Journal, 36*(2), 102–116. https://doi.org/10.2307/20444595

Deledalle, G. (2000). *Charles S. Peirce's philosophy of signs, essay in comparative semiotics.* University of Indiana Press.

Doniger, W. (1973). *Śiva: The erotic ascetic.* Galaxy Books 650. Oxford University Press.

Dwyer, R. (2006). *Filming the gods: Religion and Indian cinema.* Routledge.

Eck, D. L. (1998). *Darśan, seeing the divine image in India* (3rd ed.). Columbia University Press.

Ehrat, J. (2005). *Cinema and semiotic: Peirce and film aesthetics, narration, and representation.* Toronto Studies in Semiotics and Communication. University of Toronto Press.

Ehrat, J. (2021). A semiotic concept of religion for the social sciences. forthcoming. https://doi.org/10.13140/RG.2.2.19522.20168. Retrieved May 23, 2022, from https://www.researchgate.net/publication/348676245_A_semiotic_concept_of_religion_for_the_social_sciences

Falcone, J. M. (2016). Dance steps, nationalist movement: How Hindu extremists claimed Garba-raas. *Anthropology Now, 8*(3), 50–61. https://doi.org/10.1080/19428200.2016.1242910

Heidegger, M. (1975). *Gesamtausgabe.* Klostermann.

Hiltebeitel, A. (1994). Are mantras meaningful? *Journal of Ritual Studies, 8*(1), 125–130.

Katju, M. (2003). *Vishva Hindu Parishad and Indian politics.* Orient Longman.

Kiti'āsā, P. (Ed.). (2008). *Religious commodifications in Asia: Marketing gods.* Routledge.

Kuiper, F. B. J. (1970). Cosmogony and conception: A query. *History of Religions, 10*(2), 91–138. https://doi.org/10.1086/462623

Leone, M. (2014). The semiotic ideology of semiotics: A vertiginous reading. *Religion, 44*(1), 92–98. https://doi.org/10.1080/0048721X.2014.866721/

Liszka, J. J. (1996). *A general introduction of the semiotic of Charles Sanders Peirce.* Indiana University Press.

Lutgendorf, P. (1990). Ramayan: The video. *TDR (The Drama Review), 34*(2), 127–176. https://doi.org/10.2307/1146030

Miller, C. R. (1984). Genre as social action. *Quarterly Journal of Speech, 70*(2), 151–167. https://doi.org/10.1080/00335638409383686

Nagel, T. (2001). Theology and the Qurʾān. In J. D. McAuliffe (Ed.), *Encyclopaedia of the Qurʾān.* V (pp. 256–275). Brill.

Nagel, T. (2010). *Mohammed: Zwanzig Kapitel über den Propheten der Muslime.* Oldenbourg.

Parmentier, R. J. (2016). *Signs and society: Further studies in semiotic anthropology.* Indiana University Press.

Parry, J. (1986). The gift, the Indian gift and the "Indian gift". *Man, 21*(3), 453–473. https://doi.org/10.2307/2803096

Peirce, C. S. (1960). *Collected papers* [= quoted as CP]. C. Hartshorne, & P. Weiss (Eds.). Belknap Press of Harvard University Press.

Peirce, C. S. (1991). *Peirce on signs, writings on semiotic.* J. Hoopes (Ed.). University of North Carolina Press.

Peirce, C. S. (1992–1998). *The essential Peirce: Selected philosophical writings* [= quoted as EP]. N. Houser, & C. J. W. Kloesel (Eds.). Indiana University Press.

Rio, K., MacCarthy, M., & Blanes, R. (Eds.). (2017). *Pentecostalism and witchcraft: Spiritual warfare in Africa and Melanesia.* Springer International Publishing; Palgrave Macmillan.

Schäfer, P. (2010). *Die Geburt des Judentums aus dem Geist des Christentums: Fünf Vorlesungen zur Entstehung des rabbinischen Judentums.* Tria corda 6. Mohr Siebeck.

Scholem, G. (1954). *Major trends in Jewish mysticism.* Schocken Books.

Siegert, F. (2008). The sermon as an invention of Hellenistic Judaism. In A. Deeg, W. Homolka, & H.-G. Schöttler (Eds.), *Preaching in Judaism and Christianity: Encounters and developments from biblical times to modernity* Studia Judaica 41 (pp. 25–44). de Gruyter.

Stecconi, U. (2009). Semiotics. In M. Baker, & G. Saldanha (Eds.), *Routledge encyclopedia of translation studies* (pp. 260–263). Routledge.

von Stockhausen, A. (2008). Christian perception of Jewish preaching in early Christianity? In A. Deeg, W. Homolka, & H.-G. Schöttler (Eds.), *Preaching in Judaism and Christianity: Encounters and developments from biblical times to modernity* Studia Judaica 41 (pp. 49–70). de Gruyter.

Sullivan, B. M. (2010). Kerala's Mahabharata on stage: Texts and performative practices in Kūtiyāttam Drama. *Journal of Hindu Studies, 3*(1), 124–142. https://doi.org/10.1093/jhs/hiq001

Wilke, A., & Moebus, O. (2011). *Sound and communication: An aesthetic cultural history of Sanskrit Hinduism.* de Gruyter.

Selected Readings

Geertz, C. (Ed.). (1973). *The interpretation of cultures: Selected essays.* Basic Books.

Netton, I. R. (1993). *Allah transcendent: Studies in the structure and semiotics of Islamic philosophy, theology, and cosmology.* Curzon Press.

Parmentier, R. J. (2016). *Signs and society: Further studies in semiotic anthropology.* Indiana University Press.

Ponzo, J. (2019). *Religious narratives in Italian literature after the Second Vatican Council: A semiotic analysis* (Vol. 2). de Gruyter.

Raposa, M. L. (2020). *Theosemiotic: Religion, reading, and the gift of meaning.* Fordham University Press.

Singer, M. B. (1984). *Man's glassy essence: Explorations in semiotic anthropology.* Indiana University Press.

Yang, M. M. (Ed.). (2008). *Global, area, and international archive, Chinese religiosities: Afflictions of modernity and state formation.* University of California Press.

25

Religious Rituals, Pilgrimages, Festivals, and Media
Exploring the Interface

Gnana Patrick

Study of Ritual–Media Interface: The Contemporary Turn

Religious rituals, pilgrimages, and festivals have existed in combination with different forms of media from time immemorial. Starting with ancient oral forms, passing through print and contemporary electric/electronic forms to digital/virtual worlds, media have related to religious communication in myriad forms. Some of the longstanding media forms integrated with rituals include sacred objects, images, texts, manuscripts, oral traditions, and performances. Though studies on such primordial media forms of religious phenomena are limited, they are not unavailable. Berkwitz et al. (2009) "offers cross-cultural and comparative insights into the transmission of Buddhist knowledge and the use of texts and images as *ritual objects* in the artistic and aesthetic traditions of Buddhist cultures" (p. i, italics added). The work dwells upon the way the texts of the Buddhist manuscripts obtained the nature of rituals by generating their own artistic, aesthetic, and religious senses. Meyer (2009) highlights something similar, noting the formation of the aesthetic sense through the practice of religion and the role of media in it. Aesthetics has formed an important ingredient in the transforming of religious objects into "ritual events" for a long time.

From such a context wherein religion and media remained merged with one another, we have come a long way. The modern era, characterized by technological innovations and "objectivized" thought processes, differentiated media and religion, freeing the former to develop with its own autonomy, acquiring secular attributes. Religion too, in its private realm, functioned with relative independence. So much so, until the middle of the twentieth century, the prevailing assumption, as Stewart Hoover (2006, p. 9) observes, had "been that we can (could) and should look at religion and media as separate realms." However, the two did overlap as religious communication utilized modern media facilities as tools for communication – an approach termed a "functionalist" approach to the religion–media interface (Hosseini, 2008).

Today, while studying phenomena like religious rituals, pilgrimages, and festivals in relation to media, the almost "paradigmatic" change occurring on the interface strikes one immediately. A "culturalist approach," associated with cultural studies, has gained high visibility today. Differentiated from the earlier sociological, anthropological, and even psychological approaches that carried a certain modernist bias against religion, the culturalist approach explores the interface between religion and media more openly and nonreductively. In a religion–media continuum, the culturalist approach negotiates its way between "religious essentialism" – a manner of treating media as essentially religious on the one hand – and "media essentialism" – a manner of treating religion as essentially a form of media on the other (Hosseini, 2008).

The culturalist turn, opening up a new horizon of understanding, treats media as part and parcel of the life-world, performing life concerns in ritualist manners. This is a change from an externalized modernist instrumentalist approach to an embedded, organic, and integrally performative perspective today (Carey, 2009; Couldry, 2003, 2005; Grimes et al., 2011; Hoover, 2002, pp. 25–36; Hoover & Lundby, 1997; Lövheim, 2013a, 2013b; McLuhan, 1962). As Chris Arthur (1993) suggests, this change helps us go beyond the popular tendencies of either using the media as a mere tool for religious communication on the one hand or critiquing it as a source of profanation on the other (p. 2). As Ronald L. Grimes (2006) observes, "once there was a clear-cut segregation between the fields of media and rituals and the former was treated, oftentimes, as a 'profane' zone which dissipated in varied ways the religious import of rituals" (p. 3). Religionists hesitated to embark upon the world of media, fearing loss of the religious vitality of rituals. However, scholars have begun to look at the interface differently today.

Such a change is paralleled also in anthropological studies related to rituals. For example, Catherine Bell (2009) has explored rituals more as realities embedded in everyday construction of relationships, power, and so on rather than as rites set apart as institutions of religions. She privileges a "practice-theory" of rituals wherein rituals are considered as constitutive of self, otherness, relationship, and power in everyday life processes. One finds therefore certain convergence between studies of media and that of religion in the fact that they are being approached today more organically and dynamically, and as part of the very process of life, rather than as externalized entities ready for instrumental usage.

This chapter will first focus on ritual to introduce some of the scholars exploring the connection between media and ritual, review salient research orientations, then highlight the chief dynamics of the interface between media and religion. Utilizing these theoretical foundations, the chapter examines case studies occurring in pilgrimages and festivals.

Some Notable Scholars Exploring the Ritual–Media Interface

A good number of scholars explore this interface: James W. Carey, Ronald L. Grimes, Adam Seligman, Stewart M. Hoover, Nick Couldry, Heidi Campbell, Christopher Helland, Mia Lövheim, Pari Pork, Jonathan Z. Smith, and Peter Simonson are prominent among them. Most study rituals in relation to media primarily as events, process, performance, patterned-symbolic structures, etc. from the perspective of cultural studies, drawing upon anthropological insights. Here is a quick look at some salient insights of a few of these scholars.

James W. Carey (1934–2006), a teacher at the Universities of Illinois and Columbia, was a forerunner in proposing a ritual view of communication, in contrast to the traditional "transmission view of communication." The latter, according to Carey, dwelt upon the spread of the message across space from a sender to a receiver (as per Harold Lasswell's classical communication theory); the former is a participation in a process of construction of community, fellowship, shared beliefs, and so on. Hoover (2006) succinctly paraphrased Carey:

> Carey describes a distinction between "transmission" and "ritual" understandings of communication. The transmission model, he suggested, had inordinately blinded media scholars to the more subtle and profound ways in which communication is integrated into the fabric of daily life. Using

the term "ritual" almost metaphorically Carey called for a "ritual" view of communication that would understand it in this more organic, culturally rooted way. (pp. 15–16)

Though Carey (1988) distinguished the two views, he held, "[B]oth definitions (views) derive, as with much in secular culture, from religious origins, though they refer to somewhat different regions of religious experience" (p. 18). The ritual view of communication originates from "sacred ceremony that draws persons together in fellowship and commonality" (p. 15) and is indebted to religion not so much to its aspects of sermon, instruction and admonition as its prayer, chant and ceremony (p. 15), resulting in maintenance of social order and community. Thus we find that a religious dimension can be identified in the ritual view of communication as understood by Carey.

Peter Simonson, professor of communication in the College of Media, Communication and Information at the University of Colorado Boulder, also speaks of the process of communication in ritual terms. Agreeing with Carey on his distinction between the transmission and ritual models of communication, Simonson (2002, p. 33) takes communication to be "a process of re-enacting shared cultural understandings and social relationships." In one of his essays, he relates the ritual view of communication to the field of bio-ethics and argues that the media constitutes bio-ethics in two ways: one, grumbling about media, which helps take a symbolic distance from the field of bio-ethics, and the other, legitimizing the very same bio-ethics by media presentations that undermine the symbolic distance it takes through grumbling about bio-ethics (pp. 32–33). He emphasizes here the ritual mode of communication attendant upon media that play vital roles in contemporary societies. Relating the ritual view of communication to the Christian religion, Simonson points out that the transmission model finds expression in Christian evangelism and in Protestantism, while the ritual model finds "resonance in traditions of liturgy and formalized worship" (p. 33).

Ronald L. Grimes (b. 1943), Director of Ritual Studies International and co-editor of the Oxford Ritual Studies Series, has authored several books on the ritual–media interface. He speaks of 11 ways of relating ritual to media (Grimes, 2002, p. 220): "media presentation of a rite," "ritual event extended by media," "ritual actions in virtual space," "subjunctive ritualizing," "magical rite with media device as fetish," "ritualized behavior towards electronic objects," "media delivered ritual object," "certifying a ritual event" (as it happens in documentaries), "ritual use of media" (as technology is contained in performing traditional rituals), "mediated ritual fantasy," and "media as model or critique of ritual." These are the salient ways by which, according to Grimes, media and rituals relate to one another (for an elaboration of these types, cf. Grimes, 2006, p. 4). His insights on media rituals correspond well with the dynamics of religious rituals too.

Nick Couldry (b. 1958), Professor of Media, Communications and Social Theory in the Department of Media and Communications at London School of Economics, explores the symbolic power concentrated on rituals. His *Media Rituals* explores how the sociality is constructed through ritualized media forms (media rituals), and what role our beliefs and practices play in that process (Couldry, 2003, pp. 1–2). Through media rituals, we act out, indeed naturalize, the myth of the media's social centrality. Whatever is "in" the media obtains a social value, whereby a standard sociality is constructed by the media, even while embedding itself firmly into that sociality. He says: "media rituals direct our attention to a transcendental value associated with 'the media', that is, the media's *presumed* ability to represent the social whole" (Couldry, 2003, p. 13). He goes on to argue that such media construction of sociality keeps reproducing the hierarchy prevalent in a given context. "Media rituals," he says, "are the key mechanism through which the concentration of symbolic power in mediated institutions is reproduced for its legitimacy" (2003, p. 2). Couldry's contribution to understanding the role of media rituals in reproducing the symbolic power structure of a given society is significant.

Stewart M. Hoover (b. 1951), Director, Center for Media, Religion and Culture in the College of Media, Communication and Information at the University of Colorado Boulder and the founding president of the International Society for Media, Religion, and Culture, is a votary of the culturalist approach and envisions a close proximity between religion and media. As he argues, "media and religion have come together in fundamental ways. They occupy the same spaces, serve many of the same purposes, and invigorate the same practices in late modernity. Today, it is probably better to think of them as related than to think of them as separate" (Hoover, 2006, p. 9). He studies the interface in terms of practices in actual social contexts wherein they mediate social and religious meaning to social living (Lundby, 2013, pp. 225–237).

Adam Seligman and his colleagues (2008) argue, in the vein of the culturalist turn, that rituals are more deeply part of our living than what we generally perceive. It is, according to them, the post-Reformation Enlightenment thinking that had isolated the rituals from our quotidian life contexts and had searched for their essence outside of them in meanings, values, etc. Rituals, on the other hand, are part of a process of ortho-praxis, a manner of doing rather than thinking. The authors bring in an insight to understand the rituals as "shared subjunctives," collective "as if" or "could be," which produce a collective imaginary within which our lives occur. They act as spheres of creative imagination that offer their "own capacities for human realization and fulfilment" (p. 8); they allow us "to face the unavoidable ambiguities and ambivalences of our existence" (p. 180).

Similarly, Mirella Klomp and Martella van der Meulen (2017) reflect upon rituals as ludic experiences, which create a subjunctive sphere – an imaginative sphere of playfulness that helps in facing the perplexities and challenges of life. They state: "[S]cholars in cultural studies argue that, since the 1960s, playfulness has increasingly become a feature of our culture. We may even speak of a 'ludic turn' or, in the first decade of the 21st century, a global 'ludification of culture'" (p. 391). The subjunctive aspect of rituals, as reflected upon by the abovementioned scholars, may be found to inform religious rituals as well, but within the sphere of the experience of the sacred.

A more recent work critically exploring the concept of media rituals comes from Christopher Peyton Miller (2020). Observing the ubiquity and inescapability of media presence in the lives of individuals, Miller raises a critical alarm regarding the overdetermination of human living by the incessant arrival of media images. He observes that the media ritual images flood our subjective experiences to the point of pushing our relationship with others to that of sheer information sharing. Under the impact of this media ritual process, human selves are violated.

The ritual–media relationship, as seen earlier, is complex and ranges from complete identification, on the one side, to total distinction on the other. Many explorations tend today to move toward the former pole, dwelling upon several aspects of continuity and even identity. As Grimes cautions, treating them as identical does not help the explorations: "Meaningful ritual-and-media discussion becomes possible when the two domains are neither equated nor segregated but rather differentiated and conceived as sharing a common boundary" (Grimes, 2006, p. 11).

Salient Research Orientations on the Interface

One finds several orientations in research on the interface between ritual and media. Let us examine some of them.

Media as Rituals

First, as we have seen earlier, a group of media scholars study the media and communication themselves as rituals. Carey was one of the early media scholars to move away from a "transmission" view of media to adapt to a culturally rooted organic view with the help of the concept of ritual, which came from the domain of religious studies. Others like Grimes, Hoover, Couldry, and Seligman followed his lead. This view, discussed earlier, treats rituals as part of everyday, quotidian life, named in some circles as part of secular culture. However, their insights verge on a religious understanding of rituals. For example, their insights on the way rituals create a "hyper-reality," "an imaginary structure of consciousness" (Carey, 1989/2009), and so on, within which the everyday activities take place, and their reflections upon the dynamics of rituals in relation to experiences of community and transcendence are very pertinent to understanding religious rituals in relation to media.

Descriptive Orientation

Second, there are studies that dwell upon the presence of religious rituals in the media sphere in the two ways suggested by Nadja Miczek (2008) – "online rituals" and "ritual online," a distinction inspired by Christopher Helland's (2000) "online religion" and "religion online." While the former presents myriad forms of data on rituals, the latter provides multidimensional facilities for online performance or enactment of rituals. Studies based on this distinction primarily describe the media–ritual interface. For example, a work by Tim Hutchings (2019) gives an ethnographic account of the online churches, besides giving the history of online churchgoing from its origins in the 1980s and tracing the major themes of debates – academic and religious – around the topic of online churches. By exploring the "transformative third space" created by online churches, Hutchings shows the significance and impact of digital media in the religious and social lives of people. A volume by Rachel Wagner (2011) is another example that presents studies on how religions and rituals work in cyberspace. Wagner studies the characteristics of virtual religion in its multiple forms.

Similarly, Erica Baffeilli (2018) dwells on how new religions in the Japanese context take to media by way of spreading their new religious phenomenon known as *Soka Gakkai*. The volume speaks about how Buddhist rituals are televised across the country while being performed in indoor contexts. It speaks of two indoor rituals: "Agonshū: *tsuitachi engi hōshō goma* (a fire rite), held on the first day of each month at the Tokyo center, and *meitokusai* (a rite for the ancestors), performed on the 16th of each month at the Yamashina temple in Kyoto. Both rituals are transmitted to other Agonshū centers throughout Japan, where members assemble in front of large video screens and participate in the rite being performed on the other side of the country" (p. 74).

Along the same lines, Heidi Campbell's (2013) edited volume brings together case studies from different parts of the globe. Besides exploring the concept of ritual in a separate chapter, the two essays under the section on rituals showcase a Hindu ritual called pūjā and a Buddhist meditation ritual. In the chapter "Hindu worship online and offline," Heinz Scheifinger (2013) gives a brief account of the way pūjā is performed in a physical environment and in an online environment. The question of the possibility of experiencing the sacredness associated with pūjā performance in online environment is discussed. Louise Connelly (2013) presents a case study of practicing Buddhist meditation rituals through the online Second Life platform. Connolly records the positive estimation by practitioners of Buddhism on using the online platform. She underlines the observation made by Ostrowski as: "It is in Second Life that the interaction with others and participation in online ritual provides meaningful experiences – an opportunity to engage with, learn about and participate in Buddhist rituals – whereas offline, these opportunities may not be available" (p. 128).

Analytical Orientation

Third, some studies analyze the changes occurring on religious rituals as they take to or become adapted to the media sphere. Hoover (2006), for example, speaks about a "flattening of symbols" whereby the religious symbols get "submerged in the general universe of symbols of the media sphere" and consequently tend to lose their power of transcendental signification. Similarly, Adan Medrano speaks of the "naturalization" of religious symbols when adapted to the media sphere (cited in Hoover, 2006).

There are also studies that dwell on the very possibility or the impossibility of transferring rituals to the online sphere. Brenda Brasher (2001), for example, is highly critical of the possibility of the transfer of rituals to online mode, and avers that it alienates them from their religious dimension. According to her, the experience of the sacred/holy is technologized in the process, resulting in total estrangement. On the contrary, Mark MacWilliams (2002) considers the transfer not merely possible, but an experience unique to our age when the experience of the sacred/holiness can reach wider sections of humanity through the online medium.

As Carmen Becker points out, successful ritual transfers would imply that the rituals are efficacious in the transferred conditions. Becker (2011) posits three criteria to ascertain the efficacious transfer of rituals: (i) they must keep the sacred protected from the profane; (ii) they need to be a communal endeavor wherein a significant part of the community of believers participates and/or accepts them as legitimate; and finally (iii) they must maintain and reproduce the core values and fundamental beliefs of a religion (p. 1186). Manifesting the sense of the holy, bonding a religious community, and reproducing the core beliefs of a religion are the three aspects that, Becker thinks, give effect to a ritual. Whether these criteria can be successfully obtained in an online platform depends also upon what Becker calls "the interplay between the affordances of the technologies and the exigencies of the ritual segments" (p. 1186).

Functional Orientation

Fourth, some studies dwell on the functional aspects of religious rituals as found in the media sphere. They speak of "functions" not in the sense in which traditional functional schools of sociology of religion did, but in a nonreductive way that explores the dynamic functions both in terms of how the religious rituals in the media sphere construct a religious universe, identity, religious praxis, etc., and in terms of how they engage human beings in their everyday life contexts, especially in conditions of power operations. Some of the salient theoretical keys around which the social functions of religion are generally explored and debated in social sciences are social cohesion (solidarity, communitarian bond, identity, identity politics, etc.), social conflict (violence, hatemongering, inimical othering, etc.), social domination/hegemony (legitimation, maintenance of power, exploitation, oppression, etc.), and social empowerment (interrogation, contestation, mobilization, alternate identity construction, etc.). These traditional keys generally dwell on the typical social dimension of the social functions, that is, functions in relation to the social systems, structures, relationships, etc. However, in more recent times, we witness also the social constructions of selves, subjecthood, consciousness, and so on as part of the social functional theoretical explorations. Thus, the perception of social functions keeps changing. The same takes place in studies in relation to media as well.

For example, Tamar Liebes and James Curran (1998) explore the role of media in the construction of social identities and in shaping democratic politics by participating in the processes of civil society. Three articles in their volume explore the role rituals play in the societal and political processes. Carey (1998) speaks directly of "political ritual," a theme inspired by Daniel Dayan and Elihu Katz's (1992) well-known volume *Media Events – the Live Broadcasting of History*, wherein they explore the concepts of "ceremonial politics" carried through media events not merely for legitimizing certain forms of authority but also for "transformative" politics.

Other studies examine the role of rituals, including the media-present rituals, for innovation and development of economic activities. For example, a study by Carsten Hermann Pillath and Man Guo (2021) on "interaction ritual chains" in the context of Chinese popular religion shows how the Internet becomes the ritual space with socioeconomic implications. Based on their study in Shenzhen, the authors discuss how observance or celebrations of popular religious rituals enables people to resituate themselves within the newly emergent globalization, along with its challenges like migration and anomie on the one hand and opportunities like commerce and economic gains on the other. The already prevalent ancestor rituals that maintain kinship bonds between the people become also conduits for commerce, including religious markets, by way of multiplying "interaction ritual chains." It is an interesting study that brings up the role of popular religious rituals, as performed in virtual spaces, to augment the social, religious, and economic aspirations in the contemporary context of globalization.

Similarly, Semontee Mitra (2016) writes about the role of media in marketing religious goods to the Indian American diaspora, who, through ritual or festal enactments, "dig into" their cultural and religious roots, even while constructing a distinct identity for themselves in the American soil. The virtual media, in the author's estimation, have come to play a vital role in merchandising the religious symbols and artifacts (pp. 113–121).

Methodological Orientation

Fifth, studies focus on methodological concerns. For example, how to study the way religious rituals relate themselves to any form of media is an important methodological question. The classical methods of social sciences (qualitative and quantitative approaches) are indeed relevant. Under the qualitative approach, multiple levels of descriptive studies or "thick descriptions" are being undertaken. Christine Hine (2000) provides a good example in *Virtual Ethnography*. We find also participant observations on online religious forums as well as studies that deal with websites as texts, applying textual interpretative methods, including hermeneutical methods on the media texts.

An important interpretative key used to study the ritual–media interface comes from performance theory. "In my view," Grimes (2006, p. 12) opines, "performance-oriented theories offer the most provocative approaches to the interface of ritual and media. If performance is the 'showing of a doing' or 'twice-behaved behavior,' ritual and media are species of performance having much to do with one another." Felicia Hughes-Freeland and Mary M. Crain (1998) explain how approaching rituals as "ritualized performances" rather than as "ritual process" helps in understanding the participatory role rituals play in a given context:

> Instead of a ritual process which moves from one moment to another in time and space, ritualized performative practices embody creativity and constraint to be thought of as simultaneous, co-present, and co-dependent, and embodied in different forms of participation. This entails a shift in focus from form and meaning in ritual, to the different aspects of participation. It also provides insight into the analysis of spectatorship as participation. (p. 3)

The emplacement theory proposed by Jonathan Z. Smith, who speaks about the "spatial theory of rituals," provides another methodological key. "Emplacement" is the way a ritual occupies a space in ordinary events of life, thereby substituting the ordinary, the quotidian life (Grimes, 2006, p. 102).

There are studies that examine the content analyses of the ritual–media interface. Treating the contents of the online sites – including the linguistic, symbolic, and aesthetic contents – as texts by themselves, several studies undertake interpretive or hermeneutical explorations to delve into the semantic axes of the layers of meanings emerging from the online ritual sites.

Ideological Orientation

Sixth, studies undertaken from ideological perspectives include those asking how religious rituals as present in media environment reinforce hierarchy, patriarchy, racism, casteism, consumerism, etc. More scholars ask such ideologically oriented questions today. How the aspect of hierarchy plays out in the interface between rituals and media forms another common line of enquiry. Similarly, some scholars of this interface observe that media presentation of religious rituals, especially the presentation of religious rituals in computer-mediated communication platforms, is dominated by Christianity. Discussing ritual dynamics in chat rooms and discussion forums, Becker (2011, p. 1183) states that: "there is a Christian bias in contemporary research on religious practices in CMEs in which researchers largely draw their conclusion from Christian rituals and practices online like prayers and worship services."

The abovementioned orientations are indicative of the several perspectives being followed in the study of ritual–media interface. While they are not exhaustive, or distinct and discreet from one another, they do provide heuristics to classify work.

Some Notable Dynamics of the Interface

The dynamics of the religious ritual–media interface form a prominent research area today. Ritualization is perhaps the most fundamental dynamic process involved in any ritual. It is a repetitive enactment of a set of symbolic actions patterned in a specific manner, poised for an experience of vitality in view of the future. As Grimes (2014, p. 192) avers, ritualizing "transpires as animated persons enact formative gestures in the face of receptivity during crucial times in founded places." It is a poignant activity taking place in quotidian contexts of life in innumerable ways. However, when it takes place in a religious realm, with a religious intention and motivation, it becomes a liturgy, a sacred enactment.

The traditional approach to ritualization, even within the field of anthropology, carried a certain cognitive bias in that it looked for what ideas, meanings, values, etc., were communicated by rituals. It separated rituals from life processes and understood them as forms of media, transmitting ideas, meanings, etc. In contrast, scholars of ritual studies, like Bell (2009, pp. 69–70), took an experiential approach whereby rituals are understood as "structured patterns that trigger experiences that reproduce concepts in the minds of the participants." According to this view, the communicative dimension of ritual is "only secondary to a primary function of inducing or sustaining an experiential aspect of living" (p. 70).

This experiential aspect of ritualization is associated with the creation and maintenance of a transcendental realm or a "hyper-reality," which functions as the context for self-consciousness and construction of identity. This ability to create a hyper-reality was taken by Bell (2009, p. 245) to be the "mythologizing ability of the media," by which she meant the "ability to suggest cultural themes, simplicities, and stereotypes in organizing a story and orchestrating an experience." Such a "mythologizing ability" of the media makes it the very ritual by itself.

A question that comes to mind at this juncture lies in the very genuineness of the experience or the nature of realism attendant upon media presentation of reality. Helland (2013) addresses himself to similar questions like "Are online religious rituals real?", "Can a virtual pilgrimage be a real sacred journey?", "Can online religious rituals bring about real transformations?", and "Can online religious rituals give substantive religious experience?" (p. 25). All such questions, according to him, hinge on themes of authenticity and authority. The question of authenticity of online rituals, as Helland surmises, is relative to whether one is an insider or an outsider. Claiming to look at it from an insider's perspective, Helland argues that online rituals are authentic experiences of the sacred/the holy – the core of religion. He further argues that the experience of liminality associated with rituals (Van Gennep, Victor Turner), an experience between and betwixt, is also to be found in the online space, especially for an insider.

Helland's confidence in finding authentic online religious rituals is shared by other scholars. Stephen Jacobs (2007), for example, based on a semiotic analysis of two websites – one a Christian virtual church and the other a Hindu virtual temple – explores the potential of online space and online architecture to serve as "hermeneutical conversational events" to mediate sacredness. Premising upon the Durkheimian understanding of religion as that which separates the sacred from profane, Jacobs argues that cyber-rituals and cyber-architectures of temples can "set-apart the virtual sacred spaces for the performance of cyber-rituals" (p. 1104). Moreover, like the ritual architectures by which the believers cross over from the profane to the sacred in offline situations, virtual "ritual architectural events are as possible in computer-mediated contexts as they are in geographical space," and virtual sacred spaces may well have the potential to "constitute inexhaustible funds of otherness" (p. 1105). Thus we find a considerable measure of confidence among scholars with regard to the genuineness or authenticity of mediated religious experiences.

Another major theme discussed in this regard is whether the religious ritual–media interface is transformative. Drawing inspiration from Victor Turner's understanding of the ritual process, wherein rituals play emphatic transformative roles, media theorists like Carey understand the ritual–media interface as transformative and creative, generating moments of liminality, thereby even "temporarily dissolving social hierarchies."

In this context, it is instructive to read Marleen de Witte (2003) wherein she narrates the way media are transformatively integrated with charisma in the charismatic Christianity of Ghana. De Witte notes that there is a certain power, charisma, that emerges on "televisualizing" the interface of charismatic prayer and worship with media technology. This is created by the manner in which the pastor presents himself on the "altar" with attractive attire and by his captivating performance on the stage, the effects of which are enhanced owing to the presence of the media technology. Moreover, the interface in the context of Ghana creates a charismatic Christianity for the Ghanaian public sphere integrated with patriotism, and civic virtues of citizenship and participation.

However, there are other scholars like Couldry who are less confident in the transformative potential of the ritual–media interface; for them, the interface, oftentimes, reinforces hierarchical status quo, maintains the existing unequal power relations, or even hides the conflict generated in the operation of hierarchy. In a study on the dynamics of televising religious rituals in Tansen, Nepal, Michael J. Wilmore (2006) explores the role televised religious rituals and festivals plays in the maintenance of power relations in a given social and political context (pp. 317–342). He presents materials on three festivals televised by a local cable organization called RCTV, and shows how these televised festivals, patronized by different fractions of the town's population, go on to construct different cultural identities in the public with the use of old and new media technologies.

Pilgrimages

This and the following sections illustrate the more theoretical material presented earlier, first by examining pilgrimages and then by a look at festivals.

Religious pilgrimages are on the increase today. Media are closely integrated with pilgrimages at different levels in various ways. We have found several studies examining different aspects of pilgrimages in relation to their interface with media. First of all, as seen in relation to ritual, some studies treat pilgrimages in nonreligious contexts, though the term pilgrimage is taken from the religious provenance. Couldry (2000), for example, speaks also of "media pilgrims," that is, tourists who visit media production sites, like the sets used for popular movie or entertainment soaps. Stijn Reijnders (2010) studies the "media pilgrimages" undertaken by fans of James Bond. On the basis of interviews with some of these pilgrims, Reijnders argues that by visiting the tourist sites associated with James Bond, these pilgrims enter the liminal space to embody or imbibe an imagined masculinity associated with the actor. Such pilgrims, Reijnders avers, also negotiate social relations in favor of masculinity.

We find several types of pilgrimages related to the media. Tilson and Chao (2002) study the pilgrimage of the relics of Saint Therese, the Little Flower, which toured from 1995 to 2001 across Europe and the United States. One might note that relics play an important role in the Christian tradition of pilgrimage. However, the same cannot be said of the Hindu tradition, though some Eastern religions like Buddhism do have such relics, for example, the tooth temple of Buddha in Sri Lanka. Pori Park's (2012) remapping of sacred geography in contemporary Korean Buddhism is illustrative of the way relic-centered or Bodhisattva-centered pilgrimages are on the rise today. The Buddhist centers housing some elements of Buddha's relics do not merely showcase them, but conduct religious teachings, meditations, and so on in the vicinity of the shrines. In order to attract more and more visitors, these Korean Buddhist centers have also paid attention to developing the nearby facilities for board and lodging. Park opines that the number of pilgrimages has increased alongside an increase in means among the population that began in the 1980s.

Virtual Pilgrimages

Initially, the role of media was to provide information on different aspects of pilgrimages, but a relatively recent phenomenon is the use of media to conduct virtual pilgrimages (Couldry, 2007). Notwithstanding questions such as "Can an online pilgrimage really be counted as a pilgrimage at all?," "Is the experience of the sacred substantively the same in online and offline contexts?," and "Can the central aspect of the journey be undertaken virtually?" etc., people have taken to online pilgrimages with varying levels of satisfaction. Major pilgrimage sites like Jerusalem, Lourdes, Mecca, and Varanasi have constructed virtual pilgrimage sites. Connie Hill-Smith (2011) engages with the questions of what is involved in the making of cyber-pilgrimages and how authentic are they. In an era wherein cyber/virtual reality has become part and parcel of the spiritual quest of humanity everywhere, Hill-Smith avers that the genuineness of the spiritual experience associated with cyber-pilgrimage cannot be undermined.

MacWilliams (2002), in a study of the virtual pilgrimage website Jesus2000.com, offers some reflections on how a virtual pilgrimage works. First of all, he gives an account of the variety of services the website offers (pp. 315–335). It is interesting to note that the website offers not merely information and facilities for undertaking virtual pilgrimage to places like Jerusalem, the place where Jesus carried out his ministry and died, but also sells religious and nonreligious goods. MacWilliams suggests that virtual pilgrimage offers a pertinent example for studying how religion has changed in the present-day postmodern context, integrating elements of advanced technologies. He reflects on the reasons for the appeal of virtual pilgrimages and how they satisfy a religious or spiritual need of modern-day humanity. He states that:

> in order to understand the new ways of being religious in the postmodern world, virtual pilgrimages must be taken into account. They exploit the new technological possibilities of the internet to re-imagine the sacred by constructing an immaterial reality from four components. First, they create a mythscape, a highly symbolic sacred geography, largely based upon oral or scriptural traditions. Second, they use interactive visual-auditory techniques to evoke experiences of divine presence. Third, they provide liminoid forms of entertainment for the traveler/viewer. Fourth, as a leisure activity done at home or office computers, virtual pilgrimages allow individuals to join online traveling communities, which they often describe using the discourse of *communitas*. (p. 320)

The four elements go into the dynamics of creating a virtual experience of pilgrimages today. Virtual pilgrimages, which embody these dynamics, exhibit characteristics that appeal to the religious sensitivity of people today. Though MacWilliams is broadly positive about the experience of virtual pilgrimages, he cautions us about their limitations as well:

> Nevertheless a virtual pilgrimage is not the same as "the real thing." First, it is instantaneous. Travel to the site is a click of the button away. Second, it takes place figuratively not literally. The arduous journey to a distant place, the ascetical practices that are so important in penitential pilgrimages, do not exist virtually. The virtual journey is a disembodied act of the imagination that cannot fully simulate the physical rigors of the RL original. (p. 326)

Similarly, Brasher (2001) is also critical of the efficacy and authenticity of the virtual pilgrimage. In her words:

> [T]he journey to the site is gone. There is no wait to get into the temple. There is no interaction with other pilgrims en route. The temple itself is gone. The heavy smell of flower and fruit offerings has vanished. In sum, in the transition from temple to screen, a radical alteration of the sense stimulation integral to Hindu worship has silently taken place. Consequently, the religious experience itself has been altered, numinous, or holy, experience that cyberspace makes possible by way of Digital Avatar is almost entirely an affair of the mind. (p. 4)

Thus, we find critical voices alerting us to the inauthenticity or inefficacy of virtual pilgrimages, even while the volume of such pilgrimages is growing in leaps and bounds.

Becker (2011) discusses virtual pilgrimages such as the Hajj undertaken by Muslims. She observes that though there is a general impression that Muslims easily take to online rituals or pilgrimages, she finds from some websites devoted to Islam that virtual pilgrimages are not an adequate substitute for the actual pilgrimage. At most, they prepare people to undertake their rituals in offline mode. Based on interviews with Muslim participants, she observes that:

> When prayer time draws near, participants in forums and chat rooms tell each other that they will have to leave the keyboard in order to perform the prayer ritual in their homes. For a few moments, activities cease while the chat room connects the different personal prayer spaces of the participants at home. Being confused by my questions about why they do not pray communally in a chat room, most answers hint at the impossibility to enact and feel the embodied movements of the ritual in CMEs. (p. 1196)

She points out that there is also a *fatwa* issued on IslamOnline.net that a virtual Hajj is only an educative and informational tool, and cannot replace the actual one. She further observes that:

> [M]any researchers point to the hajj, the Muslim pilgrimage to Mecca, as an example of a Muslim rit-
> ual that has recently been transferred to CMEs like Second Life. However, reading the press releases
> of IslamOnline.net, the Islamic Portal that maintains the virtual hajj in Second Life, and asking my
> Muslim interlocutors how they understand the practice of virtual hajj, the picture that emerges is dif-
> ferent. Interlocutors stress the usefulness of the virtual hajj for the preparation of the "real." (p. 1196)

Ian Reader (2007) discusses the way the Japanese media have taken to religion and pilgrimage more enthusiastically, contrary to the apparent perception that Japanese media are indifferent, if not actively hostile, to religion. Reader mentions that the Meiji Restoration period led to skepticism of both religion and pilgrimage because they were considered to be in opposition to the modernizing project of the state. However, current thinking on the topic has changed and one now finds "mass media representations of the Shikoku pilgrimage (*Shikoku henro* or *Shikoku hachijûhakkasho*), a pilgrimage that circles Shikoku, Japan's fourth largest island, and takes the pilgrim to 88 Buddhist temples along a 1400-kilometer route" (p. 15). Reader further testifies that: "My recent study of the Shikoku pilgrimage shows that the increase in Shikoku pilgrim numbers since the mid-1990s has been boosted by the massive interest shown by the mass media in the topic, and by the extremely positive images that have been presented therein as a result" (p. 15). However, Reader notes that pilgrimages are treated "primarily as symbols of culture and tradition rather than as manifestations of religion" (p. 14).

Jeremy Dell's (2013) study of pilgrimage videos circulated among American Murid communities makes another point regarding the valuable role played by media in fulfilling the religious aspirations of people to undertake pilgrimages. Though the pilgrimage videos do not replace the actual pilgrimages, they go a long way in satisfying the religious needs of the participants. In the words of Dell, they "approximate the pilgrimage experience via their internal organization and formal characteristics" (p. 50).

Peter Sutherland (2007) gives an ethnographic account of an interfaith pilgrimage that walked in reverse the path by which slaves were transported to the colonies in earlier centuries (pp. 31–62). The walk was planned as an interfaith endeavor to heal the wounds of history. Sutherland does not merely describe the walk but also theorizes upon it relating the experience to Victor Turner's insights on pilgrimage. While so doing, he speaks of the emergence of "virtual communitas" formed with the facility of the Internet. It makes for an interesting study on the virtual dimension of the pilgrimage.

Festivals

Religious festivals have been mediatized in a big way. Starting with the traditional media, festivals have come on board with the latest digital media too. There are various ways in which religious festivals use media: (i) offline festivals are mediated live through the media; (ii) offline festivals are reported with video and audio clips after they've taken place; (iii) media become part and parcel of offline festivals (e.g. using films, series, etc., or electronic and digital media equipment become part of the festival process); and (iv) online festivals, religious or cultural, celebrated by specific groups with online performances.

Chiara Cocco and Aleida Bertran (2021) present a virtual ethnographic study of the festival of Sant'Efisio celebrated through social media in the region of Sardini, Italy, bringing to light the process of festivals' moving from the streets to the Internet during the pandemic. Originating as a festival during the seventeenth century in the context of an epidemic wherein Sant'Efisio was beseeched to ward off evil, the festival consists of carrying the statue of Sant'Efisio on the streets for about 8 km. The Covid-19 pandemic moved this festival to hybrid media like Facebook and

YouTube, and the participants became individualized and private rather than collective and public. The festival became less and less an occasion of corporeal participation and more and more reflective and distanced. However, the participants joined in the festival with the utmost seriousness and fulfilled a religious duty. This case study is an example of the way festivals continued to be celebrated virtually even during the pandemic.

Festivals of different kinds are integrated with various types of media. Religio-cultural festivals, with political overtones, are increasingly being mediatized. Diwali, the festival of lights celebrated all over India, is a typical example. Though it is related to certain religious beliefs, it has come to be presented as a national festival with political underpinnings.

Then there are purely religious festivals celebrated by particular religious communities at regional, national, and global levels, and media play an important role in strengthening the communitarian bond across regions. They contribute significantly also to the process of construction of identity and political mobilization.

Conclusion

Contemporary times have brought about a change in the understanding of the interface between media and religious rituals, pilgrimages, and festivals. Moving away from the traditional understanding of media as a technique or facility to transmit messages, present-day scholars understand media itself as a ritual, deeply embedded in social relations, negotiating power in multiple forms. While such a move occurs in the domain of media studies, studies on religious rituals, including pilgrimages and festivals (as conglomerate rituals) also approach them as embedded realities in everyday life, rather than as special occasions to fulfill religious aspirations or obligations. Thus, there is a convergence in both domains to approach them more dynamically, nonreductively, and as part of the life process.

It is gratifying to see that several perspectives or orientations appear in exploring the interface between media and religious rituals. While approaching media itself as a ritual is one such orientation, others emphasizing descriptive-ethnographic, analytical, functional, methodological, and ideological aspects are some of the other salient perspectives to be found today. A number of outstanding scholars from both media and religious studies evince continued interest in exploring the interface. The increasing number of publications that we witness in the domain is an indication of the importance this field is gaining today. And the new insights into the workings of the interface keep enriching the field.

Similarly, pilgrimage and festival studies have become associated with media studies in fruitful ways. Concepts like media pilgrimages and media festivals are on the rise, leading to multifaceted integration of media with religious pilgrimages and festivals. One of the salient functions of this integration seems to be construction of identities, leading to identity politics in several regions of the world. With that being the case, the ways pilgrimages and festivals transform their nature, functions, and dynamics in relation to the ever-renewing media present creative and increasing scope for future study and research.

References

Arthur, C. (Ed.). (1993). *Religion and the media: An introductory reader*. University of Wales Press.

Baffeilli, E. (2018). *Media and new religion in Japan*. Routledge.

Becker, C. (2011). Muslims on the path of the Salaf Al-Salih: Ritual dynamics in chatrooms and discussion forums. *Information, Communication & Society, 14*(8), 1181–1203. https://doi.org/10.1080/13691 18X.2011.597414

Bell, C. (2009). *Ritual perspectives and dimensions*. Oxford University Press.

Berkwitz, S. C., Schober, J., & Brown, C. (Eds.). (2009). *Buddhist manuscript cultures: Knowledge, ritual and art*. Routledge.

Brasher, B. E. (2001). *Give me that online religion*. Jossey-Bass.

Campbell, H. A. (Ed.). (2013). *Digital religion: Understanding religious practice in new media worlds*. Routledge.

Carey, J. W. (1988). *Media, myths, and narratives: Television and the press*. Sage Publications.

Carey, J. W. (1998). Political ritual on television: Episodes in the history of shame, degradation, and excommunication. In T. Liebes, & J. Curran (Eds.), *Media, ritual, and identity* (pp. 42–69). Routledge.

Carey, J. W. (2009). *Communication as culture: Essays on media and culture*. Routledge. (Original work published 1989).

Cocco, C., & Bertran, A. (2021). Rethinking religious festivals in the era of digital ethnography. *Social Analysis: The International Journal of Anthropology, 65*(1), 113–122. https://doi.org/10.3167/sa.2021.650107

Connelly, L. (2013). Virtual Buddhism: Buddhist ritual in Second Life. In H. Campbell (Ed.), *Digital religion: Understanding religious practice in new media* (pp. 128–133). Routledge.

Couldry, N. (2000). *The place of media power: Pilgrims and witnesses of the media age*. Routledge.

Couldry, N. (2003). *Media rituals: A critical approach*. Routledge.

Couldry, N. (2005). Media rituals: Beyond functionalism. In E. W. Rothenbuhler, & M. Coman (Eds.), *Media anthropology* (pp. 59–69). Sage Publications.

Couldry, N. (2007). Pilgrimage in mediaspace: Continuities and transformations. *Etnofoor, 20*(1), 63–73. https://www.jstor.org/stable/25758130

Dayan, D., & Katz, E. (1992). *Media events: The live broadcasting of history*. Harvard University Press.

de Witte, M. (2003). Altar media's "Living Word": Televised charismatic Christianity in Ghana. *Journal of Religion in Africa, 33*(2), 172–202. https://www.jstor.org/stable/1581654

Dell, J. (2013). Re-creating Touba: Pilgrimage videos in the American muridiyya. *Islamic Africa, 4*(1), 49–68.

Grimes, R. L. (2002). Ritual and media. In S. M. Hoover, & L. Schofield Clark (Eds.), *Practicing religion in the age of the Media: Explorations in media, religion, and culture* (pp. 232–247). Columbia University Press.

Grimes, R. L. (2006). *Rite out of place: Ritual, media and the arts*. Oxford University Press.

Grimes, R. L. (2014). *The craft of ritual studies*. Oxford University Press.

Grimes, R. L., Husken, U., Simon, U., & Venbrux, E. (Eds.). (2011). *Ritual, media, and conflict*. Oxford University Press.

Helland, C. (2000). Religion online/online religion and virtual communitas. In J. K. Hadden, & D. E. Cowan (Eds.), *Religion on the internet: Research prospects and promises* (pp. 205–224). JAI Press/Elsevier Science.

Helland, C. (2013). Ritual. In H. Campbell (Ed.), *Digital religion: Understanding religious practice in new media worlds* (pp. 25–40). Routledge.

Hill-Smith, C. (2011). Cyber-pilgrimage: The (virtual) reality of online pilgrimage experience. *Religion Compass, 5*(6), 236–246. https://doi.org/10.1111/j.1749-8171.2011.00277.x

Hine, C. (2000). *Virtual ethnography*. Sage Publications.

Hoover, S. M. (2002). The culturalist turn in scholarship on media and religion. *Journal of Media and Religion, 1*(1), 25–36. https://doi.org/10.1207/S15328415JMR0101_4

Hoover, S. M. (2006). *Religion in the media age*. Routledge.

Hoover, S. M., & Lundby, K. (Eds.). (1997). *Rethinking media, religion and culture*. Sage.

Hosseini, S. H. (2008). Religion and media, religious media, or media religion: Theoretical studies. *Journal of Media and Religion, 7*(1–2), 56–69. https://doi.org/10.1080/15348420701838350

Hughes-Freeland, F., & Crain, M. M. (Eds.). (1998). *Recasting ritual: Performance, media, and identity*. Routledge.

Hutchings, T. (2019). *Creating church online: Ritual, community and new media*. Routledge.

Jacobs, S. (2007). Virtual sacred: The performance of asynchronous cyber-rituals in online spaces. *Journal of Computer Mediated Communication, 12*, 1103–1121. https://doi.org/10.1111/j.1083-6101.2007.00365.x

Klomp, M., & van der Meulen, M. (2017). The passion as ludic practice: Understanding public ritual performances in late modern society: A case study from the Netherlands. *Journal of Contemporary Religion, 32*(3), 387–401. https://doi.org/10.1080/13537903.2017.1362879

Liebes, T., & Curran, J. (Eds.). (1998). *Media, ritual, and identity*. Routledge.

Lövheim, M. (2013a). Media and religion through the lens of feminist and gender theory. In M. Lövheim (Ed.), *Media, religion and gender: Key issues and challenges* (pp. 43–76). Routledge.

Lövheim, M. (Ed.). (2013b). *Media, religion, and gender: Key issues and challenges*. Routledge.

Lundby, K. (2013). Theoretical frameworks for approaching religion and new media. In H. Campbell (Ed.), *Digital religion: Understanding religious practice in new media worlds* (pp. 225–237). Routledge.

MacWilliams, M. W. (2002). Virtual pilgrimages on the internet. *Religion, 32*, 315–335. https://doi.org/10.1006/reli.2002.0408

McLuhan, M. (1962). *The Gutenberg galaxy: The making of typographic man*. University of Toronto Press.

Meyer, B. (Ed.). (2009). *Aesthetic formation: Media, religion and the senses*. Palgrave Macmillan.

Miczek, N. (2008). Online rituals in virtual worlds. Christian online services between dynamics and stability. *Heidelberg Journal of Religions on the Internet, 3*(1), 144–173. https://heiup.uni-heidelberg.de/journals/index.php/religions/article/view/392/367

Miller, C. P. (2020). *Pixilated practices: Media, ritual and identity*. Wipf & Stock.

Mitra, S. (2016). Merchandising the sacred: Commodifying Hindu religion, gods/goddesses, and festivals in the United States. *Journal of Media and Religion, 15*(2), 113–121. https://doi.org/10.1080/15348423.2016.1177351

Park, P. (2012). Devotionalism reclaimed: Re-mapping sacred geography in contemporary Korean Buddhism. *Journal of Korean Religions, 3*(2), 153–171.

Pillath, C. H., & Guo, M. (2021). Interaction ritual chains and religious economy: Explorations on ritual in Shenzhen' identities. *Identities: Global Studies in Culture and Power, 28*. https://doi.org/10.1080/1070289X.2021.1911474

Reader, I. (2007). Positively promoting pilgrimage: Media representations of pilgrimage in Japan. *Nova Religio: The Journal of Alternative and Emergent Religions, 10*(3), 13–31.

Reijnders, S. (2010). On the trail of 007: Media pilgrimages into the world of James Bond. *Area, 42*(3), 369–377. https://www.jstor.org/stable/40890889

Scheifinger, H. (2013). Hindu worship online and offline. In H. Campbell (Ed.), *Digital religion: Understanding religious practice in new media worlds* (pp. 121–127). Routledge.

Seligman, A. B., Weller, R. P., Puett, M. J., & Bennet, S. (2008). *Ritual and its consequences: An essay on the limits of sincerity*. Oxford University Press.

Simonson, P. (2002). Bioethics and the rituals of media. *The Hastings Center Report, 32*(1), 32–39.

Sutherland, P. (2007). Walking middle passage history in reverse: Interfaith pilgrimage, virtual communitas and world-recathexis. *Etnofoor, 20*(1), 31–62. https://www.jstor.org/stable/25758129

Tilson, D. J., & Chao, -Y.-Y. (2002). Saintly campaigning: Devotional-promotional communication and the U.S. tour of St. Therese's relics. *Journal of Media and Religion, 1*(2), 81–104. https://doi.org/10.1207/S15328415JMR0102_1

Wagner, R. (2011). *Godwired: Religion, ritual and virtual reality*. Routledge.

Wilmore, M. J. (2006). Gatekeepers of cultural memory: Televising religious rituals in Tansen, Nepal. *Ethnos, 71*(3), 317–342.

Selected Readings

Carey, J. (2009 [1989]). *Communication as culture – Essays on media and culture*. Routledge.

Couldry, N. (2003). *Media rituals – A critical approach*. Routledge.

Grimes, R. L. (2006). *Rite out of place: Ritual, media and the arts*. Oxford University Press.

Hine, C. (2000). *Virtual ethnography*. Sage Publications.

Hoover, S., & Clark, L. S. (Eds.). (2002). *Practising religion in the age of the media – Explorations in media, religion, and culture*. Columbia University Press.

Hutchings, T. (2019). *Creating church online: Ritual, community and new media*. Routledge.

26

Death, Spirituality, and Digital Afterlife

Johanna Sumiala

Introduction

"Death loves to be represented," asserts Philippe Ariès (1985, p. 11), historian of death in Western society. During the Covid-19 pandemic we saw a global representation of death: bodies lying in the streets, mass graves, people mourning and using media in various ways to commemorate death, funerals without mourners present, and the imposition of new antipandemic regulations (Sumiala, 2021) all attest to a public representation of death on a global scale and suggest the cultural, social, and political implications of this representation.

This chapter investigates the idea of representation of death from within the framework of the academic field of media and religion. As the ultimate fate of individual life, death is a major concern for human existence in society. According to anthropologist Maurice Bloch (1992), nature begins with life and ends in death, but culture begins with death and transforms death into a life-affirming event; therefore, representation of death in culture is of central significance (see also Parry & Bloch, 1982). As widely acknowledged in death studies, religions as institutions have historically played an important role in the way individuals, communities, and societies perceive and experience death and negotiate the relationship between the living and the dead in society, as well as in ideas related to the afterlife and immortality (Ariès, 1977; Davies, 2002; Howarth, 2007; Kellehear, 1984; Walter, 2020). The latest developments in media and communication technology – in particular the hybridization of media and the use of artificial intelligence in digital communication – broaden the scope of death studies and also profoundly challenge the authority of religious institutions to define rituals and relationships between the living and the dead in today's society of deep mediatization (Couldry & Hepp, 2017; Hepp, 2020), especially in so-called Western societies.

Death in the media is always a representation, since physical death cannot be directly observed through media (cf. Meyer, 2009). Still, many researchers of media and death argue that the way the media represent death offers us clues to how a society views and experiences death and organizes relationships between the living and the dead (Hanusch, 2010, p. 14; Hviid Jacobsen, 2021; Walter, 2017). Death representations in media depend on a complex set of historical, religious, and cultural norms, ethics, hierarchies, and conventions, not to mention media technologies and journalistic conventions (see Seaton, 2005). Therefore, we must study death representations in media (and in society) as a historically changing, multifaceted phenomenon. We must also acknowledge that media can mean many different things. As Nick Couldry argues (2012, p. 2),

The Handbook on Religion and Communication, First Edition. Edited by Yoel Cohen and Paul A. Soukup.

media can refer to infrastructures, institutions, or content. It matters a great deal what type of media we are discussing in relation to death and its mediated representation. This chapter investigates death representation in the context of news media and social media. I have excluded fictional death representation, whether in books, in film, or in TV series, and instead concentrate on "real" death reported and represented in news media and social media. This decision is made primarily in the interest of space and is not a philosophical claim about the ontological value and relevance of one type of death representation over another in human culture (see Han, 2019).

Carey (1989) provides a way to structure our thoughts about the representation of death in news media. He identifies two perspectives: the transmission view of communication focuses on how death is transmitted and disseminated in media, and the ritual view of communication focuses on the media practices that make sense of death and foster a sense of community and belonging among the public in the wake of death. The structure of this chapter combines the transmission approach and the ritual approach to examine the representation of death in media from three interconnected perspectives. It draws on an interdisciplinary research tradition of the study of media, religion, and culture (see Hoover & Lundby, 1997; Hope Cheong et al., 2012; Lynch et al., 2012; Morgan, 2008) and analyzes in particular certain points of intersection between media and religion in the representation of death.

The chapter begins with a brief history of the representation of death in communication media asking how and for what purpose death is represented in news media beginning with early newspapers, the visual representation of death in photography, television, and finally the Internet and social media. Second, the chapter turns to Carey's ritual view of communication and investigates death representation in different media from the perspective of symbolic and religiously and spiritually inspired communication. This category includes the analysis of rituals of mourning in media in relation to witnessing, martyrdom, and sacrifice. The concepts of martyrdom and sacrifice, which typically originate in anthropology (see Turner, 1969) and the study of religions (see Davies, 2002), serve as conceptual tools that help scholars to understand the religious implications of media representation of death. Finally, the chapter considers the emerging research field of digital death (Ess, 2017; Hutchings, 2019; Lagerkvist, 2019; Sumiala, 2021) pointing out some questions for current scholarly thinking about how the digital representation of death in hybrid media may challenge existing philosophical, sociological, and theological categories of life and death (see also Ess, 2017; Lagerkvist, 2019; Papacharissi, 2019).

Representing Death in Media – A Brief Historical Overview

The Roman Games

Hanusch (2010, p. 32) reminds readers that humans have a long history of recording and commemorating death in society, while Seaton (2005, p. xix) concurs that modern news representation of death is "only the latest manifestation of the long history of the public representation of cruelty." Importantly, Seaton argues that religious forces have often shaped public representation of death; she tracks this idea to the early history of public spectacle, for example, Roman games. Drawing on literary and archeological evidence, she explains that the Roman games evolved out of the Etruscan tradition of sacrificing enemy war prisoners to honor the war dead. Seaton continues: "Following the Etruscan patterns, the Roman games started as solemn occasions, associated with funeral rites. They were redemptive sacrifices, expiatory offerings, at a time of stress, and at first they took place in a public place – the forum" (pp. 53–55). The idea of public sacrifice has an explicitly religious meaning (see Girard, 1977). The spectacular nature of the Roman games expressed both their religious meaning and their social-hierarchical meaning (Seaton, 2005, pp. 54–56) – for not only did they include sacrifice, but they were a gift from the rich to the poor: "bread and circuses" for the common people.

The role of Christian martyrs in public death spectacles connects the games as public representations of death to religion:

> Christian martyrs successfully took control of the meaning of the arena away from the bemused Roman officials and used the emotional and political impact of the games for their own purposes. The Christian martyrs understood that to be seen to die in terror legitimized authority, but that to refuse to be frightened, to control the time and place of death, to die willingly, and to master the performance of death, constituted an attack on death itself, and became a challenging subversion. It was a battle of meaning, carried out through a performance. Through their exploitation of the meaning of the dominant entertainment the Christian martyrs unequivocally won the struggle for control of public opinion. (Seaton, 2005, p. 71)

What was at stake in such public representations of martyrdom were the meanings of death, solidarity, and power – in other words, morality and values. These are the enduring elements expressed in the mediation of death and the public response to it. Their configurations and contents change through time, but the underlying issues of morality and values remain, and they continue to carry weight even as the media environment changes.

Death in Newspapers – A Morality Play

From the beginning print media have played a significant role in the public representation of death. According to Zelizer (2010), Seaton (2005), and Hanusch (2010), early newspapers represented death as a morality play, which both informed and confirmed (cf. Carey, 1989) popular ideas about morally and socially virtuous or reprehensible ways of life (see Spierenburg, 1984). Media historians have identified printed representations of death dating back to the seventeenth century. Such representations included pamphlets that offered sensational accounts of "witches being tortured and burnt" (Arnold et al., 2018, p. 17). Discussing the early history of American news about death, Nord (2001) explains that the idea of an exceptional and remarkable death had deep roots in the religious culture of New England. He notes that in seventeenth-century newspaper reports on drownings, hangings, and murder trials, references to higher powers, such as spiritual beings and devils, often set the tone for reporting on death. The US colonial era was characterized by "melancholy accidents and deplorable news"; reports of death caused by crimes, disasters, accidents, sex scandals, and executions functioned as cautionary tales of moral corruption, serving to confirm society's morals (Copeland, 1997, p. 85). However, there was more to these phenomena than the moral lessons; the sensationalism and explicit grotesqueness of these news reports were compelling; they exploited people's hunger for the macabre (Copeland, 1997).

In addition to public representation of the death of criminals and accident victims, newspapers also published obituaries to celebrate the lives of distinguished members of society (Fowler, 2007), a type of public representation of notable lives and deaths originating in the seventeenth century. Obituary developed as a newspaper genre that typically provided a biography including religious instruction and moral lessons inspired by the virtuous life of the deceased (Arnold et al. 2018, p. 17). While news of public executions functioned as morality plays with warnings of the consequences of breaking society's moral order, obituaries functioned as an indicator of the kind of life one should pursue. Early obituaries told a story of a life well lived and focused on individuals high in the social and political hierarchy, such as royalty, aristocrats, and other upper-class (male) figures (p. 18; cf. Staudt, 2001). Public representations of death in obituaries served to maintain the status quo in society's power structure and moral order.

The arrival of mass-circulation newspapers in the nineteenth century (the penny press in the United States) provided readers with an increasing number of public representations of death, typically in the form of news stories of violent, unexpected death and destruction (Stephens, 2007; Thompson, 2004). The penny press, as an early capitalist news institution, was driven by spectacle and sensationalism; gory stories addressing the public's voyeuristic desires helped sell newspapers. This development intensified with the expansion of the tabloid and sensational presses in the twentieth century (Hanusch, 2013).

Hybridization – A Revolutionary Development

In the contemporary period, the most radical change in public representation of death stems from the changing media environment – the growth of the Internet and social media. Today, death representations in print news have expanded, and death has become omnipresent in news media (Hanusch, 2010, p. 2), with online newspapers constantly updating their stories, where death is part of a nonstop cycle. Consequently, death stories and related public representations of death have become not only digitalized and multiplied, but also globalized on a new scale (Sumiala, 2021). The hybridization of media forms a critical part (Chadwick, 2013), a trend in which the logics of journalistic media and social media merge and new actors enter the public realm of making and sharing death news (Sumiala et al., 2018).

This has two consequences: On one hand, scholars of media and death say that the rise of hybrid media has deprived journalistic news media and religious authorities of their gatekeeping power over public representation of death (Sumiala, 2021), and the ensuing chaos has caused a disintegration of the moral codes and conventions defining acceptable ways to represent death. Pushing the argument further, critics have introduced the concept of "death porn" (Tait, 2008) to describe blasphemous, instrumentalized, and disrespectful public portrayal of death in hybrid media. On the other hand, death events and near-death events that may otherwise have been kept secret from the public owing to various political, economic, or religious interests may now gain public attention because of the public's new access to the power of representation. The death of Iranian Neda Agha-Soltan is one example (see Reading, 2011). Agha-Soltan, a philosophy student in her 20s, was killed by the Iranian police in 2009 in Tehran while participating in a demonstration against the government. Her killing was captured on mobile phone cameras, and the footage of her death was uploaded onto YouTube soon after the event. The viral video immediately began to circulate in global journalistic news media, including CNN and many other major outlets. In addition to the video clip, a still image taken from the video, showing Neda's bloody face, became a symbol for the movement demanding free elections and democracy in Iran (Semati & Brookey, 2014, p. 137). This still image is also, as Reading (2011) reminds readers, an iconic symbol of public representation of death in what she calls (using a term coined from "global" and "digital") "the globital memory field."

Present-day pluralized societies immersed in hybrid media communication do not have a single, unified moral community guiding the work of journalists in their assessment of public representation of death (Sumiala, 2021). However, as the case of Neda Agha-Soltan demonstrates, this does not mean a total loss of collective values regarding the morally and socially acceptable representation of death but rather an ongoing public debate about how society should draw moral boundaries concerning death, as well as the role of media producers and audiences in this process. This debate appeared regarding the assumed murder attack of the Russian opposition leader Alexei Navalny and his ideological, political, and moral legacy (cf. Hanusch, 2010, p. 162).

Visual Representation of Death

As Seaton (2005) argued, visuals play an important role in the intersections between religion and mediated representation of death. Christian imagery and the news hold in common a certain relationship to truth. Both are produced by institutions that claim not merely to represent reality, but to reveal the truth about the events they depict; hence, they share a special relationship with the real, a relationship that carries an almost compulsive power (p. 92). Photography in the nineteenth century holds special importance in this context, as it brought about new possibilities for the visual representation of death in the news and elsewhere in society (Mirzoeff, 2009) and provided an index of death (cf. Zelizer, 2010). Illustrated magazines and photojournalism played a significant role in Europe and the United States in magnifying public representation of death in newspapers. Goldberg (1998) discusses how the illustration of death gained new significance as death became more distant from people's everyday lives. In her analysis, the transfer of physical death from public life into the private realm (e.g. hospices) and the simultaneous growth of vivid depictions of death in newspapers were closely interrelated. As fewer people had actually witnessed physical death, people sought new ways to manage their fears and thoughts related to dying. Thus, the role of death images, and the emotions associated with them, gained new significance in newspaper depictions of death (Goldberg, 1998, p. 29).

One particularly well-known photojournalistic motif in of the dead and dying is the Christian *pietá* motif (Zelizer, 2010). The Italian word means "compassion" and the motif refers to the Virgin Mary grieving as she holds the lifeless body of Jesus. Famously depicted by Michelangelo in 1499, this type of image, modified over and over again in the history of the Western visual culture, is common even in today's news; it powerfully communicates the suffering associated with death, whether caused by human violence or natural disasters (Hanusch, 2010, p. 22). Seaton (2005) highlights the cultural relevance of this visual trope by noting how "Modern news photography and television (like modern reporting) draw directly or indirectly on this tradition." While Islamic and Judaic cultures do not stress pictorial images, "In Western culture, by contrast, there is an unbroken tradition from Graeco-Roman imagery to the refinements of the Renaissance and the Enlightenment through to the birth of photography that as seen physical representation as simultaneously instructive, uplifting and entertaining" (p. 85). In addition to revealing the truth about death, visual representations, including the Christian *pietá* motif, play a vital role in mourning and commemorating the dead – in other words, in maintaining relationships between the living and the dead (Walter, 2017).

A striking example of the postmortem relationship appearing early in modern media is the phenomenon of postmortem photography. This nineteenth-century practice involved taking pictures of deceased babies and children (Troyer, 2007; see also Zelizer, 2010, pp. 335–336). The practice of taking postmortem photographs of loved ones remained relatively common until the early twentieth century, when embalming began to gain popularity in the United States. Even then, pictures taken after embalming typically imitated the aesthetics of pictures taken immediately after death, aiming to give the deceased subject the appearance of "deep sleep" (Troyer, 2007, pp. 30–31). "The visual index of corpses produced mechanically by photographers created a new way of seeing the dead body for the general public" (p. 30). Remaining somewhat unaltered until the 1940s and 1950s, the practice of photographing embalmed corpses began to be taboo (see Norfleet, 1993; Zelizer, 2010, p. 336). Ruby (1995) explains the social power of photographs to separate the dead from the living:

> Photographs commemorating death can be seen as one example of the myriad artifacts humans have created and used in the accommodation of death. Because the object created, i.e., the photograph, resembles the person lost through death, it serves as a substitute and a reminder of the loss for the individual mourner and for society. (p. 7)

Photography also bears witness as the powerful example of public representation of death in the Holocaust shaped an ultimate symbol of horror in modern history. Holocaust visualization has become an integral part of our collective understanding of the atrocities of World War II and news photographs explicitly contributed to how we see the Holocaust and collectively remember it. Pictures taken during the liberation of Nazi concentration camps, which were circulated through US and British news media in the aftermath of the war became a significant genre (Zelizer, 1998, p. 1). These "atrocity photos" have become "a lasting iconic representation of war atrocity and human evil" (p. 1) – the public representation of death *par excellence*.

The emergence of television expanded the public representation of death in news media (Hanusch, 2010). By introducing a new modality of representing death: the moving image (cf. Ellis, 2009). While news clips in movie theaters had represented death on screens before the advent of television (Pantti & Sumiala, 2009), television was the definitive medium that brought death as a public matter into the private lives of ordinary people. Through television the death of an unknown person, a stranger, became newly "intimate" (Ellis, 2009). This sense of intimacy was compounded by certain televisual means of communication, including close-up images of bodies, live coverage of death reports (cf. Zelizer, 2010), and sound.

Today, Instagram, Facebook, YouTube, and Twitter are the digital heirs of traditional photography. As the media of mobile photographs, snapshots, and selfies (Hjorth & Hendry, 2015; Zuromskis, 2013), such sites form today's *memento mori*, visual reminders of the inevitability of death (cf. Sontag, 1977/1990). In social media this function involves ordinary people posting and sharing photographs of the dead. Through this practice, a social media user can claim the public and socially recognized status of a person in mourning. By posting pictures of themselves with the deceased (taken when they were still alive) and posting selfies taken at funerals, people maintain mediated and ritual relationships with the dead. Consequently, they participate in the cultural and social negotiation to determine which lives and deaths are worthy of collective attention and representation (Cann, 2014, pp. 69–86).

Death as a Media Event – Funerals

One televisual genre of special significance for public representation of death is the media event: the live broadcast of an historic event (see Morse, 2018; Sumiala, 2013). As a paramount example of the ceremonial media event (Dayan & Katz, 1992), public funerals play an important role in managing death and conveying the deceased into a new category in social life through mediation. Media funerals have the potential to create a collective ritual through which onsite and home participants become momentarily united in a ceremony that pays tribute to the deceased, providing a space to manage emotions through the symbols associated with a public death. Traditionally funeral media events marked the death of political leaders and major public figures. Although globally broadcast, they had a strong nationalist emphasis. In Western media history, the funeral of John F. Kennedy (1963) stands out as a paradigmatic example (Hoover, 2006; Zelizer, 1992) of the televised funeral. Other examples include the funerals of Indian Prime Minister Indira Gandhi (1984), North Korean leader Kim Jong Il (2011), Palestinian leader Yasser Arafat (2004), and South African leader Nelson Mandela (2013), all of which received considerable media attention. From the perspective of religion, such funeral media events include elements of civil religion (Bellah, 1967/2005). In a broad understanding of this concept, funerals as national ceremonies and civil rituals communicate the special meaning and destiny of a nation and its people through the ritual farewell to the leader.

Similarly, media events surround the deaths of prominent nonpolitical public figures, such as members of a royal family, celebrities, pop icons, and sport heroes. The funeral of Princess Diana in 1997 became an iconic example of the power of media to bring people together in the face of death (Turnock, 2000; Walter, 1999). We may also think of the death of pop stars such as Michael Jackson or David Bowie (Bennett, 2010; Sanderson & Cheong, 2010; Sumiala, 2013; van den Bulck & Larsson, 2019) and the massive amount of media attention they received. Han (2019, p. 80) looking at such death events through the lens of celebrity and fan culture, interprets them as coronations that produce a hero-figure, or "Great Man" (see Katz & Dayan, 1985, p. 307). This glorification of the deceased as superstars, legends, and icons sometimes appears in popular culture literature as a form of popular religiosity, idol worship, and celebrity adoration (Burgess et al., 2018; Han, 2019; Walter, 2011).

The death of Argentinian football legend Diego Maradona in late 2020 is a paradigmatic example of the present-day veneration of the dead (see Giles, 2017). The idolization of Maradona had already begun during his lifetime. While Maradona's career had many widely reported ups and downs, his famous victories on the pitch overcame his faults in the public eye. Following his death at the age of 60, *The Guardian* referred to Maradona as "the greatest player of all time" (Tondo, 2020). The public mourning was massive, especially in Argentina, where the president declared three days of national mourning. In Naples, Italy, the home of one of Maradona's former teams, he was named a patron saint of the city and the *Daily Mail* (November 25, 2020) suggested, "Maradona is a god in this city. People are walking around the streets like zombies, weeping at the news" (Cagnazzo, 2020). News reports showed Maradona's supporters, fans, and compatriots all over the world weeping while expressing their thoughts about their idol. One Instagram photo depicted Maradona wearing his legendary number 10, with the text reading "Ad10s" (Sumiala, 2021), became a symbol of the public mourning afforded this hero's death.

The death of a religious leader or teacher and role model is a special category in which the religious implications of media representation explicitly appear (cf. Cohen & Hetsroni, 2020). The broadcast funerals of Martin Luther King Jr. (1968), Pope John II (2005), and Mother Teresa (1997) belong to this category. These globally broadcast death events gathered people all over the world together from all ethnic, national, and religious backgrounds. The death and funeral of Pope John II in 2005 has received special scholarly interest (see Kennedy, 2015). Rosenthal (2012) analyzed the funeral as a transnational media event. Fitting the classic model of media event (Dayan & Katz, 1992), the broadcast was a cooperative production of major media networks and the religious elite, namely the Vatican press office. Rosenthal (2012) argues that the whole carefully scripted event began with the media following the crowds of people moving toward St. Peter's square, the public center of the Vatican and integrating diverse audiences on the screen, including both Catholic and non-Catholic viewers, with a nonconflictual and highly reverential reportorial tone. Reporting stressed themes of Pope John Paul II's role in contributing to political change in Poland and Eastern Europe, his achievements in promoting interfaith tolerance and dialogue, his skill in appealing to secular media, his strong bonds with Catholic youth, and his worldwide travel (p. 148). Rosenthal concludes:

> As a quintessential media event, the funeral momentarily united a fractious audience, creating a ritual moment that transcended the screen. For both the networks and the Vatican, the televised funeral was a successful, solidarity-promoting event that emphasized both the importance of the contemporary Roman Catholic Church and the ritual importance of television… At the funeral, the

Catholic Church employed television broadcasts to enhance and reinforce the authority of institutional religion. (p. 150)

As a ritual event the funeral aimed at manifesting the power and unity of a religious community and the bond between lay people and their religious leader; it also sought to address a larger global media audience in the name of institutional religion (Kertzer, 1988; cf. Sumiala et al., 2021). It functioned on many levels as a classic media event of "coronation" (Dayan & Katz, 1992), urging imagined community among the ritual participants (see also Han, 2019; Rosenthal, 2012).

Recent research on funerals as media events has noted the impact of the hybridization of the media environment (cf. Han, 2019), which has profoundly altered the conditions of producing funeral media events as performances of unity and has transformed media events into a new type of hybrid and networked phenomenon (Sumiala et al., 2018). In that environment, the professional news media, journalists, and political and religious elites have lost their exclusive power to orchestrate and manage such media events; instead, ordinary social media users have become media actors with power to produce material for and actively participate in such events, thus shaping their circulation. Consequently, funerals as hybrid media events have moved away from the original television-centered view observed by Dayan and Katz (1992) onto multiple digital platforms. Han (2019, p. 81) argues that this development calls for a scholarly rethinking of funeral media events to include the *total* media environment and not only the broadcasting of a single funeral event (see also Couldry et al., 2010), a challenge that future scholarship of media and religion will have to address in more detail.

How to Overcome Death in Media? – A Ritual View

Mourning

In addition to funeral media events, with their strong ritual dimension (Sumiala, 2013), media also represent death in the context of mourning rituals taking place outside of funeral events. Anthropological research on ritual has greatly enriched the study of mediated mourning (see Metcalf & Huntington, 1997; Turner, 1969; van Gennep, 1909/1960). Morse (2018) argues that media-related mourning rituals are best described as performative practices that "assemble a community in order for the dead to be farewelled." The ritual participants "accompany the dead in their trajectory from dying to afterlife … mourning rituals mark the departure of members of the community" (pp. 36–37). Mourning rituals also constitute a substantial subcategory of life-crisis rituals (Metcalf & Huntington, 1997). Anthropologically speaking, mourning rituals function to move the deceased symbolically into another category of social life, which can comprise ancestors, spirits, angels, or memories (see Metcalf & Huntington, 1997; Parry & Bloch, 1982). This repositioning of a deceased individual may include emotional demonstrations by a ritual participant – a mourner – such as grieving and lamenting or celebrating and paying tribute to the life and legacy of the deceased. In this way, mediated mourning rituals – when successful – help individuals and communities overcome the fundamental fear of death by providing culturally coded ways to express emotionally laden responses to loss. Thus, mourners are armed with collective strength to continue with a renewed social life; in this way, mourning rituals also demonstrate society's values and strengthen its institutions (Metcalf & Huntington, 1997; Morse, 2018, p. 36).

The great majority of the existing research on mediated mourning centers around public death events as media or news events; this category includes various types of events, such as high-profile terror attacks and deaths of public figures (Burgess et al., 2018; Morse, 2018). Mourning as a ritual practice is generally examined as a response to these events, with a strong emphasis on the analysis of media representations of ritual mourning. Walter (2011, 2016) provides an example of the use of angels as vernacular religious expressions of mourning and symbols of perduring bonds between the living and the dead.

Witnessing

Mediated ritual mourning, in any media, also involves mediated witnessing of someone's suffering. Witnessing as a mediated ritual practice is a way of looking at someone else's suffering and death from a mediated distance (e.g. Ellis, 2009; Frosh & Pinchevski, 2009; Katz & Liebes, 2007; Liebes & Blondheim, 2005; Peters, 2009). Throughout history, this morally engaging spectatorship of death, performed and experienced in diverse media, has played an important role in death events (cf. Ong, 2012). Witnessing suffering and death always involves a moral obligation to act, for instance, by taking part in public mourning and commemoration, and hence publicly acknowledging the value of the life lost (Sumiala et al., 2020).

For many scholars (e.g. Chouliaraki, 2006; Moeller, 1999; Ong, 2012; Silverstone, 2007; Tester, 2001), research on mediated witnessing contains a normative moral dimension that gives a voice to the voiceless and visibility to the victims, while still relying on a ritual means of managing the event. Boltanski's (1999) work has influenced the articulation of the mediated relationship between the suffering individual and the onlooker (see also Sontag, 2003), referring to "distant suffering" and claiming that the moral relationship becomes weaker as the mediated distance – whether temporal, spatial, or cultural – between the two increases. Moeller (1999) proposed the concept of "compassion fatigue," through which the public experiences apathy and indifference after witnessing "too much" suffering in the media. Ellis (2009) calls a type of everyday mediated witnessing "mundane witnessing," pointing to the passivity of viewers as they sit in front of TV screens. Chouliaraki's (2013) work on "ironic spectatorship" sees the relationship between the suffering or dead individual and the onlooker in terms of the "politics of pity." She proposes a position of solidarity between the spectator and the suffering individual as agonistic, a concept Chouliaraki (2013, 2011) borrows from Arendt (1958/1990). In this type of solidarity, a "proper distance" – a concept first introduced by Silverstone (2003) – is maintained between the onlooker and the suffering individual.

The critical element in solidarity as agonistic is the recognition of the asymmetry of power between the two individuals. In a global, digital age, this recognition is the only way to make a proposal of solidarity morally acceptable to the vulnerable regardless of religious, political, or cultural background (Chouliaraki, 2011, p. 364). The death of the small Syrian boy Alan Kurdi, whose drowned body was found on a Turkish beach in September 2015, stands out as an example of solidarity as agonistic. The pictures of the body evoked powerful feelings of pity. In various mediations, the pictures filled the front pages in global newspapers and occupied social media. Kurdi's death images became a visual symbol of the 2015 refugee crisis. The propagation of this image expanded possibilities for solidarity and the related politics of pity – although ambivalence remained – well beyond national boundaries. Mortensen and Trenz (2016) call the visually enriched mediated engagement with the suffering and death of Kurdi an act of moral spectatorship.

Modern Martyrdom and Sacrifice

Another example of mediated witnessing comes from martyrdom in media, a topic briefly discussed in the context of the Roman games. The discipline of sociology approaches martyrdom as an altruistic act that overcomes the human need to survive. It anchors two symbolic aspects: strength and purity. In sacrificing their life, martyrs show self-discipline and self-mastery (Hatina, 2014, p. 4). Durkheim's classic work *Le Suicide* (1951 [1897]) offers a valuable framework for understanding martyrdom in relation to community dynamics. In Durkheimian thinking, "altruistic suicide" is a radical expression of group solidarity. The martyr's sacrifice helps the community to identify with its collective values (Hatina, 2014, p. 4). In the present-day hybrid media environment, martyrdom is typically witnessed in the context of political unrest. In the Arab Spring of 2011, the deaths of the Tunisian fruit seller Mohammed Bouazizi and the young Egyptian Khaled Saeed stand out as examples of martyrdom constructed, witnessed, and circulated in hybrid media with explicit political implications (Sumiala & Korpiola, 2017). Kraidy (2016) calls such acts of martyrdom creative insurgency; a radical means of bodily communication intended to be represented in hybrid media to raise public awareness of injustice and to challenge the moral and ethical justification of those in power by sacrificing one's physical inviolability and integrity.

Digital Death

Mediated acts of public mourning, witnessing, and martyrdom and sacrifice – all of which have religious or spiritual connotations – have undergone radical change owing to the hybridization and consequent transformation of the contemporary media environment. We may identify two crucial, interconnected developments. Because the hybrid media environment allows for the pluralization of the actors, sites, and events around which death is publicly represented, the conventions of the ritual management of death and their social and cultural functions are also now in flux. New vernacular acts of mediated ritual engagement with death have evolved and expanded as ordinary media users have gained the capacity to create and share such acts through social media. Today, hashtags such as "#prayfor" or "#jesuis" and their countless variations vividly circulate between journalistic media and social media (in particular, Twitter and Instagram) in the aftermath of news of death. Diverse actors on YouTube use identifiers such as "tribute" or "RIP" to indicate ritual mourning and commemoration. On Facebook people use gestures such as changing a profile picture to pay respect to often unknown victims of violence or natural disasters (Sumiala, 2021). These mediated practices both pluralize public representation of death in the present hybrid media environment and make death more visible in our contemporary social lives, immersed as they are in mediated communication (Deuze, 2012). They also contribute to the vernacularization of ritual practices surrounding death and thus challenge traditional religious institutions and their authority to delineate the way death should be represented in public (Campbell, 2012). In the contemporary world of deep mediatization, tradition no longer controls meaning-making strategies and their related symbolic communication (Couldry & Hepp, 2017). Drawing from Hjarvard's (2016) idea of banal religion, we may call this development the expansion of the banal ritualization of death.

Hybrid media and the development of digital communication, in particular artificial intelligence (AI) and data mining, have prompted scholars of media and religion to ask new questions about the public representation of death as it relates to ritual relationships between the living and the dead. If traditional journalists, in concert with prominent political and, especially, religious institutions, previously had the primary authority to define those relationships and orchestrate the transition by which the dead were moved into a new category in social life (such as afterlife or immortality), today hybrid media poses new challenges for the definition of such postmortem relationships (see Hutchings, 2019; Savin-Baden & Mason-Robbie, 2020).

Contemporary technologies, including AI and data mining, newly enable a kind of communication between the living and the dead and offer possibilities for immortalization novel in human history. These technological advancements also enable the dead, in a certain sense, to talk back to us. Today, there exists the ability to produce new sentences, new conversations, and new idea exchanges in digital interactions between the dead and the living (see Savin-Baden & Mason-Robbie, 2020).

This development transforms the very idea of public representation of death and the permanence of death – articulated in the saying "rest in peace" – into something far more ephemeral that is carried out through hybrid media platforms best described as unstable and unsustainable (Arntfield, 2014, p. 91). This observation is not a merely theoretical one. According to some calculations, by the second half of the twenty-first century, the dead will outnumber the living on Facebook (Kasket, 2019, p. 59). What follows from this new circumstance is an ongoing temporality (in contrast to the idea of permanence) and animation (in contrast to the idea of repose) (see Nansen et al., 2014, p. 113) in public representation of death and its ritual management. Hence, the dead as digital beings – now as immortals – continue to participate in various ways across various hybrid media platforms. By engaging in such practices, the living allow for the communal presence of the dead in society and retain death as part of society in new ways, independent of religious institutions (Bassett, 2015; Savin-Baden & Mason-Robbie, 2020). Bassett (2015, p. 1134) designates these immortal, semi-spiritual creatures as "digital zombies" – beings whom she defines as physically dead but virtually alive and, more importantly, socially active. Thus, digital zombies allow for the reanimation and resurrection of death in society. Brubacker and Vertesi (2010) call this development "technospirituality," a condition in which media, religion, and death become interconnected in a new manner.

How does this digitalization of the line between life and death influence public representation of death and its ritual handling? Are we now – at least in the Western part of the world – moving toward a culture and society in which eschatology (to use theological terminology) is being transformed into communication technology (cf. Bassett, 2015)? If this is the case, immortality will become more and more profoundly linked to the mediated lives of people immersed in hybrid media and digital communication. We may describe this form of immortality as temporary, impermanent, and effervescent (cf. Nansen et al., 2014, p. 113). If this transformation is our future, researchers of media and religion will need new theoretical concepts and tools through which to understand its implications for the existing philosophical, sociological, and theological categories of life and death. Scholars must now pose novel questions about the diminishing authority of journalistic and religious institutions and about the meaning of immortality and the afterlife.

References

Arendt, H. (1990). *The human condition*. University of Chicago Press (Original work published 1958).

Ariès, P. (1977). *L'homme devant la mort*. Éditions du Seuil.

Ariès, P. (1985). *Images of man and death*. Harvard University Press.

Arnold, M., Gibbs, M., Kohn, T., Meese, J., & Nansen, B. (2018). *Death and digital media*. Routledge.

Arntfield, M. (2014). eMemoriam: Digital necrologies, virtual remembrance, and the question of permanence. In C. M. Moreman, & A. D. Lewis (Eds.), *Digital death. Mortality and beyond in the online age* (pp. 89–110). Praeger.

Bassett, B. (2015). Who wants to live forever? Living, dying and grieving in our digital society. *Social Sciences*, 4(1), 1127–1139. https://doi.org/10.3390/Socsci4041127

Bellah, R. N. (2005). Civil religion in America. *Dædalus*, 96(1), 1–21 (Original work published 1967).

Bennett, J. (2010). Michael Jackson: Celebrity death, mourning and media events. *Celebrity Studies*, 1(2), 231–232.

Bloch, M. (1992). *Prey into hunter: The politics of religious experience.* Cambridge University Press.

Boltanski, L. (1999). *Distant suffering: Morality, media, and politics.* Cambridge University Press.

Brubacker, J. R., & Vertesi, J. (2010). Death and the social network. *Proceedings of the ACM CHI/Workshop on Death and the Digital.* Atlanta, Georgia.

Burgess, J., Mitchell, P., & Münch, F. V. (2018). Social media rituals. The uses of celebrity death in digital culture. In Z. Papacharissi (Ed.), *A networked self and birth, life, death* (pp. 224–239). Routledge.

Cagnazzo, A. (2020). The view from Naples: Maradona is a god in this city. People are walking around the streets like zombies, weeping at the news that Diego is dead. The Daily Mail. Retrieved May 24, 2022, from https://www.dailymail.co.uk/sport/sportsnews/article-8987079/THE-VIEW-NAPLES-Naples-weeps-city-having-lost-favourite-son-Diego-Maradona.html

Campbell, H. A. (2012). *Digital religion: Understanding religious practice in new media worlds.* Routledge.

Cann, C. K. (2014). Tweeting death, posting photos, and pinning memorials: Remembering the dead in bits and pieces. In C. M. Moreman, & A. D. Lewis (Eds.), *Digital death. Mortality and beyond in the online age* (pp. 69–86). Praeger.

Carey, J. W. (1989). *Communication as culture.* Unwin Hyman.

Chadwick, A. (2013). *Hybrid media system: Politics and power.* Oxford University Press.

Chouliaraki, L. (2006). *Spectatorship of suffering.* Sage Publications.

Chouliaraki, L. (2011). "Improper distance": Towards a critical account of solidarity as irony. *International Journal of Cultural Studies, 14*(4), 363–381. https://doi.org/10.1177/1367877911403247

Chouliaraki, L. (2013). *The ironic spectatorship: Solidarity in the age of post-humanitarianism.* Polity Press.

Cohen, Y., & Hetsroni, A. (2020). Monotheism and television: A comparative content analysis of religion in prime-time programming in the USA, Israel, and Turkey. *Atlantic Journal of Communication, 28*(2), 103–114. https://doi.org/10.1080/15456870.2019.1613405

Copeland, D. (1997). *Colonial American newspapers: Character and content.* University of Delaware Press.

Couldry, N. (2012). *Media, society, world. Social theory and digital media practice.* Polity Press.

Couldry, N., & Hepp, A. (2017). *The mediated construction of reality.* Polity Press.

Couldry, N., Hepp, A., & Krotz, F. (2010). *Media events in a global age.* Routledge.

Davies, D. (2002). *Death, ritual and belief: The rhetoric of funerary rites.* Continuum.

Dayan, D., & Katz, E. (1992). *Media events: The live broadcasting of history.* Harvard University Press.

Deuze, M. (2012). *Media life.* Polity Press.

Durkheim, E. (1951). *The elementary forms of religious life.* K. E. Fields (Trans.). The Free Press (Original work published 1897).

Ellis, J. (2009). Mundane witness. In P. Frosh, & A. Pinchevski (Eds.), *Media witnessing: Testimony in the age of mass communication* (pp. 73–88). Palgrave Macmillan.

Ess, C. (2017). Can we say anything ethical about digital religion? Philosophical and methodological considerations. *New Media & Society, 19*(1), 34–42. https://doi.org/10.1177/1461444816649914

Fowler, B. (2007). *The obituary as collective memory.* Routledge.

Frosh, P., & Pinchevski, A. (2009). Introduction: Why media witnessing? Why now? In P. Frosh, & A. Pinchevski (Eds.), *Media witnessing: Testimony in the age of mass communication* (pp. 1–19). Palgrave Macmillan.

Giles, D. (2017). The immortalisation of celebrities. In M. Hviid Jacobsen (Ed.), *Postmortal society: Towards a sociology of immortality* (pp. 97–113). Routledge.

Girard, R. (1977). *Violence and the sacred.* Johns Hopkins University Press.

Goldberg, V. (1998). Death takes a holiday, sort of. In J. Goldstein (Ed.), *Why we watch: The attractions of violent entertainment* (pp. 27–52). Oxford University Press.

Han, S. (2019). *(Inter)facing death: Life in global uncertainty.* Routledge.

Hanusch, F. (2010). *Representing death in the news. Journalism, media and mortality.* Palgrave Macmillan.

Hanusch, F. (2013). Sensationalizing death? Graphic disaster images in the tabloid and broadsheet press. *European Journal of Communication, 28*(5), 497–513. https://doi.org/10.1177/0267323113491349

Hatina, M. (2014). *Martyrdom in modern Islam: Piety, power, and politics.* Cambridge University Press.

Hepp, A. (2020). *Deep mediatization.* Routledge.

Hjarvard, S. (2016). *The mediatization of culture and society.* Routledge.

Hjorth, L., & Hendry, N. (2015). A snapshot of social media: Camera phone practices. *Social Media + Society*, *1*(1), 1–3. https://doi.org/10.1177/2056305115580478

Hoover, S. (2006). *Religion in the media age*. Routledge.

Hoover, S. M., & Lundby, K. (1997). *Rethinking media, religion and culture*. Sage publications.

Hope Cheong, P., Fisher-Nielsen, P., Gelfren, S., & Ess, C. (2012). *Digital religion, social media and culture: Perspectives, practices and futures*. Peter Lang.

Howarth, G. (2007). *Death and dying: A sociological introduction*. Polity Press.

Hutchings, T. (2019). Angels and the digital afterlife: Death and nonreligion online. *Secularism & Nonreligion*, *8*(7), 1–6. https://doi.org/10.5334/snr.105

Hviid Jacobsen, M. (Ed.). (2021). *The age of spectacular death*. Routledge.

Kasket, E. (2019). *All the ghosts in the machine: Illusions of immortality in the digital age*. Robinson.

Katz, E., & Dayan, D. (1985). Media events: On the experience of not being there. *Religion*, *15*(3), 305–314. https://doi.org/10.1016/0048-721X(85)90017-X

Katz, E., & Liebes, T. (2007). No more peace! How disaster, terror and war have upstaged media events. *International Journal of Communication*, *1*, 157–166. http://ijoc.org

Kellehear, A. (1984). Are we a 'death-denying' society? A sociological review. *Social Science & Medicine*, *18*(9), 713–721.

Kennedy, M. C. (2015). The death of a pop-star pope: Saint John Paul II's funeral as media event. *Journal of Communication & Religion*, *38*(1), 95–112.

Kertzer, D. I. (1988). *Ritual, politics and power*. Yale University Press.

Kraidy, M. M. (2016). *The naked blogger of Cairo: Creative insurgency in the Arab world*. Harvard University Press.

Lagerkvist, A. (Ed.). (2019). *Digital existence. Ontology, ethics and transcendence in digital culture*. Routledge.

Liebes, T., & Blondheim, M. (2005). Myths to the rescue: How live television intervenes in history. In E. W. Rothenbuhler, & M. Coman (Eds.), *Media anthropology* (pp. 188–198). Sage Publications.

Lynch, G., Mitchell, J., & Strhan, A. (2012). *Media, religion and culture: A reader*. Routledge.

Metcalf, P., & Huntington, R. (1997). *Celebrations of death: The anthropology of mortuary ritual*. Cambridge University Press.

Meyer, B. (2009). Material mediations and religious practices of world-making. In K. Lundby (Ed.), *Religion across media. From early antiquity to late modernity* (pp. 1–19). Peter Lang.

Mirzoeff, N. (2009). *An introduction to visual culture*. Routledge.

Moeller, S. (1999). *Compassion fatigue: How the media sell disease, famine, war and death*. Routledge.

Morgan, D. (Ed.). (2008). *Keywords in media, religion, and culture*. Routledge.

Morse, T. (2018). *The mourning news. Reporting death. Reporting violent death in a global age*. Peter Lang.

Mortensen, M., & Trenz, H.-J. (2016). Media morality and visual icons in the age of social media: Alan Kurdi and the emergence of an impromptu public of moral spectatorship. *Javnost – The Public*, *23*(4), 343–362. https://doi.org/10.1080/13183222.2016.1247331

Nansen, B., Arnold, M., Gibbs, M., & Kohn, T. (2014). The restless dead in the digital cemetery. In C. M. Moreman, & A. D. Lewis (Eds.), *Digital death. Mortality and beyond in the online age* (pp. 111–124). Praeger.

Nord, D. (2001). *Communities of journalism: A history of American newspapers and their readers*. University of Illinois Press.

Norfleet, B. (1993). *Looking at death*. David R. Godine.

Ong, J. C. (2012). "Witnessing" or "mediating" distant suffering? Ethical questions across moments of text, production, and reception. *Television & New Media*, *15*(3), 179–196.

Pantti, M., & Sumiala, J. (2009). Till death do us join: Media, mourning rituals and the sacred centre of the society. *Media, Culture & Society*, *31*(1), 119–135. https://doi.org/10.1177/0163443708098251

Papacharissi, Z. (Ed.). (2019). *A networked self and birth, life, death*. Routledge.

Parry, J., & Bloch, M. (1982). *Death and the regeneration of life*. Cambridge University Press.

Peters, J. D. (2009). Witnessing. In P. Frosh, & A. Pinchevski (Eds.), *Media witnessing: Testimony in the age mass communication* (pp. 23–41). Palgrave Macmillan (Original work published 2001).

Reading, A. (2011). *Gender and memory in the globital age*. Palgrave Macmillan.

Rosenthal, M. (2012). Commercial television news, crisis, and collective memory. In D. Winston (Ed.), *The Oxford handbook of religion and the American news media* (pp. 141–156). Oxford University Press.

Ruby, J. (1995). *Secure the shadow: Death and photography in America.* MIT Press.

Sanderson, J., & Cheong, P. H. (2010). Tweeting prayers and communicating grief over Michael Jackson online. *Bulletin of Science, Technology & Society, 30*(5), 328–340. DOI:10.1177/0270467610380010

Savin-Baden, M., & Mason-Robbie, V. (Eds.). (2020). *Digital afterlife: Death matters in a digital age.* CRC Press/ Taylor & Francis.

Seaton, J. (2005). *Carnage and the media. The making and breaking of news about violence.* Allen Lane.

Semati, M., & Brookey, R. A. (2014). Not *for Neda*: Digital media, (citizen) journalism, and the invention of a postfeminist martyr. *Communication, Culture & Critique, 7*(2), 137–153. DOI:10.1111/cccr.12042

Silverstone, R. (2003). Proper distance: Towards an ethics for cyberspace. In G. Liestol, A. Morrison, & T. Rasmussen (Eds.), *Digital media revisited: Theoretical and conceptual innovations in digital domains* (pp. 469–490). MIT Press.

Silverstone, R. (2007). *Media and morality. On the rise of the mediapolis.* Polity Press.

Sontag, S. (1990). *On photography.* Strauss and Giroux (Original work published 1977).

Sontag, S. (2003). *Regarding the pain of others.* Strauss and Giroux.

Spierenburg, P. (1984). *The spectacle of suffering: Executions and the evolution of repression: From a preindustrial metropolis to the European experience.* Cambridge University Press.

Staudt, C. (2001). *Picturing the dead and dying in the nineteenth-century L'illustration.* PhD dissertation. Columbia University Press.

Stephens, M. (2007). *A history of news.* Oxford University Press.

Sumiala, J. (2013). *Media and ritual: Death, community and everyday life.* Routledge.

Sumiala, J. (2021). *Bella ciao* clangs on the balconies: The art of ritual practice during lockdown 2020 – Some digital media ethnographic notes. *Comunicazioni Sociali. Journal of Media, Performing Arts and Cultural Studies, 43*(1), 87–93. DOI:10.26350/001200_000115

Sumiala, J. (2021). *Mediated death.* Polity.

Sumiala, J., & Korpiola, L. (2017). Mediatized martyrdom? Witnessing global compassion and solidarity during the 'Arab Spring'. *New Media and Society, 19*(1), 52–66. https://doi.org/10.1177/1461444816649918

Sumiala, J., Lounasmeri, L., & Lukyanova, G. (2021). Almost immortal? The ritual transition of power and the dynamics of history in three Cold War media events. *Media History, 28*(2), 261–277. https://doi.org/10.1080/13688804.2021.1958671

Sumiala, J., Tikka, M., & Valaskivi, K. (2020). Just a 'stupid reflex'? Digital witnessing of the Charlie Hebdo attacks and the mediation of conflict. In P. Budka, & B. Bräuchler (Eds.), *Theorising media & conflict* (pp. 57–75). Berghahn Books.

Sumiala, J., Valaskivi, K., Tikka, M., & Huhtamäki, J. (2018). *The Charlie Hebdo attacks and the global circulation of terrorist violence.* Emerald.

Tait, S. (2008). Pornographies of violence? Internet spectatorship on body horror. *Critical Studies in Media Communication, 25*(1), 91–111. https://doi.org/10.1080/15295030701851148

Tester, K. (2001). *Compassion, morality and the media.* Open University Press.

Thompson, S. (2004). *The penny press: The origins of the modern news media.* Polity Press.

Tondo, L. (2020). Italians mourn death of Diego Maradona, the 'naughty rascal' of Naples. The Guardian. Retrieved May 24, 2022, from https://www.theguardian.com/world/2020/nov/26/naples-mourns-death-of-diego-maradona-their-little-rascal

Troyer, J. (2007). Embalmed vision. *Mortality, 12*(1), 22–47. https://doi.org/10.1080/13576270601088525

Turner, V. (1969). *The ritual process: Structure and anti-structure.* Routledge and Kegan.

Turnock, R. (2000). *Interpreting Diana. Television audiences and the death of a princess.* BFI Publishing.

van den Bulck, H., & Larsson, A. O. (2019). 'There's a Starman waiting in the sky': Mourning David #Bowie on Twitter. *Convergence: The International Journal of Research into New Media Technologies, 25*(2), 307–323. https://doi.org/10.1177/1354856517709670

van Gennep, A. (1960). *The rites of passage.* University of Chicago (Original work published 1909).

Walter, T. (Ed.). (1999). *The mourning of Diana.* Berg.

Walter, T. (2011). Angels not souls: Popular religion in the online mourning for British celebrity Jade Goody. *Religion, 41*(1), 29–51. https://doi.org/10.1080/0048721X.2011.553138

Walter, T. (2016). The dead who become angels: Bereavement and vernacular religion in the 21st century. *Omega: Journal of Death & Dying, 73*(1), 3–28. https://doi.org/10.1177/0030222815575697

Walter, T. (2017). How the dead survive: Ancestors, immortality, memory. In M. Hviid Jacobsen (Ed.), *Postmortal society. Towards sociology of immortality* (pp. 19–39). Routledge.

Walter, T. (2020). *Death in the modern world.* Sage Publications.

Zelizer, B. (1992). *Covering the body: The Kennedy assassination, the media, and the shaping of collective memory.* University of Chicago Press.

Zelizer, B. (1998). *Remembering to forget: Holocaust memory through the camera's eye.* The University of Chicago Press.

Zelizer, B. (2010). *About to die. How news images move the public.* Oxford University Press.

Zuromskis, C. (2013). *Snapshot photography. The lives of images.* MIT Press.

Selected Readings

Arnold, M., Gibbs, M., Kohn, T., Meese, J., & Nansen, B. (2018). *Death and digital media.* Routledge.

Cann, K. C. (Ed.). (2018). *The Routledge handbook of death and the afterlife.* Routledge.

Fishman, M. J. (2017). *Death makes the news: How the media censor and display the dead.* New York University Press.

Hviid Jacobsen, M. (Ed.). (2020). *The age of spectacular death.* Routledge.

Morse, T. (2018). *The mourning news. Reporting violent death in a global age.* Peter Lang.

Sisto, D. (2020). *Online afterlives: Immortality, memory, and grief in digital culture.* Polity.

Sumiala, J. (2021). *Mediated death.* Polity.

Part VII
Cultural Perspectives

27

Incipient Diversity
Gender and Race in Media and Religion Research

Chiung Hwang Chen

Although gender and race/ethnicity have long been crucial concerns within academic research in many disciplines, the field of media and religion has only slowly begun to catch on. Following calls for integrating cultural studies into the larger media research agenda (Dines, 1995), Hoover proposed a "culturalist turn" within media and religion scholarship to shift research paradigms away from media-effect-centered positivist approaches toward cultural studies-based and audience-oriented frameworks (Hoover, 2002a, 2002b; Hoover & Venturelli, 1996). This approach introduces possibilities of a more critical view toward ideologies in media texts and mediated lived experience. It also allows more scholars to tackle gender and race/ethnicity issues, as this subject matter is a central concern of cultural studies. This chapter reviews and assesses studies on gender and race/ethnicity in media and religion research over the past two decades. I utilized the EBSCO search engine and eight of the field's leading journals[1] to locate relevant work published between 2000 and 2020. The chapter identifies emerging scholarship in three areas: gender, race/ethnicity, and the intersection between the two. It concludes by pointing out an imbalance in scholarly attention and expressing the hope the study will help shape future research prospects.

Scholarship on Gender

In surveying edited books and journal articles from the late 1990s to 2000s, Lövheim (2013a) sees a "blind spot" in media and religion research, finding disappointingly few studies foregrounding gender issues. She thus invites fellow researchers to incorporate feminist and gender theories in their analyses (Lövheim, 2013b). Sterk (2010, p. 208), a former editor of *Journal of Communication and Religion*, similarly suggests that gender is an "underdeveloped area of scholarship," as she reviews the authorship and themes of articles published in the journal. A recent study by Chen and Yorgason (2022) provides a more thorough picture of gender issues within religion and media scholarship. Looking at publications in five leading journals since the turn of the twenty-first century, they report that, the percentages of male and female authors are 63% vs. 37%. While white males still dominate the conversations (56% of authors), the percentage of white female researchers has increased significantly and steadily (up to 30% overall). The representation of non-white women continues to lag behind their male counterparts, except for Asian female scholars

The Handbook on Religion and Communication, First Edition. Edited by Yoel Cohen and Paul A. Soukup.
© 2023 John Wiley & Sons Ltd. Published 2023 by John Wiley & Sons Ltd.

who outnumber Asian male authors. Nevertheless, percentages for all nonwhite authors remain very low. In terms of themes discussed within articles, the number relating to gender has increased consistently but only modestly, reaching about 10% of media and religion articles. These studies illustrate that media and religion scholarship still is not fully giving gender issues their due, either in authorship or thematic content. Nevertheless, an impressive body of literature on gender has emerged. This section points to key works in this area over the past two decades.

Kellner (2011) suggests three approaches to critical media cultural studies. Textual analysis looks at media representations and ideologies embedded in cultural/media products. Audience research examines media impacts and audience gratification. Political economy observes systems of media production and distribution. I follow his categorizations below in organizing the literature pertaining gender issues. However, I replace the political economy category with religious media in order to better understand the dynamic between institutional faiths and their followers (and because of the lack of political economic approaches within the media and religion literature on the media system itself). In this section, I focus primarily on women, as most gender-related studies do likewise. However, discussions of masculinity and sexuality are also included toward the end of the section.

Media Text

In relation to media texts, Lövheim (2013b) identifies three major areas in the emergent literature exploring intersections of gender and religion: news, entertainment, and (new) technology. The vast majority of studies I surveyed relating to journalistic accounts focus on Islam and women, especially the symbolic meaning of the veil. Klaus and Kassel (2005), for example, critique the German press narrative on (un)veiling as symbols of freedom and bondage as paths that legitimize the foreign invasion of Afghanistan. MacDonald (2006, p. 9) further questions "colonial obsessions with 'unveiling'" and the Western media's sidelining of Muslim women's subjectivity and agency (see also Korteweg, 2008; Moll, 2007). Quoting Vis (2011, p. 176), Lövheim sees these feminist and postcolonial analyses "as indications of a move 'beyond the hijab debates' [focused on questions of oppression] toward addressing 'the interconnectedness between religion, media, conflict, gender and race' and how this contributes to various forms of agency among Muslim women" (Lövheim, 2013b, p. 21). Aside from the veil, scholars also explore other aspects of Muslim women's identity. For instance, Randhawa (2019) analyzes how "the women's pages" in a Malaysian newspaper teach working women to be devout Muslim wives and mothers, whereas Brown (2011) dissects accounts that "other" Muriel Degauque, the so-called first European female suicide bomber, in the English-language news media.

The second and probably most prominent area of textual analysis relates to gender and religion in popular/entertainment media. Unlike in news media, Christianity has especially been extensively explored in this category. While a few studies deal with symbols of feminine divinity and spirituality (Briggs, 2009; Knight, 2005; Paule, 2012) and gender dynamics and ideologies (Frank, 2011; Frykholm, 2005; Hinojosa Hernández, 2019; Lövheim, 2015; Shoemaker, 2017), many scholars focus on the material body as a medium for religious communication. Lelwica (2000), for example, looks meticulously at the religion of thinness and weight loss as means to salvation (see also Höpflinger, 2015 for displaying death; Wimmler, 2014 for God manifested through the female body). Another research thread on the female body examines suffering. Taking an ecofeminist perspective, Sawyer (2020) provides a critical reading of biblical passages and Tracy Chapman's song, "The Rape of the World." Maddux (2008) and Birzache (2014) similarly analyze suffering female bodies in films such as *The Passion of the Christ* and *The Passion of*

Joan of Arc. One exception to the Christianity-centered literature is Cañas's (2008) analysis of *The Little Mosque on the Prairie*, a Canadian comedy designed to challenge Orientalist perceptions and Western feminism.

The third area of textual analysis deals with emerging new media. Earlier research tended to address gendered debates between technology and theology (Graham, 1999). Studies within the surveyed period have begun to explore how technologies and digital media affect or expand women's religious authority and participation (Moore, 2011; Piela, 2013; Schulz, 2012). Notable examples include Krishnan's (2017) exploration of the use of the Kannada Goddess image in social media to reaffirm and unite regional identity in southern India, Vis et al.'s (2011) feminist reinterpretation of a Dutch anti-Islam YouTube video, and Dickerson's (2020) Womanist take on the digital "Beloved Community" as a type of religious liberation within US Black experiences.

Audience Research

Clark and Chiou (2013) have reviewed methodological aspects of gender-related literature. They find that earlier quantitative empirical studies on audience research tended to use gender merely as a demographic variable to understand media use and attitudes. In responding to Hoover's call for a "culturalist turn," mentioned earlier, several scholars have employed ethnography and in-depth interviews to examine how audiences make sense of media content; unfortunately, most do not often use gender as a vantage point.

Feminist cultural studies research does so more directly by foregrounding gender-based interpretive analysis and taking women's frames of reference more seriously. One way this occurs is by giving voice to women's mediated lived experience. For example, Elsayed (2016) examines young Egyptian women's articulation of Muslim identity through transnational television. Olson (2017) similarly analyzes online hijab meaning negotiation (see also Aly, 2009). On Christianity, Pype's (2012) participatory ethnography explores a reimagined and reconstructed Pentecostalism through the creation of a popular television melodrama in Kinshasa, while Petersen (2013) looks at gratifications of romance and spirituality among *The Twilight Saga*'s Danish female fans. Other studies explore voices of women in minority and alternative religions: Tunç (2012) on Greek Orthodox in Turkey; Neriya-Ben Shahar (2017) on Amish and Orthodox Haredi in the United States; Berger and Ezzy (2009) on witchcraft practices the United States, UK, and Australia; and Boutros (2013) on online Vodou.

Religious Media

Political economy analyzes systems of production in order to understand media content, as mentioned earlier. Instead of taking this approach to explore the mainstream media, this section shifts the institutional focus toward media use of and content produced by religious groups. Scholars have given significant attention to the ways in which gender is embedded in this phenomenon as well as to women's reaction to the processes and messages involved. Clear attention to oppression by and resistance to patriarchal systems emerges within the surveyed literature, especially within the North American Christian context. My own analysis of the "I'm a Mormon" ad campaign, for example, argues that the ads buttress conservative ideals of motherhood and shape Mormon women's feminine identity (Chen, 2014). Sumerau et al. (2015) similarly document the reinforcement of gender roles and hierarchy in both religious and secular magazines. Highlighting the "war on yoga pants" online debate, Michael (2019) specifies the meaning of modesty in white evangelical Christian culture and shows how it is used to sur-veil women's piety and purity. Hobbs (2015), on the other hand, finds that within Christian news sites feminism is often associated with abortion, promiscuity, sexual deviation, as well as anti-family and anti-Christian stances. Outside North America, institutionally mediated construction of Christian femininities has also been tackled. Examples include Armanios and Amstutz (2013) on Coptic films in Egypt, Pype (2016) on Pentecostalism in Congo, and Newell (2005) on Christian pamphlets in Ghana and Nigeria. Beyond Christianity, two studies are worth men-tioning. One is a discourse analysis on women's bodies as the bearer of Iranian identity through compulsory dress codes (Rahbari et al., 2019). Another investigates a men's movement that functions as a backlash to feminism in India (Lodhia, 2014).

The theme of women's resistance to male-dominated religious culture shows that women do not merely see themselves as victims; many fight the system in order to achieve empowerment. In examining the Latter-day Saints' faith, Johns (2008) decodes female Mormon missionaries' rhe-torical strategies to define their own role in the faith, while Lampert-Weissig (2011) repositions the female protagonist in the *Twilight* series (written by a Mormon author) and equips her with additional agency and power. Looking at American evangelism, Moore (2010) uses participant observation and interviews to reveal female churchgoers' defiance of patriarchal messages. In the same vein, Mesaros-Winckles (2010) provides a feminist critique of the Quiverfull movement while Burke and McDowell (2012) open up space for reconceptualizing God's gender. In the con-text of Iran's religion-suffused culture, AbdulRazak (2017) explores how female voices rebel against and subvert cultural-religious patriarchal power through feminist films.

Building (especially female-nurturing) community to achieve empowerment is an emerging motif. Kleman et al. (2009) analyze how women in faith communities supported each other through communication strategies (see also Dickerson, 2020). Taking a rather different tack, McLaughlin (2012) theorizes how sacred narratives might help connect women in supportive relationships across believing/nonbelieving and other ideological divides. Rifai (2020) likewise shows how digital community-making combines with subtle religious ideals and habits to create communities of support for those with what many people regard as eating disorders.

Masculinity

A few scholars have started to interrogate masculinity through a gender studies lens. Most of this research relates to men within Christianity. Hoover and Coats (2011, 2015), for instance, explore how media shape Christian men's sense of self and masculine identity. Others explore media content choices among abstinent Christian men within a heavily sexualized media landscape (Luisi et al., 2018) or gender divisions and gendered technologies within media ministries (Fenimore, 2012). Some investigate specific male movements or particular reactions to feminism within Christianity. The Promise Keepers movement was a starting point for many, especially during the first decade of the 2000s. Scholars analyzed how these conservative Christians (often complexly) define masculinity, construct political rhetoric, recruit through media strategies, or compare to other religious and male-centered phenomena (Abbott, 2006; Chapman, 2009; Harper, 2012; Sumerau et al., 2015). Du Mez's (2020) acclaimed work, *Jesus and John Wayne*, espe-cially captures the historical shift of Christian masculinity well as she documents how Christian and popular media started to perpetuate the warrior ideal of evangelical manhood in the mid-twentieth century.

Elsewhere, while Clanton (2017) theorizes Superman's religious implications, Propp (2013) compares the misogyny and men's fear of women found in the New Guinean folktale, the "The

Swan Maiden," to those themes in Dan Brown's *The Da Vinci Code*. Also moving away from a Christianity-centric focus, Iwamura (2017) critiques the fascination for and stereotyping of Asian monks in American popular culture. Shirazi (2014) conversely identifies ideals of manhood and kingship associated with the concept of Sahibqirani found in Muslim-Urdu narratives.

Sexuality

Van den Brandt (2019) calls for more attention to female sexuality and queer issues in media and religion research. Topics relating to these areas are indeed starting to be explored. Studies mentioned earlier regarding institutional messages on dress codes and women's bodies indicate attempts at religious control over female sexuality. A few publications foreground the sexual aspect of religious messages and women's efforts to define their own sexuality. Butler and Winston (2009), for example, demystify the Madonna/whore Christian dichotomy of womanhood, whereas Bochow and van Dijk (2012) argue that Christian churches in Africa provide an alternative space for women to envision marriage and sexuality. Within studies on Islam, Ibrahim (2019) examines the sexual image the "Jihadi-bride." Robinson (2015) alternatively shows how the American hijabi fashion community functions as a counterculture movement. Meanwhile, Zainal (2019) points out Malaysian audiences' preference for secular media content with physical intimacy over the state-sponsored religious messages. On other faith systems, Tsuria (2017) analyzes a Jewish website's attempt to solve pornography addiction, and Gresaker (2017) explores astrological advice to heterosexuals in a Norwegian women's magazine.

Within discussions of LGBTQ+ issues, one area of research is media portrayals of LGBTQ+ people and issues. In relation to journalism, Adamczyk et al. (2018) provide a macro analysis comparing newspaper coverage of homosexuality in various religious, economic, and political contexts. A few scholars specifically focus on news reports of conservative Christian narratives in gay-rights debates in North America (Haskell, 2011; Mosurinjohn, 2014; Rhodes & Stewart, 2016). Elsewhere, Bompani and Brown (2015) look at how Pentecostal churches affect the Ugandan press coverage of antigay legislation. On the entertainment media, most studies address the perpetuation of heteronormativity in popular culture (Hilton-Morrow, 2011; Lauricella & Scott, 2018; Pires & Revelles-Benavente, 2020; Roos, 2010; Whitney, 2017). One exception is Silverman's (2014) intriguing analysis of the performativity of LGBTQ+ identity in comparison with the performativity of Jewishness in the TV drama *Sex in the City*. In regard to digital media, Schippert (2007) highlights negotiation between sexual and national identities as the gay community attempted to canonize the sainthood of Mychal Judge, a New York City Fire Department chaplain who died in the World Trade Center during the September 11, 2001 attack. In a rather different vein, O'Riordan and White (2010) use virtual ethnography to chart the LGBTQ+ community's spiritual practices and networking on social media.

A second major theme of LGBTQ+ studies deals with homosexuality in religious settings, with significant critical attention given to Christian condemnation of queerness (Burack, 2014; Stokes & Schewe, 2016; Weaver, 2011). Trammell (2015) charts how a prominent Christian news magazine reinforces heteronormativity while trying to simultaneously find space to discuss gay and lesbian lived experience. Others examine religious messages that shape antigay prejudice (Herbert, 2019; Obadare, 2015; Perry & Snawder, 2016). A couple of studies deal with gay believers' identity issues: Weber (2019) investigates queer Mormons' struggles between their sexual desires and their Church's heterosexual tenets and demands for thoroughgoing obedience, while Taylor et al. (2014) explore how Christian LGBTQ+ youths negotiate sexual and religious identities on social media.

Scholarship on Race/Ethnicity

In comparison with gender research, scholarship on race and ethnicity has received even less explicit attention within the field of media and religion. While promoting women-centered scholarly work, Sterk (2010), Lövheim (2013a), and Clark and Chiou (2013) mostly sidestep the race/ethnicity aspect of diversity. Dines (1995) argues that the neglect of race generally reflects white feminism's bias, as race issues are often passed over. The field only recently began to pay attention to this bias. In an introduction to a special issue on race, *Journal of Communication and Religion* acknowledged that "race has been a missing element" and that the journal had fallen "woefully short" in incorporating race in analysis of religion and communication (House & Johnson, 2018, p. 5). Chen and Yorgason's (2022) survey of leading journals shows that the lack of racial/ethnic diversity among authors and topics is much more severe than is the gender imbalance. Nonwhite scholars make up only 13% of total authorship. Theme wise, race-related articles constitute only 4% of the total. Nevertheless, quality scholarship centering race/ethnicity has accumulated during the past two decades. I use categories of textual analysis, audience research, and religious media to highlight important contributions.

Media Text

The bulk of textual analysis on race or ethnic minorities/cultures deals with media portrayals, especially those in the news media. The question of representation is at the heart of such studies. Some look at the visibility of racial/ethnic/religious groups in the news (Syed, 2008); others take issue with journalistic ideologies in framing minority stereotypes and "problems" (Ait Abdeslam, 2019; Døving, 2016; Tolz, 2017; Weng & Mansouri, 2021). Categories of race/ethnicity and religion are not always clearly distinguished as they are largely intertwined in some parts of the world, although some have called for decoupling between the two (Eisenlohr, 2011; Feddersen, 2015; Gueneli, 2014; Meer, 2008). A few works specifically analyze depictions of Islam in political cartoons amid the Muhammad caricatures controversy in the European press and elsewhere (Ata, 2010; Miera & Pala, 2009; Olsen, 2009). Aside from representation, researchers also discuss press coverage of social diversity (Meadows, 2014; Susanto et al., 2020). Shaari et al. (2006), for example, find that how stories are covered depends on which ethnic/religious group a newspaper serves, while Meer et al. (2010) discuss the increasing inclusion of Muslim voices in the British press.

Regarding popular and entertainment media, some research takes on Hollywood. Alaklook et al. (2016), for instance, investigate Arab characters in *Body of Lies* and argue that the sympathetic portrayal of Muslims as victims in the post-9/11 film does not necessarily reduce Western fear toward them. Rather, the depiction becomes a tool for a new Orientalism. Dalton (2019) similarly scrutinizes the benevolent racism toward Mexicans in Mormon director Jared Hess's films. Jones and Tajima (2015) alternatively explore the Caucasianization of Jesus in blockbuster movies. Beyond Hollywood, Lewis (2019) reports on the exclusion of Black and nonthin models in the Muslim fashion industry. Additionally, Banjo and Williams (2011) examine the Black/white racial divide within gospel music in terms of narrative message, and DeSanti (2015) analyzes depictions of the Native American Algonquian windigo (a type of "monster") in various media. Outside the US context, Baderoon (2009) employs a historical view, tracing images of Islam in South Africa's popular culture, while Reid (2015) looks at Celtic stereotypes reinforced in a Scottish sport-related comedy show.

As for digital texts, Harris and Steiner (2018) analyze how Trump-era white Christian rhetoric was amplified in social and traditional media, and Williams et al. (2020) focus on the link between online anti-Black and anti-Muslim rhetoric and offline hate crimes. Alternatively, Boustos (2015) takes a minority-centered approach, examining identity building and negotiating in Black online forums, while Latif (2021) explores the engagement of Muslim scholars with media and politics in contemporary America.

Audience Research and Institutional Media

In comparison to scholarship on gender, relatively less research has been produced on race/ethnicity that either utilizes audience research or is about religious media. Among the extremely limited literature on media users, a cross-cultural study by Croucher et al. (2010) concludes that an unclear correlation between religiosity and ethnic identity exists – a relationship that depends on location. In contrast, Rinnawi (2012) finds a positive link between Arab satellite media consumption and the formation of Arab nationalism in Germany. Clark and Hinzo's (2019) interesting research places emphasis on both the processes of mediatization and what they call indigenous "survivance" (survival/resistance). They explore how the use of media in Dakota Access Pipeline protests in the United States relates to the sacralization of land, spaces, and places within different cultural contexts.

Less than a handful of studies deal with religious media and race/ethnicity. Butler (2011) discusses media strategies and aesthetics used by Afro-Pentecostal evangelists, while Devir (2019) examines the use of the Internet to promote Judaism in Central Africa. Examining faith and ethnic dynamics, Eisenlohr (2011) argues that religious messages can play a key role in achieving pluralism in Mauritius. Apart from specifically religious media, additionally, a few studies look at the music industry, especially in relation to racial/ethnic empowerment and identity. Williams and Banjo (2018), for example, detail how the rapper Lecrae Moore challenges assumptions of Christian institutional whiteness in his musical mission of social justice. Walsh (2013) similarly considers biblical themes within rap lyrics, especially the testimony they bear to human resilience and value (see also Hatch, 2002; Lauricella & Alexander, 2012). Poirier (2018) identifies both the contact zone between Native and non-Native cultures that was created by Jim Pepper's "Witchi Tai To" as well as the ways in which this 1970s jazz hit resisted non-Native cooptation. Meanwhile, Harrison's (2005) fieldwork examines racial reconciliation and inclusion within the contemporary Christian music industry.

Intersectionality

In addition to single-axis approaches, scholars have also begun to utilize intersectional analysis, which focuses on multiple strands of diversity/marginality, and to suggest the need for more such studies (Weber, 2015). Some studies include elements of both race and gender, and a few contain sexuality as well. This final short section introduces intersectional works in the field of media and religion. In relation to journalistic representations, Moody-Ramirez and Dates (2014) take on gender, race, and religion in their analysis of media coverage of African Americans, especially the Obamas. On popular media, Branfman (2020) adds a racial/ethnic dimension and queer theory to feminist comedy theory when analyzing Jewish femininity in the *Broad City* TV show, and Warren (2002) deals with the portrayals of both gender and race in relation to authority in Christian videos for children. And for the digital media, Fangen (2020) looks at gendered stereotypes of Muslim men and women in Norwegian anti-Islamic Facebook groups.

Chen and Yorgason (2020) draw on earlier scholars of intersectionality when they distinguish between two varieties of intersectionality. The weaker form incorporates more than a single kind of diversity, but the conceptual discussion does not take the multiplied effect of being a double (or triple, etc.) minority into account; instead, it merely adds one more element to the analysis. Some of the studies mentioned here utilize this type of intersectional analysis. The stronger form of intersectionality more rigorously conceptualizes each type of diversity/ marginality and attempts to understand the simultaneous impact of multiple marginalities. Many audience studies reflect this type of intersectionality as they focus on ethnic/racial minority groups' expressions of their gender and religious identities that challenge hegemonic media narratives.

Employing Womanist analysis, Dickerson (2020), for example, documents how various social media platforms enabled Black communities to nourish themselves in the midst of mainstream media representations of Black pain throughout American history as a source of entertainment and pleasure. Similarly, Tounsel's (2018) exploration of social media narratives among Black Christian women helps this community to both redefine singleness and marriage and to perform their femininities (for additional valuable work on Black women, see also Lumpkins, 2010; Lumpkins et al., 2012). Waltrop's (2013) participatory ethnography illuminates young Muslim women's mediated lived experiences in negotiating the idea of moral goodness in Copenhagen. Regarding minority masculinity, while Dwyer et al. (2008) interview Muslim men on managing the intersection of gender, ethnicity, and class in British society, Barnes and Hollingsworth (2020) explore young Black Christian gay men's spirituality and online social support.

Conclusion and Implications

This chapter reviews, assesses, and organizes scholarly work focusing on gender, sexuality, and race/ethnicity issues in relation to religion and media/communication published over the past two decades in relation to themes of media text, audience research, and institutional media. Aside from articles addressing theoretical perspectives, this chapter located and utilized 142 pertinent empirical studies (including books). I take a glass-half-full perspective here and argue that although the number is relatively low, it includes much insightful scholarship that contributes to our understanding of how gender, sexuality, and race/ethnicity intersect with religion and media. However, a few striking imbalances exist in this body of literature. First, the bulk of empirical research focuses on Christianity and Islam. Among the 142 studies, over 61% (87) focus on Christianity and about 29% (41) are on Islam. There are only six articles on Judaism and eight on others, including three on Native American religions, two on Hinduism, one on Buddhism, one on Vodou, and one on witchcraft. Second, gender research outpaces race/ethnicity by over two times, about 74.2% (74 on gender and 28 on sexuality) and 34.5% (49), respectively, with some articles including more than one element. In terms of geography, studies on North America (mainly the United States) dominate at about 60% (85). Western Europe comes in a distant second with 15.5% (22). Among others, 10 articles are on Africa, 7 on the Middle East, 7 on Asia, 7 unspecific or on cyberspace, 5 on the Pacific and 2 on others. A couple of additional observations can be made about the geography of research: all studies on Asia pertain to South Asia (India, Malaysia, and Indonesia). Eastern Asia is surprisingly entirely absent. All but one study on the Pacific is about Australia. These numerical breakdowns provide insight on where the field has been and I hope they also direct attention to where future studies might go in order to rectify the imbalances.

Note

1 These journals are *Journal of Communication and Religion* (US based), *Journal of Media and Religion* (US based), *Journal of Religion and Popular Culture* (published by the University of Toronto in Canada), *Journal for Religion, Film and Media* (affiliated with the University of Graz and the University of Munich in Europe), *Journal of Religion, Media and Digital Culture* (US based, but affiliated with the International Society for Media, Religion and Culture), *Religion and Social Communication* (affiliated with the Asian Research Center for Religion and Social Communication in Bangkok, Thailand), *Journal of Religion in Africa* (published by Brill), and *African Communication Research* (published by Daystar University in Nairobi).

References

Abbott, J. Y. (2006). Religion and gender in the news: The case of Promise Keepers, feminists, and the "Stand in the Gap" rally. *Journal of Communication and Religion, 29*(2), 224–261.

AbdulRazak, S. (2017). Female resistance in the *Legend of Sigh. Journal of Religion and Popular Culture, 29*(3), 207–216. DOI:10.3138/jrpc.29.3.1367

Adamczyk, A., Kim, C., & Schmuhl, M. (2018). Newspaper presentations of homosexuality across nations: Examining differences by religion, economic development, and democracy. *Sociological Perspectives, 61*(3), 399–425. DOI:10.1177/0731121417724563

Ait Abdeslam, A. (2019). The representation of Islam and Muslims in French print media discourse: Le Monde and Le Figaro as case studies. *Journal of Muslim Minority Affairs, 39*(4), 569–581. DOI:10.1080/13602004.2019.1688514

Alaklook, H., Aziz, J., & Ahmad, F. (2016). Ambivalence and sympathy: New Orientalism and the Arab characters in Ridley Scott's *Body of Lies. e-BANGI Journal, 11*(2), 62–77.

Aly, A. (2009). Media hegemony, activism and identity: Muslim women representing Muslim women. In C. Ho, & T. Dreher (Eds.), *Beyond the hijab debates: New conversations on gender, race, and religion* (pp. 18–30). Cambridge Scholars Publishing.

Armanios, F., & Amstutz, A. (2013). Emerging Christian media in Egypt: Clerical authority and the visualization of women in Coptic video films. *International Journal of Middle East Studies, 45*(3), 513–533. DOI:10.1017/S0020743813000457

Ata, A. W. (2010). Entrapping Christian and Muslim Arabs in racial cartoons in Australia: The other anti-Semitism. *Journal of Muslim Minority Affairs, 30*(4), 457–462. DOI:10.1080/13602004.2010.533438

Baderoon, G. (2009). Regarding South African images of Islam: From the picturesque to Pagad and after. *South African Historical Journal, 61*(1), 103–120. DOI:10.1080/02582470902812244

Banjo, O. O., & Williams, K. M. (2011). A house divided? Christian music in black and white. *Journal of Media and Religion, 10*(3), 115–137. DOI:10.1080/15348423.2011.599640

Barnes, S. L., & Hollingsworth, C. (2020). Spirituality and social media: The search for support among black men who have sex with men in Tennessee. *Journal of Homosexuality, 67*(1), 79–103. DOI:10.1080/00918369.2018.1525945

Berger, H. A., & Ezzy, D. (2009). Mass media and religious identity: A case study of young witches. *Journal for the Scientific Study of Religion, 48*(3), 501–514. DOI:10.1111/j.1468-5906.2009.01462.x

Birzache, A. (2014). You cannot be in love with a word: Theologies of embodiment in Dreyer's "The Passion of Joan of Arc," Axel's "Babette's Feast" and von Trier's "Breaking the Waves". *Journal of Religion, Media and Digital Culture, 3*(1), 8–30. DOI:10.1163/21659214-90000039

Bochow, A., & van Dijk, R. (2012). Christian creations of new spaces of sexuality, reproduction, and relationships in Africa: Exploring faith and religious heterotopia. *Journal of Religion in Africa, 42*(4), 325–344. DOI:10.1163/15700666-12341235

Bompani, B., & Brown, S. T. (2015). A religious revolution? Print media, sexuality, and religious discourse in Uganda. *Journal of Eastern African Studies, 9*(1), 110–126. DOI:10.1080/17531055.2014.987507

Boustos, A. (2015). Religion in the Afrosphere. *Journal of Communication Inquiry*, *39*(4), 319–337. DOI:10.1177/0196859915608916

Boutros, A. (2013). *Lwa like me*: Gender, sexuality and Vodou online. In M. Lövheim (Ed.), *Media, religion and gender: Key issues and new challenges* (pp. 96–110). Routledge.

Branfman, J. (2020). "Plow him like a queen!": Jewish female masculinity, queer glamor, and racial commentary in *Broad City*. *Television & New Media*, *21*(8), 842–860. DOI:10.1177/1527476419855688

Briggs, S. (2009). "Elect Xena god": Religion remixed in a (post-)television culture. In D. H. Winston (Ed.), *Small screen, big picture: Television and lived religion* (pp. 173–199). Baylor University Press.

Brown, K. E. (2011). Muriel's wedding: News media representations of Europe's first female suicide terrorist. *European Journal of Cultural Studies*, *14*(6), 705–726. DOI:10.1177/1367549411419976

Burack, C. (2014). The politics of a praying nation: The presidential prayer team and Christian right sexual morality. *Journal of Religion and Popular Culture*, *26*(2), 215–229. DOI:10.3138/jrpc.26.2.215

Burke, K., & McDowell, A. (2012). Superstars and misfits: Two pop-trends in the gender culture of contemporary Evangelicalism. *Journal of Religion and Popular Culture*, *24*(1), 67–79. DOI:10.1353/rpc.2012.0010

Butler, A. (2011). Media, Pentecost and prosperity: The racial meaning behind the aesthetic message. *Pneuma: The Journal of the Society for Pentecostal Studies*, *33*(2), 271–276. DOI:10.1163/027209611X575050

Butler, A. D., & Winston, D. (2009). "A vagina ain't a halo": Gender and religion in *Saving Grace* and *Battlestar Galactica*. In D. Winston (Ed.), *Small screen, big picture: Television and lived religion* (pp. 259–286). Baylor University Press.

Cañas, S. (2008). The little mosque on the prairie: Examining (multi) cultural spaces of nation and religion. *Cultural Dynamics*, *20*(3), 195–211. DOI:10.1177/0921374008096309

Chapman, J. (2009). Tender warriors: Muscular Christians, Promise Keepers, and the crisis of masculinity in *Left Behind*. *Journal of Religion and Popular Culture*, *21*(3), 1–26. DOI:10.3138/jrpc.21.3.006

Chen, C. H. (2014). Diverse yet hegemonic: Expressions of motherhood in "I'm a Mormon" ads. *Journal of Media and Religion*, *13*(1), 31–47. DOI:10.1080/15348423.2014.871973

Chen, C. H., & Yorgason, E. (2020). Intersectionality. In A. Hoyt, & T. G. Petrey (Eds.), *The Routledge handbook of Mormonism and gender* (pp. 38–49). Routledge.

Chen, C. H., & Yorgason, E. (2022). Deficient progression: Charting diversity in major media and religious journals. *Journal of Media and Religion*, *21*(1), 18–37. DOI:10.1080/15348423.2021.2020494

Clanton, D. W. (2017). The origin(s) of Superman: Reimagining religion in the man of steel. In B. D. Forbes, & J. H. Mahan (Eds.), *Religion and popular culture in America* (3rd ed., pp. 33–50). University of California Press.

Clark, L. S., & Chiou, G. (2013). Feminist orientations in the methodologies of the media, religion, and culture field. In M. Lövheim (Ed.), *Media, religion and gender: Key issues and new challenges* (pp. 33–51). Routledge.

Clark, L. S., & Hinzo, A. (2019). Digital survivance: Mediatization and the sacred the tribal digital activism of the #NoDAPL movement. *Journal of Religion, Media and Digital Culture*, *8*(1), 76–104. DOI:10.1163/21659214-00801005

Croucher, S. M., Oommen, D., Borton, I., Anarbaeva, S., & Turner, J. (2010). The influence of religiosity and ethnic identification on media use among Muslims and non-Muslims in France and Britain. *Mass Communication and Society*, *13*(3), 314–334. DOI:10.1080/15205430903296085

Dalton, D. S. (2019). On (Dang) quesadillas and nachos: Mexican identity and a Mormon imaginary in the films of Jared Hess. *Journal for Religion, Film and Media*, *5*(2), 141–165. DOI:10.25364/05.052019.2.8

DeSanti, B. (2015). The cannibal talking head: The portrayal of the windigo "Monster" in popular culture and Ojibwe traditions. *Journal of Religion and Popular Culture*, *27*(3), 186–201. DOI:10.3138/jrpc.27.3.2938

Devir, N. P. (2019). The role of the Internet in the promulgation of Judaism and Jewish identity in Central Africa. *Journal of the Middle East & Africa*, *10*(1), 75–94. DOI:10.1080/21520844.2019.1565198

Dickerson, D. W. (2020). "Don't get weary": Using a womanist rhetorical imaginary to curate the Beloved Community in times of rhetorical emergency. *Journal of Communication and Religion*, *43*(3), 62–74.

Dines, G. (1995). Class, gender and race in North American media studies. *Race, Gender & Class*, *3*(1), 97–112. https://www.jstor.org/stable/41675349

Døving, C. A. (2016). Jews in the news: Representations of Judaism and the Jewish minority in the Norwegian contemporary press. *Journal of Media and Religion, 15*(1), 1–14. DOI:10.1080/15348423.2015.1131039

Du Mez, K. K. (2020). *Jesus and John Wayne: How white evangelicals corrupted a faith and fractured a nation.* Liveright.

Dwyer, C., Shah, B., & Sanghera, G. (2008). "From cricket lover to terror suspect": Challenging representations of young British Muslim men. *Gender, Place & Culture, 15*(2), 117–136. DOI:10.1080/09663690701863208

Eisenlohr, P. (2011). Religious media, devotional Islam, and the morality of ethnic pluralism in Mauritius. *World Development, 39*(2), 261–269. DOI:10.1016/j.worlddev.2009.11.026

Elsayed, H. (2016). A divine cosmopolitanism? Religion, media and imagination in a socially divided Cairo. *Media, Culture & Society, 38*(1), 48–63. DOI:10.1177/0163443715615413

Fangen, K. (2020). Gendered images of us and them in anti-Islamic Facebook groups. *Politics, Religion & Ideology, 21*(4), 451–468. DOI:10.1080/21567689.2020.1851872

Feddersen, A. (2015). Same but different: Muslims and foreigners in public media discourse. *Swiss Political Science Review, 21*(2), 287–301. DOI:10.1111/spsr.12158

Fenimore, J. (2012). Boys and their worship toys: Christian worship technology and gender politics. *Journal of Religion Media and Digital Culture, 1*(1), 1–24. DOI:10.1163/21659214-90000001

Frank, G. (2011). "Ideals of stability, order and fidelity": *The Love Dare* phenomenon, convergence culture, and the marriage movement. *Journal of Religion and Popular Culture, 23*(2), 118–138. DOI:10.3138/jrpc.23.2.118

Frykholm, A. J. (2005). The gender dynamics of the *Left Behind* series. In B. D. Forbes, & J. H. Mahan (Eds.), *Religion and popular culture in America* (revised ed., pp. 269–287). University of California Press.

Graham, E. (1999). Cyborgs or goddesses? Becoming divine in a cyber feminist age. *Information, Communication and Society, 2*(4), 419–438DOI:10.1080/136911899359484.

Gresaker, A. K. (2017). "If your life feels empty, perhaps it's time to find a partner?" Constructions of heterosexual coupledom and femininity through astrological advice in a Norwegian women's magazine. *Journal of Gender Studies, 26*(5), 517–531. DOI:10.1080/09589236.2016.1150159

Gueneli, B. (2014). Reframing Islam: The decoupling of ethnicity from religion in Turkish-German media. *Colloquia Germanica, 47*(1/2), 59–82. https://elibrary.narr.digital/content/pdf/99.125005/cg20141-20059.pdf

Harper, R. (2012). New frontiers: *Wild at Heart* and post-Promise Keeper evangelical manhood. *Journal of Religion and Popular Culture, 24*(1), 97–112. DOI:10.1353/rpc.2012.0014

Harris, T. M., & Steiner, R. J. (2018). Beyond the veil: A critique of white Christian rhetoric and racism in the age of Trump. *Journal of Communication and Religion, 41*(1), 33–45.

Harrison, M. F. (2005). "ERACE-ing" the color line: Racial reconciliation in the Christian music industry. *Journal of Media and Religion, 4*(1), 27–44. DOI:10.1207/s15328415jmr0401_3

Haskell, D. M. (2011). "What we have here is a failure to communicate": Same-sex marriage, evangelicals, and the Canadian news media. *Journal of Religion and Popular Culture, 23*(3), 311–329. DOI:10.3138/jrpc.23.3.311

Hatch, J. B. (2002). Rhetorical synthesis through a (rap)roachement of identities: Hip-hop and the gospel according to the Gospel Ganstaz. *Journal of Communication and Religion, 25*(2), 228–267.

Herbert, D. (2019). Religion and the dynamics of right wing populism in Poland: Impacts, causes, prospects. *Religion and Society in Central & Eastern Europe, 12*(1), 23–37. DOI:10.20413/rascee.2019.12.1.23-37

Hilton-Morrow, W. (2011). Between a rock and a slippery slope: Negotiating the intersections of religion and sexuality on network television's *The Book of Daniel. Journal of Homosexuality, 58*(3), 355–381. DOI:10.1080/00918369.2011.546732

Hinojosa Hernández, L. (2019). Discursive constructions of motherhood: A feminist analysis of social media discourses about motherhood, religion, and *19 Kids and Counting. Journal of Media and Religion, 18*(4), 134–147. DOI:10.1080/15348423.2019.1696117

Hobbs, V. (2015). Characterizations of feminism in reformed Christian online media. *Journal of Media and Religion, 14*(2), 211–229. DOI:10.1080/15348423.2015.1116267

Hoover, S. M. (2002a). The culturalist turn in scholarship on media and religion. *Journal of Media and Religion, 1*(1), 25–36. DOI:10.1207/S15328415JMR0101_4

Hoover, S. M. (2002b). Introduction: The cultural construction of religion in the media age. In S. M. Hoover, & L. C. Clark (Eds.), *Practicing religion in the age of the media: Explorations in media, religion, and culture* (pp. 1–6). Columbia University Press.

Hoover, S. M., & Coats, C. D. (2011). The media and male identities: Audience research in media, religion, and masculinities. *Journal of Communication, 61(5)*, 877–895. DOI:10.1111/j.1460-2466.2011.01583.x

Hoover, S. M., & Coats, C. D. (2015). *Does god make the man?: Media, religion and the crisis of masculinity.* New York University Press.

Hoover, S. M., & Venturelli, S. S. (1996). The category of the religious: The blindspot of contemporary media theory? *Critical Studies in Mass Communication, 13(3)*, 251–265. DOI:10.1080/15295039609366978

Höpflinger, A. (2015). Staging the dead: The material body as a medium for gender and religion. *Journal for Religion, Film and Media, 1(1)*, 57–62. DOI:10.25364/05.1:2015.1.6

House, C. A., & Johnson, A. E. (2018). Communication, religion, and race in America: 50 years later and where do we go from here? *Journal of Communication and Religion, 41(1)*, 5–7.

Ibrahim, Y. (2019). Visuality and the "Jihadi-bride": The re-fashioning of desire in the digital age. *Social Identities, 25(2)*, 186–206. DOI:10.1080/13504630.2017.1381836

Iwamura, J. N. (2017). The Oriental monk in American popular culture. In B. D. Forbes, & J. H. Mahan (Eds.), *Religion and popular culture in America* (third ed., pp. 51–70). University of California Press.

Johns, B. (2008). Hidden strategies of resistance in female Mormon missionary narratives: Two case studies. *Journal of Communication and Religion, 31(1)*, 54–81.

Jones, C., & Tajima, A. (2015). The caucasianization of Jesus: Hollywood transforming Christianity into a racially hierarchical discourse. *Journal of Religion and Popular Culture, 27(3)*, 202–219. DOI:10.3138/jrpc.27.3.3071

Kellner, D. (2011). Cultural studies, multiculturalism, and media culture. In G. Dines, & J. M. Humez (Eds.), *Gender, race, and class in media: A critical reader* (pp. 7–18). Sage Publications.

Klaus, E., & Kassel, S. (2005). The veil as a means of legitimization: An analysis of the interconnectedness of gender, media, and war. *Journalism, 6(3)*, 335–355. DOI:10.1177/1464884905054064

Kleman, E., Everett, M. K., & Egbert, N. (2009). Social support strategies among women of faith. *Journal of Communication and Religion, 32(1)*, 157–193.

Knight, J. S. (2005). Re-mythologizing the divine feminine in *The Da Vinci Code* and *The Secret Life of Bees*. In B. D. Forbes, & J. H. Mahan (Eds.), *Religion and popular culture in America* (revised ed., pp. 56–74). University of California Press.

Korteweg, A. C. (2008). The Sharia debate in Ontario: Gender, Islam, and representations of Muslim women's agency. *Gender and Society, 22(4)*, 434–454. DOI:10.1177/0891243208319768

Krishnan, U. (2017). Goddess of the nation: Semi-religious iconography in the digital age. *Religion and Social Communication,15(1)*,45–62.https://drive.google.com/file/d/0B_kygwa402xwNHJveG16TndQdWs/view?resourcekey=0-mOLAhakzl4ugukP_LpoB8w

Lampert-Weissig, L. (2011). A latter day Eve: Reading *Twilight* through *Paradise Lost*. *Journal of Religion and Popular Culture, 23(3)*, 330–341. https://doi.org/10.3138/jrpc.23.3.330.

Latif, J. (2021). Different strokes: American Muslim scholars engage media and politics in the woke era. *International Journal of Politics, Culture and Society, 35(3)*,1–28. DOI:10.1007/s10767-021-09406-7

Lauricella, S., & Alexander, M. (2012). Voice from Rikers: Spirituality in hip hop artist Lil' Wayne's prison blog. *Journal of Religion and Popular Culture, 24(1)*, 15–28. DOI:10.3138/jrpc.24.1.15

Lauricella, S., & Scott, H. M. (2018). Anatomy of a wedding: Examining religiosity, feminism, and weddings in *Grey's Anatomy*. *Journal for Religion, Film and Media, 4(2)*, 39–53. DOI:10.25364/05.42018.2.3

Lelwica, M. M. (2000). Losing their way to salvation: Women, weight loss, and the salvation myth in culture lite. In B. D. Forbes, & J. H. Mahan (Eds.), *Religion and popular culture in America* (pp. 180–200). University of California Press.

Lewis, R. (2019). Modest body politics: The commercial and ideological intersect of fat, black, and Muslim in the modest fashion market and media. *Fashion Theory, 23(2)*, 243–273. DOI:10.1080/1362704X.2019.1567063

Lodhia, S. (2014). "Stop importing weapons of family destruction!": Cyberdiscourses, patriarchal anxieties, and the men's backlash movement in India. *Violence Against Women, 20(8)*, 905–936. DOI:10.1177/1077801214546906

Lövheim, M. (2013a). Introduction: Gender – a blind spot in media, religion and culture? In M. Lövheim (Ed.), *Media, religion and gender: Key issues and new challenges* (pp. 1–14). Routledge.

Lövheim, M. (2013b). Media and religion through the lens of feminist and gender theory. In M. Lövheim (Ed.), *Media, religion and gender: Key issues and new challenges* (pp. 15–32). Routledge.

Lövheim, M. (2015). (Re)making a difference: Religion, mediatization and gender. *Journal for Religion, Film and Media, 1*(1), 45–56. DOI:10.25364/05.1:2015.1.5

Luisi, M. L. R., Luisi, T., & Bobkowski, P. S. (2018). "A very dangerous battleground": How abstinent Christian men select and navigate media in the presence of sexual media content. *Journal of Media and Religion, 17*(1), 1–11. DOI:10.1080/15348423.2018.1463706

Lumpkins, C. Y. (2010). Sacred symbols as a peripheral cue in health advertisements: An assessment of using religion to appeal to African American women about breast cancer screening. *Journal of Media and Religion, 19*(4), 181–201. DOI:10.1080/15348423.2010.521083

Lumpkins, C. Y., Cameron, G. T., & Frisby, C. (2012). Spreading the gospel of good health: Assessing ethnic and mass women's magazines as communication vehicles to combat health disparities among African Americans. *Journal of Media and Religion, 11*(2), 78–90. DOI:10.1080/15348423.2012.688664

MacDonald, M. (2006). Muslim women and the veil: Problems of image and voice in media representations. *Feminist Media Studies, 6*(1), 7–23. DOI:10.1080/14680770500471004

Maddux, K. (2008). Playing the victim: Violence, suffering, and feminine submission in *The Passion of the Christ. Journal of Media and Religion, 7*(3), 150–169. DOI:10.1080/15348420802223023

McLaughlin, E. L. (2012). Half the sky and the image of God: Stories to transform and save women's lives. *Journal of Communication and Religion, 35*(2), 147–171.

Meadows, L. (2014). Creating, sustaining, or dispelling misconceptions: Discourse analysis of mainstream print media's coverage of Obama's religious identity. *Journal of Media and Religion, 13*(3), 138–152. DOI :10.1080/15348423.2014.909192

Meer, N. (2008). The politics of voluntary and involuntary identities: Are Muslims in Britain an ethnic, racial or religious minority? *Patterns of Prejudice, 42*(1), 61–81. DOI:10.1080/00313220701805901

Meer, N., Dwyer, C., & Modood, T. (2010). Beyond "angry Muslims"? Reporting Muslim voices in the British press. *Journal of Media and Religion, 9*(4), 216–231. DOI:10.1080/15348423.2010.521090

Mesaros-Winckles, C. (2010). TLC and the fundamentalist family: A televised quiverfull of babies. *Journal of Religion and Popular Culture, 22*(3), 170–190. DOI:10.3138/jrpc.22.3.007

Michael, K. S. (2019). Wearing your heart on your sleeves: The surveillance of women's souls in evangelical Christian modesty culture. *Feminist Media Studies, 19*(8), 1129–1143. DOI:10.1080/14680777.2018.1490 915

Miera, F., & Pala, V. S. (2009). The construction of Islam as a public issue in western European countries through the prism of the Muhammad cartoons controversy. *Ethnicities, 9*(3), 383–408. DOI: 10.1177/1468796809337430

Moll, Y. (2007). "Beyond beards, scarves and halal meat": Mediated constructions of British Muslim identity. *Journal of Religion and Popular Culture, 15*(1). DOI:10.3138/jrpc.15.1.001

Moody-Ramirez, M., & Dates, J. (2014). *The Obamas and mass media: Race, gender, religion, and politics.* Palgrave Macmillan.

Moore, D. L. (2011). Constructing gender: Old wine in new media(skins). *Pneuma: The Journal of the Society for Pentecostal Studies, 33*(2), 254–270. DOI:10.1163/027209611X575041

Moore, E. E. (2010). Braveheart, sacred heart: Exploring resistance to patriarchal discourses in mainstream media and faith in the American spiritual marketplace. *Women's Studies Quarterly, 38*(3/4), 94–115. DOI:10.1353/wsq.2010.0004

Mosurinjohn, S. (2014). Popular journalism, religious morality, and the Canadian imaginary: Queers and immigrants as threats to the public sphere. *Journal of Religion and Popular Culture, 26*(2), 244–258. DOI:10.3138/jrpc.26.2.244

Neriya-Ben Shahar, R. (2017). The medium is the danger: Discourse about television among Amish and ultra-Orthodox (Haredi) women. *Journal of Media and Religion, 16*(1), 27–38. DOI:10.1080/15348423.2 017.1274590

Newell, S. (2005). Devotion and domesticity: The reconfiguration of gender in popular Christian pamphlets from Ghana and Nigeria. *Journal of Religion in Africa, 35*(3), 296–323. DOI:10.1163/1570066054782324

O'Riordan, K., & White, H. (2010). Virtual believers: Queer spiritual practice online. In K. Browne, S. R. Munt, & A. K. Yip (Eds.), *Queer spiritual space: Sexuality and sacred places* (pp. 199–230). Ashgate.

Obadare, E. (2015). Sex, citizenship and the state in Nigeria: Islam, Christianity and emergent struggles over intimacy. *Review of African Political Economy, 42*(143), 62–76. DOI:10.1080/03056244.2014.988699

Olsen, T. (2009). The Muhammad cartoons conflict and transnational activism. *Ethnicities, 9*(3), 409–426. DOI:10.1177/1468796809337432

Olson, L. J. (2017). Negotiating meaning through costume and social media in Bulgarian Muslims' communities of practice. *Nationalities Papers, 45*(4), 560–580. DOI:10.1080/00905992.2017.1303470

Paule, M. (2012). Girls, the divine and the prime time. *Feminist Theology, 20*(3), 200–217. DOI:10.1177/0966735012436914

Perry, S., & Snawder, K. (2016). Longitudinal effects of religious media on opposition to same-sex marriage. *Sexuality & Culture, 20*(4), 785–804. DOI:10.1007/s12119-016-9357-y

Petersen, L. N. (2013). Danish female fans negotiating romance and spirituality in *The Twilight Saga*. In M. Lövheim (Ed.), *Media, religion and gender: Key issues and new challenges* (pp. 82–95). Routledge.

Piela, A. (2013). Claiming religious authority: Muslim women and new media. In M. Lövheim (Ed.), *Media, religion and gender: Key issues and new challenges* (pp. 125–139). Routledge.

Pires, F., & Revelles-Benavente, B. (2020). Co-viewing a lesbian kiss between two elderly characters: Unveiling axes of oppression through the Brazilian telenovela Babilônia. *Poetics, 80*(June). DOI:10.1016/j.poetic.2019.101430

Poirier, L. (2018). Makes me feel glad that I'm not dead: Jim Pepper and the music of the Native American church. *Journal of Religion and Popular Culture, 30*(2), 120–130. DOI:10.3138/jrpc.2017-0003

Propp, W. H. C. (2013). Is *The Da Vinci Code* true? *Journal of Religion and Popular Culture, 25*(1), 34–48. DOI:10.3138/jrpc.25.1.34

Pype, K. (2012). *The making of the Pentecostal melodrama: Religion, media and gender in Kinshasa*. Berghahn.

Pype, K. (2016). Blackberry girls and Jesus's brides: Pentecostal-Charismatic Christianity and the (im-) moralization of urban femininities in contemporary Kinshasa. *Journal of Religion in Africa, 46*(4), 390–416. DOI:10.1163/15700666-12341106

Rahbari, L., Longman, C., & Coene, G. (2019). The female body as the bearer of national identity in Iran: A critical discourse analysis of the representation of women's bodies in official online outlets. *Gender, Place & Culture, 26*(10), 1417–1437. DOI:10.1080/0966369X.2018.1555147

Randhawa, S. (2019). The limits of pious families: Religion, family and the state in the women's pages of *Utusan Malaysia* (1987–98). *International Journal of Media & Cultural Politics, 15*(2), 231–238. DOI:10.1386/macp.15.2.231_7

Reid, I. A. (2015). Just a wind-up? Ethnicity, religion and prejudice in Scottish football-related comedy. *International Review for the Sociology of Sport, 50*(2), 227–245. DOI:10.1177/1012690213480140

Rhodes, C. D., & Stewart, C. O. (2016). Debating LGBT workplace protections in the bible belt: Social identities in legislative and media discourse. *Journal of Homosexuality, 63*(7), 904–924. DOI:10.1080/00918369.2015.1116341

Rifai, E. (2020). Digital waistlands: Pro-ana communities, religion, and embodiment. *Journal of Religion, Media and Digital Culture, 9*(2), 207–227. DOI:10.1163/21659214-BJA10018

Rinnawi, K. (2012). "Instant nationalism" and the "cyber mufti": The Arab diaspora in Europe and the transnational media. *Journal of Ethnic and Migration Studies, 38*(9), 1451–1467. DOI:10.1080/1369183X.2012.698215

Robinson, R. S. (2015). Sexuality, difference, and American hijabi bloggers. *Hawwa, 13*(3), 383–400. DOI:10.1163/15692086-12341289

Roos, L. (2010). Religion, sexuality and the image of the other in *300*. *Journal of Religion and Popular Culture, 22*(1), 1–24. DOI:10.3138/jrpc.22.1.001

Sawyer, A. S. (2020). Comfort the waste places, defend the violated earth: An ecofeminist reading of Isaiah 51: 1–52:6 and Tracy Chapman's song, "The Rape of the World". *Journal for Religion, Film, and Media, 6*(2), 21–33. DOI:10.25364/05.6:2020.2.2

Schippert, C. (2007). Saint Mychal: A virtual saint. *Journal of Media and Religion, 6*(2), 109–132. DOI:10.1080/15348420701357583

Schulz, D. (2012). Dis/embodying authority: Female radio "preachers" and the ambivalence of mass-mediated speech in Mali. *International Journal of Middle East Studies, 44*(1), 23–43. DOI:10.1017/S0020743811001231

Shaari, H., Ngu, T. H., & Raman, V. (2006). Coverage of race and religion: The Moorthy and Nyonya Tahir cases in four Malaysian newspapers. *Kajian Malaysia: Journal of Malaysian Studies, 24*(1/2), 185–201. http://web.usm.my/km/24-06/KM%20ART%2010.pdf

Shirazi, Q. (2014). Sahibqirani: An ideal of kingship and manhood in the romance of Amir Hamza. *Journal of Religion and Popular Culture, 26*(2), 187–201. DOI:10.3138/jrpc.26.2.187

Shoemaker, T. (2017). Escaping our shitty reality: Counterpublics, *Orange is the New Black*, and religion. *Journal of Religion and Popular Culture, 29*(3), 217–229. DOI:10.3138/jrpc.2016-0013.r2

Silverman, R. E. (2014). Jewish performativity on *Sex and the City*. *Journal of Religion and Popular Culture, 26*(2), 173–186. DOI:10.3138/jrpc.26.2.173

Sterk, H. M. (2010). Faith, feminism and scholarship: The *Journal of Communication and Religion*, 1999–2009. *Journal of Communication and Religion, 33*(2), 206–216.

Stokes, E., & Schewe, R. (2016). Framing from the pulpit: A content analysis of American conservative evangelical Protestant sermon rhetoric discussing LGBT couples and marriage. *Journal of Communication and Religion, 39*(3), 59–75.

Sumerau, J. E., Barringer, M. N., & Cragun, R. T. (2015). I don't need a shotgun, just a look: Representing manhood in secular and religious magazines. *Men and Masculinities, 18*(5), 581–604. DOI:10.1177/1097184X14564009

Susanto, E. H., Loisa, R., & Junaidi, A. (2020). Cyber media news coverage on diversity issues in Indonesia. *Journal of Human Behavior in the Social Environment, 30*(4), 510–524. DOI:10.1080/10911359.2019.1708525

Syed, J. (2008). The representation of cultural diversity in Urdu-language newspapers in Pakistan: A study of Jang and Nawaiwaqt. *South Asia: Journal of South Asian Studies, 31*(2), 317–347. DOI:10.1080/00856400802192937

Taylor, Y., Falconer, E., & Snowdon, R. (2014). Queer youth, Facebook and faith: Facebook methodologies and online identities. *New Media & Society, 16*(7), 1138–1153. DOI:10.1177/1461444814544000

Tolz, V. (2017). From a threatening "Muslim migrant" back to the conspiring "West": Race, religion, and nationhood on Russian television during Putin's third presidency. *Nationalities Papers, 45*(5), 742–757. DOI:10.1080/00905992.2017.1282449

Tounsel, T. N. (2018). #WaitingForBoaz: Expressions of romantic aspiration and black Christian femininities on social media. *Journal of Media and Religion, 17*(3/4), 91–105. DOI:10.1080/15348423.2019.1595843

Trammell, J. (2015). "Homosexuality is bad for me": An analysis of homosexual Christian testimonies in *Christianity Today* magazine. *Journal of Media and Religion, 14*(1), 1–15. DOI:10.1080/15348423.2014.971560

Tsuria, R. (2017). From sin to sick: Digital Judaism and pornography. *Journal of Media and Religion, 16*(4), 117–128. DOI:10.1080/15348423.2017.1401407

Tunç, A. (2012). Identities in-between: The impact of satellite broadcasting on Greek Orthodox minority (Rum Polites) women's perception of their identities in Turkey. *Ethnic and Racial Studies, 35*(5), 906–923. DOI:10.1080/01419870.2011.628032

Van den Brandt, N. (2019). Religion-in-the-making: Media, culture and art/activism as producing religion from the critical perspectives of gender and sexuality. *Journal of Religion, Media and Digital Culture, 8*(3), 408–426. DOI:10.1163/21659214-00803005

Vis, F. (2011). Media, religion and conflict/beyond the hijab debates: New conversations on gender, race and religion. *European Journal of Communication, 26*(2), 172–176. DOI:10.1177/0267323111026002054

Vis, F., van Zoonen, L., & Mihelj, S. (2011). Women responding to the anti-Islam film *Fitna*: Voices and acts of citizenship on YouTube. *Feminist Review, 97*, 110–129. DOI:10.1057/fr.2010.29

Walsh, C. (2013). Shout-outs to the creator: The use of biblical themes in rap lyrics. *Journal of Religion and Popular Culture, 25*(2), 230–248. DOI:10.3138/jrpc.25.2.230

Waltrop, K. (2013). Public/private negotiations in the media uses of young Muslim women in Copenhagen: Gendered social control and the technology-enabled moral laboratories of a multicultural city. *International Communication Gazette, 75*(5–6), 555–572. DOI:10.1177/1748048513491912

Warren, H. (2002). The Bible tells me so: Depictions of race, gender, and authority in children's videos. *Journal of Media and Religion, 1*(3), 167–179. DOI:10.1207/S15328415JMR0103_3

Weaver, J. (2011). Unpardonable sins: The mentally ill and evangelicalism in America. *Journal of Religion and Popular Culture, 23*(1), 65–81. DOI:10.3138/jrpc.23.1.65

Weber, B. M. (2015). Gender, race, religion, faith? Rethinking intersectionality in German feminisms. *European Journal of Women's Studies, 22*(1), 22–36. DOI:10.1177/1350506814552084

Weber, B. R. (2019). *Latter-day screens: Gender, sexuality, and mediated Mormonism.* Duke University Press.

Weng, E., & Mansouri, F. (2021). 'Swamped by Muslims' and facing an 'African gang' problem: Racialized and religious media representations in Australia. *Continuum: Journal of Media & Cultural Studies, 35*(3), 468–486. DOI:10.1080/10304312.2021.1888881DOI:D

Whitney, E. (2017). The sex that god can't see: Heteronormativity, whiteness, and the erasure of queer desire in popular media. *QED: A Journal in GLBTQ Worldmaking, 4*(2), 143–149. DOI:10.14321/qed.4.2.0143

Williams, K. M., & Banjo, O. O. (2018). Fight the power: Lecrae – a new evangelical archetype. *Journal of Communication and Religion, 41*(1), 61–76.

Williams, M., Burnap, P., Javed, A., Liu, H., & Ozalp, S. (2020). Hate in the machine: Anti-black and anti-Muslim social media posts as predictors of offline racially and religiously aggravated crime. *British Journal of Criminology, 60*(1), 93–117. DOI:10.1093/bjc/azz049

Wimmler, J. (2014). Masters of cyber-religion: The female body as God's "Interface" in the TV series *Caprica*. *Journal of Religion, Media and Digital Culture, 3*(1), 120–154. DOI:10.1163/21659214-90000043

Zainal, H. (2019). The irony of Islamization: Sexuality, piety and power on Malaysian screens. *Continuum: Journal of Media & Cultural Studies, 33*(1), 16–36. DOI:10.1080/10304312.2018.1536778

Selected Readings

Barr, B. A. (2021). *The making of biblical womanhood: How the subjugation of woman become gospel truth.* Barzos Press.

Chen, C. H., & Yorgason, E. (2022). Deficient progression: Charting diversity in major media and religious journals. *Journal of Media and Religion, 21*(1), 18–37. DOI:10.1080/15348423.2021.2020494

Cho, S., Crenshaw, K. W., & McCall, L. (2013). Toward a field of intersectionality studies: Theory, applications, and praxis. *Signs: Journal of Women in Culture and Society, 38*(4), 785–810. DOI:10.1086/669608

Clark, L. S., & Hinzo, A. (2019). Digital survivance: Mediatization and the sacred the tribal digital activism of the #NoDAPL movement. *Journal of Religion, Media and Digital Culture, 8*(1), 76–104. DOI:10.1163/21659214-00801005

Crenshaw, K. W. (1991). Mapping the margins: Intersectionality, identity politics, and violence against women of color. *Stanford Law Review, 43*(6), 1241–1299. DOI:10.2307/1229039

Dickerson, D. W. (2020). "Don't get weary": Using a womanist rhetorical imaginary to curate the Beloved Community in times of rhetorical emergency. *Journal of Communication and Religion, 43*(3), 62–74.

Du Mez, K. K. (2020). *Jesus and John Wayne: How white evangelicals corrupted a faith and fractured a nation.* Liveright.

28

Material Religion

Felicia Katz-Harris

People of all faiths and religions construct, use, respond to, or otherwise engage material in their religious experiences and practices of belief, whether that material is tangible or intangible, human-made, natural, or divinely gifted. It has even been suggested that "all religion is material religion" (Engelke, 2011, p. 209). Indeed, the significance of materiality to religion and to understanding what it communicates about religion, its practice, and the identity and lived experience of its participants cannot be overstated.

Material religion itself is as old and as ubiquitous as religion. Yet, its study is a relatively new field and turns in the humanities and social sciences have brought materiality into focus for religious studies in different ways. This chapter presents a general overview of the ways in which scholars have defined and discussed the concept of material religion, with examples of how it manifests in different religious traditions. It provides an account of historic shifts that influenced the development of theoretical leanings. This chapter also explores how material religion is recontextualized in public, secular spaces, such as museums, which are repositories and spaces for participation and exhibition.

A Material Lens for the Study of Religion

Material religion refers to the materiality of religion ("things" related to, or the "stuff" of religion) and the material study of religion. That is not to say that material religion is one or the other, but that these are two main ways that scholars use the term: as "things" themselves and as a field of study.

As a field of study, material religion explores ways that religion (or religious doctrine and belief) finds material form and expression. This includes how religious ideas and beliefs transform secular media into sacred entities. As interesting and as valid as these sorts of questions are for material religion, they have been critiqued as conventional (Houtman, 2020, p. 117). That is, focusing on objects' ideological expression (for example) limits or obscures what can be said about objects and their use, the role that objects play in religious life and in the world, the relationships people and nonhuman entities have with materiality, and even how materiality engenders creed (Meyer et al., 2005, p. 6; Meyer et al., 2010, p. 209; Morgan, 2017, p. 14; Plate, 2015, p. 4). As S. Brent Plate suggests, "ideas, beliefs, and doctrines begin in material reality," rejecting

The Handbook on Religion and Communication, First Edition. Edited by Yoel Cohen and Paul A. Soukup.

the notion that materiality merely exemplifies religious doctrine (Plate, 2015, p. 4). Others agree that "things, their use, their valuation, and their appeal are not something added to a religion, but rather inextricable from it" (Houtman & Meyer, 2012, p. 7; Meyer et al., 2010, p. 209).

Considering these arguments, stronger studies interrogate how "religion happens materially" in the everyday lives and in the lived, religious (or spiritual) experiences of its devotees (Houtman, 2020, p. 117; Houtman & Meyer, 2012, p. 7; Meyer et al., 2005, p. 6; 2010, p. 209). This is what Primiano called "vernacular religion" – religion as it is "practiced and perceived," expressed and lived in everyday life through "mental, verbal, and material expressions" (Primiano, 1995, p. 40; 2012, p. 384). Vernacular religion situates religion as a "tradition," which Glassie (1995) describes as a dynamic process that changes over time. Even after religion becomes evident, or materializes in expressive forms, its interpretation is still subject to change to meet people's needs or the needs of a given time or place (Primiano, 2012, p. 384).

Whereas scholars of religion have traditionally focused on religious text, scripture, and history (Hazard, 2013, p. 59; Primiano, 2012, p. 382), the current approach moves materiality from its previously marginal, incidental place in religious studies to the center. A growing number of material religion scholars are focused *not* on beliefs, doctrines, or texts but on how vernacular religion is experienced through relationships, knowledges, practices, and encounters with materiality (Engelke, 2011, p. 209; Flueckiger, 2017, p. 462; Hazard, 2013, pp. 63–64; Houtman, 2020, p. 118; Hutchings & McKenzie, 2018, p. 5; Morgan, 2010, p. 18; Pintchman & Dempsey, 2016, p. 2; Plate, 2015, pp. 3–4; Primiano, 2012, p. 384).

However, Webb Keane (2008, p. 230) cautions us from completely separating belief from material religion, noting that some religious traditions "privilege belief in their own self-understandings." He also asserts that studying the material form of belief is significant for understanding how religion happens materially, over time. That is, beliefs and other ideas have to be "exteriorized," or communicated in some material way in order to be recognizable and therefore able to be passed on from one person to another, or from generation to generation.

Nevertheless, for most scholars of material religion, materiality is not a mere aspect of religion. Some look at religion as a "category for analyzing materiality" (Chidester, 2000, p. 374). It is generally agreed that religion can be best understood by attending to what people do and say with and to the material things and spaces around them, and how these things and spaces construct experience, personal and group identity, and other religious realities (Harvey, 2012, pp. 208–209; Meyer et al., 2005, p. 5).

Material religion is inherently culturally and contextually specific. Lived experience is shaped and expressed in multiple ways. The nature of those lived experiences, including vernacular religion (which is less about belief and more about the way religion is lived out, practically, on a day-to-day basis) "depends on the particularities of time and place and the exigencies of tradition," among other conditions (Engelke, 2011, p. 212). Therefore, context is essential to knowing what something is, how it is considered or known, what it means to the people who make, use, value, worship, or tend it, and how those meanings might change over time. Analyzing "religiosity in historical and contemporary settings" and in other wide-ranging contexts are the specific strengths of, and part and parcel to ethnology and folklore (Primiano, 2012, p. 383). Whereas traditional religious studies have generally excluded these disciplines (p. 382), their focus on vernacular, emic, and culturally specific modes make them the very fields with which material religion naturally aligns.

It is always important to keep in mind that while different religious communities may share ontological and epistemological perspectives regarding their material religion, individuals may have unique opinions. Particular faith communities or communities of practice are heterogeneous, made up of people with distinct thoughts, emotions, priorities, beliefs, and forms of knowledge about, and relationships with, their material religion.

The way vernacular religion happens materially can be observed through what people do; how they use their body to perform and practice in certain places, and at certain times (Morgan, 2021, p. 77, 2010, p. 15; Plate, 2015, p. 3). As Meyer et al. (2010) suggest, "Practices are bodies, things, and places put to work, put on display, put into circulation, exchanged and hoarded, heard, smelled, fondled, destroyed" (p. 209). Performance theory emphasizes the "mode of presentation in social context," which illuminates nuances of belief and practices, their verbal and material expressions, the relationships between these, and the tendency toward transformation for individuals and groups of individuals (Primiano, 2012, p. 386). As an example, when people make offerings to ancestors, spirits, deities, or other entities, in addition to the act of providing and using material items (like food, flowers, candles), devotees engage the senses and use words, gestures, and intentional thought to enact belief (see Figures 28.1 and 28.2).

In Thailand, a vast array of spirits, including a category of nature spirits (*phii*), inhabit land, water, forests, and other natural elements. Phii hold positions of varying importance in a spiritual hierarchy and they demand devotion from the human world. The propitiation of spirits predates Buddhism in Thailand. While more orthodox Buddhist doctrine does not accept spirit worship, the complex dynamics of vernacular practice allow for the coexistence of spirit houses and Thai Buddhism today.

Building a home, shop, bar, hospital, or any other structure displaces these spirits. Providing them with attractive alternative housing, with appropriate gifts, keeps them appeased. Happy spirits return the goodwill by bringing prosperity and protection to the property, while neglected or unsatisfied spirits leave or turn away, allowing misfortune to befall the residents. How the specific spirits (or kinds of spirits) are tended, and the material forms engaged by the humans that tend them, vary by region, community, and personal traditions and preferences.

Spirit houses are generally for high-ranking guardian spirits such as the Deity of the Land (Phra Phoom Jao Ti), whose house is modeled after Thai Buddhist temples, and the Ancestor Spirits of the Land (also known as the Grandparent Spirits of the Land, Ta Yai), whose house is modeled after a Thai home. Their houses are typically set up, side by side, always outside, in a ritually designated spot. Spirit houses are consecrated by a Brahmin (spiritual priest) through a series of rituals that invite the spirits to live in the house, to be happy, to protect the residents, and to bring them blessings. Rituals involve mantras and offerings. These divine gifts include foods, beverages, and cigarettes for spirits' consumption; flowers that beautify their home;

Figure 28.1   Ritual master Ajarn Tawee Kam-wong Pin performing a spirit house consecration for a private home. Chang Mai Province, Thailand, 2014.

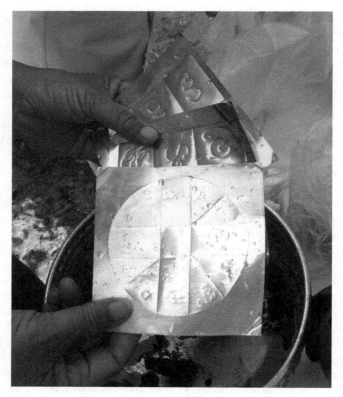

Figure 28.2   *Yant* (magic squares). Lanna culture. Chang Mai Province, Thailand, 2015. Tri-color metal foils. Gift of Ajarn Tawee Kam-wong Pin for future generations to learn about the magic of Lanna amulets and culture, Museum of International Folk Art (A.2015.70.1). Magical formulas are embossed on these metal foils for protection, blessings, and good fortune.

candlelight and incense to bring light and pleasant aromas; servant, animal, and dancer figures serve and entertain spirits; and *yant* (amuletic scripture in the form of magic squares) are embedded in the foundation upon which the spirit house is set. Daily rituals involve less elaborate rituals, but supplying fresh food and beverages, flowers, incense, and prayer is expected by the spirits. (Reichart & Khongkhunthian, 2007; personal research, 2014, 2015).

Concept and Definitions

A number of important volumes specifically on material religion emerged in the past 20 years and now form a recognized body of research. The literature offers a wide range of definitions because material religion crosses a number of academic fields, each with its own special interests. Be that as it may, Plate suggests a five-part scheme articulating his definition of material religion:

> material religion refers to (1) an investigation of the interactions between human bodies and physical objects, both natural and human-made; (2) with much of the interaction taking place through sense perception; (3) in special and specified spaces and times; (4) in order to orient, and sometimes disorient, communities and individuals; (5) toward the formal strictures and structures of religious traditions. (Plate, 2015, pp. 4–7)

Reflecting a growing interest in this subject matter, the journal *Material Religion* appeared in 2005. Rather than declaring an authoritative definition of what it is, the journal's editors articulate an interdisciplinary focus on material forms of religion, how those forms are put to use in religious practice, and their relationship to religious identity, experience, and practices of belief (Meyer et al., 2005, p. 5). A casual reading of a few issues demonstrates the vast range of material, ideas, and approaches scholars take to analyzing material religion.

Materiality

On the surface, materiality implies physical properties, but scholars generally agree that materiality is not limited to objects and images. For example, things like "actions and words" are also material, "no matter how quickly they pass from sight or sound or dissipate into the air" (Engelke, 2011, p. 209). In defining materiality, Daniel Miller (2005) begins with its colloquial use to mean "artifact," a human-made object, but suggests that thinking about materiality as an artifact is a "vulgar" and "mundane" use of the term. He necessarily expands on the definition because materiality also includes "the ephemeral, the imaginary, the biological, and the theoretical," which are not necessarily tangible, dimensional artifacts (pp. 3–4). From here, we might say that material religion is the materiality of spiritual life, meaning how people experience material in their spiritual-social lives.

Tilley et al. (2006) explain that there cannot be universal definitions for something like materiality because it comprises multiple, context-specific ideas (p. 4). Materiality, they say, includes things made by nature, things made by humans, and things made with particular media that constitute other things or components of things. They conceptualize materiality in terms of relationships that can be between things and the ideas, emotions, experiences, identities, and bodies of people(s) and/or other subjects. These relationships may reflect histories and heritage, traditions, cosmologies, ontologies, epistemologies, value systems, and how things circulate (exchange and consumption) on local and global scales (p. 4).

Ideas about materiality are potentially ways to think about how religion happens and becomes tangible in the world (Houtman & Meyer, 2012, p. 2), in the way that "religious thought and practice are variously engaged in material practices and artifacts" (Morgan, 2021, p. 77). Engelke (2011) explains that materiality is the stuff through which "the religious" is manifest and gets defined in the first place (p. 213). So, how a deity, ancestor, or spirit may be recognized or is known to be present can "materialize" through an object or image, but also through the senses.

Consider as an example the rice goddess, Dewi Sri, as she is known in Bali and other areas of Indonesia (see Figure 28.3). There are probably more shrines dedicated to Dewi Sri in Bali than any other deity (Reichle et al., 2010, p. 13), material evidence of her esteemed status. Rice is life and a divine gift from Dewi Sri, who is attended through ritual. How she takes shape and is known to be present varies by stages of rice cultivation. As rice grows and its flowers open for pollination, Dewi Sri is carried by the wind and enters the rice plant as sunlight. Her presence is known to people by the robust, intangible, dissipating scent of the flowers. Sometimes Dewi Sri is more visible, such as when (after flowering) panicles appear and the swelling of the stem is a visual sign that she is in the rice plant (Ottino, 2000, p. 71). Doll-like figures (*cili*) are made by hand, woven from palm leaves, and decorated with a variety of synthetic and natural elements. At some stages of rice production, cili are a potential receptacle for Dewi Sri; at other times the cili *are* Dewi Sri. The figure is also considered an offering in the field and on household shrines. Cili are meant to be ephemeral but they are also commonly preserved in museum collections.

Figure 28.3   Cili. Bali, Indonesia. c. 1958. Artist unknown. Dried palm leaf, cotton thread, ink. Gift of the Girard Foundation Collection, Museum of International Folk Art (A.1981.28. 895).

Sometimes Dewi Sri is present via her embodiment of handmade, physical objects, and sometimes she is known to be present through the senses like smell and sight.

Ritual

Ritual is among a number of key terms in material religion (Plate, 2015). In defining ritual, several factors are at play: materiality, sensory experience, bodily performance, transformation, and affect. For example, religious and ritual experiences are often "transacted through embodied encounters with the material world," and the materiality of ritual is usually accompanied by multi-modal sensory dynamics (Kendall et al., 2013, p. 68). In considering what rituals and ritualized activities are and what they do, not only sacred but also mundane activities are ritualized through flexible and strategic processes, including performance: the multi-modal, sensory, deliberate, self-conscious enactment of highly symbolic actions (Moore and Myerhoff, 1977; Bell, 1997). Certain feelings complement understandings of ritual. According to Durkheim, rituals deliberately stimulate passion, feelings of "collective effervescence," in which individuals experience affective responses that connect them to a larger social group (Durkheim, 1995). Durkheim's idea of collective effervescence, his rooting of religion in "the real," the sacred as something social, and his focus on ritual action over belief resonate with studies of material religion and many successive theories reverberate from his work (Durkheim, 1995). For example, Victor Turner's (Turner, 1977) writings on "liminality and communitas" draw upon Durkheim's collective effervescence, while more recent work closely examines the role of affect in ritual process and transformation (Kratz, 2010). Further, ritual is dynamic, an ongoing performative discourse with practices that are continually reinterpreted or renovated according to the context of place and/or the changing needs of its practitioners, needs that might depend on sociocultural, sociopolitical or economic conditions (Schnell, 1999, p. 4; Primiano, 2012. This explains how certain rituals maintain relevance over time.

Turning back to Plate's reference to ritual as a key term, rituals are an example of material religion and they involve religious materiality. They can occur outside religious settings, in secular spaces. For example, in museums, rituals can be publicly performed and formally staged. Religious dance, songs, and ceremonial acts are commonly produced for diverse audiences as part of public programming (discussed further in the text that follows). Museums, communities, and governments may perform repatriation rituals when sacred objects are returned to source communities. Smaller-scale religious rituals of care may occur in more private settings, like collection storage rooms, performed by source communities for sacred images or special material that they may know as sentient beings. For example, delegations of Native American communities make visits to museum collections to feed certain artifacts or to ritualize pest management practices by smudging or using botanical treatments (Rosoff, 2003). Of course, there are a whole range of such ritual possibilities.

Subject–Object Agency in Material Religion

Disrupting the notion that subjects and objects are distinct emphasizes the object-like qualities of humans, and the ways that objects take on characteristics that define human agency (Keane, 2006, p. 200). Moreover, that living beings, spirits, or other entities inhabit objects or are infused into their production, or that those objects are entities in and of themselves, acknowledges the co-constitutive nature of humans and things and that "humans, nonhumans, nature, culture, subjects, objects [...] exist on a single plane of being" (Hazard, 2013, p. 65).

Morgan (2021) explains that material religion is, in part, the study of agency, or how things act on one another (p. 6), and the ways that people imbue the material world with agency that in turn enables them (p. 7). To borrow his example, "we use tools to do things which transforms the user into a creator or builder. It is an agent that does things [and makes us become things] we could not do by ourselves" (p. 7). Bruno Latour's Actor–Network Theory (ANT), holds that nonhuman actors, "things," have the capacity to act and participate in social networks, in human–nonhuman assemblages, "tangles of heterogeneous things, and hybrid formations" (Bräunlein, 2016, pp. 378 referencing Deleuze & Guattari, 1987), and that objects, themselves, are fully agentive (Hicks & Beaudry, 2010, p. 9).

A special category of material religion embodies animated, agentive properties that elevate their status above a mere "object." They are known by their originating communities to embody a presence and/or they may be known *as* living beings. This may or may not be a divine, sacred presence and an object's status as animate is not unchanging. Laurel Kendall (2008) demonstrates that in places like Vietnam and Korea, an object can be imbued with or released from an animating presence through ritual performance. But rituals can fail, and deities have their own agency to inhabit or vacate objects (Kendall & Yang, 2015). Therefore, according to the sensibilities of various communities of practice, religiously animated objects do not necessarily fall within the dichotomy of sacred or not sacred.

Likewise, secular objects can also be animate because certain materials come from a "living earth" or because the objects have special relationships with the people who made and used them, or relationships with other powerful objects and/or experiences (Hays-Gilpin & Lomatewama, 2013, p. 268). When considering animacy in Hopi pottery, "potters identify the prosodic language of voice and embodied language of blush (the beauty of agency)" as evidence of the living, emotive nature of the pot (McChesney & Charley, 2011, p. 25). So, while a secular pot itself is not necessarily within the realm of how we typically think of material religion, sacred or agentive objects, its materiality is exactly that.

Historic Developments and Approaches in Material Religion

Just as meaning is subjective for, and communicates something about those who make, use, worship, tend, and otherwise consume material religion, the study of it and the questions we ask are subjective from, and communicate something about the perspectives, motivations, personal background, and colonial heritage of the scholar. Related to this is how material religion studies today intersect with a number of turns in the social sciences, humanities, and beyond. Situating material religion against its historical disciplinary backdrop helps to clarify its motivation and importance in religious studies.

Enlightenment and Colonial Legacies

Scholars of material religion commonly qualify its intellectual genealogy within religious studies as profoundly shaped by Christian, particularly Protestant, ideology. As such, scholarship has long placed an emphasis on religious dogma, textual genre, doctrine, and belief as opposed to vernacular practice and materiality. In addition, deep-seated biases toward the seeming "immateriality" of Euro-American Judeo-Christian religions and against the supposed "materiality" of Indigenous, Hindu–Buddhist, and other non-Judeo-Christian religions have roots in Enlightenment-period, Cartesian dualisms that influenced the historic devaluation of material studies in religion by scholars, missionaries, and laypeople, and continue to perpetuate religious, economic, and colonialist interests (Bräunlein, 2016, p. 383; Hazard, 2013, p. 58; Houtman & Meyer, 2012; Pintchman & Dempsey, 2016, p. 1; McDannell, 1995, pp. 2–7; Morgan, 2021, pp. 27–30).

   Furthermore, in the fifteenth to sixteenth centuries, European explorers, travelers, traders, and scientists amassed vast collections of objects, including sacred, religious material from distant, "exotic" places. "Cabinets of curiosity" and "royal cabinets" were employed to organize, study, and show off these assemblages to communicate collectors' scholarship, wealth, clout, and more generally to convey Euro-Christian "progress" and intellectual and religious superiority over those from whom they collected (Abt, 2006; Ames, 1992; Kreps, 2020; Pearce, 1993; van Hout, 2017). The European Enlightenment period (seventeenth to eighteenth centuries) is marked by revolts against absolute, royal and religious authority and subjugation, resulting in a widespread, radical shift away from religious orthodoxy and toward rationalism, science, and ideals of liberalism: freedoms, rights, and equality. However, in the name of science and liberty, the Enlightenment period advanced the Age of Empire with its traumatic violence of slavery and colonialism: materialist projects with exploitative, capitalist motives for people and products, as well as the rejection of Indigenous spirituality and religion (Abt, 2006, pp. 285–88; Ames, 1992, pp. 16–17; Gray, 2007; Hobsbawm, 1989; Horning, 2021, p. 2; Pearce, 1993).

   The "cabinets" largely became the collections of later museums (examples include the Louvre Museum in Paris and the British Museum in London). US museums (such as the American Museum of Natural History in New York) have similar histories. In fact, the study of material religion is an outgrowth of material culture studies, which developed simultaneously with the discipline of anthropology, within US natural history museums (Basu, 2020; Bräunlein, 2016, p. 368; Conn, 1998; Geismar, 2011; Redman, 2016; Shelton, 2006). Early anthropologists collected (sometimes stole) massive amounts of material to build museum collections while conducting ethnographic research. Items extracted from their original contexts, or from gravesites, include skeletal remains, natural specimens, crafted objects, and sacred objects (Jacknis, 1996). Generally, this period of "salvage ethnography" (late nineteenth to twentieth centuries) established important museum collections (Basu, 2020, p. 371; Jacknis, 1996), while at the same time witnessed a "profound hemorrhaging of cultural, linguistic, social, and economic structures and systems," from Indigenous communities (Field, 2008, p. 20).

These dark histories were the impetus for US Native American Graves Protection and Repatriation Act legislation in the 1990s, and international repatriation and restitution efforts that are occurring around the world today in contemporary decolonial projects.

The Postmodern Crisis

Following World War II and the end of European colonialism in Asia, the Pacific, and Africa, postcolonial studies began to take up issues left in its wake. One important critique, Edward Said's canonical *Orientalism* (1978), exposed racist attitudes and colonialist perspectives propagated by academic cultural studies in the way it represented people in Asia and the Middle East, particularly in discussions of religion (Wang, 2018, p. 61). Postcolonial critique generally led to the "postmodern crisis" of the 1980s, a reckoning with the far-reaching, negative impact of the Enlightenment enterprise and colonialism. Scholars interrogated scientific methods and positivist claims to knowledge that displaced other forms of knowledge and justified racism and cultural violence. It became widely acknowledged that Euro-American values and "ethical stance" are "constituted in specific historical relations of dominance" and that we are hindered by "colonial modes of representation" (Clifford, 1983, p. 119). This applies to how Indigenous religions and material expressions were understood and treated.

This postmodern crisis of representation and Enlightenment thought galvanized major paradigm shifts from positivist to more ontological approaches across the disciplines. Postmodernist methods remain guiding principles for much of the social sciences and humanities: collaboration; shared authority; multiple interpretations; privileging Indigenous voice; and critical theory and reflexivity as a central aspects of these engagements. These approaches aim to lessen hegemonic processes and power relationships that exist in research and representations of people and religion and recognize and acknowledge historic and ongoing injustices, especially related to colonialism that exist in so many aspects of our lives (Ames, 1992; Clifford, 1988; Harvey, 1990, p. 41, pp. 39–65; Hicks, 2010, p. 27; Tuhiwai Smith 2012; Lonetree, 2012).

Out of postmodernism, a number of turns developed in contemporary approaches, seeking ways to address the problems and challenges that still vex us. The next sections review a few of these in relation to material religion.

The Material Turn and New Materialism

Material culture studies lost popular favor in ethnology (with some exceptions) as functionalism and structural functionalism took center stage (Basu, 2020, p. 373; Bauer, 2019, p. 337; Geismar, 2011; Tilley et al., 2006). It eventually made a comeback as the material turn.

While earlier material culture studies usually examined physical aspects of material objects, commodity exchange, symbolism, functions, and so forth, the material turn (or new materialism) takes a more object/artifact-oriented approach. Material religion took shape within this framework, perhaps beginning with Colleen McDannell's "Material Christianity" (Horning, 2021, p. 13; Hicks, 2010, p. 26; Bräunlein, 2016, p. 368; McDannell, 1995).

Applying material culture studies to the study of religion, McDannell (1995) wrote that people practice religion (as a pianist would practice piano) and through that practice (through "doing, seeing, and touching"), people learn religious language. She writes that "Experiencing the physical dimension of religion helps *bring about* religious values, norms, behaviors, and attitudes" (p. 2, author's emphasis). She places ways of thinking in the body of doing. Her analysis looks for ways the material deciphered meanings about religious life in America and how faith is communicated, expressed, lived, and perpetuated over time.

As religious studies turned to more ethnographic methods, religion scholars moved into the lived worlds that people inhabit to better consider the perspectives of communities of practice. Rather than viewing religion strictly as discourse about ideology, textual analysis, and morality (which remains important), there was a growing interest in the vernacular: physical, sensory, and visual phenomena; materiality. Looking at how religion happens materially, the places where it happens, and what counts as religion, greater attention was given to religious and ritual objects, their social circulation, use in practice and performance, how they are perceived, and what they communicate. In this way, material religion widened understandings of human religion (Meyer et al., 2010; Morgan, 2017; The Editors, 2009). McDannell (1995) insists that "objects are not merely interesting forms to be described and collected. The material world [...] is not neutral and passive; people interact with the material world thus permitting it to communicate specific messages" (p. 2).

Arjun Appadurai's *The Social Life of Things* (1986) proposed the idea that objects, like people, have social lives and that by following objects and tracing their stories, we can learn how their meanings and values are transformed through their circulation and changing social contexts. This work birthed a whole area of studies that focused on "things in motion" (Appadurai, 1986; Bauer, 2019; Forshee, 2002; Hazard, 2013; Horning, 2021; Hoskins, 1998; Joyce & Gillespie, 2015; Kendall, 2008; Kopytoff, 1986; Myers, 2001). While Appadurai's idea that things have social lives was incredibly influential when it came out, more recent turns in social theory address more nuanced entanglements, reframing his ideas toward object biographies, sacred–social lives, object itineraries, actor–networks, new materialism, and so forth (Appadurai, 1986; Bauer, 2019; Forshee, 2002; Hazard, 2013; Horning, 2021; Hoskins, 1998; Kendall, 2008; Kopytoff, 1986; Myers, 2001).

One criticism of Appadurai tackles his argument that inanimate things "have no meanings apart from those that human transactions, attributions, and motivations endow them with" (Appadurai, 1986, p. 5; as quoted in Hazard, 2013, p. 60). Sonia Hazard (2013) reasons that this "symbolic analysis" only asks what things communicate to us about human subjects. As such, it is an anthropocentric approach, flawed in its centering of humans because it risks losing sight of "the various activities of things beyond the horizons of human sense or knowing" (p. 59). Anthropocentrism is a common criticism of the dominant approaches to material religion in their privileging of the human perspective in material analysis. Instead, Hazard advocates for "New Materialism" (p. 60), a move away from anthropocentrism and toward analyses that focus on materiality and the agentive nature of objects. New materialism rejects Cartesian dualisms that divide subjects and objects, humans and nonhumans, mind and matter. Rather, these aspects co-constitute each other (Hazard, 2013, pp. 60, 66; Horning, 2021, p. 14; Bräunlein, 2016, p. 379; Chidester, 2000, p. 374). New materialism rethinks subject–object relationships through "assemblage" which may comprise human and nonhuman subjects and objects. (Bräunlein, 2016, p. 379).

The Ontological Turn

The ontological turn is a study of reality that is not limited to the human world. It postulates that nonhuman beings have realities, and that their perspectives must be taken seriously. Whereas belief and worldview are often discussed as being dependent on cultural context, or on particular religious orientations, proponents of the ontological turn argue that people do not have different cultural or religious "beliefs" but different "realities"; they experience entirely different worlds. The ontological approach rejects the notion of "one world, many worldviews" in favor of accepting "multiple worlds" (Bräunlein, 2016, p. 377). Eduardo Kohn (2015) describes the turn as "a response to a conceptual, existential, ethical, and political problem – how to think about human life in a world in which a kind of life and future that is both beyond the human and constitutive of the human is now in jeopardy" (p. 315). John Kelly (2014) likens the ontological turn to its predecessor, the "epistemological turn" (related to the postmodern crisis), dominated by postcolonial approaches, with particular emphasis on reflexive contemplation (p. 264). It acknowledges alternate ways of knowing, perceiving, and representing unique truths.

The ontological turn has been hotly debated over the years, with the main critiques being that it is essentialist, radically relativist, and structuralist. It denies unique cultural and historical trajectories and relationships of power. Further, its focus on alterity only otherizes people and paints a false picture of cultural homogeneity (Bessire & Bond, 2014; Ramos, 2012). Despite these shortcomings, the idea of alternate realities elevates the notion of belief from subjective ideas or opinions to real experiences. As Peter Bräunlein (2016) points out, plurality of ontologies is not necessarily relativist if it is considered in terms of 'perspectivism' (p. 377, referencing Viveiros de Castro, 2012). Acknowledging difference in this way can validate the experiences and perspectives of others (both human and nonhuman beings). Indigenous and vernacular expressions of alternative ontologies and epistemologies, particularly around materiality, must be taken seriously if we (as scholars) are to engage with diverse communities with sincerity, let alone to attempt to understand the experiences of our interlocutors. In terms of material religion, some things are recognized to have their own agency; attending to this gives legs to artifact-oriented studies beyond traditional material culture analyses (Harvey, 2012, p. 208, referencing Henare et al., 2007, p. 1).

Material Religion and Museums

Most museums exhibit or otherwise have some objects or larger collections related to religion in their holdings, whether that includes ritual material, manuscripts, amulets, images, effigies, or objects known by their devotees as deities. When museum exhibitions, collections storage and care, and educational programming involve material religion, or material related to religion, it becomes clear how museums are important sites of religious performance, understanding, and dissemination of religion (Paine, 2012). Thus, museums are a significant topic for material religion.

A host of others have written on the important, deeply entangled history of museums and colonialism and imperialism. Because of their work, museums have been confronting and acknowledging their pasts, and radically altering praxis. Examples of how museums are changing to be more sensitive, inclusive, and decolonial include collaborations (in exhibition development, collections care, and programs), sharing collections, sharing authority, and repatriating cultural patrimony.

But what about material religion, specifically? While material religion includes intangible material and lived experience, for many religious systems, physical objects themselves remain central to religious activity (Sullivan, 2015, p. 1). As material objects endure spatially and temporally, and are appreciated and owned by people outside the source community, they they may be interpreted differently in varied contexts (Keane, 2008, p. 230). So, a sacred object can also be an exalted work of art; an educational tool used to teach about different cultures, traditions, and worldviews; and a symbol of world heritage to be preserved for human posterity (Paine, 2013). It can also be all of these things at the same time. This is how museums come to collect, use, interpret, and present their "assemblages."

Using the frame of ritual described earlier and as one of the "Key Terms in Material Religion" (Plate, 2015), the following section presents an example of how religion happens, materially in museums.

Rituals and Museum Exhibitions

"Sacred Realm: Blessings & Good Fortune across Asia" was an exhibition at the Museum of International Folk Art (MOIFA), Santa Fe, NM, United States, about material religion. It explored the diverse ways that materiality works to communicate with the sacred realm. The exhibition demonstrated ways that people employ amulets and talismans, divine communication (variations of prayer practice), and ritual performance to achieve blessings and good fortune for themselves, their loved ones, and their communities.

Any exhibition about a region as diverse as Asia, or about religion, is automatically complex and multicultural. By their very nature museums remove objects from their original context. Limited by space, conservation issues, and other factors, museums recontextualize sacred items for public audiences. They are not displayed or used in the same way they would be in their intended context. To address these issues, the museum collaborated with local and international communities to select, research, interpret, and display sacred and ritual objects. (To give the reader an idea of the scope of this work, collaborators and consultants included: from New Mexico, three Jewish rabbis from different congregations, the Imam and other members of the New Mexico Islamic Cultural Center, the Hindu Temple Society of Albuquerque, monks from Wat Buddhamongkolnimit (a Therevada Buddhist temple in Albuquerque), and members from the local Tibetan community (Tibetan Association of Santa Fe); from international locations, a Tibetan Rinpoche from the Drepung Loseling Monastery (India), a Balinese Hindu Brahmin (who is also a master maskmaker), an Iban artist from Sarawak, magical masters, spirit mediums, and Buddhist monks in Thailand, community members, gallerists, and friends in Thailand and Vietnam, and scholars of Islam, Hinduism, Yao shamanism, religious studies, anthropology, visual culture, and Asian and Middle Eastern amulets.)

As the exhibition curator, I reached out to Wat Buddhamongkolnimit, a local Therevada Buddhist temple in Albuquerque, New Mexico, to discuss the exhibition with some of the resident monks, conduct interviews and learn about their practice, and ask for their opinions and wishes for exhibition topics involving Therevada Buddhism. Three of the temple's monks attended the opening and, feeling inspired by the exhibition's content, they asked if they could perform a blessing for the exhibition's success and for the well-being of visitors.

Howard Morphy (2006) writes that museums engage in "processes of value creation" through collecting, preserving, interpreting, and displaying objects, and that through collaborative projects and cultural performances, Indigenous people influence those processes (p. 471). Like collections and exhibitions, cultural performances in museums have a problematic history, and have been critiqued as decontextualized, inauthentic, culturally appropriated, and a means to perform and exoticize difference (p. 474). However, Morphy reminds us that we need to recognize

Indigenous agency and respect cultural performers' decisions to participate in these processes of value creation. Through these processes, "museums become sites of persuasion which people attempt to use to get their version of history, and their regime of value acknowledged and disseminated to wider audiences" (pp. 471–472; see also Myers, 2001, p. 6) (see Figure 28.4). Through performing rituals for outsiders, cultural performers can engage those outside their community and/or persuade them to recognize their cultural value (Morphy, 2006, pp. 479, 480).

Particularly with regard to agency, and with respect to the fact that the religious artifacts on display inspired the monks to respond with ritual performance, MOIFA gladly obliged the monks' desire to bless the exhibition. The gallery was designed for clockwise visitor traffic flow, and the monks began circumambulating the exhibition, clockwise, in the fashion they would walk around a temple. They did not wait for introductions: their intention was to bless the space, not necessarily to receive the pomp and circumstance given by museum visitors. However, the sound of their chanting reverberated around the gallery, their bodies moving together in unison around the space, and their gold-colored robes set them apart from the crowd, identified their cultural and religious affiliation, and communicated their material and performative religious practice. Hundreds of visitors quieted, and many silently followed them around the exhibition space. After several circulations, the monks sat in the exhibition lobby, each in prayer-mudra posture, and chanted mantras (see Figure 28.5). Because the blessing was not on the agenda of the exhibition's opening program, the audience and museum staff were somewhat disoriented.

Figure 28.4   Monks from the Drepung Loseling Monastery, India, on tour with the Mystical Arts of Tibet program create *dul-tson-kyil-khor* (mandala of colored powders, or sand) as a public ritual performance, in conjunction with the exhibition, *Sacred Realm: Blessings and Good Fortune* at the Museum of International Folk Art, Santa Fe, August 13, 2016. After a week of focused production, the monks brush away the sand mandala and cast it to a body of water. Promotional materials state that the monks share their cultural traditions through art and performance to contribute to world peace and to create greater awareness of the Tibetan situation. In this way, through material religion, even as ephemeral as a sand mandala, the museum becomes a "site of persuasion," a place for Tibetan monks living in exile (in south India) to participate in "processes of value creation" where they can perform their identity and where their sociopolitical situation is seen and recognized (Morphy, 2006).

Figure 28.5   Therevada Buddhist monks from Wat Buddhamongkolnimit, Albuquerque, New Mexico, blessing an exhibition at the Museum of International Folk Art in Santa Fe, February 28, 2016.

Visitors questioned one another; some watched; some participated. When the monks finished their recitations, they thanked us and then they left. Visitors slowly dispersed, clearly in that liminal state. People, strangers to one another when they came in, were talking about their shared experience and feelings of communitas as the crowd dispersed.

In line with Steph Berns's (2017, p. 203) exploration of how museums facilitate encounters with the "materially mediated divine," Therevada Buddhist images and artifacts, although situated in the secular space of a museum exhibition, prompted spiritual response and engagement from the monks. The blessing ritual performed by the monks engaged material elements such as sound, sight, bodily movement, and words, and their performance communicated value and blessings to others, which further elicited response from those who witnessed or participated in the action of doing.

Future Trajectories

Material religion, like religious studies, has generally been moving toward more interdisciplinary and multidisciplinary approaches (Chidester, 2017, p. 74). Much of today's research, as discussed earlier, focuses more than it did in the past on vernacular, lived religious experience, intangible expressive forms, things in motion, relational networks, commodification, and so forth. Studies of material religion will likely continue along these lines, more commonly engaging ethnographic methods.

One area of research within material religion that is picking up steam is media and technology. This includes consideration of how the technologies we use in daily life influence practices of belief. For example, Gertrud Hüwelmeier (2016) discusses material religion and the role of new media and technologies of mediation. On special occasions in Vietnam and in Vietnamese communities, votive offerings such as paper versions of necessities and luxury goods are, by way of burning, transferred to the sacred realm through a kind of divine reciprocity. Keeping ancestors and other beings happy and entertained or providing for their needs brings them peace. In return, they protect their descendants from harm and bring them blessings and good fortune. Hüwelmeier argues that this "practice of mediation" bolsters communication between people of this world and the otherworld (p. 298, referencing Meyer, 2006). She further notes that a growing range of paper offerings include new media form (cell phones, computers, iPads, and the like). In addition to assisting ancestors with their continued work in the afterlife and facilitating communication between spirit mediums and the spirit world, these new media forms are related to wider processes such as globalization and migration (pp. 297–298).

Another growing area of material religion and technology research is the digitization of museum collections that include sacred material. A number of museum databases are built to integrate Indigenous ontologies into their catalogues and research has started to look at how communities of practice use images or otherwise access religious material through online databases (Bohaker et al., 2015; Glass, 2015). In the past few years, collaborative work between the Tlingit tribe of Alaska and the Smithsonian Museum of Natural History has utilized technologies in important ways. An example of their work is the creation of objects through CT (computerized tomography) scans, 3D digitization, and printing technologies at the request of the tribe. In some projects, technologies were employed as a form of insurance. That is, scanned data provides reference information for community members to re-create, by hand, lost or damaged objects. However, those data can also be used, and have been used to create 3D printed objects as replacements. In other projects, such 3D printed material was used by the Tlingit for ritual and/ or for education, keeping the older, original, repatriated materials safe within the community (Hollinger & Partridge, 2017a, 2017b).

Media of technologies such as the Internet, virtual reality, and video games, as well as the lived, spiritual experiences of online communities of practice, are other exciting areas of material religion that will only continue to grow (Aupers, 2012; Houtman & Meyer, 2012; Zandbergen, 2012). As the pace of technological change advances at lightning speed, and its impact on people, things, and practices of belief presents so many areas of research, new and overlapping fields of study emerge. "Digital religion studies" more specifically seeks to understand spirituality and religiosity by considering emerging technology and its relationship to lived, material religion (Campbell & Evolvi, 2020).

Conclusion

Context is key to understanding how material religion works and is significant for people (King, 2010, p. 136). As sacred objects circulate and enter into new or different contexts, they may take on new meanings, and elicit different responses, from varied communities. Rituals (as an example of material religion) that take place in museums potentially give Indigenous communities, and other communities of practice, agency to create, negotiate, and advocate for recognition of their identity and cultural value and the value of their materially expressed religion.

Material religion communicates dynamic social contexts and the lived experience of religion. This includes a wide range of media that will only continue to advance and enhance peoples' religious and spiritual experiences. The way religion happens materially, will therefore continue to change and stay relevant with new societal developments and contextual changes over time.

References

Abt, J. (2006). The origins of the public museum. In S. Macdonald (Ed.), *A companion to museum studies* (pp. 115–134). Blackwell Pub.

Ames, M. M. (1992). *Cannibal tours and glass boxes: The anthropology of museums*. UBC Press.

Appadurai, A. (Ed.). (1986). *The social life of things: Commodities in cultural perspective*. Cambridge University Press.

Aupers, S. (2012). Enchantment, Inc.: Online gaming between spiritual experience and commodity fetishism. In D. Houtman, & B. Meyer (Eds.), *Things: Religion and the question of materiality* (pp. 339–355). Fordham University Press.

Basu, P. (2020). Material culture: Ancestries and trajectories in material culture studies. In J. G. Carrier, & D. B. Gewertz (Eds.). *The handbook of sociocultural anthropology* (1st ed., pp. 370–390). Routledge. https://doi.org/10.4324/9781003086987-25

Bauer, A. A. (2019). Itinerant objects. *Annual Review of Anthropology*, 48(1), 335–352. https://doi.org/10.1146/annurev-anthro-102218-011111

Bell, C. (1997). *Ritual: Perspectives and dimensions*. Oxford University Press.

Berns, S. (2017). Mobilising Mecca: Reassembling blessings at the museum. In T. Hutchings, & J. McKenzie (Eds.), *Materiality and the study of religion: The stuff of the sacred* (pp. 203–218). Routledge.

Bessire, L., & Bond, D. (2014). Ontological anthropology and the deferral of critique. *American Ethnologist*, 41(3), 440–456. https://doi.org/10.1111/amet.12083

Bohaker, H., Corbiere, A. O., & Phillips, R. B. (2015). Chapter 3. Wampum unites us: Digital access, interdisciplinarity and indigenous knowledge – Situating the GRASAC knowledge sharing database. In R. A. Silverman Ed., *Museum as process: Translating local and global knowledges* (Museum Meanings pp. 45–66). Routledge.

Bräunlein, P. J. (2016). Thinking religion through things. *Method & Theory in the Study of Religion*, 28(4–5), 365–399. https://doi.org/10.1163/15700682-12341364

Campbell, H. A., & Evolvi, G. (2020). Contextualizing current digital religion research on emerging technologies. *Human Behavior and Emerging Technologies*, 2(1), 5–17. https://doi.org/10.1002/hbe2.149

Chidester, D. (2000). Material terms for the study of religion. *Journal of the American Academy of Religion*, 68(2), 367–380. https://doi.org/10.1093/jaarel/68.2.367

Chidester, D. (2017). Beyond religious studies? The future of the study of religion in a multidisciplinary perspective. *NTT Journal for Theology and the Study of Religion*, 71(1), 74–85. https://doi.org/10.5117/NTT2017.71.074.CHID

Clifford, J. (1983). On ethnographic authority. *Representations*, 1(2) 118–146. https://doi.org/10.2307/2928386

Clifford, J. (1988). *The predicament of culture: Twentieth-century ethnography, literature, and art*. Harvard University Press.

Conn, S. (1998). *Museums and American intellectual life, 1876–1926*. University of Chicago Press.

Duncan, C. (1995). *Civilizing rituals: Inside public art museums*. Routledge.

Durkheim, E. (1995). *The elementary forms of religious life* (K. E. Fields, Trans.). Free Press.

The Editors. (2009). Visual culture and material culture paradigms for the study of religion. *Material Religion*, 5(3), 355–356. https://doi.org/10.2752/175183409X12550007730020

Engelke, M. (2011). Material religion. In R. Orsi (Ed.), *The Cambridge companion to religious studies* (pp. 209–229). Cambridge University Press. https://illiad.unm.edu/illiad/ill/illiad.dll?Action=10&Form=75&Value=830547

Field, L. W. (2008). *Abalone tales: Collaborative explorations of sovereignty and identity in native California*. Duke University Press.

Flueckiger, J. B. (2017). Standing in cement: Possibilities created by Ravan on the Chhattisgarhi Plains. *South Asian History and Culture*, 8(4), 461–477. https://doi.org/10.1080/19472498.2017.1371489

Forshee, J. (2002). Tracing troubled times: Objects of value and narratives of loss from Sumba and Timor Islands. *Indonesia*, 74, 65–77. https://doi.org/10.2307/3351526

Geismar, H. (2011). "Material culture studies" and other ways to theorize objects: A primer to a regional debate. *Comparative Studies in Society and History*, 53(1), 210–218. https://doi.org/10.1017/S001041751000068X

Glass, A. (2015). Indigenous ontologies, digital futures: Plural provenances and the Kwakwaka'wakw collection in Berlin and beyond. In R. A. Silverman (Ed.), *Museum as process: Translating local and global knowledges* (pp. 19–44). Routledge.

Glassie, H. (1995). *The spirit of folk art*. Harry N. Abrams.

Gray, J. (2007). *Enlightenment's wake: Politics and culture at the close of the modern age*. Routledge.

Harvey, D. (1990). *The condition of postmodernity: An enquiry into the origins of culture change*. Blackwell Publishers.

Harvey, G. (2012). Things act: Casual indigenous statements about the performance of object-persons. In M. Bowman, & Ü. Valk (Eds.), *Vernacular religion in everyday life: Expressions of belief* (pp. 194–210). Equinox Pub.

Hays-Gilpin, K., & Lomatewama, R. (2013). Curating communities at the Museum of Northern Arizona. In R. Harrison, S. Byrne, & A. Clarke (Eds.), *Reassembling the collection: Ethnographic museums and indigenous agency* (pp. 259–283). School for Advanced Research Press.

Hazard, S. (2013). The material turn in the study of religion. *Religion and Society*, 4(1), 58–78. DOI: 10.3167/arrs.2013.040104

Henare, A. J. M., Holbraad, M., & Wastell, S. (Eds.). (2007). *Thinking through things: Theorising artefacts ethnographically*. Routledge/Taylor & Francis Group.

Hicks, D. (2010). The material cultural turn. In D. Hicks & M. C. Beaudry (Eds.), *The Oxford handbook of material culture studies*. Oxford University Press. https://doi.org/10.1093/oxfordhb/9780199218714.013.0002

Hicks, D., & Beaudry, M. C. (Eds.). (2010). *The Oxford handbook of material culture studies*. Oxford University Press.

Hobsbawm, E. J. (1989). *The age of empire, 1875–1914* (1st ed.). Vintage Books.

Hollinger, E., & Partridge, N. (2017a). 3D technology may revive this ancient hunting tool. Smithsonian Magazine (blog), October 25, 2017. Retrieved May 29, 2022, from http://www.smithsonianmag.com/blogs/national-museum-of-natural-history/2017/10/25/3d-technology-may-revive-ancient-hunting-tool

Hollinger, E., & Partridge, N. (2017b). Is 3D technology the key to preserving indigenous cultures? *Smithsonian Magazine* (blog), November 29, 2017. Retrieved May 29, 2022, from http://www.smithsonianmag.com/blogs/national-museum-of-natural-history/2017/11/29/3d-technology-key-preserving-indigenous-cultures

Horning, A. (Ed.). (2021). *A cultural history of objects: In the age of enlightenment*. Bloomsbury Academic.

Hoskins, J. (1998). *Biographical objects: How things tell the stories of people's lives*. Routledge.

Houtman, D. (2020). Book review: Materiality and the study of religion: The stuff of the sacred. *Material religion*, 16(1), 117–118. https://doi.org/10.1080/17432200.2019.1696568

Houtman, D., & Meyer, B. (2012). *Things: Religion and the question of materiality*. Fordham University Press.

Hutchings, T., & McKenzie, J. (2018). Introduction: The body of St. Cuthbert. In T. Hutchings, & J. McKenzie (Eds.), *Materiality and the study of religion: The stuff of the sacred* (pp. 1–12). Routledge.

Hüwelmeier, G. (2016). Cell phones for the spirits: Ancestor worship and ritual economies in Vietnam and its diasporas. *Material Religion*, 12(3), 294–321. https://doi.org/10.1080/17432200.2016.1192149

Jacknis, I. (1996). The ethnographic object and the object of ethnography in the early career of Franz Boas. In G. W. Stocking (Ed.), *Volksgeist as method and ethic: Essays on Boasian ethnography and the German anthropological tradition* (pp. 185–214). University of Wisconsin Press.

Joyce, R. A., & Gillespie, S. D. (Eds.). (2015). *Things in motion: Object itineraries in anthropological practice*. School for Advanced Research Press.

Keane, W. (2006). Part III: Subjects and objects. In C. Tilley, S. Kuechler, M. Rowlands, & P. Spyer (Eds.), *Handbook of material culture* (pp. 197–201). Sage Publications.

Keane, W. (2008). On the materiality of religion. *Material Religion*, 4(2), 230–231. https://doi.org/10.2752/175183408X328343

Kelly, J. D. (2014). The ontological turn: Where are we? *HAU: Journal of Ethnographic Theory*, 4(1), 357–360. https://doi.org/10.14318/hau4.1.019

Kendall, L. (2008). Popular religion and the sacred life of material goods in contemporary Vietnam. *Asian Ethnology*, 67(2), 177–200.

Kendall, L., Hà, V. T., Tâm, V. T. T., Huy, N. V., & Hien, N. T. (2013). Is it a sin to sell a statue? Catholic statues and the traffic in antiquities in Vietnam. *Museum Anthropology*, 36(1), 66–82. https://doi.org/10.1111/muan.12005

Kendall, L., & Yang, J. (2015). What is an animated image?: Korean shaman paintings as objects of ambiguity. *HAU Journal of Ethnographic Theory, 5*(2), 153–175. https://doi.org/10.14318/hau5.2.011

King, E. F. (2010). *Material religion and popular culture.* Routledge.

Kohn, E. (2015). Anthropology of ontologies. *Annual Review of Anthropology, 44,* 311–327. https://doi.org/10.1146/annurev-anthro-102214-014127

Kopytoff, I. (1986). The cultural biography of things: Commoditization as process. In A. Appadurai (Ed.), *The social life of things: Commodities in cultural perspective* (pp. 64–91). Cambridge University Press.

Kratz, C. A. (2010). *Affecting performance: Meaning, movement, and experience in Okiek women's initiation* (paperback edition). Wheatmark.

Kreps, C. F. (2020). *Museums and anthropology in the age of engagement.* Routledge.

Lonetree, A. (2012). *Decolonizing museums: Representing Native America in national and tribal museums.* University of North Carolina Press.

McChesney, L. S., & Charley, K. K. (2011). Body talk: New language for Hopi pottery through cultural heritage collaboration. *Practicing Anthropology, 33*(2), 21–27.

McDannell, C. (1995). *Material Christianity: Religion and popular culture in America.* Yale University Press.

Meyer, B., Morgan, D., Paine, C., & Plate, S. B. (Eds.). (2005). Editorial statement. *Material Religion, 1*(1), 4–8. https://doi.org/10.2752/174322005778054474

Meyer, B., Morgan, D., Paine, C., & Plate, S. B. (2010). The origin and mission of material religion. *Religion, 40*(3), 207–211. https://doi.org/10.1016/j.religion.2010.01.010

Miller, D. (Ed.). (2005). *Materiality.* Duke University Press.

Moore, S. F., & Myerhoff, B. G. (1977). Secular ritual, forms and meaning. In S. F. Moore, & B. G. Myerhoff (Eds.), *Secular ritual.* Van Gorcum.

Morgan, D. (2010). The material culture of lived religion: Visuality and embodiment. In J. Vakkari (Ed.), *Mind and matter: Selected papers of the Nordik 2009 conference for art historians* (pp. 14–31). Helsingfors. Studies in Art History, No. 41 http://www.taidehistorianseura.fi

Morgan, D. (2017). Material analysis and the study of religion. In T. Hutchings & J. McKenzie (Eds.), *Materiality and the study of religion: The stuff of the sacred* (pp. 14–31). Routledge.

Morgan, D. (2021). *The thing about religion: An introduction to the material study of religions.* The University of North Carolina Press.

Morphy, H. (2006). Sites of persuasion: Yingapungapu at the National Museum of Australia. In I. Karp, C. A. Kratz, L. Szwaja, & T. Ybarra-Frausto (Eds.), *Museum frictions* (pp. 469–499). Duke University Press. https://doi.org/10.1215/9780822388296-023

Myers, F. R. (Ed.). (2001). *The empire of things: Regimes of value and material culture* (1st ed.). School of American Research Press.

Ottino, A. (2000). *The universe within: A Balinese village through its ritual practices.* Karthala.

Paine, C. (2012). Introduction: Museums and material religion. *Material Religion, 8*(1), 4–8. https://doi.org/10.2752/175183412X13286288797773

Paine, C. (2013). *Religious objects in museums: Private lives and public duties* (English ed.). Berg Publishers.

Pearce, S. M. (1993). *Museums, objects, and collections: A cultural study.* Smithsonian Institution Press.

Pintchman, T., & Dempsey, C. G. (Eds.). (2016). *Sacred matters: Material religion in South Asian traditions.* SUNY Press, State University of New York Press.

Plate, S. B. (Ed.). (2015). *Key terms in material religion.* Bloomsbury Academic.

Primiano, L. N. (1995). Vernacular religion and the search for method in religious folklife. *Western Folklore, 54*(1), 37–56. https://doi.org/10.2307/1499910

Primiano, L. N. (2012). Manifestations of the religious vernacular: Ambiguity, power, and creativity. In M. Bowman, & Ü. Valk (Eds.), *Vernacular religion in everyday life: Expressions of belief* (pp. 382–394). Equinox Publications.

Ramos, A. R. (2012). The politics of perspectivism. *Annual Review of Anthropology, 41,* 481–494. https://doi.org/10.1146/annurev-anthro-092611-145950

Redman, S. J. (2016). *Bone rooms: From scientific racism to human prehistory in museums.* Harvard University Press.

Reichart, P. A., & Khongkhunthian, P. (2007). *The spirit houses of Thailand.* White Lotus.

Reichle, N., Brinkgreve, F., & Stuart-Fox, D. J., Asian Art Museum of San Francisco. (2010). *Bali: Art, ritual, performance*. Asian Art Museum-Chong-Moon Lee Center for Asian Art and Culture.

Rosoff, N. B. (2003). Integrating native views into museum procedures: Hope and practice at the National Museum of the American Indian. In L. Peers, & A. K. Brown (Eds.), *Museums and source communities: A Routledge reader*. Routledge.

Schnell, S. (1999). *The rousing drum: Ritual practice in a Japanese community*. University of Hawaiʻi Press.

Shelton, A. (2006). Museums and anthropologies: Practices and narratives. In S. Macdonald (Ed.), *A companion to museum studies* (pp. 64–80). Blackwell Publications.

Sullivan, B. M. (2015). *Sacred objects in secular spaces: Exhibiting Asian religions in museums*. Bloomsbury Academic.

Tilley, C., Keane, W., Kuechler, S., Rowlands, M., & Spyer, P. (Eds.). (2006). *Handbook of material culture*. Sage Publications.

Tuhiwai Smith, L. (2012). *Decolonizing methodologies: Research and indigenous peoples* (Second edition). Zed Books.

Turner, V. W. (1977). *The ritual process: Structure and anti-structure*. Cornell University Press.

van Hout, I. (2017). *Indonesian textiles at the Tropenmuseum*. LM Publishers.

Wang, X. (2018). Rethinking material religion in the East: Orientalism and religious material culture in contemporary western academia. *Religions, 9*(2), 62. https://doi.org/10.3390/rel9020062

Zandbergen, D. (2012). Fulfilling the sacred potential of technology: New edge technophilia, consumerism, and spirituality in Silicon Valley. In D. Houtman, & B. Meyer (Eds.), *Things: Religion and the question of materiality* (pp. 356–378). Fordham University Press.

Selected Readings

Bräunlein, P. J. (2016). Thinking religion through things. *Method & Theory in the Study of Religion, 28*(4–5), 365–399. https://doi.org/10.1163/15700682-12341364

Buggeln, G. T., Paine, C., & Plate, S. B. (Eds.). (2017). *Religion in museums: Global and multidisciplinary perspectives*. Bloomsbury.

Hazard, S. (2013). The material turn in the study of religion. *Religion and Society: Advances in Research, 4*(1), 58–78. DOI:10.3167/arrs.2013.040104

Houtman, D. & Meyer, B. (2012). *Things: Religion and the question of materiality*. Fordham University Press.

Morgan, D. (2021). *The thing about religion: An introduction to the material study of religions*. The University of North Carolina Press.

Pintchman, T., & Dempsey, C. G. (Eds.). (2016). *Sacred matters: Material religion in South Asian traditions*. SUNY Press, State University of New York Press.

Plate, S. B. (Ed.). (2015). *Key terms in material religion* (1st ed.). Bloomsbury.

29

The Sex–Religion Matrix

Ruth Tsuria and Jason Bartashius

Religion and sexuality form a complicated but attractive topic. And we cannot understate the media's role in shaping the perceived relationship between religion and sexuality. This chapter examines the dynamics between various forms of media – magazines, film, television, and digital – and the sex–religion matrix.

Both religion and sexuality play a central role in human life, and their intersection merits close study. According to Stephen Ellingson (2002), "The importance of religion as a system of faith and ethics, and above all as a structure of meaning, has often been acknowledged" (p. 1). The importance of sexuality needs no explanations, since "sexuality is perhaps the most powerful dimension of human life... Sexuality communicates something to others and ourselves about what kind of person we are" (p. 2). The more interesting question then becomes, how do these two primary systems intersect?

Scholars have addressed this issue from a variety of perspectives, such as highlighting sexual themes in prehistoric religions (Schmidt & Voss, 2005), reviewing sexual regulations in historical religions (Jakobsen & Pellegrini, 2004), and examining current religions and sexual norms (Yip & Hunt, 2016). This chapter contributes to this last area of focus, by reviewing the intersection between religion, sexuality, and media – an intersection that could fill books.

Traditional mass media, such as film, television, and news, tend to stress the tension between religion and sexuality, showing religion as a force that is either asexual or anti-sexual (Claussen, 2002). But religion and sexuality are not always at odds with each other. In some ways, they are parallel forces and, as such, sexuality is sometimes used in religious traditions as a positive force.

All religious traditions have made some "attempt to structure sexual behaviors through divinely sanctioned or sacred moral guidelines" (Yip & Hunt, 2016, p. 4). One could think, as examples, of Christian, Jewish, or Islamic laws against premarital intimacy or homosexuality, or of sexual prohibitions for Buddhist monks and nuns, or of sacred sexual relationships in Hindu or Buddhist tantra. These attempts to tame sexuality are based on the central place that sex holds for humans. As Ellingson (2002, p. 2) puts it, "Sexuality occupies the attention of many religions because it is a powerful way to organize and relate to human beings."

Because sexuality is so powerful, many religious traditions tried to combat or repress it. For example, in Europe in the early modern period, the relationship between sexuality, motherhood, and witchcraft was always assumed (Roper, 2013). Even today, sexuality is mostly seen as a threat or sin in many Christian congregations (Robertson, 2006). In Judaism, while sexuality by-and-large is not a threat, *certain* types of sexuality most certainly are – such as homosexuality (Tsuria,

The Handbook on Religion and Communication, First Edition. Edited by Yoel Cohen and Paul A. Soukup.

2016). Similarly, in Buddhism, while sexuality is not rejected (for lay people and in certain contexts even for priests), it is most certainly bounded by a set of ethical rules (Langenberg, 2017). In Islam too, sexuality is often controlled through practices such as sexual segregation (Hidayatullah, 2003). In short, almost all religious traditions have some texts, laws, or guidelines that attempt to control sex(uality).

Religion also operates to construct and perpetuate gender norms. In Catholicism, the cult of the Virgin Mary, for instance, not only idealizes chastity but also renders divine motherhood – and by extension women's domesticity and submissiveness in patriarchal societies (Warner, 1983/1976). This desire for "traditional" gender conformance extends to the contemporary political milieu. Recent years have seen the rise of an anti-feminist/LGBT Catholic "alt-right" in the United States that claims to seek the restoration of (toxic) masculinity (Wetzel, 2020). Similar intersections between hypermasculinity, anti-feminism, and homophobia exist in a Denmark-based globalizing Tibetan Buddhist movement (Scherer, 2011). Hetero gender conformance also plays an integral role in the US Christian Right's "ex-gay" movement that attempts to change people's sexual orientation. Robinson and Spivey (2007) observe how "doing masculinity is advocated as the main treatment for adult men and is recommended to fathers as a preventative measure for their sons" (p. 664). These "preventative" measures include exhibiting dominance over wives (p. 663).

The following discussions focus on the intersections of religion and media representations of gender and sexuality. We take a bird's eye view to explore, on the one hand, how (ultra) conservative religious influences on censorship have been preoccupied – more often than not – with preserving "traditional" portrayals of the heteronormative nuclear family, and conversely how film industries and new media texts have the potential to reflect and/or reinforce socio-religious norms. Yet, on the other hand, we also demonstrate how specific texts reject or subvert religious heteropatriarchal ideologies. Brought together, the chapter provides some insight on how religious heteropatriarchy is constructed and contested in different types of media.

Censorship in the Name of God

One important aspect of the intersection between religion, sex, and media is the use of religion to promote censorship of sexuality in media. Many countries have a long history of censorship, both in the West (Western Europe and the United States) and in South and Southeast Asian (India and Malaysia) contexts. Reviewing the history of these censorship processes allows us to see the real impact of religion in media, of religious ideas of sexuality in popular culture, and of how, in the past century and around the globe, some media institutions maintain traditional notions of sexuality and some have broken away from them.

In the US context, this history began early on when in 1915 the Supreme Court ruled that film content was not protected free speech. Film's potential to reach far larger audiences than print material became a cause for moral concern. Early critics of depictions of sex and crime consisted primarily of Protestants and women's organizations. The advent of sound intensified the moral panics as the talkies permitted "sexy starlets" the chance to "rationalize their immoral behavior" (Black, 1989, p. 170). In the 1930s, for example, performances by female actor and sex icon Mae West triggered outrage. The same decade saw Catholics mobilize to lead a crusade for increased censorship. Although a religious minority, Catholics represented nearly half the population in urban cities including New York, Philadelphia, Boston, and Chicago that were the home of prominent theaters. Catholic leaders mobilized the laity to boycott films deemed immoral (a category that included sexuality, violence, and crime). The industry bowed to pressure and agreed to allow for the formation of the Production Code Administration (PCA) to be headed by the lay Catholic Joseph Breen. Having an internal spokesperson, however, did not suffice for advocates. In order to sustain pressure on the PCA and Breen, Catholic bishops founded an external organization (the National Legion of Decency) in 1935. Together with the International Federation of Catholic Alumnae the Legion produced a tier system to evaluate the moral soundness of films.

Beginning in the 1950s, however, the Legion's influence over the industry began to diminish. In 1952 the Supreme Court ruled in *Burstyn v. Wilson* that films did fall under First Amendment protections of free speech. Moreover, prominent Catholic theologians questioned the Legion's authority "under Canon Law to forbid individual Catholics from attending condemned films" (Black, 2013, p. 250). The late 1960s saw the dismantling of the PCA and the industry's implementation of a rating system. Not surprisingly, in different forums US and global Catholic bodies have continued to review films albeit without the enormous influence that the Legion enjoyed in the early to mid-twentieth century. In terms of sexuality and gender, when rating films the Legion turned to the Church's conservative positions on homosexuality, premarital sex, divorce, and abortion (Accomando, 2016).

Pope Pius XI commended the Legion in his 1936 encyclical *Vigilanti Cura*, reflecting and bolstering appeals for censorship in predominantly Catholic countries such as Italy and Ireland. Whereas US Catholics leveraged their urban demographic to threaten theater boycotts, in the Italian context a dramatic mid-century increase in local parish cinemas pressured the industry to bow to Catholic censorship (Gennari, 2013). In Ireland – a nation-state that did not legalize divorce until 1995 – strong measures were taken to ban foreign films or cut portions, sometimes substantial enough to alter the narrative, that presented any challenge to the heteronormative nuclear family. As a result, Hollywood imports that had already been subjected to censorship during the production phase by "the Irish-American influenced Legion of Decency" underwent further "'moral' editing" in Ireland (Rockett, 2013, p. 210). Kevin Rockett (2013, p. 211) notes that in cases of films that dealt with divorce and remarriage all references to the first marriage were deleted "thus making the second marriage in effect the first and only relationship, thereby ensuring that Irish audiences would not be contaminated by the concept of divorce."

Mirroring the efforts of the Legion in previous decades, the New Christian Right of the late 1970s and 1980s called for the censorship of popular culture and a ban on pornographic magazines. Methodist minister Rev. Donald Wildmon established the Coalition for Better Television, which, with the support of the Moral Majority, threatened boycotts over televised sexual content. Wildmon also appeared at the forefront of a nationwide crusade for sexually explicit magazines (e.g. *Playboy* and *Penthouse*) to be removed from 7/11 convenience stores (Mendenhall, 2002). Much controversy also surrounded the sexually charged/(explicit) music of pop icons Madonna and Prince. Among songs that served as the impetus for the formation of the Parents Music Resource Center (PMRC) in 1985, which campaigned for advisory labels on albums with explicit lyrics, were Prince's "Let's Pretend We're Married" (1982) and "Darling Nikki" (1984). Though the organization's founders denied ties with the Christian Right, the PMRC, nevertheless, received much support from religious fundamentalists (Chastagner, 1999). The music video for Madonna's "Like A Prayer" (1989) shows the singer kissing a Black saint/(Jesus) on a Catholic church altar. Pepsi used the song in a commercial, but ultimately pulled it after threats of boycotts from conservative Christians outraged by both Madonna's use of religious imagery to affirm women's sexuality and the depiction of a Black Jesus figure (Greeley, 1992). Pope John Paul II weighed in on the controversy by advocating for radio and TV stations to ban the song in Italy, giving the singer reason to dedicate the song in a 2008 concert to Benedict XVI (Reuters, 2008).

Censorship of film is not unique to the US context. In many Muslim countries, for example, censorship of film and television alike is common (Zeydabadi-Nejad, 2009). However, as noted by Zeydabadi-Nejad and other scholars, the story of censorship in the Middle East is not so simple. For example, during most of the late twentieth century, Turkey's government censored religious elements out of films. This was done in order to preserve "Kemalist secularism and a 'true' Islam (a private, enlightened, apolitical, national and Sunni Islam)" (Mutlu & Koçer, 2012, p. 70). But even in the religiously informed censorship in Iran, for example, Zeydabadi-Nejad (2009) argues that the process of censorship, because it is not fully uniform, serves as a site of the negotiation of power, and thus, cultural norms. Similarly in Malaysia, the censorship bureau is still, as noted by Wan Amizah et al. (2009, p. 48) "a work in progress." Malaysian state censorship, inspired by Muslim principles, acts to remove content that is blasphemous, immoral, violent, or "excessively sexual." As suggested by Wan Amizah et al. (2009, p. 48), "Religion, moral conduct and cultural identities hence are modulated into the pillars that hold the country with multicultural make up together; the Censorship Board then becomes a visibly conflicting manifestation of the status quo's need to be able to keep doing this."

In the 1990s Bollywood India's Central Board of Film Certification (CBFC) maintained that the impact of the "audio-visual medium … is far stronger than that of the printed word" (quoted in Bose, 2009, p. 23). The Hindu right played an active role in advocating for censorship of female characters exercising sexual agency. In the political context of the 1990s the "Indian nation was reimagined as Hindu" and religious–national discourses informed censorship (p. 30). A focal point of controversy was sexually charged film songs. Shohini Ghosh (2002) stresses the prominence of songs featured in cinema at the turn of the century:

> Film songs acquire an independent life in Indian society because they are often released on audiocassette before the film's release, and song sequences are shown on television on their own. Long after a film is forgotten, one or more of its songs may continue to be very popular, regularly played on radio and TV… The proliferation of music channels and music-based shows on television have provided the narratives of song and dance sequences even more autonomy. (p. 212)

The Hindu right protested the song "Choli ke Peechey Kya Hai" ("What is behind the blouse?") from the 1993 film *Khalnayak* (*The Villain*), and subsequently a number of tracks inspired by the song were subjected to censorship. Of significance, the song appears in two contrasting scenes in the film. Only one, however, became the target of a protest in the form of a petition that was ultimately dismissed by the High Court. The first sequence shows two women pretending to be courtesans singing "Choli ke Peechey Kya Hai" while the second depicts men singing the same song "culminating in the intimidation and physical assault of the heroine by the male protagonists" (Bose, 2009, p. 26). Though the protestors claimed the song would result in "Eve teasing" (sexual harassment) they ironically only took issue with the first sequence and dismissed the scene that actually portrayed a sexual assault. In essence, female sexual agency, rather than human rights, appeared to be the central issue for the Hindu right. Ghosh (2002, p. 214) notes that the first sequence's homoeroticism became more pronounced when it was shown out of context on television and speculates that "this might have been largely responsible for the controversy it aroused." This incident underscores the interpenetration of television and film. Further, it should be stressed, that in the milieu of the 1990s, which saw waves of sporadic censorship campaigns, much anxiety existed over the threats that Western culture vis-à-vis satellite television posed to the imagined Hindu state (see Ghosh, 1999).

Filmography as Agents for Female Sexuality and Homosexuality

Another avenue in which media are used to negotiate religious sexual and gender norms is in regard to women's place in society: their role in the family and in public, as well as in terms of their own sexuality. A Christian example of a text that subverts and negotiates traditional, religious understanding of gender is Mark Turtletaub's *Puzzle* (2018). The film centers on the protagonist Agnes' path for independence from a male-dominated household and community. Another film also replete with Catholic imagery and male surveillance of a female protagonist is *Rosemary's Baby* (1968). Notably, the film's release closely coincided with the Vatican encyclical *Humanae Vitae*, which – to the dismay of many US Catholics – reaffirmed the Church's position on abortion and birth control (Valle, 2012). The social parody proffers "a perversion of the Christian narrative of the Immaculate Conception in which Satan" rapes and "impregnates a mortal woman in order to become human and intervene in world history" (Valerius, 2005, p. 118). The film's narrative conclusion finds Rosemary – though incensed by her discovery that her husband made a Faustian agreement with a satanic cult – embracing motherhood. Karyn Valerius observes:

> Rosemary's seduction by motherhood is a profane parody of sacred maternity that is horrifying for the extreme self-sacrifice it implies. Within the terms of the film, Rosemary's assent to nurture the baby entails eternal damnation. Rather than sanctifying Rosemary's maternity, the narrative pursues the logic of "pro-life" arguments against abortion to grotesque conclusions. (p. 128)

Wadjda tells the tale of a Saudi girl's quest to buy a bicycle even though riding bikes is gendered masculine. Throughout the film, men repeatedly appear in elevated spaces, offering them the vantage point to monitor women's activities on the street. In contrast, the narrative conclusion – in which Wadjda's mother gives her a bicycle – finds both mother and daughter standing on a rooftop (Ceuterick, 2020). Wadjda's struggles are analogous to women's struggle to obtain the right to drive – a point underscored in the closing scene that finds the young girl triumphantly racing a boy on a street that dead ends and merges with a highway. In another example, Kim Ki-duk's classic film *Spring, Summer, Fall, Winter … and Spring* (2003) serves as a Buddhist example for a media text that contests Buddhist conceptions of women as temptresses (Bartashius, 2018, pp. 131–132). A young ill female character enters a Korean temple to recuperate. While in residence she and a celibate apprentice fall in love.

Mainstream films can also be used by religious communities to sustain/(propagate) heteropatriarchial norms. Ellen Moore's (2010) ethnographic work documents how evangelical Christian churches employ segments from television and Hollywood films – such as *Indiana Jones and the Last Crusade*, *Brave Heart*, and *Bruce Almighty* – in which (white) men are featured prominently while women are either absent or play subordinate roles. In these clips, men "are the ones who make important decisions (leaps of faith), who take action (fighting a war or fighting on the golf course), and who are able to talk to God directly" (p. 101). Similarly, as delineated by Rebecca Poe Hays and Nicholas Werse (2017), evangelicals concerned about the feminization of Christianity appropriate symbols, themes, and even the name of the film *Fight Club* – a text that addresses the "masculinity crisis" caused by consumerism – to serve as the basis for men's ministries designed to restore or reinforce participants' conceptions of (hetero) masculinity. Bartashius (2019) demonstrates how the film has similarly been appropriated by Buddhists to celebrate notions of hypermasculinity (p. 361).

American evangelicals' turn to the big screen for heroic emblems of toxic masculinity is, by no means, a new trend. Kristen Kobes Du Mez (2020, p. 13) examines the historic significance of Western films for the Christian Right, noting that "John Wayne became an icon of rugged American manhood for generations of conservatives."

In stark contrast an increasing number of texts (biopics and documentaries) have emerged exploring and challenging evangelical anti-gay rhetoric. Based on a *New York Times* review (Catsoulis, 2017), biopic *I am Michael* (2015) follows gay activist Michael Glatze's transformation that led him to leave his partner, renounce his homosexuality, marry a woman, and become a spokesperson for Christian fundamentalists with his own ministry. The film's strained apolitical stance and ambiguous conclusion – an uncertain Glatze lost for words takes the pulpit for the first time – put it on a slippery slope. Brian Moylan (2015), writing for *The Guardian*, aptly describes Glatze's conversion as "an ill that besets a young man without direction. And with that, it becomes, in essence, identical to some of the evangelist propaganda dished out on public transportation." In 2017, two years after its Sundance premiere, *I am Michael* was released to a general audience. The same year Netflix released a responsive 19-minute documentary *Michael: Lost and Found* executive-produced by Glatze's former partner Benjie Nycum, who was dismayed by the *I am Michael* script. The Netflix short documents Nycum's visit with Glatze and his wife Rebekah. The film finds a repentant Michael, who apologizes for his homophobic rants and affirms his past LGBT activism. The couple's nondenominational church, viewers learn, spoke out on sexism and (after being subjected to much criticism for doing so) terminated its relationship with a fundamentalist Bible college. *Come Sunday* (2018) is another biopic that follows the similar transformations of Christian minister Carlton Pearson. Through a fictional subplot exploring the relationship between Pearson and his church's closeted music director suffering from AIDS, Pearson is "converted to a still more radical understanding of the gospel: one in which absolutely no one is excluded from God's unconditional love"; one of the final scenes proffers the once staunchly conservative minister preaching at Bishop Yvette Flunder's LGBTQ+ inclusive church (Laarman, 2018).

The biopic *Boy Erased* (2018) and the documentary *Pray Away* (2021) expose the adverse detrimental effects ex-gay programs have had on participants. The former is based on LGBT advocate and "conversion" therapy survivor Garrard Conley's memoir by the same name. In the film, Conley's Baptist parents persuade him to enroll in the "Love In Action" program. The conclusion finds Conley (having left the program) beginning to write about the physical and psychological abuse he and others were subjected to – one fellow youth is beaten with a Bible and berated by program leaders and family members before taking his life. *Pray Away* not only documents the rise and fall of Exodus International (the largest ex-gay organization), but also gives glimpses of the persistence of the ex-gay movement. The subjects consist of five ex "ex-gay" leaders (read: individuals who survived therapies and served, in decades prior, as spokespersons before ultimately renouncing the movement) juxtaposed with one active "ex-gay" proponent. In the 1990s, ex-gays allowed the Christian Right to humanize its anti-gay rhetoric and proffer the idea that changing one's sexuality was possible. *Pray Away*, in contrast, visits prominent former spokespersons, who in the film are now spokespersons for opposition to the movement, relaying their own stories of complicity, struggles, and even self-harm. Lynne Gerber (2021) problematizes this by opining that *Pray Away*'s limitation is holding a handful of sexual minorities – rather than the Christian Right – accountable: "I felt like I was watching only gay people being held, and holding themselves, accountable for the anti-gay politics that put all LGBTQ lives in peril."

The issue of repressing homosexuality is by no means limited to Christianity – it exists in most of the world's religions. Therefore, media representations of these issues in Judaism, Islam, Hinduism, etc. can be found. In the case of Judaism, *Eyes Wide Open* (2009) interrogates hetero-masculinity and the repression of same-sex desires in the Mea Shearim neighborhood in Jerusalem. Despite the narrative focus on the Haredi community's response to an illicit affair between two men, homosexuality is never explicitly acknowledged in the film. The protagonist Aaron initially conceptualizes his attraction to Ezri as a spiritual challenge but gradually comes to "accept his bodily sensations and the pleasure another man evokes in him as gifts of God's creation" (Knauss, 2013, p. 12). Evaluating more broadly LGBT+ representation in Hindi films, Kaur (2017, p. 29) suggests that the "LGBT community in India which has long been deprived of their true identity and representation in the social and cultural sphere of society," has experienced recent changes in the India mediascape that have allowed for sexual minorities to find a place in Hindi cinema. Kaur's research examines the "active role which Hindi cinema can play in bringing them into the mainstream discourse through their realistic and authentic screen representation" (p. 29). The growing representation of religious LGBT+ individuals in media texts allows then for the religious communities themselves to negotiate religious norms regarding diverse sexualities (Tsuria, 2017).

The Internet as a Liberating Force

The mutual and complicated relationship between media and religion emerges especially in new media, which have been used to reframe and negotiate religious understandings of sexuality. While traditional religious media tend to support religious ideology, the Internet, because of its participatory qualities, allows for the empowerment of alternative voices (Campbell, 2010). In relation to sexuality, the Internet has impacted the religious discourse in several areas: sexual abuse, LGBTQIA +, female sexuality, and dating.

Sexual Abuse

While coverage of sexual abuse tends to depend on internal sources, it is usually an *etic* perspective – an outsider's view into a different world. Digital media allow religious or ex-religious individuals to speak about their abuse. Online pages provide resources and anonymous testimonies. By doing so, they encourage others to share their stories and normalize speaking against abuse within religious communities. Examples of using digital media to report sexual abuse in religions appear in the literature. According to Rashid and Barron (2019, p. 572), digital media have been especially beneficial in uncovering cases of abuse by Muslim imams. Similarly, changes in media spheres in conservative countries, like Bhutan, have allowed for the rise in reports of sexual abuse of children by Buddhist monks (Arora, 2013). During the #MeToo movement, a sub-movement known as #ChurchToo was present on Twitter (Tsuria, 2020a). This hashtag was used not only to expose the actual sexual abuse in churches, but also to reveal the reception victims of such abuse received. Users shared their own stories and carefully but clearly pointed to the systemic issues within their religious organizations or communities. Online, users were not only interested in the exposure and apprehension of the predators, but also called for institutional changes within the religion (Bogen et al., 2020).

LGBTQIA+ Identities

The tension between the individual and the religious organization also appears clearly in regard to LGBTQIA+ and religion. In general, digital media are important sources for LGBTQIA+ individuals for support, knowledge, community, dating, and activism (Lucero, 2017; Pullen & Cooper,

2010). According to Lucero (2017, p. 117), "Digital media have become a safe space for multiply minoritized LGBTQ youth to explore issues of sexuality and gender." For religious LGBTQIA+ individuals, who tend to live in more conservative societies that might reject these identities, digital media might be the only source of information available. For example, Burke (2014, p. 17) shows that online resources provide an avenue for Christians to explore a variety of sexual "awakening": "evangelicals use the internet to shape, interpret and make meaning of sex in ways different than what is presented in popular evangelical literature." In addition to using digital media for support and community, religious LGBTQIA+ individuals use digital media to question and negotiate the religious norms in their community that relate to their identities. One prominent avenue of this negotiation happens on social media. In their study of Christian youth in the UK, Taylor et al. (2014) found that social media play a pivotal role in understanding and communicating one's identity. Taylor et al. suggest that for these participants, their religious and sexual identities were not "separate and divergent paths," but rather two parts of one's identity that "mutually and complexly construct one another" (p. 1139).

This use of digital media is not unique to Christian LGBTQIA+ users. Other religious individuals make similar uses of social media. For example, Mokhtar et al. (2019) examined the role of social media for LGBTQIA+ individuals in Malaysia. Malaysia, while officially a secular state, is heavily guided by (Sunni) Islamic principles. According to Mokhtar et al., "In Malaysia, LGBT is considered to be a taboo subject, due to strict Islamic practices and laws" (p. 78). Similarly in Hinduism, the Facebook page LGBT Hindu Satsang (https://www.facebook.com/groups/LGBTHinduSatsang/.) states that one of its goals is to "speak out against mistreatment and injustice of LGBTQ+ in religious communities, and work with temples and satsangs to help them become affirming and welcoming of all people."

Female Sexuality

Women have been overlooked or oppressed in most religious traditions (Stopler, 2003). This oppression happens in institutional leadership (from which women are usually banned), household chores and child-raising (work that tends to be seen as a woman's responsibility), and the bedroom, where female sexuality is often ignored, disregarded, or suppressed. While many religious traditions also dictate and suppress male sexuality (e.g. by banning masturbation), female sexuality tends to be transparent in religious traditions. Since most religions were created and maintained by male leadership, it is not so surprising that they were unaware of female sexual needs. With the advent of digital media, women can, for the first time, explore their own needs, and voice them in public, for consideration within their religious community.

For example, the Israeli-Jewish website Kipa.co.il, in association with Yahel Center (2021), created an online video series speaking explicitly about intimacy and challenging existing sexual norms in the Orthodox community. The rationale for the video series was that the Orthodox society needs to be able to discuss intimacy in a "clean" way. While most users reacting to this video series were resistant (Tsuria, 2017), some users supported this effort and lauded this groundbreaking content: "Better late than never … the issue is important and necessary, this content is available throughout the web and it's best that children are exposed to it in a clean language, with modesty in mind" (Tsuria, 2017, p. 231).

Digital media can also be used to defend the right of women to have a more "liberated" sexuality. This was the case with the Pink Chaddi social media campaign in India (Chattopadhyay, 2011). According to Chattopadhyay, following an attack on women in a nightclub by a few male members of a Hindu right-wing party in 2009, a female journalist started a Facebook group titled

Consortium of Pub-going, Loose, and Forward Women (later known as Pink Chaddi). The Facebook group, which started a as joke, shortly became a hub for activism against Hindutva – a Hindu movement that promotes a gendered, sexist extremism. The Hindutva movement in India "draws on images of women as ideal mothers, chaste wives, and compliant daughters. Not surprisingly, these notions are grounded on the idea of virtue being the precondition of women's entry into the public sphere of nation-building" (p. 65). Therefore, controlling female sexuality is an important avenue for this ideological struggle. Using digital media, however, women and feminists from around the globe joined this struggle. As Chattopadhyay (2011, p. 64) explains: "online media and web services provide the space and tools for advocacy, where the personal can become political." Females' personal choices – how to dress, drink, or interact – were defended and women's freedoms advocated for in this online campaign. In these ways, digital media allow women in religious societies to discuss, enact, and protect their sexual needs and freedoms.

Similar awareness arises in other religions. According to Tomalin et al. (2015, pp. 12–13), "In recent years, ... Buddhist women's social movement activity has been conducted digitally through websites, Facebook pages, and Twitter accounts... Buddhist women globally make use of a wider range of web-based opportunities." These digital opportunities have allowed Buddhist nuns and female leaders to become more visible, and, in turn, they have begun to highlight women's needs, including their sexuality.

Dating

Online dating has allowed a shift in dating habits within religious communities. As a result, there is a growing flora of religiously specific dating websites and apps, which allow for users to date digitally, but still within the boundaries of their religious tradition and community (Richardson et al., 2020). For example, within the religious Jewish community, there seems to be a growing acceptance of online dating and dating applications (Cohen & Tsuria, 2019).

Online dating, while it might be approved by religious leaders, does challenge the traditional norms of prematrimonial relationships in religious communities. Most notably, it increases individual agency in the process. Rochadiat et al. (2017) interviewed 16 Muslim American women, who self-identified as "moderate Muslims." Using digital media tools for dating, these women reported an increased sense of personal agency. The researchers summarize their key findings thus:

> One advantage mentioned by many respondents was how increased privacy and anonymity of the Internet reduced the embarrassment associated with traditional matchmaking. Other notable advantages [were] access to a larger pool of potential romantic partners and greater control over self-presentation... Use of dating technology also created another juxtaposition by increasing Muslim women's sense of individual agency during courtship. (p. 1634)

It seems that online dating allows women more control in the process of dating. However, the women do not simply abandon traditional/religious dating norms. Instead, they engage in a delicate and complicated act of balancing new technology and agency with traditional norms, for example, keeping their families involved in the dating process (Rochadiat et al., 2017, p. 1635). While technology can support a greater individual agency, a person's religious values also play a meaningful part in how they use the technology. As Rochadiat and colleagues point out: "Given the importance placed on marriage as the ultimate goal for many Muslims, future research may assess the impact of these values on their approach to online dating" (p. 1635).

In other words, research should note how religious users bring their set of religious concepts and behavior to online dating and, in turn, how these concepts shape the use of the technology. Many religious dating websites might not function according to the same logic as a secular website. On a religious dating website, one might find categories like level of religious observance (Cohen & Tsuria, 2019) or a stronger emphasis on marriage and limiting dating or sexual "hookups" (Naji Bajnaid & Elyas, 2017). In general, religious dating websites offer religious-valued avenues for dating. While these websites adhere to religious values, these still allow users higher agency and privacy in comparison with traditional religious dating.

The Internet as a Conserving Force

The Internet is a conserving force used to enforce traditional religious approaches to sexuality. In opposition to the uses of digital media to promote sexual freedom, the following describes the ways digital media are also used to enforce traditional religious approaches to sexuality. Specifically, this enforcement can be seen in three areas: LGBTQIA+, heterosexual norms, and female sexuality.

Digital media, and more specifically, religious web platforms, are used to educate and regulate traditional religious norms. For example, the Faithful World Baptist Church (based in the United States and identified as a hate group by the Southern Poverty Law Center) declares on its website as a doctrinal statement that "homosexuality is a sin and an abomination which God punishes with the death penalty" (http://www.faithfulwordbaptist.org/page6.html). Similarly, Żuk and Żuk (2020) show how Catholic-inspired homophobia and anti-gender narratives are popular on Polish social media.

This phenomenon is further theorized by Boellstorff (2020) as "digital heterosexism." In his review of the anti-LGBT movement in Indonesia, he claims that "online media are key" (p. 8) in promoting populist and exclusionary opinions. Boellstorff shows how anti-LGBTQIA+ sentiments were mediated online and then translated into real government decisions: for example, by banning Grindr and other LGBT-related web applications. In that sense, for Indonesia, "digital spaces were becoming construed as part of the national imagined community" (p. 15) – spaces in which the larger community can dictate correct sexual behavior. Such online *dakwah* then promote an anti-LGBTQIA+ attitude, using the logics of digital culture to disseminate traditional approaches to sexuality (Haridi et al., 2016; Weng, 2015). For example, an anti-LGBT social media campaign in 2014 called Wear White was the combined effort of Christian and Muslim participants in Singapore. According to Han (2018), the Wear White campaign was launched on Facebook in 2014 as a reaction to the Pink Dot Pride Parade. The campaign's goal was to "send a message to LGBT activists that there is a conservative majority in Singapore who will push back and will not allow them to promote their homosexual lifestyle and liberal ideologies" (p. 44). The use of social media was especially powerful, as it allowed both Christian and Muslim individuals to participate simply by using the hashtag #wearwhite. While the examples here are explicitly against homosexuality, digital media are also used implicitly to police heterosexual norms within religious communities. This mostly happens through normalizing discourse (Tsuria, 2016). According to Tsuria, digital media use within communities can work as a site of push and pull, of negotiation of norms. However, more often, those already empowered – religious leaders, for example – tend to have a stronger pull. The participatory uses of technology are then applied to show support for traditional norms and leadership, not resistance to it. Examining the attitudes of Jewish religious websites to sexuality, Tsuria (2016) provides various examples in which the

Q&A section serves as a regulatory tool. Analyzing 60 sexually related Q&A sections from three leading Jewish religious websites, Tsuria concludes that:

> Online Q&As play a double part, as do the Christian confessions for Foucault, as spaces of power-knowledge, as a practice where (traditional/communal/external) authority is empowered, and at the same time, the (individual/internal) self is "created" and (self-)disciplined. I suggest this process is informed by cultural norms and social contexts, and it is mediated and made possible through the technology of online Q&A websites. (p. 9)

Digital media, and more specifically, religious web platforms, are used to educate and regulate traditional religious norms. Another stark example is the US Christian efforts against online pornography and the general encouragement toward modesty and premarital celibacy. While many of such efforts happen offline, there are also growing online efforts. The root of such efforts tends to be a religious adherence to avoid masturbation and to maintain purity. The increase accessibility of the Internet and the plethora of pornographic material online has led Christian religious leaders to declare that "pornography may be the greatest area of immorality inflicted on and pursued by Generation Z" (White, 2017, p. 60). This is true for Christians in the United States as well as in the Global South. Examining the issue for Pentecostal Christians in Democratic Republic of the Congo, Pype (2013) writes that: "Pentecostals deem that Christian households, and the Christian community at large are endangered by this new technology." To combat this "danger," several churches have created online resources to help individuals avoid consuming pornography.

Digital media are used to maintain traditions even on the path to heterosexual marriage. While the previous section discussed the autonomy and agency given to individuals through online dating, online dating also reinforces religious traditional views of marriage. For one thing, many religious dating websites and applications only allow for heterosexual relations (Cohen & Tsuria, 2019). Another interesting example is the issue of caste in Hindu dating. Caste is a cultural–religious construct that is preserved through Hindu religious traditions. On various Hindu digital dating platforms, caste is not only one of the profile categories one has to self-describe; it is usually a major category. Thus, as Titzmann (2019, p. 35) argues, digital media "emphasize … caste as an important social criterion to be considered in matchmaking." Through these design choices, digital dating platforms uphold religious heteronormative assumptions.

While many online sources are used to empower women to ask and speak about their sexuality, digital media are also used by women and men alike to urge a more traditional approach to female bodies. The Vishva Hindu Parishad, the organization whose members attacked the women at the bar that started the online Pink Chaddi campaign, is an example of a traditional, extremist religious organization that uses digital media to oppress women. According to Chattopadhyay (2011, p. 65), "new media plays a significant role for supporters of Hindutva as well." In fact: "the internet, … help[s] maintain over five hundred VHP Web sites through which to spread their messages about Hindutva, Hindu history, and Muslim-bashing" (Chopra, 2006, p. 194) as well as, in this case, actions against liberated female sexuality.

But acts against female sexual liberation do not have to be so explicit or violent, and they can also be promoted by women themselves. One such example is ModLi, a modest swimwear and fashion line created by Nava Brief-Fried, a Jewish Israeli woman. ModLi is described by its founder as "Etsy for conservative women" – in other words, it is based on conservative, traditional values and attitudes toward female bodies and sexualities. While such a fashion line celebrates multiculturalism, it also reinforces traditional attitudes toward female bodies – mainly, that female bodies should be hidden. What makes this case even more complex is the fact that this line, and other modest fashion companies, are fueled by digital media. According to Weinswig (2017), a Forbes journalist: "Modest fashion is gaining momentum, driven by E-commerce, social media, and other non-traditional channels." And modest fashion is not limited to Judaism. In fact, Wienswig also noted that "Modest fashion purchases by Muslim women were estimated at $44 billion that year." Indeed, there are many Muslim social media influencers that promote modest fashion, and they have gathered a following in the millions (Peterson, 2020). For example, Saufeeya Goodson (@safiyahhh) has more than three million followers on her Instagram page, where she posts Muslim messages and fashion. The photos all include women dressed according to Muslim law, thus promoting a traditional religious view of female bodies.

Aside from issues of modesty, religious digital media also portray female masturbation as a sin. The sexual liberation movement recognized female sexual needs, including masturbation, which allowed women to engage with sexuality more fully and in a healthier way, and feel less objectified. Women who masturbate also enjoy higher self-esteem and greater marital and sexual satisfaction (Hurlbert & Whittaker, 1991). In other words, it allows them to be a subject in the sexual act, not just an object. While most religious traditions have no explicit language against female masturbation (probably since female sexuality was largely dismissed), contemporary religious texts online tend to object to it (Tsuria, 2020b), as, for example, Today's Christian Woman website and Covenant Eyes, another Christian website, oppose female sexual expression. Through this type of discourse, female masturbation and female sexuality are framed as sinful and problematic.

Conclusion

In this chapter we surveyed the relationship between media and religious heteropatriarchy. We provided multiple examples from various forms of media – film, television, magazines, and new media – that impact this intersection. As noted in the introduction to the chapter, religion and sex and gender is already a complicated intersection. However, we can roughly posit that throughout history and globally, religious traditions constantly seek to control sexuality and reify gender norms, to some degree. In this chapter we showed how this attempt can be noted through and by religious actors themselves, either in trying to control media's sexual exposure through censorship, or in using media to maintain religious heteronormativity. But contemporary media texts are also used to negotiate and subvert traditional religious ideas of sexuality and gender by, for example, creating representations of religious LGBT+ individuals, exposing gendered or sexual abuse in religious communities, or by crafting narratives that empower women and sexual minorities.

This chapter then serves as a map, providing various viewpoints through specific examples. This map highlights the influence of religion on media, and, in turn, of mediated representations of sexuality. The map also points to the way media is used to negotiate sexual norms within religion (Tsuria, 2020a). As readers traverse this map they may ask themselves how they see sexuality and gender in media, and what role religion plays in that view.

References

Accomando, B. (2016, March 3). C is for 'condemned': A nun looks back on 47 years of unholy filmmaking. WBUR. Retrieved from https://www.wbur.org/npr/469041022

Arora, V. (2013). Bhutan's Buddhist monks accused of sexually molesting boys. *The Washington Post*, June 28. Retrieved June 1, 2022, from https://sojo.net/articles/bhutans-buddhist-monks-accused-sexually-molesting-boys

Bartashius, J. (2018). Subverting patriarchal Buddhism in *Spring, Summer, Fall, Winter … and Spring. Religion and Culture, 19*(1), 127–138. DOI:10.1080/14755610.2017.1416647

Bartashius, J. A. (2019). White Samurai in a fascistic house of mirrors: Fight Club, Zen, and the art of (re)constructing ethno-nationalism. *Religion and Culture, 20*(4), 351–370. DOI: 10.1080/14755610.2020.1842475

Black, G. D. (1989). Hollywood censored: The production code administration and the Hollywood film industry 1930–1940. *Film History, 3*(3), 167–189. http://www.jstor.org/stable/3814976

Black, G. D. (2013). The Legion of decency and the movies. In D. Biltereyst, & R. V. Winkel (Eds.), *Silencing cinema: Film censorship around the world*, (pp. 241–254).Palgrave Macmillan.

Boellstorff, T. (2020). Om toleran Om: Four Indonesian reflections on digital heterosexism. *Media, Culture & Society, 42*(1), 7–24. https://doi.org/10.1177/0163443719884066

Bogen, K. W., Haikalis, M., Meza Lopez, R. J., López, G., & Orchowski, L. M. (2020). It happens in# ChurchToo: Twitter discourse regarding sexual victimization within religious communities. *Journal of Interpersonal Violence, 37*(3–4), 1338–1366. https://doi.org/10.1177/0886260520922365

Bose, N. (2009). The Hindu right and the politics of censorship: Three case studies of policing Hindi cinema, 1992–2002. *The Velvet Light Trap, 63*, 22–33. https://www.utexaspressjournals.org/doi/abs/10.5555/vlt.2009.63.22

Burke, K. (2014). What makes a man: Gender and sexual boundaries on evangelical Christian sexuality websites. *Sexualities, 17*(1–2), 3–22. https://digitalcommons.unl.edu/sociologyfacpub/590/

Campbell, H. (2010). *When religion meets new media*. Routledge.

Catsoulis, J. (2017). Review: 'I am Michael' portrays a gay activist seeking to be straight. *New York Times*, January 26. Retrieved June 1, 2022, from https://www.nytimes.com/2017/01/26/movies/i-am-michael-review-james-franco-zachary-quinto.html

Ceuterick, M. (2020). *Affirmative aesthetics and willful women: Gender, space and mobility in contemporary cinema*. Palgrave.

Chastagner, C. (1999). The parents' music resource center: From information to censorship. *Popular Music, 18*(2), 179–192 http://www.jstor.org/stable/853600.

Chattopadhyay, S. (2011). Online activism for a heterogenous time: The Pink Chaddi campaign and the social media in India. *Proteus: A Journal of Ideas, 27*(1), 63–67. www.ship.edu/uploadedFiles/Ship/Proteus/2011Proteus.pdf

Chopra, R. (2006). Global primordialities: Virtual identity politics in online Hindutva and online Dalit discourse. *New Media & Society, 8*(2), 187–206. https://journals.sagepub.com/doi/10.1177/1461444806061942

Claussen, D. S. (Ed.). (2002). *Sex, religion, media*. Rowman & Littlefield.

Cohen, Y., & Tsuria, R. (2019). A match made in the clouds: Jews, Rabbis and online dating sites. In A. Hetsroni, & M. Tuncez (Eds.), *Internet-infused romantic interactions and dating practices* (pp. 177–190). Institute of Network Cultures.

Du Mez, K. K. (2020). *Jesus and John Wayne: How white evangelicals corrupted a faith and fractured a nation*. Liveright Publishing.

Ellingson, S. (2002). Introduction. In S. Ellingson, & M. C. Green (Eds.), *Religion and sexuality in cross-cultural perspective* (pp. 1–18). Routledge.

Gennari, D. T. (2013). Blessed cinema: State and Catholic censorship in postwar Italy. In D. Biltereyst, & R. V. Winkel (Eds.), *Silencing cinema: Film censorship around the world* (pp. 255–271). Palgrave Macmillan.

Gerber, L. (2021, August 10). Netflix's 'Pray Away' confronts the lies of the ex-gay movement. Religion and Politics. Retrieved June 1, 2022, from https://religionandpolitics.org/2021/08/10/netflixs-pray-away-confronts-the-lies-of-the-ex-gay-movement

Ghosh, S. (1999). The troubled existence of sex and sexuality: Feminists engage with censorship. In C. Brosius, & M. Butcher (Eds.), *Image journeys: Audio-visual media and cultural change in India* (pp. 231–259). Sage Publications.

Ghosh, S. (2002). Queer pleasures for queer people: Film, television and queer sexuality in India. In R. Vanita (Ed.), *Queering India: Same-sex love and eroticism in Indian culture and society* (pp. 207–221). Routledge.

Greeley, A. M. (1992). Like a Catholic: Madonna's challenge to her church. *Black Sacred Music, 6*(1), 244–249. DOI:10.1215/10439455-6.1.244

Han, S. (2018). Wear white: The mediatized politics of religious anti-LGBT activism in Singapore. *Nordic Journal of Religion and Society, 31*(1), 41–57 https://www.idunn.no/doi/abs/10.18261/issn.1890-7008-2018-01-03

Haridi, N. H., Abd Rahman, K. A., & Wazir, R. (2016). Metodologi dakwah terhadap golongan lesbian, gay, biseksual dan transgender (LGBT). *Jurnal Pengajian Islam, 9*(2), 103–118. https://scholar.google.com/citations?view_op=view_citation&hl=en&user=Az-JKiEAAAAJ&citation_for_view=Az-JKiEAAAAJ:YsMSGLbcyi4C

Hidayatullah, A. (2003). Islamic conceptions of sexuality. In D. W. Machacek & M. M. Wilcox (Eds.), *Sexuality and the world's religions* (pp. 255–292). ABC-Clio.

Hurlbert, D. F., & Whittaker, K. E. (1991). The role of masturbation in marital and sexual satisfaction: A comparative study of female masturbators and nonmasturbators. *Journal of Sex Education & Therapy, 17*(4), 272–282.

Jakobsen, J. R., & Pellegrini, A. (2004). *Love the sin: Sexual regulation and the limits of religious tolerance.* Beacon Press.

Kaur, P. (2017). Gender, sexuality and (be) longing: The representation of queer (LGBT) in Hindi cinema. *Amity Journal of Media & Communications Studies (AJMCS), 7*(1), 22–30. https://amity.edu/UserFiles/asco/journal/ISSUE50_3.%20Pushpinder.pdf

Knauss, S. (2013). Exploring Orthodox Jewish masculinities with Eyes Wide Open. *Journal of Religion and Film, 17*(2), 1–35. https://digitalcommons.unomaha.edu/jrf/vol17/iss2/7/.

Laarman, P. (2018, April 17). Netflix's Carlton Pearson biopic, 'Come Sunday' reveals Christianity's struggle for its soul. Religion Dispatches. Retrieved from https://religiondispatches.org/netflixs-carlton-pearson-biopic-come-sunday-reveals-christianitys-struggle-for-its-soul

Langenberg, A. P. (2017). *Buddhism and sexuality.* Oxford University Press.

Lucero, L. (2017). Safe spaces in online places: Social media and LGBTQ youth. *Multicultural Education Review, 9*(2), 117–128. https://www.tandfonline.com/doi/abs/10.1080/2005615X.2017.1313482

Mendenhall, R. R. (2002). Responses to television from the new Christian right: The Donald Wildmon organization's fight against sexual content. In D. S. Claussen (Ed.), *Sex, religion, media* (pp. 101–114). Rowman and Littlefield Publishers.

Mokhtar, M. F., Sukeri, W. A. E. D. W., & Abd Latiff, Z. (2019). Social media roles in spreading LGBT movements in Malaysia. *Asian Journal of Media and Communication (AJMC), 3*(2), 77–82. https://journal.uii.ac.id/AJMC/article/view/14310

Moore, E. E. (2010). "Braveheart," sacred heart: Exploring resistance to patriarchal discourses in mainstream media and faith in the American spiritual marketplace. *Women's Studies Quarterly, 38*(3/4), 94–115. http://www.jstor.org/stable/20799367

Moylan, B. (2015, January 25). Sundance 2015 review: I am Michael – James Franco's gay pastor hits the straight and shallow. *The Guardian.* Retrieved June 1, 2022, from https://www.theguardian.com/film/2015/jan/25/sundance-2015-review-i-am-michael-james-franco

Mutlu, D. K., & Koçer, Z. (2012). A different story of secularism: The censorship of religion in Turkish films of the 1960s and early 1970s. *European Journal of Cultural Studies, 15*(1), 70–88. https://journals.sagepub.com/doi/abs/10.1177/1367549411424948

Naji Bajnaid, A., & Elyas, T. (2017). Exploring the phenomena of online dating platforms versus Saudi traditional spouse courtship in the 21st century. *Digest of Middle East Studies, 26*(1), 74–96. https://onlinelibrary.wiley.com/doi/10.1111/dome.12104

Peterson, K. M. (2020). The unruly, loud, and intersectional Muslim woman: Interrupting the aesthetic styles of Islamic fashion images on Instagram. *International Journal of Communication, 14,* 20.

Poe Hays, R., & Werse, N. R. (2017). Evangelicals and the film Fight Club: A cultural comparison and masculine ideology. *The Projector: A Journal on Film, Media, and Culture, 17*(2), 15–31. https://www.theprojectorjournal.com/_files/ugd/d3b63e_5bd27920c99947fc8f7f909e3c5baaf4.pdf

Pullen, C., & Cooper, M. (Eds.). (2010). *LGBT identity and online new media.* Routledge.

Pype, K. (2013). Cursing the mobile phone: Pentecostal understandings of urban sociality, sexuality and social media in contemporary Kinshasa. *Sexuality and Social Media in Contemporary Kinshasa.* Retrieved September 6, 2022, from https://ssrn.com/abstract=2253735

Rashid, F., & Barron, I. (2019). Why the focus of clerical child sexual abuse has largely remained on the Catholic church amongst other non-Catholic Christian denominations and religions. *Journal of Child Sexual Abuse, 28*(5), 564–585. https://doi.org/10.1080/10538712.2018.1563261

Reuters. (2008, September 7). Madonna dedicates "Like a Virgin" to pope. Reuters. Retrieved June 1, 2022, from https://www.reuters.com/article/us-italy-madonna-idUSPAR75048420080907

Richardson, M., Cannon, S., Teichert, L., Vance, A., Kramer, I., Barter, M., King, J., & Callahan, C. (2020). Religion-focused dating apps: A Q methodology study on the uses of mutual. *Telematics and Informatics*, *55*(3), art. 101448. https://doi.org/10.1016/j.tele.2020.101448.

Robertson, C. K. (2006). *Religion & sexuality: Passionate debates*. Peter Lang.

Robinson, C. M., & Spivey, S. E. (2007). The politics of masculinity and the ex-gay movement. *Gender and Society*, *21*(5), 650–675. https://journals.sagepub.com/doi/10.1177/0891243207306384

Rochadiat, A. M. P., Tong, S. T., & Novak, J. M. (2017). Online dating and courtship among Muslim American women: Negotiating technology, religious identity, and culture. *New Media & Society*, *20*(4), 1618–1639. https://doi.org/10.1177/1461444817702396

Rockett, K. (2013). Irish film censorship: Refusing the fractured family of foreign films. In D. Biltereyst, & R. V. Winkel (Eds.), *Silencing cinema: Film censorship around the world* (pp. 207–220). Palgrave Macmillan.

Roper, L. (2013). *Oedipus and the devil: Witchcraft, religion and sexuality in early modern Europe*. Routledge.

Scherer, B. (2011). Macho Buddhism: Gender and sexualities in the diamond way. *Religion & Gender*, *1*(1), 85–103. https://brill.com/view/journals/rag/1/1/article-p85_5.xml?language=en

Schmidt, R. A., & Voss, B. L. (2005). *Archaeologies of sexuality*. Routledge.

Stopler, G. (2003). Countenancing the oppression of women: How liberals tolerate religious and cultural practices that discriminate against women. *Columbia Journal of Gender and Law*, *12*, (1), 154–221. https://heinonline.org/HOL/P?h=hein.journals/coljgl12&i=164

Taylor, Y., Falconer, E., & Snowdon, R. (2014). Queer youth, Facebook and faith: Facebook methodologies and online identities. *New Media & Society*, *16*(7), 1138–1153. https://doi.org/10.1177/1461444814544000

Titzmann, F.-M. (2019). Hindu religious identification in India's online matrimonial market. In X. Zeiler (Ed.), *Digital Hinduism* (pp. 35–49). Routledge.

Tomalin, E., Starkey, C., & Halafoff, A. (2015). Cyber sisters: Buddhist women's online activism and practice. *Annual Review of the Sociology of Religion*, *6*, 11–33. https://brill.com/view/book/edcoll/9789004302549/B9789004302549-s003.xml

Tsuria, R. (2016). Jewish Q&A online and the regulation of sexuality: Using Foucault to read technology. *Social Media + Society*, *2*(3), 1–10. https://journals.sagepub.com/doi/full/10.1177/2056305116662176

Tsuria, R. (2017). New media in the Jewish bedroom: Exploring religious Jewish online discourse concerning gender and sexuality. PhD dissertation, Texas A&M University.

Tsuria, R. (2020a). Get out of church! The case of# emptythepews: Twitter hashtag between resistance and community. *Information*, *11*(6), 335. https://doi.org/10.3390/info11060335

Tsuria, R. (2020b). The discourse of practice – Online Q&A as normalizing gender and sexual behaviors. *International Journal of Communication*, *14*(2020), 3595–3613. https://ijoc.org/index.php/ijoc/article/view/13811

Valerius, K. (2005). 'Rosemary's baby,' gothic pregnancy, and fetal subjects. *College Literature*, *34*(3), 116–135. https://www.jstor.org/stable/pdf/25115290.pdf

Valle, M. (2012, May 14). Another 'hot-text' for the war on women: Rosemary's Baby. Religion Dispatches. Retrieved June 3, 2022, from https://religiondispatches.org/another-hot-text-for-the-war-on-women-irosemarys-babyi

Wan Amizah, W. M., Kee, C. P., & Aziz, J. (2009). Film censorship in Malaysia: Sanctions of religious, cultural and moral values. *Jurnal Komunikasi: Malaysian Journal of Communication*, *25*, 42–49. http://journalarticle.ukm.my/305/

Warner, M. (1983). *Alone of all her sex: The myth and the cult of the Virgin Mary*. Vintage Books (Original work published 1976).

Weinswig, D. (2017, March 31). Is modest fashion the next big thing? *Forbes* Retrieved June 1, 2022, from https://www.forbes.com/sites/deborahweinswig/2017/03/31/is-modest-fashion-the-next-big-thing/?sh=3866e3999e97

Weng, H. W. (2015). Dakwah 2.0: Digital dakwah, street dakwah and cyber-urban activism among Chinese Muslims in Malaysia and Indonesia. In H. W. Weng (Ed.), *New media configurations and socio-cultural dynamics in Asia and the Arab world* (pp. 198–221). Nomos Verlagsgesellschaft mbH & Co. KG.

Wetzel, D. (2020). The rise of the Catholic alt-right. *Journal of Labor and Society, 23*(1), 31–55. https://brill.com/view/journals/jlso/23/1/article-p31_3.xml?language=en

White, J. E. (2017). *Meet generation Z: Understanding and reaching the new post-Christian world.* Baker Book House.

Yahel Center. (2021). About. Yahel Center. Retrieved June 1, 2022, from https://merkazyahel.org.il/en

Yip, A. K., & Hunt, S. J. (2016). *The Ashgate research companion to contemporary religion and sexuality.* Routledge.

Zeydabadi-Nejad, S. (2009). *The politics of Iranian cinema: Film and society in the Islamic Republic.* Routledge.

Żuk, P., & Żuk, P. (2020). 'Murderers of the unborn' and 'sexual degenerates': Analysis of the 'anti-gender' discourse of the Catholic Church and the nationalist right in Poland. *Critical Discourse Studies, 17*(5), 566–588. https://doi.org/10.1080/17405904.2019.1676808

Selected Readings

Bartashius, J. (2020). The *Fight Club* Path to Buddhist Heteronormativity. 文学部紀要」文教大学文学部 34–351号 2020年 47–74.

Du Mez, K. K. (2020). *Jesus and John Wayne: How white evangelicals corrupted a faith and fractured a nation.* Liveright Publishing.

Lövheim, M. (Ed.). (2013). *Media, religion and gender: Key issues and new challenges.* Routledge.

Scahill, A. (2010). Demons are a girl's best friend: Queering the revolting child in The Exorcist. *Red Feather Journal, 1*(2), 39–45.

Tsuria, R. (2016). Jewish Q&A online and the regulation of sexuality: Using Foucault to read technology. *Social Media + Society, 2*(3). DOI:10.1177/2056305116662176.

30

Authority, Religion, and Media

Míriam Díez Bosch and Alba Sabaté Gauxachs

In the present day, the media have acquired some of the societal functions that were previously the preserve of religious organizations (Hjarvard, 2011, p. 4). This chapter will explore this phenomenon by analyzing its causes, effects, and consequences. Soukup (2017) and Zsupan-Jerome (2017) highlight that authority nowadays resides in whoever has a voice, so the chapter also deals with the issue of voices of authority and the nature of authority itself, by contemplating what communication and media signify for religious communities and institutions.

The Concept of Authority

The definition of the term authority is itself contested (Campbell, 2021; Hackett & Soares, 2015; Soukup, 2017; Zsupan-Jerome, 2017). Hannah Arendt (1954) affirms that "since we can no longer fall back upon authentic and undisputable experiences common to all, the very term [of authority] has become clouded by controversy and confusion." For her, there is no possible definition of "authority in general" (p. 91) – something that Giddens (1990) affirms by noting that notions of authority are continuously codified.

A number of authors address the issue in different fields and from different perspectives. Weber (1922) defines authority as a legitimized dominance, through which certain specific commands must be obeyed by given groups of people. Campbell (2021) considers authority as role based whereas Foucault (1977) sees authority as power based, focused on a structure's ability to control others. Hofstede (2011) defines a tightly or loosely coupled power between different individuals and powerbrokers. Both Weber and Foucault touched on notions of relationality in their approach to authority, an aspect used by social psychologists. Those taking the relational point of view consider authority in terms of individuals' willingness to accept a leader's directives and assertions of power (Campbell, 2021). This category could also include definitions of the concept like Zelizer's (1992), who regards authority as a construct of community, functioning as the glue that binds the community together.

Most of the authors dealing with this concept (Campbell, 2021; Hoover, 2016; Schofield Clark, 2012; Soukup, 2017) follow Weber's (1922) definition of the ideal types of authority to better explore the term: legal authority (based on a system of rules), traditional authority (based on the legitimacy of "what has always existed" and on a claim by the leaders, and a belief on the part of their followers, that there is virtue in the sanctity of age-old rules and powers; Ritzer, 1999), and charismatic authority (based on the leader's appeal). Weber (1947) notes that authority cultivates legitimacy; he finds it useful to classify the types of authority according to the kind of claim to legitimacy typically made by each type. Authority, then, exists when people voluntarily obey. Matheson (1987) deals with Weber's concept of legitimacy and proposes eight major sources of legitimization. Soukup (2017) updated and extended Weber's list by proposing that the current decentralized model of communications dilutes the legal and traditional models of authority, and identifies 10 more models: the authority of power or coercive forces, the authority of knowledge, the authority over knowledge, the authority of presence, the authority of ritual, political authority, participatory or democratic authority, community authority, institutional authority, and leadership authority.

Monteiro (2017) thinks that authority and power are not synonymous, but rather closely related and more a way to express care for others, for example, by helping someone to be better. Nevertheless, he links Weber's approach to Kant's view, in which human beings can think and feel coherently only in categories. For Mosca (1939), authority is essential for a society to function. Seligman (2000) highlights that modernity is hostile to authority, arguing that individuals now look to themselves as the root of morality, and this morally conscious self has become the cornerstone of civic order (Schofield Clark, 2012). Ruggiero and Winch (2005) talk about "cultural authority" and Starr (1982), also defining "cultural authority," affirms that it is the force that defines and describes reality, highlighting the relevance of the role of journalists in this respect. For Schofield Clark (2012), cultural authority is the right of some parts to express the perceived norms of the whole. As regards communication, Zsupan-Jerome (2017) distinguishes between the application of external measures of authority and the internal sense of authority within a religious organization specifically, through the prescriptions of the Rule of Benedict and how the rules construct the ethos of this community.

Some scholars studying the sociology of religion have also favored studying authority and, according to Campbell (2021), their definition of the term religious authority suffers from lack of clarity, as they use it as an overarching term rather than a clearly defined category. Even the term religion itself creates controversy among anthropologists and sociologists (Ferré, 1970; Horton, 1960). This chapter recognizes religion as a force in society, culture, and politics, both domestically and internationally (Hoover, 2016). Here, the term "religion" encompasses all traditions; thus, discussions of religious authority take into account all religions and beliefs. As Hoover (2016) affirms, proof of this is the presence of religions in new forms beyond the formal domains of discourse.

Authority appears regularly in the religious sphere since globally religions have historically embedded ideas of hierarchy, bonds, and loyalty (Hackett & Soares, 2015; Horsfield, 2016; Schofield Clark, 2012) in their structure. Authority moves between the necessary contingency of religion and the pull toward a divine or spiritual authority given to the most sacred aspects of religion. While religious authority could have different purposes in different religious traditions, obedience holds particular importance (Weber, 1947; Zsupan-Jerome, 2017), and so is a prominent aspect of religious studies. Zsupan-Jerome (2017) sees authority as problematic in our contemporary cultural context, "as it often implies a potentially oppressive imbalance of power" (p 79) and, in some contexts, could be linked to the power of some authoritarian states (Keyes et al., 1994). Zsupan-Jerome (2017) balances this with a focus on the Benedictine notion of obedience, rooted in the act of listening and the less linear and more networked value of openness.

Weber identified religious, sacred, and spiritual forms of authority as traditional authorities (Schofield Clark, 2012). Chavez (1994) argues that the distinguishing feature of religious authority is an influence legitimized by calling on some supernatural referent. Some, like De Pillis (1966), refer to a divine authority granted to religious structures or, like Wiles (1971), suggest that the divine authority is manifested in appointed gatekeepers representing the sentiments and decision-making of God on Earth. Chavez (2003) and Barnes (1978) refer to religious authority as a trust-based relationship given to institutional professionals or self-appointed leaders by their followers or resting in systems of knowledge able to define what constitutes religious authenticity, especially in relation to religious identity and membership.

However, in our current society values and authenticity appear more liquid, even volatile (Bauman, 2005), and religious experience enters into the dynamic that shapes society: competition. Horsfield (2016, p. 55) sees authority as fluid, constructed, and sustained symbolically, as it "needs to continually establish itself through language and communication within a marketplace of competing claims and interests."

As institutions, religions share the global arena with other kinds of organizations and religious leaders must seek "airtime" opportunities to promote their views in broadcast media (Hoover, 2016). This situation is part of a broader crisis in which reason, science, technology, and bureaucratic rationality sideline religious, spiritual, and sacred considerations (Thomas, 2003) – a secularization that exemplifies the decline of religious authority (Chavez, 1994). This also appears in contexts where religious authority had links to political authority, situations where the complexity of the general model of authority increase. In this context, Keyes et al. (1994) look at Asian visions of authority, through a "crisis of authority" model, which emerged as a consequence of the modernization and nation-building projects of Asian states and the subordination of religious authority to the state authority. Feener (2014) analyzes diverse models of Muslim religious authority in modern Asia to highlight the rapid and dramatic social, economic, and political transformations of the past two centuries that have resulted in complex reconfigurations of religious authority in many Muslim societies. These changes have involved new profiles of leadership. Similarly, Gifford (2005, p. 380) notes that religions in Africa have not remained unaffected by the changing contexts and "the elements of authority within a religion, the way they are balanced, perceived, experienced, are among the things that have changed."

The only way of moving forward occurs through innovation, and through changes in the entities that compete for authority (Weber et al., 2005). But this competition could lead to a rise of fundamentalism and radicalization, given that authority in these cases is concentrated in a small number of individuals (Almond et al., 2003). According to Díez Bosch et al. (2017), competition should not be confused with lack of cooperation. Though the interaction of different parts of all systems spontaneously sets off the collective dynamic of competition, at the highest levels competition encourages cooperation and stimulates progress. This is the case when religious authority is challenged. Communication practices have taken on social, hermeneutic, and transcendental functions such as religions once had in different contexts, providing people with a sense of community that may help them to live with a sense of identity, as religions once did (Lynch, 2005). Such authority is not an entity in itself, but rather an artifact of the communications process (Lincoln, 1994). Historically, communication progress has offered both a challenge and an opportunity for religions and religious authority (Campbell, 2021; Cowan, 2005; Hoover, 2016; Soukup, 2017; Stout, 2012).

Media: The Key to Religious Authority

Religions have embraced communication as an ally to construct, rethink, and reinforce their authority, as most of them quickly adopted the tools, channels, and platforms required in the different eras, with the objective of connecting with their members (Schofield Clark, 2012; Soukup, 2017; Spadaro, 2012). Schofield Clark (2016) detects the roots of historical links between media, religion, and authority in the early Christian and Muslim scriptures. Religions built their authority by taking control of the main communication channels (Campbell, 2021; Hoover, 2016; Soukup, 2017) and technologies.

Having control of communication technologies and of the distribution of messages gave religious groups power because such control implicitly conveys a recognition of legitimacy (Monteiro, 2017). Homilies, decrees of the ecumenical council, scriptures, rituals, music, art, and architecture constituted a kind of "soft authority." In his reflection on theological implications of communication after the Second Vatican Council, Dulles (1988) affirms that communication among Catholics defines the dynamics of authority – distributed among five "models" (hierarchical/institutional, kerygmatic/herald, sacramental, community/communion, and servant). Eilers (1994) follows this by underlining the need for an awareness of influences of media in people's lives, asking who and how they present values and how the presentations change or determine personal and societal life.

Several have traced the ways religions have adapted to existing technology to construct and reinforce authority. Hoover (2016, 2006) analyzes how media presence affects and influences religious authority, particularly in Christianity, while Turner (1974) applies Weber's theory on authority and legitimacy to Islam. Horsfield's (2015) examination of the historical links between Christianity and the media shows how media processes and technologies have shaped the historical development of Christianity. Cohen (2012) does the same for Judaism by analyzing the links between Jewish authority and media. For instance, delving into what he calls the dual loyalties dilemma, he affirms that the modern Orthodox Jew is characterized by a symbiosis between the Torah and the modern world. Grieve and Veidlinger (2015) and Cheong et al. (2011) do something similar with Buddhist organizations. Cohen (2021) reviews studies on Asian mass media and their relationship with religious authority. Radde-Antweiler and Zeiler (2019) also look at the mediatization of religion in Asia, taking into account the interrelation of media, religion, and culture in different Asian regions with heterogeneous cultural, linguistic, ethnic, and religious backgrounds – including China, India, Korea, Japan, Siberian regions of North Asia, Central Asia, the Middle East, the Arabian Peninsula, the Philippines, Malaysia, and Indonesia. Chinese media coverage of religion plays a role (Yao et al., 2011) as do Korean media (Min-Soo, 2013) in their respective countries. Kumar (2003) examines the coverage of religion and spirituality in Indian newspapers. For Africa, Ihejirika (2009) reviews the landscape of research on this field and highlights that recent developments in African cultures and politics show the influence of religion in media. More specifically, White (2009) applies the role of these changing media to democratic governance in Africa, evaluating the effectiveness of the media in Africa in political education.

Soukup (2017) reminds us of older media: of the trust religions put in scriptures, specifically citing the Bible as an example. The book historically became the channel of Christian authority and helped the Catholic institution shape and consolidate its authority. During the Reformation each Christian church codified its teaching authority, as the legitimacy of the printed book magnified the influence of its content. Gifford (2010) and other scholars similarly show how organized faiths draw on scriptures, tradition, and charisma to produce religious experiences, all of which serve as sources of authority. Golan and Martini (2020) point out that the power of symbolic artifacts (Jewish mezuzah, talismans, and arabesques) sometimes supplements the literal meanings of the canon. All the authors mentioned remark that the close links between religious authority and media mean that the many kinds of religious authority are challenged every time the communication landscape changes (Campbell, 2007; Soukup, 2017). Meyer and Moors (2006) agree that the adoption of the mass media, although suitable for the spread of religious ideas, raises important questions concerning the maintenance of religious authority. This can vary. For "in contexts as Africa, perhaps more than anywhere else, the new does not replace the old" (Hackett & Soares, 2015, p. 8). This remains true of religion as well as media, where the old and the new not only coexist and are interdependent but are often inextricably entangled.

Hjarvard (2016) argues that the impact of mediatization (see Chapter 18) on religion is so powerful that it moderates global religious authority. For him mediatization is defined as the phenomenon by which people experience religions through the mediation of communication media. Information about religion is molded in accordance with the demands of various popular media genres, so journalistic news media play a significant role in framing religion and religious issues and actors follow journalistic praxes to garner attention. Schofield Clark (2012) and Hoover (2006) argue that journalists are not the only ones acting out this role, as it is also exploited by the entertainment industry. A paradox results: people practice religion and speak of the sacred in an openly secular and inexorably commercial media context (Hoover & Clark, 2002).

Perhaps Hoover has reflected the most on this phenomenon as he highlights the evidence that the media define the terms through which religious and spiritual interests are formed and talks about their power of legitimation (Hoover, 2006). "Media are positioned so centrally in the social world that people, cultures, events or beliefs are often thought not to be authentic, legitimate or real unless they are mediated by modern mass communication" (Hoover & Emerich, 2011, p. 211). In an edited volume, Hoover (2016), with more than 10 colleagues, analyzed the relationship between the mediation of religion and religious authority, judging it complex, layered, and nuanced. They sought to promote a rethinking of these matters and claim that the media directly confront religious authorities' ability to control their own symbols and resources both by relativizing some religious symbols and by the coverage of the great number of "religious and quasi-religious" imbrications and truth claims. The questions of the mediation of religion impinge on Weber's thinking because the Weberian concept of traditional authority and charismatic authority draws on religion. Similarly, media affect the Weberian concept of plausibility, which is necessarily linked with transparency and authenticity, because "to assign things the category of the authentic is the primary power that religious authorities hold, and their claim for this power is their necessary currency of exchange" (Hoover, 2016, p. 5).

This also affects religious fundamentalism. Hoover and Kaneva (2009) argue that fundamentalisms cannot be fully understood without media, as media authority reinforces the power, actions, and image of some movements. For example, fundamentalism in the United States became known through their media as occurred with the political evangelicalism of televangelism (Hadden & Shupe, 1988; Marsden, 1983). Media serve as instruments of construction and dissemination of meaning and provide the contexts in which competing sets of symbols are proposed, promoted, circulated, and consumed (Hoover & Kaneva, 2009).

Communication media also affect the sacred. Authority occurs in what we sacralize (Schofield Clark, 2012). In an analysis of the concept of the "sacred" in the context of the postmodern media, Sumiala-Seppänen et al. (2006) underscore how the concept depends on production and reception of communication, building on the Durkheim and Eliade works on the sacred. Zeiler and Radde-Antweiler (2018) trace this in the ascription processes within news media, noting how news media ascribe meanings to key terms. Focusing on "sacred," "secular," and "authority," they find that "authority" is essential to decipher the process of to whom power is endorsed and to understand how this very framework functions.

Others use different entry points. Linderman (2016) begins with the term vicarious religion, first proposed by Grace Davie. Cohen (2018) tackles the concept of authority from the newsroom approach, reviewing the evolution of religious coverage. Kazi (2021) reflects on religious TV and authority in Pakistan and Eisenlohr (2014) talks about media, citizenship, and religious mobilization among Mumbai's Muslims. Radde-Antweiler (2018) works on mediatization in relation to local rituals in the Philippines, and Burhani (2018) focuses on plural Islam and contestation of religious authority in Indonesia. Ho (2010) applies the model to the negotiation of Islam in

China's cyberspace, while Hirschkind (2006) writes about radio preachers, public piety, and popular media in Egypt. Bucar (2017) explores the religious authority of Muslim women's fashion. Zeleke and Bruzzi (2015) study women's involvement and leadership in Sufism, specifically in Ethiopia and Eritrea. Dipio (2009) looks at gender and religion in Nigerian popular films. Kamate (2009) talks about Pentecostalism in Kinshasa and Asamoah-Gyadu (2009) about mediating supernatural power through enchanted texts and tapes in Africa. Ukah (2008) thinks about the authority and the regulation of religious broadcasting in Nigeria, and Adama (2007) reflects on Islamic communication and mass media in Cameroon. Miroslav Volf (2015) approaches this concept of authority from the globalization perspective. For him, religions are part of the dynamics of globalization, and he considers religions the original globalizers and affirms that they still remain as drivers of globalization processes.

However, Turner (2007) considers that the rapid development and cultural acceptance of new media (for a definition, see Campbell, 2021) as shaping the social conditions that produce authority. The digital environment adds new ways of understanding the concept of authority (Campbell, 2007; Soukup, 2017) by bringing new languages, leadership positions, and dynamics of interaction that revisit the Weberian and other classical models of authority.

Authority, Religion, and Media in the Digital Age

Scholars speculate how digital culture transforms accepted understandings and patterns of authority (Anderson, 1999; Turner, 2007). According to Turner (2007, p. 117), "multimedia entertainment and communications systems challenge both the print-based authority of secular governments and the traditional authority of the world religions." Indeed, the Internet allows religious community members to make private institutional and theological discussions public (Barker, 2005) and poses a challenge to religious authority in established communities (Herring, 2005; Piff & Warburg, 2005). Campbell (2021) reports that some scholars like Dawson and Hennebry (1999) assumed that the appearance of new forms of authority online would displace traditional authorities and lead to struggles over membership, but there appears no unified understanding of the concept of authority in studies of the Internet.

Campbell (2021) herself has often reflected about how digital media challenges religious authority. She asks what religious authority looks like in the age of digital media, and whether recognized religious leaders and the structures they work within recognize it. For her, "in the digital culture, authority is established in a very different way, as it does not come from external sources and protocols, but it is cultivated by and comes from within the media system" (p. 8). She considers authority in this context as a scaffolding by which the abilities of certain individuals or structures gain or maintain influence over a particular group of people within digital spaces. Earlier, Campbell (2007) looked into the attributes of authority at play in the online context and distinguished between different layers of authority in terms of hierarchy, structure, and ideology, exploring how different religious traditions approach questions of authority in relation to the Internet and how traditional authority is affected by the Internet. In the course of that work Campbell reviewed existent work on online authority and suggested a categorization of authors dealing with the concept within Internet studies. This classification aligns with the three most dominant uses of the term. First, Ahuja and Carley (1998) and Wang and Archer (2004) link it to organizational and community structures, systems, and hierarchies; second, Breen (1997) and Greenleaf (1996) consider it as leadership-specific roles and positions of influence; and third, Mnookin (1996) relates it to an ideological notion such as moral or higher authority relative to issues of governance. Still others consider authority as a general concept synonymous with "power," and even refer to nonhuman sources of authority such as documents, texts, or historical events (Campbell, 2021).

For Hoover (2016) the entire meaning of religious authority may be shifting away from structure and toward practice. He talks about how religions are present online in a kind of a marketplace, and of the challenges of placing them in (new) media in this more-or-less horizontal way. In this sense, Campbell (2021) looks at authority online as an algorithm. Schofield Clark (2012) also reflects on "algorithmic authority," a term borrowed from Shirky (2009), to describe an authority resting in consensus-based collective evaluation systems. These "consensus-based interpretative authorities" mark systems whose authority rests upon their ability to articulate perspectives that are widely appreciated and that provide a reasonable interpretation of current events (Schofield Clark, 2012). This kind of authority is not new in religion but has roots in the ascetic Puritans (sixteenth and seventeenth centuries), during whose time moral and religious authority rested on consensus, as the group had to agree to grant authority to a leader.

Soukup (2017), however, highlights that "the digital world encompasses millions of believers in alternative de facto structures of religious authority." Online media became a place to look for authoritative messages and, in this marketplace, "authority not only depends on who has a position of authority, but on who has a voice, the ways in which people craft messages, the ways in which those messages fit into the ecosystem, the frequency of messaging and the 'horizontal' communication" (pp. 31–32). In the digital world, the criteria for transmitting information may either originate from algorithms that act mechanically, or in human judgments about newsworthy elements, so it is important to learn the language of new media and to understand the nature of authority in the digital age. "The kind of authority that matters to people is the authority that they themselves grant" (p. 32). For this reason, the very variety of authorities should motivate the Church and religions in general to think carefully about their communication plans (Soukup, 2017). Hjarvard (2016) affirms:

> The Church and other religious actors may also use various media to seek to reach fellow believers and disseminate information about their religion, but the traditional religious media, genres, and texts (e.g., sermon and Bible) play a less central role for the circulation of information about religion. In effect, centralized control of information by religious organizations has become increasingly difficult both because of mass media's predominantly secular orientation toward this kind of information as a result of the distributed, networked-like character of various interactive media. (p. 10)

Often the authority ascribed in digital practice is one earned in the process of interaction on specific topics or issues, a type of authority more common in oral-dominant communities than in the aloof, institution-based authority that most churches have carried into this third millennium (Horsfield, 2015). For Hoover (2018), the mode of practice in the digital age enforces feedback loops and conversations. This means that new forms of religious and spiritual interaction take place on and in the media. Is there a need for religious authority in this setting? Monteiro (2017) reflects that, for some, this may reflect a sacramental need as part of a sense of being religious; for others it exists for the sake of the orderliness of the online community. But Cheong (2013, p. 4) characterizes religious authority in the digital sphere by "the logic of disjuncture and displacement." Monteiro (2017, p. 61), in turn, underlines that the Internet challenges authority by "expanding access to religious information in a way that can undermine the plausibility structure of religious systems."

Spadaro (2012, p. 66) frames things differently, arguing that the main problem of authority is that the Internet allows a direct connection with a center of information, with no mediation. This situation of horizontal network communication challenges the dynamics of the testimonial transmission of information in the specific case of the Catholic Church. Spadaro (2017, p. 63) quotes Archbishop Celli, the former head of the Pontifical Council on Communication, who argues that the model of the pulpit is no longer sufficient for religious authority. Instead, people need "a model of the Church able to engage and to share, able to inflame hearts and to welcome people, understanding expectations, doubts, hopes, and questions, not a Church which is a container of doctrine or a broadcaster of faith," something that Viganò (2017) claims characterizes Pope Francis' communications. Such new media dynamics also open access to religion to the "underchurched" (Vassallo, 1998). Some evidence from papal documents supports the claim that the Catholic Church gradually legitimized social media and proclaimed the need to adopt their language (Arasa et al., 2018) – a finding confirmed by Golan and Martini (2020), who found that the Catholic Church perceives social media as an effective platform for transmitting core religious values and devout behavior. Other scholars see more challenges (Carroggio, 2016; Tridente & Mastroianni, 2016). Following the Benedictine model, Zsupan-Jerome (2017) identifies in it a less linear and more networked obedience, aligned with digital culture. The Benedictine option includes three areas of relevance for authority – listening, obedience, and mutuality – that link directly with social media values of dialogue, gift of self, and encounter (McGrane, 2013). In any event, social networks are fast becoming principal venues of shaping religious discourse, performing rituals, and ultimately developing new modes of authority (Golan & Martini, 2020), such as "networked theology" (Campbell & Garner, 2016) or an authority built on media ecology, the complex relationship between new media, faith, and digital culture (Soukup, 2017).

These issues of authority arise in other religious traditions. Stout (2012) tackles how Islam addresses authority online. The multiplicity of online voices lead Muslims to draw on a culturally embedded decision-making process that strives for consistency between "Islamic primary sources" and online discussion of such sources in light of contemporary conditions, something made possible by familiarity with ancient writings and teachings. Stout et al. (2003) analyze the phenomenon in the Mormon context, reviewing how the denomination controls Mormon websites in order to protect its hierarchy and structure. Similar studies address Judaism (Golan, 2015), Asian religions (Han & Nassir, 2016), Jainism (Shah, 2015), Japanese religions (Baffelli et al., 2011), and Hinduism (Helland, 2010; Scheifinger, 2011; Zeiler, 2020). A few studies turn to Africa. Hackett and Soares (2015, p. 7) note how in Africa individuals acting alone or as members of religious communities use the Internet to "evoke, sense, and access the divine presence on their own terms and without always feeling that they need the enabling presence or blessings of the hierarchy of the churches, mosques or temples." Bezabeh (2015) analyzes the digital activity of Muslims, Orthodox Christians, and Indian gurus in Ethiopia.

Who Owns Religious Authority in the Digital Age?

The question of "who" becomes more and more important. Both media studies and religious studies analyze people who use media to establish their authority within a culture, linking authority, media, and the digital sphere. The mediatization of our world offers more possibilities for individual participation in defining norms (Rorty & Vattimo, 2005). The nature of new media provides creators and users new opportunities to construct and present information, as well as share media content within a network of individuals that may lie outside the traditional boundaries of their established communities and institutions. Authority online rests primarily on visibility within media culture and on digital expertise in the media ecosystem, rather than on external mediated or monitored sources (Campbell, 2021). Instead of considering authority inductively, Hoover (2006) urges for authority to be thought of in terms of its constitution.

Evidence shows that people endow authority on people who can articulate or embody what they hold most meaningful, truthful, and valuable (Schofield Clark, 2012).

These conclusions emerge from four waves of research: descriptive research in which scholars document new forms of religious practice emerging on the Internet; categorization of key trends within religious Internet practice; a theoretical turn that identifies common methods and frameworks for analyzing online as well as offline and religious communities; and studying religious actors' negotiation between their online and offline lives and activities, asking how such intersections create new, hybrid places for religiosity (Campbell, 2021; Lövheim & Campbell, 2017). To illustrate the fourth wave, Campbell (2021) asks how Christian organizations employ digital media experts to help build and manage religious online presence and facilitate public discourse about faith through social media. She coined the term "Religious Digital Creatives" (RDCs) to describe individuals whose digital media work and skills grant them unique status and influence within their religious communities. "They are not simply digital workers with a religious goal in mind, but individuals who intentionally and unintentionally exert influence within religious institutions due to their digital work" (p. 5). For this reason, they have become religious authorities for their faith communities. RDCs often simultaneously support and challenge traditional structures of authority. For this reason, technological contrivances often force recognized religious leaders to rethink the extent of their influence in a digital age as they must negotiate between multiple spheres of religious practice and meaning found online, offline, and within newly created digital "third spaces" of religion (Campbell, 2021; S. Hoover & Echchaibi, 2014).

Cheong (2016) offers a complementary perspective as she reports that, rather than forcing a debate over authority in an informational age, religious leaders have asserted authority through the construction of norms of credibility in navigating online resources, blogs, and social networking sites. Religious leaders typically increase their use of the Internet for information gathering and facilitating spiritual or religious experiences (Campbell & Garner, 2016). This sets the stage for a discursively constructed authority tied to a performative communication approach with microblogging practices by clergy of mega-churches (Cheong, 2016). Something similar occurs with rabbis in the media, who act as decision makers and guides in their communities (Cohen, 2012). Asian pastors and priests have become savvy in their use of Twitter to consolidate their positions as religious leaders (Cheong et al., 2011), as have Buddhist priests through personal blogs (Lee, 2009). Members of Christian e-mail communities let their online experience guide the evaluation and expectations of their offline faith communities (Campbell, 2005); religious bloggers use their blogs to affirm different forms of religious authority online (Campbell, 2010a); and debates within the Anglican Communion over the legitimacy of online worship in Second Life offer another view of authority (Campbell, 2010b).

Not everyone agrees. Several earlier studies held to the idea of the Weberian charismatic leader, asking about the symbolism and characteristics of charisma a leader needs (Antonakis & Atwater, 2002) or the emotional, expressive, and communicative attributes of such charisma (Stark, 1965). Some conservative religious leaders with an implicit preference for charismatic leadership regard the Internet, particularly Web 2.0, as superfluous at best and unbridled at worst. Many ban their communities from using it. Some of their concerns reflect a hesitation to bring theological discussions of religious leaders into public forums; others worry about leaders monitoring and controlling their community members' online activities (Campbell, 2021).

Schofield Clark (2012) focuses on the religious consequences of the institutionalization of Weber's (1947) rational-legal authority in the profit-driven media systems that increasingly rely upon consensus, a seemingly democratic culture promoting sometimes unlikely candidates as its authorities. Following this logic, media industries have contributed to the rise of celebrities. In American popular culture, celebrities have superseded religious figures as moral authorities (Portmann, 2019). As trust in religious institutions has waned, the entertainment fringe has become the moral center. Unlike traditional elites whose authority resides in specialized education or proximity to political and religious authority, or religious charisma, celebrities often achieve their celebrity based on their ability to articulate and represent ordinariness. They serve as reference points for others as they are "like us" (Furedi, 2010; Schofield Clark, 2012). The strategic use of media empowers certain groups with the right and ability to speak out in a public setting (Lincoln, 1994).

In her RDC model, Campbell distinguishes between "media influencers," "thought leaders," and "digital leaders." She defines the first as individuals who use social media or blogs and who have achieved a notable following online. For Booth and Matic (2011, p. 184) "the nobodies of the past are now the new somebodies." Campbell (2021) clarifies that those who had a strong media presence before social media and now use these new media are also influencers. However, thought leaders have recognized that the specialist knowledge that they have in a specific field makes them an expert in an area, so they focus more on the knowledge they possess (Brosseau, 2014). The third group mentioned, digital leaders, are those whose authority emanates from a place of exhibiting traditional leadership skills (Kane, 2018). To explore this, several scholars offer case studies. Micó-Sanz et al. (2021) analyzed the top influencers for Catholic youth; Kinard (2020) analyzed how influencers could be considered as saints posting their gospel online. Lövheim and Lundmark (2019)'s work on bloggers and vloggers delved into how women's authority to speak on religion is forged in digital media building. These groups of online religious authorities manifest authority in algorithmic culture and offer insights into how technology creates new spaces of influence and how the strategies used by different digital actors to leverage those opportunities (Campbell, 2021). It is suggested by Campbell (2021) that the classification and strategies she uses apply to digital media actors in other religious traditions.

Conclusion

Despite its central role in religious studies, authority's definition remains elusive as authors look at it from different contexts, disciplines, and approaches. Weber's definition (authority as a legitimized dominance) acts as a starting point (Campbell, 2021; Hoover, 2016). In the religious context, its links with the concepts of leadership, power, and obedience both reinforce and puzzle (Schofield Clark, 2012). The liquid (Bauman, 2005) and accelerated (Rosa, 2015) context in which religious authority is performed today brings the dynamics and experience of religion into the dynamics of competition, as religious authority continually needs to establish itself through language and communication in a media-dominated marketplace (Horsfield, 2016).

Religions have embraced media as allies to reinforce their authority and have adopted communication tools to be close to their members or believers. This occurs in different geographical contexts and with different religions. In this Hoover (2016), Campbell (2021, 2020, 2007), and Schofield Clark (2012) lead the way in exploring how Christian churches frame authority within religious media and communication dynamics. They situate the media's role through which religious and spiritual interests are formed, based on Hjarvard's (2016) mediatization of religion; the work of Sumiala-Seppänen et al. (2006) on the sacred; and Linderman's (2016) "vicarious religion." Radde-Antweiler and Zeiler (2019) explore the mediatization of religion in Asia, with its heterogeneous cultural, linguistic, ethnic, and religious backgrounds. White's (2008) analysis of changing media in Africa's democratic turn applies as well to religious groups. In a related move Hackett and Soares (2015) focus on the interdependence of media and religion in Africa.

Most agree on the crucial role of the media in reinforcing religious authority. However, the evolution of the media and the emergence of the digital sphere has transformed accepted understandings and patterns of authority in the religious field. This new paradigm establishes authority as not arising from external sources but as cultivated within the media system (Campbell, 2021). Here the term "algorithmic authority" defines a situation in which authority rests in a consensus-based collective evaluation system (Schofield Clark, 2012). The risk that arises in this environment stems from the digital world's vast numbers, where millions of believers live in alternative de facto structures of religious authority (Soukup, 2017); these dynamics both support and challenge traditional structures of authority (Campbell, 2021), made up of "media influencers," "thought leaders," and "digital leaders." While these labels can refer to traditional religious leaders using digital media, they also apply to other individuals not affiliated with traditional religion who have achieved a notable influence. Scholars have explored these constructions of online authority in different contexts: Twitter-savvy Asian pastors and priests consolidating their positions as religious leaders (Cheong et al., 2011); Buddhist priests' personal blogs on cultivating the Self (Lee, 2009); and online rabbis (Cohen, 2012).

The pandemic of 2020–2021 highlighted the competitive context that religious authority occupies online. A number of scholarly studies address this: Cadge (2020) remarks on how religious professionals had to play expanded roles. Baker et al. (2020) and Campbell (2020, 2021) look at how religious leaders framed the crisis, its challenges, and opportunities in the online sphere. Sabaté Gauxachs et al. (2021) documented the online response of the Catholic Church in Spain during the first months of the pandemic and draw a fragmented map of different levels of online authority depending on the diocese. Silverkors (2021) looked into religious ministry online, reflecting on how users could minimize the authority of the leader by simple actions like lowering the volume of the computer or switching off the camera. These initial studies on the pandemic-inflected negotiation of religious authority open up new areas for further in-depth research and discussion.

References

Adama, H. (2007). Islamic associations in Cameroon: Between the umma and the state. In B. Soares, & R. Otayek (Eds.), *Islam and Muslim politics in Africa* (pp. 227–241). Palgrave Macmillan.

Ahuja, M., & Carley, K. (1998). Network structure in virtual organizations. *Journal of Computer-Mediated Communication, 3*(4). https://onlinelibrary.wiley.com/doi/full/10.1111/j.1083-6101.1998.tb00079.x

Almond, G., Appleby, S., & Emanuel, S. (2003). *Strong religion. The rise of fundamentalisms around the world.* The University of Chicago Press.

Anderson, J. (1999). The internet and Islam's new interpreters. In D. Eickleman (Ed.), *Media in the Muslim world: The emerging public sphere* (pp. 41–55). Indiana University Press.

Antonakis, J., & Atwater, L. (2002). Leader distance: A review and a proposed theory. *The Leadership Quarterly, 13*(6), 673–704. https://www.taylorfrancis.com/chapters/edit/10.4324/9781315250601-11/leader-distance-review-proposed-theory-john-antonakis-leanne-atwater

Arasa, D., Cantoni, L., & Narbona, J. (2018). The Catholic church and Twitter. In Y. Cohen (Ed.), *Spiritual news. Reporting religion around the world* (pp. 325–346). Peter Lang.

Arendt, H. (1954). What is authority? In *Between past and future* (pp. 91–141). Penguin Classics.

Asamoah-Gyadu, J. K. (2009). Signs, wonders, and ministry: The gospel in the power of the spirit. *Evangelical Review of Theology, 33*(1), 32–46. https://theology.worldea.org/wp-content/uploads/2020/12/ERT-33-1.pdf

Baffelli, E., Reader, I., & Staemmler, B. (2011). *Japanese religions on the internet. Innovation, representation, and authority.* Routledge.

Baker, J., Martí, G., Braunstein, R., Whitehead, A. L., & Yukich, G. (2020). Religion in the age of social distancing: How COVID-19 presents new directions for research. *Sociology of Religion, 81*(4), 357–370. https://doi.org/10.1093/socrel/sraa039

Barker, E. (2005). Crossing the boundary: New challenges to religious authority and control as a consequence of access to the Internet. In M. Hojsgaard, & M. Warburg (Eds.), *Religion and cyberspace* (pp. 67–85). Routledge.

Barnes, D. (1978). Charisma and religious leadership: An historical analysis. *Journal for the Scientific Study of Religion, 17*(1), 1–18. https://www.unil.ch/files/live/sites/issr/files/shared/8._Telechargement/Cours_BA_printemps_2013/Douglas_Barnes.pdf

Bauman, Z. (2005). *Liquid life*. Polity Press.

Bezabeh, S. A. (2015). Living across digital landscapes: Muslims, orthodox Christians, and an Indian guru in Ethiopia. In R. I. J. Hackett, & B. F. Soares (Eds.), *New media and religious transformations in Africa* (pp. 266–283). Indiana University Press.

Booth, N., & Matic, J. A. (2011). Mapping and leveraging influencers in social media to shape corporate brand perceptions. *Corporate Communications, 16*(3), 184–191. https://doi.org/10.1108/13563281111156853

Breen, M. (1997). Information does not equal knowledge: Theorizing the political economy of virtuality. *Journal of Computer-Mediated Communication, 3*(3). https://doi.org/10.1111/j.1083-6101.1997.tb00076.x

Brosseau, D. (2014). *Ready to be a thought leader? How to increase your influence, impact, and success*. Jossey-Bass.

Bucar, E. (2017). *Pious fashion. How Muslim women dress*. Harvard University Press.

Burhani. (2018). Islam nusantara as a promising response to religious intolerance and radicalism. *Trends in South East Asia, 21*, 1–29. https://www.iseas.edu.sg/wp-content/uploads/pdfs/TRS21_18.pdf

Cadge, W. (2020). The rise of the chaplains, May 17. *The Atlantic*. Retrieved June 6, 2022 from https://www.theatlantic.com/ideas/archive/2020/05/why-americans-are-turning-chaplains-during-pandemic/611767

Campbell, H. A. (2005). *Exploring religious community online*. Peter Lang.

Campbell, H. A. (2007). Who's got the power? Religious authority and the internet. *Journal of Computer-Mediated Communication, 12*, 1043–1062. DOI:10.1111/j.1083-6101.2007.00362.x

Campbell, H. A. (2010a). Bloggers and religious authority online. *Journal of Computer-Mediated Communication, 15*(2), 251–276 https://www.jstor.org/stable/41348770.

Campbell, H. A. (2010b). *When religion meets new media*. Routledge.

Campbell, H. A. (2020). *Religion in quarantine. The future of religion in a post-pandemic world*. Network for New Media, Religion and Digital Culture Studies.

Campbell, H. A. (2021). *Digital creatives and the rethinking of religious authority*. Routledge.

Campbell, H. A., & Garner, S. (2016). *Networked theology: Negotiating faith in digital culture*. Baker.

Carroggio, M. (2016). Lo scenario digitale: Una comunicazione a cerchi concentrici. In M. Tridente, & M. Mastroianni (Eds.), *La missione digitale. Comunicazione della chiesa e social media* (pp. 19–39). Edizioni Santa Croce.

Chavez, M. (1994). Secularization as declining religious authority. *Social Forces, 72*(3), 749–774. https://www.jstor.org/stable/2579779

Chavez, M. (2003). Religious authority in the modern world. *Society, 40*(3), 38–40. https://doi.org/10.1007/s12115-003-1034-8

Cheong, P. (2013). Authority. In H. Campbell (Ed.), *Digital religion. Understanding religious practice in new media worlds* (pp. 72–87). Routledge.

Cheong, P. (2016). Religious authority and social media branding in a culture of religious celebrification. In S. M. Hoover (Ed.), *The media and religious authority* (pp. 81–102). Pennsylvania State University Press.

Cheong, P. H., Huang, S., & Poon, J. P. (2011). Religious communication and epistemic authority of leaders in wired faith organizations. *Journal of Communication, 61*(5), 938–958. https://doi.org/10.1111/j.1460-2466.2011.01579.x

Cohen, Y. (2012). *God Jews and the media: Religion and Israel's media*. Routledge.

Cohen, Y. (2018). *Spiritual news. Reporting religion around the world*. Peter Lang.

Cohen, Y. (2021). Asian media: A pillar of religious authority? In K. Radde-Antweiler, & X. Zeiler (Eds.), *The Routledge handbook of religion and journalism* (pp. 122–135). Routledge.

Cowan, D. (2005). *Cyberhenge: Modern pagans on the internet*. Routledge.

Dawson, L. L., & Hennebry, J. (1999). New religions and the internet. Recruiting in a new public sphere. *Journal of Contemporary Religions, 14*(1), 17–39. https://doi.org/10.1080/13537909908580850

De Pillis, M. S. (1966). The quest for religious authority and the rise of Mormonism. *Dialogue: A Journal of Mormon Thought, 1*(1), 68–88. https://www.dialoguejournal.com/wp-content/uploads/sbi/articles/Dialogue_V01N01_70s.pdf

Díez Bosch, M., Micó Sanz, J. L., & Sabaté Gauxachs, A. (2017). Scientific authority, academic leadership, axiological reference. In M. Díez Bosch, P. Soukup, J. L. Micó, & D. Zsupan-Jerome. (Ed.), *Authority and leadership: Values, religion, media* (pp. 13–19). Blanquerna Observatory on Media, Religion and Culture.

Dipio, D. (2009). Gender and religion in Nigerian popular films. *African Communication Research, 2*(1), 85–116. https://ccms.ukzn.ac.za/?mdocs-file=1820

Dulles, A. (1988). *The reshaping of Catholicism: Current challenges in the theology of the church.* Harper and Row.

Eilers, F. J. (1994). *Communicating in community. An introduction to social communication.* Logos Publications.

Eisenlohr, P. (2014). Media, citizenship, and religious mobilization: The muharram awareness campaign in Mumbai. *The Journal of Asian Studies, 74*(3), 687–710. doi:10.1017/S0021911815000534

Feener, R. M. (2014). Muslim religious authority in modern Asia: Established patterns and evolving profiles. *Asian Journal of Social Science, 42*(5), 501–516. https://doi.org/10.1163/15685314-04205002

Ferré, F. (1970). The definition of religion. *Journal of the American Academy of Religion, 38*(1), 3–16. https://www.jstor.org/stable/1461697

Foucault, M. (1977). *Discipline and punish.* Pantheon Books.

Furedi, F. (2010). Celebrity culture, symposium: Celebrity around the world. *Society, 47*(6), 493–497. https://doi.org/10.1007/s12115-010-9367-6

Giddens, A. (1990). *The consequences of modernity.* Polity.

Gifford, P. (2005). Worlds of power: Religious thought and political practice in Africa. *Journal of Religion in Africa, 35*(2), 246–248. https://www.jstor.org/stable/1581539

Gifford, P. (2010). Religious authority: Scripture, tradition, charisma. In J. Hinnells (Ed.), *The Routledge companion to the study of religion* (pp. 379–410). Routledge.

Golan, O. (2015). Legitimation of new media and community building among Jewish denominations in the U.S. In H. Campbell (Ed.), *Digital Judaism* (pp. 125–144). Routledge.

Golan, O., & Martini, M. (2020). Religious leadership on social networks: The visual language of Pope Francis. In M. Díez Bosch, A. Melloni, & J. L. Micó Sanz (Eds.), *Perplexed religion* (pp. 77–88). Blanquerna Observatory on Media, Religion and Culture.

Greenleaf, G. (1996). A proposed privacy code for Asia-Pacific cyberlaw. *Journal of Computer-Mediated Communication, 2* (1). https://doi.org/10.1111/j.1083-6101.1996.tb00184.x

Grieve, G. P., & Veidlinger, D. (2015). *Buddhism, the internet, and digital media: The pixel in the lotus.* Routledge.

Hackett, R. I. J., & Soares, B. F. (2015). *New media and religious transformations in Africa.* Indiana University Press.

Hadden, J., & Shupe, A. (1988). *Televangelism: Power and politics on God's frontier.* Henry Holt and Co.

Han, S., & Nassir, K. M. (2016). *Digital culture and religion in Asia.* Routledge.

Helland, C. (2010). (Virtually) been there, (virtually) done that: Examining the online religious practices of the Hindu tradition: Introduction. *Online-Heidelberg Journal of Religions on the Internet, 4*(1), 148–150. https://doi.org/10.11588/rel.2010.1.9389

Herring, D. (2005). Virtual as contextual: A net news theology. In L. Dawson, & D. Cowan (Eds.), *Religion and cyberspace* (pp. 149–135). Routledge.

Hirschkind, C. (2006). *The ethical soundscape: Cassette sermons and Islamic counterpublics.* Columbia University Press.

Hjarvard, S. (2011). The mediatization of religion: Theorizing religion, media and social changes. *Culture and Religion, 12*(2), 119–135. https://doi.org/10.1080/14755610.2011.579719

Hjarvard, S. (2016). Mediatization and the changing authority of religion. *Media, Culture & Society, 38*(1), 8–17. https://doi.org/10.1177/0163443715615412

Ho, W. (2010). Islam, China and the internet: Negotiating residual cyberspace between hegemonic patriotism and connectivity to the ummah. *Journal of the Institute for Muslim Minority Affairs, 30*(1), 63–79. https://doi.org/10.1080/13602001003650622

Hofstede, G. (2011). Dimensionalizing cultures: The Hofstede model in context. *Online Readings in Psychology and Culture, 2*(1), 1–26. https://doi.org/10.9707/2307-0919.1014

Hoover, S., & Echchaibi, N. (2014). Media theory and the "third spaces of digital religion." Finding religion in the media: Work in progress on the third spaces of digital religion. https://doi.org/10.13140/RG.2.1.3315.4641

Hoover, S. M. (2006). *Religion in the media age*. Routledge.

Hoover, S. M. (2016). *The media and religious authority*. Pennsylvania State University Press.

Hoover, S. M. (2018). Religion and the news in the age of media change. In Y. Cohen (Ed.), *Spiritual news: Reporting religion around the world* (pp. 15–29). Peter Lang.

Hoover, S. M., & Clark, L. S. (2002). *Practicing religion in the age of the media: Explorations in media, religion, and culture*. Columbia University Press.

Hoover, S. M., & Emerich, M. M. (2011). *Media, spiritualities and social change*. Bloomsbury Publishing.

Hoover, S. M., & Kaneva, N. (2009). *Fundamentalisms and the media*. A&C Black.

Horsfield, P. (2015). *From Jesus to the internet. A history of Christianity and media*. Wiley Blackwell.

Horsfield, P. (2016). The media and religious authority from ancient to modern. In S. Hoover (Ed.), *The media and religious authority* (pp. 37–66). Pennsylvania University Press.

Horton, R. (1960). A definition of religion and its uses. *The Journal of the Royal Anthropological Institute of Great Britain and Ireland, 90*(2), 201–226. https://doi.org/10.2307/2844344

Ihejirika, W. C. (2009). Research on media, religion and culture in Africa: Current trends and debates. *African Communication Research, 2*(1), 1–60. https://ccms.ukzn.ac.za/Files/articles/ACR/Media%20and%20Religion%20in%20Africa.pdf#page=5

Kamate, R. (2009). Pentecostalism in Kinshasa: Maintaining multiple church membership. *African Communication Research, 2*(1), 145–166. https://ccms.ukzn.ac.za/?mdocs-file=1820

Kane, G. C. (2018). *Common traits of the best digital leaders*, June 9. MIT Sloan Management Review. Retrieved June 7, 2022 from https://sloanreview.mit.edu/article/common-traits-of-the-best-digital-leaders

Kazi, T. (2021). *Religious television and pious authority in Pakistan*. Indiana University Press.

Keyes, C. F., Kendall, L., & Hardacre, H. (1994). *Asian visions of authority: Religion and the modern states of East and Southeast Asia*. University of Hawaii Press.

Kinard, H. (2020). Social religion: Posting. Undergraduate Research Symposium. Old Dominion University. Retrieved June 7, 2022 from https://digitalcommons.odu.edu/undergradsymposium/2020/artexhibit/11.

Kumar, K. (2003). Spirituality in the Indian media. *Religion and Social Communication, 1*(1), 32–37.

Lee, J. (2009). Cultivating the self in cyberspace: The use of personal blogs among Buddhist priests. *Journal of Media and Religion, 8*(2), 97–114. https://doi.org/10.1080/15348420902881027

Lincoln, B. (1994). *Authority: Construction and corrosion*. University of Chicago Press.

Linderman, A. (2016). Media and (vicarious) religion. In S. M. Hoover (Ed.), *The media and religious authority* (pp. 67–80). Pennsylvania State University Press.

Lövheim, M., & Campbell, H. (2017). Considering critical methods and theoretical lenses in digital religion studies. *New Media and Society, 19*(1), 5–14. https://doi.org/10.1177/1461444816649911

Lövheim, M., & Lundmark, E. (2019). Gender, religion and authority in digital media. *ESSACHESS Journal for Communication Studies, 12*, 23–38. https://www.essachess.com/index.php/jcs/article/view/462/487

Lynch, G. (2005). *Understanding theology and popular culture*. Blackwell.

Marsden, G. (1983). Preachers of paradox: The religious New Right in historical perspective. In M. Douglas, & S. M. Tipton (Eds.), *Religion and America: Spirituality in a secular age* (pp. 150–168). Beacon Press.

Matheson, C. (1987). Weber and the classification of forms of legitimacy. *The British Journal of Sociology, 38*(2), 199–215. https://doi.org/10.2307/590532

McGrane, C. M. (2013). Practising presence: Wisdom from the rule on finding balance in a digital age. *American Benedictine Review, 64*(4), 370–383. http://pascal-francis.inist.fr/vibad/index.php?action=getRecordDetail&idt=28024675

Meyer, B., & Moors, A. (2006). *Religion, media, and the public sphere*. Indiana University Press.

Micó Sanz, J., Díez Bosch, M., Sabaté Gauxachs, A., & Israel-Turim, V. (2021). Mapping global youth and religion: Big data as lens to envision a sustainable development future. *Trípodos, 48*, 33–52. https://doi.org/10.51698/tripodos.2020.48p33-52

Min-Soo, K. (2013). The rediscovery of religious silence in social media era: A Korean case. *Religion and Social Communication, 11*(2), 138–154.

Mnookin, J. (1996). Virtual(ly) law: The emergence of law in LambdaMOO. *Journal of Computer-Mediated Communication, 2*(1). https://doi.org/10.1111/j.1083-6101.1996.tb00185.x

Monteiro, B. G. (2017). Authority in digital ecology: A Christian perspective. In M. Díez Bosch, P. Soukup, J. L. Micó, & D. Zsupan-Jerome (Ed.), *Authority and leadership: Values, religion, media* (pp. 53–62). Blanquerna Observatory on Media, Religion and Culture.

Mosca, G. (1939). *The ruling class.* McGraw-Hill.

Piff, D., & Warburg, M. (2005). Seeking for truth: Plausibility on a Baha:'I email list. In M. Hojsgaard, & M. Warburg (Eds.), *Religion and cyberspace* (pp. 86–101). Routledge.

Portmann, J. (2019). *Celebrity morals and the loss of religious authority.* Routledge.

Radde-Antweiler, K. (2018). The papal election in the Philippines: Negotiating religious authority in newspapers. *Journal of Religion, Media, and Digital Culture, 7*(3), 400–421. https://doi.org/10.1163/21659214-00703009

Radde-Antweiler, K., & Zeiler, X. (2019). *Mediatized religion in Asia: Studies on digital media and religion.* Routledge.

Ritzer, G. (1999). *Resisting McDonaldization.* Sage Publications.

Rorty, R., & Vattimo, G. (2005). *The future of religion.* (S. Zabala Ed.; W. McCuaig, Trans.). Columbia University Press.

Rosa, H. (2015). *Social acceleration. A new theory of modernity.* Columbia University Press.

Ruggiero, T., & Winch, S. (2005). The media downing of Pierre Salinger: Journalistic mistrust of the internet as a news source. *Journal of Computer-Mediated Communication, 10*(2). https://doi.org/10.1111/j.1083-6101.2005.tb00245.x

Sabaté Gauxachs, A., Albalad Aiguabella, J. M., & Díez Bosch, M. (2021). Coronavirus-driven digitalization of in-person communities: Analysis of the Catholic church online response in Spain during the pandemic. *Religions, 12*, 311. https://doi.org/10.3390/rel12050311

Scheifinger, H. (2011). Hinduism and cyberspace. *Religion, 38*(3), 233–249. https://doi.org/10.1016/j.religion.2008.01.008

Schofield Clark, L. (2012). Religion and authority in a remix culture. How a late night TV host became an authority on religion. In G. Lynch, J. Mitchell, & A. Strhan (Eds.), *Religion, media and culture: A reader* (pp. 111–121). Routledge.

Schofield Clark, L. (2016). Afterword. The media and religious authority. In S. M. Hoover (Ed.), *The media and religious authority* (pp. 253–267). Pennsylvania State University Press.

Seligman, A. (2000). *Modernity's wager: Authority, the self, and transcendence.* Princeton University Press.

Shah, K. (2015). Oral traditions of Jainism discourse in the wake of digital and social media: A communications study of Jain mendicants. *Religion and Social Communication, 13*(2), 158–173. https://2127847f-212d-4d74-9161-d5e5241ea7f0.filesusr.com/ugd/5c600f_c78f97afea4d4acdaed6925c630d8161.pdf

Shirky, C. A. (2009). *Speculative post on the idea of algorithmic authority*, November 15. Blog Clay Shirky. Retrieved June 7, 2022, from https://stoweboyd.typepad.com/message/2009/11/a-speculative-post-on-the-idea-of-algorithmic-authority-clay-shirky.html

Silverkors, D. (2021). Reflections on doing church ministry online and AFK (away from keyboard) during the pandemic. In H. Campbell (Ed.), *Revisiting the distanced church* (pp. 24–30). OAK Trust.

Soukup, P. A. (2017). Authority, new media, and the church. In M. Díez Bosch, P. Soukup, J. L. Micó, & D. Zsupan-Jerome (Ed.), *Authority and leadership: Values, religion, media* (pp. 31–40). Blanquerna Observatory on Media, Religion and Culture.

Spadaro, A. (2012). *Cyberteologia.* Vita e Pensiero.

Spadaro, A. (2017). The authority of Pope Francis and the internet culture. In M. Díez Bosch, P. Soukup, J. L. Micó, & D. Zsupan-Jerome (Ed.), *Authority and leadership: Values, religion and media* (pp. 63–67). Blanquerna Observatory on Media, Religion and Culture.

Stark, W. (1965). The routinization of charisma: A consideration of Catholicism. *Sociological Analysis, 26*(4), 203–211. https://doi.org/10.2307/3709920

Starr, P. (1982). *The social transformation of American medicine.* Basic Books.

Stout, D.. (2012). *Media and religion: Foundations of an emerging field.* Routledge.

Stout, D., Scott, D., & Martin, D. (2003). Mormons, mass media, and the interpretative audience. In D. Stout, & J. M. Buddenbaum (Eds.), *Religion and mass media: Audiences and applications* (pp. 243–258). Routledge.

Sumiala-Seppänen, J., Lundby, K., & Sakolangas, R., Eds. (2006). *Implications of the sacred in (post)modern media*. Nordicom.

Thomas, K. (2003). *Religion and the decline of magic: Studies in popular beliefs in sixteenth and seventeenth-century England*. Penguin.

Tridente, G., & Mastroianni, B. (2016). *La missione digitale: Comunicazione della chiesa e social media*. Edizioni Santa Croce.

Turner, B. S. (1974). *Weber and Islam*. Routledge & Kegan Paul.

Turner, B. S. (2007). Religious authority and the new media. *Theory, Culture and Society, 24*(2), 117–134. https://doi.org/10.1177/0263276407075001

Ukah, A. F. K. (2008). Seeing is more than believing: Posters and proselytization in Nigeria. In R. I. J. Hackett (Ed.), *Proselytization revisited: Rights talk, free markets and culture wars* (pp. 167–198). Routledge.

Vassallo, W. (1998). *Church communications handbook*. Kregel Publications.

Viganò, D. (2017). *En salida. Francisco y la comunicación*. Herder.

Volf, M. (2015). *Flourishing: Why we need religion in a globalized world*. Yale University Press.

Wang, S., & Archer, N. (2004). Strategic choice of electronic marketplace functionalities: A buyer-supplier relationship perspective. *Journal of Computer-Mediated Communication, 10*(1). https://doi.org/10.1111/j.1083-6101.2004.tb00236.x

Weber, B. H., Depew, D., & Smith, J. D. (2005). *Entropy, information and evolution*. The MIT Press.

Weber, M. (1922). The three types of legitimate rule (trans. H. Gerth). *Berkeley Publications in Society and Institutions, 4*(1), 1–11.

Weber, M. (1947). *The theory of social and economic organisation*. Oxford University Press.

White, R. A. (2008). Media and democratisation in Africa. *African Communication Research, 1*(3), 269–431.

White, R. A. (2009). New research methodologies in media and religion: An international survey. *African Communication Research, 2*(1), 167–202. https://ccms.ukzn.ac.za/?mdocs-file=1820

Wiles, M. F. (1971). Religious authority and divine action. *Religious Studies, 7*(1), 1–12. https://doi.org/10.1017/S0034412500000160

Yao, Q., Stout, D. A., & Liu, A. (2011). China's official media portrayal of religion (1996–2005): Policy change in a desecularizing society, *Journal of Media and Religion, 10*(1), 39–50. https://doi.org/10.1080/15348423.2011.549399

Zeiler, X. (2020). *Digital Hinduism*. Routledge.

Zeiler, X., & Radde-Antweiler, K. (2018). Introduction to the special issue on journalism, media and religion: How news media ascribe meanings to the terms 'sacred,' 'secular,' and 'authority.'. *Journal of Religion, Media and Digital Culture, 7*(3), 261–268. https://doi.org/10.1163/21659214-00703001

Zeleke, M., & Bruzzi, S. (2015). Women, gender and religions in Ethiopia / Femmes, genre et religions en Ethiopie. *Annales d'Éthiopie, 30*, 11–19. https://www.persee.fr/doc/ethio_0066-2127_2015_num_30_1_1580

Zelizer, B. (1992). *Covering the body: The Kennedy assassination, the media and the shaping of collective memory*. University of Chicago Press.

Zsupan-Jerome, D. (2017). Authority and obedience: Engaging Benedictine spirituality for digital communication. In M. Díez Bosch, P. Soukup, J. L. Micó, & D. Zsupan-Jerome (Ed.), *Authority and leadership: Values, religion, media* (pp. 79–93). Blanquerna Observatory on Media, Religion and Culture.

Selected Readings

Buckley, D. T., Gainous, J., & Wagner, K. M. (2021). Is religion the opiate of the digital masses? Religious authority, social media, and protest. *Information, Communication & Society*. https://doi.org/10.1080/1369118X.2021.1971279

Campbell, H. A., & Tsuria, R. (2021). *Digital religion. Understanding religious practice in digital media*. Routledge. https://doi.org/10.4324/9780429295683

Cheong, P. H. (2021). Bounded religious automation at work: Communicating human authority in artificial intelligence networks. *Journal of Communication Inquiry*, *45*(1), 5–23. https://doi.org/10.1177/0196859920977133

De Sousa, M. T., Tudor, M. A., & Evolvi, G. (2021). Media, religion, and religiosity in the digital age. *Tropos. Comunicação, Sociedade e Cultura*, *10*(1), 1–14. https://periodicos.ufac.br/index.php/tropos/article/view/5194

Evolvi, G. (2021). Religion, new media, and digital culture. In *Oxford research encyclopedia of religion*. Oxford University Press. https://doi.org/10.1093/acrefore/9780199340378.013.917

Lorea, C. E., Mahadev, N., Lang, N., & Chen, N. (2022). Religion and the COVID-19 pandemic: Mediating presence and distance. *Religion*, *52*(2), 177–198. https://doi.org/10.1080/0048721X.2022.2061701

31

Religion and Development Communication

Robert A. White

The central question that the present chapter explores is how religious media can contribute to socioeconomic development in our contemporary world. Let us begin by explaining the meaning of the basic terms in discussion: religious organizations, social development, and communication, with emphasis on the use of media for development.

Religions

Currently Christianity is the largest single religion in the world with an estimated 2.3 billion adherents (31.1%), followed by Islam (24.1%), Hinduism (15.1%), Buddhism (6.9%), and folk religions (6.9%) (https://en.wikipedta.org/,wiki/Major_religious_groups). The continent with the most Christians is Africa with more than 631 million, followed by Latin America with 601 million, and Europe with 571 million. The second largest religious group is Islam with approximately 1.8 billion making up 24% of the world's population. Muslims are concentrated, 1,703,146, in South Asia (mainly in Indonesia and Bangladesh), 507 million in the Middle East and North Africa, and 257 million in East Asia. The third largest religious group is Hinduism with 1.2 billion adherents concentrated largely in India and Nepal. Buddhism is the fourth largest religious group with 448 million adherents throughout the world: 244 million largely in western China with further large numbers in the South Asian countries of Cambodia, Thailand, Myanmar, Bhutan, and Sri Lanka. Although Buddhism is not strictly speaking a religion in the sense of a focus on the cult of a supreme being, it is concerned with a worldview and way of life that is considered religious (Forrest, 2020).

All the major religious traditions have attempted to contribute to national socioeconomic development and all have incorporated or work with the major forms of mediated communication – pictorial, print, radio, TV, and new media, or combinations of these media. Socioeconomic development based on new productive technology, heavy capitalization, and emerging nationalism took shape largely in Europe, interacting with European Christianity, and influenced the development of a religion much concerned with social equity. Often the dominant religious institution in a country or region has a highly developed world-wide organization, such as the Christian Churches, and most directly interacts with a given national development policy using media.

The Handbook on Religion and Communication, First Edition. Edited by Yoel Cohen and Paul A. Soukup.
© 2023 John Wiley & Sons Ltd. Published 2023 by John Wiley & Sons Ltd.

The Meanings of Socioeconomic Development

In the late 1940s after World War II a socio-political consensus emerged that colonialism by North Atlantic nations was not only politically unjust, but also denied colonized peoples their socio-cultural rights. Colonialism prevented the occupied peoples from exercising the right to develop their own political, economic, cultural, and social systems according to their own consensus. The assembly of the United Nations was one of the main institutions that would guarantee this autonomous process of development, but the right to national independence was generally agreed on by all national governments in the world. The end of colonialism saw political movements to establish independent governments and other national public service institutions emerge in former colonial dependencies. A new elite, with opportunities for education and professional experience in the colonial period, often led these movements. The leaders of the independence movements often formed a governmental and economic ruling class with access to the wealth and other resources from government offices, local economic enterprise, and external financial aid (McMichael, 2012, pp. 47–50; Wanyama, 2006, pp. 73–108). The new nations attempted to provide education, health, and other services to the whole nation, but in effect the new governing and local entrepreneurial leadership sought superior educational, health, and other services for their own class. Although attempts to provide schools, health services, and assistance to improve agricultural productivity existed in rural areas, an urban bias dominated development efforts (McMichael, 2012, pp. 76–78), and the vast majority of rural people continued to scrape a meager living from semi-subsistence farming (Mehrotra & Delamonica, 2007, pp. 57–68). In the developing nations a dual system of education and other services developed: one sector for the urban-based, higher social status with standards emulating the developed world, and another much inferior system serving the subsistence farming communities in the interior (Barrett et al., 2007, pp. 1–12; Hartmann & Crawford, 2008, pp. 7–32; Taylor & Mackenzie, 1992, pp. 217–221).

With the emergence of the developing nations a tradition of development science evolved, often based on the models of development of the North Atlantic nations (Melkote, 1991, pp. 37–73). Most of these theories assumed the interest of the political economic elites would become involved in the rural areas to provide development education and technical assistance. However, many of the developing nations could not afford the professional salaries demanded for work in outlying rural areas. So, the demands of the urban political elites of the new nations, the expanding government employees, and vocal urban youth asking for employment dominated the governments (Hall & Midgley, 2004, pp. 44–80; McMichael, 2012, pp. 48–51). Often religious organizations, more present in rural areas, provided health and agricultural services in rural areas (Chambers, 1983; Ndiritu et al., 2004, pp. 261–286).

Agriculture both for the domestic food consumption by the increasing population and for export to gain resources for needed modernization imports mainly sustained economic development, but the new governments lacked the organizational and communication capacity to reach out into the rural areas to improve agricultural production. In many new nations of Africa, Latin America, and Asia the traditional organization, often religious in its leadership, provided the major community leadership and communication for productive and other rural improvements (Boafo, 2006; Quebral, 2006). Religious leadership often provided the administrative structure for introducing agricultural and other improvements. In many cases the religious culture often provided the motivation to introduce a variety of development improvements, especially among women (Gifford, 2016, pp. 151–155). As the new nations of the developing world improved their transportation and communication, religious organizations were often able to use the improved communication to revitalize their communication and administration throughout their nations. The Christian denominations as well as other major world religions such as Islam, Hinduism, and Buddhism began a significant resurgence in many parts of the developing world. Since these religious organizations were strongest in the rural areas of the countries of the South, the religious revitalization often had its greatest impact on the improvement of the rural areas of the new nations.

The Commitment to Socioeconomic Development by Major Religious Groups

One can ask how religious traditions become involved in socioeconomic development. Virtually all the founders of the great religions of the world received an inspiration that impelled them to announce the need for a transformation of personal lives and of society in general. Mohammad, after the revelation experience of the embracing angel, began to preach the need not only for a change of life but a new social order (Quasimi, 1987, p. 65). Jesus, also, after his own conversion experience, moved about Palestine calling people to commitment to establishing a new social order of service to the poor, just government, uplifting women, and participatory community action. Buddhism, a religion of inner personal transformation, implies social development, and Hindu spiritual leaders foster socioeconomic development aspirations.

Using media to communicate the movement is also found in all the religions. Within a generation Christian founders had put their central transformative vision in written, copied form. The communication of the message in all forms of media – oratory, traveling preachers, witnessing lives, handwritten manuscripts, books, paintings, sculpture – became an integral part of the Christian movement. Mohammed and his followers emphasized the spread of their teachings in written and other mediated form (Nasr, 1987). Other great religious traditions used writings, artistic expression, and other forms of mediation to spread their devotions.

In virtually all the developing nations, the religious beliefs and religious organizations became a factor in national development. Although the long-term economic goal of the new nations has been industrialization, the immediate economic challenge involved the improvement of agricultural production in the early stages of socioeconomic development (McMichael, 2012, pp. 52–54). Subsistence farming of these new nations remains deeply intertwined with the traditional religious beliefs of the people for all the major religious traditions. In the religious perspective a good harvest to sustain the food and income of the community depends on the favor and support of supernatural power and the traditional religious rituals (Zalot, 2002, pp. 30–36). Thus, as national socioeconomic development became a more central goal in all nations, religious motivations became part of the national development process. Religion provided a motivational support for capitalization and organization in the process of industrialization as Weber explained in his analysis of religion and expansion of industrial capital investments in Europe (Peet & Hartwick, 2009, pp. 24–33; Weber, 1958). Also, as worker and farmer movements entered into the national development process, they called on the churches to support the recognition of their rights and well-being, with those disadvantaged by industrialization the major constituents of religious organizations. Just as in Europe, the working class and rural social movements sought religious support to defend social justice (Hinton, 1983). In response, religious leaders developed teachings on human rights and development of disadvantaged sectors. Thus, most major religions developed a tradition of analysis of social problems and systematic teaching on government social policy and the resulting social conditions. From the nineteenth century demands for improved workers' salaries and small farmer welfare became important in the development goals of all religious groups.

The major development institutions such as the World Bank often formed coalitions with the major religious traditions (Belshaw et al., 2001). The religious traditions made the well-being of the people forming new nations an integral part of their teachings and supported the goal of the independence leaders to form governmental systems of public services (McMichael, 2012, pp. 50–54). Generally, however, in virtually all developing nations the dual system of education, health, and other services took shape: one for urban elites and an inferior system for the large rural population and the poverty-stricken immigrants from rural areas moving into the urban slums (Boyle, 1999; Mehrotra & Delamonica, 2007, pp. 57–68). Thus, the religious institutions, more present in rural areas, especially supported efforts to introduce education and health services into the rural and other disadvantaged sectors of the new nations (Zalot, 2002).

The Central Role of Religion in the Development of Rural People

Rural people of developing nations tend to continue to be more deeply religious, and, in the developing nations, the strongest adherents of the major religions of the world are mainly rural people and rural people migrating into urban lower status areas. In Latin America, for example, the rural people tend to be traditionally Catholic with their festivals centered around patron saints or feasts of the Church year. In Africa, the rural culture of both Islamic and Christian peoples is deeply religious (Chu Ilo, 2014, pp. 213–223). The same is true of areas where a religious dominance of Buddhism (Marshall, 2011) and Hinduism (Mondal, 2021) exists. With independence many new nations affirmed their national Indigenous cultures, and many of the major religions entered into the process of reaffirmation of the indigenous social and political institutions. There was also an effort to maintain the religiosity of the people in the face of the secularization emphasis that accompanied the model of industrialization coming from the North Atlantic nations. One of the aspects of development was the improved communication and transport into the outlying areas of the nation (Melkote, 1991). Thus, an integral part of this modernization of the religious beliefs was the use of media and intensification of communication contacts especially with the rural populations, which were among the main religious adherents.

How the Religions Organizations Support Socioeconomic Development

Christianity and Socioeconomic Development

Although socioeconomic development as it is defined today did not exist in early Christianity, following the emphasis of Jesus led Christian communities to reach out to the poor, the sick, and the needy. Christianity promoted the distribution of wealth within its own communities and to those in the vicinity of its communities. Personal service to the poor and the sick became a Christian ideal and helped in the spread of Christianity throughout Europe and its world-wide extension (Stark, 1996). With the Industrial Revolution in Europe in the eighteenth century, many workers sought better wages and working conditions and asked the Christian churches to support their demands. In the nineteenth century, churches responded by helping in the organization of the working classes and acting to improve working and living conditions. For example, the Catholic Church proved influential in the field of public policy with its 1891 statement of moral guidelines for industrialization, *Rerum Novarum*, outlining the obligations of industrialists, governments, and others to improve wages, living conditions, and other aspects of the life of workers. At the practical level the churches set up educational institutions to train workers and farmers in their rights and how to strengthen organizational capacity and influence national policy (Dronen, 2014).

With decolonization and the formation of new nations in the early 1960s, independence leaders appealed to the churches for support. The churches not only supported independence, but also used their base in the developed nations to get resources to build schools, health services, agricultural training institutions, and provide other assistance for national development. Virtually all of the Christian Churches responded with policy statements emphasizing development priorities. One of the first major statements regarding the moral obligations of socioeconomic development came from the Catholic Church in 1961: *Mater et Magister* (*Mother and Teacher*) issued by Pope John XXIII. Significantly, the document dealt almost entirely with the moral obligations of those planning and facilitating rural development. The churches focused on the rights of the poor and the rural people, criticizing the self-serving interests of the new elites (Hansen & Twaddle, 1995; Oyugi, 1994, pp. 10–14). The leadership of the Catholic Church has regularly called for more technical assistance in agriculture for the small farmers in the new nations, better health services, and much improved educational facilities. Pope Benedict XVI's *Charity in Truth* (2009) again emphasizes the basic objective of rural welfare (Chu Ilo, 2014).

From the late 1940s the Catholic Church and other Christian Churches in the developed nations began to set up development programs to channel their resources to the developing nations. The Churches usually source their development assistance in nations of the North and distribute their help through their churches in the developing nations. The Catholic Church works through the international organization of Caritas (https://www.caritas.org). Virtually every one of the 4000 Catholic dioceses in the world has a Caritas office and in the developing nations the Caritas organizations provide socioeconomic development support, as occurs throughout Africa (https://caritas-africa.org/?s=development+support). An example of how the Christian Churches enter into the development process appears in the Caritas development projects in the Diocese of Mbeya, one of the 34 Diocesan Caritas offices in Tanzania (Issa, 2004, pp. 203–225). Discussion of farmers in one parish with the directors of the Mbeya Diocese Caritas office led to the design of an agricultural project involving small farmers in a series of Small Christian Communities in one parish. Supported by Caritas Netherlands through the national Caritas office in Tanzania, the project provided credit, purchasing improved breeds of livestock and improved varieties of crops and farm animals. Approximately 150 small farmers, men and women, entered into the project, producing improved varieties of maize, potatoes, beans, milk cows, and pigs. Government extension agents provided technical training and guidance. A learning experience in farm management with some mistakes, the project not only taught farmers better farming methods, but also focused on soil conservation methods such as terracing and planting trees to prevent erosion, and introduced better storage and marketing of produce. Generally, production was improved and both food consumption and incomes improved. Many farmers harvested 5–10 bags of maize instead of just 2. The religious organizations offer an organizational structure reaching down into rural communities and motivation to improve development action.

Other Christian Churches also support socioeconomic development as a priority in church planning and funding (Zalot, 2002, pp. 156–178). The Christian Churches have been especially important for defending the poor in the framing of national constitutions, especially in Africa (Mugambi, 1997, pp. 139–148). Christian organizations of different denominations are a major provider of health services in Africa. In Tanzania the Christian Social Service Commission, involving all denominations, operates 90 hospitals, some 40% of the hospitals of the country. In addition, there are both Christian and Muslim dispensaries all over Tanzania (Paivansalo, 2014, p. 116).

The World Council of Churches and each of the major Christian denominations also sponsors a series of international social assistance and social development programs. Lutheran World Relief has programs emphasizing agriculture in Africa in Tanzania, Ethiopia, Nigeria, Liberia, and Ghana. Lutheran churches also have development programs in Latin America, the Middle East, south India, Papua New Guinea, and the Philippines. In each of these countries Lutheran World Relief maintains radio stations to support the development programs funding development projects, primarily in rural communities (https://lwr.org/about-lwr). The Anglican International Development agency, although smaller in scope, provides development assistance especially in the African countries of South Sudan, Uganda, and Kenya (https://anglicaninternationaldeve lopment.org). The US Presbyterian Mission Agency, the United Methodist Committee on Relief, the United Church of Christ, the Disciples of Christ, and other ecumenical partners have various projects in Africa, especially in Sierra Leone and Liberia. The fastest growing Christian groups in Africa, Latin America, and the Philippines (Freeman, 2015), Pentecostal and charismatic movements appeal to more urban lower middle class persons who make a living with small businesses and seek God's blessings on their personal business endeavors (Hasu, 2012).

Agriculturists in the developing world now increasingly use social media and the Internet to increase their productivity. A study of farmers in Kenya using the Internet found that 42.9% received information for their small farmers from Facebook, 13% from Twitter, 10.4% from WhatsApp, 24% from YouTube, 6.4% from Google+, and 2.6% from LinkedIn (Wangu, 2014, p. 57). Religious organizations in rural communities encourage small farmers to take advantage of this new technology.

The Islamic Religious Tradition and Socioeconomic Development

Humanity's seeking the will of Allah and following the will of Allah in all aspects of life guides Islamic religious devotion. The will of Allah, in the socioeconomic order, "should liberate men and women from the crippling pressure of unfulfilled physical needs, from abject poverty and hunger. All forms of oppression and tyranny, institutional or otherwise should be eliminated" (Siddiqi, 2001). This is a major concern in Islamic countries such as Bangladesh (43% below the poverty line), Pakistan (32.6%), and Sierra Leone (70.2%). Concretely, Islamic social ethics requires as a religious obligation that the more successful economic sectors make a special effort to assist the poor and needy. A specific example of this is the financing of village-level micro enterprises, especially among women's groups (Obaidulluh, 2019).

Muslim religious approaches to development play an important role in the conception and planning of national development programs as, for example, in Bangladesh (Oded, 2000). Muslim international voluntary assistance programs such as Muslim Relief World Wide and Islamic Aid are also an expression of the Muslim religious tradition of *Zakat*, the donation of wealth to the poor, and of assistance to marginal areas.

The Buddhist Religious Tradition and Socioeconomic Development

Buddhism originated in the north of India about 300 BCE, and spread gradually to what is now Sri Lanka, Thailand, Vietnam, China, Korea, and Japan with adherence also among some in the North Atlantic nations. In China Buddhism is concentrated in the Tibetan region. Buddhism does not focus on worship of a supernatural creator but is a practice of reflective exercises to achieve a virtuous personality. Although Buddhist ideals have many variations, Buddhism emphasizes moderation in lifestyle, simplifying desires, and the redistribution of wealth in a society. The "small is beautiful" philosophy derives from Buddhism (Hershock, 2021).

In countries such as Thailand Buddhist teaching forms the foundation of national development policy. Development efforts from a Buddhist perspective do not emphasize simply increased incomes but concrete efforts to improve education, health services, and raising agricultural production especially in rural villages (ICDV Conference, 2011) New programs in countries such as Thailand train the ubiquitous Buddhist monks as social workers promoting schools, health centers, and agricultural education (Marshall, 2011). In countries such as Japan, Korea, Vietnam, and parts of China where Buddhism is a dominant religious influence on the culture, Buddhism cultivates the economic values of hard work, organizational dedication, social generosity, and moderation in consumption that underlies the rapid industrial development in those countries (Schumacher, 1974). Where Buddhism influences the national development model as in Japan, a country in which Buddhism has been a major socio-cultural influence, the emphasis is on shared prosperity (not personal wealth acquisition), harmonious cooperation of major actors, and respect for the environment (Schumacher, 1974).

Hinduism as a Religion and a Factor in Socioeconomic Development

Hinduism can best be described as the religion of the culture of India. Hinduism in India is not so much a creed that one believes or not, but is a way of life, a worldview of one's social position in society, motivating a person's socioeconomic endeavor. India's constitution states that it is a secular state, but the vast majority (79.8%) practices Hinduism, with the next highest (14.2%) adhering to Islam (Wikipedia, 2020). Most Hindus commemorate a local deity on some days, carry out the Hindu rituals for a newborn baby, and perform Hindu rituals at weddings and funerals. Although religious practices may be slackening among the youth, seeking success in life and in families is closely tied to practice of the traditional rituals. The Hindu caste system continues as a major influence on social position and socioeconomic development practice. Studies show that just 10% of upper caste Hindus own 60% of the total wealth of India, and this concentration of wealth and economic control in India is growing (Paliath, 2019). Socioeconomic initiative is expected of the virtuous, religious higher caste people.

The devotional practices of religious life in India relate very much to socioeconomic endeavor in India. Many adopt a religious patron and establish a small shrine in the home to seek the favors of that patron in economic life. Periodic rituals and pilgrimages are carried out to further economic success in life (Chowdhury, 2017).

How the Major Religions Use Communication Media for Development

Christianity: Using Media to Promote Development

Through the ages Christianity has emphasized the use of the media technology of the period to communicate not only its own doctrinal message but knowledge and contemporary learning. Monastic institutions, which from the year 500 onwards were the centers of the spread of Christianity, emphasized libraries and reading and writing. In the sixteenth century the churches were major promoters of the early printing press, and as the Christian institutions spread in the areas of America, Africa, and Asia they brought the new media with them.

With socioeconomic development growing more important, the Christian Churches began to use their media for development in Latin America, Africa, the Philippines, and Oceania. The Catholic Church, other Christian Churches, and other religions tend to use radio and to some small extent television rather than new media and the Internet because the audience the Churches want to reach is largely in rural areas and in lower status urban areas that the Internet does not reach. The Catholic Church has more than 400 radio stations in Latin America, and many Catholic dioceses in Africa and the Philippines have radio stations. The Lutheran Church also has radio and television stations in Latin America, especially in Central America and in Brazil (Lutheran Church, Missoui Synod, 2000).

One of the notable initiatives in Church-related development radio in Latin America is the Latin American Association of Educational Radio (ALER: Assoc. Latinoamericana de Educacion Radiofonica) (White, 1978, 1983). By the early 1970s the Catholic Church in Latin America had some form of educational programming on virtually all its 400 or more radio stations supporting local rural development projects. Typically, these stations broadcast programs in literacy training, agriculture, health, community improvement, and other areas of rural development. These radio stations often became the most listened to stations with debate, call-ins, drama, and other entertainment formats. The Church encouraged the educational radio stations to form national associations of educational radio so that each Latin American nation would have a central office providing training of broadcast personnel and development of attractive radio formats. The organizational structure of the Catholic Church at the national, subnational, diocesan, and the parish levels as well as small Christian groups in rural communities support this radio educational system. The radio stations are financed by advertising, by the education departments of local Latin American governments, grants given by European and North American development agencies, and grants from the Catholic churches and development agencies in Europe and North America. The ALER organization, specialists in methods of educational radio, maintains a central team to train the local stations throughout Latin America in educational broadcasting. The ALER training team also receives funding by international funding agencies such as the European Union. A similar organizational structure to support the Church's radio-based rural education has been developed in Africa, the Philippines, and other parts of the world where the Catholic diocesan structure exists.

This movement of radio education coincided with the widespread introduction of the educational methods of Paulo Freire in Latin America, and many of the radio educational systems incorporated the Freirean methods to develop a critical awareness of the exploitation of peasant farmers by large landowners and political leaders. This objective has motivated peasant farming peoples to form local and national organizations to introduce legislation favorable to the rural lower status population.

Many development movements sparked by the rural and urban poor found support in the media of Christian Churches in Latin America, Africa, the Philippines, and areas of Oceania such as Papua New Guinea (Hansen & Twaddle, 1995); governments often use Church media for the development programs of the new nations (Leonard, 1991, pp. 248–274). Often the moves away from dictatorial government to constitutional government have found strong support in the media of the Churches (Hansen & Twaddle, 1995). In Kenya, the protests against the brutality of the Moi regime were led by religious leadership, Protestant, Catholic, and Muslim (Zeleza, 2014, p. 30).

In India the Christian Churches, though a small minority, have been active through "small media" such as audio and video cassettes in urging the government to enforce laws that provide special benefits such as government jobs and positions in educational institutions for the Dalits, who do not share in the privileges of the higher castes (Gomes, 2018).

The Churches and Development Communication
in Africa and Asia

Although all religious groups are involved in development initiatives in Africa, the Catholic Church has made an especially significant effort toward rural development in Africa. In Kenya, for example, in 2013 the Catholic Church sponsored 5766 public primary schools out of Kenya's total of 19 059 (Gifford, 2016, p. 86). In 2010, the Catholic Church in Kenya operated 16 178 health centers including 1074 hospitals, 5373 out-patient clinics, 186 leper colonies, 753 homes for the elderly, and 979 orphanages (Gifford, 2016, p. 90).

The Lutheran Church in Africa operates radio stations or radio services in Liberia, Ghana, Nigeria, and Ethiopia, with a particularly influential radio center in Tanzania, all providing development programming to support the community-based development programs of the Lutheran Church. The Lutheran Church also broadcasts over a series of radio stations in Guatemala and in Brazil, supporting its development work in those countries.

The Catholic Church's Caritas network in Africa, mentioned earlier, has more than 300 diocesan Caritas organizations with development projects supported by the Caritas organization in the developed countries of Europe and America (see, for example, https://caritas-africa. org/?s=development+projects). Where governments allow nongovernmental media, the dioceses in Africa have also moved to have a small radio broadcasting unit in every diocese and often two or three radio stations where dioceses are very large. In the East African region, Kenya has 24 diocesan radio stations and 2 television stations; Tanzania has 12 diocesan radio stations and 2 national television stations; Uganda, 18 diocesan radio stations and 2 television stations; and Zambia has 9 diocesan radio stations and 2 television stations (Fr. Andrew Kaufa, Communications Officer, East African Episcopal Conference, personal communication, 2020). These radio programs are often closely coordinated with the agricultural training courses given by the Catholic development program of Caritas. Productive innovations often originate from the farmers themselves and are circulated by local radio stations in close contact with the projects promoted by the churches at the grassroots level (Scoones & Thompson, 1994, pp. 16–31). These training courses in agriculture and radio interviews reporting innovations directly from the farmers provide a stimulus for agricultural innovations (Mallery et al., 2001; Nasr et al., 2001). These diocesan radio stations are frequently the most listened to stations in the area because they often mention the leaders of community organizations or send messages to friends and relatives. Rural Africans like religious programming and music in the traditional languages and dialects. Typically, the stations report progress of the community development projects in agriculture and health. In many parts of Africa there continues to be conflict over land or other disputes among clans and tribes, and the radio stations support a program of reconciliation. Currently, the Catholic Church, through its world-wide Center for Applied Research in the Apostalate organization and other Christian groups, is moving to introduce means of sharing information regarding local agricultural and other development projects through various forms of social media, especially video cassettes (Nyamnjoh, 2020).

In Asia and Oceania, Catholics and other Christian groups have more than 60 radio stations in the Philippines, several radio stations in Papua New Guinea, and several international shortwave radio stations providing radio services throughout Asia and Oceania (Torres, 2017).

Christian Churches are also rapidly moving into mobile phone communication (Smith, 2018). Agricultural development agencies increasingly communicate new technology through mobile phones (Masuki et al., 2010) and the Catholic Church in southern Africa is organizing its development communication via mobile phones (White, 2009). Because mobile phones occupy so much personal attention, they are a major locus of personal religious experience. People exchange religious views on mobile phones apart from institutional religion, and, given the decline in association with religion as worship sites, the mobile phone is increasingly a place of religious practice (Cho & Campbell, 2015).

The Importance of Pentecostal Movements in Countries of the South

The expansion of Pentecostal Christianity is noteworthy in Latin America, Africa, the Philippines, Korea, and Papua New Guinea (Gifford, 2016). Pentecostal practice is especially attractive among the immigrants in the exploding cities of the South. Pentecostal movements welcome the more urban popular culture in music, dress, exuberant religious worship, and use of popular media (Kalu, 2008, pp. 103–122). Pentecostalism is a democratizing religion in that it promotes personal religious beliefs over official religious doctrine and emphasizes personal evangelizing through big media star preachers (Kolapo, 2019). Pentecostalism also embraces social media, which permits users to insert their own personal religious beliefs and personal life successes (Saxena, 2018).

Evangelical Pentecostal movements, with their value emphasis on prosperity in business efforts, are particularly strong all over Africa and Latin America, where everybody survives with their own small business on the side. Forms of Pentecostalism have made a significant contribution to the development culture and motivation in contexts where big development efforts are so difficult. The evangelical religious emphasis on personal inspiration for economic success mirrors the classical Protestant ethic, stressing economic prosperity and entrepreneurial effort as a major emphasis in life (Gifford, 2016). Pentecostal programs on radio and television tell stories of small businesses success through Pentecostal prayer, doing away with witches and spells, and promoting personal abstemious practice (Freeman, 2015). The Pentecostal Jesus as a factor for life success in business is also highlighted in enormously influential video films not only in Nigeria but throughout Africa (Merz, 2015). Pentecostal religious experience is presented on the world wide web as a dominant experience throughout the world and a factor of personal success especially in the developing world of Latin America and Africa (Asamoah-Gyadu, 2015).

Pentecostalism fits into the urban lives of many developing nations. In many parts of the world, but especially in Africa and in Latin America, major mass production manufacturing industries have not developed. The evangelical preachers and the videos they distribute promise success in businesses through prayer to Jesus with examples of how prayer to Jesus bought instant financial success (Gifford, 2016, pp. 3–28). The Pentecostal prosperity gospel forms a major attraction to people in Latin America and offers an explanation of the growth of Pentecostalism in Latin America (Masci, 2014).

Increasing evidence shows that the Pentecostal ethic influences socioeconomic development in Africa, Latin America, and other parts of the world (Freeman, 2012, pp. 1–38). Pentecostalism sees business as a form of Christian service that gains God's blessing, often miraculously, on entrepreneurial risk (Freeman, 2012, pp. 20–21). Pentecostalism attacks the destructive machismo of fighting, gangs, drugs, and alcohol common in both Latin America and Africa with the male ideal of entrepreneurial risk supported by God's euphoric blessing (van Dijk, 2012, pp. 87–108). Pentecostalism encourages followers to tithe and give generously to the Church's activities, which often includes setting up a loan fund to assist members' entrepreneurial activities at virtually no interest. Personal prosperity in business and living a life of prosperity in dress and life style are an external show of personal piety and the blessings of an integral religious practice (Kalu, 2008, pp. 255–266) The Pentecostal ethic often strengthens the entrepreneurial spirit of its followers (Masci, 2014).

Pentecostal television and video cassettes, following the Nollywood film style, have adopted narrative approaches, making them very entertaining and attractive. For example, Pentecostal video brings in elements of the traditional religious culture, witches, apparitions, and miracles (Merz, 2015). Every country of Africa has its own popular video production centers and Pentecostal videos imitate local styles, with storylines following the typical local narrative style of different countries (Pype, 2015). Sound and video cassettes are important media for Pentecostal adherents but radio stations in Latin America and in Africa also play a role in the spread of the Pentecostal religion and Pentecostal business ethic (Kay, 2009). The Pentecostal radios are extended and reinforced by the wide distribution of audio and video cassettes.

The Islamic Contribution to Development Communication

The Islamic scholarly tradition has focused on development research and policy throughout the centuries, but currently there is more emphasis on an Islamic perspective in development studies (Atiyya Saqr, 2020; Azislam.com, 2020). One of the more notable contributions in current development policies and program design is the small loan system of the Grameen Bank (Grameen is Bengali for "village") initiated by Muhammad Yunus and his colleagues at the University of Chittagong in Bangladesh, but now a model spread throughout the world (Armendariz & Morduch, 2005). The program was pro poor in that it gave loans demanding no collateral and favored women especially. A major factor in its success is interpersonal and small media communication: to get a loan a person must join a group of about seven poor people that meets regularly and advises members on the use of the loan with communication advice from the Grameen Bank overseer of the group. The loans are paid daily with eligibility for a further loan (Grameen Bank, 2020). As of 2017, the Bank had about 2600 branches and nine million borrowers, with a repayment rate of 99.6%. Some 97% of the borrowers are women. The worldwide success of the Grameen Bank system has led to its replication in 64 countries of the world including a World Bank initiative to finance similar schemes following the Grameen model. The Grameen Bank, following the inspiration of its founder, Yunus (a devout Muslim), follows many of the Islamic principles of socioeconomic development. For example, the basic motive of socioeconomic activity focuses not on personal wealth coming from entrepreneurial activity, but on social benefits and general social usefulness, with an overall concern for the poor and unfortunate. The Muslim principles of *"zakat"* (purifying), meaning "giving or purifying of one's money or goods," demand a distribution of one's economic success to the poor and less fortunate (30 Days of Prayer, 2010).

In the Islamic countries of sub-Saharan Africa, local radio, cassettes, and other media are much used for development purposes. In Burkina Faso, women, not normally brought into the leadership of development, were instructed in the process of planting trees to stop the advancing Sahara by video cassettes (Sankare & Konate, 2006). Also in Burkina Faso, villagers' explanations of their development innovations were broadcast over the radio (Ouattara & Ouattara, 2006).

The use of Twitter, Facebook, and other social media has developed especially among the youth in the debate on socio-political development of Islamic countries (Access now, 2020). Many listen to and discuss in groups the newer more radical Islamic views of socio-political development and use this as the basis of their entry into movements for national development (Hirschkind, 2009).

Buddhism and Communication for Socioeconomic Development

Buddhism encourages all adults to engage in forms of meditation in homes and in villages. In a Buddhist country such as Thailand, one sees Wats (temples) and saffron robed monks everywhere (Facts and Details, 2019). The challenge has been to integrate the practice of reflection and meditation with life in industrial and development organizations. Buddhist social movements in Thailand, Sri Lanka, Japan, and other areas promote and teach a socioeconomic development theory that emphasizes moderation and distribution rather than accumulation, interdependence rather individual initiatives, and promotion of widespread participation rather than individualism (Essen, 2019). Although people in Buddhist countries experience the pressure of industrial development, they seek to find space for Buddhist ideals, cultivating an atmosphere of "spirit building" or prayer and reflection (ICDV Conference, 2011). In various parts of the Buddhist world, especially in Thailand, Cambodia, and Sri Lanka, monks are now being trained for improvement in the communities where they are located. Their activities focus on health improvement, family counseling, and dispute resolution, improvement in local agriculture and natural resource management. The social action is coordinated with local radio programs on development issues (Buddhism for Development, 2022).

Media, Religion, and Development in India

Indian religious beliefs and practices continue to be communicated by household shrines, traditional ceremonies, and ubiquitous temples. However, Indian holy men with a very modern style that borrows from international televangelism propagate a new version of Hinduism (see Chapter 11). The content of their television programs deals with simple herbal remedies (to cure ring worm, for example) but focuses especially on tips for success in business affairs and announcement of coming religious festivals. The gurus also use various forms of social media – Facebook, Twitter, YouTube, and WhatsApp – and appeal especially to the upwardly mobile young middle class workers in the pharmaceutical and biological technology industries linked to the world economy. The fact that some of the gurus have their own business empires only adds to their attractiveness. Some organize social media camps mixing ancient Indian knowledge with technology training and advice for success in business (Chouhan, 2016). Their audiences are estimated to reach hundreds of millions. A recent survey by the Centre for the Study of Developing Societies found 30% of the respondents, devotees of the new gurus, felt that they were becoming more religious and more spiritual. They are particularly attracted by the message of the gurus regarding the mix of religion, consumer styles, getting ahead in business, and the power of Indian new technology nationalism (Das, 2022).

Although Christians are a very small minority in India, they have established their media centers distributing video, films, and print materials quite widely. A particularly good example of this is the Lutheran media center in Chennai.

Conclusion

The central question of this chapter addresses how major religious traditions have used media to contribute to socioeconomic development and improve access to the basic necessities of life.

The Judeo-Christian tradition has perhaps the most explicit emphasis on socioeconomic development in its use of media because of its priority of seeking the well-being of the poor and marginal people of the society and because of its traditional emphasis on media beginning with its written gospels and letters. Christian Churches, together, now have more than 500 educational radio and television stations in Latin America, Africa, and other areas such the Philippines. The fastest growing sector of Christianity, the evangelicals, in addition to their use of radio, video cassettes, and television, are expanding their use of social media, computers, and mobile phones, emphasizing small business, entrepreneurial promotion.

Islam also emphasizes putting religious teaching in publications and other forms of media. With a long scientific and socioeconomic development tradition, Islam has a tradition of concern for the poor and less developed parts of its societies. The expectation that individual adherents of Islam will give away part of their economic success for the benefit of the poor and less fortunate provides added motivation. One of the most notable contributions to development from an Islamic background is the system of credit to the poor, the Grameen Bank, initiated by Mohammed Yunus in Bangladesh.

Buddhism emphasizes heightened inner consciousness of well-being, reconciliation, compassion, and the overcoming of hate and selfishness. Buddhism communicates its message through the plastic arts, especially the ubiquitous images of Buddha. Where Buddhism is the dominant religious tradition (as in Thailand), the Buddhist temples and monks are centers promoting socioeconomic improvement at the local community level and national radio has programs for development purposes.

Hinduism, located largely in India, is essentially a social worldview that assigns one's socioeconomic status in life. Wealth and entrepreneurial initiative are part of the culture of the higher castes, and people of the higher castes are often leaders in development initiatives in India. Although religious communications and development involvement are still a matter of household deities, Indian holy gurus now sponsor television programs that attract an upwardly mobile technological class with tips on getting ahead in business, personal wealth, and upper class styles.

References

30 Days of Prayer. (2010). Muslim's money, and "zakat". 30 Days of Prayer. Retrieved June 8, 2022, from https://www.pray30days.org/zakat

Access now. (2020). Open letter to Facebook, Twitter, and YouTube: Stop silencing critical voices from the Middle East and North Africa. Access now. Retrieved June 9, 2022, from http://www.accessnow.org/facebook-twitter-youtube-stop-silencing-critical-voices-mena

Armendariz, B., & Morduch, J. (2005). *The economics of microfinance*. The MIT Press.

Asamoah-Gyadu, J. K. (2015). "We are on the internet": Contemporary Pentecostalism in Africa and the new culture of online religion. In R. I. J. Hackett, & B. F. Soares (Eds.), *New media and religious transformations in Africa* (pp. 157–170). Indiana University Press.

Azislam.com (2020). 5 principles of the Islamic economic system. Azislam.com. Retrieved June 9, 2022, from https://azislam.com/principles-of-the-islamic-economic-system

Barrett, C. B., Mude, A. G., & Omiti, J. M. (Eds.). (2007). *Decentralization and the social economics of development: Lessons from Kenya*. CAB International.

Belshaw, D., Calderisi, R., & Sugden, C. (Eds.). (2001). *Faith in development: Partnership between the World Bank and the churches of Africa*. Regnum Books International.

Boafo, S. T. K. (2006). Participatory development communication: An African perspective. In G. Bessette (Ed.), *People, land, & water: Participatory development communication for natural resource management* (pp. 41–48). Earthscan.

Boyle, P. (1999). *Class formation and civil society: The politics of development*. Ashgate Publishers.

Buddhism for Development. (2022). Buddhist radio TV: Socially engaged Buddhism. Buddhism for Development. Retrieved June 9, 2022, from https://bfdkhmer.org/?page_id=30

Chambers, R. (1983). *Rural development: Putting last first*. Pearson.

Cho, J., & Campbell, H. (2015). Religious use of mobile phones. In Z. Yeng (Ed.), *Encyclopedia of mobile phone behavior* (Vol. 1, pp. 308–321). IGI Global.

Chouhan, S. (2016). Social media the new mantra for Indian gurus. Reuters. Retrieved June 9, 2022, from https://www.reuters.com/article/idIN310130821820160428

Chowdhury, E. R. (2017). Shradh puja: Five facts you should know about death anniversary ritual in Hinduism. Newsgram. Retrieved June 8, 2022, from https://www.newsgram.com/general/2017/09/03/shradh-puja-five-facts-you-should-know-about-death-anniversary-ritual-in-hinduism

Chu Ilo, S. (2014). *The church and development in Africa*. Pickwick Publications.

Das, M. K. (2022, June 20). Televising religion in India: Telebabas, the new age gurus. *Hindustan Times*.

Dronen, T. S. (2014). *Religion and development*. Peter Lang.

Essen, J. (2019). Thrifty, Part 1: Find your sufficiency sweet spot. Global Wellbeing Institute. Retrieved June 28, 2022, from https://globalwellbeinginstitute.org/thrifty-part-1-find-your-sufficiency-sweet-spot

Facts and Details. (2019). Buddhism and Religion in Thailand. Facts and Details. Retrieved June 9, 2022, from https://factsanddetails.com/southeast-asia/Thailand/sub5_8b/entry-3212.html

Forrest, J. (2020). Is Buddhism a religion? Retrieved June 9, 2022, from https://www.patheos.com/blogs/thebuddhasaid/2020/08/is-buddhism-a-religion

Freeman, D. (2012). The Pentecostal ethic and the spirit of development. In D. Freeman (Ed.), *Pentecostalism and development* (pp. 1–38). Palgrave Macmillan.

Freeman, D. (2015). Pentecostalism and economic development in sub-Saharan Africa. In E. Tomalin (Ed.), *The Routledge handbook of religions and global development* (pp. 114–126). Routledge.

Gifford, P. (2016). *Christianity, development, and modernity in Africa*. Oxford University Press.

Gomes, R. (2018, November 5). Indian Christians to celebrate Dalit liberation Sunday on Nov 11. Vatican News. Retrieved June 8, 2022, from https://www.vaticannews.va/en/church/news/2018-11/india-christians-cbci-ncci-dalit-liberation-sunday-november-11.html

Grameen Bank (2020). Grameen Bank. Grameen Bank. Retrieved June 9, 2022, from https://en.wikipedia.org/wiki/Grameen_Bank

Hall, A., & Midgley, J. (2004). *Social policy for development*. Sage Publications.

Hansen, H. B., & Twaddle, M. (1995). *Religion and politics in East Africa*. James Currey.

Hartmann, C., & Crawford, G. (2008). *Decentralisation in Africa: A pathway out of poverty and conflict?* Amsterdam University Press.

Hasu, P. (2012). Prosperity gospels and enchanted worldviews: Two responses to socio-economic transformation in Tanzanian Pentecostal Christianity. In D. Freeman (Ed.), *Pentecostalism and development* (pp. 67–86). Palgrave Macmillan.

Hershock, P. (2021). *Buddhism and intelligent technology: Toward a more humane future*. Bloomsbury.

Hinton, J. (1983). *Labour and socialism. A history of the British Labour movement 1867–1974*. The University of Massachusetts Press.

Hirschkind, C. (2009). *Ethical soundscapes: Cassette sermons and Islamic counterpolitics*. Columbia University Press.

ICDV Conference. (2011). Buddhist virtues in socio-economic development. Retrieved June 8, 2022, from http://www.undv.org/books/Symposium2011_final.pdf

Issa, F. H. H. (2004). *The present and potential role of non-governmental organizations in agricultural and rural development in Tanzania*. Shaker Verlag.

Kalu, O. (2008). *African Pentecostalism*. Oxford University Press.

Kay, W. K. (2009). Pentecostalism and religious broadcasting. *Journal of Beliefs and Values*, 30(3), 245–254. https://doi.org/10.1080/13617670903371555

Kolapo, F. J. (2019). Nigeria's Pentecostal churches and the tribunal of social media. *Social Media*, 26. http://www.pctii.org/cyberj/cyberj26/kolapo2.html

Leonard, D. K. (1991). *African successes: Four public managers of Kenyan rural development*. University of California Press.

Lutheran Church, Missoui Synod. (2000). Latin American mission. Lutheran Church, Missoui Synod. Retrieved June 8, 2022, from https://cyclopedia.lcms.org/display.asp?t1=L&word=LATINAMERICA MISSION

Mallery, Z., Temu, A., Kinabo, N., Mwigune, S., & Mwageni, A. (2001). Sowing maize in pits: Farmer innovation in southern Tanzania. In C. Reij, & A. Waters-Bayer (Eds.), *Farmer innovation in Africa* (pp. 267–280). Earthscan.

Marshall, K. (2011). Monks as social workers: How Buddhism helps development. Huffpost. Retrieved June 9, 2022, from https://www.huffpost.com/entry/buddhism-for-development-_b_814969

Masci, D. (2014). Why has Pentecostalism grown so dramatically in Latin America. Pew Research Center. Retrieved June 9, 2022, from https://www.pewresearch.org/fact-tank/2014/11/14/why-has-pentecostalism-grown-so-dramatically-in-latin-america

Masuki, K. F. G., Tukahirwa, J. M. B., Kamugisha, R. N., Mowo, G. J., Tanui, J. K., Mogoi, J. B., & Adera, E. O. (2010). Mobile phones in agricultural information delivery for rural development in eastern Africa: Lessons from western Uganda. World Agroforestry Centre. Retrieved June 10, 2022, from https://www.worldagroforestry.org/publication/mobile-phones-agricultural-information-delivery-rural-development-eastern-africa

McMichael, P. (2012). *Development and social change*. Sage Publications.

Mehrotra, S., & Delamonica, E. (2007). *Eliminating human poverty: Macroeconomic and social policies for equitable growth in the Third World: Theory and practice*. Sage Publications.

Melkote, S. (1991). *Communication and development in the Third World: Theory and practice*. Sage Publications.

Merz, J. (2015). Mediating transcendence: Popular film, visuality and religious experience in West Africa. In R. Hackett, & B. F. Soares (Eds.), *New media and religious transformations in Africa* (pp. 99–115). Indiana University Press.

Mondal, P. (2021). Rural religions: Characteristics and functions of rural religions. Your Article Library. Retrieved June 9, 2022, from https://www.yourarticlelibrary.com/religion/rural-religion-characteristics-and-functions-of-rural-religion/34951

Mugambi, J. N. K. (1997). *Democracy and development in Africa: The role of the churches*. All African Council of Churches.

Nasr, N., Hdaidi, E. A., & Ben Ayed, A. (2001). A bridge between local innovation, development and research: The regional radio of Gafsa, Tunisia. In C. Reij, & A. Waters-Bayer (Eds.), *Farmer innovation in Africa* (pp. 293–299). Earthscan.

Nasr, S. H. (1987). The Quran as the foundation of Islamic spirituality. And the life, traditions and sayings of the Prophet. In S. H. Nasr (Ed.), *Islamic spirituality* (pp. 3–10 and pp. 97–110). Crossroads Publications.

Ndiritu, C. G., Lynam, J. K., & Mbabu, A. (Eds.) (2004). *Transformation of agricultural research systems in Africa*. Michigan State University Press.

Nyamnjoh, H. (2020). "When are you going to change those stones to phones?": Social media appropriation by Pentecostal churches in Cape Town. In F. Nyamnjoh, & J. Carpenter (Eds.), *Christianity and social change in contemporary Africa* (Vol. 1, pp. 201–235). Langaa RPCIG.

Obaidullah, M. (2019). *Introduction to the Islamic microfinance*. International Institute of Islamic Business and Finance. Retrieved June 9, 2022, from https://akhuwat.org.pk/introduction-to-islamic-microfinance

Oded, A. (2000). *Islam and politics in Kenya*. Lynne Rienner Publishers.

Ouattara, S., & Ouattara, K. (2006). From information to communication in Burkina Faso: The brave new world of radio. In G. Bessette (Ed.), *People, land & water: Participatory development communication for natural resource management* (pp. 181–190). Earthscan.

Oyugi, W. O. (1994). The state in post-colonial East Africa. In W. O. Oyugi (Ed.), *Politics and administration in East Africa* (pp. 3–32). East African Educational Publishers.

Paivansalo, V. (2014). Fragile health justice: Cooperation with faith organizations. In T. Sundnes Drønen (Ed.), *Religion and development: Nordic perspectives on involvement in Africa* (pp. 109–125). Peter Lang.

Paliath, S. (2019) Income inequality in India: Top 10% upper caste households own 60% wealth. Business Standard. Retrieved June 9, 2022, from https://www.business-standard.com/article/current-affairs/income-inequality-in-india-top-10-upper-caste-households-own-60-wealth-119011400105_1.html

Peet, R., & Hartwick, E. (2009). *Theories of development*. Guilford Press.

Pype, K. (2015). Fictional melodrama: A new religious genre. In R. Hackett, & B. Soares (Eds.), *New media and religious transformations in Africa* (pp. 116–136). Indiana University Press.

Quasimi, J. (1987). The life of the Prophet. In S. H. Nasar (Ed.), *Islamic spirituality Foundations* (pp. 65–110). Crossroads Publishing.

Quebral, N. (2006). Participatory development communication: An Asian perspective. In G. Bessette (Ed.), *People, land & water: Participatory development communication for natural resource management* (pp. 35–40). Earthscan.

Sankare, A., & Konate, Y. (2006). From Rio to the Sahel: Combatting desertification. In G. Bessette (Ed.), *People, land & water: Participatory development communication for natural resource management* (pp. 94–105). Earthscan.

Saqr, S. A. (2020). *Islam and development*. Islamic Research Foundation International, Inc. Retrieved June 9, 2022, from www.irfi.org/articles/articles_501_550/islam_and_development.htm

Saxena, S. (2018). 7 key differences between social media and traditional media. Easymedia. Retrieved June 9, 2022, from https://www.easymedia.in/7-differences-social-media-traditional-media

Schumacher, E. F. (1974). *Small is beautiful*. Harper and Row.

Scoones, I., & Thompson, J. (1994). Knowledge power and agriculture – Towards a theoretical understanding. In I. Scoones, & J. Thompson (Eds.), *Beyond farmer first: Rural people's knowledge, agricultural research and extension practice* (pp. 16–31). Intermediate Technology Publications.

Siddiqi, M. N. (2001). Economics: An Islamic approach. Islamic Markets. Retrieved June 8, 2022, from https://islamicmarkets.com/education/economic-philosophy-of-islam

Smith, T. (2018). Top 10 ways thriving churches communicate. Church Tech Today. Retrieved June 9, 2022, from https://churchtechtoday.com/top-10-ways-thriving-churches-communicate

Stark, R. (1996). *The rise of Christianity*. Princeton University Press.

Taylor, D. R. F., & Mackenzie, F. (Eds.). (1992). *Development from within: Survival in rural Africa*. Routledge.

Torres, J. (2017). *Philippine Catholics fear silencing of 54 radio stations*. Retrieved June 10, 2022, from https://www.ucanews.com/news/philippine-catholics-fear-silencing-of-54-radio-stations/80584

van Dijk, R. (2012). Pentecostalism and post-development: Exploring religion as a development ideology in Ghanaian Pentecostal Christianity. In D. Freeman (Ed.), *Pentecostalism and development* (pp. 87–108). Palgrave Macmillan.

Wangu, K. C. (2014). Use of social media as a source of agricultural information by small holder farmers: A case study of lower Kabete, Kiambu County. Unpublished MA Thesis, School of Journalism and Mass Communication, University of Nairobi Kenya.

Wanyama, F. (2006). Local organization and sustainable development in Kenya. In J. Kamenju, & P. O. Okoth (Eds.), *Power play and policy in Kenya* (pp. 73–108). Oakland Books.

Weber, M. (1958). *The Protestant ethic and the spirit of capitalism*. Charles Scribner's Sons.

White, R. (1978). *Un modelo alternativo de educacion basica: Radio Santa Maria*. UNESCO.

White, R. (1983). The Latin American Association of Radiophonic Education. *Media in Education and Development*, 16(3), 122–128.

White, R. (2009). Research on communication for development in Africa: Current debates. *African Communication Research*, 2(2), 203–252.

Wikipedia. (2020). Religion in India. Retrieved June 9, 2022, from http://en.wikipedia.org/wiki/Religion_in_India

Zalot, J. (2002). *The Roman Catholic Church and economic development in sub-Saharan Africa*. University Press of America.

Zeleza, P. T. (2014). The protracted transition to the Second Republic in Kenya. In G. Muranga, D. Okello, & A. Sjogren (Eds.), *Kenya, the struggle for a new constitutional order* (pp. 17–43). Zed Books.

Selected Readings

Buddhism for Development. (2022). *Buddhist radio and TV: Socially engaged Buddhism*. Retrieved June 9, 2022, from https://bfdkhmer.org/?page+_id=30

Chouhan, S. (2016). Social media new mantra for Indian gurus. Reuters Retrieved June 9, 2022, from https://www.reuters.com/article/idIN310130821820160428

Dronen, T. S. (2014). *Religion and development*. Peter Lang.

Freeman, D. (2015). Pentecostalism and economic development in sub-Saharan Africa. In E. Tomalin (Ed.), *The Routledge handbook of religions and global development* (pp. 114–126). Routledge.

Gifford, P. (2016). *Christianity, development and modernity in Africa*. Oxford University Press.

Masci, D. (2014). Why has Pentecostalism grown so dramatically in Latin America. Pew Research Center. Retrieved June 9, 2022, from https://www.pewresearch.org/fact-tank/2014//11/14/why-has-pentecostalism-grown-so-dramatically-in-Latin-America

Part VIII

Approaches in New Technologies

32

Internet, Mobile Technology, and Religion

Miriam Díez Bosch and Josep Lluís Micó

This chapter explores and analyzes the impact of the Internet and mobile technology upon the major religions of the world. Reviewing the present digital times (Díez Bosch et al., 2015a; Grant et al., 2019) and the evolution of digital technologies, we present an overview of the meaning of these technologies and what they might mean for religions in the future. This chapter reviews the link between religion and the Internet, and then considers how this relationship between the online sphere and religions became mobile through the role of communities, social media, and especially mobile applications, looking at how phenomena such as robotics and artificial intelligence could become a very close next step.

Religion and Technology, a Historical Link

The technological enterprise has historically been a religious endeavor infused with spiritual belief (Nobel, 1997); "because religion remains a factor, influencing public as well as private life, it is important to include it in analyses focusing on social and cultural forces shaping Internet consumption and design" (Campbell, 2005b, p. 313). Wuthnow and Berger acknowledge that several different symbolic universes compete with each other in their ability to participate in the social construction of shared everyday reality (Sumiala-Seppänen, 2006), creating a new reality that opens up the possibilities for an encounter with religion and metaphysical truths (Roof, 2001).

Combining both a culture of individualism and a desire for a worldwide *oikos* or *ecumene* (Hillis, 2009), the Internet demands critical investigation as to how far new technologies serve a real dialogue, the true core of any human communication (Eilers, 1994). The Christian faith brings an inalienable public dimension to this critique – "Christians aren't Christ's followers only in their private and communal lives; they are Christ's followers in their public and political lives as well" (Volf & McAnnally-Linz, 2016, p. 3), even though contemporary spiritual searching is largely a private matter involving loosely associated social networks and small groups (Roof, 2001).

Online religious activity will not disappear: 62% of churchgoers in 2022 hope that, even post-Covid-19, churches will keep using digital means of bringing people together, a jump from the 8% of adults and 12% of teenagers using the Internet in their religious or spiritual experiences in

The Handbook on Religion and Communication, First Edition. Edited by Yoel Cohen and Paul A. Soukup.
© 2023 John Wiley & Sons Ltd. Published 2023 by John Wiley & Sons Ltd.

2001 (Barna, 2020). Pew Research (2014) found that 20% of Americans shared their faith online. However, the trend includes not only the Internet, but also religious experience through mobile technologies and other platforms and devices. In the first Internet age, 64% of Americans reported searching for religious information or engaging in religious practice online (Hoover et al., 2004). These figures suggest that religion and digital media influence each other (Hoover, 2016), as several authors note.

Internet, New Media, and Religion

At first, scholars investigated whether the Internet would change religious practice and ideology, because of the increase in online communities and the integration of religious practices into the digital sphere (Campbell, 2005a). Computer-mediated communication and Internet studies led the way (Baym, 2005). Campbell (2005a), whose work focuses on this topic, traces religious use of the Internet to the early 1980s, with scholarly attention to the link between the Internet and religion starting in the 1990s. Rheingold (1993) found the first religious-oriented activity online, on bulletin board systems, follows by several forums on religion, linked to various offline religious communities. Lochhead (1997) places the emergence of discussions about religion on Usenet at the same moment. The "net.religion" discussion list was the "first networked forum for discussions on the religious, ethical, and moral implications of human actions" (Ciolek, 2004, p. 799); other online groups also formed, led by "religious computer enthusiasts" (Campbell, 2005a). Ess (1996, p. 9) asserted that "if computer-mediated-communications only partially affects the revolutionary transformations of values and social structures envisioned by its enthusiasts, then religion – as humanity's oldest expression of values and community – is likely both to impact and to be impacted by these transformations." Lochhead (1997) pointed out that a Usenet online memorial service for the crew of the Challenger in 1986 demonstrated the power of the computer medium to unite a community in times of crisis.

O'Leary and Brasher (1996) provided an overview of how religion appeared in and influenced online environments through the public advocacy of faith. Others also explored the possibilities of online spirituality (Cobb, 1998; O'Leary, 1996; Schroeder et al., 1998; Zaleski, 1997) and the plurality of expressions of religion online (Dawson & Hennebry, 1999; Fernback, 2002). However, the study by Haddon and Cowan (2000) is considered the first noteworthy academic text tackling different theoretical approaches to studying religion on the Internet (Campbell, 2005a), as it is the first systematic inquiry into the nature, scope, and content of religion in cyberspace.

The early 2000s saw a growing number of studies: Brasher (2001), the concept of cyber-religion; Houston (1998), ethics and virtual reality; Wertheim (1999), how technology reconnects people with spiritual beliefs; Bunt (2000), the adaptations of traditional religious practices online; and Davis (1998), the identification of new religious expressions. McKay (2004) explored the effect of the Internet on public citizenship and social life and the challenge of ICT use to traditional religious culture, while Ess (2004) looked at the challenge involved in the transformation of the written word, that is, how reference texts such as the Bible should be revamped. Schultze (2002), Brooke (1997), and Dixon (1997) reflected on a number of concerns and critiques on the role and religious activity online. A key insight emerged in Helland's (2000) distinction between "religion online" – directly importing traditional forms of religion to the digital sphere – and "online religion" – adapting religion to create new forms of networked spiritual interactions. Dawson and Cowan (2004) summarize much of the work on traditional and progressive religious movements online and provide a theoretical base illustrated with case studies.

Hoover and his colleagues (Hoover et al., 2004), see a reshaping of ideas of what it means to be religious or spiritual in society. Hoover (2006, p. 48) affirmed that "the Internet was bringing a more fluid and multifaceted situation to the relationship between media and religion." He also detected that Internet and web-based practices are particularly individualistic and, in the case of the Web specifically, are thought to be "fundamentally interactive." This foreshadows how religion is being introduced in the digital sphere of mobile devices. Hoover also identified a range of websites according to their religious content or function, including those "directed self-consciously at traditional religious movements"; the pan-religious or meta-institutional; those focused on the fringe or emerging religious or spiritual movements; those intended to become new religious movements or sensibilities; and some highlighting their religious podcasting. He also found "quasi-religious" sites and even "antireligious" or "irreligious" sites (p. 48). The latter group focused on blogging, podcasting, instant messaging, and gaming (on gaming and religion, see Hess, 2017; Kristiadi et al., 2019; Sulistiyo et al., 2019).

Campbell (2005b) also reviews the state of the art, beginning with religious computer-mediated communication research. She argues that Internet studies from a religious approach are necessary because they offer a wide view of society. For her, "a complete picture of life online must include a consideration of how issues of religion, faith, and religious culture influence both specific online communities and the global network of humanity found online" (p. 313). In 2007, she explored the attributes of authority in the online context (see Chapter 30).

While Campbell (2005b) explored these issues from a Christian US and European perspective, Asamoah-Gyadu (2008) worked on the online religious action of Christian African communities, such as Pentecostal, charismatic, and Methodist churches, as did Faimau and Lesitaokana (2018), who highlight a serious digital divide. Within Judaism, Campbell (2015) and Cohen (2012) reflected on how the Internet is integrated into the lifestyle of the Jewish community. Marín (2015) addresses Muslim online platforms in Spain; Rahimi (2018), the influence of the Internet on Islamic news organizations. Prebish (2004) studies the cybersangha – the term describes the entire Buddhist community online – exploring its online appearance and defining the organizational structure of various Buddhist sites. Helland (2015) analyses "Virtual Tibet" and Fukamizu (2007), the role of the Internet in postmodern Buddhism in Japan underlining that, in postmodern faith, horizontal interaction among religious followers takes on an increasingly important role in comparison with the vertical (top-down) structure of traditional doctrines. Patrick (2007) focuses on Hinduism in cyberspace and Jayachandran (2019), on online spiritualism in India. Campbell and Fulton (2013) explore the challenges and choices made by the Baha'í community in the online sphere.

Online Religious Practices

Scholars have focused on the study of identity, authority, and the creation of community (Campbell, 2005a) because the Internet and mobile technology have influenced religious practices mainly in terms of rethinking those three aspects of religious environments and groups. Changes in the dynamics of practicing religion, learning about religion, believing, and engaging with religion and with groups of other believers have challenged several communities. We can analyze them under three main categories of religious online practices: Religious online platforms, social media, and apps.

This section analyzes each practice, organizing them by confessions. The practices are directly aligned with the three aspects identified already (identity, authority, and community), with content helping to promote and reinforce the aspects. Table 32.1 shows how.

Table 32.1   Alignment of religious online practices, contents, and aspects of religious communities reinforced

Religious online practice	Aspect reinforced	Religious online content
Religious online platforms	Community	Religious content
		Online rituals and practices
		Other religious services
		Links with communities
Social media	Authority	
Apps	Identity	

As seen in detail in Chapter 30, the contents and services offered on different platforms and their sources (religious institutions, religious leaders, lay associations, online religious influencers, etc.) establish an authority capable of constructing a community in which the members share the same religious values that build their identity (Campbell, 2005a; Lövheim & Linderman, 2005; Wolf, 2003). One key to understanding the effectiveness seems to reside in the intersection and interaction of online and offline networks (Campbell, 2005a; Campbell & Lövheim, 2011). "No longer are the online and offline seen as completely distinct fields of practice, as for many they are integrated spheres of interaction: the internet constitutes the space where individuals and groups live out their social and spiritual lives, and offline boundaries and relations often inform the online sphere" (Campbell & Lövheim, 2011, p. 1083). Wellman and Haythornwaite (2002) agree that online platforms are not simply "virtual" but are also embedded in the real or offline world: the two influence each other (Katz & Rice, 2002; Lundby, 2011). Dawson and Cowan (2004) propose the analogy that the Internet acts as both mirror and shadow of the offline world. Campbell and Garner (2016) and Garner (2017) talk about networked theology, tackling the networked relationships between physical and digital worlds in religious communities.

Religious Online Communities

Several characteristics of online religious communities emerge in published studies of different religious confessions. All wrestle with questions of authority (Campbell, 2021; Hoover, 2016; Soukup, 2017; Spadaro, 2012). Hoover (2018) notes that new online voices of authority are "increasingly interactive," with digital feedback loops and conversations and circulating in such spaces where it is legitimated through practices of circulation. Díez Bosch et al. (2015b) affirm that religions are not exempt from legitimation if they are to endure in these new digital times when competitors battle to fill the intersection between the sacred and the secular.

A four-year ethnographic study of five online churches revealed a fluid and multilayered relationship between online and offline activity of Christian users of blogs, forums, chat rooms, video streams, and virtual worlds (Hutchings, 2011). Stewart (2011) also found that relationship between the online and the offline expressions of religion, specifically in the case of Christian women in Brighton, UK. Even the practice of Voodoo links offline and online spheres (Boutros, 2016).

Catholic online communities stand between the religion online and the online religion stage (Helland, 2000), still more focused on being an extension of offline spheres than on becoming autonomous online platforms (Díez Bosch et al., 2018), confirming results from an earlier study

(Díez Bosch et al., 2017a). A third study (Díez Bosch et al., 2015b) asks what it means for Catholics to be online, since even if researchers know Catholics are online, it is not always evident whether they are forming online communities or merely adapting themselves to the new space and time. In line with these previous studies, Kołodziejska (2020) analyses the mediated identity of Catholic users in Poland.

Campbell and Golan (2011) first raised the question of the motivation behind bounded groups' creation of digital enclaves online. Campbell (2005a) noted that online church communities can provide a sense of belonging and being valued even if one never meets the other members in person. She also found that religious bloggers use their blogs to affirm different forms of religious authority online (2010a); debates within the Anglican Communion over the legitimacy of online worship in Second Life also raise the issue of community identity (2010b). Motivation occurs in other Christian groups (Young, 2004) and in pagan ones (Griffin, 2004). O'Leary and Brasher (1996) and Bunt (2000) probed Christian and Muslim communities and their responses to new media as ways to reach new groups, despite its challenges to offline institutional control over traditional practices and theology.

In other studies of online Islam, Al-Saggaf and Begg (2004) explore the online communities' challenge to offline ones, while Stanton (2014) looks into the elements of Islamic online community building. Blondheim (2015) situates new media in the Jewish communication tradition, and Golan (2015) asks about the legitimation of new media and community building among Jewish groups in the United States. Mishol-Shauli and Golan (2019) do something similar for Jewish ultra-Orthodoxy in Israel. More general studies of online Jewish groups examine online content (Gottlieb, 2011) and webmasters and content managers (Tsuria & Campbell, 2018).

Foulks McGuire (2015) analyses Buddhist blogs on the web, and Price Grieve and Veidlinger (2015) study the virtual world of Second Life from the perspective of Buddhism. Hinduism also engages with new media, with sites devoted to ritual practices, teaching, and Hindu identity on cyberspace (Pamplany, 2020; Stroope, 2011). Zavos (2015) focuses on the role of digital communities on Hindu activism in the diaspora, specifically in the UK. Similarly, Ackroyd (2006) documents the use of the Internet by American Hindus, showing how the digital sphere shapes Hindu communities in America by allowing massive, simultaneous communication among large groups of practitioners and extended families. Gittinger (2021) argues that for Hindus living in the United States (particularly for those distant from a local diaspora community), the Internet plays an important role in mediating cultural and religious identity. Eilers (2017) did some similar exploration on the role of religions in the digital world in Asia.

Social Media

"There is evidence Internet use may transform the ways people conceive of religious community and local church, particularly in a new conception of religious community as a social network" (Campbell, 2005a, p. 192). This social network, located online, creates what Campbell (2013) calls digital religion, a technological and cultural space that occurs when online and offline religious spheres have become intertwined. Digital religion rests on social media. "Digitalization has produced many more channels and platforms and proliferated the ways and contexts where religion is represented and circulated in national and global contexts" (Hoover, 2018, p. 25). Where religion and media were two separate concepts before, Hoover (2018) argues that with new media religions are not only mediated, but they have been able to mediate themselves.

Campbell (2010b, 2013) explores how this comes about, first how specific religious groups perceive and respond to new forms of technology, both the positive and the elements they consider negative or a risk. In the second book, Campbell addresses religious engagement with a wide range of these new media. Soberón (2015) asks what religious communities could learn from secular social media to "mediate themselves." She highlights the sensibility for sharing and creating new knowledge and the decision of some secular communities in social media to deliberate for solving some problems. For her, these social media have passed "from the inter-activity between the web and the users, to an extended conversation between all the partici-pants going towards deliberation" (p. 35). On this matter, Cheong (2016) wonders how spiritual role models and leaders respond to social media dynamics. Chen et al. (2014) study the reli-gious landscape in the United States on Twitter considering atheism, Buddhism, Christianity, Hinduism, Islam, and Judaism.

The Catholic Church has received moderate attention, with studies examining its "digital mission" through social media (Tridente & Mastroianni, 2016); its engagement through Facebook, Flickr, YouTube, Instagram, Pinterest, and Instapray (Valladares & Herrera, 2015); its papal doc-uments that gradually legitimized social media (Arasa et al., 2018); its call for a new language for new media (Viganò, 2017); and the response of Filipino youth to Catholic messages on Facebook presented randomly alongside the secular ones (Roman, 2015). In the wider Christian sphere, Cheong (2016) analyses how pastors of mega-churches construct their authority on Twitter.

Scholars have not ignored Islam. Shehu et al. (2017) look at the challenges of social media to the global Islamic community; among them, Almenayes (2014) identifies the relationship bet-ween religiosity and psychological consequences of social media usage in a Muslim country based on secularization theory. Slama (2018) focuses on Islamic social media practice and behavior in Indonesia. Pennington (2018) studies the experience of 188 Muslim bloggers on Tumblr to understand how this platform can facilitate third spaces where these bloggers can explore the hybrid nature of their identities while connecting to others. Mohamad (2021) turns to micro-celebrity practices in three Muslim-majority countries, Brunei, Malaysia, and Indonesia. Muslim women have also taken to social media to reclaim narratives around space, embodiment, and power (Hirji, 2021); to undertake digital activism on visual platforms such as YouTube (Islam, 2019); and to support Indonesia's Hijabers' Community through Instagram (Bauch & Pramiyanti, 2018). In a comparative study Ferguson et al. (2021) examine the Muslim and Jewish responses to social media and how they transform faith communities in less embodied ways.

Regarding Judaism, Abrams (2015), Yadlin-Segal (2015), and Osterbur and Kiel (2020) explored the use of Facebook and Twitter by Jewish communities, while Altmann (2017) studied how social media provides the possibility to unite different opinions and sections of Judaism.

Connelly (2014) studied how social media (specially Facebook and blogs) are used by Buddhists. Karapanagiotis (2019) delves into Hindu rituals on Facebook and Sundaram (2019) examines how hashtags convert Hindu social media posts into cultural products on Facebook and Instagram.

All these works manifest the emergence of digital religion studies, which encompasses the research on how digital media are used by religious groups and users to translate religious prac-tices and beliefs into new contexts, as well as the reimagining of religion offered by unique affor-dances within these new mediums and spaces (Campbell, 2017). Campbell and Vitullo (2016) offer an assessment of the evolution of the study of these religious online communities. The Internet and social media form the basis of what Campbell (2021) defines as new media, a range of different digital and mobile technologies whose main characteristics include dynamism, mal-leability, interactivity, and transformation, bringing with them social acceleration (Rosa, 2013; Tridente & Mastroianni, 2016). At the same time, this becomes problematic for several religious groups bound by theological convictions based on traditions. In contexts in which religion has high political power, some groups may want to prevent their communities succumbing to the fluidity inherent in these devices. Campbell (2005a) gives an example of the "kosher cell phone," one modified to prevent Internet usage, text messaging, and video. However, as Wagner (2013) argues, the fluidity evident in digital worlds need not lead to fragmentation. Turkle (1995) observes a more fluid self allows a greater capacity for acknowledging diversity. The next section on mobile technology and religion reflects on this aspect.

Apps: Mobile Religion – Content or Practice

Religion has embraced mobile apps. Tkach (2014) compiled 30 000 applications which pertain to religious belief and practice that spanned 81 world religion search terms. A decade earlier Eck (2003) affirmed that the authenticity of religious experience rested not only in the hands of recognized religious authorities or in fixed rituals, but also in our hands and in the mobile devices we hold in those hands. Spadaro (2012), too, affirms that portable devices become an easily accessible religious window to the world of the Internet. The simplicity of using a smartphone or a tablet erases what he considered the "technological aura," providing more direct, versatile, and immediate contact: "the object becomes transparent for the person who uses it" (p. 66).

Stout (2018) distinguishes a "media vs. religion" paradigm from a "convergence paradigm" in which previously separated technologies (text, video, audio, and photos) are integrated into computers, tablets, mobile devices, and other new media. For the religious person navigating a saturated media environment such copious sources of information hold great salience (pp. 111–112).

The consequences, challenges, and opportunities the Internet offers for shaping religious identity, authority, and communities also appear in the digital sphere in mobile devices. People participate in religion using mobile phones, tablets, and all kinds of portable wearables. Special applications created for this purpose make this possible but people can also directly use social media for religious purposes in mobile devices, something Horsfield (2015) terms the "omnipresence" of the digital experience – a flow of constant information, interactivity, and acceleration, aspects that can, however, disrupt some of the foundational elements of religious traditions.

Noting the increasing use of mobile media and apps for religious purposes (Campbell, 2010b), Bellar et al. (2019) and Cheong (2014) explore the intersection of religion and mobile technology. Rinker et al. (2016) examine the use of religious applications for smartphones and tablets and argue that owing to their portability, the nature of religion has shifted from a primarily public location (i.e. institutions) to the more private spaces of everyday life. Wagner (2013), citing Campbell (2005a), underlines that religious social media apps can serve as portals into communities as well as signify a desire for such grounding; to install a religious app expresses a wish for involvement with the real people behind it. Because of this, Wagner (2013) links mobile device applications with the construction of the identity and considers how people see and define themselves through the use of these apps, noting that this could raise new challenges to traditional religion, suggesting a new kind of individualized, personalized authenticity of religious experience. She also addresses a concern about apps and religion – the classification and categorization of the available applications linked to religious communities or practices. As a religious app designer, Daily (2013) expressed frustration with the limitations of iTunes categories as being too broad, with no clear definitions or evaluations provided. To describe the situation more clearly Wagner (2013) proposed six categories for the religiously oriented apps found in the iTunes store: prayer apps, ritual apps, sacred apps, religious social media apps, self-expression apps, and focusing/meditation apps. These categories reveal challenges to authenticity and authority in different ways: (i) the inability to clearly identify a recipient of an app's prayer or to officially sanction its performance; (ii) The unsupervised performance of rituals via apps; (iii) the individualized interpretation of sacred texts using app-based tools; (iv) industrially rather than institutionally shaped forms of religious social media apps; (v) the out-of-context use of sacred texts and symbols for personal expression via apps; and (vi) user-determined use of focusing applications on apps (Wagner, 2013).

Individual experiences challenge accepted assumptions about religious authority in traditional contexts, and redefine authenticity, as in these platforms "authority shifts from the institution to the individual" (Wagner, 2013, p. 202). Following these dynamics, religions are institutionally subject to market forces and must access and manage their resources from the external environment to survive in the "religious marketplace" (Finke & Stark, 1988). Hoover (2018, 2016) also warns of the so-called marketplace of religions that the Internet promotes through these new media devices, a view shared by Lövheim and Linderman (2005), who see the possibility for an individual seeker to find information about established as well as alternative religious organizations, and apps become a conduit for this information. Furthermore, "on our smartphones, religious apps are installed alongside secular ones, and games and rituals coexist, so they show what people care about" (Wagner, 2013, p. 203). Gilmore (2012, p. 56) talks about DIY spiritualities in this context and reflects on how new media can host "authentic fakes," referring to some pop culture phenomena analogous to religion through their rhetoric, symbolism, and rituals. These "fake religions" are doing real religious work if they are "engaged in negotiating what is to be human" (p. 56).

Campbell et al. (2014) provide a new methodological approach to studying religious-oriented mobile applications available in English through the review of 451 religious applications. They aim to set a starting point for scholars interested in this topic and for developers desiring to integrate religious goals in their designs. Because religious motivation shapes a unique use of technology, in terms of specific values (Campbell, 2005b), Campbell and her colleagues (2014) extended Wagner's (2013) list of categories from 6 to 11, grouping them in 2 parent classifications: apps oriented around religious practice (those that provide instruction for specific religious practice and help to facilitate religious experiences); and apps embedded with religious content, providing access to a specific form or religious information or materials, but not always to facilitate religious practices. Their categories are Prayer, Focus/Meditation, Ritual, Sacred Textual Engagement, Devotional Worship, Religious Utilities, Religious Social Media, Religious Games, Religious Wisdom and Leaders, Religious Media Outlets, and Religious Apps for Kids. In the course of their work, Campbell and her colleagues (2014) detected some trends depending on the app's target religion or denomination. Among these, they stressed how apps from the Abrahamic faiths (Christianity, Islam, and Judaism) tend to facilitate engagement with their sacred texts or reference materials and appeared in the iTunes categories of Education, Books, Reference, and Utilities.

Bellar (2012) explored questions of app design rooted in how evangelical Christian users actually used religious iPhone apps, and Riezu (2014) analyzed the reasons why believers used the application Rezandovoy (Pray as you go) through the uses and gratifications theory. Padrini (2015) explored the iBreviary app, a Catholic application for praying in portable devices, defining it as a real spiritual assistant, able to offer a text and a place to experience prayer, giving concrete suggestions through a spiritual diary. Hutchings (2014) researched the Protestant and Catholic approaches to the Digital Bible in the Bible app. "Confession: A Roman Catholic App" caused some controversy: first granted official approval by the Bishop of Fort Wayne-South Bend, Indiana (United States), "though it was not designed to be a substitute for face-to-face confession, the app caused quite a stir among many Catholics and Church officials around the world, including the Vatican." It was not in conflict with Church teachings but it "could in no way substitute for the embodied act of confession, which can only be heard and forgiveness granted by a priest" (Campbell, 2021, p. 2).

Religious apps do encourage individualism across denominational and religious groups, as a survey of youth in 13 different groups in Catalonia found (Díez Bosch et al., 2017b). This aligns with Wagner's (2013) conclusion, "the flow of religious apps mimics the flow of religious options generated every day, as users decide what to pay attention to and how to practice what they believe" (p. 203).

The same holds true with Islamic apps. The Aa Gym app, created by an Islamic televangelist in Indonesia, reshaped the way Indonesians engage with Islamic teaching and embedded mediatization into Indonesian Islam (Fakhruroji, 2019). The individualism also affects culturally important religious practices, such as dating (De Rooij, 2020), where uses and gratifications theory also played a role, and food practices (Fewkes, 2019). Despite this move away from community, many still work to develop "Islamic-friendly" apps for Android (Komarudin et al., 2020).

In Hinduism, seeking innovative ways to spread the teachings and practices of Buddhism has led programmers to translate elements of Buddhist belief and practice into apps, thus removing a communal element (Wagner & Accardo, 2015). The iTunes store selling Buddhist apps categorizes them as Lifestyle, even though they might focus on ritual (Campbell et al., 2014), thus shifting them toward individualism. Campbell and her group note that many Catholic, Islamic, and Buddhist apps stressed religious wisdom and content from famous religious leaders, highlighting the personal use. Despite these trends, Tkach (2014), based on a study of religious applications, insisted that there was no clear measurable method for categorizing, calculating, and organizing smartphone applications pertaining to religious belief and practice, and that all scholarship focused only on the iPhone and related platforms. One can only ascertain which religions are represented in these platforms and how often they are represented in comparison with each other.

Conclusion

The Internet and mobile technology have challenged the dynamics of religious communities. While accepting the benefits of new media in religious confessions, several communities still hesitate to implement the various tools or platforms (Campbell, 2021). How this negotiation takes place has provided a focus for the work of researchers in the digital religion studies field. They have identified main challenges dealing with identity, authority, and community (Hoover, 2016). At the same time, different existing online religious practices have reinforced these aspects and opened a new link between online and offline spheres in religious communities (Lundby, 2011). Research to date has shown that the construction of online religious platforms, the use of social media, and the use of mobile apps have done the most to extend online religious practices. All religious groups participate in these spaces at different levels and this chapter shows examples of online trends and practices within Christianity, Islam, Judaism, Buddhism, and Hinduism.

In this context, Torma and Teusner (2011) studied what happens when the cultural and social values of the mobile technology intersect with religious values. It varies. In the African context, new media have benefited the provision of information but have also been detrimental "as it can influence and alter the values and principles that underpin societal traditions and cultures" (Faimau & Lesitaokana, 2018, p. 2). The technology can seem to replace religious functions, too. Some religious communities opposed the augmented reality smartphone game Pokémon Go because it could seem a religion itself promoting techno-animism. But even if players become attached to the world within the game, that does not necessarily mean that changes in religious behavior outside the game really take place (Gabriel, 2017).

All the platforms, channels, and applications require professionals behind them, experts in designing these spaces and tools and in managing and monitoring them. These RDCs (Campbell, 2021) provide the professional technological and communicative skills that religious organizations need to manage their online presence and to facilitate public conversation about faith in social media. Campbell highlights how these professionals could become religious authorities themselves – a change of intended function. Hoover (2018), too, raises the great possibilities offered by the online sphere for autonomous producers of knowledge, as digital spaces encourage their practitioners to think of themselves. With skills and knowledge going further than the "religious computer enthusiasts" of the 1990s, they shift the skillsets needed for religious ministry. Their creativity and the innovation they spearhead will take this discussion further, as new devices and applications appear daily and through them new religious experiences emerge (Torma & Teusner, 2011). Machines appear by the day more in charge of activities that once seemed only possible to humans (Micó & Díez Bosch, 2021). For example, Kimura (2017), delves into the social-religious significance found in the emerging relationships between humans, robotics, and artificial intelligence. Transhumanism, modifying the body with brain implants to increase intelligence or implement genetic engineering to achieve more skills to avoid death, is also a trend in scholarly debates linked with religion and media, challenging some religious traditions (Smith, 2017). The phenomenon of posthumanism has the same effect, but in this case, addresses the extinction of the common individual to produce a special entity with exceptional characteristics to become a superior specimen. Some regard both phenomena as "saviors" and nurture the utopia that human beings can become a kind of God (Bennett, 2019).

As technology keeps expanding, religious communities will tend to follow it, adopting most of the innovation while addressing new challenges. The Internet of Things, robotics, data science, and cloud computing will open up new and further discussions owing to the increasing conviction that is possible to believe both in technology and in God at the same time (Lennox, 2020; Micó & Díez Bosch, 2021).

References

Abrams, N. (2015). Appropriation and innovation: Pop-up communities: Facebook, grassroots Jews and offline post-denominational Judaism. In H. A. Campbell (Ed.), *Digital Judaism: Jewish negotiations with digital media and culture* (pp. 40–55). Routledge.

Ackroyd, B. B. (2006). Hinduism in cyberspace. PhD Thesis, University of Florida.

Almenayes, J. J. (2014). Religiosity and the perceived consequences of social media usage in a Muslim country. *Journal of Arts and Humanities, 3*(5), 108–117. https://doi.org/10.18533/journal.v3i5.439

Al-Saggaf, Y., & Begg, M. M. (2004). Online communities versus offline communities in the Arab/Muslim world. *Journal of Information, Communication, and Ethics in Society, 2*(1), 41–54. https://doi.org/10.1108/14779960480000242

Altmann, C. (2017). 'Judaism to go': Hastening the redemption through Web 2.0. *Heidelberg Journal of Religions on the Internet, 12*(1), 5–17. https://doi.org/10.17885/heiup.rel.2017.0.23765

Arasa, D., Cantoni, L., & Narbona, J. (2018). The Catholic church and Twitter. In Y. Cohen (Ed.), *Spiritual news. Reporting religion around the world* (pp. 325–346). Peter Lang.

Asamoah-Gyadu, J. K. (2008). "'Get on the internet!' says the LORD": Religion, cyberspace, and Christianity in contemporary Africa. *Studies in World Christianity, 13*(3), 225–242. DOI:10.1353/swc.2007.0026

Barna. (2020). 2 in 5 churchgoers are open to inviting others to digital church services. Barna. Retrieved March 4, 2022, from https://www.barna.com/research/digital-service-invitation

Bauch, E., & Pramiyanti, A. (2018). Hijabers on Instagram: Using visual social media to construct the ideal Muslim woman. *Social Media + Society, 4*(4), 1–15. https://doi.org/10.1177/2056305118800308

Baym, N. (2005). Is "internet research" a virtual field, a proto-discipline, or something else? Special issue: ICT research and disciplinary boundaries *The Information Society, 21*(4). https://kuscholarworks.

ku.edu/bitstream/handle/1808/8720/Baym_2005_Intro-Internet-Research.pdf;jsessionid=26E39DB B8ABFE6AB20ADCE29B788CE9C?sequence=1

Bellar, W. (2012). *Pocket full of Jesus: Evangelical Christians' use of religious iPhone applications*. Syracuse University.

Bellar, W., Cho, K. J., & Campbell, H. A. (2019). *The intersection of religion and mobile technology*. IGI Global.

Bennett, G. (2019). Silicon Valley's original sin. Sojourners. Retrieved March 4, 2022, from https://sojo.net/ magazine/january-2019/silicon-valley-s-original-sin

Blondheim, M. (2015). The Jewish communication tradition and its encounters with (the) new media. In H. Campbell (Ed.), *Digital Judaism: Jewish negotiations with digital media and culture* (pp. 16–39). Routledge.

Boutros, A. (2016). Techno-Vodou: Transnational flows in the spiritual marketplace. In S. M. Hoover (Ed.), *The media and religious authority* (pp. 193–208). Pennsylvania State University Press.

Brasher, B. (2001). *Give me that online religion*. Jossey-Bass.

Brooke, T. (1997). *Virtual gods*. Harvest House.

Bunt, G. (2000). *Virtually Islamic: Computer-mediated communication and cyber Islamic environments*. University of Wales Press.

Campbell, H. (2005a). *Exploring religious community online: We are one in the network*. Peter Lang.

Campbell, H. (2005b). Making space for religion in internet studies. *The Information Society, 21*(4), 309–315. https://doi.org/10.1080/01972240591007625

Campbell, H. A. (2010a). Bloggers and religious authority online. *Journal of Computer-Mediated Communication, 15*(2), 251–276. https://www.jstor.org/stable/41348770

Campbell, H. A. (2010b). *When religion meets new media*. Routledge.

Campbell, H. A. (2013). *Digital religion. Understanding religious practice in new media worlds*. Routledge.

Campbell, H. A. (Ed.). (2015). *Digital Judaism. Jewish negotiations with digital media and culture*. Routledge.

Campbell, H. A. (2017). Surveying theoretical approaches within digital religion studies. *New Media and Society, 19*(1), 15–24. https://doi.org/10.1177/1461444816649912

Campbell, H. A. (2021). *Digital creatives and the rethinking of religious authority*. Routledge.

Campbell, H. A., Althenhofen, B., Bellar, W., & Kyong, J. C. (2014). There's a religious app for that! A framework for studying religious mobile applications. *Mobile Media and Communication, 2*(2), 154–172. https://doi.org/10.1177/2050157914520846

Campbell, H. A., & Fulton, D. (2013). Bounded religious communities' management of the challenge of new media: Baha'í negotiation with the internet. In M. Gillespie, D. E. J. Herbert, & A. Greenhill (Eds.), *Social media and religious change* (pp. 185–200). De Gruyter.

Campbell, H. A., & Garner, S. (2016). *Networked theology: Negotiating faith in digital culture*. Baker.

Campbell, H. A., & Golan, O. (2011). Creating digital enclaves: Negotiation of the internet among bounded religious communities. *Media, Culture and Society, 33*(5), 709–724. https://journals.sagepub.com/ doi/10.1177/0163443711404464

Campbell, H. A., & Lövheim, M. (2011). Introduction: Rethinking the online-offline connection in the study of religion online. *Information, Communication & Society, 14*(8), 1083–1096. https://doi.org/10.1080/1 369118X.2011.597416

Campbell, H. A., & Vitullo, A. (2016). Assessing changes in the study of religious communities in digital religion studies. *Church, Communication and Culture, 1*(1), 73–89. https://doi.org/10.1080/23753234.20 16.1181301

Chen, L., Weber, I., & Okulicz-Kozaryn, A. (2014). U.S. religious landscape on Twitter. International Conference on Social Informatics. 6th International Conference, SocInfo 2014, Barcelona, Spain, November 11–13, 2014. Proceedings.

Cheong, P. (2016). Religious authority and social media branding in a culture of religious celebrification. In S. M. Hoover (Ed.), *The media and religious authority* (pp. 81–102). Pennsylvania State University Press.

Cheong, P. H. (2014). From cyberchurch to faith apps: Religion 2.0 on the rise? In A. M. Brazal, & K. Abraham (Eds.), *Feminist cyberethics in Asia* (pp. 141–158). Palgrave Macmillan.

Ciolek, T. M. (2004). Online religion: The internet and religion. In H. Bidgoli (Ed.), *The internet encyclopedia* (pp. 798–811). John Wiley and Sons.

Cobb, J. (1998). *Cybergrace. The search for God in the digital world*. Crown.

Cohen, Y. (2012). *God, Jews, and the media: Religion and Israel's media*. Routledge.

Connelly, L. (2014). Virtual Buddhism: Online communities, sacred places and objects. In S. Brunn (Ed.), *The changing world religion map* (pp. 3869–3882). Springer.

Daily, E. (2013). The promise of mobile technology for public religious education. *Religious Education, 108*(2), 112–128. https://doi.org/10.1080/00344087.2013.767653

Davis, E. (1998). *Techngnosis*. Random House.

Dawson, L. L., & Cowan, D. E. (2004). *Religion online: Finding faith on the internet*. Routledge.

Dawson, L. L., & Hennebry, J. (1999). New religions and the internet. Recruiting in a new public sphere. *Journal of Contemporary Religions, 14*(1), 17–39. https://doi.org/10.1080/13537909908580850

De Rooij, L. (2020). The relationship between online dating and Islamic identity among British Muslims. *Journal of Religion, Media and Digital Culture, 9*(1), 1–32. https://brill.com/downloadpdf/journals/rmdc/9/1/article-p1_1.xml

Díez Bosch, M., Micó, J. L., & Carbonell, J. M. (2015a). *Catholic communities online*. Blanquerna Observatory on Media, Religion and Culture.

Díez Bosch, M., Micó, J. L., & Carbonell, J. M. (2015b). *Negotiating religious visibility in digital media*. Blanquerna Observatory on Media, Religion and Culture.

Díez Bosch, M., Micó, J. L., Carbonell, J. M., Sánchez Torrents, J., & Sabaté Gauxachs, A. (2017a). Open wall churches. Catholic construction of online communities. *Prisma Social, 19*, 298–323. https://revistaprismasocial.es/article/view/1734/2336

Díez Bosch, M., Micó, J. L., & Sabaté, A. (2017b). Typing my religion. Digital use of religious webs and apps by adolescents and youth for religious and interreligious dialogue. *Church, Communication and Culture, 2*(2), 121–143. https://doi.org/10.1080/23753234.2017.1347800

Díez Bosch, M., Micó, J. L., & Sabaté, A. (2018). Construction of online communities based on consolidated face-to-face communities: The case of Catholic church on the internet. *El profesional de la información, 27*(6), 1699–2407. http://profesionaldelainformacion.com/contenidos/2018/nov/09.pdf

Dixon, P. (1997). *Cyberchurch, Christianity, and the internet*. Kingsway.

Eck, D. (2003). *Encountering God: A spiritual journey from Bozeman to Benares*. Beacon Press.

Eilers, F. J. (1994). *Communicating in community. An introduction to social communication*. Logos Publications.

Eilers, F. J. (2017). Religions in the digital world of Asia: Some considerations. *Religion and Social Communication, 15*(1), 3–14.

Ess, C. (1996). *Philosophical perspectives on computer-mediated communication*. SUNY Press.

Ess, C. (2004). *Critical thinking and the Bible in the age of new media*. University Press of America.

Faimau, G., & Lesitaokana, W. O. (2018). *New media and the mediatisation of religion: An African perspective*. Cambridge Scholars Publishing.

Fakhruroji, M. (2019). Digitalizing Islamic lectures: Islamic apps and religious engagement in contemporary Indonesia. *Contemporary Islam, 13*, 201–215. https://link.springer.com/article/10.1007/s11562-018-0427-9

Ferguson, J., Ecklund, E. H., & Rothschild, C. (2021). Navigating religion online: Jewish and Muslim responses to social media. *Religions, 12*(4), 258. https://doi.org/10.3390/rel12040258

Fernback, J. (2002). Internet ritual: A case study of the construction of computer-mediated neopagan religious meaning. In S. Hoover, & L. Schofield Clark (Eds.), *Practicing religion in the age of the media* (pp. 254–276). Columbia University Press.

Fewkes, J. H. (2019). "Siri, is alligator halal?": Mobile apps, food practices, and religious authority among American Muslims. In J. H. Fewkes (Ed.), *Anthropological perspectives on the religious uses of mobile apps* (pp. 107–129). Palgrave Macmillan.

Finke, R., & Stark, R. (1988). Religious economies and sacred canopies: Religious mobilization in American cities. *American Sociological Review, 53*(1), 41–49. https://doi.org/10.2307/2095731

Foulks McGuire, B. (2015). The way of the Blogisttva: Buddhist blogs on the web. In G. Price Grieve, & D. Veidlinger (Eds.), *Buddhism, the internet, and digital media: The pixel in the lotus* (pp. 204–220). Routledge.

Fukamizu, R. K. (2007). Internet use among religious followers: Religious postmodernism in Japanese Buddhism. *Journal of Computer-Mediated Communication, 12*(3), 977–998. https://doi.org/10.1111/j.1083-6101.2007.00359.x

Gabriel, S. (2017). Pokémon Go. How religious can an augmented reality hunt be? *Heidelberg Journal of Religions on the Internet, 12*, 18–31. https://doi.org/10.17885/heiup.rel.2017.0.23766

Garner, S. (2017). Are you my neighbor? Theology, networks, and encounters with God and others. In M. Díez Bosch, P. Soukup, Jo. Lluís Micó, & D. Zsupan-Jerome. (Eds.), *Authority and leadership: Values, religion, media* (pp. 111–122). Blanquerna Observatory on Media, Religion and Culture.

Gilmore, L. (2012). DIY spiritualities, Reverend Billy, and Burning Man. In G. Lynch, J. Mitchell, & A. Strhan (Eds.), *Religion media and culture: A reader* (pp. 49–58). Routledge.

Gittinger, J. L. (2021). Cultural regrouping in the diaspora: Mediating Hindu identity online. In X. Zeiler (Ed.), *Digital Hinduism* (pp. 68–87). Routledge.

Golan, O. (2015). Legitimation of new media and community building among Jewish denominations in the U.S. In H. A. Campbell (Ed.), *Digital Judaism: Jewish negotiations with digital media and culture* (pp. 16–39). Routledge.

Gottlieb, O. (2011). Moving beyond the limited reach of current "social media" approaches: Why Jewish digital communities require rich and remixable narrative content. *CCAR Journal: The Reform Jewish Quarterly* (Spring), 82–99.

Grant, A. E., Stout, D. A., Chen, C. H., & Sturgill, A. F. C. (2019). *Religion online: How digital technology is changing the way we worship and pray*. Praeger.

Griffin, W. (2004). The goddess net. In L. Dawson, & D. Cowan (Eds.), *Religion online: Finding faith on the Internet* (pp. 189–204). Routledge.

Haddon, J. K., & Cowan, D. E. (Eds.). (2000). *Religion on the internet: Research prospects and promises*. JAI.

Helland, C. (2000). Online-religion/religion-online and virtual communitas. In J. K. Hadden, & D. E. Cowan (Eds.), *Religion on the internet: Research prospects and promises* (pp. 205–223). JAI Press.

Helland, C. (2015). Virtual Tibet: From media spectacle to co-located sacred space. In G. Price Grieve, & D. Veidlinger (Eds.), *Buddhism, the internet, and digital media: The pixel in the lotus* (pp. 155–172). Routledge.

Hess, M. (2017). Gameful learning and theological understanding: New cultures of learning in communities of faith. In M. Díez Bosch, P. Soukup, Jo. Lluís Micó, & D. Zsupan-Jerome (Eds.), *Authority and leadership: Values, religion, media* (pp. 191–200). Blanquerna Observatory on Media, Religion and Culture.

Hillis, K. (2009). From capital to karma: James Cameron's Avatar. *Postmodern Culture, 19*(3). https://doi.org/10.1353/pmc.2009.0007

Hirji, F. (2021). Claiming our space: Muslim women, activism, and social media. *Islamophobia Studies Journal, 6*(1), 78–92. DOI:10.13169/islastudj.6.issue-1

Hoover, S., Clark, L. S., & Rainie, L. (2004). Faith online: 64% of wired Americans have used the Internet for spiritual or religious information. Pew Internet and American Life Project. Retrieved June 17, 2022, from https://www.pewtrusts.org/-/media/legacy/uploadedfiles/wwwpewtrustsorg/reports/society_and_the_internet/pewinternetfaith0404pdf.pdf

Hoover, S. M. (2006). *Religion in the media age*. Routledge.

Hoover, S. M. (2016). *The media and religious authority*. Pennsylvania State University Press.

Hoover, S. M. (2018). Religion and the news in the age of media change. In Y. Cohen (Ed.), *Spiritual news. Reporting religion around the world* (pp. 15–29). Peter Lang.

Horsfield, P. (2015). *From Jesus to the internet. A history of Christianity and media*. Wiley Blackwell.

Houston, G. (1998). *Virtual morality*. Apollos.

Hutchings, T. (2011). Contemporary religious community and the online church. *Information, Communication and Society, 14*(8), 1118–1135. https://doi.org/10.1080/1369118X.2011.591410

Hutchings, T. (2014). Now the Bible is an app: Digital media and changing patterns of religious authority. In K. Granholm, M. Moberg, & S. Sjö (Eds.), *Religion, media and social change* (pp. 143–161). Routledge.

Islam, I. (2019). Redefining #YourAverageMuslim woman: Muslim female digital activism on social media. *Journal of Arab and Muslim Media Research, 12*(2), 213–233. https://doi.org/10.1386/jammr_00004_1

Jayachandran, J. (2019). New media and spiritualism in India: Understanding online spiritualism in convergence cultures. In X. Zeiler (Ed.), *Digital Hinduism* (pp. 207–229). Routledge.

Karapanagiotis, N. (2019). Automatic rituals and inadvertent audiences: ISKCON, Krishna and the ritual mechanics of Facebook. In X. Zeiler (Ed.), *Digital Hinduism* (pp. 51–67). Routledge.

Katz, J. E., & Rice, R. E. (2002). *Social consequences of internet use: Access, involvement, and interaction*. MIT Press.

Kimura, T. (2017). Robotics and AI in the sociology of religion: A human in imago roboticae. *Social Compass*, *64*(1), 6–22. https://doi.org/10.1177/0037768616683326

Kołodziejska, M. (2020). Mediated identity of Catholic internet forum users in Poland. *Journal of Religion, Media and Digital Culture*, *9*(1), 59–81. DOI:10.1163/21659214-bja10007

Komarudin, F., Pranata, D., & Nurhasanah, S. (2020). Developing Islamic-friendly android mobile apps for understanding mathematical concepts. Proceedings of the 1st Raden Intan International Conference on Muslim Societies and Social Sciences (RIICMuSSS 2019).

Kristiadi, D., Vinday, Sambera, R., Julianto, A., Warnars, H. L. H. S., & Hashimonto, K. (2019). Mobile game application for religion engagement. Speech presented at 2019 IEEE International Conference on Engineering, Technology and Education (TALE), Yogyakarta, Indonesia Retrieved June 17, 2022, from https://ieeexplore.ieee.org/stamp/stamp.jsp?tp=&arnumber=9144827

Lennox, J. C. (2020). *2084: Artificial intelligence and the future of humanity hardcover*. Zondervan.

Lochhead, D. (1997). *Shifting realities: Information technology and the church*. WCC.

Lövheim, M., & Linderman, A. G. (2005). Constructing religious identity on the internet. In M. Hojsgaard, & M. Warburg (Eds.), *Religion and cyberspace* (pp. 121–137). Routledge.

Lundby, K. (2011). Patterns of belonging in online/offline interfaces of religion. *Information, Communication and Society*, *14*(8), 1219–1235. https://doi.org/10.1080/1369118X.2011.594077

Marín, F. X. (2015). Islam and virtual reality. How Muslims in Spain live in the cyberspace. In M. Díez Bosch, J. L. Micó, & J. M. Carbonell (Eds.), *Negotiating religious visibility in digital media* (pp. 69–80). Blanquerna Observatory on Media, Religion and Culture.

McKay, J. (2004). *Netting citizens: Exploring citizenship in the internet age*. Saint Andrew Press.

Micó, J. L., & Díez Bosch, M. (2021). *Beatus technological. Industria 4.0, coronavirus, valores y espiritualidad*. Mínima.

Mishol-Shauli, N., & Golan, O. (2019). Mediatizing the holy community – Ultra-Orthodoxy negotiation and presentation on public social-media. *Religions*, *10*(7), 438. https://doi.org/10.3390/rel10070438

Mohamad, S. M. (2021). Micro-celebrity practices in Muslim-majority states in Southeast Asia. *Popular Communication. The International Journal of Media and Culture*, *19*(3), 235–249. https://doi.org/10.1080/15405702.2021.1913492

Nobel, D. (1997). *The religion of technology*. Alfred A. Knopf.

O'Leary, S. (1996). Cyberspace as sacred space: Communicating religion on computer networks. *Journal of the American Academy of Religion*, *64*(4), 781–808. https://www.taylorfrancis.com/chapters/edit/10.4324/9780203497609-4/cyberspace-sacred-space-communicating-religion-computer-networks-stephen-leary

O'Leary, S., & Brasher, B. (1996). The unknown God of the Internet. Religious communications from the ancient agora to the virtual forum. In C. Ess (Ed.), *Philosophical perspectives on computer-mediated communication* (pp. 233–269). State University of New York Press.

Osterbur, M., & Kiel, C. (2020). Tweeting in echo chambers? Analyzing Twitter discourse between American Jewish interest groups. *Journal of Information, Technology and Politics*, *18*(2), 194–213. https://doi.org/10.1080/19331681.2020.1838396

Padrini, P. (2015). iBreviary as a new concept of religious app. In M. Díez Bosch, J. L. Micó, & J. M. Carbonell (Eds.), *Catholic communities online* (pp. 49–58). Blanquerna Observatory on Media, Religion and Culture.

Pamplany, A. (2020). Hinduism and new media. Identities being deconstructed and constructed. In G. Isetti, E. Innerhofer, H. Pechlaner, & M. de Rachewiltz (Eds.), *Religion in the age of digitalization* (pp. 1–14). Routledge.

Patrick, G. (2007). Hinduism in cyberspace. *Religion and Social Communication*, *5*(1 & 2), 71–81.

Pennington, R. (2018). Social media as third spaces? Exploring Muslim identity and connection in Tumblr. *International Communication Gazette*, *80*(7), 620–636. https://doi.org/10.1177/1748048518802208

Pew Research Center. (2014). Religion and electronic media. One-in-five Americans share their faith online. Retrieved March 7, 2022, from https://www.pewforum.org/2014/11/06/religion-and-electronic-media

Prebish, C. S. (2004). The cybershangha: Buddhism on the internet. In L. Dawson, & D. Cowan (Eds.), *Religion online: Finding faith on the internet* (pp. 189–204). Routledge.

Price Grieve, G., & Veidlinger, D. (2015). *Buddhism, the internet, and digital media: The pixel in the lotus*. Routledge.

Rahimi, B. (2018). Internet news, media technologies, and Islam: The case of Shafqna. In Y. Cohen (Ed.), *Spiritual news. Reporting religion around the world* (pp. 367–381). Peter Lang.

Rheingold, H. (1993). *The virtual community*. Harper-Perennial.

Riezu, X. (2014). Uses and gratifications of a Spanish digital prayer project: Rezandovoy. *Trípodos, 35*, 29–42. http://www.tripodos.com/index.php/Facultat_Comunicacio_Blanquerna/article/view/191

Rinker, C. H., Bailey, E., & Embler, H. (2016). Religious apps for smartphones and tablets: Transforming religious authority and the nature of religion. *Interdisciplinary Journal of Research on Religion, 12*(4), 1–14. http://www.religjournal.com/pdf/ijrr12004.pdf

Roman, A. (2015). God in Facebook, like it or not: Filipino youth response to socially mediated religious message. In M. Díez Bosch, J. L. Micó, & J. M. Carbonell (Eds.), *Catholic communities online* (pp. 59–76). Blanquerna Observatory on Media, Religion and Culture.

Roof, W. C. (2001). *Spiritual marketplace: Baby boomers and the remaking of American religion*. Princeton University Press.

Rosa, H. (2013). *Social acceleration: A new theory of modernity*. Columbia University Press.

Schroeder, R., Heather, N., & Lee, R. (1998). The sacred and the virtual: Religion in multi-user virtual reality. *Journal of Computer Mediated Communication, 4*(2). https://doi.org/10.1111/j.1083-6101.1998.tb00092.x

Schultze, Q. (2002). *Habits of the high-tech heart*. Baker Academic.

Shehu, M. I., Othman, M. F. B., & Osman, N. B. (2017). The social media and Islam. Sahel Analyst. *Journal of Management Sciences, 15*(4), 67–80. https://www.academia.edu/35463318/THE_SOCIAL_MEDIA_AND_ISLAM

Slama, M. (2018). Practising Islam through social media in Indonesia. *Indonesia and the Malay World, 46*(134), 1–4. https://doi.org/10.1080/13639811.2018.1416798

Smith, W. J. (2017). What's love got to do with transhumanism? First Things. Retrieved March 7, 2022, from https://www.firstthings.com/web-exclusives/2017/06/whats-love-got-to-do-with-transhumanism

Soberón, L. (2015). What we can learn from secular social media networks. Deliberating together: A new paradigm of dialogue in the net. In M. Díez Bosch, J. L. Micó, & J. M. Carbonell (Eds.), *Catholic communities online* (pp. 35–48). Blanquerna Observatory on Media, Religion and Culture.

Soukup, P. A. (2017). Authority, new media, and the church. In M. Díez Bosch, P. Soukup, J. L. Micó, & D. Zsupan-Jerome (Eds.), *Authority and leadership: Values, religion, media* (pp. 31–40). Blanquerna Observatory on Media, Religion and Culture.

Spadaro, A. (2012). *Cyberteologia*. Vita e Pensiero.

Stanton, A. J. (2014). Islamic emoticons: Pious sociability and community building in online Muslim communities. In T. Benski, & E. Fisher (Eds.), *Internet and emotions* (pp. 80–98). Routledge.

Stewart, A. R. (2011). Text and response in the relationship between online and offline religion. *Information, Communication and Society, 14*(8), 1204–1218. https://doi.org/10.1080/1369118X.2011.592206

Stout, D. A. (2018). Convergence, digital media, and the paradigm shift in religion news in the United States. In Y. Cohen (Ed.), *Spiritual news. Reporting religion around the world* (pp. 111–124). Peter Lang.

Stroope, S. (2011). Hinduism in India and congregational forms: Influences of modernization and social networks. *Religions, 2*(4), 676–692. https://doi.org/10.3390/rel2040676

Sulistiyo, E., Vindy, Anwar, N., Warnars, D. T. S., Wibawa, S. C., Brotosaputro, G., Kristiadi, D. P., Hendric, H. L., & Warnars, S. (2019). Implementation of mobile game for religion learning. Paper presented at 2019 IEEE International Conference on Engineering, Technology and Education (TALE) in Yogyakarta, Indonesia, December 10, 2019. Retrieved June 17, 2022, from https://ieeexplore.ieee.org/document/9225918

Sumiala-Seppänen, J. (2006). Implications of the sacred in media studies. In J. Sumiala-Seppänen, K. Lundby, & R. Sakolangas (Eds.), *Implications of the sacred in (post)modern media* (pp. 11–29). Nordicom.

Sundaram, D. (2019). Instagram your Durga Puja! Social media, hashtags and state-sponsored cultural marketing. In X. Zeiler (Ed.), *Digital Hinduism* (pp. 107–121). Routledge.

Tkach, A. (2014). Faithapps.net: Measuring the dispersal of religious smartphone applications. *Trípodos, 35*, 11–28. http://www.tripodos.com/index.php/Facultat_Comunicacio_Blanquerna/article/view/190

Torma, R., & Teusner, P. E. (2011). iReligion. *Studies in World Christianity, 17*(2), 137–155. https://doi.org/10.1177/1461444820970180

Tridente, G., & Mastroianni, B. (2016). *La missione digitale: Comunicazione della chiesa e social media*. Edizioni Santa Croce.

Tsuria, R., & Campbell, H. A. (2018). Understanding Jewish digital media in Israel. Between technological affordances and religious-cultural uses. In K. Radde-Antweiler, & X. Zeiler (Eds.), *Mediatized Religion in Asia: Studies on digital media and religion* (pp. 190–207). Routledge.

Turkle, S. (1995). *Life on the screen: Identity in the age of the Internet*. Simon and Schuster.

Valladares, X., & Herrera, S. (2015). Social media and religion: New ways of engaging and sharing in Catholicism. In M. Díez Bosch, J. L. Micó, & J. M. Carbonell (Eds.), *Negotiating religious visibility in digital media* (pp. 35–56). Blanquerna Observatory on Media, Religion and Culture.

Viganò, D. (2017). *En salida. Francisco y la comunicación*. Herder.

Volf, M., & McAnnally-Linz, R. (2016). *Public faith action. How to think carefully, engage wisely and vote with integrity*. Brazos Press.

Wagner, R. (2013). Religious authenticity and identity in mobile apps. In H. A. Campbell (Ed.), *Digital religion: Understanding religious practice in new media worlds* (pp. 199–205). Routledge.

Wagner, R., & Accardo, C. (2015). Buddhist apps: Skillful means or dharma dilution? In G. Price Grieve, & D. Veidlinger (Eds.), *Buddhism, the internet, and digital media: The pixel in the lotus* (pp. 134–153). Routledge.

Wellman, B., & Haythornwaite, C. (2002). *The Internet in everyday life*. Blackwell.

Wertheim, M. (1999). *The pearly gates of cyberspace*. Virago.

Wolf, M. (Ed.). (2003). *Virtual morality: Morals, ethics and new media*. Peter Lang.

Yadlin-Segal, A. (2015). Communicating identity through religious internet memes in the "Tweeting Orthodoxies" Facebook page. In H. A. Campbell (Ed.), *Digital Judaism: Jewish negotiations with digital media and culture* (pp. 110–124). Routledge.

Young, G. (2004). Reading and praying online: The continuity in religion online and online religion in internet Christianity. In L. Dawson, & D. Cowan (Eds.), *Religion online: Finding faith on the Internet* (pp. 93–106). Routledge.

Zaleski, J. (1997). *The soul of cyberspace: How technology is changing our spiritual lives*. Harper.

Zavos, J. (2015). Digital media and networks of Hindu activism in the UK. *Culture and Religion, 16*(1), 17–34 https://doi.org/10.1080/14755610.2015.1023814.

Selected Readings

Campbell, H. A., & Shepherd, T. (2021). What should post-pandemic religion look like? OAK Trust. https://doi.org/10.21423/postpandemicreligion

De Wildt, L., & Aupers, S. D. (2021). Eclectic religion: The flattening of religious cultural heritage in videogames. *International Journal of Heritage Studies, 27*(3), 312–330. https://doi.org/10.1080/1352725 8.2020.1746920

Mercer, C., Trothen, T. J., & Cole-Turner, R. (2021). *Religion and the technological future*. Springer International Publishing.

Nwankwo, A. O. (2022). Connectivity and communion: The mobile phone and the Christian religious experience in Nigeria. *New Media & Society, 24*(5), 1161–1178. https://doi.org/10.1177/1461444820970180

Singler, B. (2022). Origin and the end: Artificial intelligence, atheism, and imaginaries of the future of religion. In B. Sollereder, & A. McGrath (Eds.), *Emerging voices in science and theology*. Routledge.

Tsuria, Bellar, W., Campbell, H., & Cho, K. J. (2021). Transferred, mediated or transformed: Considering the design, features, and presentation of sacred text mobile applications. *Journal of Contemporary Religion, 36*(1), 57–78. https://doi.org/10.1080/13537903.2021.1878633

33

Online Religion

Rohit Chopra

Introduction

As a fundamental aspect of human existence, religion has been profoundly impacted by the radical changes wrought by the Internet on the social world. At the same time, given the symbiotic relationship between media and society, cyberspace, through its evolution, has continued to reflect the importance of religion to social life. As Krotoski (2011) notes, "The concept of religious ritual is so deeply embedded in our social fabric that it is natural for it to have made the leap to virtuality." Even before, but especially since, the invention of the world wide web in 1989, the Internet has functioned as a radically new modality for the expression, development, and, indeed, flourishing of religion. Most aspects of religion, other than those embodied in in-person rituals, appear online, whether we understand religion as a manifestation of community or of individual commitment; a historical and sociological phenomenon; an expression of faith, belief, or conscience; a set of ethical and philosophical doctrines and precepts; a "structure of feeling" in Raymond Williams' illuminating term; a source of cultural identity; an organized institutional structure; or an array of particular individual or collective practices or both (Mathews, 2001; Simpson, 1992, pp. 15–16). Even in-person practices of communal worship can be supplemented with the possibilities offered by the Internet, such as virtually connecting separate physical congregations for an act of worship or a shared experience of listening to a speech by a religious figurehead that is streamed on YouTube or Facebook.

Expressions of religion online encompass major and minor communities of faith, from the ancient to the new, including Christians, Buddhists, Jews, Hindus, Muslims, and Wiccans, as well as denominations within each of these groups. Each religious tradition has charted its own trajectory on the Internet, though we can also find common patterns as we track the genealogies of particular religions online. Evangelicals and newer, unconventional, religious communities, for instance, were quicker to adopt the web than older faiths like Islam and Christianity, possibly since the latter two did not need the new medium to bolster their numbers as the world's two largest religions by followers (Krotoski, 2011). Diasporic communities from all backgrounds were also swift in their adoption of the Internet for communication and community but Hindus based in Silicon Valley were, arguably, among the most proactive of these groups, likely as a result of their location and vocation. Working in high-tech industries and living in the Bay Area meant their lives were integrated with the development of the Internet itself; and, along with visiting

The Handbook on Religion and Communication, First Edition. Edited by Yoel Cohen and Paul A. Soukup.
© 2023 John Wiley & Sons Ltd. Published 2023 by John Wiley & Sons Ltd.

local temples, Hindu communities could also participate in shared religious rituals with family members across the globe or view religious services at a temple of particular significance in India (Chopra, 2008).

A new medium, especially one with the potential to radically amplify the volume and modality of communication, would intuitively seem to bolster the sheer presence and significance of religion in society. Scholars have suggested, in fact, that the Internet, in terms of its impact on religion, is as significant as the printing press (O'Leary, 1996). A 2001 study published by the Pew Research Center found that 28 million Americans, about one-quarter of all American Internet users at that point, had turned online to get religious information or to reach out to other members of their religious groups. These "religion surfers," as Larsen terms them, exceeded in sheer count the number of Americans who had "gambled online, used Web auction sites, traded stocks online, placed phone calls on the Internet, done online banking, or used Internet-based dating services" (Larsen, 2001). Yet, a more recent, 2014, study published in the *MIT Technology Review* pointed out that since the 1990s, the Internet was one factor among three accounting for a drop in religiosity (Emerging Technology, 2014). In short, the overall impact of the Internet on religion escapes easy summary. Suffice it to say that any general understanding of religion in the present historical moment needs to take cognizance of the impact of the Internet. To put it in somewhat different terms, we cannot articulate generalizations about the universe of religion over the past 30 years without acknowledging the central role of the Internet in reshaping that landscape.

The Landscape of Online Religion

The complex and variegated terrain of religion online includes, first and most simply, a range of informational resources on different religious traditions, largely, if not always exclusively, consisting of writings, repositories of scripture, accounts of historical developments, sayings of religious figures, and the like. Examples include Hinduwebsite.com, a comprehensive portal along these lines, founded in 1999, which covers Hinduism as well as other subcontinental religions like Sikhism; Avesta (www.avesta.org), a similarly comprehensive archive on Zoroastrianism; Sahih Muslim (Sunnah.com), a collection of hadith or sayings of the Prophet Muhammad; Buddhanet (www.buddhanet.net), which defines itself as the "world's largest database of Buddhist non-sectarian organizations"; and Christianity.com (www.christianity.com), which dedicates itself to a message of "accessible orthodoxy." These sites all share the foundational imperative of registering the presence of the faith itself and making available an archive of information related to it. The sites, however, also often reflect very specific visions of the faith, on the spectrum from radically conservative to radically liberal, as well as an implicit, if not overt, perspective on the relationship of the religious tradition in question to broader understandings of cultural, ethnic, or national identity. Hinduwebsite.com, for example, as is also the case with numerous Hindu online resources, defines Hinduism, Sikhism, and Zoroastrianism as indigenous faith traditions of India while omitting Islam and Christianity, which are and have long been Indian religions.

China's unique system of religious organization, which consists of five government-sanctioned religions, several categories of official religious organizations, as well as illegal or banned religious associations, is reflected online as well. One of the seven official associations, the BAC or national association for Buddhism (www.chinabuddhism.com.cn), mediates the relationship between the Chinese government and the Buddhist community in accordance with official guidelines (Xu & Campbell, 2021, pp. 339–340). As of March 2020, the BAC had a staggering six million webpages, including news activities and webpages, as well as the interactive feature of the WeChat app, testifying to the fact that Chinese authorities use the Internet highly effectively to manage religious social life in a manner that does not undermine the official atheism of the Chinese government and the Chinese Communist Party (p. 341). The Japanese do not always label or describe religious activities as such, in part because of the negative connotations of the term (Kawabata & Tamura, 2007, p. 1002). Religious websites, at least as of the first decade of the twenty-first century, appeared to have a limited presence online. Yet, there were still several thousand websites as of 2007, with Buddhism dominating and Shinto, or traditional Japanese religion, accounting for the smallest number of sites (p. 1005).

Beyond providing a new platform for storing and disseminating information, online modalities have enabled new kinds of mediated engagement for and among members of religious groups. The Internet has been especially valuable in allowing religious believers and adherents to participate virtually in rituals, religious practices, and forms of worship as well as to remotely visit sacred sites. Through sites like Saranam, one can pay for a *pūjā* or worship dedicated to the goddess Kali at the famous Kalighat temple of Kolkata for a little under US$11 (Saranam.com, n.d.). In 2020, the Osaka Tenjin festival went online, a first in its 1000-year history, and a Shinto ritual conducted at the Tenmangu shrine was livestreamed on YouTube (Sankei Shimbun, 2020). The Western Wall in Jerusalem and the Temple Mount, which is the holiest site in Judaism, can be viewed at all times through a webcam (Skyline Webcams, n.d.). The development of the mobile web, a revolution within a revolution, has resulted in an explosion of religious apps, for all believers and faiths. The MuslimPro app helps practicing Muslims keep track of prayer times and points them in the direction of the Kaaba, while The Bible App offers an astonishing 1500 versions of the Bible for users (Al-Heeti, 2017).

Major platforms like Facebook and Reddit as well as websites or portals focused on particular religions foster religious community online. Reddit has numerous communities or sub-reddits covering religion in general, particular religions, and atheism as well (Reddit, n.d.). The sub-reddit communities range in size from less than a hundred to several hundred thousand members.

Religious extremist and fundamentalist groups have weaponized the Internet, though religious radicalization cannot be attributed solely to the Internet but stems from a complex constellation of historical, political, and sociological factors. At initial view at least, conspiracy theorist communities like QAnon seem to draw disproportionately from religious believers, especially of evangelical persuasion (Jaradat, 2021). Radical Islamist groups, like Al-Qaeda and ISIS, have used the Internet, through chat rooms and online forums related to Islam, as a tool to radicalize and recruit potential members for carrying out terrorist activity, just as Hindu nationalists in India have used WhatsApp to deadly effect to whip up mob hysteria and violence against Muslim minority groups in India and white supremacist groups have used the Internet for global recruitment (Dornbierer, 2021; Hoskin, 2020; Purohit, 2019).

Theoretical Considerations and Historical Survey

I understand online religion as a distinct conceptual entity, yet one that does not rest on a dichotomy between the online and offline; between the virtual and the real. It would be a theoretical error to conceptualize the online manifestation of religion as a mere supplement to a more authentic in-person correlate. Online religion, in other words, is part of the spectrum and larger world of religion, yet possesses a coherence of its own and can be described, observed, and analytically dissected as such. Online religion, further, is informed as much by the character of online communication, conventions, and discourse as it is by the character of religious practice, commitment, belief, and authority.

An early and important scholarly examination of religion on the Internet by Helland (2000) presented a conceptual distinction between religion online, according to which the Internet essentially was a means to religious activity in the physical embodied world, and online religion, in which religious practice or activity took place in the online realm itself. In a subsequent work, Helland (2005) modified this distinction to develop a more sophisticated and nuanced understanding in which the spectrum of religious activity on the Internet can be seen in terms of a combination of both kinds of practice, and consuming religious information, a seemingly passive act, can be seen as reflecting religious agency in itself. In accordance with Helland's updated and refined model, I understand online religion to encompass both these imperatives. A website that is primarily a repository of religious texts may occasion religious contemplation, reflection, or meditation, which, depending on the faith, is as much a religious practice as participating in a ritual. An action or event in the offline, brick-and-mortar world may spur an individual to write a blog post or initiate a discussion in an online forum dedicated to religion.

The framework that I employ in this chapter in mapping the terrain of online religion broadly mirrors four main phases in the development of the Internet, following the eras, respectively, of the preweb Internet, the static web, the interactive web, and the social web. The first *era before the web* refers broadly to the Internet before the creation of the world wide web in 1989. The second phase in the schematic employed in the chapter may be termed *the era of the static web*. This period began with the emergence of the postweb Internet, the moment when the Internet truly became a global phenomenon, and lasted about a decade or so. The third phase, *the era of the interactive web*, emerged in the resurgence of the Internet in the aftermath of the dot-com bust of 2001, and lasted till approximately 2010. The fourth phase is *the era of the social web*, for which we can take the second decade of the twenty-first century as an approximate starting point.

I offer a description of what I consider the main thematic concerns related to research on online religion in each phase. My methodological approach does not seek to exhaustively describe all the categories and subcategories of scholarship on online religion across these phases. Instead of deploying a taxonomic logic along these lines, I have chosen instead to highlight significant lines of inquiry in each phase, outlining the contours of research trends, illuminating these through a brief engagement with representative works, and drawing attention to the larger questions that they raise. Through this approach, I indicate abiding questions that continue to animate the study of online religion as well as emphasize new issues and themes raised by recent developments in the area. Importantly, I seek to embed the discussion of developments in online religion in terms of broader and deeper trends in the development of the Internet itself.

A final note in this section is that the schematic employed here is somewhat idealized, as schema tend to be, and that the features associated with one phase of online religion, or the Internet at large, may well be found in subsequent phases as well. Characteristics particular to each phase are often subsumed but not entirely superseded by later developments. This would include initiatives such as livestreaming services that may have failed to quite take off in the immediate, early years of the Internet, but are now central to the experience of being online.

Online Religion in the Preweb Era

The Internet can be dated to at least 1969, though, as Campbell notes, it is since "the 1980s that there has been a steady rise in the performance and practice of religion in online environments"

(Campbell, 2011, p. 233; Tarnoff, 2016). These early communities and sites of religious users took the form of Usenet and email discussion groups and virtual locations for worship. Campbell and Vitullo (2016) locate the Bulletin Board System discussion area titled "Create Your Own Religion," founded in the early 1980s, as possibly "the first religious-oriented activity online" (p. 73). This early moment also brought to the fore new challenges regarding religious authority that deepen and magnify as the web developed. The Usenet newsgroup alt.religion.scientology was blocked by the Church of Scientology, who claimed that it did not have the approval of religious authorities (Brown, 1998). Although the group was founded in 1991 (i.e., very soon after the invention of the web), the controversy reflected the structure of online discourse from this earlier era of Usenet groups and text-based discussion forums. It is worth noting here that the Internet had not yet broken through as a mass medium, in the way that it would after the invention of the world wide web, and its use was mostly restricted to communities with access, such as those of academics, scientists, and technologists. This nascent moment of the emergence of online religion thus did not seem to have had overwhelming significance in shaping the future development of online religion.

Online Religion in the Era of the Static Web (c. 1990–2000)

Scholarship centered on online religion in this era approaches the Internet through the frame of foundational general concepts such as the "virtual community," the "virtual public sphere," and the "network society" or the network (Castells, 1996; Garton et al., 1997; Poster, 1997; Rheingold, 1993). While these texts did not focus on religion necessarily, their arguments provide important heuristic insights for the study of religion online. Spatiality functions as an organizing metaphor in many of these concepts, for example, in informing the very notion of a website as a specific location in the ether of the online realm or in the use of the term "cyberspace" to describe the online world. Implicit in the very metaphor of a web, the frame of the network enables an understanding of how social networks travel, translate, and are transformed online. Such overarching and foundational concepts for understanding social life online have continued to inform scholarship since this initial phase. As may be expected, perspectives on community, online publics, spatiality, virtuality, and networks have become more nuanced, richer, and, indeed, more contested as a massive body of scholarship about the Internet has accumulated. Other important issues about the character and complexities of online social practice and behavior highlighted in this early phase of scholarly inquiry have held enduring interest in Internet studies. These include the digital divide, the impact of the Internet on axes of identity, whether race, gender, ethnicity, and other markers of difference, and the effect on the Internet on community, especially the question of whether it has strengthened social and communal bonds or led to us being more isolated.

Much of the scholarly work related to social life online during this phase can be termed *extensionist*, in that such scholarship frames activities in online space as extensions of their correlates in offline space even if social and behavioral practices may manifest themselves somewhat differently offline. In the extensionist model, online communities and networks, including religious communities and networks, are measured implicitly, or even overtly, against their brick-and-mortar counterparts. Hackett (2006) provides a succinct description and useful taxonomy of the multidimensionality and multimodality of religious life online in an inquiry of how the Internet has impacted both religion and scholarship of religion. Hackett draws attention to "the ambiguous, fluid, almost volatile, nature of the internet, as well as its composite character," in other words, its complexity, which calls for careful attention in any kind of analysis (p. 67). While Hackett's brief essay dates from the mid-2000s, the developments to which it refers span much of what I have categorized as the first phase of the static web. Hackett argues that as far as religion is concerned (and perhaps by implication, more broadly as well), the Internet is not just about "communication and information" but goes well beyond it (p. 68). She lists the modes and dimensions of religious experience that the Internet enables and amplifies as, respectively: communicating, proselytizing, informing, learning, practicing, seeking, commodifying, advocating, and healing and problem-solving. Dawson (2000, p. 26) identifies several important theoretical questions germane to this still early moment of the study of online religion. Is the Internet, for instance, analogous to other media, in terms of its impact on social structures and practices or is it a form of media so unique that it deserves to be treated as a different kind of creature altogether? Dawson notes that "the work done to date on the internet is quite limited, though promising" and calls for any work on religion to be embedded in an examination of "the general sociology of the internet" (p. 26). In her description of the early history of Buddhism on the Internet, Ostrowski (2006) points out that while the term "cybersangha" was introduced as early as 1991 to refer to the Buddhist community online, Buddhism's early manifestation on the Internet was largely in the form of textual and pedagogical archives and resources, with interactive spaces increasing in relative significance later by the late 1990s (p. 93). Schroeder et al. (1998), in their study of the electronic church, describe a multiuser Christian virtual reality environment that is part of a network of other such virtual environments. In comparison with other virtual reality environments that are not religious, the e-church has more structure, cohesion, hierarchy, and stronger distinctions between insiders and outsiders, though member behavior also contains playful elements that may not appear in a physical church setting. The authors argue that the connections seen in the virtual space, however, are "weak" and "unidimensional" and do not rise to the level of the complex, rich, and multilayered interaction of face-to-face in-person communication among a group of religious believers (n.p.).

Azzi (1999, p. 104) observes that the "Islamic input on the internet is still in its infancy." While his own political views lead Azzi to put forth the problematic proposition that Muslims have an obligation to present the "correct" or "authentic" view of Islam online, the descriptive aspects of his analysis provide some useful facts about Islam online (p. 104). Azzi is right in noting that the early presence of Islam owed much to Muslim communities in the West, where the ability to communicate and express ideas in a public space was much less restricted than in non-Western parts of the "Muslim world." Larsson's (2011) brief overview of scholarship about the relationship of Islam and the Internet notes that early Muslim users and adopters of the Internet emphasized their "Muslimness" in their use of the new technological space. This suggests that a religious self-consciousness may have been a prime motivating factor for Muslims to announce their voices online and to ensure the presence of Islam in cyberspace. Larsson also highlights several other vital characteristics of Islam online, notably, its globality and transnationality, reflecting the existence of new Muslim communities of immigrants in the West; its deployment by religious authorities as a theological space and instrument; and the subversive potential of the Internet to challenge the status of the pronouncements of such theological authorities. Bunt's (2000) exhaustive work on CIEs or "cyber-Islamic environments" offered an early model for how the networked nature of online space was transforming the scope and meanings of Islam for Muslims across the globe.

Initial adoption of the web by adherents of Hinduism reveals some of the same patterns. Early Hindu online groups were significantly peopled by members of the transnational religious and cultural Hindu diaspora, many of whom were located in Western countries and based in technology hubs like Silicon Valley. Scholarship on this initial moment of online Hinduism, roughly from the early or mid-1990s to the turn of the century, highlighted the networked nature of the online Hindu community, linking together comprehensive informational resources such as Hindunet, sites associated with particular temples or sects, listservs, and discussion groups.

Importantly, how Hindus across the globe, particularly those of a conservative and nationalist bent, envisioned the web as a space to be captured and dominated, curiously anticipated a trend that would be seen in America decades later, peaking during the Trump presidency in 2016–2020. The Internet was understood by Hindu groups as a space where community members could fashion and present accounts of Hindu religion and culture, unhindered by the authority of gatekeepers whether academia, governments, or organizations. Similarly, the Internet was a platform where Hindus could articulate their vision of Hinduism as an ancient, scientific faith that, nonetheless, was uniquely attuned to modernity. Less innocently, though, dozens of websites, many located in and run by diasporic Hindus based in Silicon Valley, promoted an ethno-nationalist and religious majoritarian vision of Indian civilization as uniquely Hindu in its ethos, defining and excluding Muslim and Christian Indians as outsiders (Chopra, 2008, 2019; Lal, 2001; Mazumdar, 2003). A final thought here is that scholarship in the postweb phase of the Internet already drew attention to some of the troubling aspects of online culture, foretelling the problems that we now recognize as intrinsic to social media culture a quarter of a century later. These unfortunately persistent aspects of online culture include the erasure and marginalization of minority and vulnerable voices in cyberspace, cyberbullying and online shaming, and attacks on women and minorities (Stein, 2016). The amplification of inequities of power online, an ironic inversion of the aspirational hope that the Internet would foster an egalitarian culture, has ballooned into an international scourge of mass trolling, whether by enraged mobs, angry misogynist gamers, or organized political actors employed by state and nonstate actors. Religious and secular users and communities alike are involved in these unsavory aspects of global online culture, as both abusers and victims.

Online Religion in the Era of the Interactive Web (c. 2000–2010)

By this stage, interactivity had become the normative, defining, experience of the web, with the Internet offering the perennial possibility of producing, circulating, and consuming content, products, and services in ever more sophisticated ways. The dream of perfect community and connection had always been part of the utopian promise of the web, along with unfettered information for all, as the term "information superhighway" might have suggested. Technological limitations and the realities of unequal access, however, had kept this dream largely in the realm of aspiration in the first decade after the emergence of the web as a global communication medium. While the techno-utopianism inherent in the idealized vision of cyberspace as a promised land meant that it could never realistically be wholly fulfilled, by the second decade, with the establishment of Web 2.0 and rapid global spread of the web, it became clearer at least which hopes and concerns about the web had been justified and which ones were unfounded. By this point, arguably, the Internet and web had been adopted by religious communities in all their diversity and complexity, reflecting the wide range of meanings that users attached to religion. Indeed, Internet usage and practice by this point reveal that the assumed dichotomy between religion as an atavistic drive ostensibly rooted in a premodern ethos and the Internet as an embodiment of technological modernity did not quite hold. As Barzilai-Nahon and Barzilai (2005) note about the Internet and religious fundamentalism:

> The interaction between innovative information technology (IT) and religion is often perceived as contradictory, especially when it is religion at its most conservative practice. The most prominently perceived conflict is between religious fundamentalism and telecommunications, since cyberspace, through the development of both local and global networks, and software, has expanded immensely. Yet religions remain as meaningful ways of life around the globe and are not excluded from the Internet. (p. 255)

Focusing on fundamentalism among ultra-Orthodox Jews as expressed in cyberspace, Barzilai-Nahon and Barzilai note that the Internet and religious fundamentalism hold a symbiotic, if agonistic, relationship. While communities may resist, or seem to resist, the Internet out of commitments that appear grounded in the desire to follow the pure, premodern tenets of a religion, they also use the Internet to reshape the nature of fundamentalism. This latter use is consistent with the understanding of fundamentalism as an essentially modern movement, contrary to its self-image as a return to an unsullied premodern past. The complex relationship between religion and the Internet, however, does not only apply to extreme manifestations such as fundamentalism. From the early 2000s onward, we see an expansion of scope and interest in numerous aspects of online religion, taking shape in the form of nuanced and fine-grained theoretical and empirical analyses. The *Heidelberg Journal of Religions on the Internet*, for instance, has covered a broad range of topics on online religion over the course of more than a decade, including the role of religion in digital gaming, online jihad, Western adoption of Asian religions on the Internet, mobile expressions of religion, and religion in augmented reality. Importantly, the journal was inaugurated in the mid-2000s with a special issue dedicated to examining questions of method and theory for studying online religion (Krüger, 2005).

We also see an expansion of scholarship on online religion in different geographical contexts, a trend that continues well into the 2010s. Kluver and Cheong (2007) find that in Singapore, technological modernization, exemplified by Internet usage, was not seen as threatening and indeed embraced by most faith communities, including "Buddhism, Taoism, Christianity, Islam, Hinduism, and traditional Chinese religions" (p. 1122). Religion, in fact, has a positive symbiotic relationship with technology, and religious community leaders are proactive in ensuring that the Internet does not increase strife between communities (pp. 1122–1123). Asamoah-Gyadu (2007) undertakes a comparative analysis of how traditional Christian denominations and newer ones that he classifies as Pentecostal/charismatic use the Internet, finding the latter to be self-consciously global in their self-understanding and in how they use the new technology of the Internet. A study of the attitudes of Russian Internet users toward religion and God found that these users situated their faith in terms of family and self and the power of affect rather than with reference to the wider frame of society (Khroul, 2015). Religion, in other words, appeared to become a matter more of self-interest than of a sense of belonging to a larger public.

A distressing development appeared during the era of Web 2.0, revealing an especially troubling use of the Internet with regard to religion. This phase sees attacks by self-proclaimed guardians of religious groups on those perceived to be offensive to the faith, including journalists, satirists, and academics – in general, those who critically examine religion and question received wisdom. Offense at books or critics of religion is not unique to the Internet age or even the modern era, of course. And the momentum for such attacks and culture of hounding people online had been gradually building up since the postweb years. Yet, in scale and scope, the Internet amplifies such controversies and their consequences. First, as a global medium, the Internet allows for allegations of offense, insult, heresy, blasphemy, and the like to circulate very rapidly and globally, to go viral, in other words. Secondly, the Internet itself becomes a space, instrument, and weapon for online mobs to attack alleged offenders. The Internet was central to the Danish cartoon controversy in 2005, and the attacks on Wendy Doniger and Paul Courtright, scholars of Hinduism, by right-wing Hindus, during the decade (Braverman, 2004; Hervik, n.d.). The issue, as Hinduism scholar Patton (2019) notes, concerns who "owns" religion and who, therefore, has the right to represent it. With the increased reach of the Internet, religious, cultural, and other forms of difference become more visible and more threatening. This situation engenders and magnifies anxieties about identity, representation, and the question of control over the representation of identity, resulting in policing and disciplining of both insiders and outsiders deemed to be disrespectful or abusive of faith groups. The Internet also allows politicians to exploit accusations of religious bias for domestic political capital and gains. In the Indian context, for instance, scholars who critique Hinduism are routinely accused by Hindu right-wing organizations of "anti-Hindu" prejudice. Regrettably, these trends have continued through the 2010s, that is, during the era of the social web.

Online Religion in the Era of the Social Web

In the present, ongoing era of the social web, scholarship builds on existing foundations and extant lines of inquiry, deepening and enriching the field. Collections of scholarship in the area of online religion from its origins to the present, embodying what one may call a cumulativist perspective on online religion, point to the maturity of the field and delineate new possibilities and vistas for inquiry. Such anthologies may focus on one religion, such as Grieve and Veidlinger's (2015) volume, *Buddhism, The Internet, and Social Media: The Pixel in the Lotus.* Or they may address online religion at large, such as Campbell's three-volume, *Religion and the Internet* (2017), which gathers a large number of important perspectives on religion and the Internet. The text classifies scholarly work under different headings as follows: Volume 1 examines the rise of religious practice in cyberspace; Volume 2, divided into three parts, looks at religious community, identity, and authority online; and Volume 3, in two parts, addresses theoretical and methodological questions.

In addition to work on well-established topics in the field and collections that provide a sense of the range of perspectives on online religion, social media is a new area that has drawn significant interest during this period. Given their massive reach and the fact they have rapidly permeated and become integrated with routine practices of sociality, economic transactions, and work, social media platforms are inescapably intertwined with religious practice in the present. The centrality of social media networks and platforms to the Internet in its present incarnation and to its future development have naturally led scholars to examine their impact on religion. As Sutton (2018) observes, in his brief reflection on how Facebook is transforming religion, "It would seem that Facebook is here to stay." More detailed studies offer more precise insights. Brubaker and Haigh (2017, p. 1) note that social media platforms like Facebook allow for forms of engagement that may not be possible in face-to-face interaction. Their study of religious Christians' use of Facebook showed that the community employs the platform for a range of reasons, prime among which are proselytization, seeking guidance, entertainment, and obtaining information. McClure's (2016) study on how social networking sites, with their potential to expose emerging adults to pluralistic belief and an array of belief systems, finds that engagement with social networks increases syncretism and the idea of religion as a choice among these users. However, it is not necessarily the case that they see all religions as equal online. In other words, while religious preference may become a matter of choice, all religious content is not equally flattened out online. Aeschbach and Lüddeckens (2019) investigate the potential of Twitter, the micro-blogging social network platform, on the articulation of religious community. Their study of a hashtag, #WhatBritishMuslimsReallyThink, reveals that Twitter can foster affective sentiment, leading to ephemeral, temporary communities grounded in religion that coalesce around particular themes.

Influencer culture, an essential aspect of social media culture and the contemporary landscape of the Internet, has also amplified the aspect of performativity in online religion. To present oneself via social media platforms, in the specific modality of the platform in question, such as filtered images on Instagram or posts on Facebook intended to reach members of one's network, has become a way of affirming one's religious identity. Performance and affirmation also become an important form of informal religious practice, extending the ambit of practice beyond the orthodox or conventional.

Social media platforms and spaces, relatedly, become important sites for challenging traditional structures of religious authority such as through the expression of female agency. A study of Muslim sportswomen's use of social media, undertaken by Ahmad and Thorpe (2020), for instance, found that they deployed social media as a highly effective narrative tool to subvert stereotypes about Muslim women. Employing interviews as well as digital ethnographies of Muslim sportswomen on Facebook, Instagram, Snapchat, and Twitter, the study identified granular techniques such as the use of hashtags through which Muslim women rendered themselves visible on social media. A study of the visual self-presentation of Indonesia's hijabers' community (Baulch & Pramiyanti, 2018) on Instagram identified two imperatives that animate hijabers' posts: the expression of a modern sensibility that draws on a global online cultural milieu and a desire to extend the community of Islam by inviting potential believers into the fold, a phenomenon termed *dakwah*. The posts by hijabers constitute a new intervention in the field of the norms of Islamic communication even as they are consistent with the forms through which other, nonreligious, influencers may use the platform. Baulch and Pramiyanti (2018) highlight the agency of women involved in such practices, stating: "These women ride high on the myth of social media's epochal transformative power, using their cellphones and other social media affordances to produce themselves, and design paths for circulating their self-productions, sparking dialogues across distant sites among female strangers commonly engaged in crafting the ideal look for the modern Muslimah" (p. 2). The authors argue that even as the presentation of Indonesian hijabers as modern, fashionable, and self-assured women reinforces rather than challenges postfeminist gender norms, their use of Instagram in administering *dakwah* or the invitation to Islam represents a foray into an activity that has traditionally been the domain of men (p. 2).

Each social media network or platform has its own appeal for the faithful. Facebook offers a customized platform for faith groups to form their own communities (https://faith.facebook.com). The social media behemoth, Culliford (2021) notes, "sees worshippers as a vital community to drive engagement on the world's largest social media platform" and, accordingly, earlier this year, it offered US-based religious users a prayer tool. Other popular social media sites and networks with a massive global following, such as Etsy and Pinterest, are home to a universe of religious-themed items for purchase and images of religious art or objects. Instagram is home to religious facts, wisdom art, and teachings from traditions as diverse as Buddhism (Prom, 2018), Wicca (Instagram, n.d.a), and the Bahá'í faith (Instagram, n.d.b).

Conclusion: Online Religion in the Time of Covid-19 and After

Over most of 2020 and much of 2021, with the Covid-19 pandemic radically distorting life as we knew it, the Internet has become central to social interaction in a range of areas including religion. While we are still in the throes of the pandemic, with ebbs and flows of outbreaks, globally, the impact of the pandemic on religious life, broadly, and online religious life has already received some scholarly attention. The presence of religion online, in particular, seems to have become pointedly more significant (Selsky, 2020). Confined to their homes, cut off from normally available avenues for socializing, isolated from friends and family, large sections of humanity have spent an increasing proportion of their life online. In times of crisis, it is a natural instinct to turn to faith for solace, strength, or answers to thorny, intractable issues. This unique mix of factors may explain the enhanced salience of online religion during this peculiar, particular phase of recent human history. As Parish (2020, p. 286) points out, "Religions are some of the oldest organizational forms, yet the breadth and depth of the impact of COVID-19 on their communities has required radical change in the face of an escalating crisis." Scholars of religion and the Internet have, accordingly, turned their attention to this urgent question. The Berkley Center for Religion, Peace and World Affairs at Georgetown University, for instance, launched an initiative related to the challenges posed by the Covid-19 crisis to faith communities, as well as the potential for mobilizing faith and belief to meet these challenges (Berkley Center, n.d.). A recent essay by Baker et al. (2020, p. 358) examines how the pandemic has significantly reshaped the universe of religion at large, with a focus on how "religious institutions, congregations, and individuals are responding to the social changes wrought by COVID-19." The Internet plays a central role in this transformation of the nature of religious engagement in the era of Covid-19 and, by implication, the post-Covid-19 era as well. The authors note that at "a minimum, religion scholars will want to pay attention to how religious professionals have altered their leadership to accommodate social distancing, switching to a largely remote working environment" (p. 359). In addition to religious gatherings in so-called "superspreader" events, the complex relationship between religion and science, and the importance of religious values in caring for the vulnerable, the authors also identify online modalities of communication and the use of digital media and technologies as important aspects of the post-Covid-19 religious landscape that call for study. They highlight the growth of asynchronous participation in religious rituals during this period, enabled by communication technologies, which attenuates the communal, shared aspect of religious life and the mediated nature of social events, like marriage, which also may bear a religious significance (pp. 364–365). Kühle and Larsen (2021) examine the near-total religious lockdown in Denmark, a policy measure taken in response to Covid-19, which forced religious activities, at both the individual and communal level, to move to the digital realm. The authors assess the impact of the shift to the online realm for both majority religion and minority religions, like Islam, highlighting the deeper questions such shifts raise about religion in public life. While all religions were forced to go online, churches in the Danish context count as public institutions, reflecting their role as secularized, social, and civic spaces in what the authors term a "post-secular" society (p. 496). Christianity, then, was not addressed as a religion in the same sense as Islam in this shift.

During and after the pandemic, each religious tradition looked within itself, so to speak, to find resources that could help not just its own adherents but the global community to deal with matters of belief, solidarity, dignity, suffering, and compassion brought to the fore by the pandemic. Parish's (2020) study of a virtual Christian community in the time of a pandemic and social distancing investigates the meaning of participating in worship and ritualistic practice in the absence of the material space of the church. Parish notes that the virtualization of religious services, practices, and faith profoundly altered the meaning of religious participation in at least two fundamental ways: one, though a physical absence of presence or not being able to congregate in person in a material space; and two, through a psychological presence of that absence, that is, the deeply felt psychological impact of being isolated from religious community. For Muslim communities, the crisis wrought by the pandemic has compelled an examination and consideration of appropriate ethical responses to the situation. Shabana (2021, p. 4) points out that there is a historical precedent for this in the Islamic tradition in the form of "a significant body of literature that addresses the issue of the plague." The ethical issues raised by the crisis pertain to three areas: preventive measures, treatment of those stricken by the virus, and ensuring the dignity of those who have died (p. 4). Shabana's analysis shows that responses to the pandemic, rooted in this tradition, seek to balance scriptural and metaphysical imperatives with practical concerns. Buddhist organizations and religious figures have called for the Buddhist religious values of "meditation, compassion, generosity and gratitude" to guide and shape the response of both state and society to the pandemic (Salguero, 2020).

The Covid-19 pandemic and its impact in reshaping online religious life could not have been predicted in advance by anyone. It would, similarly, be foolhardy to attempt to predict either the direction in which the Internet will evolve or the dominant forms that religion will take in either the near term or long term. To do so would be to fall prey to the temptations of both technological and social determinism. Whatever the developments in both arenas of human life and social existence, though, it is hard to envision the future of religion without the Internet and the future of online life without the participation of communities of religious practice and belief. With more than three decades of a distinct presence on the Internet, online religion offers a rich archive for various kinds of analysis, whether from the perspective of religious studies, historical, sociological, and anthropological frameworks, or interdisciplinary inquiry. Even as religion continues to flourish in earlier kinds of online spaces, such as websites, discussion forums, and listservs, it also makes its presence felt through newer forms of Internet structures, such as social media platforms or mobile networks. As an inextricable part of human existence, religion does not appear to be at any risk of withering away, either with increased modernization, the spread of globalization, or the latest disruptions of capitalism. The size and dominance of Internet corporations, the more than two billion active users of Facebook, and the pervasiveness of Internet use suggest that the Internet too is likely to continue to be part of our lives for as long as we can envision. The relationship between the two promises to continue to provide fertile ground for scholars to study, engendering fascinating and challenging theoretical, empirical, and methodological questions.

References

Aeschbach, M., & Lüddeckens, D. (2019). Religion on Twitter: Communalization in event-based hashtag discourses. *Heidelberg Journal of Religions on the Internet, 14*, 108–130. https://doi.org/10.17885/heiup. rel.2019.0.23950

Ahmad, N., & Thorpe, H. (2020). Muslim sportswomen as digital space invaders: Hashtag politics, and everyday visibilities. *Communication & Sport, 8*(4–5), 668–691. https://doi.org/10.1177/2167479519898447

Al-Heeti, A. (2017, December 14). Religious apps with a higher purpose. Cnet. Retrieved June 16, 2022, from https://www.cnet.com/tech/services-and-software/religious-apps-christian-jewish-muslim

Asamoah-Gyadu, J. K. (2007). '"Get on the internet!" says the LORD': Religion, cyberspace, and Christianity in contemporary Africa. *Studies in World Christianity, 13*(3), 225–242. https://muse.jhu.edu/article/224396

Azzi, A. (1999). Islam in cyberspace: Muslim presence on the internet. *Islamic Studies, 38*(1), 103–117. https://www.jstor.org/stable/20837028

Baker, J. O., Marti, G., Braunstein, R., Whitehead, A. L., & Yukich, G. (2020). Religion in the age of social distancing. *Sociology of Religion: A Quarterly Review, 81*(4), 357–370. https://doi.org/10.1093/socrel/sraa039

Barzilai-Nahon, K., & Barzilai, G. (2005). Cultured technology: The internet and religious fundamentalism. *The Information Society, 21*, 25–40. https://doi.org/10.1080/01972240590895892

Baulch, E., & Pramiyanti, A. (2018). Hijabers on Instagram: Using visual social media to construct the ideal Muslim woman. *Social Media and Society, 4*(4), 1–15. https://doi.org/10.1177/2056305118800308

Berkley Center. (n.d.). Covid-19. Berkley Center. Retrieved September 8, 2022, from https://berkleycenter. georgetown.edu/topics/covid-19

Braverman, A. M. (2004). The interpretation of gods. *University of Chicago Magazine, 97*(2). https:// magazine.uchicago.edu/0412/features

Brown, J. (1998, July 15). A web of their own. Salon. Retrieved June 16, 2022, from https://www.salon. com/1998/07/15/feature_299

Brubaker, P. J., & Haigh, M. M. (2017). The religious Facebook experience: Uses and gratifications of faith-based content. *Social Media + Society, 3*(2), 1–11 https://doi.org/10.1177/2056305117703723.

Bunt, G. (2000). *Virtually Islamic: Computer-mediated communication and cyber Islamic environments.* University of Wales Press.

Campbell, H. A. (2011). Internet and religion. In M. Consalvo, & C. Ess (Eds.), *The handbook of internet studies* (pp. 232–250). Wiley-Blackwell.

Campbell, H. A. (Ed.). (2017). *Religion and the internet.* Routledge.

Campbell, H. A., & Vitullo, A. (2016). Assessing changes in the study of religious communities in digital religion studies. *Church, Communication and Culture, 1*(1), 73–89. https://doi.org/10.1080/23753234.2016.1181301

Castells, M. (1996). *The rise of the network society.* Blackwell.

Chopra, R. (2008). *Technology and nationalism in India: Cultural negotiations from colonialism to cyberspace.* Cambria Press.

Chopra, R. (2019). *The virtual Hindu Rashtra: Saffron nationalism and new media.* HarperCollins.

Culliford, E. (2021, July 21). Facebook decided faith groups are good for business. Now, it wants your prayers. Reuters. Retrieved June 16, 2022, from https://www.reuters.com/technology/facebook-decided-faith-groups-are-good-business-now-it-wants-your-prayers-2021-07-22/#:~:text=COVID%20gave%20new%20urgency%20to,also%20a%20pastor%20in%20Florida

Dawson, L. (2000). Researching religion in cyberspace: Issues and strategies. In J. K. Hadden, & D. E. Cowan (Eds.), *Religion on the internet: Research prospects and promises* (pp. 25–54). JAI Press.

Dornbierer, A. (2021, September 13). How al-Qaeda recruits online. The Diplomat. Retrieved June 16, 2022, from https://thediplomat.com/2011/09/how-al-qaeda-recruits-online

Emerging Technology from the arXiv. (2014, April 4). How the internet is taking away America's religion. MIT Technology Review. Retrieved June 16, 2022, from https://www.technologyreview.com/2014/04/04/13684/how-the-internet-is-taking-away-americas-religion

Garton, L., Haythornthwaite, C., & Wellman, B. (1997). Studying online social networks. *Journal of Computer-Mediated Communication, 3*(1). https://doi.org/10.1111/j.1083-6101.1997.tb00062.x

Grieve, G. P., & Veidlinger, D. (2015). *Buddhism, the internet, and social media: The pixel in the lotus.* Routledge.

Hackett, R. I. J. (2006). Religion and the internet. *Diogenes, 211,* 67–76. https://doi.org/10.1177/0392192106069015

Helland, C. (2000). Religion online/online religion and virtual communitas. In J. K. Hadden, & D. E. Cowan (Eds.), *Religion on the internet: Research prospects and promises* (pp. 205–224). JAI Press/Elsevier Science.

Helland, C. (2005). Online religion as lived religion: Methodological issues in the study of religious participation on the internet. *Heidelberg Journal of Religions on the Internet, 1*(1). http://archiv.ub.uni-heidelberg.de/volltextserver/5823/1/Helland3a.pdf

Hervik, P. (n.d.). Danish cartoon crisis/controversy. Oxford Islamic Studies Online. Retrieved June 16, 2022, from http://www.oxfordislamicstudies.com/article/opr/t343/e0198

Hoskin, M. N. (2020, December 16). Google's The Current reveals the new face of violent online white supremacist organizations and how to get out of these radical groups. Forbes. Retrieved June 16, 2022, from https://www.forbes.com/sites/maiahoskin/2020/12/16/googles-the-current-reveals-the-new-face-of-violent-online-white-supremacist-organizations-and-how-to-get-out-of-these-radical-groups/?sh=5126706c37b1

Instagram. (n.d.a). Buddhism daily. Retrieved September 8, 2022, from https://www.instagram.com/buddhism_daily/?hl=en.

Instagram. (n.d.b). Wiccagram. Retrieved September 8, 2022, from https://www.instagram.com/wiccagram/?hl=en.

Instagram. (n.d.c). Bahaiteachings. Retrieved September 8, 2022, from https://www.instagram.com/bahaiteachings/?hl=en.

Jaradat, M. (2021, March 28). Why would Christians embrace conspiracy theories? Deseret News. Retrieved June 16, 2022, from https://www.deseret.com/indepth/2021/3/28/22334183/what-group-of-christians-most-likely-believe-conspiracy-theories-white-evangelicals-qanon-faith

Kawabata, A., & Tamura, T. (2007). Online-religion in Japan: Websites and religious counseling from a comparative cross-cultural perspective. *Journal of Computer-Mediated Communication, 12*(3), 999–1019 https://doi.org/10.1111/j.1083-6101.2007.00360.x.

Khroul, V. (2015). The religious identity of Russian internet users. *Digital Icons: Studies in Russian, Eurasian and Central European New Media*, *14*, 133–143. https://www.digitalicons.org/wp-content/uploads/2016/01/DI_14_7_Khroul.pdf

Kluver, R., & Cheong, P. H. (2007). Technological modernization, the internet, and religion in Singapore. *Journal of Computer-Mediated Communication*, *12*(3), 1122–1142. https://academic.oup.com/jcmc/article/12/3/1122/4583048

Krotoski, A. (2011, 16 April). What effect has the internet had on religion? The Guardian. Retrieved June 16, 2022, from https://www.theguardian.com/technology/2011/apr/17/untangling-web-aleks-krotoski-religion

Krüger, O. (2005). Methods and theory for studying religion on the internet: Introduction to the special issue on theory and methodology. *Online Heidelberg Journal of Religions on the Internet*, *1*(1). https://heiup.uni-heidelberg.de/journals/index.php/religions/article/view/379

Kühle, L., & Larsen, T. L. (2021). 'Forced' online religion: Religious minority and majority communities' media usage during the COVID-19 lockdown. *Religion*, *12*(7), 496. https://doi.org/10.3390/rel12070496

Lal, V. (2001). The politics of history on the internet: Cyber-diasporic Hinduism and the North American Hindu diaspora. In M. R. Paranjpe (Ed.), *In diaspora: Theories, histories, texts* (pp. 179–221). Indialog Publications.

Larsen, E. (2001, December 23). Part 1: Defining the religion surfers. Pew Research Center. Retrieved June 16, 2022, from https://www.pewresearch.org/internet/2001/12/23/part-1-defining-the-religion-surfers

Larsson, G. (2011). Islam and the internet. Oxford Bibliographies. Retrieved June 16, 2022, from https://www.oxfordbibliographies.com/view/document/obo-9780195390155/obo-9780195390155-0116.xml

Mathews, S. (2001). Change and theory in Raymond Williams's structure of feeling. *Pretexts: Literary and Cultural Studies*, *10*(2), 179–194. https://doi.org/10.1080/10155490120106032

Mazumdar, S. (2003). The politics of religion and national origin: Recovering Hindu Indian identity in the United States. In V. Kaiwar, & S. Mazumdar (Eds.), *Antinomies of modernity: Essays on race, orient, nation* (pp. 223–260). Duke University Press.

McClure, P. (2016). Faith and Facebook in a pluralistic age: The effects of social networking sites on the religious beliefs of emerging adults. *Sociological Perspectives*, *59*(4), 818–834. https://doi.org/10.1177/0731121416647361

O'Leary, S. D. (1996). Cyberspace as sacred space: Communicating religion on computer networks. *Journal of the American Academy of Religion*, *64*(4), 781–808. https://www.jstor.org/stable/1465622

Ostrowski, A. (2006). Buddha browsing: American Buddhism and the internet. *Contemporary Buddhism*, *7*(1), 91–103. https://doi.org/10.1080/14639940600878117

Parish, H. (2020). The absence of presence and the presence of absence: Social distancing, sacraments, and the virtual religious community during the COVID-19 pandemic. *Religions*, *11*(6), 276. https://doi.org/10.3390/rel11060276

Patton, L. (2019). *Who owns religion? Scholars and their publics in the late twentieth century*. University of Chicago Press.

Poster, M. (1997). Cyberdemocracy: The internet and the public sphere. In D. Holmes (Ed.), *Virtual politics: Identity and community in cyberspace* (pp. 212–228). Sage Publications.

Prom, A. (2018, November 13). *How this young Buddhist monk uses Instagram to connect with Khmer youth*. KUOW/NPR, Retrieved September 14, 2022, from https://www.kuow.org/stories/cambodian-american-buddhist-monk-instagram

Purohit, K. (2019, December 19). The WhatsApp groups spewing anti-Muslim hatred amid India's citizenship dispute. Ozy. Retrieved June 16, 2022, from https://www.ozy.com/around-the-world/the-whatsapp-hate-groups-belying-modis-calls-for-calm-amid-citizenship-row/258641

Reddit.com. (n.d.). r/ReligionHub. Retrieved September 8, 2022, from https://www.reddit.com/r/ReligionHub/comments/kohy3/directory_of_religionrelated_subreddits

Rheingold, H. (1993). *The virtual community: Homesteading on the electronic frontier*. Addison-Wesley.

Salguero, P. (2020, 15 May). How do Buddhists handle coronavirus? The answer is not just meditation. The Conversation. Retrieved June 16, 2022, from https://theconversation.com/how-do-buddhists-handle-coronavirus-the-answer-is-not-just-meditation-137966

The Sankei Shimbun (2020, August 4). [Hidden wonders of Japan] Osaka's Tenjin festival Celebration goes online for the first time in 1,000 years. JapanForward. Retrieved June 16, 2022, from https://japanforward.com/hidden-wonders-of-japan-osakas-tenjin-festival-celebration-goes-online-for-the-first-time-in-1000-years

Saranam.com. (n.d.). Kalighat Temple. Saranam.com. Retrieved September 8, 2022, from https://www.saranam.com/temple/8/kalighat-temple

Schroeder, R., Heather, N., & Lee, R. M. (1998). The sacred and the virtual: Religion in multi-user virtual reality. *Journal of Computer-Mediated Communication*, 4(2). https://doi.org/10.1111/j.1083-6101.1998.tb00092.x

Selsky, A. (2020, 17 May). Houses of worship gain audience online. Federal News Network. Retrieved June 16, 2022, from https://federalnewsnetwork.com/technology-news/2020/05/houses-of-worship-gain-audience-by-going-online-during-virus

Shabana (أيمن شبانة), A. (2021). From the plague to the coronavirus: Islamic ethics and responses to the COVID-19 pandemic. *Journal of Islamic Ethics* (published online ahead of print 2021). https://doi.org/10.1163/24685542-12340060

Simpson, D. (1992). Raymond Williams: Feeling for structures, voicing "history". *Social Text*, 30, 9–26.

Skyline Webcams. (n.d.). Jerusalem Western Wall live cam. Skyline Webcams. Retrieved September 8, 2022, from https://www.skylinewebcams.com/en/webcam/israel/jerusalem-district/jerusalem/western-wall.html

Stein, J. (2016, August 18). How trolls are ruining the internet. Time. Retrieved June 16, 2022, from https://time.com/4457110/internet-trolls

Sutton, A. T. (2018, July 12). How Facebook is transforming religion. Sightings. Retrieved June 16, 2022, from https://divinity.uchicago.edu/sightings/articles/how-facebook-transforming-religion

Tarnoff, B. (2016, July 15). How the internet was invented. The Guardian. Retrieved June 16, 2022, from https://www.theguardian.com/technology/2016/jul/15/how-the-internet-was-invented-1976-arpa-kahn-cerf

Xu, S., & Campbell, H. A. (2021). The internet usage of religious organizations in mainland China: Case analysis of the Buddhist Association of China. *Human Behavior and Emerging Technologies*, 3(2), 339–346.

Selected Readings

Bunt, G. R. (2018). *Hashtag Islam: How cyber-Islamic environments are transforming religious authority*. University of North Carolina Press.

Campbell, H. A. (2010). *When religion meets new media* (1st ed.). Routledge.

Dawson, L. L., & Cowan, D. E. (Eds.). (2004). *Finding faith on the Internet*. Routledge.

Ess, C., Cheong, P. H., & Fischer-Nielsen, P. (Eds.). (2012). *Digital religion, social media and culture: Perspectives, practices and futures*. Peter Lang.

Zeiler, X. (Ed.). (2020). *Digital Hinduism*. Routledge.

Index

www.ingramcontent.com/pod-product-compliance
Lightning Source LLC
LaVergne TN
LVHW081257161224
798528LV00005BA/17